Israel Handbook

Vanessa Betts
Dave Winter

There is, perhaps, no other place on earth as famed, as historic, as loved, and yet as controversial as Israel. It is the 'promised land' of milk and honey to the Jews; the site of the Prophet Mohamed's ascent to heaven for Muslims; and the setting for Jesus Christ's ministry, crucifixion, death and resurrection. As the centre of the world's three great monotheistic religions, this land has also been at the heart of continuous conflict throughout the millennia. The intractable dispute between Israeli and Palestinian is ever-present, but provides a unique opportunity to learn, listen and debate. Leave your preconceived notions behind when stepping off the plane.

Whether you want a sun-and-sea beach break, are on a religious pilgrimage searching out spirituality, have your backpack strapped on and a limited budget in your pocket, or are a fitness fanatic craving strenuous hiking and biking, this land really does have it all. Smaller than Belgium, Wales or the state of New Jersey, the range and diversity of attractions crammed into Israel and the Palestinian Territories is incredible. Within just one day you can lie on the beach in Tel Aviv, pray at the site of Christ's crucifixion and finish off with a beer in Ramallah.

Jerusalem – the name alone conjures up images and feelings that awaken the senses before one even arrives. But though the tangible sense of history and the wealth of archaeology are almost overwhelming, Israel sees past and present living side by side. For every holy site in Jerusalem, Tel Aviv has a pavement café-bar. And the contrasts don't end there: seasonal skiing on Mount Hermon, diving and snorkelling in Eilat all year round, camel treks into desert expanses, and soaks in the steamy Dead Sea waters are all part of the experience in the Holy Land.

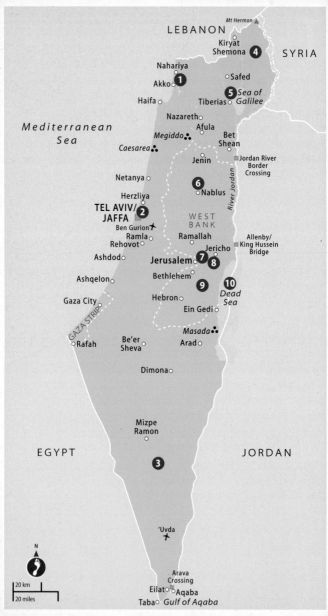

Israel highlights

See colour maps in centre of book

1 Wander around Akko's crusader city, where churches and mosques mingle on the edge of the Mediterranean Sea. ›› page 519

2 Cool café-bars, miles of beachfront promenade, noisy markets and elegant Bauhaus buildings make Tel Aviv the perfect place to kick back and relax. ›› page 393

3 Take on the Negev desert, where ibex traverse the craters and wadis that line the ancient spice routes between Nabatean cities. ›› page 295

4 Visit the heights of the Golan for dramatic landscapes, crashing waterfalls and some unforgettable hikes through the wilderness. ›› page 669

5 Linger on the shores of the Sea of Galilee, a shimmering splash of blue edged by historic religious sites, peaceful little villages and the refreshing brashness of holiday-town Tiberias. ›› page 591

6 Venture into the timeless markets of Nablus to eat the famed kanafe and experience an authentic hammam. ›› page 256

7 The site of Christ's crucifixion, burial and resurrection: the Church of the Holy Sepulchre is the holiest place in Christendom. ›› page 107

8 The iconic image of the Dome of the Rock becomes inseparable from any visitor's memories of Jerusalem. ›› page 79

9 Explore the Herodium, a stunning palace-fortress that is one of Herod the Great's most ambitious building projects and the location of his tomb. ›› page 215

10 Reach the lowest point on earth, and float for a while in the salty waters of the Dead Sea. ›› page 269

Top Church of the Holy Sepulchre, Jerusalem.
Mid-left The Dead Sea.
Mid-right A street in Nablus.
Above Sea of Galilee.
Right Gamla Nature Reserve, The Golan.

Contents

Contents

Footprint features

Essentials

Planning your trip

Where to go

Israel has so much to offer that it can be hard to know where to begin; it really does have a bit of everything. The vast majority of visitors base themselves in Tel Aviv or Jerusalem, then visit the rest of the country in a series of extended day trips. Though most foreign tourists come on pre-arranged package tours, Israel is very easy to explore independently, with accommodation, transport, dining and entertainment suited to any budget. Even relying on public transport it should be possible to see a large percentage of the key highlights in just two weeks, though the more time you have to spend the better; a month dedicated to sightseeing would allow you to see just about everything.

One week

Head straight to **Jerusalem** and immerse yourself in the Old City, with its narrow market streets and its holy places. The Western Wall, the Dome of the Rock and the Holy Sepulchre are all mesmerising, plus a visit to the Holocaust museum (Yad Vashem) or the Israel Museum to see a selection of the 'Dead Sea Scrolls' is recommended. Spend day three at the **Dead Sea**; start by exploring the mountain-top fortress of Masada with its spectacular views and remains from one of the defining events in Jewish history. Make sure of a float in the salty opaque waters, and those with transport could squeeze in a short hike at Ein Gedi and stop to see the views of Wadi Qelt along the way. Then make your way north to the **Sea of Galilee** for a night in holiday-town Tiberias. Either visit the Christian sites on the lake where Jesus fed the 5000 and walked on water or, if you prefer nature, hike down the Arbel cliff to enjoy the enchanting scenery and classic views of the magical lake. Squeeze in a half-day in **Nazareth** with its Arab old quarter and atmospheric churches (be sure to be there at lunchtime to sample the best restaurants in the Galilee) on the way to **Tel Aviv**. You'll want the last two days to enjoy Old Jaffa, tastefully restored and with a concentration of galleries, antique shops and restaurants, as well as time in the modern city, where street cafés, shopping, museums, Bauhaus style and Israel's best nightlife make the perfect way to round off your week.

Two weeks

Spend two days in **Jerusalem**, as above, but add on an extra day to visit **Bethlehem's Church of the Nativity**, the place of Jesus' birth and now behind the separation wall. Spend a couple of nights by the Dead Sea, also visiting Jericho and Wadi Qelt in the **Judean Desert**, before continuing south to **Eilat** (via colourful Timna Park) for some sun, sea, snorkelling and party fun. Otherwise, mix nature and history in stunning **Sde Boker** where you find spectacular hiking in Ein Avdat (and that rarest of desert commodities, water pools) and can visit the nearby ruins of Avdat, the best-preserved example of a Nabatean-Roman-Byzantine city in the Negev. Moving back up north, choose between a visit to **Caesarea**, Herod's magnificent port city, or the ruins of **Bet Shean** where the extensive Roman-Byzantine town needs little imagination. Have a night in **Haifa** to see the beautiful Shrine of the Bab and the luxuriant gardens before continuing to **Old Akko**, the last bastion of Crusader rule in the Holy Land with a compact, labyrinthine quarter packed with historic remains and timeless Arab life. Safed, one of the four holy cities of the Jews and the spiritual capital of Jewish mysticism, is equally attractive to the secular

Packing for Israel

Most travellers tend to take too much, particularly when you bear in mind that practically everything that you need is available in Israel. However, with few exceptions, most things bought in Israel will be more expensive than back home. There are a few things that you might like to bear in mind before packing your bag.

Taking appropriate clothing is essential. When selecting what to take, you should remember cultural and religious factors as well as climatic considerations. When passing through either Arab or religious Jewish areas, conservative dress is a must. This means no shorts or bare shoulders on either men or women, closed necklines, and loose unrevealing clothes. In Jewish religious areas women are requested to wear long skirts as opposed to trousers. At Jewish religious sites both men and women are requested to cover their heads; yarmulkes and scarfs are often provided, though it is as well to bring some sort of head-covering or hat of your own. You will be denied entry into churches, mosques and synagogues alike if you are inappropriately dressed. In summer light loose-fitting cottons are best, though desert and upland areas can get remarkably cold at night. With the exception of day-time in Eilat, the Negev and the Dead Sea Region, winter in Israel can get very cold and wet so bring appropriate warm clothing.

Toiletries, including tampons, sanitary towels and condoms, are readily available, though they tend to be more expensive than at home. Those staying in hostels should definitely bring their own cotton sleep-sheet and ear-plugs, and consider bringing an eye-mask.

who come to admire the views, wander around the narrow streets of the old quarters or browse amongst the galleries and workshops of the Artists' Colony. At least one night by the **Sea of Galilee** is essential, but also take a day trip to the **Golan** to see Nimrod Fortress, the best-preserved medieval fortress in Israel, with breathtaking views across the whole area, and to far-flung **Gamla** where birds of prey swoop past the ruins from one of the most dramatic events in the First Jewish Revolt against Rome (66-73 CE). Don't forget to make sure of some quality beach time in **Tel Aviv**, and save some money to enjoy the great restaurants and hip café-bar scene.

One month

Spend a few days thoroughly exploring **Jerusalem** and surrounds, including quaint Ein Karem, the cave-complexes at Beit Guvrin and the Cave of Machpelah/Haram el-Khalil in Hebron, considered the traditional site bought by the patriarch Abraham as a family burial tomb and of profound significance to Muslims also. Then head to **Ramallah** for the night where you'll find a surprisingly lively bar-restaurant scene that costs half the price of the capital. Spend the next day in **Nablus**, visiting the Samaritan community on Mt Gerizim and wandering some of the most authentic markets in the Middle East. Spend some time around the **Dead Sea**, based either in lush Ein Gedi or little Neot HaKikar on the Jordanian border, before visiting the quirky kibbutzim of the Arava en route to **Eilat**. See how long the sea, sport and sunshine detain you then head north through the heart of the Negev to **Makhtesh Ramon**, a deep erosion crater often described as the Israeli equivalent to America's Grand Canyon, featuring vivid and spectacular rock formations. Hiking here, or in the Negev's two smaller erosion craters (Makhtesh HaGadol/Makhtesh HaKatan), is a highlight of many people's trips. Go off the beaten track and veer west, after Sde Boker, to the **Egyptian border** where Nabatean cites lie shrouded in sand, and remote little **Ezuz** has wonderful accommodation. After the desert, the lush **Galilee** and lofty **Golan** call, so take Route 90 and stop at Belvoir Castle and the hot springs of Hammat Gader on the way to Mt Hermon at the most northerly point of Israel. Spend at least two days hiking, either on the Cross Golan Trek or along the Jesus Trail taking in rolling landscapes, prehistoric and historic ruins and places of unique religious significance along the way. As well as the Galilean highlights mentioned above, seek out the perfect mosaics of Zippori and the splendidly isolated church atop Mt Tabor, and explore Tel Dan Nature Reserve's lush waterscape, where unique flora and fauna flourish among Canaanite and Israelite remains. Return via the coast road, all the way from Rosh HaNikra, with a stop at the beach in either Dor or Netanya, to finish up with some r'n'r in **Tel Aviv**.

When to go

There are two key factors to bear in mind when timetabling a visit to Israel: climate and religious holidays/festivals.

Climate

The climatic seasons in Israel are the same as those in Europe (and the northern hemisphere). Thus spring is roughly March-May, summer is June-August, autumn (fall) is September-October and winter is November-February. As a very general guide, winter tends to be rather wet and overcast, becoming colder and wetter the further north or the higher up you go. Many visitors are unprepared for just how cold it gets in Jerusalem and Bethlehem in the winter. Nevertheless, the Dead Sea Region and the Negev are particularly appealing at this time of year, with very comfortable day-time temperatures. Since Israel is so small, it does not take much travelling to escape from a cold and wet Jerusalem to a dry and sunny Eilat. Indeed, winter is an ideal time to take a beach holiday in Eilat.

Climatic conditions in spring are ideal across most of the country, notably in the Negev and Dead Sea Region, where day-time temperatures have not climbed too high. Temperatures are beginning to pick up on the Mediterranean coast and Jerusalem area, though there will be some rainy days. Galilee (notably Upper Galilee and Golan) may still be cloudy and wet.

Early summer is the best time to visit Galilee and the northern areas, with the cooling influence of the sea making the Mediterranean coast an appealing option. At the height of summer, however, the Dead Sea Region and Negev can get far too hot to be comfortable.

As summer turns to autumn around September, the entire country becomes an attractive proposition, with comfortable temperatures and little rainfall. As autumn draws to an end, however, the northern areas such as Galilee and Golan become cloudier and wetter.

Holidays

Unless you are coming to Israel specifically to celebrate a religious holiday (whether Jewish or Christian), the main holiday periods are best avoided. Flights to and from Israel just before or after religious holidays tend to be heavily booked, and you will almost certainly end up paying more for your ticket. Likewise, accommodation prices rocket (sometimes double), and in some places it can be difficult to find a room without an advance reservation.

The key Christian festivals are of course Easter and Christmas, though the accommodation shortfalls and problems of over-crowding at major sites only really affect visitors to Jerusalem and Bethlehem. Note, however, that different branches of the Church celebrate these events at different times, and hence the Christmas and Easter rush can become quite an extended period. Nevertheless, there is a special atmosphere in Jerusalem and Bethlehem at these times (even if you are non-observant).

Jewish holidays and festivals are numerous, though the key ones are Rosh Hashanah, Yom Kippur, Sukkot and Pesach. Though the holidays are generally brief (usually one day), you should bear in mind that the holiday affects all aspects of life in Israel. Not only do accommodation prices sky-rocket, but almost everything else closes down (including places to eat, sights, banks, post offices and transport). When several holidays come along together it can have a major impact on your visit. Dates of Jewish holidays follow the lunar calendar and thus change each year, though the approximate time of year remains the same. Thus, September/October may be a time to avoid since Rosh Hashanah, Yom Kippur and Sukkot all come along together. Likewise, April/May tends to feature Pesach, Independence Day and Holocaust Memorial Day. For full details of holidays and festivals see the section starting on page 32.

What to do

Bird-watching
Israel is a superb place for bird-watching because of its location on the main migratory route between Europe and Africa. The **International Birding & Research Centre** in Eilat (T08-6335339, www.geocities.com/ibrce) is a good place to enquire for further information. The eco-friendly **Kibbutz Lotan**, www.kibbutzlotan.com, in the Arava, have successfully created wetlands that now accommodate winter migratory birds. There are also 'twitching' sites in Upper Galilee and the Golan, notably the Hula Nature Reserve and nearby Agamon Lake where vast numbers of migratory birds halt for a rest in the winter months.

Cycling
Cycling has really taken off in Israel in the last few years, both in terms of tour-biking and mountain-biking. The Negev is well set-up for tourists to hire bikes and set off on marked trails, either with or without a guide. In particular, **ibike**, ibike.co.il, in Makhtesh Ramon, and **Geofun**, www.geofun.co.il, in Sde Boker, are recommended places for renting equipment and receiving excellent advice from specialists, plus they are located in some of the finest mountain biking regions in the world. Also **HooHa Cyclists**,

www.hooha.co.il, based next to Mt Tabor in the southern Galilee, and the **Cyclists Inn**, www.weekend.co.il/negev/cycle/indexe.html, in Ne'ot HaKikar next to the southern tip of the Dead Sea.

Diving
The Gulf of Aqaba is justifiably rated as being home to some of the world's best dive sites and, though most potential divers head to the Sinai (Egypt), there are plenty of diving opportunities in Eilat. All the dive centres in Eilat offer 'introductory dives', which you can do with no previous experience (usually around $60, though a medical may be compulsory). These dives are to a maximum of 6 m, with a qualified instructor taking full charge.

However, if you really want to appreciate the fascination of diving, the only thing for it is to learn. Beginners' (Open Water) courses with PADI, SSI, CMAS or NAUI are available at all the dive centres. They usually last 5 days and include at least 10 dives. Once you have completed the course (and passed) you are free to dive within the limits set by your Open Water qualification. After that there are Advanced courses, usually only 2-3 days, followed by Rescue courses and a whole host of speciality courses, including wreck

Diving code of conduct

Don't touch, kneel on or kick corals. They are delicate animals, which are damaged when touched.

Don't stir up the sand. Sand settling on coral inhibits its feeding and limits growth; in suspension it reduces the sunlight's penetration with the same effect.

Don't collect souvenirs. Many dive sites are heavily visited and could become rapidly depleted of their resources.

Don't feed the marine life. Feeding interferes with the reef's natural food chains. It can produce dependency and in some cases aggression in normally non-aggressive species.

Don't catch marine life. Fishing and spearfishing is prohibited in National Parks/Protected Areas.

Do control your buoyancy and body/equipment placement. Much damage is done unknowingly. Proper buoyancy control is crucial; practise away from reefs. Be aware of trailing gauges and alternative air sources, which can drag along the reef.

Do respect aquatic life. For the most part, the fish appear indifferent or mildly inquisitive towards divers. However, excessive attention, or activities such as hitching lifts on dolphins or turtles, can cause stress and interfere with mating behaviour.

Do collect any rubbish you see. Litter is a significant and blatantly unnecessary cause of damage to the reef.

Do inform divers if they are damaging the reef or acting irresponsibly. Many people act out of ignorance; speaking up helps raise environmental awareness.

Do report damage to the reef, injured marine life or other disturbances. As a diver, you are in a position to contribute towards the monitoring of reef ecosystems.

---

diving, deep diving, night diving, navigation, etc. Finally, there is the Divemaster course, which is the minimum qualification needed to work as a dive guide. This takes from 2 to 4 weeks. When enquiring after diving courses, check whether the price quoted includes certification and log book.

All dives include tanks and weightbelt. All the other equipment can be rented from the dive centre you go with. If you are going for a full day, or for longer, hire of all the equipment usually costs around $40 per day. It is worth checking the state of the equipment you are hiring. Most of it comes under heavy use and begins to wear out quickly; broken fastenings on a buoyancy control jacket or bad-fitting/damaged flippers can be very distracting when what you want to do is give your full attention to the marine life around you. The major dive centres have underwater camera equipment available for hire, and also run underwater photography courses. Eilat also has decompression chambers for dealing with diving accidents. Diving is available along the Mediterranean coast, though most prefer the underwater attractions of the Red Sea.

Hiking

Israelis love to hike, and Israel is a great country for hiking. Carefully marked colour-coded trails crisscross the country, and it's possible to follow the Israel National Trail for 950 km all the way from the Syrian/Lebanese border down to the Gulf of Eilat! The best hiking resource is the **SPNI (Society for the Protection of Nature in Israel)**, who have offices and field schools across the country. They are generally staffed by dedicated hikers who are keen to share their enthusiasm with you. SPNI also sell detailed 1:50,000 hiking maps (84NIS). Unfortunately all but the Eilat sheet are only available in Hebrew, but staff are more than willing to translate the relevant details. For further

Hiking code of conduct

Water Few hikes have sources of potable (drinkable) water en route, so you must carry your own supply. The amount you carry will really depend upon the length of the hike and the season, though it should never be less than two litres per person (three litres per person is a better figure). A good way of carrying your water (and keeping it cool) is to buy a thermally insulated jacket that fits around a standard one-litre mineral water bottle. They are available in camping stores across Israel and generally keep water cool for up to six hours.

Clothing Comfortable footwear is essential. This does not necessarily mean walking boots, though the added ankle support is useful. A wide-brimmed hat is a must to help to prevent sun-burn, or worse sun-stroke. High protection factor sun-block must also be worn.

Season/timing The best time to hike depends upon the location, though in desert regions it is between October and April when the day-time temperatures are more manageable. In winter, however, there is the danger in some areas of flash floods. Hiking is not recommended if it looks like it is about to rain, or has rained in the past few days. If it rains whilst you are walking, avoid entering canyons or seemingly dry river beds. Always take local advice before commencing your trek. Hiking in summer is best avoided in the desert. High midday temperatures, even in winter, mean that you should make an early start, if necessary resting up during the middle of the day.

Routes The best routes are all marked by colour-coded trail markers. Stick to them. This not only offers you a degree of security, it also provides protection to the environment by controlling the activities of visitors.

Maps . The hiking maps provided within this book are for general information, and are not intended to serve as an alternative to the SPNI-prepared 1:50,000 hiking maps. If making an ambitious hike, you are strongly advised to buy the relevant sheet of the SPNI map. These generally cost around 85NIS and are available from most SPNI offices, particularly those in the larger towns. Unfortunately, only the Eilat area sheet has been translated from Hebrew into English, though staff at most SPNI offices and Field Schools are more than happy to translate the relevant data for you.

Expert advice SPNI offices and Field Schools offer expert advice, particularly on local areas, and you are well advised to make use of this free resource. Before attempting a particularly adventurous trek, it is worth 'clearing' it with the local SPNI Field School.

Security This aspect is particularly relevant if you are hiking alone (bad idea). Before commencing your trek, it is strongly advised that you leave details of your planned route and expected return time with somebody, for example the SPNI office or Field School, hostel or hotel manager. You should then 'check-in' with them when you return.

Environmental awareness There is a code of conduct to follow when hiking, some aspects of which are enshrined within Israeli law. In reserves and parks it is a requirement to stick to the marked trails. It is generally forbidden to pick, or even touch, plants and flowers. Swimming in most waterholes is usually forbidden. Camping and lighting of fires can only be done in designated areas. Carry out all your waste and be sure not to litter. The old maxim for hiking in Israel is "leave only footprints, take only photos".

information and accommodation booking, see www.aspni.org and www.teva.org.il.

Serious hikers should buy Ya'akov Shkolnik's *Hiking in Israel* with 36 selected hikes (2008, The Toby Press, available at most branches of Steimatsky Bookshops), or for treks in the Galilee get the new *Hiking the Jesus Trail* guidebook (2010, www.villagetovillage press.com) by Anna Dintaman and David Landis, also see box on page 670.

Horse-riding

This is available at a number of places, though notably in the Galilee and Golan region, see **Vered HaGalil**, just north of the Sea of Galilee, www.veredhagalil.com; for horse-riding trails above the dramatic crater of the Makhtesh Ramon in the Negev see the Alpaca Farm, www.alpaca.co.il; for some steep hills and Kinneret views visit the **Cowboy Ranch** in the Lower Golan, near Givat Yoav, T04-2419966, www.habokrim.co.il.

Skiing

Israel has 16 graded ski runs and 25 km of slopes at the **Mt Hermon Ski Centre** in Upper Golan. The skiing receives mixed reviews, though at least the option is there (between Dec and late Apr). See www.skihermon.co.il for a full price list.

Snorkelling and Snuba

Again, Eilat is the place in Israel for snorkelling. In fact, it can offer an even better means of viewing the coral reefs since they tend to grow relatively close to the surface (making diving unnecessary). A further alternative to diving is Snuba-ing, where the air supply remains on a floating raft on the sea's surface and is piped down to you. Eilat has a long-established centre for Snuba, at the South Beach near Taba, see www. snuba.co.il.

Watersports

A full range of watersports, from water-skiing, sailing, kayaking, wind-surfing, jet-skiing, and being towed along on an inflatable yellow banana, are all available in Eilat and at the Mediterranean coastal resorts.

Getting there

Air

The majority of visitors to Israel arrive by air. Most arrivals are at **Ben-Gurion Airport** (at Lod, some 22 km southeast of Tel Aviv), though some charter flights land at **'Uvda Airport** (60 km north of Eilat). Ben-Gurion Airport can get very crowded during holidays when it can take almost an hour to clear immigration on arrival. For further details on Ben-Gurion Airport, including getting there and away, see the box opposite.

At peak periods not only do air-fares rise dramatically, but it can also be difficult getting a flight in or out of Israel. Such peak periods include the time around Jewish and Christian holidays, plus the peak periods associated with school holidays in the country of the flight's origin. You are advised to book tickets for these periods well in advance.

Ben-Gurion Airport

General Ben-Gurion Airport is located at Lod, some 22 km southeast of Tel Aviv. For general 24-hour airport information call T03-9755555 or *6663, or see www. iaa.gov.il. Recorded information for departures/arrivals/transportation, T03-9723332, in English, 24 hours. All international flights arrive at Terminal 3, and the vast majority also depart from there, save for a couple of low-cost airlines which check in at Terminal 1. Domestic flights also depart/arrive from the old Terminal 1.

To/from the airport Trains go from Tel Aviv's four terminals to the airport, and are the only form of public transport to/from the city (buses leave from outside the airport grounds, a long impractical walk away). The train service operates 24 hours. From Hagana train station in Tel Aviv it is a short walk to the Central Bus Station, from where buses/sheruts 4 and 5 pass most of the hostels.

Sheruts (24 hours) are the only means of public transport to/from Jerusalem, leaving from outside the arrivals hall (Nesher, T03-9759555, 1 hour). For Haifa/the north there are 24-hr sheruts (Amal, T04-8662324, 1½ hours), or the train service through Tel Aviv carries on to northern destinations. Taxis are also available 24 hours, departing from the ground floor next to Gate 2.

Arrival formalities You have to fill out a landing card on arrival. Immigration will stamp this card and not your passport, but only if you ask in advance. The card is then taken from you after passport control, leaving you with no record of your entry date. This generally only poses a problem when you cross borders (to the West Bank, Egypt, Jordan) when Israeli security officials might ask where your stamp is. A phone call to an authority figure follows, and then you will be allowed to pass. Do not mention any travel plans to the West Bank if questioned on arrival at Ben-Gurion, as this will only arouse suspicion.

Departure formalities Ensure that you arrive no less than three hours before your flight departs. Be prepared for thorough questioning by the security staff before you check in (which can be lengthy). Bear in mind that this is done for your own safety. On exiting passport control, if you avoided an Israeli stamp when you arrived you can avoid getting one now, but only if you ask.

Airport facilities There are limitless opportunities for frenzied duty-free shopping upon arrival or departure. There is free Wi-Fi throughout Terminal 3. All the major car-hire firms have offices at the airport, most of which are open 24 hours. A number of companies offer cellular phone hire. Banks here do not offer the best deals: change just enough to tide you over until you can go to more competitive places in Tel Aviv or Jerusalem. VAT refunds are processed at the **Bank Leumi** in the Departures lounge. There's a post office and the **Buy & Bye** shopping area (including **Steimatzky** bookshop, cafés, restaurants) before exiting through passport control. Baggage storage facilities, T03-9754436, are found at the short-term car park, ground level, Sunday-Thursday 0800-1945, Fri 0800-1430, 20NIS per 24 hours.

Flights from the UK

A one-year open return can cost between £190 and £230 depending upon the season. Shorter stay tickets can be even cheaper. **British Airways** (BA; T03-606 1555; www.british airways.com), **Jet2** (from Manchester) and **EasyJet** (London Luton) offer cheap charter seats to Israel.

Flights from Europe

Discount flights to Israel can be picked up from most major cities in mainland Europe, though they tend to be slightly more expensive than flights from the UK. Airlines include **Air France**, www.airfrance.com; **Alitalia**, www.alitalia.it; **Austrian Airlines**, www.aua.com; **Iberia**, www.iberia.com; **KLM**, www.klm.com; **Lufthansa**, www.lufthansa.com. The cheapest deals tend to be with Eastern European airlines.

Flights from the USA and Canada

It is possible to fly to Israel from Atlanta, Chicago, Los Angeles, Miami and Toronto, though the best deals and widest choice of flights are from New York. There are several daily direct flights from New York's JFK to Israel with **El Al**, www.elal.co.il. There are also flights with **American Airlines**, www.aa.com; **United**, www.united.com; and **Air Canada**, www.aircanada.com. Look out for special deals, though don't expect much change from $800.

Flights from Australasia

Flying from Australia/New Zealand will require either stop-overs or plane changes. The cheapest deals are with the national carriers operating via Cairo, Athens or Rome, though expect to pay between A$1,700 and A$2,500 during the low season. A better deal may be to include Israel as part of a round-the-world ticket.

Flights from Egypt

There are flights between Tel Aviv and Cairo, operated by **Air Sinai**. There are also flights on **El Al** linking Ben-Gurion airport to Cairo (US$100 one way).

Flights from Jordan

Flights between Tel Aviv and Amman on **Royal Jordanian**, www.rj.com) go daily (around US$130 one-way). El Al offer a similar service.

Airline security

For obvious reasons, airline security on planes flying in and out of Israel is probably the tightest in the world. Whether you are flying in or out of Israel, you should check-in at least three hours prior to departure. El Al also use their own airline security staff abroad.

Prior to checking-in at Ben-Gurion or 'Uvda Airport to board a flight out of Israel, you will be questioned thoroughly by the airline security service. How long this cross-examination lasts depends upon a number of factors: your name and ethnic background, the stamps in your passport, your appearance, and where in Israel you admit to having been. Dave Winter's personal record is one hour and 55 minutes!

Road

Israel has land borders with Lebanon, Syria, Jordan and Egypt, though currently it is only possible to cross overland into the latter two. Information on all the border crossings can be found at www.iaa.gov.il.

Driving in Israel

No two ways about it, Israelis are aggressive drivers. Much pseudo psychological/philosophical rubbish is written to explain Israeli driving habits, generally focusing on the question of the impact of living in a place that is in a perpetual state of war (psychologically at least) with hostile neighbours. The simple truth is that many Israeli drivers are impatient, inconsiderate and downright dangerous.

Those who thought that Athenian and Parisian drivers were quick on the horn when traffic lights change to green are in for a shock here. And if you hire a car, be aware that under-taking is commonplace and watch out for people whipping past on the inside when you least expect it. Don't take this particular style of driving as a personal challenge or insult, but remain calm, safe and hyper-aware until you get used to the different rules of the road.

To/from Jordan

Jordanian visas can be obtained upon entry at most of Jordan's air, sea and land entry/exit points, though visitors arriving at the Allenby/King Hussein Bridge crossing from Israel will not be given visas on arrival. See 'The entry-exit stamp game' box for further notes on travelling in the region (see next page). Fees vary according to nationality. Visas issued at point of entry are valid for a period of two weeks, but can be easily extended in Amman. Alternatively, you can apply to the Jordanian Embassy in your own country. Security procedures for entering Israel from Jordan are very strict and it may take some time to cross the border. Israeli immigration will stamp entry-exit stamps on a separate piece of paper if you so request.

Jordan River Border Crossing/Jisr Sheikh Hussein This is located in the north, 6 km east of the Lower Galilee town of Bet Shean. Though the least-used of the three crossing points, it is actually closer to Jerusalem than the Arava crossing. Leaving Israel you will have to pay 98.5NIS departure tax. Jordanian visas are available on the border, and a Jordanian entry stamp will appear in your passport. From the Jordanian side, irregular service taxis run to Irbid and then on to Amman. Leaving Jordan, a JD departure tax must be paid and a Jordanian exit stamp will be entered in your passport (even if you previously entered via the Allenby/King Hussein Bridge crossing, where the entry stamp was put on a separate sheet of paper). There are currency exchange facilities on both sides of the border. Four buses per week (**Nazarene Tours**, T1-599-599-599, www.ntt-buses.com) run from the border to Afula and on to Nazareth; you need to book in advance. An over-priced taxi to Bet Shean will cost 30NIS. The crossing is officially open Sunday-Thursday 0700-2200, Friday-Saturday 0800-2000, closed on Yom Kippur and Jordanian holidays (though it's best to try and cross before 1700 on Friday-Saturday).

Allenby/King Hussein Bridge Closest to Jerusalem (16 km east of Jericho), there are special regulations in force at this crossing point. Leaving Israel, the departure tax is a staggering 163NIS (since both Israel and the Palestinian Authority collect a share). Jordanian visas are not available on the border, you must arrange them in advance. The Jordanian entry stamp will not be entered on your passport, but on a separate piece of paper. If you also leave Jordan through this crossing point, the only evidence of your visit to Jordan will be a visa (but no entry/exit stamps). If you leave Jordan through any other

The entry-exit stamp game

Anybody intending to travel beyond Israel into Arab and/or Muslim countries may like to avoid having Israeli entry and exit stamps in their passport. Fortunately, Israeli immigration officials are quite happy to assist here and will, on request, stamp a separate sheet of paper rather than your passport. This is fine if you fly in or out of Israel, though if you leave or arrive by land it is difficult to avoid an Egyptian or Jordanian entry-exit stamp. An entry stamp that says that you arrived in Egypt at Taba, for example, means that you can only have come from one place – Israel. In the wider world this is no great hassle, though it will almost certainly prevent you from ever using the same passport to get a Syrian, Lebanese or Sudanese visa (amongst others). Even entering Jordan through the Allenby/King Hussein Bridge, where

the Jordanian entry stamp is given on a separate piece of paper, does not appear to help matters. The Syrians will scan your passport for a Jordanian entry stamp, with the lack of one (presuming you've hidden the piece of paper) telling the Syrians where you have come from.

It helps to get such visas as far in advance as possible, preferably in your home country. Note that it is difficult to get a Syrian visa in Jordan, even if you have never been to Israel. If you do have Israeli or Israel-Jordan/Israel-Egypt entry/exit stamps, getting a new passport is one solution, though again, the Syrians, Lebanese and Sudanese are suspicious of new passports issued at embassies in Cairo and Amman. The easiest solution is to plan your trip carefully so that you visit Lebanon and Syria before Israel.

exit, you will get a Jordanian exit stamp in your passport. From the crossing point there are buses and taxis to Amman. Leaving Jordan, a JD departure tax must be paid. There are currency exchange facilities on both sides of the border. For details of transport between Jerusalem and this crossing point, see 'Transport' in the 'Jerusalem' chapter (page 193). The crossing is open Sunday-Thursday 0800-2330, Friday-Saturday 0800-1300, closed on Yom Kippur and Jordanian holidays, though aim to cross as early in the day as possible. Note that you cannot walk across the bridge (but have to pay an extortionate amount for a five-minute bus ride). Israelis are not permitted to cross at this border.

Yitzah Rabin/Arava Crossing This is located about 4 km north of Eilat on the Israeli side and 10 km northwest of Aqaba on the Jordanian side. From Eilat it can be reached by taxi (30NIS) or by bus (get dropped by the Eilot turning from where it's 1.5 km walk); see 'Transport' in the 'Eilat' section on page 362. The border is open Sunday-Thursday 0700-2200, Friday-Saturday 0800-2000, closed on Yom Kippur and Jordanian holidays. For details on crossing the border from the Israeli side, T08-6300555. If leaving Israel, a departure tax of 98.5NIS must be paid. Jordanian visas are available on the border and a Jordanian entry stamp will appear in your passport. If leaving Jordan, a JD departure tax must be paid and a Jordanian exit stamp will be entered in your passport (even if you previously entered via the King Hussein/Allenby Bridge crossing, where the entry stamp was put on a separate sheet of paper). There are currency exchange facilities on both sides of the border.

To/from Egypt
Rafah crossing This border crossing is closed to travellers indefinitely, so all overland travellers to Egypt go through Eilat/Taba at present.

Eilat/Taba crossing Tourists who intend visiting Sinai only need a 14-day Sinai permit, which is issued at the border crossing. Those wishing to travel beyond Sinai require a full tourist visa which must be arranged in advance in Tel Aviv or Eilat. It is easiest and quickest in Eilat, where it takes about 15 minutes (see page 363 for Egypt Consular details). The Eilat/Taba crossing is open 24 hours a day. For details on reaching the crossing point from the Israeli side, see under 'Transport' in the section on Eilat (and also page 362). The Taba bus station is less than 1-km walk from the border, on the left after the Moevenpick Hotel. Buses to Cairo leave at 1030 and 1430 (60LE), and for Sharm el-Sheikh/Suez at 1500. Mini-bus taxis also wait immediately after the border crossing. To Cairo they cost $100 (or 80LE per person if all 14 seats are taken); these are also useful for getting to destinations in Sinai if the bus times don't suit. Leaving Israel, you have to pay 98.5NIS departure tax, followed by 75LE Egyptian entry tax (paid on the bus at a checkpoint five minutes after leaving Taba bus station). You do not have to pay these taxes if you are just visiting the Taba Hilton casino. Leaving Egypt there is a 2LE departure tax (unless you have overstayed your visa which then costs 153LE). There are money-changers on both sides of the border, though rates to buy Egyptian LE are slightly better on the Egyptian side. Security procedures for entering Israel from Egypt are not particularly strict, but it still may take some time to cross the border. Israeli immigration will stamp entry-exit stamps on a separate piece of paper if you so request. For further details on the Israeli side, T08-6360999.

Mazada Tours ⓘ *141 Ibn Gvirol, Tel Aviv, T03-5444454; 9 Koresh, Jerusalem, T02-6235777, www.mazada.co.il, runs buses to Cairo on Sunday and Thursday, $90 single, $110 return, departs 0830, takes around 12 hours, prices exclude border taxes of $55.* Their Cairo office is at the Cairo Sheraton (T00202-33488600). Buses back to Israel are on Sunday and Thursday at 0800. Buses to Amman daily (minimum three persons required), each way $88, departs 0830, takes six hours, prices exclude border taxes of $49. Pick-up from both Tel Aviv and Jerusalem.

Private vehicles

For full details on bringing a private vehicle into Israel, check with your nearest Israeli embassy or tourist office. A *Carnet de Passage* is required.

Departure tax

Departure tax for foreigners flying out of Israel is incorporated in the ticket price, but leaving Israel for Egypt by land, foreigners must pay 98.5NIS departure tax at the Eilat/Taba crossing. Leaving Israel for Jordan by land, foreigners pay 98.5NIS departure tax at the Jordan Valley and Arava crossings, and 163NIS at the Allenby/King Hussein Bridge.

Getting around

Air

Given Israel's compact size, very few visitors travel around the country by air, though the domestic airline **Arkia** have flights connecting Eilat with Tel Aviv, Ben-Gurion and Haifa. For booking see www.arkia.co.il or call T09-8633480.

Rail

Israel State Railways run a limited passenger network, but for travel along the coast it is the quickest, easiest and most pleasant route. Many trains are express, meaning travel time between Tel Aviv and Akko, for example, is as short as 1 hour 20 minutes. Inland, train stations often tend to be inconveniently located away from the town centres (eg Lod). Fares are comparable with the bus service, though slightly more, and those with a student card get 10% discount, making it even more attractive.

The service between Tel Aviv and Jerusalem is slower than the bus, and the station in Jerusalem is inconveniently situated. The ride, however, is a pleasant one.

Road

Bicycle

Israel is an ideal country to explore by bicycle, though some careful planning is required. El Al does not charge extra for bringing a bike, see www.elal.com for details. Freewheeling down into the Jordan Valley basin and the Dead Sea Region is exhilarating; climbing back out on the road up to Jerusalem is not. Likewise, be prepared for some stiff climbs when exploring Upper Galilee and the Golan. The climate is also another major consideration, notably high day-time temperatures in summer, especially in the Negev and Dead Sea Region. Make an early start, rest up during the hottest part of the day, and carry and consume plenty of water. Most roads (particularly the main highways) have wide hard shoulders so you should be able to remain safe. It may also be possible to put your bicycle on a bus for longer/difficult journeys (at 50% of the passenger fare). Those who don't arrive in Israel with their own bicycle can pick up an 18-21 speed form of 'mountain bike' for around 400NIS (see under 'Shopping' in major cities). Look for bicycle itineraries on www.goisrael.com, and the **Israeli Cycling Federation**, www.ofanaim.org.il.

Bus

The **Egged Bus Company** provides the back-bone of the Israeli transport system, linking not just the major towns and cities but also all the remote villages, kibbutzim and moshavs. Because of the small size of the country, the longest journey you will conceivably undertake is five-six hours (Eilat to Haifa, or Jerusalem to Kiryat Shmona), and costs remain reasonable (under 80NIS for the two longest journeys). As a very general rule, Egged services operate from around 0530 until about 2230 Monday-Thursday. **NB** Remember that on Friday and on the eve of Jewish holidays, services stop at around 1500 and don't resume until sunset on Saturday. Plan your journey carefully if travelling at these times. Relying on the bus in the Negev, Golan and Dead Sea Region also requires careful planning since services are less regular.

Efficient bus information can be obtained by dialling *2800, and then pressing '9' or '0' to bypass the recorded message to a human voice. Keep requests simple – to/from, price, travel time – and you should have no problems. The helpful website, www.egged.co.il, takes a little getting used to but you will soon be familiar with it. Eilat is the only destination to which you can book advance tickets online. The information kiosks at the main bus stations have a very poor reputation for service, but often there is a free-phone booth in the bus station where an operator can provide you with immediate and accurate information. Large electronic boards give full details of all departures, including next and last bus and platform number. If travelling to remote areas (notably Negev, Golan and Dead Sea Region), double-check bus times.

Intra-city services around town are operated by **Egged**, though other companies also operate local services. **Dan Bus Company** (T03-6394444, www.dan.co.il) run the buses in/ around Tel Aviv; **Metropoline** (T5900*) operate around Be'er Shevam/Mizpe Ramon; Veolia (6686*) operate around Tiberias; **Nateev Express** and **Nazareth** (T1-599-599559) operate in the north; **Kavim** (T03-6066055) operate in the centre/north; and **Superbus** (T08-9205005) operate in the centre. Be warned: urban bus drivers will shut the doors and pull away as soon as everyone is deemed to be on board. Elderly passengers, the disabled and blind, and those carrying children, heavy shopping or backpacks are likely to be sent flying. The driver will then collect the fares and give change whilst weaving through the traffic.

Arab buses Travel around the West Bank starts with the Arab bus services operating mainly out of the bus stations opposite Jerusalem's Damascus Gate. As a rule of thumb, green and white buses leaving from the bus station on Nablus Street are heading north to Ramallah, while the blue and white buses leaving from the station on Sultan Suleiman Street go south to Bethlehem and Beit Jala. From Ramallah, you can change to services to Nablus, while from Bethlehem you can change to services to Hebron.

Car hire

Hiring a car in Israel makes a lot of sense, particularly for exploring the Negev and Upper Galilee and Golan areas where public transport connections are poor. When divided between two, three or four passengers, a hire car can be excellent value. All the major international rental agencies are represented in Israel, along with a number of local firms.

It pays to shop around, but you should also be clear as to what exactly it is that you are getting. Ask about insurance and mileage charges before you commit. As a very general rule of thumb, the cheapest cars cost about $30 per day including insurance. You only generally get unlimited mileage if you hire for three days or more. Check exactly what the insurance covers. Depending upon what time of year you visit, and where you intend going, think very seriously about getting a car with a/c. Most rental agencies require drivers to be over 21, though this rule is sometimes waived. You will require a clean (-ish) licence (international licence not generally necessary) and a credit card. You have to keep your passport, driving licence and rental agreement with you at all times when driving in Israel. It is usually possible to drive the car one-way and drop it off in a different city from where you rented it. Rental cars cannot be taken into Sinai (Egypt) or Jordan, whilst most Israeli agencies forbid you from taking the car inside the West Bank (as they are not insured for this). Those intending to travel extensively around the West Bank should consider hiring a car from a Palestinian agency (see entries under various West Bank towns and East Jerusalem).

Israeli traffic drives on the right-hand side of the road. It is compulsory for the driver and all passengers (including those in the back seats) to wear seat belts. Children under 14 must be seated in the back seat, and those under four must be strapped in to a suitable car seat. Urban speed limit is 50 kph (31 mph), and 90 kph (56 mph) on inter-city roads. On main arterial roads (eg Routes 1 and 4) 100 kph (62 mph) is permitted. It is compulsory in Israel to drive with headlights on at all times from 1 November to 31 March. Most traffic signs are self-explanatory, or similar to those used in Europe and North America. Other road regulations are similar. When in doubt, give way.

Regarding parking, where the kerb is painted red and white, parking and stopping is prohibited at any time. A blue-and-white painted kerb indicates parking permitted with a parking card (available from kiosks, post offices, etc) or by feeding a meter. Parking may be limited to one hour 0700-1700, though a sign should indicate this. Red-and-yellow painted kerbs are for buses and taxis only. Whenever possible, use a designated car park. Do not drive the wrong way in or out of a car park: the car trap will wreck your tyres.

Hitching

Hitch-hiking (*tremping*) remains a popular way of getting around Israel, especially in the Golan and the Negev where bus services are infrequent. As with any other country in the world, there are inherent risks attached. A number of measures can be taken to reduce these risks, such as never hitching alone and being selective about whom you get into a car with. It is strongly recommended that women should never hitch without male company. To hitch a ride point down to the road with your index finger (don't use the 'thumb' system used elsewhere).

Taxi

Taxis that operate around towns are metered, though fares are not particularly cheap. Israeli taxi drivers are like taxi drivers the world over: always keen to rip-off foreign tourists with tales of 'broken meters' and inflated fares. They are obliged to use their meters, so insist upon it, and even ask the name of the company and the driver if you suspect they might be 'trying it on'. Taxis can add a surcharge for a call out, for baggage, and may add 25% for night (2100-0530) and Shabbat services. It is possible to organize a 'special', whether for a tour around a particular town or a visit to a remote site that is poorly served by public transport. Be certain what the exact deal is (eg waiting time, etc), otherwise you are likely to be ripped off. Hotel and hostel receptionists, or the tourist office, may be able to give you some idea of what the fare should be.

Sherut An alternative to the intercity bus network is provided by the 'sherut' or service taxi network. They operate on fixed routes between towns for a fare only slightly more than the Egged bus fare (sometimes it is even less). The advantage is that this service is quicker, plus you can get out where you wish. These shared taxis do not run on a fixed schedule but depart when full, though it is surprising how quickly they fill up. In certain areas, service taxis are the only form of transport within or between towns on Shabbat.

In Tel Aviv, sheruts operate on the same route as certain buses, displaying the same number. Though costing marginally more than the bus, they can be hailed or stopped anywhere along the fixed route. Many also run on Shabbat (though the fare is 25% more).

Sleeping

Hotels

Israel has a very broad range of hotels and, as a general rule, the LL-L category hotels live up to their price tag, with facilities and service to match their 'luxury' pricing. Things can be a little more variable in the lower categories, with many of the hotels here holding themselves in too high esteem. If you are looking to stay in the 'top end' accommodation, it may be worth noting that the suites in some hotels offer very good value. For a guide to the classifications used, see box on next page or inside the front cover.

There are a number of considerations to bear in mind when booking/checking in to a hotel in Israel. Firstly, there is a huge variation in room charges according to the season. 'High' season generally coincides with Jewish and Christian religious festivals, and can see prices increase by between 25-50%! Note that the weekend (Friday-Saturday) is usually considered 'high' season.

Sleeping price codes

LL	over US$200	L	US$151-200
AL	US$101-150	A	US$66-100
B	US$46-65	C	US$31-45
D	US$21-30	E	US$12-20
F	US$7-11	G	under US$6

Price of a double room in high season, including taxes.

Despite this blatant rip-off, in some places (notably Eilat, Tiberias and Jerusalem) it can be hard to find a bed during the 'high' season. Most of the rest of the year is designated 'regular' season, with a couple of weeks of 'low' season when tourist bookings are slack. The classifications in this Handbook are for the 'regular' season. Note that the prices used here are spot/rack rates: if you book as a group or through a travel agency, you may be getting a significant discount. With all hotel classifications, look out for hidden taxes. An Israeli breakfast is included within the price at many hotels.

Remember that by paying in a foreign hard currency you avoid paying the 17% VAT. High-end hotel prices are almost always quoted in US dollars, and this is the preferred means of payment. Many hotels have specific characteristics that reflect the Jewish nature of Israel, such as in-house synagogues, Shabbat elevators (that stop at every floor and don't require buttons to be pressed) and kosher restaurants.

NB All accommodation in Israel (from five-star hotels down to backpacker hostels) is required by law to provide a free safe for depositing valuables.

Kibbutz guesthouses
Kibbutz guesthouses represent a relatively recent diversification by the beleaguered kibbutz movement. Almost all are located in rural environments, and on the plus side tend to be peaceful and quiet, well run, and with full access to kibbutz facilities such as swimming pools and private beaches, children's entertainment and restaurant/dining hall. The down side is that few are served by regular public transport.

Hospices
Christian hospices often provide excellent value. They are run by various denominations of the church and tend to be located close to major Christian pilgrimage sites. Advance reservations are recommended, and essential during major Christian holidays. They tend to be impeccably clean, though most have early curfews, early check-out times, and non-married couples might not be able to share a room. Half- and full-board deals can be good value.

Hostels
Jerusalem's hostels provide the cheapest accommodation in Israel (at $10-15), though generally you should expect to pay around $18-20 for dormitories in the other large cities. There is a big jump in price for double rooms, with the cheapest generally $45-$50. Some hostels in Israel allow you to sleep on the roof for less or give discounts for longer stays. Standards are highly variable. Dorm sizes vary between three and 46 beds, with some being single-sex and others mixed. Some hostels pride themselves on their 'party atmosphere', the idea being that they act as a meeting place for backpackers who want to go out and get drunk together.

A more than welcome addition to the hostelling scene is the **ILH organization**. This independent group of hostels/guesthouses has enrolled members whose beds are guaranteed to be clean, with a mix of dorm and private rooms, who nearly always provide kitchen facilities, have prices that are very fair and are in locations that are always interesting – and so might be the accommodation (in wood cabins, country kibbutzim or camel ranches). ILH hostels accommodate a range of budgets, are suitable for all ages, and are a good place to meet like-minded travellers, see www.hostels-israel.com. They are a real blessing for backpackers (and all independent travellers) in Israel.

You don't need to be a 'youth' to stay at any of Israel's Hostelling International (HI) hostels; in fact most have a number of family rooms. In some of the more remote places of interest, **IYHA** hostels provide the cheapest (or only) accommodation at about $30 per night. Without exception, they are spotlessly clean, offering a choice of spacious air-conditioned dormitories (usually single-sex); family rooms, sleeping four-eight; a/c; and private rooms; all with en suite shower. Sheets and blankets are provided. Breakfast is almost always included, and evening meals tend to be generous and reasonable value (but only available if enough people are staying). Bookings are recommended during holidays and weekends, though these hostels can get very noisy with kids at these times. For further details see www.iyha.org.il.

The **Society for the Protection of Nature in Israel** (SPNI) operates Field Schools throughout Israel, many of which have accommodation similar to IYHA hostels, though they are usually more basic, see www.aspni.org.

Camping

There are a number of fully equipped campsites in Israel, though they are only really for those who are dedicated to sleeping under canvas. Camping in a hostel grounds is cheaper than sleeping in a dorm and may be a good compromise. You can generally camp for free on beaches, though theft and security remain major risks. When trekking for a few days, 'wild' camping is an acceptable option (though of course you have to carry all your gear and camping equipment).

Private homes

Accommodation in private homes is available in a number of towns, notably Netanya, Nahariya, Safed, Eilat and Jerusalem. You can respond to advertisements in the paper, notes on the wall in hostels, or signs hung outside homes for rent, though it is recommended that you make enquiries through the local tourist office (who should have a list of licensed places). Daily rates vary from $40 to $60 per person, though weekly and monthly deals can be struck. Make sure that you see the place before handing over any money, and be sure that the deal is clear (eg heating, blankets, breakfast, etc).

Eating and drinking

Despite a common bond (Judaism) Israelis have a diverse cultural and ethnic background. Not surprisingly, therefore, the dining experience in Israel reflects this diversity. Dining out in Israel can, however, be an expensive business. The cheapest eating options are provided by the ubiquitous falafel and *shwarma* stands, though eating at these three times a day is neither good for your health nor morale. Expect to spend $20-$25 a day for une decent meal plus two 'street meals' (less – if you don't eat meat, and stick to falafel and pizza). Hostels with their own kitchens can reduce your food bill.

Eating price codes

ⵇⵇⵇ over US$30   ⵇ US$15-30   ⵇ under US$15

For a two-course meal for one person, excluding drinks or service charge.

Israel is (for those with a bit of money) a gastronomic paradise. Everyone you meet will recommend the best place in town to eat, and they usually know what they are talking about. Yes, it costs money, but the size of portion and the quality of the meal is way above what many visitors are used to. Diners in Israel can choose from a global menu, with Argentinean, Mexican, Italian, French, Chinese, Southeast Asian and Indian restaurants in the main cities. In many cases, the owners/chefs have strong links to the country that their restaurant claims to represent.

The staple of many Arab restaurants is barbecued meat on skewers (*shashlik*), *shwarma* (known elsewhere as doner kebab) and grilled chicken. Accompaniments include salad, falafel, hummus, bread, and possibly chips (fries), though put together these side dishes can provide a filling meal. One of the most delicious (and cheap) meals served in Israel is *fuul*: a plate of mashed fava beans served in garlic-flavoured oil with hummus and bread. More specialist dishes include *mansaaf*, usually a whole leg of lamb served on a bed of rice with nuts and lemon juice. A diet-busting Arab sweet dish, often served in Jerusalem's Old City for breakfast, is *kanafeh*, a mild cheese mixed with pistachios and baked in a honey syrup shell.

Budget eating

It is possible to eat on a budget in Israel, though it is very easy to fall into a predictable diet of nutritionally poor food. The backpacker staple, considered to be Israel's national dish, is the falafel. This comprises ground-up chickpeas blended with herbs and spices, rolled into balls and then deep fried. They are usually served stuffed into a pitta bread with *tahini* (a thin paste made from sesame seeds) and salad. Such a sandwich costs 6NIS for a half and about 10NIS for a full sandwich, or even 15NIS (depending upon where you buy it). At many such streetside stalls you do the salad-stuffing yourself. A variation of this is the *shwarma*, where the falafel balls are substituted by a form of processed lamb or turkey cut from a revolving spit. Blokes who go down the pub in England know such a dish as a doner kebab. It's funny how a dish that in some cultures would only be eaten after consuming 10 pints of lager can become a staple in others.

Traditional Jewish

Some dishes associated with the Ashkenazi, or Eastern European, Jewish immigrants include good old fashioned Hungarian goulash, Viennese schnitzel, chicken livers and gefilte fish. Perhaps more appealing are the Sephardi/Mizrachi, or 'Oriental', restaurants that are becoming more and more popular. Food here reflects the Sephardi roots in the Middle East, with many dishes such as the grilled meats and chicken being very similar to those found in Arab restaurants. Goose livers, baked sinia and stuffed vegetables are all specialities. Falafel (see 'budget eating' above) and hummus (a thick paste made from ground chickpeas, garlic, seasoning and tahini) are also served as side dishes.

Vegetarian

Vegetarians, though not necessarily vegans, are pretty well catered for in Israel, usually as a by-product of the kashrut dietary laws. In addition to the chain of 'dairy' restaurants that

Kosher

The eating habits of observant Jews are governed by the *kashrut* dietary laws laid down by God to Moses (*kosher* being the noun of *kashrut*). Given the standards of hygiene likely to have been practised at this time, many of them make good sense, particularly in the area of prevention of cross-contamination. Many people are familiar with the *kosher* prohibitions against eating pork and serving meat and dairy products at the same meal, though there is far more to the *kashrut* laws than just this.

Beasts that are clovenfooted and chew the cud can be eaten (*Leviticus 11:1-47*; *Deuteronomy 14:6-7*). Hence you can eat a cow, which fulfils this criteria, but not a camel (since it chews the cud but is not cleft-hooved). Conversely pigs, despite being clovenfooted, do not chew the cud and so are forbidden. Only birds that do not eat carrion can be considered 'clean', whilst fish must have fins and scales; thus shellfish is forbidden (*Deuteronomy 14:8-19*). However, to be considered *kosher*, animals have to be killed instantly and according to methods supervised by the religious authorities. Animals that

have died of disease, or in pain, are not considered *kosher*.

A *kosher* kitchen, whether in a restaurant or private home, will keep separate plates and dishes for cooking and serving meat and dairy products and will not serve the two together (*Exodus 23:19*; *Deuteronomy 14:14-21*). Such have been the culinary habits developed by Israelis over the years, however, you will not simply be given a black coffee to finish off your meal – a milk substitute will be provided. It is permitted for *kosher* restaurants serving dairy products also to serve fish.

Visitors should note that many restaurants (especially in Jerusalem) are closed on Shabbat, though - bar a few extreme cases - finding somewhere to eat should not be a problem. Note that a restaurant that offers a *kosher* menu will not be given a *kashrut* certificate if it prepares or serves food on Shabbat.

Despite the strict regulations regarding *kashrut* dietary laws, few visitors to Israel will be inconvenienced by them, whilst the dining experience of vegetarians will be positively enhanced.

can be found across Israel, Jerusalem and Tel Aviv have a number of notable restaurants that are preparing imaginative vegetarian dishes. In less cosmopolitan areas vegetarians may have to fall back on the tried and tested falafel and hummus formula, though many hotels prepare good-value eat-all-you-want breakfast salads.

Drink

You pay around $5-7 for a beer in a regular bar, though these prices can be almost halved if you look out for happy hours and backpacker-oriented bars.

It is still said that Israelis are not big drinkers, though the recent massive influx of Eastern Europeans into the country appears to have replaced one stereotype with another. The most popular locally produced beers are Goldstar (4.7%) and Maccabee (4.9%), the latter of which is considered marginally better. Locally brewed-under-licence Carlsberg, Tuborg and Heineken are readily available at similar prices. A half-litre glass in a regular bar will cost 18-22NIS, or 10-12NIS if you drink in one of the bars catering to the backpacker crowd. The German-style Ramallah-brewed Taybeh beer (see page 252) wins a lot of friends, though is not widely available outside of the West Bank.

A number of very good wines are produced in Israel, with notable labels coming from the Golan Heights Winery of Katzrin (see 'Lower Golan' on page 680), the Carmel Wine Cellars in Zichron Ya'akov (see 'North of Tel Aviv' on page 470) and the Carmel Winery in Rishon LeTzion (see 'South and southeast of Tel Aviv' on page 442). Imported wines tend to be expensive. A variety of spirits and fortified wines are also produced locally, with Israeli vodka renowned for its, er, cheapness.

Drinking coffee is a popular Israeli habit, with a wealth of cafés to choose from. Coffee served in Arab cafés tends to be the thick, bitter Turkish-style drink, complete with half a cup of sludge. It is usually served with a palate-cleansing glass of water. The tea served in Arab teahouses is particularly refreshing; it is served black, in a glass, often with a sprig of mint and plenty of sugar. Carbonated drinks are readily available. Expect to pay 6NIS for a can of Coke, while bottled water costs 4-5NIS for a litre (less in a big supermarket).

Entertainment

Bars, cafés and nightclubs

Rather than English-style pubs or American bars, Israel is much more at home with its European style café-bars. In addition to coffee and alcoholic drinks, most also serve light meals. In the more fashionable ones 'being seen' is as important as the quality of the food and drink. Tel Aviv has the greatest concentration of such places, though the rest of the country is catching up.

The larger cities all have a selection of nightclubs, though hotel nightclubs are rather staid and somewhat dull unless busy. Those aimed at holiday-makers (Israeli and foreign) are extremely variable (see 'Essentials' information in each town for the low-down). To really penetrate the 'Israeli scene' you need local contacts. Most of the 'happening' places are in rather remote locations (notably industrial estates on the edges of towns), and you probably won't find out about them unless you ask around locally (try record shops or 'trendy' bars). Entry is typically 100NIS, drinks are expensive, and most have a selective door policy (dress up).

Cinemas

Almost all towns of any size have at least one multi-screen cinema complex, with many US-produced films screened here before they are shown in Europe. Almost all non-Israeli films are shown with their original soundtrack, with Hebrew subtitles added. The diet is standard Hollywood stuff, though there are a few art-house cinemas in Jerusalem and Tel Aviv. Expect to pay around 35NIS to go to the cinema.

Israelis are great theatre- and concert-goers, though performances tend to be in Hebrew (sometimes with English subtitles), with the latest interpretation of Chekov, Beckett or Miller eagerly awaited. See 'Tel Aviv' and 'Jerusalem' sections for main theatre and concert hall listings, see the weekly English language newspapers for listings. The Palestinian al-Hakawati theatre group perform regularly in East Jerusalem.

Sport

Israelis are generally keen on sports, however, as a nation Israel is yet to really leave its mark on the sporting world stage (perhaps a reflection of its relatively small population).

The most popular spectator sports are basketball and football ('soccer'). Although Israeli sides have had some success in Europe with the former, they have regularly underachieved with the latter. Most towns of any size have a decent tennis centre, with the beach version, matkot, also being hugely popular. There is currently only one 18-hole golf course in Israel, and it's not cheap. For full details of activities such as hiking, skiing, diving, water-sports and horse-riding, see page 15.

Festivals and events

Holidays and religious festivals in Israel and the Palestinian Authority areas present a very confusing picture. Not only are there 'secular', Jewish, Christian and Islamic holidays, but the dates that they fall on are variously governed by the Hebrew lunar calendar, the solar Gregorian calendar, plus sightings of the new moon at Mecca! It should also be noted that the various branches of the Christian Church celebrate key events on different days.

Jewish holidays

Israel works on the lunar Hebrew calendar (as opposed to the solar Gregorian calendar), and thus all Jewish religious and secular holidays fall on different dates of the Gregorian calendar each year. However, they always remain at roughly the same time of year. Most of the main Jewish holidays fall within the autumn season ('fall'). Unless you are coming to Israel specifically to celebrate one of these holidays, this is a good time to avoid visiting. Transport, banks, offices, shops and restaurants are all affected, whilst accommodation can be difficult to find in spite of the sky-rocketing prices. If you are here for one of the major holidays (Rosh Hashanah, Yom Kippur, Sukkot, Pesach), plan ahead. For details of the Jewish Sabbath (Shabbat) see under 'Business hours' above. Dates are given here for 2010 (where appropriate), 2011 and 2012. The holidays below are listed in the order in which they occur during the Hebrew calendar year, and not in order of importance.

Rosh Hashanah

Rosh Hashanah celebrates the beginning of the Hebrew calendar year, though it is also a time of introspection as religious Jews examine their conduct over the previous 12 months. Because it is the only holiday in Israel that lasts for 2 consecutive days, it is considered to be the main vacation period.

It is celebrated on the 1st and 2nd of Tishri. 2010: Sep 9-Sep 10; 2011: Sep 29-Sep 30; 2012: Sep 17-18.

Yom Kippur

This is the holiest day of the year and the most important date in the Hebrew calendar. It marks the end of 10 days of penitence and moral introspection that began with Rosh Hashanah, and finishes with God's judgement and forgiveness: the Day of Atonement. Yom Kippur is characterized by a sunset to sunset fast that is usually observed by even the most 'secular' Israelis. Virtually everything in Israel closes down for Yom Kippur and the roads are totally empty. Since 1973 it has also acted as an unofficial memorial day, commemorating those who died in the surprise war that the Egyptians and Syrians launched on that date. It takes place on the 10th of Tishri. 2010: Sep 18; 2011: 8 Oct; 2012: 26 Sep.

Sukkot

Sukkot commemorates the 40 years spent wandering in the wilderness after the Moses-led Exodus out of bondage in Egypt. Many Jews recreate the succah, or moveable shelter, in which the Israelites lived during their wanderings, taking all their meals there for a period of 7 days. Small plywood structures with a roof of loose thatch and branches are built in courtyards,

Months of the Hebrew calendar

Tishrey (Sep/Oct); **Cheshvan** (Oct/Nov); **Kislev** (Nov/Dec); **Tevet** (Dec/Jan); **Shvat** (Jan/Feb); **Adar** (Feb/Mar, Adar bet in a leap year); **Nisan** (Mar/Apr); **Iyar** (Apr/May); **Sivan** (May/Jun); **Tamuz** (Jun/Jul); **Av** (Jul/Aug); **Elul** (Aug/Sep).

on balconies, in gardens, on roof-tops, and in corners of rooms, all across the country. Many hotels also build a symbolic succah in reception. An oft-told story, said to derive from a case in the United States, tells how a Jew who had built a succah on his balcony was taken to court by a bigoted neighbour, who claimed it was an eye-sore. The judge (who was himself Jewish) found in the plaintiff's favour, ordering the Jew to remove the structure within 7 days! Sukkot is often referred to as the Feast of Tabernacles. Zionist tradition associates Sukkot with the celebration of the Harvest Festival. It takes place on the 15th to 21st of Tishri. **2010:** 23-29 Sep; **2011:** 13-19 Oct; **2012:** 1-7 Oct.

Simchat Torah

This is probably the only Jewish religious holiday in Israel that has no accompanying Zionist tradition. It celebrates the giving of the Torah (first five books of the Bible: *Genesis, Exodus, Leviticus, Numbers, Deuteronomy*); literally the Rejoicing of the Law. It falls 1 week after Sukkot, at the end of Tishri. **2010:** 1 Oct; **2011:** 21 Oct; **2012:** 9 Oct.

Hanukkah

Not an official public holiday, since it does not mark an event mentioned in the Torah, Hanukkah celebrates the Maccabean Revolt that began in the 2nd century BCE when the Jews rose up against the pagan reforms of the dominant Hellenistic culture. The revolt culminated in a return to Jewish self-rule under the Hasmonean dynasty (c.152-37 BCE). Hanukkah is celebrated by the nightly ceremonial lighting of the menorah, or 7-branched candelabra, and is thus often known as the Feast or Festival of Lights. British readers who used to watch Blue Peter

at Christmas will understand. It falls during Kislev. **2010:** 2-9 Dec; **2011:** 21-28 Dec; **2012:** 9-16 Dec.

Tu B'Shevat

This is not a public holiday, though in recent years it has been used as an occasion for tree-planting. Its origins are in the Mishnah, when the 'New Year for Trees' was celebrated by eating fruit and nuts. **2011:** 20 Jan; **2012:** 8 Feb.

Purim

Purim is probably the most bizarre holiday in the Hebrew calendar. It celebrates events in ancient Persia when the Jews were sentenced to death for refusing to bow to the secular authority. Their main persecutor was a man named Haman, though eventually it was Haman whom the authorities executed, whilst the Jews were left unmolested. For some reason Purim, or the Feast of Lots, has been turned into a sort of Jewish Halloween, with children dressing up and adults encouraged to get uncharacteristically drunk. **2011:** 20 Mar; **2012:** 8 Mar.

Pesach

Pesach, or Passover, celebrates the Exodus out of Egypt. The festival lasts for a whole week and, even though only the first and last days are official public holidays, many shops (including food stores) close for the entire 7 days. Be prepared. During the Israelites' escape from Egypt, the Bible recalls how there wasn't even time for them to wait for their bread to be baked. As a symbolic gesture, no products containing yeast or other leavening agents are eaten. Anyone spending Pesach in Israel will have to content themselves with a special unleavened bread called *matzah*, a rather tasteless substitute in most people's minds. Even McDonald's produces a special bun! The Passover meal also has a symbolic significance in the Christian tradition. Pesach is celebrated from the 15th to 21st of *Nisan*. **2011:** 19-25 Apr; **2012:** 7-13 Apr.

Mimouna

This takes places on the 22nd of *Nisan*, the day after the last day of Pesach. It is only really celebrated by Sephardi Jews, noticeably those from North Africa, and, though its exact origin is unclear, it is a good excuse for a party – usually in the form of a big barbecue. **2011:** 26 Apr; **2012:** 14 Apr.

Lag B'Omer

Lag B'Omer is really a multiple celebration. Taking place on the 18th of *Iyar*, it marks the end of a 33-day period of mourning and represents a sort of rite of spring when a plague was lifted from the Jewish nation. There's really only one place to celebrate this event, and that's at the Tomb of Rabbi Shimon bar Yochai at Meiron, near Safed (see 'Galilee' section for full details). His teachings in the 2nd century CE were compiled into printed form some 1100 years after his death, with Lag B'Omer also used as a celebration of the giving of this *Zohar*, or central text of kabbalah. **2011:** 22 May; **2012:** 10 May.

Shavuot

In its original form, Shavuot commemorated the 7 weeks that it took the Israelites to reach Mt Sinai, and is thus something of a celebration of the receiving of the Torah. In Hebrew shavuot means 'weeks', though many readers will know this festival as the Jewish Pentecost. Under the Zionist influence of the early kibbutzniks, however, Shavuot has come to represent something of a celebration of the productive capability of the land, and is often referred to as the 'kibbutz holiday'. It takes place on the 6th of *Sivan*. **2011:** 8-9 Jun; **2012:** 27-28 May.

Tisha B'av

This is a solemn occasion commemorated mainly at the Western Wall in Jerusalem. It remembers the occasions upon which the First and Second Temples were destroyed. It falls on the 9th of *Av*. **2011:** 9 Aug; **2012:** 29 Jul. Some observant Jews also fast on the 17th of *Tamuz*, the date upon which the Romans destroyed Jerusalem's city walls.

Israeli 'secular' holidays

Yom HaSho'ah (Holocaust Memorial)

Since 1951, the 27th of *Nisan* has been set aside as a day to remember both the victims of the Holocaust and the heroes of the Jewish resistance. Its official title is in fact Memorial to the Holocaust and the Heroism. At 11 o'clock sharp a siren is heard throughout the country, signalling all traffic (human and vehicular) to stop whilst 2 minutes of silence is observed. It really is a very unusual (and moving) sight, particularly if you are on a normally busy street at the time. Israeli television broadcasts a special service from Yad VaShem. Note that most businesses and places of entertainment close the evening before. **2011:** 27 Jan; **2012:** 27 Jan.

Yom Ha'Atzmaut (Independence Day)

David Ben-Gurion declared Israel's independence on 14 May 1948. Or rather he declared it on the 5th day of the month of *Iyar*. Every 19 years the event can be celebrated on the same day, though otherwise the Hebrew calendar is used. Note that most businesses and places of entertainment close the evening before. **2011:** 9 May; **2012:** 26 Apr.

May Day

May Day reflects the socialist leanings of the early Zionists, though International Labour Day is now only celebrated on some kibbutzim (1 May).

Christian holidays

All the major Christian festivals are celebrated in Israel, though none are official public holidays; Israeli life proceeds as normal. The key festivals are celebrated on different dates by the 'Eastern' Orthodox, 'Oriental' Orthodox and 'Western' Churches ('Latin' ie Roman Catholic, and Protestant).

Christmas

Christmas Day is celebrated on **25 Dec** by the 'Western' Church, with the highlight being the midnight mass held at the Church of the Nativity in Bethlehem on the night of Christmas Eve (**24th**). For full details see the 'Bethlehem' section. The Orthodox ('Eastern') Church celebrates Christmas on **7 Jan** (except Greek Orthodox which also uses 24-25 Dec) whilst the Armenian Christmas falls on **19 Jan**. These dates remain consistent.

Easter

Easter is celebrated on different dates by the 'Western' Church, 'Oriental' and 'Eastern' Orthodox Churches, with the date also changing from year to year. 'Good Friday' commemorates the Crucifixion, with impressive crowds walking the Via Dolorosa. 'Easter Sunday' (two days later) celebrates the Resurrection. Note that the Orthodox 'Holy Saturday' is the day when the 'Miracle of the Holy Fire' is celebrated (arguably Jerusalem's most intense Christian celebration). 2011: 'Western' Good Friday, 22 Apr; 'Eastern' Orthodox Good Friday, 22 Apr (note that they both fall on the same day, which will be intense); 2012: 'Western' Good Friday, 6 Apr; 'Eastern' Orthodox Good Friday, 13 Apr.

Feast of the Annunciation

This festival celebrates the revelation by the archangel Gabriel to the Virgin Mary that she was pregnant with Jesus. The most spectacular celebration is held at the Basilica of the Annunciation in Nazareth (25 Mar).

Other

For details of various Christian festivals and holidays contact **Christian Information Centre** (Catholic), PO Box 14308, opposite Citadel, Jaffa Gate, Jerusalem, T02-6272692, www.cicts.org, and **Franciscan Pilgrim Office** (same location), T02-6272697.

Muslim holidays

The Islamic calendar

The Islamic calendar begins on 16 July 622 AD, the date of the *Hijra* ('flight' or 'migration') of the Prophet Mohammad from Mecca to Medina in modern Saudi Arabia, which is denoted 1 AH (Anno Hegirae or year of the Hegira). The Islamic or Hijri calendar is lunar rather than solar, each year having 354 or 355 days, meaning that annual festivals do not occur on the same day each year according to the Gregorian calendar.

The 12 lunar months of the Islamic calendar, alternating between 29 and 30 days, are; *Muharram, Safar, Rabi-ul-Awwal, Rabi-ul-Sani, Jumada-ul-Awwal, Jumada-ul-Sani, Rajab, Shaban, Ramadan, Shawwal, Ziquad* and *Zilhaj*. To convert a date in the Hijra calendar to the Christian date, express the former in years and decimals of a year, multiply by 0.970225, add 621.54 and the total will correspond exactly with the Christian year!

Ras as-Sana/Al-Hijra

(Islamic New Year) 1st *Muharram*. The first 10 days of the year are regarded as holy, especially the 10th. 2010: 5 Apr; 2011: 26 Nov; 2012: 15 Nov.

Moulid an-Nabi

Birth of the Prophet Mohammad: 12th *Rabi-ul-Awwal*. 2011: 15 Feb; 2012: 4 Feb.

Leilat al-Meiraj

Ascension of Mohammad from the Haram al-Sharif in Jerusalem: 27th *Rajab*. 2011: 28 Jun; 2012: 16 Jun.

Ramadan

The holiest Islamic month, when Muslims observe a complete fast during daylight hours. Businesses and Muslim sites operate on reduced hours during Ramadan. 21st *Ramadan is the Shab-e-Qadr* or 'Night of Prayer'. 2010: 11 Aug-10 Sep; 2011: 1-30 Aug; 2012: 20 Jul-19 Aug.

Eid el-Fitr

Literally 'the small feast'. 3 days of celebrations, beginning 1st *Shawwal*, to mark the end of Ramadan. 2010: 10 Sep; 2011: 30 Aug; 2012: 19 Aug.

Eid el-Adha

Literally 'the great feast' or 'feast of the sacrifice'. 4 days beginning on 10th *Zilhaj*. The principal Islamic festival, commemorating Abraham's sacrifice of his son Ismail, and coinciding with the pilgrimage to Mecca. Marked by the sacrifice of a sheep, by feasting and by donations to the poor. 2010: 17 Nov; 2011: 6 Nov; 2012: 26 Oct.

Palestinian 'secular' holidays

There are a number of dates that are celebrated as 'secular' holidays in Palestinian areas, some of which have been designated public holidays by the PA (marked with an asterisk).

Fatah Day 1 Jan*
Jerusalem Day 22 Feb
Palestinian Land Day 30 Mar
Deir Yassin Day 19 Apr
Black September Day 18 Sep
Balfour Day 2 Nov
Independence Day 15 Nov
UN Palestine Day 29 Nov

Shopping

There's a saying along the lines of "you have to kiss a lot of frogs to find a prince". Something similar could be said with regard to shopping in Israel. Most visitors to Israel seek some sort of **souvenir** of their visit to the Holy Land, though you will have to wade through piles of pilgrim/tourist junk before you find that gem. There's some real *Life of Brian* stuff on offer, including your very own crown of thorns. Another perennial favourite is the 3-D effect picture that is Jesus at one angle, the Virgin Mary at another angle, and the Virgin Mary with a beard if held somewhere in the middle. It is worth seeking out a plastic model of the Dome of the Rock whose alarm clock wakes you up with a blast of "Allah oh-Akhbar". Jerusalem's Old City remains the main centre for the mass-produced pilgrim trash, though there are some nice pieces there if you look hard enough. Some of the **ceramic** work, **copper** and brassware, and **Judaica** is quite interesting. If you can afford them and know what you are dealing with, there are some fabulous icons on sale. Haggling (bargaining) is an integral part of the buying process.

Tel Aviv, Netanya and Tiberias all have showrooms where you can indulge your passion for **diamonds**, whilst Eilat is renowned for its 'gems'. Be careful. As a general rule, anything that Israel exports will be cheaper in your home country, whilst anything that is available in Israel and your own country will be cheaper at home. If buying expensive luxury items, look out for shops participating in the 'VAT refund for tourists' scheme (see page 44).

The Steimatzky chain is the best source of English-language **books**, though prices tend to be more expensive than in the UK and USA at least. Israelis are in fact second on the worldwide list of book readers, despite the prices. There is, however, a wide range of material on Judaism, Israeli and Palestinian culture, and the Arab-Israeli conflict. Second-hand bookshops in Tel Aviv and Jerusalem (listed under Essentials in the relevant chapters) are a good place to source cheap English fiction.

National parks and nature reserves

Most of Israel's key archaeological and scenic attractions are enclosed within national parks and nature reserves, managed by the **Israel Nature and Parks Authority** (www.parks.org.il). Entrance to these is usually between 20-30NIS for an adult.

If you intend visiting more than five national parks within a 14-day period, it makes sense to buy the **Green Card**. Costing 130NIS, in theory you can visit all 65 national parks once, as long as you can do so within a two-week period. Alternatively (and more realistically) you can buy entrance for six sites of your choice for 90NIS. The Green Card is available from the Parks Authority head office, 3 Am Ve'Olamo Street, Givat Shaul Jerusalem, T*3639, F02-5005471, or at the 'major' national parks. For up-to-date information on fees, email moked@npa.org.il.

Responsible travel

Bargaining

Israel provides almost unlimited shopping potential, particularly in the field of 'souvenirs' for pilgrims/tourists looking for some memento of their visit to the Holy Land. Much of the stuff is garbage, and much is concentrated in Jerusalem's Old City, where nothing has a price tag and you are expected to haggle a deal. There is great potential for the tourist to be heavily ripped off. Most dealers recognize the gullibility of travellers and start their offers at an exorbitant price. The dealer then appears to drop his price by a fair margin but remains at a final level well above the local price of the goods.

To protect yourself in this situation be relaxed in your approach. Talk at length to the dealer and take as much time as you can afford inspecting the goods and feeling out the last price the seller will accept. Do not belittle or mock the dealer; take the matter seriously but do not show commitment to any particular item you are bargaining for by being prepared to walk away empty handed. Also, it is better to try several shops if you are buying an expensive item such as a carpet or jewellery. This will give a sense of the price range. Walking away from the dealer normally brings the price down rapidly.

Clothing

Israelis tend to dress informally, particularly in Tel Aviv, Eilat and the coastal resorts. A highly visible exception to this rule are the ultra-orthodox Jews, who dress as per the Eastern European Jewish community of the 18th century. As mentioned elsewhere, visitors to Israel (both men and women) should be prepared to dress conservatively when visiting Arab areas, ultra-orthodox Jewish neighbourhoods, and religious and holy sites of any creed. Though light, loose-fitting cottons are excellent for the summer heat, you should bring some sort of jumper whichever season you visit, and cold weather gear if visiting Jerusalem at Christmas.

Conduct

Without descending into stereotypes, there are aspects of the Israeli psyche that often take foreign visitors some getting used to. A rare thing in Israel is a polite standard of service in shops, post offices, banks, and even some tourist information offices and hotels. Likewise, queuing at bus stops, holding doors open and saying 'please' are just not part of the Israeli make-up. There are lots of witticisms floating around that are supposed to sum up the Israeli personality (eg two Israelis in a room means three different opinions), though the reference that native-born Israelis prefer for themselves is sabra – the cactus fruit that is tough and thorny on the outside but remarkably sweet on the inside.

The rules of conduct that most affect foreign visitors to Israel concern visits to holy places, ultra-orthodox Jewish neighbourhoods and Arab areas. The modest dress that you should adopt when visiting such places is discussed elsewhere, though there are a few other rules of etiquette that should be remembered. When visiting mosques, remember to remove shoes before entering. Women are generally permitted entry, though they should cover their heads. In synagogues, both men and women are required to cover heads. In churches, it's hats off for men. Public displays of affection at any religious site should be completely avoided.

Photography

Ultra-orthodox Jews dislike having their photograph taken. Ask first, and be prepared for a refusal. Carrying cameras in certain areas on Shabbat is 'forbidden' (Western Wall, Mea She'arim, Safed). Arab women also dislike being photographed. Again, ask first and be prepared to be disappointed. Soldiers in uniform are an exception to this rule; however, be wary of taking photos of Israeli soldiers in confrontational situations with Palestinians.

Essentials A-Z

Accident and emergency

Medical emergency: T101 (Hebrew) or T911 (English). A special medical helpline for tourists can be reached on T177-0229110. **The Jerusalem Post** carries a daily list of late-night and all-night pharmacies. **Police**: T100. **Fire**: T102.

Children

Children rule the roost in Israel and seem to be ever present. They are frequently taken to restaurants and cafés, so most places have high chairs and changing facilities. Many museums provide activities aimed at children and youth (particularly science museums) as they are used to entertaining school groups. There are playgrounds in every park, and of course beaches, nature reserves and numerous subterranean caverns and tunnels that kids will enjoy. Only very few hotels say no to hosting children. They are also very welcome in the Palestinian Territories, especially seeing as they are such infrequent visitors there.

Customs and duty free

Persons over the age of 17 are each allowed to bring in duty free 1 litre of spirits, 2 litres of wine, 250 cigarettes or 250 g of tobacco, and personal gifts up to the value of $200. You may have to declare video equipment, personal computers and diving equipment, and pay a deposit, which is refunded when you re-export the goods. Do not lose the receipt.

There are no restrictions on the amount of foreign and local currency that you can bring into Israel.

Prohibited items

It is prohibited to bring fruit and vegetables, plants, fresh meat, animals and firearms into Israel.

Disabled travellers

Israel makes more attempt to cater to disabled visitors than most 'Western' countries, though that's not really saying much. Because visitors to Israel are often elderly pilgrims, most hotels have access ramps and wheelchair-friendly lifts. Many hotels and guesthouses have rooms specially designed for the disabled. A great deal of effort has been made to make many archaeological sites wheelchair accessible, and some national parks (eg Gamla, Tel Dan) have trails that are suitable for wheelchairs. The public transport system remains largely off-limits, however. In the Palestinian Territories it is much harder for disabled travellers, as pavements are more crowded and the land is generally much more hilly, although by travelling in a hire car you will be able to pass through checkpoints without having to disembark. A useful guide is the **Access Project** (PHSP) website, which has a page on Israel, see www.accessproject-phsp.org. Also see **Access Israel**, www.access-israel.com, and Access Unlimited, www.access-unlimited.com, which both give excellent information on where and what is accessible.

Drugs

Possession of narcotics in Israel is illegal and those caught in possession risk prison and/or deportation. That said, they are widely available, should you be looking. Given the thoroughness of Israeli security checks, attempting to bring drugs into the country is even more foolish than it would be in normal circumstances.

Electricity

220 volts, 50 cycle AC. Plugs are of the round 2-pin variety. Adapters can be bought, though they are probably cheaper in your home country.

Embassies and consulates

See www.mfa.gov.il for the websites of further embassies and consulates overseas.

Australia, 6 Turrana Ave, Yarralumla, Canberra, ACT 2600, T61-2-62154500, http://canberra.mfa.gov.il.

Canada, 50 O'Conner St, Suite 1005, Ottawa, Ontario KIP 6L2, T613-5676450, http://ottawa.mfa.gov.il; 1 Westmount Sq, Suite 650, Montreal, Quebec H3B 4S5, T514-9408500, http://montreal.mfa.gov.il; 180 Bloor St West, Suite 700, Toronto, Ontario M5S 2V6, http://toronto.mfa.gov.il.

France, 3 Rue Rabelais, 75008 Paris, T01-40765500, http://paris1.mfa.gov.il.

Germany, Auguste-Viktoria Str 74-76, Berlin 14193, T30-89045500, http://berlin.mfa.gov.il.

Ireland, Carrisbrook House, 122 Pembroke Rd, Ballsbridge, Dublin 4, T01-2309400, http://dublin.mfa.gov.il.

Netherlands, 47 Buitenhoff, The Hague 2513 AH, T70-3760500, http://thehague.mfa.gov.il.

New Zealand, BD Tower, The Terrace 111, PO Box 2171, Wellington, T04-4722362.

South Africa, 428 Kings Highway, Lynnwood, Pretoria, T012-470-3500, http://pretoria.mfa.gov.il.

UK, 2 Palace Green, London, W8 4OB, T0207-9579500, http://london.mfa.gov.il.

USA, 3514 International Drive NW, Washington DC 20008, T202-3645500, www.israelemb.org, plus 9 other consulates.

Gay and lesbian visitors

Israel's GLBT scene is actively marketed by the Tel Aviv tourist board, so popular is Tel Aviv as a destination. Information on gay and lesbian issues, as well as tourist activities, can be found at www.glbt.org.il. Remember that in conservative religious areas (whether Muslim or Jewish) homosexuality is not accepted.

Health

See your GP or travel clinic at least 6 weeks before departure for general advice on travel risks and vaccinations. Make sure you have sufficient medical travel insurance, get a dental check, know your own blood group and, if you suffer a long-term condition such as diabetes or epilepsy, obtain a Medic Alert bracelet/necklace (www.medicalert.co.uk). Also, get advice from your doctor and carry sufficient medication to last the full duration of your trip. You may want to ask your doctor for a letter explaining your condition. If you wear glasses, take a copy of your prescription.

Travellers should consider carrying a small first-aid kit that contains such basic items as headache treatments (eg Paracetamol), preparatory treatments for diarrhoea such as Loperamide (eg Imodium, Arret), oral rehydration proprietary preparations (ORS), plus sticky plasters and corn plasters (eg Band Aid). A good insect repellent may also come in handy, particularly those with around a 40-50% concentration of Diethyltoluamide (DET). There are also repellents available that use more natural ingredients. All of these items are available in Israel, though you will probably find that they are cheaper at home.

Vaccinations
Confirm your primary courses and boosters are up to date. It is advisable to vaccinate against diphtheria, tetanus, poliomyelitis, hepatitis A and typhoid. Other vaccinations that may be advised are hepatitis B and rabies.

Health risks
The standard of healthcare in Israel is very high (it leads the world in some fields). There are no special health precautions that visitors should take, except to avoid **dehydration** and **sunburn/stroke**. A wide-brimmed hat plus high-factor sun-cream should be worn as protection against the sun, whilst 4 litres of water should be drunk per day to avoid dehydration. Dark-coloured urine, perhaps coupled with a feeling of lethargy, is often a sign of dehydration. Tap water in Israel is safe, though the delivery system in the Old City of Jerusalem may be questionable. Bottled water is widely

available. Sunglasses with 100% UV protection are a must. Note that not all clothes offer protection against the sun. As a general rule of thumb, if you can see through it when you hold it up to the light, then you can burn through it.

Travellers continuing on to countries such as Egypt should arrange **malaria** prophylaxis (prevention) before leaving home. Remember that most courses must be started 2 weeks before arriving in the infected area, and continued for 4 weeks after leaving. Consult your doctor or travel clinic.

If swimming or diving in an area where there are poisonous fish such as stone or scorpion fish (also called by a variety of local names), sea urchins on rocky coasts, or coral, tread carefully or wear plimsolls. The **sting** of such fish is intensely painful but can be helped by immersing the stung part in water as hot as you can bear for as long as it remains painful. This is not always very practical and you must take care not to scald yourself. It is highly recommended that you take immediate local medical advice in order to ascertain whether any coral or sting remains in the wound. Such injuries take a long time to heal and can be liable to infection. The main diving resorts in Israel (and across the Egyptian border in Sinai) have medical facilities equipped to deal with diving accidents.

If you get sick
Contact your embassy or consulate for a list of doctors and dentists who speak your language, or at least some English. Doctors and health facilities in major cities are also listed in the Directory sections of this book. Make sure you have adequate insurance (see below).

Useful websites
www.btha.org British Travel Health Association.
www.cdc.gov US government site that gives excellent advice on travel health and details of disease outbreaks.

www.fco.gov.uk British Foreign and Commonwealth Office travel site has useful information on each country, people, climate and a list of UK embassies/consulates.
www.fitfortravel.scot.nhs.uk A-Z of vaccine/health advice for each country.
www.numberonehealth.co.uk Travel screening services, vaccine and travel health advice, email/SMS text vaccine reminders and screening returned travellers for tropical diseases.

Insurance

It is strongly recommended that you take out insurance, in particular health insurance. Health care in Israel is of a high standard, and the costs are equally high. Receiving the bill from a night's stay in hospital may induce an instant relapse! Check exactly what your medical cover includes, eg ambulance, helicopter rescue or emergency flights back home.

When you take out travel insurance, make sure that it is a policy that suits your needs. Whilst many policies that cover theft appear to offer comprehensive coverage, they have very low ceiling limits on individual items (often limited to £250). If you are carrying expensive equipment you may need to get separate cover for those items unless they are covered by existing home contents insurance.

Check for exclusions such as diving, skiing, mountain biking and even hiking. Also check the payment protocol. You may have to pay first before the insurance company reimburses you. Always carry with you the telephone number of your insurer's 24-hr emergency helpline and your insurance policy number.

A policy where the insurance company pays the bill direct (rather than you paying, then claiming back the fees later) is probably a better deal, though generally more expensive. Keep all receipts for any treatment that you receive.

Internet

Given Israel's contribution to the world of computer technology, there are in fact remarkably few cyber cafés in the country (everyone has a computer at home). Most of the major cities have a few, with the going rate being around 8NIS for 30 mins and 12NIS for 1 hr. Perhaps as a reflection of their perceived isolation, Palestinians have really taken to the internet and its potential for access to the outside world. Cyber cafés are springing up in all the major Palestinian towns, and at a very competitive price too (4NIS per hour in most places).

Language

If the State of Israel represents the in-gathering of the Jewish people from the Diaspora, then the Hebrew language represents one of the main unifying factors. In fact, the very pronunciation of modern Israeli Hebrew (a compromise between Sephardi and Ashkenazi elements) symbolizes its unifying influence.

For several thousand years Hebrew was just used for Jewish liturgy. Indeed, there are some elements in Israeli society (most notably the ultra-orthodox community from Eastern Europe) who believe that it is blasphemous to use Hebrew outside of liturgy, and thus they continue to use native tongues (frequently Yiddish). The modern usage of Hebrew was revived largely through the efforts of Eliezer Ben Yehuda (1858-1922), with the modern Hebrew movement becoming appended to the early Zionist movement. Theodor Herzl is alleged to have wistfully remarked, "Can you imagine buying a train ticket in Hebrew?".

Hebrew is a West Semitic language related to Assyrian and Aramaic. As a general rule, an Israeli could read a Hebrew Bible with relative ease, whilst someone brought up on biblical Hebrew would have some difficulty reading an Israeli newspaper.

The second most widely spoken language in Israel and the Palestinian Territories is Arabic. It belongs to a branch of the southwestern branch of the Semitic language group, though there are a number of different dialects.

Road signs in Israel are almost always written in Hebrew and English, and in most areas Arabic too. English is widely spoken and understood, particularly by those involved in the tourist industry. The Diaspora experience is reflected in the number of other languages spoken in Israel, including Ethiopian, German, Yiddish, Polish, Romanian, Hungarian, Spanish, and notably Russian.

Media

Newspapers
Though there are many newspapers in Israel to suit all political leanings, ethnic and linguistic groupings, and prejudices, there is only one English-language daily, *The Jerusalem Post*. For many years a flag-waving banner-carrying member of the Labour party grouping, *The Post* lurched decidedly to the right about 10 years ago and its editorials are now markedly right-wing. On certain days its 'Letters to the Editor' page is full of bigoted, racist rantings (usually originating outside of Israel). However, the Fri supplement can be very useful for listings of 'What's On' in Jerusalem, Tel Aviv and elsewhere. It is not published on Saturday.

The left-wing *Ha'Aretz* daily also has a weekly English edition with an excellent listings section. If you don't want to get stressed by right-wing view-points, then this is the paper for you. Foreign newspapers (generally a day old) and magazines can be bought in larger branches of Steimatzky and at 'top end' hotels.

Radio
The best frequency for receiving the **BBC World Service** is 1323 kHz (MW), though it is also available on SW bands. **Voice of America** is on 1260 kHz. The FM dial is packed with Israeli stations playing Western music.

Television
Israel has a few TV stations. The Israel Broadcasting Authority (IBA) broadcast Channel 1 (and a number of radio stations). In addition there are two nationwide commercial channels: Channel 10 and Channel 2. There is persistent talk of a wide reform in the public Broadcasting Authority. Commercial Channel 2 and Channel 10 have a legal monopoly on all TV advertising, whilst Channel 1 relies largely on an annual licence fee (about $105). Without advertising, it's unlikely that a commercial Channel 1 would be viable, whilst any attempts to allow it to show adverts would be challenged in court by the commercial channels! Other critics suggest that Channel 1 is not run by the management but by the unions and that most of the income generated by the licence fee is allocated to salaries, instead of quality TV shows. Channel 1 shows news in English at 0630, 1230 and 2030, plus in many other languages. Visit www.iba.org.il/world/ to see the schedule and find on-demand and recorded shows. Many homes, hotels and hostels now have cable channels, including BBC World, MTV, Sky and CNN (Cable Netanyahu News, as it used to be known). There are two companies, Yes and Hot, both of whom can supply hundreds of channels, depending on how much you are willing to pay.

Money

Currency
The unit of currency in Israel is the New Israeli Shekel, written as NIS. It has in fact been 'new' for over 20 years. The Hebrew plural of shekel is shekelim, though the generally used expression is 'shekels' (or 'sheks'). The new shekel is divided into 100 agorot. There are notes of 200, 100, 50, 20NIS, plus coins of 10, 5, 2 and 1NIS. There are also coins of 50 and 10 agorot. .

Note that by paying in foreign hard currencies (preferably US dollars) for hotel accommodation, car hire, airline tickets and expensive purchases, you avoid paying the 17% Value Added Tax (VAT). For details on VAT refunds, see page 44. Though almost all foreign hard currencies are accepted, US Dollars remain the best option. It is always useful to have some hard currency cash with you, particularly when you are crossing borders. A mix of high and low denomination US dollars is probably the best bet.

Credit cards

Credit cards are accepted pretty much everywhere in Israel (though not everywhere in the West Bank). Banks with ATMs are found in even the smallest towns. Debit/credit card withdrawals are the easiest and best way to access your travelling funds.

Changing money

Travellers' cheques can be cashed at banks and money-changers, though commission charges are excessive. Good places to exchange TCs are post offices (which all offer commission-free foreign exchange at good rates). You will need to bring your passport.

Licensed Arab money-changers inside Jerusalem's Damascus Gate (and in most Palestinian towns) may give you marginally better than bank rates for cash and TCs. They are also a good source of Jordanian dinars and Egyptian pounds for those travelling beyond Israel (something worth considering).

If you need to transfer money, most main post offices act as agents for Western Union. Commission charges are high, though. For further details, see www.westernunion.com.

Cost of travelling

Public transport in Israel is reasonably good value. As an example, the 1-hr bus ride from Tel Aviv to Jerusalem is $5 (20NIS), whilst the country's longest bus journey, the 6 hrs from Haifa to Eilat, is $20. For further details on getting around see page 23.

Your daily budget will be influenced by how much sightseeing you intend doing. Israeli museums, galleries, religious sites, national parks and general sights charge anywhere between nothing and $10 for admission, though the average is around $5. Don't let admission fees deter you from visiting; if you are on a very tight budget, then pick and choose carefully.

With careful budgeting it should be possible to eat, sleep and see something of the country on $40-$50 per day. You do meet some people surviving on $20 a day or less, though they invariably seem to be miserable and tend to leave Israel having seen next to nothing of the country.

Opening hours

Few first-time visitors to Israel are prepared for the impact of Shabbat, or the Jewish Sabbath. Beginning at sun-down on Fri and finishing at sun-down on Sat, it sees all Israeli offices, banks, post offices, and most shops, restaurants and places of entertainment close down completely. Almost everywhere, both the inter-city and urban transport systems grind to a complete halt. If you don't want to go hungry or get stranded somewhere, plan in advance for Shabbat. Note that in many work environments, the 'weekend' is now adding Fri to the Sat day of rest. The picture is further confused by the fact that shops and businesses in Muslim (Arab) areas observe Fri as their Sabbath, whilst Sun is the day of rest for Christians. Anyone who claims their religion to be 'monotheism' (as opposed to just Judaism, Christianity or Islam) should in theory be entitled to a very long weekend! The following are a general guide only:

Banks Sun, Tues and Thu 0830-1230 1600-1700, Mon, Wed and Fri 0830-1200.
Post offices Sun-Thu 0700-1900, Fri 0700-1200 (though branch offices generally close 1230-1400).
Government offices Sun-Thu 0800-1300 and 1400-1730, Fri 0900-1400.
Shops Mon-Thu 0800-1300 and 1400-1900, Fri 0900-1400.

Post

Outgoing mail from Israel is notoriously slow, taking 4-5 days to Europe and 7-10 days to North America and Australia. Incoming mail is rather quicker. Almost all post offices offer poste restante (doar shamur), and holders of Amex cards and TCs can use the American Express Clients' Mail service at their offices. Post offices also offer commission-free foreign exchange at good rates for TCs.

Safety

Israel and Palestine rarely appear to be out of the news, though this is hardly surprising when you consider that even in the quieter periods Israel plays host to one of the largest press contingents in the world. Many outsiders' perception of Israel and the Palestinian Territories is focussed on suicide bombings, political assassinations, stone-throwing Palestinians and rubber-bullet firing Israeli soldiers. Unsurprisingly, the two intifadas resulted in tourists staying well away for several years. It would be dishonest to claim that violent events are completely detached from 'normal' life in Israel. However, from the foreign visitor's perspective (and to be totally cynical), most clashes take place well away from the main tourist centres, and there has been no deliberate targeting of foreign tourists. There is a unique security situation in Israel, and a highly visible one at that, though it should also be remembered that levels of street crime are far lower than in places such as North America and much of Europe. The general advice is to be alert and aware of potentially serious situations, but not to be overly paranoid; relax and enjoy your trip.

Student travellers

Anyone in full-time education is entitled to an **International Student Identity Card** (ISIC). These are issued by student travel offices

and travel agencies across the world, and by **issta** in Israel (see under 'Tour companies and travel agents' in major city entries). ISIC cards are particularly useful in Israel, where they entitle you to 10% discount on Egged bus fares over 26NIS, 10% discount on train fares, and approximately 30% discount on museum entrance and 20% off national park entry fees.

Taxes

Departure tax for foreigners flying out of Israel is incorporated within the ticket price, but leaving Israel for Egypt by land, foreigners must pay 98.5NIS departure tax at the Eilat/Taba crossing. Leaving Israel for Jordan by land, foreigners pay 98.5NIS departure tax at the Jordan Valley and Arava crossings, and 163NIS at the Allenby/King Hussein Bridge.

Tax refunds

Though there is a 17% Value Added Tax on many goods in Israel, tourists are entitled to a VAT refund on certain products (generally not electrical, photographic or computer equipment). Shops that participate in the scheme generally have a large sign in the window, also see www.cpl.co.il. You should get a 5% discount on the marked price of the goods. Make sure that the VAT paid is marked clearly on the invoice (in shekels and US dollars). The goods should then be placed in one of the special clear-sided bags, with the invoice prominently displayed. You cannot open the bag prior to leaving Israel. At Ben-Gurion Airport, a booth in the 'departures' lounge will stamp the invoice and pay the refund, minus a commission.

Telephone

Telecards are available at post offices, shops and kiosks. Telecard-operated public phone boxes can be used for international direct dial (IDD) calls. The standard international access code of 00 has been replaced with the access numbers of three private firms, 012, 013, 014.

Peak rates are Mon-Fri 0800-2200. There is a 25% discount Mon-Fri 2200-0100 and all day Sat and Sun. There is a 50% discount Mon-Sun 0100-0800.

Mobile phones can be rented on arrival at Ben-Gurion Airport, or see www. israelphones.com for rental phone delivery anywhere in Israel. Calls cost about 1.20NIS per minute. Most foreign providers operate here (but it's worth checking your mobile package from home). To buy a SIM card, plus activation, usually costs 200NIS. In Israel, Cellcom and Orange both offer fixed-line (local user) and pay-as-you-go services.

Time

Israel is 2 hrs ahead of Greenwich Mean Time (GMT+2); 7 hrs ahead of American Eastern Standard Time; 8 hrs behind Australian Eastern Standard Time. Clocks go forward 1 hr for daylight-saving ('summer time') in Mar, and back again at Rosh Hashanah (usually Sep).

Tipping

In common with many other countries in the world, bar staff, waiters and waitresses in Israel receive fairly low wages, relying on tips to top up their salaries. If service is good then add 10%, if not leave nothing. It is not customary to tip taxi drivers. Tipping guides and tour bus drivers is a matter of personal choice. If someone cleans your room the right thing to do is leave a tip (5NIS per day is perfectly acceptable).

Tour operators

There are plenty of tour companies featuring Israel as a destination, and just about any travel agent you walk into will be able to book you on to some sort of package deal. In the UK, the weekly Jewish Chronicle

frequently has last-minute flight deals as well as competitively priced packages (especially to Eilat, where the advert generally also states which hotel you will be in and whether your room faces a building site or not!). Below is just a small selection of UK-based tour operators offering trips to Israel.

In the UK

Accessible Journeys, www.disablitytravel. com. Escorted tours and packages for disabled tourists, with three different levels of care dependent on ability.
Bible Land Journeys, T0845-4562413, www.biblelandjourneys.com. Religious/ Christian holidays.
C-L Ministries, www.clministries.org.uk. Around 3 Bible Tours per year, in conjunction with Worldwide Christian Travel.
Explore Worldwide, www.explore.co.uk. Regular 5-day tours to Israel or 11 days combined with Jordan.
Jet2, www.jet2.com. Some of the cheapest available flights to Israel, from Manchester twice a week.
Israel Travel Service, T0161-8391111, www. itstravel.co.uk. Family tours, pilgrim tours, packages to Eilat; long established.
Isstadirect, T0208-2020800, www. isstadirect.com. Loads of package deals, cheap flights and full services all over Israel.
Longwood Holidays, T0208-4182516, wwwlongwoodholidays.co.uk. Flexible guided tours or package deals, variety of budgets and interests catered for. High-end hotels and tailor-made itineraries possible.
McCabe Travel, T0800-1073107, www. mccabe-travel.co.uk. Family-run company, they are one of Britain's foremost religious tour operators to many holy lands. Recommended.
Rosary Pilgrimage Apostolate, T0845-1308550. Roman Catholic pilgrimages.
Superstar, T0207-1211500/0161-8346553, www.superstar.co.uk. Part of El Al; tailor-made tours, with or without guides, and city-breaks, at very competitive prices. They also cater for disabled tourists.

Thomson Holidays, www.thomson.co.il. Full packages or just hotel bookings.
TravelLink, T0208-9318000, www.travel. linkuk.com. Long-time specialists in travel to Israel, also kibbutz hoidays.

In North America
Gate 1 Travel, www.gate1travel.com. American company that organizes guided and independent tours at reasonable prices, plus decent hotel accommodation.

Tourist information

Visit www.visitisrael.gov.il, www.goisrael. com and www.peacecentre.org. The best source of online information for the Territories is www.thisweekinpalestine.com.

Almost all Israeli towns have at least one tourist information office (sometimes a government office and a municipal office), though the standard of service is highly variable. They are generally a good source of free (or cheap) city maps, may be able to assist in booking accommodation, and should stock some sort of free 'What's On' guide to the region that you are in. Beyond this, the help that you get depends upon the dedication of the staff member that you see.

Overseas tourist offices
Canada, 180 Bloor St West, Suit 700, Toronto, T1416-9643784, www.goisrael.com.
France, 94 Rue Saint Lazarere, Paris 75009, T01-42610197, www.otisrael.com.
Germany, Friedrichstr 95, 10117 Berlin, T030-20399720, www.goisrael.de.
Italy, Via Carducci 19, 20123 Milan, T02-804905, www.goisrael.it.
Japan, 3 Nibancho Chyoda-Ku, Tokyo 102-0084, T03-32640911.
Netherlands, Stadhouderskade 2, 1054 ES Amsterdam, T020-6128850, www.goisrael.nl.
South Korea, Hanaro Building, 10th Floor, 194-4 Insa-Dong, Jongro-Gu, Seoul 110-794, T02-7380882, www.israel.co.kr.
Spain, C/ Fuencarral 101, 28004 Madrid, T091-5943211, www.tuisrael.com.

Sweden, Sveagagen 28-30, 4 tr., Box 7554, 10393 Stockholm, T08-213386, www. goisrael.nu.
UK, 180 Oxford St, London W1N 9DJ, T0207-2991111, www.thinkisrael.com.
USA, 800 Second Ave, New York, T212-4995650, www.goisrael.com; 6380 Wiltshire Blvd 1718, Los Angeles, T213-6587463.

Visas and immigration

On arrival (by air, land or sea) you will be requested to fill in a landing card. If you request (but only if you specifically ask), the immigration official will stamp this card and not your passport. This card is then surrendered to an official before collecting your baggage. The lack of a stamp will only cause you difficulties when crossing the border into Egypt or Jordan, when officials may delay you while they check everything is in order. This usually just involves a few phone calls being made. Also, you may face questions when entering/exiting the West Bank. Note that you may have to provide evidence of a return ticket, though this is very rare.

Passports
All visitors require a passport that is valid for 6 months beyond the date of their entry into Israel. You should carry your passport with you (in a secure place) at all times. You may be required to show it when checking in to hotels. You will be asked for your passport at checkpoints if travelling around the West Bank.

Visas
Almost all nationalities are granted a free 3-month **tourist visa** on arrival, whether via land or air. The exceptions to this rule include most African countries, Arab/Muslim nations, India and many of the former Soviet republics. Be aware that at a land border you may be asked how long you intend to stay; then the exact figure you state could well be what you are issued with. Tourist

visas do not permit you to work. They can be extended (see below). Visas expire on exit from Israel. For further details on arrival protocol see page 19.

If you are intending to work on a kibbutz or moshav, it is possible to apply for a 6-12 month volunteer visa once you are already inside Israel with the help of your kibbutz or moshav. Applicants should be aware that this visa is non-transferable, so if you move kibbutz you need a new visa.

A 12-month **student visa** is available to those who have been accepted by a university/education institute, though it is non-transferable and does not allow you to work. It is recommended to apply for the visa before arriving in Israel from an Israeli embassy abroad, though it is possible to obtain after arrival in the country if necessary. You require a letter of acceptance and proof of sufficient funds to cover tuition and living costs.

Work visas are arranged either before arrival through an Israeli embassy abroad, with a letter from your employers in Israel, or when already in Israel with a tourist visa. When in Israel, employers arrange working visas on your behalf, certified by the Ministry of the Interior. A work permit is non-transferable between jobs or employers and you will be liable for tax and national insurance contributions.

Jewish visitors considering returning to Israel permanently may be eligible for **temporary residence**. It is advisable that you contact one of the relevant agencies to guide you through this process: Association of **Americans and Canadians in Israel** (AACI), Jerusalem, T02-5661181, www.aaci. org.il; **British Olim Society**, 37 Pierre Koenig, Talpiyyot, Jerusalem, T02-5635244; 76 Ibn Gvirol, Tel Aviv, T03-6965244, www.ujia.org.il.

Visa extensions

Tourist visas can be extended for further 3-month periods at offices of the Ministry of the Interior. Appointments must be made in advance by calling *3450 Sun-Thu

0800-1200, with later shifts on Wed and Sun (1600-1900), though there can be a 2-week wait before you can even get an appointment. You should remember that granting visa extensions is at the discretion of the Ministry of the Interior and you are in no position to begin demanding your rights.

It costs 145NIS for an extension (plus 75NIS for multiple entry) plus one passport photo. It pays to dress smartly and act in a polite manner, and it's recommended to bring proof of sufficient funds. Having an itinerary of places that you still wish to visit in Israel may assist your application.

The **Ministry of the Interior** can be found at: 24 Hillel, Jerusalem, T02-6294726; 125 Menachem Begin, Tel Aviv, T03-5193305; Municipality Building, HaTemarim Blvd, Eilat, T08-6381333; 23 Zaki Elkhadif, Tiberias, T04-6729111. It is a nightmare renewing a visa at one of the main offices (even getting an appointment is an ordeal). Better to go to one of the regional offices,such as Netanya, Rishon LeTzion or Ramat Gan. You will need a hotel receipt that shows an address in the place where you are renewing your visa. Then it is possible to obtain a renewal in 1 day.

Many people feel it is simpler to leave Israel just before your visa expires (eg go to Sinai, Egypt, or Jordan) and get a new visa upon re-entry. However, crossing into Egypt for an hour, then returning, tends to raise the suspicions of immigration officials. Spending a weekend in Amman is a workable option (for cheap package deals to Jordan see **Flying Carpet**, www.flying.co.il). There is now a Jordanian consulate in Ramallah which can provide a Jordanian visa so that you can cross at the Allenby/King Hussein Bridge Crossing, rather than travelling all the way to the Rabin Crossing in Eilat.

Expired visas

There can be severe penalties for overstaying your visa, though how rigorously they are enforced appears to be a rather hit-or-miss affair. You may be obliged to pay a monthly charge for each month (or part thereof) that you have overstayed. Some travellers who have over-stayed their visa report being interrogated for hours at the airport/land border with the possibility of a deportation order being issued at the end. Others who have over-stayed by only a few days report no fines and no such problems. If you attempt to leave Israel at a land border with an expired visa you will almost certainly be refused exit and referred back to the Ministry of the Interior. Be polite and repentant. If you overstay your visa, you may be blacklisted and denied re-entry to Israel for 5-10 years (though this normally only applies to those who overstay by 6 months or more).

Women travellers

Women travelling alone face greater difficulties than men or couples. Despite the fact that levels of conventional crime are considerably lower in Israel than in parts of North America and Europe, women travellers in Israel occasionally experience a degree of sexual harassment. Instances of physical assault are thankfully very rare, though verbal harassment or suggestive comments more commonplace. It is probably best to steadfastly ignore rude comments directed at you but aimed at boosting the caller's ego, though if you feel yourself to be in any immediate danger, don't be afraid to shout and make a scene. Dressing conservatively certainly minimizes the hassle and is in any case required for visiting holy sites, so it is perhaps a good habit to get in to. In many parts of Israel you are free to wear whatever you like, as young Israeli women in Tel Aviv and Eilat so clearly demonstrate. Note, however, that going topless on the beach is still quite rare and can attract unwanted attention.

Working in Israel

Without the proper work permits, it is not really possible for foreign travellers to get work in Israel, since authorities started cracking down on illegal employment around 2006. There is a dependency on foreign workers in the construction and agriculture sectors, as there are difficulties in attracting Israelis to these menial and low-paid manual labour jobs, and Palestinians can no longer get work permits very easily. Therefore, construction workers, home-helps, agricultural workers, etc, are granted a 5-year period that is strictly regulated, and illegal workers are actively tracked down. Most foreign workers in the cities are Chinese, Filipino or Indian, while in moshavim you will see large numbers of Thai farmers working the land.

Kibbutz
Several points need to be made about the kibbutz system straight away. You won't make much money, and it is doubtful whether it is a great way to conserve your travelling funds either (with many volunteers drinking away their savings). It is also not a good way to get to see Israel since you have to work six days a week, your day off is on the day that the buses don't run, they are usually situated in remote locations and you generally have to stay for more than 3 months to qualify for the kibbutz outings. However, it will offer a unique experience, and, according to what your expectations are and what sort of people you share the experience with, it may well be a memorable one. (**NB** The concept and functioning of the kibbutz and moshav is discussed below).

To join a kibbutz as a volunteer you have to be aged 18 to 32, in good mental and physical health, have proof of health insurance (not always asked for) and be willing to submit to a HIV/Aids test (not always enforced). Your work regime will be 6 days per week, 8 hours per day (generally starting very early in the morning), and you will be expected to accept whatever task is assigned to you. There is every reason to believe that volunteers are given the most menial and tedious chores on the kibbutz. Gardening is considered to be a good job. Getting up at 0430 to pick up all the dead chickens that died overnight is not.

In return for your labour you will receive free accommodation (usually in a special volunteers' block well away from the regular kibbutzniks), meals, a number of basic requisites such as toiletries, plus a personal allowance of around US$100 per month. Volunteers generally have access to all the recreational facilities at the kibbutz. You may believe that with all your basic needs provided for it would be possible to save your monthly personal allowance – not necessarily true. It's very easy to drink away both your monthly allowance and your travelling funds that you're holding in reserve. On the positive side, like-minded kibbutz volunteers can become lifelong friends (and partners).

You can organize a kibbutz placement in your home country (begin preparations for this at least 1 month in advance) or wait until you arrive in Israel. A list of kibbutz representatives overseas and in Israel is provided below.

To organize a kibbutz placement when already in Israel go to the kibbutz representative in Tel Aviv, 6 Frishman (cnr with HaYarkon), T03-5246154/6, www.kibbutz.org.il, but as you will need a volunteer visa you may end up waiting a while. July/August is a bad time to try this approach as student numbers are high, whereas harvest period is a good time. Acting like a sober, diligent, hard worker is a good way of getting a placement. It is also possible to apply directly to an individual kibbutz; many offer advice for volunteers on their websites.

Kibbutz representatives

overseas Austria, Schimmelgasse 16, 1030 Vienna, T0676-83181466, pnina.

schreiber@chello.at. **Belgium**, Bureau de Volontaires, 68 Ave Ducpetiaux, 1060 Bruxelles, T0475-891324. **France**, T01-48040866, paris@hachomer.net. **Germany**, Schadowstr 9, 60596 Frankfurt, T69-61993460, lydia.boehmer.gmx. de. **Netherlands**, Oppenheim Travel, Cronenburg 164, Amsterdam 1081GN, T20-4042040, arjan@oppenheim.nl. **UK**, Kibbutz Representatives, 1A Accommodation Rd, London NW11, T020-84589235; Kibbutz Representatives, 222 Fenwick Rd, Glasgow, T0141-6202194; Kibbutz Representatives, Harold House, Dunbabin Rd, Liverpool, T0151-7225671; Kibbutz Representatives, 11 Upper Park Rd, Salford, Manchester M7 0HY, T0161-7959447; Project 67, 10 Hatton Garden, London EC1N 8AH, T020-78317626. **USA** and **Canada**, 114 West 26th Street, New York, T212-4622764, www.kibbutzprogramcenter.org.

Moshav

Whilst many kibbutzim are diversifying into light industry and tourism, agriculture remains the backbone of the moshav system. Moshav volunteers are usually assigned to one particular farmer, and the success (or otherwise) of your moshav experience will almost certainly depend upon this relationship. Moshav farmers generally have a reputation for being slave-driving bullies. Moshav work tends to be far harder than that on a kibbutz ('back-breaking' is an often-used term), though the financial rewards are greater. Overtime is often compulsory, though getting paid for it can be a problem. The after-hours social scene varies considerably from moshav to moshav; you may be billeted with other volunteers, though don't be surprised if you are on your own. Moshav volunteers generally provide their own food (better get used to tomatoes), though if your farmer supplies your meals expect wages to be halved.

Moshav volunteers have to be aged 18 to 35 and have medical insurance. Don't apply unless you are physically fit and prepared for hard manual labour. To join a moshav go to the representatives office at 19 Leonardo de Vinci St, Tel Aviv, T03-5258473 (bus 70 from central bus station). Good luck!

Archaeological digs
If you want to work on an archaeological dig in Israel, contact the Israeli Antiquities Authority as early in the year as possible and request their list of forthcoming excavations that are open to volunteers (see www.antiquities.org.il, and look under 'public information'/'join a dig'). Bear in mind that you will have to pay for this experience. The **Institute of Archaeology** at the Hebrew University, Mount Scopus, (http://archaeology.huji.ac.il) provide a similar opportunity. Half-day digs are available at Beit Guvrin National Park through **Archaeological Seminars**, T02-5862011, www.archsem.com, price $30 for adults, $25 children (between the ages of 5-14 years), does not include entrance fee to the National Park.

Volunteering in the Palestinian Territories
A number of organizations arrange volunteer opportunities inside the West Bank. A registration fee is normally required if arranging the placement from overseas, as well as proof of medical insurance. You pay your own flight and transport costs, though accommodation and meals are usually provided.

Organizations offering such placements include: **Canadian and Palestinian Cultural Exchange**, (CEPAL), volunteers work and live in camps in cooperation with CEPAL's Palestinian NGO partners, 323 Chapel Street, Ottawa, Ontario, Canada, www.cepal.ca. **Cinema Jenin**, Jenin, an interesting project to re-open the cinema, www.cinemajenin. org. **International Voluntary Service** (IVS) GB, Thorn House, 5 Rose Street, Edinburgh, EH2 2PR, T0131-2432745, http://ivsgb.org/info. The **Israeli Committee Against House Demolitions** (ICHAD), Jerusalem-based direct action organization, www.icahd.org. **Palestine Red Crescent Society**, medical volunteers for a recommended minimal stay of three months, non-medical volunteers for a recommended minimal stay of six months, PO Box 1928, Jerusalem, T02-628.6694, www.palestinercs.org. **Universities Trust for Educational Exchange with Palestine (UNIPAL)**, short-term summer teaching English assignments and other work/activities as needed, BCM UNIPAL, London, WCIN 3XX, www.unipal.org.uk. **Project Hope**, Nablus, opportunities for skilled/unskilled volunteers, www.projecthope.ps . Also see www.sciint.org and www.volunteerabroad. com for further volunteer opportunities in Palestine and Israel.

Contents

Footprint features

Jerusalem

It would not be much of an over-statement to say that Jerusalem is the most famous city in the world. In many minds it is also the most important. Here is a city that is of fundamental spiritual importance to one third of humanity, sacred to Jews, Christians and Muslims alike. Three faiths based on a common creed that now present mutually exclusive claims to the same city.

A visit to Jerusalem can be an intense experience, yet it is one that should not be missed. In fact, almost all foreign tourists visiting Israel come to Jerusalem at some stage during their trip, on average spending around half of their time in the city. And there is plenty to justify a prolonged stay, with even the most ardent of non-believers becoming enthralled by its unique atmosphere. Not only is the first sight of the Dome of the Rock far better in reality than in the imagination, but the chaotic, crowded streets of the Old City retain a timeless exoticism despite the passage of many centuries of pilgrims and tourists. Layered beneath the city are remains of civilizations stretching back 3000 years, which can be explored via tunnels under the Old City itself or at countless other archaeological and architectural sites. Should the pervasive air of history and religion get too intense, there are excellent museums and nightly cultural activities – as well as a fine bar and dining scene in both East and West Jerusalem.

Such is the fascination of the city that many people find themselves altering their plans to fit in a couple more days in Jerusalem at the end of their trip.

Jerusalem is a fairly easy city in which to orientate yourself, though it is a little more complex than just an 'Old' and a 'New' city. The places of interest in this chapter have been grouped according to location, though most of the attractions are in or close to the walled Old City. In fact, it's not difficult to see all the key attractions in just three to four days.

Ins and outs

Getting there and away Coming from Ben Gurion Airport, sheruts (shared mini-bus taxis) can drop you off at your destination/hotel in Jerusalem. Many visitors arrive from Tel Aviv by bus, to the multi-storey Central Bus Station to the west of the New City centre, from where buses connect to the Old City. Sheruts from Tel Aviv's Central Bus Station arrive in the New City at Zion Square within walking distance of the Old City. There are also two bus stations in East Jerusalem: Suleiman Street bus station (outside Damascus Gate) serves destinations in East Jerusalem and Ramallah; Nablus Road bus station (also near Damascus Gate) serves southern destinations in the West Bank; usually you must change in Bethlehem.

Trains run between Jerusalem and Tel Aviv in 1½ hours, 10 per day, but the station is inconveniently located in Malha suburb to the southwest of the city. The express train line that will connect Jerusalem to Ben Gurion Airport in less than 30 minutes is not expected to be completed until 2017.

Getting around Though many of Jerusalem's sights are within walking distance of each other (notably in and around the Old City), you will almost certainly have to use the city bus service at some stage; few enjoy the walk from the Central Bus Station to the Old City carrying a backpack. Fares are currently 5.9NIS whether you go one stop or all the way across town. Buses from outside the Central Bus Station to the Old City leave from the opposite side of Jaffa (Yafo) Road from the bus station. To get to Jaffa Gate take 20; to Damascus Gate take 6 or 1 (the latter of which carries on to Dung Gate for the Western Wall).

Known as the '**Jerusalem City tour**' ① *Line 99, T1-700-70-75-75, www.egged.co.il, 2 hrs, 5 tours per day Sun-Thu, 3 tours on Fri, buy tickets on board*, links many of Jerusalem's main sights on one continuous loop, with the one-day (80/68 NIS) or two-day (130/110 NIS) ticket allowing you to hop on and off at any designated stop. Audio guides are available in eight languages.

When it is completed (supposedly 2011) the Light Rail tramway will be a handy, if controversial, connection between Mt Herzl in the west and the northern suburbs, going along the length of Jaffa Road passing the Central Bus Station and Damascus Gate.

Tourist information Municipal Tourist Offices ① *Jaffa Gate, T02-6271422, www.tour. jerusalem.muni.il, Sat-Thu 0830-1700, Fri 0830-1330.* Usefully located, make this your first point of call to pick up one of the detailed maps of the Old City, which clearly shows every street. They also have brochures, information, audio-guides, etc. The Municipality also run free walking tours every Saturday at 1000 (English and Hebrew) to various Jerusalem sites and areas, recommended particularly for long-stay visitors (leaving from Safra Square, Jaffa Street: meet near the palm trees; full list of destinations on website). The Municipality hotline is T106 (from outside Jerusalem T02-5314600).

Christian Information Centre ① *Jaffa Gate, T02-6272692, www.cicts.org, Mon-Fri 0830-1730, Sat 0380-1230.* Come here for information relating to churches for all denominations, throughout the Holy Land.

Jewish Student Information Centre ① *5 Beit-El, Jewish Quarter, T02-6282634, www. jeffseidel.com.* Free tours, hostel accommodation and more for Jewish youth.

Also see Tour Operators, page 192, and www.holypass.co.il, which can save up to 25% on sightseeing around many of the Old City sights.

Background

The ancient city extended over a series of hills or ridges intersected by deep valleys, though several thousand years of building, destruction and reconstruction has introduced a man-made topography. The eastern border, the Kidron Valley, remains largely unchanged, dividing the Old City from the low north-south ridge that includes Mount Scopus and the Mt of Olives. The western border of the Old City is the Valley of Hinnom, which then turns southeast, skirting Mount Zion to form the southern border. The ancient city, located on the southeast ridge to the south of the low hill that was to become the Temple Mount, was defined by the Kidron Valley to the east and the Valley of Hinnom to the south. Its western boundary was formed by the Tyropneon (Cheesemakers') Valley, which runs broadly north to south from the area around the present-day Damascus Gate, along the west side of the Temple Mount, joining with the Kidron Valley and Valley of Hinnom at a point south of the ancient city. The Tyropneon Valley formerly divided the Temple Mount from the Southwestern Hill (upon which the first-century BCE to first-century CE Upper City was founded, now occupied by the Armenian and Jewish Quarters), though the valley has subsequently been filled in by two millennia of building activity. The northern boundary of the city is less well defined, with the series of hills and ridges upon which Jerusalem is built merging imperceptibly with those further north. For this reason, the north approach has always been the least defensible.

History

Pre-Davidic settlement The relative lack of archaeological finds and epigraphic evidence make it rather difficult to reconstruct the pre-Israelite settlement here. However, sufficient finds have been discovered that suggest a continuity of settlement from the Chalcolithic period (c. 4500-3300 BCE) up until **David**'s conquest in the 10th century BCE. The location of the walled stronghold that David conquered is in no doubt (see page 141) though who its inhabitants were is less certain. It is generally concluded that the so-called Jebusites (who are described in the biblical account of David's capture of the stronghold) were related to the Hittites, and formed an enclave within Israelite-controlled land.

The City of David Following David's capture of the stronghold of **Zion** on this southeast ridge late in the 10th century BCE (*II Samuel 5:6-9; I Chronicles 11:4-7*), the true history of Jerusalem may be said to have begun. This relative backwater, so long ignored by the Israelites, suddenly became their new political capital. The choice of location perhaps reflects David's military and political astuteness, selecting a site midway between the northern and southern tribal territories of the Israelites, and on the main north to south axis between the two. Yet it was not just a political capital that David established. Having brought the **Ark of the Covenant** here (the symbol of the unity of the tribes of Israel and of the covenant between the tribes and God), David effectively made Jerusalem the only legitimate focus of cult for the tribes. The city was now the religious and cultural capital of the Israelites. Following God's command, David bought the threshing floor of Araunah the Jebusite on what was to become the Temple Mount (and much later the Haram al-Sharif), and set up an altar there. It was not unusual for elevated spots close to a city to be used as the local cultic spot, and the Temple Mount was clearly considered sacred prior to David's transaction. In fact the site was linked with the **Mt Moriah** upon which the patriarch **Abraham** offered his son Isaac for sacrifice (*Genesis 22*, though Muslims believe that Ishmael was the offered son), and thus David was considered to be rebuilding the altar of Abraham.

First Temple period Some suggest that David was considered to have had too much blood on his hands to build the First Temple on Mt Moriah, though it is more likely that he simply wanted to avoid turning Israel into a royal temple-state. Thus, the task of building the Temple fell to his successor, **Solomon**.

During the coregency of David and Solomon the city was centred upon the southeast ridge, though plans were made to expand the city by building the Temple on Mt Moriah and a new palace and royal court complex to the south. It was not until after David's death that construction on the Temple began, though it was to take 20 years for all the building plans to be realized.

Solomon's death c. 928 BCE saw a radical change in Jerusalem's standing. The collapse of the United Monarchy saw the establishment of rival cultic centres in the northern kingdom of **Israel**, (as well as rival political centres), whilst Jerusalem's status was reduced to that of capital of the southern kingdom of **Judah**. It also appears to have been considerably impoverished by the loss of tax revenues from the north.

The key event during the rule of the subsequent **Kings of Judah** was the rise to the east of the **Assyrian empire**. Clashes with the Assyrians during the reign of Uzziah (769-733 BCE) had led to a considerable flow of refugees to Jerusalem, and with the Assyrian destruction of the northern kingdom of Israel c. 722 BCE, Jerusalem now found itself hosting a substantial refugee population. Archaeological evidence points to the incumbent king of Judah, **Hezekiah** (727-698 BCE), making considerable efforts to refortify the expanded city, particularly in the face of the Assyrian king Sennacherib's advance (701 BCE). See for example the 'Broad Wall' in the present Jewish Quarter of the Old City (page 118), or Hezekiah's efforts at defending the city's water supply (page 144). Under Hezekiah's successor, Manasseh (698-642 BCE), further strengthening of the city's defences took place, though under Assyrian supervision.

Jerusalem: topography

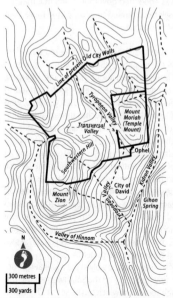

During Josiah's rule (639-609 BCE) the Assyrian empire fell (613 BCE), though this only served to suck the kingdom of Judah (and Jerusalem) into the power vacuum that the Egyptians and **Babylonians** were trying to fill. Having sided with the Egyptians, Judah saw the victorious Babylonians sack Jerusalem in 597 BCE, and then totally destroy it in 586 BCE. The Babylonians burnt down the Temple, razed the city, and the Israelites were led off in chains: the Exile had begun.

Post-Exilic and Persian periods How many of Jerusalem's population survived the Babylonian sacking and avoided exile is a matter of some debate, though the claim that only the "poorest of the land" (*II Kings* 25:8-12) remained is seemingly supported by the archaeological evidence. The fall of the Babylonian empire in 539 BCE ushered

Jerusalem: origins of the name

The earliest written reference to Jerusalem, or more correctly Rushalimum, appears in the Egyptian Execration texts of the 20th and 19th centuries BCE, whilst the 14th-century BCE el-Amarna letters refer to *Urusalim*. The pre-Israelite city was known as *Jebus*, taking its name from the ethnic group who lived here, and whose last king was Araunah the Jebusite. Araunah's stronghold of Zion (see 'Ancient City of the SE Ridge', page 141) was captured by the Israelites (II Samuel 5:6-7), with David subsequently calling it 'City of David' (*II Samuel 5:9; I Chronicles 11:7*).

The earliest Hebrew pronunciation appears to be *Yerushalem*, with its meaning presumed to come from the West Semitic elements *yrw* and *slm*, and is generally interpreted as "Foundation of (the God) Shalem" (Mazar, *New Encyclopedia of Archaeological Excavations in the Holy Land*, 1993). The etymological link between this pagan deity after which the city may have been named, and the Semitic words for peace (Hebrew: *Shalom*, Arabic: *Salaam*), has led many to refer to Jerusalem as the "city of peace", though, as can be seen from studying the city's history, this is a most inappropriate name. The Arab name, al-Quds, 'the Holy', is equally unlikely. Perhaps the best description of the city was given by the 10th-century CE Jerusalem-born Arab geographer al-Muqaddasi, who referred to Jerusalem as "a golden basin filled with scorpions".

in Persian (Achaemenid) rule, and in the following year a proclamation by the Persian ruler Cyrus II (539-529 BCE) allowed Jews to return to Jerusalem and rebuild the Temple (*Ezra 1:2-3*). However, it was not until **Nehemiah** was appointed governor in 445 BCE that the city wall was rebuilt. Even so, Post-Exilic Jerusalem continued to occupy little more than the original southeast ridge and the Temple/Mt Moriah area.

Hellenistic and Hasmonean periods Though Alexander the Great conquered Jerusalem in 332 BCE, his rule was short-lived and impact negligible. By 301 BCE Jerusalem was in the hands of the **Ptolemies of Egypt**, though little is known about their tenure. However, the power struggle between the Ptolemies of Egypt and the **Seleucids of Syria** led to the capture of the city in 200 BCE by the Seleucid ruler **Antiochus III** (223-187 BCE), who began reorganizing the city along the lines of a Greek polis. Antiochus III was fairly subtle in introducing such changes, recruiting the city's wealthy Jews and aristocratic priestly families to his cause, but his successor **Antiochus IV Epiphanes** (175-164 BCE) attempted to bludgeon through fairly radical measures. In particular, the Jews of Jerusalem (and all across the country) objected to the renaming of the city Antiochia, the looting of the Temple treasures, the installation of a graven image in the Temple sanctuary, and its desecration by sacrificing a pig on the sacred altar! The subsequent **Hasmonean (Maccabean) Revolt** reached its climax in 164 BCE when **Judas Maccabeus** entered Jerusalem and cleansed the Temple (an event celebrated in the Jewish festival of Hannukah). However, the Acra fortress that Antiochus IV had built in the city (and garrisoned with mercenaries) remained in Seleucid hands, and it was not until 141 BCE that **Simeon the Hasmonean** could be said to have firmly established Jewish (Maccabean) control over Jerusalem.

The Hasmonean period saw the expansion of the city, most notably in the move away from settlement on the southeast ridge towards the new Upper City on the Southwestern hill. This new area was protected by the so-called First Wall, sections of which can be seen today within the Citadel and at various places in the Jewish Quarter. The successional dispute among the Hasmoneans brought their period of rule to an end in Jerusalem, and saw republican Rome's first real intervention in the city's affairs. In 63 BCE **Pompey** captured Jerusalem for Rome, subsequently setting up Antipater the Idumean as the head of the Roman client state.

Herodian period and the Second Temple period It was under Antipater the Idumean's second son, **Herod the Great**, that Jerusalem entered into a golden age of prosperity, with building projects on a grandiose scale including the construction of the Antonia fortress (page 96), a new palace defended by three gigantic towers (page 65), an extension of the upper-class Upper City (page 120), and of course the Second Temple (page 77). (**NB** Though the First Temple that was destroyed by the Babylonians in 586 BCE was subsequently rebuilt, the term 'Second Temple' is used to refer to the temple that Herod the Great built.) The result was a beautified city that was also able to provide substantial employment opportunities, particularly within the construction industry. Herod's sons,

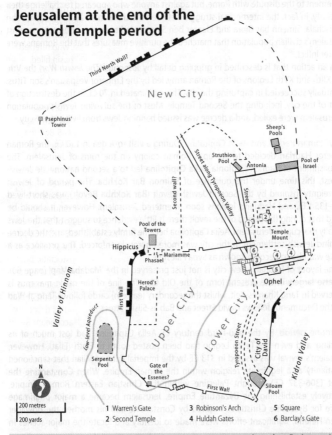

Jerusalem at the end of the Second Temple period

1 Warren's Gate   3 Robinson's Arch   5 Square
2 Second Temple   4 Huldah Gates   6 Barclay's Gate

however, upon inheriting their father's 'kingdom', proved themselves to be generally weak rulers, and Jerusalem found itself ruled by a Roman procurator based in the Roman province's capital at Caesarea. Possibly the most famous of these Roman procurators was **Pontius Pilate**, who ruled 26-36 CE.

The First Revolt and the destruction of the Second Temple The first half of the first century CE saw growing tension between the Jewish population of the Roman province and their Roman rulers, as well as increased resentment between various classes of the population. In particular, Zealot groups emerged, and messianic expectations were heightened. It was into such an atmosphere of uncertainty and expectation that **Jesus** emerged.

By 66 CE minor disturbances had escalated into a full-scale rebellion against Rome, gripping the entire country. Jerusalem's preparations for the inevitable Roman reprisals were not helped by the factional in-fighting that consumed the city's population, with the Zealot leaders conducting a reign of terror not just against those who proposed a peaceful settlement to the dispute with Rome, but against anyone who appeared to challenge their authority. In fact, the internecinal struggle between the three main Zealot leaders, John of Gischala, Simeon bar Giora and Eleazar ben Simeon, led to scenes of brutality against Jerusalem's civilian population that matched the punitive measures that the Romans were to later inflict.

In an action that is described in gripping detail by Josephus (*The Jewish War*) the Vth, Xth, XIIth and XVth Legions of the Roman army, led by the Emperor Vespasian's son **Titus**, eventually succeeded in capturing the city. This culminated in 70 CE in the destruction of most of the city, including the Second Temple. Most of the surviving Jewish population of Jerusalem were exiled, and a decree was issued banning Jews from living in the city.

Early Roman Period and Aelia Capitolina During a visit to Judea in 130 CE, the Roman emperor **Hadrian** decided to set up a Roman colony on the ruins of Jerusalem. The establishment of Hadrian's **Colonia Aelia Capitolina** led to a second nationwide Jewish protest, this time under the guidance of **Shimon Bar Kokhba**. The period of Jewish sovereignty inspired by the Second Jewish Revolt (**Bar Kokhba Revolt**) was short-lived (132-135 CE), and Hadrian's legions soon re-entered Jerusalem. However, it should be noted that during the period of the revolt there is little evidence to suggest that the Jews actually reoccupied Jerusalem. Aelia Capitolina became firmly established, and the decree banning Jewish settlement in the city was more rigorously enforced. The province as a whole was also to become known as Syria Palestine.

The layout of Hadrian's new city is not just preserved in the 'Madaba Map' (page 60), but also largely in the present form of the Old City. The line of the cardo maximus is preserved in Tariq Khan es-Zeit, whilst the secondary (eastern) cardo follows Tariq al-Wad and the Decumanus follows David Street and Bab as-Silsila Street.

Byzantine period By the mid-third century CE Aelia Capitolina had lost much of its standing, and even the Tenth Legion had been posted south to Elath (Eilat). However, Jerusalem's revival was assured in 313 CE by the Imperial Edict of Milan that sanctioned Christianity as a legitimate religion within the Roman Empire. When **Constantine the Great** (306-337 CE) brought Palestine within the Christian Eastern Roman Empire, effectively establishing the **Byzantine Empire**, Jerusalem became a major pilgrimage centre for Byzantine Christians. Inspired by Constantine and his mother, the dowager queen **Helena**, significant efforts were made to identify and locate the major scenes in

Christ's Passion. Numerous churches and religious institutions were established, most notably the Constantine Church of the Holy Sepulchre (page 107).

In the fifth century CE **Eudocia**, wife of the emperor Theodosius II (408-450 CE), was responsible for establishing a number of churches, as the Byzantine passion for identifying the locations of both major and minor gospel scenes reached the point of obsession. It is also clear that by this time Jews were permitted to settle in the city, though the exact date of recolonization is unknown. The zenith of Byzantine Jerusalem was the sixth century CE, during the reign of **Justinian I** (527-565 CE). The Byzantine cardo maximus (still visible today, page 119), was extended southwards to link the Church of the Holy Sepulchre with Justinian's Nea Church (page 122). The decline of the Byzantine empire precipitated the **Persian** invasion of 614 CE, in which the invading Persian forces, aided by the Samaritans and Jews, razed most of the city's churches and religious institutions, massacring some 33,000 Christians in the process. Though the city was returned to the Byzantines by treaty, and attempts were made to restore the city to its former glory (including destroying any remaining Jewish symbols, such as the walls of the Temple Mount), the Byzantines were in no position to resist the advancing **Arabs**, and in 638 CE the city was surrendered to the Muslim army.

Early Arab period The Arab conquest of Palestine, and in particular their subsequent control over Jerusalem, created reverberations through the region that can still be felt today. Though the caliph **Omar** himself entered the city in 638 CE, famously refusing to

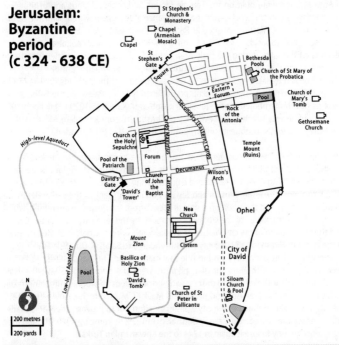

Jerusalem: Byzantine period (c 324 - 638 CE)

The Madaba Map

Established as a Christian village by the beginning of the fourth century CE at the latest, the small settlement of Madaba (some 30 km south of the Jordanian capital of Amman) gained international fame following the discovery in 1897 of the so-called 'Madaba Map'. The map is in fact part of the mosaic floor of a Byzantine church that is now generally agreed to have been laid in the sixth century CE. The map shows a stylized image of Palestine and may have been intended as a guide for pilgrims to the Holy Land. Of particular interest is the large (54 cm by 93 cm) inset showing a bird's-eye view of Jerusalem, confirming how the basic axis of the present Old City largely follows that of the Byzantine city before it, which in turn is based upon Hadrian's Aelia Capitolina. Landmarks of the city are clearly discernable on the map, such as the Cardo Maximus and the Church of the Holy Sepulchre.

pray at the Church of the Holy Sepulchre, little is known about these early years of Arab rule except that the Christian shrines and sanctuaries were left unmolested, and Jews and Arabs were subject to jizya (a kind of poll-tax levied on non-Muslims). In fact, early Arab rule was considerably more enlightened than previous and subsequent Christian rule.

The reshaping of Jerusalem along the lines of a Muslim city could be said to have begun under the **Umayyad** dynasty of caliphs (661-750 CE), when the Dome of the Rock and the al-Aqsa Mosque were built on the Temple Mount, and other religious and institutional buildings were constructed. Despite the importance of Jerusalem within Islam, the capital of the province of Filastin remained at Ramla on the coastal plain. Even the Umayyad's successors, the **Abbasids** (749-974 CE), ruled Palestine from their capital at Baghdad. A series of earthquakes during the Early Arab period further reduced Jerusalem's status to little more than that of a poor (albeit important) religious pilgrimage centre.

The Abbasid dynasty was soon to be replaced by that of the Fatimids (909-1175 CE), based in Cairo. A Shi'ite dynasty, ruling predominantly Sunni Palestine, the Fatimids are perhaps best remembered for the fanatical caliph **al-Hakim** (996-1020 CE), who in 1009 went out of his way to remove all evidence of Christianity from Jerusalem. Muslim rule of the 'Holy Land' was subsequently interrupted by the arrival of the Crusaders.

Crusader period The various periods of Crusader rule in Jerusalem are marked by the construction of grandiose institutions, as well as a large measure of religious intolerance. In fact the first thing that the Crusaders did on capturing Jerusalem on 15 July 1099, was to massacre almost the entire Muslim and Jewish population. Many of the earlier Byzantine churches that marked the traditional sites of scenes from the gospels were rebuilt, whilst the defensive capabilities of the city were enhanced by the reconstruction of the Citadel and the remodelling of the city walls. Nevertheless, following the defeat of the Crusaders at the Horns of Hittim in 1187, the city was surrendered to **Salah al-Din** (Saladin).

The subsequent period of **Ayyubid** rule saw many of the Christian institutions turned over to Muslim use, though Christian pilgrims were still permitted to visit the Holy Sepulchre. Salah al-Din refortified the city, with further defensive programmes undertaken by his brother el-Malik el-'Adil and nephew el-Malik el-'Mu'azzem 'Isa. However, in 1219 the latter dismantled much of the city walls in an effort not to provoke another Crusader attack. In fact, the Crusaders did regain Jerusalem in 1229, this time by treaty, though they were subsequently to lose it again in 1244 to the **Khwarizmian Turks**.

Jerusalem: Further reading

The definitive archaeological guide (with virtually a description of every building in the Old City) is the *Blue Guide* by Kay Prag (2002, Norton and Black). Perhaps the best biography of the city is to be found in Amos Elon's hugely entertaining *Jerusalem: City of Mirrors* (1989, Flamingo, London). This book also contains a good bibliography of Jerusalem-related matters. A politically incorrect account can be found in PJ O'Rourke's *Holidays in Hell* (1988, Picador). Events in Jerusalem in the period of the first century BCE to the first century CE are brilliantly told in Josephus' *The Jewish War* (various edition). Wandering around the Old City with this book is a lot of fun. An overall picture of the historical complexities alongside the city's buildings, which isn't heavy

weather and can be used for walking tours, is Simon Goldhill's *Jerusalem: City of Longing* (Harvard University Press, 2008). For a Zionist view of Jerusalem this century try Martin Gilbert's *Jerusalem in the Twentieth Century* (1996), or for a more balanced view, Karen Armstrong's *A History of Jerusalem: One City, Three Faiths* (1996, HarperCollins). The 1948 battle for Jerusalem is told in gripping, though hardly impartial, style in Collins and Lapierre's *O Jerusalem* (1972, various reprints).

Of course a Bible or Torah is not a bad accompaniment to a visit to Jerusalem! Most of these books are available in Jerusalem bookshops.

For a comprehensive list of books about Israel see Background, page 743.

Late Arab period Jerusalem soon passed into the hands of the **Mamluks**, the former slave guards of the Ayyubid dynasty who had risen to power in Egypt. Their most notable rulers were the sultan **Baibars** (1260-77) and **al-Nasir Mohammad** (c. 1294-1340), the latter of whom largely rebuilt the Citadel. There are also a number of distinctive tombs and religious institutions dating to the Mamluk period, most notably in the area to the west of the Haram al-Sharif. However, descriptions of Jerusalem in the latter part of the Mamluk period suggest a city decimated by disease, high taxation, internal division and Bedouin incursions.

Ottoman period The conquest of Syria by Selim the Grim (1512-20) brought Jerusalem under the control of the expansive **Ottoman** empire, though it was **Sulaiman II** ('the Magnificent') who restored Jerusalem to something approaching its former glory; the walls of the Old City that you see today are largely the result of his efforts. However, the Ottoman period in Jerusalem is seen as a metaphor for the rest of Palestine, and widely regarded as a period of corruption, high taxation and neglect. The Ottoman period in Jerusalem was brought to an end on 10 December 1917, when General Allenby's **British** forces captured the city.

British Mandate The British Mandate for Palestine was formalized by the League of Nations in 1922. Though Jerusalem benefitted greatly from the early years of British rule, the Mandate period is generally associated with the growing antagonism between the Arab population of Palestine and the increasing numbers of Jewish immigrants. As calls for the establishment of a Jewish state became louder, confrontations between the Jews and the British, Jews and Arabs, and Arabs and the British became more common. Though this was occurring all across Palestine, major events specific to Jerusalem included the conflict over access to the Western Wall (see page 85) and the bombing of the King David Hotel (see page 181).

War of Independence and the Six Day War With the termination of the British Mandate in May 1948, and the declaration of the State of Israel, Jerusalem became engulfed in war as the neighbouring Arab armies invaded in an attempt to snuff out the infant Jewish state. The upshot of the war was a divided city, with the Old City and most of East Jerusalem in **Jordanian** hands, and the rest in **Israeli** hands. This tense situation, monitored by the United Nations, continued for almost 20 years, until the Israelis captured the whole of the West Bank and Jerusalem in the **Six Day War** of 1967. The Israelis subsequently declared Jerusalem to be "reunified" (though Palestinians would disagree), making it their "eternal, undivided capital".

Present and future status of Jerusalem In Israeli eyes the status of Jerusalem as the 'United Capital' is unequivocal, yet most nations have refused to accept Israel's annexation of East Jerusalem, and as a mark of protest retain their diplomatic missions at Tel Aviv. Likewise, the Palestinians view East Jerusalem as the capital of a future Palestinian state, a fact that is non-negotiable. Thus, the status and borders of Jerusalem, including the Temple Mount/Haram al-Sharif, is probably the biggest sticking point in discussions on a future two-state solution.

Old City

Start your visit to Jerusalem with these highlights: a wander around the walled Old City, taking in the Citadel, Church of the Holy Sepulchre and the Via Dolorosa; the Temple Mount/Haram al-Sharif area, featuring the Western (Wailing) Wall and Dome of the Rock; and the Mount of Olives, for its views and important Christian sites.

Old City Walls and Gates

Amongst Jerusalem's most striking features are the pale-yellow stone walls that encircle the Old City: for many visitors, the first vision of these walls is a lasting one. They are equally impressive close up, where you can fully appreciate the sheer size of some of the masonry slabs, or from afar, most notably from one of the surrounding hills such as Mount Scopus or the Mt of Olives.

Ins and outs
A complete circuit of the city walls is highly recommended, including sections where you can walk along the top of the walls themselves ('Rampart Walk'). Jerusalem's city walls run for 4.02 km and are breached by eight gates (seven of which are open to passage). Visitors should note that each gate has three names: an Arabic/Muslim version, a Hebrew version, and an Anglicized version that is in common usage (and used here).

Background
Relative to Jerusalem's long and ancient history, the city walls and gates that you see today are a recent addition, having been completed by **Sulaiman the Magnificent** (Sulaiman

II) between 1537 and 1541. The previous city walls had been dismantled in 1219 by al-Malik al-Mu'azzam in order to discourage the reoccupation of the city by the Crusaders. However, certain stretches of the walls follow the course of far older fortifications, dating back to Crusader and Ayyubid, Byzantine, Herodian/Roman and even Hasmonean times, and in places the earlier defences can still be seen.

Ramparts Walk

ⓘ *Sat-Thu 0900-1600 (-1700 in summer), Fri 0900-1400. NB on Fri only southern ramparts open. Tickets cannot be bought on Sat or holidays: buy the day before. Adult 16NIS, student 8NIS, valid for two days. You also can buy a combination ticket for 55NIS, allowing entry to the Ramparts Walk, Jerusalem Archaeological Park, Zedekiah's Cave and the Roman Plaza, valid for 3 days (saving 18NIS). The main ticket office is by Jaffa Gate, T02-6277550, www.pami. co.il, but you can also buy tickets and enter from Damascus Gate or the entrance beyond the Citadel. Exit-only points are at Herod's Gate, New Gate, Zion Gate, Dung Gate and Lions' Gate, but (confusingly) after 1600 you cannot exit from Jaffa, Damascus or the Citadel.*

Some sections of the ramparts are closed, notably between Lions' Gate and Dung Gate, and the section within the Citadel. The route is split into two sections: the southern ramparts (Jaffa-Dung, 30 minutes) and the northern ramparts (Jaffa-Lions, 1-1½ hours). It is particularly nice to walk in late afternoon sunlight, and is of human as well as historical interest, giving glimpses into the hidden everyday life in the Old City.

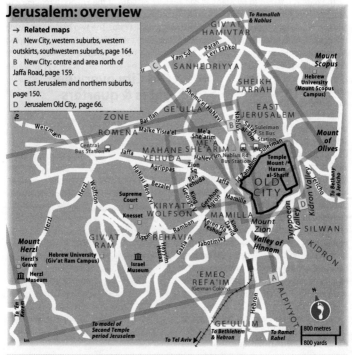

Jerusalem: overview

→ **Related maps**
A New City, western suburbs, western outskirts, southwestern suburbs, page 164.
B New City: centre and area north of Jaffa Road, page 159.
C East Jerusalem and northern suburbs, page 150.
D Jerusalem Old City, page 66.

Warnings The stone path along the ramparts is particularly slippery when wet. And, although all sections are securely fenced, vertigo sufferers might be affected. Security staff patrol the area between Damascus and Lions' Gate (in case children throw stones) until around 1500; however, we have not received any reports of problems by tourists when walking alone after that time.

Northern Ramparts Walk (Jaffa Gate to Lions' Gate)

Jaffa Gate Though Sulaiman II's original 1538 gate remains, and is still used for pedestrian access, a section of the curtain wall to the south was demolished in 1898 (and the moat filled in) to allow Sultan 'Abd al-Hamid II's guests, the German **Kaiser Wilhelm II** and his wife, to drive into the city in the splendour of their carriage. **General Allenby** also entered the city with the victorious British Army at this point in December 1917, though he consciously chose humbly to proceed on foot (following the cabled recommendation of the British War Office: "Strongly suggest dismounting at gate. German emperor rode in and the saying went round 'a better man than he walked.' Advantages of contrast will be obvious"). This also contrasts with the entry into Jerusalem of Gustave Flaubert in 1850, who commented: "We enter through the Jaffa Gate and I let a fart escape as I cross the threshold very involuntarily. I was even annoyed at bottom by this Voltaireanism of my anus" (*Les oeuvres complètes de Gustave Flaubert: Vol.19, Notes de voyage*, edited by L. Conrad, Paris 1910).

The gate is referred to by Arabs as *Bab el-Khalil*, or 'Gate of the Friend'; a reference to Abraham, the 'Friend of God', whose tomb lies south of here in Hebron. The Hebrew name, *Sha'ar Yafo*, reflects the gate's orientation towards Jaffa (Yafo). The two graves just inside the gate (behind the railings near the tourist office) are said to belong to two of Sulaiman II's architects, executed for displeasing him with their penny-pinching (see Jaffa Gate to Zion Gate, page 69).

Jaffa Gate to New Gate One point along this stretch of the walls is labelled "Watchtower"; a reference to the period between 1948 and 1967 when Jordanian soldiers stationed here looked down upon the no-man's land that divided the Jordanian-controlled Old City from Israeli-held Jerusalem. Amos Elon recounts an amusing incident when a nun on the Israeli side of the line managed to 'cough' her dentures into the no man's land: "A brace of blue-helmeted UN truce supervisors, brandishing white flags, combed the debris-covered terrain where few persons had ventured for years and fewer still had come back alive. The false teeth were successfully retrieved" (Jerusalem: City of Mirrors, 1989).

Just before New Gate, inside an angle in the wall, is the small Ottoman-period (16th-century) **al-Qaymari mosque**. Also at this

Old City overview: gates & quarters

East Jerusalem

Old City Walls

Herod Gate

St Stephen's Gate

Damascus Gate

Muslim Quarter

Haram al-Sharif/Temple Mount

Golden Gate

Church of the Holy Sepulchre

Dome of the Rock

New Gate

Christian Quarter

al-Aqsa Mosque

Jewish Quarter

Ophel

Jaffa Gate

Citadel

Dung Gate

Armenian Quarter

Ancient City on the southeast ridge

Zion Gate

300 metres

300 yards

northwest corner, just outside the Old City walls, are the remains of a substantial tower (35 m by 35 m) built of re-used Herodian blocks, though almost certainly dating to the Crusader period. The north wall of the tower is best seen in the small 'archaeological garden' outside the Ottoman period walls, whilst parts of the huge internal piers are preserved within the Christian Brothers' College (viewing is discretionary, and by appointment only). The structure is commonly referred to as **Tancred's Tower**, after the Crusader knight who assisted Godfrey of Bouillon in capturing Jerusalem in July 1099. A medieval legend claims this as the spot where David slew Goliath (*I Samuel 17*), with the tower referred to in some sources as the *Castle of Goliath* (Arabic: *Qasr Jalut*). A further identification is with Herod Agrippa I's *Psephinus Tower* (described by Josephus in his *Jewish War V: 160*), though not only is the archaeological evidence against such an interpretation, the written evidence is also contrary (Josephus describes an octagonal, as opposed to square, tower). The tower was probably razed in 1219 by al-Malik al-Mu'azzam, nephew of Salah al-Din.

New Gate to Damascus Gate As its name suggests, New Gate (Arabic: Bab al-Jadid, Hebrew: Sha'ar He-Hadash) is a relatively recent access point into the walled city, cut in 1887 by the Ottoman Sultan 'Abd al-Hamid II in order to facilitate communications with the expanding 'New City' to the northwest. It remained sealed from 1948 until 1967. The stretch of wall from New Gate to Damascus Gate is particularly fine Ottoman period work, though excavations suggest that Sulaiman II's architects followed the line of the third- or fourth-century CE Byzantine walls.

Damascus Gate The most impressive gate in the city walls, Damascus Gate (Bab al-'Amud in Arabic, Sha'ar Shechem in Hebrew) is also considered to be one of the best examples of Ottoman architecture in the region. Flanked by two defensive towers, it is solid yet highly decorated with elaborate *crenellation* (battlements) above. It is not unknown for the *machicolations* above the gate, originally designed for dropping molten lead or boiling oil on to attackers, to have been used for dispensing tear gas canisters! The gateway is set back within a pointed arch of carved wedge-shaped blocks (known as *voussoirs*) and is reached via a bridge built in 1967 as a temporary structure. The entrance passage to the gate makes a double turn before leading into the heart of the Muslim Quarter. The street inside the gate and the plaza outside are used as informal market places (though the majority of the fruit vendors have recently been relocated, more's the pity). Still, it's a lively and busy thoroughfare and arguably the most interesting way to enter the Old City. The steps are certainly one of the best place to sit and absorb the atmosphere of Jerusalem, particularly in the hour before Shabbat.

Sulaiman II's structure is built precisely upon the lines of the former Roman period gate, with excavations in the area revealing remains from most periods of Jerusalem's history. To view closely the Roman and Crusader remains (and for access to the Roman Plaza Museum and Ramparts Walk), take the steps that go under the bridge (to the right of the entrance as you look at Damascus Gate from the outside).

Beneath the modern bridge (now a scruffy café) it is possible to observe the kerbstones of the medieval roadway that entered the gate on precisely the same line as the modern entrance, though at a lower level. The Byzantine and Roman gates also stood at this spot, again at a lower level still, with Roman remains evident in the building bearing the mark of the **Tenth Legion** (Fretensis).

Emerging on the east side beneath the modern bridge, the remains of the **East Tower** and **East Gate of the Triple Gate** are clearly distinguishable. This round-arched triple gate flanked by two towers is thought to have been built by the emperor Hadrian in 135 CE

Jerusalem Old City

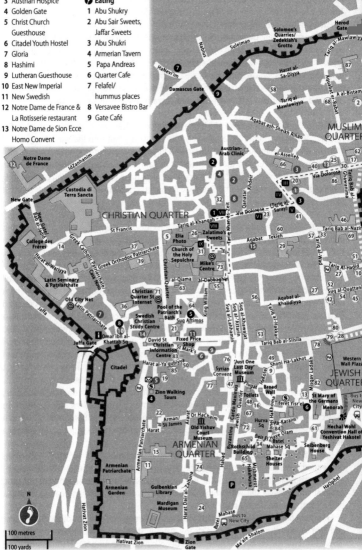

😴 Sleeping
1. American Guesthouse
2. Al-Arab
3. Austrian Hospice
4. Golden Gate
5. Christ Church Guesthouse
6. Citadel Youth Hostel
7. Gloria
8. Hashimi
9. Lutheran Guesthouse
10. East New Imperial
11. New Swedish
12. Notre Dame de France & La Rotisserie restaurant
13. Notre Dame de Sion Ecce Homo Convent
14. Petra Hostel
15. Hebron Hostel

🍴 Eating
1. Abu Shukry
2. Abu Sair Sweets, Jaffar Sweets
3. Abu Shukri
4. Armerian Tavern
5. Papa Andreas
6. Quarter Cafe
7. Felafel/ hummus places
8. Versavee Bistro Bar
9. Gate Café

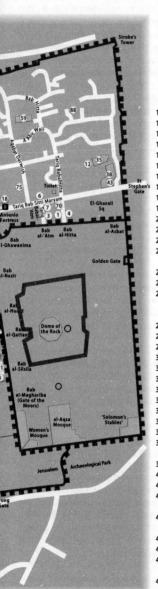

at the north end of the cardo maximus of his city of Aelia Capitolina. The fact that no traces of any first-century CE walls have been found goes far to support the theory that this triple gate was more a triumphant arch than a defensive structure. However, there is enough archaeological evidence to support the view that **Hadrian** merely rebuilt a gate begun by **Herod Agrippa I** (c. 40-41 CE) as part of the 'Third North wall', possibly reusing some of the drafted stones from the Temple (destroyed in 70 CE). Hadrian's gate opened on to a **monumental paved plaza** at the top of the cardo maximus, at the centre of which stood an honorific column, probably bearing a statue of his likeness. In fact, the Arabic name for Damascus Gate, *Bab al-'Amud*, actually means 'Gate of the Column', though like everything in Jerusalem, the interpretation is not straightforward. Murphy-O'Connor reminds observers (*The Holy Land*, 1992) that Ottoman-period gates invariably take their name from something outside them, and consequently the 'column' in question may refer to the huge column drums found within St Stephen's Church, about 200 m to the north. In the Crusader period the gate was referred to as St Stephen's Gate, with tradition associating the stoning to death of the first Christian martyr just outside. Following the defeat of the Crusader's Latin Kingdom in 1187, Christian pilgrims were forbidden from gathering close to the vulnerable north wall of the city, so the name was conveniently 'moved' to the gate on the east side of the city (see page 69). The Hebrew name for the gate, *Sha'ar Shekhem*, refers to the gate's orientation towards Shechem (Nablus).

Within the Roman Triple Gate is the **Roman Plaza** ① *Sat-Thu 0900-1600 (summer -1700), closed Fri, adult 10NIS (or with combined ticket, see page 53)*. In the eastern guard tower, first used by Roman soldiers, there are the remains of an oil press from the early Arab period. Venturing further below brings you to a small excavated section of the Roman/ Byzantine plaza with polished stone slabs bearing the carved markings of a gaming-board similar to the ones found at the Convent of the Sisters of Sion (page 98). There is also a copy of the sixth-century CE Madaba Map, and photos and diagrams of the Damascus Gate through the ages. But you don't get much for your money, to be honest.

Damascus Gate to Herod Gate Between Damascus Gate and Herod Gate the bed-rock is exposed at the surface. At the mid-point between the two gates, an ancient quarry extends beneath the city walls, known as **Zedekiah's Cave** or **Solomon's Quarry** ① *Sat-Thu 0900-1600 (summer -1700), closed Fri, buy tickets a day in advance for Sat. Adult 16NIS (or a combined ticket, see page 53)*. It is generally well-lit, though you might want to bring a torch to explore more thoroughly. Discovered in 1854 by an adventurous dog, the origins of the cave are still open for debate. The malaki limestone found here was almost certainly exploited by Herod the Great and/or Herod Agrippa I, and may well be the 'Royal Caverns' that Josephus mentions (*Jewish War V: 147*). However, it is not unreasonable to speculate that the tradition associated with Solomon (*I Kings 5:17-18*) is also plausible. The cave complex extends for, well, who knows? It's certain that the main passageway leads some 230 m from the cave entrance, though Jewish tradition relates how Zedekiah escaped the besieging Babylonian army in 586 BCE through this hidden network of passages all the way to Jericho! The size of the quarry is remarkable, as is the concept of walking deep beneath the Muslim Quarter. As the cave descends, the shapes hewn from the rock vividly bring the blocks of the Temple wall to mind. The main hall has been used to hold Freemasons ceremonies, a notion pioneered by Sir Charles Warren.

Herod Gate This small gate in the north wall originally took its name from the rosette panel above the arch (*Bab al-Zahra*, or Gate of Flowers). Some time in the 16th or 17th century, Christian pilgrims mistakenly confused a nearby medieval house, *Dair Abu 'Adas*, with the palace of the man who condemned Jesus, Herod Antipas (Abu 'Adas/Antipas?), since when the name Herod Gate has stuck. Like Lions' Gate, this gate has been modified to allow direct access.

Herod Gate to Lions' Gate It was through a breach in the medieval-period walls just to the east of where Herod Gate is now located that the Crusaders first entered Jerusalem, at noon on 15 July 1099. The northeast corner of the Old City has always been considered to be Jerusalem's weak spot since the terrain is relatively flat and the protective ravines that defend the other sides are absent. Attempts have been made to improve the defences on this side by digging a deep ditch from the rock, and building a large number of insets and off-sets into the walls (thus increasing the field of fire). The northeast corner is occupied by the Stork Tower (or Burj Laqlaq), one of the more impressive towers in the ramparts.

Lions' Gate Built in 1538 by Sulaiman II, the name that he gave, *Bab al-Ghor* or Gate of the Valley (of Jordan), has never caught on, though the Hebrew name, *Sha'ar ha-'Arayot* or Lions' Gate (referring to the carved lions that adorn either side of the arch) has. Many Muslim sources still call the gate by its Arabic name, *Bab Sitti Maryam*; an obvious reference to the Church and Tomb of the Virgin Mary just to the east. During the Crusader period the name changed from the 'Gate of Jehoshaphat' to 'St Stephen's Gate' for reasons given above (see under 'Damascus Gate', on previous page), and is often still referred to as such. The gate was modified during the British Mandate period to allow access to motor vehicles. It was through Lions' Gate that the Jordanian Arab Legion entered the Old City in 1948, but also through here that Colonel 'Motta' Gur led an Israeli parachute brigade in capturing the city on 7 June 1967. Lions' Gate is the end point of the northern section of the walls, and the starting point for the tour of the Muslim Quarter (page 93).

Southern Ramparts Walk (Jaffa Gate to Dung Gate)

Jaffa Gate to Zion Gate To the south of Jaffa Gate is the **Citadel** (see page 71). Ascend to the Ramparts Walk at the stairs 100 m south of Jaffa Gate by the Citadel (signed). There are a number of points of historical interest along the stretch of wall between the Citadel and the southwest corner (before the wall turns east towards Zion Gate), though most of these features are best seen from outside (as opposed to on top of) the city walls.

This section of the city walls follows the line of far older defensive fortifications. Sections of the Hasmonean **city walls** (c. 164-63 BCE) are clearly visible in places, as are the slightly later **Herodian tower and walls**. One tower along this stretch is particularly noteworthy, featuring bulging Herodian stones at its base, medieval blocks above, and Ottoman-period work at the top. It was just to the south of here, close to the first-century CE city gate, that the Roman army finally broke through into the Upper City in 70 CE, during their suppression of the Jewish Revolt (see Josephus' *Jewish War VI: 374-99*).

At the southwest corner of the Old City walls, just beyond the remains of what must have been an impressive medieval tower, the line of the walls turns sharply east towards Zion Gate. Legend has it that Sulaiman II's walls should have been extended south to encompass the supposed site of the Tomb of David on Mount Zion. However, to save time and money this extension of the walls was not undertaken; a decision taken by the architects that is said to have cost them their lives when a furious Sulaiman II found out.

Zion Gate Completed in 1540, Sulaiman II's *Bab al-Kabi Da'ud* (or 'Gate of the Prophet David') was severely damaged in the 1948 battle for the city: in fact, when the Jewish Palmach forces breached the gate with over 70 kg of explosives on the night of 18/19 May 1948, they did something that according to Collins and Lapierre "no Jewish soldier had done since the days of Judas Maccabaeus [c. 164 BCE] – they had breached the walls of Jerusalem" (*O Jerusalem*, 1972). Their success was short-lived, however, with the Palmach forces being forced to withdraw almost immediately. Zion Gate still bears the scars of the 1948 fighting, and some of the ornamentation seen here is not original.

Zion Gate to Dung Gate Extensive excavations have taken place along the stretch of wall between Zion Gate and Dung Gate, with visible remains from most periods of Jerusalem's history. Some of the main points of interest are within the line of the current city walls, though most are outside.

Continuing east from Zion Gate, it is possible to see part of the **Ayyubid tower** built in 1212, but dismantled just seven years later. To the east of the Ayyubid tower, inside the city walls, is a short section of wall dating to the Crusader period, whilst further east still is the **Sulphur Tower** (Arabic: *Burj al-Kibrit*). An inscription on the south side dates it to 1540, though the mixed remains of the tower projecting beneath it date to the medieval period. Close to the Sulphur Tower can be seen a section of the first-century BCE **aqueduct** that brought water from Solomon's Pools near Bethlehem to the Temple at Jerusalem. With various repairs, including the insertion of the ceramic pipes in the early Ottoman period, the aqueduct remained in use until early in the 20th century!

Just beyond the angle in the wall lie the remains of a sixth-century CE building, possibly a hospice, that is thought to be connected with the **Nea Church** just inside the walls, whilst further along the wall itself a small section of the Nea Church's southeast apse protrudes beyond Sulaiman II's walls (see page 122). The massive size of the four revealed courses (the upper of which has been restored) hint at the monumental size of this structure, and serve to confirm its status as the largest basilica in Palestine.

The rest of the section between here and Dung Gate is occupied mainly by rock-cut **cisterns** and **ritual baths** that formed part of first-century CE houses. Flanking Dung Gate to the west is a large **medieval tower** that is usually associated with the Crusader *Tanner's Gate*, or *Gate of the Leatherworkers*. Its foundations rest upon a section of **paved Byzantine road** that led down to the Pool of Siloam (see page 146).

Dung Gate This was probably a small Ottoman postern gate (built 1540-1541), but was greatly enlarged between 1948 and 1967 by the Jordanians to allow motor vehicles to enter the Old City (Jaffa and New Gates being sealed during this period). The name in common usage (Hebrew: *Sha'ar ha-Ashpot*) is said to refer to its proximity to a former waste dumping site, though its official name of *Bab al-Maghariba* (Gate of the Moors) is derived from its position close to the former Moorish (North African) colony.

Dung Gate to Lions' Gate For details of the southeast section of the Old City, where it abuts the south wall of the Haram al-Sharif/Temple Mount, see under the **Jerusalem Archaeological Park**. Unfortunately, the sensitive religious and political nature of the Haram al-Sharif/Temple Mount means that it is impossible to visit the Golden Gate on the east side of the Old City. Details of this structure are included within the Haram al-Sharif/Temple Mount section (see page 75).

The Citadel (Tower of David)

ⓘ T02-6265333, 24-hr information T02-6265310, www.towerofdavid.org.il. Sep-Jun: Sun-Thu 1000-1600, Fri closed, Sat and hols 1000-1400. Jul-Aug: Sat-Thu 1000-1700, Fri 1000-1400. Adults 30NIS, student 20NIS, children 15NIS. Entrance fee includes a free guided tour, English: Sun-Thu at 1100, (in Jul/Aug also Fri at 1100); French: Tue at 1100. Personal audio guides available in English at the ticket office. There is a wheelchair route, though it does not reach all of the viewpoints and museum displays. Cafés, toilets. There's also a sound and light show: The Night Spectacular, adult 50NIS, students/children 40NIS; combined tickets for the Citadel and the Night Spectacular: adults 65NIS, students/children 55NIS. Book in advance on website or 24-hr tel no, although it's possible to get tickets on the night. A bit overpriced for only 45 mins, but children especially will enjoy the clever lighting effects giving a potted history of Jerusalem, and the optical illusions set against the Citadel walls are memorable. Bring warm clothes (even in summer); no photography.

Located on high ground on the west side of the Old City (just south of Jaffa Gate), the Citadel of Jerusalem has been the city's stronghold for around 2000 years. Built largely upon the site of Herod the Great's first-century BCE palace/fortress and incorporating the substantial remains of one of three massive towers that he built, successive rulers of Jerusalem from the Romans, Arabs, Crusaders, Mamluks and Ottomans all rebuilt, modified and reused this defensive stronghold. Following the capture of Jerusalem by the Israelis in 1967, the Citadel was turned into a magnificent museum, and tells the history of the city through a superb assembly of scale models, maps, paintings, photographs, holograms, video footage and artefacts found during numerous excavations. Given the superb views from the ramparts, and the clear and concise museum presentation, the Citadel is an ideal place to begin a visit to Jerusalem. A thorough visit takes 1½-2 hours.

Ins and outs

Getting around There are three marked 'theme-routes' around the Citadel, of which the **Exhibition** tour (**red**) provides an excellent introduction to the city and gives the greatest rewards when undertaken in chronological order. The tour described here begins with the Exhibition (red) tour, and tries to provide background details on the building within which each exhibit is displayed rather than merely repeating the historical information provided by these museum displays. The **Panorama** (**blue**) tour around the towers and battlements requires little explanation, with noticeboards posted at key vantage points. The tour of the Citadel concludes by descending to the garden in the centre for a closer examination of the **Excavations** (**green**). Note, however, that in order to gain some perspective on this "jumble of masonry" it is wise to take advantage of the aerial perspective provided from the top of the Northeast (Phasael) tower (**7**). Bold numbers in brackets refer to a point marked on the map.

Background

Early history Evidence suggests that the site here was used as a stone quarry as early as the seventh century BCE, but was included within the northwest angle of the city walls by the late second century BCE. The dating of this 'First Wall' (which can be seen in the garden on the 'Excavation' tour) remains contentious, though the weight of opinion is behind the argument that it was built by the **Hasmoneans**, probably John Hyrcanus (134-104 BCE).

What is clear, however, is that **Herod the Great** built three monumental defensive towers here in the first century BCE to protect the magnificent palace that he constructed for himself just to the south. The base of Herod's **Phasael Tower**, named after the king's brother who had fallen in battle, can still be seen today on the northeast side of the

Citadel, though there is the possibility that this could be the **Hippicus Tower** named after Herod's great (dead) friend. The latter tower is described by Josephus as being "superior in size, beauty, and strength to any in the whole world" (*Jewish War, V: 162*). The third tower was named after Herod's wife **Mariamme**, whom the king "had himself killed through passionate love" (*ibid*).

Josephus provides us with a flowery description of Herod's **palace**, repeatedly referring to its "magnificence", "splendour" and "beauty", concluding that "no words are adequate to portray the Palace" (V: *176*). Parts of the palace were destroyed at the outbreak of the Jewish Revolt in 66 CE, when the rebels gained access by undermining one of its towers and torched the building (*Jewish War II: 430-440*). The Roman garrison took refuge in the three great towers and, having agreed to surrender, were then treacherously murdered by the Jews (*Jewish War, II: 431-56*). Josephus suggests that by this act "the city was stained by such guilt that they must expect a visitation from heaven if not the vengeance of Rome" (*ibid*).

Excavation in the 'Armenian Garden' to the south of the Citadel suggest that the palace would have stretched almost to the line of the present south wall of the Old City. Following **Titus'** conquest of Jerusalem in 70 CE, this area became for the next 200 years part of the camp of the Tenth Legion Fretensis.

Of course, much of the interest in Herod's palace lies in its relevance to the Christian tradition of the Crucifixion. Most experts now believe that the Roman Procurator of Palestine, in this case **Pontius Pilate**, would have stayed here in Herod's palace (as opposed to the Antonia fortress on the opposite side of the city, see page 96) whilst visiting from the Roman capital at Caesarea. Thus, this would be the site of the **Praetorium** where Pontius Pilate judged Jesus (for example *Mark 15:1-15*). If so, as is probably the case, this completely undermines the authenticity of most of the modern route of the Via Dolorosa.

Later history Remains are scant from the Early Arab period of occupation (638-1099 CE), though parts of an **Umayyad** palace have been excavated here (and in the 'Armenian Garden' to the south). When Jerusalem fell to the **Crusaders** in 1099, the **Fatimid** garrison in the Citadel withstood the attack and negotiated their surrender and safe passage from here. The Citadel was subsequently rebuilt into the fortress-palace of the newly established Crusader kings of Jerusalem, but was surrendered to **Salah al-Din** (Saladin) when he took the city in 1187. The fortifications were rebuilt and then dismantled a number of times in the ensuing years, but only when it was clear that the Crusaders were not going to return imminently did the Muslim rulers feel comfortable about extensively refortifying the city. By this time the **Mamluks** had replaced the Ayyubids as the rulers of Palestine, and it was the Mamluk sultan **al-Nasir Mohammad** who gave the Citadel much of its present form (c. 1310-11). Further additions were made between 1531 and 1532 by the Ottoman ruler **Sulaiman II** ('the Magnificent'), who was later to build the Old City walls that you see today. In recent years the Citadel has been used as barracks by the Jordanian army (1948-67) before being turned over to its present use as a museum following the Israeli capture of the city during the Six Day War.

The museum's full title, **The Tower of David Museum of the History of Jerusalem**, perpetuates the use of the popular name for the Citadel that arose in the fourth century CE when Byzantine Christians incorrectly identified the site as the palace of David. The Crusaders revived this erroneous identification, with their reused Herodian tower referred to as the 'Turres David'. In the 19th century the minaret (still standing) of the mosque became known as the **Tower of David**, and the name is now generally applied to the whole Citadel complex.

Sights

The current **entrance** to the Citadel is on the northeast side, a short way inside Jaffa Gate. The **outer steps (1)** here are those from which the British commander General Allenby declared the liberation of Jerusalem from Turkish rule in 1917. This ornamental entrance dates to the period of Sulaiman II's rebuilding project (1531-1532) and bears his name in a number of inscriptions. A bridge passes over the medieval **moat (2)** and enters the **outer barbican (3)** that the Mamluks, and then Sulaiman II, adapted from the original Crusader gate system. On the left is the **open air mosque (4)** built by Sulaiman II, whilst to the right a series of steps lead down into the moat and café.

The main **entrance gate (5)** dates to the 12th century and comprises a guardroom (complete with original stone benches), a portcullis, and the usual L-shaped right-angled turn that was designed to slow down enemy attackers. This Crusader gate complex was also restored by the Mamluk sultan al-Nasir Mohammad. The entrance gate leads into a **hexagonal chamber (6)** built in the 14th century, where the main ticket office is located. It is possible to proceed into the courtyard garden from here, though it is recommended that you follow the blue and red arrows up the stairs to the top of the **Northeast (Phasael) tower (7)**. A small room within this tower shows the Italian artist Emmanuele Luzzati's 14-minute animated film "Jerusalem" (every half an hour between 1010 and 1640; Hebrew with English translation).

Citadel (Tower of David)

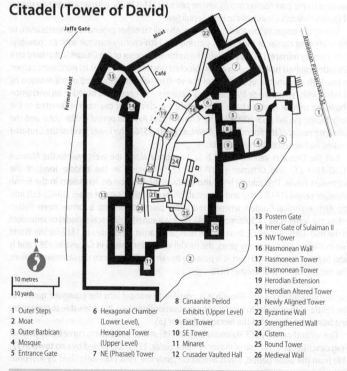

1 Outer Steps	6 Hexagonal Chamber	8 Canaanite Period
2 Moat	(Lower Level),	Exhibits (Upper Level)
3 Outer Barbican	Hexagonal Tower	9 East Tower
4 Mosque	(Upper Level)	10 SE Tower
5 Entrance Gate	7 NE (Phasael) Tower	11 Minaret
		12 Crusader Vaulted Hall

13 Postern Gate
14 Inner Gate of Sulaiman II
15 NW Tower
16 Hasmonean Wall
17 Hasmonean Tower
18 Hasmonean Tower
19 Herodian Extension
20 Herodian Altered Tower
21 Newly Aligned Tower
22 Byzantine Wall
23 Strengthened Wall
24 Cistern
25 Round Tower
26 Medieval Wall

The base of this tower is solid all the way through, with the original Herodian construction comprising eight courses above the bedrock rising to just under 19 m. The smaller masonry at the top of the tower dates to al-Nasir Mohammad's building efforts in the early 14th century.

Exhibition (red) tour From the top of the **Northeast tower** follow the red arrows down to the adjacent roof of the 14th-century Mamluk **hexagonal tower** (6). The top of this tower provides a good aerial perspective of the mixed remains in the garden below, with an information board indicating the key points of interest.

To the south of the hexagonal tower, on the same level and still outdoors, there is some information on Jerusalem in the *Canaanite period (c. 3000-1200 BCE)* (8). To the south of this exhibit is the **East tower** (9), probably built during the Mamluk period on Crusader foundations. The chamber that you enter on this level is devoted to the *First Temple period (c. 1000-586 BCE)*, and features among other things a model of the City of David in the 10th century BCE. The lower level of the east tower (follow the red arrows) is devoted to the *Hellenistic, Hasmonean and Second Temple period (332 BCE-70 CE)*, featuring an excellent model of Robinson's Arch.

Continue to the **Southeast tower** (10), also built between 1310 and 1311 by al-Nasir Mohammad and restored between 1531 and 1532 by Sulaiman II. The chamber inside is devoted to the *Late Roman and Byzantine periods (131-638 CE)*, with an interesting model of Queen Helena's Church of the Holy Sepulchre.

Exiting the tower, follow the line of the south wall (at either ground or ramparts level) to the southwest corner of the Citadel, passing the 14th-century mosque with its (possibly) 16th-century **minaret** (11) to your left. The southwest corner of the Citadel is occupied by a **Crusader vaulted hall** (12), with a now-blocked **postern gate** (13) at its northwest corner. In the 14th century the upper level of the vaulted hall was converted into a mosque by al-Nasir, with repairs made by Sulaiman II between 1531 and 1532 noted in an inscription above the minbar (pulpit chair). The exhibition in this upper chamber is devoted to the *Early Islamic period (638-1099 CE)*, the *Crusader and Ayyubid period (1099-1291)* and the *Late Arab period of the Fatimids and Mamluks (1291-1516)*. The lower level of the Crusader vaulted hall occasionally has exhibitions.

Exit the Crusader vaulted hall (12) and continue along the west wall to the *Mamluk (1260-1517 CE)* and *Ottoman (1517-1917 CE)* exhibition in the middle level of the northwest tower. This middle level also contains information on Jerusalem in the *British Mandate period (1917-1948)* and the establishment of the State of Israel (1948). Exit into the Archaeological Garden, where a red arrow points down into a former deep cistern below the **inner gate of Sulaiman II** (14). Here is a superb 1:500 scale model of Jerusalem in the mid-19th century CE, built by the Hungarian artist Stefan Illes in 1872 for the World Fair in Vienna. Lost for many years, the model was rediscovered in Geneva in 1984 and is now here on an extended loan. It is possible to exit the Citadel from the Northwest Tower. The red Exhibition tour finishes here.

Excavations (green) tour Though it is possible to wander into the courtyard garden in the centre of the Citadel to examine the excavations up close, it is advisable to view them first from from the roof of the **hexagonal tower** (6).

The second-century BCE **Hasmonean wall** (16) makes a sweeping curve through what Prag describes as a "jumble of masonry" (*Blue Guide*, 1989). Defended by two **towers** (17) (18) from the same period, this is almost certainly the 'First Wall' described by Josephus

(Jewish War, V: 142-5). Its continuation can be seen at the start of the tour of the Jewish Quarter (see page 118). The periods of Hasmonean building can be distinguished from later periods by the general use of smaller blocks. The rooms abutting the Hasmonean wall (**16**) became buried beneath the podium that Herod built to support his palace. He also built an **extension** (**19**) to one of the Hasmonean towers, whilst reducing the size of the other (**20**). For some unexplained reason this tower had to be rebuilt early in the first century CE, on a slightly different alignment (**21**). Evidence of the damage caused to the palace during the Jewish attack of 66 CE was identified just here.

To the north side of the Northeast (Phasael) tower is a section of the **Byzantine wall** (**22**) added in the fourth century CE; perhaps part of Herod Agrippa's Third North Wall. The original Hasmonean wall (**16**) was also strengthened (**23**) and the Herodian tower (**21**) rebuilt. The **cistern** (**24**) also dates to this period. Later additions include the **round tower** (**25**), generally thought to be part of an eighth-century CE Umayyad palace, and the stretch of medieval wall (**26**). If you have any time left at the end, it is recommended to do the Panoramic tour for the excellent views.

Temple Mount/Haram al-Sharif

ⓘ *Entry hours are restricted to Sun-Thu 0730-1030 and 1330-1430. During the holy month of Ramadan visiting is only Sun-Thu 0730-1000, and the Haram al-Sharif may be closed completely during certain Islamic festivals. Non-Muslims can only enter the Haram al-Sharif through the Bab al-Maghariba (Gate of the Moors, via the covered ramp leading up from the Western Wall Plaza), though you can leave by any of the functioning gates. Non-Muslims are not permitted to enter the Dome of the Rock nor Al-Aqsa Mosque, and this is very unlikely to change in the near future. The Islamic Museum, on top of the mound, remains shut.*

The Temple Mount/Haram al-Sharif is an artificially raised platform built upon a low hill on the eastern side of the Old City. Whilst representing the architectural and visual focus of Jerusalem, it could also be said to be one of the most contested pieces of real estate on earth. The site of the First and Second Jewish Temples, the latter where Jesus taught, it is now home to a shrine and mosque that make it the third most important place of pilgrimage within the Islamic world. Whilst the status of Jerusalem divides Israelis and Palestinians like no other matter, the custody of the Temple Mount/Haram al-Sharif provides a vivid and terrifying focus to this confrontation. When trouble flares up in the Old City, it invariably is centred around this area, and consequently the Western Wall Plaza will be closed to visitors. Though there are no standing remains of the Temple, Jews still visit the Western (Wailing) Wall to mourn its destruction. The central Islamic buildings stand on the Haram al-Sharif/Temple Mount itself and include Jerusalem's main congregational mosque (al-Aqsa Mosque), plus one of the world's most beautiful architectural monuments, the Dome of the Rock. Non-Muslims are not permitted entry to either structure.

Ins and outs
Getting there and away There are any number of ways of approaching the Temple Mount/Haram al-Sharif, though most arrive via the Western Wall Plaza (on foot from just about any direction in the Old City, or by buses 1, 3 or 38). There is (free) 24-hour access to the Western Wall Plaza.

Temple Mount or Haram al-Sharif?

Even for a guidebook that is attempting to be non-partisan, problems arise when it comes to deciding by which name to refer to certain contested sites.

In the main, the name commonly used in Western sources has been selected, based largely on the premise that most of the readership is drawn from here and thus the 'common' name used will strike a chord of familiarity. Thus, there is a chapter called 'West Bank' and not 'Judea and Samaria' or 'Occupied Territories'. With regard to the platform on which the Jewish Temple once stood, but is now occupied by the Dome of the Rock, al-Aqsa Mosque, and a number of Muslim shrines, when referred to in a Jewish context this Handbook will use the term Temple Mount; and when referred to in a Muslim context, it will be referred to as the Haram al-Sharif. In a general context the Handbook will call it the Temple Mount/Haram al-Sharif (though the placing of 'Temple Mount' before 'Haram al-Sharif' signifies nothing). The Hebrew name for the Temple Mount is *Har Ha-Bayit*, though it is sometimes referred to as *Har Ha-Moriyya* (Mt Moriah) or *Beth Ha-Maqdas* (the Holy House). The Arabic name Haram al-Sharif means 'Noble Sanctuary', though *Bait al-Maqdis* (the Holy House) is occasionally used.

Getting around It is important to dress modestly when visiting both the Muslim and Jewish holy places around the Temple Mount/Haram al-Sharif. This means no shorts (on men or women), with women in particular being reminded to wear loose, non-revealing clothes. Some form of head covering is advisable for both sexes (paper kippas are provided at the male entry point to the Western Wall). Photography is not permitted in the Western Wall Plaza on Shabbat or Jewish holidays (and should be treated as a privilege and not a right at other times), nor is smoking, using mobiles or taking notes. Decorous behaviour is also essential in both the Jewish and Muslim areas, with public displays of affection being wholly inappropriate. Al-Qasr Mosque and the Dome of the Rock are off-limits to non-Muslim visitors, and so are some other areas of the Haram al-Sharif (there are no signs indicating where you can and cannot go, though someone will soon tell you). Anyone offering to be your guide is definitely best avoided.

Background

Mount Moriah Tradition links the low hill upon which the Temple Mount/Haram al-Sharif stands with the Mt Moriah upon which **Abraham** offered his son Isaac as a sacrifice, as a sign of his obedience to God (*Genesis 22*). There are at least two other versions of this story, with Muslims believing that it was Ishmael, and not Isaac, who was offered by Abraham, whilst Samaritans believe that the biblical description of the sacrifice site – "Abraham lifted up his eyes, and saw the place afar off" (*Genesis 22:4*) – better fits Mt Gerizim (near Nablus) than the low rise here in Jerusalem. Tradition also places here the "threshing floor of Araunah the Jebusite" that **David** purchased in the 10th century BCE as the site upon which to build an altar to God (*II Samuel 24:18-25*). Other traditions central to Judaism, Christianity and Islam appear to have been placed at this spot retrospectively, with the rock at the spiritual centre of the Temple Mount/Haram al-Sharif also being associated with the place where God took the dust for the creation of Adam, where Adam was buried, where Cain and Abel offered their gift to God, and where Noah raised an altar after leaving the ark.

Solomon's Temple Though it was David who brought the symbol of the Israelites covenant with God (the Ark of the Covenant) to Jerusalem, it is generally claimed that his militaristic past meant that he had too much blood on his hands to build the first Jewish Temple, and thus the task was left to his son **Solomon**. Johnson (*A History of the Jews*, 1987), however, suggests that this argument does not stand up since "war and the Israelite religion were closely associated", citing as an example how the Ark of the Covenant was sometimes carried into battle like a flag or standard. He argues that David chose not to build the Temple since this would have changed the essential nature of the balance between state and religion, and he wished to avoid turning Israel into a royal temple-state.

Work began on Solomon's Temple c. 961/960 BCE, taking seven years to complete, and though no trace remains it is possible to make a tentative reconstruction from the description in the Old Testament (*I Kings 5-8*). It was built of stone and timber, with the Phoenician king of Tyre, Hiram, sending his hands to assist in its construction (*I Kings 5:1-18*). He also sent experts in casting bronze to make the ceremonial vessels. The Temple was tripartite in plan, with an inner **Holy of Holies** housing the Ark of the Covenant. Whether the Ark stood on the 'rock', or the 'rock' served as an altar in the Holy of Holies is unknown. The entrance to the Temple was to the east, flanked by two free-standing columns named for unknown reasons *Jachin* and *Boaz* (*I Kings 7:21*). The Temple was looted of its treasures on a number of occasions before being destroyed in the **Babylonian** sack of Jerusalem in 586 BCE. However, it is important to note that the building style of the Temple, similar to Canaanite temples excavated at Lachish and Bet Shean, would have been "put up and equipped in a manner quite alien to the Israelites" (Johnson, *ibid*). In fact, Johnson goes on to argue that "What is clear is that Solomon's Temple, in its size and magnificence, and its location within the fortified walls of a royal upper city or acropolis, had very little to do with the pure religion of Yahweh which Moses brought out of the wilderness" (*ibid*). What Johnson is suggesting is not that Solomon was building a pagan place of worship, but that he was introducing a religious reform that was based upon royal absolutism. This centralization of religious power and cult worship did not survive the death of Solomon, leading to the dissolution of the United Monarchy and the return to the northern (Israel)/southern (Judah) rivalry.

Post-Exilic Temple Following the return from Exile, the Temple was rebuilt by **Zerubbabel** c. 537-515 BCE, probably on the same plan as Solomon's effort but without the ornamentation. The Ark of the Covenant, however, had been lost. **NB** Though the Post-Exilic Temple in reality represents the second Temple built on this site, the term 'Second Temple' is generally used to refer to Herod the Great's creation (see below).

Herod's Temple The decision of **Herod the Great** to construct a grand new temple on the Temple Mount says much about his character as a propagandist and a showman. The fact that he built the Antonia fortress (page 96) and the three great towers (Phasael, Hippicus and Mariamme, see page 70) before commencing work on the Temple further illustrates Herod's standing amongst a suspicious Jewish population. With his Idumean background, his Hellenizing reforms and his dependence for legitimacy on his Roman backers, Herod had to be very careful in how he went about building his Temple since this would require the dismantling of the Post-Exilic Temple then standing on the Temple Mount. He did this by summoning a national council of religious leaders in 22 BCE and laying his plans before them. At every step of the way he was extremely sensitive to charges of desecration, even going so far as to train up to 1000 priests as builder-craftsmen to work in areas forbidden to the ritually impure. Though the temple structure itself took less than two years to complete, such was the monumental scale of the entire complex that it was barely finished when the Romans tore it down in 70 CE.

In order to fulfil his ambitions of creating a temple that would not only rival Solomon's effort but also exceed it in splendour, it was necessary to enlarge the Temple Mount platform. This was done by bridging the valleys surrounding the Mt Moriah of Solomon's Temple, and filling them in. The Herodian Temple Mount enclosure was shaped like an uneven rectangle, with the following dimensions: west wall 485 m, east wall 470 m, north wall 315 m, south wall 280 m. Thus, the enclosure covered an area in the region of 144,000 sq m; a remarkable achievement.

The magnificence of Herod's building project can still be appreciated, despite the fact that no trace of the Temple building itself actually remains standing in place. Large sections of the retaining wall can still be seen, rising in various numbers of courses above the bedrock. The most easily visible, and famous, section of Herod's retaining wall is preserved at the so-called Western Wall, where seven courses rise above the level of the present plaza with more courses reaching down to bedrock below. See the line drawing on below to help you visualize the scene. The southeast corner of the mound perhaps best displays the scale of the enclosure, with 35 original courses extending 42 m above the bedrock.

A fairly accurate picture of the Temple building and the enclosed plan has been reconstructed by examining the fragments found on or near the site, the subterranean features remaining in situ, and the detailed descriptions found in contemporary accounts (most notably Josephus' *Jewish War V, 1-226* and *Antiquities XV, 380-425*). Standing on a vantage point overlooking the Temple Mount and reading the relevant passage in *The Jewish War* is an enlightening experience. The Temple enclosure probably had nine gates, and was surrounded on three sides by a portico, with a *double (Royal) portico* to the south. It is suggested that this is where the moneychangers and usurers, whose tables Jesus upset, would have been located. The outer *Court of the Gentiles* could be entered by non-Jews, though entry to the sacred area was prohibited on pain of death (parts of two tablets, one in Latin and one in Greek, declaring this fact have been

Herod the Great's Temple: the Second Temple

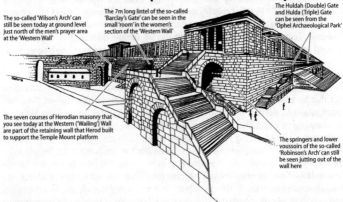

The so-called 'Wilson's Arch' can still be seen today at ground level just north of the men's prayer area at the 'Western Wall'

The 7m long lintel of the so-called 'Barclay's Gate' can be seen in the small 'room' in the women's section of the 'Western Wall'

The Huldah (Double) Gate and Hulda (Triple) Gate can be seen from the 'Ophel Archaeological Park'

The seven courses of Herodian masonry that you see today at the Western ('Wailing') Wall are part of the retaining wall that Herod built to support the Temple Mount platform

The springers and lower voussoirs of the so-called 'Robinson's Arch' can still be seen jutting out of the wall here

found). Within the sacred area itself, the *Beautiful Gate* led from the *Court of the Women* to that of the men (*Court of Israel*), and from thence into the *Court of the Priests*. This is perhaps where the young Jesus was presented (*Luke 2:22-39*). Like the Solomonic Temple, Herod's construction was on a tripartite plan, with the inner chamber veiled by a purple curtain (that tradition says was rent in two during the Crucifixion: *Matthew 27:51*; *Mark 15:38*; *Luke 23:45*). The curtain concealed the inner *Holy of Holies*. Though the exact location of the Holy of Holies is unknown (a factor which prevents religious Jews from visiting the Temple Mount for fear of violating it), it is generally assumed that it stood on the site of the rock that is now enshrined within the Dome of the Rock. The destruction of the Second Temple by the Romans in 70 CE is vividly brought to life by Josephus (*The Jewish War VI, 230-442*).

The 12th-century CE rabbi and sage Maimonides ruled that, despite the destruction of the Temple, the site still retained its sanctity and hence any Jew wishing to visit had to be ritually pure. Unfortunately, this is not that simple. The ritual purification process is laid out explicitly in The *Fourth Book of Moses, Called Numbers* and features, amongst other things, the "ashes of the burnt heifer of purification for sin" (*Numbers 19:17*). The heifer had to be red and "without spot, wherein is no blemish, and upon which never came yoke", and if only two hairs of the heifer were not red, it couldn't be used. As a further complication, the preparation had to be carried out by Eleazar, the heir apparent of Aaron. Thus, when the Temple was destroyed, no new ashes could be produced, and so purification is not possible until the Messiah arrives to prepare a new supply. As a result, rabbinical consensus is of the opinion that all Jews are now ritually impure.

Haram al-Sharif The Temple platform appears to have been largely neglected and ignored by the Byzantines, and it is with the arrival of the Arab armies in 638 CE that the course of the enclosure's history is irreversibly changed. The holiness of the site to Muslims is immediately apparent from the early decision of the caliph Omar to build a mosque on the Temple Mount platform, within a year of the Arab conquest of Jerusalem. The mosque is described as a simple crude affair by the Christian pilgrim Arculf (c. 670 CE), perhaps reusing the columns from Herod's ruined Royal Portico. However, many right-wing Israelis suggest that the Arab conquerors of the city 'invented' the religious significance to Muslims of the site as a means of superseding the influence of previous Jewish or Christian claims to Jerusalem (see box on the next page).

By the end of the seventh century CE/start of the eighth century CE, the Muslims had built the Dome of the Rock (c. 691-2 CE) and the al-Aqsa Mosque (c. 705-15 CE) on the Temple Mount platform, renamed the enclosure the Haram al-Sharif, and banned non-Muslims from entering it. Subsequent centuries saw the Crusaders occupy the Temple Mount/Haram al-Sharif, turning the Dome of the Rock into a Christian prayer hall and the al-Aqsa Mosque into a palace for the king, and then the headquarters of the Templars. Salah al-Din's conquest of Jerusalem in 1187 saw the main buildings revert to their former use, followed by the continuous additions of Muslim shrines and monuments through the Mamluk and Ottoman periods. Despite the capture of all of Jerusalem by the Israelis in 1967, the Haram al-Sharif has remained in Muslim hands since the 12th century.

Sights

Dome of the Rock The Haram al-Sharif, like most views of Jerusalem, is dominated by the graceful lines of the Dome of the Rock (Arabic: *Qubbat al-Sakhra*). The building's dimensions rest upon a mathematical precision that is related to the piece of rock that it encloses. If it

The sanctity of the Temple Mount/Haram al-Sharif: competing religious interests

Whilst the sacredness of the site to Jews is well known (the scene of Abraham's sacrificial offering; David's purchase of the threshing-floor and construction of an altar; site of Solomon's, and then Herod's, Temple) the sanctity within Islam is perhaps less well known to the non-Muslim audience.

Abraham, Solomon and Jesus are all revered within Islam, and though the Muslim belief is that Ishmael and not Isaac was offered by Abraham for sacrifice, and that Jesus was a prophet but not son of God, the 'holy' link between Jerusalem and Islam is easily established.

Jerusalem, and more importantly the Haram al-Sharif, was the place where the prophet Mohammad stopped to behold the celestial glories on his isra', or nocturnal flight to heaven. Though the Qur'an does not specify a location by name, the masjid al-aqsa, or 'furthermost sanctuary' has come to be associated with Jerusalem. As a further link between Islam and Jerusalem, the qibla (direction of prayer) in the early days of Islam was not towards Mecca, but to Jerusalem.

A recurring theme within the right-wing Israeli press has been the premise that Islam merely incorporated Jewish (and to a lesser extent Christian) notions of the 'heavenly' Jerusalem. Though the fact that Mohammad almost certainly did not visit Jerusalem during his lifetime is irrelevant. As Amos Elon puts it, that the fact that the attachment of Islam to Jerusalem is 'late' in no way undermines the significance of that attachment: "the legend of Mohammad's ascent to heaven from the Temple Mount of Jerusalem is by now as central an element in Islam as the Exodus is in Judaism and the cult of Mary is in Christianity" (*Jerusalem: City of Mirrors*, 1989).

does, as some believe, stand at the centre of the world, then it is a fitting monument. Not only is it the first great building of Islam, it is an architectural masterpiece in its own right.

It was built between 688-692 CE by the fifth Umayyad caliph, 'Abd al-Malik, following the Arab capture of Jerusalem (638 CE). Though Muslims emphasize that the Dome of the Rock was built to commemorate the prophet Mohammad's night ascent to heaven (*Sura XVII*), there are several less-divinely inspired considerations that must have been in 'Abd al-Malik's mind. In fact during the succeeding (and rival) Abbasid caliphate, attempts were made to discredit the Umayyad caliph 'Abd al-Malik by suggesting that he built the Dome of the Rock in order to lure the lucrative pilgrim trade away from the Ka'ba at Mecca. There is an element of truth in this, though it is generally believed that 'Abd al-Malik was seeking to consolidate a rival political, as opposed to religious, centre in the Jerusalem-Damascus region. However, there are fairly strong grounds to believe that 'Abd al-Malik was seeking to build a striking monument that would reaffirm Islam as the successor to its imperfect predecessors.

This point is underlined by the founding inscription around the ambulatories inside the building, quoting a verse from the Qur'an: "O you People of the Book, overstep not bounds in your religion, and of God speak only the truth. The Messiah, Jesus, son of Mary, is only a Messenger of God, and his Word, which he conveyed into Mary, and a Spirit proceeding from him. Believe therefore in God, and his prophets, and say not three. It will be better for you. God is only one God. Far be it from his glory that he should have a son" (Sura IV, verse 169). The emphasis on this rejection of the Christian Trinity is aimed at the Byzantine church that had been established for almost four centuries in Jerusalem. The magnificence

Haram al-Sharif / Temple Mount overview

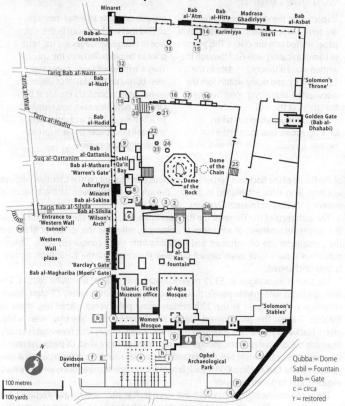

Minaret

Bab al-'Atm · Bab al-Hitta · Madrasa Ghadiriyya · Bab al-Asbat

Bab al-Ghawanima

Karimiyya · Isra'il

14 · 13 · 15

Tariq Bab al-Nazir

Bab al-Nazir

'Solomon's Throne'

12

Tariq al-Hadid

Bab al-Hadid

10 · 11 · 18 · 17 · 16 · 19 · 20 · 21

Golden Gate (Bab al-Dhahabi)

22 · 24 · 23

Bab al-Qattanin

Suq al-Qattanin

9

Sabil Qa'it Bay

Dome of the Chain

Bab al-Mathara 'Warren's Gate'

Ashrafiyya

Minaret Bab al-Sakina

Dome of the Rock

25

Tariq Bab al-Silsila

8 · 7 · 5 · 4 · 3 · 2

Bab al-Silsila 'Wilson's Arch'

Entrance to 'Western Wall tunnels'

6 · 1

26

Western Wall plaza

al-Kas fountain

'Barclay's Gate'

Bab al-Magharba (Moors' Gate)

c

d

Islamic Ticket Museum office

al-Aqsa Mosque

'Solomon's Stables'

b

a

Women's Mosque

k

l

m

Pol

N

Davidson Centre

f · e · h · i · g

Ophel Archaeological Park

n · o · s

100 metres
100 yards

p · q · r

Qubba = Dome
Sabil = Fountain
Bab = Gate
c = circa
r = restored

1 South Qanatir (c 10th cent)	11 Sabil Sha'lan (c 1216, r 1429, 1627)	21 Qubbat al-Arwah (c 16th cent)
2 Minbar of Burhan al-Din (c 1388, r 1843)	12 Sabil Basiri (c 1456)	22 Masjid al-Nabi (c 1700)
3 Qubba Yusuf (c 1681)	13 Qubbat Sulaiman (c 1200)	23 Qubbat al-Mi'raj (c 1200)
4 Qubba Nahwiyya (c 1207)	14 Sabil al-Sultan Sulaiman (c 1537)	24 Qubbat al-Nabi (c 1538, r 1845)
5 SW Qanatir (c 1472)	15 Pavilion of Sultan Mahmud II (c 1817)	25 E Qanatir (c 10th cent)
6 Qubba Musa (Dome of Moses) (c 1249)	16 NE Qanatir (c 1326)	26 SE Qanatir (c 1030, r 1211)
7 Mastabat al-Tin (c 1760)	17 N Qanatir (c 1321)	a 'Robinson's Arch'
8 Sabil Bab al-Mahkama & Birka Ghaghanj (c 1527)	18 Cell of Muhammad Agha (c 1588)	b Pier
9 Mihrab 'Ali Pasha (c 1637)	19 NW Qanatir (c 1376, r 1519,1567)	c Herodian Street
10 Sabil al-Shaikh Budayr (c1740)	20 Qubbat al-Khadir (c 16th cent)	d Umayyad Courtyard
		e Umayyad Palace
		f Umayyad Hospice?
		g Medieval Tower
		h Byzantine House

i 'Excavation's Gate'
j Herodian Plaza
k Double Gate
l Triple Gate
m Single Gate
n Mikvehs (Ritual Baths)
o Byzantine Building
p 7th–6th century BCE remains
q Herodian Building
r Byzantine Homes
s Byzantine City Wall

God goes online

Inspection of the stone blocks of the Western Wall reveals thousands of slips of paper stuffed into the cracks. This practice of communicating with God through the written word is thought to date to the 18th century, and many visitors join the worshippers in pushing notes between the stones of the wall.

This communication has taken on a significant new form in the last decade. By visiting www.thekotel. org you can write an email message to God that will be placed in the wall, free of charge. Messages are not read prior to being stuffed into the crevices. They are removed twice a year and then buried on the Mount of Olives, on consecrated ground. US President Barak Obama's note, however, was removed by a Yeshiva student and published in an Israeli newspaper (to widespread condemnation) in 2008.

of the Dome of the Rock was certainly a conscious effort to 'out do' the Christian religious buildings long-since established in the city, though it may have been aimed as much at wavering Muslims as towards Christians.

The architects of the Dome of the Rock are unknown, though the architectural style is a successful synthesis of a number of influences, reflecting the spread of Islam and the consequent use of craftsmen and traditions from these conquered lands. Though numerous repairs have been carried out over the centuries, the basic form remains largely unchanged.

The base is an **octagon** (c. 53.75 m in diameter) built of local limestone courses. The walls are faced with marble panels, though the original seventh-century CE glass mosaic coverings were replaced in the 20th century using polychrome glazed tiles made in Kütahya, Turkey. The predominant colour is a beautiful turquoise-blue, with white, green, black and yellow tiles adding to the overall effect. The stylized floral motifs closely resemble the original patterns, though the colours are far more vivid. Of particular note is the band of blue and white tiles that extends all the way round the octagon, and features verses from the Qur'an (*Sura XXXVI*). Each face of the octagon features five grilled windows, allowing light to penetrate inside.

The original dome collapsed in 1016 and was rebuilt in 1022, though many repairs have been made since. The original lead casing proved to be too heavy, leading to instability, and was replaced in 1961 with the brilliant gold-coloured anodized aluminium that you see today. When the Crusaders occupied the Temple Mount/Haram al-Sharif following their capture of Jerusalem in 1099, the Dome of the Rock became the *Templum Domini* (Temple of Our Lord), and a tall cross stood at the pinnacle of the dome. It was replaced with a crescent by Salah al-Din in 1187.

Inside, a single line of Kufic script, the 'founder's inscription', runs along the top of both sides of the inner octagon. It originally featured 'Adb al-Malik's name, the founding date (AH 72, or 691 CE), and *Sura IV*, verse 169 (see above), though the later Abbasid caliph al-Ma'mun (813-830 CE) inserted his name instead, but without altering the founding date. The interior of the drum is lavishly decorated, with al-Zahir (c. 1027), Salah al-Din (c. 1198) and al-Nasir Mohammad (1318) all leaving their mark.

At the centre of the inner octagon is the **Holy Rock**. The rock is associated with Abraham's sacrificial offering (*Genesis 22:2-19*), and the place where David built an altar to God (*II Samuel 24:18-25*), and thus is generally believed to be the site of the Holy of Holies in the

Solomonic Temple where the Ark of the Covenant stood. Muslims believe that Mohammad began his Night Ascent from this rock, and his footprint has been left in the rock in the southwest corner. Tradition relates how the rock attempted to follow Mohammad on his journey, and thus the handprint next to the footprint is where the angel Gabriel held down the rock. During the Crusader period the footprint was venerated as that of Christ, with the result that visiting pilgrims chipped away parts of the rock to keep as souvenirs or sell as relics. By the late 12th century the rock had to be paved with marble, and a beautiful wrought-iron screen built around it to keep the souvenir-hunters away.

At the southeast angle of the rock a Crusader-period marble entrance gives way to a **cave** beneath. Muslim tradition holds that the rock overlies the centre of the world, lying above a bottomless pit whilst the waters of Paradise flow beneath the cave. The spirits of the dead can supposedly be heard here awaiting Judgement Day, and hence the popular name of the **Well of Souls** (Arabic: *Bir al-Arwah*). Similar themes can be found within the Jewish Talmud.

Dome of the Chain Immediately to the east of the Dome of the Rock is a small dome supported by 17 columns (all of which can be seen from any point). Referred to as the Dome of the Chain (Arabic: *Qubbat al-Silsila*), built from 691 to 692 CE by 'Adb al-Malik, the function of which is still a matter of scholarly debate. Much has been made of the fact that it, and not the Dome of the Rock, stands at the centre of the Temple Mount/Haram al-Sharif platform, and it has been speculated that it stood above the Solomonic (and then Herodian) sacrificial altar. Its position on the platform has also been used to suggest that it marks the *omphalos*, or navel of the world. In all likelihood it was built to house the treasury of the Haram al-Sharif, though the traditions surrounding it may have created a sense of sacredness that may have acted as a deterrence to would-be thieves. The popular name derives from the tradition that a chain once stretched across the entrance, hung there by either David, Solomon, or God. Those who swore falsely whilst holding the chain were either struck by lightning, or a link would fall, thus giving judgement on them as a liar.

Platform of the Dome of the Rock The Dome of the Rock stands on a **platform**, with eight **staircases** ascending from the esplanade. At the top of each staircase is a *qanatir*, a series of arches or arcade. They are popularly referred to by Muslims by the Arabic word *mawazin*, meaning 'scales'; a reference that derives from the tradition that on the Day of Judgement, scales will be hung from them to weigh the souls of the dead. The oldest is the west qanatir, dating to 951-52 CE, with the rest dating to the 10th, 14th and 15th centuries (with later refurbishments). Also of interest on the dome platform itself is the **Qubbat al-Mi'raj**, or Dome of the Ascension of the Prophet. Murphy-O'Connor proposes that the "mere existence of this structure shows that the original purpose of the Dome of the Rock was not to commemorate the Ascension of Mohammad" (*ibid*), though this argument can be challenged on two counts. Firstly, as Prag points out (*Blue Guide*, 1989), this commemorates not the spot from which Mohammad ascended, but rather where he prayed prior to his Ascension. Secondly, the identification of the Temple Mount/Haram al-Sharif with *al-Masjid al-Aqsa al-Mubarak*, "the furthermost Blessed Mosque" where Mohammad made his Night Ascent, is very old, with the pilgrim Arculf describing a rudimentary mosque here by 680 CE, and the Dome of the Rock being constructed a little over 10 years later. The Qubbat al-Mi'raj, by contrast, dates to 1200-01, and thus any tradition surrounding it is far later. Also of note on the dome platform is the exquisite **Minbar of Burhan al-Din**, next to the south qanatir, a 14th-century pulpit (restored in 1843) which is associated with praying for rain.

Al-Aqsa Mosque Whilst the Dome of the Rock is a shrine and place of pilgrimage, **al-Aqsa Mosque** serves as Jerusalem's Jama'i Masjid, or main Friday congregational mosque. Though not an unattractive building, it loses out in inevitable comparison with the Dome of the Rock, though the two do rather complement one another. However, its architectural history is far more complex than that of its near neighbour and, as a result of its numerous restorations, its original form is far more difficult to discern.

The date of the first mosque built on the former Temple Mount platform is uncertain. It is not entirely clear whether the caliph **Omar** built a mosque here following the Arab capture of the city in 638 CE, though the Christian pilgrim Arculf describes a rudimentary mosque standing in the ruins of Herod's Royal Stoa (portico) in 680 CE. A mosque certainly was standing here by 715 CE, presumably built by the Umayyad caliph **al-Walid I**. This mosque may well have formed the basis of the plan of the mosque seen today. By c. 775 CE the mosque had been enlarged to a fifteen-aisled basilica-like structure, though whether the work was carried out by the Umayyads or the Abbasid caliph **al-Mahdi** (775-785 CE) is also uncertain (though the general consensus is that the work was Umayyad). The main entrance to the mosque was via the Double Gate and the passage beneath the mosque (see Jerusalem Archaeological Park, page 89). The steps down can be seen outside the main entrance to the mosque, though they are not open to the public. Two major earthquakes in 747/48 CE and 774 CE caused extensive damage, though every set-back saw repairs swiftly made. By the ninth century the mosque probably had seven aisles on either side of a central nave, a central door in the north wall, with a marble portico along the north façade, and a large lead-sheathed dome.

The earthquake of 1033 devastated the mosque, with the relative impoverishment of the city at this time meaning that al-Aqsa was restored as a more modest five-aisled building. Crusader rule in Jerusalem saw the mosque used first as a palace of the king, then as a headquarters of the **Order of the Knights Templar**. They made a number of structural alterations, including the construction of the Templar Hall to the west (now occupied by the Women's Mosque and Islamic Museum). In 1187 **Salah al-Din** restored the building to its original purpose, making a number of changes including endowing the mosque with a beautiful **minbar** (pulpit) of carved, inlaid and gilded cedar wood. In 1969, a mad Australian started a fire in the al-Aqsa and the pulpit was destroyed (see box, page 89).

Other features on the Haram al-Sharif

There are a number of other points of interest on the Haram al-Sharif, though not all are accessible to tourists. The **Golden Gate** (Arabic: *Bab al-Dhahabi*), date unknown, has links with Eudocia (mid-fifth century CE) and the triumphant entry into Jerusalem by the Emperor Heraclius (631 CE), though there are architectural features that are distinctly Umayyad. It is very similar in style to the Double Gate in the south wall, which is generally believed to be Herodian with Umayyad (amongst others) modifications. Its north entrance is often referred to as the **Gate of Mercy** (Arabic: *Bab al-Rahma*), and the south entrance the **Gate of Repentance** (Arabic: *Bab al-Tawba*). The gate, blocked in the eighth century CE, is the source of a number of traditions. It is variously believed that the just will enter through this gate on the Day of Judgement – hence its popularity as a burial site. A Muslim tradition seems to suggest that a Christian conqueror will enter through this gate; perhaps a byproduct of the tradition that Jesus entered this gate on Palm Sunday, and will appear here at the Second Coming. The theory has also been proposed that the purpose of the Muslim cemetery is to deter any Jewish or Christian messiah!

Just to the north of the Golden Gate is '**Solomon's Throne**' (Arabic: *Kursi Sulaiman*), a small rectangular structure with twin shallow domes. A Muslim tradition holds that when Solomon died, his body was propped up here so as to conceal his death from the demons, and thus avoid fulfilling the prophecy that said the Temple would be destroyed following his death. The structure probably dates to the 16th century CE, with the fact that it may have been built by Sulaiman II ('the Magnificent') perpetuating the tradition.

The so-called **Solomon's Stables** complex are in fact part of the subterranean vaulting system that Herod the Great built to support his Temple Mount, and have no connection whatsoever with Solomon. Much of the upper parts and arches were actually built by the Crusaders (who introduced the Solomonic link) when they used the vaulted chambers as a stables for their war-horses. In 1996 the halls were opened as a prayer chamber capable of accommodating 10,000 people, with the 'Solomon's Stables' name being dropped in favour of the **Marwani Mosque** title. Over 200 architectural units have been recorded on the Haram al-Sharif. Amongst the minor features that can be inspected close, the most interesting include the following three. The **Sabil Qa'it Bay**, to the west of the Dome of the Rock, is an attractive structure built in the late 15th century CE, but largely restored in 1883. Though it is built in the style of a funerary monument, it is in fact a public fountain drawing water from what may well be a Herodian cistern below. This is possibly the same cistern that is described in relation to the 'cave' synagogue close to Warren's Gate (see 'Western Wall Tunnels' tour, page 87). The isolated structure to the north of the Dome of the Rock is the **Qubbat Sulaiman**, possibly an Ayyubid-modified Crusader building (c. 1200 CE) that tradition links with the spot at which Solomon prayed after completing the Temple. Also of note between al-Aqsa Mosque and the Dome of the Rock is **al-Kas**, the main fountain at which Muslims perform their ritual ablutions before praying at al-Aqsa.

Western Wall ⓘ *Access 24 hrs, every day of the year (free), www.thekotel.org.* The focus of Jewish prayer and pilgrimage, the Western Wall (Hebrew: Ha-Kotel Ha-Ma'aravi) is not part of the Temple building itself, but an exposed stretch of the retaining wall that Herod the Great constructed c. 20-17 BCE to support the platform on which the Second Temple was built. Approximately 60 m of the 485-m-long western retaining wall is exposed here, allowing Jews and non-Jews alike to appreciate something of the monumental scale of Herod's building project. See the line drawing on page 78 to put the scene before you into historical and archaeological perspective.

Though seven courses of Herodian masonry are visible, there are in fact a further 19 courses below the level of the current pavement. The Herodian blocks are characterized by their carefully drafted edges and are cut with such precision that they are set without mortar. Though most of the stones are around 1 m high and weigh around 1,800-4,500 kg), there are some notable exceptions: one stone of the 'mastercourse' in the southeast corner is estimated to weigh 90,000 kg, whilst another stone to the north of the Western Wall area (and visible on the tour through the Western Wall Tunnel, page 87) is 13.6 m long, 3.5 m wide, 3.5 m high, and estimated to weigh around 570,000 kg! Above the seventh Herodian course the stones are Umayyad (c. seventh century CE), whilst the smaller ones at the top are part of the restoration effort that followed the 1033 earthquake.

It is not entirely clear when Jews first began to gather here to lament the destruction of the Temple, though it is reasonable to assume that it may well have closely followed Hadrian's death in 138 CE. By the third to fourth century CE it was certainly common practice, though following the Arab conquest in 638 CE and the subsequent construction of Islamic monuments on the platform itself it appears that the Western Wall itself became the focus of Jewish pilgrimage. Because of the Jewish lamentations here, it became known as the **Wailing Wall**. Though only a small section of the Wall was available to Jews, as the Jewish population of Jerusalem increased in the 19th century they attempted to change long-standing practices at the Wall (such as bringing chairs for the elderly to rest, and putting up a temporary screen to divide the male worshippers from the women). Though these introductions seem innocent enough, the Muslim leaders opposed any change in the status quo for fear that they would lead to further concessions. Matters were brought to a head on Yom Kippur in 1928 when, following complaints from the Supreme Muslim Council, British policemen forcibly removed a screen from the Wall. Complaints were made to the League of Nations and the British parliament by leading Zionist officials, with Chaim Weizmann writing an open letter to the Yishuv (Jewish community in Palestine) stating that the only solution to this problem of access was to "pour Jews into Palestine". As the Muslims had feared, the matter had moved from being a religious one to a political and racial question, and they were quick to link the confrontation at the Wall with the greater question of Jewish designs on Palestine. In mid-August 1929 members of Betar, the youth organization of Jabotinsky's Revisionist party, marched on the wall, raising the Zionist flag and singing the Zionist anthem. The following day at Friday prayers Muslims were exalted to defend the Haram al-Sharif. The following Friday (23 August 1929) saw a full-scale riot ensue in which Jewish quarters in Jerusalem, Hebron and Safed were attacked. Zionist groups responded, and by the end of the week 133 Jews and 116 Arabs had been killed, with many more injured.

The square, or **Western Wall Plaza**, in front of the Wall took its present form after the Israeli capture of the whole of Jerusalem in the Six Day War of 1967. Until this time the houses and buildings of the Magharibi or 'Moors Quarter' virtually abutted the western retaining wall of the Temple Mount/Haram al-Sharif platform. These, including the 12th-century CE mosque and shrine of Shaikh 'A'id (the Afdaliyya Madrasa), were bulldozed in June 1967 to allow greater Jewish access. The Western Wall is now divided into two distinct areas for prayer: men have the larger area to the north, whilst women are separated by a screen to a smaller area to the south. At the southern end of the women's prayer area (and accessible only to modestly dressed women) is the so-called Barclay's Gate. Erroneously identified with the Kiponos Gate of the Mishnah, Barclay's Gate allowed access to the Temple Courts on the Temple Mount platform via a ramp from the street below. All that can be seen today is part of the 7-m-long lintel of the gate, made from a single stone.

The 1990s saw hostile confrontations between orthodox and liberal Jews, as a group of women attempted to assert their rights at the Western Wall. The 'Women of the Wall' gathered here to sing from the Torah for an hour or two per month, maintaining that no halachic ruling stated that the Wall belongs only to men. However, the Supreme Court in 2002 voted against their right to worship as they please by the actual Western Wall, and a special prayer hall for women was created by Robinson's Arch (where the sounds of their chanting from the Torah cannot be heard).

Just to the north of the men's prayer area (and accessible only to modestly dressed men), a gateway leads to a further prayer area beneath the so-called **Wilson's Arch** (see drawing on page 78). This structure (described in further detail as part of the 'Western Wall Tunnels' tour, below) is generally agreed to be easternmost of the series of arches that supported the causeway spanning the Tyropoeon Valley, linking the Upper City with the Second Temple.

Western Wall Tunnels ⓘ *Sun-Thu 0700-evening, Fri 0700-1200. Advance bookings must be made with the Western Wall Heritage Foundation, T1599-515888, have a credit card ready. Tickets are collected from a pre-paid booth by the entrance, no refunds (though it is possible to enter at a later time if you miss your slot). Yarmulkes (provided) or some form of head-covering must be worn. Modest dress is essential. The first section is wheelchair accessible, though some prior arrangements should be made. During daylight hrs the tour emerges in the Muslim Quarter; the guide will escort those who feel that they need this service back to the Western Wall Plaza. Or after darkness, visitors walk the tunnels in reverse to exit via the main door (recommended if you want to spend longer inside). Tours take about 1 1/4 hrs.*

The Western Wall Tunnels complex features a number of places of major archaeological, historical, religious and (arguably) political interest. The key sites date to several important periods in Jerusalem's history, most notably the Hasmonean and Herodian eras, though a number of questions still need to be answered and further excavations are necessary. Unfortunately, fear of desecration (by Jews and Muslims), and the fact that the complex has been turned into a political issue (by Israelis and Palestinians), means that any excavations here cause invariably prompt unrest. However, some of the more fanciful legends and traditions surrounding the 'tunnels' may be rendered obsolete or mundane if archaeology wins the day, so it is perhaps best that some of the questions remain unanswered.

Tour The entrance to the Western Wall Tunnels complex is on the northwest side of the Western Wall Plaza (marked by the 'Western Wall Heritage' sign). Turning right you enter a **vaulted passage** (named the 'secret passage' by Warren) that passes a series of arches and vaulted chambers. This is in fact the route of the causeway over the Tyropneon Valley that connected the Temple with the Upper City on the Southwestern Hill. The original causeway leading to the Temple was destroyed by the Hasmoneans in their defence against Pompey in 63 BCE, rebuilt by Herod the Great when he constructed the Second Temple, and then destroyed again in 70 CE as the Jewish Zealots retreated into the Temple in the face of the Roman advance (see Josephus' *Jewish War II, 344; Antiquities XIV, 58*). The present vaults support Tariq Bab al-Silsila (the Street of the Chain), though their date of construction is uncertain. According to some tour guides, it took six people 24 years to excavate this section, since they worked with their hands only for fear of alerting the Muslim householders above!

Towards the end of this passage, to the right, a low window-grille reveals a vaulted chamber at a lower level. Warren explored this so called **Masonic Hall** in 1867, suggesting that it was at least as old as the Western Wall (in other words Herodian), though possibly older (Hasmonean). Measuring 14 m by 25.5 m, it is well built with a paved floor and a single central column (now broken but still visible) supporting the vaulted roof. Its original function is unknown, though it is said to have been used by Masons who connected it with Solomon's works in the Temple.

At the point where the causeway meets the Temple Mount/Haram al-Sharif platform, it is supported by **Wilson's Arch**. Explored and described by Wilson in 1864, it is very similar to 'Robinson's Arch' to the south (see page 89), and excavations appear to confirm Wilson's assertion that its lower courses and pier at least date to the Second Temple period. The upper courses are probably Umayyad. There is a prayer room here for women that offers a good perspective on Wilson's Arch, while men can get a better view via the small entrance to the north of the men's prayer area at the Western Wall.

Turning north, the narrow passage opens out into a high **cruciform chamber**. The hall is part of four interlocking vaults that were built by the Mamluks (c. 14th century CE) as the substructure supporting the buildings above. The purpose of these vaults was to raise the street level to such an extent that their buildings would be on the same level as those inside the Haram al-Sharif. There is some evidence to suggest that these substructures were used as cisterns. Dominating this hall today is a mechanical **model of the Second Temple** which brilliantly illustrates the levels of construction around the Western Wall area. From this hall a series of steps lead down to a **section of the Herodian Western Wall**. The 'mastercourse' can be examined here, including one monster stone (c. 13.6 m by 3.5 m by 3.5 m) said to weigh 570 metric tons! Though quarried locally it is not known how it was moved into position, particularly considering that there are a further 15 rows to the wall that are hidden below ground level.

Continuing north alongside the Western Wall, at a point a little over 40 m north of Wilson's Arch is **Warren's Gate**, which was discovered by Charles Warren in 1867 whilst exploring a cistern on the Temple Mount esplanade. The cistern was in fact originally an underground staircase leading from street level outside the platform, up to the esplanade, and there is reason to suppose that it served the Jewish population as a synagogue during the Early Arab period (638-1099 CE). Its location was chosen due to its presumed proximity to the site of the **Holy of Holies** (which is generally thought to have stood on the west side of the Temple Mount and explains why Jews pray at the west, as opposed to the other walls). In fact, at a point just to the north of Warren's Gate is a section of the wall that is continually wet. Jewish tradition suggests that the wall is crying over the destruction of the Temple. People stop here to post notes into the cracks of the wall or sometimes to pray. A little further to the north of here is another Mamluk period **cistern** that utilizes the space created by the substructure supporting the buildings above.

As the tour continues north, the so-called **Western Wall Tunnel** exposes the entire length of Herod's magnificent Western Wall of the Temple Mount platform. At a point nearing the northwest angle, the retaining wall moves out by some 2 m as the **bedrock** is exposed. Part of an open **Hasmonean cistern** can be seen, protected by a large stone serving as a **guard-rail**. Beyond this a number of **Herodian columns and paving stones** that belong to the Herodian street that ran along the outside of the western retaining wall remain in situ. It is also possible to see a section of a **quarry** from which stone for the retaining wall was cut.

The tour continues down the narrow canyon-like **Hasmonean aqueduct**. Though certainly used by the Hasmoneans to channel water to the Temple from a source in the vicinity of where Damascus Gate now stands, the aqueduct may be older (though links with Solomon are highly unlikely). It was certainly last used by the Hasmoneans since Herod's construction of the Antonia fortress (c. 37-35 BCE) cut off its source of supply. The tunnel now terminates at the **Struthion Pool**, a second-first-century BCE rock-cut storage pool. The pool appears to have taken its present form in the second century CE during Hadrian's construction of Aelia Capitolina. The pool is split by a dividing wall, the rest of it falling within the property of the Sisters of Sion to the north (see page 98). The Roman blocked steps to the west lead up to a grocery store in the Muslim Quarter, whilst the exit (to the right) emerges on to the Via Dolorosa in the Muslim Quarter beneath the steps that lead to the Umariyya Boys' School (see page 96).

Generations Centre ① *Book via T*5958 or T02-6271333, www.thekotel.org, Sun-Thu 0800-evening, adults 20NIS, children 10NIS, 1-hr guided tour included. Headphones available for languages other than English and Hebrew.*
A trip through time, the "Chain of Generations" traces 2000 years of the Jewish national story. It's pretty kitsch with glass sculptures, illuminations and sound-and-light visuals.

Plots against the Haram al-Sharif

The Temple Mount/Haram al-Sharif is more than just a symbol of nationalism between the Israelis and the Palestinians, whilst those who have played a part in trying to alter the status quo have not necessarily been Jewish or Muslim. In August 1969, a 29-year-old Australian by the name of Denis Michael Rohan set fire to al-Aqsa Mosque, and then proceeded to take photos of his handiwork. By the time Rohan was apprehended the mosque had been badly damaged and the 12th century CE minbar presented

by Salah al-Din completely destroyed. He was to claim later that the "abominations" on the Temple Mount were delaying the rebuilding of the Temple, and thus putting the Second Coming on ice. Rohan's aim was to see the Jewish Temple rebuilt "for sweet Jesus to return and pray in". In an oft-quoted aside, then Prime Minister Golda Meir's comment to her cabinet colleagues that "we must condemn this outrage" was met by Menachem Begin's "yes of course, but not too much".

Jerusalem Archaeological Park ① *T02-6277550, www.archpark.org.il, Sun-Thu 0800-1700, Fri and hol eves -1400, adult 30NIS, student 16NIS (or combined ticket including Ramparts Walk, Roman Plaza and Zedekiah's Cave 55NIS). For guided tours in English (1 hr, 160NIS, includes 'Virtual Reality' of life in the Second Temple period) phone ahead. Audio guide included (recommended).*

Excavations to the south and southwest of the Temple Mount/Haram al-Sharif enclosure have revealed remains from several key periods in the city's history. The whole area, variously referred to as the Jerusalem Archaeological Park or the Davidson Centre, has elevated walkways, explanatory signs, and a marked walking route making it more tourist friendly. The excellent Davidson Centre, which uses computers, artefacts and films to bring archaeology to life, is recommended as a first stop before touring the area. The tour outlined below highlights areas which are not mentioned by the audio tour.

From the entrance to the park head to the southwest angle of the Temple Mount/Haram al-Sharif platform. About 12 m north of this corner, look up towards the small section of Herodian masonry jutting out from the face of the wall. These are the springers and lower *voussoirs* (wedge-shaped stone blocks that form an arch) of the so-called **Robinson's Arch** (a) (named after the American who discovered them in 1835). The discovery of the **base of a pier** (b) to the west, and a careful study of Josephus (*Antiquities XV, 410-11*), suggests strongly that the arch supported a series of monumental staircases that led south to the Lower City. In the piers that supported Robinson's Arch four Herodian shops were discovered, opening on to the Herodian street that ran beneath the arch. A neatly preserved section of the **Herodian street** (c) can be seen running in front of the wall. Also to be seen here is an Umayyad period **courtyard** (d) that stands over a former pool from a Byzantine house. As some indication of the quantity of debris that built up here, Robinson's Arch, originally 17.5 m above the level of the Herodian street, was virtually at ground level in 1968.

Much of the Archaeological Park is covered by the remains of an eighth-century CE **Umayyad palace** (e) (85 m by 95 m), made more interesting by the fact that it does not appear to be mentioned in any written source. The plan of the palace featured a central open court, probably partly paved and partly planted with trees, whilst covered porticoes ran around the outside of the court. It is generally agreed that a building with an identical plan, though smaller, stood directly to the west of the Umayyad palace, possibly serving as an **Umayyad hospice (f)**. It appears that these buildings were badly damaged in the Abbasid period, the masonry being reused for construction elsewhere in the city (as is the constant theme in Jerusalem).

To the east of the Umayyad palace, built against the south side of the al-Aqsa Mosque, is what appears to be a **medieval tower (g)**. Possibly built in the 12th century by the Crusaders, it may have been refurbished by Salah al-Din (c. 1191) before finding its present form under the Mamluks (15th century). A flight of modern steps provides a good perspective of the excavations in the Park. Spiral steps descend to the remains of a partly reconstructed Byzantine house **(h)**, whose mosaic floors have been preserved in several rooms.

Passing through the '**excavation gate' (i)** in the wall, to the left is a section of restored pavement and steps cut from the rock belonging to the **Herodian plaza (j)**. The retaining wall of the Temple Mount/Haram al-Sharif platform can be examined in some detail here. A continuous section of the Herodian 'master-course' can be traced all the way to the southeast corner of the platform. Of particular note in this south wall of the Temple Mount/ Haram al-Sharif platform are the three gates. About two-thirds of the **Double Gate (k)** is obscured by the medieval tower **(g)**, though a section of its eastern part can still be seen. This is certainly the western *Huldah Gate* (Arabic: *Abwab al-Akhmas*) of Herod's Temple, one of the main entrances from the Lower City, though much of the work that you see today is Umayyad. In the third course above the arch's cornice is a reused statue base (upside-down) that mentions the second-century CE Roman emperor Hadrian, or possibly his adopted son Antoninus. The **Triple Gate (l)** marks the position of Herod's original eastern Hulda Gate, and part of the western door jamb can still be seen, though again this gate largely dates to the Umayyad period. Further east is the **Single Gate (m)**, a postern gate cut by the Crusaders but blocked by Salah al-Din since 1187. It leads to one of the chambers within 'Solomon's Stables' (see page 85). The southeast angle of the Temple Mount/Haram al-Sharif platform, perhaps originally 41 courses of Herodian masonry high (26 above ground, 15 below), is traditionally linked with the *Pinnacle of the Temple (Matthew 4:5; Luke 4:9)*.

Immediately to the south of the wall between the Double and Triple Gates are a number of Herodian or Roman period **mikvehs (n)**, or Jewish ritual baths. The large building to the southeast of the Triple Gate is Byzantine **(o)**; a number of vessels that obviously belonged to a Byzantine church, including a bronze cross and door knocker, were discovered here. Other remains that can be seen in this section of the Park include a tower, gate and **storerooms (p)** dating to the seventh-sixth centuries BCE (being excavated); a **Herodian building (q)** doubtfully linked with Queen Helena of Adiabene (see page 153); further **Byzantine houses (r)** and sections of the **Byzantine city wall (s)**.

Via Dolorosa and the Stations of the Cross

The Via Dolorosa, or 'Way of Sorrows', is the traditional route along which Jesus carried his cross on his way from his Condemnation to his Crucifixion. It remains a major draw for Christian pilgrims, many of whom carry crosses and prostrate themselves at the various 'Stations'. Because of the confused, sometimes amusing, process by which the modern route came into being, it is easy to mock the hordes of pilgrims who continue to walk the route. Yet the Via Dolorosa remains a triumph of faith over fact, and if you go with the philosophy that "these are probably not the places where the actual incidents happened, but that is not important: what is important is that the incidents did happen, and that is what we are here to commemorate", then the experience can be a means of renewing a relationship with God.

Ins and outs

The first seven Stations of the Cross fall within the Muslim Quarter of the Old City, and full details of the various sites are described within the description of this quarter beginning below (and see the map on page 66). The VIIIth and IXth Stations are on the 'border' between the Christian Quarter and the Muslim Quarter, with full details of these stations found in the description of the latter beginning on the next page. The final five Stations are all found within the Church of the Holy Sepulchre (see page 107). You can walk the entire route in as little as 30 minutes, though most prefer to spend more time (human traffic jams can also make this walk considerably longer).

Background

The origins of recreating Jesus' steps as part of an act of pious remembrance are very old indeed, with Egeria describing such a procession (from the Eleona Church on the top of the Mt of Olives, via the place of Jesus' arrest at Gethsemane on the evening of Maundy Thursday, arriving at Calvary on the morning of Good Friday) as far back as 384 CE. Though the latter section of the route was largely the one followed today, there were no devotional stops at various 'Stations' marking specific incidents on Christ's journey. Within a couple of centuries such devotional stops had been introduced, though the route itself had substantially changed. However, it was the medieval pilgrims who took up this devotional walk with relish. The various sects into which the Christian church had long since split each provided their own version of the Via Dolorosa, the route of which generally reflected where in Jerusalem their churches were located. Yet it was not just in Jerusalem, or indeed the Holy Land, that the Via Dolorosa was created; by the 15th century cities all across Europe had their own symbolic Via Dolorosas! This was later to become a source of some confusion for visiting pilgrims: they were used to 14 'Stations' or devotional stops and were surprised to find that the Jerusalem Via Dolorosa had just eight. The solution was simple: they added six more! The modern route was established in the 17th century, though some 'Stations' were not fixed at their present point until the 19th.

Whilst the authenticity of the site of the Crucifixion and Tomb of Christ at the Church of the Holy Sepulchre is strongly supported, retracing Jesus' route to Calvary depends entirely upon locating the Praetorium where he was condemned. The modern route is based upon the assumption that Pilate would have stayed at the Antonia fortress (page 96) when visiting the city from the Roman capital at Caesarea. However, most scholars now agree that Pilate would almost certainly have resided at the palace that Herod built just to the south of the present Citadel, on the opposite side of the city (see page 71). Gospel descriptions of the trial setting (*Matthew 27:19*; *Luke 23:4*; *John 18:28*) match other descriptions of the Herodian palace, such as those found in Josephus (*Jewish War II, 301*). Thus, a more likely route would involve Jesus heading east along what is now David Street, perhaps turning north towards Calvary at the three parallel souqs at the current junction of David Street, the Cardo and Tariq Khan es-Zeit. In fact, it is a miracle that the trinket salesmen on David Street have not campaigned more rigorously to have this route introduced!

Tour

The following is just a brief summary of the Via Dolorosa; fuller details can be found within the sections on the 'Muslim Quarter' and the 'Church of the Holy Sepulchre'. The route is marked by the dotted lines on the 'Old City: Sights' map on page 66.

Ist Station This commemorates the spot where Jesus was condemned to death by Pilate. The present tradition suggests that this took place at the Antonia fortress, a site now occupied by the 'Umariyya Boys School (page 96).

IInd Station The site where Jesus traditionally took up the cross, this event was previously commemorated in the street outside, though is now more commonly associated with the courtyard of the **Monastery of the Flagellation/Chapel of Condemnation** (page 97). The route then passes beneath what is known as the Ecce Homo Arch (page 98).

IIIrd Station Where Jesus fell for the first time, marked by a small carving outside the **Polish Catholic Chapel** at the junction of the Via Dolorosa and Tariq al-Wad (page 99).

IVth Station Where Jesus met his mother, commemorated by a carving of the event outside the **Armenian Catholic Patriarchate and Church of Our Lady of the Spasm** on Tariq al-Wad (page 99).

Vth Station Jesus falls again and Simon of Cyrene is compelled to carry the cross; the station is marked by a small 'V' at the junction of Tariq al-Wad and Tariq al-Saray (also known as the Via Dolorosa, see page 99).

VIth Station A Roman numeral VI on the door of the **Church of the Holy Face and St Veronica** commemorates the spot where Veronica wiped the face of Jesus with her handkerchief, the imprint of the face remaining on the cloth (page 100). The present location is part of the 13th-century tradition.

VIIth Station At the top of the street, at the junction with Tariq Khan es-Zeit, a small VII above a doorway opposite marks the VIIth Station (page 100). This is sometimes commemorated as the spot where Jesus fell for a second time, though it also marks the **Porta Judicaria** where legend relates that the death decree was posted. This Station was seemingly introduced in the 13th century to prove to confused medieval pilgrims that the Holy Sepulchre site was indeed outside the city walls at the time of the Crucifixion. The door here is sometimes open, revealing an altar set next to a pillar from the Constantine Church of the Holy Sepulchre, as well as a small chapel.

VIIIth Station Located a little way up Aqabat al-Khanqah Street (see page 100) , this Station marks the traditional site where Jesus addressed the women of Jerusalem: "Daughters of Jerusalem, weep not for me", and is is marked by a VIII on the wall of the **Monastery of St Caralambos**. Now return to Tariq Khan es-Zeit and continue along it, ascending the steps to the right just beyond Zalitimo's Sweets. Follow the narrow street to the end.

IXth Station Where Jesus fell for a third time, marked by a IX on the pillar at the entrance to the **Ethiopian Monastery** on the 'roof' of the Church of the Holy Sepulchre (page 100). From here there are a number of options. If open, you can descend via the Chapel of the Ethiopians to the 'Parvis' (courtyard outside the present entrance to the Church of the Holy Sepulchre). Alternatively, retrace your steps to Tariq Khan es-Zeit, take the first right on to Harat al-Dabbaghin, and this also leads to the Parvis.

Xth and XIth Stations Located in the **Latin Chapel of the Nailing to the Cross** on Calvary (inside the Church of the Holy Sepulchre, page 113), the Xth and XIth Stations commemorate where Jesus was stripped of his robes and nailed to the cross.

XIIth Station The **Greek Chapel of the Exaltation or Raising of the Cross** marks where the cross was raised and Jesus died (inside the Church of the Holy Sepulchre, page 113).

XIIIth Station The **Stabat Mater altar** between the two chapels is where Jesus' body was taken down from the cross and handed over to Mary (inside the Church of the Holy Sepulchre, page 114).

XIVth Station The **Tomb of Christ** at the centre of the Rotunda is the final Station of the Cross (inside the Church of the Holy Sepulchre, page 114).

Muslim Quarter

The Muslim Quarter is both the largest quarter in the Old City (c. 28 ha) and one of the most densely populated parts of Israel (with population estimates of around 25,000 residents). For many visitors it is also their first experience of a truly Middle Eastern city, and a surprisingly vibrant and real experience despite the many tourist shops. Although there are a number of fine Islamic institutions (notably those dating to the Mamluk period), the majority of visitors are primarily interested in the Christian sites associated with the route of the Via Dolorosa.

Ins and outs

Getting in and getting away Most visitors arrive via the Christian Quarter (along David Street from Jaffa Gate), or from East Jerusalem via Damascus Gate. Although many begin their tour of this quarter at the Chapel of the Condemnation on Via Dolorosa/Tariq Bab Sitti Maryam (because it's the Ist Station of the Cross), there are a number of points of interest towards Lions' Gate further east. With most visitors following the route of the Via Dolorosa, the main dilemma comes when you reach the Vth Station of the Cross. The description below follows the most popular choice: it details the rest of the sites along the Via Dolorosa as far as the Church of the Holy Sepulchre (subsequently described in the 'Christian Quarter' on page 107), and then gives details of the various points of interest on Tariq al-Wad, Aqabat Tekieh, Tariq al-Khalidiyya and Tariq Bab al-Silsila (the area to the west of the Temple Mount/Haram al-Sharif, see map on page 66).

Warning The Muslim Quarter is a conservative area and you should dress accordingly: you will probably be denied access to both Muslim and Christian sites if your dress is not deemed to be modest enough (no shorts/bare shoulders/revealing clothes on either sex). **NB** 'bab' = gate; 'tariq' = street; 'madrasa' = Islamic religious school; 'sabil' = fountain; 'ribat' = hospice; 'turba' = tomb; 'hamman' = bathhouse.

Background

During the Umayyad period (seventh to eighth centuries CE), the division of the Old City into well-defined 'quarters' was far less regimented (or political) than today, and there is considerable evidence to suggest that the main Muslim residential and commercial districts lay west and southwest of the Haram al-Sharif (the current Jewish Quarter!). Though there is evidence of continued Muslim activity in this northeast corner of the Old

City, by the Fatimid period (10th to 12th centuries CE) this was in fact the Jewish Quarter. Following the arrival of the Crusaders through a breach in the medieval walls near Herod Gate in 1099, the present Muslim Quarter was occupied largely by Christian Crusaders, with several major churches constructed.

This northeast quarter of the Old City can be said to have become firmly Muslim in the 12th century CE, when the Ayyubid Caliphs (12th to 13th centuries CE), and then the Mamluks (13th to early 16th century CE) established large numbers of schools, mosques and foundations in the quarter. The Mamluks in particular developed the areas adjacent to the Haram al-Sharif, building many fine madrasas, tombs and town houses, the exteriors of which can still be viewed today (since most are in private use, it is not generally possible to view the interiors).

The period of Ottoman rule in Jerusalem (1512-1917) saw the establishment of the Ottoman administration in the Muslim Quarter (including the governor's palace), as well as commercial interests (most notably in the caravanserais to the west of the Haram al-Sharif). It also saw the return of many of the Crusader-period buildings (particularly along the Via Dolorosa) to Christian use. The fact that this northeast quarter of the Old City has been the key 'Muslim Quarter' for the last 800 years or so explains why Palestinian Muslims find it so provocative when Jewish groups buy or lease property in the area, then move in to establish a 'Jewish presence'. However, the latter group argue that Jews continued to live in the 'Muslim Quarter' throughout this period, until being driven out by Arab mobs in 1936.

Sights

Around Lions' Gate Immediately inside Lions' Gate is the **Hamman Sitti Maryam**: a bathhouse named for the Virgin Mary and still in use until quite recently. The adjacent **Sabil Sitti Maryam** ('fountain of the Virgin Mary') was built by Sulaiman II in 1537. The doorway just beyond the fountain belongs to the **Greek Orthodox Church of St Anna** and displays a sign claiming it as the "birthplace of the Virgin Mary". For a small donation you will be led down a few steps inside the doorway to the right, and shown a small room with a mosaic floor that is claimed to be the spot in question.

Bethesda Pools ① *Daily 0800-1200 and 1400-1800, winter-1700, adult 7NIS (entrance to the Church of St Anne is free). Small souvenir shop and toilets.*
Entering this Greek Catholic complex, you emerge into an attractive square court containing a number of fragments of masonry excavated in the vicinity, set amongst flower beds that are carefully tended by the French White Fathers who occupy the seminary. The bust at the centre of the court is of Cardinal Lavigerie, founder of the order. Beyond this medieval cloister is the Greek Catholic Church of St Anne (details below) and the Bethesda Pools (but don't expect to find any water in them).

A pool here is thought to have been first cut around the eighth century BCE to channel rainwater to the First Temple, and may well be the '**upper pool**' referred to in the Bible (*II Kings 18:17*). The high priest Simon the Just is thought to have added the second pool c. 200 BCE. By the Early Roman period healing properties had been attributed to the pools, with additional baths and pools having been dug from the bedrock just to the east. The sick, blind, lame and paralysed gathered here awaiting the 'disturbing of the water', as recounted in John's gospel, and this was the scene of Jesus' miracle that so infuriated the Jewish elders since it was performed on the Sabbath (*John 5:1-12*, see box above).

Hadrian's paganizing of Jerusalem (into Aelia Capitolina) in 132-135 CE saw the construction of a small temple/shrine to Serapis (Aesculapius) featuring five colonnades,

The healing of the paralytic

"Now there is at Jerusalem by the sheep market a pool, which is called in the Hebrew tongue Bethesda, having five porches. In these lay a great multitude of sick folk, blind, lame, paralysed, waiting for the moving of the water. For an angel went down at a certain season into the pool, and troubled the water: whosoever then first after the troubling of the water stepped in was made whole of whatever disease he had.

"And a certain man there was, who had been crippled for 38 years. When Jesus saw him lie, and knew that he had been now a long time in that condition, he saith to him, 'Wilt thou be made whole?' The crippled man answered him, 'Sir, I have no man, when the water is troubled, to put me into the pool: while I am coming, another steppeth down before me.'

"Jesus saith unto him, 'Rise, take up thy bed, and walk.' And immediately the man was made whole, and took up his bed, and walked." (*John 5:2-9*).

which Origen described following his visit c. 231 CE (though he mistakenly believed that he was describing the five 'porches' mentioned in the gospel account). By the mid-fifth century CE a small church on the site commemorated the miracle, whilst shortly afterwards the tradition developed linking this spot with the birthplace of the Virgin Mary (with a subsequent church taking her name). The early church was probably destroyed during the Persian invasion of 614 CE, though ninth-century CE records record some form of church on the site.

The church seems to have survived the anti-Christian edicts of the Fatimid sultan al-Hakim in the early 11th century CE, and there appears to have been a church standing on the site when the Crusaders arrived in 1099 (though it may not have been serving a Christian purpose). A small chapel was erected on the site of the Byzantine church and a convent church for Benedictine nuns was also built. In fact, the Crusader king Baldwin I placed his repudiated Armenian wife Arda into the care of the Benedictine nuns here. The Crusader period saw the revival of the tradition concerning the birthplace of the Virgin Mary, and the house of her parents Anne and Joachim. In the early 12th century CE the Church of St Anne that you see today was constructed.

Greek Catholic Church of St Anne Many commentators consider the Greek Catholic Church of St Anne to be the finest example of Crusader ecclesiastic architecture in the Old City, and it is easy to see why. In spite of an extension to the church that saw the façade shifted west by 7 m (you can clearly see the 'join'), the church retains the clean lines of classic Romanesque architecture. The rather plain and austere interior is also renowned for its superb acoustics. There is a fine entrance portal, above which remains the inscription of Salah al-Din that records the conversion of the church into the Salahiyya Madrasa in 1192. Franciscans were granted permission to continue to hold Mass in the madrasa on the annual Feasts of the Immaculate Conception and the Nativity.

The present church was probably built sometime around 1140, in a basilica style with three naves. From the south aisle a number of steps lead down into the crypt of the earlier Byzantine chapel that tradition holds was built over part of Joachim and Anne's home (the parents of the Virgin Mary). One of the small chambers holds an altar above which stands a statue of the Virgin Mary, whilst a second chamber contains an icon depicting the 'Nativity of the Virgin'.

By the mid-19th century, the property was all but abandoned, with some sources saying that the Muslims believed it to be haunted. In 1856 the Ottoman Sultan 'Abd-al-Majid I offered the site to Napoleon III in recognition of French support for the empire during the Crimean war. The building had previously been offered to Queen Victoria for similar services rendered, though she chose to take Cyprus as a gift instead: much to the continued regret of the Anglican Church!

Mamluk-period buildings around Tariq Bab Sitti Maryam At the top of Tariq Bab Hitta (at its junction with Tariq Bab Sitti Maryam) is the **Ribat al-Maridini**, a mid-14th-century hospice built to house pilgrims from Mardin (now in southeast Turkey). Further down Tariq Bab Hitta on the same side of the street is the **al-Awhadiyya**, the supposed tomb of Salah al-Din's great-great-nephew al-Malik al-Awhad (d. 1298). The recessed arch entrance is guarded by two recessed re-used Crusader columns, now painted with graffiti. Opposite is the **al-Karimiyya**, a madrasa built in 1319 by a former Inspector of the Privy Purse in the Mamluk administration. A Copt converted to Islam, Karim was responsible for a number of religious endowments in Cairo and Damascus, though he was later disgraced and forced to leave office (supposedly for protecting Christians). The road finishes at the *Bab Hitta* (Muslims only).

Continuing west along Tariq Bab Sitti Maryam, the vault spanning the road belongs to the former **al-Mujahidin mosque**, built in 1274. As recently as the 1860s a square Syrian-style minaret was still standing, as depicted by C.W. Wilson in his *Picturesque Palestine* (1880). Only its base can now be seen. Attached to the north side of the mosque is the **Mu'azzamiyya madrasa**, established in 1217.

Under the vaulted arch, a vaulted street (Tariq Bab al-'Atm, sign-posted as 'King Faisal Street') leads left (south) towards the al-'Atm Gate to the Haram al-Sharif (*Bab al-'Atm*). At the top of the street on the left is the al-Sallamiyya madrasa, built by an Iraqi merchant c. 1338. It is noted for its attractive recessed entrance doorway with typically Mamluk style red-and-cream door jambs, and for the three grilled windows of the assembly hall (another architectural feature typical of the period). Further down the street on the same side is the al-Dawadariyya Khanqah, now a day-centre for disabled youth (visitors welcome). Built in 1295 by a Mamluk amir who served under six different sultans, this is amongst the finest Mamluk buildings in the quarter although recent modernisation has changed its appearance somewhat. The road finishes at the *Bab al-'Atm* (Muslims only).

Continuing west along Tariq Bab Sitti Maryam, it is possible to take a short diversion north along Aqabat Darwish Street, though in reality there is very little to see at the three main sites on this diversion: **Church of St Mary Magdalene** (Ma'muniyya School), **St Agnes Church** (Mawlawiyya Mosque) and **Greek Orthodox Church of St Nicodemus** (handpainted sign reads "Apostle Peter's Prison") but the street itself is very attractive and is blissfully free of traffic.

Antonia fortress The site upon which the Antonia fortress used to stand, (now occupied by the 'Umariyya Boys' School), has been of military significance since the time of Nehemiah at least (c. 445 BCE), and may have been the location of his 'tower of Hananeel' (*Nehemiah 3:1*). It is also likely that a stronghold existed on this site during the overlapping periods of Ptolemic (304-30 BCE), Hasmonean (152-37 BCE) and Seleucid (311-65 BCE) rule. The Antonia fortress was built some time between 37 and 35 BCE by **Herod the Great** in order to protect, but perhaps also to control, the Temple. It was named on behalf of his patron Mark Anthony and is described in some detail by Josephus: "[it] was built on a rock

75 feet high and precipitous on every side … the interior was like a palace in spaciousness and completeness … it was virtually a town, in its splendour a palace … in general design it was a tower with four other towers attached, one at each corner; of these three were 75 feet high, and the one at the SE corner 105 feet … the city was dominated by the Temple and the Temple by Antonia … " (*Jewish War V: 237-245*). Captured by the rebels in 66 CE, the conquest of Antonia became a priority for Titus and was one of the principal foci of attack for the Roman Fifth and Twelve Legions. Josephus graphically describes the bitter two-month campaign that finally led to its capture on 24 July 70 CE (*Jewish War V: 466; 523; VI: 5*). Titus ordered his soldiers to "lay Antonia flat" (*VI: 93*) to allow his troops easy access to the Temple, and now all that remains is a section of the 4-m-thick south wall.

Christian tradition identifies Antonia with the **Praetorium** (seat of Roman procurators in Jerusalem) where Pilate judged and sentenced Jesus (*Mark 15:1-15*), though archaeologists generally dispute this claim. However, the former site of the Antonia fortress marks the traditional **First Station of the Cross**.

NB A window from the upper terrace of the 'Umariyya Boys' School commands possibly the best view Dome of the Rock in the whole city. Entrance is via the steps up the outside wall. The iron door in the alcove under the flight of steps is the exit to the 'Western Wall Tunnel' (see page 87). Entrance is via the steps up the outside wall, and visits are possible outside of school hours.

Chapels of the Flagellation and Condemnation ① *T02-6280271/6282936, daily Apr-Sep 0800-1145 and 1400-1800, Oct-Mar 0800-1145 and 1300-1700, free.*
Within this complex stands the Chapel of the Flagellation (to the right, east), the Chapel of the Condemnation (to the left, west) and the Monastery of the Flagellation (straight ahead, north). The latter is an eminent Franciscan school of biblical and archaeological studies and houses a small museum with a number of interesting finds.

It remains unclear as to when Christian tradition first placed events in Christ's Passion at this site, though Crusader churches commemorating the Flagellation and Condemnation certainly once stood here. During the Ottoman period it is reported that the buildings were being used as stables, and later as a private house, until the whole complex was given to the Franciscans by Ibrahim Pasha in the early 19th century.

The current **Chapel of the Flagellation** was built between 1927 and 1929 to a design by the Italian architect Antonio Barluzzi. A simple single-aisled chapel, the gold dome above the altar features a representation of the crown of thorns (*Matthew 27:29; Mark 15:17*), plus images of Jesus being scourged at the pillar (*Mark 15:15; John 19:1*), Pilate washing his hands (*Matthew 27:24*), and the release and triumph of Barabbas (*Matthew 27:26; Mark 15:15; Luke 23:24-25*).

The **Chapel of the Condemnation** is an early 20th-century structure built upon the site of a medieval three-aisled chapel. The most interesting feature of the chapel is a section of pavement that continues under the wall into the property of the Sisters of Sion next door. This is part of the *lithostrotos* (Greek for 'pavement', *Gabbatha* in Aramaic, see *John 19:13*) upon which Pilate is said to have set up his judgement seat. You can see games carved into the flagstones by bored Roman soldiers. For full details of the *lithostrotos*, see the 'Convent of the Sisters of Sion', below.

The Chapel of the Condemnation is the **First Station of the Cross** in the Franciscan's procession, whilst the **Second Station of the Cross**, where Jesus took up the Cross, is the courtyard outside. Every Friday at 1500 the Franciscans lead a procession carrying a heavy wooden cross from here along the route of the Via Dolorosa.

Convent of the Sisters of Sion ⓘ T02-6277292, Mon-Sat 0830-1230 and 1400-1700, adult 8NIS. Toilets. NB this place is an absolute nightmare when packed with several tour groups; however, in the late afternoon you may be alone.

The Convent of the Sisters of Sion contains several very interesting items connected to the tradition of this area as the site of the Passion of Christ. These include the Struthion pool, sections of the pavement (lithostrotos) laid over the pool that have an earlier connection with Christ's condemnation, and a lateral section of the 'Ecce Homo Arch' that passes over the Via Dolorosa outside. There is also a small museum that you will pass through during the visit.

Struthion pool The Struthion ('sparrow') pool is a rock-cut cistern that dates to the end of the second/beginning of the first century BCE. Originally an open pool measuring around 52 m by 14 m, it was fed by a channel from the region of what is now Damascus Gate, itself supplying the Temple via a Hasmonean aqueduct. The construction of the Antonia fortress from 37 to 35 BCE cut the aqueduct to the Temple and led to a change in the plan of the pool.

The pool was roofed over in the second century CE, with the outstanding barrel vaults that supported Hadrian's pavement above still clearly visible. It was discovered during the construction of the convent in the early 1860s, though until 1996 it was only possible to view a small section of the pool. The controversial decision to extend the 'Western Wall Tunnel' by excavating the former Hasmonean aqueduct means that it is now possible to view the whole pool: though you have to visit two different sites to do so!

Lithostrotos This impressive pavement of large smooth slabs is associated with the Christian tradition of Pilate's condemnation of Jesus: "When Pilate therefore heard that saying, he brought Jesus forth, and sat down in the judgement seat in a place that is called the Pavement, but in the Hebrew, Gabbatha" (John 19:13). The fact that incised gaming-boards of a dice game called 'King's Game' are carved into the lithostrotos recalls to Christians the scene of the Roman guards' mockery of Jesus (John 19:2-3) and the casting of lots for his garments after his crucifixion (John 19:23-24). The flaw in this argument is the fact that this pavement was laid by the emperor Hadrian in 135 CE as part of the eastern forum for his city of Aelia Capitolina. However, some sources suggest that Hadrian's pavement may have used re-cut and re-laid Herodian flagstones, and thus there is still hope that Jesus may have walked on these stones.

Ecce Homo Arch The arch spanning the Via Dolorosa outside the Convent of the Sisters of Sion is popularly known as the 'Ecce Homo Arch'. Christian tradition has it that this is the spot at which Pilate presented Jesus in his crown of thorns and purple robe to the baying crowd, and declared "Behold the man!" (in Latin, Ecce Homo, see John 19:5). However, it is not claimed that this is the actual arch from which Pilate made his declaration. The arch that you see spanning the Via Dolorosa today is part of the central arch of a triple-arched gate that is attributed to Herod Agrippa I (41-44 CE). The northern lateral arch of what was probably Herod Agrippa I's east gate to the city can be seen within the Basilica of the Ecce Homo. To see this section, pass under the Ecce Homo Arch on the Via Dolorosa and climb the steps on your right to the Basilica. A glass screen allows sightseers to view the northern lateral arch without disturbing proceedings within the Basilica, while a map on the wall puts things into context.

The Ethiopians in Jerusalem

The Ethiopians have a long association with Jerusalem dating back to King Solomon; in fact, the Ethiopian emperors claimed a line of descent from Solomon as a result of his union with the Queen of Sheba. They have fared badly in the sectarian squabbles for control of the Holy Sepulchre, with rising debts forcing them to relinquish control of most of their sites within the church itself in favour of their bitter rivals the Copts. Their rivalry with the Copts is all the more ironic because both groups belong to the Monophysites who believe in the single composite nature of Christ (as opposed to the dual composite nature). The Ethiopians now largely occupy the 'roof' of the Holy Sepulchre, where their simple annual Searching for the Body of Christ ceremony forms one of the gentlest and most interesting annual religious festivals. More details on the Ethiopian church can be learned at the Ethiopian Compound on Ethiopia Street, between the Russian Compound and Me'a She'arim in the New City.

Greek Orthodox Prison of Christ ① *Mon-Sat 0900-1600, Sun 0900-1300.*
Just to the west of the Ecce Homo Arch is the Greek Orthodox Prison of Christ, which serves as the **Ist Station of the Cross** in the Orthodox Church's Easter procession. Visitors are shown three 'cells' (one for Jesus, the other two for the criminals he was crucified with).

Polish Catholic Chapel (IIIrd Station of the Cross) ① Just to the south of the junction of the Via Dolorosa and Tariq al-Wad is the **Polish Catholic Chapel** (so named because it was restored in 1948 with donations from Polish soldiers who had served in the Palestine campaigns of World War II). The tiny chapel outside, marked by two fallen pillars, commemorates the **IIIrd Station of the Cross** where Jesus fell for the first time. The scene is depicted in a small carving above the chapel.

IVth Station of the Cross About 25 m south of the Polish Catholic Chapel is the **Armenian Catholic Patriarchate and Church of Our Lady of the Spasm**, marking the **IVth Station of the Cross** where Jesus met his mother. A small bas-relief of Mary touching Jesus' face recalls the scene.

Vth Station of the Cross At the junction of Tariq al-Wad and the street variously known as Tariq al-Alam or Tariq al-Saray (though invariably referred to and signposted as the Via Dolorosa), a Roman numeral 'V' marks the modern site of the **Vth Station of the Cross** where Simon of Cyrene took up the cross. Before turning along here, if you look ahead down Tariq al-Wad, the house built over the road was referred to as the 'House of the Rich Man' in the 14th century. Next door, the 'House of the Poor Man' was the site of the 14th-century Vth station.

NB The rest of this section on the Muslim Quarter first details the rest of sites along the Via Dolorosa as far as the Church of the Holy Sepulchre, and then returns to the points of interest on Tariq al-Wad, Aqabat Tekieh, Tariq al-Khalidiyya and Tariq Bab al-Silsila.

VIth Station of the Cross Continuing up the slight incline on the Via Dolorosa, at the point where a vault stretches over the street, the Roman numeral 'VI' on the left indicates the **VIth Station of the Cross**. Tradition claims this as the site of the home of St Veronica, who used her veil or handkerchief to wipe the face of Christ. A medieval tradition claims that an imprint of his face was left on the cloth, which has subsequently been involved in a number of miracles and is now the property of St Peter's in Rome (though the Greek Orthodox Patriarchate in the Christian Quarter also has one!). The identification of this site as the VIth Station is medieval. Bullfighting fans will know that a 'Veronica' is a pass made with the cape, so called because the cape is grasped in two hands in the manner in which St Veronica is shown in religious paintings as holding the veil/handkerchief with which she wiped the face of Christ. The **Church of the Holy Face and St Veronica** ① *Mon-Sat 0930-1300*, just beyond the 'VI', is another example of Antonio Barluzzi's work (restoring the 19th-century chapel), with fine stained-glass windows and vaulted ceilings.

Porta Judicaria (VIIth Station of the Cross) The point where the Via Dolorosa meets Tariq Khan es-Zeit is one of the most congested spots in the Old City, with a crush of Palestinian shoppers meeting hoards of bewildered and disorientated tourists walking the Via Dolorosa. The junction marks the **VIIth Station of the Cross**, though views vary as to which event this station commemorates. Some hold that this is where Jesus fell for a second time, whilst others refer to it as the **Porta Judicaria** (or 'Gate of Judgement') where the death sentence notice would have been posted. The latter argument was seemingly introduced in the 13th century to remind pilgrims that this was the former city limit in the first century, thus confirming that the place of crucifixion ('Golgotha') was outside the city walls.

VIIIth Station of the Cross Located a little way up Aqabat al-Khanqah on the left, the VIIIth Station is marked by a small 'VIII' on the wall of the **Monastery of St Caralambos**, and commemorates Jesus addressing the women of Jerusalem: "Daughters of Jerusalem, weep not for me". It is possible to to view the interior from the rear, through a window.

Returning to Tariq Khan es-Zeit, you come to a wide stone staircase on the right. In the angle beneath the stairs is a private shop selling traditional Arab sweets: **Zalatimo's Sweets** (*no sign, daily 0700-1400*). Within the storeroom here lies the superb remains of Constantine's massive doorway between the propylaea and east atrium of his fourth-century CE Church of the Holy Sepulchre (see page 107). **NB** It is customary to make a purchase if seeking permission to view the doorway, or pay 5NIS (he'll ask for 10NIS).

IXth Station of the Cross Ascending the staircase, follow the winding street (Aqabat Dair al-Sultan) to its dead end. The column on the left marks the IXth Station of the Cross where Jesus is said to have fallen for the third time. Passing through the gate on to the 'roof' of the Holy Sepulchre, you encounter the **Ethiopian Monastery** ① *gate open 0800-1800, winter -1700*, occupying the ruins of the 12th-century Canons' Cloister (itself built upon the ruins of the Constantine basilica). Unable to fulfil their tax obligations to the Ottoman sultan in the 16th-17th centuries, they lost their ownership to various parts of the Holy Sepulchre to the Copts, and were forced up to these small cells on the 'roof'. The dome that you see at floor level is the same one that you see from the Chapel of St Helena below.

A doorway in the southwest corner of the roof leads into the narrow **Chapel of the Ethiopians**, from where steps descend via the Coptic Chapel of St Michael to the courtyard (Parvis) outside the Church of the Holy Sepulchre. This is probably the most interesting and affecting way to enter the Church of the Holy Sepulchre, where the last five Stations of the Cross are all found. If the gate to the roof is closed, retrace your steps to Tariq Khan es-Zeit, continue south to the next right turn (Harat al-Dabbaghin), and follow this street to the Parvis.

Coptic Orthodox Patriarchate and Coptic Church and Cistern of St Helena ① *Daily 0900-1630 or 1700. A small donation may be requested.*

Next to the pillar marking the IXth Station of the Cross is the Coptic Orthodox Patriarchate, whilst opposite is the Coptic Church of St Helena. From this tiny church, about 70 steps descend to the large (and generally full) '**Cistern of St Helena**'. The wonderfully spooky cistern has not yet been dated. It's a must.

St Alexander's Chapel and Russian Excavations ① *Daily 0900-1800, adult 5NIS. Prayers are said for Tsar Alexander III on Thu at 0700 in the chapel. Women will be given a skirt to wear; bags must be left at the entrance; no photos allowed.*

Located at the junction of Tariq Khan es-Zeit and the main Muslim-Quarter souqs is the so-called St Alexander's Chapel and Russian Excavations (also known as the Russian Mission in Exile). Beneath this 19th-century building lay a number of remains from Constantine's fourth-century CE church, as well as Hadrian's second-century CE building. The site was

St Alexander's Chapel and Russian excavations

1 Column
2 Stairs
3 Pier of 2nd century Arch
4 Walls of Hadrian's Platform
5 Gate
6 Blocks
7 Pavement of Cardo Maximus
8 Columns
9 Door cut by Constantine
10 Main Entrance (Zalatimo's Sweets)
11 Modern Chapel
12 Medieval Arch

acquired by Russia in 1859 (for the very fact that it contained elements of the original Holy Sepulchre), with the present structure built to protect them, following the visit of the Grand Duke Sergei Alexandrovitch in 1881. The building subsequently became known as the Alexandrovsky Hospice (of the Orthodox Palestine Society). There is a small museum on the right-hand side as you enter the building.

Tour The column (1) at the bottom of the stairs (2) is part of a poorly built triumphant arch built by the (poor) Christian community of Jerusalem to show their gratitude to Constantine Monomachos for his 11th-century rebuilding efforts. It was probably modelled on the far more impressive Hadrianic arch that previously marked this spot, part of which can still be seen (3). Some of the walls of Hadrian's monumental structure can still be seen (4). These utilized some Herodian blocks, and were in turn reused in Constantine's basilica. According to legend, the gate (5) ahead was the gate through which Jesus was led out of the city on his way to Golgotha (hence the protective glass over the sill), though it is in fact a Constantinian entrance to the south cloister (that may previously have been a Hadrianic arch). At a later date this gate was modified, possibly being enlarged by cutting back the walls on either side and inserting the two blocks (6). Beyond this gate was the pavement of

Hadrian's cardo maximus (**7**), flanked by a row of columns of which part of two remains (**8**). To the left (west) is a door (**9**) that Constantine cut through the Hadrianic wall (**4**) as a minor entrance into the basilica. The main entrance lies (**10**) just to the north and can be seen within Zalatimo's Sweet shop (see page 100). From the modern chapel (**11**) a medieval arch (**12**) led to the Canons' Cloister, now occupied by the Ethiopian Monastery (see page 100)

Muslim Quarter souqs Jerusalem's most atmospheric **bazaar** stands at the junction of the Muslim, Christian and Jewish Quarters, at the point where Tariq Khan es-Zeit, David Street, Tariq Bab al-Silsila and the Cardo converge. Three parallel streets are linked by narrow lanes along the route of the Roman-Byzantine town's cardo maximus, though much of the structure that you see here is Crusader. For much of the 12th century, the central street of the covered market was the property of St Anne's Church (see page 95), and the monogram 'SA' appears in the masonry above some of the arched entrances to the shops. When St Anne's Church was converted into the Salahiyya Madrasa by Salah al-Din in 1192, he also transferred the title deed. The other two streets on either side were waqf of al-Aqsa Mosque. The street on the west was the vegetable market in Crusader Jerusalem, but it is now the **Souq al-Lahhamin** (or 'Street of the Meat Sellers'). Visiting tourists tend to find this street particularly nauseous. The central street is the **Souq al-'Attarin** ('Street of the Spice Sellers'), though it previously fulfilled all the Crusaders' drapery needs. The east street is **Souq al-Khawajat** ('Street of the Merchants'). If you continue south on the most westerly of these souqs (Habad, see 'Old City: Sights' map on page 66), a flight of iron steps to the left leads up to the **rooftops** above these souqs. There are excellent views from here (as well as some peace and quiet).

Muslim Quarter: area to the west of the Haram al-Sharif

Dar al-Sitt Tunshuq ('Palace of the Lady Tunshuq') Considered by some to be one of the finest Mamluk monuments in the city, it is in some need of restoration though it is still possible to admire some typical features of Mamluk building style. The entrance portals are of particularly good work, notably the now-blocked east door, whilst some of the inlaid work is well executed. Little is known about 'Lady Tunshuq', except that she died in 1398 ten years after the palace was built. It is suggested that she fled to Jerusalem to escape the campaigns of Timur (Tamerlane), though to be able to build such a palace, she was no ordinary refugee. In later years (c. 1552) the building was incorporated within a charitable foundation ('Imaret of Khassaki Sultan') established by a wife of Sulaiman II, and was then used in the 19th century as the residence of the Ottoman governor. Part of the palace was subsequently used as an orphanage. Opposite the palace is the **Mausoleum of Sitt Tunshuq**, which also features some nice detail, and now houses a wood-workers.

Maktab Bairam Jawish Though an early Ottoman structure, built in 1540 by the Amir Bairam Jawish as either a school or pilgrim hospice, the inference is that the architects and craftsmen were Mamluk trained since it incorporates so many features from this earlier period. Its most notable points are the lead plates that bond the courses (the source of the madrasa's name 'Rasasiyya'), and the decorative arch. This building is at the east end of Aqabat Tekiek, at its junction with Tariq al-Wad.

Sights along Tariq Bab al-Nazir From the Aqabat Tekieh/Tariq al-Wad junction, proceed straight ahead (east) into the narrow street opposite that leads to the Haram al-Sharif. The top of this street is marked by a **fountain** built by Sulaiman II in 1537 (called 'Sabil Tariq Bab al-Nazir' or 'Sabil al-Haram'). The street leads to the Bab al-Nazir ('Gate of the Inspector': hence the street name), though confusingly this gate is sometimes referred to as the Bab al-Habs ('Gate of the Prison') and hence the street has a second name (Tariq Bab al-Habs).

Fifty metres down Tariq Bab al-Nazir, on the left, is the **Hasaniyya madrasa**, built by Husam al-Din al-Hasan in 1434. Next door is the Ribat **'Ala' al-Din Aydughdi al-Basir**, built as a pilgrim hospice around 1267, and probably the oldest Mamluk building in the city. An official in the Mamluk administration, such was the reputation of 'Ala' al-Din Aydughdi that, despite his blindness in later years, he was referred to as 'al-Basir' ('the clear sighted'). Following the loss of his vision he was made Superintendant of the Jerusalem and Hebron Harams ('sanctuaries'). The building was later used as quarters for the Sudanese Muslims who guarded the Haram al-Sharif, and then during the Ottoman period as a prison (hence the gate/street name).

Opposite, occupying much of the south side of Tariq Bab al-Nazir, is the **Ribat al-Mansuri**. This was also built as a pilgrim hospice (c. 1282), but later used as barracks for the Haram guards, and then as a prison. Many North African Muslim families still live here, and though an invitation into their home is a rarely extended privilege, it is a fascinating experience. The road continues to the Bab al-Nazir (Muslims only).

Sights along Tariq al-Hadid About 50 m along quiet Tariq al-Hadid, at the point where the path divides, located on the right is the **Hanbaliyya madrasa**, founded in 1380 by the Mamluk official Baidamur al-Khwarizmi. Taking the left fork, the lane runs all the way to the *Bab al-Hadid* (Muslims only). Just before the gate on the right is the impressive **Jawhariyya madrasa and ribat** that is now occupied by the offices of the Administration of Waqfs and Islamic Affairs. It was built in 1440 by an Abyssinian eunuch by the name of Jawhar al-Qunuqbayi who later became Steward of the Royal Harem. The entrance portal has the now familiar red and cream masonry, whilst the upper windows are well worked. The upper storey extends above the adjacent **Ribat Kurt al-Mansuri** (hospice built in 1293 by the renowned soldier Sayf ed-Din Kurt who died fighting the Tartars in 1299), linking it to the Haram al-Sharif complex itself. Other buildings from the period close to the Bab al-Hadid include the **Arghuniyya madrasa** (c. 1358), with striking carving above the door and windows, the **Khatuniyya madrasa** (c. 1354) and the **Muzhiriyya madrasa** (c. 1480).

Souq al-Qattanin (Market of the Cotton Merchants) This superb 95-m-long Mamluk covered bazaar has been substantially restored, and is an impressive sight featuring 50 or so shops, two bathhouses and a caravanserai. Unfortunately, only half of the shops are open for trade (others are used for storage), and at times it has a somewhat abandoned feel. Burgoyne, who extensively surveyed the Mamluk buildings in the Muslim Quarter between 1968 and 1975, believes that the arcade represents two distinct construction periods, going as far as to suggest that the east section was built merely to fill the space between the market and the walls of the Haram al-Sharif. Even to the untrained eye it is easy to see that this is the case, though the block to the east is in no way inferior. It is now generally assumed that the west half was originally a Crusader market (the lower four courses of masonry are certainly Crusader) that was repaired at the same time that the east section was built. The 'join' in the middle is particularly well executed. The market is generally attributed to **Tankiz al-Nasiri**, with a number of inscriptions in the structure mentioning his gift, including on the doors of the *Bab al-Qattanin* at the east end and on the lintel above these doors. Two of these inscriptions indicate 1336 as the date of construction.

To the north side is the vaulted hall of the **Khan al-Qattanin** (a caravanserai) founded c. 1453-1461. Further along the north side, about half-way, stairs provide access to the living accommodation above the shops. At the east end the steps lead up to the elaborate *Bab al-Qattanin* (Muslims only) through which you can get a stunning view of the Dome of the Rock.

On the south side of the bazaar is the entrance to the **Hamman al-Shifa** (closed), a bathhouse built in 1330 in the Roman-Byzantine style. A 26-m-deep well-shaft draws water from a source below, though it is renowned for its poor quality. Also on the south side of the bazaar, between bays eight and nine, is the entrance to the Khan Tankiz, which is now the Al-Quds University Centre for Jerusalem Studies which runs Arabic language courses (see page 196) and excellent tours.

The **Hamman al-'Ain** is a typical Mamluk bath built c. 1330, also accessed via Al-Quds University. It has been partially restored, though progress was halted. Just to the south of the bathhouse entrance on Tariq al-Wad is the **Sabil Tariq al-Wad**, a fountain constructed by Sulaiman II in 1536.

Crusader Church of St Julian Diagonally opposite Souq al-Qattanin is a street heading west called Aqabat al-Khalidiyya. Just 15 m along the street on the right is a small workshop/furniture maker's showroom. Examination of this structure in 1978 by Bahat and Solar tentatively identified it as the **Crusader Church of St Julian** (though some other sources claim that it may have been dedicated to St John the Evangelist). Despite a number of structural changes throughout the years, this is still identifiable as a three-aisled basilica with three apses.

Tariq Bab al-Silsila This historic street has remained the main east to west artery of the Old City throughout history. The eastern part follows the course of the Hasmonean causeway that crossed the deep Tyropneon valley (the ravine that ran along the side of the Temple Mount/Haram al-Sharif but has now been filled by centuries of construction). Herod the Great enlarged the vaulted causeway (sections of the Hasmonean/Herodian causeway can be seen in the 'Western Wall Tunnels', page 87), and the Mamluks built over it further. In between time, the current Tariq Bab al-Silsila formed one of the main east to west routes in Hadrian's Aelia Capitolina, and the Street of the Temple during Crusader rule. It now leads to one of the main gates to the Haram al-Sharif, Bab al-Silsila (usually Muslims only). There are several noteworthy buildings located just outside the gate, including the ornate **Tomb of Turkan Khatun** (c. 1352), the **Tomb of Sa'd al-Din Mas'ud** ('al-Sa'diyya', c. 1311), and the splendid **al-Tankiziyya madrasa** (c. 1328), though a checkpoint denies access to these on Friday and Saturday.

The **Tashtamuriyya** is an interesting complex on Tariq Bab al-Silsila that was built c. 1382 by Sayf al-Din Tashtamur, a former First Secretary of State to the Mamluk sultan. Not only a residence, the Tashtamuriyya was also built as a tomb, religious school and charitable institution. It's now divided into a number of private residences (some Jewish) and, though not open, it is still possible to admire the impressive façade.

Further along the street on the same side is the **Tomb of Baraka Khan**. A chief of one of the Tartar Khwarizmian tribes that swept through Syria and Palestine in the early 13th century, he ended his days with his severed head impaled on the citadel gate at Aleppo (c. 1246). His memory was rehabilitated when one of his daughters married the Mamluk sultan Baibars. One of his sons is thought to have built this tomb some time between 1265 and 1280. A number of structural alterations have been made to the building, including its conversion into the Khalidi Library in 1900 (home of many ancient Islamic texts), and little remains of its original splendour bar the façade. Almost next door you can see the arched entrances to the **Dar al-Qur'an al-Sallamiyya**, a Koranic school built in 1360. Note the British Mandate period post-box in the wall. The building opposite, at the junction with Tariq al-Wad, is the **Tomb of Baybars al-Jaliq**, a Mamluk official who died c. 1281, though the windows are blocked preventing you from peering inside.

Other minor sights The **Khan al-Sultan** (just off Tariq Bab al-Silsila) is a former Crusader caravanserai that was restored in 1386 by the Mamluk sultan al-Zahir Sayf-al-Din Barquq, and continued to be used in this role during the Ottoman period (with some structural modifications). It still pretty much retains this function, with the lower floors used for storage (though no longer as stables), and the upper floors providing living accommodation.

The **Madrasa al-Lu'lu'iyya** (on Aqbat al-Khalidiyya) was built c. 1373. The street that it stands on is noted for some fine views back to the Dome of the Rock.

Christian Quarter

The Christian Quarter is the second largest of the four divisions of the Old City (c. 18 ha), with a permanent resident population estimated at around 5,200 (3,850 Christian, 1,200 Muslim, 150 Jewish). Spiritually (though certainly not physically or aesthetically) it is dominated by the central shrine of Christendom, the Church of the Holy Sepulchre – revered as the scene of Christ's Crucifixion and Resurrection. The quarter contains numerous other Christian institutions (churches, hospices, convents, patriarchates, seminaries, etc) built to serve the various Christian sects. Today, in excess of 20 different major Christian denominations compete for influence within the quarter, often displaying a distinct lack of Christian brotherly love in the process. Meanwhile, the predominantly Muslim traders along two of the Old City's main shopping streets, David Street and Christian Quarter Road, compete for the tourist dollar.

Ins and outs

Getting there and away Most visitors arrive through Jaffa Gate, though many enter from the Muslim Quarter whilst following the route of Via Dolorosa. **Warning** Given the high tourist flow through this area (notably Omar ibn al-Khattab Square inside Jaffa Gate), it is popular with hustlers offering their services as guides, or trying to tempt you to various shops where you will get a 'special discount' (and they will get a commission). Some of the offers are genuine, and many of the guides are very knowledgeable and speak a number of foreign languages fluently. However, there is no way of sorting the 'wheat from the chaff', and it is wise to err on the side of caution and dispel any offers. **NB** David Street's gently sloping incline, with graded steps and ramps, can be treacherous when wet.

Background

Though the line of Herod Agrippa I's 'Third North Wall' around the first century-CE city is still a matter of speculation, the lack of archaeological evidence for pre-second century-CE construction on the spot now occupied by the Christian Quarter seems to confirm that this whole area was undeveloped until the construction of Hadrian's city of Aelia Capitolina in 135 CE. The Christian Quarter really owes its historical foundation to the rapid expansion of the Christian community in Jerusalem during the Byzantine period, who clustered their institutions around the Holy Sepulchre. This is also true of the Crusaders, who built in this quarter on a monumental scale.

Sights

Pool of the Patriarch's Bath For the best view of this sight you will need to ask permission to climb up to the roof of the **Petra Hostel**. Surrounded on all sides by later period buildings, the Pool of the Patriarch's Bath takes its current name from its medieval function as a source of water for the baths located close to the palace of the Crusader patriarch. However, despite a lack of systematic archaeological investigation, it is clear that the origins of the pool are far older. The area was extensively quarried in the seventh century BCE and a small rain-fed pool could well have existed at that time: hence the alternative name, **Pool of Hezekiah**. It is equally likely that the pool has its origins in the Hasmonean (152-37 BCE) or Herodian (37-4 BCE) quarries that were dug in this vicinity, and it may well be the 'Amygdalon' or 'Tower Pool' mentioned by Josephus in his account of the Roman suppression of the Jewish Revolt in 70 CE (*Jewish War V: 468*). The Crusader period saw the water from the pool used by the patriarch, and later by the nearby bathhouse. Measuring 72 m by 44 m, this large pool is probably only worth seeing if it has recently rained (unless of course you like looking down upon several generations' worth of accumulated trash).

Church of St John the Baptist Visitors to the church are welcome, though it may be necessary to ring the bell in the little courtyard to summon the priest, who may or may not come.

This small church has a complex history, which is not surprising given the fact that it is one of the oldest churches in Jerusalem. Its crypt and foundations date to the fifth century CE, and it is quite possible that it was built to mark the presence in Jerusalem of relics related to John the Baptist. Largely destroyed in the Persian invasion of 614 CE (when the relics were looted and large numbers of Christians massacred), it was restored shortly after, pretty much on the same plan, by the Patriarch of Alexandria. It has what is known as a trefoil shape, with three apses to the north, east and south. The upper storey (ie, bar the crypt and foundations, most of what you see today) belongs to the 11th-century CE reconstruction that was undertaken by the merchant community of Amalfi, Italy. The façade and two small bell-towers are a later addition still.

The Crusader period saw much confusion arise as to the tradition of the site upon which the church is built. The tradition that the church stood on the site of the house of Zechariah, father of John the Baptist, was challenged by the Latins in the 14th century, who claimed that it in fact stood above the former residence of Zebedee, father of St John the Evangelist. The Greek Orthodox, who are now the custodians of the church, have been rejecting this claim since the 17th century.

Whilst the crypt was being cleared of accumulated debris in the 19th century, a magnificent reliquary (an object used to hold religious relics) was located hidden amongst the masonry. Inlaid with precious stones and bound with gilded copper bands, it was made from a piece of rock crystal formed into the shape of a mitre. Amongst the relics it held were 'fragments of the True Cross' and items associated with St Peter, John the Baptist and most of the apostles. It is now held in the Greek Orthodox Treasury of the Church of the Holy Sepulchre.

Christian Quarter Street This thoroughfare features numerous shops selling religious icons and Christian-related souvenirs. Some of the large, smooth **paving stones** along this street date to the Roman/Byzantine city of the third to fourth century CE, and were discovered some metres below the present surface during work on the sewers in 1977.

'Mosque of Omar' **NB** This is not considered a 'tourist site' by the Muslim community, and non-Muslims are not allowed entry. Do not confuse this mosque with the title 'Mosque of Omar' erroneously applied to the Dome of the Rock on the Haram al-Sharif.

The present mosque was built in 1193 by **Afdal 'Ali** following the defeat of the Crusaders six years earlier by his father Salah al-Din. It takes its popular name from the seventh-century CE story relating to the Caliph Omar's refusal to pray inside the Church of the Holy Sepulchre (see 'Church of the Holy Sepulchre' on page 107), though it was originally referred to as the Mosque of Afdal 'Ali. The original mosque reuses much Crusader masonry from the Muristan (page 117), perhaps from the Hospital of the Knights itself, though much of the work was completed later.

The outer entrance gate dates to the mid-19th century, whilst the minaret had to be rebuilt after the 1458 earthquake (possibly in 1465). The top of the minaret has much in common with its counterpart on the al-Khanqah Mosque (page 118), 100 m to the north; in fact, they are at exactly the same height and a line drawn between them is absolutely parallel to the ground. Further, a line drawn between the two minarets has its mid-point at the entrance to the tomb of Christ in the Holy Sepulchre. Murphy-O'Connor (The Holy Land, 1992) believes that there is no doubt that this was intentional, and may have been a crude effort to 'nullify' the resurrection of Jesus, which Muslims reject.

Church of the Holy Sepulchre

① *T02-6273314, daily 0400-2000, -1900 in winter, free. For details of service times, contact the Christian Information Centre opposite the Citadel – midnight mass is highly recommended here, with an atmosphere totally different to the camera-clicking disturbances of the daytime.* The Church of the Holy Sepulchre is built upon the traditional site of the Crucifixion and Resurrection of Jesus, and is thus the most important site within Christendom. The church that you see today dates to a number of periods, having been partially destroyed and rebuilt on a number of occasions, reflecting the Christian experience in the Holy Land. It is admittedly a rather confusing place, and getting to grips with the complexity of not only the setting and history (not least of all the events that it was built to celebrate), as well as the confusing architectural elements, is not easy in the crush of bodies milling around here. If you can, make a series of visits at different times of the day, and it may be an idea to read the account below before entering the church.

Ins and outs There are three approaches to the Church of the Holy Sepulchre, though the only entrance is via the Parvis (courtyard) on the south side (1). Those walking the Via Dolorosa route will, on reaching the Ninth Station of the Cross, have two options. Either to descend to the Parvis via the Ethiopian Monastery on the 'roof' (through the Chapel of the Ethiopians at the upper level, and the Coptic Chapel of St Michael (7) at the lower level). Note that this route is not suitable for large processions (or those carrying crosses), and is probably the most interesting way to arrive. Or to retrace their steps to Tariq Khan es-Zeit, turn right on to Harat al-Dabbaghin, and follow this street through the low doorway into the Parvis. The final approach is from Christian Quarter Road, via Qantarat al-Qiama (St Helena Street), and into the Parvis from the west side. **NB** Modest dress is essential to enter the church.

Church of Constantine Work begun on the Church of Constantine in 326 CE, and it was dedicated on 17 September 335 CE. This truly was a monumental edifice, dwarfing all later efforts including what you see today. It comprised four main elements (atrium, basilica, court and rotunda), and at its longest and widest points it measured around 180 m by

100 m (see plan). The main entrance was from the cardo maximus to the east, into the slightly irregularly shaped **atrium**. This led into the basilica itself, often referred to as the **Basilica of Constantine** or **Martyrium** ('place of witness') which comprised five aisles. The roof was lead, and the ceiling was lined with gold that according to Eusebius "like some great ocean, covered the whole basilica with its endless swell". To the west of the basilica was a porticoed court, with the block of stone venerated as Golgotha in the southeast corner. The court gave on to the Rotunda (or Anastasis, meaning 'Resurrection') around the Tomb of Christ. Construction of this great circular edifice required substantial quarrying and levelling of the rock around the tomb itself, and there is evidence to suggest that it was not completed when the church was dedicated (though certainly by 384 CE, and possibly by 340 CE). A dome (probably wood with a lead covering) capped the **rotunda**, supported by 12 columns 10.5 m high and 8 piers. The exact form of the structure over the tomb (**The Edicule**) is not entirely clear, though attempts have been made to reconstruct it from representations on souvenirs brought back from the Holy Land by early pilgrims.

The **Persian** invasion of 614 CE saw the church burnt, the wooden roof destroyed, the relics looted and the monks murdered. Repairs were undertaken by **Modestus**, Abbot of St Theodosius, though the description of the church given by the pilgrim Arculf in 680 CE varies little from the descriptions of the original Constantine church. The **Arab** conquest of Palestine in 638 CE placed Jerusalem under Muslim control, and led to an amusing, though subsequently fateful, incident in the building's history. Following a tour of the church conducted by the Christian patriarch Sophronis, the Muslim Caliph **Omar** was invited to pray in the church. Omar considerately declined, stating "if I had prayed in the church it would have been lost to you, for the believers would have taken it saying 'Omar prayed here'". Ironically, had it been converted into a mosque it is unlikely that it would have fallen victim to the subsequent desecration at the hands of the Fatimid **Caliph al-Hakim**.

There is evidence that various desecrations of the church took place in the 10th century CE, often at the hands of combined Muslim and Jewish mobs, but the vandalism of 1009 was the most systematic and complete. Al-Hakim ordered Yaruk, governor of Ramla, to "demolish the church of the Resurrection … and to get rid of all traces and remembrance of it". Thus, Constantine's grand church was all but destroyed, though much of the Rotunda remained intact, and the lower levels of the Edicule and much of the rock-cut tomb itself may have been protected from the hammer-wielding vandals by the sheer volume of accumulated debris.

The church rebuilt Until recently it was assumed that the church was rebuilt between 1042 and 1048 by the Byzantine emperor **Constantine Monomachos**. However, it is now clear that the Christian community of Jerusalem began rebuilding the church in 1012, just three years after the al-Hakim- inspired attack. Indeed, as early as 1020 al-Hakim himself had permitted the resumption of Christian liturgies at the site. The subsequent church was a much more modest affair, occupying just the court, Rotunda and some minor chapels and courts of the former building. The original basilica and atrium disappeared (though fragments of these sections of Constantine's church can be seen at 'St Alexander's Chapel and Russian Excavations', page 101, and 'Zalatimo's Sweets', page 100). The columns of the rotunda were cut in half and re-erected (giving the visitor today some sense of the scale of the original Constantine church), and several other modifications made, including the construction of a new apse on the east side. The entrance was as it is today: from the courtyard to the south. This is more or less how the Crusaders found the church when they captured Jerusalem in 1099.

Crusader Church of the Holy Sepulchre There are further misconceptions with regard to dating the Crusader modifications to the church. It has largely been assumed that the 50th anniversary of Crusader rule in Jerusalem was celebrated on 15 July 1149 by the dedication of the modified and restored Crusader Church of the Holy Sepulchre. This assumption has been drawn from the wording of a (now disappeared) Latin inscription above or around the western arch that led to the Chapel of Golgotha (now the Chapel of Adam (**17**). However, it is now clear that this date of dedication refers solely to the Chapel of Golgotha and not the whole **Church of the Holy Sepulchre**. In fact, it is more likely that the Crusader Church of the Holy Sepulchre was not completed until around 1163-1169.

The work undertaken by the Crusader masons was substantial. In addition to rebuilding the chapels around Calvary, they extended the church to the east across Constantine's previously open court by building a choir with an ambulatory and three radiating chapels in the finest late Romanesque style. This was linked to the Rotunda by a crossing covered by a dome and flanked to the north and south by transepts. The principal entrance was (as today) through the portal in the south transept. To the east of the choir, upon the site of Constantine's basilica and atrium, was built the complex needed to house those tending the church.

Although Jerusalem was surrendered to Salah al-Din in 1187, the Church was left unmolested. Pilgrims were permitted to return under the truce signed between Richard Coeur de Lion and Salah al-Din in 1192, and Latin priests were able to join the Syrian priests who had remained since 1187. However, much of the Church was badly damaged in 1244 when the **Khwarismian Turks** rode into the city, and the Edicule itself is said to have been in a particularly parlous state by the time **Boniface of Ragusa** began his restoration programme in 1555.

Recent history A major fire in 1808 had a catastrophic effect on the Church, destroying seven out of ten of the remaining original fourth- and 11th-century columns in the Rotunda, with the collapsing roof badly damaging the exterior of the Edicule. In 1809 the Greek Orthodox community obtained permission from the Ottoman sultan to restore the Church, with the subsequent work being completed in a little over 18 months under the supervision of the Greek architect **Nikolaos Komnenos**. In Biddle's words, "Komnenos' work has not commended itself to non-Orthodox critics" (*ibid*), with the rebuilt Edicule having been described as a "gaudy newspaper kiosk" (Amos Elon). There is even evidence to suggest that the Greeks systematically removed the tombs of the various Crusader kings simply to remove as much trace as possible of the church's Latin past (though it is not really known what state these tombs were in following their looting by the **Khwarismian Turks** in 1244). It should also be noted that Komnenos' restoration was not a structural success either, with the dome of the Rotunda having to be rebuilt in 1868. The whole Church was further weakened by a major earthquake in 1927, and it took until 1959 for a mutually acceptable restoration plan to be agreed by all sides. In the meantime, the Public Works Department of the British Mandatory Government in Palestine (in 1947) had to strap the whole place (including the Edicule) together with iron girders to prevent it collapsing.

Much has been made of the sectarian squabbles within the Holy Sepulchre. The split between the 'Eastern' and 'Western' churches dates to the fifth or sixth centuries, though the theological split subsequently became influenced by political and geopolitical manoeuvres, notably during the Crusades. As a result, the Church of the Holy Sepulchre now finds itself not united by a common belief in Christ's Resurrection, but divided in a territorial battle between Latins, Greeks, Copts, Armenians, Ethiopians and Syrian Jacobites

The Tomb of Christ: is this the place it claims to be?

The first question that many visitors ask concerns the authenticity of the site. Amos Elon records the alleged remark of one young visitor, no doubt repeated by numerous other visitors since: "I didn't know that our Lord was crucified indoors!" (*Jerusalem: City of Mirrors*, 1989).
The information that the gospel accounts give us is useful but limited. They refer to "a place called Golgotha, that is to say, a place of a skull" (*Matthew 27:33; Mark 15:22; John 19:16*), whilst John further adds that "there was a garden; and in this garden a new sepulchre" (19:41). Looking at the church today, such a scene is hard to imagine (and compare with the 'Garden Tomb', page 151).

Of course, a first century CE Jewish graveyard would have been outside the city walls, though proving that this site once fitted this criteria is not difficult. Evidence for the alignment of the city walls in the early first century CE has admittedly been rather elusive, but extensive archaeological examination of this northwest corner of the Old City has revealed no significant construction that predates the early second century CE. Therefore it is more than reasonable to assume that the site of the present Church

of the Holy Sepulchre did indeed stand outside the limits of the first century CE walls.

Thus, when Bishop Makarios of Jerusalem (with the permission of the emperor Constantine) began his search for the burial place of Christ in 325/6 CE, he concentrated his excavations on this site here, within the city walls. Why he chose this particular spot is still not certain, though there is the very real possibility that this place was still being pointed out as the site of the Crucifixion. Tradition records that the early Christian population of Jerusalem continued to venerate the site of the Crucifixion and Resurrection right through the early years of persecution, including the destruction of Jerusalem by the Romans in 70 CE. It is also important to note that although the actual Tomb of Christ may have been 'lost', the rock of Golgotha was still being pointed out to visitors.

Much has also been made of the fact that Hadrian chose to redevelop this site around 135 CE, the inference being that he deliberately built a large pagan temple here in order to snuff out reminders of the nascent Christian faith. However, it is doubtful whether the nature of Hadrian's

for control of a piece of real estate. Physical fights have broken out over such trivial matters as the positioning of a Greek Orthodox rug a few centimetres into Armenian 'space', or "the sweeping of Greek dust with brooms held by Franciscan hands" (Amos Elon, *ibid*); the wooden ladder seen resting against the outer façade of the main entrance is perhaps the best illustration of such territorial wars (see (**14**) below).

Tour

The exterior The tour of the Church of the Holy Sepulchre begins in the **Parvis** (**courtyard**) (**1**) on the south side. Standing in the **Parvis** looking towards the entrance doorway of the Holy Sepulchre (north), one can see three Greek Orthodox chapels to your left (west) that were built on the former site of the Constantine baptistery in the 11th century CE. The first (south) is the **Chapel of St James the Less** (**2**), the brother of Christ. In the centre is the Chapel of the Forty Martyrs (**3**), formerly referred to as the Chapel of the Trinity. The north chapel, adjoining the Holy Sepulchre, is dedicated to **St John the Baptist** (**4**). The bell-

monumental public building will ever be determined, and claiming that a statue of either Venus or Aphrodite was placed above the Tomb of Christ is mere speculation. The fact that Bishop Makarios was prepared to go to the expense of demolishing Hadrian's building, excavating the former quarry, and then shifting all the debris when it would have been far easier (and cheaper) to use the large open space just to the south as the site for his church is cited as evidence that the precise location of Golgotha was known.

However, when Bishop Makarios did find a typical Jewish burial cave of the first century CE during his excavations in 325/6 CE, it is still not clear why it was immediately accepted as the Tomb of Christ. In fact, another rock-cut tomb typical of the first century BCE/first century CE can be seen in the west exedra of the Rotunda in the present church (see (27) on map). Amos Elon notes how in Eusebius' account of the discovery of the holy tomb at this spot, he describes it as being "contrary to all expectation" (*Life of Constantine, 3: 28*). Elon asks: "Why contrary? Could it be that, in ordering the basilica to be built on the site of

the greatest pagan shrine in Jerusalem, Constantine, with the zeal of a new convert, was catering as much to politics as to theology?" (*ibid*). There could be a far simpler explanation for this discovery being "contrary to all expectation"; as Biddle notes, the tomb hadn't been seen in 200 years and "Makarios dug more in hope than expectation and was, to Eusebius's surprise, proved 'right'" (*ibid*). Biddle also speculates that Makarios was able to proclaim his find as the Tomb of Christ because it "could have been marked in some way, possibly with cut or painted graffiti which were legible in 325/6", noting how the tomb of St Peter in the Vatican was also identified in this way.

Thus, in conclusion, the authenticity of the claim that this is the site of the Tomb of Christ is best summed up by Dan Bahat, former City Archaeologist of Jerusalem: "We may not be absolutely certain that the site of the Holy Sepulchre Church is the site of Jesus' burial, but we certainly have no other site that can lay a claim nearly as weighty, and we really have no reason to reject the authenticity of the site" (*Biblical Archaeology Review*, May/June 1986).

tower was added in 1170, though it had become so unstable by the early 18th century that almost half of it had to be removed. These three chapels are generally closed.

To your right (east) are entrances to three other buildings. The first, furthest away from the Holy Sepulchre, is the **Greek Monastery of Abraham (5)**, from where there is (restricted) access to the upper storey of the Holy Sepulchre (including the 'Church of Abraham'). In the centre is the **Armenian Chapel of St James (6)** (sometimes open), whilst in the northeast (top right) corner of the courtyard is the **Coptic Chapel of St Michael (7)**. A staircase inside this chapel leads up to the Chapel of the Ethiopians, the Ethiopian Monastery up on the roof, and the nearby Ninth Station of the Cross (see page 100).

The structure with the small dome in the northeast corner of the courtyard is known as the **Chapel of the Franks (8)**. This was originally designed as a 12th-century Crusader ceremonial entrance to Calvary/Golgotha, which is on an upper level inside the Holy Sepulchre. It was closed following the fall of Jerusalem in 1187, though the stairs up (9) can still be seen. The lower storey is referred to as the **Greek Chapel of St Mary of**

Egypt, whilst the upper storey is the **Latin Chapel of the Agony of the Virgin**. You can see into the latter from a window in the Latin chapel on Calvary inside (**15**).

Before entering the Holy Sepulchre, it's worth taking a few minutes to admire some of the finer points of the **Crusader façade**, particularly the delicately carved stonework on the upper storeys. The entrance doors are flanked by marble triple columns, topped by

Church of the Holy Sepulchre: 12th century to present day

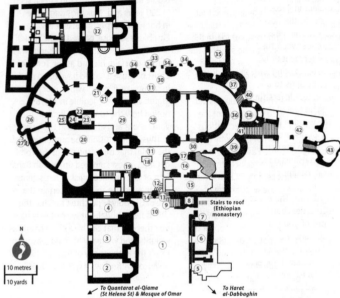

1 Courtyard (Parvis)
2 Chapel of St James the Less
3 Chapel of the Forty Martyrs
4 Chapel of St John the Baptist
5 Greek Monastery of Abraham
6 Armenian Chapel of St James
7 Coptic Chapel of St Michael (and stairs to Ethiopian Monastery)
8 Chapel of the Franks
9 Stairs
10 Tomb of Philip d'Aubigny
11 Redundant wall
12 Steps up to Golgotha
13 Blocked doorway
14 Entrance
15 Latin Chapel of the Nailing to the Cross (upper level)
16 Greek Chapel of the Exaltation or Raising of the Cross (upper level)
17 Chapel of Adam (lower level)
18 Stone of Unction
19 Three Mary's Place
20 Rotunda
21 11th century columns
22 Tomb Monument
23 Chapel of the Angels
24 Chapel of the Holy Sepulchre
25 Coptic Chapel
26 Syrian Chapel
27 Rock-cut Tomb
28 Greek Orthodox Catholicon
29 Arch of the Emperor Monomachos
30 Crusader period side aisles
31 Mary Magdalene Altar
32 Chapel of the Apparition
33 North Aisle
34 'Seven Arches of the Virgin'
35 Prison of Christ
36 Ambulatory
37 Chapel of St Longinus
38 Chapel of the Parting of the Raiment
39 Chapel of the Derision
40 Doorway to Canon's Monastery
41 Step
42 Chapel of St Helena
43 Chapel of the Invention or Finding of the Cross

carved capitals. You may see Greek Orthodox worshippers kissing the central of the three columns on the left side of the main doorway (14). This tradition relates to the miracle of 'The Descent of the Holy Fire' (see page 114). Seemingly, members of the Armenian community locked the Greek Orthodox Patriarch outside the Church so that only their group would be able to receive the Holy Fire inside the Tomb of Christ. But according to Greek Orthodox tradition, the Holy Fire suddenly burst forth from the central of the three columns outside, lighting the torch of the Patriarch. If you closely examine the column in question you will find that it is blackened by fire!

The right (east) door (13) was sealed shut by the Muslim rulers following the fall of Jerusalem in 1187. The original 12th-century carved marble lintels above the doorway are now in the Rockefeller Museum (see page 149). If you look above the sealed east door, you will see a small wooden ladder. This is probably the most potent symbol of the tension between the different sects that control the Holy Sepulchre. Under the 'status quo' agreement of 1757 (implemented by the Ottomans and reapplied during the British Mandate), existing arrangements within the church cannot be changed. Thus, this ladder which belongs to one sect cannot be removed since it stands on property 'owned' by another sect. In fact, the ladder even appears in the watercolours painted by David Roberts during his tour of the Holy Land in 1839!

The wooden boards just outside the entrance cover the **tomb of Philip d'Aubigny (10)** (d. 1236), discovered by accident in 1867 when a bench concealing it was removed. It thus escaped the fate of the other tombs of the Crusader knights that the Greeks removed during their reconstruction work after the 1808 fire. He was an English knight and councillor to King John at the time of the signing of the Magna Carta, and also Tutor to Henry III.

The interior The entrance (14) to the Holy Sepulchre leads into the south transept of the Crusader church. Notice how the clear view across the church is blocked by the wall in front of you (11). This wall was first constructed shortly after the catastrophic fire of 1808 and was designed to support the badly damaged arch. The Greek Orthodox subsequently used it to hang their icons (and it now features an unimaginative mosaic of Christ's Passion). However, recent restoration of the arch above has made this wall superfluous and it now serves no structural purpose whatsoever. The logical thing to do would be to remove it, allowing the clear view across the church that was originally intended, but then the Greeks would have nowhere to hang their icons! Hence the wall stays. The south transept is dominated by the Stone of Unction (18), though we shall come to this shortly.

Having entered the Holy Sepulchre, the logical route is to take the steps (12) up to **Calvary/Golgotha** immediately to the right. The steps were built subsequent to the blocking of the doorway (13) in the 12th century. They lead to an upper floor that reveals the top of the rock outcrop upon which tradition claims Jesus and the two thieves were crucified – Calvary or Golgotha. The first chapel (south) is the **Latin Chapel of the Nailing to the Cross (15)**, and forms the **Xth and XIth Stations of the Cross** where Jesus was disrobed and nailed to the Cross. Most of the mosaic decoration here is relatively modern, though the ceiling medallion depicting the Ascension is 12th century. It is possible from here to see through the window grille into the Latin Chapel of the Agony of the Virgin (see page 113). The second chapel (north) on Calvary is the **Greek Chapel of the Exaltation or Raising of the Cross (16)**, and represents the **XIIth Station of the Cross**. The slots cut in the rock for the three crosses can be seen in the east apse here, whilst it is also possible to touch the rock itself beneath the Greek altar (leading to some very unholy scenes involving

Miracle of the Descent of the Holy Fire

Every year the Church of the Holy Sepulchre is the scene of what Amos Elon describes as "a barbaric ceremony that is part Greek-Dionysiac, part Christian and part Zoroastrian fire worship" (Jerusalem: City of Mirrors, 1989). The origins of the 'Miracle of the Descent of the Holy Fire' are obscure, though it may be derived from the story of Solomon's consecration of the First Temple. On 'Holy Saturday' (the day after the Orthodox Good Friday) the Greek Orthodox Patriarch and an Armenian prelate are locked inside the Tomb of Christ. Then, by miracle, fire descends from heaven, the Patriarch receives it, and proceeds to light a great torch with it before passing it out to the crowd. What this has to do with Christianity is questionable, though it is usually justified by some line about a supernatural event marking the spot of the Resurrection (and is often seen by the Orthodox Church as a symbol of God favouring them).

'Holy Saturday' is arguably the most exciting time to be in Jerusalem. Up to 15,000 people cram into the Church of the Holy Sepulchre on this day, with thousands more locked outside (all streets to the Church are closed off by the Israeli police from about 0700 onwards). If you can't get inside the Church, then Christian Quarter Street or Tariq al-Khanqah are not bad places to spend your day (particularly when the Catholic Scouts and sword swirling Armenians march past). When you eventually manage to get into the Church (often not before 1500), there are still plenty of believers milling around waving dripping candles and struggling get inside the Tomb of Christ.

The ceremony can be a considerable source of tension between the various Orthodox communities: in 1834 over 300 worshippers were said to have died in the mêlée. The whole event, like everything else in the Church, is governed by the 'status quo' agreement of 1757. For example, the spaces between columns 18 and 15 and 11 and 8 of the Rotunda are reserved for Armenians, whilst 14 to 12 and 8 to 5 are for the Greek Orthodox. A knife fight broke out in the Church in 1998 when members of the Syrian Church "displayed religious exuberance" at the Miracle, and were subsequently attacked by Armenians; under the 'status quo' only the Greek Orthodox are allowed to display religious zeal when the Miracle is performed!

cameras). The Latin **'Stabat Mater altar'** (Our Lady of Sorrows) between the two chapels is said to mark the spot where Mary received the body from the cross, and is the **XIIIth Station of the Cross**.

Descending the stairs from the Greek chapel, it is possible to see further sections of the rock of Golgotha (behind perspex) in the **Chapel of Adam** (17). Early tradition claims that Christ died where Adam was buried, so hence the name. The concept of the blood of Christ on the Cross dripping on to the first guilty head is particularly strong within the Greek Orthodox, and may explain why many Greek depictions of the Crucifixion feature a skull at the foot of the Cross. You can choose the explanation for the large fissure seen in the rock here according to your personal spiritual leaning. It is either a natural fault in the rock that led the workmen to abandon this section of the quarry prior to its use as a place of execution/burial, or it is the direct result of the earthquake that occured at the time of the Crucifixion. The tombs of the first two Crusader 'kings' of Jerusalem, Godfrey of Bouillon and Baldwin I, previously lay just inside this chapel, though they were removed by the Greeks during the restoration programme that followed the 1808 fire.

Beyond this chapel, dominating the entrance to the Holy Sepulchre, is the **Stone of Unction (18)**, commemorating the anointing of Jesus' body by Nicodemus prior to its burial (*John 19:38-40*). The previous 12th-century stone was lost in the fire of 1808 and the present limestone slab dates only to 1810. The lamps hanging above it belong to the Armenians, Copts, Greeks and Latins. It is not uncommon to find worshippers prostrating themselves on this 19th-century stone, scooping up the now 'holy' water that they have poured on to it, and wiping cloths and scarves across it.

Ahead, to the left, the small canopy supported by four pillars marks the traditional site where the three Marys are said to have watched the Crucifixion **(19)**. The steps lead up to the Armenian Chapel (closed).

From here you enter the **Rotunda** or **Anastasis (20)** that was originally part of Constantine's fourth-century CE church, and later restored in the 11th, 12th and 20th centuries. The columns and piers are thought to closely follow the line of the fourth-century CE supports, whilst two of the columns to the northeast **(21)** are originals from the 11th-century reconstruction. This was originally a single column used in Constantine's church (and possibly reused from Hadrian's structure), cut in half for the 11th-century rebuilding programme. It gives some idea of the scale of second- and fourth- century CE monumental building projects in Jerusalem. In 1997, the walls and columns were restored, along with the dome, which has a 'starburst' on its interior representing the Twelve Apostles and the spreading out of the Church in the World.

At the centre of the Rotunda is the **Tomb of Christ**, covered by the Edicule **(22)** (or tomb monument, see box on page 117) which is surrounded by bunches of burning candles. The entrance to the marble tomb monument is to the east, and the approach is lined by tall electric candles belonging to the Armenians, Greek and Latins. The queue to enter usually goes half way around the Edicule, and access is rigorously controlled by the officials and monks in charge. The interior is divided into two tiny chapels. The first, the **Chapel of the Angels (23)** (3.4 m by 3 m), is said to contain a part of the rolling stone used to seal Christ's tomb (and subsequently rolled away by the angels). A low doorway leads from the Chapel of the Angels into the tiny **Chapel of the Holy Sepulchre (24)** (2 m by 1.8 m), the **XIVth Station of the Cross**. There's just about room inside for four or five people at a time, who are given 30 seconds or so to have a quick pray. The streaked honey-coloured marble slab covering the burial couch is actually one stone, and dates to at least 1345. Legend suggests that the cut in the slab was deliberately made in order to deter looters from removing it. Marble shelves run around the west, north and east sides of the burial slab. The central part of the shelf is 'owned' by the Greek Orthodox, the left-hand part and left angle by the Latins, and the right-hand part and right angle by the Armenians. The marble icon in the centre (north) belongs to the Greek Orthodox, and is part of the 1809-10 restoration. The silver-coated picture to the left belongs to the Latins, and the painting to the right to the Armenians. The positioning of the candlesticks, vases and pictures is strictly governed by the 'status quo' agreement. On the west wall is a hinged painted icon of the Virgin that opens to reveal a rough masonry wall (possibly part of the 11th-century Byzantine reconstruction).

Leaving the tomb monument, walk round to the far (west) side. It is thought that the miniature and atmospheric **Coptic Chapel (25)** here was built against the west wall between 1809/1810 and 1818. The cupboard under the altar reveals what is generally believed to be the west face of the west wall of the rock-cut Tomb Chamber.

Opposite the Coptic Chapel, in the west exedra of the fourth-century CE Rotunda, is the **Syrian Chapel (26)**. Inside the candlelit hole in the wall on the left (south) side it is possible to see part of the first century-BCE to first-century CE rock-cut tomb (27) that was a deciding factor in the argument aimed at establishing the authenticity of the site. The north, west and south exedras of the fourth-century CE Rotunda have all survived, and much of the west rear wall (not visible from the interior) is original up to a height of 11 m.

Return to the entrance to the tomb monument. Facing east you are confronted by the central aisle of the 12th-century Romanesque Crusader Church, now functioning as the **Greek Orthodox Katholikon (28)**. It is entered through the incorrectly attributed **Arch of the Emperor Monomachos (29)** that was originally built to support the east apse of the 11th-century restoration programme. The 'eastern' influence in the Crusader Church is not necessarily solely the result of the Greek Orthodox ownership (and subsequent decorative style). Much of the Crusader sculpture, as well as the cupola, displays the conscious decision of the Crusader craftsmen to merge their work with the existing 'eastern' stylistic elements that were already in place in the church. The partition walls (11) that divide the Katholikon from the Crusader side aisles (30) are now redundant following recent renovations. The 'omphalos' (navel) on the floor relates to the tradition of the site of the Crucifixion and Resurrection as being at the centre of the world.

Return to the tomb monument and turn right (north). Beyond the two original 4th- and 11th-century pillars (21), is an **altar** dedicated to **St Mary Magdalene (31)**, commemorating Christ's appearance to her on the morning of the Resurrection. The double-doors ahead lead to the **Chapel of the Apparition (32)**, sometimes referred to as the **Chapel of St Mary**. The principal Franciscan chapel in the Holy Sepulchre, it honours the ancient tradition of Jesus' appearance to his mother after the Resurrection (though the gospels do not record the event). In the **north aisle (33)**, the 12th-century architect went to considerable lengths to preserve the portico of the 11th-century courtyard (built using Byzantine pillars), though what resulted is described as a "remarkable jumble" of decorative pillars and weight-bearing piers that is referred to as the **Seven Arches of the Virgin (34)**. At the east end of this aisle is the so-called **Prison of Christ (35)**, a small chapel with smoke-blackened walls that honours the eighth-century tradition that Christ was held in a small room with the two thieves whilst their crosses were being prepared. Continuing around the ambulatory (36) of the Crusader church, there are three small chapels set in the three apses. The first (northeast) is the **Greek Chapel of St Longinus (37)**, dedicated to the Roman soldier who pierced Jesus' side with a spear whilst on the Cross (John 19:34). A fifth-century CE tradition relates how Longinus (who noted at the time "surely this man is the Son of God") was cured of his blindness in one eye by the blood that spurted out. He subsequently repented and became an early Christian convert. The Armenian chapel in the centre (east) apse is the **Chapel of the Parting of the Raiment (38)**, whilst the third (southeast) apse is occupied by the **Greek Chapel of the Derision** or the **Crowning with Thorns (39)**.

The 12th-century doorway (40) between the first northeast and east apses led to the Canon's Monastery, built on the ruins of the Constantine basilica. The flight of steps (41) between the east and southeast apses leads down into the **Chapel of St Helena (42)** (known to its Armenian custodians as the Chapel of St Krikor, or Gregory). Note the crosses carved into the walls by early pilgrims. The chapel is generally thought to date to the Crusaders' 12th-century building programme (the vaulted ceiling certainly does), though the north and south walls are almost certainly part of the foundations of Constantine's basilica. The dome above is the one that you meet at floor level when visiting the Ethiopian Monastery (see page 100).

A further 22 steps in the southeast corner of the Chapel of St Helena lead down to the **Chapel of the Invention or Finding of the Cross (43)**. Remarkably, in his account of the

The Edicule over the Tomb of Christ

Probably the greatest authority on the Edicule is Professor Martin Biddle, whose publication The Tomb of Christ (Sutton, 1999) broke new ground in the study of the Holy Sepulchre. Having been granted unprecedented access to the Tomb, and using all resources at his disposal (such as photogrammetry), Biddle's insight is largely as a result of applying one of the basic rules of systematical archaeological enquiry: starting with what is there at the present and working your way backwards! Remarkably, this fundamental approach has never before been used here, largely because it was always assumed that nothing could be learnt from the relatively modern Edicule. However, Biddle believes that the anomalies in the form of the present Edicule reveal clues to the form of previous monuments.

The exterior of the present Edicule (22) dates to the 1809-1810 restoration, and is thought to be perilously close to collapse (partly as a result of the 1927 earthquake). In fact, it is largely held together by the timber and steel cradle put there in 1947 by the British Mandate government. It appears that the east and west walls are largely unsupported, and Biddle estimates that "elements in the east front [have] moved as much as 3cm in the years 1990-1993" (ibid). Because the spike on the top of the cupola has moved no more than 2 mm between 1989 and 1992, it is believed that the outer cladding is moving independently of the vault and cupola over the Tomb Chamber.

Since the state of the Edicule is so 'parlous', it is hoped that a restoration plan that is acceptable to all the interested parties can be worked out. This will require dismantling stone by stone the present Edicule, though such a programme will reveal what is actually left of the original Tomb Chamber.

discovery of the tomb of Christ (*Life of Constantine*, written c. 337-40) Eusebius neglects to mention how Constantine's mother, the Empress Dowager Helena, discovered the True Cross in a cistern close to the rock of Golgotha. Perhaps it slipped his mind! In fact, the tradition did not appear until 351 CE, 16 years after the completion of Constantine's church. Nevertheless, this spot is revered as the place where Helena found the True Cross. Custody of the chapel is divided between the Greeks and Latins.

Returning up the steps to the ambulatory of the Crusader Church (**36**), continue west along the south aisle, passing the Chapel of Adam (**17**), and ending the tour of the Church of the Holy Sepulchre back at the entrance.

Muristan

The Muristan was developed in the early 11th century by wealthy, but pious, traders from **Amalfi** in Italy. They constructed, or reconstructed, a number of churches and hospices including the Church of St John the Baptist (page 106) and the Church of St Mary of the Latins (the site now being occupied by the Lutheran Church of the Redeemer, see below.

The turning point in the development of the area came with the conquest of the city in 1099 by the **Crusaders**. Many of the knights wounded in the assault were admitted to the small hospital for sick pilgrims that was attached to the Church of St John the Baptist. Some of these knights were to go on to serve the hospital, primarily protecting the sick pilgrims, and with generous endowments from the first two Crusader kings of Jerusalem (Godfrey of Bouillon and Baldwin I) within a short space of time an order known as the **Knights of**

St John of the Hospital had been established. This later became the military order known as the **Hospitallers**; subsequently one of the most powerful and wealthy medieval orders whose military role "almost overshadowed its primary charitable purpose". A huge hospice housing 400 knights was built during the mid-12th century, whilst according to one contemporary source, over 2000 patients of both sexes were being treated in the enlarged hospital in the 1170s.

The fall of Jerusalem in 1187 saw the Hospitallers involved in negotiating the terms of surrender with Salah al-Din and, though the Order lost their property, the hospital continued to function until the 16th century. The present name, Muristan, is taken from the Persian word for 'hospital' or 'hospice'. Reports from the 15th century suggest an area in terminal decline, with most of the buildings in a state of dilapidation and decay, and by c. 1524 the whole area appears to have been abandoned. Most of the Crusader structures were plundered for masonry to be used in Sulaiman the Magnificent's 16th-century city walls and as Prag notes (*Blue Guide*, 1989), "It requires considerable imagination to visualize the area as the well-built and busy 12th-century headquarters of a great hospital and military order". The area is now geared towards tourists, with several cafés and restaurants on the fountain square.

Lutheran Church of the Redeemer ① *T02-6276111/6282543, Mon-Sat 0900-1200 and 1300-1500, cloisters 2NIS, tower 5NIS. Prior arrangement is needed to view the medieval excavations below.* Built in 1898 on the lines of the Church of St Mary of the Latins, the 178-step tower of the Lutheran Church of the Redeemer can proudly boast one of Jerusalem's best views. The mosaic in the apse shows Christ the Redeemer, and modern modifications include the striking stained-glass windows.

Greek Orthodox Patriarchate and Museum ① *Tue-Fri 0900-1300 and 1500-1700, Sat 0900-1300, adult 5NIS.* This museum presents an insight into the history of one of Jerusalem's largest Christian groups, and displays some items of archaeological interest including sarcophagi from Herod's family tomb (see page 172). There is also access via the Patriarchate to the roof of the Holy Sepulchre, with spectacular views into the dome above the Rotunda.

Al-Khanqah Mosque Formerly the palace of the Latin Patriarch in Jerusalem, it became a khanqah (convent for Sufi mystics) following the Crusader surrender of the city to Salah al-Din in 1187. The minaret was built c. 1417 (see also 'Mosque of Omar', page 84).

Jewish Quarter

The Jewish Quarter is the smallest of the four divisions of the Old City (c. nine hectares), and the population is exclusively Jewish. The Israeli High Court ruled in 1981 that non-Jews could not buy property there (to preserve the quarter's homogeneity), though similar legislation does not apply to the Old City's other three quarters. The quarter was badly neglected during the period of Jordanian occupation (1948-1967), even systematically looted, and was devastated during its capture by the Israelis in the Six Day War of 1967. One positive consequence of this devastation was the opportunity afforded to archaeologists to excavate here thoroughly before the bulldozers of the rebuilding contractors moved in. The time and effort invested by the archaeologists has been amply rewarded, and there are now a number of important and interesting sites to be seen. However, the heavily-restored buildings and residential nature of the quarter make it the least atmospheric to wander around. A 'combined ticket' is available for entrance into several of the sights, and will save you money.

Ins and outs

Getting there and around Visitors arrive from the 'Western Wall Plaza', from Zion Gate, at the southern tip of the Armenian Quarter; or along the Byzantine cardo maximus, from its north end. **NB** Photography and smoking are frowned upon here on Shabbat, and the bank ATM machine closes.

Background

The ancient city that David established on the southeast ridge (see page 141), and Solomon expanded northwards with the construction of the Temple, gradually developed to occupy the land now comprising the Jewish Quarter during the period of Hezekiah's rule (727-698 BCE). In fact, remains of Hezekiah's fortification of the area can be seen today. The Babylonian sacking of the city in 586 BCE led to the virtual abandonment of this land for the next three centuries or so. Hasmonean and then Herodian rule in Jerusalem saw the rapid expansion of the city, and by the end of the first century BCE the main focus of the Upper City was shifted here. The evidence of this is presented at the Wohl Archaeological Museum in the quarter (see page 121).

The devastation wreaked upon the Upper City by the Romans in 70 CE is also evidenced by the archaeological remains and, following the second rebellion by the Jews (Bar Kokhba Revolt 132-135 CE), much of what is now the Jewish Quarter was occupied by the Roman Tenth Legion (Fretensis). There is little evidence of occupation of this area by Jews in the Byzantine, Early Arab or even Crusader periods (though it should be remembered that the Crusaders massacred most of the Muslim and Jewish population upon their capture of the city in 1099). However, there is considerable weight of evidence to suggest that Jerusalem's only medieval synagogue was built here (see Ramban Synagogue, page 123). It was during the Ottoman period that this south central area of the Old City became known as the Jewish Quarter. The Sephardi community became established here at the beginning of the 16th century, with the Ashkenazi Jews firmly planting roots around 1700. The Karaites sect had been long established by then. All were driven out by the war in 1948.

The reconstruction of the Jewish Quarter following its capture by the Israelis in 1967 has been carefully planned. Although most of the new buildings are modern in design and function, an old bye-law dating to the early years of the British Mandate was invoked, requiring all new buildings to be faced with dressed, natural Jerusalem stone.

Sights

Byzantine cardo maximus Whilst the three parallel streets of the covered bazaar just to the north overlie the Roman-Byzantine cardo maximus of Hadrian's city of Aelia Capitolina, the section of the cardo maximus exposed here is a later southern extension of the main north to south thoroughfare. At the time of the construction of Aelia Capitolina (135 CE), the area in which we are now standing (and indeed most of the present Jewish and Armenian Quarters) was occupied by the camp of the Tenth Legion (Fretensis), and would not have been considered part of Aelia Capitolina itself. Thus, Aelia Capitolina's cardo maximus ran roughly from the present site of Damascus Gate to the junction of Tariq Khan es-Zeit, David Street and Tariq Bab al-Silsila.

The section of restored cardo maximus presented for viewing here represents the **Byzantine** extension of the city, and is usually attributed to **Justinian** (527-565 CE). It is generally believed that the cardo was extended in order to link the two principal churches of the city: the Church of the Holy Sepulchre and Justinian's own Nea Church (page 122). A "magnificent street" some 22.5 m wide, it comprised a broad uncovered roadway (12 m wide) flanked by two rows of 5-m-high columns forming a *stoa* (covered passageway) on either side. The road was paved with large well-dressed stones laid in parallel rows at right angles to the street, with a raised ridge along the centre assisting with drainage. About 180 m of the cardo maximus has been exposed here.

The northern section was laid upon earth fills that covered sections of the **Hasmonean wall** (second to first century BCE) and earlier seventh-century BCE **Israelite wall**. In fact, glass-covered shafts allow visitors to look down upon excavated remains that the Byzantine cardo maximus overlies, thus giving some idea of how the successive levels of construction and destruction of Jerusalem have changed the city's landscape.

'Broad Wall' The section of wall exposed here is part of Hezekiah's expansion of the fortified city (c. 727-698 BCE). The original wall is thought to have run west from the Temple Mount to the present location of the Citadel, though only a 65-m section is exposed here. It takes its popular name from the fact that it is 7 m wide, though what you see here is merely the foundations of partly hewn stones that have been laid without mortar. A line drawn on the adjacent modern building indicates how high the original wall may have been. The function of the wall was to protect the area of the city that had grown up outside the original Solomonic city walls, quite possibly as a result of the Assyrian invasion of Samaria in 722 BCE and the subsequent flow of refugees. The wall was hastily built in advance of Sennacherib's march on Jerusalem in 701 BCE (see *II Kings 18:13*), and required the demolition of a number of eighth-century CE private houses that stood in its way. The archaeological evidence fits perfectly with the written record: "And ye have numbered the houses of Jerusalem, and the houses have ye broken down to fortify the wall" (*Isaiah 22:10*). A map here shows the plan of Jerusalem in the First Temple period. A multi-media tour about Jerusalem during the First Temple period and a scale model can be found in the Ariel Visitor Centre, a little further along **Plugat HaKotel** ① *T02-6286288. Sun-Thu 0900-1600, adult 18NIS, student/child 14NIS*, call ahead (even if it is the same day) for a guided tour in English.

Israelite Tower and Hasmonean defences At the junction of Plugat HaKotel and Shonei HaLakhot is a section of a massive Israelite Tower and Hasmonean defences preserved beneath a modern building (the sign on the door says 'Israelite Tower'). The Israelite Tower is part of a gate dating to the seventh century BCE, and possibly built by Manasseh (698-642 BCE). In fact, a number of arrowheads dating to the Babylonian sack of Jerusalem in 586 BCE were found in the vicinity, scattered amidst signs of the burning that followed the conquest. However, the site is closed for the foreseeable future.

Burnt House (Beit Katros) ① *T02-6287211, Sun-Thu 0900-1700 (last video show at 1620), Fri 0900-1300, adult 25NIS, student 13NIS, child 12NIS*. The archaeological evidence to support Josephus' graphic description of the Roman sacking of Jerusalem following the destruction of the Temple in 70 CE can be seen here at the 'Burnt House'. Josephus relates how the Romans "poured into the streets sword in hand, cut down without mercy all who came within reach, and burnt the houses of any who took refuge indoors, occupants and all" (*Jewish War VI: 403*). Such was the scale of slaughter that the city was deluged with gore "so that many of the fires were quenched by the blood of the slain" (*ibid*). Though the latter is a typical Josephus exaggeration, the debris-filled rooms of this house contained charred wooden beams and fallen stones scorched by fire, thus confirming part of Josephus' account. The date of the fire was further confirmed by the discovery of a coin dated 69 CE amongst the debris, as well as an iron spear leaning against a wall and the bones of a young woman's hand and arm.

The plan of the house is that of a large complex belonging to a fairly wealthy family, though you should bear in mind that what you see today is merely the remains of the basement. The identity of the owner was established following the discovery of a stone weight inscribed "[belonging] to the son of Katros". The Babylonian Talmud refers to such a priestly family who served in the Temple, though the line in question (*Pes. 57a; Tosefta, Men 13:21*) suggests that they were not the most popular people in town. The museum includes a display of household items discovered in situ, the labelled plan of the 'Burnt House', and a video which tells of the destruction of the Temple through a rather lame soap-opera about Katros's family (shown every 40 minutes).

St Mary of the Germans During the medieval period, this area was regarded as the German quarter of Crusader Jerusalem (and Misgav Ladakh was the 'Street of the Germans'). A complex containing a church (St Mary of the Germans), a hospice and hospital was built here around 1128 by the **German Knights of the Hospitallers Order** (from which developed the Order of the Teutonic Knights in the next century) to serve the needs of German-speaking pilgrims. Modifications were made to the building during the Mamluk period, and there is even evidence to suggest that the church was used as a residence for dervishes. The complex was excavated following the Israeli capture of the Old City in 1967, and the crusader-style arches restored.

The steps descending from St Mary of the Germans lead via one of Jerusalem's best **viewpoints** down to the Western Wall Plaza, past a replica of the giant golden menorah from the Second Temple.

Wohl Archaeological Museum ① *T02-6265900 (ext 102), Sun-Thu 0900-1700, Fri 0900-1300, adult 15NIS, student 13NIS, child 7NIS*. This museum contains the well-presented remains of a residential area dating to the first century BCE/first century CE, generally referred to as the **Herodian Quarter**.

The area covers some 2700 sq m of the Upper City of Jerusalem. During the Herodian period (37 BCE-70 CE) Jerusalem experienced great prosperity and rapid growth, with the Upper City becoming the most exclusive residential address. The value of the excavated section that is presented in this museum is that it "provides evidence of an urban plan for a residential neighbourhood, house plans, domestic architecture and art, the living conditions of the city's inhabitants, and various aspects of everyday life in the city in the Second Temple period" (Avigad, New Encyclopedia of Archaeological Excavations in the Holy Land, 1993).

Tour Now located some 3 to 7 m below the present street level, the site here presents the remains of a series of six houses from the Herodian period. Descending the steps, you arrive at an elevated walkway around the **Western Building**. The plan before you here is only the basement of the house, though it superbly illustrates the layout of the water installations and service rooms of a wealthy household. It comprises a number of cisterns, a vestibule, a bathroom, and two mikvehs (ritual baths), of which one is preserved intact. Parts of the mosaic floor from the bathroom remains. The tour continues along the corridor, where finds from the Second Temple period are displayed, including pottery with geometric designs (imagery being forbidden). The '**Middle Complex**' comprises the remains of two separate houses, apparently divided by a common wall. There is a fine mosaic preserved in the large living room, though when first discovered it was covered by a layer of debris directly related to the fire of 70 CE (see 'Burnt House' on page 120). Amongst the artefacts recovered from the house were a number of stone tables: the first pieces of furniture from the Second Temple period ever found. The walkway descends into "the largest and most magnificent of the buildings discovered in the Jewish Quarter" (Avigad, *ibid*) – the '**Mansion**'. The topography of this residential quarter of the Upper City dictated that the floor level here is some distance lower than that of the houses in the Middle Complex (and 7 m below the present street level). This large mansion comprises two storeys, though experts speculate that there may originally have been a third. The number of *mikvehs* found in the complex, including one where the vaulting, double entrance and mosaic-paved corridor were found in a superb state of preservation, has led to speculation that this large villa may have been the residence of members of the family of a high priest at the Temple. Other experts have challenged this assumption, looking to the stylistic Hellenistic influences to dismiss this argument. The 1:25 scale model of the reconstructed mansion allows the visitor to picture the building in its prime.

Batei Mahasseh Square This large square, often filled with Jewish schoolchildren playing, has a number of fragments of columns, capitals and Attic bases scattered about. None was found *in situ* and their exact origins are unclear, though it is certain that they formed part of some monumental structure(s) built nearby during the Hasmonean or Herodian period. The building along the west side of Batei Mahasseh Square, the **Rothschild Building**, dates to 1871, whilst the complex of buildings along the south side, the **Shelter Houses**, were built nine years earlier to house poor immigrant Jews from Holland and Germany. Their basements provided shelter for the quarter's residents during the last weeks of the battle for the Old City in 1948. This area was also badly damaged in the fighting for the city in 1967, though the subsequent archaeological excavations that ensued led to the discovery of remains of the Nea Church beneath the square.

Nea or New Church of Justinian Next to nothing remains of Justinian's Nea Church, dedicated to 'St Mary, Mother of God', though when dedicated in 543 CE it was (and remains) the largest basilica built in Palestine. Its external measurements are something in the region of 116 m by 57 m, which is not so difficult to imagine when you see that the seemingly meagre remains (part of the northeast apse, vaults to the south, external southeast corner) have walls up to 4-m thick.

   Though the approximate location of the church just to the east of the south end of the Byzantine cardo maximus was known from the sixth-century **Madaba Map** (see page 60), and sections of it had been exposed during the construction of the Batei Mahasseh complex in 1862, it wasn't until Avigad's excavations (1970-82) that the true identity of the structure was firmly established. It was probably badly damaged in either the Persian invasion of 614 CE or the Arab conquest of 638 CE, and finally destroyed in the ninth century CE.

   To view the preserved section of the **northeast apse**, walk down the steps away from the Rothschild Building to the southeast corner of Batei Mahasseh Square. Descend the steps to the right and turn left under the arch on Nachamu Street. Descend a further seven steps, then take the double flight of stairs down. Behind the green metal grille is the entrance to the northeast apse (not always accessible). Sections of the vaulted cistern and external structures can be seen in the archaeological garden to the south (just inside the present Old City walls). The remains can also be seen from above when walking the ramparts.

Four Sephardi Synagogues ⓘ *Sun-Thu 0930-1600, Fri 0930-1230, adult 3NIS*. Construction of synagogues to serve the Sephardi community on this site date to 1610, with the completion of the **Ben Zakkai Synagogue** (named after the first-century CE rabbi and noted sage). A study hall was added on the northwest side in 1625, and converted into the **Prophet Elijiah Synagogue** some 70 years later. Further modification to the complex saw the **Middle Synagogue** added some point later, and the **Stambouli Synagogue** completed by 1857. The entire complex became badly neglected during the period of Jordanian occupation of the Jewish Quarter (1948-67), though subsequent restoration work has been completed using items recovered from Italian synagogues destroyed during World War II.

Ramban and Hurva Synagogues The west side of Hurva Square is occupied by the Hurva and Ramban Synagogues, and the Sidi 'Umar Mosque. Visiting Jerusalem in 1267, the noted Jewish scholar **Rabbi Moses ben Nachman** (known as **Ramban** or **Nachmanides**) discovered that there were only enough Jews in Jerusalem for a game of chess (out of a total population of around 2000). He settled in the city (meaning that the Jewish population were now just one short for a hand of bridge) and founded a synagogue on Mount Zion. Some time in the 14th century CE the **Ramban Synagogue** was moved to the present site, occupying the ruins of a Crusader church (possibly 'St Peter in Chains' or 'Church of St Martin'). The building collapsed in 1474 but was rebuilt in 1523 (possibly as the only synagogue in Jerusalem). Ottoman edicts subsequently banned its use as a Jewish place of worship.

In 1700 a group of Ashkenazi Jews (from Eastern Europe) arrived in Jerusalem and established themselves on a site just to the north of the Ramban Synagogue. Their attempts to build their own synagogue were complicated by internal squabbling following the death of their leader, and the half-built structure was confiscated by the Ottomans to settle the group's debts. Hence the synagogue's name: **Hurva**, or 'the Ruin'. The Hurva was returned to the Ashkenazi community by Ibrahim Pasha in 1836, finally completed in 1856 but destroyed in the fighting of 1948. Recently rebuilt, the Hurva Synagogue reopened in March 2010, triggering unrest among Palestinian groups concerned that it signalled Jewish intent to build a Third Temple on the Temple Mount.

The small **minaret** nearby belongs to the **Sidi 'Umar Mosque** (also known as **Jabi Kabir**), which may well have occupied a former Crusader structure (Church of St Martin?) some time in the 14th century. The minaret shows a number of 15th-century characteristics and is built in the square Syrian style.

Armenian Quarter

Marginally bigger than the Jewish Quarter (c. 10.5 ha), the Armenian Quarter occupies the southwest corner of the Old City. Visitors should note that many of the quarter's would-be attractions are behind high walls and closed doors, and are not open to the casual visitor. The heavy gates are locked at night, as they were in the Middle Ages. It is a 'walled city within a walled city', perhaps explaining why this is the only ethnic/religious quarter of the Old City that occupies the same site as it did in the fifth century CE.

Ins and outs

Getting there and around The two main approaches to the Armenian Quarter are from Jaffa Gate or from Zion Gate. Perhaps the most interesting time to visit the quarter is at the end of April, when the community commemorates the genocide of the Armenian people at the hands of the Turks during World War I. Following a moving service at the atmospheric Cathedral of St James, the Patriarch leads a silent procession along Armenian Patriarchate Street to the Armenian Church of the Holy Saviour on Mount Zion.

Background

Much of this quarter was formerly occupied by Herod the Great's palace, though next to no traces remain. The Armenians were quick to establish a presence in Jerusalem following the adoption of Christianity as the state religion in 301 CE (the first nation to do so), and the period of exile that followed the collapse of the Armenian state in the fourth century CE seemed to strengthen the Armenian community in the Holy Land. Indeed, by the seventh century CE an Armenian visitor to Jerusalem noted 70 Armenian convents/monasteries in the city. Many of these were established by St Gregory (Krikor) the Illuminator, though most were destroyed during the Persian (614 CE) and Arab (638 CE) invasions, and their remains are now scant.

The re-established Armenian kingdom in Cilica (c. 1098-1375) had close links with the Latin kingdom in Jerusalem (with Baldwin I, Jerusalem's second Crusader ruler, also being the Count of Armenian Edessa), and the Armenian revival in the Holy Land was further cemented by the purchase of the Church of St James from the Georgians (some time in the 12th century prior to 1151). Armenian fortunes in Jerusalem fluctuated in subsequent centuries, though not necessarily reflecting fortunes in the home land. However, the genocide committed by the Turks early in the 20th century has galvanized the Armenian community in Jerusalem, who now see themselves not only as the custodians of the religious centre of the Armenian diaspora, but also as the guardians of the Armenian cultural identity.

Sights

Christ Church ⓘ *T02-6277727, www.cmj-israel.org. Church daily 0900-1700, services Sat 1000 (except 1st Sat in month) and Sun 0930; museum daily 0900-1700, free.*
Consecrated in 1849, the Anglican Christ Church is the oldest Protestant church in Jerusalem (though the meaning of its claim to be the "first major 'modern' building in Jerusalem" is less clear). After obtaining permission from the Ottoman sultan to build a "prayer hall" for workers next to their consul, the British constructed a church that in fact dwarfed the consul building. Though the initial impression of the church is one of simplicity, closer inspection reveals a number of details that are a clue to the church's unusual history and function. Note the Hebrew writing and Jewish symbols on the stained-glass windows, the Star of David on the table and menorah on the altar.

The church was built by an Anglican missionary society called the **London Society for Promoting Christianity** amongst the Jews (later the **Church's Ministry among the Jews**, or **CMJ**). The society, founded in 1809, drew its inspiration from a line in the *epistle of Paul to the Romans*, which declared: "For I am not ashamed of the gospel of Christ: for it is the power of God unto salvation to every one who believeth; *to the Jew first*, and also to the Greek" (*Romans 1:16*, emphasis added). Like other evangelical groups of the period (and indeed today), the CMJ's founders believed that before the Messiah returned, the Jewish people would be restored to the promised land and that a good many of them

The Armenian genocide: a rehearsal for Hitler?

On 24 April each year a day of mourning is held in the Armenian Quarter to commemorate what many Armenians refer to as the first European Holocaust. In the period 1915-1918, over 1,000,000 Armenian civilians were murdered by the Turks, not, as Fisk points out, using the "sophisticated machinery that the Nazis were to employ against another minority community less than 30 years later", but "shot or knifed to death, the women often raped before being murdered" (*Pity the Nation: Lebanon at War*, 1990). A further 75,000 Armenians were murdered during Turkey's 1918 invasion of the Caucasus, whilst Walker estimates that 250,000 more may have died between 1919 and 1922

(*Armenia: The Survival of a Nation*, 1980). The fact that the genocide was largely ignored by the rest of the world was tragic not just for the people of Armenia, but also for European Jewry. Describing the Armenian genocide as "a rehearsal for Auschwitz", Amos Elon quotes an Armenian spokesman as saying "The Armenian holocaust was forgotten or ignored. If it had not been ignored, perhaps Auschwitz would not have happened" (*Jerusalem: City of Mirrors*, 1989). This may not necessarily be true, yet Hitler is said to have told those generals who questioned the possible international reaction to his Final Solution, "Who remembers today the fate of the Armenians?"

would acknowledge Jesus Christ as the Messiah. The CMJ's presence was established in Jerusalem in 1833 both in anticipation, and to precipitate, such events. The organization did much to support the first Aliyah of Russian Jews to the Holy Land in 1882. The founders of Christ Church incorporated Jewish symbols into the church design so that Jews would feel comfortable about entering, and could see how the Christian church acknowledged its Jewish origins. The history of the building and of the CMJ are presented in the small museum on site, along with topographical models of the Old City, worth a quick visit. The church also runs a very attractive guesthouse to the rear and has a nice courtyard café (see page 177).

Ya'qubiyya This small mosque (rarely accessible to visitors) occupies a former 12th-century CE Crusader church dedicated to St James (the Less). The site may originally have been the site of a monastery founded c. 430 CE by Peter the Iberian to house the relics of **St James Intercisus** (or St James the Cut-up), a Persian Christian martyred in 422 CE. Muslim documents of the 14th century CE refer to the building as the Zawiya (tomb) of Shaikh Ya'aqub al-'Ajami (James the Foreigner), and this medieval dedication has been preserved in the name of the mosque today. Parts of 12th-century CE Crusader masonry can be seen in the arch and choir.

Syrian Orthodox Church and Convent of St Mark ① *T02-6283304, Mon-Sat 0900-1700, Sun 1200-1700 (if closed, telephone), free, donations accepted.* A remarkable number of traditions are related to this site, occupied intermittently since the 12th century by the Syrian Orthodox (or **Jacobite**) community. A Byzantine tradition links the site to Mary of Jerusalem, mother of (John) Mark (St Mark), and suggests that i) the Last Supper was eaten here (*Matthew 26:17-30*; *Mark 14:12-36*; *Luke 22:7-38*; *John 13-17*); ii) the Descent of the Holy Spirit at Pentecost took place here (*Acts 2:1-47*); iii) the Virgin Mary was baptized in the stone font against the present south wall; and iv) that St Peter came here after his miraculous release from prison by the Angel (*Acts 12:12*)! Little wonder that the site was chosen for a church during the Byzantine period.

The present church was built in the 12th century, with numerous later modifications, though its constructors have not been positively identified. The confusion arises from the fact that the Jacobites fled Jerusalem prior to its capture by the Crusaders in 1099, with much of their property being passed to a Frankish knight. His apparent death in Egypt in 1103 saw the property returned to the Jacobites, though his subsequent reappearance in 1137 (alive and well) further confused the rights to the title deeds. A settlement in favour of the Jacobites was eventually reached.

The entrance portal of the convent is 12th century, and leads to a much more recent courtyard. The key feature is the stone font opposite the door in which the Virgin Mary is said to have been baptized, now adorned with gilt and flowers. The portrait of the Virgin and Child above the font is attributed to St Luke, though it is generally agreed that it dates only to the Byzantine period. Other points of interest include the inscription on the west pillar inside the entrance (said to be sixth-century CE) and the crypt beneath, where the Last Supper possibly took place.

Armenian Convent of St James This large complex, containing the Cathedral of St James, the residence of the Patriarchate, a pilgrim hospice, accommodation for nuns and monks, a seminary, library, museum, printing press, and various other related buildings, is the centre of the Armenian Christian community. On entering, note the impressive complex of locks and bolts on the inside of the main door from Armenian Patriarch Street.

Cathedral of St James ① *T02-6282331, daily during afternoon service, 1500-1530 (the priest will give visitors a short tour afterwards), and morning services 0600-0630. Stand at the rear. Free, donations accepted.* Those who make the effort to visit or worship in the Cathedral of St James are rarely disappointed: it is the finest church in town with an atmosphere during services and festivals that is very moving. Laden with incense, the interior of the cathedral is at its best on fine days, when "sunlight from the high windows and the lights of all the lamps create a dazzling and memorable reflection on the rich vestments, ornaments, tiles and other treasures" (Prag, 1989).

The central part of the present cathedral dates to the 11th century, though it is believed that a friend of the Byzantine empress Eudocia may have endowed some form of Christian establishment near here as early as 444 CE, and installed an Armenian as abbot. It was almost certainly destroyed during the Persian invasion of 614 CE. Between 1072 and 1088 the **Georgian** Christian community established a church and monastery here dedicated to St James the Great. An early Christian martyr, St James (son of Zebedee) was one of the first of the apostles, and was executed c. 44 CE on the orders of Herod Agrippa I. The fortunes of the Georgians took a turn for the worse in the 12th century, and they were forced to sell the church to the **Armenians**. A number of alterations were made to the church, though the Armenians retained the link with St James (in fact the principal relic is said to be his severed head).

During the Ottoman period the Armenian church fell into heavy debt through both mismanagement of its finances and its financial commitments to the Church of the Holy Sepulchre. The arrival of **Gregory the Chainbearer** in 1721 (so called because he wore a chain around his neck for three years whilst begging for restoration donations in the doorway of the Church of the Holy Mother of God in Constantinople) saw the debts repaid and the cathedral lavishly restored. Most of the precious stone and metal ornamentation dates to this period. The appearance of the cathedral was further enhanced by the addition of the decorative blue and white tile work (in the Kütahya style) between 1727 and 1737. **NB** Only the monastic compound and main church (excluding the chapels to the north) are open to visitors.

Armenian Garden The walled compound of the Armenian Garden contains a number of institutions related to the Armenian community, though the area is not open to the public. This area to the south of the Citadel was previously occupied by Herod's palace, though precious little survived the 70 CE sacking.

Armenian Museum Closed for renovation at time of writing, possibly reopening in 2010. Housed in a very attractive former seminary (built 1843), this museum explains the history and culture of Armenia, and also houses some of the gifts that pilgrims have given to the cathedral. The nearby Gulbenkian Library is unfortunately closed to tourists.

Church and Convent of the Holy Archangels (Convent of the Olive Tree) It is sometimes possible (on request) to visit the Church and Convent of the Holy Archangels (also known as the Convent of the Olive Tree) within the grounds of the Armenian Convent, to the

Cathedral of St James

5 metres
5 yards

N

1 Vestibule (with Mamluk inscription)
2. Armenian inscription
3 Khatchkars
4 Small Court
5 Armenian inscription
6 Porch
7 Hidden staircase (to Chapel of the Apostles)
8 Chapel of the Apostles (upper level)
9 Chapel of St Menas (lower level)
10 Altar of St Menas (lower level)
11 Altar of St Sargis (lower level)
12 Chapel of St James the Less
13 Chapel of St Makarios
14 Chapel of St Nishan (upper level)
15 Church of St Stephen
16 Baptismal Font
17 Altar of St Cyril
18 Altar of St Stephen
19 Altar of St Gregory the Illuminator
20 Altar of St John the Baptist
21 Hidden staircase leading to Chapel of St Paul (upstairs)
22 Main Apse
23 Altar of the Virgin Mary
24 Chapel of St Peter (upstairs)
25 Patriarchal Throne
26 Grave of St James the Less
27 Opus Sectile Floor
28 Hidden staircase
29 Original entrance to 12th-century church
30 Tiles
31 Etchmiadzin Chapel
32 Altar of Sinai

To Citadel & Jaffa Gate
Armenian Patriarchate St
To Zion Gate

southeast of the Cathedral of St James. With a very beautiful interior, a 14th-century CE tradition places the 'House of Annas' here, where Jesus was taken after his arrest prior to being sent to the House of the High Priest Caiaphas. The olive tree against the north wall of the church is said to mark the site of the scourging. Women still come to eat three olives from the tree, as then they fall pregnant. The outer wall of the church is also said to contain one of the stones that would have cried out aloud had the disciples not praised God (*Luke 19:40*). This may seem risible to some, though as Murphy-O'Connor has pointed out, it is a tradition that "no one can ever prove false"!

Mount Zion

The area now referred to as Mount Zion is a low hill just below the southwest corner of the Old City, outside the current walls. Tradition links it with a number of important Christian events, including the Last Supper, the imprisonment of Jesus in the House of the High Priest Caiaphas, Peter's denial of Jesus (thrice), the Descent of the Holy Spirit at Pentecost, the falling asleep (death) of the Virgin Mary, and the location of the earliest Christian church. Also sited here is the 'Tomb of David', though it is 99.9% certain that he is not buried on this hill, but rather on the 'Ancient City of the Southeast Ridge' – the real Mount Zion.

Ins and outs
Getting there and around For those arriving on foot, the principal point of access to Mount Zion is from Zion Gate (a natural continuation of the tour of the Armenian Quarter). There is also parking available at the main entrance to the hill's attractions.

Background
Evidence strongly suggests that the hill now referred to as Mount Zion was enclosed within the city walls as early as the second century BCE, with the walls remaining in place until the Roman sack of Jerusalem in 70 CE, and thus this area was part of the walled city at the time of the crucifixion of Jesus. The hill probably marked the southern limit of the Tenth Legion (Fretensis) camp after the establishment of Aelia Capitolina (135 CE), and remained unwalled until the Byzantine empress **Eudocia** rebuilt the ruined walls around the hill between 444 and 460 CE.

By this time many (though not all) of the Christian traditions associated with this site had been firmly established, and several churches had been built and rebuilt. Though the New Testament does not specify the exact location of many of the key events in the final days of Jesus' life, identifying and locating the sites became a fixation amongst **Byzantine Christians**, who sought to localize every detail of the gospels.

Thus, by the fifth century CE Mount Zion had become associated with the Descent of the Holy Spirit at Pentecost, Jesus' imprisonment in the House of the High Priest Caiaphas on the night before the Crucifixion, Peter's three denials of Jesus before the crowing of the cock (and his subsequent weeping on the rock), and as the site of the seat of the patriarchal throne of James the Less (brother of Jesus) and hence the location of the first church. By the end of the sixth century the tradition surrounding the Upper Room (where the Descent of the Holy Spirit at Pentecost had taken place) had been extended to include the Last Supper in this same room. The tradition surrounding the location of the House of John, where the Virgin Mary fell asleep (and died), was also added to the list. All of these sites were marked by Byzantine churches, and a detailed picture is provided by the sixth-century CE Madaba Map (see page 60). By the end of the 10th-beginning of the 11th century CE, this hill now referred to as Mount Zion had also become associated (incorrectly as it happens) with the burial place of King David.

Having been sacked by the Persians in 614 CE, the various churches on Mount Zion were rebuilt, but stood outside the city walls in a state of ruin when the Crusaders took Jerusalem in 1099. The Crusaders restored and refurbished the venerated New Testament sites, and built the **Monastery and Church of St Mary**. The upper level commemorated the room of the Last Supper (the Cenacle, or Coenaculum), whilst the Tomb of David was located below. Salah al-Din's capture of Jerusalem in 1192 saw Mount Zion once again enclosed within the city walls, though al-Malik al-Mu'azzam's subsequent dismantling of the city's fortifications in 1219 may have also included many of the defensive features that the Crusaders had incorporated into the church.

The **Franciscans** acquired permission to establish a presence on Mount Zion in 1335, and within 10 years had obtained control of most of the venerated places including the Cenacle. Within 50 years they had built a number of hospices on the hill and a cloister along the south side of the Cenacle. The **Tomb of David**, which had only created minor interest amongst the Crusaders, suddenly became a contested site in the late 14th century CE, with both Muslims and Jews laying claim to it. The reason for this sudden interest, according to Murphy-O'Connor, was the "legend of treasures buried with the king" (*ibid*), and by 1450 the Muslims had gained control of the site and built a mosque into the lower storey of the

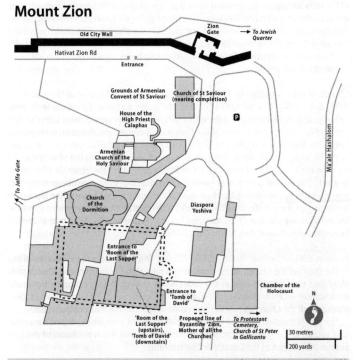

Mount Zion

church. Franciscan (and other Christian, as well as Jewish) rights of access were gradually eroded over the following years, culminating in the 1523-24 decree of **Sulaiman II** ('the Magnificent') that forbade all Jewish and Christian access. In fact, access to the site for non-Muslims remained difficult right up until 1948 when the **Israelis** captured the hill. Between 1948 and 1967, when Jewish access to the Western Wall was impossible, the 'Tomb of David' became the *de facto* main Jewish pilgrimage site in Jerusalem.

Armenian Church of the Holy Saviour The property of the Armenian church has been thoroughly excavated and has revealed a number of interesting finds. In addition to remains of first-century BCE homes and Byzantine-period streets and houses, part of a fifth-century CE apse was also excavated: tentatively linked with the 'Zion, Mother of all the Churches', though most experts believe that this was located slightly further south (see line superimposed on map of Mount Zion). Far more likely is a church associated with the site of the **House of the High Priest Caiaphas**, where Jesus was tried before the High Priest on the night before his Crucifixion, and where Peter thrice denied Jesus before the crowing on the cock, as prophesied. Note that there is an alternative proposed site on Mount Zion for these same scenes (see next page, and another in the Armenian Quarter, page 126).

The 12th-century Crusader church that commemorates these events stands in the southeast corner of the compound. It was acquired by the Armenians in the 14th century CE, repaired and rebuilt in the next century, and is now referred to as the **Armenian Church of the Holy Saviour**. Its key points of interest are the 'Chapel of the Second Prison of Christ' in the southeast corner, and the piece of the 'Stone of Angels' taken from the Church of the Holy Sepulchre in the 13th century CE and placed in the altar here. The church was badly damaged during the 1948 war (and was used by the Israelis as a gun emplacement, 1948-1967), and a new **Church of St Saviour** is laboriously being constructed in the northeast corner of the compound.

Church of the Dormition ① *T02-6719927, Mon-Fri 0830-1200 and 1240-1800, Sat 0830-1730, Sun 1030-1145 and 1240-1730, free, donations accepted. Toilets, souvenir shop, cafeteria.* Built in Romanesque style, with a tall circular tower capped with a grey conical roof and four turrets, the Church of the Dormition is one of Jerusalem's most prominent landmarks. Built between 1901 and 1910 on land presented to the German Catholic Society of the Holy Land by William II of Prussia, the church commemorates the fifth-century CE tradition of the site of the House of John on Mount Zion where the Virgin Mary fell asleep (ie died). Though the church is elaborately decorated, and some careful examination of the detail is highly rewarding, the main draw of the church is the **Chapel of the Dormition** in the circular crypt. A life-sized statue shows a sleeping Mary, with the golden mosaic in the dome above showing Christ receiving her soul, surrounded by six women of the Old Testament (Eve, Miriam, Jael, Judith, Ruth, Esther).

Room of the Last Supper ① *Daily 0900-1700, free.* The whole block of medieval buildings to the south of the Church of the Dormition is part of the 'Monastery and Church of St Mary' that the Crusaders built in the 12th century, though it has undergone significant modification since then. Much of this complex overlies the site of the fifth-century CE **Zion, Mother of all the Churches** (see the superimposed plan on the map of Mount Zion).

The pointed-arched entrance leads to a small courtyard, from where steps in the corner take you up to the groin-vaulted hall. Tradition relates that this is the **Room of the Last Supper** (also known as the **Cenacle** or **Coenaculum**).

Mount Zion has been associated with the site of the Last Supper (*Matthew 26:17-30*; *Mark 14:12-36*; *Luke 22:7-38*; *John 13-17*) since the sixth century CE, though this belief may well have developed from the site's association with the tradition of the Upper Room of the Descent of the Holy Spirit at Pentecost (*Acts 2:1-47*) that developed a century or so earlier. Note that the Syrian Orthodox Church of St Mark in the Armenian Quarter also claims this honour (see page 125). The hall here was probably built in the 12th century, but significantly restored in the 14th century when the Franciscans gained control of the Cenacle. The altar and choir to the east were removed during the later construction of the dome over the 'Tomb of David' in the level below, and a sculptured mihrab (indicating Muslim direction of prayer) was added to the south wall during the early Ottoman period. The coloured-glass windows also date to this period. The pelicans adorning the canopy over the steps in the corner are a medieval Christian symbol of charity. The steps descend to an antechamber of the tomb below, though access is not permitted. Be sure to go up on to the roof for good views of the minaret and steeple close by, as well as a good perspective on the separation barrier and the distant hills.

'Tomb of David' ⓘ *T02-6719767, Sun-Thu 0800-1800, Fri 0800-1400 (closes 1 hr earlier in winter), free. Men must cover heads; cardboard yarmulkes provided for use.* Retracing your steps to the lane outside, turn left and pass beneath a second pointed arch. The cloister that you enter is the one built by the Franciscans c. 1377 after gaining rights to the Cenacle. To the left is the so-called 'Tomb of David'.

As explained in the introduction, King David is not buried here, however, the late 10th-early 11th-century CE tradition has survived, following the revival of interest in the legend in the 14th century CE. A second revival of interest in the site as the Tomb of David stemmed from the Jordanian occupation of the Old City between 1948 and 1967, when Jews denied access to the Western Wall chose this Israeli-held position at which to pray.

The controversy surrounding the site does not end there, though. The relationship between the lines of the 12th-century CE Crusader 'Church of St Mary on Mount Zion' that you see today and the fourth-century CE 'Zion, Mother of all the Churches' has not been definitively established, and thus it is also claimed that the ancient foundations of the present Crusader church are in fact part of a first- or fourth-century CE **synagogue**. A synagogue on Mount Zion is mentioned by both the Bordeaux pilgrim (c. 333 CE) and Epiphanius of Salamis (c. 374-94 CE). A particular point of contention is the **niche** in the wall behind the cloth-draped **cenotaph** itself. It has been suggested that the niche, orientated 'correctly' towards the Temple Mount, would have held the Torah Scrolls of the synagogue. Another view is that the niche is an inscribed arch of the fourth-century CE church. And finally, in order perhaps to allow all competing interests to find an answer that suits their prejudices, it may also be part of an earlier Roman pagan building whose remains were incorporated within the fourth-century CE 'Zion, Mother of all the Churches'. The **Museum of King David** in the cloisters is no longer open but, on exiting the cloister, across the path you can visit the **Chamber of the Holocaust** ⓘ *T02-6715105, Sun-Thu 0900-1545, Fri 0900-1330, suggested fee adult 12NIS, student 6NIS, but any donation acceptable*, a memorial to the six million Jews murdered by the Nazis. This began as a symbolic cemetery in 1949, a place for survivors to come and mourn. Now there are remembrance tablets to over 2000 communities in Europe.

Protestant cemetery A number of prominent Christians are buried here, including three important Middle East/Holy Land archaeologists, **Sir WM Flinders Petrie**, **Leslie Starkey**,

CS. Fisher; and the German industrialist **Oskar Schindler**. The cemetery is on the lower southwest slope of Mount Zion. To find Schindler's Grave (immortalized in the Spielberg film), enter the cemetery gate, then drop down to the second (lower) level. The grave is fairly central (it has no headstone so can be hard to find, though it is usually adorned by small piles of stones). If the cemetery is closed, try calling T052-5388342.

Church of St Peter in Gallicantu ① *T02-6731739, Mon-Sat 0830-1700. Souvenir shop, toilets.* Although now venerated as the site of the **House of the High Priest Caiaphas** (again!), and thus the place where St Peter thrice denied Jesus before the crowing of the cock, it is still not certain when tradition first placed this event at this particular spot. Excavations at the site have revealed a rock-cut crypt (now referred to as the 'First Prison of Christ') above which was built a monastic church some time in the Byzantine period (probably sixth century CE). However, the earliest mention of this as the place where Peter "went outside, and wept bitterly" (*Luke 22:62*) is recorded several centuries later. By the 11th-12th centuries CE the site was firmly on the pilgrim trail, billed (as today) as the 'Church of St Peter in Gallicantu', though this structure had been destroyed by the mid-15th century CE. The present church was built from 1928 to 1932 and has a fine view over the 'City of David (the 'real' Mount Zion; see page 141).

As a further challenge to the identification of this site as the location of the House of the High Priest Caiaphas, the question has been raised as to the positioning of the home of such an important figure on the lower slopes of Mount Zion. Though one can be fairly sure that the city walls enclosed Mount Zion at the time of Jesus' crucifixion, it is less sure that they extended this far down to the edge of the Tyropneon Valley. Thus, would such an important figure as the High Priest have his house outside the city walls? Further, such a wealthy and influential man as Caiaphas would surely have had his property on the very top of the hill, thus making the case of the alternative site to the north of the Church of the Dormition (within the Armenian St Saviour compound) a more compelling one. Either way, the exact position remains pure conjecture.

Mount of Olives

The Mount of Olives stands to the east of Jerusalem, separated from the Old City by the Kidron Valley (see page 140). It is part of a ridge of soft sandstone that has Mount Scopus at its northern end, the Mount of Olives at the centre, and the low rise above the Arab village of Silwan to the south. Much of its west and south slopes are covered by a vast ancient Jewish cemetery, whilst several major events in the life of Jesus in the days leading up to the Crucifixion are commemorated in a number of churches located here. The top of the Mount of Olives marks the beginning of the Last Path, leading on to Via Dolorosa, which many people (both religious and secular) find a spiritual and holistic experience. The various viewpoints high up on the Mount of Olives also offer arguably the best panorama of the whole city.

Ins and outs
Getting there and around The logical place to begin a tour of the Mount of Olives is at the top, thus avoiding a steep upward climb. From East Jerusalem, minibus 75 goes to Al-Tur, the village at the top (4NIS) or spend 25NIS on a taxi. If you are part of a guided tour you will probably be dropped at the summit, though the majority of independent sightseers will reach the Mount of Olives at the bottom: from Lions' Gate in the Old City

walls; from the junction of Jericho Road and Sulaiman Street at the northeast corner of the Old City; or by making their way up from the tombs in the Kidron Valley below. Hence, the description below is from the bottom up.

Warning Lone women should be careful in the high-walled cemeteries and along the east side of the hill from Bethphage; it may be wise not to come here unaccompanied. **NB** Suitably modest clothing must be worn when visiting these sites.

Background

The earliest history of the Mount of Olives relates to a function still undertaken here today: that of a **burial place**. Burial shafts dating to the late third millennium have been found on the east and south slopes of the ridge, whilst by the Late Bronze Age (c. 1550-1200 BCE) the west slope of the Mount of Olives formed part of the main cemetery of Jerusalem. This tradition of burial here on the southwest slopes of the Mount of Olives, and on the other side of the Kidron Valley beneath the east side of the Temple Mount/Haram al-Sharif, stems from the belief that the Kidron is in fact the **Valley of Jehoshaphat** where the whole of humanity will assemble to be judged by God: "I will also gather all nations, and will bring them down into the valley of Jehoshaphat" (*Joel 3:2*), and "Then shall the Lord go forth, and fight against those nations, as when he fought in the day of battle. And his feet shall stand in that day upon the mount of Olives, which is before Jerusalem on the east, and the mount of Olives shall cleave in the midst thereof toward the east and toward the west, and there shall be a very great valley" (*Zechariah 14:3-4*). As well as the Jewish cemeteries here, there are also Muslim and Christian graveyards. Many of the Jewish tombs here were systematically desecrated during the Jordanian occupation of part of Jerusalem (1948-67), when the graves were allegedly broken up for use as paving stones in the latrines. One notable burial in the large Jewish cemetery here is Robert Maxwell (whose grave would make an excellent latrine). For further information on famous Zionists and Jews buried here, see www.mountofolives.co.il which outlines some self-guided tours.

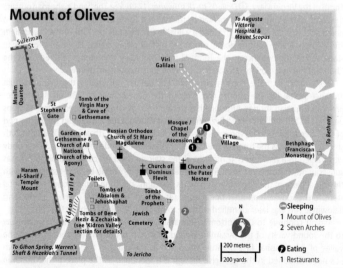

Mount of Olives

There is some evidence to suggest that the Mount of Olives was the site of an Iron-Age Jewish sanctuary, possibly David's 'Nob' (*II Samuel 15:30-32*) or Solomon's temples to foreign gods on the Mount of Corruption (*II Kings 23:13*): the low rise above Silwan. After the construction of the Temple by Solomon, the Mount of Olives became associated with the Ceremony of the Red Heifer (*Numbers 19:1-10*).

The importance of the Mount of Olives to Christians stems from the episodes in the life of **Jesus** that were enacted here, most notably in the days leading up to his arrest and Crucifixion. It is highly probable that on his visits to Jerusalem, particularly during festivals when the costs of accommodation in the city would sky-rocket (as today), Jesus stayed with friends at Bethany (see West Bank chapter, page 228). Thus the road between Bethany and the Temple (pretty much following the route of the tour outlined below) would have been well known to him. It was from Bethphage on the top of the Mount of Olives that Jesus begun his triumphal entry into Jerusalem before the Passover (*Matthew 21:1-11; Mark 11:1-11; Luke 19:28-40; John 12:12-15*); where Jesus foretold the future of the city (*Matthew 24-25; Mark 13:1-4*) and wept over it (*Luke 19:37, 41-44*); and in the garden at the foot of the slope, Gethsemane, that he was betrayed and arrested (*Matthew 26:36-56; Mark 14:32-50; Luke 22:39-54; John 18:1-12*). Luke's gospel also places the Ascension on the Mount of Olives (*Luke 24:50-52*).

The early **Byzantine** period saw numerous churches established on the Mount of Olives to commemorate these events, and by the sixth century CE a Christian visitor (Theodosius, c. 518) noted 24 churches on the hill. Many were destroyed during the Persian invasion of 614 CE, though some were rebuilt immediately afterwards and others later by the Crusaders. However, subsequent years of neglect left the area in a state of ruination and many of the churches that you see today are primarily the result of late 19th-and early 20th-century restoration efforts.

Sights

Tomb of the Virgin Mary ⓘ *Daily 0530-1830 (winter -1730), free.* The bend in the road outside the Tomb of the Virgin Mary is marked by the reputed **Tomb of Mujir al-Din** (1456-1522), a noted Arab scholar who has provided a valuable commentary on 15th-century Jerusalem and Hebron. A 20th-century dome, supported by four pillars, stands above a simple white stone shrine. The entrance to the Tomb of the Virgin Mary (sometimes referred to as the Church of the Assumption) is located off an open square courtyard below.

Descending into the sunken courtyard (1), before you stands the Crusader-built entrance portal (2). The church was built by the Benedictines c. 1130 on the ruins of previous Christian shrines. After one has passed through the Crusader entrance, 44 steps descend to the remains of the Byzantine church. Much of the masonry at the upper end of this staircase, including the steps themselves, dates to the 12th century CE. At the 20th step, to the right, is the **tomb of the Crusader Queen Melisande** (died 1161) (3). Her body was moved to a new tomb at the foot of the stairs in the 14th century, though this has subsequently become lost. In later years Queen Melisande's tomb became associated with the burial place of the Virgin Mary's parents, **Joachim** and **Anne**. Almost opposite, several steps further down, is another burial niche (4), related to the family of the Crusader king Baldwin II. This was later identified with the tomb of the Virgin's husband, Joseph.

As you continue to the bottom of the stairs, the pointed Crusader arches give way to the round vaults of the Byzantine period church. It is not entirely certain when the Valley of Jehoshaphat first became associated as the place of the Virgin Mary's death (it's not mentioned in the gospels), though it is identified as the place of her burial in the anonymous second-third-century CE *Transitus Mariae* (Assumption of Mary). A church may have been built above a rock-cut tomb on this site as early as 455 CE, with a bench *arcosolium* being venerated as the burial place of Mary. Though the seventh century CE saw Mount Zion identified as the site of the Dormition (see page 130), the church here was certainly still functioning in the ninth century CE. It was probably destroyed by the caliph al-Hakim in 1009 before the Benedictines rebuilt the church and added a large monastery. This was largely effaced by Salah al-Din in 1187, with many of the stones from the monastery finding their way into the sultan's new city wall.

The Byzantine **crypt (6)** at the bottom of the steps is 10.6 m below the level of the entrance. The built apse to the left belongs to the Ethiopians, whilst the rock-cut apse to the right (east) is under the custodianship of the Armenians, Greeks, Copts and Syrians. The Eastern Orthodox influence is manifested in the darkness of the church and the incense-thickened atmosphere. At the centre of the east apse (right) is a small square chapel marking the supposed site of the **tomb of the Virgin (7)**. As with the tomb of Christ in the Church of the Holy Sepulchre, this tomb has been cut away from the surrounding rock. To its north, a niche **(8)** stands at the entrance to another tomb of the first-century CE style **(9)**. To the south of the Virgin's tomb a *mihrab* **(10)** marks the direction of Mecca: Muslims revere Mary as the mother of the prophet Jesus.

Tomb of the Virgin Mary

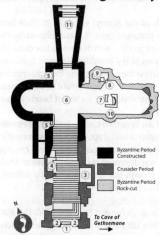

N

| 10 metres |
| 10 yards |

1 Sunken Courtyard
2 Crusader entrance portal
3 Tomb of the Crusader Queen Melisande
4 Burial niche of family of Baldwin II
5 Byzantine period entrances
6 Byzantine period crypt
7 Tomb of the Virgin
8 Niche
9 1st century CE style tomb
10 Mihrab
11 Original entrance to Cemetery

■ Byzantine Period Constructed
■ Crusader Period
■ Byzantine Period Rock-cut

To Cave of Gethsemane →

Grotto of Gethsemane ① *Daily 0830-1200 and 1430-1700 (on Sun and Thu -1540), free.* Returning to the courtyard, a passageway to the east leads to the Grotto of Gethsemane (or 'Cave of the Oil Press'). Quite possibly a natural cave, it contains a pre-Christian water cistern (below) that seems to have been used later as a Byzantine and then Crusader burial place. At the time of Jesus it appears that an oil press (Hebrew: *Gat Shemen*) was operating here, whilst the cave may have been used as a shelter at other times. During the Byzantine period the cave became associated with a number of traditions surrounding Jesus, including the site where the Disciples rested whilst he prayed "a stone's throw away" (*Luke 22:41*), and where he was betrayed and arrested.

Garden of Gethsemane and Church of All Nations ① *Daily 0800-1200 and 1430-1730 (summer-1800), but go at 1400 as you will probably avoid large crowds, free.* Before entering the Garden of Gethsemane, it is worth continuing a short distance south along the Jericho Road in order to admire the superb west façade of the church. Above the colonnaded portico of Corinthian columns is a glittering gold

Jesus weeps over the city

"When Jesus came in sight of the city, he wept over it and said, 'If only you had known this day the way that leads to peace! But now it is hidden from your sight. For a time will come upon you, when your enemy shall cast a trench about you, and encircle you and hem you in on all sides. And they will bring you to the ground, you and your children within your walls, and not leave you one stone standing on another, because you did not recognize the time of God's visitation'." (*Luke 19:41-44*)

mosaic depicting Christ as mediator between God and man, and assuming the suffering of the world (hence the alternative name, Church of the Agony). The quote is from the *Epistle of Paul the Apostle to the Hebrews* (*Hebrews 5:7*). The newly landscaped section of the Kidron Valley in front of the church was where Pope Benedict XVI celebrated mass with many thousands of devotees in May 2009.

The garden was identified as early as the fourth century CE as the place where Jesus prayed, was betrayed by Judas and arrested (*Matthew 26:36-56; Mark 14:32-50; Luke 22:39-54; John 18:1-12*), though the tradition may be earlier. The dating of the gnarled olive trees in the garden varies between 300 and 2300 years old, though this upper limit seems unlikely since the Romans are widely believed to have stripped the entire region around Jerusalem bare during their siege of 70 CE.

The present **Church of All Nations (Church of the Agony)** was built in 1924 from subscriptions collected worldwide (hence the popular name). It was designed by the Italian architect **Antonio Barluzzi** as a triple-aisled basilica, with the twelve low domes in the ceiling being decorated with the coats of arms of the countries that gave donations towards the church's construction. The purple glass in the windows dims the light entering the church, perhaps representing the "hour when darkness reigns" (*Luke 22:53*) of Jesus' arrest. The focal point of the church, in front of the altar, is the section of bedrock upon which Jesus is said to have prayed prior to his arrest.

The present church largely follows the line of the Byzantine basilica built here between 379 and 384 CE by Theodosius I; in fact the two internal lateral apses include some courses of the Byzantine church, plus sections of the original mosaic floor (under glass) can also be seen. It is generally believed that the church was destroyed in the earthquake of 747/8 CE. The Crusaders rebuilt the church c. 1170, though this time on a slightly different orientation. The church appears to have been abandoned by 1345.

Russian Orthodox Church of St Mary Magdalene ⓘ *Tue and Thu 1000-1200*. This eye-catching church was built by Czar Alexander III in 1888 and is most noted for its seven Kremlin-style gold onion-shaped domes, which are a Jerusalem landmark. Only limited access to the church is possible. Buried within the convent grounds is Princess Alice of Greece, mother of Prince Philip, Duke of Edinburgh.

Church of Dominus Flevit ⓘ *Daily 0800-1145 and 1430-1700, free. Toilets*. This attractive 20th-century church is built on a site that was associated by medieval pilgrims with the tradition of Jesus weeping over the city as he rode towards it (on Palm Sunday). However, the land upon which the church was built shows signs of far earlier usage, the evidence of which can be seen just inside the gate of the grounds, to the right.

Excavations in the early 1950s revealed the remains of a **cemetery** first used in the Late Bronze Age (c. 1550-1200 BCE) that later became the **largest necropolis** of the Roman period thus far discovered in Jerusalem. Covering 0.6 hectares, the necropolis contained at least 20 arcosolium burial caves (arched recesses) and 38 pit tombs, most dating to the third-fourth centuries CE, though the site continued in use during the Byzantine period. Seven hard limestone sarcophagi were found, some of which were elaborately decorated. In addition, over 120 ossuaries (secondary burial receptacles into which bones are put after the flesh has decayed) were discovered, about a third of which bear inscriptions (in Aramaic, Hebrew and Greek). The first two tombs on display just inside the gate are thought to date to the period 100 BCE-135 CE, and were generally used for secondary burial in ossuaries. The Late Bronze-Age tombs could not be preserved, though they provided a very rich assemblage of pottery, plus some alabaster and faience vessels and Egyptian scarabs.

Continuing along the path brings you to the **Church of Dominus Flevit** ('the Lord wept'), built in 1955 to a tear-shaped design (discernable from above) by Antonio Barluzzi. The altar points to the west in the direction of the Temple, where Jesus would have faced whilst he prayed. Consequently, the church's most notable feature, the chalice window, beautifully frames a view of the Dome of the Rock and Temple Mount. The present church stands on the site of a Byzantine-style chapel, of which mosaics on the floor remain, though experts are quick to point out that it almost certainly dates to the Early Arab period, c. 675 CE. From at least the seventh century CE onwards a liturgical procession began at the top of the Mount of Olives on Maundy Thursday, arriving in Jerusalem on the morning of Good Friday. This may be when the tradition of this site as the place where Jesus wept began. However, the fourth-century CE pilgrim Egeria also mentions such a procession, and excavations have also revealed the remains of a fourth-century CE monastery here. Its dedication has not been established. The small terrace in front of the Church of Dominus Flevit provides an excellent viewpoint for secular visitors, and a quiet place for prayer and meditation for pilgrims.

Tombs of the Prophets ⓘ *Mon-Thu 0900-1500. Admission is free in theory, though you may be expected to pay a tip if you don't have your own torch and have to be shown round.* Despite the claim that these are the tombs of the prophets **Haggai**, **Zechariah** and **Malachi**, who lived c. sixth-fifth centuries BCE, this tomb complex is in fact part of the first-century BCE-135 CE necropolis that you may already have seen within the grounds of the Church of Dominus Flevit. In fact, these style tombs (*kokhim*) did not come into use for Jewish burials until the first century BCE. Its radiating fan-shape is unusual, however. Some of the inscriptions discovered here suggest that the complex was reused for the burial of foreign Christians in the fourth and fifth centuries CE.

Rehav'am Viewpoint One of Jerusalem's best panoramas, the sun is best placed for photography early in the morning. Those who like to pose sitting on a camel in front of a spectacular backdrop will not be disappointed here.

Church of the Pater Noster ⓘ *Mon-Sat 0830-1200 and 1430-1700, 7 NIS.* Early Christian visitors such as Eusebius (c. 260-340 CE) and the Bordeaux Pilgrim (c. 333 CE) record that the Emperor Constantine ordered a church built on the Mount of Olives above a cave that was venerated as a place at which Jesus taught the disciples. The site also became identified with the Ascension (*Luke 24:50-52*), though most early sources refer to it by its popular name, **Eleona** ('Church of the Olive Groves': an Aramaic 'a' added to the Greek 'elaion' creates 'of olives'). Visiting the church in c. 384, the pilgrim Egeria noted that the site was identified with Jesus' teaching on the ultimate conflict between good and evil (*Matthew 24, 25*), and no mention is made of the Ascension, the site of which had supposedly been moved further up the hill.

Following the destruction of the church in 614 CE by the Persians, the fate of the site is not entirely clear. A "Church where Christ Taught his Disciples" is mentioned in a ninth-century CE list, and it is now thought that the site here lay in ruins until the arrival of the Crusaders, when the cave became associated specifically with Jesus' teaching to the Disciples of the **Lord's Prayer**. Early in the 12th century CE a modest oratory was built, followed by a succession of churches destroyed and rebuilt as the fortunes of the Crusaders and Muslims ebbed and flowed.

The property was bought in 1857 by the Princesse de la Tour d'Auvergne, who spent the rest of her life searching for the cave. She is responsible for the cloister here (1868) and the adjacent Carmelite convent (1872). In 1910 the White Fathers discovered the remains of the Byzantine Church of Eleona, and further excavations were made by the Dominicans in 1918. Subsequent appeals were made to raise a basilica above the ancient foundations, though work stopped when funds ran out. The unfinished structure remains as it was left and is now referred to as the **Church of the Pater Noster** ('Our Father').

The site is perhaps most famous today for the 60 plus renditions of the Lord's Prayer inscribed on to ceramic tiles, each in a different language. The collection originally occupied the cloister, though recent additions have expanded into the church, vestibule, and all available walls. More recent translations include Gujarati, Hausa and Igbo. It is also possible to view the cave at the centre of the reconstructed (but unfinished) basilica. The 20th-century basilica was supposed to recreate the fourth-century CE building, though the fact that it was never finished perhaps avoided the controversy over what form the original building actually took. The crypt of the basilica was built around the cave, and it is still possible to descend inside today. It is not thought that the cave itself was originally part of a tomb, though it certainly cuts part of a first-century CE kokhim tomb.

Mosque/Chapel of the Ascension ① *Daily 0800-1430 (summer-1730). 5NIS; if locked call the tel no on the sign and the custodians will come to open up. Small souvenir stall.* Of the four gospels, only Luke mentions the Ascension of Jesus into heaven (*Luke 24:50-52* and *Acts 1:9*). Of course the actual site is not specified, though the Byzantine pilgrims in their zeal to localize every detail of the gospels came to venerate a cave on the Mount of Olives as the scene. The choice of a cave as the place to venerate the Ascension arises probably not from some unusual interpretation of the gospels, but rather from the realities of life in Jerusalem for early Christians: the fear of persecution meant that it was probably safer to congregate in a cave than in the open. As mentioned in the background to the Church of Eleona/Church of the Pater Noster (see previous page), the cave was rapidly forgotten as the place of the Ascension and the venerated site 'moved up the hill'. In c. 384 CE the pilgrim Egeria records that the Ascension was celebrated at the site now occupied by the Mosque/Chapel of the Ascension.

The first church on this site appears to have been built some time before 392 CE by Poimenia, a wealthy and pious Roman woman. It was almost certainly destroyed by the Persians in 614 CE and then restored by Modestus. The round building, open to the sky, is described c. 680 CE by Arculf, including the footprints of Jesus in the dust. Arculf's

The Ascension

"Jesus led the disciples out as far as to Bethany, and he lifted up his hands, and blessed them. And it came to pass, while he blessed them, he was parted from them, and carried up into heaven." (*Luke 24:50-52*)

description is largely confirmed by excavations undertaken in 1960 by the Franciscan Fathers. The present octagonal form dates to the Crusader restoration of 1102, when several other alterations were made. At the end of the 12th century Salah al-Din granted the site to two of his pious followers (Wali al-Din and Abu'l Hasan), and the custodians have been Muslim ever since.

The small mosque and minaret at the entrance to the site date to 1620. The original Crusader shrine featured an outer colonnaded cloister within which stood an octagon of columns and arches, open to the sky. A stone dome on an octagonal drum now covers the octagonal Crusader chapel, and the arches have been blocked. Of particular note are the 12th-century CE Crusader capitals on the columns surrounding the octagon, especially the two featuring bird-headed winged quadrupeds. A sectioned-off area of the floor bears the supposed imprint of Jesus' right foot; the imprint of his left foot was removed to the al-Aqsa Mosque some time around 1200 CE.

Russian Orthodox Convent of the Ascension and Viri Galilaei ① *Tue and Thu 0900-1300, free.* A little to the north of the Mosque/Chapel of the Ascension is the Russian Orthodox Convent of the Ascension, whose tower provides one of the best views from the top of the Mount of Olives. To find it, turn right down the alley just after Royal Taxis. Also to the north is the site of **Viri Galilaei** (see Mount of Olives map), where tradition relates that the disciples were referred to as 'Men of Galilee' immediately after the Ascension (Acts 1:11). The site is marked by a Greek Orthodox Church, though a Byzantine chapel may well have stood here originally.

Bethphage ① *T02-6284352, daily 0700-1145 and 1400-1730, closes one hour earlier in winter, ring the bell for admission. Free, though gatekeeper may expect a small tip.* Bethphage is mentioned in the gospels as the place where Jesus mounted the donkey to make his triumphal entry into Jerusalem, an event that Christians now celebrate as 'Palm Sunday' (*Matthew 21:1-11; Mark 11:1-11; Luke 19:28-40; John 12:12-15*). Though the gospels do not reveal the specific place where the procession began, the Franciscan monastery that now commemorates the event is in all likelihood pretty much 'in the vicinity' of Bethphage.

Within the courtyard of the monastery (ring the bell for admission) is a late 19th-century church (1883) built upon the remains of a medieval chapel. Enshrined within the Crusader chapel is a stone block that is venerated as the mounting-stone that Jesus used to mount the donkey. As Murphy-O'Connor dryly observes (*The Holy Land*, 1993), a mounting-stone may have been necessary to mount a huge battle-charging Crusader steed, but would it really have been necessary for your average Palestinian donkey? Nevertheless, the Franciscans Palm Sunday procession begins from this chapel.

The Kidron Valley (Arabic: Wadi Jauz) forms Jerusalem's eastern border, dividing the Old City and East Jerusalem area from Mount Scopus, the Mount of Olives and the Arab village of Silwan. The valley is at its deepest between the Temple Mount/Haram al-Sharif and the Mount of Olives, where it is often referred to by its biblical name, the Valley of Jehoshaphat ('Yahweh judges'). The Kidron owes its importance to this identification as the place where the Last Judgement is due to take place (see for example *Jeremiah 31:40*; *Joel 3:2*; *Zechariah 14:3-4*), and this is why so many cemeteries and burial grounds are located on the valley's slopes. There are a number of tombs and monuments of particular note in the Kidron Valley, though a succession of legends, traditions and popular stories have served to obscure many of their original functions.

Ins and outs

Getting around A path leads down opposite the Garden of Gethsemane and Church of All Nations to the tombs; or they can be reached by the modern flight of steps (signed 'Abshalom's Pillar') at the southeast corner of the Old City. For a map showing the position of these tombs, see the 'Mount of Olives' map on page 133.

Tombs of Absalom and Jehoshaphat

The most imposing monument here is the so-called Tomb of Absalom. Resembling a bottle-shape at the top, the upper section is masonry whilst the base below the cornice is cut directly from the rock. It stands 20 m high and is probably the most complete tomb monument in the country. The square, rock-hewn base features an unusual combination of styles, including Ionic columns at each corner, a Doric frieze above, and an Egyptian-influenced cavetto cornice. The upper masonry section features a concave conical roof resting on a stone pedestal (*tholos*). The entrance to the tomb within is on the south side, high up above the level of the cornice, whilst the other holes hacked in the side were made by grave-robbers. It is generally believed to have been built in the second half of the first century BCE.

The dating of the tomb has negated the popular association with **Absalom**, son of David, who lived almost 1000 years before this tomb was cut. In fact, this association with Absalom was probably first made by Benjamin of Tudela c. 1170 from the reading of a line in the *Second Book of Samuel*: "Now Absalom in his lifetime had taken and reared up for himself a pillar, which is in the king's valley" (*II Samuel 18:18*). In fact, an 18th-century CE commentator relates how passers-by used to throw stones at the tomb because of Absalom's treachery towards his father.

Though the Tomb of Absalom is a tomb in its own right, it also forms part of the **Tomb of Jehoshaphat** that is located behind (cut into the rock). In fact, the Tomb of Absalom may well have acted as a nephesh, or memorial cenotaph, for the burial complex cut in the cliff behind. For whom the eight-chambered catacomb-like burial complex was built is not certain, and it is now popularly known as the Tomb of Jehoshaphat. Its entrance, sealed off by a metal grill, features a finely carved pediment. The style of intricate carvings inside suggests a Herodian period dating (c. 37 BCE-70 CE). The Byzantine period saw these catacombs occupied by hermits.

Tombs of the Bene Hezir and Zechariah

Just to the south is a further burial complex, also featuring a *nephesh* (funerary monument) and a catacomb burial complex. The Tomb of the Bene Hezir is the rock-cut catacomb that you come to first. It has a Doric façade comprising two free-standing and two engaged columns with Doric capitals supporting a Doric frieze. A Hebrew inscription on the architrave (beam resting on the capitals) above the Doric columns identifies individual members of the priestly family of the **Bene Hezir** (see *I Chronicles* 24:15). It almost certainly dates to the late second-early first century BCE, though a 12th-century CE tradition linked it with **St James the Less**, and you still sometimes see it referred to as his tomb.

Just to the south is the nephesh belonging to the Tomb of the Bene Hezir. This freestanding monument was carved directly out of the rock and comprises a cube base supporting a pyramid. All four sides of the cube are decorated with Ionic columns and an Egyptian cavetto cornice. The decorative style strongly suggests that it is contemporary with the Bene Hezir complex, though it is still referred to as the **Tomb of Zechariah**.

Silwan

The village of Silwan (from 'Siloam') occupies the east side of the Kidron Valley, and looks upon the City of David. Sometimes referred to as the 'Tomb of the Pharaoh's Wife/ Daughter', the **Monolith of Silwan** is located on the edge of an escarpment as you enter the village. It comprises a large free-standing cube cut from the rock, and previously capped by a pyramid (presumably similar to the 'Tomb of Zechariah'). The pyramid was removed in the Roman period (for an unknown reason) and the Monolith now blends in with the rest of the houses making it difficult to locate without local help. It is a funerary monument probably dating to the ninth-seventh centuries BCE, with a distinct Phoenician-Egyptian influence. The hole cut through the Hebrew inscription was made by the Byzantine hermit who made his home inside.

City of David (Ancient City on the Southeast Ridge)

The low ridge to the south of the Temple Mount/Haram al-Sharif (sandwiched between the Tyropoeon Valley to the west and the Kidron Valley to the east) is the site where David built his capital early in his reign, effectively founding the new city of Jerusalem. Generally referred to as the 'City of David', the site today presents an insight into 4000 years of continuous occupation, of which David's episode was just a small part. Remains from most periods of occupation can be seen in the Royal Quarter, while further down the ridge are a number of interesting sites related to the sophisticated water-supply system that served the city, most notably Warren's Shaft and the extraordinary Hezekiah's Tunnel.

Ins and outs

Getting there and around Exiting the Old City through Dung Gate, turn left (east) along HaOphel Road. Almost immediately on your right, a road (Ma'alot Ir David) leads south down into the Tyropoeon Valley. Take this road downhill, looking out for the entrance to the City of David Archaeological shortly on your left.

Background

Archaeological, epigraphic and biblical evidence of pre-Davidic Jerusalem does not allow a detailed reconstruction of the city's development and history prior to the Israelite conquest, though the exact location of the early city has been irrefutably established – here on the southeast ridge. The exact year of **David**'s conquest is unknown, though it is generally believed to have been fairly early in his reign (997 BCE is often mentioned). The capture of the city is graphically described in biblical sources (*II Samuel* 5:6-9), though some of the key action events are also ascribed to Joab (*I Chronicles 11:4-7*). What is clear, however, is that the resident population, known as the **Jebusites**, were not murdered or expelled but continued to live amongst their Israelite conquerors (*Judges 1:21*).

David subsequently shifted his capital here, and as the city developed to the north and west during the reigns of David's successors (Solomon, then the kings of Judah), the seat of power shifted also. However, this southeast ridge remained settled and within the city walls until the first century CE at least. The subsequent centuries saw the settlement on this ridge alternately enclosed, then excluded from the confines of the city walls, and since about the 11th century CE it has been located outside. It remained an important part of Jerusalem, however, not least because of the complex water-supply system built here that drew water from the Gihon Spring in the Kidron Valley and supplied it to the city. Extensive excavations were begun by Warren in 1867, and have continued intermittently until the present day. Opposite the main entrance to the City of David (over the road in the Giv'ati parking lot) recent digs have uncovered what archaeologists believe to be the palace of Queen Helena of Adiabene (in northern Mesopotamia, now in northeast Iraq). Helena settled here and built herself a palace in the Lower City (Josephus, *Jewish War, V, 253*). She died in Adiabene in 65 CE, though her body was sent to Jerusalem for burial (in the Tombs of the Kings in East Jerusalem, see page 153). Also at this site a large hoard of gold coins (267 pieces) has been unearthed, dating from the early years of the reign of Heraclius (610-641 CE). It is hoped the site will open to the public around 2012.

The site

ⓘ *T*6033, www.cityofdavid.org.il (see www.ticketnet.co.il for booking tours). Adult 25NIS, student 21NIS, child 13NIS, additional 10NIS for 15-min 3D movie. Open Sun-Thu 0800-1900 (in Aug -2100, winter -1700), Fri-1500. Last entrance to Hezekiah's Tunnel 2 hrs before closing. Two excellent guided tours available, adult 60NIS, child 45NIS, book in advance. First Temple Period tour includes Hezekiah's Tunnel and lasts 3 hrs (summer 1000 & 1600, winter 1000 & 1400); Second Temple Period tour includes underground streets and lasts 2 hrs, at 1400. If entering the tunnel, be prepared to get wet and bring a torch (or rent one for 4NIS).*

'Large stone structure' (remains of David's palace?) The foundations of this monumental building, discovered in 2005, are believed by some archaeologists to be the palace of David/the Israelite kings. There is still dispute, however, over whether the fieldstones that you see here which supported the structure (nothing of the upper levels has survived) are 9th or 10th century BCE. Certainly the huge buttress found lower down the slope is hefty enough to support a monumental building of particular importance. In the vicinity, two bullae (clay seals bearing impressions) were found, both measuring 1 cm in diameter and lettered in ancient Hebrew with the names of two court ministers from the time of Jeremiah who are mentioned in the same verse of the Old Testament (*Jeremiah 38:1*). It is also worth noting that, as yet, no epigraphic evidence has been uncovered from the reigns of either David or Solomon in the City of David).

Royal Quarter The so-called Royal Quarter (also known as Area G) represents a century's worth of archaeological excavation of some 14 centuries of settlement (see map below). Archaeologists believe that the houses built on the ridge c. 1800 BCE were constructed on the natural slopes and terraces. Some time in the 13th-12th centuries BCE a 'stepped stone structure' was built to flatten the ridge and to make construction easier. This was done by building stone compartments, filling them with rubble, then building above them. It

City of David, Kidron Valley & Tyropoean Valley

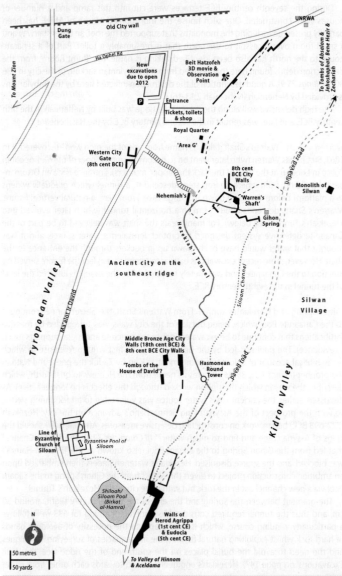

Dung Gate

Old City wall

UNRWA

Ha Ophel Rd

To Mount Zion

New excavations due to open 2012

Beit Hatzofeh 3D movie & Observation Point

To Tombs of Absalom & Jehoshaphat, Bene Hezir & Zechariah

Entrance

Tickets, toilets & shop

Royal Quarter

'Area G'

Western City Gate (8th cent BCE)

8th cent BCE City Walls

Monolith of Silwan

Nehemiah's

'Warren's Shaft'

Gihon Spring

Ancient city on the southeast ridge

Hezekiah's Tunnel

Siloam Channel

Silwan Village

Middle Bronze Age City Walls (18th cent BCE) & 8th cent BCE City Walls

'Tombs of the House of David'?

Hasmonean Round Tower

Kidron Valley

Line of Byzantine Church of Siloam

Byzantine Pool of Siloam

Shiloah/Siloam Pool (Birkat al-Hamra)

Walls of Herod Agrippa (1st cent CE) & Eudocia (5th cent CE)

N

50 metres

50 yards

To Valley of Hinnom & Aceldama

is thought the podium was extensively modified and repaired by David, then Solomon (10th-9th centuries BCE), and strengthened by means of the massive stone ramp or glacis that you can clearly see here today.

During the seventh century BCE terraces were cut into this ramp and a number of houses were constructed. One such house, the four-roomed 'House of Ahiel', has been partially preserved including the monoliths that supported the roof, an outer stairway and a small room over a cesspit to the north that is presumably a toilet. Part of a separate house to the north has also been identified, taking is name, the 'Burnt Room', from the destruction debris found here that resulted from the Babylonian sacking of the city in 586 BCE (*II Kings 25:9*). A good description of the destruction inflicted here by the Babylonians is provided by Nehemiah (Nehemiah 2:13-16).

The high defensive wall along the crest of the ridge was built by Nehemiah in the fifth century BCE, and later was rebuilt in the second century BCE by the Hasmoneans.

Warren's Shaft 'Warren's Shaft' takes its name from one of the men who 'discovered' it in 1867, Sir Charles Warren (who later went on to become Commissioner of the Metropolitan Police in London at the time of the 'Jack the Ripper' murders). Entrance is via an Ottoman-period building, from where 80 iron steps descend to a tunnel which gradually widens to a platform before dropping down to a large cave. From here, a natural vertical fissure, 'Warren's Shaft', descends about 13 m to a horizontal tunnel (which later evolved into 'Hezekiah's Tunnel', see below). For many years the shaft was believed to be part of the Canaanite defensive system designed to protect Jerusalem's water source, and it was thought that water would have been drawn up in buckets through the entrance to the shaft. However, more recent excavations have ascertained that in fact the fissure served no function to the Canaanites and was merely revealed when the Israelites lowered the level of the tunnel in the eighth century BCE.

Gihon Spring and Hezekiah's Tunnel From Warren's Shaft, the 'Secret Tunnel' continues to the Canaanite Pool which, being outside of the city walls, was surrounded by massive fortifications that continue to be excavated (hence the concrete and metal supports much in evidence). The pool was fed by the Gihon Spring, the first written reference to which is the biblical account of Solomon's anointment as king by Zadok the priest and Nathan the prophet (*I Kings 1:33, 38, 45*). It takes its name from the Hebrew 'to gush forth', which describes the way in which the siphon worked (though this effect is no longer active). As discussed earlier, the ancient city's water source was vulnerable to attack during sieges, so with the prospect of the Assyrian king Sennacherib's advance on the city, **Hezekiah** (727-698 BCE) began work on constructing defensive measures. After all, "why should the kings of Assyria come and find so much water?" (*II Chronicles 32:4*). The Siloam Channel that led from the Gihon Spring to the Siloam Pool (also known as the 'Birkat al-Hamra') was blocked, and the source disguised. Hezekiah's water engineers then embarked upon an ambition construction project to divert the waters from the Gihon Spring to the Siloam Pool via a new channel cut in the rock, but within the city walls: **Hezekiah's Tunnel**.

The gradient between the spring and the end of the tunnel is very slight, around 30 cm, and thus the tunnel required considerable planning. Running for 533 m, it follows a particularly winding course, which is attributable to the necessity of avoiding bands of hard rock whilst exploiting natural fissures, the inadequacies of surveying techniques and the need to avoid the burial places on the south end of the ridge (see 'the Weill Excavations' on page 147). Hezekiah's engineers worked towards each other from either

The 'Siloam Inscription'

"Behold the tunnel. This is the story of its cutting. While the miners swung their picks, one towards the other, and when there remained only three cubits to cut, the voice of one calling his fellow was heard – for there was a resonance in the rock coming from both north and south.

So the day they broke through the miners struck, one against the other, pick against pick, and the water flowed from the spring towards the pool, 1200 cubits. The height of the rock above the head of the miners was 100 cubits."

end; a process described in the so-called **Siloam Inscription** found mounted on the wall at the south end of the tunnel. This contemporary account, written in Hebrew, is now in the Istanbul Museum, though the Israel Museum in Jerusalem has a copy.

It's possible to walk along the entire length of the pitch-black tunnel, emerging at the 'Byzantine Pool of Siloam' after about half an hour. For the most part the water is about 50 cm deep, though it is deeper (about 70 cm) for a short while at the beginning of the tunnel. You will be walking in this water so some form of flip-flop is recommended, as well as lightweight trousers/skirt that will dry easily. Bringing a torch is essential, especially if you are entering independently rather than with a guided tour. It is impossible to get lost, though women should probably not attempt this walk unaccompanied. Do not attempt the tunnel walk if you are any way claustrophobic, and bear in mind that it is a very cold walk in winter.

Two flights of steps, probably medieval, lead down to the tunnel. About 20 m into the tunnel it takes a sharp turn to the left. The chest-high wall here blocks a channel that leads to Warren's Shaft. The point where the two groups of miners met is clearly visible, though the group working from the south had to lower the level of the floor because they had started too high. The tunnel eventually emerges into the Byzantine Pool of Siloam, which was until very recently believed to be 'the' Shiloah/Siloam Pool (see below) at which Jesus performed the miracle of curing the bind man (*John 9:1-12*; one of only two miracles he performed in Jerusalem, the other being at the Bethesda Pools). By the mid-fifth century CE this pool had become firmly linked with Jesus' miracle, and the Empress Eudocia had the pool rebuilt with the Church of Siloam constructed above it. Sections of pillars from the Byzantine building can be seen submerged in the water. The church stood to the north, with an aisle that overhung the end of the pool, with the Piacenza pilgrim (c. 570 CE) describing the church as a "hanging basilica". All that remains to be seen today is a narrow stone-lined pit (c. 18 m by 5 m) occupying a fraction of the Byzantine pool, with Hezekiah's Tunnel entering from the north. The church was destroyed by the Persians in 614 CE, the whole area being left in a state of desolation and villagers from Silwan occasionally shifting the accumulated debris so that they could draw water. The mosque was built in the late 19th century CE.

From the Byzantine Pool of Siloam, the route passes a Second Temple Period 'stepped street' (and the main sewer running beneath it) which leads up to the Temple Mount. Note that every two steps are followed by a platform area, giving some breathing space for the people climbing up to the Temple.

Only discovered in 2004, the true **Shiloah (Siloam) Pool** now contains an orchard owned by the village of Silwan and is fenced off. What you see here is the eastern edge of the pool where large stone steps lead down to the square area of the pool itself. Long before its association with Jesus' miracle, the Shiloah pool was used by Jews for ritual purification ceremonies, particularly around the Feast of Tabernacles when water from

Jerusalem's early water-supply system

The primary source of water for the City of David was the Gihon Spring. This rises to the surface in the Kidron Valley beneath the east slope of the ridge upon which the ancient city stood. Though perennially full, the Gihon Spring is an intermittent spring, gushing forth into the Kidron several times a day and thus requiring the construction of a series of reservoir pools to store the water. The main drainage channel linking these pools was the 'Siloam Channel' (part channel, part tunnel) that ran for some 400 m along the floor of the west side of the Kidron Valley, filling the reservoirs and irrigating the crops grown on the floor of the valley. A 120-m section of this channel has been cleared.

The overwhelming disadvantage of this system is that the majority of it lay outside the city walls, and so was vulnerable when the city was under siege. Thus, two further tunnels were cut or enlarged as part of Jerusalem's early defensive water system. The dating of the first, 'Warren's Shaft', remains a matter of conjecture. Early opinion suggested that this shaft was cut by the Jebusites prior to David's capture of the city on the ridge, and may even have been the zinnor (gutter) up which the young king, or his general Joab, gained entrance to the city (*II Samuel 5:8; I Chronicles 11:6*). However, Yigal Shiloh, who was responsible for the most complete excavation of Warren's Shaft, rejects this

view suggesting that the identification of the shaft as a Canaanite (Jebusite) water system "is unsubstantiated by any concrete archaeological evidence" and has been "rejected for various reasons – textual, architectural, and archaeological – by most scholars" (New Encyclopedia of Archaeological Excavations in the Holy Land, 1993). Shiloh suggests that the shaft is characteristic of the Israelites, and dates it to the 10th or 9th century BCE.

The purpose of Warren's Shaft, (a natural fissure in the rock enlarged to form a vertical shaft) was to allow buckets to be lowered to the spring below without the water-drawers having to leave the city walls. This explanation took a long time to become accepted, and it wasn't until Kenyon's excavations of 1961-1967 that it could be proved that the entrance to the shaft was indeed within the Canaanite and Israelite city walls.

The second tunnel of the defensive water system, 'Hezekiah's Tunnel', is far less controversial. It was, according to Shiloh, "planned and executed as part of a comprehensive design by Hezekiah's town planners" (*ibid*) in the eighth century BCE, with the archaeological evidence matching the biblical record (*II Kings 20:20; II Chronicles 32:3-4, 32:20*). It replaced the lower section of the Siloam Channel, and brought the water-supply system within the city walls.

the pool was carried up to the Temple in a gold ewer. It is hoped that eventually the pool will be excavated in its entirety.

From the Siloam Pool, there is a choice from three routes back to the top of the slope. You can take a seat in one of the minibuses waiting on the road for 5NIS. Alternatively, on exiting the pool area, turn left to walk up the fairly steep path through the Arab village of Silwan, passing a couple of sites of minor interest on the way (detailed below). Or you can walk through the underground stepped street to emerge on Ma'alot Ir David street (from where an escort will accompany you back to the site entrance).

If you continue south from here you would eventually come to the Monastery of St Onuphrius (Aceldama) in the Valley of Hinnom (see below).

The Weill Excavations (Tombs of the House of David) On the lower slopes of the Southeast Ridge is a large area that has been substantially, but inconclusively, excavated. The area has undoubtedly been worked as a quarry, probably some time between the second century BCE and second century CE (though experts can't agree), but there are also some far older shafts cut into the bedrock that are suggested as the Tombs of the Israelite kings.

As discussed in the description of the so-called Tomb of David on the Mount Zion tour, all the written evidence suggests that David and his sons and successors were buried within the walls of his city (I Kings 2:10). Weill, who excavated this area in 1913-14, proposed that the two 'tombs' located here belonged to David and his family members. The most impressive one is entered by a deep shaft leading to a vaulted tunnel 16.5 m long and 4 m high. A stone bench with a niche may have been intended for a coffin. In addition to the area being used as a quarry, the 'tombs' had been looted in antiquity, which fits in neatly with Josephus' observation that Hyrcanus took 3000 talents from the Tomb of David to finance his mercenary army and pay off Antiochus VII Sidetes in the early second century BCE (The Jewish War, I, 61). The jury is still out on this one.

Ancient walls Sections of the **Middle Bronze Age city wall** (18th century BCE) can be seen on the above-ground route back to the site entrance. The ancient wall is distinguishable by the massive blocks of roughly cut masonry, overlain by sections of the **eighth century BCE city walls**, preserved in places to a height of 3m.

Beyond here is the Tyropoeon Valley, which defines the western limits of the ridge upon which the City of David stood. In antiquity it was a considerably deeper ravine, extending as far north as the present location of Damascus Gate, though centuries of building, destruction and rebuilding have filled it in somewhat. The name translates as Cheesemakers' Valley, though the origins are unclear. It may have been the inspiration for the "Blessed are the Cheesemakers" line in Monty Python's Life of Brian, though as the Samaritan observes, "it's not supposed to be taken literally, and obviously refers to any manufacturer of dairy products".

Valley of Hinnom

The Valley of Hinnom begins to the northwest of the Old City, in the vicinity of the Mamilla Pool in Independence Park. It sweeps down in a gently curving northwest to southeast arc, defining the western boundary of the Old City, before turning east to join up with the Tyropneon and Kidron Valleys at a point to the south of the Old City (see topographical map of Jerusalem, page 66).

Much of the west side of the Valley of Hinnom is now occupied by the New City, so the various places there are included within the description of the 'New City, Southwestern suburbs' (see page 170). Described below are the points of interest on the east side of the valley, notably the Sultan's Pool and the Monastery of St Onuphrius (Aceldama).

Ins and outs

Getting there and around To reach the sights described here on the east side of the Valley of Hinnom, exit Jaffa Gate and head south along the busy Hativat Yerushalayim. Just before the junction where Hativat Yerushalayim swings east (left) in a loop around Mount Zion, and the Hebron Road heads southwest (right), to the right of the road is the Sultan's Pool. Take the smaller road straight ahead to reach the Greek monastery on the site of Aceldama (600 m).

Background

The Valley of Hinnom has traditionally marked the boundary between the tribes of Benjamin and Judah (*Joshua 15:8, 18:16*), and was often the site of cultic places for the worship of non-Israelite gods (*II Kings 23:10*; *Jeremiah 32:35*). This is probably the reason why the valley became associated with the 'Valley of Slaughter' on the 'Day of Vengeance' that Jeremiah describes so vividly: "And the carcases of this people shall be meat for the fowls of the heaven, and for the beasts of the earth; and none shall fray them away" (*Jeremiah 7:32-33*). This tradition evolved into the Jewish concept of the 'hell of fire', or Gehenna (the latter word being the Greek and Latin form of 'Hinnom Valley'). The valley was used as a burial place in Roman and Byzantine times, notably at the southern end, and from this developed the tradition of Aceldama (see below). The 20th century CE has seen the construction of much of the 'New City' of Jerusalem on the west side of the valley.

Sights

Sultan's Pool The 'Sultan's Pool' (Arabic: *Birkat al-Sultan*) takes its name from Sulaiman II ('the Magnificent') who restored much of Jerusalem in the 16th century CE, including the present city walls and this pool. However, the origins of the pool here are much older, perhaps being part of the Herodian low-level aqueduct system that brought water to the city from 'Solomon's Pools' close to Bethlehem. The pool here was known to the Crusaders as the 'Germain's Pool', and was also restored by al-Nasir Mohammad in the 13th century CE. Despite Sulaiman II's restoration work, it soon fell into disrepair and by the 19th century it was generally referred to as just a muddy pool. It has now been filled in, and contains the Merrill Hasenfield Amphitheatre as the centrepiece to a large public park. This is one of Jerusalem's most atmospheric venues for live music, and tends to be the place where major international acts perform. Check listings in the *Jerusalem Post* and *Hello Israel*, which can be found in Ramparts Walk ticket office.

Monastery of St Onuphrius (Aceldama) ⓘ *Flexible hours. Free, though donations expected.* St Onuphrius was a Byzantine-period Egyptian hermit whose claim to fame was the length of his beard, worn long to hide his nakedness! This site became associated with a number of traditions in the Byzantine period (and revived by the Crusaders), most notably as the Aceldama or 'Field of Blood' that the high priests bought as a burial place for foreigners with the 30 pieces of silver with which Judas betrayed Jesus. 'Field of Sleeping' is a more accurate translation of the Aramaic, and thus the site is also claimed as the traditional place where Judas hung himself. The monastery features a small cave (now used as a chapel) that a 16th-century CE tradition claimed as the place where eight of the apostles hid during the Crucifixion. The cave is part of a series of first-century BCE to first-century CE rock-cut Jewish tombs that are to be found in the vicinity. Two distinct burial complexes close to the monastery are associated with Aceldama, one belonging to the Western Church and one belonging to the Eastern Church. Also nearby is the medieval charnel house built by the Order of the Knights of the Hospital of St John for the burial of pilgrims.

East Jerusalem

To Palestinians, the term 'East Jerusalem' refers to the whole of the walled Old City, the districts just to the north such as Sheikh Jarrah, and those to the east and southeast including the Mount of Olives, Kidron Valley, Silwan, Tyropneon Valley and Mount Zion. These various districts would be the desired capital of a Palestinian state. For most tourists and visitors to Jerusalem (and for the purposes of this book), 'East Jerusalem' is considered to be the area of the city just to the north of Damascus Gate.

Ins and outs
Getting there and around Buses 6 and 1 from the Central Bus Station go to Damascus Gate at the heart of East Jerusalem, whilst minibuses for Ramallah, Bethlehem and destinations in East Jerusalem go from/to the two bus stations near Damascus Gate. Most visitors to the various sites in East Jerusalem arrive from the Old City via Damascus Gate.

Sights
Pontifical Institute Notre Dame of Jerusalem Centre ① *T02-6279111, notredamecenter. org, daily 0930–1230 and 1430–1830.* Founded as a centre for pilgrims by the Augustinian Fathers of the Assumption in 1887, this imposing building is very much a statement about 19th-century Catholic France. It was built with subscriptions raised in every parish in France so that the French presence in the Holy City "would no longer be a nomad camped under a tent ... but ensconced in her own palace, equal to her rivals" (quoted in Collins and Lapierre, *O Jerusalem*, 1972).

The building's solid granite walls and defensive capabilities meant that it was immediately pressed into service during the battle for Jerusalem in 1948; in fact it was to play a pivotal role. As former President of Israel Chaim Herzog observes, "a few hundred yards from the centre of the Jewish city in Jerusalem, the Arab Legion was halted. The Jewish city had been saved by the stubborn struggle of the defenders of Notre Dame" (*The Arab-Israeli Wars*, 1982).

The considerable damage inflicted in 1948 was eventually repaired and Notre Dame now functions again as a very pleasant pilgrim hostel, despite having had to shut for 6 months during the second intifada. Since 2006, it has housed a permanent exhibition on the Holy Shroud of Turin. The 5-m-high statue of the Virgin Mary presenting her child to Jerusalem remains the building's crowning glory.

Schmidt's College This large building opposite Damascus Gate (on the corner of Nablus Road) was built as the German Catholic Hospice and College in 1886, though it later served as the temporary headquarters of the British administration following General Allenby's capture of the city in 1917, and later as the HQ of the Royal Air Force.

Rockefeller Museum ① *Sultan Suleiman, T02-6282251, www.imj.org.il. Sun, Mon, Wed and Thu 1000-1500, Sat 1000-1400. Free. Toilets; small bookshop. Guided tours on Mon and Wed, shuttle bus leaves from Israel Museum at 1100 (as part of entrance fee to Israel Museum, call to ask about English). No photos.* This magnificent limestone building (constructed 1927-1929) was built using funds from J.D. Rockefeller to house the antiquities of Palestine that had been gathered together by the Department of Antiquities of the Mandate Government. Built in neo-Gothic style, the architect incorporated aspects of local Byzantine and Islamic design, most notably the peaceful garden courtyard at the heart of the building. The exhibits are superb, though the presentation has changed little since the museum opened, and there is no sense of the dynamism that is a feature of most museums in Israel – consequently it is often mercifully peaceful. The exhibits are presented in chronological order, starting in the south octagon and following a clockwise route. Notable features include the eighth-century CE wooden panels from al-Aqsa Mosque; stucco work and other decorative fragments from Hisham's Palace in Jericho; and the 12th-century CE marble lintels from the Church of the Holy Sepulchre.

East Jerusalem & northern suburbs

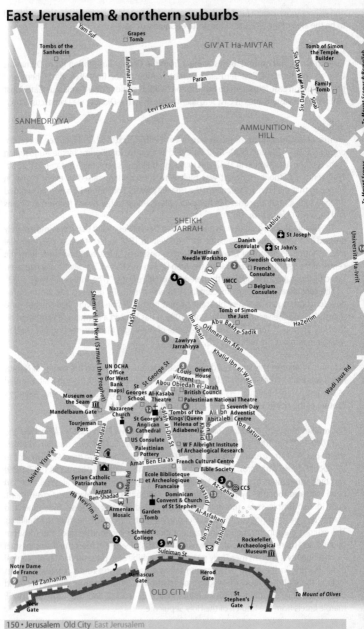

Yam Suf

Grapes
Tomb

GIV'AT Ha-MIVTAR

Tombs of the
Sanhedrin

Tomb of Simon
the Temple
Builder

Six Days War

Six Days War

Family
Tomb

Sinai

To Mount Scopus & Ramallah

Paran

Mishmar Ha-Gvul

Levi Eshkol

SANHEDRIYYA

AMMUNITION
HILL

To Mount Scopus

Universita Ha-Ivrit

SHEIKH
JARRAH

Nablus

St Joseph

Danish
Consulate

St John's

Palestinian
Needle Workshop

Swedish Consulate

French
Consulate

Pol

❷

JMCC

Belgium
Consulate

Shemu'el Ha-Nevi (Samuel the Prophet)

HaShalom

❹ ❶

Tomb of Simon
the Just

Abu Bakr e-Sadik

Othman Ibn Afan

HaZeitim

Ibn Jubair

Khalid Ibn el-Walid

Wadi Jauz Rd

❶ Zawiyya
Jarrahiyya

UN OCHA
Office
(for West
Bank)
maps)

Louis
Vincent

Orient
House

St George St

Abou
Obiedah

el-Jarah

British Council

Museum on
the Seam

Georges
School

Al-Kasaba
Theatre

Palestinian National Theatre

Mandelbaum Gate

❶❷

Nazarene
Church

Seventh Day
Adventist
Centre

Tourjeman
Post

❺

St George's
Anglican
Cathedral

Tombs of the
Kings (Queen
Helena of
Adiabene)

Ali Ibn
Abitaleb

Ibn Batura

❶❶

HaAyin

US Consulate

W F Albright Institute
of Archaeological Research

Palestinian
Pottery

French Cultural Centre

Bible Society

Amar Ben Ela'as

Ecole Biblioteque
et Archeologique
Francaise

❸ ❹ @ CCS

Syrian Catholic
Patriarchate

Az-Zahra

❶❸

Shivtei Yisra'el

❽

Dominican
Convent & Church
of St Stephen

Ibn Sina

Rashid

Antara
Ben-Shadad

Armenian
Mosaic

❶

Garden
Tomb

Al-Asfahani

Ha Nevi'im St

❷

Ha Ayin

Schmidt's
College

❺ ❼

Suleiman St

Rockefeller
Archaeological
Museum

Notre Dame
de France

❾

Id Zanhanim

Damascus
Gate

Herod Gate

OLD CITY

New
Gate

St Stephen's
Gate

To Mount of Olives

Garden Tomb ① *T02-6272745, Mon-Sat 0900-1200 and 1400-1730 (busiest on Sat). Admission and guided tours free (mainly English, but also in Arabic, Dutch, French, German, Hebrew). Toilets; souvenir shop.* The Garden Tomb is proposed as an alternative site for the crucifixion and resurrection of Jesus Christ, and many visitors prefer its landscaped and ordered efficiency to the mayhem of the Holy Sepulchre. There is indeed a very pleasant garden (*John 19:41*), and a tomb cut in the rock-face (*Matthew 27:60; Mark 14:46; Luke 23:53; John 19:41*), complete with what appears to be a groove for a rolling stone (*Matthew 27:60; Mark 15:46; Luke 24:2*), and from the vantage point overlooking the Sulaiman Street Arab bus station, the cliff-face does appear to resemble a skull (*Matthew 27:33; Mark 15:22; John 19:16*). Yet this is where imagination must be tempered with the hard facts of reality. Notwithstanding the convincing evidence that suggests that the Church of the Holy Sepulchre does in fact stand upon the site of Christ's crucifixion, the archaeological evidence supporting the claim of the Garden Tomb is conspicuous by its absence. The tomb chamber features none of the characteristics of a first-century CE burial place, such as *arcosolia* (rock-cut troughs or burial benches beneath an arched opening), with the configuration of the tombs that you see today characteristic of the ninth-sixth centuries BCE. Thus, it cannot have been the "new" or "unfinished" tomb that the gospels describe. There is also evidence to suggest that the body benches here were cut back significantly in the Byzantine period, and this would have been highly unlikely if the early Christians had considered this to be the tomb of Jesus. Further modifications were also made by the Crusaders, when the site was used as a stable!

Though the rock-face above the Sulaiman Street Arab bus station had already been identified as a possible Golgotha (Thenius 1842; Fisher Howe

N

200 metres
200 yards

1871; Conder 1878), it was the "feverish mind" of **General Charles George Gordon** ('of Khartoum') who popularized the Garden Tomb as Christ's sepulchre. As Amos Elon points out, it was not the form of the cliff face that so convinced Gordon this was the 'place of the skull', but rather the 1864 British Military Ordnance Map of Jerusalem! Apparently, the contour line marking 2549 feet makes a perfect "death's-head, complete with eye-sockets, crushed nose and gaping mouth" (Amos Elon, *Jerusalem: City of Mirrors*, 1989)!

Cynics would argue that the speed with which the Anglican Church rushed to endorse Gordon's identification had more to do with the absence of any Protestant-owned 'holy sites' within the city than with actual belief in his claims. The Garden Tomb is now administered by the (British) Garden Tomb Association, and not only provides a pleasant place for prayer or contemplation, it also acts as a valuable visual aid in recreating an image of the Crucifixion.

Dominican Convent and Church of St Stephen ⓘ *T02-6264468. The Ecole has an excellent research library (Mon-Sat 0900-1145), and organizes a programme of lectures.*

The present Church of St Stephen (1900) is part of a complex founded some 10 years earlier as the first graduate school in the Holy Land dedicated to the study of the Bible and biblical archaeology: **Ecole Biblique et Archéologique Française de St Etienne**. The school, run by Dominican monks and financed in part by the French government, has been instrumental in deciphering the Dead Sea Scrolls.

The first church on this site was built c. 455-460 by the Empress Eudocia to house the shrine for the bones of St Stephen, the first Christian martyr (*Acts 6:5 to 8:1*), whilst the empress herself was later buried here. The sixth-century CE monastery built here was destroyed by the Persians in 614 CE and, though a small chapel was built here soon after, it was the Crusaders who substantially redeveloped the site. The Knights Hospitallers restored the chapel in the 12th century CE, though the whole complex, including large stables, was pulled down in 1187 so as not to provide the advancing Salah al-Din with a strategically placed stronghold. The stables were redeveloped in 1192 as a hospice to house pilgrims, since the Ayyubids forbade Christians from lodging within the city walls. It was at this time that the name 'St Stephen's Gate' (more commonly called Lions' Gate) was shifted from its original position (the present 'Damascus Gate') to its present one at the northeast gate in the walls. Excavations within the walls of the Dominicans' property have revealed the plan of the **Byzantine church** (upon which the present church is built, and incorporating some of the original mosaics), some of the **Hospitallers' stables**, the **Byzantine and medieval chapel**, and a **Byzantine tomb complex**. It is suggested that the presence of the many reused columns found here is the reason why Sulaiman II chose the title *Bab al-'Amud* ('Gate of the Column') for the entrance now referred to as Damascus Gate. He notes that Ottoman-period gates invariably took their name from something outside them, and thus the association with the column of Hadrian's Roman paved square *inside* Damascus Gate may be erroneous.

Armenian Mosaic ⓘ *The mosaic is not easy to find, and the building is rarely open (officially daily 0700-1700, but don't rely on this). On HaNevi'im Street, just south of the (closed) Ramsis Hostel, is a small cul-de-sac behind rusted iron gates. The entrance is behind the grill on the left.*

Of outstanding workmanship, the mosaic (measuring 6.3 m by 3.9 m) was discovered in 1894 during the digging of the foundations of a new house. Its decorative style has led to a sixth-century CE dating, though the exact year that it was laid is not certain. An Armenian inscription reading "To the memory and for the salvation of all the Armenians the names of whom the Lord knoweth", together with the discovery of several burial caves in the vicinity, have led to the assumption that this was a Byzantine mortuary chapel (though it has been identified by some as the Church of St Polyeucht). The multi-coloured tesserae feature a number of birds, including peacocks (drinking the elixir of life, and thus symbolizing life after death), ducks, storks, pigeons, fowl, an eagle (symbolizing evil), and a caged bird representing an interpretation of the relationship between the body and the soul.

Mandelbaum Gate and Tourjeman Post The huge swathe of 'empty' land on either side of Shivtei Isra'el Street and Shemu'el HaNevi Street was the no-man's land between the Israelis and Jordanians in the years that control of the city was divided (1948-1967). The only crossing point between the two spheres of influence was the UN-supervised spot that became known as the Mandelbaum Gate: the crossroads were marked not by a gate, but by a house belonging to a wealthy businessman – Mandelbaum. The house (marked by a plaque) is located at the meeting point of the following roads: Shivtei Israel, Samuel the Prophet (Shmuel HaNevi), Hel Hahandasa (Engineer Corps) and St George.

Just across the road is the Tourjeman Post. Formerly a small museum offering a Zionist perspective on the years 1948-1967, it is now the **Museum on the Seam** ⓘ *4 Chel Hahandasa, T02-6281278, www.mots.org.il, Sun-Thu 1000-1700, Tue 1000-2100, Fri 1000-1400, adult 25NIS, student 15NIS*, a "socio-political contemporary art museum" which has excellent changing exhibitions by international and local artists. The bullet-holed and battle-scarred building has been left as it is.

St George's Anglican Cathedral ⓘ *No set opening hours, free.* Built in 1898, this beautifully maintained church now acts as the cathedral of the Anglican Episcopal Diocese of Jerusalem and the Middle East. There are many British links to the past, including a font donated by Queen Victoria and a tower dedicated to the memory of Edward VII, though the years 1910-17 saw the complex occupied by the Ottoman army's High Command. Following General Allenby's capture of the city on 9 December 1917, the instrument of Turkish surrender was signed in the bishop's study here. Within the complex is a highly recommended guesthouse, see listings page 177.

'Tombs of the Kings' ⓘ *Closed at the time of writing, with no date set to reopen.* The so-called 'Tombs of the Kings', the most magnificent Roman period tomb in Jerusalem, has been labouring under a misnomer for over a century now. Although mentioned in several ancient sources including Josephus (*Jewish War V, 147; Antiquities XX: 17-96*), and well known to travellers from the 16th century CE onwards, the tomb was excavated in 1863 by de Saulcy, who was so struck by the magnificence of the monument that he identified it as the Tombs of the Kings of Judah, hence the popular name. The tomb was in fact cut c. 50 CE and belongs to **Queen Helena**, the dowager queen of Adiabene in northern Mesopotamia (now in northeast Iraq), a town with a sizeable Jewish merchant community who had converted the royal family to Judaism. Some time between 44 and 48 CE the dowager came on a pilgrimage to Jerusalem, her visit coinciding with the great famine that struck the city. Helena immediately threw herself into a one-woman famine relief programme, procuring food from such far-away places as Egypt and Cyprus. She died in Adiabene c. 65 CE, but her body (along with that of her sone Izates) was sent to Jerusalem for burial. The tomb is closed to the public at present, but bring a flashlight in case this situation has changed.

American Colony Hotel The 'American Colony' was one of several new suburbs of Jerusalem established outside the old walled city at the end of the 19th century. Its founding members were the American lawyer and church leader Horatio Spafford and his Norwegian wife Anna, whose religious consciousness had been raised in a tragic shipwreck in 1874 in which their four young children were drowned. In 1881, with a group of friends, the Spaffords settled in the Holy Land, occupying a large house in the Old City between Damascus Gate and Herod Gate and devoting their lives to charitable work amongst Jerusalem's poor.

Fifteen years later they were joined by a large group from the Swedish Evangelical Church, the story of their journey being fictionalized and told in Selma Lagerlof's Nobel-prize-winning *Jerusalem*. The large influx of new settlers required more space, and so the group rented (and later bought) a large mansion built outside the walled city by a rich Arab landowner, Rabbah Daoud Amin Effendi el Husseini. The community soon expanded further, requiring adjacent properties also to be rented, and in a very short space of time the whole area was being referred to as the American Colony.

In the opening years of the 20th century, the foundations of the subsequent American Colony Hotel were laid when Baron Ustinov (grandfather of Peter Ustinov) made an arrangement to lodge visiting pilgrims there. The main function of the building, however, continued to be charitable, with hospital and clinic facilities being run through the Turkish occupation, World Wars I and II, the Israeli-Arab war of 1948 and subsequent Jordanian occupation, and the Six Day War of 1967. It was not until the Colony became a de facto part of Israel that the hospital facilities were deemed no longer necessary, and the building became upgraded to form the *American Colony Hotel*. This remains one of Jerusalem's most prestigious addresses, having played host over the years to (in alphabetical order): General Allenby, Lauren Bacall, Joan Baez, Gertrude Bell, Saul Bellow, Carl Bernstein, John Betjeman, John Le Carré, Marc Chagall, Graham Greene, Alec Guinness, Gayle Hunnicutt, T.E. Lawrence, Malcolm Muggeridge, Peter O'Toole, Dominique LaPierre, Donald Pleasance, John Simpson, Leon Uris, Peter Ustinov and Richard Widmark. The hotel is a favourite haunt of journalists and Palestinian officials.

Nearby, along Abu Obiedah ibn el-Jarrah Street, is **Orient House**, which used to be the *de facto* headquarters in Jerusalem of the PLO. It was forcibly closed by the Israeli authorities in August 2001 during the second intifada, but has recently been put to use again by the World Health Organization Office for the Palestinian Territories. Just to the north of the American Colony Hotel, on Nablus Road, is the **Zawiyya Jarrahiyya**, or tomb of Amir Husam al-Din al-Jarrahi (died c. 1201, an early 13th-century CE holy man). The shrine is meant to bring good fortune to those who pray here (with special good luck available to those involved in raising chickens and egg production!). The mosque was added in 1895.

Tomb of Simon the Just Jewish tradition relates that this is the tomb of Simon the Just (Hebrew: *Shimon Hatsadik*), a High Priest at the Temple in the fourth century BCE who was renowned for his piety. The rock-cut tomb undoubtedly dates to the Middle to Late Roman period, with a Roman inscription mentioning a Roman woman by the name of Julia Sabina, and is certainly not that of Simon. Nevertheless, the tomb remains a place of Jewish pilgrimage, particularly popular amongst Sephardi (Oriental) Jews. To reach the tomb head north along the Nablus Road past the American Colony Hotel. Where the road dips before the hill up to Sheikh Jarrah, take the road to the right (east). Take the left fork and then the next left fork, and the tomb is on the left. Head coverings must be worn. There is little to see here, however, apart from the surprising sight of Orthodox Judaism in the midst of a Palestinian neighbourhood.

Northern suburbs

There are several points of interest in the Northern suburbs of Jerusalem, to the immediate north of the area covered in the 'East Jerusalem' section. The location of the various places of interest here can be found on the 'East Jerusalem and northern suburbs' map (see page 150).

Sights

Ammunition Hill To the north of the American Colony Hotel is the suburb of Sheikh Jarrah. Taking its name from the small Arab village established here at the end of the 19th century CE, the district is now home to a number of administrative buildings and foreign embassies. It is Sheikh Jarrah where demolitions (and the threat of demolition) of Palestinian houses are proving a consistent obstacle to peace (for more information see Israeli Committee Against House Demolitions, www.icahd.org). The low hill to the north, between Sheikh Jarrah and the newer Jewish suburbs of Sanhedriyya and Giv'at Ha-Mivtar, is Ammunition Hill.

During the period 1948-1967, when most of East Jerusalem (including the Old City) was controlled by Jordan, this low hill not only controlled the road leading to the Israeli enclave on Mount Scopus, but also the road between Ramallah and the Old City. The Jordanians, recognizing the strategic importance of the hill as well as remembering the fierce battles that had taken place here in 1948, had heavily fortified what had come to be known as 'Ammunition Hill'. The night of 5/6 June 1967, saw Israeli paratroopers take the hill in a particularly bloody and hard-fought battle. The hill is now a war memorial to the 183 Israeli dead, and features an **underground museum** ① *T02-5828442. Sun-Thu 0900-1800 (winter -1700), Fri 0900-1300, entrance free, buses 4, 8 or 28 to bottom of hill. Wheelchair access.* This is basically the Jordanian command bunker, with an auditorium (screening a number of films that explain the Israeli version of history), an outdoor museum (tanks, pillboxes, trenches) that explains the battle for Ammunition Hill, plus picnic gardens.

Giv'at Ha-Mivtar To the north of Ammunition Hill is the Jewish suburb of Giv'at Ha-Mivtar. A couple of minor tombs – **Tomb of Simon the Temple Builder** and **The Family Tomb** – are hidden within this residential district. This suburb has also revealed the world's only archaeological evidence of crucifixion. Despite the fact that thousands were crucified by the Romans, archaeological evidence for this form of execution was completely lacking until **Yehohanan ben Hagkol** ('The Crucified Man from Giv'at Ha-Mivtar') was excavated here in 1968. Nothing is known about him except his name and the fact that he died some time between 7 and 70 CE, with the iron nail driven through his heel bone confirming how he died. A replica is displayed in the Israel Museum (the real bones having been given a Jewish burial).

Tombs of the Sanhedrin (The Judges) A small park in Jerusalem's northern suburb of Sanhedriyya contains a number of tombs characteristic in style and workmanship of Jewish tombs from the first century CE. Because the number of burials is approximate to the 70 judges of the Sanhedrin who met in the Temple and monitored and maintained Jewish religious law, the site became known as the Tombs of the Sanhedrin. There are in fact 55 kokhim (roughly oven-shaped rock-cut burial places), four arcosolia (rock-cut bench burials beneath arched openings) and two cave/ossuaries (secondary burial containers), though there is nothing to suggest that the tombs have any connection with the Sanhedrin; in fact, they appear to be standard family burial places.

The most notable of the tombs in this quiet fir-strewn park are tomb 14 towards the northwest corner and tomb 8 to the east. The former has an intricately carved pediment.

The so-called 'Grapes Tomb' is part of the same tombs complex, though located outside the park some 200 m to the east. At a point along Red Sea (Yam Suf) Road, opposite Mishmar Ha-Guvl Street, take the steps down between apartment blocks 8 and 10 (sign-posted 'Doris Weiler Garden'). At the bottom of the steps is another first-century CE Jewish burial cave, comprising a porch, central chamber, three rooms with *loculi* and one chamber with arcosolia. The pediment above the entrance is decorated with vine tendrils and bunches of grapes (hence the name). An interest in first-century CE Jewish tombs would have to be your reason for coming here (bus 39 from the city).

Mount Scopus

Mount Scopus is a low hill (903 m) to the northeast of the Old City, part of the soft sandstone ridge of which the Mount of Olives is also a part. It is a strategic highpoint overlooking the city (the name deriving from the Greek *skopus*, meaning 'look out'), and the list of generals and armies that have camped out on this high ground is long and impressive. The Roman general Cestius camped here in 66 CE during the early stages of the Jewish Revolt (Josephus, *Jewish War II*, 528), though he was subsequently forced to beat a hasty and costly retreat. Titus was more successful four years later, launching his attack on the city from this vantage point (*Jewish War*, V, 67). The Crusaders also camped here in 1099, whilst more recent conquerors have included the British in 1917 and Moshe Dayan's Israeli forces in 1967. The 20th century saw a number of institutions established on Mount Scopus.

Ins and outs

Getting there and away Egged Buses 23 and 28 run to Mount Scopus, plus Bus 82 from the Nablus Road Bus Station.

Sights

Hebrew University Though proposals for a modern Jewish university in Jerusalem had existed since the end of the 19th century, and land for this purpose had been bought on Mount Scopus in 1913, it was not until 1925 that the university was formerly opened. Though the Hebrew University set itself the task of resurrecting Hebrew culture, it was also charged with, in the words of its first president, Dr Judah Magnes, "reconciling Arab and Jew, East and West". Its success as a centre of learning is unquestioned, though whether it has fulfilled the latter requirement is a point of contention. In the late 2000s, around 10% of its students were Arab, with virtually all of these being 'Israeli Arabs' drawn from Galilee.

From 1948, the university spent 20 years isolated from the rest of Jerusalem: a pocket under Israeli control at the centre of the Jordanian-held West Bank. The new campus was subsequently established in the suburb of Giv'at Ram, on Jerusalem's western side. Following the Israeli victory in the Six Day War of 1967, the campus on Mount Scopus not only reopened, but also expanded significantly, with many new faculties being added.

Tombs on Mount Scopus Excavations on Mount Scopus have revealed a number of tomb complexes, several of which can be found within the recently 'renovated' Botanical Gardens of the Hebrew University.

The **Five Tombs complex** dates to the first century CE, and forms part of the vast Jewish necropolis that spread across this hill. The tombs are in fact separate entities, though overcrowding on the necropolis meant that they were so close together, the *kokhim* actually interconnected.

Dating to the same period is the **Tomb of Nicanor**, located approximately 50 m to the southeast. A Greek inscription on one of several decorated ossuaries that were found when the cave was excavated in 1902 mentions "the sons of Nicanor of Alexandria" (who is said to have donated one of the gates of the Temple). The burial cave is one of the largest of the period in Jerusalem, and features a 17-m-long façade entered through a pillared porch. The burial catacomb is complex, featuring four burial chambers containing loculi on several levels.

The **Tomb of a Nazirite Family** was discovered in 1967 during the extension of the university, and was subsequently dismantled and moved to its present position on the southeast side of the Botanical Gardens. The tomb comprises a central chamber roofed with a barrel vault, with three side chambers branching off. No burial installations are cut in the tomb, though two sarcophagi and fourteen ossuaries were found. An inscription in Hebrew on one names "Hananiah son of Jehonathan the Nazirite", whilst another mentions "Salome wife of Hanahiah son of the Nazirite". Both are thought to date to the second half of the first century CE. Comparisons are often made between this tomb and the Tomb of Herod's Family near the King David Hotel in the New City (see page 181).

Brigham Young University ① T02-6265666, http://ce.byu.edu/jc/. Buses 23 and 28. Also know as the Jerusalem Centre of Near Eastern Studies, this Mormon university (whose establishment religious Jews opposed) is architecturally acclaimed, with gardens, terraces, alleyways and courtyards that can be explored on a tour (one hour, free, phone to book). The views are spectacular, and free concerts are held every Sunday at 2000 (recommended, book as far in advance as possible).

British World War I cemetery On the northwest slope of Mount Scopus is the British World War I cemetery, superbly maintained by the Commonwealth War Graves Commission.

Augusta Victoria Hospital On the south side of Mount Scopus, on the road to the Mount of Olives, is the **Augusta Victoria Hospital** ① T02-6279911, daily 1200-1600. Built in 1898 by Emperor Wilhelm II of Germany, and dedicated to his wife, the Empress Augusta Victoria, the most striking feature of the hospital and hospice complex is the 60-m-high tower. When open, it provides excellent views of the city and surrounding area.

New City

The area to the northwest, west and southwest of the walled Old City is variously described as the New City, or West Jerusalem. There are numerous places of interest within the New City; some very ancient and others post-dating the establishment of the State of Israel. The sites are fairly spread out, the information below attempts to broadly group the various places of interest by location.

City centre and area north of the Jaffa Road

Russian Compound

Though now containing the City Hall, police district headquarters, and law courts, the large area to the northwest of the Old City was previously owned by Imperial Russia, and is still referred to as the Russian Compound. The four-ha plot was bought with a grant from the Imperial Treasury following a visit to the Holy Land by the Grand Duke Constantine Nicholaevitch in 1859. Growing numbers of visiting Russian pilgrims through the course of the 19th century meant that the traditional hospices and monasteries within the Old City could no longer cope with the demand, and the Grand Duke's assessment was that new facilities needed to be provided. Of course, the construction of grand edifices such as the Cathedral of the Holy Trinity (consecrated in 1864) would also reflect Russia's sense of its standing in the world, and thus the building here was on a grand scale. Within 20 years the high-walled enclosure of the Russian Compound housed a cathedral, consulate, monastery, hospital and hospice capable of accommodating 2000 Russian pilgrims annually.

The mass flow of Russian pilgrims, generally poor peasants, continued, and in 1881 additional accommodation was provided by the 'Alexandrovsky Hospice' (see page 101). By the beginning of the 20th century, each Easter saw the arrival of up to 9000 Russian pilgrims, though events soon took a dramatic turn. The Russian Revolution saw the number of pilgrims slow to a trickle, and the buildings of the Russian Compound were taken over by the British Mandate administration who used them as a police headquarters and prison. This is the complex that became known to Jews fighting for an independent state as 'Bevingrad', after the British Foreign Secretary Ernest Bevin. The Israeli government purchased the estate in 1955, though its British function remains largely unchanged. Recent renovation has produced an 'open-plaza' feel to the public space (Safra Square), which has been planted with palm trees. To the north of the Russian Compound (on the north side of HaMalka Street and east side of Monbaz Street) are some of Jerusalem's trendiest bars.

The **Cathedral of the Holy Trinity** still stands at the heart of the Russian Compound, and is open to visitors. The grand Kremlin-style onion-shaped domes are executed far better on the Russian Orthodox Church of St Mary Magdalene (on the Mount of Olives).

An interesting feature near the church (by the police station) is the large **monolithic column** still lying in its quarry bed. Its size (12.15 m long, approximately 1.75 m in diameter) is comparable with the description of the columns in the Royal Portico of Herod the Great's Temple, and it is suggested that this is what it was intended for until the fault at one end was discovered.

The former British prison nearby now houses the **Underground Prisoners Museum** ① *T02-6233166, Sun-Thu 0900-1700, adult 15NIS student/child 10NIS*, dedicated to the memory of Jewish freedom-fighters (or terrorists, according to your viewpoint) from the British Mandate period.

Me'a She'arim Quarter

To the north of the Russian Compound is the Me'a She'arim Quarter: Jerusalem's principal ultra-Orthodox Jewish neighbourhood. The name literally means 'hundred gates': a reference to the defensive architectural style of the quarter that sees the outer walls of the houses providing a continuous protective façade, with the '100 gates' leading to the main, and then private courts. These design practices provide not only privacy, but also defensive

New City: centre & area north of Jaffa Road

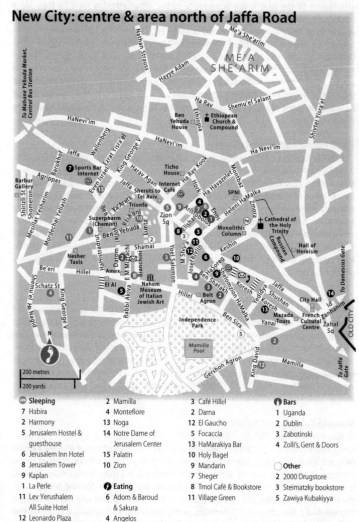

◉ Sleeping			
7 Habira	2 Mamilla	3 Café Hillel	🎵 Bars
2 Harmony	4 Montefiore	2 Darna	1 Uganda
5 Jerusalem Hostel & guesthouse	13 Noga	12 El Gaucho	2 Dublin
6 Jerusalem Inn Hotel	14 Notre Dame of Jerusalem Center	5 Focaccia	3 Zabotinski
8 Jerusalem Tower	15 Palatin	4 HaMarakiya Bar	4 Zolli's, Gent & Doors
9 Kaplan	10 Zion	10 Holy Bagel	
1 La Perle		9 Mandarin	⚪ Other
11 Lev Yerushalem All Suite Hotel	🍴 Eating	7 Sheger	2 2000 Drugstore
12 Leonardo Plaza	6 Adom & Baroud & Sakura	8 Tmol Café & Bookstore	3 Steimatzky bookstore
	4 Angelos	11 Village Green	5 Zawiya Kubakiyya

measures, considered essential when the quarter was built away from the walled Old City in 1874. The name is also a pun; an invocation of fruitfulness and plenty drawn from a line in the First Book of Moses, *Genesis*: "Then Isaac sowed in that land, and received in the same year an hundredfold: and the Lord blessed him" (*Genesis 26:12*).

Yet it is not just the architectural features that conjure to mind the *shtetl* (Jewish ghettoes) of pre-Holocaust Eastern Europe: it is the quarter's residents. The most visible attachment to the past is the appearance of the ultra-Orthodox men (in their black frock-coats, wide fur-brimmed hats, stockinged feet, and speaking Yiddish), who would appear to be more at home in a ghetto of 18th-century Poland or Lithuania than a 21st-century Mediterranean/Middle Eastern nation. Many of the more confrontational ultra-Orthodox groups who oppose the modern State of Israel, such as the radical Neturei Karta ('Guardians of the City', www.nkusa.org), have a popular base in Me'a She'arim and conduct their campaigns through the inflammatory posters that are present throughout the quarter. In fact, more than one observer has suggested were it not for the posters that hold the old stone blocks of the houses together, the whole quarter would have fallen down years ago!

Ticho House and Ethiopia Street
ⓘ *9 HaRav Kook Sreet, T02-6245068, imj.org.il, Sun, Mon, Wed and Thu 1000-1700, Tue 1000-2200, Fri 1000-1400, free.*
Most visitors now know Ticho House (Beit Ticho) for its superb restaurant, though this former home of prominent ophthalmologist Dr Abraham Ticho and his artist wife features a gallery showing some of Anna's beautiful work as well as high-quality temporary exhibitions. It is an excellent place for sitting and relaxing, especially on one of the nights when there are concerts accompanying dinner or brunch. After lunch, head to charming Ethiopia Street and visit the **Ethiopian Church** ⓘ *daily 0600-1300 and 1400-1700, free, leaves shoes by the door*, built between 1896 and 1904. Be aware that the inner sanctum is only for the priests.

Zion Square
The focus of the New City is Zion Square (Kikar Zion), although the construction of the Jerusalem light rail system and the seven-storey department store being built do tend to kill the atmosphere somewhat. However, the pedestrianized streets that radiate from Zion Square (Ben Yehuda, Yoel Salomon, Josef Rivlin, Dorot Rishonim and Mordechai Ben Hillel) are all lined with shops, cafés, restaurants, bars and nightclubs where young Jerusalemites and foreigners gather to shop, eat, drink and be seen. On Friday and Saturday afternoons, when the weather is fine, there's barely enough elbow space to hold your knife and fork, though early Friday and Saturday evenings see the whole area eerily deserted.

Mahane Yehuda and Nahalot
ⓘ *Sun-Wed and Thu -2000, Fri -1500.*
In the heart of the predominantly Sephardi Orthodox neighbourhood of Mahane Yehuda (about 1 km northwest of Zion Square) is a market that provides a fitting contrast to the 'civilized' shopping experience of Ben Yehuda Street: this is a true Middle Eastern market. It is particularly exhilarating and crowded in the pre-Shabbat rush. Mahane Yehuda is on the edge of the attractive old streets and alleys of Nahalot, which are well worth a wander. You will find a few interesting little shops, pretty courtyards and squares, and the **Barbur Gallery** ⓘ *T077-7500619, www.barbur.org, Sun-Thu 1400-2000, Fri 1000-1400, also see*

Visiting Me'a She'arim

There are a number of important things to bear in mind if you decide to visit Me'a She'arim. Quite naturally, the people who live in this quarter do not consider themselves to be a 'tourist attraction', and find nothing unusual in the way that they dress and conduct themselves; in fact, they consider themselves to be the norm.

Thus, visitors to Me'a She'arim should conduct themselves, and dress, in a modest manner. Men should wear long trousers, and preferably a long-sleeved shirt. Women must wear a long, loose-fitting skirt (even long trousers are unacceptable), a long-sleeved, loose-fitting shirt, and it may also be wise to cover hair (though shaving it off and wearing a wig is not necessary). Public shows of affection should be avoided.

Both male and female residents of the quarter dislike being photographed, so discretion, or better still abstinence, is recommended. Photography should be avoided on Shabbat (Sabbath) at all costs (and it's probably best not to visit on Shabbat either). Thursday evenings are, however, an interesting time to visit when the streets are packed and the restaurants pumping out traditional food.

The reaction to those who do not act or dress in an appropriate manner is unpredictable. Immodestly dressed women may find men crossing the road to avoid them, or being hissed at and called a 'whore', though spitting and stone-throwing are not unknown. Those who sneak photographs with long lenses risk expensive repair bills.

page 189, which has some thought-provoking exhibitions. Information plaques on many of the buildings will inform you about the area's history as one of the first neighbourhoods built outside the Old City walls in the 19th century.

Museum of Italian Jewish Art
ⓘ *27 Hillel, T02-6241610, Sun-Thu 1000-1300, Wed 1600-1900, adult 5NIS.*

The Museum of Italian Jewish Art is a collection of religious art and artefacts from Italy housed in the former 18th-century synagogue from Conegliano Veneto near Venice. At the end of World War II Conegliano Veneto no longer had a Jewish population, so in 1952 the interior of the town's synagogue was carefully dismantled and shipped to Israel. The polished wood benches, brass chandeliers and gold altar decorated with foliate designs are unusually ornate. A Shabbat service in Italian is still held here.

Artists House
ⓘ *12 Schmeul Hanagid, T02-6253653, www.art.org.il/www.schatz.co.il, Sun-Thu 1000-1300 and 1600-1900, Fri 1000-1300, Sat 1100-1400, free.*

This beautiful period house, built in the Islamic style, was the home of the Bezalel school of art until 1990 (ask them to put on the short film showing the history of the building and its founders), and now hosts quality rotating exhibitions. There is also an appealing **restaurant** ⓘ *T02-6222283, Sun-Thu 1700-0200, Fri and Sat 1200-0200*, which is quite a social hub, and excellent gallery/shop (closed Wednesday).

Western suburbs

The western suburbs of the New City, particularly Giv'at Ram, are home to most of Israel's public institutions, most notably the Parliament building (Knesset), Supreme Court, Prime Minister's Office and the newer campus of the Hebrew University. This large, green, open space also contains a number of places of interest, such as the Israel Museum, Bible Lands Museum, Monastery of the Holy Cross, and some of the city's more upmarket hotels. Allow a full day to explore all these sites (though the Israel Museum alone could probably justify a day in itself).

Ins and outs

Getting there and around There are buses direct to most of the buildings and museums, though many visitors with spare time on their hands choose to take a bus to the Central Bus Station, cross the road, then work their way north to south through the landscaped park. For orientation, refer to the 'New City (including Western suburbs, Western outskirts and Southwestern suburbs)' map on page 164.

Supreme Court

ⓘ *Qiryat Ben-Gurion, T02-6759612/3, marcia@supreme.court.gov.il, Sun-Thu 0830-1440, free guided tours in English at 1200, also guided tours for the blind (call to book). NB you must bring your passport.*

The **Israeli Supreme Court** opened within a new architectural masterpiece in 1992, after operating from a rented building in the Russian Compound for 44 years. Contrasting elements of light and dark, circles and planes, old and new materials all represent themes related to the city of Jerusalem or the system of justice. These are explained during the tour. Between the Supreme Court building and the Knesset to the south is the pleasant **Wohl Rose Park**, featuring many species of roses.

Knesset (Israel Parliament)

ⓘ *Off Ruppin, T02-6753538, www.knesset.gov.il. Guided tours in variety of languages Sun and Thu 0830-1430. Public gallery Mon-Tue 1600-2100, Wed 1100-1300. Enter from north side. NB you must bring your passport and be prepared for a thorough body/bag search. Buses 31 and 32a from Central Bus Station, Buses 9, 24 and 28 from Jaffa Road.*

The Israeli Parliament, or Knesset, stands at the centre of Sacher Park, to the south of the Israeli Supreme Court building. A modern, futuristic building (inaugurated in 1966), the rather austere exterior belies the lavishly decorated interior. Of particular interest are the tapestries and mosaics designed by Marc Chagall. The public gallery is open to visitors when the Knesset is in session and, though the debate is in Hebrew, the body language and decibel level translates into any tongue. Guided tours of the building are also available. The large bronze menorah opposite the entrance (to the north) was a gift from the British Parliament.

Israel Museum

ⓘ *Rehov Rupin, PO Box 71117, T02-6708811, www.imj.org.il. Sun, Mon, Wed and Thu 1000-1700, Tue 1600-2100; the Shrine of the Book Sun-Thu 1000-2200, Fri 1000-1400, Sat 1000-1700. Adult 36NIS, student 26NIS, child 18NIS, repeat visit within 3 months 18NIS, family 100NIS. Audio guides available. Shuttle bus on Mon and Wed at 1100 from Israel Museum to Rockefeller Museum for guided tour – must be reserved in advance. Buses 9, 17, 24, 31, 31 and 99 run from the city centre to the museum.*

The Israel Museum in Jerusalem has the country's foremost collection of antiquities and art, with the historical, archaeological and monetary value of many of the exhibits too vast to contemplate. At the time of writing, the museum complex was undergoing a 'campus renewal program' due to finish in summer 2010. Until then, all the permanent exhibitions are closed except for the Second Temple Model and the Shrine of the Book. Check the website for the latest situation, and to view the programme of lectures, films, concerts and temporary exhibits. When it reopens, visitors to Israel who intend exploring the country's major archaeological sites should either begin or end their journey here.

Model of Second Temple ① *Tours in English Sun, Mon, Wed and Thu at 1100. Audio guides available (also in Arabic, French, Russian, Spanish).* This 1:50 scale model re-creates Jerusalem at the end of the Second Temple period, as the First Jewish Revolt was beginning in 66 CE. It is an extremely useful tool for helping to visualize how the city would have appeared at this time, when it was twice as large as the present Old City.

Shrine of the Book ① *Free tours of the Shrine of the Book in English take place on Sun, Mon, Wed and Thu at 1300, Tue 1630, Fri and Sat 1100. Audio guides available (languages as above). No photography allowed inside.* A highlight of the Israel Museum complex, the Shrine of the Book houses part of the collection of manuscripts known as the **Dead Sea Scrolls**. The distinctive white-tiled roof of the building is designed to resemble the lid of one of the jars in which the scrolls were stored. A film detailing the story of the scrolls shows every hour in the complex adjacent to the shrine, and is recommended. For further details of the scrolls, see page 274.

The Shrine of the Book building is divided into three sections: the corridor, the main hall and the lower exhibition area. Displayed in the dark corridor are a number of remarkably well-preserved artefacts dating to the time of the Bar Kokhba Revolt (132-135 CE) that were retrieved from a cave in the Nahal Hever near Qumran. The centrepiece of the main hall is a huge facsimile of the Isaiah scroll, whilst in the wall cases are fragments from the **Habbakuk Commentary, War of the Sons of the Light and the Sons of Darkness**, and the **Community Rule**, amongst others. Some are originals whilst others are accurate copies. The lower exhibition hall currently contains the Aleppo Codex exhibition, the 10th-century manuscript that travelled to Egypt and Syria before returning to Israel in the 1950s.

Bible Lands Museum
① *25 Granot, opp Israel Museum, T02-5611066, www.blmj.org. Sun, Mon, Tue and Thu 0930-1730, Wed 0930-2130, Fri 0930-1400. Adult 32NIS, student 20NIS. English tours at 1030, additional on Wed 1730. Buses 9, 24 and 28.*
The Bible Lands Museum features one of the largest (and most valuable) private collections of antiquities from the Middle East. Presentation is excellent, with artefacts arranged chronologically from the time of hunter-gatherers until the Byzantine Era, encompassing wonderful ancient Egyptian, Iranian and Persian period pieces on the way, The museum also hosts a wide range of events, from cheese and wine evenings to workshops, courses and concerts. The changing exhibitions are of a similarly high standard, as is the gift shop (but the café is average). Look out for the events programme in hotels/tourist information centres.

Hebrew University To the west of the Israel Museum is the Giv'at Ram campus of the Hebrew University. When studies were suspended at the original Hebrew University on

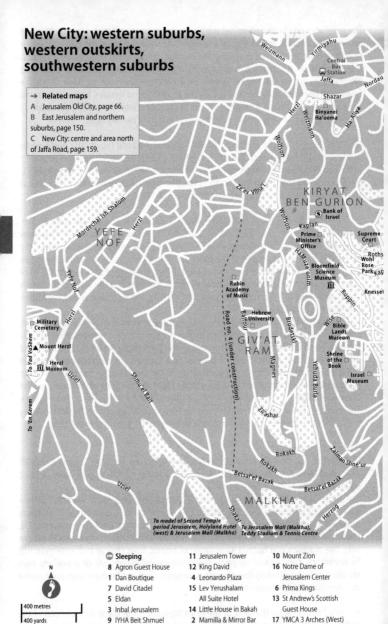

New City: western suburbs, western outskirts, southwestern suburbs

→ **Related maps**
A Jerusalem Old City, page 66.
B East Jerusalem and northern suburbs, page 150.
C New City: centre and area north of Jaffa Road, page 159.

Sleeping
8 Agron Guest House
1 Dan Boutique
7 David Citadel
5 Eldan
3 Inbal Jerusalem
9 IYHA Beit Shmuel

11 Jerusalem Tower
12 King David
4 Leonardo Plaza
15 Lev Yerushalam All Suite Hotel
14 Little House in Bakah
2 Mamilla & Mirror Bar

10 Mount Zion
16 Notre Dame of Jerusalem Center
6 Prima Kings
13 St Andrew's Scottish Guest House
17 YMCA 3 Arches (West)

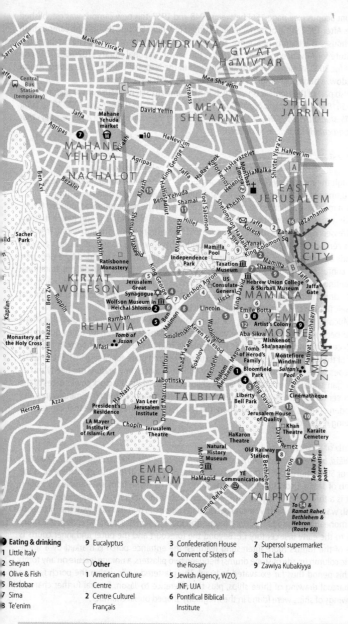

Eating & drinking

1 Little Italy
2 Sheyan
4 Olive & Fish
5 Restobar
7 Sima
8 Te'enim

9 Eucalyptus

Other

1 American Culture
Centre
2 Centre Culturel
Français

3 Confederation House
4 Convent of Sisters of
the Rosary
5 Jewish Agency, WZO,
JNF, UJA
6 Pontifical Biblical
Institute

7 Supersol supermarket
8 The Lab
9 Zawiya Kubakiyya

Mount Scopus (see page 156) between 1948 and 1967, this new campus was established here. After 1967 some of the faculties returned to Mount Scopus, though the campus here still houses the Faculty of Science, the Science Library, the Institute for Life Sciences, the Institute for Advanced Studies, as well as the Jewish National Library (T02-6585027), and halls for 3000 students. Of particular interest in the National Library is the superb **Ardon Window**, a huge stained-glass window featuring Kabbalistic symbols.

Also part of the Hebrew University is the **Bloomfield Science Museum** ① *Ruppin Street, T02-5618128, www.mada.org.il, Mon-Thu 1000-1800, Fri 1000-1400, Sat 1000-1600, adult 30NIS, student/child 25NIS, buses 9 and 28, featuring interactive "science is fun" displays that are particularly appealing to children.*

Monastery of the Holy Cross
① *Hayyim Hazaz, daily 1000-1500, entry 15NIS, shop, cold drinks, toilets.*

Though the monastery complex is incongruously set next to a major road on the edge of the upmarket suburb of Rehavia, it is still sufficiently isolated to give some impression of how it may have appeared some 950 years ago. When the monastery was founded (1039-1056) it was quite remote from the defensive walls of the Old City, and hence its thick buttressed walls, fortress-like appearance and tiny entrance way. Though dating from the 11th century, the monastery that was founded here by King Bagrat of Georgia actually stands upon the site of a fifth-century CE Byzantine church (also founded by a Georgian, the confusingly named Peter the Iberian). The original church marked the traditional Byzantine site of the tree from which the cross used in Jesus' crucifixion was made. The Byzantine church was destroyed by the Persians in 614 CE, though a section of the original mosaic floor to the right of the altar can still be seen.

Much of the church that you see today dates to the 11th century, though alterations have been made throughout the years. The Georgians fell upon hard times during the 16th century and the church was subsequently sold to the Greek Orthodox in the latter half of the century (though it is still an extremely sacred place for Georgians). The unusual frescoes were added in the 17th century ('unusual' since they feature the heady mix of Christian saints, pagan gods and Greek philosophers!), whilst the clock-tower dates to the 19th century. There is a little museum displaying millstones, immense metalwares and wooden effigies. Go upstairs to where the refectory, with a marble table that can seat 66, is being restored.

Tomb of Jason
① *Alfasi, between Ramban and Azza, Rehavia. Mon-Thu 1000-1300. Nearest buses 9, 17 and 22.*

About 500 m northeast of the Monastery of the Holy Cross, in the suburb of Rehavia, is the Tomb of Jason. Excavated in 1956, the tomb takes its name from an Aramaic inscription that is a three-line lament to Jason. Though robbed in antiquity, it is suggested that the tomb was actually used by several generations (about 25 burials in all), with the mixture of Hasmonean and Herodian pottery suggesting that it was in use from the early first century BCE to the early first century CE. Beyond the forecourt and the outer and inner courts is one of the tomb's more interesting features: the entrance porch is marked by a single Doric column (made of stone drums) between two pilasters, a unique feature on any tomb of this period thus far excavated in Israel. The plastered walls within the porch feature a charcoal drawing of three ships, plus the reference to Jason. Several further charcoal drawings of ships were found in the irregularly shaped burial chamber.

There are a number of notable places of interest in the western outskirts of the New City that visitors to Jerusalem should make every effort to see. In particular, the Holocaust Memorial at Yad Vashem should be on everybody's 'must visit' list.

Ins and outs

Getting there and around Public transport access to the various sights in the western outskirts is extremely straightforward, all being on the route of Bus 27. For orientation, refer to the 'New City (including Western suburbs, Western outskirts and Southwestern suburbs)' map on page 164.

Sights

Biblical Zoo ① T02-6750111, www.jerusalemzoo.org.il, Sun-Thu 0900-1700/1800/1900 winter/spring/summer, Fri 0900-1630, Sat 1000-1700/1800 winter/summer, last tickets an hr before closing, adults 45NIS, students/children 35NIS. Souvenir shop, toilets, snack bar. Buses 26, 33 and 99. Recently expanded and re-vamped, the zoo features animals now rare in Israel that are mentioned in the Bible, as well as other species in danger of extinction. It's a good family excursion, being both educational and well-run. The zoo is located just to the southwest of Jerusalem (Malkha) Mall, not far from the train station.

Mt Herzl ① Cemetery Sun-Thu 0800-1645, Fri 0800-1300, Sat 0900-1645, free, map provided. Toilets, small café. Buses 13, 17, 18, 20, 23 and 27 stop outside. The hill on the western outskirts of Jerusalem, Mt Herzl (Har Herzl), is home to the **Military Cemetery** as well as the tombs of Israel's past prime ministers and presidents, including Levi Eshkol, Golda Meir and Yitzhak Rabin. One 'Great Leader of the Nation' who is not buried here is Menachem Begin who requested to be buried on the Mount of Olives, where he lies near his wife and to fellow members of the Etzel and Lehi resistance movements. The centrepiece of the cemetery is the grave of **Theodore Herzl**, whose body was moved here in 1949, a stark black tomb in the Ceremonial Plaza with a handful of rocks placed on top (as per the custom). His life and works, including a reconstruction of his Vienna study, are presented through an audio-visual tour in the **Herzl Museum** ① T02-6321515, museum@wzo.org. il Sun-Thu 0845-1515, Fri 0845-1215, adult 25NIS, student/child 20NIS, call ahead to book a place on a 80-min tour (English/French/German/Spanish/Russian available) just inside the gates. This takes the form of a mini-movie (as too many Israeli audio-visuals in museums are wont to do). Visitors move through 'sets' whilst Herzl's immense contribution towards the creation of a Jewish state is lightly sketched out, followed by a 10-minute propaganda film that makes 'modern' Israeli society look decidedly unattractive. The western slopes of Mt Herzl are occupied by the extensive **Jerusalem Forest** (good picnic spots) and the memorial to the Holocaust, **Yad Vashem** (see below). A pathway connects Mt Herzl cemetery to Yad Vashem.

Yad Vashem (Holocaust Memorial) ① T02-6443802, www.yadvashem.org, Sun-Wed 0900-1700, Thu 0900-2000, Fri 0900-1400 (last entrance an hr before closing times), free. Take buses 13, 17, 18, 20 or 27 to Mt Herzl, from where it is signed; 99 is the only bus to go right to the museum entrance. It's a 5-10-min walk from the main road, or there's a free shuttle bus every 15 mins. Allow at least 2 hrs for the main museum, plus an hour for other outlying buildings and memorials. NB Respectful dress should be worn. There are guided tours in English at 1100

Theodore Herzl (1860-1904)

Herzl is described by Johnson as "one of the most complex characters in Jewish history" (*A History of the Jews*, 1989). He was born to wealthy parents in Budapest in 1860 (his father subsequently loosing everything in the crash of 1873), and studied for the bar, though writing was to remain his first great love. To his dying day he was to lament his lack of appreciation as a playwright. The turning point in Herzl's life came in the last decade of the 19th century, when the Dreyfus trial in Paris served to convince him that Jews would never fully be accepted into European society because anti-Semitism was so deeply engrained.

Herzl's publication of Judenstaat in 1896, in which he called for the establishment as a Jewish state on the grounds that Jews were a distinct race as opposed to just being a religious grouping, effectively marked the birth of what is known today as political Zionism. It was not a concept that Herzl invented; instead he was the catalyst that began a chain of events that eventually led to the foundation of the State of Israel some 44 years after his death. But as Johnson remarks, "he gave Zionism a lead of nearly twenty years over its Arab nationalist equivalent, and that was to prove absolutely decisive in the event" (*ibid*).

for 30NIS, or an audio tour is available for 20NIS. Cafeteria has pleasant terrace with views.
The most moving experience for many visitors to Israel, Yad Vashem ("a memorial and a name", from Isaiah 56:5) pays homage to the six million Jews who died in the Holocaust. Entering from the east, you pass along the **Avenue of Righteous Gentiles** – a memorial garden to non-Jews who risked their lives protecting Jews – to the **Holocaust History Museum**. This museum features harrowing photographs and testimony documenting the Holocaust in Europe, and the factors that created it, though some of the presentation is controversial. Children under 10 years old are not permitted to enter. To the west of the museum is the **Hall of Names**, where 'Pages of Testimony' by Holocaust survivors and their families fill over three million pages.

The same building also features an **art museum** of work produced in the concentration camps and Jewish ghettoes. To the west of here is a **railway boxcar** that was used to transport Jews to the camps, and now serves as a memorial monument. Below is the **Valley of the Destroyed Communities** that commemorates the Jewish communities in Europe that were eliminated during World War II. North of the Historical Museum is the **Hall of Remembrance**, where an eternal flame (*ner tamid*) is a memorial to the six million Jewish victims of the Holocaust, with the names of the 21 major concentration and death camps engraved on the floor.

Ein Karem

Though Jerusalem continues its relentless expansion westwards, the former Arab village of Ein Karem retains a rural feel, with cyprus and olive trees filling its stony hillside terraces. The village is traditionally associated with the home of Zechariah and Elizabeth, the parents of John the Baptist, and consequently as the birthplace and early home of John. The Virgin Mary's visit to her cousin Elizabeth is also commemorated here. Now something of an artists' colony, the village is dotted with glassmakers/jewellery/ceramic workshops as well as souvenir stalls (pay a visit to Yitzhak Greenfield's gallery, signed, whose paintings and prints have Jerusalem themes).There are also a number of attractive restaurants and cafés; in fact, Ein Karem is a good place to visit on Friday evenings/Saturday lunch when most of West Jerusalem is deadly quiet (though you'll need to take a taxi).

Getting there and away Bus 17 runs through the village from Jerusalem Central Bus Station. Alternatively, it is possible to follow the signed track down from the Jerusalem Forest by Yad Vashem/Mt Herzl (see page 167). In the centre of the village, where the restaurants are clustered, signs point down alleys on either side of the road to the places of tourist interest.

Sights

Franciscan Church of John the Baptist ① *T02-6413636, daily 0700-1145 and 1430-1745, closes 1 hr earlier in winter, Sun mornings only, free. Souvenir shop, toilets.* Most of the present church dates to the late 17th century, though it stands on far older foundations. Its somewhat fortress-like appearance reflects its remote location away from Jerusalem and its eventful past. Parts of a fifth- to sixth-century CE church underlie the present structure, hinting at the Byzantine tradition linking the village with John the Baptist, though the remains of a Roman marble statue of Venus/Aphrodite found here suggest that an earlier pagan temple may well have once stood on this spot. The original Byzantine church was damaged and rebuilt a number of times until the Crusader Knights Hospitallers, and then the Templars, took it over. Following the Crusader defeat in 1187 it was occupied by the Muslims, not returning to Christian hands until the Franciscans acquired it in 1621. However, they were unable to establish a presence and restore the church until 1674: the year to which much of the present structure belongs. It was expanded in 1860, the main doorway to the west added in 1885, and a new bell-tower constructed in 1895. The main feature of the church is the **Grotto of St John**, reputedly built over the house of Zechariah and Elizabeth, and thus the Baptist's birthplace (*Luke 1:5-25, 57-66*).

Two fifth- to sixth-century CE chapels are also built against the southwest wall of the present church. The most interesting of these is the **Chapel of the Martyrs**, to the north. Discovered in 1885 during the construction of the west doorway, the chapel contains a mosaic with a Greek inscription offering "Greetings, Martyrs of God". It is still unclear as to whom this dedication refers.

Notre Dame de Sion ① *Mon-Fri 1000-1200 and 1400-1700 (summer -1730), Sat 0900-1700 (summer -1730), Sun closed, 2NIS. Music in the church every Sat at 1200 (around 45NIS).* Beautiful gardens with views across the wadi to the Russian Monastery and the Church of the Visitation – the classic image of Ein Karem – and a peaceful enclave that is a joy to wander around. The Congregation of Our Lady of Sion was founded in France in the mid-19th century by one Theodore Ratisbonne, who was born a Jew but became a Catholic priest after a religious experience. His brother Alphonse came to Jerusalem in 1855 where he built the Ecce Homo Convent on the Via Dolorosa (see page 90). The house in Ein Karem dates from 1861, and here Christian orphans from Lebanon and the local Arab community were looked after by the sisters. After the Arab villagers were ousted in 1948, the house became a guesthouse and remains so to this day (see Sleeping, page 178). The Sion Community now, as then, seeks to "witness God's faithful love for the Jewish people and remember that the roots of Christianity are in the Jewish tradition" – note the Hebrew script utilised in the church and cemetery.

Virgin's Spring About 400 m to the south of the Church of John the Baptist (follow the sign) is a small abandoned mosque built over a spring. A 14th-century CE tradition notes this as the place where the Virgin Mary drew water during her three-month stay with her cousin Elizabeth.

Church of the Visitation ⓘ *T02-6417291, daily 0800-1145 and 1430-1800, closes one hour earlier in winter, free. Toilets.* Climbing the hill to the right past the Rosary Sisters Orphanage, steps lead to the Church of the Visitatio Mariae, or Church of the Visitation. The 'upper' church was built in 1955 over 'lower' Crusader and Byzantine remains. The west façade of the church features a mosaic depicting the Virgin Mary mounted on a donkey meeting with her cousin Elizabeth (the 'Visitation', *Luke 1:39-56*). The modern 'upper' church features a number of paintings depicting events in the life of Mary, plus the glorification of the Virgin throughout the centuries. The artist must have been proud of them, as he even included himself in one of the pictures (when facing the altar, look at the painting on the right wall, second along from the altar, to spot him). However, it is the older 'lower' church that is of the greatest interest. The Crusader church is built above the Byzantine remains around a cave that pious legend links with the story of Elizabeth hiding the baby John from Herod's soldiers. The shape of a baby is vaguely visible in the rock.

Hadassah Medical Centre ⓘ *Chagall Windows T02-6776271. English-language tours Sun-Thur 0830-1230, Fri 0930-1130; synagogue Sun-Thu 0800-1315 and 1400-1545, Fri 0800-1245, adults 10NIS, students 5NIS. Buses 19 and 27.* The Hadassah Medical Centre was built here in 1963 when the original hospital of the same name on Mount Scopus was inaccessible (1948-1967). It is one of the world's foremost teaching hospitals, with a reputation for also providing treatment to Israel's Arab neighbours. Those without medical insurance who intend using the facilities should bear in mind that a night here can cost more than a night at the King David Hotel!

The hospital is worth visiting to see the magnificent **stained-glass windows** by **Marc Chagall** in the synagogue. Depicting the 12 tribes of Israel (based on *Genesis 49* and *Deuteronomy 33*), four of the windows were badly damaged in the 1967 war, requiring delicate repair work by the artist himself. Chagall decided to remember the war by leaving some of the bullet holes in place.

Southwestern suburbs

The Southwestern section of the New City largely comprises the suburbs Yemin Moshe, Talbiyeh, 'Emeq Refa'im and Rehavia. These suburbs are divided from the walled Old City by the Valley of Hinnom. The background to the Valley of Hinnom, and the sites on the east and southeast side of the valley, are included in the section that begins on page 147. The places described below are largely associated with the expansion of Jerusalem beyond the confines of the Old City at the end of the 19th century CE.

Ins and outs
Getting there and around Most of the sites detailed below can be reached by heading to the east end of Independence Park, then heading down King David Street (all pretty much within walking distance of the Old City and New City centre).

Sights

Independence Park At the centre of Independence Park is the **Mamilla Pool** (89 m by 59 m by 5.8 m deep), probably once part of the Herodian aqueduct system that brought water to the head of the Valley of Hinnom from Solomon's Pools near Bethlehem. A number of traditions surround this location, invariably involving massacres of innocents by various groups. The Mamilla Pool became part of the Mamluk water system sometime in the 15th century CE, with a channel linking it to the Pool of the Patriarch's Bath in the Christian Quarter. At the time of writing the Pool was fenced off.

In the 13th century CE the main Muslim graveyard was established here, continuing in use until the 20th century. In a grove to the east of the park, about 100 m from the Mamilla Pool, is the **Zawiya Kubakiyya** – the burial place of Amir Aidughidi al-Kubaki (d. 1289). A former slave in Syria, al-Kubaki rose to become Governor of Safed under the Mamluk sultan Baibars, though in later years he fell from grace and was banished to Jerusalem. The cube-shaped tomb, supporting a low dome on a drum, uses much secondary Crusader material, and it has been suggested that it was originally the mortuary chapel used to bury the Canons of the Church of the Holy Sepulchre. In fact, in the centre of the mausoleum stands a Romanesque Crusader sarcophagus. **NB** Independence Park has something of a reputation as a meeting place after dark for gay men.

Opposite the park is the **Jerusalem Great Synagogue** ① *58 HaMelekh George Street, T02-6230628, tours Sun-Thu 0900-1300, Fri 0900-1200*, seat of the Chief Rabbinate and with wonderful windows by Marc Chagall. Next door is the **Wolfson Museum** (Hechal Shlomo), ① *4th floor, T02-6247908/6247112, adult 15NIS, student/child 10NIS, Sun-Fri 0900-1300*, which features a small but interesting collection of Jewish liturgical art and folklore, plus a Torah library. Slightly further up the road is the **Jewish Agency** ① *48 HaMelekh George, T02-6202222*, the headquarters of the World Zionist Organization (and its archives), the Jewish National Fund (JNF) and United Jewish Agencies.

Mamilla Avenue The Alrov Mamilla Avenue opened in 2007, a huge renovation project and seemingly a great success for an historic street that was very decrepit. Designed by Israeli architect Moshe Safdie to incorporate the existing 19th-century structures, the whole length of Mamilla Avenue was narrowed and each brick moved to its new location (you can still see the numberings on many of them). The result is a busy shopping mall that has several designer shops, cafés and restaurants. Look out for the Stern House (slated for demolition, but saved) where Theodore Herzl stayed for a short while during his one visit to the Holy Land in 1945. It's now a Steimatzsky's Bookshop with a small basement museum about Herzl, and was left in its original position, thus demonstrating the original width of the street.

Hebrew Union College ① *13 King David, T02-6203333*. The Skirball Museum at the Hebrew Union College (at the north end of King David Street) has a small collection of items excavated by the Biblical Archaeology School here, however, it was closed at the time of writing (indefinitely). The College, part of the Reform Movement within Judaism, runs regular Ulpan courses.

Jerusalem International YMCA Three Arches Not your run-of-the-mill YMCA, this Jerusalem landmark (nick-named 'Yimka' in Hebrew) was built in 1933 to a design produced by the firm of architects responsible for the Empire State Building, and with funds provided by the New Jersey millionaire James Jarvie. Considering the synthesis of styles, the building is remarkably attractive, as well as being a nice place to stay (see Sleeping on page 182). The three aspects of the YMCA philosophy – mind, body, spirit – are represented by the three different buildings: the right (when facing the front) is the theatre/concert hall, the left is the pool/gym, and in the centre is the soaring **Jesus Tower** ① *Sun-Thu 0800-2000, Fri 0800-1300, 10NIS, minimum of 2 persons required*, which, at 90 m high, provides good views of the city. Note the sculptures by the doorway of the Samaritan woman and the pascal lamb, as well as the exquisitely carved column capitals depicting native flora and fauna along the aisles.

King David Hotel The King David Hotel was long considered the most prestigious residence in Jerusalem, though these days there are new pretenders to the throne. However, in a head-to-head contest, its celebrity guest list of former residents easily matches the American Colony Hotel in East Jerusalem (see page 179).

The King David Hotel is less famous for its celebrity roll-call (such as the scene in the film version of Leon Uris' *Exodus* in which Paul Newman and Eva-Marie Saint share a drink on the terrace), than for the events of 22 July 1946. Around lunchtime on that day over 300 kg of explosives placed in a milk-crate detonated, demolishing one wing of the hotel. The bomb had been placed by the Irgun – the Jewish resistance (or 'terrorist', according to your viewpoint) movement headed by the future Prime Minister of Israel, Menachem Begin. Its target was the British Mandate administration, whose offices occupied most of the building. The victims included 28 Britons, 41 Arabs, 17 Jews and five 'others' dead, with hundreds injured; most were civilians. The controversy over the bombing, including details of the sequence of events, continues to this day. Begin publicly mourned the Jewish victims alone, blaming the British for failing to act on the telephone warning in time (which was phoned through by a 16-year-old girl). Other sources suggest that the bomb detonated six minutes early, but, even so, insufficient time had been given to evacuate the building. The Jewish establishment condemned the outrage, and the British called it the "ninth worst terrorist act this century", yet it achieved its objective: the cost of a continued British presence in Palestine was too much to bear, and the decision on the future of Palestine was handed over to the United Nations.

'Tomb of Herod's Family' Just to the south of the King David Hotel, Aba Sikra Street leads to the north end of Bloomfield Park and the so-called **'Tomb of Herod's Family'**. Though Herod himself was buried at the Herodium (see page 215), Josephus mentions a family tomb belonging to Herod to the west of the city (*Jewish War I, 228; I, 581; V, 108; V, 507*). However, the evidence that this is indeed the burial place of Herod's family is purely circumstantial, based on Josephus' vague description and the fact that the tomb lies directly across the Valley of Hinnom from Herod's former palace. The tomb was robbed in antiquity, which has not helped in its identification.

However, the tomb itself is well constructed and contained sarcophagi rather than mere niches for the bodies, suggesting that it was indeed the burial place of someone rich or important. Although the catacomb itself is closed, the tomb is interesting for the large rolling stone which seals the entrance – currently the only place in Jerusalem where this feature can be be seen (as the King's Tombs are closed, see page 153). There is some uncertainty concerning the dating of the tomb. Some of the features could be of the second half of the first century BCE, thus making it reasonable that Herod's father Antipater (d. 43 BCE) was buried here, as suggested by Josephus. However, some of the features are certainly later, though this could simply mean that the tomb was intended for later descendants.

Yemin Moshe and the Montefiore Windmill Yemin Moshe is a small neighbourhood of some 130 houses, the first quarter to be established outside the walls of the Old City in 1891. It was virtually abandoned and became a slum during the period of Jordanian occupation (1948-1967), but has subsequently been redeveloped. Running to the south of the Yemin Moshe Quarter, at the bottom of the hill, are two rows of terraced houses known as Mishkenot Sha'ananim ('tranquil settlement'). These were amongst the first houses to be built outside the city walls (c. 1860), and formed part of an attempt to provide affordable, comfortable accommodation for poor Jewish immigrants in the 19th century. Their benefactor was the Anglo-Jewish philanthropist, Sir Moses Montefiore. The houses were restored in 1973 and now function as a conference centre and guesthouse (but only for the accommodation of artists, writers and scholars), and indeed the whole area has something of the 'artists' colony about it.

The incongruous **Montefiore Windmill** ① *Sun-Thu 0900-1600, Fri 0900-1300, free*, was built to enable the community to produce their own flour, though the scheme never really came to fruition. It is now a museum detailing the campaigns and achievements of Montefiore.

Sunset from this point (or anywhere in Bloomfield Park) is particularly scenic, as the walls of the Old City gradually change colour as the sun goes down.

Liberty Bell Park and the 'German Colony' Popular with strollers and picnicking families, this park was laid out to commemorate the bicentennial of Israel's patron and ally, the United States of America. It contains a replica of the Liberty Bell in Philadelphia.

The suburb to the southwest of Liberty Bell Park, '**Emeq Refa'im**, was the main German Colony of 19th-century Jerusalem, with many of the houses displaying a northern European influence. The colony was founded by the same 'Templars' German Protestant Christian group who established the German Colony in Haifa some three years earlier. Most of the community were expelled during World War II.

There are several notable museums located in this district, including the highly recommended **L A Mayer Institute of Islamic Art** ① *2 HaPalmach, T02-5661291/2, www.islamicart.co.il, Sun, Mon and Wed 1000-1500, Tue and Thu 1000-1900, Fri and hol eves 1000-1400, Sat 1000-1600, adult 40NIS, student 30NIS, child 20NIS, bus 15*. Known for the extraordinary story of the theft of the museum's world-famous watches and clocks collection, which were stolen over 25 years ago but now returned almost intact: the unique Marie Antoinette watch, valued at many millions of dollars, proved too hard for the thief to sell on. The museum is a good place to be on a Saturday afternoon when virtually nothing else is open and it's almost empty.

Natural History Museum ① *6 Mohilever, T02-5631116, Sun, Tue and Thu 0900-1330, Mon and Wed 0900-1800, Sat 1000-1600, adult 15NIS, student/child 12NIS. Buses 4, 14 and 18*. This museum displays indigenous (stuffed) animals of Israel, as well as information on life sciences, the environment and the human body.

St Andrew's Church St Andrew's Church of Scotland, was built in 1930 to commemorate the Allied victory in World War I, and the Scots who died during the capture of the Holy Land. The church was designed by Clifford Holliday and is said to reflect his interest in the Armenian style of monastic architecture. The church operates a highly recommended pilgrim guesthouse (see Sleeping, page 182) and a handicraft shop from which profits go to a number of Palestinian self-help groups.

Security and safety in Jerusalem

There are a number of security and safety considerations that should be borne in mind when visiting Jerusalem. Though acts of terrorism have been rare in recent years, it remains a volatile city and violence can flare up as a result of any political provocation. Recently, incidents have centred on the Haram Al-Sharif/Temple Mount area and you might find access to the Western Wall Plaza denied if trouble is anticipated. Attacks on Jews in East Jerusalem and the Old City are very unusual and security forces are much in evidence, however choice of wearing a kippa or making other outward displays of Jewishness is something that ought to be considered (though of course there is the argument that you shouldn't be intimidated by racist attacks). Likewise, tourists who wander around in 'amusing' IDF t-shirts should not be surprised if they are greeted with hostility (or worse) when wandering around the Muslim Quarter. Note that not all terrorist attacks in Jerusalem are committed against Jews/Israelis by Palestinians; you need to be equally vigilant in the vicinity of institutions (bus stations, government offices, places of worship) where the likely targets of any attacks are Palestinians.

Women may experience varying levels of harassment in the East Jerusalem/Old City area, ranging from disparaging or suggestive remarks to actual physical touching. The Old City should be considered unsafe for lone females at night (who might feel quite vulnerable and isolated after dark). Wandering around the Old City (particularly the Muslim Quarter) at any time whilst dressed in skimpy clothes remains a bad idea; wearing baggy and androgynous clothing can make for a more stress-free experience. It may seem like a fine idea to wear your shorts when you get on the bus at Eilat or Tel Aviv but, by the time you have reached the Old City and are wandering around looking for a hostel, you will realize your mistake. Beware of pressing crowds when the human traffic jams on Tariq Khan es-Zeit reach their peak.

As with any city that attracts huge numbers of tourists, Jerusalem (and the Old City in particular) has its share of pickpockets and confidence tricksters. On the whole, however, despite the religious and political tensions, Jerusalem is considerably safer than most cities in the 'West' (and of course has a considerable 'security presence'). Being sensible and vigilant, though not over-paranoid, is the best way to approach the issue of safety in Jerusalem.

Khan Theatre The road that heads south, passing on the west side of St Andrew's Church, leads to the old railway station (opened in 1892 when the line to Jaffa was completed). The station has been derelict for a number of years, but is now slated to become a new café/theatre/shopping complex. Just before the station, housed in a former Ottoman period caravanserai, is the **Khan Theatre** ⓘ *2 David Remez Square, T02-6718281, www.khan.co.il*, shows are in Hebrew but some have English subtitles or these can be arranged by prior request – see website for program; the pleasant café-bar is only open on performance night; buses 4, 6, 8, 10, 14, 18 and 21.

Cinémathèque ⓘ *T02-656433, www.jer-cin.org.il; full listings on website, or consult newspapers.* Just below the Hebron Road is the Jerusalem Cinémathèque, which features nightly screenings, annual film festivals, theme nights, and 'movie marathons'. The café here is a good vantage point over the Himmon Valley to Mount Zion.

Abu Tor Observation Point Further southeast along Hebron Road is the cable car monument, a site that was previously occupied by the St John's Ophthalmic Hospital (built 1882), part of which now forms the old wing of the Mount Zion Hotel. It is possible to arrange a visit in advance (T02-6277550, daily 0900-1600). Continuing south along Hebron Road, just before the Dan Boutique Hotel, a road leads left (east) to the Abu Tor Observation Point. In Crusader times this hill was known as the 'Hill of Evil Counsel', from the tradition that this was the site of the House of the High Priest Caiaphas (yes, another one!) where Jesus was taken the night before his crucifixion. The present name is taken from the tradition that one of Salah al-Din's warriors, to whom the hill was given, used to ride into battle on the back of a bull. His tomb on the hill became a place of Muslim pilgrimage, though most visitors nowadays come to admire the view across to the Old City.

Southern section of the New City

There is a scenic viewpoint and an archaeological site in this southern section of the New City (directly south of the Abu Tor Observation Point, see above). The Talpiyyot industrial estate here is home to some of Jerusalem's trendiest nightclubs.

Haas Promenade
Another fine view of the Old City, Valley of Hinnom and Mount Zion can be had from the south of the city, on the Haas Promenade. This is a particularly popular spot in the early evening or night-time. It is reached by heading south towards the suburb of Talpiyyot on the Hebron Road, and turning left (east) just beyond the 'Peace Forest'.

Ramat Rahel
Running parallel to the Hebron Road as it runs south through the suburb of Talpiyyot is the Betar Road. This road leads to **Kibbutz Ramat Rahel**, an independent collective within the municipal borders of Jerusalem. In addition to its agricultural activities, the kibbutz also has a rather luxurious **guesthouse** (L) ① T02-6702555, www.ramatrachel.com, and leisure/ recreation centre, plus some interesting archaeological remains. The kibbutz was also the scene of heavy fighting in the 1948 war, with control of the hill fluctuating between the Jews and the Arabs.

The modern kibbutz occupies a prominent hill (818 m above sea level) at a point roughly equidistant from the Old City and Bethlehem. Not a great deal is known about the ancient site, though many scholars now support an identification with the biblical **Beth-Haccherem** *(Jeremiah 6:1, 22:13-19; Nehemiah 3:14)*. The earliest settlement suggests a stronghold dating to the ninth or eighth century BCE, though the most prominent ancient remains are from a magnificent **citadel-palace** built by one of the later kings of Judah, probably **Jehoiakim** (608-597 BCE). Sections can still be seen here, though the best-preserved decorative remains (three complete proto-Aeolic capitals and several incomplete fragments) have been removed to the Israel Museum. The citadel-palace complex was almost certainly destroyed during the Babylonian invasion of 586 BCE.

Though remains have been found from the Babylonian-Hellenistic periods (586-37 BCE), and the Herodian period (37 BCE-70 CE), the next significant finds date to the third century CE. These comprise a **Roman bathhouse** and **villa** built by the Tenth Roman Legion c. 250 CE. Both were renovated and used during the Byzantine period. Also in the Byzantine period, c. 455 CE, a large **church** and **monastery** were built on the hill by Lady

Ikelia, possibly to mark the traditional site where Mary rested on her way to Bethlehem. The plan of the church is readily identifiable, though only a small section of the mosaic floor was preserved. The site appears to have been abandoned since the seventh to eighth century CE.

Abu Ghosh

An interesting Crusader church, a more rural setting and excellent Middle Eastern restaurants make Abu Ghosh good for a half-day out from Jerusalem. The present name of the village (13 km northwest of Jerusalem), preserves the name of a 19th-century CE sheikh who used to levy tolls on pilgrims using this route to Jerusalem. The former Arabic name for the village, Qaryet el-Enab, in turn preserves the biblical name, Kirjath-jearim, a small village on the border of the tribes of Judah and Benjamin. It was at Kirjath-jearim that the Ark of the Covenant was kept during the 20-year period between its restoration by the Philistines (*I Samuel 6:21-7:2*) and its removal to Jerusalem by David (*II Samuel 6; I Chronicles 13:5-14*). The village from this period occupied the hill-top area (Deir el-Azhar) and is now marked by a large statue of the Virgin Mary and the infant Jesus in the grounds of the Notre Dame de l'Arche d'Alliance. This **modern church** ① *daily 0800-1130 and 1330-1800; free, donations accepted; ring the bell if locked*, (1924) stands on the site of a Byzantine chapel that was built to mark the traditional site of the house of Abinadab, where the Ark was kept (*I Samuel 7:1*). Parts of the chapel's fifth-century CE mosaic floor can still be seen.

In the second century CE, the settlement moved to a new site on the valley floor when the Romans built a reservoir over the spring here. The reservoir was entered via two stepped passages hewn from the rock (and now incorporated into the Crusader church, see below). In the mid-ninth century CE, a caravanserai was built east of the Roman reservoir, water from which supplied a pool beneath a pavilion at the centre of the caravanserai's courtyard, whilst a large reservoir was built on the east side. The caravanserai continued in use up until the Crusader period, and was later restored by the Mamluks some time between 1350 and 1400.

During the Crusader period, the village became associated with the gospel story of the resurrected Christ's appearance to two disciples on the road to Emmaus (*Luke 24:13-35*). The reason for the Crusaders locating the biblical Emmaus here was based largely on circumstantial evidence; they simply selected the nearest village that was located the necessary 60 stadia (11.5 km) from Jerusalem, believing that the spring and reservoir would have been a suitable place for Jesus and the disciples to stop for their meal. In 1142, the village and all its land were granted to the Order of the Hospitallers, and a large Crusader church was built above the reservoir. The eastern reservoir built in the ninth century CE was turned into a great vaulted hall, whilst the Early Arab period caravanserai was considered to be the place where the meal took place. In latter years the Crusaders located Emmaus at el-Qubeibeh (see below). The **Crusader church** ① *T02-6342798, Mon-Wed, Fri and Sun 0830-1100 and 1430-1700; free, donations accepted; the church is marked by the sign 'Eglise de Croisse – Crusaders Church'; Superbus 185 runs to Abu Ghosh from Shazar in Jerusalem (one street south of the Central Bus Station, parallel to Jaffa*, is very well preserved, particularly the crypt over the Roman reservoir, thanks in part to extensive renovations carried out at the end of the 19th century CE. The church was presented to Napoleon III at the conclusion of the Crimean War, and subsequently entrusted to the French Benedictine Lazarus Fathers. To find the church in the village head for the tall minaret of the adjacent mosque.

El-Qubeibeh

The **church** ⓘ T02-952495 extn 4; daily 0800-1145 and 1400-1700; free, donations accepted, (to the northwest of Abu Ghosh) is the venue of a popular pilgrimage on Easter Monday. Though el-Qubeibeh lies the necessary distance from Jerusalem to qualify as Emmaus, the association with the gospel tradition is rather nebulous. Located on the Roman road to Jerusalem (parts of which can still be seen), in the eighth or ninth century CE a number of houses (still visible) were built here by Arab settlers, who thus founded a village. Some time in the first half of the 12th century CE the Canons of the Holy Sepulchre in Jerusalem acquired the land, ostensibly for tax farming purposes. The village probably took its name, Parva Mahomeria, from the small Muslim shrine that stood in the village (el-Qubeibeh means 'little cupola'). A small fortress and hospice were built to service the needs of Christian pilgrims using this route to Jerusalem. It is now widely believed that later Christians became confused as to why a church had been established here; the only tradition that seemed to fit the location was the gospel story of Christ's resurrection appearance at Emmaus and, given that the distance matched certain versions of Luke's gospel, the tradition stuck. The present Franciscan church here was consecrated in 1902, though the foundations of the Crusader-period church are still visible. Visitors are shown a wood panel in the floor to the left of the nave, which is claimed to be part of the house of Cleopas (though this is highly unlikely).

Jerusalem listings

For Sleeping and Eating price codes and other relevant information, see Essentials pages 26-31.

● Sleeping

The majority of upmarket accommodation is found in the New City, whereas budget hotels, hospices and hostels tend to be in the Old City and East Jerusalem. The Old City/East Jerusalem area is more atmospheric, but starts shutting down after dusk. The New City is blander but has better shopping, dining out and nightlife options. You pays your money and takes your choice (though in reality the two areas are little more than a 30-min walk apart). Advance booking is highly recommended during holidays (all denominations, all price categories), and essential at hospices and places orientated to pilgrimage-tours. Even budget places will require reservations backed up by credit card during peak Christmas/Easter seasons. Note that tour groups get significant discounts on the 'spot rates' used here. The Old City backpacker hostels offer the cheapest accommodation

in Israel (around 50-70NIS per night for a dorm bed). The rates quoted are regular season, and presume breakfast is included unless otherwise stated.

Old City p62, map p66

AL Austrian Hospice, 37 Via Dolorosa, T02-6265800, www.austrianhospice.com. This busy, well-maintained hospice has been a landmark since 1863. Single/double/triple rooms are expensive but there are also high-standard large dorms (**C**). Plum walls with golden framed paintings in the hallways, black-and-white tiled floors. Curfew (but key available); half-board option. Some of the best Old City views from the roof; popular garden café. Reservations essential.

AL Christ Church Guesthouse, Omar ibn al-Khattab Sq, Jaffa Gate, T02-6277727, www.cmj-israel.org. Sedate but welcoming atmosphere, lovely lounge areas and corridors hung with rugs and artefacts conjure up imperial times. Rooms in the older wing more characterful and colonial but new wing has a/c. Flowery courtyard and café where breakfast is served; some family rooms (**L**); meals available (Shabbat dinner); 2300 curfew; check-out 1000; church on your doorstep; unmarried couples cannot share.

AL Gloria, 33 Latin Patriarchate, Jaffa Gate, T02-6282431/2, www.gloria-hotel. com. Great location and fine views from restaurant and rooftop. Unexciting rooms with sizable bathrooms, but plasticky fittings and endless off-putting dark corridors upstairs. Arabesque decor in public areas is much nicer. Good value; no religious vibes.

AL Lutheran Guest House, 7 St Mark's, T02-6266888, www.guesthouse-jerusalem. com. Very well-run guesthouse, with spotless 1-4 person rooms set around a peaceful courtyard; new rooms just built at roof level; lovely stone walls throughout. Meals available. Mainly German guests. Booking essential.

AL-D Armenian Guest House, 36 Via Dolorosa, T02-6260880, armenianguesthouse@hotmail.com. Doubles/triples can be a great deal, apartment-style with kitchen, washing machine, dining room. Decor is fairly spartan but inoffensive. Single EURO55, double EURO74, dorms EURO20. Courtyard restaurant is OK; no curfew.

A East New Imperial, Jaffa Gate, T02-6282261, imperial@palnet.com. Historic building (previous guests include Kaiser Wilhelm II in 1898), with hallways so packed with memorabilia and antique furniture it's like a museum. Cheapish doubles, all with bath (though these tend to be recent additions 'into' the room); 5 have 'the' front balcony views on to the Citadel and Jaffa Gate. Some suites (**AL**) can fit families. Very friendly, free internet, breakfast $5. Recommended (but not for those who want high-spec fixtures and fittings).

A Notre Dame de Sion Ecce Homo Convent, 41 Via Dolorosa, T02-6277292, www.eccehomoconvent.org. Romantically located above the Lithostrata, next to a basilica and by the Ecce Homo arch. Spotless rooms (doubles $80),

some with marvellous views; huge public terraces; single-sex dorm $24 (partitions separate the beds). Austere atmosphere, not for backpackers. B&B; half-board available. Advance bookings only. Ask about their curfew.

A-D Hashimi, 73 Souq Khan es-Zeit, near Damascus Gate, T02-6284410, hashimihotel. com. Better backpacker choice for those after some peace and quiet. Single-sex dorms (100NIS with breakfast) are newly kitted out in dubious taste, public areas marbled, awesome views of the Al Aqsa from the roof terrace and indoor dining area, Private rooms (**A**) are overpriced, strictly no unmarried couples, and alcohol forbidden. 1030 checkout, curfew 0230-0600. Internet 15NIS per hr or free Wi-Fi, use of kitchen.

A-E Citadel Youth Hostel, 20 St Mark, T02-6284494, citadelhostel@mail.com. A rocky rustic cave on the lower 2 levels, the rooms become more modern and less enticing as you ascend. Single/double/triples, with/out bath, and a couple of cramped 10-bed dorms (60NIS). Shared shower/toilets truly are cubby holes. But decor is appealing - Bedouin style - and so is the atmosphere and rooftop views, Beds changed daily but only private rooms get towels. Free Wi-Fi (or 10 mins use of pc). No breakfast, but use of kitchen (hot drinks 4NIS) and no curfew (quiet requested after 2330). Recommended to book ahead, only 11 rooms. Day trips on offer to the usual places for $50.

A-F Petra Hostel, 1 David St, T/F6286618, www.newpetrahostel.com. Excellent location just inside Jaffa Gate with fabulous views from the roof (if you look beyond the wasteland of Hezekiah's Pool). The rambling historic building has basic rooms (all en suite) – nothing special, minimal tasteless furnishings, fans. Pay more for balcony views (200-300NIS). Better for backpackers: dorms are pleasant, old-style, with balconies (6-8 beds, 70NIS); June-Oct sleep on the roof (40NIS). Clean linen, free use of kitchen, fridges on each floor; internet access (10NIS per hr); 24-hr reception; no curfew; 1000 check-out; baggage storage. 'Interesting' clientele (lots of 'Jerusalem Syndrome' types); takes credit cards.

B-E Golden Gate, 10 Souq Khan al-Zeit, T/F02-6284317, goldengate442000@yahoo.com. Single sex dorms sleep 6-9 (some with single beds rather than bunks), private rooms all en-suite, new and tiled throughout (blankly decorated), small outdoor terrace (no views), not on the main backpacker circuit. Breakfast and free tea/coffee. No alcohol and 2400 curfew.

B-F Hebron Hostel, 8 Aqabat Etkia, off Souk Khan El Zeit, T02-6281101, ashraftabasco@hotmail.com. One of the Old City's nicest hostels and one of Jerusalem's most popular backpacker options, with variety of rooms and dorms. 18 per room in mixed/female dorms (40NIS) but feels spacious enough and rock walls/arches add appeal. Very hot showers and clean toilets. Some private rooms (doubles 180/150 NIS with/out baths), but check a few as they vary. Roof terrace; tearoom below has cheap meals, drinks and internet (10NIS per hr). Competitively priced tours. Check-out 1100, curfew 0100, friendly staff. Recommended.

D-F Al-Arab, Tariq Khan es-Zeit, near Damascus Gate, T02-6283537. Long-established backpacker favourite and cheapest in town. Rather run down: grubby toilets and showers (irregular hot water and peep-holes), variously sized dorms (including one with 46 beds on the roof!), private rooms (**D**). Kitchen not terribly hygienic; no curfew. Popular despite its shortcomings.

E New Swedish, 29 David, T02-6277855, www.geocities.com/swedishhostel. Cramped 14-bed mixed dorm, and 6 pokey rooms (**B**, but much cheaper low season and decent discount for long stays). All share clean showers and very cosy kitchen; free tea/coffee; TV room. Friendlier than competitors, but not a place for anyone who values privacy. In peak season, backpackers find themselves on a mattress behind reception. No alcohol. Internet 6NIS per hr.

East Jerusalem p148, map p150

LL American Colony, 1 Louis Vincent, off Nablus, T02-6279777, www.americancolony.com. Historical building now houses East Jerusalem's (many would say, Jerusalem's) classiest hotel. There's a certain simplicity to the interior decor, while antiques and wall-hangings dotted about the public places add classic Arabian style. Small heated pool (in summer) and gym; palm- and flower-filled garden, attractive courtyard (for a great Sat brunch). To appreciate your stay fully, go for the more luxurious Pasha Deluxe rooms ($510) with sleek tiled bathrooms, although smaller standard rooms will be refurbished in 2010. An intimate feel throughout and excellent restaurant. Recommended.

LL Olive Tree, 23 St George, T02-5410410, www.olivetreehotel.com. Rooms are just big enough, with modern-retro decor (but beginning to get scuffed), stone-tiled bathrooms, flat-screen TVs. No pool; charge for internet. Book online for 10% discount.

L Ambassador, Nabus, Sheikh Jarrah, T02-5412222, www.jerusalemambassador.com. Favoured by tour groups, but don't let that put you off because rooms here are spacious, decorated in a modern style with classic furniture, a/c, TV, free Wi-Fi, wide beds and big bathrooms. Those with balconies facing the Old City are best. Welcoming restaurant serves Middle Eastern/French/Italian food and has outdoor seating in summer. Bedouin tent in the garden, fitness centre and sauna. A bustling social place.

L Legacy (formerly YMCA East), 29 Nablus, T02-6270800, jerusalemlegacy.com. A halls-of-residence exterior belies a beautifully refurbished interior – all cream and white, contemporary sofas, subtle lighting and clean wooden lines. Rooms vary in size (some have fabulously large balcony), fridges, flat-screens, safes, fluffy dressing gowns and smellies. Indoor pool, squash, basketball and gym. Nice outdoor coffee shop in summer, and Cardo restaurant on the top floor is a great spot (see Eating page 184).

L Jerusalem, 4 Antara Ben-Shadad, off

Nablus, T6271356, F6283282. Attractive old building, with well-furnished rooms (some with excellent balcony views) in the Arab style which are quaint but with modern amenities. Busy patio restaurant attracts interesting folk; friendly management. Recommended and advance booking is essential, especially as there aren't many rooms.

L-AL Christmas, 1 Ali Ibn Abitaleb, T02-6282588, christmas-hotel.com. Modest hotel catering largely for pilgrims but without a stuffy atmosphere and always bustling with activity. Rooms are cosy and pleasantly furnished and there's a good garden restaurant/bar. No seasonal price increases.

AL AzZahra, 13 Az-Zahra, T02-6282447, azzahrahotel.com. It's not luxurious but a/c rooms in a romantic old building have Arabesque lamps, high ceilings, old doors and atmosphere (some with good balcony). 15 rooms, mostly twin bed, with kettle, fridge, TV. Large bathrooms, but a down point is "shower" attachment on the tubs. Courtyard/restaurant is a good place for a beer and has decent menu.

AL Golden Walls, Sultan Suleiman, T02-6272416, www.goldenwalls.com. Excellent though noisy location between Damascus and Herod gates: pleasant lobby lounge, good views from rooftop café (breakfast and BBQs up there when weather's hot). Many rooms recently refurbed in modern Arabic style, bright and airy with sparkling bathrooms – request one of these, they're priced the same (db $130-150 depending on season).

AL Ritz, corner of Ibn Khaldun/Ibn Batura, T02-6269900, jerusalemritz.com. 104 functional a/c rooms are newly decorated and very clean, though with no sense of style. Other options with this price tag are more interesting and atmospheric, but staff here are nice and efficient. Free Wi-Fi.

AL St George's Cathedral Pilgrims Guesthouse, 20 Nablus Rd, T02-6283302, stgeorges.gh@j-diocese.org. Tranquil setting around cloistered courtyard; most rooms were part of the choir school and are simple yet very spacious with attractive stone walls. Sensibly run, mostly pilgrim groups but independent travellers welcome, reservations recommended (no choice as to which room you are allocated, some upstairs ones lack the Jerusalem stone walls). Reasonable value by Jerusalem standards with no seasonal price hikes. Alcohol available, a/c, tv, and cathedral and lovely gardens on the doorstep. Good choice.

A Victoria, 8 al-Masoudi, T02-6274466, www.4victoria-hotel.com. Modest rooms (some triples), with TV/fan, newish furniture and clean bathrooms, but hand-held shower fittings. Some have balcony. Pleasant staff, breakfast hall a bit dingy; alcohol available. Scope for negotiation on price.

B-E Palm Hostel, 4-6 HaNevi'im, T/F02-6273189, newpalmhostel@yahoo.com. A real travellers hang-out, this is where to come for political chat, a friendly hectic atmosphere, crowded dorms (some with attached bath) and grotty but cheap rooms. Recently the Palm has overtaken premises next door (previously the Faisal), where the atmosphere is more staid but rooms are freshly renovated and tiled (though tiny) with a/c-cum-heater. Flexible midnight curfew; free internet; breakfast and hot drinks included.

Northern Suburbs *p155, map p150*

LL Regency Jerusalem, 32 Lehi, Mount Scopus, T02-5331234, www.regency.co.il. Bold, modern design featuring hanging gardens and waterfalls in the lobby, palm-fringed pool area, plus true 5-star facilities (including Jerusalem Spa complex, with indoor pool). Amazing views of the city from Mount Scopus. Recommended.

A-B Mount of Olives, 53 Mount of Olives Rd, Al-Tur, Mount of Olives, T02-6284877, www.mtolives.com. Friendly family-run place; mainly pilgrims but without the pious atmosphere. A few of the 55 basic rooms have awesome views, 7 have been revamped with new furnishings and bathrooms, TVs, and are more spacious – all equally competitively priced. It has appeal for its Arab village location and proximity to some of the city's holiest sites. B&B, alcohol available. Minibus 75/sheruts go to Damascus Gate till 1700, otherwise it's a taxi or a real schlep uphill. **NB** Lone women are not advised to roam the area at night.

New City *p158, map p164*

LL Dan Boutique, 31 Hebron, T02-5689999, www.danhotels.com. Formerly the Ariel, some distance south of city centre, this hotel has undergone a recent refurb and become part of the Dan group (though is less pricy than others in the chain). Boutique here means mod cons meet retro, it's trying to be hip and almost hits the mark. Black, cream, silver and gold trimmings, flock wallpaper, TVs in the public spaces showcasing animation, 'funky' bar, fitness centre, cartoon art in the bedrooms, decent sized bathrooms with nice toiletries - and everything new. Jewish vibes. Try the central reservations T03-5202552 for seasonal discounts.

LL David Citadel, 7 King David, T02-6211111, www.TheDavidCitadel.com. Bustling with Bar Mitzvahs, this high-end hotel in a premier location meets professional standards. Restaurants (nice terrace) are slick without a hint of stuffiness, plush rooms, big pool with plenty of loungers – in fact, everything's on a giant scale and light reflects off every marble surface. All the services and facilities that you would expect, for the money. Recommended.

LL Inbal Jerusalem, 3 Jabotinsky, T02-6756666, inbalhotel.com. The full facilities you would expect for the price, with a fresh contemporary feel and sociable airy public spaces. Good shops, very professional staff. Recommended.

LL King David, 23 King David, T02-6208888, www.danhotels.com. Flagship of the Dan chain with a famous history, this place used to ooze style but it's starting to look dated in comparison to the swanky new upstarts. The

quiet grassy grounds have an inviting pool, the veined marble tables, parquet floors and dark furnishings are classic. To appreciate the experience fully you really need to stay in one of the 'deluxe' or 'executive' rooms facing the Old City ($700+). Tennis, fitness centre.

LL Leonardo Plaza, 47 King George, T02-6298666, www.leonardo-hotels.com. Ex-Sheraton, excellent service and facilities that you would expect. Regular rooms are spacious and better than many others at the same price; expect to pay more for an Old City view or extra $70 for balcony or 'smart room'. Good restaurants and sushi bar, seasonal swimming pool, popular with Jewish families.

LL Mamilla Hotel, mamillahotel.com. Luxurious new hotel in keeping with the upmarket shopping street of the same name that it adjoins. The stylishly lit lobby sets the tone for the spacious rooms, with glass-walled (liquid gel) bathrooms, soft-pile carpets and minimalist sophisticated decor. The basic studio costs US$360 but can go up to $480 on Jewish holidays. Holistic spa (due to open Sep 2010) and sublime pool; dairy restaurant and brasserie on roof both excellent; and the Mirror Bar is one of 'the' places for the Jerusalem elite to be seen (or there's the Winery for a less dressy drink). However, some staff don't yet seem to be quite at the same level as the top-class facilities.

L Eldan, 24 King David, T02-5679777, www.eldanhotel.com. Beginning to get shabby and scratched around the edges. Rooms have picture windows and all the amenities, comfy beds, but bathrooms a bit disappointing. Bustling coffee shop; sloppy staff. Worth considering if there's a cheap online deal (which there frequently is).

L Harmony, Yoel Moshe Salomon, Nachalat Shiva, T02-6219999, www.atlas.co.il. Typical Atlas hotel styling and features, which comes as a pleasant change in Jerusalem. Grey and white decor splashed with bright colours, contemporary furnishings, art installations and books to browse. Rooms with a/c, fridge, tea/coffee, safe, hairdryer, free Wi-Fi. Entrance is via the Salomon Centre, a weirdly empty mall, but otherwise an excellent location next to hippest restaurants of the new city, easy walk to the Old City and East Jerusalem. Price includes afternoon refreshments (exc Shabbat), which can be taken in the trendy lounge/foyer.

L Prima Kings, 60 King George, T02-6201201,www.inisrael.com/primahotels/kings. The best flower-filled balconies in the city; fair-sized rooms, attractive restaurant and lively lobby coffee shop. Half-board available. Good central location for both old and new city.

L YMCA 3 Arches, 26 King David, T02-5692692, www.YMCA3arch.co.il. Famous Jerusalem landmark, in very appealing building with ornamental public areas (the foyer-salon is especially glorious). Though renovated, the 56 rooms are rather sombre, but there's use of the indoor pool, fitness room, squash and tennis. Nice restaurant/terrace.

AL Jerusalem Tower, 23 Hillel, T02-6209209, www.jthotels.com. Perfect location if you want the city-centre vibe, with great views from the 12th floor of the concrete tower. Rooms rather small but recently refurbed in an almost-art-deco way, though bathrooms disappoint. Public areas cheap and dated.

AL La Perle, 6 Hahistadrut St, T77-5525251, laperle-hotel.com. Intimate new hotel (6 doubles, 6 singles) with a central location and subtly decorated rooms. 15% discount for stays over 3 nights, includes continental breakfast at the café next door. Management are accommodating about check-in/out times – and in all other matters. Good choice, book ahead.

AL Lev Yerushalayim All Suite Hotel, 18 King George, T2530-0333, levyerushalayim. co.il. Part of the Royal Plaza chain, this apartment hotel has 1-2-bed suites with kitchenette (dishes for rent), lounge/dining area (20% discount for monthly

stays with no breakfast). Good value for money, suitable for families and excellent location – but rooms are a bit gloomy. Expensive internet.

AL Little House in Bakah, 1 Yehuda, T02-6737944, littlehouse@o-niv.com. Quite a unique little place, in a renovated Ottoman mansion. Smaller than most with just 35 rooms; large garden with pine trees. Polly restaurant is homely and comes recommended; breakfast is good; free Wi-Fi and tea/coffee. Bakah is nice old neighbourhood, not far from the nightlife of the German Colony, and a short drive to Bethlehem. An interesting choice.

AL Montefiore, 7 Schatz, T02-622111, www.montefiorehotel.com. On a pedestrianized street (near cool Bezalel Street), this welcoming and modern hotel has shiny new furniture, big, comfy beds, nice bathrooms, cool-ish restaurant; safe/fridge/etc. Just squeezes into this price bracket at $149 per double. A good choice.

AL Notre Dame de Sion Ein Karem, 23 HaOren, Ein Karem, T02-6430887, www.sion-ein-karem.org. Idyllic setting in the walled gardens of a convent. Rooms to accommodate 1-5 persons, pricier in the Hermitage. Communal fridges; half/full board available. By reservation only; complicated rules about check-ins/outs.

AL Palatin, 4 Agripas (entrance on Even Israel), T02-6231141, palatinhotel.com. Popular and cosy; most rooms recently renovated with attractive stone-tiled floors, muted furnishings, plenty of mirrors, small shower rooms. Older cheaper rooms with carpets are scruffier. Check-out 1200; nice management (book ahead, will negotiate on price).

AL St Andrew's Scottish Guest House, 1 David Ramez, T02-6732401, www.scotsguesthouse.com. Quiet rooms ($140-150, $10 more for room with Old City view; other rooms look over the garden), furnishings are tasteful though simple, excellent bathrooms, no TVs, heater-a/c, kettle. A grand 1930s building where

Ottoman tiles mix with colonial charm; feels remote, yet both old and new city are walkable, as are restaurants on Emek Refajm. Dinner available; free Wi-Fi; relaxing Allenby lounge for sunset drinks; rooftop; charming library/tv room; church adjacent. No curfew, mixed clientele, lovely staff. 1 suite ($180), 1 bland apartment ($240/300 for 4/6 people); pre-booking essential. Can pay to use the pool at the Mount Zion hotel, nearby (100NIS).

AL-A Jerusalem Inn Hotel, 7 Horkanos, T02-6252757, jerusalem-inn.com. Close to city centre but mercifully on a quiet backstreet, recently remodelled rooms are spotless and tastefully and modestly furnished, plus older cheaper rooms are popular ($95 double); a/c/heaters, fridge, TV, generous breakfast. Best to book through website.

A Habira, 2nd Fl, 4 HaVatzelet, (crn Frumkin), T02-6255754, hotelhabira@gmail. com. Set back from noisy Jaffa Street, but still surrounded by cheap eats and cool nightlife. A homely little place, with TV, a/c, fridge, big beds, plenty of furniture; no curfew. S/D/T/Q 250/350/450/600NIS. Considered an historical site by fans of Menachem Begin.

A Kaplan, 1 HaHavazelet, T02-6254591, natrade@netvision.net.il. Small rooms in an old-school guesthouse (jigsaw art, primrose and blue paint, hard beds), but it's cheaper than most for a private room (doubles $70); TV, a/c, 4-bed room for 300NIS; some rooms with balcony; clean, central location. Free internet and tea/coffee, use of kitchen; extremely pleasant management.

A Mount Zion, 17 Hebron, T02-5689555, www.mountzion.co.il. Excellent views (especially at sunset) from most rooms; best in the 19th-century Ottoman-period 'citadel' wing; some balconies. Deceptively large hotel, but still feels friendly. Unique oriental furnishings can border on bad taste in some suites. Ask for a renovated room, as older ones are tired and shabby. Outdoor pool (closed in winter), Turkish bath, health centre, average breakfast. Possible to walk to both old/new city. Despite minor faults, the vast majority of people enjoy their stay here.

A Zion, 10 Dorot Rishonim, T02-6232367, F6257585. Hard to find a more central location. Lovely period building but disappointing interior; a/c, fridge, tiny balconies; management lackadaisical; no breakfast.

A/B-E Jerusalem Hostel & Guesthouse, nr Zion Sq, 44 Jaffa, T02-6236102, jerusalem-hostel.com. The only 'hostel' in West Jerusalem has an excellent central location (though extremely noisy at time of research due to the tram-line construction outside). Shame the old building retains few features: stone floors are covered by carpets and decor is 80s-style. All rooms have en suite showers; cheaper plastic 'bungalows' on roof are tiny (need to stoop, shared bath, NIS180); cramped but clean 16-bed dorms (NIS70) are popular. Kitchen facilities, sociable dining room; centrally controlled a/c, TV, towels, free internet; long-stay discounts possible; no curfew.

A-B Noga, 4 Bezalel, T02-6254590/5661888. More apartment than hotel, with self-contained rooms (sleep 2-4) with kitchenette, heating; minimum 2-night stay; advance booking essential. It's a good deal, and a cool street to 'live' on. Call Kristal to book a room.

A-C Agron Guest House, junction Keren Ha-Yesod/Agron, T02-6558400, www.iyha. org.il. Don't be put off by the large lettering stating "Conservative Judaism" on the front of the building - the hostel is not affiliated and are keen to point out all races and creeds are welcome. Spacious modern dorms (114NIS, essential to book ahead) or private rooms (doubles 340NIS, each extra adult 100NIS) are functional but spotless. Those on the 4th floor have balconies (some with Old City view).Heating, a/c, fridge, kettle, TV, free internet; check-out 1000; nice and informative staff. Buses 7, 8, 9, 31 and 32.

A-C Beit Shmuel Hotel and IYHA Hostel,
6 Shamma, behind Hebrew Union College,
T02-6203455/6, www.beitshmuel.com. Part
of World Union for Progressive Judaism but
welcomes all-comers. 6-bed 'dorms' ($219)
in the 'hostel' section which feels quite
studenty but is very clean. Private rooms (A)
in the 'hotel' half are Scandinavian-styled
and spacious, with cool colours, sofa, fridge
etc; some have Old City views. Check-out
1100; no curfew; luggage storage. Young
friendly staff are a big plus; check for
discounts online.

Ein Karem *p168*
**AL Notre Dame of Jerusalem
Center**, 3 HaZanhanim, T02-6279111,
notredamecenter.org. Historic castle-like
building opposite New Gate, aimed primarily
at Roman Catholic pilgrims (though others
welcome). Fine views, grand public areas,
well-kept rooms, free Wi-Fi. Recommended
high-class restaurant (La Rôtisserie,
see Eating page 184). Reservations
recommended – despite there being
150 rooms (doubles $150, or rather
magnificent suites).
E IYHA Ein Karem Youth Hostel, off Ma'ayan,
Ein Karem, T02-6416282. A wonderful rural
setting with valley views, peeling and dusty
exteriors, very much for long-stayers – rooms
are booked out months in advance or ask to
pitch a tent. Bus 17.

🍴 Eating

Restaurants are listed in Jerusalem's Menus
(free from the tourist office; bear in mind
that the places mentioned have paid to
appear in these brochures, but the discount
coupons are attractive). As a general rule,
restaurants in the New City and Jewish
Quarter of the Old City are kosher and close
on Shabbat (whilst those in East Jerusalem
and the rest of the Old City aren't and
don't!). Most places in the New City take
credit cards, whilst those in the Old City
tend not to.

Old City and East Jerusalem
p62 and 148, maps p66 and 150
The cheapest places to eat are probably the
'hummus and fuul' places on HaNevi'im,
just outside Damascus Gate. There are
plenty of 'falafel and shwarma' places in East
Jerusalem and in the Muslim Quarter. Across
the road from Damascus Gate are plenty of
fruit and veg stands.
🍴🍴 **Arabesque**, American Colony Hotel, 1
Louis Vincent, off Nablus, T02-6279778. Good
food, in pleasant surroundings. Sat brunch in
the courtyard is wonderful if you're feeling
flash (1200-1530, around 140NIS).
🍴🍴 **La Rôtisserie**, Notre Dame of Jerusalem
Centre, 3 HaZanhanim (opposite New
Gate), T02-6279114. Recently renovated,
this elegant restaurant in a beautiful old
space attracts Jerusalem's elite. Soft greys
and white linens sit well against stone walls
and decadent lighting. Up-lit pillars split
the room to give an intimate feel. Pleasant
pre-dinner drinks area and bar to prop up.
The Spanish-inspired menu is interesting,
dominated by fish and seafood, also pork;
well reviewed and expensive. Daily 1230-
1530 and 1900-2200.
🍴🍴-🍴🍴 **The Cardo**, 5th Floor at Legacy Hotel,
29 Nablus Rd, T02-6270827. Pretty good
value Mediterranean cuisine (eg salads
35NIS, mains 55NIS and up) and worth it for
the surroundings: simple appealing decor,
sweeping views to the Mount of Olives from
the huge windows or terrace, long bar to
tempt drinkers. Promise to replace your meal
should you be dissatisfied. Daily 1200-2400.
🍴 **Armenian Tavern**, 79 Armenian
Patriarchate, Armenian Quarter, T02-
6273854. Atmospheric setting in part of
Crusader-period church: vast pieces of
metalware, mother-of-pearl, mirrors, icons,
etc adorn ceilings. Try the stuffed vine leaves;
salads 15-35NIS, main dishes 50-60NIS,
pasta 35-45NIS. Recommended. No credit
cards. Mon-Sat 1200-2200. Mainly meat, gets
mixed reviews.
🍴 **Askadinya**, 11 Shimon Hatzadik, T02-
5324590. An East Jerusalemite favourite

for a mix of Italian/Western cuisine but using traditional local ingredients. Cobbled courtyard with cosy rooms off it, live (loud) music on Thu nights, daily 1200-2400 (bar stays open longer if there are still drinkers).

† Azzahra Hotel and Restaurant, 13 Az-Zahra, East Jerusalem, T02-6282447, azzahrahotel.com. Surprisingly pleasant and relaxed venue; indoor or courtyard nicely lit at night. Good place to unwind with relatively cheap booze. Everything from pizza to Palestinian food you can peruse the menu online). Tue-Thu 1200-2300.

† Borderline/Pasha's Restaurant, 13 Sheikh Jarrah, East Jerusalem, T02-5825162, borderlineofjerusalem.com. Reliable oriental food (mezze 10NIS, mains 45-90NIS) and relaxed atmosphere (beer 20NIS). Shady yard with drifts of nargilla smoke, good mix of people (popular spot with NGO types). Food served 1200-2300, but stays open later for drinking (-0100).

† Papa Andreas, 64 Souq Aftimos, Muristan, T02-6284433. Pleasant rooftop restaurant, with nice atmosphere even if it is strictly for the tourists. St Peter's Fish, spinach pie and salad, shishlik, mezze with salad and hot pitta. Good lunchtime specials, or just smoke a nargila.

† Philadelphia, 9 Az-Zahra, East Jerusalem, T02-6289770. Well-reputed restaurant that has been here since the time of Jordanian control, and is a great place to eat authentic Palestinian food. Long and famous clientele list (newspaper clippings adorn the walls), decor is Christmas colours and plastic plants. A bit of a den (seedy staff at times: lone women beware); also good for cheap beer and mezze. Daily 1200-2400.

†-† Hong Kong House, 9 Az-Zahra, East Jerusalem, T02-6263465. Chinese lanterns mixed with office furniture and pictures of Al Aqsa, but good cheap fix of hot'n'sour soup or egg rolls. Also take-away. No alcohol. Sat-Thu 1200-2100.

† Abu Shukri, 63 Tariq al-Wad, Muslim Quarter, T02-6271538. One of the Old City's best-known hummus places. Daily 0730-1730.

† Abu Shuky, Tariq al-Khanqah. Almost the same, but even better. Possibly the best hummus in Jerusalem? Stuff yourself for 15NIS. No English sign: ask around. Closes early (0900-1530 except Sun), but if you are late there is always Lina just up the street (blue sign) which stays open till at least 1630 – though the hummus ain't a patch.

Abu Sair Sweets and **Jaffar Sweets** on Tariq Khan es-Zeit are two good places to get your daily sugar fix. However, for kanafeh (mild cheese, baked in strands of honey syrup mixed with pistachios) save yourself for **Eiffel Sweets**, Sultan Sulieman St, T02-6263614, where it is dangerously good and very authentic.

† Gate Café, just inside Damascus Gate. Good little spot for watching the world go by (without being spotted yourself), run by the right-on Hytham, fair prices, and free wireless connection. All are welcome.

New City *p158, map p164*

The New City's shwarma and falafel places are located on and around Ben Yehuda, though they're slightly pricier than those found in the Old City. Cheapest fruit and veg is found in Mahane Yehuda Market.

†††-†† Adom, Feingold Courtyard, 31 Jaffa, T03-6246242. Veteran Jerusalem restaurant. Menu is French-Italian: risotto is excellent, as is the fish; specials menu changes daily. Unfussy and unpretentious.

†††-†† The Colony, 3 Beit Lehem (Bethlehem) Street, German Colony. Secluded location with balcony. Delicious food and superb service.

†††-†† Darna, 3 Horkanos, T02-6245406, www.darna.co.il. Kosher Moroccan cuisine (tagines, cous-cous and plenty of lamb), but not for vegetarians. Beautiful interiors in this rambling 200-yr-old building with tiled floors, a tented area, trees, lamps and candles. Business lunch is a good deal at 70NIS. Sun-Thu 1200-1500 and 1830-2400, Sat after Shabbat.

†††-†† El Gaucho, 22 Rivlin, Nahalat Shiva, T1800-422000. Big steaks and kebabs in this reliable Argentinean chain. Not cheap but the meat is excellent.

¶¶¶-¶¶ Eucalyptus, Hutzot Hayotzer (Artists' Colony), Yemin Moshe, T6244331. New location (its 7th) but continued rave reviews. Moshe Basson is one of Israel's most renowned chefs and never fails with his innovative Middle Eastern menu. The upper level (Sabras café) serves dairy and vegetarian dishes. Recommended.

¶¶¶-¶¶ Olive & Fish, 2 Jabotinsky, T02-5665020. A faithful grill restaurant, with plenty of out-of-towners, the setting is warmly comfortable and familiar and the food commendable. They also run 'Olive' restaurant in the German Colony, on Emek Rafa'im, which is equally attractive.

¶¶¶-¶¶ Restobar, 1 Ben Maimon (corner with Azza St), T02-5665126, www.restobar.co.il. One of few places open on Shabbat – when consequently it's heaving (best book a table on Fri night). Mood changes depending on time of day: laidback café for brunch-time, morphing into a bar at night (though you wouldn't say it's 'hip'). Either way, the atmosphere is relaxed and buzzy, and the food fresh and good quality. Outdoor decking or a welcoming oval bar to eat, drink and chat over. Wi-Fi. Daily 0830-0200, or later.

¶¶ Angelo, 9 Horkenos, T02-6236095. Possibly the best homemade pasta in town and good pizza. Kosher so good for veggies, main dishes around 50NIS. Daily 1600-2400.

¶¶ Cafe Hillel, 36 Jaffa. There are many in the Hillel chain, but this corner location is always buzzing and very convenient.

¶¶ Focaccia Bar, 4 Rabi Akiva, T02-6256428. Busy Mediterranean/Italian café/restaurant; good patio scene. Worth knowing, as it's open every day 0900-0200.

¶¶ Lavan Café Restaurant, T02-6737393, 11 Hebron Road (in the Cinematheque). Perfect spot with a view of the Old City (especially lovely at sunset) through huge windows. Italian staples 45-60NIS (all veg/fish), great risotto, salads around 45NIS, bread made in-house. Breakfasts served till 1700 (1300 on

weekends). Or just sip (very good) wine on the outdoor bar stools facing the view. The service is decent. Daily 1000-2400.

¶¶ Little Italy, 38 Keren Ha-Yesod, T02-5617638. Excellent Italian vegetarian food, plus some fish; main dishes 50NIS+. Sun-Thu 1200-2300, Fri 1200-1400.

¶¶ Mandarin, 2 Shlomzion HaMalka, T02-6252890. One of Israel's oldest Chinese restaurants, with Hong Kong/Chinese chefs. Main dishes are reasonably priced.

¶¶ Sheyan, 8 Ramban, T02-5612007, www.sheyan.co.il. Black and red softly lit Chinese decor, and outdoor seating below the Rahavia windmill, all make for a pleasant dining environment. Mixture of loosely Asian dishes, lots of sweet'n'sour, sushi, veg options (tofu), spring chicken skewers. Around 100NIS per person. Sun-Thu 1230-1500 and 1800-2300, Sat after Shabbat.

¶¶ Te'enim, Confederate House, 12 Emil Bota, Yemin Moshe, T02-6251967. A worthy long-timer of the Jerusalem veggie scene, Te'enim ("figs") has a café-feel and a menu with vegan options too. Tofu is used creatively in oriental offerings, in addition to the more commonplace soups and salads. Bit hard to find, tucked away on the edge of historic Yemin Moshe (approach from Emile Bota Street, next to King David Hotel). Sun-Thu 0900- 2300, Fri 0900-1430.

¶¶ Ticho House, 9 HaRav Kook, T02-6244186. Innovative salads (with bread) are a meal in themselves; also exciting range of fish/veg dishes; or just stop in for coffee and cake. Currently a delightfully tranquil setting with garden terrace, but threatened by the luxury apartment block being constructed next door. Sun-Thu 1000-2300, Fri 1000-1500, Sat dusk-2400. Also live music (reservations necessary), Tue Jazz 2030, Fri chamber music 1100 and Sat dinner to Jewish tunes.

¶¶ Tmol Café and Bookstore, 5 Salomon, T02-6232758, www.tmol-shilshom.co.il. Set on a quiet courtyard, this mainly vegetarian café is a delight. Lovely 1st-floor terrace or cosy cluttered interiors; nice staff; attracts the intelligensia. Pasta/salads 40-50NIS, fish 80NIS, Fri buffet is expansive, 55NIS, 0900-1230. Sun-Thu 0900-2400 or later, Fri 0900–late afternoon, Sat eve.

♥♥-♥ Holy Bagel, Jaffa, www.holybagel.com. With several branches around the city, this chain has become a phenomenon (but who knows for how long). Their bagels are delicious and come in every form and filling. A cheap eat (just).

♥♥-♥ Sheger, on alley between Jaffa/Agrippas. Delicious Ethiopian meals in this white-washed cubby hole with tiny tables; veg (30-35NIS), meat (35-40NIS), beers 10-12NIS. Flags painted on the walls, simple and authentic. At 10 Agrippas, look for the Arcadia sign and go down the alley.

♥♥-♥ Sima, 82 Agrippas, T02-6233002. Handily on the edge of Mahane Yehuda market, this popular place has reasonably priced salads and hummus (8-20NIS), and a line up of steaks, kebabs, shishlik and liver which come with rice/veg/salad on a plate (44NIS) or in a pitta (35NIS). Half-way between a café and a restaurant, it's a proper Jewish experience.

♥♥-♥ Village Green, 33 Jaffa, T02-6253065, www.village-green.co.il. Excellent and wholesome veggie dishes, pies, quiches, great soups; self-service canteen style, outdoor/indoor. Pay by weight so don't pile your plate too high; about 40NIS for a huge feed. Excellent salads, lots of seeds, dressings, hot and cold mixes to choose from. Can take-away. Check website for coupon giving 10% discount. Sun-Thu 0900-2200, Fri 0900-1430.

♥ HaMarakiya, 4 Koresh, T02-6257797. Devoted solely to soup, this little place rotates the flavours: six different vegetarian varieties per night (28NIS). It's very groovy, full of hand-me-down furniture, communal tables, red walls, trendy clientele and the local city's LGBT community. Alcohol is served; the basement is a den; prices very reasonable. Sun-Fri 1800-last customer.

Sakura, Feingold Courtyard, off 31 Jaffa, T6235464. Israel's best Tokyo-style sushi bar; main dishes around 60NIS. Recommended.

Ein Karem p168

There's are several excellen[t] clustered together in the villag[e] open during Shabbat – and hen[ce] (though of course, you will have to g[et] by car/taxi). Best are:

♥♥ Karma, 74 Ein Karem, T02-6436643, www.karma-rest.co.il. The standard menu of pasta/pizza/salads (38-48NIS) is given an interesting twist, plus casseroles and meat entrées (50-70NIS). Upstairs terrace; sleek indoors; lots of windows; stylish yet friendly. Sun-Wed 1000-2400, Thu-Sat 1000-0100.

♥♥ Mala Bar, Ein Karem, T02-6422120. Glowingly inviting indoor cave or intimate street-side tables, it's the place to be seen (in a good way), always buzzing. Wonderful salads/pasta, good drinks selection. No English sign, look for the chandelier and candles. Weekdays 1730-0200, or from morning at weekends.

Also **Trezoro** for Italian/gelato (daily 0830-2400), the Lebanese Restaurant for a more casual experience, and **Karem** for meaty kosher delights (1130-2330 except Shabbat).

Abu Ghosh p176

♥♥-♥ Lebanese Food Restaurant, 88 Ha'shalom, Abu-Gosh, T02-5702397, www.abo-gosh.co.il. Exit off Road 1 at the Hemed Junction, or take Bus 185, and it's the first restaurant at the entrance to the village on the left; you can't miss it. The labaneh with mint/garlic is possibly the best around; hummus and other salads also fantastic (11NIS). Meaty mains 30-70NIS. Eat under the ancient mulberry tree. Despite its rambling size and many tables, it's hard to get a seat on Shabbat. Daily 0900-2300. No alcohol.

◑ Bars and clubs

Jerusalem's nightlife used to be a standing joke, particularly amongst Tel Avivians, though this is certainly no longer the case. There is now a selection of bars and nightclubs to suit most tastes and pockets,

, staying open until the early ...urs. With very few exceptions, most bars are located in the New City, while the fashionable nightclubs tend to be out in the suburbs, notably Talpiyyot to the south.

Bars

Artel Jazz Club, 9 Heleni Hamalka 9, Russian Compound, T077-9620165. Live jazz every night at 2200; good range of drinks (the food is great too). Wi-Fi .

Austrian Hospice, 37 Via Dolorosa. The tranquil gardens and cloisters are perfect for a late afternoon beer. Nip up to the roof for the call to prayer and sunset over the Dome of the Rock. Daily 1000-2200.

Baroud Bar-Restaurant, Feingold Yard, 31 Jaffa, T02-6259081. Friendly: good for hanging out at the bar and a place solo women feel comfortable. The food is OK (particularly the calamari) but it's better for a drink. Mon-Sat 1230-very late.

Borderline, 13 Sheikh Jarrah, East Jerusalem, T02-5825162. Very popular place for boozing; naturally weekends are particularly good.

Cellar Bar, American Colony Hotel, 1 Louis Vincent, off Nablus, T02-6279777. For those on expense accounts, notably journalists, aid workers and Palestinian officials. A stylish and beautifully lit arched grotto, from 1800.

Dublin, 4 Shammai/Darom, T02-6223612. A mega-pub, plenty of Israeli rock music (yes!) or even karaoke, plus trance. Big, busy and social. You can't miss the Guinness signs outside signalling the way in. Open until very late.

Mirror Bar, Mamilla Hotel, 11 King Solomon, T02-5482222, www.MamillaHotel.com. Art-deco styling in this new venue popular with the 'in-crowd'. Black walls covered with sheets of mirrored glass, stretched bar of lit alabaster, adjacent cigar bar, retro furniture. Fusion food is reasonably priced (3 courses 58NIS). Daily 1900-the last customer (usually about 0230, or at weekends 0400); DJ every night.

Uganda, 4 Aristobulos, T026236087. You know it's cool coz they serve Taybeh.

Versavee Bistro Bar, Greek Catholic Patriarch, Old City, www.versavee.com. Courtyard is always busy due to their prime location, but it's attractive with a well-stocked bar, high ceilings and pleasant atmosphere. Happy hour 1600-1800; free Wi-Fi. Good place to hang out. The food's not that cheap. Daily 0830-late.

Zabotinski, 2 Ben Shattach, T054-4928878. Familiar pub-feel, if that's what you are after. Always a few hardened drinkers sitting outside. Cheap drinks offers all day. Not a bad place at all and very handy location right in the centre.

There are a number of bars and pubs on Yoel Salomon and Josef Rivlin, many of which have some sort of 'happy hour', including: **Doors**, **Gent** and **Zolli's Pub**.

Clubs

Haoman 17, 17 Haoman, Talpiyyot Industrial Area. Thu and Fri nights only 2400- after sunrise. DJs from around the world; house-techno music. Dress up. Cover is 80-120 NIS. Long-standing Jerusalem favourite; there's also a mega-huge bar.

The Lab, 28 Hebron, T02-6292001. Dance club/bar in the grounds of the old Jerusalem railway station, a restored old Ottoman building. It's pretty laid-back. Music is quite rocky, though there is a mix. Also good for just drinking as opposed to 'clubbing'.

Yellow Submarine,13 HaRechavim, Talpiyyot, T02-6794040, www. yellowsubmarine.org.il. In Hebrew 'Tzolelet Tzehubah', this venue for underground alternative music is found among the industrial warehouses of Talpiyyot. It might be punk-rock or salsa or a night of jazz, every night of the week till the early hours. See the website for schedules.

😊 Entertainment

For full details of cultural, cinematical and theatrical performances, check www. jerusalem.com, the 'entertainment' section of Friday's *Jerusalem Post*, *Hello Israel*, *Time*

Out (http://digital.timeout.co.il/), *This Week in Palestine*, and other such freebies that can be picked up at tourist offices and hotel receptions.

Cinemas

Barbur Gallery, 6 Shirizli Street, Nachlaot, www.barbur.org. Seriously art-house movies in a shed-like gallery space, Tue at 2000. In English or with English subtitles. By donation.

Cinémathèque, 11 Hebron Rd, T02-5654333 www.jer-cin.org.il. Jerusalem's main art-house cinema; highly recommended for interesting yet approachable films; check website for complete listings. Also hosts the annual **International Film Festival** (Jul) and **Jewish Film Festival** (Dec). Adult 36NIS, student 28NIS.

Cultural centres

American Cultural Centre, 19 Keren Ha-Yesod, T02-6255755, www.usembassy-israel.org.il/ac. Sun-Thu 1000-1600, Fri 0900-1200. Free Wi-Fi.

Beit Avi Chai, 44 King George, T02-621-5900, http://www.bac.org.il. Hosts frequent music concerts/lectures/events. All relate to Jewish or Israeli culture, but are held in an open as well as artistic milieu.

British Council, 31 Nablus, East Jerusalem, T02-6267111, www.britishcouncil.org/ps. Mon-Thu 0730-1530, Fri 0730-1330; or 3 Shimshon, New City, T6736733. Mon-Thu 1000-1300 and 1600-1900, Fri 1000-1300.

Centre Culturel Français Romain Gary, 9 Kikar Safra, T02-6243156, www.ccfgary-jerusalem.com. Library with good stock of DVDs/CDs as well as books/periodicals; free internet. Sun and Tue-Thu 1400-1800, Mon 1000-1200 and 1400-2000, Fri 1000-1300; membership adult/student 350/280NIS a year. Also run French language courses and cultural events (various venues, listed on website).

Centre Culturel Français, 21 Salah al-Din, East Jerusalem, T02-6282451, www.consulfrance-jerusalem.org. Mon-Thu

1000-1300 and 1400-1800, Fri and Sat 1400-1800. Housed in a beautiful old building, hosts films, exhibitions, concerts, plus a worthwhile Christmas fair.

Music

The world-renowned Israel Philharmonic Orchestra performs at the **Binyanei Ha'Uma** (International Convention Centre) opposite Central Bus Station, T02-6558558/6237000, www.ipo.co.il, box office Sun-Thu 0900-1900, Fri 0900-1300; whilst the Jerusalem Symphony Orchestra and Israel Chamber Ensemble often play the **Jerusalem Theatre/Jerusalem Centre for the Performing Arts**, 20 David Marcus, T5617167.

Classical music concerts and recitals are also held at **Beit Shmeul**; **Beit Ticho**, off Harav Kook.

Eden-Tamir Music Centre, 29 Hamaayam (by Mary's Spring), Ein Karem, T02-6414250, www.einKaremusicenter.org.il. A season of concerts (Fri and Sat) in enchanting surroundings.

Edward Said National Conservatory of Music, Regent Hotel, 20 Az-Zahra Street, East Jerusalem, T02-6271711, http://ncm.birzeit.edu. Concert series twice yearly (spring and autumn, check website for schedules) in Jerusalem and West Bank towns; a good opportunity to hear Arabic music. Also has branches in Ramallah and Bethlehem.

YMCA (West), 26 King David, T02-5692692, www.jerusalemymca.org, 600-seat theatre, not just classical concerts.

Zionist Confederation House, 12 Emil Botta, Yemin Moshe, T02-6245206, www.confederationhouse.org. Organises the annual Oud Festival and is home to the Ethiopian Hullegeb Theatre; also Israel Museum, see 'Sights' on page 162, every Tue at 1800.

Live outdoor concerts (classical/folk/rock) are occasionally held at the **Sultan's Pool**, just to the southwest of Jaffa Gate.

Theatres
The Khan, 2 David Remez, T02-6718281. Theatre, music, stand-up comedy, restaurant, art gallery; but most performances in Hebrew.

Palestinian National Theatre, Nunza (near American Colony Hotel), T02-6280957, info@pnt-pal.org. Critically acclaimed (and highly politicized) theatre, usually in Arabic but sometimes English/Turkish/Greek.

O Shopping

It's difficult to exhaust Jerusalem's potential for shopping, though if you're looking for a trinket or souvenir you will have to wade through a sea of rubbish before you find anything tasteful in the Old City. As a general rule, shops in the New City tend to be fixed-price, with prices prominently displayed. In the Old City it's a free-for-all, with protracted bargaining required to make the most of your spending power. In the Old City, David Street/Street of the Chain and the Via Dolorosa are crammed with small shops staffed by multi-lingual merchants with a keen eye for the tourist dollar. Initially stunned by the bright colours, unusual objects and accumulated junk, closer inspection usually reveals that all the stalls are pretty much selling the same stuff. There's some choice rubbish aimed at the pilgrim market, most notably the 3-D picture of Jesus with the winking eyes, or your own personal crown of thorns. Shops listed below are just a tiny selection of what's on offer.

Arts, crafts and Judaica
Quality Judaica pieces can be very expensive; they are generally more tasteful in the New City rather than the shops along the Cardo in the Jewish Quarter.

Eight Ceramists, 6 Yoel Salomon, T02-6255155. Handmade ceramics from pottery cooperative, much in demand.

Frank Meisler Galleries, Annex of King David Hotel, 21 King David, T6242759. Beautiful Judaica.

Gallery Anadiel, 27 Salah al-Din, T02-6282811. Contemporary Palestinian art.

Gift Box, American Colony Hotel, T6734046. Daily 1000-1200 and 1730-2000, closed Sat morning. Nice range of classy gifts and beautiful antiques, but at a price.

House of Quality, 12 Hebron, near Mount Zion Hotel, T02-6717430. In a romantic building opposite Mount Zion Hotel, new and established Israeli artists and quality crafts, ceramics etc, well worth investigating. Sat-Thu 1000-1300, Sun, Mon, Tue and Thu 1700-1900, Fri 1100-1300. Not cheap. Selection of work by artists in their studios.

Palestinian Pottery/Armenian Ceramics, 14 Nablus, opposite US Consulate, T02-6282826, www.palestinianpottery.com. Hand-painted designs. Family business since 1922, fixed price.

Sunbula, 7 Nablus, opposite Mt Scopus Hotel, Sheikh Jarrah, T02-6721707, www.sunbula.org. Quality embroidery work, rugs, clothing, olive oil, soaps, jewellery, gifts etc, with profits going to 14 Palestinian cooperatives spread over the West Bank and Gaza. Mon-Sat 1000-1800. The original venue at St Andrew's Scottish Guest House, 1 David Remez, was closed for refurbishment at the time of writing but should soon reopen on Sun only 1000-1400 (or by appointment).

Trionfo, 9 Dorot Rishonim, T/F02-6232368, trionfo.webs.com. Sun-Thu 1000-1900, Fri 1000-1400. Tempting Aladdin's cave of Judaica and Israeliana, plus antique books (Hebrew and English), old photos, posters, prints, maps and heaps of LPs in the basement. Unique but expensive (save for the second-hand books).

Bookshops
Book Gallery, 6 Schatz, T02-6231087. Multi-levelled labyrinth packed with books in several languages, from first editions to second-hand basics.

Dani Books, 3 Even Israel, T2624-8293, Sun-Thu 0900-1900, Fri 0900-1400. Good selection of new and old fiction; will buy/ swap; sells second-hand books for around 30NIS.

Educational Bookshop, Salah El-Din, East Jerusalem. A good information point, plus there's a café. You can pick up the Alternative Tourism Group (ATG) guide *Palestine and the Palestinians*, an excellent guide for travelling in the West Bank.

Elia Photo Service, 14 Al-Khanqah, Christian Quarter, T02-6282074, www.eliaphoto. com. Sells superb black-and-white photos of Jerusalem in the 1930s-60s; prices fixed (large beautiful silver-coated prints cost 250NIS). Owner Kevork Kahvedjian also signs copies of the book Through My Father's Eyes, a collection of many of his late father's famed photos. Mon-Sat 0900-1900.

Gur Arieh, 8 Yoel Salomon, T02-6257486. An eclectic collection of second-hand stuff, some (overpriced) travel books and new stock. Plenty in English. Sun-Thu 1000-2000, Fri 1000-1500, sometimes Sat evening.

Libraire Française, Jaffa, sells French-language books, newspapers and magazines.

Munther's, American Colony Hotel, Louis Vincent, East Jerusalem. T02-6279777. Wide selection of books on the region; also readings by authors. Daily 0900-2000.

Sefer ve-Sefel ('Book and Mug'), 2 Ya'Avetz/49 Jaffa, T/F02-6248237. New and second-hand odds and ends; good selection, largely in English. Sun-Thu 0900-1900, Fri 0900-1400.

Steimatsky, 7 Ben Yehuda, 33 Jaffa, and 9 Mamilla. The latter (in the historic house where Hertzl slept) is the biggest, with best choice of travel and fiction by Israeli/Arab authors in English. Café and toilets. Sun-Thu 1000-2200, Fri 1000-1400, Sat 1 hr after Shabbat-2300.

Trionfo, 9 Dorot Rishonim, T/F02-6232368, trionfo.webs.com. Great antique maps, posters, plus some old (but cheap, 5NIS) English titles in the basement. Sun-Thu 1000-1900, Fri 1000-1400.

Camping gear

Camping Jerusalem, Ben Hillel. Army surplus, lots of knives, etc. Less about tents and camping gear.

Orc'ha, 12 Yoel Moshe Salomon, T02-6240655. Here in Jerusalem for the last 32 years, it's where the locals go for all their equipment needs.

Steve's Packs, 11 Ben Hillel, T02-6248302. Outdoor and camping gear, also has a branch in Jerusalem Mall, Malkha T02-6482003.

Supermarkets

Supersol, Gershon Agron. Sun-Tue 0700-2400, Wed 0700-0100, Thu 24 hrs, Sat end of Shabbat-2400.

2000 Drugstore, Shamai. Booze, fags, groceries, but controversially open 24 hrs, 7 days per week.

On the corner of Lunz, there is a 24-hr supermarket which is useful (as they say, they "don't have a door").

▲ Activities and tours

Children

Time Elevator, Beit Agron, 37 Hillel, T02-6248381, time-elevator-jerusalem.co.il. An "interactive experience" (three giant screens, moving seats and stage) takes you through 3000 years of Jerusalem's history (eight languages, frequent showings). Not recommended for pregnant women or children under five! Sun-Thu 1000-2000, Fri 1000-1400, Sat 1200-1800, adult 49NIS, student/internet booking 42NIS.

Hiking

Those intending to hike in the Jerusalem area (and elsewhere in Israel) are advised first to consult with the SPNI (see under 'Tour companies and travel agents' below).

Leisure centres

Cybex Fitness Centre, David Citadel Hotel, T02/6211111. One of the nicest in town.

Jerusalem Spa, Regency Hotel, French Hill, T02-5331234. Full facilities and fitness centre, fabulous setting.
YMCA West, 26 King David, T02-5692692. Aerobics classes, swimming, squash, tennis, etc.

Swimming

Jerusalem Pool, 43 Emek Refaim, T02-5632092. The city's only Olympic-sized pool (which is under threat of closure) has sauna, fitness room, lawns. Adult 500NIS, child 40NIS. Buses 04 and 018. Daily 0700-1900.
Mitzpeh Ramat Rahel Pool, Kibbutz Ramat Rahel, T6702920. Balloon-covered heated pool, weight and fitness room, tennis; coffee shop; year and half-year membership.

Tour operators

For tours that present a Palestinian perspective, in Jerusalem and the West Bank, also see box, page 201. **NB** Tours generally do not include entry fees to sites. Remember to take your passport with you.
Al Quds Tours, Centre for Jerusalem Studies, Khan Tankiz, Souq Al-Qattanin, T02-6287515, www.jerusalem-studies.alquds. edu. Jerusalem/Bethlehem tours from a Palestinian perspective, call for schedules.
Alternative Tours, c/o Jerusalem Hotel, off Nablus, T/F02-6283282, mobile 052-2864205, www.alternativetours.ps. Experienced and reliable Abu Hassan runs a variety of Palestinian-orientated tours including Bethlehem (3 hrs, 120NIS), Hebron (5-6 hrs, 150NIS), Jericho (half-day, 140NIS), Nablus (1 day, 180NIS), plus refugee camps (3 hrs, 100NIS), and Qalqilya/the wall, (full day, 180NIS). Also organises transport to airport/Allenby Bridge etc. Recommended.
Archaeological Seminars, Jaffa Gate, T02-5862011, www.archesem.com. A variety of walking tours with a Jewish slant for up to 10 people, half ($200) or full ($350) day, plus dig-for-a-day at Beit Guvrin archaeological park ($30 plus 20NIS entrance fee, 3 hrs).
Ateret Cohanim, T02-6284101, www.ateret. org.il. This organization is involved with 'settling' Jews in the Christian and Muslim Quarters of the Old City. They arrange short tours in the old city and will explain their viewpoint.
issta, 4 Herbert Samuel, T02-6211888. Good for student-priced flights, etc.
Green Olive Tours, T03-7219540/054-6934433, www.toursinenglish.com. Tours around East Jerusalem, West Bank and Israel, single or multi-day, some political and others focussed on sights. Comprehensive list on website, easily booked online. Fred runs his office out of the Gate Café, by Damascus Gate. Recommended.
Holycopter, T050-2411339/050-9313144, www.holycopter.co.il. Helicopter flights over the city for $150 per person.
Jerusalemp3 Tours, www.jerusalemp3. com. Take yourself around, with a free downloadable audio tour. Lots of interesting (and less run-of-the-mill) destinations are covered, eg Ein Karen, Nachalot.
Mazada Tours, 9 Koresh, T02-6235777, www.mazada.co.il. Runs buses to Cairo on Sun and Thu, $90 single, $110 return, departs 0830, takes around 12 hrs; prices exclude border taxes of $55; buses also pick up in Tel Aviv. Their Cairo office is at the Cairo Sheraton (T00202-33488600); buses back to Israel Sun and Thu at 0800. Buses to Amman daily (min 3 persons required), each way $88, departs 0830, takes 6 hrs; prices exclude border taxes of $49; buses also pick up in Tel Aviv. Also run tours to Egypt and Jordan from Jerusalem/Tel Aviv, and from Eilat to Petra/Wadi Rum, plus choice of other tours.
Mike's Centre, nr Station IX (off Souq Khan al-Zeit), T02-6282486, www.mikescentre. com. 1-day tours to Galilee $65 (Wed and Sun) and Masada (Mon, Tue, Thu and Sat) $50; half-day (Tue and Fri) to Bethlehem $40.
Sandemans New Europe, c/o Steimatzky's Bookshop, Mamilla Avenue, T02-6244726, www.neweuropetours.eu. You can't miss the guys in red t-shirts just inside Jaffa Gate offering free tours (on a tips basis) at 1100 and 1430 every day, lasting around 3 hrs. It's

'Masada Sunrise Tour'

For those visitors to Israel with limited time, the 'Masada Sunrise Tour' offers a cheap and convenient way of seeing some of Israel's most spectacular (but remote) sights. Packed into a non-stop 12 hours you will get to climb Masada for sunrise, float in the Dead Sea, hike in Ein Gedi , pass by Qumran and enjoy the panoramic view of Jerusalem from the Mount of Olives. And, unless you are on a tour led by an Israeli, you'll probably visit Jericho and see St George's Monastery in Wadi Qelt as well. All this for just $50 (excluding entrance fees). Too good to be true? Of course there are both advantages and disadvantages to seeing Israel in this way. For a start, the tour is extremely rushed. Mount of Olives, St George's Monastery, Jericho and Qumran are little more than 'photo stops' (with most people too knackered to even bother getting out the minibus at the latter), whilst the short time spent at Ein Gedi Nature Reserve does not allow you to get away from the hordes of visitors who just pop in for an hour or so. Further, the 0300 departure time is a real killer (and

very cold if the minibus is late), whilst some people feel the "sunrise over the Dead Sea" is not all it's cracked up to be! That said, there are enough advantages to make this tour worthwhile, particularly to those on a tight budget. For example, the cheapest accommodation at Masada and Ein Gedi is some $30 per night, so you're half-way to saving the tour price already. Also, you need not worry about the Dead Sea Region's irregular transport connections; to do the same tour by public transport would probably take three to four days. And finally, by travelling as a group you gain the advantage of reduced admission prices.

If you do take the tour, make sure that you bring some warm clothes for the Masada climb (and wait for the bus), drinking water and food (most the places you pass are expensive), swimming costume and towel for the Dead Sea, and money for admission fees. And backpackers, please, organise all these things the night before so you don't wake up the rest of the dorm with the rustling of those bloody bags!

a jovial introduction to the old city with a fair sprinkling of history. Office Sun-Fri 1200-1900, Sat 1200-1330.

Society for the Protection of Nature in Israel (SPNI), 13 Heleni HaMalkha, T02-6244605, tourism@spni.org.il, www.teva.org.i/englishl. SPNI organize a series of excellent guided tours in Israel, all of which involve some hiking, with accommodation in field schools: 3-day Galilee and Golan ($395), 3-day Upper Galilee crossing ($395), 4-day Negev and Eilat ($485), 2-day Masada, Ein Gedi and Dead Sea ($295), 1-day Wadi Qelt ($125), and Jerusalem Old City, Mt of Olives ($95). Individuals can join but a minimum of 10 persons is required; email them for schedules.

Zion Tours, off 19 Hillel, T02-6254326, mark.feldman@ziontours.co.il. Cheap airfares, Sun-Thu 0830-1730.

Zion Walking Tours, near Jaffa Gate (opp entrance to Citadel), T/F02-6261561, 052-5305552, zionwt.dsites1.co.il. Long-established tour company; tours last 3 hrs: Old City $30, Mount of Olives $40, 'Underground' City $35 (good way to see the Western Wall Tunnels, book in advance), Bethlehem $40, Mount Zion and City of David, plus others.

Transport

Air

The vast majority of airlines only have offices in Tel Aviv. **Arkia**, T*5758, for reservations in

Israel; www.arkia.co.il). No flights on Shabbat within Israel, and few charter flights abroad. Call for schedules, as they vary according to demand. **Israir**, T0516-5931785, www.israirairlines.com. Domestic flights. **El-Al**, 12 Hillel. T02-9771111, Sun-Thu 0830-1830, Fri 0830-1300. **SAS**, 14 Az-Zahara, T02-6283235.

For details of air tours around Jerusalem, see above. There are buses from Jerusalem's Central Bus Station to Ben-Gurion Airport (see page 19), as well as taxis (see page 26).

Bus

Jerusalem's Central Bus Station is located on Jaffa Rd, to the west of the New City centre. See Ins and outs, page 53. Information booths are relatively helpful. The multi-storey bus station has a plethora of shops, toilets and places to eat. **Central Egged bus** information www.egged.co.il, T03-6948888 or speedial T*2800, Sun-Thu 0700-2000, Fri 0800-1500, Sat 30 min after conclusion of Shabbat to 2300.

Akko: go to Haifa and charge. **Ashkelon**: 437, Sun-Thu half-hourly 0630-2200, Fri last at 1630, Sat first at 1800, 1½ hrs, 24NIS. **Be'er Sheva** direct: 470, Sun-Thu every 1-2 hrs 0600-2200, Fri last at 1600, 1½ hrs, 31.5NIS. **Be'er Sheva** via **Kiryat Gat**: 446, Sun-Thu 2 per hr, Fri last at 1545, Sat first at 2045. Bet Shean: 961, every hr Sun-Thu 0700-2030, Fri until 1530, Sat 2040 and 2245, 2 hrs, 44NIS. **Bet Shemesh**: 417, Sun-Thu 2 per hr 0550-2400, Fri last at 1630, Sat first at 2100, 1 hr, 15NIS. **Bnei Brak**: 400, Sun-Thu every 15 mins 0630-2330, Fri last at 1600, Sat first at 1915. **Eilat**: 444, Sun-Thu 0700, 1000, 1400 and 1700, Fri 0700, 1000 and 1400, Sat 0000, 5 hrs, 73NIS, book 2-3 days in advance. **'En Gedi**: 421 and 486, 7 per day 0800-2030, Fri 5 per day, Sat bus 487 2200, 1 ½ hrs, 36NIS, or bus 444 (see 'Eilat, above) 1 hr. **Haifa** direct: 940, Sun-Thu every hr 0600-2000, Fri last at 1630, Sat first at 2100, 3 hrs, 44NIS. **Haifa** via **Hadera** and **Netanya**: 947, every 30 mins Sun-Thu 0600-2100, Fri last at 1630, Sat first at 2040. **Kiryat Arba** (for Hebron): 160, Sun-Thu every 30 mins 0530-2200, Fri

last at 1630, Sat first at 2125, 1¼ hrs. **Kiryat Shemona**: 963, Sun-Thu 5 per day 0630-2330, Fri 0715, 1130 and 1400, Sat 2130 and 2330, 4 hrs, 61NIS. **Latrun**: 404, 432, 433 and 434, frequent service, Sun-Thu 0630-2330, Fri until 1640, Sat from 2000, 30 mins, 17NIS. **Masada**: see "En Gedi' and 'Eilat' buses above. **Nahariya**: go to Haifa and change. Netanya: 947, see 'Haifa via Netanya' above. **Ramla**: 433, 435 and 404, frequent service, 1 hr. Safed: 982, Sun-Thu 7 per day 0920-2320, Fri 7 per day until 1320, Sat 21250 and 2320, 3½ hrs, 44NIS. **Tel Aviv** direct: 405, Sun-Thu every 15 mins 0550-2350, Fri last at 1700, Sat first at 2030, 1 hr, 20NIS. Tiberias 962 and 963, Sun-Thu hourly 0630-2330, Fri last at 1600, Sat first at 2040, 2 hrs, 40NIS. For buses to Cairo see Tour operators, above.

For the West Bank mini-buses are the main transport link to **Ramallah** (north) and **Bethlehem** (south) from Jerusalem. Bus 18 to Ramallah (30 mins, 6NIS) departs from Suleiman, just outside Damascus Gate (exit Damascus Gate, turn right). For **Nablus**, go to Ramallah and change. For **Bethlehem** (45 mins, 4-6.5NIS), take minibus 21 to **Beit Jala** from where it is a 15 min walk to the centre of town, or minibus 124 to the large checkpoint on the outskirts of Bethlehem from where you need to get a taxi or walk about 30 mins. For **Jericho** change in Ramallah or Azariya; for **Hebron** change in Bethlehem.

Car hire

Most of the car hire firms have their offices on King David, near the Hilton Jerusalem. Note that most will not cover damage or theft that occurs on the West Bank (including East Jerusalem). Offices are generally open Sun-Thu 0800-1800, Fri 0800-1400. Book online to get special deals. **Avis**, 22 King David, T02-6249001, www.avis.co.il.
Budget, 23 King David, T03-9350015, www.budget.co.il.
Eldan, Eldan Hotel, 24 King David, T02-6252151/2, www.eldan.co.il/en.
Goodluck, Nablus (next to American

Colony), East Jerusalem, T02-6277033, reservation@goodluckcars.com. Cars are insured for travel in the West Bank.
Nesher Taxis, 21 King George, T02-6257227. The best way to get to Ben-Gurion Airport (45 mins); book ahead and they will pick you up. Allow plenty of time since the taxi may drive all over Jerusalem picking up other pre-booked passengers. In the Old City they will usually only arrange to pick you up from outside the tourist office at Jaffa Gate. The Ben-Gurion sherut operates on Shabbat, but reservations aren't taken: you'll need to book on Fri morning if travelling between Fri afternoon and Sun morning.

Another option is **Mike's Centre**, nr Station IX (off Souq Khan al-Zeit), T02-6282486, www.mikescentre.com. 24-hr service, leaving from Jaffa or New Gate, 4 hrs before departure, 65NIS per person.

Sheruts

Sheruts to and from Tel Aviv arrive and depart from the junction of HaRav Kook and Jaffa, close to Zion Square (50 mins). They also wait outside the Central Bus Station for departures to Tel Aviv. Sheruts run on Shabbat.

Train

Jerusalem's train station is inconveniently located in Malha to the southwest of the city. Route and fare information can be found at www.rail.co.il; T03-6117000 or speed dial T*5700, Sun–Thu 0600–2300, Fri 0600–1500, Sat from half an hour after Sabbath until 2300. On weekdays there are 10 services to Tel Aviv (1½ hrs, 20.5NIS one way) and, though it's slower than the bus, it's a very pleasant journey.

ⓘ Directory

Banks Banking hours are Sun, Tue and Thu 0830-1230 and 1600-1700, Mon, Wed and Fri 0830-1200. All banks have 24-hr ATM machines offering shekel advances on most cards. Hotels are bad places to change money. Note that post offices offer commission-free foreign exchange for travellers' cheques. There are also a number of legal money-changers inside Damascus Gate who offer good deals on travellers' cheques and cash. Those travelling on to Egypt or Jordan are recommended to buy a supply of Jordanian Dinars/Egyptian Pounds in advance. **American Express**, 18 Shlomzion HaMalka, T02-6240830. Sun-Thu 0900-1700, Fri 0900-1300, member services including clients' mail. **Embassies and consulates** Many nations still refuse to recognize Jerusalem as Israel's "eternal undivided capital", and so retain their embassies in Tel Aviv. Some, however, maintain consulates in Jerusalem, though you may be referred to Tel Aviv for certain matters. **Belgium**, 5 Biber, Sheikh Jarrah, East Jerusalem, T02-5828263; **Denmark**, 10 Bnei Brith, T02-6258083; **France**, 5 Emil Botta, T02-6259481, and Sheikh Jarrah, East Jerusalem, T6282387 626-2236, www.consulfrance-jerusalem.org; **Italy**, 16 November, T02-5618966; **Spain**, 53 Rambam, T02-5633473; **Sweden**, 58 Nablus, East Jerusalem, T5828117 02 582-8212/13; **UK**, 19 Nashashibi, Sheikh Jarrah, East Jerusalem, T02- 6717724, and 5 David Remez, West Jerusalem, T02 -6717724, www.britishconsulate.org; **US**, 27 Nablus, East Jerusalem, T02- 622-7221/6287137 (come here for visa services), or 18 Agron, T02-6227230, http://jerusalem.usconsulate. gov/. **Ministry of Foreign Affairs**, Press Office, T5303343. Ministry of Information, Beit Agron, 37 Hillel. The place to come for your Israeli press card. Visa extensions from the Ministry of Interior, 24 Hillel Street, T02-6294726, *3450. **Hospitals** The world-famous **Hadassah Hospital** in 'En Karem (T02-6777333, www.hadassah.org.il), or its sister on Mount Scopus (T02-5818111), are capable of dealing with all emergencies, though you should make sure that your medical insurance is up to it. **Bikur Cholim Hospital**, 74 HaNevi'im, T02-6461111, www.bikurholim.org.il, may be a better bet for the budget-minded. **Terem Immediate Medical Care**, Magen David Adom Building, 7 HaMemGimel, T1-599-520520, www.terem.com, offers what its name suggests.

Internet Café Net, 3rd Fl, Central Bus Station, T02-5379192. Sun-Thu 0530-2400, Fri 0530-hr before Shabbat, Sat hr after Shabbat-2400. Cheap, fast, half-price happy hour Sun-Thu 2300-2400. **CCS**, 17 Zahra, East Jerusalem, T02-6261705. Computers for use 10NIS 1hr, Sat-Thu 0700-1800. **Internet**, 31 Jaffa St (opp Holy Bagel), T02-6223377. Good for night-owls, 15min 5NIS, 1 hr 14NIS, 10 hr member 110NIS. Sun-Thu 0900-0600, Fri 0900-1600, Sat 1930-0600. **Internet Café**, 2 HaRav Kook (corner with Jaffa), T052-4831038. Fast computers, new and relatively quiet, but only 1030-2400, closed Fri and Sat. 15 min 5NIS, 1 hr 14NIS, 2 hrs 25NIS. **Mike's Centre**, nr Station IX (off Souq Khan al-Zeit), T02-6282486, www.mikescentre.com. Cheapish: 5 mins 1NIS, 1 hr 10NIS. Daily 0900-2300. **Old City Net**, Latin Patriarchate, Jaffa Gate. Nice setting. **Sandemans New Europe**, c/c Steimatzsky's Bookshop, Mamilla, T054-8831447/02-6244726. Free internet in this friendly independent travellers' centre where there's also bike hire. **Sports Bar**, 10 Agrippas. Up-to-date technology; alcohol available (happy hour daily till 2000); smoking section; sports on LCD screens, 1 hr 14NIS (8NIS with flyer). Sun-Thu 0900-0300, Sat after Shabbat -0300. **YE Communications**, 31 Emek Refa'im,

T050-5242091, www.asim.co.il. Sun-Thu 0900-1900, Fri 0900-1300. 30 mins 10NIS.

Language Courses Al-Quds University Centre for Jerusalem Studies, Khan Tankaz, Suq Al-Qattanin, Old City, T02-6287517, www.jerusalem-studies.alquds.edu. Regular 2-month Arabic courses. **Gerard Behar Centre** (Beit Ha'am), 11 Bezalel, T02-6240034/6254156. Intensive courses only, 5 times per week. **Hebrew Union College**, 13 King David, T02- 6203333, hsaggie@hotmail.com. 3-month ulpan twice a week; tourists accepted. **Milah**, 4 Mevo HaMatmid, T02-623 3164/6249834. www.milah.org. Intensive course 4 days a week. **YMCA**, 26 King David, T5692673/05-2674770, www.simplehebrew.com. 3 days per week, 900NIS for 3 months; geared towards English speakers. **Laundry** Mike's Place, nr Station IX (off Souq Khan al-Zeit), T02-6282486, www.mikescentre.com. 2.5kg 17NIS, 4.5kg 30NIS, wash only (add 10NIS for drying). Daily 0900-2300. **Post office** Post offices are generally very busy and operate on a numbered ticket system. GPO, 23 Jaffa, T02-6244745. Sun-Thu 0700-1900, Fri 0700-1200. Poste restante, parcel mail. There are branch offices in the New City on Ezra M Mizrachi, in East Jerusalem on Salah al-Din (Sun-Thu 0800-1800, Fri 0800-1200), in the Old City opposite Citadel (open till 1400) and the Jewish Quarter.

Contents

Footprint features

West Bank

The area known as the 'West Bank' (of the Jordan River) is the heart of the biblical regions of Judea and Samaria, and contains some important historical-archaeological sites. However, the population is overwhelmingly Arab Palestinian (Muslim and Christian), a population that rejects the Israeli rule that has been imposed upon it since the Six Day War of 1967.

Most of the international community regard the West Bank as territory 'occupied' by Israel, thus making any Israeli (Jewish) settlement here illegal; whilst Palestinians view the West Bank as the heart of the future Palestinian state. Tourists will have to deal with some practical difficulties when visiting the various West Bank sights, but as a foreigner can enjoy the peculiar privilege of free movement – something neither a Palestinian nor an Israeli can do.

Highlights of the West Bank include the Church of the Nativity in Bethlehem, the birthplace of Jesus, and the surreal Herodium, Herod's palace-fortress in the wilderness. The Haram el-Khalil/Cave of Machpelah in Hebron is an unforgettable experience, an active place of worship split in two that seems to sum up the craziness of Middle East politics. To the east, the beauty of the Wadi Qelt ravine and lonely St George's Monastery lead you to Jericho, the world's oldest walled city. Make sure you spend a Thursday night out in Ramallah, and seek out the views from Mt Gerizim, near Nablus, where time seems to have stood still.

Ins and outs

This chapter refers to this area as the 'West Bank' simply because this is the term most familiar to an English-speaking audience. Used in the context of this Handbook it has no political connotations. If this Handbook was written in Hebrew it would use the expression 'Judea and Samaria', and in French 'Cisjordanie'. For a brief summary of the politicization of the geographical nomenclature, see 'History' below.

Tourists generally use Jerusalem as a base to visit the various West Bank sites in a series of extended day trips, but there are decent enough hotels in all big West Bank towns, and budget travellers should be able to find something in their price range, allowing the Palestinian economy to benefit from the much-needed tourist dollar. Transport arrangements are complicated somewhat by checkpoints and the separation barrier (see box, next page), though as a tourist you are free to cross in and out, even if it takes some time.

Most of the Jewish settlements are served by Egged buses from the Central Bus Station in Jerusalem (you pay an added extra for the bullet-proof glass) which as a foreigner you are also able to use. The Palestinian towns and villages are best served by minibuses from two bus stations outside Jerusalem's Damascus Gate. Green and white buses leaving from Nablus Street are heading north to Ramallah, while the blue and white buses leaving from Sultan Suleiman Street go south to Bethlehem and Beit Jala. Some of the sites described in this 'West Bank' chapter are fairly remote, and are not served by public transport. Those travelling in a hire car should note that Israeli car rental agencies are not insured for their vehicles to travel beyond the 'Green Line' (this can also apply to East Jerusalem). You can overcome this by renting in East Jerusalem or Ramallah, though the cost of the vehicle is consequently higher. Therefore, often the best way to reach these outlying sites is to hire a taxi at the nearest town.

For the best (and only) selection of maps for the West Bank, visit the **UN OCHA office** ⓘ *MAC House, 7 St George, T02-5829962*, in East Jerusalem (just past the Museum on the Seam, on the right-hand side if you're heading north). The maps are given out free of charge, or are downloadable at www.ochaopt.org.

Background

Geography Covering a total land area of 5,860 sq km, the West Bank has a surprising diversity of geographical features. Topographically it is dominated by the Central Range made up of the rolling hills of Judea and Samaria, a beautiful patchwork of rocky hilltops and fertile valleys, scattered with age-old silver-green olive trees. And though the West Bank is today largely demarcated by the separation wall which generally follows the 'Green Line', there are also very clear physical boundaries. To the north, the Jezreel Valley (Plain of Esdraelon) divides the Central Range between Samaria and Judea to the south, and Galilee to the north; to the west the West Bank is defined in topographical terms by the Maritime Coastal Plain, and to the southwest by the Shephelah; to the south the hills of the Central Range around Hebron meet the Negev arid area; to the southeast is the stark yet beautiful Judean Desert, whilst the eastern limits of the West Bank are defined by the Jordan River itself. Much of the Jordan Valley and the northern section of the Dead Sea are included within the political boundary of the West Bank's 'Green Line'.

Climate Most of the West Bank falls within a Mediterranean climatic zone, with dry hot summers and mild humid winters. Aspect and altitude have an important influence, with winter snows not uncommon on the higher ground, and rainfall higher on west-facing

Warning: travelling around the West Bank

Situations can change very quickly here, and thus you are advised to seek up-to-date advice on recent events in the places that you are intending to visit. Though your embassy or consulate is a good place to start, they tend to provide the most pessimistic view of safety levels, and may even attempt to discourage you from going. A good bet is to ask other travellers who have visited these places, starting with the New Palm Hostel opposite Jerusalem's Damascus Gate, or any other of the East Jerusalem hotels. If you don't want to travel independently, there are several excellent tour operators to the West Bank who can provide fascinating insights into the situation and handle the transport difficulties for you (see boxed text, opposite). As a very general rule, in towns such as Bethlehem or Jericho that are part of the tourist trail, there are no special security precautions. In smaller towns you might be looked on as something of an oddity, but are likely to be treated very cordially for having bothered to visit at all. Hebron remains the most volatile West Bank town, and you should seek further authoritative advice before visiting, and scan recent news to see if there has been any trouble.

Transport arrangements are complicated by the fixed checkpoints into (but mostly out of) West Bank towns and cities. All the checkpoints are open to foreign tourists (large red warning signs forbid Israelis from entering). Keep an eye on the situation at Qalandiya checkpoint into Ramallah, which is a flashpoint for violence as it is next to the Qalandiya refugee camp (note that Fridays in particular often see stone-throwing). Getting caught up in a 'situation' is a frightening experience. The Hizmah checkpoint (used by Jewish settlers) allows quicker and easier access to Ramallah and the northern West Bank for those in their own vehicle. You may also encounter a 'flying checkpoint', which consists of two jeeps parked on the road and searching cars. Drive slowly on the approach to any checkpoint; if it is dark turn off your headlights and put the interior light on. There is no need to lie to soldiers; greet them with "shalom", be polite and honest, and you should have no problems.

Most of the Jewish settlements are served by Egged buses from the Central Bus Station in Jerusalem. The Palestinian towns and villages are best served by service-taxis or minibuses, which can be picked up from near Damascus Gate. Some of the sites described in this West Bank chapter are fairly remote, and are not served by public transport. The best way to reach these outlying sites is to hire a taxi at the nearest town. Those renting a vehicle should note it needs to be insured for travel in the West Bank, and that standard car-hire firms in Israel do not offer this option. You will need to rent a vehicle in East Jerusalem or Ramallah, and the price will be somewhat higher, at around $40 per day. Yellow (Israeli) licence-plated vehicles are becoming more common in the West Bank, while green or white plates are allowed in the West Bank only.

When visiting Palestinian towns and villages, it is worth making your 'foreign tourist' status very clear, though this does not necessarily mean flashing expensive cameras around or wearing a Hawaiian shirt. Appearing non-Israeli/Jewish is the key, unless of course you are visiting Jewish settlements. In effect, caution and common-sense should be your watchwords. **NB** You must **carry your passport at all times**. Backpackers who have overstayed their visa should forego visiting the West Bank since a random ID check may ultimately result in deportation. All visitors to the West Bank should remember to dress conservatively, with upper arms and legs covered. Women should bring some form of scarf, which comes in handy when visiting religious sites.

Palestinian perspectives

Alternative Tourism Group, 74 Star Street, Beit Sahour, Bethlehem, T02-2772151, www.atg.ps. Political tours to West Bank destinations. Also recommended are the "Nativity Trail" walking tours, which cover 160 km in 11 days. Going mostly through the West Bank (Nazareth to Bethlehem), bags are transported between the nightly stops. Also have volunteer opportunities.

Alternative Tours, c/o Jerusalem Hotel, off Nablus, T/F02-6283282/052-2864205, www.alternativetours.ps. Long-established tour operator going to all West Bank towns, plus Qalqilya and the wall. Political half-day and one-day tours.

Al Quds Tours, Centre for Jerusalem Studies, Khan Tankiz, Souq Al-Qattanin, T02-6287515, www.jerusalem-studies.alquds.edu. Jerusalem and Bethlehem tours from a Palestinian perspective. Breaking the Silence, www.breakingthesilence.org.il. Tours taken by ex-IDF soldiers who have something to say about their role and the work of the IDF in the West Bank. Tours go to Hebron or the South Hebron Hills. Fascinating and highly informative.

Green Olive Tours, T03-7219540/054-6934433, www.toursinenglish.com. Tours all over the West Bank and Israel, Fred is pretty unique in that he's an Israeli working with Palestinian tour guides. Single or multi-day trips, some are very political while others focus more on the sights. Also a great link to homestays and guesthouses around Bethlehem and elsewhere.

Palestinian Association for Cultural Exchange (PACE), Nablus Road, Al-Bireh, Ramallah, T02- 2407611, www.pace.ps. Half-day through to 10-day tours of the West Bank.

Also see www.visitpalestine.ps

---

slopes than on the relatively arid east-facing slopes. The further east you move, the greater the fluctuations in temperature, with an extreme climate in evidence in the Jordan rift valley and Judean Desert regions.

History The idea of 'the West Bank' as a single political or geographical unit is a comparatively recent phenomenon. Prior to the founding of the State of Israel in 1948, Palestinians living on the West Bank tended to refer to themselves as citizens of a particular city, town or village. The UN Partition Plan of 1947 (Resolution 181), however, envisaged the bulk of what is now known as the 'West Bank' as forming the heart of a future Arab state, though most Palestinians rejected this as a 'division of the homeland'. Following Israel's independence war, the term 'West Bank' was used to describe the area to the west of the Jordan River that King Abdullah incorporated into Transjordan (subsequently the Hashemite Kingdom of Jordan). It is important to note that Abdullah deliberately avoided using the term 'Palestine' in an attempt to stifle nascent Palestinian identity, thus hoping to legitimize his rule over the 'West Bank'. Right-wing Israelis, such as the prime minister Benjamin Netanyahu, suggest that Abdullah "invented" the term "West Bank" "in order to obliterate the historic and on-going Jewish connection to the land" (*A Place Among the Nations: Israel and the World*, 1993). Only Britain and Pakistan recognized Abdullah's claim to the West Bank.

However, there are far older names for the West Bank. As much as Palestinians and left-wing Israeli 'doves' would like to dispute the point, this is the land of *Eretz Yisrael*, the centre of the biblical Israelite kingdoms of **Judea** and **Samaria**. Those looking for the heart of the Jewish connection to the land need not look to Galilee, the Mediterranean coast, or the Negev: it is here, on the West Bank. Thus, the Israeli religious-right who want the right to settle anywhere in the land of *Eretz Yisrael* don't want to live in Tel Aviv or Eilat; they want to settle in Shechem, Samaria, Shiloh and Hebron. The more secular settlers have tended to develop towns in the commuter belt, closer to the 'Green Line', and within easy access of the Israeli towns where they work. Israel's settlement of the West Bank/Judea and Samaria was facilitated by its capture in the Six Day War of 1967. The revival by Israel of the terms Judea and Samaria to describe the West Bank is often described as a politicization of the geographic nomenclature, though in reality the name West Bank is equally loaded.

The Israeli claim to this land is of course complicated by the fact that, for the past millennium, the population of West Bank has been predominantly (Muslim) Arab. The current population estimates for the West Bank suggest fewer than 350,000 Jewish settlers (plus about 210,000 in East Jerusalem) and 1,500,000 Palestinians. Few nations recognize the Israeli claim to the land (though Israel has not attempted to annex it, unlike East Jerusalem), with most states regarding the West Bank as being 'occupied territories', thus making any settlement activity there illegal under international law. To the international community, biblical arguments are irrelevant.

Israeli-Palestinian Interim Agreement (Oslo II) The Oslo II Accords divide the West Bank into three categories. In Area A, consisting of the main urban areas (and 17% of the land), the PA has powers and responsibilities for internal security and public order. In Area B, the PA has responsibility for public order for Palestinians while Israel maintains overriding responsibility for security with the purpose of protecting Israeli nationals and confronting the threat of 'terrorism'. Areas A and B cover about 41% of the land area in the West Bank and 96% of the population. Area C covers Jewish settlements and areas of 'strategic importance', with Israel responsible for civil affairs and all security. The percentage of the West Bank's population that are Jewish settlers (excluding East Jerusalem) is around 4%.

Bethlehem

→ *Colour map 2, grid C4.*
In appearance Bethlehem is a typical Palestinian Arab town; but one whose economic base is distorted out of all proportion by its dependence on the pilgrim and tourist trade arising from the fact that this is the site of the birth of Jesus. The town's key attraction is Christendom's oldest complete and working church, built over the traditional site of the Nativity. A number of other sites in and around the Bethlehem area are also based upon (less well-founded) biblical traditions. The old market centre, though it has been repaved and sanitised, is still full of character and life, while the out-lying villages of Beit Sahour and Beit Jala have a mellow atmosphere all of their own.

Ins and outs

Getting there and away Bethlehem is easily visited as a short excursion from Jerusalem, just 8 km away. Mini-bus 21 (6.5NIS) from Sultan Suleiman bus station (near Damascus Gate) goes to Beit Jala, west of Manger Square. This avoids having to stop

Bethlehem

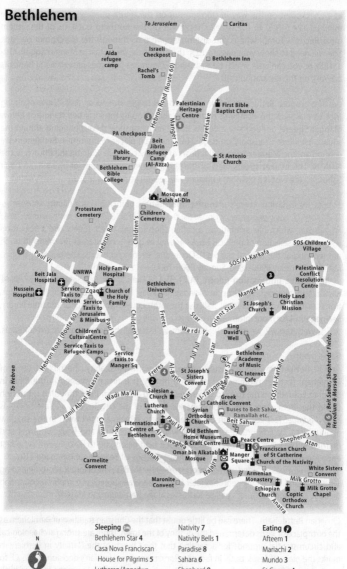

To Jerusalem

□ Caritas

□ Aida refugee camp

Israeli Checkpost

□ Bethlehem Inn

Rachel's Tomb

Hebron Road (Route 60)

Manger St

Palestinian Heritage Centre

✝ First Bible Baptist Church

Havelsake

③

PA checkpost

Beit Jibrin Refugee Camp (Al-Azza)

✝ St Antonio Church

Public library

Bethlehem Bible College

Mosque of Salah al-Din

Protestant Cemetery

Children's Cemetery

Children's

Hebron Rd

SOS Children's Village

Paul VI

⑦

SOS/Al-Karkafa

Palestinian Conflict Resolution Centre

Beit Jala Hospital

UNRWA

Holy Family Hospital

Bab Zqaq

Church of the Holy Family

Bethlehem University

Manger St

③

Holy Land Christian Mission

St Joseph's Church

Hussein Hospital

Service Taxis to Hebron

Service Taxis to Jerusalem & Minibus

Children's

Orient Star

Wardi Ya

King David's Well

Bethlehem Academy of Music

Ⓢ

Frères

Star

Jul Jul

Service Taxis to Refugee Camps

Children's CulturalCentre

⑨

Service taxis to Manger Sq

Al-Batin

St Joseph's Sisters Convent

Al-Taraqma

Ⓢ

ICC Internet Cafe

SOS/Al-Karkafa

To Hebron

Frères

Al-Batin

②

Salesian Church

Wadi Ma'Ali

Lutheran Church

Paul VI

Al-Fawagh

Greek Catholic Convent

Syrian Orthodox Church

①

Buses to Beit Sahur, Ramallah etc.

Beit Sahur

To Beit Sahur, Shepherds' Fields; Herodium & Marsaba

Jamil Abdel al-Nasser

Al-Saff

Carmel

International Centre of Bethlehem

Old Bethlem Home Museum & Craft Centre

Shepherd's St

Atan

Carmelite Convent

Qanah

Omar bin Alkatab Mosque

Peace Centre

①

Manger Square

Franciscan Church of St Catherine

Najala

④

✉

Church of the Nativity

Maronite Convent

Anatra

Armenian Monastery

White Sisters Convent

Ethiopian Church

Coptic Orthodox Church

Milk Grotto Chapel

Milk Grotto

N

100 metres

100 yards

Sleeping 🛏

Bethlehem Star **4**
Casa Nova Franciscan House for Pilgrims **5**
Lutheran/Annadwa & Il'iliyeh **2**
Jacir Palace **3**

Nativity **7**
Nativity Bells **1**
Paradise **8**
Sahara **6**
Shepherd **9**

Eating 🍴

Afteem **1**
Mariachi **2**
Mundo **3**
St George **4**

at a checkpoint on the way in (though not on the return journey). Alternatively, take minibus 124 (4NIS) to the Israeli checkpoint on the northern outskirts of Bethlehem (near Rachel's Tomb) where you disembark and pass through the checkpoint on foot. You will need to show your passport. On the other side, take a taxi to Manger Square (10-15NIS), or you can walk which takes around 20 minutes and goes past some of Banksy's artwork on the separation wall.

Getting around Bethlehem is compact enough to get around on foot. Those planning trips to places in the vicinity of Bethlehem should go to the local bus stand just below **Manger Square**, or negotiate a deal with the numerous taxi drivers hanging around the square itself (see 'Transport' on page 214). The main places of interest in Bethlehem are centred around **Manger Square**, the heart of the town, where you find the Church of the Nativity. The market streets west of the square have some points of interest, and Beit Sahour to the east is a pleasant Christian village with attractions that are worth visiting.

Tourist information There's a **tourist information point** ⓘ *Peace Centre, Manger Sq, T02-2766677, www.peacenter.org, open 0900-1530 (or until 1800 when events are on), closed Fri and Sun*, which has exhibitions, a coffee shop (closes 1600), toilets and a bookshop with a good selection of political books as well as gifts. Free internet (in theory, though not working at the time of our visit). Occasional evening concerts. The building is open Monday-Saturday 0900-1800, Sunday 0900-1600.

Alternative Information Centre (AIC) ⓘ *111 Main Street, Beit Sahour, T02-2775444, www.alternativenews.org.* Drop in Monday-Saturday 1000-1700 to pick up information from the local and international staff, use the internet (with your own PC) and little library. See page 214 for more information on their activities.

The website www.whatsinbethlehem.com has lists of all the hotels, stores and restaurants.

Background
Jewish Bethlehem Though usually associated with Christianity, the biblical town of Bethlehem features prominently in Jewish history. It is first mentioned in the Bible in defining Ephrath, on the road to which Rachel died and was buried, though it is through **David** that Bethlehem rises to prominence. A son of the city, he was anointed here as king (*I Samuel 16:1-23*), though Bethlehem was to remain a small town in the shadow of Jerusalem. David's grandfather, Obed, was the son of Ruth and Boaz, who met and married in the town (*Ruth 4:17*). The supposed field belonging to Boaz, in which he first encountered Ruth, is an attraction in the nearby village of Beit Sahour (see page 210).

Bethlehem was included within Rehoboam's (929-911 BCE) line of fortifications defending Jerusalem, and some nine centuries later it again became strategically important guarding the road to Herod the Great's palace-fortresses at the Herodium and Masada.

Christian Bethlehem There can be little doubt that the Christian tradition of Bethlehem as the birthplace of Jesus determined the destiny of the town. There are strong archaeological and circumstantial grounds for accepting that the Church of the Nativity in Bethlehem marks the place of Jesus' birth. In fact, the Roman emperor Hadrian's decision in 135 CE to plant a grove dedicated to the pagan god Adonis at the traditional cave site of Jesus' birth did not so much divert Christian attention away from the spot as mark the site out for the next two centuries. However, it is fairly safe to assume that Luke's gospel account of the events leading up to the birth of Jesus is fundamentally flawed (see box opposite).

Luke's gospel and the birth of Jesus

Luke's assumption that Mary and Joseph lived in Nazareth prior to Jesus' birth (*Luke 2:4*) is largely based on the premise that since Jesus was brought up there as a child (*Matthew 13:54; Luke 4:16*), and had relatives there (*Matthew 13:55-56*), his parents must have lived there before his birth. A reading of Matthew's gospel, however, suggests that Mary and Joseph were in fact natives of Bethlehem (*Matthew 2*), only later moving to Nazareth in order to avoid the murderous designs of the Herodian dynasty, or perhaps seeking work at the grand building project at Sepphoris (Zippori). This presented Luke with a dilemma since he needed to place the couple at Bethlehem for the birth of Jesus. He did this by invoking the census of Quirinius (Cyrenius, governor of Syria), suggesting that Joseph had to come to Bethlehem since he was "of the house and lineage of David" (*Luke 2: 4*). However, this census did not actually take place until 6 CE.

Luke's gospel is largely responsible for the image of the Nativity that most adults from some form of Western Christian background grow up with: the Christmas carol picture of "no room at the inn" and Jesus' subsequent birth in a stable. However, this whole image could largely be based upon a flawed translation of the gospel, with the Greek underlying the line "she laid him in a manger because there was no room for them at the inn" (*Luke 2:7*) also capable of being translated as "she laid him in a manger because they had no space in the room". Though there is no specific mention of a cave in the gospel account of the Nativity, it may be possible that in order to avoid the overcrowding within the house that Joseph shared with his parents, the couple moved to the cave area at the back of the house that was a feature of most of the homes in the Bethlehem area at the time. The manger element of the story is probably derived from the fact that such a cave would have been used as a shelter for the domestic animals during periods of bad weather. Interestingly, second-century CE Christian references to the Nativity all speak of Jesus' birth in a cave, whilst the area beneath the Church of the Nativity that is today venerated as the birthplace of Christ is part of a cave complex.

The first church built to commemorate the site of the Nativity was constructed by the emperor **Constantine**, and dedicated by his mother **Queen Helena** in 339 CE. Just under 50 years later, **St Jerome** settled in Bethlehem with a group of Roman matrons (including St Paula and St Eustochium), thus founding an important monastic tradition in the town. During his period of residence in Bethlehem, St Jerome translated the Bible from Greek and Hebrew into Latin, creating *The Vulgate*, or authoritative version of the Bible that the Roman Catholic Church used right up until the 20th century. The 'study' that he used whilst working on the translation is said to be one of the caves in the complex beneath the Church of the Nativity.

The subsequent history of Bethlehem is effectively the history of the Church of the Nativity. Like the rest of the town it was largely damaged in the Samaritan revolt of 529 CE, before being rebuilt on a much grander scale by the emperor **Justinian I** (527-565 CE). Remarkably, the church survived the Persian invasion of 614 CE that brought destruction to most churches in the country (Jerusalem in particular). Legend suggests that the invaders recognized the dress of the Magi ('three wise men') in the mosaic on the west façade, and spared the church out of respect for their ancestors. It even survived al-Hakim's destructive

Christmas in Bethlehem

Bethlehem hosts three Christmases. The (Latin) Roman Catholic and Protestant celebrations are held on 24 to 26 December, and the Greek Orthodox church also uses this date. Those wishing to attend the midnight mass will require a special ticket, available from the Franciscan Pilgrim's Office (T02-6272697) at the Christian Information Office opposite the Citadel, inside Jerusalem's Jaffa Gate (T02-6272692, www.cicts.org). It's free, though you may have to pretend that you are Catholic (and you should have your passport with you when you go to the service). The Orthodox churches (except for the Greek) celebrate Christmas on 6 January, whilst the Oriental Orthodox (Armenian, Coptic, Ethiopian, Syrian, etc) church holds its services on 18 January. Visitors should note that accommodation rates in Bethlehem sky-rocket, and those without confirmed reservations may find 'no room at the inn'. However, as traditional Christmas preparations start two weeks before the Western calendar date of 25 December, with a Christmas tree and lights in Manger Square and the surrounding streets, you can always go and soak up the atmosphere ahead of time.

Christmas in Bethlehem can be very cold, and heavy snow is not unknown.

edict of 1009, probably because Muslims had been allowed to perform devotions here for several centuries (Jesus is a prophet within Islam, though not the son of God).

The Church of the Nativity was held particularly dear to the **Crusaders**, with Baldwin I crowning himself king there on Christmas Day 1100. When the Latin Kingdom collapsed following defeat at the Horns of Hittim in 1187, the Ayyubid dynasty respected the sanctity of the church, though subsequent dynasties such as the Mamluks and Ottomans systematically looted the place. The **British** captured the town from the Turks without a shot being fired three days before General Allenby entered Jerusalem in 1917. The town was occupied by the **Jordanians** following the termination of the British Mandate in 1948, finally coming under **Israeli** control during the Six Day War of 1967.

Recent history In December 1995 Bethlehem became autonomous of Israel under the remit of the Palestinian Authority, an event marked at the traditional Christmas Eve celebrations in the Church of the Nativity by the presence of a beaming Yasser Arafat. With its economic well-being relying almost entirely on the pilgrim and tourist trade, Bethlehem is a very vulnerable town. This sector of the economy was very badly hit by the lack of visitors during the *intifadas*, and, coupled with the closure of other work opportunities beyond the separation barrier, unemployment in the town currently runs at about 60%. The urban population of Bethlehem (c. 75,000) was previously evenly split between Christian Arabs and Muslim Arabs, though the recent exodus of Christian families has now put the Muslims very much in the majority. The Christian population is now estimated at 15% when once it was 80% (in 1948). The siege in the Church of the Nativity in 2002, which lasted 39 days, brought international condemnation of Israel for their attacks on a holy site where Palestinian militants had taken refuge. The situation was eventually resolved by negotiation, and the militants were sent into exile in Gaza and Europe (eight had been killed).

Sights

Greek Orthodox Monastery of Mar Elias

ⓘ *Mon-Sat 0800-1100 and 1300-1700 (ring bell on right side of main door), Sun 0900 and 1730 for services. Modest dress essential.*

On the Hebron Road between Jerusalem and Bethlehem is the **Greek Orthodox Monastery of Mar Elias**, on the left 5 km after Jerusalem. This marks the traditional site where the prophet Elijah rested, although there are some later traditions associated with this spot. Mar Elias is believed to answer the prayers of barren women and sick children. The exterior's imposing walls exhibit enclosed stone balconies, while the interior has been modernised with some high quality paintings on the iconostasis.

Church of the Nativity

ⓘ *Summer 0600-1800, winter 0800-1730, free, donations accepted. Modest dress essential.*

From the outside, the Church of the Nativity bears a greater resemblance to a medieval citadel than a place of worship, neatly encapsulating the history of competing faiths in the Holy Land. It is hard to distinguish which of the solid walls hides the actual Nativity church when viewing it from Manger Square, but roughly speaking it is the middle section. The northern (left) portion is the comparatively modern Franciscan Church of St Catherine, whilst on the south (right) side is the Armenian Convent, and the higher tower to the right belongs to the Greek Orthodox Convent.

Church of the Nativity

1 Lintel, 6th century
2 Lintel, 6th century
3 19th-century Buttress
4 Main Entrance / Door of Humility
5 Narthex
6 Doorway
7 Nave
8 St Canute
9 St Olaf
10 St Cathal
11 Baptismal Font
12 South Aisle
13 Greek Orthodox High Altar
14 North Aisle
15 South Wall
16 North Wall
17 4th-century Mosaic below trapdoors
18 South Transept
19 Altar commemorating Circumcision
20 Steps to Grotto of the Nativity
21 Steps up from Grotto of the Nativity
22 North Transept
23 Door in North Aisle
24 Entrance to Cave Complex
25 Toilets

Caves beneath Church
(see 'Grotto of Nativity' map)

The entrance to the church through the **western façade** has been considerably altered down the years, though evidence of the three sixth-century CE entrances can still be seen. When standing a few metres back, the tips of the **lintels** (1) (2) of two lateral doors can be seen projecting beyond the 19th-century **buttress** (3). It is easy to see how the **main entrance doorway** (4) has been reduced in size, firstly by the Crusaders and then in the Mamluk or Ottoman period. The entrance is often referred to as the **Door of Humility** (4), though this probably has far less to do with the idea of all visitors having to bow their heads to enter than with the very practical measure of defence: not only did it prevent horsemen from riding directly into the church, it also stopped looters wheeling their carts all the way in!

The Door of Humility leads into the Justinian **narthex** (5), though the partitions are of a later date. Only one doorway (6) now leads into the central **nave** (7). A few carved panels are all that remain of the heavy wooden entrance door made by an Armenian carpenter in 1227. The main body of the church remains largely unchanged since Justinian had it built in the sixth century CE, though, in the tradition of the Eastern Orthodox church, the nave is devoid of furniture. The graceful red limestone **pillars** were probably part of the original fourth-century CE Constantine church, with the stone having been quarried locally. Many of the pillars were decorated with paintings of saints during the Crusader era, with the most notable images being those of Canute of Denmark and England (8), Olaf of Norway (9) and Cathal of Ireland (10). The passage of time means the pictures are hard to make out. One of the columns bears an image of Christ, with reports in December 1996 suggesting that it was "weeping for the sins of the world". The original **octagonal baptismal font** (11) from the Justinian church occupies a new position in the south aisle (12). It was probably moved here during the Crusader restoration of the church, having previously stood above a cistern close to the present high altar (13).

The interior walls of the north (14) and south (12) aisles of the nave were decorated with mosaics during the Crusader period, small sections of which remain intact. The **south wall** (15) featured depictions of the seven ecumenical councils, below which were images of the genealogy of Jesus according to the Gospel of Matthew (*Matthew 1:1-17*). The **north wall** (16) bore themes representing six of the provincial councils (Antioch, Ancyra, Sardica, Gangra, Laodicea and Carthage) above figures illustrating the genealogy of Jesus according to the Gospel of Luke (*Luke 3:23-38*). A series of **trapdoors** (17) in the floor of the nave reveal parts of the mosaic floor of the original fourth-century CE Constantine church.

The **high altar** (13) is hidden by the iconostasis, or ornately carved screen hung with icons. The **altar** (19) in the south transept (18) belongs to the Greek Orthodox Church and commemorates the Circumcision. Two flights of steps lead down to the **Grotto of the Nativity** (those to the south (20) for going down, those to the north (21) for coming up). It can get ugly round here, with unruly battles between pilgrims all struggling to fit through the small doorway all at the same time.

The **Grotto of the Nativity** is part of a complex of caves that marks the traditional site of the birth of Jesus. At the bottom of the steps (20) a large silver star (a) in the floor, encircled by oil lamps and icons, marks the scene of the Nativity. The present star belongs to the (Latin) Catholic church and dates to 1717, though it was removed by the Orthodox church in 1847 following a dispute. Though the Ottoman authorities ordered the star returned some six years later, this trivial quarrel was one of the factors that led to the Crimean War between Russia and the alliance of Britain, France and Turkey (1853-56). Like the

Grotto of the Nativity

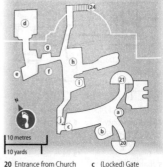

10 metres
10 yards

20 Entrance from Church of the Nativity
21 Exit from Church of the Nativity
24 Entrance from Franciscan Church of St Catherine
a Silver Star marking Birth Place
b Representation of the Manger
c (Locked) Gate
d Cave of St Jerome
e Tomb of St Jerome
f Tombs of St Paula & St Eustochia
g Tomb of Eusebius
h Chapel of the Holy Innocents
i Altar to Joseph's Dream
j St Jerome's Passage

Church of the Holy Sepulchre in Jerusalem, different sects of the Christian church battle it out for guardianship of this holy place. Fortunately here there are only three players (Greek Orthodox, Roman Catholics, Armenians), though this has not prevented some bitter and bloody battles over such trivial matters as cleaning rotas and prayer times. Close to the star marking the Nativity is a representation of the Manger (**b**). A narrow passage reputedly cut by St Jerome leads to other points of interest within the cave complex, though this passage is blocked by a locked door (**c**). They are accessible, however, through the entrance (**24**) in the Franciscan Church of St Catherine (see below). Return to the main church above via the steps (**21**).

Exit the Church of the Nativity via the door in the north transept (**22**) into the Franciscan Church of St Catherine, or via the door in the north aisle (**23**) into the attractive Franciscan cloister.

Franciscan Church of St Catherine
① *T02-2742425, daily 0530-1730, free, donations accepted; toilets. Modest dress essential.*
Based on an original Crusader construction, this Roman Catholic church was rebuilt in 1882 and then modified again in 1949. The midnight mass held here on Christmas Eve is broadcast around the world. The medieval cloister to the west of the church is particularly attractive.

A number of steps in the south aisle lead down to the cave complex connected to the Grotto of the Nativity. Amongst these are: the **Cave of St Jerome** (**d**), where he reputedly completed the translation of the Hebrew and Greek Bibles into the Vulgate; the **tomb of St Jerome** (d. 420 CE) (**e**); the **tombs of St Paula** (d. 404 CE) and **St Eustochia** (d. 419 CE) (**f**); the **tomb of Eusebius** (**g**); the **Chapel of the Holy Innocents** (**h**), dedicated to those massacred by Herod (*Matthew 2:16*); and an altar commemorating Joseph's dream that he should flee to Egypt (**i**); and finally the passageway (**j**) to the Grotto of the Nativity reputedly cut by St Jerome. These identifications have no archaeological value.

Armenian Monastery
① *Daily 0530-1800, closes one hour earlier in winter, free, donations accepted.*
It is sometimes possible to visit the Armenian Monastery, adjacent to the Church of the Nativity. It is particularly noted for its use of blue tile-work on the chapel, as well as the splendid view from the roof.

Milk Grotto Chapel
① *Daily 0600-1145 and 1400-1700, free, donations accepted; toilets.*
Five minutes' walk along Milk Grotto Street from the Church of the Nativity, this Franciscan chapel is built above the cave where the Holy Family reputedly hid prior to their flight into Egypt. It takes its name from the white-coloured rock on the floor that supposedly turned that colour when a drop of Mary's milk fell on it whilst she was nursing Jesus. The chapel is popular with women praying for fertility (testimonies decorate the walls), and presumably good lactation. The present chapel dates to 1871, though the tradition dates to the sixth century CE. The seductively lit cave interior is a rather attractive spot, from which passages lead off to the impressive modern space for services.

Old Bethlehem Home Museum
① *Off Paul VI Street, T02-2742589, Mon-Sat 0800-1200 and 1400-1700, closed Thu pm, 8NIS.*
This small museum attempts to recreate 19th-century Bethlehem, using exhibits of costumes, furniture, handicrafts, photographs and jewellery displayed in two old

Palestinian houses. It is a mild diversion and it's interesting to see the building's interior as much as to view the artefacts. It is also home to the Arab Women's Union craft centre, see Shopping, page 214.

King David's Well
ⓘ *Off Manger Street, known here as King David Street, daily 0700-1200 and 1400-1900.*
The Second Book of Samuel tells how David declared "O that someone would give me water to drink from the well of Bethlehem which is by the gate!" (*II Samuel 23:15*), but then refused to drink because of the risks taken by three of his followers when they broke through the Philistine lines to fetch the water. Instead he offered it to God. During the Crusader period the cistern in the Church of the Nativity above which the octagonal baptismal font originally stood became associated with this tradition, though now the revered site is a series of three restored cisterns.

Palestinian Heritage Centre
ⓘ *Manger St, www.palestinianheritagecenter.com, T02-2742381/052-2227844, Mon-Sat 1000-1800, or call to arrange a visit out-of-hours.*
Director Maha Saca seeks to promote and preserve the cultural heritage of Palestine, as well as to employ local women as embroiderers (goods are for sale in the gift shop). There is a re-creation of life in a Bedouin tent, a Palestinian living room, and the (obligatory) dressing up in Arab costume for a photo souvenir.

Rachel's Tomb
ⓘ *Sun-Wed 0030-2230, Thu open all night, Fri until 3 hrs before Shabbat, Sat open 1 hr after Shabbat, free. Bus 124 from East Jerusalem stops at the checkpoint just to the north of the tomb, from where you walk to the nearby yellow barrier, show your passport and hitch a lift with a passing pilgrim. Alternatively, armoured Bus 163 goes from the Central Bus Station in West Jerusalem every couple of hours.*
The traditional site of the tomb of Rachel, Jacob's fourth wife, is located on the northern outskirts of Bethlehem, the town to which she was travelling when she died giving birth to Benjamin (*Genesis 35:16-19*). Rachel is venerated by Jews, Christians and Muslims alike, though within Jewish tradition she is regarded as something of a 'mother of the nation', and the shrine here is particularly busy with Jewish women praying for fertility and safe birth. The tomb itself is probably medieval, though substantial repairs were carried out in the 19th century and minor renovations done in 2006. The cenotaph draped with shiny gold-embroidered cloth inside the tomb is certainly not the one described in the Bible (*Genesis 35:20*). Sexes are segregated by a screen; modest dress must be worn, and men must wear one of the cardboard yarmulkes provided. A violent flashpoint since the mid-1990s, particularly during the second intifada, the area is heavily militarised, and the tomb itself is now annexed by a series of walls which create a corridor of access for Jewish pilgrims. Muslims, who know the tomb as Masjid Bilal, can no longer enter the area.

Beit Sahour

Ins and outs
Getting there and around Bus 47 runs to Beit Sahour from the bus stand behind and below the Manger Square police station in Bethlehem (five minutes, 1NIS). The square where Bus 47 terminates (before returning to Bethlehem) is where you may be able to get

a service taxi (and definitely able to get a 'special' taxi) to the **Herodium**. From here the sites are marked, but if you want to save a walk the clunking local bus first passes the Greek Site and then goes on to the Roman Catholic site.

Field of Ruth and Shepherds' Fields
The small Arab village of Beit Sahour lies 1.5 km east of Bethlehem and is the scene of a number of biblical traditions. It is supposedly the setting for much of the *Book of Ruth*, including the scene in which Boaz (David's great-grandfather) first observed **Ruth** in his field gleaning the ears of corn (*Ruth 2:2-3*). A particular site in the village is referred to as the **Field of Ruth**, whilst the Hebrew translation of Beit Sahour means 'Village of the Watching'.

Beit Sahour is also home to the Christian tradition of the **Shepherds' Fields** where, according to Luke's gospel and the Christmas carol, the shepherds "watched their flocks by night" and were then greeted by the angel with the news of Jesus' birth (*Luke 2:8-20*). The site was first noted in the fourth century CE by Christian pilgrims, anxious to see the spot where the angel appeared to the shepherds, and there are now competing Greek Orthodox and Roman Catholic sites marking the traditional spot.

Greek Orthodox site
ⓘ *Daily 0800-1130 and 1400-1700, free. Ring the doorbell by the main gate to gain admittance.*
The Greek Orthodox site is marked by an attractive raspberry pink-domed church completed in 1989. The earliest remains here date to the fourth century CE, and comprise one of the earliest Christian mosaic floors excavated in the country. The floor is believed to belong to the "splendid cave with an altar" first described by the pilgrim Egeria in 384 CE, and later enlarged in the fifth century CE with the construction of a simple church above it. Vigils were held in this 'Church of the Shepherds' (known locally as **Kaniset er-Ru'at**) on the eve of Epiphany in the early fifth century CE. In the following century a new basilica was built above the existing church. Its northern aisle became a burial place for nuns and monks serving the church, with over a hundred skeletons having been excavated (a couple of skulls are on display). A much more elaborate basilica was built in the sixth century CE, emphasizing the importance of the site to the early-Christian church. The basilica was destroyed in the Persian invasion of 614 CE, rebuilt in the seventh century CE, before finally being destroyed in the 10th century CE. In addition to the ancient remains, the modern church is also worth visiting.

Roman Catholic site
ⓘ *T6472413, daily 0800-1130 and 1400-1730.*
The Roman Catholic site is administered by the Franciscans, and is known locally as **Siyar el-Ghanam**. The compound includes the remains of a church built in the late fourth or early fifth centuries CE, later converted into a monastery in the sixth to eighth centuries CE. Most observers now believe that this complex was simply another Byzantine monastery in the Judean Desert, and not specifically connected with the tradition of the Shepherds' Fields. The modern **Chapel of the Angels**, completed in 1954, is another attractive ecclesiastical design by the Italian architect Antonio Barluzzi.

Bethlehem listings

For Sleeping and Eating price codes and other relevant information, see Essentials pages 26-31.

Sleeping

Bethlehem's hoteliers have suffered badly since the Al Aqsa uprising, the 2002 siege and the building of the wall. Most pilgrim groups make a whistle-stop visit to the Church of the Nativity, while independent travellers frequently opt for day tours from Jerusalem. However, there is much to be gained from a night or two's immersion in Bethlehem and, although choice in the budget price range is limited, haggling out of season can get results. A good choice for budget travellers are home-stays with local families, which can be very good value and also offer half-board for between 100-150NIS per night (arrange through www.toursinenglish.com and www. alternativetours.ps/). Bethlehem's hotels tend not to be as overpriced as those in Jerusalem, though don't expect great luxury. Advance booking is essential over the Christmas period, when prices sky-rocket (24-26 December add at least 50% to the prices quoted below). Breakfast is included, unless stated otherwise.

L Jacir Palace Intercontinental, Hebron Rd, T02-2766777, www.intercontinental.com. This is an Arabesque fantasy of mellow stone – it makes a sharp contrast to the nearby graffiti-ed slabs of the separation wall. The original building dates from 1910, with a modern extension added with 250 extra rooms. It is good value for money ($180 per couple) for such a beautiful place. Zeitouneh restaurant serves excellent food (bit of a wait), the bar is nice, and there is an outdoor pool and spa. Recommended.

A Nativity Bells, Nativity, T02-2748880, www.nativitybellshotel.com. Brand new hotel designed rather like a mall, near main bus station, 10 mins' walk to Manger Square. Spacious rooms, some 4-bed, plain unfussy furnishings, quality furniture, shiny

bathrooms. Some rooms have balconies, and views of Nativity Church (plus building constructions!) or to Shepherd's Fields. Bar, a/c-heater, TV.

A Paradise, Manger St, T02-2743769/42, www.paradisebethlehem.com. Large 5-storey hotel. Modern a/c rooms are plainly furnished, with TV and radio, fridge, a/c-heater. There's a restaurant and bar.

A Shepherd, Jamil Abdel al-Nasser, T02-2740656-8, www.shepherdhotel.ws. Cosier, more homely than most, lobby bar is welcoming, rooms rather flowery, central a/c and heating, large bathrooms with fussy curtains, TV, phone. Decent choice.

B Bethlehem Star, Freres, T02-2743249, www.star-inn-hotels.com. Slightly depressing brown-themed rooms and corridors (single $40, double $60) with central a/c, TV, and breakfast room with panoramic views. Free Wi-Fi in lobby. Good management makes it a reasonable choice.

B Casa Nova Palace, Manger Sq, T02-2742798, www.casanovapalace.com. Franciscan pilgrim house, with superb setting right next to the Church of the Nativity (a door leads from the lobby into cloisters of St Catherine's Church). Nicely furnished a/c rooms in vaguely Arabesque style, comfortable beds, TV, phone, internet connection (singles $45, doubles $60). Pleasant terrace restaurant/bar.

B Lutheran Guest House/Annadwa, 109 Paul VI, T02-2770047, F02-2770048, nodeh@ annadwa.org. Part of the International Centre of Bethlehem complex, in the heart of town, this 13-room guest house is cosier than most hotels. Rooms are very small, simply but pleasantly furnished, bathrooms are best around, TV, heaters, a/c, internet point. Enjoy the peaceful interior and outdoor spaces of the Centre, which has a little café-bar (Al-Kuz). Contact Mr Naim Odeh to book a room; prices fluctuate ($45-60) depending on demand.

B Nativity, Paul VI, T02-2770650, www. nativityhotel.com. Large hotel with large rooms, comfortable if characterless, a/c-heater,

TV. Close to the Bab Zqaq minibus stop (for Jerusalem/Hebron) and the attractive village of Beit Jala, though it's a 20-min walk to Manger Square). Bar with pool table, very pleasant staff. Ring ahead to negotiate on price and ask for room at rear with views of olive trees rather than the main road.

B Sahara, Shepherds' Fields, Beit Sahour, T02-2772428, sahara.hotel@live.com. Located next to the Roman Catholic site, this new hotel has sparkly rooms with flat-screen TVs, great bathrooms, and no fussy furnishings. Restaurant and bar; rooftop area planned. Good discounts given, nice staff. Good choice.

C Al Beit Guest House, Beit Sahour, www. arabwomenunion.org. Run by the Arab Women's Union in order to generate income to fund their many worthy projects, this is a nice little place with modest prices. All rooms have bathrooms and have been recently renovated, and there's an outside terrace. It's about a 15-min walk from the bus station in Beit Sahour.

D Bustan Qaraaqa, Beit Sahour, T02-2748994, www.bustanqaraaqa.org. The Bustan Qaraaqa works with the local community to raise environmental awareness and look for sustainable means of production. They are setting up a permaculture project (volunteers are welcomed). Accommodation-wise, their guesthouse is an excellent budget choice: a dorm bed is 100NIS full-board (mattresses on floor) in a pleasant stone room. Wonderful rural setting. Call at least a week in advance to see if there is space.

D Everest, Paul VI, Beit Jala, T02-2742604, makkrum@yahoo.com. Small, modest hotel in the attractive village of Beit Jala, with good-value rooms ($25 for a couple) and the all-important heater. Internet connection. Restaurant (grills, salads, etc). Different vibe out here at the tip of Beit Jala among the pine trees.

Eating

In addition to the hotel restaurants (notably Zaitouneh in the Jacir Palace), there are a few places around Manger Square that you may care to consider, and some quainter choices in Beit Sahour.

¶ Al Andalus, T02-2743519, serves basic Middle Eastern fare, plus 'Western' favourites such as burgers and hot-dogs.

¶ Dar Al Balad, Beit Sahour, T02-2749073. Quality Mediterranean/Italian/Middle Eastern food in a beautiful old house (one of the town's oldest). The building also houses an 'artisana' on the first floor, with space for craftspeople.

¶ Il'iliyeh Restaurant, International Centre of Bethlehem, 109 Paul VI, T02-2770047. Daily from around 1800. Lovely upstairs outdoor terrace in summer.

¶ Mariachi, Grand Hotel, Freres, T02-2741440. Mexican restaurant; the lobby bar is more authentic than most.

¶-¶ Citadel (Al-Qala'a), Beit Sahour, T02-2775725. Crypt-like smoky bar is good for a beer, or the restaurant is strangely appealing with its bad art, Bedouin clothing on walls and stone floors. Choice of Chinese or burgers, but it's the Arabic salads/shish kebabs/fish and other Palestinian delicacies you should be sampling. Outdoor patio seating in good weather. Daily 1200-2400.

¶-¶ Grotto, Arafat St, Shepherds' Fields, Beit Sahour, T02-2748844, www.grotto-restaurant.com. Not at all like a grotto (very roomy), Bedouin patterns, big windows and Har-Homa views, welcoming Carlsberg sign. Nargila 15NIS, beer 12NIS, fish, shish kebab and salads. Daily 1130-2300.

¶-¶ Mundo, Manger St, T02-2742299. Flags, neon and wooden interior give a vaguely US feel to this busy pizza joint (22-65NIS), with big-windowed back terrace. Family-friendly. Daily 1100-2300.

¶-¶ St George, T02-2743780. Receives good reviews for its Middle Eastern cuisine. The interior layout is not appealing, but prices are fair and the location handy; serves alcohol. Daily 0800-1730.

¶-¶ The Tent, Arafat St, Shepherds' Fields, Beit Sahour, T02-2773875. The original tent is open 1200-2400 every day; the same vibe and food as the Grotto (above). Popular for tour groups and locals alike.

¶**Afteem**, Manger Sq, T02-2747940, afteemrestaurant@yahoo.com. From the outside it just looks like a typical falafel stall, but surprisingly pleasant under-the-arches style interior. Has served the usual salads, hummus and (great) falafel since 1948. Clean, busy and friendly. Mon-Sat 0730-2130 (opens on Sun during Christmas). Recommended.

Bars and clubs

Bethlehem is not a place to head if you're after wild nightlife, but most of the hotels have a bar, the coffee shop scene is good, and there is a lively cultural scene to tap into if you hit the right night.

AICafé, Alternative Information Centre (see below). Café Tue and Sat from 1830 for coffee and beers, before (and after) events hosted here. Gathers together the international community of Bethlehem as well as local faces. Taybeh 15NIS.

Al-Kuz Coffee shop/bar, International Centre of Bethlehem. Drinks and snacks in a pleasing little space, glass art on the stone walls, Taybeh/Carlsberg 15NIS. Daily 1000-2030 (ish).

Al Makan bar at the **Jacir Palace** is swish, and the Bethlehem Star bar attracts a few drinkers.

The Citadel in Beit Sahour is a perfect spot for a clandestine beer.

Entertainment and events

Alternative Information Centre (AIC), 111 Main Street, Beit Sahour, T02-2775444, www. alternativenews.org. A joint Israeli-Palestinian activist organization, seeking to disseminate information, involved in advocacy and practical grassroots activism. Every Tue and Sat at 1930 the café has an interesting film/ discussion/lecture on relevant topics. Library free for anyone to join. From the bus station in Beit Sahour, look for the orange signs for 'Adal', and AIC is just next door.

Al-Liqa' Centre for Religious & Heritage Studies in the Holy Land, T/F2741639;

Bethlehem Academy of Music/Bethlehem Music Society, Manger St, T02-2777141; **International Centre of Bethlehem**, 109 Paul VI, T02-2770047, www.annadwa. org, holds a concert and play each month, plus films. Look out around town for their *Where to Go leaflet* which lists the month's events. The complex contains the 'Cave' where art/photo exhibitions are held and documentaries can be shown on request (there is also literally a cave). Toilets, coffee shop, space to hang out.

National Conservatory of Music, T02-2745989.

Shopping

Most of the tacky tourist stuff is found on Manger Square, Milk Grotto Street, al-Nizhma (Star) Street and Paul VI Street, but there's a few tasteful scarves and kaffiyehs in the mix. The old tradition of mother-of-pearl carving still continues, introduced to Bethlehem by monks in the 14th century, with crosses, earrings and picture frames being popular items.

Arab Women's Union, off Paul VI, T02-2742589, www.arabwomenunion. com. Beautiful selection of cross-stitch embroidery pieces in many designs, often using non-typical colour schemes. Bags, shawls, and many a placemat. Prices range from 5NIS for a key-ring to 500NIS-plus for decorative galabiyyas. Mon-Sat 0800-1200 and 1400-1700 (except Thu pm).

International Centre of Bethlehem Gift Shop, 109 Paul VI, T02-2770047. Has some pretty pottery, jewellery, prints by Palestinian artists, among other things. Mon-Thu 0900-1600, Sat 0900-1300 (also opens on request, just ask at ICB reception).

Transport
Bus

The main bus station is on the junction of Beit Sahour/Shepherd's Street, below street level at the back of the mall (access by elevator). No 47 runs to Beit Sahour (1NIS, 5 mins); there are also minibuses to **Ramallah**.

Service taxis to **Beit Jala** (2.5NIS, 10 mins) go from outside the front of this mall (by the Housing Bank) and these can drop you near the north checkpoint for transport back to Jerusalem, or just carry on to Bab Zqaq (junction of Hebron/Paul VI) to pick up bus 124 back to Sultan Suleiman in Jerusalem. Regular transport to **Hebron** also leaves from Bab Zqaq, on the opposite side of the road.

Car hire

Orabi, T02-5853101; Petra, T02-5820716. Most hotels can arrange car (and driver) hire. See www.whatsinbethlehem.com for a list of car rental agencies.

Taxis

The taxi stand just below (north of) Manger Square is the place to enquire about hiring a taxi to visit places such as the Herodium, Chariton, Mar Saba, Solomon's Pools and Hyrcania. Haggle like mad and make sure the conditions are clear (price, waiting time, etc). If you want to book a taxi try **Holyland Taxi**, T052-2372779 (Walid).

Directory

Banks There are plenty of money-changers at the Manger Square end of Paul VI Street. Housing Bank (by the bus station) has an ATM; another by the post office on Manger Square. **Hospitals** Holy Family, Paul VI, T02-2741151. There are other hospitals in Bethlehem, though your best bet is to get to Jerusalem. **Internet** ICC Internet Café, Manger Street (see map). **Post offices** Main Post Office, Manger Square (Mon-Fri 0800-1700, Sat 0800-1430).

Around Bethlehem

The Herodium, the most visually stunning of all Herod's palaces as well as the location of his tomb, is worth any transport hassles to reach there. Meanwhile, Solomon's Pools (just a short excursion from Bethlehem) are little visited yet never fail to amaze the rare tourist by the sheer scale and ingenuity of their construction.

The Herodium → *Colour map 2, grid C4.*

ⓘ *T057-7761143/057-7762251, www.parks.org.il, daily 0800-1700, winter -1600, closes one hour earlier on Fri, adult 25NIS, student 21NIS, child 13NIS. Entrance to Lower Herodium free (though you are not encouraged to visit). Snack shop, toilets. Israeli citizens should call in advance.* Located some 10 km southeast of Bethlehem is a volcano-like hill, on the summit of which is the Herodium (Herodion, or in Arabic Jebel Fureidis). This palace-fortress complex represents one of Herod the Great's most ambitious building projects. At the base of the hill is a series of palace annexes and entertainment facilities known as Lower Herodium. The site is well preserved, and highly recommended not just for its historical/archaeological value, but for the fine view that it affords across the surrounding Judean Desert as it drops down to the Dead Sea.

Ins and outs

Getting there and away It's a bit of a pain to reach the Herodium by public transport. You can take Bus 47 from Bethlehem to Beit Sahour, and then wait around in the parking lot that serves as a bus stop until there are enough people to fill a service taxi heading in the direction of (Arab) Tekoa (the local price is 3NIS). Disembark at the roundabout near the site. Alternatively you can hire a taxi privately ('special'). Bargain hard, though expect to pay around 150NIS for the vehicle to take you there, wait, and return (or 50NIS one-way). Make sure you specify how long you wish to stay at the site; at least one hour is needed to explore the upper and lower sites. From Jerusalem, Egged Bus 166 to (Jewish) Tekoa passes reasonably close to the site (Sun-Thu every two hours 1200-2300, Fri and Sat very restricted service). Make sure the driver knows where you want to get off. It's a 10-minute uphill walk from the stop.

Background

Much of our knowledge of the Herodium's history is derived from the writings of Josephus (*The Jewish War*; *Antiquities*), with a series of excavations at the site confirming many of the details he gives. It is worth standing facing the site and reading Josephus' description (*Antiquities XV*, 324-325).

Dating construction here can be narrowed down to a period of nine years between Herod's wedding to Mariamne (24 BCE) and the visit to Judea (including the Herodium) of Marcus Agrippa, son-in-law of Herod's patron the emperor Augustus (15 BCE). It was built at the site of one of Herod's key victories over the Hasmoneans during his flight from Jerusalem to Masada in 40 BCE. The site appears to have been particularly dear to Herod for, not only did he give it his name, he also requested that he be buried there. Josephus gives great detail of Herod's funeral cortège (*Jewish War I*, 670-673; *Antiquities XVII*, 196-199), and very recently Herod's tomb has been discovered.

The fortress was in Jewish hands at the beginning of the First Jewish Revolt (66 CE) but fell to the Romans after the capture of Jerusalem (70 CE). It was also a command post for the Jewish rebels during the Second (Bar Kokhba) Revolt of 132-135 CE. In the fifth to seventh centuries CE Byzantine monks established a monastery in the palace-fortress and built at least three churches in the Lower Herodium area.

Sights

Herodium Palace-Fortress Herod's palace-fortress complex is reached by a winding staircase around the outside of the mound. The original **monumental staircase (1)** was a far grander affair, comprising 200 white marble steps descending in a straight line from the summit's northeast corner. After a minute's walk, a left turn (after the memorial) leads to a view over a newly excavated semi-circular theatre (I) and then continues to the Bar Kokhba secret tunnels and water cisterns (a). You can choose to walk through the tunnels to ascend the mound (steep steps) now or exit from the top via this route, at the end of your visit.

Continuing around the exterior of the mound, just before the summit there is a sign on the left to Herod's tomb (m). Discovered in 2007, the finding of the tomb solves one of Israel's great archaeological

Herodium Palace-Fortress

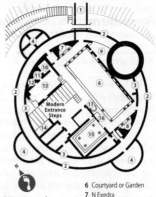

	20 metres
	20 yards

1 Herodium Monumental Staircase
2 Outer Wall
3 Inner Wall
4 N, W, S Semi-circular Towers
5 Monumental Tower or Keep
6 Courtyard or Garden
7 N Exedra
8 S Exedra
9 Underground Entrance
10 Apodyterium
11 Tepidarium
12 Frigidarium
13 Caldarium
14 Byzantine Chapel
15 Triclinium
16 Mikveh
17 Furnace

mysteries and ends 30 years of concentrated searching. The square base has been uncovered and you can view the tomb from the outside. His ornate limestone sarcophagus was found smashed inside, presumably by rebels during the first Jewish revolt. Excavations of the mausoleum continue, so you cannot enter as yet.

The palace-fortress comprises **two parallel circular walls (2) (3)**, defended by **three semi-circular towers (4)** at the north, west and south compass points. To the east stood a 45-m high monumental tower or **keep (5)**, the base of which is extremely well preserved. Both the circular walls and defensive towers are built on a series of vaults that were built to produce an artificially flat top to this natural hill.

The palace appears to have been divided into two distinct areas. The eastern section beneath the keep was occupied by a large **garden** or **courtyard (6)**, and enclosed to the north, south and west by columns, and by a wall with pilasters to the east. Two symmetrical exedrae lie to the north and south **(7) (8)**. In the northeast corner is an **underground entrance (9)** that probably dates to the First Jewish Revolt (66-73 CE); this leads into a series of secret tunnels that end up at the Herodian cisterns outside **(a)**.

The western section of the palace comprised dwellings and service rooms around pools and gardens. Of particular note here is the bathhouse, featuring an *apodyterium* **(10)**, a circular *tepidarium* **(11)** topped with a hemispherical dome, a small *frigidarium* **(12)** and a large rectangular *caldarium* **(13)**. During the Byzantine period the monks mainly occupied the still-roofed bathhouse, setting up their oven in the *caldarium*. They also built a small chapel to the south of the bathhouse **(14)**. In the southern part of the western section stood a rectangular *triclinium* **(15)**, with four columns supporting the roof (the base of one remains). This dining hall appears to have been converted into a synagogue during the Bar Kokhba Revolt, with a **mikveh (16)** being added. The Jewish rebels were also responsible for the **furnace (17)** in which they used to make arrow and spear heads.

Herodium: overview

N 200 metres / 200 yards

a Tunnels & Cisterns
b Pool
c Circular Pavilion
d Ornamental Garden
e Bath House
f Artificial Course (funerary path)
g Monumental building
h Palace
j Byzantine Churches

Lower Herodium

The Herodian structures at the foot of the hill were undoubtedly built at the same time as the palace-fortress. They are supposedly closed to the public for the next two years or so, though it is possible to explore them on your own. Standing at the top of the hill provides a good perspective. In the centre of Lower Herodium is the **pool complex**, featuring a large uncovered **pool (b)** that was fed by aqueduct from the Artas spring near 'Solomon's Pools' (see page 219). The presence of the **circular pavilion (c)** at the centre of the pool suggests that the pool's primary function was not as a reservoir, but as an artificial lake for swimming and sailing that acted as the architectural focal point of the complex. The pool was contained within a large rectangular **ornamental garden (d)**. At the southwest corner stood a large **bathhouse (e)**, built in the Roman-

Monasteries, laurae, coenobium, anchorites and archimandrites

From the fourth century CE onwards, monasticism spread throughout Palestine, with monasteries being established close to holy places generally connected with the life of Jesus. However, the monasteries that developed in more isolated environs, most notably in the Judean Desert, were rather different in character. These desert monasteries can be divided into two types, the laura and the coenobium, according to a number of factors such as the type of life practised there and the plan and architecture of the complex. Most, however, began with the decision of a single hermit to withdraw from the world (usually to a cave with water close by), with other monks perhaps joining at a later stage and thus forming a community. Whether the community became a laura or a coenobium was generally a decision of the founding hermit (**archimandrite**).

The laura was a monastery for an **anchorite** community (a term used to describe religious hermits), with monks living in solitude in individual cells but meeting for communal meals and prayers perhaps once per week. The laura comprised a series of dispersed cells connected to each other or a central building by a path. In a **coenobium** the monks tended to meet on a daily basis for prayers and meals, whilst the various monastic buildings (often including a hostel for visitors, a sick-bay, church, storerooms and workshops) were enclosed within a wall.

Mar Saba is a particularly fine example of a Byzantine period Judean Desert monastic complex, since it appears that it gradually evolved from a laura into a coenobium; the original individual cell of its founder can still be seen.

style with mosaic floors and frescoes similar to those found at Masada, Jericho and Cypros. Extending west–east from the southeast corner of the ornamental garden is a large **artificial course** (f), some 350 m long and 30 m wide, that could possibly have been used for army parades. At its western end is a **monumental building** (g), which had walls thick enough (3 m) to support a vaulted ceiling, and quite conceivably a pyramidal roof. Along part of its south side stands the remains of a large **palace** (h). Three **Byzantine churches** (j) have also been excavated in Lower Herodium.

Chariton

This little-visited monastery was founded in the mid-fourth century CE by the monk Chariton and, despite considerable hardship and persistent attacks, monks continued to occupy the monastery until the Crusader period, possibly finally abandoning it in the Mamluk period. About 1.5 km to the south of the monastery, beyond the 'Ein en-Natuf spring, is a small opening in the cliff face some 15 m above ground level known as the **Hanging Cave of Chariton**. Decorations on the cave's walls suggest that it could indeed be Chariton's cave, occupied in later years by another monk, Cyriac of Corinth (449-557 CE). Precious little remains of the monastery itself.

Bus 166 goes from Jerusalem every three hours or so to the Jewish settlement of Tekoa, about 2 km further along the road past the Herodium. Ask for directions on arrival. Obviously, do not travel in an Arab taxi to this site. A white/black trail signed to Hariton Cave passes a number of prehistoric caves before arriving at the ruins of the Chariton Monastery (3 km). The path makes a loop back to the settlement, about 1½ hours' walk.

Mar Saba Monastery

ⓘ *Daily 0700-1100 and 1330-1700, though Sun and meal times are a bad time to call, free, but donations expected. Modest dress is essential. Women are not permitted inside the monastery, only the tower (see below); Israelis can only visit on Sat.*

Few of the Byzantine desert monasteries can match Mar Saba as a spot for solitude and quiet contemplation in a stark and austere landscape. Located some 15 km east of Bethlehem, the monastic complex here clings to the cliff-face of the Kidron Valley, sprawling down from top to bottom and stretching along either side of the ravine for some 2 km.

The monastery is named after **St Sabas** (439-532 CE), who settled in a cave on the opposite side of the valley from the present main complex (look for the cave with the cross and letters 'A' and 'C') around 478 CE. Such was his fame that his period of seclusion lasted just five years, and by 483 CE so many other anchorites had sought to settle close to him that a de facto monastic community had come into being. By 486 CE as many as 70 monks were living here. Within the next 20 years the community doubled in size and two churches were built and dedicated. From 494 CE he was recognized as the archimandrite of Palestine's anchorite community (see box).

The monks here suffered greatly during the Persian invasion of 614 CE, yet despite repeated attacks throughout the Early Arab period (638-1099 CE) the laura reached its golden age during the eighth and ninth centuries CE. Mar Saba had a reputation during this period as a centre of scholarly and literary activity.

The core of the laura is still inhabited, though Mar Saba is now a coenobium covering an area some 60 m by 100 m. Many of the buildings are relatively recent, following the destructive earthquake of 1834. The **body of St Sabas** can be seen in the principal church, as can rows of skulls of martyred monks, whilst his tomb is in the paved courtyard outside. The **chapel of St Nicholas** marks the site of the first church founded here by St Sabas. If it is open, it is possible to enter the 18-m-high **Tower of St Simeon** (built c. 1612). The tower is sometimes referred to as Justinian's Tower, though the inscription dating it to 529 CE in the reign of the emperor Justinian is a forgery. Women are allowed to enter this tower, plus the **Women's Tower** (c. 1605) built outside the monastery walls, but not the rest of the complex. Be sure to drop down into the Kidron Valley and climb the other side for a memorable view of Mar Saba Monastery.

The road from Bethlehem to Ubeidiya (for Mar Saba Monastery) passes **St Theodosius' Monastery**. Founded by St Theodosius in the late fifth to early sixth century, it stands above the reputed site where the Magi (three wise men) rested on their way back from visiting the infant Jesus at Bethlehem. By the time of the founder's death in 529 CE there were said to be some 400 monks living at the monastery, though many of the residents here were massacred during the Persian invasion of 614 CE. The monastery (also known by the Arabic name of Deir Dosi) was largely restored in 1893, but visitors are rarely admitted.

The only practical way to get to Mar Saba Monastery is to hire a taxi from Bethlehem (around 160-200NIS for the return trip and waiting time, after serious bargaining). Make sure it is clear how long waiting time will be; you will need a couple of hours here if you wish to cross the ravine to get the best view.

Bethlehem to Hebron

Solomon's Pools and Artas

ⓘ *The pools are about 5 km southwest of Bethlehem, just east of Route 60. To get there, take Minibus 1 from Bethlehem to the nearby Arab village of Dashit. A good way to appreciate the*

Artas area is on a tour organized by the Bethlehem Artas Folklore Centre, T02-2760533/059-9992509, artasfcenter@gmail.com, or through www.dahertravel.com. They can also fill you in on the annual Artas Lettuce Festival (Apr).

The erroneously named Solomon's Pools are the closest perennial springs to Jerusalem at an altitude above that of the city, and have provided one of the oldest and most reliable supplies of water. A low-level aqueduct taking water from here to Jerusalem dates at least to the time of Herod the Great (first century BCE), sections of which can be seen here and around the 'Sultan's Pool' in Jerusalem (see page 148). A second, higher aqueduct was built in the late second century CE by the Romans to bring water to Jerusalem. The entire aqueduct system is a remarkable technical achievement, dropping as it does only one metre every kilometre. In later years this water-supply system was repaired by the Mamluks, then refurbished by the Ottomans, who built the fort here to defend the pools. The British also exploited the water from Solomon's Pools, and they continued to supply Jerusalem until well into the 20th century.

The **Ein Salah** spring in the nearby village of **Artas** (2 km away) fed the aqueduct that Herod built to supply the Herodium, though a Crusader period tradition has associated this village with the "enclosed garden of Solomon" from the *Song of Songs*. Such biblical traditions associated with Artas saw several Europeans, including a son of Queen Victoria, buy land in and around the village. In 1894 the Italian Order of the Sisters of Mary of the Garden built the **Hortus Conclusus Convent** in Artas.

Hebron

→ *Colour map 2, grid C4.*
The City of the Patriarchs, Hebron is the burial-place of Abraham, Isaac and Jacob, and consequently sacred to Jews, Muslims and Christians alike. Built on a series of hills and wadi beds in the Judean Hills, the city is home to a Jewish community of some 400-500 people living amongst a Palestinian population of 170,000 mainly Muslim Arabs. Around 1000 Israeli soldiers and 400 Palestinian policemen attempt, with limited success, to keep the two communities apart. In many ways Hebron can be seen as a microcosm of the Israeli-Palestinian conflict and, after Jerusalem, is perhaps the biggest potential flashpoint between the two sides.

Ins and outs

Getting there and away Hebron is most easily reached by Egged Bus 160 (8.80NIS, one hour) from Jerusalem's Central Bus Station to the 'centre' of town next to the Ibrahimi Mosque/Cave of Machpelah, going via the Jewish settlement of Kiryat Arba (see Transport, page 226 for details). Alternatively, take Bus 21 from Damascus Gate and change in Bethlehem at Bab Zaqaq (the driver will tell you where, ask for Al-Khalil) to another service taxi/mini-bus to Hebron. You will get dropped near Bab Zahwiyya in H1 zone in Hebron (see map). A private taxi direct from Damascus Gate will cost 70-100NIS. From Hebron there are service taxis to Ramallah (two hours, 25NIS; change here for destinations further north), Bethlehem (15 minutes, 7 NIS), and south to es-Samu' (see page 227).

Getting around Central Hebron, where the Mosque/Cave and Old City are found, is extremely compact and easily tackled on foot. The outer reaches of the Palestinian city are a bit of a hike, but there are plenty of taxis and service taxis from Bab Zahwiyya to get you around. Note that many roads in the Old City and between the H1 and H2 areas are closed off. You should carry your passport with you at all times (you will be asked to show it at various roadblocks).

Tourist information It goes without saying that Hebron is one of the most fascinating cities in the Holy Land and a visit is highly recommended. However, there are several factors that should be borne in mind. The situation around the old market area will always be tense, as settlers live above the streets where the Arabs work. The perpetual closure to Palestinians of Shuhada Street, where hundreds of Palestinian business were located, is a focal point for weekly protests, and the February 2010 declaration by Israel that the Cave of Machpelah/Ibrahimi Mosque was to be part of a "national heritage restoration plan" has caused outrage and led to violence. Acts of seemingly random violence are perpetrated by both Arabs and Jews. It may be as well to take advice from embassies, tourist offices, and other travellers before visiting Hebron. You can get good advice from the Christian Peacemaker team (www.cpt.org) or the **Ecumenical Accompaniment Programme in Palestine and Israel (EAPPI)** ① *T02-6289402, www.eappi.org* for the current situation. Expressing pro-Israeli views in the Arab areas is obviously not recommended. Likewise, fraternizing with Israeli soldiers and Jewish settlers may not be a good idea for the casual visitor. As with all other West Bank towns, men and women should dress conservatively.

Any problems that you encounter should be reported to the (largely Norwegian) TIPH representatives, seen around town with TIPH armbands. **Temporary International Presence in Hebron (TIPH)** ① *Dahiyyet Al-Rame, T02-2224445, to report an incident (24 hrs) T1-800-100600, www.tiph.org, Sun-Wed 0900-1200.*

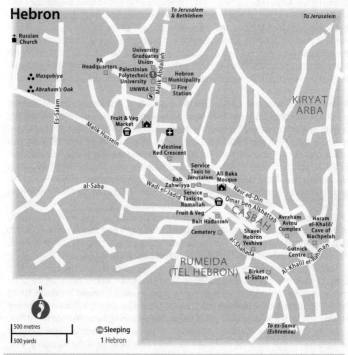

Hebron

To Jerusalem & Bethlehem

To Jerusalem

✝ Russian Church

Masqobiya

Abraham's Oak

Es-Salam

PA Headquarters

University Graduates Union

Palestinian Polytechnic University

UNWRA

Malik Abdallah

Hebron Municipality

Fire Station

KIRYAT ARBA

Malik Hussein

Fruit & Veg Market

Palestine Red Crescent

al-Saba

Wadi el-Jadid

Bab Zahwiyya

Service Taxis to Jerusalem

Ali Baka Mosque

Nasr ed-Din

Service Taxis to Ramallah

Omar ben Alkhattab

Fruit & Veg

CASBAH

Avraham Avinu Complex

Haram el-Khalil/ Cave of Machpelah

Beit Hadassah

Cemetery

Shavei Hebron Yeshiva

al-Shahada

Gutnick Centre

RUMEIDA (TEL HEBRON)

Birket el-Sultan

Al-Khalil er-Rahman

N

500 metres

500 yards

To es-Samu (Eshtemoa)

🛏 **Sleeping**
1 Hebron

Background

According to the Bible, it was at Hebron that Abraham, the progenitor of the Jewish people, first bought land in Eretz Yisrael (Genesis 23). Johnson, in his acclaimed study *A History of the Jews* (1987), suggests that this "is where the 4000-year history of the Jews, in so far as it can be anchored in time and place, began". Indeed, the purchase by Abraham of the Cave of Machpelah as a burial place for his wife Sarah and ultimately himself is probably the first actual, witnessed event in the Bible.

Abraham was buried in the Cave of Machpelah alongside Sarah, as were Isaac and his wife Rebecca, and Jacob and Leah (*Genesis 49:30-31; 50:13*). With so many important events in Jewish history having taken place here (*II Samuel 2:1-4; II Samuel 5:1-3; Samuel 15:7-12*), it is little wonder that Jews have such a spiritual and physical attachment to Hebron. Ironically, some of the antagonism between Muslims and Jews in Hebron is derived from the common origins of their faith: Hebron is holy to Muslims because Abraham (Ibrahim) is regarded in the Qur'an as "the first Muslim". Indeed in Arabic, Hebron is referred to as 'Al-Khalil' (the friend) in honour of Ibrahim's closeness to God.

Following the destruction of the Temple in 70 CE, Jews were banned from living in Hebron. The date of the Jewish return to Hebron is unclear, though Eusebius' *Onomasticon* (written before 340 CE) describes Hebron as a "large Jewish village". It is also clear that both Christian and Jewish pilgrims were visiting Hebron in the Byzantine period, whilst the superb Herodian enclosure built around the Cave of Machpelah now incorporated a Christian basilica.

The bishop Arculf (who visited c. 680 CE) describes a half-ruined town, though the Tomb of the Patriarchs/Cave of Machpelah complex remained undamaged; it subsequently became the Ibrahimi Mosque, and is now referred to in all Muslim sources as the Haram el-Khalil. Jews continued to settle in Hebron and pray at the Cave of Machpelah, but were then banned from the town by the Crusaders before being permitted to return under the Mamluks (though in 1266 they were banned by ordinance from entering the cave to pray). In 1588 the Jewish population suffered a massacre at the hands of the Ottoman Turks.

Recent events Twentieth-century Hebron has seen a depressing cycle of violence resulting from competing Jewish and Muslim, Israeli and Palestinian, claims to the holy city. A word that visitors to Jewish areas in Hebron will repeatedly hear is 'tarpat', the Hebrew name for the Jewish year 5689. In the Gregorian calendar this is the year **1929**: the year of the Arab riots all across British Mandate Palestine, and the year in which 67 members of the Jewish community of Hebron were massacred by their Muslim neighbours. What made this attack all the more despicable was that the majority of the victims were the old and defenceless, women and children. The Arab revolt of 1936 saw the British authorities evacuate the remaining Jewish population of Hebron.

The importance of the 1929 massacre in the minds of the present Jewish community in Hebron is as real today as yesterday. Indeed, a large sign on a Jewish property next to Hebron's central casbah reads "This market was built on Jewish property, stolen by Arabs, after the 1929 massacre" (see Casbah in 'Sights' on page 226).

Following Israel's victory in the Six Day War of 1967, Hebron, by now a wholly Arab town, came under Israeli control. Out of sensitivity to Muslim wishes, however, the Israeli military were under strict instructions not to allow Jewish settlement in Hebron. On 12 April 1968, **Rabbi Moshe Levinger** led 32 Jewish families into the Park Hotel in downtown Hebron and rented all 40 rooms from its owner. The original rental period was for 10 days, ostensibly to celebrate Passover, though there was an agreement between Levinger and the owner that the lease could be extended indefinitely: "Until the Messiah comes",

Levinger is said to have muttered under his breath in Hebrew, according to the journalist Robert I. Friedman (*Zealots for Zion*, 1992). The incident is said to have deeply embarrassed the Israeli government, though the truth of the matter is that Levinger's plan was perhaps the worst kept secret in Israel. A month later the cabinet voted to allow the community to remain in Hebron, subsequently moving them into a military compound. After some bitter negotiations the Israeli government eventually established (in 1970) the new Jewish settlement of **Kiryat Arba** (see page 227) on the slopes overlooking Hebron.

In March 1979 Levinger's wife Miriam led a group of 40 women and children down from Kiryat Arba and occupied the old derelict Jewish health clinic in Hebron (Beit Hadassah, see page 226), thus reestablishing a Jewish presence in the city proper. They have remained ever since and, even though their numbers are small, their impact is large, as they are among the most radical of the Israeli religious right-wing.

In February 1994, during the Oslo Peace Process, Kiryat Arba resident Dr Baruch Goldstein launched an attack on Muslim worshippers at the Ibrahimi Mosque. Twenty-nine were murdered and scores injured when Goldstein, wearing his IDF uniform and carrying his IDF-issued gun, opened fire on worshippers as they prayed. A further 30 Palestinians were killed by Israeli soldiers following the demonstrations across the country that Goldstein's act triggered. To the Israeli religious right Goldstein is a hero (his grave in Kiryat Arba mentions a "martyr" who died "sanctifying God's name") whilst Hebron's Jews dismiss comparisons between the massacres of 1929 and 1994, stating that the massacre of Jews was perpetrated by the Arab masses rather than one individual.

The long-delayed Israeli redeployment in Hebron that was a condition of the Oslo Accords eventually took place in 1997 after a long and tense period of uncertainty. Hebron was divided into **H1**, under Palestinian Authority control, and the Israeli controlled **H2** enclave at the centre of the old town. This situation remains in effect to the present day, hence connecting roads between the two areas are blocked either by gates or military checkpoints.

Sights

Cave of Machpelah/Ibrahimi Mosque The central focus of Hebron is the complex built around the traditional burial place of Abraham, Sarah, Isaac, Rebecca, Jacob, Leah and Joseph (the latter to Muslims only, with Jews believing that he is buried in Shechem, see 'Nablus' on page 256). There is also a tradition that Adam and Eve are buried here. In Jewish sources it is referred to as the **Cave of Machpelah** or **Tomb of the Patriarchs**, whilst Muslims refer to it as **Ibrahimi Mosque** or **Haram el-Khalil**. Both faiths rank the site second only to the Western Wall and Dome of the Rock respectively as a sacred site in the Holy Land.

The architectural highlight is the superb enclosure wall that Herod the Great built around the Cave of Machpelah in the first century BCE. The workmanship is excellent, with the surface of the exterior wall neatly broken up by the pilasters. The two minarets were added in the 12th century CE by Salah al-Din, though there were originally four. The top section of the exterior wall is later still, though as Murphy-O'Connor observes, "Oblivion is too kind a fate for the unknown responsible for the crenellated monstrosity that still disfigures the summit of the Herodian wall" (*The Holy Land*, 1993). It is difficult not to think of a medieval citadel when you first see the Ibrahimi Mosque/Cave of Machpelah.

From the 13th century CE onwards Muslims forbade Jews from worshipping at the Cave of Machpelah; they were limited to praying on the steps outside. The Israeli victory of 1967 saw a compromise worked out that meant the complex would remain within Muslim hands, but would allow Jews free and easy access. This all changed following Goldstein's shooting spree in 1994, and now the shrine is divided into Jewish and Muslim sections with two separate entrances. For 10 days per year the whole complex is open to Jews only, and for a further 10 days it is open to Muslims only (see www.machpela.com for contact numbers regarding the days). Security is obviously very tight, and you may well be searched two or three times before you are allowed inside. Sharp objects in your possession will probably be confiscated for the duration of your visit. Make sure that you are carrying your passport. **Modest dress is essential**.

Muslim section ① *Sun-Thu 0700-1900, Sat 1130-1900, no non-Muslims on Friday or during prayer times. Women are given a hooded cloak to wear, leave shoes outside.*

The Muslim entrance is via the **Mamluk period staircase (1)** on the west side of the Haram el-Khalil. Your attention is drawn to the fine Herodian blocks adjacent to the staircase, some of which still have the projecting knobs that protected them on their journey from the quarry to here. At the top of the staircase, on the north side of the Herodian enclosure, is the **Djaouliyeh mosque**, built c. 1318-20. The Muslim section is entered through a break in the Herodian wall **(2)**, a passageway cut sometime before 918 CE. Within the enclosure to the right (west) a slim partition **(3)** (and armed soldiers) divide the Muslim and Jewish sections. A small window grille straight ahead allows you to peer into the **tomb of Sarah (4)**.

Haram el-Khalil / Cave of Machpelah

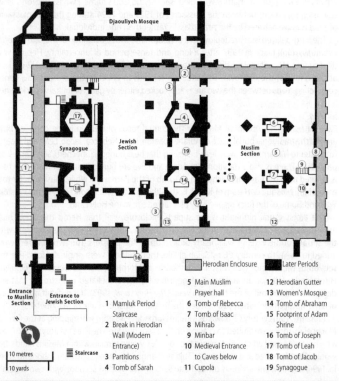

Djaouliyeh Mosque

Synagogue

Jewish Section

Muslim Section

Entrance to Muslim Section

Entrance to Jewish Section

10 metres
10 yards

≋ Staircase

N

1 Mamluk Period Staircase	5 Main Muslim Prayer hall
2 Break in Herodian Wall (Modern Entrance)	6 Tomb of Rebecca
3 Partitions	7 Tomb of Isaac
4 Tomb of Sarah	8 Mihrab
	9 Minbar
	10 Medieval Entrance to Caves below
	11 Cupola
	12 Herodian Gutter
	13 Women's Mosque
	14 Tomb of Abraham
	15 Footprint of Adam Shrine
	16 Tomb of Joseph
	17 Tomb of Leah
	18 Tomb of Jacob
	19 Synagogue

■ Herodian Enclosure   ■ Later Periods

Entering the Muslim main prayer hall (5) it is easy to see the Mamluk influence in the use of coloured inlaid marble. The hall has changed hands and hence form through the centuries, revealing Byzantine, Crusader and Mamluk influence. The cenotaphs marking the **tomb of Rebecca (6)** and the **tomb of Isaac (7)** date to the visit in 1332 of Tankiz, Mamluk viceroy of Syria, though like all the other cenotaphs here they are merely symbolic, with the true burial place being somewhere in the caves below. Tankiz was also responsible for much of the decorative marble work on the walls. To the right of the **mihrab (8)** is the beautifully carved **minbar (9)**, or pulpit. It was originally carved c. 1091 for a mosque in Ashkelon, though it was brought here in 1191 by Salah al-Din. Following the destruction in 1969 of a similar minbar in Jerusalem's al-Aqsa mosque, this is the finest period piece in the country. Close to the minbar is the **medieval entrance (10)** to the cave complex beneath the Haram el-Khalil. The first recorded exploration of the original Cave of Machpelah was made by the Augustinian Canons in 1119. They were lowered down via a rope from this spot, though a staircase was later built. They described a Herodian passage leading to a circular chamber, from which a door opened out into a large cavern. A further doorway gave access to a square rock-cut tomb chamber. A more recent clandestine Israeli investigation described a straight corridor linking the stairs with the tomb chamber. The medieval entrance (10) was sealed in 1394. A small **cupola (11)** covers the padlocked entrance to the rock-cut tomb below.

Though now obscured by carpets, the paved floor is also Herodian. There is a slight slope from east–west terminating in a gutter (12), suggesting that the enclosure built by Herod was unroofed. A small chamber of the main hall is now referred to as the **Women's Mosque (13)**. A window grille allows you to peer inside the tomb of Abraham (14). Through the window (and bullet-proof barrier) you can see the Jewish visitors praying on the other side. Like the other tombs it is draped with a richly embroidered cloth, though again the cenotaph is merely symbolic. It almost certainly dates to the ninth century CE. Muslim tradition attributes the **footprint (15)** in the stone to Adam, a result of his persistent praying here. It is marked by a small shrine.

Jewish section ① *Daily 0400-2200 (winter -2100), closed to non-Jews on Fri, Sat and Muslim and Jewish holidays.*
The designated entrance to the Jewish section of the Cave of Machpelah is via the Crusader buttresses adjacent to the original entrance. In the 10th century CE this entrance was blocked by the construction of the **tomb of Joseph (16)**, with the cut in the Herodian wall (2) providing the new access point. The Crusader adaptations to the building retain the façade of the Byzantine church (built after 570 CE), though nothing else of this structure remains. Perhaps the architectural highlight of the Jewish section is the unimpeded view of the Herodian wall and paved floor, with the former attracting scenes similar to those seen at the Western Wall in Jerusalem. The **tomb of Leah (17)** and **tomb of Jacob (18)** both date to the Mamluk period (14th century CE), whilst the cenotaphs marking the symbolic **tomb of Abraham (14)** and **tomb of Sarah (4)** are both ninth century CE. Between the two latter tombs is a small **synagogue (19)** built after 1967.

Jewish Community of Hebron The Jewish population of Hebron is approximately 600 persons, comprising some 45 families and a relay of 150 yeshiva students (many from North America). They are concentrated in a number of buildings and housing complexes in the centre of the city. The largest settlement is the complex of buildings adjacent to the **Avraham Avinu** courtyard, which includes a synagogue, two kindergartens, the municipal committee offices and a guest house. The synagogue was rededicated in 1981, having been rebuilt and restored according to plans drawn in the 1940s; the Jordanians had razed the building in 1948 and turned it into an open market. Seven families live in Tel Rumeida, whilst twelve families live in Beit Hadassah, the former Jewish clinic. There is supposedly a museum to the 1929 massacre inside the **Beit Hadassah** complex, though a prior appointment is probably necessary (see 'Visit Hebron' below). **Beit Romano** is home to the Shavei Hebron yeshiva and a military camp.

Casbah The town's main casbah (or souq) was once a typically fascinating Arab bazaar featuring, amongst other things, a number of butcher shops selling camel meat. After 2002, 9000 of the 10,000 residents left, and it's due mainly to the work of the Hebron Rehabilitation Committee - who have restored buildings and provided cheap rents, free utilities and other incentives - that about 4000 Arabs have been coaxed back to the old quarter. There is ample opportunity to engage in discussion with local residents about life in Hebron/West Bank and, although most of the shops now cater to the tourist market, their wares are often more attractive (and certainly better priced) than those you find in the souqs of Jerusalem or Bethlehem. The market gets livelier the further east you go, with clothes, shoes, home-wares and fruit and veg beginning to dominate the scene.

Masqobiya and Abraham's Oak A very dead-looking oak tree on Shariah al-Masqobiya (to the west of the town centre) competes with Mamre for the title of 'Abraham's Oak'. The Russian Orthodox church has a 19th-century monastery here.

Birket el-Sultan The Birket el-Sultan (Sultan's Pool) is the traditional site where David had the murderers of Saul's last son, Ish-bosheth, executed (*II Samuel 4:7-12*), though there is little to see.

Hebron listings

For Sleeping and Eating price codes and other relevant information, see Essentials pages 26-31.

Sleeping and eating

Most people visit Hebron as a day trip from Jerusalem, though there are a couple of hotels and plenty of good, cheap restaurants should you decide to stay – which is such an unusual move as to make it interesting.

The stalls around the Casbah sell some of the cheapest falafel in the country (2.5NIS!), whilst good value grilled chicken, hummus, salad, etc is available at a number of places in the market area. Ask around for Khafisha, which has been recommended.
B-C Hebron, Sharia Malik al-Faisal (next to the University Union), T02-2254240/1, hebron_ hotel@hotmail.com. Comfortable rooms, cavernous (as are bathrooms) with internet cable, fridge, heater-a/c, TV, but in need of a

wipe-down – as it's certainly not busy. Dull brown colour scheme. Friendly, breakfast (but not tax) included, coffee shop, room service.

Transport
Car hire
Holy Land, T02-2220811.

Taxis
A recommended driver from Jerusalem to Hebron is Mr Hani Balbisi, T054-6664902.

Directory
Cultural centres Association D'Echanges Culturels Hebron-France, T02-2224811/229, www.hebron-france.org/; British Council, Palestine Polytechnic University, T02-2293717, information@ps.britishcouncil.org. **Hospitals** Al-Ahli, T02-2220212; Amria Alia, T02-2228126; Red Crescent Society, T02-2228333. **Post office** On Shahrah Malik al-Faisal.

Kiryat Arba

Ins and outs

Getting there and away Egged Bus 160 runs from the stop outside Jerusalem's Central Bus Station to Kiryat Arba (Sunday-Thursday every 30 minutes or so 0630-2300, Friday last at 1530, Saturday first at 2100).

The Jewish settlement of Kiryat Arba, built on a low rise to the north of the Cave of the Machpelah, preserves a biblical name for Hebron: Kiriath-Arba. Meaning literally 'town of the four', it alternatively stands for the four couples who tradition says are buried here (Adam and Eve, Abraham and Sarah, Isaac and Rebecca, Jacob and Leah), or as evidence that the ancient town was divided into four quarters or clans.

The population of Kiryat Arba is over 7000, with many of its residents followers of the right-wing messianic *Gush Emunim* movement, and the settlement is considered the most militant on the West Bank. Kiryat Arba's most notorious former resident is Baruch Goldstein, the Jewish settler who murdered 29 Muslims at the Haram el-Khalil in 1994. His grave stands at the entrance to the settlement, in a park named after the assassinated founder of the now illegal fascist party *Kach*, Meir Kahane (for an enlightening biography of Kahane see Robert I. Friedman's *The False Prophet: Rabbi Meir Kahane – From FBI Informant to Knesset Member*). Since the massacre, Goldstein's family has laid a tile floor around the grave, put in bookshelves, a wash-basin and lights, whilst the wording on the tomb refers to a "martyr" who died "sanctifying God's name". There have been moves to have the grave shifted to a less prominent spot, though the IDF have already once refused permission for him to be buried in the Jewish cemetery in Hebron.

South of Hebron

es-Samu'/Eshtemoa

From Hebron, Route 60 continues southwest to es-Samu' (take a service taxi from Hebron). This is believed to be the site of the biblical city of Eshtemoa, a town in the territory of Judah (*Joshua 15:50*) that was granted to the Levites (*Joshua 21:14; I Chronicles 6:42*). The Bible recalls how David sent part of the spoils of his campaign against the Amalekites to the elders of Eshtemoa (*I Samuel 30:26-28*), whilst excavations at the site in 1968 revealed a hoard containing 26 kilogrammes of silver. Unfortunately, the dates do not quite match. A large synagogue, complete with mosaic floor and walls preserved in places to seven metres, has been excavated, with tentative dating suggesting that it was in use around the fourth to fifth centuries CE. The present Palestinian village is famed for its carpets.

Khirbet Susiya

Located approximately 5 km east of es-Samu' is a site known by the Arabic name of Khirbet Susiya. Identification is not certain, though this may be the biblical town of **Carmel** in the territory of Judah (*Joshua 15:55*) that was the birthplace of one of David's mighty men (*II Samuel 23:24*). There are a number of remains at the site, the best preserved of which is the **synagogue** founded in the third or fourth century CE that continued in use until the eighth or ninth century CE, when it was replaced by a mosque.

East of Jerusalem

Travelling east from Jerusalem the drive along Route 1 to Jericho is only 40 km, yet it is spectacular. The landscape becomes increasingly barren and austere as the road rapidly drops down to the Jordan Valley via the Judean Desert. Amos Elon suggests that a "traveller with a historical bent might be forgiven if he or she insisted on approaching Jerusalem from the desert in the east. The early Hebrews came in this way – from the desert to the sown – after their crossing of the Jordan; and the Romans and Arabs after them. It is the most spectacular route. The stage is set. The colour is switched on. The hills suddenly part like curtains. The drama of the scene, like a trumpet blast in Fidelio, is enhanced by its suddenness" (Jerusalem: City of Mirrors, 1989).

There are a number of notable sights along this route, including a rewarding hike, though most are only accessible if you have your own transport.

Bethany (al-Azariyya) → *Colour map 2, grid B4.*

Bethany (known to everyone as al-Azariyya) is generally associated with the village in which Jesus' friends Martha, Mary and Lazarus lived (*Mark 10:38-42*), with whom Jesus and the Disciples usually stayed when visiting Jerusalem. It was to this village that Jesus returned after his triumphant entry into Jerusalem (*Mark 11:11-12*), and also the home of Simon the Leper, where Jesus was anointed by Mary. But perhaps the best known gospel scene associated with Bethany is Jesus' raising of Lazarus from the dead (*John 11:1-44*). A number of religious buildings in the village commemorate these events.

East of Jerusalem

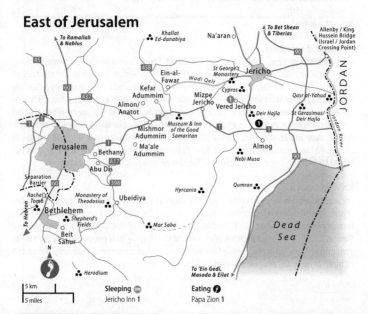

| 5 km / 5 miles | **Sleeping** 🛏 Jericho Inn 1 | **Eating** 🍴 Papa Zion 1 |

Ins and outs

Getting there and away The village of Bethany lies on the lower east flanks of the Mount of Olives, and can be reached by walking down from Bethphage on the Mount of Olives. **NB** This walk is not recommended for unaccompanied females. There is no public transport from Jerusalem: you need to change in Bethlehem to a service taxi (ask for the Arabic name, 'al-Azariyya') or there are service taxis from Jericho that leave when full.

Background

Bethany was known to early Christians (for example, Eusebius, c. 330 CE) by its Greek name Lazarion, 'place of Lazarus', a name that was also used by Byzantine and medieval pilgrims. This name is also preserved in the Arabic name in common usage today, '**al-Azariyya**'.

Christians appear to have venerated this site from an early stage, with Egeria (384 CE) describing a service held at the 'Lazarium' (tomb of Lazarus and guest room of Mary and Martha) commencing the Easter service. Egeria's mention of the large numbers gathered here, who "fill not only the Lazarium itself, but all the fields around", may have inspired the construction of the first church here.

The church/Lazarium appears to have been destroyed in an earthquake, and was subsequently replaced by a new church in the fifth century CE. The Byzantine church was refurbished by the Crusaders, and a completely new church built over the tomb of Lazarus. This almost certainly served as the chapel for the vast new Benedictine convent that the Crusader Queen Melisande built adjacent to the tomb in 1138-1143. Though this was to become one of the richest convents in the Crusader kingdom, it was abandoned following the Crusader surrender of Jerusalem in 1187, and by all accounts the whole complex was lying in ruins by the 14th century. The tradition of the raising of Lazarus appears to have been revived in the 15th century, and in the 16th century the Muslims built the Mosque of al-'Uzair above the forecourt of the Byzantine church, adjoining the tomb (since Islam also venerates the raising of Lazarus). Between 1566 and 1575 the Franciscans cut the present stepped entrance to the tomb so that Christians could also have access. The present Franciscan Church was completed in 1954 whilst the Greek Orthodox Church is a little over 10 years younger.

Sights

Franciscan Church ① *T02-6749291, daily 0800-1125 and 1400-1700, closes 1 hr earlier in winter.*
The **Franciscan Church** (1) is one of a number of churches in the Holy Land designed by the Italian architect Antonio Barluzzi. It is cruciform in shape, and features a mosaic depicting Martha, Mary and Lazarus on the façade. The apse of the **fourth-century church** (2) can be seen beneath trapdoors immediately inside the modern entrance. Further grilles and trapdoors reveal mosaics from the fourth-century church, whilst the apse of the **fifth-century church** (3) is clearly defined in white marble close to the modern east altar. Masonry from the fourth-century church can be seen in the courtyard outside the **modern church** (4), plus piers from the **fifth-century church** (5) and masonry from the **fifth-century façade** (6). To the south are some Crusader remains relating to the **Benedictine convent** (7) (8). Return to the street by the stairs (9).

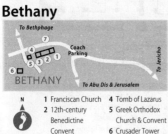

Bethany

To Bethphage

Coach Parking

To Jericho

BETHANY

To Abu Dis & Jerusalem

N

100 metres
100 yards

1 Franciscan Church
2 12th-century Benedictine Convent
3 Mosque of al-'Uzair
4 Tomb of Lazarus
5 Greek Orthodox Church & Convent
6 Crusader Tower
7 'Oldest House in Bethany'

Mosque of al-'Uzair The 16th-century **mosque** (12) is not generally open to non-Muslims. The **courtyard** of the mosque (11) occupies what previously had been the atrium of the fourth- and fifth-century churches. An earlier (though not necessarily the original) entrance to the tomb of Lazarus can be seen in the **west wall** of the mosque (13). Opposite the mosque is what is billed as the "oldest house in Bethany" (visitors welcome for a 'donation').

Tomb of Lazarus The current entrance to the **tomb of Lazarus** (14), via 26 steep, rock-hewn **steps** (15) cut by the Franciscans in the 16th century, is through a small doorway a little further up the street. The owners of the shop opposite hold the key, and generally ask for a few shekels to unlock the tomb. At the bottom of the shaft, further steps lead under a low slab into a small antechamber. You have to be something of a contortionist to get in here, and visitors should also note that getting stuck in here with a tour group is a real nightmare. Next to none of the original rock-cut walls of the tomb are visible (they are obscured by Crusader masonry) and the floor level of the tomb has probably been raised substantially. Thus, what you are really seeing is a Crusader-built chamber.

Greek Orthodox Church and Convent The Greek Orthodox complex incorporates part of the Crusader chapel built over the tomb of Lazarus. Behind the church are the remains of a Crusader tower that was part of the 12th-century convent.

Ma'ale Adumim → *Colour map 2, grid B5.*

This Jewish settlement is named after the biblical Ma'ale Adumim, or 'ascent of the red rocks', that provided a pass leading up to Jerusalem from Jericho on the border of the tribes of Benjamin and Judah (Joshua 15:7). The settlement is a rather striking sight, modern white apartments perched on a high, reddish hill above the Judean wilderness,

Church, Mosque & Tomb of Lazarus, Bethany

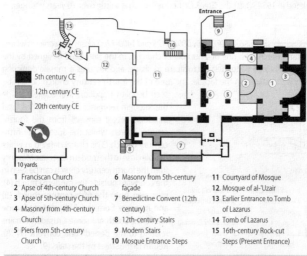

1 Franciscan Church
2 Apse of 4th-century Church
3 Apse of 5th-century Church
4 Masonry from 4th-century Church
5 Piers from 5th-century Church
6 Masonry from 5th-century façade
7 Benedictine Convent (12th century)
8 12th-century Stairs
9 Modern Stairs
10 Mosque Entrance Steps
11 Courtyard of Mosque
12 Mosque of al-'Uzair
13 Earlier Entrance to Tomb of Lazarus
14 Tomb of Lazarus
15 16th-century Rock-cut Steps (Present Entrance)

though not necessarily an attractive one. Flowering roundabouts, grassy laws and palm trees are planted at every opportunity, despite the barren environment and the chronic water-shortage. Consistent expansion means Ma'ale Adumim now houses around 33,000 people, acting as a Jewish overspill from Jerusalem. Incongruously located in the heart of Ma'ale Adumim's residential centre is the large Byzantine Martyrius Monastery, while near the industrial area you find the Monastery of St Euthymius.

Ins and outs

Getting there and away This settlement is about 8 km east of Jerusalem along Route 1. Egged buses 174, 175, 176 and 177 go to Ma'ale Adumim from Jerusalem. Note that in addition to the Jerusalem–Jericho road (Route 1) there is an 'Israeli' road linking the town to the Jewish northern suburbs of Jerusalem. Entering the city from Road 1, take the south entrance and the monastery is reached by following orange signs to the 'Archaeological Site' along Midbar Yehuda Road.

Sights

Martyrius Monastery The Martyrius Monastery (Arabic: *Khirbet Murasas*) was established by **Martyrius the Cappadocian** in the fifth century CE, though founding such an extensive monastic complex does not appear to have been the monk's original intention.

Martyrius Monastery

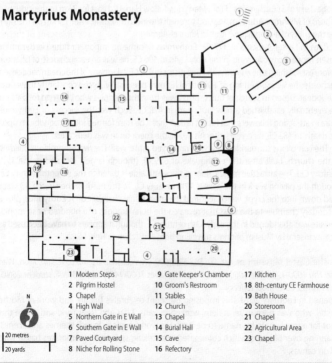

1 Modern Steps	9 Gate Keeper's Chamber	17 Kitchen
2 Pilgrim Hostel	10 Groom's Restroom	18 8th-century CE Farmhouse
3 Chapel	11 Stables	19 Bath House
4 High Wall	12 Church	20 Storeroom
5 Northern Gate in E Wall	13 Chapel	21 Chapel
6 Southern Gate in E Wall	14 Burial Hall	22 Agricultural Area
7 Paved Courtyard	15 Cave	23 Chapel
8 Niche for Rolling Stone	16 Refectory	

N

20 metres
20 yards

He arrived in the Holy Land from Egypt in 457 CE, settling at the laura of St Euthymius some 4 km to the east. However, it appears that he found that laura too overcrowded, and thus retreated to a cave that has been identified here. He subsequently founded the monastery that bears his name, though during this early phase it was not particularly large and was certainly not walled. Martyrius was later appointed priest of the Church of Anastasis (The Holy Sepulchre) in Jerusalem, and patriarch of Jerusalem (478-486 CE), a position that he used to develop the monastery to become one of the central monasteries in the Judean Desert.

Martyrius' Monastery reached its peak in the late sixth century CE, under the archimandrite Genesius. A new pilgrim hostel was built outside the monastery walls, the refectory was constructed, alterations were made to the church, and new chapels were added. Also during this period, the mosaics that cover almost all the floors were laid (which are now in varying states of repair and restoration). Most notable are the geometric designs in the large refectory, and the grey wolf and colourful birds in the main church. A white marble table from the refectory, complete with wine cups and dining utensils, is displayed in the Museum of the Good Samaritan (see page 233). Also note the broken sealing stone for the north gate: impressively huge, although only half remains. The monastery was abandoned after the Arab conquest of 636 CE. There is supposedly a guard with keys on site, but in reality you may have to scale the fence to gain access.

Monastery of St Euthymius From Martyrius, follow Hagai Rd east for 2 km to the industrial suburb of **Mishmor Adumim**. Passing through the industrial zone, after 1.5 km on the right are the ruins of a monastery (Arabic: *Khan el-Ahmar*).

Born in Lesser Armenia in 377 CE, **Euthymius** became an important figure in Byzantine desert monasticism. Arriving in the Holy Land in 406 CE, he was an early disciple of Chariton before establishing a new laura with Theoctistus in 411 CE. Like many of the charismatic desert anchorites he was something of a victim of his own personality, forced constantly to wander the Judean Desert in search of quiet spots away from the disciples who chose to follow him. He eventually established a new laura here in 428 CE. Such was the success of Euthymius' laura in attracting followers that he left orders that it be transformed into a coenobium upon his death. In 482 CE, nine years after his death, the coenobium was dedicated.

The complex is surrounded by a well-preserved ashlar wall. The most prominent building is the **church**, built after the earthquake of 659 CE (though largely restored in the 12th century CE). The attractive mosaic floor in the south aisle is dated to the seventh century CE, though the paving work in the nave is 12th century CE. To the north of the church, 13 steps lead down into the crypt, which featured the main burial chamber of **St Euthymius**, plus a secondary chamber to the west that revealed the burial troughs of a hundred or so monks. The site was abandoned in the early 13th century CE, though it appears to have been used as a caravanserai by Muslim pilgrims travelling from Jerusalem to Nebi Musa.

Moshe Castel Museum of Art ① *T02-5357000, www.castelmuseum.co.il, Sun, Mon, Wed and Thu 1000-1700, Tue 1000-1900, Fri and hol eves 1000-1400, adults 36NIS, student 26NIS, child 18NIS. Café, shop, toilets.*
Opened in February 2010, this imposing museum celebrates the life and work of Moshe Castel, who was born in Jerusalem, worked in Paris, Tzfat and New York, and chose this spot for a museum in his name to be built. His works explore Jewish themes and scenes, spanning over 60 years, which culminated in a striking style that incorporates basalt with oil on canvas.

Khallad ed-Danabiya This little-visited site is located along Route 458, a turning north off Route 1 (see 'East of Jerusalem' map). A steep and difficult path leads down the cliff. Very little is known about the laura complex here, and even an identification with any of the 41 Byzantine desert monasteries known from contemporary literary sources is not possible. However, the series of small cells linked by a network of stairways on the narrow ridge above the deep ravine of the Wadi Makkuk is quite an impressive sight, leading to comparisons with Peru's Machu Picchu! The focus of the laura, presumably founded in the fourth century CE, is a small cave with a natural apse known as the 'cave-church'.

Museum and Inn of the Good Samaritan ① *Sun-Thu 0800-1500, Fri 0830-1300, T02-5417555, entrance free.*

The desire of Christian pilgrims from the Byzantine and Crusader periods to localize every event mentioned in the gospels leads to the often spurious adoption of many places as the traditional site of events in the life of Jesus. It is not entirely certain when this spot first became associated with the story of the Good Samaritan (*Luke 10:30-37*), but what makes it all the more ridiculous is that Jesus was not recounting an actual event or describing a specific inn, but rather using the inn as a setting for a parable in response to the question "Who is my neighbour?" Excavations in the vicinity have, however, revealed remains from the first century BCE, second Temple period caves and a sixth-century CE basilical church. The building you now see dates to the Ottoman period and variously served as a caravanserai and police-post, and has recently been revamped as an attractive mosaic museum-cum-chapel.

Here you will see pieces collected from various West Bank sites, beautifully restored and displayed. Inspired by the parable of the Good Samaritan, the collection is based on the places of worship of the three faiths: Jew, Samaritan and Christian. From St Martyrius' Monastery (see above) is the marble table from the refectory and 'Paul's' tombstone. Also of interest are lovely marble columns and pillars from the Byzantine Church of St Mary on Mt Gerizim, near Nablus, as well as mosaics from the Samaritan synagogue located there which have a distinct and complex style. The open-air display of extraordinary mosaic floors from both churches and synagogues is as impressive as the indoor exhibits.

On the hill above the Inn of the Good Samaritan (on the north side of the road) lie the unspectacular remains of the Crusader-built **Tour Rouge** fortress, constructed by the Templars to protect pilgrims on the Jerusalem-Jericho road. It stands on the site of the **Maledomni** fortress, built in the early Byzantine period for the same purpose.

Wadi Qelt → *Colour map 2, grid B5.*

Wadi Qelt is a seasonal stream (Hebrew: Nahal Prat) that drains an area of 180 sq km on its course from close to Jerusalem, all the way to the Jordan River to the east of Jericho. 28 km long, the ravine of the Wadi Qelt forms three distinct stages, each providing a challenging hike. A beautiful section is along the Lower Wadi Qelt, taking in St George's Monastery, and terminating at the Tulul Abu el-'Alayiq site to the southwest of Jericho. The palm trees and lush growth in the wadi, the giant crosses dotting the ravine close to St George's, and the harsh desert hills all around make a lasting impression.

Ins and outs

Getting there and away The turning for Lower Wadi Qelt is at the major bend in the road just before Route 1 drops down to sea-level after the Inn of the Good Samaritan (look for a sign indicating "Mizpe Jericho" and a big brown sign announcing "Al-Wadi Qelt"). Bus 125 goes every couple of hours from Jerusalem to Mizpe Jericho, first one at 0710 (except Saturday). Several buses return back from the junction until at least 2200. From the turning, head left towards the cluster of small white buildings until you get to the T-junction. There are two options here. Hikers attempting the Lower Wadi Qelt hike should turn left (see below for details). Those visiting St George's Monastery should take the (old Roman) road to the right, which has a sign signalling no entry, although cars and bikes are fine to travel on it (coaches are not, as it is poorly maintained). This Roman road runs parallel to Wadi Qelt, and has a car park with a viewpoint nearby from where there are excellent views down to St George's Monastery. There is also a steep walking path down, which takes about 20 minutes, plus 30 minutes for the climb back up. Bedouins with donkeys might follow you to try to tempt you into a 20NIS ride up again. The Roman road is blocked beyond the car park, and to reach Cypros you have to walk for about 20 minutes. **NB** Do not leave any valuables in the car here.

Lower Wadi Qelt hike

There are several important points that must be remembered before tackling this hike. Do not enter the canyon if rain is forecast since there is very real danger of flash-floods. Take plenty of drinking water since there is none en route. There are also security concerns that should be considered before making this hike. Take advice from the SPNI in Jerusalem before making the trip. It is almost certainly safe, though it does not hurt to ask around beforehand. Israelis can only visit on Saturdays accompanied by a ranger. Women should certainly not hike here without male companions, and nobody should hike alone. SPNI in Jerusalem offer guided hikes (US$125). This hike takes six to eight hours (about 12 km), depending upon how long your stops are at the various points of interest.

Head left (**1**) along the road parallel to the main Jerusalem-Jericho road for about 1 km towards the group of white buildings. At the T-junction (**2**) turn left (the turning right follows the old Roman road to Jericho).

After a very short distance, opposite a group of ruined buildings (**3**), an unpaved road heads north. As it curves down to the left, a viewpoint (**4**) on the right provides an excellent view across the northern Judean Desert before you. Begin to follow the unpaved road as it drops down, though to make the hike more interesting follow the trail indicated by the small green sign to the left. This leads down via a twisting and turning wadi, and is more scenic than the

Lower Wadi Qelt hike

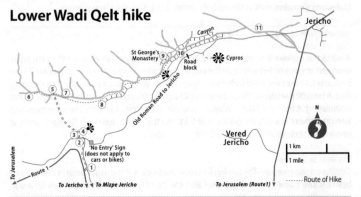

St George's Monastery

Clinging to the side of the Wadi Qelt ravine, this monastery takes its name from St George of Koziba; a monk born in Cyprus c. 550, but who spent much of his life at various lauras in the Judean Desert. The caves in the Wadi Qelt cliffs were originally occupied by anchorites in the early fifth century CE, though it was John of Thebes who transformed the small oratory here into a monastery complex (c. 480 CE). Though the height of the monastery's fame coincided with George of Koziba's period of residence in the late sixth century CE, it is almost certain that St George's Monastery was one of the victims of the Persian invasion of 614 CE. It was restored by the Crusaders in the 12th century, with several new traditions being introduced as well. The story of Elijah hiding in a cave and being fed by ravens during his flight to Sinai is now credited to the Church of the Cave at the upper level, whilst the legend of Joachim weeping over the sterility of his wife Anne, and the angel subsequently announcing to her the impending conception of the Virgin Mary, are both commemorated at churches on the middle level. All these buildings are relatively recent, however. A pilgrim passing in 1483 recalls seeing the entire complex in ruins, and it was not until the Greek Orthodox church's reconstruction programme of 1878 to 1901 that St George's Monastery took its present form. The large bell-tower was added by Timothy the First in 1952. Inside the dark and gloomy interior of the main church are boxes containing the bones and skulls of saints, but the pièce de résistance is the mummified abbot in the smaller rear church. Just 10 monks currently reside at St George's.

The monastery is open daily 0800-1800. Donation accepted. There's a souvenir shop. Modest dress is required and women are admitted.

unpaved road. After some walking you pass through what appears to be a natural rock arch supporting a former aqueduct that was built to supply Cypros (see next page). Ahead of you is the British-built pumping station (5) that used to pump water to Jerusalem, but now supplies Jericho. A path and then steps to your left (green-and-white arrows) lead to a bridge across the wadi. Though signs here say no wading or diving, few hikers can resist taking off their shoes and socks and wading up the Ein Qelt canyon. Water flows here via an aqueduct from En Fawar, and though the waterfall (6) is man-made, this is still a very attractive spot.

Return to the pumping station, then follow the course of the aqueduct eastwards. The red-and-white route climbs upwards, linking with the Central Wadi Qelt hike; ignore these trail-markers and follow the signs along the aqueduct marked "picnic site – circular trail". Beyond the buildings attached to the pumping station are a number of picnic tables set amongst some shady trees. Follow the aqueduct until it crosses a small tributary on a bridge (7). There are two options here: you can either follow the course of the aqueduct or, better still, drop down into the Wadi Qelt canyon itself. Continuing along the course of Wadi Qelt (red trail markers again), it shortly becomes more and more canyon-like (8). Note that there is one reasonably tricky descent shortly after entering the canyon. After about 2 km scrambling along the canyon, the floor of the wadi becomes increasingly thick with vegetation, and the aqueduct crosses above you to the southern bank. As you round a corner **St George's Monastery** (9) comes spectacularly into view.

Beyond the monastery there are a number of options. The least interesting is to return the way you came. The next option is to cross the bridge across the canyon, and climb the path up the cliff to the south side of Wadi Qelt. This path leads to the parking lot and viewpoint (**10**) from which most tour groups view the monastery. From here you can continue east along the Roman road towards Jericho (passing the site of Cypros after about 20 minutes), or return along the road to the hike's starting point (**2**). You may be able to hitch a lift from the car park. Note that it is not recommended that you leave your car unattended here whilst you complete the loop trip, and certainly not with any valuables in.

The most interesting option, however, is to continue along Wadi Qelt to Jericho. Follow the red markers up the steps beyond the monastery, following the path along the north side of the canyon. Eventually the path begins to drop down again, passing the ruins of Tulul Abu el-'Alayiq (**11**) on either side of you. From here it is a fairly unrewarding 2-km walk into Jericho.

Cypros

Often described as a 'mini-Masada', most of the building remains here are attributed to Herod the Great, and form one of the Judean Desert palace-fortresses that he was so keen on building. Despite having a magnificent palace at Tulul Abu el-'Alayiq just below, it was relatively exposed, and thus it is believed that Cypros (Arabic: Tell el-'Aqaba) was built as the nearest citadel in which Herod could take refuge during periods of revolt. It appears that Herod's fear of revolt was only matched by his fear of having to suffer any hardship, and hence the construction of two very fine Roman-style **bathhouses**, one on the summit and one on the lower level. The complex takes its name from Herod's mother.

Excavations at the site suggest that the hill was a fortified stronghold in Hasmonean times, and may very well be either one of the two fortresses (**Threx** or **Taurus**) that the Syrian general Baccides built during the Maccabean wars. Strabo recounts their destruction by Pompey in 63 BCE during the Roman invasion. Certainly the round tower on the lower level is pre-Herodian. To build his palace-fortress Herod enlarged the summit by means of packed earth fills supported by retaining walls, whilst the lower level was also built up. Archaeological evidence supports Josephus' account of the palace-fortress' destruction at the beginning of the First Jewish Revolt (66-73 CE), though the picture is confused slightly by the buildings of a group of monks in the Byzantine period (324-638 CE). The square building on the lower level is believed to be a Byzantine period chapel.

Nebi Musa → *Colour map 2, grid B5.*

ⓘ *Daily 0800-1900, free, but donations accepted.*

This important Muslim shrine has an interesting and colourful history. Situated on one of the old roads up to Jerusalem from the Jordan Valley, tradition has it that Muslim pilgrims on their way to/from Mecca used to stop here to look across the Jordan Valley to Mt Nebo, site of Moses' death (Deuteronomy 34:1-7).

Ins and outs

Getting there and away Shortly after the turn off for Wadi Qelt along Route 1 (and 8 km short of Jericho), a road branches off to Nebi Musa (look for the brown sign). A bus between Jerusalem and the Dead Sea will drop you here, though there is no public transport for the 2 km to the site. Perhaps the best way to reach Nebi Musa is to hire a Palestinian service taxi ('special') from Jericho. The path heading west from Nebi Musa leads all the way to the Monastery of St Euthymius, though it may not necessarily be safe to follow this route.

The shrine

In 1269 CE the Mamluk sultan Baibars built a small shrine to Moses here (Arabic: *Musa*), and in time the shrine came to be venerated as the tomb of Moses himself. The legend was helped by several factors, one of which was the fact that the line in *Deuteronomy* describing Moses' death on Mt Nebo does not claim that he is buried there, instead stating that "no man knows the place of his burial to this day". This site was also convenient in that it was exactly one day's march from Jerusalem on the pilgrimage to Mecca.

Early in the 19th century CE the Ottoman Turks initiated a complete restoration of the shrine, hospice and auxiliary pilgrim-related buildings here, and Nebi Musa then became the venue for a 7-day pilgrimage (*mawsim*) that coincided with the Christian Holy Week. The timing of this event was no coincidence, it even being set annually not by the Islamic lunar calendar but by the Christian calendar; to all intents and purposes, it was in competition with Easter. In later years the week-long festival, which began with a procession from al-Aqsa Mosque in Jerusalem to Nebi Musa, became a focus for political agitation, with tight controls on the event being imposed by the British Mandate authority. The festival was cancelled altogether in the period of Jordanian occupation of the West Bank (1948-1967), and following the Yom Kippur war of 1973 the shrine was used as a military base by the Israelis. The mawsim was briefly revived in 1987 but was quickly stopped by the Israelis. Nowadays the festival takes the form of a celebration lasting throughout April, with the main activities and crowds coming each Friday. This is also the only time when believers are permitted inside the shrine to the enormous tomb, covered with green velvet and embroidered with gold Koranic script.

Wadi Og trek

This is a nice little trek, with a couple of ladder descents, along a picturesque wadi with some dramatic scenery. It takes less than an hour.

To get there from Route 1, take the turn-off to Almog, opposite the Jericho turning. Look out for a red/white trail marker on the sharp left bend before the entrance gate to Almog. This is the start of the walk, but if driving it's best to leave your vehicle inside the village where security-men will keep it safe. **NB** Get local advice to ensure there is no danger of flash floods.

From the red/white marker walk 50 m before turning to follow a blue/white way-marker, up to a viewpoint over the sheer walls of the wadi. It's a 10-minute walk along the edge of the wadi, before beginning a short descent. Down in the wadi, the force of flash floods is told by the polished rocks and battered metal drums that have been washed down. Continue walking between the 10-m-high walls of the wadi, zig-zagging along. Depending on the season, you might have to cross a couple of shallow pools. You will reach a sheer drop where, using the handholds wedged into the rock, you descend 7 m. Here, the wadi opens up with some dramatic overhangs of rock looming above. After a short distance, there's another descent of 10 m or so. This is a bit tricky as there is a negative incline and with sweaty hands the metal is slippy. The metal rings in the rock nearby are for abseiling, should you have the equipment. Carry on until you meet a sign-post for Qalya/Ha'eteqim Cliff in red/white and Lower Og Canyon in green. Follow the dirt road back uphill to the starting point of the walk. The trail is clearly way-marked throughout. (The loop can be done in reverse, but views are better going down the wadi than up).

Jericho

→ Colour map 2, grid B5.

Located on the wide plain of the Jordan Valley some 40 km east of Jerusalem, Jericho's position at 250 m below sea-level makes it the lowest city in the world. Jericho's benign winter climate and productive soils made this spot an obvious choice for human settlement, and by general consensus the defensive walls built around this settlement c. 8000 BCE make Jericho the oldest walled city on earth.

Not surprisingly, the area in and around Jericho is rich in archaeological-historical sites from just about every period you care to mention. The modern town of Jericho sprawls somewhat throughout the oasis, though the fact that it is almost entirely low-rise, and there remain plenty of splashes of green, make it rather attractive in a ramshackle kind of way. The kind of place where horses and carts remain a viable form of transport and every transaction is accompanied by the offer of Arabic coffee.

Ins and outs

Getting there and away Many visitors come to Jericho as part of an organized tour. There is no direct public transport from Jerusalem. Take a bus from Damascus Gate to the town of Azariya, then change into a shared (service) taxi to Jericho. Or there are services from Ramallah (30 minutes) and Bethlehem (one hour). These will drop off in Palestine Square. Alternatively, you could get dropped off by an Egged bus at the turn-off to Jericho, on Route 1. From there, it's easy to pick up a local mini-bus on to the city centre (2NIS).

Getting around With an early start it is possible to see all of Jericho's main attractions in one day, though a second day is needed if you wish to explore the other sites in the Jericho area (see page 247 onwards). The sites in Jericho itself are fairly spread out, involving a 6-7-km walk to see them all, though they do neatly fit into a loop that begins and ends at the main square. Taxis can be hired for a tour around Jericho's attractions for around 150NIS, though you'll need to bargain hard and establish exactly what the deal is. You may also be able to negotiate a deal to take you to Nebi Musa. An excellent way to explore the Jericho area is on a bike (see page 246).

Background

The beginnings The evidence of early human settlement at this oasis is seen most vividly at the 8000 BCE walls and tower at Tel Jericho/Tel es-Sultan. Early settlers were no doubt attracted by the plentiful water supply, productive soils and benign winter climate, with a succession of cultures establishing themselves here in the Mesolithic, Pre-Pottery Neolithic, Pottery Neolithic, Early and Middle Bronze Age periods. It seems that the wandering hunter-gatherers made the shift to sedentary agriculture some 11,000 years ago.

The Israelites The most famous incident in Jericho's history comes with the return of the Israelites from the Exodus, c. 1250 BCE. The prophet-general Joshua commanded the priests to carry the Ark around the walled city for six consecutive days. On the seventh day the priests blew their trumpets and "Joshua said unto the people 'Shout; for the Lord hath given you the city.' ... So the people shouted when the priests blew the trumpets; and it came to pass, when the people heard the sound of the trumpet, and the people

Jericho

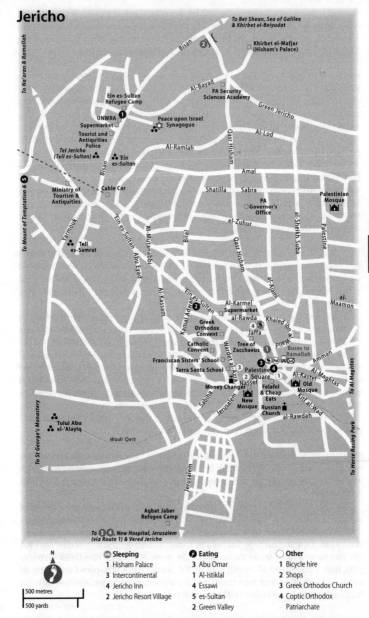

To Na'aran & Ramallah

To Bet Shean, Sea of Galilee & Khirbet el-Beiyudat

Bisan

Khirbet el-Mafjar (Hisham's Palace)

Al-Bayad

PA Security Sciences Academy

Green Jericho

Ein es-Sultan Refugee Camp

UNWRA Supermarket

Peace upon Israel Synagogue

Tourist and Antiquities Police

Tel Jericho (Tell es-Sultan)

'Ein es-Sultan

Al-Ramlah

Qasr Hisham

Al-Lod

Bisan

Ministry of Tourism & Antiquities

Cable Car

Amal

Shatilla

Sabra

Palestinian Mosque

To Mount of Temptation & St

Yarmouk

Tell es-Samrat

Ein es-Sultan

Abu Eyad

Al-Mutanabbi

Bilal

PA Governor's Office

el-Zuhur

Qasr Hisham

al-Sheikh Suba

Palestine

Al-Kassam

Ein es-Sultan

Kamal Adwan

Ware al-Askar

al-Alami

al-Maamon

Al-Karmel Supermarket

al-Rawda

Jaffa

Khaled Ibn al-Walid

Amman

Greek Orthodox Convent

Tree of Zacchaeus

Buses to Ramallah

Catholic Convent

Franciscan Sisters' School

Terra Santa School

Palestine Square

Al-Kastel

Old Mosque

Al-Maghtas

To Al Maghtas

Money Changer

Nasser

Felafel & Cheap Eats

Sabina

Jerusalem

New Mosque

Russian Church

al-Rawdah

Kitt al-Wad

Tulul Abu el-'Alayiq

Wadi Qelt

To St George's Monastery

Jerusalem

Aqbat Jaber Refugee Camp

To New Hospital, Jerusalem (via Route 1) & Vered Jericho

To Horse Racing Park

N

500 metres

500 yards

🛏 Sleeping		🍴 Eating		○ Other	
1	Hisham Palace	3	Abu Omar	1	Bicycle hire
3	Intercontinental	1	Al-Istiklal	2	Shops
4	Jericho Inn	4	Essawi	3	Greek Orthodox Church
2	Jericho Resort Village	5	es-Sultan	4	Coptic Orthodox
		2	Green Valley		Patriarchate

shouted with a great shout, that the wall fell down flat" (*Joshua 6:16-20*). Ancient Jericho never recovered its former importance (a fact confirmed by archaeological evidence from Tel Jericho), with the ancient city being abandoned from the time of the Babylonian Exile (586 BCE). Subsequent centres of Jericho established themselves elsewhere in the oasis.

Hasmoneans and Herod Jericho's fortunes were revived in the first century BCE by the Hasmonean dynasty, who began to establish a number of winter palaces here (Tulul Abu el-'Alayiq, see page 247). The Jericho plain was soon to feature prominently in the struggle between the Hasmoneans and the upstart Herod. It is possible that at this time Jericho was considered to be Roman property, so much so that Mark Anthony saw fit to make a present of the estate to his paramour Cleopatra. In turn she leased part of the estate to Herod, allowing him to build the first of his three palaces here. With the death of Cleopatra c. 31 BCE, the Roman emperor Octavian (Augustus Caesar) granted Jericho to Herod. In a dramatic 25-year period Herod built two further palaces, had the surviving male heir to the Hasmonean dynasty drowned here, and planned his final tyrannical act (see Tel es-Samrat, page 242), before finally dying in Jericho in 4 BCE. Jericho subsequently reverted to Roman rule, though was largely destroyed in the recriminations that followed the First Jewish Revolt (66-73 CE).

Byzantines, Arabs and British In the Byzantine period it appears that the oasis of Jericho was heavily populated, with the new town established largely on the area of the present settlement. Jericho had a large Christian population at this juncture, though the presence of the 'Peace Upon Israel' synagogue (see page 242) suggests that a Jewish community continued to exist here.

Jericho was one of the first cities taken in the Arab conquest of Palestine and, judging by the opulence of the palace of Khirbet el-Mafjar (Hisham's Palace), it enjoyed the same reputation as a winter playground of the wealthy as it had eight centuries before.

The town was captured by the Crusaders in 1099 and still carries several reminders of this European heritage (Mount of Temptation, amongst others). Though Jericho returned to Muslim rule following Salah al-Din's victories in 1187, the town's lack of defences (it was unwalled) and its apparent wealth (based on agriculture) made it a persistent target for Bedouin raids. The decline continued throughout Ottoman rule and it was not until the British repaired the aqueducts and irrigation facilities that Jericho once again became a centre of agricultural production, specializing in dates and fruit.

Modern history Jericho fell to Transjordan in the war of 1948, with the town's population being boosted by Arab refugees from areas now controlled by Israel. Jericho's reputation as a winter resort continued, with many of the wealthy classes from Amman taking their holidays here.

The 1993 Declaration of Principles signed by Israel and the PLO envisaged a degree of autonomy in areas that Israel had occupied since the Six Day War of 1967. Since the Gaza Strip alone did not appear to be a sufficient inducement to entice the Palestinians, Jericho was included within a package that became known as 'Gaza-Jericho first', and in May 1994 the Jericho area came under the control of the newly established Palestinian Authority (PA). With a population of around only 20,000, Jericho has a slow-paced and sultry air compared with other West Bank towns, and the enticement of the Intercontinental Hotel is attracting Arab Israeli holiday-makers as well as foreign tourists.

Sights

Mount of Temptation (Jebel Quruntul) ⓘ *Supposedly Mon-Sat 0800-1400 and 1500-1700, winter -1600, early visit recommended (though it's not unknown for it to be inexplicably closed and for the knocking of pilgrims and priests to go unheeded). Modest dress essential. Free; donation expected.* It's a cable car ride up to the monastery from the Sultan Tourist Centre, then 5-10 mins up the steps to the monastery. A taxi to the start of the cable car from Jericho centre should cost no more than 10NIS, or 15NIS to get as far up the mountain as the road allows. Walking takes 30-45 mins and is hard work in the heat, though the path up the cliff is not as steep as it first appears. Take plenty of water, a hat and sun-screen.

The **Télépherique and Sultan Tourist Centre** ⓘ *Ein es-Sultan, T02-2321596, www.jericho-cablecar.com, daily 0800-1800,* on the northwest side of Jericho, is the start of the cable car up the mountain. A ride takes less than 10 minutes (a bit pricey at 55NIS return; you may be able to get a locals' price of 25NIS), but it's an enjoyable dangle over the remains of ancient Jericho, banana tree plantations and magnificent views.

The association of this cliff with the first and third temptation of Christ (*Matthew 4:1-11*) dates only to the 12th century CE. The Crusaders built two churches at the site: one in a cave halfway up the cliff face and one on the summit. The present Greek Orthodox monastery halfway up the cliff dates to 1874-1904 and contains the medieval cave church within its grounds. Visitors are shown the traditional site of the conversation between Christ and the devil, including the stone upon which the former sat!

Permission should be sought (and a small fee paid) to continue up the path to the summit (30 minutes). The Crusader church here had been destroyed by the 14th century, whilst a 19th-century attempt to rebuild it did not come to much. This is the site of the second-century BCE Fortress of Doq, built by the Syrian general Baccides and scene of the murder of Simon Maccabeus in 134 BCE by his son-in-law Ptolemy. Little remains of the fortress bar parts of a ditch, retaining wall and tower. The view down to the Plain of Jericho and across to the Dead Sea certainly makes the climb up here worthwhile. The present name of the hill, Quruntul, is an Arabic translation of the Crusader name Mont Quarantana, meaning 'Mount of Forty', a reference to the 40 days and 40 nights that Jesus spent in the wilderness.

Tel es-Sultan (Ancient Jericho) ⓘ *Daily 0800-1700, closes one hour earlier on Fri, 10NIS adult, 7NIS student, 5NIS child. Toilets, souvenir shops, café and restaurant.*

It is now generally accepted that this site is the location of the oldest city at Jericho, though early excavations here were not promising. Charles Warren's dig in 1868 had no success, with Warren himself concluding that there was nothing of significance to be found here. It later transpired that one of the shafts that he sunk missed the stunning Pre-Pottery Neolithic stone tower by just one metre! Subsequent excavations, the latest being an Italian-Palestinian cooperation ending in 2000, have revealed up to 23 levels of occupation.

In truth, those without a deep interest in archaeology may fail to be impressed by the significance of the finds here, since Tel Jericho is not the most visually exciting historical site. Information boards with site maps help to explain mud-bricks amid drifting grey dunes that you gaze upon. The earliest remains date to around 9600-7700 BCE, though a major change took place in the late ninth millennium BCE with the construction of a town wall. Such a step suggests a move in human society from food-gatherer to food-producer, with this Pre-Pottery Neolithic date suggesting that Jericho was one of the first places on earth to experience this shift (and thus justifying to a certain extent the mantle of 'world's oldest city'). The focus of this wall is the **stone tower** built against the inner side. Built of solid stone, except for the centre where a preserved staircase winds its way to the very top (hidden by a grill), the tower is preserved to a height of 7.75 m. Murphy-O'Connor suggests that "this supreme achievement of a Stone Age people is without parallel elsewhere in the world" (*The Holy Land*, 1992). The sedentary population at this stage must have been in the region of 2000, largely dependent upon agriculture.

Different communities came and went during the Bronze Age, each leaving their mark, such as the Middle Bronze Age (2200-1550 BCE) **defensive wall** that featured a 17-m-high curtain wall standing on top of an artificial glacis, one of the best-preserved sights on view today. Jericho's destruction in the Late Bronze Age II ties in with the Israelite entry into the country after the Exodus. Whether the walls of Jericho were sent tumbling by the blasts from the Israelites' trumpets is another matter (*Joshua 6*). The site here remained largely abandoned until the seventh century BCE, though subsequent occupation appears to have only lasted until the Babylonian Exile (586 BCE). Thereafter Tel es-Sultan was abandoned.

Ein es-Sultan The perennial spring opposite Tel Jericho is the reason why this site was first occupied around 8000 BCE, and some 10,000 years later it is still a vital source of water to the oasis of Jericho. The spring is also identified with the story of Elisha purifying Jericho's water supply by adding salt (*II Kings 2:19-22*), and is sometimes referred to as Elisha's Spring. A restoration project is currently beautifying the area creating a plaza of local stone and bridges over the water channels; when it's finished it will be a pleasant place to rest under the shady trees.

Tel es-Samrat Located 600 m southwest of Tel Jericho is a small artificial mound known as Tel es-Samrat. Excavations here have revealed remains of a large **racetrack** adjoined to the north by a theatre. Behind the theatre is a large **square structure** that appears to have been some sort of residence or reception room connected with the racecourse, or perhaps a gymnasium. All have been positively identified with the Herodian period and general consensus suggests that this site is associated with the last days of Herod (d. 4 BCE) that Josephus recounts in such detail (*Antiquities XVII, 161, 173-179, 193-195; Jewish War 1, 647-73*). Josephus describes Herod as being "melancholy-mad, and in a virtual challenge to death itself he proceeded to devise a monstrous outrage." Having locked up the head men of every village in Judea at the racetrack here he summoned his sister Salome, telling her "I know Jews will greet my death with wild rejoicing; but I can be mourned on other people's account … These men under guard – as soon as I die, kill them all … then all Judea and every family will weep for me – they can't help it." Fortunately for the head men Salome ignored his dying wishes, instead choosing to release them.

Shalom al-Yisrael/Peace Upon Israel Synagogue This synagogue was constructed in the late sixth or early seventh century CE, and remained in common use until the eighth century CE. It is noted for its fine **mosaic floor** featuring a six-line Aramaic inscription set below a pattern of alternating interwoven squares and circles. The centrepiece is an image of the Ark of the Law supported on four legs, with a stylised conch above. Below is a panel containing a seven-branched menorah flanked by a lulab and shofar. The Hebrew inscription, 'Peace upon Israel', gives the synagogue its common name. This is a sensitive area, as right-wing Jews occasionally enter the synagogue without PA permission in order to conduct prayers. Visitors are unlikely to be able to do more than peer through the window (if permitted near the building at all).

Khirbet el-Mafjar (Hisham's Palace) ① *T02-2322522, daily 0800-1700, 10NIS adult, 7NIS student, 5NIS child. Toilets.*

Visitors disappointed by Tel es-Sultan are far more likely to be impressed by Khirbet el-Mafjar, popularly known as **Hisham's Palace**. It was built as a hunting-lodge or spring/winter resort in the Umayyad period, though surprisingly little is known about its history, whilst its ancient name is unknown and it has not been identified in ancient literature.

The popular name comes from an association with the Umayyad caliph **el-Hisham ibn Abd el-Malik** (724-43 CE), though the palace's "sumptuous architecture" that provides a "congenial setting for the life of esthetic hedonism" (Hamilton, 1993) better suits the known character of el-Hisham's nephew and successor **el-Walid ibn el-Yazid II** (743-744 CE). It is generally agreed that, though the bath area was constructed during el-Hisham's reign, the palace was still being built when el-Yazid assumed the caliphate. When the latter's career was cut short by assassination in 744 CE, it appears that the palace was abandoned with only the bath complex fully completed. It was probably badly damaged in the major earthquake of 749 CE and subsequently became a source of cut stones for the local population.

A major restoration project is underway at the complex, which at the time of our visit meant the baths were off-limits to visitors while the mosaic floor is being restored (though views from some distance are possible). A small museum by the entrance contains findings from the site, and here you can pick up a leaflet about the palace and its restoration. Much of the stucco (carved plaster) reliefs are on display at the Rockefeller Musuem in East Jerusalem (see page 149).

Tour The **modern entrance (1)** leads into a **forecourt (2)** where a number of architectural fragments brought down by the earthquake of 749 CE have been rearranged. The palace was originally a two-storied square building around a central courtyard, enclosed by four arcaded galleries. A **vaulted porch (3)** set in the base of a projecting tower to the east formed the main entrance, with the architectural style exhibiting an Iraqi influence. At the centre of the unroofed **courtyard (4)** is a **stone sculpture (5)** that was erected by the excavators from fragments found *in situ*. The **rooms (6)** around the courtyard appear to have been used to accommodate guests and servants. Hamilton suggests that the preponderance of non-domestic rooms in the palace suggests "a numerous retinue and hospitality lavishly dispensed" (*ibid*). A **small mosque (7)** complete with *mihrab* stands to the south of the courtyard. A flight of **steps (8)** in the western gallery leads to an underground vaulted room. The water spout, wall benches and brick-lined waterproofed space confirms that it was a *sirdab* (bathing hall) **(9)**. Unfortunately this is locked, despite the striking geometric floor having been wonderfully restored. The large hall in the northern gallery may have served as a **banqueting hall (10)**.

The bath is connected to the palace by a **path (11)** that may have been for the exclusive use of the caliph. The **bath complex (12)** is in fact the architectural highlight of Khirbet el-Mafjar. It contained a **domed porch (13)**, a large **frigidarium (14)** and a **swimming pool (15)** (that el-Yazid reputedly filled with rosewater mixed with musk and turmeric). The floors are paved with a spectacular coloured stone mosaic divided into separate panels or carpets, designed to give the optical effect of a series of large rugs. The complex of rooms to the north includes a **diwan** or **reception hall (16)**, an unheated room **(17)** that led into a small inner chamber **(18)** containing two hip-baths, two caldaria or hot rooms **(19)** heated by a hypocaust connected to two furnaces **(20)**, plus a latrine **(21)**. Of particular note is the diwan **(16)**, decorated with one of the best-preserved mosaics in the country, whilst the benches, vaults and dome feature extensive use of carved plaster. Stairs (accessed from the exterior) give a view from above of the famous mosaic depicting a lion attacking a deer beneath a luxuriant fruit tree. Also of note are the **hip-baths (18)**: according to legend el-Yazid used to fill these with wine, immerse himself fully, then drink until the level of the bath was 'distinctly lowered'!

To the south of the bath complex is the **large mosque (22)**. The southern section closest to the mihrab **(23)** appears to have been sheltered by a roof, though there is evidence to suggest that the mosque and roof were never completed. The tour finishes at the **ornamental pool (24)**, which featured an octagonal pavilion set on a series of piers as the centre-piece.

Khirbet el-Mafjar (Hisham's Palace)

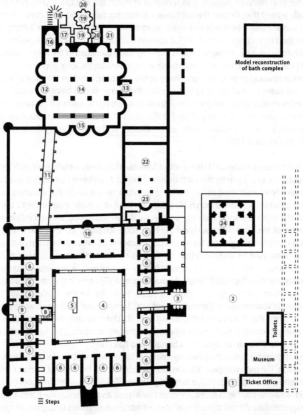

Model reconstruction of bath complex

1	Modern Entrance	7	Small Mosque	13	Domed Porch	19	Hot Rooms
2	Forecourt	8	Steps	14	Frigidarium	20	Furnaces
3	Vaulted Porch	9	Sirdab	15	Swimming Pool	21	Latrine
4	Courtyard	10	Banqueting Hall	16	Diwan	22	Large Mosque
5	Stone Sculpture	11	Path	18	Unheated Room	23	Mihrab
6	Guestrooms	12	Bath Complex	18	Inner Chamber	24	Ornamental Pool

Tree of Zacchaeus Jericho is the scene of several events in the life of Jesus. It is here that he healed the two blind beggars (*Matthew 20:29-34*), healed blind Bartimaeus (*Mark 10:46-52*), and where he dined with the rich tax collector Zacchaeus, who had climbed a sycamore tree to see Jesus better (*Luke 19:1-10*). There is a sycamore tree on 'Ein es-Sultan Street that is called the 'Tree of Zacchaeus', but it's not really 2000 years old.

Jericho listings

For Sleeping and Eating price codes and other relevant information, see Essentials pages 26-31.

Sleeping

AL InterContinental Jericho, Jericho-Jerusalem Rd, T02-2311200, www.intercontinental.com. Bargain prices for great rooms with generous bathrooms, some suites (**LL**). Decor in rooms is more muted than the opulent lobby with fountain, marbles, Mamluk-striped arches and comfortable bar. Large freshwater pool, plus Dead Sea pool, outside jacuzzi, tennis, squash, some fitness equipment; spa includes sauna and steam rooms (non-residents can use for 100NIS), Turkish bath 50NIS extra. The 2 restaurants lack ambiance but serve good food; Flintstones poolside bar.

AL Jericho Resort Village, Qasr Hisham, T02-2321255, www.jerichoresorts.com. This hotel is good value (with facilities that you would pay double the price for in Jerusalem). Standard rooms are large and well furnished with TV, balconies, either pool-views ($20 extra) or dramatic views of the mountains from the other side. Bungalows accommodating up to 4 are by the pool, which is large with a bar. Also a kid's pool, tennis, outdoor grill, buffet restaurant, friendly service. Recommended.

A-D Jericho Inn Guesthouse, Vered Jericho, T02-9941599/052-8600969, www.itour.co.il/eng.jericho_inn. Close to Jericho, but outside the city limits in a Jewish settlement. 4 cosy stone chalets have well equipped kitchenettes, a/c, satellite TV. Garden lit by coloured lamps, with hammocks, water features, shaded tables on the terrace, all very tempting and relaxing. Beds in colourful spotless dorm with big kitchen, a/c, TV (100NIS). Super Israeli breakfast (40NIS) or continental (25NIS). Unobtrusive and easy-going hosts. The kibbutz has a swimming pool (seasonal) and the Rose Bar (Thu and hols only), but no grocery shop. To find them, go straight after the village gate, left at the roundabout, the 3rd turn on the right.

B Al-Zaytouna Guest House, Deir Hajla Monastery, Route 90, T02-9943038/050-348892. The monastery on the edge of town (see 'Around Jericho' section, page 247) offers accommodation for pilgrims only. It's a charming place with rooms around the monastery's cluttered courtyard and lovely gardens. Not much English spoken but you might be able to swing a room if they like the look of you.

E-F Hisham Palace, Ein es-Sultan, T02-2322414, F02-2323645. You could be forgiven for thinking that this British Mandate period hotel closed down (during the British Mandate!). It's extremely shabby, with renovations proceeding at a snail's pace. Inspect the rooms first, be clear what the deal is (ie paying for the whole room or just 1 bed); 'shower' is a pipe overhead, balcony overlooks pile of rubbish. Strictly for hardcore travellers on tightest of budgets and nostalgic for old times, but no doubt the cheapest room you'll find, at 50NIS for a double.

Eating

Most visitors stay just long enough to have a meal or snack at the tourist complex at the Mount of Temptation. This is a shame since there are some decent restaurants in Jericho and they are excellent value.

Cheap falafel and shwarma can be found around Palestine Square.

¶¶ Papa Zion's Grill Restaurant, Route 1, Almog Junction, T/F02-5715860. Outside of town on Road 1. Chicken shishlik is recommended, good vine leaves, great hummus massawshar, generous with the salads. Functional indoor area, walls adorned with old radios and musical instruments. Bedouin seating outside (though road is busy). Impressive array of alcohols, lovely waiters. From Jerusalem, pass Almog Junction then restaurant is on lefthand side just before the giant pots for sale.

¶¶-¶ Abu Omar Sweet & Restaurant, Ein es-Sultan (nr Palestine Sq), T02-2323429. Busy take-away at all hours, or seating in the back is vaguely Bedouin-themed. Excellent falafel, hummus, salads, along with more substantial chicken, lamb and kebab meals. Good for early risers – open 0600-2400.

¶¶-¶ Al-Istiklal, Ein es-Sultan. Pleasant gardens, reasonably priced food, nargillas 12NIS. Food served 0700-late. Also see Swimming, below.

¶¶-¶ Essawi, Palestine Sq, T02-2322160. Excellent food, hummus, salads, kebab, shwarma, chicken, etc. 1st floor balcony is a good spot to dine and watch the world below; come sunset you'll struggle to find a seat. You can't miss their red and black signage in the centre of town. Daily 0600-2300. No alcohol.

¶¶-¶ es-Sultan, the restaurant/coffeeshop at the end of the cable car on Mt Temptation has fabulous views from its cliff-edge terraces and has reasonably priced food. Mainly Middle Eastern, plenty of cheap salads and starters, some Western dishes (pasta). Daily from 0900.

¶¶-¶ Green Valley, Ein es-Sultan, T02-2322349. A shady outdoor restaurant offering a spread of grilled meats, chicken, liver, hummus, salads (8NIS). A real bargain and they serve alcohol (beer 15NIS). Daily 0930-2100.

Bars and clubs

The **Jericho Resort Village** has a bar, although it is aimed primarily at residents. The Green Valley (see above) is a rare chance to enjoy a drink.

Activities & tours
Football

Following recognition by FIFA, the Palestinian national team played their first sanctioned international at the 7000-capacity **Jericho International Stadium**. The pitch is currently under renovation.

Horse-racing

There is a horse-racing track to the southeast of Palestine Square, along the Al Maghtas road.

Swimming

Al-Istiklal, Ein es-Sultan, has a small pool, which you can use for the price of a meal in the garden restaurant. However, women bathers will feel conspicuous. Pool daily 0700-2000.

Transport

To return to Jerusalem, service taxis from Palestine Square run to **Bethlehem**, **Ramallah** (also buses) or **Azariya**. Or take a mini-bus to near Route 1 and pick up a bus from there. Service taxis from Palestine Square also run to the **Israel/Jordan border** at Allenby/King Hussein Bridge. Note that if travelling direct between Jerusalem and the border crossing it is quicker and cheaper to miss out Jericho. It's no problem to find a private taxi in the centre of town to drop you off at the sites.

Bicycle

Bicycles can be hired from **Abu Samaan Bike Rental** on the main square, T02-2324070/059-9820341, 5NIS per hour, 20NIS all day, 0700-2100; cash deposit preferable to leaving passport.

Directory

Banks Banks and money-changers are on Palestine Square, and at the southern end of Qasr Hisham (including Cairo Amman, with ATM). Jordanian dinars are available. **Cultural centres** Jericho Culture & Art Centre, Wardet al-Azra, T/F02-2321047. **Hospitals** Jericho New Hospital, Jerusalem St, T02-2321967/8. **Post office** Main post office is on Amman. This is a good place to buy PA stamps.

Tulul Abu el-'Alayiq

Located to the west of the modern city of Jericho, at the eastern end of the Wadi Qelt gorge, is the site known by the Arabic name of Tulul Abu el-'Alayiq. Initially confusing and spread over a considerable area, this site represents the winter playground of the first-century BCE Jewish aristocracy. Attracted by Jericho's benign winter environment, when Jerusalem was shivering, the Hasmonean (and later Herodian) court decamped to their palaces here.

Ins and outs It should be noted that the site is poorly maintained and rather confusing. The description below concentrates on the main sights that can still be discerned; without the site plans printed here you will almost certainly be lost. There is no public transport to the site, and most taxi drivers seem not to have heard of it. Entrance is officially 10NIS, though there's rarely anyone here to collect it.

Background The site was first extensively developed by the Hasmonean king Alexander Jannaeus (103-76 BCE), who built a large winter palace complex on the north side of

Tulul Abu el-'Alayiq

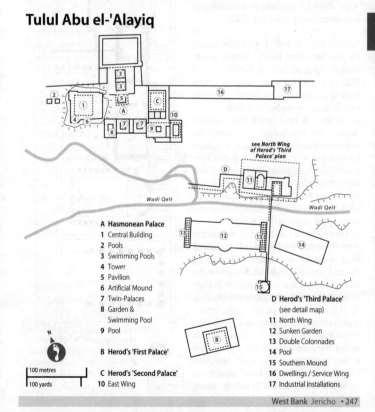

A Hasmonean Palace
1 Central Building
2 Pools
3 Swimming Pools
4 Tower
5 Pavilion
6 Artificial Mound
7 Twin-Palaces
8 Garden &
   Swimming Pool
9 Pool

B Herod's 'First Palace'

C Herod's 'Second Palace'
10 East Wing

D Herod's 'Third Palace'
(see detail map)
11 North Wing
12 Sunken Garden
13 Double Colonnades
14 Pool
15 Southern Mound
16 Dwellings / Service Wing
17 Industrial Installations

100 metres
100 yards

the Wadi Qelt, though the plan is somewhat confused by later modifications. Alexander Jannaeus' palace may also have been severely damaged by the earthquake of 31 BCE.

During the period 35-30 BCE Herod the Great built the first of three palaces here, located on the south side of Wadi Qelt, presumably whilst Alexander Jannaeus' palace was still standing and in the possession of the Hasmonean family. Following the earthquake of 31 BCE and the death of Cleopatra following the battle of Actium, it appears that Herod took control of the Hasmonean palace complex and built his own second palace over the top of it (30-25 BCE). Some time between 15-10 BCE, Herod's third palace was built: a magnificent complex straddling Wadi Qelt. However, as Netzer notes, "Herod's three palaces at Jericho should be viewed as a single unit that developed in stages; all three palaces probably coexisted in the last years of his reign" (*New Encyclopedia of Archaeological Excavations in the Holy Land*, 1993).

Herod's third palace Herod's third palace (D) may have been built to commemorate Marcus Agrippa's visit to Palestine in 15 BCE. As a mark of appreciation it seems likely that a Roman construction team was sent to assist in the building work, since it is certain that local and Roman builders worked on the palace simultaneously. Any differences in styles were disguised by covering all the walls with a fine lime plaster. The third palace was built on both sides of Wadi Qelt rather in the Roman style of building homes and palaces alongside lakes and seas; here the residents were able to enjoy the seasonal flow at least.

The key feature on the south side of the wadi is the **sunken garden (12)**. It features rows of **double colonnades (13)** flanking the east and west ends, set 2 m above the level of the garden, with a portico in front of the colonnades acting as a viewing area. To the east is a **large pool (14)**, whose waters cooled the atmosphere. The bridge across Wadi Qelt has not survived. The plan of the northern wing of the third palace is clearly discernible. The **main reception hall (18)** would have been capable of accommodating several hundred guests

Northern wing of Herod's 'Third Palace'

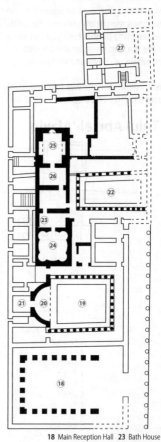

18 Main Reception Hall	23 Bath House
19 Peristyle Courtyard	24 Laconicum
20 Exedra	25 Caldarium
21 Throne Room	26 Tepidarium
22 Smaller Peristyle Courtyard	27 Adjacent Wing

10 metres
10 yards

and served as the palace's central triclinium (used for banquets, ceremonies and receptions). Three rows of columns ran parallel to the west, north and east walls, with an opening to the south providing a view of the sunken garden. Though the large paving stones from the floor are missing, their impressions remain. The walls of the hall would have been decorated with frescoes and stucco mouldings.

To the east of the main reception hall is a **peristyle courtyard** (19) with a semi-circular exedra (20) on its north side. Several guest rooms open on to the courtyard, with the one to the north perhaps being the **throne room** (21). A garden stood at the centre of the courtyard, and a number of embedded flowerpots have been found here. A second, smaller **peristyle courtyard** (22) is located to the east. The Roman-style **bathhouse** (23), built mainly of Roman 'concrete', features a circular room with four semicircular niches that may have served as a **laconicum** (24). Similar examples have been excavated at Pompeii. The rectangular room at the east end of the bathhouse served as a **caldarium** (25) and was heated by the same hypocaust as the adjacent **tepidarium** (26). The frigidarium was probably part of another Herodian building that predated the third palace. The adjacent wing (27) was built on a lower level and may in fact be part of an earlier villa incorporated into the third palace.

Herod's first palace Herod's first palace (B) is located to the south of the site, and comprises a rectangular building facing inwards around a peristyle court. There's not a great deal left to see.

Hasmonean palace complex (and Herod's second palace) The plan of the Hasmonean palace complex (A) is rather confusing. This is due to the fact that significant alterations were made during the Hasmonean period, and then again under Herod. The **central building** (1) of the original palace has only been partially excavated, mainly because it was later filled in to form an artificial mound for another structure. The structure to the southwest is a **tower** (4) that predates the Hasmonean palace. The two **pools** (2) to the west of the central building may also predate it, having probably been built by John Hyrcanus I (134-104 BCE).

Early in the reign of Alexander Jannaeus a new complex was built to the east of the central building. The focus of this complex was the two large **swimming pools** (3), with a colonnaded **pavilion** (5) built in the Doric style to the south. Later, in the period of Herod's rule (c. 35 BCE), these pools were to be the scene of a typically Herodian act. On a hot evening Herod encouraged the seventeen-year-old high priest Aristobulus III, the last in the Hasmonean line, to take a cooling dip in the pool here. He didn't get out of the pool alive (see Josephus, *Antiquities XV, 50-61; Jewish War I, 435-437*).

During the middle part of Alexander Jannaeus' reign (c. 92-83 BCE), the increasingly turbulent situation saw the need to fortify the palace complex here. This was done by filling in the central building (1) area to create an **artificial mound** (6), and cutting a fosse to defend it. Nothing of substance remains of the fortified structure built on the artificial mound. Alexander Jannaeus' successor, his wife Salome Alexandra (76-67 BCE), extended the palace complex, building a new wing to the east. The key features here are the **twin-palaces** (7), so called because they were built next to each other as mirror images. A decorative **garden and swimming pool** (8) stood to the west, with a larger pool (9) built later in the east court. This latter pool was incorporated into Herod's second palace.

Though the main Hasmonean palace complex was badly damaged in the earthquake of 31 BCE, it is still not entirely clear whether it was repaired, rebuilt, or just left to crumble. Some time in the period 30-25 BCE Herod took over the site and begun construction of his second palace (C). Amongst the alterations he made was to turn the two large swimming pools (3) into a single pool, with the second palace featuring an ample provision of gardens.

Qasr al-Yehud

Some 10 km southeast of Jericho is Qasr al-Yehud, one of five traditional sites on the Jordan River where John is said to have baptized Jesus (*Matthew 3:13-17; Mark 1:9-11; Luke 3:21-22*). This one is marked by a Greek Orthodox monastery and a Franciscan chapel. However, Qasr al-Yehud is within a (land-mined) closed military area and hence public visits are restricted to the Greek Orthodox and Roman Catholic Epiphanies (in January and October, respectively). Contact the **Christian Information Centre** ⓘ *(Catholic), opposite the Citadel, Jaffa Gate, Jerusalem, T02-6272692, www.cicts.org,* for further information. Rumours claim that Qasr al-Yehud is primed to reopen to pilgrims soon. Al Maghtas, the Jordanian rival site across the river, has taken the chance to heavily promote their claims to the baptism in the meantime.

Monastery of St Gerasimus/Deir Hajla

ⓘ *Free. Shop, toilets.*

The **Greek Orthodox Monastery** of St Gerasimus, also known as Deir Hajla, with its large silver dome and isolated position, is a striking landmark for travellers on Route 90. The current monastery dates to the end of the 19th century, though it stands on foundations laid by the patriarch of Jerusalem in the 12th century CE. Founded by the eminent monastic figure of the Judean wilderness, **St Gerasimus** (c. 455 CE), there is a main church-crypt (complete with cabinet of skulls) and the upper church (beneath the dome) equally chock-full of icons, candelabras and atmospheric gloom. Accommodation is available at the monastery (see under 'Jericho' on page 245), or take Turkish coffee in the attractive garden.

Allenby/King Hussein Bridge

A mere 16 km east of Jericho is the Allenby/King Hussein Bridge, one of the main crossing points between Israel and Jordan. For full details see page 21 in 'Getting there: overland'.

North of Jerusalem

The area to the north of Jerusalem is probably the part of the West Bank least visited by foreign tourists, yet in an historical, cultural or political context it is as important as any other part. It is the main Arab population centre, and would form the core of any proposed Palestinian state. It is also the heartland of the Jewish region of Samaria, with numerous biblical sites deserving some attention. In addition, it is a region of natural, rugged beauty.

Nabi Samwil The **prophet Samuel** was supposedly buried in Rama (*I Samuel 25:1*) but, since the sixth century CE at least, his tomb has been marked at this spot. A Crusader church was built on top of the existing Byzantine crypt (the Crusaders called this spot 'Mountjoy'), but since the 15th century the tomb has been housed within a mosque. The views from the minaret are particularly rewarding. The village of Nabi Samwil is located a few kilometres north of Jerusalem, off Route 436.

Gibeon (al-Jib) The Palestinian village of al-Jib recalls the biblical Gibeon (*Joshua 9:3-21; 10:12*), noteworthy for its superbly preserved 12th-11th-century BCE water system (see *II Samuel 2:13*). In addition to the rock-cut pool and 10th-century BCE tunnels, you can also see the eighth to seventh-century BCE wine cellars. Al-Jib is several kilometres north of Nabi Samwil (within walking distance). To reach the excavations from al-Jib, take the Biddu road and continue up the hill to the parking lot. Follow the path from there.

Situated on the crest of a hill just 16 km north of Jerusalem, Ramallah's cooling breezes formerly made it a popular resort during the Jordanian occupation (1948-1967). The Arabic name Ramallah means 'Heights of God'. Blessed with good olive plantations and viticulture, plus an expanding industrial base, it is the West Bank's most affluent town. Now that East Jerusalem is in economic decline, most businesses and government institutions have shifted to Ramallah, and the city is experiencing something of a renaissance. Rightly considered by young Palestinians to be the West Bank's 'hippiest' town, it is an excellent place for an alternative night out. Restaurants are significantly better value than Jerusalem, there are numerous bars and watering holes, and it's a

Ramallah

N

200 metres
200 yards

Sleeping
1 Al-Hajal
2 Al-Wehdeh
3 Ankars
4 Best Eastern
5 Merryland
6 Royal Court

Eating
7 Al-Bardauni
3 Angelo's
2 Azure
2 Café de la Pais, Pronto
14 Diwan
4 Espresso Cann
13 Le Grotto
8 Nazareth
6 Sangria
5 Stones
11 Taboun
12 Zeman
10 Ziryab

Taxis
1 Service taxis to/from Jerusalem
2 Service taxis to/from Nablus
3 Service taxis to/from Jericho
4 Service taxis to/from Bir Zeit
5 Taxis around town

good place to socialise with a mix of people. It was previously a predominantly Christian town, though its population of some 27,000 Arabs is now about 70% Muslim and 30% Christian.

Ins and outs

Getting there and away Ramallah is best reached by minibus 18 from Damascus Gate in Jerusalem (30-45 minutes, 6.5NIS), passing through Qalandiya checkpoint (you will need your passport). It also acts as a place to change to a service taxi for Nablus. Shout out where you want to go and someone will quickly propel you in the right direction (see also under 'Transport' on page 255). If driving yourself, it is best to use Hizmah rather than Qalandiya checkpoint, as checks are far less rigorous. The city is compact enough to get around on foot, with most services in and around the main square, Midan-Bireh. Most of the government offices (and more upmarket residences) are in the Al-Bireh suburb to the north/northeast.

Sights

There's not a great deal to see in Ramallah itself, though its population extends a warm welcome to visiting foreigners. In fact, there is a fairly high ex-pat population living in Ramallah, and a foreign face doesn't attract as much attention here as in other cities of the West Bank, making it a relaxing place to be. It's an excellent place for dining and drinking – Thursday nights are particularly recommended.

There's not much left of it, but Ramallah's old city is still worth an hour's wandering. It is very peaceful compared to the hectic bustle of the main city centre, with some attractive Ottoman-era houses still intact. Look out for the **Greek Orthodox Church** ① *daily 0900-1200,* and the Al-Omari Mosque (entrance by request). North of the modern city's main square of Midan Manara is the tomb of **Yasser Arafat** ① *Al-Ith's Street, T02-2986465 in the Al-Muqata compound,* which welcomes visitors.

An excursion from Ramallah to the brewery in the village of **Taybeh** ① *15 km to the northeast, T02-2898868, www.taybehbeer.com, Mon-Sat 0800-1600,* is recommended, this is the Biblical 'Ephraim', and it is the last 100% Christian village left in Palestine. In Arabic, Taybeh means "delicious" and anyone who has been out drinking in East Jerusalem or Ramallah will already know the German-style Taybeh beer is just that. The first weekend in October sees the annual two-day Oktoberfest, with exhibitions, rap bands, crafts, local products and more – an excellent day out. Nadim Khoury started the business in 1994, and the lovely family give free guided tours, which last about 30 minutes and include sampling (not necessary to book, unless you're a big group). Good directions to the brewery can be found on their website.

For those wishing to show support against the separation wall, weekly demonstrations are held in **Be'lin** (20 minutes away) and **Nai'lin** (40 minutes). Shared taxis leave from the main Midan Manara at 1200 each Friday (you won't have trouble spotting one as they are the only transport around on Fridays). These are non-violent demonstrations, reminiscent of the First Intifada, but a visit is not to be taken lightly. Expect tear-gas, at least, to be used to disperse the crowds; it is wise to remain at the back. There is ample opportunity to interact and get explanations. This is not an activity to mention to the authorities when questioned at the airport leaving the country, and bear in mind that you could get into trouble and all sorts of visa problems could ensue. See www.stopthewall.org for more information.

Ramallah listings

For Sleeping and Eating price codes and other relevant information, see Essentials pages 26-31.

Sleeping

There's a fair spread of hotels in Ramallah, with new ones opening up all the time. In the higher categories, you get much more for your money than you would in Jerusalem. The lower end rooms are a bit rundown, but, again, they are relatively cheap.

AL Ankars Suites & Hotel, Al-Masyoon, T02-2952602, www.ankarsuites.com. Rooms, suites with kitchenettes and VIP suites (doubles $100/120/150) in this attractive new place with lovely staff and good facilities. Lots of space, some have balcony; price includes Wi-Fi, breakfast, daily cleaning. Also available for long-term rents. Has good restaurant on 8th floor and posh bar on the 9th Floor, 24-hr room service.

AL Grand Park, T02-2986194, www.grandpark.com. Large, luxurious hotel on the edge of town, with grand public areas, some suites in the L category, swimming pool, very nice terrace restaurant. Adios bar is good (see listings, page 254). Doubles 462NIS B&B.

A Best Eastern, El-Ersal, Al-Bireh, T02-2958451, info@besteasternhotels.com. Located near the Ministry of Information in the upmarket Al-Bireh suburb, this hotel features large standard rooms, slightly bigger deluxe rooms ($20 extra), plus some suites. All have a/c, cable TV, phone. Hotel has nice restaurants but no bar, pool is open in summer; taxi service, helpful and friendly staff. Doubles $90 B&B.

A Royal Court Suites Hotel, Jaffa, T02-2964040, www.rcshotel.com. Excellent-value standard rooms have been recently remodelled with good beds, big pillows, grey carpets, fridge, decent bathrooms. Also 'deluxe plus' (with balcony) and 'businessman suites' (2 balconies, kitchenette, desk, tables, huge) in the higher price bracket. Breakfast buffet and nice patio out the front.

B Al-Hajal, T02-2986759/2987858. Plain hotel with absolutely no adornment. Rooms have comfy beds, fan, TV and plenty of space, bathrooms old and unappealing but clean. B&B, rates negotiable.

C Al-Wehdeh, 26 Al-Nahda, T02-2980412. Clean, functional rooms, basic en suite, TV; discounts for longer stays otherwise a double for 1 night is 120NIS.

D-E Merryland, Al-Ma'ahed (near Diwar Al-Sa'ah), T02-2987176/059-8398044. Basic place above a noisy shopping complex, rooms a bit grubby (check the sheets), some have ensuite, TV, fans. Very cheap.

Eating

Ramallah has a particularly good selection of restaurants, with funky interiors and noticeably cheaper prices than Jerusalem. There are also the muntazaat (outdoor restaurants) where both local dignitaries and Palestinian families come to eat and relax. Perhaps the most famous of these is **Al-Bardauni**, Jaffa, T02-2951410, where all the 'big nobs' on expense accounts come to dine and entertain. There is also a cluster of café/bars on Al-Rasheed, near its junction with Jaffa.

♔ **Azure**, Al-Nuzha. Serves very good food, from $10 upwards; the Mongolian beef or the Azure Burger are good choices for meat-eaters. Or you can come just to watch football and have a drink.

♔ **Café de la Pais**, Al-Rahseed, Highly recommended for their food (the warm beef teriyaki salad is excellent); no alcohol. Just up the road from Pronto's.

♔ **Pronto's Resto-bar**, Al-Rahseed, T02-2987312. The best pizza in town, this relaxing place gathers all and sundry for chat as well as good Italian food. The front terrace is a good place for a pint of Taybeh.

♔ **Stones**, Al-Rahseed, T02-2966038. A huge menu of good international food. Funky building with lots of glass.

♔-♔ **Espresso Cann**, Jaffa, T02-2972125. A civilised modern café with red walls, nice sunny terrace, Western-styling. Light meals include salads (20-30NIS), wide choice of sandwiches, granola breakfast and of course coffee. A lemon-mint narghilla is 20NIS. Daily 0700-2300 (or later),

₸-₸ Zeman, Al-Tira Sq, just west of the Old City. A new little café-bar, with tables outside, good coffee and sandwiches guaranteed, and they serve alcohol. Best for hanging out during daylight hours.

₸-₸ Ziryab, Salah Building, Main St, T02-2959093. Gazan owner. Little coffee-shop, which is also a registered art gallery and displays his works on the walls. It also serves alcohol and does a mean chicken stroganoff.

A selection of slightly cheaper restaurants can be found on Rokab (AKA Main Street), as it runs west from the central square (Midan Manara), and also along Ahliyyah College St. These include:

₸-₸ Mr Fish, T02-2959555, has a 20NIS deal on fish and chip sandwiches that are too big to handle, daily 0900-2100.

₸ Diwan, Maktaba. Café with backgammon (Arabic: Tawla), nargillah, card-games, mix of clientele where it's cool for women to hang out. Near to Azure resto-bar.

₸ Nazareth, cheap and cheerful, run by four brothers; **Osama's** and **Angelo's**, T02-2956408, nearby, both do a surprisingly good pizza; and **Taboun**, T02-2980505, is also a reliable choice.

Those on a tight budget will find very cheap falafel and shwarma in the places close to Midan Manara.

Bars and clubs
Unlike most of the other towns on the West Bank, you will find that many of Ramallah's restaurants also serve alcohol (cocktails, wine, beer and some locally produced arak). Alcohol is also sold in shops and supermarkets.

Adios, Grand Park Hotel, Rafat, Al-Masyoon, T02-2986194, www.grandpark.com. Cosy bar, with all the sports channels: a perfect venue for catching a football, cricket or rugby match. Sometimes, if you are lucky, it gets a bit wild and morphs into a dance club with pumping tunes.

Almonds, Ramallah Hotel, Al-Masyoun, T02-

2957028. The most pub-like of Ramallah's many drinking establishments, there are 2 large pool tables and reasonable pub grub. Suitable for some serious drinking.

Chez Vatche, Al-Masyoon, T02-2965966. Popular with rich Palestinians drinking Black Label.

Le Grotto, Al-Rasheed. Aptly named hideaway in an old stone building, run by a kindly art teacher. Bedouin draperies, rock walls decorated with paintings, sandwiches and simple snacks. Recommended for a quiet drink.

Sangria, Jaffa, Al-Muntazah, T02-2956808. Lovely back garden (open May-Sep), is a winner.

Snowbar, Ein Saman, T02-2965571. The place to go in summer (only open Apr-Oct), there is a beautiful landscaped garden and swimming pool (lone females will feel comfortable). Quality food, the black and blue burger is delicious (black pepper, blue cheese). Daily until late; in the evenings they sometimes have a bonfire and you'll hear Palestinian rap bands if you get lucky. It is a 10-min taxi ride from the city centre.

Up Town/Sky Bar, Ankars Suites (see Sleeping). Sleek marble bar, with great views from the open windows of the 9th floor. Menu has mix of Arabic/Mediterranean food, narghila available. You will find rich Ramallah-ites here.

Zan Bar, near Midan Manara. Come on a Thu night when it's packed, and there's usually DJs and good music. A haunt for ex-pats and NGO workers.

Entertainment
Concert halls
Edward Said National Conservatory of Music, Al-Isral, T02-2959070.

First Ramallah Group, T02-2952706, www.sirreyeh.org, Al-Tira, has a pool and large gardens that are popular for a nargilla.

Cultural centres
Ramallah has a vibrant cultural scene and is also the base for a number of organizations geared towards raising awareness of Palestinian culture and heritage. See This

Week in Palestine for details and look out for adverts in cafés and bars.

British Institute, T2958763; Cultural Palace, Tokyo St, T02-2984704, www.ramallahculturalpalace.org, hosts a film festival.

Franco-German Cultural Centre, Rukab, T02-2981922/7727, info@ccf-goethe.org.

In'ash Al-Usra Society (Centre for Heritage & Folklore Studies, T2956876, has a small museum and can make traditional food for visitors (phone in advance, ask for Inam Shaedi).

Al Kasaba Theatre and Cinematheque, Hospital St, near Manara Sq, T02-2965292/3, www.alkasaba.org, for film screenings and a very active scene; also has a nice bar-restaurant and holds the annual Palestine International Festival. A visit is recommended.

Khalil al-Sakakini Cultural Centre, T2987374, www.sakakini.org, a good place to start to tap into the scene.

Popular Art Centre, T2953891, F2952851, most notable for screening Hollywood films.

Activities and tours

For information on Palestine-focussed tours, see box page 201.

Transport
Car hire

There are several car hire firms insured for travel within the West Bank. **Orabi**, Main St, T02-2403521, is probably the most reputable (good for Palestinian-plated cars for touring the West Bank, though yellow Israeli plates also available).

Mini-buses/service taxis

The main bus station is on Nadha, just to the east of Midan Manara. There are services to **Nablus** and East Jerusalem's Suleiman Street bus station (note that passing back through Qalandiya you will be required to disembark and walk through the checkpoint, and rejoin your bus on the other side – ensure you have your passport with you). Buses to **Bir Zeit** run from the stand on Al-Adha'a, opposite Mukhmas Shopping Centre. Service taxis arrive/depart from a variety of places close to Midan Manara, depending largely upon where you have come from/are going to. The easiest option is to call out where you want to go and then allow yourself to be propelled in the right direction.

Taxis

Al-Bireh, T02-2402956. Al-Wafa, T02-2955544. Al-Itihad, T02-2955887. The taxi rank for journeys around town is on Al-Adha'a.

Directory

Banks HSBC (AKA the British Bank), junction of Jaffa/Rasheed, ATM machine. There are numerous banks and money-changers in and around Midan Manara. **Embassies and consulates** Austria, T02-2401477; Canada, T02-2978430; Germany, T02-2984788; Jordanian, T02-2974625 (here you can get a Jordanian visa in a day). Netherlands, T02-2406639. **Hospitals** Sheikh Zayed, Hospital Street, T02-2988088 (near the government hospital) is the best in town. **Internet** International Centre, Rokab; Old City Net, T02-2950873 (opposite Al-Omari Mosque), open 24/7. There are a number of cybercafés around town offering very cheap internet access (4NIS for 1 hr). **Post offices** The main post office is on Al-Mutaza.

Around Ramallah

Beitin

Located about 5 km northeast of Ramallah is the small Arab village of Beitin, almost certainly the site of the biblical **Bethel** or 'House of God' (formerly Luz, see *Judges 1:23*). It is best known as the scene of Jacob's dream (*Genesis 28:12*), and a low hill here is referred to as 'Jacob's Ladder' though it is indistinguishable from the other low hills in the area. Bethel was captured by Joshua c. 1240-1235 BCE, but subsequently conquered by the Canaanites.

Ephraim recaptured it for the Israelites (*Judges 1:22-26*), though it was soon overshadowed by the rise of nearby Jerusalem. It continued to be occupied during the rule of the kings of Judah, and was also settled in the Hellenistic, Roman and Byzantine periods. The minimal Bronze- and Iron-Age remains are hardly worth a visit. The controversial Jewish West Bank settlement of **Beth-El** is located nearby, where the Israeli Head of Civil Administration office is (for Palestinians to apply for permits to travel outside the West Bank).

Bir Zeit

This Palestinian town some 20 km north of Ramallah is best known as the home of **Bir Zeit University**, the premier further education centre on the West Bank. It is a relaxing village to visit, with a campus atmosphere and many international students taking (comparatively cheap) courses in Arabic or about the conflict. The university has a noted Development Studies Institute; full details of the university can be found on its web site (www.birzeit. edu). Regular buses and service taxis run to the university from Ramallah.

Jifna

The PA have restored a Crusader period **Manor House** at Jifna (just off Route 60 about 5 km north of Ramallah on the road to Bir Zeit). For further details see *Pringle's Gazeteer of Secular Crusader Buildings in the Holy Land*.

Shiloh

The site of Shiloh is located about 1 km off Route 60 at a point some 30 km north of Jerusalem (signed). It is the scene of a number of biblical traditions (*Joshua 18:1; 18:8-10; 21:2; Judges 21:19; I Samuel 1-3; 4:1-22; Jeremiah 7:12-14; Psalms 78:60*). Archaeological excavations have confirmed a number of the biblical descriptions.

Remains from the **Middle Bronze Age IIB** (1750-1550 BCE) have been found, plus a few finds from the **Late Bronze Age** (1550-1200 BCE), though it appears that the site was used more as a cultic place than a permanent residential settlement. **Iron Age IA** (1200-1150 BCE) structures have also been identified, though few visitors to Shiloh will be impressed by the sight before them. The later remains are more substantial, particularly the mosaic floors in the Byzantine **Pilgrim's Church** and **basilica**. There are also several structures from the Early Arab period (638-1099 CE), including the **Jama' es-Sittin** (Mosque of the Sixty) which re-uses fragments from earlier churches, and may well originally have been a synagogue.

Nablus (Shechem)

→ *Colour map 2, grid A4.*

Biblical references to the various sites here abound, with the ancient town of Shechem filling a significant spot within Jewish history (Israeli sources, including road signs, still refer to the town by this name). Nablus has been an important Arab settlement since the seventh century CE, and one of the main centres of Palestinian resistance to Israeli rule. During and after the Second Intifada, Nablus was under a virtual siege (some say from 2001-2007). Road blocks prevented movement in and out of the city, and the 130,000 residents lived with a perpetual night curfew. Fortunately, the situation has eased in the last couple of years, entrance is via one checkpoint, and the atmosphere has lightened perceptibly. There are plenty of points of interest in and around the town, plus seemingly endless authentic markets where life is unaffected by any tourist trap; or you can come just to discuss the 'Arab-Israeli Question'.

Ins and outs

Getting there and away The easiest way to reach Nablus is by service taxi from Ramallah (10NIS). Service taxis and buses to destinations on the West Bank arrive/depart from the stand to the west of the town centre (see map, and 'Transport' on page 260).

Getting around The town centre is compact enough to get around on foot, and most of the sights around Nablus (including Tell Balâtah, Jacob's Well and Joseph's Tomb) are probably easier to reach by walking rather than by service taxi. A walk up to the top of Mount Gerizim or Mount Ebal will take about two hours each, or a 100NIS taxi ride (wait and return). The main focus of the new town is Palestine Square (Midan Filistin), also known as Midan al-Hussein.

Warning Visitors should note that it is a conservative city, so modest dress and behaviour are essential. Nablus was very much a 'no-go' area during the intifadas, but now is considered safe for foreign tourists to visit, and unwanted attention is minimal.

Tourist information The Ministry of Tourism is housed on the eighth floor of a building on Hamdi Kan'an (see map), though they are genuinely surprised to receive visitors. Check out www.nablusguide.com for listings and information.

Background

Ancient Shechem The long history of settlement at this spot is a function of its location on a major north–south route through the central hill country, and at the mouth of the

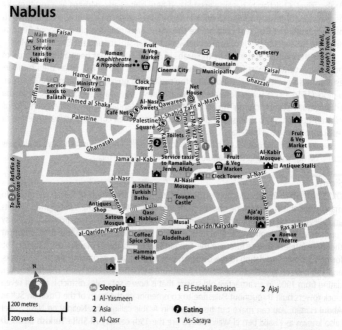

Nablus

Sleeping
1 Al-Yasmeen
2 Asia
3 Al-Qasr
4 El-Esteklal Bension

Eating
1 As-Saraya
2 Ajaj

region's only east–west pass. It was at this spot c. 1850 BCE that the patriarch **Abraham** entered the land of Canaan, and where "the Lord appeared unto Abraham, and said, 'Unto thy seed will I give this land'" (*Genesis 12:7*). It was also at Shechem that Jacob bought land for himself and his family (*Genesis 33:18-20*), whilst his son Joseph, following his death in Egypt, was buried here (*Joshua 24:32*). At the end of the United Monarchy (928 BCE) the city became the capital of the northern kingdom ('Israel' as opposed to 'Judah'), but its political significance was soon eroded when the capital was switched to Samaria (see page 264). Shechem suffered greatly from the Assyrian invasion of 724-722 BCE but experienced something of a revival in the Early Hellenistic period (332-167 BCE), and most notably in the wake of the construction of the **Samaritan** temple on nearby Mt Gerizim in the fifth to fourth century BCE (see page 263). The temple was razed during the Hasmonean ruler John Hyrcanus' sack of Shechem in 108/107 BCE, when the town was largely destroyed. Insubstantial remains of ancient Shechem, most notably from the Hellenistic period, can be seen at **Tell Balâtah** about 2 km southeast of the modern town of Nablus.

Neapolis Following the suppression of the First Jewish Revolt by the Roman army (66-73 BCE), a new Roman colony was established just to the west of the site of ancient Shechem: Neapolis. The fertile lands around Neapolis were divided amongst veterans of Titus' army, whilst a temple to Zeus was built on Mt Gerizim (see Tell er-Ras, page 264). Later centuries saw the construction of a hippodrome, amphitheatre and theatre, though the remains are not well presented today.

Arab arrival Christianity became established here quite early, perhaps as a result of the gospel story of Jesus stopping to drink at Jacob's Well (*John 4:5-42*). In 484 CE the Church of Mary Mother of God was built on the site of the Samaritan temple on Mount Gerizim, resulting in several periods of conflict between the Samaritans and the Byzantine rulers.

Since the capture of the city by the Arabs in 636 CE Nablus has been a thriving Muslim population centre (apart from a brief interregnum from 1099-1187 when the Crusaders established a presence here). It became the capital of a governorate during the Ottoman period (1516-1917) when Jerusalem was a relative backwater, and later became the administrative centre during the period of the British Mandate. It has always been a focus of Arab opposition to Zionism, and subsequently to Israeli control, and was a centre of resistance during the intifadas.

Nablus' economy today is (as it has been for hundreds, if not thousands, of years) largely based on agriculture and the manufacture of soap and olive oil.

Sights

Old City Nablus' main attraction is the Old City, just to the south of Palestine Square. In many ways this is a welcome change from Jerusalem's Old City: the same narrow streets and alleyways are here but without the rampant commercialism. Milling around in the busy souqs or strolling through the quiet back streets is a fine way to spend some time. Amongst the more interesting structures are the **Touqan Castle** and the **Al-Manara clock tower**. The former is a mansion dating to the Ottoman period. It remains occupied, despite the cracks, and you can still appreciate the building from the rubbish-filled courtyard. The clock tower, dating from 1906, in an attractive old square that is now a sofa-sales district, is one of seven clock towers built throughout Palestine to commemorate the reign of the Ottoman Sultan Abdul Hamid; you can make out his insignia in Arabic calligraphy. Nearby on Nasir Street (also known as Khalid ben el-Walid Street) are the 15th-century **Al-Shifa Turkish baths** ①

T09-2381176. Daily 100-2400. Women only Tue and Sun 1000-1800. Baths 30NIS (includes sauna, steam, and soaps), massage 15NIS (at least 1 hr), the oldest working hammam in the country. The **Hamman al-Hana (AKA As-Sumara)** ① *T09-2385185,* nearby offers similar services, with women only Tuesdays 1000-1800; the neon-paint decorations on the reception ceiling are an unfortunate stab at modernisation, however, the interior rooms of the hammam retain the old blocks of coloured glass set in domed ceilings. On Al-Qaridn Street, look out for the Qasr Nabulsi, a fine old building (where families still live on the upper floors) that is in the process of being restored. It is also worth passing by the nice folk at '**Toaster and Grinders Break Coffee'** ① *Al-Yasmeena Street, T09-2336488, daily 0700-1900 (exc Fri),* where you can purchase any number of fragrant spices and see their dusty collection of Palestinian artefacts at the rear.

Of the city's many mosques the **al-Kabir mosque** is the most impressive, featuring a columned vaulted hall that was originally part of a Crusader church (built c. 1168). The mosque is easily identified by the tall minaret with silver cupola and crescent moon. The interior is undergoing a major renovation in 2010, and it is possible to see through the windows and admire the many columns and capitals. Nearby is the green-domed al-Nasir mosque. Neither is open to non-Muslims. Ask people to direct you to the last remaining soap factory, **Al-Gamal** (the camel), which is maintaining a centuries' old industry. Apparently Nabulsi soap was Queen Elizabeth I's choice of cleanser.

Roman theatre The second-century CE Roman theatre is located on the northern slope of Mt Gerizim, just above the old city (see map). With a projected diameter of around 110 m it would have been one of the largest in the country, with three cavea (spectator seating areas). Unfortunately it was plundered by the Mamluks during the building of Nablus, and all that remains is a section of the lower cavea and some architectural fragments in amongst the undergrowth. The guy in the neighbouring metalwork shop has the key to the gate and will happily let you in.

Roman amphitheatre and hippodrome Insubstantial remains of the second-century CE hippodrome lie on the southwest slope of Mt Ebal, formerly at the western approach to the Roman city. Superimposed on the circular end of the hippodrome are the remains of the third-century CE amphitheatre, though both are in a bad state of preservation and totally overgrown, located in waste ground encircled by a fruit and vegetable market.

Former British prison The former British prison, once used to house Arab and Jewish opponents of the British Mandate authority and then the Palestinian Authority's Ministry of the Interior, was destroyed by F-16s during the last intifada. The area is now surrounded by an unattractive concrete wall, and re-building may start sometime soon.

Nablus listings

For Sleeping and Eating price codes and other relevant information, see Essentials pages 26-31.

Sleeping
AL Asia, Rafidia, T09-2392321/T09-2348480, www.asiahotel.ps. Modern hotel on the western outskirts. Boxy a/c rooms are

decently (if boringly) furnished with small balconies, TV, phone. There's a lobby coffee shop, restaurant and internet facilities.
A Al-Qasr, Omar Ibn al-Khattab, Rafidia, T08-2385444, F2385944. Located on the western outskirts of town, this is the nicest hotel in Nablus, with 40 renovated and furnished a/c rooms, with TV and minibar. 2 restaurants plus roof terrace and lobby bar.

B Al-Yasmeen, Old City, T09-2333555, www. alyasmeen.com. Comfortable well-furnished 1-4-bed rooms ($55-90), big windows, green and cream decor, carpets, TV, Wi-Fi, 24-hr hot water, very fairly priced (breakfast included); it's not surprising that every NGO worker in Nablus is staying here. The suite ($120) and mini-suite ($90) have balconies and lots of space, public areas are bright and airy, and staff friendly. It's located right next to the main Khan al-Tujjar.

F El-Esteklal, 11 Hitten, T09-2383618. Light and airy (but not very private) basic dorms with 4-6 beds, shared bath clean enough, cleanliness of sheets dubious. Old style and friendly; women allowed but may feel uncomfortable and will certainly want to insist on a room of their own. A bed costs 30NIS.

Eating

Sticky sweets, most notably kanafe (soft cheese in an orange wheat flake jacket and covered in honey), are Nablus's speciality and can be tried at numerous stalls and shops in the Old City area. This is 'the' place to eat kanafe, and you can't come to Nablus without indulging. Ask people to point you to the most famous sweetshop, called Al-Aqsa. There are any number of restaurants in the town centre (mainly around Palestine Square) offering good-value kebabs, grills, falafel and shwarma. For a more conventional dining experience try:

†††-† As-Saraya, Saleem Afandi Restaurants, Hitten, T09-2335444. On the edge of the old city souqs, Saraya is the perfect place to re-group after a day in Nablus. Entered through the courtyard at the rear, it's in an old mansion with dark-green awnings. Vaulted ceilings, a variety of rooms to relax in, open-air terrace, padded comfy chairs, Syrian styling, plus a mix of clientele (local ladies who lunch). Food is very reasonably priced: salads 5-10NIS, BBQ meats all come with fries (40-60NIS), fish and a few Western dishes; nargilla 15NIS. Efficient staff. Daily 1000-2400.

††-† Zeit ou Zaata, at the Yasmeen Hotel (see Sleeping, above). Mix of Continental food, Palestinian dishes (lots of good chicken), Lebanese grills, mains 25-90NIS, mezze 6-10NIS, vegetarian 20-30NIS. Famed for Palestinian pastries (5-6NIS). There are a couple of nice terraces, and alcohol is served. Recommended.

† Ajaj, Salahi. This is an Omelette Institution. Accompanied by pickles, yoghurt salad and 'hubs' (bread), veg omelettes are cooked to perfection in this cubby hole in the old city, which has been running for 60 years or more. Flexible opening hours, but afternoons are a safe bet. Cheap and recommended.

Entertainment
Cinema

The huge new **Cinema City** mall, in the centre of the city, has been welcomed by the citizens of Nablus.

Cultural centres
Arafat Soap Factory/Cultural Heritage Enrichment Centre, 29, An-Najah Al-Qadim, Old City, T09-2337077, has a library and exhibition space.

French Cultural Centre, An-Najah Al-Qadim, T09-2385914, F2387593, www. consulfrance-jerusalem.org. An active programme includes cine-club, theatre, concerts and discussion, Sat-Thu 1000-1800.

Shopping
Toaster and Grinders Break Coffee, Al-Yasmeena, T09-2336488, daily 0700-1900 (exc Fri), see Old City page 258. For genuine antiques try the little shop on Al-Yasmeena (coffee-pots, metalware and the like), open afternoons only (see map).

Activities and tours
For tours in the West Bank, see box page 201.

Transport
Bus/service taxis
Nablus' main bus station is a parking lot to the west of the town centre (see map). The easiest way to reach Nablus is by service

taxi. Coming from Jerusalem you will have to change at Ramallah from where it takes 1 hr. From Nablus, service taxis leave for **Ramallah** (last service at around 1800) and **Jenin** run from outside the main bus station to the west of the town centre (see map). Service taxis to **Sebastiya** (for the site of **Samaria** (Sebaste), 20 mins) run from a spot on Suffian, near its junction with Hamdi Kan'an (see map). Service taxis along Faisal St to **Tell Balatah**, **Joseph's Tomb** and **Jacob's Well** (1NIS) run from just north of Palestine Square (ask for 'Balatah').

Car hire
Orabi, T09-2383383.

Taxis
Al-Ittimad, T09-2371439; Al-Madina, T09-2373501.

Directory
Banks There are branches of most of the Arab banks (plus a few money changers) in and around Palestine Square; Bank of Palestine has an ATM. **Hospitals** Al-Watani, T09-2380039; Rafidia, T09-2390390; Red Crescent Society, T09-2382153. **Internet** Café Net, 2nd floor, Palestine St (see map), T09-2392843. 10NIS per 1 hr. **Net House**, Na'em Abdul Hadi Building, Omar Mokhtar (though entrance is on Omar Khayyam), T/F09-2392086, 10NIS per 1 hr. **Post offices** Central Post Office on Faisal (Sat-Wed 0800-1300 and 1500-1700, Thu 0800-1300, Fri closed) sells PA stamps.

Around Nablus

Jacob's Well

ⓘ *Daily 0800-1200 and 1400-1700, free. To reach the site, head southeast from Nablus, take the left fork down the hill and look out for the white-walled compound with the Greek and Palestinian flags above the gate.*

The first church built on this site dates to the end of the fourth century CE, and was built to commemorate the story of Jesus' meeting with the Samaritan woman where he spoke about the "living water" (*John 4:4-30*). The incident is said to have taken place at the site of the well dug by Jacob when he purchased land in the area (*Genesis 33:18-20*), with the 41-m-deep well forming the centrepiece of the crypt beneath the high altar. The church is mentioned by St Jerome in 404 CE, though it was largely destroyed in the Samaritan revolt against the Byzantine rulers in 529 CE. Despite being repaired by the Emperor Justinian it was again levelled during the Persian invasion of 614 CE. The Crusaders constructed a new church on the Byzantine foundations in the 12th century CE, though this church too stood in ruins until the Russian Orthodox church acquired it in 1860. Unfortunately, their reconstruction efforts were interrupted by the Russian Revolution, and it is now owned by the Greek Orthodox church. The church is some 6 m below the present ground level, and is entered via the arched gate to the west. Two flights of steps lead down from the main aisle of the basilica to the crypt, where the well is located. If enough people are present the Greek Orthodox priest will draw water from the well; it is remarkably cool and sweet.

Ancient Shechem (Tell Balâtah)

Today, ancient Shechem is little more than a series of unimpressive remains occupying three dips in an area of open ground, usually populated by lounging Palestinian policemen and kids playing football. Excavations at the site have revealed 24 distinct strata of occupation dating from the Chalcolithic period (c. 4000 BCE at the earliest) until the

The Samaritans

Best known to the Christian world through Jesus' parable of the "Good Samaritan" (*Luke 10:30-37*), the Samaritans are a dissident sect of Judaism numbering around 700 adherents. Almost the entire community live in Nablus or Holon (near Tel Aviv). Recognizing only the first five *Books of Moses* as their Torah, plus its immediate sequel, the *Book of Joshua*, the Samaritans consider themselves as true Jews. Their origins lie within the demise of the United Monarchy following the death of Solomon (928 BCE), and the subsequent split between the northern kingdom of Israel and the southern kingdom of Judah. They claim to be the descendants of the Israelites who stayed in the northern kingdom, rather than those who were exiled to Babylon. The final break between the Samaritans and the Jews came in the second century BCE.

Samaritan power was concentrated around the site of their sacred mountain, Mt Gerizim, though the rise to prominence of Christianity in the area brought them into open conflict with the Byzantine empire. The first shot in this war was fired by the Byzantine emperor Zeno (474-491 CE), who in 484 CE built the Church of Mary, Mother of God on the Samaritan sacred area on Mt Gerizim. Skirmishes between the two communities continued, reaching a bloody climax in the Samaritan revolt of 529 CE. The emperor Justinian's response to the Samaritans' nationwide church-burning and Christian-massacring spree was swift and equally brutal, effectively reducing the Samaritan community to the relatively insignificant relic that it remains today.

In the modern era, Samaritans occupy an unusual place in society, belonging to both, and yet to neither, the Palestinian nor the Israeli "side". They speak Hebrew and Arabic, and use the ancient language of Aramaic during religious services. They have Israeli citizenship and those who live in Holon serve in the IDF, yet in Nablus they are full Palestinian citizens and, until recently, had a seat reserved in the Palestinian Legislative Council. From an all-time low of 146 members in 1917, the population is growing again with most members under the age of 25, although rates of genetic disease are above average. A decreasing female population has led to a few Samaritan men marrying outside the community (notably, Ukrainian women), though previously marriage had only been permitted within the Samaritan religion. A trial period allows a woman the chance to decide if she can accept the strict interpretation of some Biblical laws before joining the community.

Late Hellenistic period (the sacking by John Hyrcanus c. 107 BCE). The most impressive (or is that the least unimpressive?) remains are on the north side of the tel, and feature the defensive **Cyclopean wall** (c. 1650 BCE), the **northwest gate complex**, and the migdal or **fortress temple**. The **east gate** is also reasonably well preserved.

Service taxis pass the modern village of Balâtah that surrounds the site, though it is in fact probably easier to walk. Balâtah is the largest of the West Bank refugee camps, with a population of about 23,000.

Joseph's Tomb

Though comparisons are frequently made between the similar architectural styles of Joseph's Tomb in Nablus and Rachel's Tomb near Bethlehem, this small domed structure bears a closer resemblance to a concrete bunker. Along with the Temple Mount in Jerusalem and the Cave of Machpelah (Tomb of the Patriarchs) in Hebron, this is one of the three places that Jews claim as theirs by right of historically documented purchase. The *Book of Joshua* recalls how, following his death, "the bones of Joseph, which the children of Israel brought up out of Egypt, buried they in Shechem, in a parcel of ground which Jacob bought of the sons of Hamor the father of Shechem for an hundred pieces of silver: and it became the inheritance of the children of Joseph" (*Joshua 24:32*). After centuries of Muslim control, from 1975 to 1995 the tomb was in the hands of the Israelis, or more accurately the Israeli army. In the protests that followed the controversial opening of the Hasmonean tunnel in Jerusalem in September 1996, the Israelis and Palestinians turned their guns on each other at Joseph's Tomb, leaving six Israeli soldiers dead, and the yeshiva here ransacked. Then in 2000, another clash left 18 Palestinians and one Israeli dead, and the government decided to pull the IDF out and forbade access to Jewish worshippers. Since then, Breslav Hassidim have made night-time visits to the tomb, there have been reports that Palestinians have defiled and vandalised the site, and Jews can now only visit under heavy IDF guard once per month. Clearly, the site remains tense and foreign visitors are unlikely to be allowed access. Modest dress must be worn (including head coverings for both sexes).

Mt Gerizim

Nablus has one of just two Samaritan communities in the world, the other being at Holon, near Tel Aviv. Until the first (Al-Aqsa) intifada, a number of Samaritans lived in a small quarter of the old city, just to the west of the town centre, in the shadow of their sacred mountain Gerizim. The uprising and its ensuing violence caused them to move, and join the larger community on top of the mount (in the modern houses on the plateau below the summit). Community members from Holon travel up to Nablus each week to celebrate Shabbat with the Gerizim community.

Mt Gerizim stands 868 m above sea-level, and 500 m above Nablus below. Those who make the two-hour hike to the summit (or 100NIS taxi ride, return journey) will not be disappointed by the view across Samaria; on a clear day the Mediterranean coast to the west is clearly visible. The Jewish settlement of Braka has been built on the slopes of the mountain, below the Samaritan village of Kiryat Luza, hence the area has an army presence. In the Samaritan enclave, the **Gerizim Centre and Museum** ⓘ *Sun-Fri 0800-1400*, has what is claimed to be the world's oldest Torah scroll; it used to be housed in the small synagogue in the old city (now abandoned). Samaritan religious celebrations reach their peak with the 40 days of Passover, when the community ritually slaughters a sheep in the manner laid down by Moses (*Exodus 12:1-51*). The men make a wonderful sight on Shabbat, with flowing white robes and red tarbushes on their heads, though being treated as a tourist attraction is, naturally, resented.

The Samaritan community believe that it was on Mt Gerizim and not Mt Moriah (Temple Mount) in Jerusalem that Abraham offered his son Isaac for sacrifice. Josephus (*Jewish War; Antiquities*) provides much of the early history of settlement on Mt Gerizim, documenting the various disputes between the Samaritan and Jewish communities. A walled city of about 40 hectares was built on the upper ridge during the Hellenistic period, with the thick layer of ash on the floor of all the buildings confirming the city's destruction by John Hyrcanus c. 108/107 BCE. Of the buildings from this period still discernible, the most impressive are remains of the **residential quarters**, the **sacred precinct** (modelled on the Temple Mount in Jerusalem), and the so-called **Twelve Stones** (part of a second-century BCE building).

Following the destruction of the settlement on Mt Gerizim, Samaritans continued to ascend the mountain to pray. According to the writings of Procopius (*Buildings 1-17*, v, vii) this was because they worshipped the summit itself, and not because they had ever built a temple there. During the struggle between the Samaritans and the (Christian) Byzantine

Empire, the Emperor Zenon built a large octagonal church on the summit. It is clear that the siting of the **Church of Mary, Mother of God** on an area sacred to Samaritans was deliberate, possibly as an attempt to convert them but definitely as a demonstration of superiority. The church was partially destroyed on a number of occasions in the ensuing conflict between the Byzantines and Samaritans, with many of the later additions to the church comprising defensive fortifications. Looking at the plan of the remains today, the lines of the octagonal church within a wall fortified by defensive towers are immediately apparent. Columns and pillars from the church are displayed in the Museum of the Good Samaritan, on Route 1 between Jerusalem and Jericho (see page 233). It was largely destroyed by the Arabs in the eighth century CE, and the fortress walls dismantled. The modern tomb at the northeast corner belongs to Abu Ghanen, a Muslim holy man.

Tell er-Ras (Roman temple)

Mt Gerizim actually comprises two perpendicular ridges: the lower one running east–west and the upper one running north–south. Facing Nablus on the north face of the lower ridge are the remains of a **temple** dedicated to **Zeus Hyposistos** (the supreme). The remains stand upon an artificial mound that is now referred to as Tell er-Ras. Nearly all the coins minted at Neapolis between the mid-second century CE and the mid-third century CE depict the temple, reached by a long monumental staircase. Later writers (such as the Bordeaux Pilgrim c. 333 CE and Epiphanius c. 315-403 CE) mention the 1300-1500 step staircase ascending Mt Gerizim, though only 65 or so of the stairs remain intact.

Mt Ebal

Whilst Mt Gerizim stands to the south of Nablus, the town is defined to the north by Mt Ebal. The former is blessed, whilst the latter is considered cursed (*Deuteronomy, 11:29*). Though a site dating from the Iron Age I (1200-1150 BCE) has been found on the northeast slope (and variously interpreted as an Israelite cultic site or a fortified tower), most visitors to Mt Ebal come for the view. As the great biblical geographer George Adam Smith observed, "No geography of Palestine can afford to dispense with the view from the top of Ebal".

Samaria (Sebaste)

→ *Colour map 2, grid A4.*
Located on the low hill above the Arab village of Sebastiya, 12 km northwest of Nablus, is the site of the city of Samaria: the former capital of the northern kingdom of Israel and centre of the region of Samaria. The site has been extensively excavated and contains remains from a number of periods of occupation. It's a romantic site where you are pretty much guaranteed to be alone.

Ins and outs

Getting there and away The easiest way to reach the site is to take a Jenin-bound service taxi from Nablus to the Arab village of Sebastiya, and then climb the hill. Make sure the driver knows where you want to get off (20 minutes). To return, flag down any passing traffic.

Background

A city was founded here by **Omri** c. 876 BCE (*I Kings 16:23-24*), and subsequently added to by his son and successor **Ahab** (871-852 BCE). The masonry used for the Israelite construction at Samaria is renowned for its high quality of workmanship, largely learnt from the Phoenicians.

It was during the reign of **Jeroboam II** (784-748 BCE) that Samaria reached its peak of prosperity, though the evolution of a privileged ruling class was to raise the ire of the prophet Amos (*Amos 3:9-15*). Jeroboam's death saw a decline in fortune of the Israelites at Samaria, with increasing **Assyrian** influence being felt in the region, most notably in the large numbers of foreigners that they settled here (*Il Kings 17:24*). This was one factor in the rise to prominence of the **Samaritan** community, and their subsequent split from the Jews.

Samaria remained the administrative capital of the province of the same name, with successive Assyrian, Babylonian and Persian governors, until **Alexander the Great** conquered the city (332 BCE). Large numbers of Macedonians were settled in Samaria, giving it a largely Greek ethnic, cultural and political feel, whilst the Samaritan community were expelled to Shechem. Hellenistic influence was terminated by the arrival of the Hasmonean ruler **John Hyrcanus**, who razed the city and sold its inhabitants into slavery (c. 108/107 BCE).

The city was subsequently granted to **Herod the Great** in 30 BCE by the Romans. He completely rebuilt the city, naming it **Sebaste** after his sponsor (Sebaste being Greek for Augustus), and it soon developed into a great and splendid city. The rise of neighbouring Neapolis (Nablus) saw Samaria enter into a terminal decline, despite some modest building projects at the site by the **Byzantines** and **Crusaders** (related to the tradition that John the Baptist, or his head at least, lay buried here).

Samaria (Sebaste)

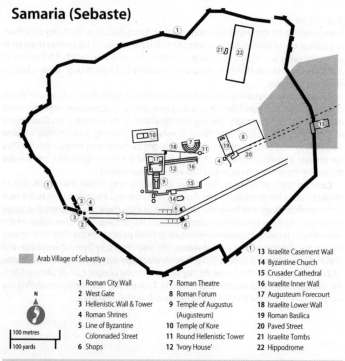

Arab Village of Sebastiya

1 Roman City Wall
2 West Gate
3 Hellenistic Wall & Tower
4 Roman Shrines
5 Line of Byzantine
   Colonnaded Street
6 Shops
7 Roman Theatre
8 Roman Forum
9 Temple of Augustus
   (Augusteum)
10 Temple of Kore
11 Round Hellenistic Tower
12 'Ivory House'
13 Israelite Casement Wall
14 Byzantine Church
15 Crusader Cathedral
16 Israelite Inner Wall
17 Augusteum Forecourt
18 Israelite Lower Wall
19 Roman Basilica
20 Paved Street
21 Israelite Tombs
22 Hippodrome

100 metres
100 yards

Sights

Remains from almost all building periods can still be found at Samaria. The most striking remains from the various periods are as follows:

Israelite The **casement wall** (13) around the acropolis; the artefacts from the **Ivory House** (12), with the group of ivory objects found here comprising the most important collection of Iron-Age miniature art found in Israel (see *I Kings 22:39* and *Amos 6:4*).

Hellenistic The **round tower** (11), described by the site's excavators as one of the most impressive remnants of the Hellenistic period found in Israel.

Roman The **Temple of Augustus (Augusteum)** (9), theatre (7) and forum (8).

Byzantine and Crusader The **small church** (14) on the south side of the hill began life as a three-aisled monastic chapel in the sixth century (celebrating the finding of John the Baptist's head), but underwent substantial alterations in the Crusader period; the **Crusader cathedral** (15) in the village of Sebastiya itself was built on the site of a Byzantine church commemorating the reputed burial place of John the Baptist, though in later years it was converted into a mosque by Salah al-Din. ① *T09-2342235. Sat-Thu 0800-1700, Fri 0800-1600, closes one hour earlier in winter. Adult 10NIS, student 6NIS.*

Moving on

From Sebastiya, Route 60 continues north through 'Emeq Dothan, or the **Valley of Dothan**. The biblical city of Dothan has been identified with the mound of **Tel Dothan** rising 60 m above the valley at a point 22 km north of Nablus. The city is associated with the story of Joseph being sold into slavery by his brothers (*Genesis 37:15-36*), though there is little to see at the site today.

Route 60 continues through the dusty town of Jenin (44 km from Nablus), another victim of long curfews and road-blocks that is only now emerging to become somewhere that tourists might stop for a night. This is greatly facilitated by the **Cinema Jenin Guesthouse** ① *1 Azzaytoon, T0-42502455/059-9075778, www.cinemajenin.org*, a wonderfully restored old building where rock-bottom prices are charged to guests who venture this far. They can provide a wealth of information about Jenin and the surrounding area, and are also renovating the old cinema (a project that welcomes volunteers).

Carry on north to Ta'anach, the history of which is very closely linked with that of Megiddo, just 8 km to the northwest. Taanach is located on a low mound just to the west of the modern village that bears the same name. In truth there is not a great deal to see at the site, and there are no information markings. The dominant structure visible on the mound today is the comparatively recent Late Abbasid palace from the 10th-11th century CE. This was the scene of the battle between the Israelites, led by Deborah and Barak, and Sisera's Canaanite army (*Judges 5:19*). Though seemingly conquered by Joshua (*Joshua 12:21*), it appears that the Canaanite city was too strong (*Judges 1:27-28; Joshua 17:11-13*), though tribute was exacted. Like Megiddo, Taanach was also conquered during the campaigns of Thutmose III (1468 BCE) and Pharaoh Shishak I (918 BCE).

Contents

Footprint features

The Dead Sea

Visitors to the Dead Sea Region are attracted by its combination of the "natural" and the "historical". It is a region of stunning, almost shocking, beauty, where white salt and desert sands meet the still blue waters of the hazy lake. It is also the setting for Masada, scene of the legendary last stand of the Zealots in the First Jewish Revolt, where 1000 rebels chose mass suicide above a life of slavery. Masada is one of those rare species – a site whose archaeological importance is matched by its visual impact: panoramic views from the mountain-top location and Herodian remains that bring the past alive. This is a site in Israel that no-one should miss.

The Dead Sea Region also contains Qumran, hardly the most dramatic of ruins, but hugely important as being the place where the famous (and controversial) Dead Sea Scrolls were discovered. Further south, the region's natural beauty can be appreciated in a number of hikes through idyllic Ein Gedi Nature Reserve, while the less chartered wadis and mountains of Sodom are easily accessed from the friendly moshav of Ne'ot HaKikar, right on the border with Jordan.

And then of course there is the Dead Sea itself. Fighting for survival, with the water receding year by year, the lowest point on earth still calls people to experience its therapeutic and cosmetic benefits as it has done for millennia. Even if you don't avail yourself of a treatment in one of the numerous spas, make time to float in the salty waters – a most peculiar sensation.

Ins and outs

The Dead Sea Region is linked via Route 90 (then Route 1) to Jerusalem to the northwest, and by Route 90 to Eilat to the south. Although the main sites have good bus connections to Jerusalem (1½ hours) or Eilat (two to three hours), travelling around the Dead Sea region itself by public transport requires some advanced planning. Of course, a hired car is the ideal way to explore the region. Those on a tighter budget may like to try one of the day package tours organized from Jerusalem, although these provide only very limited time at each spot.

It should be noted that most of the accommodation in the region is in the upper-end price categories, with the cheapest options being the camps in Neʻot HaKikar or youth hostels at Ein Gedi and Masada.

Geography

The Dead Sea, in reality a lake, is a substantial body of water some 65 km in length, up to 18 km wide, and situated at 420 m below sea level. Its surface area is contracting, but generally put at around 800 square km, and the deepest point is estimated at 380 m. The Dead Sea is divided into two unequal sectors: a larger northern area of very salty receding lake, and a shallow, smaller artificial southern basin that is rising. Both the Jordanian and Israeli sides exploit the southern area for salt, potash and other minerals, and it is segmented into evaporation pools from which the different minerals are extracted. The water in this southern basin is pumped into the pools by the Dead Sea factories, as the natural water supply had completely dried up. An accumulation of salt and mineral deposits on the floor of these pools amounts to about 20 cm per year, hence the water level here is actually increasing – in some of the Ein Boqeq hotels you can see that the water level is above the ground floor of the building. Between the two is a dried-out, gradually expanding, isthmus or Interlaken – the 'Lisan'. The land surrounding the Sea is arid and bleak, with the heavily saline soils requiring innovative methods to encourage agriculture.

The Dead Sea is fed primarily by the Jordan River, and the effect of upstream exploitation (such as the Israeli National Water Carrier and the King Abdullah Canal in Jordan) has led to a significant fall in water levels in the northern lake. Only 5% of the river's natural flow actually reaches the Dead Sea, and consequently the water level is now dropping by as much as 1m per year (certainly it has receded 30m since 1900). Apart from the environmental concerns that this drastic change raises, one recent effect are the dangerous 'sink-holes' appearing along the shore (see Boxed text page 277). With no outlet, water from the Dead Sea is lost via evaporation; as much as 25 mm per 24 hours during the summer peak. A multi-billion dollar proposal is being investigated that imagines water from the Red Sea being channelled 180 km to replenish the Dead Sea, though few people think it will come to fruition.

The Dead Sea has special chemical characteristics given its low altitude and the lack of external drainage. Evaporation has helped to increase the salt content of the sea, while the wadis that run into it include heavily sulphurous spring waters. The waters of the Dead Sea are saline and increase in salt content with depth. In the surface layer of water to a depth of 40 m the salt content of the water is approximately 300 parts per 1000 and temperatures are some 20°C-37°C. Few people can submerge themselves in densities of this kind, so the effects of the lower layers are academic! The surface layer is very rich in bicarbonates and sulphates (and heavy in health-giving iodine, bromine and magnesium if Dead Sea resort literature is to be believed) and the Sea is underlain by natural salts and a mud layer of silts brought down by the Jordan River. Certainly, the high salinity of the Dead Sea means that there are few bacteria in the water, which is therefore safe for bathing and other forms of immersion.

Background

Despite the seemingly inhospitable nature of the Dead Sea region, there is in fact a long record of human activity in the surrounding area. The history of the Dead Sea region is very closely intertwined with the history of the Judean Desert that lays to the northwest and west. Human occupation along the shores of the Dead Sea did not end with God's destruction of Sodom and Gomorrah (*Genesis 18, 19*).

The region has primarily been seen as both a place of refuge and as a centre for commercial exploitation. The Dead Sea Works that was established here by the British in 1930 is merely a continuation of a process of commercial exploitation that may have begun almost 2,500 years ago with the Nabateans, who sold the surface bitumen to the Egyptians for use in the embalming business, an industry that continued well into Roman times. Whilst the Dead Sea Works continue to produce significant quantities of potash, bromine, magnesium, chloride and salts (as well as being an important employer of residents of towns such as Dimona), the Dead Sea region increasingly looks towards tourism as its major source of revenue and employment. But once again, like the industrial exploitation of the Dead Sea's resources, this is not a new phenomenon. A great deal of the Dead Sea's tourism industry is geared towards the apparent 'health and beauty' potential of the local environment. Much is made of the increased oxygen in the air (a function of the Dead Sea's position vis-à-vis sea level), the pollution-free environment (if you ignore the Dead Sea works!), and the medicinal properties of the various bromine, magnesium, iodine and mud treatments. Yet, as stressed before, this idea of the Dead Sea region as a 'refuge' from the rigours of the modern world is not new. Communities of hermits and ascetics (possibly including groups such as Essenes or individuals like John the Baptist) appear to have sought refuge in the region over 2000 years ago, in addition to political refugees who include amongst their number King David, Herod the Great and the Jewish Zealots (at Masada and possibly Qumran). Thus the fat old men and women who jostle you for position in the Ein Gedi Spa may be the latest link in a chain that began three millennia ago with King David.

Northern Dead Sea beaches

Ins and outs

These beaches are located 2 km off Road 90, shortly after 90 heads south along the Dead Sea. Egged buses 444/486/487 stop at Kalia Jct, be sure to tell the driver where you want to get off. It's about a 2-km walk from the bus stop.

Past the rusting remains of a failed water park and the empty shells of a Jordanian village, north of Qumran, are three beaches that can be visited for the day or overnight. The shore here is mud (don't imagine golden sand) and part of the experience is smearing it all over yourself. Bring a towel, as this is not included in entrance fees for day-visitors. During the week these beaches are popular with Palestinians, while at the weekend Israelis tend to take over.

New Kalia Beach ① *T02-9942391, adults 40NIS, student/child 30NIS, summer 0730-1700, winter 0800-1600*, is the first you come to and has perhaps the nicest beach area. There's good shade, a snack-bar, a shop selling Dead Sea products and the "lowest bar in the world" at -418 m. It's generally just for day visits, although groups of 20 can be accommodated in a tent.

Next along is **Biankini** ① *Siesta Beach, T02-9400266/050-7616162, biankini1@walla.co.il, entry 50NIS per day*. Here you'll find a Moroccan kasbah with three apartments sleeping up to six people, 21 (and expanding) colourful and well-equipped chalets with jacuzzis (ask for one with view, much preferable, 650/750NIS per couple B&B week/weekend) and a tent sleeping up to 50 (100NIS per person). Those turning up after 1600 with a tent can sleep for 50NIS each. Beach is small but well-maintained, restaurant serves 26 kinds of tagine (45-49NIS, can feed two people) plus ethnic salads and dairy menu. The enormous outdoor terrace is a fine location overlooking the Dead Sea, food is served 0800-2400 (winter -2000).

Next door (but cut off by a fence) is **Neve Midbar** ① *T02-9942781, www.nevemidbarbeach.com, day entry 35NIS, overnight with a tent 50NIS per person,* where there is a Middle Eastern restaurant and accommodation in the form of "husha" huts (190NIS per couple) that have mattresses and no more. The beach is open to day visitors 0800-1900 (winter -1800). The camping spot overlooking the water is ideal, there's a bar, and sand has been imported to make the top beach more appealing.

Qumran

→ *Colour map 2, grid C5.*
Though this site is rather unprepossessing, its significance derives from the fact that this is where most of the Dead Sea Scrolls were discovered (see box, page 274). There are few sites in Israel/ Palestine that create more controversy and ill-feeling between theologians, archaeologists and historians than Qumran, yet few issues surrounding the site and the treasures found here have been satisfactorily resolved. For example, there is still ferocious debate with regard to the date of the founding of the community, the nature of the community settled here, their period of occupation, their reason for abandoning the site, and the date that the occupation finished. In fact, every single aspect of life at Qumran!

Ins and outs
Getting there and away Most visitors come as part of a tour. All buses between Jerusalem and Ein Gedi, Masada, Eilat etc on Route 90 stop opposite the turning to the site (five-minute walk uphill), though you should take care to remind the driver to stop. Qumran is also accessible by service taxi from Jericho. For bus timings, see entries under the destinations mentioned on page 269.

Getting around The compact nature of the site, and the fact that it is clearly labelled, means that a detailed tour description is not necessary. A short film starts a visit, followed by the small museum and then the archaeological remains outside. **NB** It is not possible to explore many of the caves in which the Dead Sea Scrolls were found. Cave 6 to the northwest is the most readily accessible, whilst Cave 4 is clearly visible in the cliff face across the ravine from the observation point. There is no fee for trekking in the Qumran National Park. It's possible to ramble around the hills (about 30 minutes to the top) or follow a trail to En Feshka (around five hours). Get hiking advice from staff at the entrance kiosk, where you can also check that there is no danger of flash floods (if so, paths are closed off).

The site

① *T02-9942235. Daily 0800-1700, winter 0800-1600, closes 1 hr earlier on Fri and hol eves. Adult 20NIS, student 17NIS, child 9NIS, combined ticket with Einot Tzukim 36NIS. Huge souvenir shop, toilets, restaurant.*

The 'consensus' view has long been that Qumran was occupied by a Jewish break-away group referred to as the Essenes. This sect, or sub-sect, of Judaism is generally characterized as celibate, ascetic, reclusive, pacifist, and divorced from the mainstream of religious, political and social thought; hence Qumran would appear to be a perfect location for such a group. Such an image of the Essenes is derived from their depiction in the works of Josephus, Philo and Pliny, with the inference being that they closely resemble the modern idea of a monastic order.

This image has been challenged over the years by a number of commentators (most spectacularly Baigent and Leigh, *see Dead Sea Scrolls Deception* box opposite), who question the 'Qumran-Essene Hypothesis' on a number of points. For example, if the community here were celibate, why are there graves of women and children in Qumran's main burial ground? And why is there no reference to the term 'Essene' in the Dead Sea Scrolls? In fact, some scholars argue that the scrolls may have had nothing to do with the community living at Qumran itself, but were placed in the caves for safe-keeping by rebels fleeing from the Romans during the First Revolt (66-70 CE). They were not written here, but brought from the Temple and libraries of Jerusalem. It has also been hypothesised that the glassware and range of coinage discovered points to a community concerned with worldly matters of trade and commerce, and not with sectarian religiosity. The latest controversial view is that of Prof Rachel Elior, who doubts the very existence of

Qumran

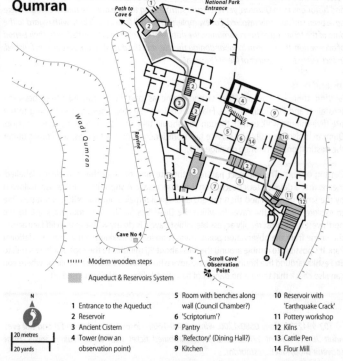

.... Modern wooden steps

[shaded] Aqueduct & Reservoirs System

1 Entrance to the Aqueduct	5 Room with benches along wall (Council Chamber?)
2 Reservoir	6 'Scriptorium'?
3 Ancient Cistern	7 Pantry
4 Tower (now an observation point)	8 'Refectory' (Dining Hall?)
	9 Kitchen
10 Reservoir with 'Earthquake Crack'	
11 Pottery workshop	
12 Kilns	
13 Cattle Pen	
14 Flour Mill	

20 metres
20 yards

"The Dead Sea Scrolls Deception"

Amongst the huge body of literature on the subject of the Dead Sea Scrolls, probably the most accessible and entertaining read is provided by Michael Baigent and Richard Leigh's "*The Dead Sea Scrolls Deception*" (1991, plus later reprints). On the question of why so much of the Qumran material is being withheld from scholarly examination, Baigent and Leigh conclude that the prime reason is some form of conspiracy surrounding the Catholic Church. (Sound familiar? A comparable theme was expounded in their 1982 book *The Holy Blood and the Holy Grail*, which some claim formed the basis of Dan Brown's The Da Vinci Code). The authors suggest that the scroll material reveals some unpalatable truths about the origins of Christianity, which is why the "international team" have sought to distance the scrolls (by dating and chronology) from the early Christian church. They propose that at the centre of the scrolls material is the story of the community's leader, none other than Jesus' brother St James, "whose dispute with Paul precipitated the formulation of the new religion subsequently known as Christianity"! They further suggest that Paul (who was perhaps a Roman agent or informer) effectively moved in the completely opposite direction to Jesus' teachings of the supremacy of the Law (*Matthew 5:17-19*), instead propagating the Pauline philosophy of supremacy of faith (*Romans 1:17; Galatians 3:11*) – now a basic tenet of Christianity.

the Essenes as a group, postulating that the sect was invented by Josephus and that the scrolls were written by a class of Jerusalem priests banished from the Temple in the second century BCE.

There are no clear answers. However, if it proves nothing else, the argument over Qumran shows how open to interpretation the field of archaeology is. When visiting the site of Qumran, you will find the community are now often referred to as 'Yahad' ('together' in Hebrew) or perhaps as the 'Sect of the Wilderness of Judea', rather than simply as Essenes.

Make sure you go to the viewpoint to look over the caves, or even take a walk in the hills of the National Park. The restaurant in the visitors' complex is acceptable, with buffet meals at not too ridiculous prices (eg main course, soup and salad for 60NIS).

En Feshka (Einot Tzukim) Nature Reserve

ⓘ *T02-9942355. Daily 0800-1700, winter 0800-1600, closes 1 hr earlier on Fri and hol eves. Adult 25NIS, child 13NIS, combination ticket with Qumran adult 36NIS. Snack shop, toilets, picnic areas, BBQs. Buses stop next to the reserve entrance.*

This oasis features a series of winding streams and pools amongst the reeds and trees, and is unique in having natural freshwater bathing spots so close to the Dead Sea. However, as signs indicate, the waters are not as close as they used to be – staff at the reserve will explain the frightening recession of the northern Dead Sea. There are short walks though the rushes, a swimming pool at weekends and a number of ruins from the Second Temple period (where balsam was produced) which are not hugely impressive but worth a look. To protect flora and fauna, the southern part of the reserve can only be visited at weekends and it's best to time a visit to coincide with a **tour** ⓘ *Sep-Jun Fri at 1000 and 1200, and Sat 1000, 1200 and 1400, about 1 hr, included in entrance fee to park, in Hebrew but concessions made for Eng speakers.* In any case, the wading pools and scenic setting make for a refreshing stop.

The Dead Sea Scrolls

A chance discovery in 1947 by a young Bedouin shepherd boy, Mohammad adh-Dhib of the Ta'amireh tribe, became one of the greatest archaeological finds of this century. Whilst searching for a stray goat in caves on the northwest shore of the Dead Sea, adh-Dhib came across a number of earthenware jars containing leather scrolls wrapped in linen. Once it became apparent that something of value had been found here, a series of excavations and bounty-hunting expeditions began (though it's difficult to distinguish between the archaeologists and the Bedouins as to who were the bigger trophy-hunters). A veritable corpus of material has now been gathered from caves in the region, much of it in fragments, but other sections, such as the "Isaiah Scroll" being several metres long. Most of the material has been divided into two broad categories, 'religious' and 'secular', though most scholars now consider the latter category as more interesting (and controversial) since it seems to indicate much about the community at Qumran and elsewhere.

The Copper Scroll: Discovered in Cave 3, and so named because the scroll is actually a roll of copper with the writing punched into the metal, this is an inventory of buried treasure concealed at 64 sites (none of which has been identified). If the figures listed are to be believed, the treasure comprises almost 25,000 kg of gold and over 59,000 kg of silver. If the inventory was compiled in anticipation of the Roman invasion following the outbreak of the Jewish

Revolt (66 CE), it gives a CE date to the Dead Sea Scrolls, with major implications for dating the Qumran community.

The War Scroll: Found in Caves 1 and 4, this scroll operates on two levels. On the one hand it is clearly a manual for conducting war, whilst on the other hand it is an order of battle for an apocryphal war between the "Children of Light" and the "Children of Darkness". As such, it challenges the 'consensus' view of a pacifist group settled at Qumran.

The Temple Scroll: Possibly found in Cave 11, though this is not certain, this scroll deals with both rituals and rites of observance at the Temple in Jerusalem, plus details of design, furnishings, fixtures and fittings. As such, it suggests that contrary to the 'consensus' view, the community at Qumran were not divorced from mainstream Jewish life or contemporary religious affairs.

The Habakkuk Commentary: Found in Cave 1, this document appears to be a chronicle of the life and times of the Qumran community, and hence dating this text would go a long way towards proving who exactly they were, and when they occupied this site. Its reference to the victorious Roman troops sacrificing to their standards (as opposed to gods) again suggests the imperial Roman invasion, as opposed to the republican Roman invasion, and thus a CE and not BCE date. Interestingly, Josephus describes such a practice following the fall of the Temple in 70 CE (*Jewish War, VI, vi*).

Metzoke Dragot → *Colour map 2, grid C5.*

Metzoke Dragot perches at the top of the Dead Sea cliffs, a dramatic drive up a snaking road that finishes in awe-inspiring views. There is a centre for 'adventure desert tourism' in the area, although activities are only offered to groups of 10 or more these days.

However, should that apply, two-day rock-climbing, abseiling and rescue courses cost 680NIS per person, not including accommodation (contact T02-9944777). **NB** The centre does not give advice about trekking, contact T*3639 for advice, and for a contact for tours and rappelling (abseiling) see Activities, below. The main reason to come up here is for the stunning view and to spend a night at the guesthouse (see below). This area is also the home of the Wadi Murabba'at Caves, where a number of important artefacts have been found. The turning is 17 km south of Ein Feshka along Route 90 (signposted). Any bus between Jerusalem and Eilat will drop you at the turning (give the driver plenty of warning), although it is at least a one-hour walk uphill – you will probably want to hitch.

Ahava Visitors' Centre and Mineral Beach

A couple of kilometres south of the turning to Metzoke Dragot, you will see signs for the Ahava Visitors' Centre. If you are keen on the much-vaunted Ahava products, you might pick up a good deal in the **showroom** ① *T02-9945117, Sun-Thu 0800-1700, Fri 0800-1600, Sat and hols 0830-1700*. There is also an information centre, with a presentation explaining production methods, and a coffee bar.

Mineral Beach ① *T02-9944888, www.dead-sea.co.il, winter 0900-1700 mid-week 0800-1700, weekend, summer and hols add 1 hr, entry 45NIS mid-week, 55NIS weekends*, provides good access to the Dead Sea, as well as café, beach bar and freshwater and hot sulphur pools. Entrance to the beach is free with a 50- or 80-min massage (prices from 220-370NIS depending on massage type/length/day of week!). It's a fair deal for the facilities on offer, especially when compared to other beaches in the northern Dead Sea and at Ein Boqeq.

Metzoke Dragot listings

For Sleeping and Eating price codes and other relevant information, see Essentials pages 26-31.

Sleeping
Metzoke Dragot Desert Village, T02-9944777, metzoke@zahav.net.il, www.metzoke.co.il. Truly outstanding views of the Dead Sea with hills of Jordan reflected in the glassy waters. This 'resort' on the edge of the cliff is rather like a holiday camp, with hammocks and seating dotted about. Rooms are very small, basic and featureless, but clean and have a/c – still expensive for what you get at 400-600NIS including breakfast (depending on season/no of persons/type of room); some renovated rooms have fridge, kettle, storage, new showers. Also 6 Bedouin tents can sleep 50-100 people in each. Essential to book in advance, frequently taken by groups, mattress only – bring a sleeping bag (adults 60NIS, child 40NIS). Restaurant serves dinner at weekends or by arrangement for groups, and there's a small coffeeshop/bar.

Activities and tours
Gyora Eldar, T052-3971774, eldarara@017.net.il. Organizes rappelling and jeep tours in the Metzoke Dragot area.

Ein Gedi

→ *Colour map 2, grid C5.*
Ein Gedi is a large oasis on the western shore of the Dead Sea, taking its name from a perennial spring that rises some 200 m above shore level. It was held as a biblical symbol of beauty (Song of Solomon 1:14), retaining that image today as a vibrant splash of greenery, rich vegetation, pools and

waterscapes amongst the austere hills of the Judean Desert and the sterile depths of the Dead Sea. The Ein Gedi Nature Reserve includes the excellent hiking trails around Wadi David and Wadi 'Arugot, one of the Dead Sea's best-established bathing beaches (Ein Gedi Beach), and a health and beauty resort providing therapeutic bathing (Ein Gedi Spa). There are also a number of accommodation options, which make Ein Gedi a good spot from which to explore the Dead Sea Region.

Ins and outs

Getting there and away The Ein Gedi region is accessible by bus from Jerusalem, Eilat, Arad and Be'er Sheva (see page 281 for timings), although many visitors come on a day trip that does not really do justice to the region.

Getting around Getting between the various sites is a bit of a pain without your own transport, as buses are a bit too infrequent to make them practical.

Background

The most celebrated story concerning Ein Gedi recalls David's flight from Saul, when he sought sanctuary in the "wilderness of En-gedi" (*I Samuel 24:1*). David passed up the opportunity to kill Saul when the latter went into a cave to "cover his feet" (*I Samuel 24:3*), ie take a dump. David chose instead to prostate himself at Saul's feet (after he'd finished his business), leading to the reconciliation of the two. There is significant evidence of settlement throughout the region in the Chalcolithic period (4500-3300 BCE), most notably at the Chalcolithic temple above Wadi David, whilst 'En-Gedi is then listed amongst the wilderness cities of Judah (*Joshua 15:62*) prior to reaching its fame during Saul's reign (c.1020-1004 BCE).

In later years it is mentioned by Josephus in the context of raids by the Sicarii during the First Jewish Revolt (66-73 CE, see *Jewish War IV, 402*), with documents found in the Cave of Letters in Nahal Hever to the south suggesting that it was also a centre of Jewish activity during the Bar Kokhba Revolt (132-136 CE). Ein Gedi remained a large Jewish village cultivating dates and balsam-producing plants throughout the Byzantine period, though subsequent occupation has been far more intermittent.

Sights

Ein Gedi Nature Reserve

ⓘ *T08-6584285, www.parks.org.il. Daily 0800-1700, winter 0800-1600. Adult 25NIS, student 21NIS, child 13NIS; synagogue only 13NIS, child 7NIS, ticket valid for 1 day. The leaflet for the site contains good information and further choices of hikes to those given here. Snack bar, drinking water and toilets at the entrance.*

Ein Gedi region

To Qumran

SPNI Field School

Nahal David

Main entrance to Ein Gedi Nature Reserve

Nahal 'Arugot

To Nahal 'Arugot National Park

Ein Gedi Beach

Dead Sea

Kibbutz Ein Gedi & Guesthouse/ Holiday Resort

N

500 metres
500 yards

To Ein Gedi Spa, Masada

Sleeping
1 Ein Gedi Youth Hostel

Eating
1 Pundak Restaurant

Sinkholes

The parched landscape of the Dead Sea has evolved some new features in recent years, making it even further resemble the surface of the moon. About 3000 craters have opened along the shoreline – sinkholes, which as the name implies, pose a physical as well as environmental hazard.

It's not unknown for an unwary hiker to plunge down a hole or for the ground to open up and swallow a building. Warning signs and fenced off areas now dot sections of the coast, and it is wise to heed them. The problem is concentrated in the northern lake – the sinkholes are clearly visible from the road as you travel between Ein Feshkha and Masada.

Also found on the Jordanian side, sinkholes are a direct result of the receding water levels. This leaves a layer of subterranean salt at the newly exposed shoreline, which then gets dissolved by fresh water coming in. Thus a hole can form underground and, when it collapses in on itself, whatever lies above has to take its chances.

Who knows how many more lie below the surface? This is surely one more reason for governments to reconsider the constant draining of the water supply to the Dead Sea.

Many people spend insufficient time here and end up following the hordes of visitors who pop in, head up to **David Falls** (15 minutes), continue to **Dodim Cave** (40 minutes), head up to the Chalcolithic temple (10 minutes), on to **Ein Gedi Spring** (five minutes), and then leave again after little more than an hour. If you come on one of the 'see the Dead Sea in one day' type tours, this is what you will end up doing, though for those with children or unable to walk long distances this will probably be enough. If you can spare the time, base yourself locally and spend four to six hours on the **Dry Canyon hike** that takes in all the main sites and gets you away from the crowds. **NB** This hike is not suitable for all, and involves some steep ascents and descents. Do not forget to bring plenty of drinking water, but not food: it is forbidden to eat within the reserve. Sightings of Nubian ibex and Syrian hyraxes are more than common.

Dry canyon hike

This hike begins at the SPNI Field School (2) above the Ein Gedi Youth Hostel (1). Follow the road up to the small amphitheatre and exit through the gate in the fence. There is nobody here to collect your admission fee. Follow the black trail in a steep upwards direction (it is sign-posted "Ma'ale Har Yishay"). After a short distance the trail divides, with the black trail continuing up to Har Yishay to the right (at least one hour), and the red trail continuing straight ahead. Follow the red trail towards the four-metre-high cliff (3), and continue up it. After ascending the low cliff, take the lower path to your left towards the edge of the cliff above the Nahal David canyon. Continue along the path above Nahal David and David Falls (which you can hear below) until you reach a small gully (4). Drop down into the gully and follow it round to the left where it enters the **dry canyon** above the Nahal David. **NB** Do not enter this canyon if there is the slightest possibility of rain, since it is subject to flash-floods. Also note that the rocks in this canyon have been worn treacherously slippery by water action.

Not far into the dry canyon, shortly after it has become steeper and narrower, a number of metal stakes have been hammered into the rock to your right (5) to show you the route out of the canyon, and to assist your ascent. Climb the metal stakes back out of the canyon to the south. You soon hit a green trail running parallel to the dry canyon. Follow it to the left (southeast), and then continue to the top of the small hill in front of you. The hill looks down upon the whole Ein Gedi area, with the **Chalcolithic temple (6)** below you. Remains found at the temple include a clay statuette of a laden bull, animal bones, horns and pottery. Follow the path down from the Chalcolithic temple, taking the right (south) at the trail intersection **(7)** to **Ein Gedi Spring (8)**. The spring provides welcome relief on a hot day, though it has to be noted that it is only mid-shin deep, and is impossibly crowded if more than five people are gathered here. There are several options from here: i) Continue south along the trail, taking in Tel Goren **(13)** and the Ancient Synagogue **(14)**, before returning to Route 90 **(15)** at a point 500 m south of the Youth Hostel **(1)**; ii) Follow the loop trail to the north, visiting Dodim Cave **(10)**, then David Falls **(11)**, before exiting the Nature Reserve at the main gate **(12)**; iii) Visiting Dodim Cave **(10)** and David Falls **(11)** as described in option ii), then returning to Ein Gedi Spring **(8)** to pursue option i). The route described here follows option iii).

Head north from Ein Gedi Spring, taking the right fork at the intersection **(7)**, and passing beneath the ledge upon which the Chalcolithic temple stands **(6)**. After several

Wadi David (including the 'dry canyon hike')

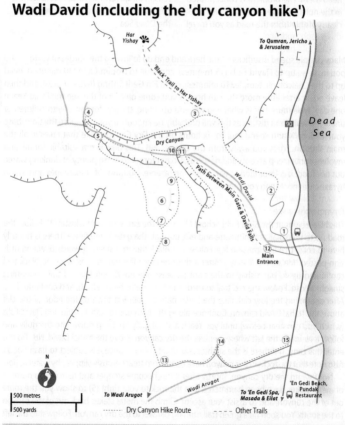

500 metres
500 yards

To Wadi Arugot
Wadi Arugot
To 'En Gedi Spa, Masada & Eilat
'En Gedi Beach, Pundak Restaurant

·········· Dry Canyon Hike Route   - - - - Other Trails

'Swimming' in the Dead Sea

With a salt concentration of over 20%, the Dead Sea actually supports one's body on the surface, and prevents 'swimming' as such: 'floating' is a far more accurate description. Before taking the almost obligatory dip in the Dead Sea, bear these points in mind: Firstly, it is best to use one of the recognized 'beaches' since these have fresh-water showers that allow you to wash off the residue that is left on your skin after bathing. Secondly, avoid getting water in your eyes since it will sting like hell and may cause inflammation. If you do get water in your eyes, rinse immediately and continuously with fresh water. For this reason, noticeboards at the beaches outlaw splashing. Thirdly, the water of the Dead Sea also tastes extremely unpleasant, and may make you feel sick if swallowed.

Lastly, the salty water causes agony in every minute scratch and cut (including some that you may not know you have); thus the Dead Sea region is a haven for designer stubble fans since shaving prior to a dip in the sea is really not advisable.

Because floating in the Dead Sea is such an unusual experience, it is not recommended that you attempt to lie on your front in the water; flicking yourself over on to your back is not as easy as it sounds, and might be a cue to splash water in your eyes/mouth. In fact most of the beaches have noticeboards giving information on how to get into the water (walk backwards and then assume a sitting position). Children should be supervised, with the 'ground-rules' carefully explained to them.

minutes walking, you reach another trail intersection (9). To visit the Dodim Cave take the signposted trail down to your left. Leopards are said to inhabit this area occasionally, though it is extremely unlikely that you will meet any. You are likely to come across ibex here, though, whose rustling in the reeds may scare the life out of you. The trail soon reaches the banks of Nahal David, though it is forbidden to follow it up to its source for fear of disturbing the flora and fauna. Note above you the 'mouth' of Window Falls. Descend to Nahal David using a series of ladders-cum-steps cut from the rock, before crossing the stream. Follow the path along the north bank to a large boulder. On the path below you it is possible to see swarms of visitors making their way up to David Falls. To reach Dodim Cave (10) (sometimes called Shulamit Cave), climb down the series of metal steps and grab rails. Unless you climb down (there are two separate ladders), the cave is largely hidden, though a full descent really means getting wet in the lovely pool here.

From here, retrace your steps to the intersection (9), then follow the path in a loop round to **David Falls** (11). Though the streams and falls here are very pleasant, unless you're very lucky this section of the Nature Reserve tends to be very busy. From David Falls you can either follow the path back to the main entrance (12), or climb back up to the intersection (9) to return to Ein Gedi Spring (8) and continue the tour.

From Ein Gedi Spring, follow the sign for 'Tel Goren' heading south. Though the low mound of Tel Goren (13) is not terribly impressive, five levels of occupation have been identified here, dating from the first Israelite settlement in the seventh century CE to the Late Roman and Byzantine periods (second to sixth century CE).

Beyond Tel Goren is the exit to the Nahal David Nature Reserve, where you hit the surfaced road. A right turn (west) here leads to Wadi Arugot (see below), whilst by following the road to the left (east) you soon come to the **Ancient Synagogue** (14) (separate entrance fee) which has its mosaic floor intact.

Ancient Synagogue at Ein Gedi

It is believed that several synagogues have stood on this site, the first possibly dating to the end of the second or beginning of the third century CE, and prominently featuring the swastika as either a decorative element or as a symbol of good luck. Substantial changes were made to the building some time between the mid-third and the beginning of the fourth century CE, at a time when Ein Gedi was described as "a very large Jewish village" (Eusebius, *Onomasticon*). Again, the synagogue was rebuilt in the late fifth century CE, and a colourful new mosaic pavement laid. An interesting feature of the mosaic pavement from this period is the fact that, although it includes the names of the signs of the zodiac in inscriptions, unlike contemporary synagogues at Hammat-Tiberias and Beit Alpha, it does not bear their images. This has led some to suggest that the community here was rather conservative. A cache of 5000 coins were discovered near the niche for the Holy Ark. Dating the synagogue's demise is not conclusive, though it could date to the persecutions of the early years of Justinian I's reign (527-565 CE).

From the Ancient Synagogue, follow the paved road until it hits the main road, Route 90 (**15**). From here it is approximately 500 m back to the Youth Hostel (**1**).

Wadi Arugot

ⓘ *The entrance is about 2 km along the turn-off from Route 90, 1 km south of the Ein Gedi Youth Hostel. Oct-Mar, last entrance 1400.*

Less famous than its neighbour, Wadi Arugot receives far fewer visitors than Wadi David, and it is easier to get away from the crowds. The most popular walk is up to the Hidden Waterfall, 1-1½ hours from the entrance (follow the marked trail along the stream), though you can continue up to the Upper Pools (about another 30 minutes).

Ein Gedi Beach

The main (though not necessarily the best) bathing spot in the northern Dead Sea Region is the Ein Gedi Beach, a little over 1 km south of the Ein Gedi Youth Hostel. The beach is rather stony and unattractive, but has changing rooms, toilets, umbrellas and freshwater showers. A lifeguard is on duty 0800-1600. **NB** Keep an eye on your possessions whilst bathing here. The **Pundak Ein Gedi Restaurant** ⓘ *1000-1800, including Sat and hols,* offers kosher bland cafeteria-style food (eg schnitzel and chips) in an equally bland environment, though everything is fresh. There is also a 24-hour snack-bar on the beach.

There's a bus stop at the beach; for onward travel, see below (though you will have to add or subtract five minutes or so).

Kibbutz Ein Gedi

Kibbutz Ein Gedi is located about 1.5 km off Route 90 and about 1.5 km south of Ein Gedi Beach. Though agriculture plays a large part in the economy of the kibbutz, it is sustained through tourism (most notably through the hotel it runs, see below). The **Botanical Gardens** ⓘ *T08-6584444, daily 0830-1600, Fri 0830-1400, adult 25NIS, student/child 22NIS, (free for guests at the kibbutz hotel). Night tours on Tue/Thu at 2000, individuals phone ahead to book with credit card,* here are really something special. There are over 800 rare species of plant from all over the globe thriving in the desert air, including exotic rainforest plants alongside Biblical frankincense and myrrh. However, it's the cacti collection that really catches the eye: towering examples of these flourish all over the kibbutz.

Ein Gedi Spa

ⓘ T08-6594813, Sun-Fri adults 69NIS, students 55NIS, Sat 79/63NIS, entrance plus lunch deal 110NIS. Sat-Thu 0800-1800, winter 0800-1600, closes 1 hr earlier on Fri.

Four kilometres south of the turning for Kibbutz Ein Gedi is the Ein Gedi Spa. The spa offers the famed Dead Sea black mud and natural minerals treatments, as well as therapeutic bathing in sulphurous pools, massages and a (seasonal) freshwater swimming pool. Now that the waters of the Dead Sea have receded so far, a trolley is necessary to ferry clients more than 1 km down to the shore. Twenty-five years ago when it was built, the spa was on the lake-shore. Facilities are free for guests of the Country Hotel. There's a bus stop at the spa; for onward travel see below (though you will have to add or subtract five minutes or so).

Ein Gedi listings

For Sleeping and Eating price codes and other relevant information, see Essentials pages 26-31.

Sleeping and eating

LL Ein Gedi Country Hotel, Kibbutz Ein Gedi, T08-6594220/1/2, www.ein-gedi. co.il. Standard or deluxe rooms in a rural setting. All mod-cons. Most pleasing are the standard "Desert Rooms" decorated by local artists. Accommodation is half-board only, and includes free entrance to Ein Gedi Spa. Relaxing on the grass by their big beautiful pool on the edge of a cliff above the Dead Sea is as good as it gets. Wellness Centre has Ayurvedic treatments. The 'Botanical Garden' restaurant has a good spread of Middle Eastern-Mediterranean cuisine, buffet-style (non-guests welcome, but phone in advance, daily 0700-1000, 1230-1400 and 1830-2100). There is also a pleasant bar and café area.

A-D IYHA Beit Sarah Ein Gedi Youth Hostel, T02-5945600, www.iyha.co.il. With a wonderful setting, rooms are also a step up from your typical hostel. Dorms rooms all have TV, a/c, tea/coffee (114NIS), roomy doubles, some have balconies with views (340NIS). Breakfast included, meals available, cafeteria, internet, basketball, 10 mins walk to the Dead Sea. Enormous though the guesthouse is, it's necessary to

book as far in advance as possible.

A-D SPNI Field School, T08-6584288. The first of Israel's field schools, founded in 1959, has great views over the Dead Sea and also into the National Park. Simple rooms but entirely adequate, for space in 5-bed a/c dorm it's 99NIS including breakfast, 74NIS without (women separate). Private doubles are 365NIS including breakfast. Advance booking definitely recommended. Fri night dinner available.

Transport

Although the bus times given here may change during the life-span of this book, they give some idea as to the frequency of services. The timetables are usually posted at the Youth Hostel reception, or check with staff. All the buses heading south stop at **Ein Gedi Spa**, **Masada Junction** (2.6 km from Masada, with some continuing to the site itself) and **'Ein Boqeq**.

To **Arad** and **Be'er Sheva**: Bus 384, Sun-Thu 0800, 1230, 1530, 1800, Fri 0800, 1230. **Eilat** (via Masada, 'Ein Boqeq and Arava Rd): Bus 444, Sun-Thu 0800, 1100, 1500, 1800, Fri same but last at 1500, Sat 0100. **Jerusalem**: Buses 427/444/486/487, depart every couple of hrs, Sun-Thu 0600-1930, Fri same but last at 1415, Sat 1900, 1945, 0045. Add or subtract about 5 minutes if catching the bus at Ein Gedi Beach, Kibbutz Ein Gedi or Ein Gedi Spa.

Ein Gedi to Masada

Approximately 7 km south of Ein Gedi the **Nahal Hever**, one of the deepest canyons in the Judean Desert, drains into the Dead Sea. During the Bar Kokhba Revolt (132-136 CE), Jewish fighters sought refuge from the Romans in the deep caves on both sides of Nahal Hever's valley. Two caves in particular have revealed priceless remains, artefacts and documents. The **Cave of Horrors** revealed the skeletons of 40 men, women and children who had been starved to death by the Roman siege of the cave. In the nearby **Cave of Letters** archaeologists discovered an 'archive of Babata' and 'Bar Kokhba Letters'. Neither cave is accessible to visitors.

A further 6 km south on Route 90, one of the longest canyons in the Judean Desert, **Nahal Ze'elim**, flows into the Dead Sea. A number of caves in this valley revealed items from the Chalcolithic (4500-3300 BCE), Iron Age II (1000-586 BCE) and Bar Kokhba (132-136 CE) periods.

Masada

→ *Colour map 3, grid A6.*

The high fortress at Masada must be one of the greatest and most exciting viewpoints in the Middle East, overlooking vast areas of the Dead Sea/Rift Valley and the Jordanian Heights. Yet Masada is more than just a spectacular location. The extensive excavations carried out have confirmed as fact much of the Jewish historian Josephus' account of the extraordinary events here in the first century CE. As the last outpost of resistance in the Jewish Revolt of 66-73 CE, it was here that 967 Jewish rebels preferred mass suicide to submission to Rome. Today, Masada is one of Israel's most visited archaeological sites, though within the Israeli psyche Masada represents far more than just an ancient place of archaeological interest. Many visitors to Masada take advantage of the early opening hours (0430) to climb to the top so that they can watch the sun rise over the Dead Sea and the Jordanian Heights. A truly magical experience. It is an easier (and shorter) climb in the dark from the western side than from the main entrance on the east. It is advisable to bring warm clothes since it can be rather cold waiting for the sun, even in summer.

Ins and outs

Getting there and away Masada is located just off Route 90, around 18 km south of Ein Gedi and 15 km north of 'Ein Boqeq. Some of the buses between Jerusalem and Eilat (via Ein Gedi) take you all the way to the site, whilst others will only drop you at the turn-off (from where it's 2.6 km to the site). Make sure that the driver knows you want to get off at Masada.

Getting around The fortress has immense natural barriers, and land access is possible only by two steep paths. Most visitors take the cable-car both up and down (and this is advisable for the very young or old). It is a taxing 45-minute step climb up the Snake Path from the main east entrance, a real killer in the heat (the path is in fact closed, going up, from 1000). Walking up the western Roman ramp takes 15-20 minutes and is a more gradual and shorter ascent.

Background

The main written historical sources on Masada are the works of Josephus (*Antiquities; The Jewish War*), though like everything else from this source, a healthy degree of scepticism is required when examining details. There still remains some doubt as to the nature of the site here during the Hasmonean period, and things only become clearer during the Herodian era.

Most of the remains seen today at Masada date to the reign of **Herod the Great** (37 BCE-4 BCE), though some structures were certainly built later by the rebels. Herod's association with Masada began in 40 BCE, when he was fleeing with his family from the pretender Antigonus and the Parthian army. Herod's brother Joseph, with 800 men, resisted Antigonus' siege, though they are only said to have survived dying of thirst by a fortuitous cloud-burst that filled the rock-cut cisterns on the summit. When Herod returned from Rome in 39 BCE, he rescued his family and then set about adding to Masada's considerable natural defences. It should be noted that Herod viewed Masada as less of a strategic stronghold protecting his kingdom, and more as a place of refuge for himself.

Masada's history subsequent to Herod's death in 4 BCE is unclear, though it was certainly occupied by a Roman garrison at the outbreak of the Jewish Revolt in 66 CE. Though Josephus does not give details, Masada was captured "by stealth" by the Jews, and its Roman garrison exterminated (*Jewish War*, II, 408). It subsequently became a refuge for the duration of the Revolt, ruled by the "tyrant" or "autocrat" **Eleazar ben Yair**. Joined by other groups fleeing Jerusalem in 70 CE after the destruction of the Temple, the rebels increased the level of fortification at Masada (72-73 CE) and held out against a 6000-8000 man Roman army for two years. It took the construction of a massive ramp up the western slope of the mountain for the Romans to gain entry by force. Eventually it became obvious that the defences would be overwhelmed, as the outer Herodian stone wall was breached and then the inner wooden retaining walls were set on fire. The rebels made a decision to take their own lives, something expressly forbidden by Jewish law, rather than become slaves. So, after killing their wives and their families, 10 men were allocated the task of dispatching the others. Then one man was allotted the task of dispatching the remaining nine, before killing himself. Out of the rebel garrison estimated at nearly 1000 persons, when the Romans finally entered Masada they found only two women and five children alive, who had hidden in a water cistern. A section of Eleazar ben Yair's speech that incited the mass suicide, as reported by Josephus, is included in the free brochure and site plan that you are given upon entry to the National Park. It is generally believed that Josephus used considerable artistic licence in his account of Eleazar ben Yair's stirring words (some suggest that he made the entire thing up), though archaeology has largely confirmed the events that he outlined. Eleven small ostraca discovered close to the Water Gate may even contain the original 'lots' that were cast to decide who should kill whom (*Jewish War*, VII, 396). These can be seen in the new museum (see page 286).

The site was occupied by a Roman garrison for some years after the siege and mass suicide of 73 CE, perhaps as late as 111 CE if the evidence of coinage found here is taken into consideration. Pottery finds have also suggested that Nabatean soldiers were included amongst the Roman siege troops and subsequent garrison. Christian monks occupied Masada during the fifth and sixth centuries CE, constructing a church and living as hermits on the summit. Following their demise, Masada appears to have been largely forgotten until being correctly identified by Robinson and Smith in 1838 (from Ein Gedi, via a telescope!).

Masada – overview

Roman Camp
Roman Camp
Roman Siege Wall
Roman Ramp
Snake path
Roman Camp
Roman Camp
Fortress
N
Roman Camp
Cliffs
Roman Camp

800 metres
800 yards

The site

ⓘ *T08-6584207/8, www.parks.org.il. Daily sunrise-1700. By foot, adult 25NIS, student 21NIS, child 13NIS. Cable-car operates 0800-1700 (Fri 0800-1500) every 15 mins; one-way adult 49NIS, student 45NIS, child 26NIS; return adult 67NIS, student 63NIS, child 38NIS; price excludes admission fee. Handheld audio-guide available in 6 languages, 20NIS (includes entrance to the museum). There is a short film shown on a loop. Self-service cafeteria (fairly pricey, closes early), souvenirs, toilets at the bottom and top, (free) cold drinking water at the top. There is an official campsite on the western side (see Listings, below).*

Viewed from the north, Masada is an enormous rock pinnacle standing out from the main ridges and peaks of the hills of the western Dead Sea coast. The site is separated from its surroundings on all sides by precipitous slopes: 120 m on the west where it connects to the hill range behind, 400 m on its northern and southern sides and more than 434 m on the coastal cliff. In addition, the approach to Masada from the west is through the bleak and poorly watered hills of Judea or from the east through the wilderness of the Wadi Arava. Both were difficult to penetrate and gave the site a unique strength, exploited in the Jewish revolts against Roman rule.

The site is well labelled so a detailed tour description in this *Handbook* is not necessary. However, some further details of the key places of interest are included below. If you want some peace and solitude head over to the southern side of the site, which few visitors bother exploring. **NB** The black line indicates the height of the walls found *in situ*, whilst construction above this line represents reconstruction made by archaeologists using masonry found scattered nearby.

The walls The great walls of Masada comprise the outer walls of the site built by the Romans during the siege of 72-73 AD, which straggle round the foot of the escarpments with garrison camps at intervals (see 'Masada, overview' map). On the heights is the main fortress wall with its 30 towers and bastions running for some 1,400 m. It is constructed of two encasing limestone block walls infilled with rubble, giving an overall width of some four metres. The 70 or so rooms in the casement wall were used as living quarters by the Zealots and their families, and have revealed a large number of artefacts.

Northern Palace-Villa The most spectacular building on the site, and described in some detail by Josephus, it is built in three tiers on the northern edge of the cliff. The upper terrace comprised a semi-circular balcony with the living quarters to the south, whilst the middle terrace some 20 m below featured some form of entertainment complex. A further 15 m down is the lower terrace, where a central hall surrounded by porticoes also served some form of entertainment purpose. Remains of the sandstone columns, with fluted drums and Corinthian capitals, can still be seen, along with replicas of the decorative frescoes (originals are now in the museum). A small bathhouse stands to the east, the ultimate location for a sauna. During the period of the Revolt, the living quarters on the upper terrace retained their original function, whilst the lower levels were used as part of the strategic defence of the water source. A thick layer of ash suggests that the middle and lower terraces were consumed by fire, with remains from the Revolt including numerous arrowheads, plus the skeletons of a man, woman and child. The woman's scalp was complete with braids.

Western Palace The largest residential structure on Masada, covering almost 4000 sq m, the Western Palace served as the ceremonial and administrative centre. The royal apartments in the southeast contain several well-preserved mosaics, which should not be missed

'Masada Complex'

The suicide of the Jewish Zealots at Masada has given rise to a phrase, 'Masada complex', that is considered by some to have become the symbol of the modern State of Israel: a state of psychology under siege where death by one's own hand is better than defeat. However, if anything, the sentiment of modern Israel is not so much reflected in a 'you'll never take us alive' attitude, but more in the 'no more Masadas' sentiment. The importance of Masada within the Israeli consciousness is manifested in the swearing-in ceremonies that some units of the IDF hold here, whilst the site is a compulsory stop for all Israeli children in what is less of an educational visit, and more an exercise in nation building. To see Masada at sunrise is a rite of passage for many people.

The storehouses There appear to be two types of storehouses for food and weapons at Masada: public storehouses, and storehouses attached to specific buildings such as palaces and administrative centres. The largest **public storeroom complex** is located just to the south of the Northern Palace-Villa's upper terrace. It is believed that oil, wine, flour and other foodstuffs were each stored in separate rooms in special jars. Most of the storehouses containing foodstuffs were burnt at the climax of the siege, though some were left undamaged in order to prove to the Romans that the mass suicide was not a result of starvation.

The bathhouse This magnificent bathhouse comprises a large open court and four rooms: the *apodyterium* (entrance room), tepidarium (warm room), *frigidarium* (cold room) and the *caldarium* (hot room). The remains of the *hypocaust* (under-floor heating system) and *praefurnium* (furnace) are preserved. Immersion pools and *mikvehs* were added to many buildings during the period of the Revolt (66-73 CE), and the large bathhouse underwent significant alterations.

The water system The key element at Masada, at an elevation of over 400 m in the middle of a harsh desert, was the provision of water. The Israeli excavations have shown that the water system included setting up a water catchment to bring water to the vicinity of the fortress from the Ben Jair and Masada wadis, carried in places on aqueducts to storage pools. Water was stored in square cisterns, 4000 cubic m in volume, cut into the rock: eight above and four below. Water was also carried to the site by animal and led to the cisterns by channels running from the Water Gate in the north of the fortress. Small scattered cisterns for storing rain water falling in the summit area were also in use and were important, if minor, supplies. The huge southern water cistern can be entered, via 64 steps, and gives a vivid picture of the vast water supplies that allowed the rebels to sustain themselves under siege for so long.

The Roman siege remains Outside the fortress are the structural remains of the Roman siege, led by Flavius Silva (see 'Masada, overview' map). In addition to the siege wall built to contain the site, there are clear signs of the Roman camps which were like fortified cities in themselves, with walls, towers and shops to accommodate the merchants who followed the Roman army. The extraordinary ramp built by the Roman general, close to the Western Gate, enabled a siege tower to destroy the entrance to the citadel. In all they are a memorial to the dedication of Flavius Silva to his task, and the effectiveness of Roman military engineering.

The Yigael Yadin Museum

ⓘ *Daily 0800-1600, entrance 20NIS, or free with a hand-held audio-guide.*

Billing it as 'an exciting museological experience' is a bit unnecessary, but this state-of-the-art museum is very worthwhile (perhaps best enjoyed after a visit to the summit when the dim cool interior is a relief). Most people don't bother with it, so a visit is peaceful and takes about 30 minutes. The sensor-activated guide gives a potted version of the information on the walls, from the time of Herod through to the Roman siege. Finds include the amphoras that brought exotic food and wines to Herod, gold jewellery and Jewish coins, a braid of hair found at the Northern Palace, belt buckles of the Roman soldiers and – most famous of all – the 'lots', perhaps those drawn to decide the fate of the rebels.

Sound and light show

ⓘ *Bookings through T08-9959333, F08-9959333, rontal.n@npa.org.il. Performances take place Mar-Aug 2100, Sep-Oct 2000, adult 45NIS, child 35NIS.*

Each Tuesday and Thursday a 50-minute sound and light show takes place at the amphitheatre by the Roman ramp (western) side of Masada. This is only accessible via Arad, from where travel time is about 30 minutes. The route is clearly signed along road 3199 from the west side of town. Aim to arrive at least half an hour before the performance starts, as they shut the road when the show starts. Though commentary is in Hebrew, headphones provide simultaneous translation into English, French, German, Spanish or Russian. There is a cafeteria by the car park.

Masada listings

For Sleeping and Eating price codes and other relevant information, see Essentials pages 26-31.

Sleeping and eating

See also Kfar Hanokdim, page 313, for accommodation on the west side of Masada.
A-C IYHA Masada Youth Hostel/Isaac H Taylor Hostel, T08-9953222, www.iyha.org.il. Beautifully maintained hostel that resembles more of a hotel; a/c dorms with attached bath and TV (131NIS), or doubles (368NIS). Breakfast included, other meals order in advance, There's a great (seasonal) swimming pool, immense balcony-terrace, internet area, safe. Advance reservations absolutely essential (ideally weeks in advance). On request, reception staff may separate those who are rising early to climb Masada from those after an undisturbed lie-in.
E Masada Campsite, west side of Masada, T08-6280404, ext. 3. Toilets and showers, can pitch your own tent (adult/child 50/40NIS) or sleep in their big one (65/55NIS),

There are cooking facilities, campfires are permitted, and the proximity to Masada when you wake up is a delight. Necessary to book in advance.

Transport

The bus times are posted on the window of the office next to the bus stop near Masada Youth Hostel. Note that all Jerusalem-bound services also stop at **Ein Gedi** and **Qumran**, whilst southbound services stop at **Ein Boqeq**. **Be'er Sheva** and **Arad**: Bus 384, Sun-Thu 0825, 1255, 1555, 1825, Fri 0825, 1255, 2 hrs. **Eilat**: Bus 444, Sun-Thu 0815, 1115, 1515, 1800, Fri same, last at 1513, 3 hrs. **Ein Gedi**: Sun-Thu about 10 per day, 0830-1915, Fri last at 1435, Sat 1845, 1923, 0023, 30 mins. **Jerusalem**: Buses 444/486, Sun-Thu, about 10 per day 0830-1950, Fri last at 1550, Sat 1815, 1920, 2 hrs. **Tel Aviv** (Arlozorov): Bus 421, Sun-Fri 1415, 3 ½ hrs.

Ein Boqeq

→ Colour map 3, grid A6.

Ein Boqeq (Ein Bokek) is Israel's major tourist resort on the Dead Sea, where upmarket hotels provide private beaches, spas and health facilities. A couple of kilometres to the south at Hamme Zohar are three further hotels with spas, and the area between is mooted to be developed so that eventually the two will be linked.

Ins and outs

Tourist information ⓘ *Tourist Office, Ein Boqeq "Solarium -400", T/F08-9975010, www. deadsea.co.il, Mon-Thu 0900-1600, Fri 0900-1500*. Good spread of leaflets and flyers for the region, helpful staff.

Sights and activities

The public beaches at Ein Boqeq are among the most attractive on the Dead Sea, though they can be prone to overcrowding. While there are no budget places to stay, the hotels all offer day-use for their spas, swimming pools, heated Dead Sea water pools, saunas, jacuzzis and gyms. It's a good idea to browse and see which takes your fancy; prices almost always include lunch, massages cost (a lot) extra and use of sulphur pool costs 50-60NIS more. There are endless types of massage to chose from (180-650NIS, depending on type and length), mud wraps 180-290NIS, hydro-baths 85NIS, facials 170-380NIS, body peeling 200-320NIS, plus various other weird and wonderful treatments.

Next to the 'Solarium -400"' in the centre of Ein Boqeq is a stretch of public beach with free showers and sun-shades, toilets nearby (for changing) and no rocks underfoot. It is a fairly attractive spot with café-bars, mini-markets and a great ice-cream parlour nearby – a good place for budget travellers to take a dip.

Mezad Boqeq and Officina

Ein Boqeq was probably first settled in the Hasmonean period (152-37 BCE), though its fame dates from the Herodian period (37 BCE-70 CE) when it became a centre for the manufacture of cosmetics and pharmaceuticals. A small Roman fort on the north side of the Wadi (Nahal) Boqeq valley was probably built as part of the Limes Palaestinae eastern frontier defences. A short section (two metres out of one kilometre) of the **aqueduct** that served Ein Boqeq is visible to the northwest of the fort, as are two of the **cisterns** that stored water at the oasis. Less easy to find, to the east of the fort (nearer to the main Route 90), are the remains of the Herodian workshop, or **officina**. This building contained ovens, basins and vessels used in the perfume, cosmetic and pharmaceutical production process. It is speculated that raw materials such as buds, blossoms, seeds, fruits, resins, twigs, bark and leaves of aromatic plants were perhaps provided from the Far East and Arabia by the Nabatean trade caravans.

Wadi Boqeq Hike

This short hike brings you to fresh water pools – excellent respite from the heat of summer months and, unlike Ein Gedi Nature Reserve, entry is free (at least for now). Take flip flops, plenty of water, sun-screen and a hat. If driving, park by the Meridien David at the entrance to Ein Boqeq. Bus 444 stops on Route 90 at the start of the trek: disembark by the Meridien hotel.

From the Meridien, cross Route 90 (or go through the tunnel under the road from the hotel parking lot) and follow the brown sign to Ma'ale Boqeq a short way uphill, to where a signpost indicates "Ma'ale Boqeq Ascent". For a very short walk (that can be done in flip flops), turn left (south) here and head into the wadi (following the sign to Wadi Boqeq) where you pick up a black/white trail marker. After about 15 minutes walking (either in the stream or alongside it) you will reach the first of two shallow pools of clean water, an excellent place to cool off and have a picnic. Only here and at Ein Gedi will you find freshwater pools all year round. For a longer alternative, at the signpost follow the red/white trail up the "ascent". Shortly you will pass Roman remains, then it's a steep climb uphill to meet a black marked trail going left along the ridge (the red trail continues up, but follow the black). Look out for ibex (Hebrew: 'yael') around here, they are a fairly common sight. A couple of minutes' walk, with the contradictory views of 5-star hotels on the east side and the wild escarpment to the west, brings you to a descent into the rush-filled wadi. It's a steep, rocky path down, followed by a short vertical climb using metal rungs in the rock to water level. The clear stream leads to two shallow pools (separated by slippery steps); the second pool is deeper and more appealing for a dip. To reach this point takes about an hour. Then it's just 15 minutes back along the wadi bed to the Meridien hotel. The trail is marked with black/white throughout.

Ein Boqeq listings

For Sleeping and Eating price codes and other relevant information, see Essentials pages 26-31.

Sleeping

The 14 or so hotels in Ein Boqeq are much of a muchness, offering typical resort-style rooms with all the amenities you'd expect from a top-end hotel. Room rates tend to be grossly overpriced, although look online for deals. Note that in high season you need to book some places 3-4 months in advance and at other times at least a week ahead.

LL Daniel, T08-6689999, www.tamareshotels.co.il. Tasteful modern rooms ($220/273 low/high season, plus $59 for club level). Outdoor pool in a pleasant grassy area; spa has a smaller pool than some but feels less institutional, and is among the cheapest for day use at 100NIS. Castle pub has 1+1 on drinks 1900-2100, bowling alley. Not a bad option.

LL Golden Tulip, T08-6689444. Sprawling hotel with suites, apartments and family rooms, right next to good private beach; choice of pools, plus full spa facilities. Attracts a lot of families. Located a couple of km south of the main hotel block.

LL Hod Hamidbar, T08-6688222, www.hodhotel.co.il. Exterior looking rather dated but, despite small balconies, rooms are pleasant and a fair size. Appealing sun-deck around pool, it also benefits from being beachside of the road. One of the cheaper options in town for both rooms and spa, ($35 with lunch, 60NIS without), attracts the older clientele.

LL Isrotel, T08-6689666, www.isrotel.co.il. Light, white contemporary lobby with rooms to match, smallish bathrooms, all have sea-views from balcony. Private beach (across road), tennis, appealing circular 2-tier pool in landscaped surrounds, lovely spa but expensive for day use (though includes massage as well as lunch) which makes it less crowded for hotel guests. Ranch House restaurant for steaks.

LL Lot Spa, T08-6689200, www.lothotel.co.il. Overpriced rooms, not all of which have sea-views or balconies. It's the very attractive poolside area and excellent spa that are the draw here (day use 180NIS including lunch, no weekend price hikes). Turkish bath is 30NIS extra, lovely treatments area and treatments more reasonably priced than elsewhere. Next to the beach, bar by poolside, it can get exceedingly busy and attracts a younger clientele overall.

LL Royal, T08-6688500, www.
royalhoteldeadsea.com. Public areas not
enormously flash, but rooms good for the
price (especially by comparison): nice decor,
balconies with side views of the Dead
Sea; sofa, shower and bath. Day use at spa
150NIS. Feels a bit like the local swimming
bath but is less packed-out than other
hotels. No weekend price rise.

Eating
¶¶¶ **Sato Bistro**, Crowne Plaza Hotel, T08-
6591975. Quality Asian food. Reserve a table.
¶¶ **Taj Mahal**, by the pool at the Tulip Inn,
T057-6506502, www.taj-mahal.co.il. Not
an Indian menu as you might suppose, but
Middle Eastern/Western food in a Bedouin
tent with well-stocked bar and nargilla
(25NIS). If you eat here you can use the pool
for free, and on Fri nights live music and
belly-dancer from 2300. Go to website for
10% discount coupon. Open 24 hrs.
¶¶-¶ **Aroma**, Petra Centre. There's not much
to choose from in the way of quick eats for
those passing through, and this reliable
café-chain does a good breakfast, excellent
chicken sandwich, soups, and pints of beer.
Wi-fi, or lap-top on counter for customers to
browse. Daily 0800-2200.
   Also in the Petra Centre (located under
the giant coffee cup and McDonalds arch)
you will find ATMs, a minimarket (closed

Shabbat) and money changers. Look out
for Aldo's ice-cream parlour near the public
beach, which is recommended.

Activities and tours
Pere Hamidbar, T08-9952711/050-3939394,
s@jeeptours.co.il, www.jeeptours.co.il.
Self-driving a low-slung mini-jeep (like a
beefed-up golf buggy) along the wadis is
loads of fun. They can traverse tracks only
suitable for 4WDs, a guide will lead the
way. $100 per jeep (seats 4), minimum of 2
jeeps. Leave from Neve Zohar gas station at
junction of roads 90 and 31; 7 days a week
but book a day ahead.

Transport
Jerusalem buses all stop at Ein Boqeq: there
are several stops in the main tourist centre
and one at the southern beach. For onward
public transport see page 286 (though you
will have to add or subtract 10 minutes or
so, and bear in mind that some services stop
at Ein Gedi Beach for a break).

Car hire
Hertz, in the Solarium, T08-6584530/054-
3999020.
Sunair, T054-5652883, sunairmzd@walla.
co.il. Glider flights over Ein Gedi and Masada.
Also do camel treks and abseiling.

Sodom (Sedom) Region

→ *Colour map 3, grid B6.*
*Tradition holds that this is the cursed land of Sodom and Gomorrah, though many Israelis will
tell you that the night-spots of Tel Aviv or Eilat are the modern Sodom and Gomorrah. The region
is one of austere, terrifying beauty; a fitting scene for where "the Lord rained upon Sodom and
upon Gomorrah brimstone and fire ... and he overthrew those cities, and all the plain, and all the
inhabitants of the cities, and that which grew upon the ground" (Genesis 19:24-25).*

Ins and outs
Geography The dominant geographical features are the salt flats of the Dead Sea to the
east, with their bizarre sculptured forms, and the Mt Sodom range to the west. This range,
11 km long but just 2 km wide, is the lowest mountain range in the world and is largely
composed of salt. The highest point is 240 m above the Dead Sea, but still -200 m below

sea level. The range is underlain by a salt rock layer 2750 m deep. Though annual rainfall is less than 50 mm, water leaking into the fissures between the harder rock and the salt rock has formed vertical chimneys and lateral caves and tunnels. Other formations formed by the erosive action of water resemble pillars and statues, including the famous Lot's wife (see Genesis 19:26). The cliff face lining this section of Route 90 is riddled with cave complexes, the soft limestone cliffs carved by water action into spectacular, swirling shapes. Unfortunately, **Salt (or Sedom) Cave** and the **Flour Cave** (so named because of the flour-like residue that lines the canyons) have both been deemed unsafe, and neither are accessible to tourists. Check with locals in case this situation changes, though it is unlikely to.

Dead Sea Works

This is an unattractive industrial complex (you can't miss it) that is vital to the economic needs of Israel. The original Dead Sea Works were founded on the northern shore in 1930, with those here being built four years later.

Ne'ot HaKikar and Ein Tamar

Nestled on the Jordanian border, this agricultural moshav (village) makes an excellent alternative base for exploring the Dead Sea and eastern Negev regions. Surrounded by date palms and with views of the Edom Mountains to the east, there are accommodation options for a range of budgets and easy-to-access hiking and biking routes along local wadis. A supremely friendly place: ask a local to reveal the way to the hidden spring – a freshwater pool perfect for a dip on (the many) hot days. A map of Ne'ot HaKikar and adjacent Ein Tamar is available from the tourist information centre in Ein Boqeq.

Ne'ot Hakikar & Ein Tamar listings

For Sleeping and Eating price codes and other relevant information, see Essentials pages 26-31.

Sleeping

AL Villa Villekulla, T/F08-6572759/052-8666062, barakhorwitz@gmail.com. Named after Pippi Longstocking's house, this place is perfect for a small group of friends or families. Both bedrooms have TV, 2 bathrooms, fully functioning kitchen, sofa-bed in living room, futon on veranda, space to throw down mattresses, games and books (Hebrew and English). Shady garden is the big attraction, with BBQ, passion fruit vines dangling overhead, lovely night lamps, and decking area with built-in jacuzzi. The owner, Barak, provides jeep tours (see below) and is good for info on hikes in the area.
AL-A Belfer's Dead Sea Cabins, T08-6555104/052-5450970,michalbelfer@gmail.

com. 3 cute wood cabins with views from the porch to the mountains of Jordan. The mezzanine accessed by a ladder sleeps 3, plus double bedroom, comfy sitting area, kitchenette, nice bathroom with jacuzzi, TV, wi-fi, light-coloured wood throughout. Each has picnic table and BBQ. Help yourself to herbs from the garden or tomatoes from the fields. Free bikes, jeep tours and guided walks available. A quality place run by lovely people. Small price rise at weekends.
A-D Shkedi's Camp Lodge, T052-2317371. www.shkedig.com, shkedi.camplodge@gmail.com. Two quirky a/c private huts with wooden and rock walls, coloured glass windows and bamboo ceilings (no en-suite). Dormitories offered in greenhouse-shaped tents are cheery and cosy (old-fashioned stoves for winter nights, fans in summer); sleep up to 15 (or take as 'private' for a reasonable price). Large tent sleeps up to 70, curtain split area (adult 85NIS, child 65NIS).

Bring your own sleeping bag, or borrow one of theirs. Mattresses are exceedingly comfy whichever accommodation you choose. Constant background of cool music, busy with Israeli families at weekends (expect to be invited to share *poikas* around the campfire). Shared kitchen, BBQs, excellent showers, communal area with bar, warm and welcoming hosts who make a stay very memorable. Couple of bikes for guests' use, wi-fi throughout. Jeep tours. Collection from bus stop provided. Recommended.

Eating

¶ Inbar Bakikar, T057-7743418. Close by the swimming pool, "Inbar on the Square" is open all year round for breakfast (55NIS), lunch and dinner (80-100NIS) and snacks. Tunisian-style food, both veg and non-veg. Ayala is a lovely host. Book in advance for dinner/breakfast.

¶ Yossi's Place, T052-8911658. Look for the coloured lights outside. Inside it's no frills and bamboo-lined walls. All about home-cooked food that is hearty and high quality; mainly meat (enormous steaks, mini-burger-style kebabs recommended) though vegetarians will enjoy the wonderful entrée salads (hot herzilim baladi – seared eggplant with tahina), hummus and quiche. Everything, down to the pickles, is home-made. Mains 65-90NIS, alcohol served. Sun-Thu 1400-2000 (opens Sat if bookings).

¶-¶ Pnina's Restaurant-Café, T08-6555107. Resident of the moshav since it began, Pnina serves breakfasts (40NIS), and snacks (good omelette and schnitzel sandwiches) in her garden. Her husband grills the fresh fish that he farms (about 70NIS) for lunch. Best to call in advance. Sun-Thu 1000-1600, Fri 1000-1430.

Festivals and events

Every year during the holiday of Sukkot (Sep/Oct) the HaTamar Festival is held in the desert for 5 days amid spectacular scenery, with free events and Israeli musicians. Contact the Tourist Information Centre in Ein Boqeq for more details.

Shopping

Estee's Pottery, T08-6552828/052-8991147, esteeuzi@zahav.net.il, www.deadseaceramics.co.il. Workshop/gallery in a charming setting, Estee's work is inspired by the agriculture of the moshav – her ceramic peppers and pumpkins are iconic. She also gives workshops: you can fire your own glaze designs using pit-fire or Raku (Japanese) techniques. Daily 1000-1700, but call in advance. Estee's husband Uzi (T052-8991146, www.cycle-inn.com) rents out mountain bikes and provides information on routes in the desert valleys. Groups can stay at the well-equipped Cycle Inn.

JoJo, Ein Tamar, T/F08-6551543/052-2964677, www.jojo-art.com. You may have noticed the colourful metal sculptures adorning Ein Boqeq and the region. They all stem from the funky gallery of Moroccan-born artist JoJo. He specialises in huge slender vases and peculiarly comfortable chairs, though there are also some smaller and more portable items for sale. His wife, Dganit, does lively acrylic paintings on wood in the vein of Jackson Pollock. To find JoJo, turn left from the roundabout at the entrance to the moshav and follow the vases to the warehouse-like workshop. Also has a gallery in Tel Aviv.

Activities and tours
Agricultural tours

Despite the highly saline soil, this little corner of Israel is a major exporter of peppers, melons, dates, etc to Europe and beyond. Interestingly, Thai employees on the farms now outnumber the local community by almost 2 to 1. An agricultural tour of the moshav gives a valuable and fascinating insight into the technological innovations and sheer perseverance involved. Arrange a tour through Shkedi's Camp, 200NIS for 1½ hrs.

Cycling
See Estee's Pottery, above.

Jeep tours

Barak Horwitz, T052-8666062, barakhorwitz@gmail.com, www.camel-lot.net. Barak can answer questions on pretty much any topic, and is a sure source of information about the desert region, its plants, economics and history. Jeep tours in any direction (but east!) can range from 2 hrs to 2 days. 800NIS for 8 people 2 hrs, 4 hrs 1200NIS, 6-7 hrs 1500NIS, day/night 2000NIS (camping gear provided, a/c vehicle).

Shkedi's Desert Tours (see Camp Lodge, above, for contact). Another trustworthy and experienced guide to the desert, a/c jeep (can be the best of activities on a scorching day), competitive prices.

Swimming

The moshav has a partially shaded swimming pool, open Apr-Sep, and is a glorious respite on a summer's day, adults 30NIS, children 15NIS.

Transport

The Jerusalem-Eilat bus 444 stops at Kikar Sodom junction on Road 90, 4 daily in each direction (restricted service Fri/Sat). For **Tel Aviv**, buses 393 and 394 leave from Arava junction (at least 10 daily). The bus to **Eilat** can be especially busy: it's a good idea to phone and book a seat in advance.

Moving on

From the southern end of the Dead Sea (Ha'Arava/Sodom Junction), Route 90 continues 164 km south to Eilat, a stretch of highway known as the Arava Road. It is also possible to drive along Wadi HaArava, the border with Jordan, from Ne'ot HaKikar to Hatseva. This is only permitted during daylight hours and after checking the situation with locals. There is a real danger of flash floods in winter. The small road begins at the security post on the southern edge of the moshav, by the border fence of barbed wire.

Dead Sea south to Eilat: the Arava road

Contents

Footprint features

The Negev

There is far more to the Negev than just the hedonistic beach resort of Eilat stuck on the bottom of a large stretch of desert. In fact, the Negev hardly fits most people's preconceptions of what a desert is anyway; this is more an austere, wind-eroded stone-strewn landscape than the sweeping sand dunes of 'Lawrence of Arabia' cinematography. This is an area to explore in depth, rather than viewed through the window of a bus heading from Tel Aviv to the beach at Eilat. Although public transport does serve all the key sites, careful planning must be made to ensure connections. If the option is available to you, this is the place to hire a car (or camel).

The first lesson that you will learn about the Negev is how adaptable people are. And a visit to the superbly preserved remains of the Nabatean-Roman-Byzantine cities at Avdat, Mamshit and Shivta will soon show you that, contrary to the oft-presented image, the Israelis were not the first to 'make the desert bloom'. The Negev is also a physically beautiful environment, no more so than at Ein Avdat National Park, where the contrast between icy blue pools of water and dry, brown barren hills is brought sharply into focus. Meanwhile, at the very heart of the Negev is a natural geological phenomenon that is as spectacular as Israel's more famous natural wonders, the Dead Sea and the Red Sea coral reefs: the Makhtesh Ramon erosion crater is the place to get your hiking boots on and your 'Every Boy's Guide to Rocks and Minerals' out of your luggage. And finally there is Eilat, Israel's premier resort.

Background

Geography The Negev, Hebrew for 'arid land', comprises over half of the State of Israel's land area, but is home to just 12% of the population. The Negev is shaped like an upside-down isosceles triangle, with the long sides being the Egyptian border to the west and the Jordanian border to the east, and the short side comprising a line drawn roughly between the Dead Sea to the east, and the Mediterranean Sea at Gaza to the west. The apex of the triangle is marked by the city of Eilat, on the Gulf of Aqaba.

Early history Despite the Negev's seemingly difficult and inhospitable nature, the region has been settled continuously since prehistoric times. During the Late Bronze Age-Iron Age I-II, the 19th and 20th dynasties of the **Egyptian** New Kingdom were involved in extensive copper mining and smelting activities in the southern Negev and Sinai regions, with the **Midianites** continuing this activity after the 12th century BCE.

Biblical references to Negev settlements abound, with excavations having revealed a rich assemblage of sites from the **Bronze Age** (c. 3300-1200 BCE) and the **Iron Age** (1200-586 BCE). The first five books of the Old Testament of the Bible, (*Genesis, Exodus, Leviticus, Numbers* and *Deuteronomy*) are filled with references to settlements in the Negev that have since been identified, such as Be'er Sheva (*Genesis 21:31-33; 26:23-33; 46:1-5*), Arad (*Numbers 21:1; 33:40*), Kadesh Barnea (*Genesis 14:7; Numbers 13:26; 20:14; Deuteronomy 1:46*), amongst others. This, after all, is the land of the route into Exodus, the return, and the wanderings of the Children of Israel.

By the beginning of the second millennium BCE, three main groups occupied the Negev: the **Canaanites** to the north, particularly around Arad; the **Amalekites** to the south, who were defeated by the United Monarchy's expansion into the Negev; and the **Edomites** to the east, who later moved north and northwest into the Shephelah, and subsequently became known as the Idumaeans.

The expansion of the **United Monarchy** (c. 1020-928 BCE) into the Negev Hills is reflected in a number of Iron Age IIA sites (1000-900 BCE), though the area was probably abandoned by the succeeding kings of Judah until the beginning of the Persian period (586 BCE). The reasons are not altogether clear, though the devastating invasion of Pharaoh Shishak in 924 BCE may have been a factor. Be'er Sheva (Beersheba), for example, is repeatedly mentioned in the Bible as defining the southern limits of Israel, the United Monarchy, or Judah (*Joshua 15:28; I Samuel 3:20; II Samuel 3:10, 17:11, 24:15; I Chronicles 21:2*). Other areas of the Negev remained occupied: Arad, for example, has remains of a series of Israelite citadels dating from the ninth to the sixth centuries BCE.

The Nabateans Perhaps one of the key defining moments in the history of the Negev was the arrival of the Nabateans, some time in the fourth or third century BCE. Their origins are unclear, though their impact is undisputed. As controllers of the trade route, the Spice Road, between their Edom capital at Petra and the Mediterranean Sea at Gaza, the Nabateans constructed a string of road stations across the Negev, spectacular remains of which can still be seen today. Their mastery of advanced irrigation techniques, in particular their control of surface water run-off, led to the establishment of urban centres of considerable size, such as Oboda (Avdat), Mamphis (Mamshit), Sobata (Shivta), and to a lesser extent, Elusa (Haluza) and Nessana (Nizzana).

Roman and Byzantine periods The independent Nabatean empire probably reached its peak in the first century CE, though the towns and routes that they established seem to have been little affected by the annexation of their kingdom into the Roman *Provincia Arabia* in 106 CE. In fact, the majority of the population of these towns were ethnically Nabatean and, as such, the Early Roman period (37 BCE-132 CE) may accurately be referred to here as the Middle Nabatean period.

A major administrative reorganization of the Eastern Roman Empire under **Diocletian** (284-305 CE) incorporated many of the Nabatean towns within the empire's southern defence system. New trade routes also led to the rise or demise of certain Nabatean towns.

The major development in the Negev region during the fourth century CE was the conversion of much of the population to Christianity. Thus ushered in the **Byzantine period** (324-638 CE), during which many of the former Nabatean towns flourished, with the monumental churches that can be seen today bearing testimony to this prosperity. The decline of Byzantine power allowed the Arabs to conquer the Negev in 636 CE, and for the next 1000 years or so, the region was inhabited solely by the **Bedouin**.

Modern history The Negev region remained a relative backwater of the Ottoman Empire right up until the **First World War**, when its strategic value was recognized. The British Army's Palestine campaign featured largely in the northern and western areas of the Negev, with Be'er Sheva being the first town in Palestine to fall into British hands (1917). In addition to General Allenby's campaign, this was also the stomping ground of TE Lawrence ('of Arabia'). Before his wartime efforts at disrupting Turkish communications and supply lines, Lawrence had spent much of 1914 surveying the archaeological sites of the area for the Palestine Exploration Fund. After the war, the Negev fell within the mandated area of the British, though there were few attempts to develop it. Population levels still remained extremely low, comprising mainly Bedouin tribesmen. In fact, the **Peel Commission Partition Plan** of 1937 granted the Negev region to the Arabs since they represented the only people living there.

Partially in response to this situation, and partially out of a desire to settle the region that Moses wandered through with the Children of Israel, Jewish pioneers began to establish isolated communities within the Negev. This programme was to prove significant in its foresight in later years. By the time the **United Nations Partition Recommendation** was published in 1947, the presence of these isolated Jewish communities was enough for the UN to allocate the entire Negev region (bar a narrow strip to the south of Gaza) to the Jewish State. With the Arab rejection of the plan, and the subsequent war, these Jewish settlements played an invaluable, and often heroic, role in holding up the Egyptian army's advance. In one of the final acts of the war, the Golani Brigade managed to establish control of a stretch of the Gulf of Aqaba (subsequently Eilat), that allowed Israel an outlet to the Red Sea.

There remains much controversy over Israel's claims that it has 'turned the desert green', but there can be little doubt that Israel leads the world in developing semi-arid and arid irrigation techniques. Thus, large areas of the Negev have been brought under cultivation. The results of establishing 'development towns' in the Negev are more contentious; for every 'success' (see Arad), the example of at least one 'failure' (see Dimona) is held up. **Tourism** is now providing a major source of income in the Negev region.

Northern Negev

The Northern Negev has a number of points of interest to the visitor, particularly those who have their own transport. The commercial capital of the Negev, Be'er Sheva, is an easy-going place, with several interesting attractions in the immediate vicinity. The bulk of the sights, however, lie to the east and southeast of Be'er Sheva, notably the archaeological sites at Tel Arad and Mamshit. For those with their own vehicles, the Makhtesh HaGadol and Makhtesh HaKatan (craters) provide a wonderfully scenic backdrop to a number of hikes.

Be'er Sheva (Beersheba) → Colour map 3, grid A3.

The ancient biblical city of the patriarchs, Be'er Sheva is redefining itself as the modern administrative and commercial capital of the Negev. Attractions in the town itself are limited and, though there are good transport connections, its potential as a base from which to explore the surrounding area is constrained by the limited choice of hotels. However, the Old City down-town area has a relaxed, laid-back atmosphere, with restoration of the Ottoman architecture ongoing and some nice restaurants opening up. Be'er Sheva's headlong rush for expansion can be seen in the numerous tower blocks shooting up, and modern architecture that embraces plate glass, angles and colourful panels. The university is highly regarded these days and hence the student population is swelling, which means Be'er Sheva is increasingly known as a place for a good night out.

Ins and outs

Getting there and away Most visitors arrive at the large Central Bus Station located just off Derekh Eilat. Be'er Sheva has good bus connections, with major destinations such as Eilat, Ein Gedi, Jerusalem and Tel Aviv being served by express, regular and local (Metropoline) buses. There is a train service between Be'er Sheva and Tel Aviv (and beyond), and it's a relaxing journey though more expensive than the bus. The train station is located immediately next to the bus station, with another stop near the university north of the centre.

Getting around The town centre is fairly small, so you can easily get around on foot. The local Metropoline routes around town (4NIS) leave next to the Central Bus Station, running regularly from 0520-2300. For details of Metropoline buses, T*5900.

Tourist Information The **Visitors' Centre** ⓘ *Abraham's Well, 1 Hebron Rd, T08-6234613, bavraham@br7.orgi.il, Sun-Thu 0800-1600, Friday 0830-1230*, has a good map of the city (5NIS), leaflets about sights in the area and a gift shop. Worth a visit.

Background

Ancient history and biblical references There are numerous biblical references to the early settlement of Be'er Sheva (Beersheba), with the etymology of the name being discussed in *Genesis*. The meaning of the name may refer to either the 'Well of Seven' (see 'Abraham's Well', page 300) from the Hebrew *shiv'a*, or 'Well of (the) Oath' from the Hebrew *shevu'a*, with the origin of Beersheba attributed to both Abraham (*Genesis 21:29-33*) and Isaac (*Genesis 26:15-33*). Jacob received the vision here that told him to take his family into Egypt (*Genesis 46:1-2*); the city was a place of importance under Samuel, with his sons Joel and Abiah judging here (*I Samuel 8:1-2*); and Elijah fled here from Jezreel on his journey to Mount Horeb (*I Kings 19:3*).

Many of the biblical references mention Beersheba as the limits of the kingdom of Judah (*Joshua 15:28*), the lands of Israel (*I Samuel 3:20*) and the United Monarchy (*II Samuel 3:10, 17:11, 24:15; I Chronicles 21:2*), with the most common incantations being 'from Dan to Beersheba' and 'from Beersheba to Dan'.

Excavations at a site known as **Tel Be'er Sheva**, 5 km northeast of the modern city (see page 305), have revealed levels of occupation dating back to the Iron Age. However, identification of the tel with biblical Beersheba has been problematic due to the lack of remains dating to the Late-Bronze and Late-Iron Age periods that would coincide with the Beersheba of the patriarchs.

Much of Be'er Sheva's history during the **Persian period** and the **Roman-Byzantine period** is told at the site of Tel Be'er Sheva (see page 305).

Be'er Sheva Centre & Old City

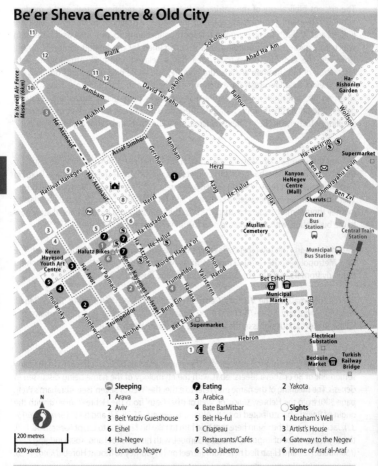

	Sleeping		**Eating**		2 Yakota
	1 Arava		3 Arabica		
	2 Aviv		4 Bate BarMitbar		○ **Sights**
	3 Beit Yatziv Guesthouse		5 Beit Ha-ful		1 Abraham's Well
	6 Eshel		6 Chapeau		3 Artist's House
	4 Ha-Negev		7 Restaurants/Cafés		4 Gateway to the Negev
	5 Leonardo Negev		6 Sabo Jabetto		6 Home of Araf al-Araf

Ottoman Empire and British Mandate The Crusaders never made it as far south as here, mistaking the site of Bet Jibrin (Bet Guvrin) for biblical Beersheba. It was the Turks who revived Be'er Sheva's fortunes at the turn of the 20th century, establishing a new town to act as an administrative centre for the Bedouin tribes of the Negev, thus strengthening the declining Ottoman Empire. Jewish settlement also began during this period. The British forces of General Allenby captured the town in 1917 as part of the World War One Palestine campaign. It subsequently expanded rapidly, with the population rising to around 7000.

The British government's White Paper of 1943 forbade the Jewish purchase of land in the Negev, though the reality of isolated Jewish settlements in the Negev convinced the architects of the 1947 United Nations Partition Plan to include most of the Negev within the proposed Jewish state. Be'er Sheva, however, was just within the boundaries of the proposed Arab state. When war broke out following the declaration of the State of Israel, Be'er Sheva was occupied by the Egyptians, who established their command centre here. The city was subsequently captured by the Negev Brigade of the Israeli army in October 1948.

Modern city The initiative for transforming the city into the administrative and commercial capital of the Negev was taken by the city's first mayor, David Tuvyahu. The population of Be'er Sheva is now around 185,000, helped in no small part by the massive influx of immigrants that followed the city's designation as an 'immigration absorption city'. In addition to Moroccan and Ethiopian Jews, the city is home to a sizeable and highly visible Eastern European community. Apparently around 160 languages are spoken in the schools and markets of the city.

Sights

Walking tour of the Old City Many of Be'er Sheva's places of interest are located in the attractive Old City area, the grid pattern of streets built by the Turks as their regional headquarters around the turn of the twentieth century. A walking tour of the Old City, taking in mainly Ottoman and British Mandate period buildings, starts at the Visitors' Centre and takes around one hour. The Be'er Sheva map, available from the Visitors' Centre (5NIS), gives additional information to that given here. You may feel that some of the 'attractions' on the walking tour are not worth the effort.

To Ben Gurion University & Tel Aviv

Montefiori

Ha-Nessi'im

issta

Henrietta Szold

Ha-Tqva

Mall

Keren Ha-Yesod

Supermarket

To big Shopping Centre (2km),
Tel Be'er Sheva (6km), Arad
47km & Dead Sea

Hebron

8	Negev Art Museum	9	Bedouin School
13	Water Tower	7	Allenby Garden
12	Turkish Railway Station	5	Bet Hasseraya
11	Turkish Station Master's House	⋯⋯	Route of walking tour of old city
10	World War 1 Cemetery		

Abraham's Well (1) ⓘ *Entrance 5NIS. See Visitors' Centre, above.* "And Abimelech said unto Abraham, What mean these seven ewe lambs which thou hast set by themselves? And he said, For these seven ewe lambs shalt thou take of my hand, that they may be a witness unto me, that I have digged this well. Wherefore he called that place Beersheba; because there they sware both of them… And Abraham planted a grove in Beersheba, and called there on the name of the Lord, the everlasting God." (*Genesis 21:29-33*). And, lo, so it came to pass that a certain well, thought to be 12th century CE, with water-drawing constructions dating to the Ottoman period, is named after the patriarch. The ticket price also includes a short movie sketching the history of Be'er Sheva to the modern day, and a guided explanation of the site (available Sun-Thu until 1400). Look out for the 500-year-old 'eshel' (tamarisk) tree just outside the walls.

Negev Artists House (3) ⓘ *55 HaAvot, T08-6273828, Mon-Thu 1000-1330 and 1600-1930, Fri 1000-1330, Sat 1100-1400.* This Mandate period building now displays work by Negev artists, both Bedouin and Jewish, new immigrants and old, in a variety of mediums. Occasionally there are musical, poetry or literary evenings. Artworks are for sale, and there is an interesting choice of ceramics, painting, jewellery, weaving, etching, etc available.

The former Turkish government building, **Bet Hasseraya (5)**, is adorned with much barbed wire and is used by the Israeli military (no photography); adjacent is the memorial at **Allenby Garden (7)**.

Ottoman period buildings On the pedestrianized Keren Kayemet Le-Israel, you pass a number of restored buildings from the Ottoman period; the most notable being the building at no 94 that now serves as the HaNegev Pharmacy. At the junction of Herzl and Ha'Atzma'ut is the former home of the Arab historian **Araf al-Araf (6)** (1892-1973), who also served as a district ruler under the Ottomans, which has been splendidly restored. A more inglorious fate has befallen the former home of Sheikh Brich Abu-Medin, Bedouin sheikh, British-appointed Mayor of Be'er Sheva, and Bedouin representative to the British government. His former house on the junction of Ha'Atzma'ut and Ha-Histadrut is now a discount clothes shop.

Negev Art Museum (8) ⓘ *Remez Gardens, 60 Ha'Atzma'ut, T08-6206570, Sun, Mon, Wed and Thu 0800-1530, Tue 0800-1400 and 1600-1800, Fri 1000-1400. Adult 14NIS, student/child 10NIS.* Housed in the former Turkish **Governor's Residence**, a mansion built in 1906 that later served as Be'er Sheva's first City Hall, the Art Museum has recently been cleverly restored and modified. The result is an attractive melding of modern glass intimate galleries into the original Turkish design. The museum features temporary art exhibitions by Israeli and international artists, in various mediums, which change every 3 months. Just next door is a renovated **Ottoman mosque (6)**, also built in 1906, with the insignia of Sultan Abdul Hamid II above the door. It is currently a controversial subject, as the Muslim community wish to use it again as a mosque while the municipality intended it for use as the archaeological wing of the museum. It used to house archaeological finds from the Be'er Sheva region, Tel Sheva in particular, which are now in the Israel Museum in Jerusalem.

Former Bedouin School (9) This building was erected by the Turks in 1913 for use as a boarding school for Bedouin boys, and during World War One was used as a military hospital. The building is undergoing a major refurbishment and will be part of a Youth Science Park.

Bedouin of the Negev

The Negev's Bedouin community numbers approximately 180,000, mainly concentrated in seven townships established by the Israeli government. These towns are designed to concentrate the Bedouin population and much of their traditional lands have been confiscated to make way for military zones, Jewish communities, and national parks. Nomadic Bedouin are a thing of the past, and the younger generation know little of the traditional ways. Many people today call themselves 'Palestinian Bedouin'.

The largest town is Rehad, 50 km north of Be'er Sheva, home to some 50,000 people. A further 65,000 Bedouin have chosen to remain in the 'unrecognized' villages that dot the roads around Be'er Sheva and Arad. The villages are deemed illegal since, although the Bedouin own their land, large tracts were not registered and are defined as 'state land' by the authorities. House demolitions are a real threat and the Israeli government sometimes destroys an entire village in one day. Generally constructed of metal sheeting, these settlements are not provided with municipal services such as electricity lines, garbage collection or running water, though some have electricity generators and a communal water supply. Their children attend school in the 'official' townships. Do visit a village if driving past, introduce yourself to whoever you meet and perhaps you'll experience the traditional Bedouin hospitality.

The Bedouin have Israeli citizenship but are exempt from army service (although 5-10% of draft age youth do volunteer for the army). Currently they have one member in the Knesset, and clan members are permitted to visit family in Sinai. However, the settlement process has not come with access to their traditional lands or permission to make a living through agriculture. They likewise have had little access to grazing land since large tracts of the Negev were declared a National Park in 1979. It is unsurprising that employment is rife and crime levels are extremely high (you are advised not to leave a car unattended in rural areas of the Negev). Most Bedouin still work the land and tend flocks of goat and sheep, however many work as construction labourers, and a few benefit from visiting tourists.

Compiled with the assistance of Fred Schlomka, www.greenolivetours.com

World War One cemetery (10) During the autumn of 1917, the Allied forces broke through the Turkish lines and captured Be'er Sheva. The battle was not without cost, and today 1,239 Allied soldiers are buried here, the biggest World War One cemetery in Israel. Many of the graves belong to members of Commonwealth regiments, with Australians and New Zealanders buried next to Welsh and English soldiers. A lot of graves are simply marked 'A Soldier of the Great War'. As with all cemeteries administered by the Commonwealth War Graves Commission, it is superbly maintained.

Turkish railway remains The northernmost section of the walking tour features a series of buildings connected with the old Turkish railway. This is the line that features so prominently in the writing and exploits of Lawrence of Arabia. The track was dismantled by General Allenby in 1917, but it is possible here to see the former **Turkish Station Master's House (11)**, and **Turkish Railway Station (12)**, now both in a poor state of repair and fenced off. The original station platform remains. Further south still, but now hidden amongst a residential area, is the **water-tower (13)** used to fill the trains' boilers.

Bedouin Market

An abundant underground water supply and a central location on the trade routes were the two main reasons that Be'er Sheva grew into an important town in antiquity. Active commerce continues unabated and there has been a weekly Bedouin market in Be'er Sheva since 1905, though the exact location has changed on several occasions. The market now takes place each **Thursday** (0700-sunset) at the grounds on the north bank of the Nahal Be'er Sheva, just off the Eilat Road. Although there are Bedouin wares on sale (jewellery, ceramics, rugs, clothes, fabrics and copperware), to many this market is no more exotic than the average car-boot sale. Long gone are the days when you could buy hashish, slaves, pure silk or women at the market, but you can get pretty much anything else. To the south of the market grounds you can see the **Turkish Bridge**. Closer to the bus station (under the arched covers) is the daily municipal market, which is also a good place to stock up on cheap goods.

Be'er Sheva listings

For Sleeping and Eating price codes and other relevant information, see Essentials pages 26-31.

Sleeping

L Leonardo Negev, 4 Henrietta Szold, T08-6405444, www.fattal.co.il. Tower-block hotel aimed at business-people. Not much to choose between 'regular' and 'business' rooms save for the decor (more modern and attractive), and LCD rather than regular TV. All have fridge, desk, minibar and nice bathrooms. Mini-suite with sitting room and 2 Presidential suites (**LL**) with kitchenette and jacuzzi. Lobby café-bar gives new meaning to the word "spacious". Fully equipped gym, sauna and jacuzzi (30NIS per day), large outdoor pool. Good facilities, without the real feel of luxury but reasonable prices.

A Beit Yatziv Guesthouse, 79 Ha'Atzma'ut, T08-6277444, www.beityatziv.co.il. Very well maintained a/c 3- or 4-bed rooms with TV and fridge, but quite expensive and not permitted to take a "dorm bed", you have to come as 3 or 4 people together (120-130NIS per person). More luxy rooms range from 250/350NIS (single/double) to 400NIS (single and double). Set in a campus of the open university with pleasant grounds, a dining room (lunch/dinner 50NIS) and functional swimming pool plus 2 paddling pools (summer only, outside guests 25-

35NIS). No curfew, 24-hr reception. Nice but not great value and the staff are very off-hand. On entering the campus, turn left to find the guest house.

B Aviv, 48 Mordey HaGeta'ot, T08-6278059, F6281961. Simple but spotlessly clean, new sheets and flowery theme, TV, a/c, private bath, front rooms with (scruffy) balconies. No breakfast but free tea/coffee in the sunny reception, nice family, some Eng spoken. Recommended for those on a budget. Single/twin/double 150/200/250NIS.

B HaNegev, 26 Ha'Atzma'ut, T08-6277026, F6278744. Double rooms 200-250NIS, those in annex are rather musty though they have TV; better rooms in new block are quite big with a/c, attached bath, towels but need to request top-sheet. None are impressive but it is more 'normal' than the other cheapies and clean enough.

B Arava, 37 Ha-Histadrut, T08-6278792. Not much English spoken but friendly, ancient Eastern Europeans seem to be main clientele (and decor to match), modest rooms a bit shabby but very clean, attached bath (at lower end of **B** price category).

C Eshel, 56 Ha-Histadrut, T08-6272917. This old fashioned time-warp place is a real oddity, but rooms are clean and cheap (singles 120NIS, doubles 150NIS) with towels, sheets, fresh paint. Communication via pen and paper. There's a shower in the room (literally), toilet outside.

Eating

There's a fair mix of interesting restaurants in Be'er Sheva. **The Kanyon HaNegev Centre** (Sun-Thu 0900-2200, Fri 0900-1500) has a handy Aroma (with wireless connection) serving the usual light meals. Inside/outside the central bus station are numerous bakeries, falafel, shwarma places. The main square at the north end of the pedestrianized **Keren Kayemet Le-Israel** is a good place to sit with your falafel or shwarma. If you're doing it yourself there are several supermarkets in both the old and new city, with fresh fruit and vegetables in abundance at the Municipal market. **Beer-Teva**, in the empty mall next to the Leonardo hotel, T1-800-225577, has organic health foods (Sun-Thu 0900-2000, Fri -1400).

††††-†† **Chapeau**, 81 Herzl, T08-6551811. Dairy restaurant, serves, excellent pastas, light meals and fish dishes. The entirely white environment sets off a goblet of red wine perfectly, and there's a covered terrace at the front with a slight trattoria vibe. No Eng menu or Eng sign. Sun-Thu 1000-0100, Fri 1000-1400, Sat from 2000.

††††-†† **Yakota**, 18 Mordey Hagetaot, T/F08-6232689. Moroccan restaurant with a gorgeously styled interior, intimate layout, lovely lamps and cushions, very romantic. Some of the dishes are positively scary, however, involving spleen, tonsils, feet and testicles. Perhaps opt for the slow-cooked casseroles, generous salad selections (35NIS, 2 persons, for 12 samples), fish (88-96NIS) or vegetarian meals (40-60NIS). Alcohol served. Daily 1200-0030.

†† **Arabica**, T08-6277801. A real everything menu, from sushi to steak via pasta and burgers. The salad bar is a good deal. A fairly anonymous setting, cavernous with echoes of a theme-pub, but it's not over-priced, is open on Shabbat and it's lively. Daily 1200-2400.

†† **Mate BaMitbar**, 22 Ha-Histadrut, T08-6233370. Within the Bet Hanegbi. This former home of the first military ruler of

Be'er Sheva after the 1948 war has been turned into a charming restaurant with garden-terrace space, simple decor, dairy kosher food and light meals. Very relaxing, especially if you make use of the spa in the same building. Sun-Thu 0900-2330, Fri 0900-1400, Sat 2000-2330.

††-† **Beit Ha-Ful**, 15 Ha-Histadrut, T08-6234253. Excellent value, with Be'er Sheva's best fuul, hummus, falafel and shwarma. Dishes come with overwhelming amounts of pickles, salads and dips. Recommended.

††-† **Saba Jabeto**, 8 Rasko Passage, T08-6272829. Handily opposite the bus station, "Grandpa Jabeto's" coffee bar is so much more than coffee. Every combination of sandwich filling you can imagine, mostly in ciabatta bread, plus Indian options, Tunisian options, stir-fry options, healthy options, all 28-35NIS. Also quiches, omelettes, great slushies, alcohol, cakes, plus a nice welcoming environment to relax. Ask staff what the special deals are. Sun-Thu 0930-2400, Fri 1000-1600, Sat 2030-2400.

Bars and clubs

When it comes to night-time entertainment, Be'er Sheva is rather deceptive. What appears to be a sleepy, quiet town has quite a number of lively bars and cafés. The whole area around **Keren Kayemet Le-Israel** has a number of pleasant evening-time watering holes, whilst those seeking a younger vibe should head north to the university area and the bars on **Ringelblum** and **Yosef Ben Mattithiau** (ask students to direct you to Pablo pub, Einstein or Inca bar). The BIG shopping mall, just east of the town centre along the Hebron road, has numerous watering holes, and **Draft Dance-bar** is recommended.

Activities and tours
Gym

Non-guests can use the gym, sauna and jacuzzis at the **Leonardo** hotel (Sun-Thu 0700-2200, Fri 0700-1800, Sat 0700-1800, 30NIS).

Swimming

Non-guests can pay to use the pool at Beit Yatziv Guesthouse, summer only (25-35NIS).

Tour companies and travel agencies

Egged Tours, Central Bus Station, T6232532; issta, 8 Henrietta Szold, T08-6650288, Sun-Thu 0900-1900, Fri 0900-1300.

Transport

Bus

The town centre is fairly small, so you can easily get around on foot. Local buses (4NIS) leave from the **Municipal bus station**, with most running regularly from 0520-2300. They also make stops in the Old City, along Ha'Atzma'ut.

Long-distance buses The **Central Bus Station** is located off Derekh Eilat, right in the middle of town. The bus information office is particularly unhelpful but the electronic display board is useful. Main destinations such as **Eilat**, **Jerusalem** and **Tel Aviv** are served by express, regular and local buses. Actual departure times may change during the lifetime of this book, but they still serve as a guide to the frequency of the services.

Arad: Bus 388 direct, 2-3 per hour, Sun-Thu 0600-2315, Fri 0600-1645, Sat from 1945, 45 mins; **Ashqelon**: Bus 363/364, Sun-Thu 0615-2130, Fri 0615-1515, Sat 2000-2245; **Dimona**: Bus 48/56/397, 2 per hour, Sun-Thu 0600-2300, Fri 0600-1630, Sat 1745-2330; **Eilat**: Bus 392/393/394/397, Sun-Thu 0730-1835, Fri last at 1735, Sat 1745-2135, 3-4 hrs; **Ein Gedi** Bus 384 Sun-Thu 0930, 1215, 1500, Fri 0945, 1250, Sat 0940, 1215, 1500; **Jerusalem**: Bus 470 direct, Sun-Thu 1 per hr 0605-1950, Fri 0615-1300, Sat 2000-2215, 2 hours; Jerusalem via **Kiryat Arba** (Hebron): Bus 440, Sun-Thu 0555, 1035, Fri 0930; Jerusalem via Kiryat Gat: Bus 446, 2 per hour, Sun-Thu 0600--2130, Fri 0720-1600, Sat 2010-2245; **Lahav**: Bus 42/47, Sun-Thu 1150, 1900; **Mizpe Ramon**: Egged bus 392 (to Eilat), Sun-Thu 0815, 0915, 1200, 1545, Fri 0800, 1 hr, and Metropoline bus 60 via

Sde Boker/Avdat1-2 per hr, Sun-Thu 0615-2300, Fri 0615-1630, Sat 1900, 2030, 2210, 2300; **Tel Aviv**: Bus 369/370/371, every 15 minutes, Sun-Thu 0510-2300, Fri 0510-1630, Sat from 1700.

Sheruts run to **Eilat**, **Jerusalem** and **Tel Aviv** from outside the Central Bus Station (same fare as bus), but they only depart when full.

Car hire

Avis, 2 Amal, Machteshim Industrial Zone, T0-6271777, www.avis.co.il; **Budget**, 1 Shazar Blvd, 03-9350017, www.budget.co.il; **Eldan**, 4 Leonard Cohen, T08-6430344, www.eldan.co.il.

Train

A comfortable and convenient option, the train station is next to the bus station. To **Tel Aviv** Sun-Thu at least 1 per hr 0525-2125, Fri last at 1220, Sat 2050, 1½ hrs; some services continue all the way to **Nahariyya**. To **Dimona**, Sun-Thu 0727, 1127, 1727, 1927, Fri 0820, 0920, 1120, 30 mins.

Directory

Banks There are numerous banks around the old town and in malls near the bus station, likewise for money changers. The post office offers commission-free foreign exchange. **Hospitals** Soroka Medical Centre, Ha-Nessi'im, nr Ben Gurion University, T6660111. **Post office** Main branch at corner of Ha-Nessi'im and Ben Zvi offers poste restante, international phone calls and foreign exchange. There are 6 other post offices, including a branch at the junction of Hadassah and Ha-Histradrut in the Old City. **Useful addresses and phone numbers** Police: T100 (emergency). **Ambulance**: Magen David Adom T101 (emergency). Fire: T102.

Around Be'er Sheva

There are a number of places of interest in the area immediately surrounding Be'er Sheva, though public transport connections are not particularly convenient.

Negev-Palmach Brigade Memorial (Andarta Memorial)
ⓘ T08-6463600.

Designed by the innovative Israeli artist Dani Karavan (also responsible for the Holocaust Memorial at Rehovot's Weizmann Institute of Science), this unusual work serves as a memorial to the Negev Brigade of the Palmach that distinguished itself in the 1948 War of Independence. Various parts of the sculpture symbolize different aspects of the campaign, with Hebrew inscriptions giving blow-by-blow accounts of the battles. The memorial is on the Be'er Sheva plateau, overlooking the Be'er Sheva Valley, though it can be difficult to reach by public transport. Off Be'er Sheva-Omer Road, several kilometres out of town to the northeast.

Tel Be'er Sheva
ⓘ T08-6467286, www.parks.org.il. Daily 0800-1700, winter 0800-1600, closes 1 hr earlier on Fri. Adults 13NIS, students/child 7NIS. Located on the Be'er Sheva to Omer-Hebron road (Route 60) 5 km northeast of the modern city. There is no public transport to the site.

The most impressive remains on view at Tel Be'er Sheva today are from the Iron Age city, of which some two-thirds have been excavated. Declared a UNESCO World Heritage Site, mud-bricks have been used to reconstruct many of the buildings and it is possible to get a clear picture of the heavily fortified Israelite city – especially from the top of the high observation tower. Good information is provided in the leaflet for the site.

Tour of the site Much of what you see today is from stratum III, and its continuation, stratum II, the latter being destroyed in a violent conflagration probably dating to the Assyrian king Sennacherib's campaign in 701 BCE. The main (and only) city gate probably dates to the 10th century BCE. Two guard rooms stand on either side, and it was protected by an outer gate. An irrigation channel runs through the city gate to a 70-m deep well outside. This well is thought to date to the 12th century BCE, though it is curious why it was not enclosed within the latter city walls. There is even a view among some scholars that this may be the Well of Abraham that is mentioned in *Genesis 21:27-32*.

The city gate emerges on to the city square, to the west of which is the Governor's Residence. Note how the entrance is built using ashlars, rectangular hewn stones laid in horizontal courses, whereas the rest of the site is built from field stones. The building contains two dwelling units, a kitchen and storerooms. The cellar below may have previously formed part of a temple site.

To the right (east) of the city gate is the largest building: three pillared structures that probably formed part of the city storehouse. Broken pottery vessels attest to their usage, with commentators suggesting that these storage facilities were part of a taxation system established by Solomon. Stones from a horned altar were found incorporated into one of the storeroom walls. The original reconstructed horned altar now stands in the Israel Museum in Jerusalem but you can see a replica here, near the ticket booth. The interesting aspect of this altar is the fact that the stones were cut (ie it was 'horned'). Biblical law is quite strict in saying that the altar should be made from uncut stone: "And there thou shalt build an altar unto the Lord thy God, an altar of stones: thou shalt not lift any iron tool upon them" (*Deuteronomy 27:5*); and again, "an altar of whole stones, over which no man hath lift up any iron" (*Joshua 8:31*). The altar was probably broken up during the religious reforms of Hezekiah, King of Judah (727-698 BCE).

Also to be seen on the tel are a number of later ruins, the most noticeable of which is the rhomboid-shaped Roman fortress around the base of the observation tower. A tour of Tel Be'er Sheva finishes with a walk through the remarkably well-preserved water system, where the reservoir walls are layered with thick plaster and the chambers are quite magnificent.

Israeli Air Force Museum, Hazerim
ⓘ *T08-6906855. Sun-Thu 0800-1700, Fri 0800-1300. Adult 30NIS, student 23NIS, child 20NIS. The museum is located 7 km west of Be'er Sheva on Route 2357. Bus 31 goes hourly to Hazerim from the bus station (15 mins, 8.5NIS). Get off when you see the planes.*

Be'er Sheva to Mizpe Ramon

This open-air museum features almost 100 assorted planes parked on a huge airfield. Guided tours, with a young soldier, last 1-1½ hours and make the experience infinitely more rewarding (phone to schedule a time), though you are welcome to visit alone and there are lots of information boards in English. There is a short film telling the story and glory of the Israeli Air Force (IAF), screened inside the belly of a Boeing 707 that played a minor role in the 1977 rescue at Entebbe, Uganda.

Lakia village

The Bedouin village of Lakia, on Route 31 about 6 km north of Be'er Sheva, is well worth a visit for anyone interested in the Bedouin way of life – and anyone interested in shopping for quality Bedouin handiwork. Two projects are in operation here, the **Centre for Bedouin Embroidery (Tatreez Al-Badiah)** (T08-6513208/052-2621161, phone to arrange a visit), provides employment and a source of income to local women, whilst preserving traditional embroidery designs and ensuring age-old skills are not lost. Tours can be arranged for groups, which include time in the Bedouin tent hearing about the lives and situation of the women and their families. There's a wide range of colourful bags, cushions, tablecloths, etc decorated with colourful designs for sale. Likewise, the **Lakia Negev Weaving Centre** ① *T08-6519883, www.lakia.org*, employs about 70 women and can be visited as part of a tour that involves weaving demonstrations, discussions with the staff and some hosting in the Bedouin tradition. Or just call in to visit the shop, which has beautiful rugs, cushions, wall hangings etc for sale, in a wide range of bright weaves and desert colours, using both contemporary and traditional designs. These workshops provide a rare opportunity to buy these desirable products which, ironically, are hard to track down in the Negev.

Joe Alon Centre: Museum of Bedouin Culture

① *Kibbutz Lahav, T08-9918597, www.lahavnet.co.il/joalon. Sat-Thu 0900-1700, Fri 0900-1400. Adult 20NIS. To reach the museum, head north from Be'er Sheva for 21 km on Route 40. Turn right at Dvira Jct on to Route 3255 and follow signs to the museum (8 km). By public transport, bus 42 runs from Be'er Sheva to Kibbutz Lahav nearby at 1150 (Sun-Thu only), but goes straight back again, so you would need to hitch back.*

Within the Joe Alon Regional and Folklore Centre is the 'Museum of Bedouin Culture', an attempt to explain aspects of the traditional Bedouin way of life (and their present day situation). Activities such as cooking, bread-baking, the coffee ceremony and carpet weaving are demonstrated, whilst displays present artefacts such as jewellery, clothing, agricultural implements and household utensils. Many of the items have been donated by the various Bedouin tribes of the Negev and the Sinai, with some of the things on display having now gone out of general usage. There is also a short movie about Bedouin life and donkey rides for children.

East and southeast of Be'er Sheva

From Be'er Sheva, it is possible to take one of two routes towards the Dead Sea Region. The east route takes in the Canaanite/Israelite city at Tel Arad and its modern neighbour Arad, before dropping below sea-level down to the Dead Sea at Neve Zohar.

The southeast route to the Dead Sea, with a number of diversions, passes the modern town of Dimona, the ancient Nabatean city of Mamshit, and the two smaller of the Negev's three main craters, Makhtesh HaGadol and Makhtesh HaKatan. If travelling with your own transport, with an early start it is possible to take in the best of both routes in one grand loop that can return you to Be'er Sheva the same day. If relying on public transport, it would take several days to cover the key sites (with some remoter areas not accessible at all).

The Cave in the Mountain
ⓘ *Drejat village, T/F08-6288660/054-7969576, gabera66@gmail.com, www.drejat.lanegev. co.il. Drejat is 3.5 km north of Route 31 (the turn off is about 5 km after Tel Arad Jct, when coming from Arad).*

On the edge of the Arad valley, at the base of the Yattir mountains, lies the Bedouin village of Drejat, established by 'falakhim' (Arab peasants) in the 19th century. The first villagers inhabited cave dwellings, and it is this heritage and way of life that Gaber Abu Hamad shares with visitors today. Discussions don't just dwell on the past, but cover the present day process of 'modernization' that Bedouin communities are undergoing: he transition from the old ways, from caves and a nomadic tent existence, to make-shift metal huts or (in some cases) plush housing. The famed Bedouin hospitality is mixed with story-telling, a visit to the remains of a Roman road, scenic observation points and of course sweet tea, bitter coffee and tabun bread (traditional 'farmers' meals can be ordered). Individual visitors are probably best to call ahead to see if they can join a bigger group. The Israel National Trail also passes the village.

Tel Arad

ⓘ *Daily 0800-1700, closes 1 hr earlier on Fri. Adult 13NIS, student/child 7NIS.*

At one time the site of the most important city in the Negev, Tel Arad has substantial remains from both the Canaanite and the later Israelite settlements. The site has been considerably restored, particularly the Israelite (and later) citadel at the top of the hill, which has been largely rebuilt using original material. The lower Canaanite city is the largest, most complete Early Bronze Age city yet excavated in Israel. The scenic views from the Israelite tower, with Bedouin villages dotting the South Hebron Hills and swathes of bright green cultivation to the east, is impressive. It is appealingly desolate and you are likely to be alone at the site, save for the numerous lizards. There is a nice picnic area and a campsite is being created.

Tel Arad

National Park entrance & car park

100 metres
100 yards

1 Israelite Citadel
(see separate plan)
2 Sanctuary/Temple
3 Sacred Precinct
(see separate plan)
4 Palace
5 City Walls
6 Projected line of city walls
7 Western Gate
8 Southwestern Gate
9 Residential Quarters &
restored 'Arad House'
10 Water Reservoir Area

Ins and outs
Getting there and away Buses between Be'er Sheva and Arad (along Route 31) will drop you at Tel Arad Junction, the turning for the site, from where it is a 2.5-km walk (or hitch) to the site. Buses from Tel Aviv also pass the junction.

Background

The Canaanite city probably reached its peak towards the beginning of the Early Bronze Age II (3000-2700 BCE). The economy of the city was based primarily on agriculture, including production and processing of barley, wheat, peas, lentils, flax and olives, plus the rearing of livestock. Another important sector of the economy involved extensive trade with southern Sinai, Egypt and other Canaanite cities. Many of the jars, cooking pots and other artefacts found at Tel Arad are now in the Israel Museum in Jerusalem. Evidence from Stratum III (c. 2950-2800 BCE) suggests that much of the town was destroyed in some major conflagration, almost certainly the result of an enemy attack. The town appears to have been rebuilt almost immediately, though occupation was not to last long, with the city being abandoned by 2650 BCE. The reasons for this are not entirely clear, though climatic change, Egyptian encroachment or political unrest throughout Canaan have all been suggested. The fact that the Canaanite city site itself was never reoccupied explains why the remains are so extensive and well preserved.

After a gap of around 1,600 years, parts of the site were reoccupied by the Israelites. The early settlement was clustered around a bamah, or cultic high place. The bamah became a royal Israelite sanctuary during the reign of Solomon (965-928 BCE), and was protected by a citadel. Five further Israelite citadels were built on the site between the ninth century BCE and the early sixth century BCE.

After the destruction of the last of the Israelite citadels at the end of the First Temple period (587-586 BCE), the site was abandoned. A brief occupation during the fifth century BCE led to some Persian building activity, though most of this was destroyed in the third to second century BCE when a large Hellenistic tower was built. The tower stood until the second century BCE.

The Romans built a fortress on the mound (c. 70-100 CE), possibly as part of the network of fortifications guarding the *Limes Palaestinae* (Dead Sea–Rafiah road). No remains were found on the tel from the Byzantine village mentioned in Eusebius' *Onomasticon*, though evidence suggests that the Roman fort was repaired and reoccupied during the Early Arab period (638-1099 CE). The mound was later used as a Muslim graveyard from the 10th to 16th centuries CE. The citadel has been rebuilt by archaeologists, with distinct sections from the tenth, ninth to eighth, and sixth centuries BCE, and the Hellenistic tower, clearly identifiable. Excavations and rebuilding continue at the site.

Tour of the site

The information leaflet provided has a map and an isometric reconstruction of the Canaanite city. A tour can begin at the top, at the Israelite citadel, which is accessible by car. However, you would still need to walk back up to collect your car. It is as well to begin at the bottom, chronologically, at the Canaanite city as the walk around is not very taxing.

Israelite citadel (Tel Hametzudot) The mound upon which the Israelite citadel stands rises above the lower (Canaanite) city to the southwest. The citadel that you see today has been largely rebuilt by the archaeologists who excavated the site, though they used the original materials. Six successive Israelite citadels stood on this site, plus later Persian, Hellenistic, Roman and Arab structures. Climbing to the observation point gives the best view of the citadel's plan, the Canaanite city below, and the surrounding countryside.

Though finds in the citadel area have revealed a hoard of silver ingots and jewellery, as well as evidence of a perfume industry, the most significant building within the citadel is the sanctuary, or temple. Its construction began in the Solomonic period (late 10th century

BCE, though the bamah and altar predate it to the late 12th to early 11th centuries BCE. The temple is orientated east–west, like the Solomonic Temple in Jerusalem, and comprises three rooms: a hall, the sanctuary, and the holy of holies. A massebá, or ritual standing stone, was found in the holy of holies. The temple remained in use until the seventh century BCE, though the use of the sacrificial altar may have gone out of use during the religious reforms of Hezekiah (727-698 BCE). Currently excavators are at work digging out the remarkably deep water cisterns that lie below the citadel foundations.

Sacred Precinct The Sacred Precinct comprises a large twin temple, a small twin temple, and a large ceremonial structure, all within a self-contained complex separated from the other city buildings by a wall. The **large twin temple** to the west consists of two large halls identical in size, both opening on to courtyards. The northern hall is divided into three cells, and a large altar and a cult basin were found in its courtyard. The southern hall proved rich in finds, most notable of which is what is thought to be a *massebá*. The **small twin temple** in the centre of the Sacred Precinct is similar in plan. A number of finds were unearthed here, including a stone altar in the courtyard of the northern hall. The **ceremonial building** to the southeast comprises a large hall opening on to a wide courtyard. All the buildings in the Sacred Precinct open to the east, with the twin temples closely resembling the twin temples at Megiddo.

The Palace complex The Palace complex was sealed off from the rest of the city buildings, with no doors or windows to the west, a main entrance to the north, and small doorways to the east and south. The location of the complex near to the Sacred Precinct was significant in determining its function as the governor's residence.

City walls and gates The **Canaanite city walls** extend for some 1,200 m, enclosing an area of 10 hectares. The wall is almost 2.5 m thick in most parts and is built of large, semi-dressed stones with a fill of smaller stones. The walls are reinforced by posterns, towers and gates, and being restored. The **western gate** was probably the main gate, suggested by its wide entrance, and is protected by a semi-circular tower to its north.

Residential quarter The Canaanite city plan was well ordered, with a functional separation of districts. Typical dwelling units comprise a main room with benches running along the walls, a stone base for a wooden pillar to support the roof in the centre of the room, a smaller subsidiary room (a kitchen or storeroom), plus a courtyard. Such is the regularity of this building within the Canaanite city, such a broadhouse is now referred to as an **Aradian House**.

Water reservoir area It should be noted that the Canaanite city lacks a natural spring or well and is thus dependent upon collection and storage of rainwater. The

Sacred Precinct, Tel Arad

Courtyard

N

20 metres	1 Large Twin Temple 3 Ceremonial
20 yards	2 Small Twin Temple Building

Eocenic rock that the mound stands upon is different in character to the Senonian rock that surrounds it and, being impervious to water, it allows the storage of water in large cisterns.

At the lowest part of the city, the water reservoir area of the Canaanite city is a distinct complex of buildings surrounding the main reservoir on three sides. The largest building in the complex comprises five long, narrow chambers, with very thick outer walls and may well have been associated with the control and distribution of this most valuable of commodities

The plan of the original Canaanite city reservoir is not clear due to the later digging of the Israelite period well in the centre. The deep well, tapping the upper aquifer, supplied water that was carried in vessels to the cistern inside the Israelite citadel. The well was restored during the Herodian period, some time between 37 BCE and 70 CE.

Arad → *Colour map 3, grid A5.*

Though there are few attractions in Arad itself, the town is a good base for easy access to the west side of Masada, and is popular with Israeli walkers as many good treks can be had in the surrounding area. Arad is also worth visiting since it is one of the few development towns in the Negev that has been deemed to have worked. Arad lies close to the ancient Canaanite city at Tel Arad (see page 308), though its main claim to fame nowadays is as home to the renowned Israeli writer Amos Oz, and as the venue for the annual Hebrew Music Festival.

Ins and outs
Getting there and away There are four buses from Tel Aviv per day and frequent services from Be'er Sheva. Arriving from the direction of the Dead Sea, there are several buses per day from 'En Boqeq, Ein Gedi and Masada.

Getting around The town centre is very compact, though if you're heading out towards the eastern edge of town it is easier to hop on bus 1 (which makes a long circuit all the way around the town).

Tourist Information There is no longer a tourist information centre in Arad, but a decent map is available from the Inbar Hotel, and you can call Anna at the **Municipality** ① *T08-9951622, Sun-Thu 1000-1530, for advice.*

Background
Earmarked as a Negev development town by the government in the early 1960s, the site for the new town was selected by a group of founding fathers. The lay-out of the town was developed by an interdisciplinary team who took into consideration physical, social, economic and demographic factors. Thus, there is a distinct separation of industrial, commercial and residential zones, with sufficient room for the town to expand in stages. Compared with other Negev development towns, Arad has been a success. As one long-time resident pointed out, "Those who planned towns such as Dimona never lived in them. The opposite is true of Arad" (Brook, *Winner Takes All*).

Arad is situated 600 m above sea-level, at the point where the Judean Hills meet the Negev desert, and the views from this plateau are excellent. With a dry desert climate, pollen-free air, and pollution-free environment, Arad has gained a reputation as a centre for the treatment of asthma and other respiratory problems.

Sights

Eshet Lot Artists' Quarter Located by the western entrance to Arad, 2 km from town, the "Lot's Wife" Artists' Quarter makes use of semi-derelict warehouses and hangars on the edge of the industrial area (a small-scale Mizpe Ramon, see page 335). The workshops and galleries tend to open only at weekends or by request, so be sure to call ahead before you visit. The **Glass Museum** ⓘ *11 HaSadan, T08-9953388*, is a highlight, exhibiting the work of Gideon Friedman plus other glass artists, and there is a shop. Close by, at 9 HaSadan, is the **Earth and Clay Culture Museum** ⓘ *T08-9939856*, where you can view installations, check out the ceramics gallery and browse the shop. The **Doll Museum** ⓘ *14 HaSadan, T052-2398918*, is an extraordinary enterprise: the sculptor-owners show their works all over the world, created in porcelain, bronze and other materials (at times unsettlingly life-like). Unfortunately, entrance is only for groups, but call to see if there is a chance you can tag along.

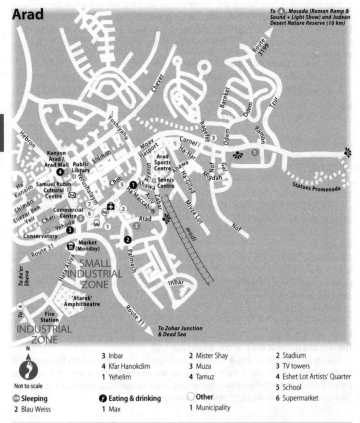

Arad

To Masada (Roman Ramp & Sound + Light Show) and Judean Desert Nature Reserve (10 km)

Not to scale

	3 Inbar	**2** Mister Shay	**2** Stadium
	4 Kfar Hanokdim	**3** Muza	**3** TV towers
	1 Yehelim	**4** Tamuz	**4** Eshet Lot Artists' Quarter
			5 School
🛏 **Sleeping**	🍴 **Eating & drinking**	⭕ **Other**	**6** Supermarket
2 Blau Weiss	**1** Max	**1** Municipality	

Access to the 'Roman Ramp' entrance to Masada

The western entrance to the fortress at Masada, (the 'Roman Ramp'), is accessible by vehicle only from Arad (though there is no public transport to the site). The west side of Masada is also the venue for the Son et Lumière (Sound and Light) show. The Roman Ramp entrance is 20 km northeast of Arad, along Route 3199. To reach Route 3199, head along Moav to the eastern limits of Arad, before turning left on to Tzur just before the *Margoa Arad Hotel*. Masada is then sign-posted along the road to the right (northeast). It's an awe-inspiring drive in the late afternoon light.

Arad listings

For Sleeping and Eating price codes and other relevant information, see Essentials pages 26-31.

Sleeping

Arad has a slim choice of hotels, though one is outstanding; package tourists will find themselves in one of the well-equipped hotels on the east side of town (not listed here).
L Yehelim, 72 Moav, T077-2028120/6 or 052-6522718, www.yehelim.com, yehelim@gmail.com. One of the most charming boutique hotels in Israel, Yehelim's 10 rooms are secluded, some with balcony overlooking the desert hills, each has a unique layout but the same cool calm colour scheme, jacuzzi, wide beds, cute garden, beautiful terrace with Moroccan lamps. Standard rooms 600NIS, deluxe 720NIS (weekend price rise), discounts for stays over 2 days. Wonderful breakfast included (outside guests welcome for breakfast, phone the day before), vegetarian/fish dinner available (guests only). Young children not allowed. Good advice on activities in the area. A peaceful haven on the eastern edge of town.
AL Inbar, 38 Yehuda, T08-9973303, www.inbar-hotel.co.il. Rather unsightly block in centre of town, though rooms are pleasantly furnished in creams with pale wood, decent bathrooms, standard amenities and fairly priced, suites significantly larger. Heated indoor pool, salt water pool and dry sauna (outside guests 40NIS for day-use, call to check opening hrs), spa and mud treatments available in adjoining spa. Kosher restaurant.

A Kfar Hanokdim, T08-9950097, wwwkfarhanokdim.co.il. An oasis in the Judean desert, stunningly located in a valley between Arad and Masada (10 km away from each). Camel rides and a 'Bedouin experience' are encouraged as part of a stay, but you can just take a room, space in a tent or even pitch your own (they try to be accommodating and can provide sleeping bags). Cabins have personality, with Bedouin rugs everywhere, pretty coverlets, coral and driftwood decor, Hebron glass baubles, coffee corner. Great thought has gone into creating unique areas to relax outdoors, with BBQs and lounging space. Bedouin hospitality includes music and chat about life before and life now. Meals in the attractive circular dining hall, with ludicrously large portions of traditional Bedouin dishes and a vast, delicious buffet breakfast. It's a good place to stay if you want to access Masada from the west, or are going to the Sound and Light show (see above).
A Blau-Weiss Guest House and Youth Hostel, 4 Atad, T08-9957150, www.iyha.co.il. Clean a/c private chalets (doubles 336NIS during week) with TV and coffee corner, breakfast included, reception open 0800-1400, no curfew. Rooms sleep 2-5 people. Be sure to call in advance, they only open up when there are bookings.

Rooms for rent

There are several zimmers and "rooms for rent" in town, including Lavi's House, 13 Irit, T08-9954791 and Villa 1000, T08-9954423.

Eating and drinking

There are no really outstanding restaurants in Arad. There are plenty of cafés, pizza parlours and kebab places in the Commercial Centre, plus a big supermarket nearby in the Kanyon Mall. For a special breakfast, call the Yehelim (see Sleeping, above).

Max, T08-9973339. Mon-Wed 1800-2400, Thu 1800-0200, Fri 1800-0300, Sat 1200-0100. This shack-like building in a rather derelict park morphs into a lively evening drinking and dining spot, with good music and a better atmosphere. Some outside tables.

Mister Shay, 32 Palmach, T08-9971956. Mon-Sat 1200-2300. Serves a large spread of Chinese food and cheap (for Israel) sushi, plus the odd Thai dish. Plenty of veg options (though rather mundane), meat eaters will be spoilt for choice, set menus for 2 from 169NIS, business lunch 40-60NIS. Tastefully and brightly decorated in Asian colours. Wireless available. The restaurant is behind a grocery shop, down some steps.

Muza, T08-9958764. (Only closes between 0600-0800 each day for cleaning!) The liveliest pub in town is definitely Muza, weirdly located behind the Alon petrol station on the western entrance to Arad. The interior is coated with football colours and license plates, with a 'real' bar and screens for watching sport. Great outdoor area, large menu of Israeli-Western food and lots of imported beers. Ask about the food/drink deals. Shabbat is raucous.

Tamuz, in the Kanyon Arad Mall. Dairy restaurant/café with a mixed menu of light meals and salads. Recommended.

Festivals and events

The population of Arad used to double during the annual **Hebrew Music Festival** (Festival Arad). After a long spell of absence, the festival was back in 2009, held during Sukkot (Sep/Oct). To get the latest information call the Municipality on T106.

Shopping

The main shopping area is the **Kanyon Arad** (Arad Mall) and the nearby **Commercial Centre** between Eliezar Ben Yair and Yehuda. **Arad Market** takes place each Mon. A branch of **Steimatzsky** in the mall sells the Jerusalem Post, but has poor fiction/travel selection.

Transport

Bus

Arad's 'Bus Station' is on Yehuda. **Be'er Sheva**, bus 388, Sun-Thu frequent service from 0530-2200, Fri until 1646, Sat from 1800, 1 hr. **Dead Sea destinations**, bus 384/385 Sun-Thu 0705 1015 1300 1545, Fri 1030 1335. **Tel Aviv** 389 direct, Sun-Thu 4 buses per day, 0600 0830 1600 1900, Fri last at 1330, Sat 1800 2100, 1½ hrs, 39NIS. **Jerusalem** 554, Sun-Thu 0730 1430 1700, Fri 1100 1345, Sat 2130 2200, 3 hrs. The best option for **Eilat** is to change at Be'er Sheva. For **Tel Arad**, take one of the buses bound for **Be'er Sheva** or **Tel Aviv** and ask to be dropped at the Tel Arad Junction (2.5-km walk to the site).

Directory

Banks There are several banks in the Mall/Commercial Centre area with ATMs; the best option for foreign exchange is probably the Post Office. **Hospitals** Soroka Hospital, T08-9400111; Bet Mazor, Yehuda, T089953339, regional rehabilitation centre for asthmatic children. Several of the hotels also have asthma treatment facilities. **Post office** The main post office is on the corner of Eliezar Ben Yair and Hebron, and offers poste restante, international phone calls and commission-free foreign exchange.

The 'Black Hebrews'

Arriving in Israel in 1969 and settling largely in Dimona (and to some extent in Arad, Mizpe Ramon and Tiberias), this sect has caused considerable controversy within Israel. The group are largely English-speakers from the United States, led by Ben-Ami Ben Israel (formerly Ben-Ami Carter), and claim to be descendants of the 'real Jews'. Amongst their beliefs is that the 'original Jews' were expelled from Israel by the Romans following the destruction of the Second Temple in 70 CE. Many settled in West Africa but were subsequently forcibly transferred to the United States as part of the slave trade. The Black Hebrews are descended from these former slaves and have now returned to Israel to reclaim the Holy Land for the 'real Jews'. Their initial claim to be Ethiopian Jews was exposed to be fraudulent by an Arad bus driver, himself an Ethiopian Jew, though nowadays they make no attempt to conceal what they consider to be their origins. Not surprisingly, their claims brought them into conflict with the Israeli government, who in the 1980s were threatening to deport them en masse.

However, the group are now tolerated and in 2003 were granted permanent residency status, with the first individual being granted full citizenship rights in 2009. The community focus on regular exercise has resulted in great success for their softball team, their gospel choir entertains heads of state, and member Eddie Butler has represented Israel in the 1999 and 2006 Eurovision Song Contests!

For more information visit www.kingdomofyah.com

Dimona → Colour map 3, grid B4.

Whilst Arad is often held up as a model for the Negev development towns, Dimona is frequently selected by commentators as the example of the one that didn't work. From modest beginnings in 1955, the population has increased to around 40,000, a sizeable proportion of whom are Jews of North African origin, plus a more recent Russian influx. The economy of the town has traditionally been sustained by four major industries, despite the fact that the remoteness of the location increases transport costs considerably. Severe staff cut-backs at the textile factories, the chemical factory, and to a certain extent at the Dead Sea Works, led to high levels of unemployment in the early 1990s though the situation has improved in recent years.

Dimona's other major 'business', sometimes euphemistically referred to as the 'chocolate factory', is the country's leading **nuclear research station**. The facility is located off the road 13 km east of the town, though sightseers are not encouraged. It's not even recommended that you stop to take a look and don't even think about getting your camera out. When a former employee at the site, **Mordechai Vanunu**, spilled the beans about Israel's nuclear capacity to the London *Sunday Times*, he was lured to Rome by a female Mossad agent, kidnapped, and brought back to Israel to stand trial. After serving 18 years in jail he was released in 2004, though his movements and speech are severely restricted (he cannot leave Israel nor talk to foreign press).

Dimona's other main talking point is the presence of the 2000-strong community of African Hebrew Israelites, popularly referred to as the **Black Hebrews** (see box). The group have established their own 'village of peace' within Dimona, and the community welcomes visitors who take a genuine interest in their beliefs and the way that they live. It is advisable to phone ahead (call **Yafah** ① *T052-3910858*, at least 24 hours in advance) and someone will show you around. Community shops cover a diverse range of activities, from the Sisterhood Boutique selling their unique style of clothing made of 100% natural fabrics, the grocery store selling organic and vegan products, to the specialist hair-braiding salon (by appointment only). The 2-day New World Passover in late May celebrates the Exodus from America, with dance, sporting events and family activities, and attracts a few hundred foreign visitors. Their compound is on Herzl, 10 minutes walk from the bus station.

Dimona listings

For Sleeping and Eating price codes and other relevant information, see Essentials pages 26-31.

Sleeping and eating
D-E Black Hebrews' Guesthouse, T08-6555400. Advance booking essential. Simple rooms, price includes half-board. Visitors are asked to respect their regulations, which means no cigarettes, alcohol or meat products to be brought into the community. Guests have access (for a small fee) to small gym, sauna, jacuzzi and exercise classes. Easily the best (and cheapest) place in town to eat is at the Black Hebrews' vegan café, which has lunch and dinner specials (eg casserole), as well as sandwiches, raw foods and tofu dishes. The (soya) ice cream is popular: flavour changes daily. Open Sun-Thu 1030-2100, Fri 0830-1400. The community also runs the Taste of Life vegan café in Tel Aviv (see page 417).

The large mall on the opposite side of Road 25 from the town centre has a branch of Aroma, which is always reliable for generously sized and tasty salads, sandwiches and the like.

Transport
Bus
Be'er Sheva, buses 48/56, 2 per hour, 30-45 minutes, 11NIS; **Eilat**, buses 393/394/397, Sun-Thu 0755-0150, Fri 0755-1800, Sat 1805-0150, 3 hrs; **Tel Aviv**, buses 393/394, every hr or so Sun-Thu 0740-2140, Fri 0740-1740, Sat 1410-2140, 2 hours 45 minutes.

Mamshit → *Colour map 3, grid B4.*

① *T08-6556478. Daily 0800-1700 (winter -1600), closes 1 hr earlier on Fri and hol eves. Adult 20NIS, student 17NIS, child 9NIS. Mamshit is 6 km southeast of Dimona along Route 25. The Dimona–Eilat bus (395/397) stops at the turning for the site, from where it is 1.5 km along the side road.*
During the reign of their King Obodas III (c. 28 BCE-9 CE), the Nabateans established a number of large settlements in the Negev, ostensibly as way-stations on the network of roads that comprised the Spice Road between their Edom capital at Petra and the Mediterranean Sea at Gaza. The extensive remains commonly referred to by the Hebrew name Mamshit (the Arabic name Kurnub sounds better to the English ear) are the site of one such Nabatean city. Mamshit was important enough to feature on the Madaba Map, and you get a good sense of this past as you walk through rooms and turn corners of clearly defined streets in the ancient city.

Background
Early Roman/Middle Nabatean period A town was probably established here during the reign of the Nabatean king Obodas III, in the Early Roman period (also known as the Middle Nabatean period, 37 BCE-132 CE). Roads almost certainly connected Mamshit to other Nabatean towns, most notably Gaza via Oboda (Hebrew: Avdat), though it should be noted that Mamshit was on a secondary and not the main trade route. Its status and

prosperity may well have increased in the Late Nabatean period when Roman engineers cut steps forming the Ma'ale Aqrabim (or Scorpions' Ascent, see page 321) to the southeast, on the road to Petra.

Much of the Nabatean kingdom was annexed by the Roman Empire in 106 CE, though this is not considered to have lessened the general prosperity of the Negev. The Nabateans had begun to establish a sophisticated system of agriculture in the central Negev, cultivating the desert by collecting rainwater in carefully constructed terraces in the narrow valleys. Potential arable land at Mamshit was scarce, however, and thus much of the town's economy was based upon the rearing of race-horses. This lack of arable land may also explain why Mamshit, with a population of around 1000, is considerably smaller than Nessana (Nizzana, population 4000) and Oboda (Avdat, population 3000).

Middle and Late Roman/Late Nabatean period One of the key features of Nabatean towns is the quality of the architecture, and Mamshit is no exception. Initially, the towns featured the characteristic Nabatean large public buildings, with only the army living in permanent quarters and most of the population living in tents. The Late Nabatean period saw a new town plan laid out, initiated largely by the construction of upper-class housing, and with the main north–south axis now dividing public buildings from the residential areas. The Nabateans used their knowledge and mastery of constructing grand building designs, and adapted it to their domestic architecture. The Middle and Late Roman periods (Late Nabatean period) saw the construction of large, spacious houses around a central courtyard, sometimes up to three storeys high. The homes were designed to be cool in summer and warm in winter. Many of the sizeable Nabatean buildings seen at the site today date to the Late Nabatean period.

During the Late Roman period, Mamshit was integrated within the southern defence system of the Roman Empire, probably guarding the Jerusalem–Aila (Eilat) road, and a fortified wall was built around the settlement. It appears that the Romans made few additions to the built environment, instead taking advantage of the high-quality building techniques of the Nabateans. It is interesting to note that much of the town's economy became based upon the payment of salaries from the imperial treasury to resident soldiers. When the Eternal Peace agreement was concluded by the Emperor Justinian in 561 CE and the military payments ceased, the economy of Mamshit went into severe decline.

Byzantine period The major change at Mamshit during the Byzantine period (324-638 CE) was that most of the population turned from paganism to Christianity. Two of Mamshit's most prominent buildings, the Eastern Church and the Western Church, date to this period. A number of buildings were destroyed by a strong earthquake in 363 CE. Mamshit was probably destroyed by local Arab tribesmen prior to the full-scale occupation of the Negev by the Arabs in 636 CE.

Tour of the site
The following tour proceeds in a roughly anti-clockwise direction from the entrance. An information leaflet, with map, is provided, plus there are useful boards around the site with diagrammatic reconstructions of how the buildings would have appeared The text below is intended to complement rather than repeat the information given at the site.

Nabatean caravanserai These large buildings standing outside the later city walls served as inns and remained buried by deep sand dunes for a long period of time. They are missing from the plan of the site that T.E. Lawrence (Lawrence of Arabia) helped prepare in 1914.

Main city gate The city's main gate was defended by two unequally sized towers, later expanded, and closed by sturdy wooden doors. Remains of the burnt doors were found in the debris of the gate. It is interesting to note that the main gate is not aligned with the main street of the Late Nabatean town.

Late Roman city walls Most Nabatean settlements were unwalled, relying instead for their defence on a series of strategically placed towers within the town itself. When the Romans absorbed the central Negev area within the southern defence system of their empire, Mamshit's compact size meant that it could be encircled by a defensive wall. The walls run for just under one kilometre, taking advantage of the contours of the land and taking into account existing buildings. They are reinforced by a number of towers.

Water-supply system Accomplished engineers as well as architects and masons, the Nabateans thrived in their desert environment through their ability to construct complex, but reliable, water-supply systems. Mamshit's water was controlled by three dams on Nahal Mamshit, a water-conservation system built above the high waterfall of a tributary of the Nahal Mamshit, plus several water-retaining pools engineered to the south and west. A small Water Gate was added to the western wall in the Late Roman period to allow water to be brought into the town from the three dams on the Nahal Mamshit (none shown on map).

Mansion The large (35 m by 20 m) building to the northeast of the tower may have been the mansion of a city official during the Late Nabatean period. The complex features a guardroom, guest quarters and offices, with the main residential area on the upper balconied storey.

Watchtower A good view of the entire city and the ancient dam in Nahal Mamshit can be had from the top of the tower, which is 5-m high. The square tower adjoins a courtyard containing a large reservoir. The tower may have served as a combined observation tower/administrative centre during the Middle and Late Nabatean periods.

Western Church The more elaborate of Mamshit's two churches in its execution, the Western Church has been well restored. The nave mosaic depicts birds, fruit, swastikas and flowers on a geometric pattern, with a central inscription within a medallion reading: "Lord, Help your servant Nilus, the builder of this place, Amen." The Western Church was destroyed in a violent conflagration. Dating the church has been problematic, with the mosaic inscriptions providing no clues. A coin found in the upper levels of the church foundations belongs to the reign of the Roman Emperor Probus (276-282 CE), whilst another coin found amongst the fill of the foundation pit dates to the late fourth century CE. Behind the church is a typical Nabatean house, with stables for 16 horses.

Eastern Church The plan of the Byzantine Eastern Church is almost identical to that of the Western Church. It is also notable for its high standard of workmanship and, unusually for a Byzantine period building, the construction methods are Roman. Dating the church precisely has not been possible, though certain clues have enabled experts to make an educated guess. The geometric mosaic pavement in the nave has two crosses incorporated into the design. Since the practice of depicting the cross on a church floor was banned in 427 CE, it is concluded that the church must predate this decree. Further, coins dating to the reigns of the Eastern Roman Emperors Diocletian (284-305 CE, in the pre-church era) and Theodosius I (379-395 CE) were discovered in the foundations, suggesting the church was built some time during the latter's reign. Part of a monastery complex, an adjacent courtyard (atrium) contains a deep cistern. Small reliquaries sunk into the floor next to the altar, and a simple grave in a side room, contain the bones of supposed saints or martyrs.

Market area The market area comprises three rows of shops lining two streets. (It is roofed with palm leaves for when a present-day "Nabatean Market" is staged, during both Pesach and Sukkot).

British police station This relatively modern building is the former headquarters of the Negev desert police (who were mounted on camels) during the British Mandate period. The construction of the police station destroyed much of what may have been the Middle Nabatean fortress building. There are good views from the top (and also from behind) down Wadi Mamshit.

"Nabatu" House One of the finest examples of the ability of Late Nabatean architects, the complex features a central courtyard with columns topped by well-formed capitals, standing on a stylobate. Stables lead off from the courtyard, each horse having a stone trough and arched stone window to their stall. The treasure room stood to the south of the courtyard, and is identifiable by the frescoes on the arches and upper walls of its vestibule. A hoard of 10,500 silver dinars and tetradrachms was found in a bronze jar concealed beneath the ruins of a staircase. The oldest of the coins date to the reign of the Nabatean King Rabbel II (70-106 CE), with the latest dating to the rule of the Roman Emperor Elagabalus (218-222 CE).

Bathhouse Dating of the bathhouse is uncertain; it was certainly in use during the Byzantine period, though it may actually have been built during the Late Nabatean period. The entrance leads to a central courtyard lined with stone benches, which probably served as the changing room. The cold room (*frigidarium*) has two sitting baths. A connecting door leads to the *tepidarium*, or lukewarm room, with the hot baths comprising three rooms (*caldarium*) sunk into the ground. Remains of the plumbing system that brought water and took away the waste can also be seen. To the east of the bathhouse, adjacent to the city walls, is a large public pool that was used as a reservoir, supplied by water carried by man and beast from the wadi to the west of the town.

Cemeteries Though not enclosed within the Mamshit National Park area (nor shown on the site map), three main cemeteries associated with the site have been excavated; the main Nabatean necropolis 1 km to the north of the city, a Roman cemetery 200 m to the northeast, and a Byzantine cemetery 500 m to the west of the city.

Mamshit listings

For Sleeping and Eating price codes and other relevant information, see Essentials pages 26-31.

Sleeping and eating
Negev Camel Ranch, T08-6552829, www. cameland.co.il. 12 excellent-value huts,

simple yet comfortable, decorated with plain coloured mats and desert colours. Heater, a/c, Bedouin seating inside and out. Dorm-style 85NIS, or 100/200NIS per single/ couple for a private hut, plus 75NIS per extra person. Bear in mind this is the desert, and dung beetles and lizards are visitors, plus a tribe of dogs and 40 female camels are near neighbours! Deliciously wholesome vegetarian "camel herder's supper": rice, lentils, veg stew, salad, bread baked on a hot stone, dates and tea to follow (adult/child 55/45NIS). Great breakfast (adult/child 35/25NIS). Beer and soft drinks available, making it a good place to come and hang out wherever you are staying. Good clean bathrooms and kitchen for guests use. Pick up from Dimona not a problem, or the Eliat bus passes nearby. Recommended.

Mamshit Campsite, cheap at 65NIS a dorm bed, but this could mean sharing with 200 people and all you get is a mattress. However, if one of the Tukuls (little huts with rush roofs and rug-interior walls) is free you will be given a place here (sleeps 5-6). Bear in mind it's geared towards school groups. Kitchen facilities, and decent shower/toilet block.

Activities and tours
Negev Camel Ranch, see sleeping and eating, provides a great opportunity to take a camel safari into the desert. Rides go on the hour every day, no minimum number and no advance arrangement required (unless you are a large group). A scenic hour's ride will pass near the ruins of Mamshit and along the cliffs above the wadi (adult/child 59/49NIS). The 2-hr and 4-hr trips are good value (adults 89/155NIS), or you can book a 2-day safari including all equipment and food (850NIS per person). Owner Ariel (and his staff) provide good information and advice on local trekking and biking, given free of charge. Anyone is welcome to drop by and it's recommended to do so before a trip, as desert conditions can be so changeable. You can pay to have someone drop you off/pick you up at the start/finish of hikes, and there is overnight accommodation, see Sleeping below. The ranch is 6 km southeast of Dimona, down the same road as Mamshit. 200 m from the main Route 25, a track branches left to the ranch.

Makhtesh HaGadol and Makhtesh HaKatan (craters)

Lying to the southeast of Be'er Sheva are two impressive erosion craters, formed by the same geological process as the Negev's more famous erosion crater, Makhtesh Ramon (see page 342). In fact, the Makhtesh HaKatan (small crater) is the most visually stunning as it can be seen in its entirety and thus the impact is more striking. There are several excellent hikes that can be made in the Makhtesh HaGadol (Great Makhtesh) and Makhtesh HaKatan area, as well as a number of archaeological remains which add interest, though many visitors just drive through and admire the views.

Ins and outs
Getting there and away Unfortunately, the sites and hiking trail heads described below are not accessible by public transport, and as none of the hikes is circular, you will need transport waiting at the finishing points or make an arrangement for pick-up/drop-off with your guesthouse.

There are several points of access to the two craters. They can be approached from the northwest via Yeroham (a Negev development town 13 km southwest of Dimona); from the north, via Rotem Junction where Route 25 meets the 204; and from the southeast, from Hazeva Junction at the meeting point of Route 90 (The Arava Road) and Route 227.

NB The usual rules about hiking in the desert apply. The map here is for information only, and should be complemented with the relevant sheets of the SPNI 1:50,000 map. The words 'wadi' and 'nahal' (river) are used interchangeably below.

Sights

Ma'ale 'Aqrabim hike (Scorpion's Ascent) The starting point for this strenuous six- to seven-hour hike is the Rogem Zafir (the starting or finishing point for a number of walks, most of which are marked on the sign-board and map). The larger of the two structures comprising Rogem Zafir is a fort, formerly two storeys high. A number of coins were found here, mostly depicting the images of Roman emperors and dating from the third and fourth centuries CE. The two structures served as a staging post on the Petra–Gaza Spice Road.

The route described here runs in a southeast to northwest direction. It follows blue trail markers for most of its journey, with a number of diversions and extensions marked in green and black. It is entirely feasible to do the walk in reverse, of course, thus descending more than ascending and enjoying the view spread out in front of you.

The route incorporates the Ma'ale 'Aqrabim, or Scorpions' Ascent, part of an ancient route linking the northern Arava with the northern Negev Hills. This area featured heavily in the wanderings of Moses and the Children of Israel, though his followers were not impressed: "And why have ye brought up the congregation of the Lord into this wilderness, that we and our cattle should die there?" (*Numbers 20:4*). This area was later described to Moses by God as the southern border of the land that the Jews should settle: "And your border shall turn from the south to the ascent of Akrabbim, and pass on to Zin ..." (*Numbers 34:4*).

The turning point in the fortunes of this route was when the Roman engineers cut a cliff road into the steep escarpment during the Late Roman period (132-324 CE). Whereas the

The Makhtesh HaGadol, Makhtesh HaKatan

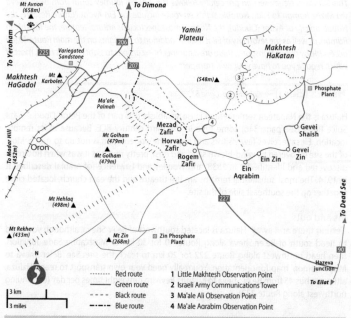

.... Red route	**1** Little Makhtesh Observation Point
——— Green route	**2** Israeli Army Communications Tower
- - - Black route	**3** Ma'ale Ali Observation Point
–·–·– Blue route	**4** Ma'ale Aqrabim Observation Point

average slope of the natural escarpment was 34°, and thus unsuitable for pack animals, the sharp curves and terraced steps that the Romans constructed reduced this gradient to a manageable 16°. As you climb up, you may wish that the Romans had reduced the gradient by a bit more. The staircase was largely rebuilt during the British Mandate period.

There is a shorter, but steeper, path off to the right, leading to the Ma'ale 'Aqrabim Observation Point, though the route described here continues in a northwest direction, between two wadis, before you encounter the first staircase. Five flights of stairs later, you arrive at the top of the Roman **Ma'ale 'Aqrabim**. The building remains here are Horvat Zafir, a Roman fortress that guarded the route. About 500 m to the south are the remains of an ancient dam.

The blue trail continues north, in the direction of the remains of the fort on the top of the hill about 1.5 km in front of you. This is Mezad Zafir, another square Roman fort. From Mezad Zafir there are several options. The red trail leads east, towards the **Ma'ale Ali Observation Point** and the **Little Makhtesh Observation Point**, intersecting the main road, Route 227, on the way (see map). The black trail heads northwest, rejoining Route 227 after about 4.5 km. The blue trail continues west-north-west, after 4.5 km either following the Ma'ale Yamin (Yamin ascent) back to Route 227, or allowing a diversion for a further 6 km along the green route of the Big Fin trail back to the **Variegated Sandstone** (some beautiful sandstone formations featuring a bold display of yellows, ochres, reds and purples).

Southern Negev

This Southern Negev section principally follows the 220-km journey south from Be'er Sheva via Mizpe Ramon to Eilat. Notable sights en route include the Ein Avdat Nature Reserve, the Nabatean city of Avdat (Oboda), the Negev's most spectacular natural feature, the Makhtesh Ramon, as well as the resort city of Eilat itself. In addition to the sights on the main Route 40 (all accessible by public transport), there are a number of excursions to sights off this road, most of which require you to have your own transport.

Haluza (Elusa) → *Colour map 3, grid B3.*

Haluza is the Nabatean settlement of Elusa, established as part of the Petra–Oboda–Gaza Spice Road (see page 346) some time in the third century BCE. Because of its remote location, Elusa receives few visitors and hence the presentation is not up to much. Most of the site is covered by wind-blown sand and dust; pretty much as it was when Robinson discovered and identified it in 1838, and Woolley and Lawrence (of Arabia) described it in 1914. The most substantial remains are the theatre and the east church, located close together on the southeast side of the site.

Ins and outs
Getting there and away Haluza is located southwest of Be'er Sheva, although you need to head south of Be'er Sheva along Route 40 for 30 km to Mash'abbe Sade Junction, then head northwest along Route 222 for 20 km to reach the site. See 'Be'er Sheva to Mizpe Ramon' map for orientation. You really need your own transport to reach Haluza, although bus 45 from Be'er Sheva to Kibbutz Revivim runs eight times per day (continuing northwest along Route 222).

Background

The principal Nabatean finds from the site date to the reigns of the Nabatean kings Aretas I (c. 168 BCE) and Aretas IV (c. 9 BCE-40 CE). However, it was during the Late Nabatean and Late Roman periods that Elusa reached its peak, eventually becoming the major Byzantine city in the Negev.

There are numerous written references to Elusa, providing some insight into the city's history. Ptolemy refers to Elusa, as does the writer Libanius in two mid-fourth century CE letters. Elusa is also listed on the Roman cartographer Castorius' 'road atlas' of the Roman Empire, *Tabula Peutingeriana* (c. 365 CE). Christian references to Elusa, however, are more problematic. The assertion by both Jerome and Nilus that Christians and idolaters lived side by side in Elusa during the early fifth century cannot be proven since the earliest Christian epitaph thus found at the site dates to 519 CE. There are also important references to Elusa in the Nessana papyri (see page 326).

The site

The **theatre** was first constructed in the Middle Nabatean period, in the first half of the first century CE. Later additions were made, and it seems to have remained in use until the middle of the Byzantine period at least. The cavea, or spectators' seating area, is about 35 m in diameter, though it is not well preserved. The 'VIP' box in the centre is still discernible, however. The *orchestra* area in front of the stage is quite well preserved, though inscriptions suggest that a new floor was laid as recently as 455 CE. The Nabatean theatre at Elusa had cultic uses, with the site's excavators believing that a Nabatean temple stood nearby.

Part of the reason that the east church was excavated so thoroughly was because it was thought that it may stand on the site of the Nabatean temple connected with the theatre. Because of this attention paid to the east church, it is probably the most impressive attraction at Elusa today. The church is particularly large (27 m by 77 m), with many limestone columns and Proconessian marble Corinthian capitals still *in situ*. The base of a bishop's throne has been identified within the central apse, suggesting that the church was in fact the region's cathedral. It has not been possible to date the church conclusively, though the building style is comparable with other churches built in the Negev between 350 CE and 450 CE.

Shivta (Sobata) → *Colour map 3, grid B2.*

ⓘ *Open all hours. Admission free.*

Though not part of the main Petra–Oboda–Gaza Spice Road (see page 346), the Nabatean town of Sobata (Arabic: Subeita) was still linked to Oboda (Avdat) and Nessana (Nizzana) by road. The principal points of interest are the churches, though parts of the Nabatean and Byzantine towns remain. Because of its remoteness, Shivta receives few visitors and entrance is still free. This, however, may soon change as the site is scheduled for restoration. Visit now, while Shivta retains its magical and isolated aura. There is a Nabatean restaurant and charming small guesthouse near the entrance.

Ins and outs

Getting there and away From Tlalim Junction on Route 40, head southwest for 20 km, then turn south for 8 km to the site (passing a number of burnt-out Egyptian tanks from the 1948 war). Metropoline bus 44 passes the turn-off, but hitching the last 8 km would be difficult, especially as the bus leaves Be'er Sheva Sunday-Thursday at 1900 and Friday at 1400.

Background

Sobata was probably founded during the time of the Nabatean king Aretas IV (c. 9 BCE-40 CE), or perhaps during the reign of his predecessor Obodas III (c. 28-9 BCE). The Romans seem to have had little impact upon Sobata, probably not even stationing a garrison and not fortifying the town. Sobata increased in importance during the Byzantine period (324-638 CE), possibly becoming a centre of Christian scholarship and pilgrimage. The Nessana Papyri (see page 326) again suggest no permanent military presence during this period, though there are plenty of references to the agricultural economy.

There is evidence to suggest that following the Arab conquest of the region (636 CE), Christians and Muslims lived in peace together here. As one of the site's chief excavators, Avraham Negev, points out, the builders of the mosque were at pains not to damage the adjoining baptistry of the South Church.

Sights

The **North Church** was probably built in two separate phases, beginning life as a single apsidal basilica in the middle of the fourth century CE. Considerable additions were made in the first half of the sixth century CE to make the church triapsidal. The church is attended by a monastery, a chapel, a baptistry and a mortuary chapel.

The **South Church** is smaller, constrained in its construction by the positioning of the double reservoir on its west side. For this reason there is no *atrium* (entrance forecourt), an unusual feature considering that the contemporary churches at Elusa, Rehovot-in-the-Negev, and the North Church here all have particularly large atriums. The apses were previously plastered and painted, with one such scene depicting the Transfiguration of Jesus, though it is hard to make out the subject of the paintings today. The well-preserved baptistry to the north of the church is adjoined by a small mosque.

Nizzana (Nessana)

→ *Colour map 3, grid B2.*
ⓘ *Open 24 hours. Admission free.*

Route 211 from Shivta continues west to one of the least populated regions in the country, where about 120 families live in five tiny villages. Groups of trees along this road signal where the Turkish built their 'Li'man': way-stations for travellers, with dams to collect run-off water and trees to give shade. Floods in February 2010 swept away the bridge connecting the villages to the outside world, along with electricity and

Shivta (Sobata)

▲ To main road, (Route 211) 8 km

Car Park

N

50 metres
50 yards

1 Entrance
2 North Church
3 Atrium of North Church
4 Town Square
5 Wine Press
6 Middle Church
7 Double Reservoir
8 Mosque
9 South Church
10 Baptistry of South Church

water cables, marooning locals for 72 hours. Nizzana is the site of the Nabatean Spice Road town of Nessana, and is famed as the place where the so-called Nessana Papyri were found (see page 326). The mound that Nessana stands upon looks impressive and mystical from a distance, though closer inspection reveals that many significant archaeological remains have been lost. The construction of the North Church in the Byzantine period obscured many of the Nabatean buildings, perhaps including the main Nabatean temple. Further, the use of the site by the Turkish administration early in the 20th century, including the 'recycling' of building material for construction of buildings throughout the area, destroyed many of the older remains.

Ins and outs

Getting there and away Nizzana lies around 20 km further west along Route 211 from the turning for Shivta (see 'Be'er Sheva to Mizpe Ramon' map for orientation). Metropoline bus 44 goes to Ezuz Sunday-Thursday at 1900, Friday at 1400, returning the next day at 0600, passing Nizzana on the way.

Nizzana (Nessana)

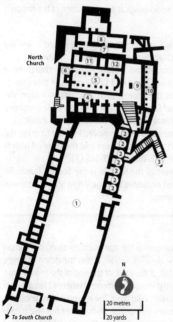

North Church

1 Roman Fortress
2 Later Period Rooms
3 Monumental Staircase
4 Southern Court
5 Mono-Apsidal Basilica
   (Church of Sergius &
   Bacchus)
6 Baptistry
7 North Court
8 Covered Gallery
9 Courtyard
10 Covered Gallery
11 Chapel
12 Sacristy

To South Church

20 metres
20 yards

N

Background

The Byzantine period (324-638 CE) was the period of Nessana's greatest prosperity, with the settlement expanding significantly and the major buildings at the site today dating from this period. The significant Nessana Papyri also date to this period, between the sixth and late seventh centuries CE (see next page). Though there was a smooth transition to Arab rule in the seventh century CE, there are no remains at Nessana (Arabic: 'Auja el-Hafir) suggesting occupation later than the eighth century CE. With no evidence of a conflagration or a violent end, it is suggested that the agricultural land that supported the settlement fell into disuse, thus accelerating the city's decline.

Sights

The Roman fortress, probably built in the first half of the fourth century CE (though this date is disputed), occupies much of the mound to the south of the North Church. There are a series of rooms along the long (85-m) west and east walls, though the rooms on the east side are thought to have been added later. The fortress is defended by a number of towers, with the main gate in the south tower and a secondary entrance in the east tower. The long monumental staircase up to the mound is now thought

The Nessana Papyri

During excavations at Nessana undertaken by the British School of Archaeology in Jerusalem, a significant discovery was made in a small room in the North Church: the Nessana Papyri. Written in Greek and bilingual Greek-Arabic, the papyri cover a number of subjects from the literary and theological to military, administrative and petty legal matters, all dating from the period of the sixth to late seventh century CE.

Though the literary and theological documents are important, and include several chapters of the Gospel of St John, details of the exploits and martyrdom of Saint George, plus a Greek dictionary accompanying Virgil's Aeneas, the nonliterary documents are particularly significant for the information that they provide on the economic, social and military life of the central Negev region during the period 512 CE to 689 CE.

Amongst the subjects discussed are marriage, divorce, inheritance, plus various bills of sale and financial contracts. There are also important references to wheat and grain yields, taxes, and payments of monthly salaries to the militias stationed at places such as Oboda and Mamshit, thus allowing a partial reconstruction of the socio-political administration of the region.

to date to the second half of the first century BCE, and not the Byzantine period as initially thought, and thus is assumed to have led to a Nabatean temple and not the fortress.

Dating the North Church is not precise, though two burials within the church have epigraphic references mentioning the dates 464 CE and 474 CE. Remains of three saints were found in a marble reliquary in one of the rooms, with inscriptions within the church dedicating it to the saints Sergius and Bacchus (with a mention of St Stephen). The Southern Court opens into the mono-apsidal basilica. To the west of the basilica is a baptistry, though at some stage parts of the east end were removed in order to make the basilica longer. Other later additions, including the North Court and the covered gallery date to the reign of the (East) Byzantine Emperor Justinian (527-565 CE).

On a separate mound some 60 m southwest of the fortress is the South Church. An inscription dates the church to 601-602 CE, and dedicates it to the Virgin Mary. The three-apse style was a feature of churches in this region.

Ezuz

Some of the stones pilfered from Nizzana can be seen in the constructions along the narrow road south to Ezuz. The Turks built a railway line down this route, across the desert to Egypt, and the old railway station can be seen to the left of the road. At the end of the road is Ezuz, formed in 1985 (and not officially recognised by the Israeli government) where 13 families live. Right on the border with Egypt, it is definitely Israel's Wild West. The reason it is so desolate is that the area is largely a fire zone, which preserves the natural environment but also means you can't do much trekking or biking (except at weekends). On the edge of the village, a Turkish railway bridge remains in its original form, and a 'bustan' (garden) has a remarkable well. Deep rope-marks have been worn into the sides where the water was brought up, before being poured into channels to water the camels. It was also channelled via an aqueduct to a large Byzantine pool in the wadi, and then used for agriculture. Leaving Ezuz, it's possible to drive down Route 10 (only during daylight and with the permission of the army) to Mitzpe: an interesting, un-travelled road. **NB** The nearest petrol station is 55 km away at Tlalim Junction.

For Sleeping and Eating price codes and other relevant information, see Essentials pages 26-31.

Sleeping and eating

AL-A Zimmer Bus, Ezuz. Truly unique accommodation in 3 old buses, which have been clad in adobe and beautifully converted into comfortable and cool 'apartments', decorated with mosaics and coloured glass. Don't think motor-home – these are very des-res. Two are perfect for families (playroom for kids in driver's compartment, a/c, fully self-catering), other suits a couple (no kitchen but can order meals). No TVs in sight.

AL-E Beer Otayim, near Ezuz, T08-6555788, www.beerotayim.co.il. A very special place. Remote, rustic, desert chic. The rush-walled dining room is made from all natural materials; mud-clad rooms have mat, mattresses and stoves (no need for locks on the palm-wood doors); hammocks and wicker seats for chilling, and a central campfire. But it's the bathrooms that will wow you, with Armenian ceramic basins facing the empty desert. No guest kitchen facilities but excellent food provided, solar power, oil-lamps, eco-conscious. In one of 16 rooms: singles/couples 210/440NIS half-board, or 120NIS per person without food. Groups in big fabric tent 50NIS per person. Desert sounds include crickets, donkeys and the occasional crump of an explosion at the distant firing range! You're sure to meet interesting people, if only the staff. Book in advance; they will pick up from bus stop. Guests get cheap rates for camel trips. Follow

the road to Ezuz from Nizzana, after about 15 km the road forks, turn right then right again (following the camel sign), the khan is 800 m along the wadi (tricky to find in the dark).

Café, Ezuz, T054-4226330. Creating a Sinai beach-vibe in the depths of the desert, this little coffee shop specialises in crêpes (owner Eyal is French), has excellent pizza, shakshuka, cous-cous, soups, and ice-cream in summer. It's basically a palm-leaf hut, with seating scattered about. Sometimes live jazz/blues at the weekend, or there's a LP collection to choose from. Booze available, good sunset spot. Open weekends and holidays from breakfast till late, otherwise phone in advance. Eyal also has a simple little hut for rent, windows all round, cosy and colourful, porch with view, outside kitchen and bathroom, compost toilet, suitable for couples (B&B, mid-week 300NIS, weekend 400NIS).

Activities and tours
Camel safaris

Beer Otayim, www.beerotayim.co.il. Trips from 1½ hrs (adult/child 80/60NIS), 3 hrs with a stop for tea, or 5 hrs with lunch. Guides are informative, and tailor trips to your interests, be it geology (fossils), history (rock art), flora (medicinal plants), or politics (the border). Cheaper rates for guests at the khan. Longer safaris, up to 10 days, also possible, eg for a group of 10 it would be 350NIS per person per day.

Cycling

There's a great single track marked out around Ezuz, though you need your own mountain bike.

Sde Boker → *Colour map 3, grid B3.*

Kibbutz Sde Boker is best known today for its association with Israel's first Prime Minister, David Ben-Gurion, who unexpectedly retired from politics in 1953 choosing instead to settle on the fledgling kibbutz. However, it is the phenomenally beautiful scenery, good hiking and excellent mountain biking that is most appreciated by foreign visitors. Midreshet Sde Boker, 3 km south of the kibbutz, is a great base for treks into the 'Wilderness of Zin'. Here you can find good accommodation, bicycle hire, and easy access to the beautiful Nahal Zin Nature Trail through the Ein Avdat National Park. There is an excellent (unique!) topographical map in English for the area showing biking, hiking and 4x4 trails, scale 1:50,000, which makes it easier to strike out into the desert.

Ins and outs

Getting there and away Sde Boker is on the main Route 40, Egged buses 392 from Be'er Sheva to Eilat stop at the kibbutz and then at the Midreshet, 4-6 buses per day, first 0815, last 1545 (but check www.egged.co.il). Metropoline bus 60 between Be'er Sheva and Mizpe Ramon stops here (about 1 per hr).

Tourist Information Anyone attempting to hike in the region (excepting the simple Nahal Zin Nature Trail in Ein Avdat National Park) should first contact the **SPNI Field School** ⓘ T08-6532016, www.boker.org.il, for advice.

Background

Kibbutz Sde Boker was founded on the fourth anniversary of the Declaration of the State of Israel, 15 May 1952. The original intention of the settlers, predominantly ex-soldiers, was to ranch cattle; hence the name Sde Boker, roughly translated from the Hebrew as 'Rancher's/Cowboy's/Farmer's Field'. Livestock rearing now plays a less important role in the agricultural economy of the kibbutz, with sophisticated irrigation techniques now producing out-of-season olives and fruits for export, as well as some cereals.

Sights

Ben-Gurion's Desert Home ⓘ T08-6560320, www.ggh.org.il, Sun-Thu 0830-1600, Fri 0830-1400, Sat 0900-1500, adults 12NIS, student/child 9NIS; guided tours by prior appointment.
Near the entrance is a **Visitors' Centre** ⓘ T08-6560469, Sun-Thu 1000-1600, Fri 1000-1400, Sat 1000-1500, adults 10NIS, child 8NIS, where you can see a short film telling the story of the kibbutz, before walking through landscaped trees to the house. Ben-Gurion's initial stay at Sde Boker was limited to just 14 months, after which time he was drawn back into politics. He finally retired to Sde Boker with his wife Paula in 1963, living here until his death (in Tel Aviv) 10 years later. His Desert Home attracts a constant stream of Israelis to pay homage to the "Old Man". A well-presented exhibition illuminates his life and relationship to the Negev through letters, photos and quotes. Following this you enter the low, green prefab home, with its red roof and narrow veranda, left exactly as it was when David and Paula lived here – from the photograph of Gandhi on the bedroom wall to the packet of band-aids on the bedside table. Although now fashionably retro, it is a humble home, unlike the large stone villa built for the couple (where their graves now stand) and which he rejected as being too grand.

Ben-Gurion University of the Negev ⓘ Sign-posted 3 km south of Ben-Gurion's Desert Home is Midrashet Sde Boker, variously referred to as Ben-Gurion College of the Negev, Sde Boker Institute of Arid Zone Research, Ben Gurion University of the Negev, etc.
Whatever title you use to refer to it, the academic speciality of this establishment is clear: the study of land and life in arid and semi-arid environments. The various institutes affiliated here attract specialists from around the world, in addition to producing much home-grown talent in this field.

Ben-Gurion Memorial National Park (Ben-Gurion's grave) The road towards the main university campus also leads to the site of David and Paula Ben-Gurion's graves. And what a place to be buried! Two simple white slabs stand amidst a landscaped park, featuring both rock and flora indigenous to the area, on the edge of a sheer rockface that provides a magnificent vista down into the canyon of the 'Wilderness of Zin'.

Ein Avdat National Park ⓘ *T08-6555684. Daily 0800-1600; winter 0800-1500; however, arrive no later than 1300 to start a trek, as access is restricted later in the day for safety reasons. Adults 25NIS, student 21NIS, child 13NIS. Admission to both the Upper and Lower entrances is permitted on one ticket, on the same day only. The Lower "entrance pavilion" is located by the gate to Midrashet Sde Boker, here you can buy the Sde Boker Desert Map (55NIS).*
The Nahal Zin Nature Trail provides a delightful walk along the bed of the Nahal (River) Zin, with the option of a gentle jaunt for the less intrepid (taking one to two hours), or a more strenuous one-way route (two to three hours), featuring a stiff climb up the rock-cut steps in the cliff face. There are some excellent picnic sites, as well as some peaceful spots beside that rarest of desert commodities, water pools.

Some advanced thought is required before commencing either of the routes. Both begin at the Lower Parking Lot (actually to the north, near to Sde Boker), with the long route finishing at the Upper Parking Lot (actually to the south) and the short route finishing where it began. After completing the long, one-way route, you cannot retrace your steps back to the Lower Parking Lot since it is forbidden to descend the rock-cut steps back to the valley bottom. You'll have to arrange for somebody to drive down Route 40 to the Upper Parking Lot to pick you up, or flag down a passing bus (60/392) or hitch a ride (walking back to Sde Boker along Route 40 is an unrewarding 7.5 km slog).

A good leaflet/map, describing the walk and sights on the way, is provided at the National Park entrance. **NB** Ein Avdat is a deservedly popular day-out, and thus is often crowded, with school groups during the week and everyone else on weekends and public holidays. Do not confuse the Ein Avdat National Park with the Nabatean-Roman-Byzantine city within Avdat National Park, some 11 km further south along Route 40 (see page 332).

Hiking around Sde Boker Other treks that are recommended (first get information from the Field School) include the Nahal HaVarim trek, which is best enjoyed at full moon when the white chalky paths glow and light the way. You are guaranteed to see lots of ibex. The blue trail starts from Route 14, where a brown sign points east to "Bor HaVarim". It's a two- to three-hour walk that finishes up near Ein Avdat. Another excellent day-trek goes from Sde Boker to Avdat (Ovdat) Nabatean ruins, taking in the Akev springs on the way. As the trail is 14 km and takes from six to eight hours, it is imperative to start as early as possible as the heat really kicks in around midday. The springs have water all year round; the upper Akev spring is a small reed-filled pool (still pleasant for a dip) while the lower Ein Akev is 20 m deep and icy.

Horvat Haluqim ⓘ *This site is to the north of Route 204, just northeast of Halukim Jct (see 'Be'er Sheva to Mizpe Ramon' map). You can walk here from Kibbutz Sde Boker.* During the United Monarchy (1004-928 BCE), a network of citadels was built in the central Negev region, each protecting state-initiated agricultural settlements. (Similarities between this process and that of the Zionist pioneers of the early 20th century are hard to ignore). Horvat Haluqim is thought to be one such 10th-century BCE fortified settlement (the original desert kibbutz?).

Today, it is still possible to see the remains of the oval-shaped fortress, with its central courtyard and seven casemate rooms, plus the remains of 25 or so private dwellings that formed the agricultural settlement. The initial settlement was probably destroyed during the pharaoh Shishak's invasion in 923 BCE, though evidence suggests that the site was reoccupied in the second-third centuries CE.

Sde Boker listings

For Sleeping and Eating price codes and other relevant information, see Essentials pages 26-31.

Sleeping

A-C SPNI Field School and Hamburg House, T08-6532016, www.boker.org.il, orders.boker@gmail.com. Youth hostel with roomy 6-bed dorms or double rooms, a/c with private bath, very clean, kosher dining hall (meals 38-47NIS), reservations essential (at least 2 months in advance for weekends/hols). Adjacent Hamburg House has a further 20 a/c rooms with added comforts (TV, fridge, tea/coffee). There are great views from most of the rooms in both places, breakfast included. Prices go up Fri nights.

A-D Krivine's Guesthouse, T052-2712304, www.krivines.com. Four attractive rooms with a sense of privacy, nicely decorated, welcoming beds and a real homely feel (down to the wonky pictures on the wall and spy novels on the bookshelves). Sociable tasty meals around a huge table in the designer "tent", garden at back (stream is planned), guests' kitchen, dorm-style accommodation possible (100NIS). British John and his French wife Marion have created a warm and relaxed place that is a real pleasure to stay in. No weekend price rise. Pick up from bus stop, will drop off at Ein Avdat. Highly recommended.

A To the Desert, T054-7245673. On the edge of the village in the new residential development, Aviva and her husband have self-built a colourful home where 2 guest rooms enjoy plenty of space (enough for families), kitchenette, breakfast 30NIS per person, TV, roof terrace, quirky garden. No weekend price rise.

A Wilderness, 08-6535087/050-8671921. A spacious ground floor apartment with quality modern furnishings, stone tiles throughout, fully equipped kitchen, feels like having your own pad. Good for families. 1 x double room and sofa bed in open plan sitting room, shady garden with seating.

Kelly can provide breakfast. Discounts on stays over 1 night, price rise at weekends.

Eating

In the Midrashet's main plaza there is a well-stocked **supermarket** (Sun-Thu 0800-1900, Fri 0800-1400). The **Mitbar pub** is in the campus area, open Tue and Fri nights 2000-2400.

Kha'dera, main plaza, T08-6532118. Locals were delighted when the 'Pot' opened its doors in 2010, thus doubling the choice for dining out in Sde Boker. Meals have a North African slant, all homemade, the menu changes daily (eg fried chicken, meatballs in sauce), BBQ, vegetarian option, 8 kinds of salad. Look for the little coffee wagon outside (great iced coffee and quality cakes). Open Sun-Thu 0900-2100, Fri 0900-1400 (take-away only).

Zin Restaurant, main plaza, is a basic canteen-style place serving up cheap meat/veg meals (23-38NIS) and beer (12NIS). Open Sun-Thu 0800-2100, Fri 0800-1400.

Activities and tours
Cycling

Geofun, Commercial Centre, Midrashet Sde Boker, T08-6553350/050-6276623, www.geofun.co.il. Mountain bike rental or guided cycling tours for all levels of experience, some suitable for very young children, some at night. Rental bikes are 80NIS per day, or 60NIS for 2 hrs plus 15NIS every extra hr during week (65NIS at weekend), map provided. Also sells bikes and accessories, and has a repair centre (the only one between Be'er Sheva and Eilat). The Sde Boker topographical map showing all trails is available here (55NIS), and the centre provides excellent information and advice – whether or not you are a customer. See website for details of week-long tours and seasonal programmes, plus they can build a full 'package' including accommodation, food, transport, etc. Open Sun-Thu 0900-1800, Fri 0830-1400, will open Sat for appointments.

Swimming

The swimming pool in the Midrashet is open Jun-Sep.

Tours

Adam Sela, organizes jeep tours around Sde Boker and Makhtesh Ramon, recommended, especially for native English speakers. **Haim**, T054-5343797. Night safaris in an 8-seater jeep (everyone gets a window), using antennae and flashlights to track animals.

Haim's speciality is predators, though you may not be lucky enough to spot one of the hyenas he has managed to 'collar'. For a full jeep 640NIS for 2-2½ hrs, cheaper if fewer numbers. Also takes scorpion walks. Tea/coffee break and lots of interesting chat.

Directory

Post office In the Midrashet's main plaza (Sun, Tue and Thu 0830-1230, Mon and Wed 0830-1230 and 1615-1800, Fri 0900-1200).

Avdat (Oboda) → *Colour map 3, grid C3.*

ⓘ *T08-6551511, F6550954. Daily 0800-1700 (winter -1600, closes 1 hr earlier on Fri and hol eves), last entrance 1 hr before closing. Adults 25NIS, students 21NIS, child 13NIS. Combined ticket with Ein Avdat 40NIS. There is an Aroma café near the site entrance, and a Visitors' Centre, souvenir shop and toilets.*

Declared a UNESCO World Heritage Site in 2005, Avdat, (referred to by the Nabateans as Oboda) is probably the best preserved of the Nabatean remains in the Negev. As one of the major way-stations on the Petra–Gaza Spice Road (see 346), Oboda also evolved as the centre of a major agricultural region. The town flourished during the Late Roman period, with the prosperity continuing into the Byzantine period. There are impressive buildings from all three periods of the town's history. The remains of the town have been substantially restored, with a line marking reconstructed areas; anything below the line indicates original remains, whilst anything above the line was reconstructed from ruins found at the site. In October 2009, however, vandals daubed paint over the churches, smashed artefacts and toppled columns, causing much damage that had not been repaired by the time of our visit. ('Avdat' is the Hebrew version of the Arabic name for Oboda, 'Abdah').

Ins and outs

Getting there and away Avdat National Park is located on the main Be'er Sheva–Eilat road (Route 40). Be'er Sheva–Eilat Egged bus 392 sets down at the park entrance, as does the slower Metropoline bus 060 that runs every one or two hours between Be'er Sheva and Mizpe Ramon. For orientation see the 'Be'er Sheva to Mizpe Ramon' map, page 306.

Background

Early and Middle Nabatean period Oboda was founded as a caravan stop on the Petra–Gaza Spice Road at the end of the fourth century/beginning of the third century BCE, though the original settlement may have comprised temporary structures only, possibly tents.

The oldest Nabatean structures date to the Middle Nabatean period, in particular the reign of the Nabatean kings Obodas III (c. 28-9 BCE) and **Aretas IV** (c. 9 BCE-40 CE). In addition to becoming a centre of pottery manufacture during this period, agriculture developed significantly. The mainstay of the local economy was still the caravan route, though the rearing of goats, sheep and camels was important. The Nabatean camel corps, used to police the Spice Road, was stationed locally. The Middle Nabatean period town came to an end during the reign of the Nabatean king **Malichus II** (40-70 CE), when Oboda was destroyed by non-Nabatean Arabian tribesmen.

Late Nabatean/Late Roman period Oboda was revived in the Late Nabatean period by Rabbel II (70-106 CE), who initiated renewed agricultural activity in the region. Even the annexation of the Nabatean's empire by Rome in 106 CE failed to interrupt Oboda's expansion; indeed, it may have given it renewed impetus. The temple was re-dedicated to the local Zeus and construction began on a new Roman town to the southeast of the mound. The Emperor **Diocletian** (284-305 CE) incorporated Oboda within the defensive system of the Eastern Roman Empire, building the fortress on the east side of the mound, and recruiting local people to serve in the militia. Much building took place during this period of prosperity, though much of the Roman quarter was destroyed by an earthquake early in the fourth century CE.

Byzantine period Many of the buildings seen at Oboda today date to the Byzantine period, with the continuing prosperity being based largely upon sophisticated irrigation techniques extending the cultivated area. Grape cultivation and wine production were important to the local economic and social scene. Most of the Byzantine town, dating approximately from the mid-fourth century CE to 636 CE, occupied the west slope of the mound, comprising 350-400 homes in both houses and caves. The Christian nature of the town is evident in the substantial remains of fine churches.

With the gradual decline of the Byzantine empire, Oboda was subject to increasingly regular incursions by Arab tribesmen, with the decline in security gravely affecting the town's economic base. Oboda was finally abandoned after the Arab conquest of 636 CE.

Tour of the park

The Visitors' Centre at the entrance to the park has a short film about the Incense Route and a display of artefacts from the site. Numbers (marked in bold) refer to points marked

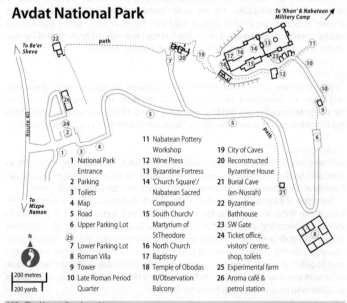

Avdat National Park

To Be'er Sheva ← path → *To 'Khan' & Nabatean Military Camp* ↗

11 Nabatean Pottery Workshop
12 Wine Press
13 Byzantine Fortress
14 'Church Square'/ Nabatean Sacred Compound
15 South Church/ Martyrium of StTheodore
16 North Church
17 Baptistry
18 Temple of Obodas III/Observation Balcony
19 City of Caves
20 Reconstructed Byzantine House
21 Burial Cave (en-Nusrah)
22 Byzantine Bathhouse
23 SW Gate
24 Ticket office, visitors' centre, shop, toilets
25 Experimental farm
26 Aroma café & petrol station

1 National Park Entrance
2 Parking
3 Toilets
4 Map
5 Road
6 Upper Parking Lot
7 Lower Parking Lot
8 Roman Villa
9 Tower
10 Late Roman Period Quarter

Route 40
To Mizpe Ramon

200 metres
200 yards

N

on the 'Avdat National Park' map. Additional detail of the mound/acropolis area is shown on the plan of 'Oboda (Avdat) Acropolis', with points of detail marked by letters in bold. From the **National Park entrance** (1), the paved road leads up a steep climb to the **upper parking lot** (6). Two points of interest, the **Burial Cave (en-Nusrah)** (21) and a **Roman villa** (8), are passed on the way up.

Burial Cave (en-Nusrah) (21) This a multi-burial site with 21 double loculi, including the graves of some women. Greek inscriptions in the vaulted entrance hall are dated to the third century CE, suggesting that the original Middle Nabatean period burial cave was later reused.

Roman villa (8) To the south of the main acropolis mound lie the remains of a Roman period villa. The plan of the building is typical of the period, with the rooms located around a central courtyard. A water cistern has been cut in the centre of the courtyard. An observation point provides an excellent view of Oboda's setting and the reconstructed Nabatean farm.

Tower This well-preserved tower stands at the southwest corner of the Late Roman period quarter. An inscription above the lintel on the tower's north wall suggests that it was built in 293-294 CE. Standing three storeys high, the tower probably served as an observation point; a function that it still retains today. Though often labelled on site plans as the 'Roman tower', it may in fact be Nabatean. The skilful architect has even contrived to make the tower earthquake proof.

Late Roman period quarter The Late Roman period quarter is probably best seen from the top of the tower. The quarter was constructed as a suburb of the early town some time in the third century CE, with building work continuing until 296 CE at least. The main street ran on a north–south axis, with most of the dwellings comprising houses built around courtyards, and constructed from well-dressed stone. The fact that there is no evidence of Christian occupation of the site suggests that the quarter had been abandoned by the Byzantine period (324-638 CE). There is a strong consensus that the quarter was destroyed by the devastating earthquake of 363 CE.

Nabatean pottery workshop (11) A brief excursion away from the main path leads right (east) to the Nabatean pottery workshop. Oboda became an important centre of pottery manufacture in the Early and Middle Nabatean periods, with a reputation for high quality and delicate workmanship. There are three distinct rooms: for clay preparation, the potter's wheel and the kiln.

Khan and Nabatean military camp There are a couple of buildings to the north and northeast of the acropolis mound that were important during the Middle and Late Nabatean periods. Neither is marked on the map.

A **khan** (caravanserai), probably dating to the Late Nabatean period and in use until the mid-fourth century CE, stands to the north of the Nabatean pottery workshop. The large building, around a central courtyard, probably stood two storeys high. The halls were used for storing goods traded along the Spice Road.

About 400 m northeast of the acropolis mound is the site of the original Nabatean military camp. The compound measures 100 square metres, with a well-built stone wall reinforced by two corner towers and two central towers on each side. The camp was the home of the camel corps during the Middle Nabatean period, with barracks and camel sheds still discernible. As with other Nabatean towns in the Negev, it appears that only the garrisons were housed in permanent structures, with the rest of the population almost certainly living in tents.

Byzantine fortress (13) Four wine-presses were discovered at Oboda; the best example (**12**), dating to the Byzantine period, is found by the **southwest gate (23)** of the fortress. The Byzantine fortress was probably built at the beginning of the fourth century CE, though much of its 2-m-thick walls was built by stone 'recycled' from the Nabatean military camp (see above) and dismantled houses. The fortress is approximately 61 m long (east–west) and 40 m wide (north–south), with twelve towers defending the walls. A deep **cistern (a)**, with a capacity of 200 cubic m, has been dug in the centre of the courtyard, supplied by two rainwater channels. In the northeast corner of the fortress is a **Late Byzantine period chapel (b)**, built of locally quarried limestone previously used at the military camp.

Church Square/Nabatean sacred compound (14) To the west of the fortress is what was the Nabatean sacred compound during the Middle and Late Nabatean period. The construction of the adjacent churches during the Byzantine period has given the compound the moniker 'Church Square'. The sacred compound was probably built during the reign of Obodas III, to serve what is thought to be the Temple of Obodas III (see below). One of the main entrances to the acropolis is the **Nabatean gate (e)** in the north wall, though the portals of the gate's tower were both altered during the Byzantine period. The **cistern (c)** provided water to the Temple of Obodas III and stands near a **Late Roman period tower (d)**.

South Church/ Martyrium of St Theodore (15) An epitaph on a tomb within the South Church, and the name of the same saint found engraved on fragments of a marble chancel screen, suggests that the church was dedicated to St Theodore. It was almost certainly built in the middle of the fifth century CE, but was destroyed by fire during the Arab invasion of 636 CE. The church is mono-basilical, with a central nave and two aisles divided

Oboda (Avdat) Acropolis

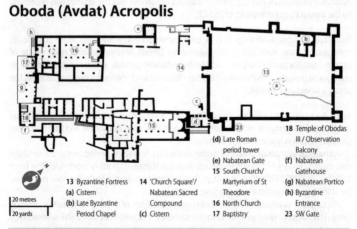

13 Byzantine Fortress	**14** 'Church Square'/
(a) Cistern	Nabatean Sacred
(b) Late Byzantine	Compound
Period Chapel	(c) Cistern

(d) Late Roman	**18** Temple of Obodas
period tower	III / Observation
(e) Nabatean Gate	Balcony
15 South Church/	(f) Nabatean
Martyrium of St	Gatehouse
Theodore	(g) Nabatean Portico
16 North Church	(h) Byzantine
17 Baptistry	Entrance
	23 SW Gate

20 metres

20 yards

by two rows of seven columns respectively. A three-dimensional model illustrates typical Byzantine church architecture. The Nabatean style of some of the capitals suggest that they were 'recycled' from the Nabatean temple.

North Church (16) The North Church is older, probably dating from some time in the mid to late fourth century. Again, it is thought that blocks from the former Nabatean temple were used in its construction. It is a basilica, with a single apse containing a pedestal for the bishop's seat. To the west of the atrium a flight of steps leads to the **baptistry (17)**. The church was largely destroyed during the Arab invasion, and was particularly damaged by the act of vandalism in 2009.

Temple of Obodas III/observation balcony (18) The present observation balcony is thought to stand largely upon the site of a former Nabatean temple. Excavations have revealed the plan of a structure similar in detail to the plan of other Nabatean temples in Moab, with dedications to the deities of Dushara and Allat. Inscriptions mention various members of the Nabatean royal family, suggesting the tentative link with Obodas III, though this connection is not assured. Parts of the modern observation platform's previous functions have been identified as a **Nabatean gatehouse (f)**, a **Nabatean portico (g)**, and a **Byzantine entrance (h)**.

City of Caves (19) From the observation balcony, stairs and a path descend through the main Byzantine town area, which comprised around 350 to 400 residencies. Given the nature of a typical house here, the area has been dubbed the City of Caves: many of the dwellings feature a cave cut into the hillside. The **reconstructed Byzantine house (20)** provides a good example. The complex comprises an enclosed court, with a hall to the north leading into two rock-cut chambers of the house-cave unit. The cave area almost certainly served as a wine-cellar cum pantry, in summer remaining beautifully cool, oblivious to the temperature outside. The entrance to the cave features some red ochre drawings of St George and St Theodore, with some Greek inscriptions.

Byzantine bathhouse (22) The Byzantine bathhouse is worth the extra walk since it is amongst the best-preserved structures from this period found anywhere in Israel. The left doorway from the courtyard leads into the *apodyterium*, or changing room. Beyond this room is the *tepidarium*, or lukewarm room.

Water was supplied to the bathhouse from a 64-m-deep well close by, with the waste water removed via a channel, parts of which can be seen to the north of the building. Though the ceiling of the hypocaust (the hollow space beneath the *tepidarium* and *caldarium* through which the hot air was circulated) has not survived, it is still possible to see the brick pillar bases that supported it. The furnace was to the south of the building, with the brick flues and clay pipes through which the hot air was circulated still in fine condition. The hot bath room, or *caldarium*, is on the west side of the building, and is built in the shape of a cross. The bathtubs were heated by channels fed from the hypocaust, whilst hot air was provided by a furnace to the west.

Mizpe Ramon (Mitzpe Ramon) → *Colour map 3, grid C3.*

Mizpe Ramon stands on the lip of arguably the Negev's greatest natural wonder, the Makhtesh Ramon (Ramon crater, see page 342). The town was only founded in 1956, primarily as a 17-man co-operative providing road services. Today the population stands at around 6000, swelled by the resettlement of Russian and Eastern European Jews. Without tourism, it's difficult to see any concrete economic base that could support the town, though Mizpe is becoming an increasingly popular choice for those seeking an alternative lifestyle to Tel Aviv. For the tourist, the town provides an excellent base from which to explore the stunning surrounding area.

Ins and outs

Getting there and away Mizpe Ramon is located on the northern edge of the Makhtesh Ramon, some 24 km south of Avdat National Park along Route 40. From Be'er Sheva, Egged

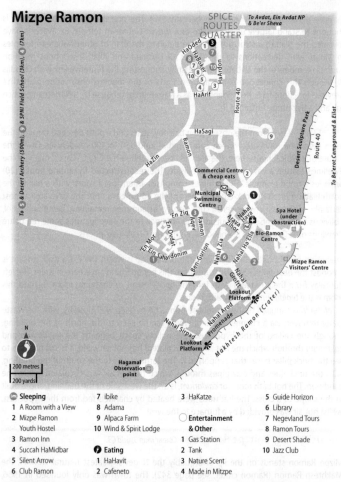

Mizpe Ramon

SPICE ROUTES QUARTER

To Avdat, Ein Avdat NP & Be'er Sheva

To Avdat, Ein Avdat NP & Be'er Sheva

To ⑤ & Desert Archery (500m), ⑨ & SPNI Field School (3km), ④ (7km)

HaOded
HaBoKer
HaKdron
HaArif

Route 40

HaSagi

Ramon
HaZin

Commercial Centre & cheap eats

Municipal Swimming Centre

'En Ziq
'En Ovda
'En Mor
'En Shardonim
Agev
Ramon
Ben-Gurion

Nahal Zia
Arava Zihot
Nahal Ha'Ela
Nahal Grom

Nahal Arod Promenade

Nahal Sirpad

Lookout Platform

Lookout Platform

Makhtesh Ramon (Crater)

Desert Sculpture Park

Route 40

To Be'erot Campground & Eilat

Spa Hotel (under construction)

Bio-Ramon Centre

Mizpe Ramon Visitors' Centre

Hagamal Observation point

200 metres
200 yards

N

Sleeping
1 A Room with a View
2 Mizpe Ramon Youth Hostel
3 Ramon Inn
4 Succah HaMidbar
5 Silent Arrow
6 Club Ramon
7 ibike
8 Adama
9 Alpaca Farm
10 Wind & Spirit Lodge

Eating
1 HaHavit
2 Cafeneto
3 HaKatze

Entertainment & Other
1 Gas Station
2 Tank
3 Nature Scent
4 Made in Mitzpe
5 Guide Horizon
6 Library
7 Negevland Tours
8 Ramon Tours
9 Desert Shade
10 Jazz Club

bus 392, four per day, and Metropoline bus 60, one to two per hour. For details on getting down into the crater, see under 'Makhtesh Ramon' on page 342. The town centre is very compact, though it is a fair walk out to some sights.

Tourist information **Visitors' Centre** (details below). Staff can offer tips on hikes and driving in the region. The only problem is, by the time the centre opens at 0800, it's almost too hot to start a hike. If possible, try to call in before it closes (1600) the day before you plan to go.

SPNI Field School ① *T08-6588615/6, Sun-Thu 0800-1600, Fri 0800-1200.* The Field School is about 4 km to the west of town. It is recommended that you call in here before taking a hike into the crater. Here you can also buy the SPNI 1:50,000 map (74NIS) before attempting anything too adventurous. It's available (in Hebrew only), though the staff are willing to translate all important details. It is also a good idea to leave a copy of your planned itinerary, as the SPNI (with their communication links to the army) your only hope of rescue if you get into difficulty.

Sights
Mizpe Ramon Visitors' Centre ① *T08-6588691/8. Sat-Thu 0800-1600, Fri and hol eves closes 1 hr earlier. Adult 25NIS, or combined ticket with Bio-Ramon Centre 30NIS, students 21/30NIS, children 13/16NIS.*
A good starting point is the eye-catching circular Visitors' Centre, built on the crater's edge. Here you can buy a map of the Makhtesh Ramon Nature Reserve (2.5NIS) showing all the trails in the crater, and get advice from staff about hiking. The price for a full visit to the centre is, however, rather steep. For your money you get a 15-minute film (a little OTT on the hyperbole); display boards about the crater's formation, geological composition, and flora and fauna; plus superb views from the roof (though no better than those from the lookout platform outside). The cliff-top around the Visitors' Centre is often occupied by a herd of grazing ibex.

Bio-Ramon Centre ① *T08-6588755. Sat-Thu 0800-1700, Fri 0800-1600 (closes 1 hr earlier in winter). Adult 13NIS, child 7NIS, combined ticket 30/16NIS. Guided tours by prior request. Toilets.*
The Bio-Ramon Centre Living Desert Museum features a tiny zoo, comprising animal, vegetable and mineral life indigenous to the crater. The collection of animal life may dissuade you from hiking in the crater: it features spiders, snakes, other reptiles, rodents and insects. Most desert creatures are nocturnal, however, and look rather wilted in their glass cages in the sun.

HaGamal Observation Point Staring into Makhtesh Ramon from the crater's rim is a pleasant way to pass the time, and is particularly rewarding at sundown as the rocks seemingly change colour. One of the best viewpoints is from the HaGamal Observation Point, to the southwest of the Visitors' Centre. It's so named because it is shaped like a camel.

Desert Sculpture Park To the north of the Visitors' Centre is the Desert Sculpture Park; an unusual collection of stone 'sculptures' inspired by the surrounding environment, and gathered here under the direction of the Israeli artist Ezra Orion.

Alpaca Farm ① *T08-6588047, www.alpaca.co.il. Open daily 0830-1800 (winter 0830-1630). Adult/child over 3 years 25NIS.*
This unique collection of llamas and alpacas, said to be the largest herd outside South America, was gathered here some 24 years ago by an Israeli couple with a love of all things

Turning the desert green: how the Nabateans beat the Israelis by 2000 years

The idea that the Israelis "turned the desert green" has its origins not in the astounding contribution towards the world's knowledge of arid and semi-arid eco-system management that Israeli scientists have made, but in a political sentiment. The implication is that prior to the return of the early Zionists, the land was 'abandoned', 'uncared for', and 'empty': thus the idea that the Palestinians had any deep attachment to the land can be negated.

However, political arguments aside, Israeli researchers have been amongst the quickest to provide evidence that they were not the first to "make the desert bloom". The Nabateans, a race probably of Arab origin, established sustainable desert agriculture in the Negev 2000 years before the foundation of the State of Israel. Their success was down to the development of sophisticated irrigation techniques.

In areas where rainfall is limited, the key factor in desert agriculture is the control of surface run-off. The loess soil of the Negev quickly develops an impermeable crust when exposed to water, thus preventing penetration into the soil of the surplus rain. By efficiently managing the control of the surface run-off, the Nabateans were able to create a system whereby each field received the water equivalent of twenty times the actual level of rainfall that falls.

Low walls dividing the water catchment area into manageable sizes also acted as conduits for directing the water. Small heaps of stones served a similar purpose, and were particularly successful in increasing the rate of water collection from light rains. Underground cisterns in adjacent farm dwellings were connected to the conduits, and allowed the prolonged storage of water. The cultivated area at the centre of the shallow wadi was terraced and walled, with the different levels of stepped terracing allowing the passage of surplus water to the field below. Along with trade on the Spice Road, the management of the water environment allowed the Nabateans to establish relatively high density settlements in this harsh desert environment.

South American. The herd has grown from 180 specimens to over 600 at times, though currently it numbers around 200. A supply of high-quality wool comes out of the on-site factory – incredibly soft and non-itchy. It's possible to feed the animals, ride the llamas, and see other animals such as goats, donkeys and a camel. During Passover, there is a shearing festival (see website for details) and you can take a "Picnicllama" for three hours (30-minute walk) into the desert with llamas loaded up with picnic hampers. The farm also has horse-riding trips to the edge of the crater, suitable for complete beginners and children (1½ hours) as well as experienced riders (two hours). Children love it here, whilst adults can enjoy some fine South American coffee in the little coffee shop. There are also four rooms available for overnight stays (see Sleeping, below).

Spice Routes Quarter The rather pretentious moniker 'Spice Routes Quarter' has not really caught on, but this is how signage refers to the old industrial part of town. Now attracting artists, entrepreneurs and those escaping the rat-race, here you can find various entertainments (see Activities, page 339), small independent shops, accommodation and plenty of practitioners of alternative medicine, acupuncture, yoga, and massage (listed on the Mizpe tourist map of the town). The disused hangars have been inventively renovated to make cool homes and offices.

Mizpe Ramon listings

For Sleeping and Eating price codes and other relevant information, see Essentials pages 26-31.

Sleeping

On the edge of town, where the road to Eilat drops into the crater, a spa-hotel is being built which may be finished by the time you read this. It will be top-of-the-range and already looks rather attractive, although such development is causing a storm between environmentalists and business people.

L Ramon Inn, 1 Aqev, T08-6588822, www. isrotel.com. Features studio apartments sleeping 2-6 adults (larger apartments are the best value) with kitchenette, salon, TV. The weekend price hike can be phenomenal, but during the week low season it's around 650NIS B&B for a couple in a studio. Cycling packages and plenty of tour options easily arranged through the front desk. Decent sized pool but not one to relax around. No lifts – boring if you are on the 4th floor.

L Succah in the Desert, 7 km southwest of Mizpe Ramon, T6586280/052-3229496, www.succah.co.il. Recreating the desert living experience of the wandering Children of Israel during their desert Exodus, accommodation is in one of 7 succahs: a portable dwelling made of stone walls and a palm-frond roof, carpeted, with mattresses and blankets. Lighting and showers are solar-powered, whilst other bodily functions are performed au naturel. A central succah is used for meals, as a meeting place, meditation centre, etc. If this is your thing, it really is superb. Reservations essential, pick up provided (it's down a rough track).

L-D Wind and Spirit Lodge, HaArdon, Spice Routes Quarter, T054-5492415. Airy accommodation in a yoga studio in one of the hangars, with 2 bathrooms and kitchen

facilities. Mattresses strewn across the upstairs gallery serve for a bedroom, and parquet expanses downstairs make it perfect for families who want plenty of their own space, or great for a group of friends. During the week, up to 8 people is 850NIS for the whole place, over 9 it's 80NIS per person. Yoga, meditation, meals and more can be arranged. Not really a place for couples.

AL Alpaca Farm, T08-6588047, www.alpaca. co.il. Chalets overlooking the alpaca farm, 2 that suit a couple and 2 for familes. Each has a shady terrace, space for campfires, roomy inside with TV, stereo, fully functioning kitchenette, a/c. Lots of light through big windows and colourful rag rugs strewn about. The isolated location means you see only stars at night. Israeli breakfast gets great reviews.

AL Club Ramon, T08-6586107, www.club-ramon.co.il, hotel@club-ramon.co.il. Rooms have an old-fashioned air but are bright and well-equipped with TV, fridge, kettle, a/c. Jon's Café serves beer and has reasonably priced pasta, sandwiches, etc. Breakfast included, central location. An unremarkable choice.

AL Room with a View, 6 Ein Sahardonim, T08-6587274. Clean, white, fresh room with, yes, a killer view from the bed, the window seat or the little garden (with loungers). Very homely and romantic, perfect for a couple. Good value and no weekend price rises; stays over 3 days get a discount. Chen's husband Yacov runs "Desert Archery", see Activities, below. Kitchenette for self-catering. Only rules are no smoking and no cooking meat. Book in advance.

A-B ibike, 4 HaArdon, Spice Routes Quarter, T052-4367878, www.ibike.co.il. Several sparkling rooms all en-suite (more being added) have fluffy duvets and on-the-mark modern decor. Intimate hospitality and spirit of joining-in makes it good for lone travellers: lots of books and games in the welcoming public areas (rugs, artwork, sofas; TV watching not encouraged!), backyard with decking, campfire, communal meals all vegetarian (soups, lasagne, all homemade and excellent quality), free tea/coffee and pc/wi-fi. Very good value (includes breakfast); small price rise at weekends. Bikers the main clientele but everyone welcome (see Activities, below). Recommended.

A-C SPNI Field School, T08-6588616/052-8746410. Great location west of town, right on the edge of the crater with direct access to trails, ibex grazing all around. Picnics tables, olive trees and shrubs beautify the area. Dorms often busy with school groups (50NIS). A/c doubles (week/Fri 315/415NIS incl breakfast) with attached bath, breakfast available (40NIS) and sometimes other meals if there are enough people. Essential to book in advance. Check-in 1400-2400, check-out 1100. Can pitch a tent (35NIS) but no shower unless room is vacant, so phone in advance to check; gives advice on best spots for wild camping. Good info for hikers (see next page).

A-D Adama, Spice Routes Quarter, T08-6595190, www.adama.org.il. Certainly a one-off (see Activities below), this dance studio offers a variety of accommodations welcome to all. Camping outside or dorm inside the big hangar (100/80NIS with/without breakfast). 10 indoor plywood 'teepees' offer more privacy and come with bedding. 3 mud-brick chalets are quirky and cute and share an eccentric bathroom. Large outdoor area is delightful in a faded kind of way. Fridge, tea/coffee, no cooking facilities but healthy meals available. Very sociable, book-swap, guests can do dance classes on Sun, Mon and Tue. For 250NIS you can do a full-day's dance on Sun, sleep in a tepee and get breakfast.

A-D Silent Arrow, T052-6611561, www.hetzbasheket.com, hetzbasheket@gamil.com. There's no electricity in this campsite

15 mins' walk from the town centre, but there is a central campfire and a million stars. A mattress in a communal tent (sleeps 35) is 80NIS (bring a sleeping bag), or private space in one of the refurbished "domes" is 120NIS per person. The sitting area –candlelit at night - is especially traveller-friendly, with plenty of comfy seats and a pot-bellied stove for winter evenings. Kitchen is excellently equipped (though of course there is no fridge, just cool boxes); free tea/coffee. There's space to pitch your own tent (but call in advance), mattresses provided and use of facilities (80NIS). Recycling is practised, bathrooms clean, all-in-all a good choice. Volunteers welcome, for a minimum stay of 2 weeks (though long-term is preferred).

B-C Mizpe Ramon Guest House and Youth Hostel, T08-6588443, www.iyha.org.il. Enormous place with clean single-sex 6-bed dorms which can be taken as private/family rooms (B), all a/c with attached shower rooms; bedding/towels provided, TV lounges, breakfast included, lunch/dinner expensive at 65NIS but plentiful. Many rooms have excellent views of the crater. Internet 10NIS for 30 mins. Can get noisy at weekends.

F Be'erot Campground, Makhtesh Ramon, T08-6586713. Pitch your own tent or stay in one of their Bedouin tents at this official campsite some 18 km inside the crater. Toilets (no showers), limited snack-bar, bookings and payment to be made at the Visitors' Centre. Day visitors can use the facilities for 10NIS.

Eating

Tel Avivian immigrants bemoan the lack of restaurants in Mizpe, but you won't starve, There is a **Supersol** supermarket (Sun-Thu 0730-2100, Fri 0700-1500) plus several falafel, shwarma and pizza places in the commercial area. The gas station is open 24/7 and has food for emergencies (it's packed on Shabbat).

†† **The Dairy Restaurant** at the Ramon Inn gets good reviews and is reasonably priced

(book ahead if not staying there). Pasta, toasts, quiches, salads, pizza, etc all 33-45NIS (NB many dishes are not available on Shabbat). Open 1300-2200.

†† HaHavit (the Barrel), next to the Visitors' Centre, T08-6588226. Offers uninspiring but decent meals, breakfast 48NIS, bagels/sandwiches 35-4NIS, pasta, hummus, labaneh, meat meals 60-100NIS (fight for a window seat or grab a picnic table outside). It's an awesome place for a drink as the sun goes down and the ibex wander past. Sun-Thu 0900-2230, Fri 1000-1400.

††-† Caféneto, Nahal Zia, T08-6587777. Tasty salads, hearty breakfasts (35-53NIS). For those on a budget the mini-sandwich (Israeli omelette is good), plus coffee deal for 26NIS fills you up. There's free wireless connection. Open Sun-Thu 0800-2300, Fri 0800-1800, Sat 0900-2200.

††-† HaKatze (the Edge), 2 HaArdon, Spice Routes Quarter, T08-6595273. A family restaurant serving filling home-cooked meals (eg green curry, goulash 48NIS) and soups (20NIS); there's usually a veggie option. Alcohol available. Recommended.

Entertainment

Desert Shade, T054-6277413, www.desert-nomads.com. Head down here for sunset on a Fri night. Locals gather, as do the ibex, and a glass of wine is enjoyed with a view of the crater and sculptures in the foreground. Good hummus and fish to eat inside after dark. Off Rd 40 at the entrance to Mizpe, opposite the Spice Routes Quarter.

Jazz Club, T050-5265628, recently remodelled venue in the old industrial area. Live music (jazz/blues) on Thu nights. You'll see posters around town, or call to see what's on. Definitely worth a visit if you're in town at the weekend.

Shopping

Nature Scent, 22 HaArdon, T08-6539333, www.Natures1.com. Eco-friendly, non-animal tested, using 100% natural ingredients, this little factory produces an enormous range of lotions and potions. The soaps are excellent, particularly the scrubs; good for gifts as well as treats. Sun-Thu 0830-1900, Fri 0830-1600.

Made in Mitzpe, 21 Har Boker, T08-6595111. New age-y place selling locally made crafts, some funky jewellery, pottery, etc. Sun-Thu 0900-1400 and 1600-1800, Fri 0900-1500.

Activities and tours
Archery

Desert Archery, T08-6587274/050-5344598, www.desertarchery.co.il, located west of town next to Silent Arrow campsite (though the 2 are not connected). Yacov has been organising desert archery for many years. It's a non-competitive, low-impact and quite spiritual activity – developing powers of concentration as well as knowledge of oneself. Same principle as golf, but using a bow and arrow; eco-friendly as it leaves the desert as you found it. Suitable for all ages, from 6 years upwards, no minimum numbers, an incredibly reasonable 40NIS for 2 hrs personal instruction (English speaking).

Cycling

ibike, 4 HaArdon, Spice Routes Quarter, T05 , www.ibike.co.il. Menachaim and Aviva provide excellent service for bikers going it alone or guided tours. Mountain bike hire a reasonable 70NIS per day. Also run a lovely guesthouse hotel (see Sleeping, above).

Dancing

Adama, Spice Routes Quarter, T08-6595190, www.adama.org.il. You probably didn't come to the Negev to dance, but the guys here might just change that. Founded 10 years ago by 2 professional dancers, Adama now has 8 staff and an average of 40 pupils at any one time (50/50 split Israeli/foreign). There are 3 studios for movement classes and workshops, for both professionals and novices; also yoga in the mornings. Five festivals per year (during Sukkot, Pesach etc) attract campers, musicians, all-day dancers. See website for details.

Swimming
Municipal Pool, corner of Ben-Gurion and 'En Ziq (1000-1800 most days).

Tour operators
Adam Sela, based in Sde Boker, but also does jeep tours of the Makhtesh Ramon. Good for English speakers.
Elisheva and Peter Bichel, T08-6588958/050-2297538. Recommended for German/Dutch speakers.
Guide Horizon, T052-3690805, www.guidehorizon.com. Desert tourism in a buggy. Stefan also does "packages" with accommodation in a cool hangar, a good to place to kick back after a desert trip with spa, ping-pong, sauna.
Midrashet Ramon, T08-6587042, part of the College for Judaic/Land of Israel studies. Special Shabbat observant weekends.
Negevland Tours, Har Boker, Spice Routes Quarter, T08-6595555, www.negevland.com. Reliable for jeep tours and biking.
Ramon Tours, T08-6539888/052-3962715, www.ramontours.com. Organized tours, etc.
SPNI Field School, T08-6588615. Organize free family-focussed tours every Sat morning, 3-5 hrs. They are in Hebrew but, should you wish to join, phone to reserve a place. Also provides information on jeep tour and guides (who is fluent in which languages). They can provide a free map of the crater showing walking routes etc, and sell the relevant SPNI map (74NIS).

Transport
Buses stop at the Gas Station on Route 40, at the Commercial Centre on Ben Gurion, or on the road outside the Youth Hostel. Metropoline bus 60 runs 1-2 times per hr (0600-2200) between **Mizpe Ramon** and **Be'er Sheva** (1½ hours), passing **Avdat National Park**, **Ein Avdat National Park**, and **Sde Boker**. Egged bus 392 between **Be'er Sheva** and **Eilat** (1½ hours) passes through in both directions 4 times per day Sun-Thu and once on Fri, though there is no guarantee that there will be empty seats.

Directory
Banks Bank HaPoalim in the Commercial Centre has foreign exchange and ATM.
Hospitals The nearest hospital is in Be'er Sheva, though there is a fully equipped **Magen David Adom** first aid station open 24 hrs on Nahal Have, T08-6588333 or T101.
Internet Free at the Municipal Library on Ben Gurion, Sun-Thu 1000-1200 and 1500-1900, Fri 0900-1200. Caféneto on Nahal Zia has wireless. **Post office** In the Commercial Centre on Ben-Gurion, T6588416 (Sun and Thu 0800-1800, Mon and Tue 0800-1230 and 1530-1800, Wed 0800-1330, Fri 0800-1200), for international phone calls and foreign exchange.

Makhtesh Ramon → *Colour map 3, grid C3-4.*

The Makhtesh Ramon can justifiably compete with the coral reefs of the Red Sea, and the unique environment of the Dead Sea, for the title of Israel's most stunning natural site. Some 40 km long, 9 km wide, and in places 400 m deep, the Makhtesh Ramon is the largest erosion crater in the world. Though comparisons with the landscapes of both the Grand Canyon and the moon are somewhat clichéd, they do serve to suggest something of the grandeur and splendour of the scenery here. Though the crater's beauty can still be appreciated from the window of a coach, this is a good place to get your walking boots on. The crater is now administered by the Nature Reserves Authority, with a number of marked walking and driving routes.

Ins and outs The main problem with hiking in the Ramon crater is that most of the trail-heads are far from Mizpe Ramon. Unless you have your own transport, take a very early bus down into the crater or are comfortable with hitch-hiking, you will expend a lot of energy just getting to the trail-head. One possibility is to stay overnight at the Be'erot Campground (see 'Sleeping', page 339). It is very important to make a preliminary visit to the Visitors' Centre or SPNI Field School in Mizpe Ramon before commencing any hikes. The SPNI 1:50,000 map is invaluable (74NIS), or at the very least equip yourself with the Parks Authority map (2.5NIS).

Geology The Hebrew word *makhtesh*, meaning mortar (as in mortar and pestle), has now entered the glossary of geological terminology since it describes a geological process that has been identified only here, in the Negev. During the Miocene geological epoch, (70 million years BP), pressure on the Earth's surface created a range of low mountains running broadly northeast-southwest through the Central Negev region. At some point the 'dome' cracked, allowing water to penetrate. Over a prolonged period the penetrating water eroded the lower, softer sandstone beneath the higher, harder limestone and dolomite, eventually creating three major erosion craters: Ramon, HaGadol and HaKatan. The term *makhtesh* is now used to describe an erosion valley surrounded by steep cliff walls and drained by a single wadi (water-course).

The layered rock beds of the cliff walls, and the bed of the makhtesh floor, display magma solidified into igneous intrusions, basalt, essexite, trachyte, clay, sandstone, mudstone, quartzite, thin layered limestone, bituminous limestone, limestone, chalk, conglomerate, flint, chert, dolomite, gypsum, ferriferous sandstone, sandstone and siltstone. What this list means to the non-geologically minded, is that the crater is full of colourful and bizarre rock formations that should not be missed.

Flora and fauna It is estimated that there are 1,200 different kinds of desert vegetation in the Makhtesh Ramon, including such flowers as sun roses, hairy storkbills, Negev tulips and asphodelines. Some floral features, such as the Atlantic Terebinth (*Pistacia atlantica*), are remnants of a wetter period and provide symbols of environmental change.

The range of fauna at home in the crater is equally remarkable. You are most likely to see the crater's ibex and gazelle population, as well as raptors and other birds of prey such as Egyptian vultures, short-toed eagle, griffin vulture, kestrel and a variety of owls.

Makhtesh Ramon, showing route of the 'Spice Road'

Less conspicuous residents are wolves, foxes, porcupines, hyenas, and a lovely selection of snakes, spiders, scorpions and rodents. You may also come across evidence of man's occupation, dating back to Byzantine, Roman, Nabatean, Israelite and Canaanite times.

Sights and hikes

The importance of getting maps and checking climatic conditions at the Visitors' Centre or Field School cannot be overstressed. Enquire the day before, particularly important from October to April when flash floods are a very real threat. The 4x4 trails generally cross the crater east-west, so for walking it's best to take a north-south trajectory to avoid vehicular traffic (it's possible to hitchhike back). For those without transport and on a budget, a half-day hike leads from Mizpe into the crater, and back via the Field School (or vice versa). Starting from the promenade near the Visitors' Centre, take the green trail then the blue.

Carpenter's Workshop and Ammonite Wall The **Haminsara** or **Carpenter's Workshop** (or 'saw-mill') can be reached by driving or walking 6 km down into the Makhtesh Ramon (crater) on Route 40 from Mizpe Ramon. Alternatively, a steep walking path leads down from the cliff-top promenade to the west of the Visitors' Centre. The name is taken from the resemblance of the rock here to pieces of sawn timber. The unusual prism shapes were created by cross-fissuring under pressure in the quartzite rock. The direction of the fissures determines the number of facets (eg triangular to hexagonal). An observation platform has been built here; this poor man's Giant's Causeway takes no more than 10 minutes to view.

You can continue from here on to the **Ammonite Wall** about 5 km away. The rock face here contains hundreds of ammonite fossils, named after the ram-headed Egyptian god Ammon, whom they resemble. From here, it's a long walk back up to Mizpe Ramon, though it is possible to hitchhike or flag down a passing bus.

Short driving tour For those with their own transport, and not wishing to travel too far on foot, it is possible to make a short driving tour of some of the crater's attractions. Leaving Mizpe Ramon to the south on Route 40, the road descends the twisting 'Atzmaut Ascent' into the Ramon crater. After 6 km, a sign indicates right for the **Haminsara**, or **Carpenter's Workshop** (see opposite page for full details).

Continuing on Route 40, take the next left at the sign for Saharonim Plateau and the **Be'erot Campground** (5.5 km away). Immediately past the campsite, the road divides. The road straight ahead leads to **Mt Ardon** (see below) after 4 km (you can drive to the base of the mountain) and to the **Ma'ale Mahmal** or 'Camel Driver's Ascent' after 10 km. This difficult ascent is one of the most dramatic sections of the Petra–Gaza Spice Road. In order to climb the face of the cliffs out of the Makhtesh Ramon, 300 m high, the Nabateans widened a natural fissure in the rock and constructed supporting terrace walls. At the top of the cliff is **Mezad Ma'ale Mahmal**, a small fort dating to the first century CE. The road is negotiable by 4WD for the first part, but the later stages are only suitable for walkers.

The right turn beyond the campsite leads to Ein Saharonim and the Saharonim Plateau. Taking the right fork, after 1.5 km the road divides again. Marked at this junction is a section of the Nabatean's Petra–Gaza Spice Road (see page 346). You have to walk a little way to see anything, with the nearest preserved 'milestone' about 2 km north.

Taking the left fork first, the road leads 1 km up to the **Saharonim Plateau** to the foot of **Harut Hill**. It's possible to walk to the top of this hill, 492 m high, and back in about two hours: well worth it for the excellent views around the crater. Other options from here include following the blue markers north to **Mt Ardon** (included in the 'Mt Ardon–Ein Saharonim' hike described below), or following the black or blue markers southeast along the Wadi Ardon towards Ein Saharonim (also included in the 'Mt Ardon–Ein Saharonim' hike described below). This latter route is also passable by 4WD vehicles.

Returning to the road junction, the left fork leads a winding 2.5 km to **Ein Saharonim**. This is the site of a small spring (Ein Saharonim) and oasis, though in summer it is often dry. Also located here are the remains of a Nabatean fortress, **Mezad Sha'ar Ramon**, that served as part of the chain of stations along the Spice Road.

Makhtesh Ramon, showing
Mt Ardon-Ein Saharonim & Mt Saharonim hikes

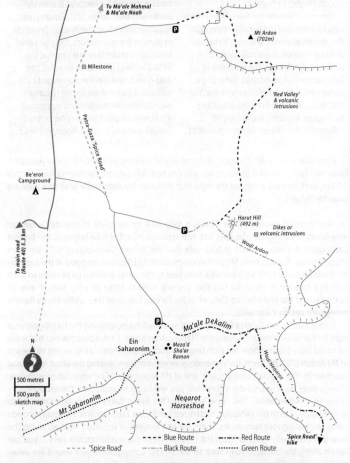

To Ma'ale Mahmal & Ma'ale Noah

P

▲ Mt Ardon (702m)

'Red Valley' & volcanic intrusions

Milestone

Petra-Gaza 'Spice Road'

Be'erot Campground

Harut Hill (492 m)

Dikes or volcanic intrusions

Wadi Ardon

P

To main road (Route 40) 5.3 km

Ma'ale Dekalim

Wadi Nekarot

N

500 metres
500 yards
sketch map

Ein Saharonim

Meza'd Sha'ar Ramon

Mt Saharonim

Negarot Horseshoe

'Spice Road' hike

- - - Blue Route   -·-·- Red Route
----- Black Route   ·········· Green Route
——— 'Spice Road'

The Petra–Oboda–Gaza Highway: The Nabatean Spice Road

Penetrating the Negev as early as the fourth century BCE, the Nabateans came to dominate the trade and transport of spices, incense, salt and bitumen between the Arabian Peninsula, through the Levant, to the Mediterranean Sea. The main route, the Spice Road, led from the Nabatean's Edom capital at Petra, via Oboda (Avdat) to Gaza.

The route taken by the Spice Road is fairly easy to determine today, not just through the identification of the various fortresses and way-stations at intervals along its path, but also through the discovery of large sections of paved road. Detecting a Roman influence, scholars believe that the Nabateans imitated these road-building techniques, including the placing of milestones; this practice became prevalent in the Roman Empire during the reign of Augustus (27 BCE-14 CE). This period is contemporary with the zenith of the Spice Road's fortunes, during the reign of the Nabatean kings Obodas III (c. 28-9 BCE) and his successor Aretas IV (c. 9 BCE-40 CE).

The Romans forced the Nabateans to relinquish their hold on the Arabian spice trade in the mid-1st century CE, severely weakening their power, and allowing non-Nabatean tribes from the Arabian Peninsula to plunder the way-stations. Despite a brief renaissance under their last king, Rabbel II (70/71-106 CE), the Spice Road fell into disuse, with new commercial routes being redirected. Some of the former Nabatean way-stations became fortified outposts of the Roman Empire following the Emperor Trajan's annexation of the Negev in 106 CE.

If you don't have a 4WD vehicle, or do not intend walking, you return the way you came. Once you have returned to Route 40, you can turn left (south), continuing for a further 2.5 km, until you see a sign on the right that indicates the **Ammonite Wall** (see previous page for details).

Mt Ardon–Ein Saharonim hike This is a long hike to complete in one day (seven to nine hours), and may best be split into two separate trips. The hike begins at the **Be'erot Campground**. Those on foot should note that the Be'erot Campground is 17 km from Mizpe Ramon. Bus 392 from Mizpe Ramon (heading to Eilat) will drop you at the junction on Route 40, but it's still a 5.5 km walk from here to the camp. It would be possible to hitch here but, bearing in mind the fact that you will need to make an early start, it may be best to spend the night before the trek at the Be'erot Campsite (see under 'Mizpe Ramon listings' for details, page 340).

Turn left out of the **Be'erot Campground** and head north, ignoring the turning on your right for Ein Saharonim and Saharonim Plateau. After about 3 km, a blue marked trail leads off to the right (east), where the path begins a gradual, and then a steep ascent to the top of **Mt Ardon** (702 m). There are tremendous views from here, making the effort more than worthwhile. The descent of the south side of Mt Ardon should be undertaken with care, though once back near to the valley floor you will begin to appreciate the extraordinary coloured rock formations. This upper section of the Ardon Valley is sometimes referred to as Red Valley, due to the profusion of dark red sandstone. Dark volcanic intrusions provide some fascinating rock formations. There are also remains of fossilized trees en route. The blue trail eventually leads to Harut Hill (492 m). There are several options here: i) you can return along the unpaved road back to the Be'erot Campground (just over 3 km away;

total trip four to five hours); ii) you can climb to the top of Harut Hill, and then return to the Be'erot Campground (total trip six to seven hours); iii) you can continue on to Ein Saharonim, adding a further four to five hours to what you have already completed.

Turning left (southeast) at Harut Hill, the trail towards Ein Saharonim follows the bed of the Wadi Ardon, passing a number of spectacular volcanic rock intrusions known as **dikes**. After 2 km or so of walking, you arrive at a three-way fork. The first left red route leads southeast, into the Wadi Neqarot, and forms part of the Spice Road hike (see below). The second path is the blue route, and involves walking in the lee of some steep cliffs (with shady caves) along the **Neqarot Horseshoe** (Parsat Neqarot), and on to **Ein Saharonim**. The third route, the red trail to the right, leads west to Ein Saharonim via the **Ma'ale Dekalim** ascent. The spring at Ein Saharonim, even after a day's hard walking, is not the sort that you would wish to dive into for some relief: it's often little more than a muddy puddle. Also sited at Ein Saharonim is the Nabatean fortress of **Mezad Sha'ar Ramon**. From Ein Saharonim, it is about 3 km back to the Be'erot Campground.

Mt Saharonim hike This four- to five-hour hike also begins at the Be'erot Campground. Turn right out of the campground, and head south along the 4WD 'Oil Road'. After 4 km, a green marked trail leads left (east), ascending Mt Saharonim, on the southern edge of the Makhtesh Ramon (crater). The walk heads along the top of the cliffs, along the crater's edge, before descending to **Ein Saharonim**. On the descent to Ein Saharonim, the green trail passes **Sha'ar Ramon** (Roman Gate), where the main wadi that flows through the crater makes its exit.

Spice Road hike This is a very long trek, covering over 40 km, and best undertaken by experienced desert hikers, preferably with a local guide, and with suitable equipment for camping out. There is no reliable drinking water supply on this route. You should consult with the SPNI in Mizpe Ramon before attempting this journey, seeking the permission of their rangers, and possibly the army. You will need the SPNI 1:50,000 map. The hike emerges on to the Arava Road (see the end of the Dead Sea Region chapter).

Borot Lotz (The Loz Cisterns)

Borot Lotz refers to a series of 17 waterholes that were thought to have been first dug around the 10th century BCE, with later modifications undertaken by the Nabateans. A 4-km walking trail has been marked encompassing the best-preserved cisterns and a number of ancient remains; the whole tour takes about two hours.

Ins and outs
Getting there and away There is no public transport to the site. To reach Borot Lotz, head north from Mizpe Ramon on Route 40, turning left (southwest) 5 km out of town at Haruhot Junction. Continue southwest on Route 171 for approximately 34 km, before turning right (northwest) on to the track at the sign for Borot Lotz. The parking lot and the beginning of the tour is 1 km along the track (taking the right fork). There are toilets, camping facilities and drinking water near the parking lot. **NB** It is forbidden to bathe in the cisterns or drink the water. Lighting fires, picking plants and flowers, and littering are all forbidden.

Background
During the reign of King Solomon (965-928 BCE), efforts were made to populate the Negev in order to provide a buffer zone between the settled kingdom and the desert nomads.

Borot Lotz was part of this settlement programme along the northern ridge of the Makhtesh Ramon. A series of cisterns were dug, primarily to store water from the winter rains, with evidence suggesting that most of the waterholes at Borot Lotz were dug during this period.

When those advanced water engineers, the Nabateans, settled in the Negev around the fourth or third century BCE, they refined the cisterns at Borot Lotz and incorporated them within their high-tech surface run-off irrigation system. Remnants of ancient farms and terraces suggest that agriculture continued at Borot Lotz until the end of the Byzantine period (seventh century CE).

Tour

Leaving the parking lot heading north, after 50 m you come to what is popularly known as the '**good water cistern**' (1), so named because of the quality of water it once supplied. The 'good water cistern' is an open cistern, cut into the soft impermeable rock and lined with a series of layers of uncut stone. Two diversion channels funnel the surface run-off water via sedimentation pools into the cistern. These pools serve to filter out silt deposits from the water.

The trail leads downhill, following an ancient drainage channel to a large cistern, 30 m in diameter, that over the years has become filled by sediment (the 'clogged cistern'). Just beyond here are the remains of a **Nabatean house** (2), probably dating to the first century CE.

Continuing downhill, in a northerly direction, lies a grove of **Atlantic Terebinth** (3) (*Pistacia atlantica*). As with other specimens of this tree elsewhere in the Negev, the presence of pistachio trees here suggests that this region was once wetter than it is now. These particular trees are thought to be several hundred years old. A diversion may be made northwest of here to climb to the viewpoint at the top of the 980-m peak known locally as the 'Fortress of Borot Lotz'.

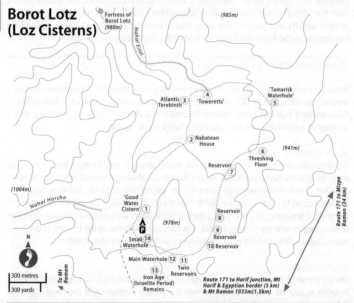

Borot Lotz (Loz Cisterns)

Fortress of
Borot Lotz
(980m)

Nahal Eliot

(985m)

Atlantic (3)
Terebinth   (4)
'Toweretts'

'Tamarisk
Waterhole'
(5)

(2) Nabatean
House

(6)
Threshing
Floor

(941m)

Reservoir
(7)

(1004m)

Nahal Horsha

'Good
Water
Cistern' (1)

Reservoir
(8)

(978m)

(9)
Reservoir
(10) Reservoir

N

300 metres
300 yards

P
Small (14)
Waterhole

To Mt
Romem

Main Waterhole (12) (11)
Twin
Reservoirs

(13)
Iron Age
(Israelite Period)
Remains

Route 171 to Harif junction, Mt
Harif & Egyptian border (5 km)
& Mt Ramon 1033m(1.5km)

Route 171 to Mizpe
Ramon (34 km)

The trail climbs slightly to the east, following the course of a seasonal wadi. Lavender cotton, cat thyme, white wormwood and wild pyretrum grow here, and were all previously used for medicinal purposes. Also present in the river-bed are fossil remains of snails, **toweretts (4)**, that previously lived here 70 million years ago. (**NB** Do not touch.)

Climbing the ridge above you, the marked trail leads to a second cistern. This one is semi-enclosed, dug into a layer of hard, impermeable rock. The tamarisk tree growing here gives it the name, the **'tamarisk waterhole' (5)**. There are remains nearby of a low stone wall; almost certainly part of the Nabatean system of surface run-off agriculture.

Ascending the next ridge, the trail leads to a **threshing floor (6)** that also probably dates to the Nabatean, or possibly Byzantine, period. It was also used in later years by Bedouins. The threshing floor stands amongst a number of ancient agricultural buildings, including livestock pens and grain storage rooms.

Crossing another dry wadi bed, the trail passes another **reservoir (7)**, though this one is in a poor state of repair and seemingly over-run by saltbushes (Atriplex halimus). A number of **reservoirs (8) (9) (10)** further on are in far better condition. They are reached by ascending the ridge from the wadi bed, passing a number of remains of Middle Bronze Age I (2200-2000 BCE) settlements. Of the **twin reservoirs (11)** ahead, the northernmost is in the best condition, having been refurbished earlier this century.

The main **waterhole (12)** to the west is the largest at Borot Lotz, being fed by four different conduits. To the southwest of the main waterhole, off the red-and-white marked trail, lie the remains of settlements from the Iron Age, or Israelite period (1200-586 BCE) **(13)**. The tour returns to its starting point, passing a **small waterhole (14)** on the way.

Eilat

→ *Colour map 4, grid C2.*

Eilat is Israel's premier resort town, frequently billed as a hedonistic alternative to the 'cultural tourism' on offer elsewhere in the country. True, the all-year-round sunshine is a major attraction, and the under-sea coral world is something that no visitor to Israel should miss, but there is some justification in the view that the tourist brochures are somewhat over-enthusiastic when describing Eilat's appeal. Development has been rapid, and though many of the larger hotels have been tastefully designed, many have not. It should also be noted that the beaches do not have the fine sand of the Mediterranean coastal resorts, but rather sand more akin to that found on the ubiquitous building sites.

However, having said all that, the town does have a very relaxed, easy-going feel, with more than enough activities available to satisfy most holiday-makers, and the north beach area is only slightly tacky. And with Israel being such a small country, attractions such as the Dead Sea or Jerusalem are never very far away.

Ins and outs

Getting there and away If arriving on a package tour or charter flight, you will arrive at 'Uvda (Ovda) Airport, the military airport some 60 km to the north. Charter airlines usually arrange transport to and from Eilat and the airport: otherwise it's a 300NIS taxi fare or an irregular bus service (392 between Eilat and Be'er Sheva, four to five per day, one hour). Domestic Arkia flights use Eilat Airport, literally in the centre of town.

The Central Bus Station is located on HaTemarim, and is within easy walking distance of the hostels (though a little further from the main hotels area). Connections are good to

Central Eilat

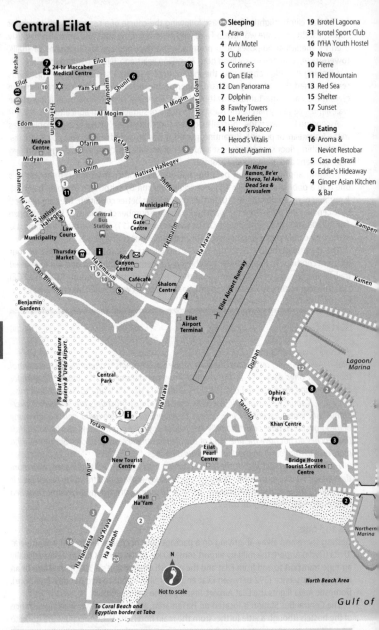

Sleeping
- 1 Arava
- 4 Aviv Motel
- 3 Club
- 5 Corinne's
- 6 Dan Eilat
- 12 Dan Panorama
- 7 Dolphin
- 8 Fawlty Towers
- 20 Le Meridien
- 14 Herod's Palace/ Herod's Vitalis
- 2 Isrotel Agamim

- 19 Isrotel Lagoona
- 31 Isrotel Sport Club
- 16 IYHA Youth Hostel
- 9 Nova
- 10 Pierre
- 11 Red Mountain
- 13 Red Sea
- 15 Shelter
- 17 Sunset

Eating
- 16 Aroma & Neviot Restobar
- 5 Casa de Brasil
- 6 Eddie's Hideaway
- 4 Ginger Asian Kitchen & Bar

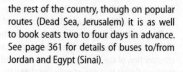

3	Gulf & @
7	Halev HaRahav
9	Il Pentileno
1	K2
10	Little Brazil
12	Pago Pago
11	Pizza Lek
8	Santa Fe
13	Shinolim
19	Three Monkeys Pub & La Cuccina
20	Wang's Grill, Ranch House

Other

2	Um Rashrash (flag)
3	Eilat Museum & Art Gallery
4	imax
5	Kings City
1	Bakery
11	24-hr supermarket
6	Shops
7	Department store
8	Left Luggage
10	Banks and moneychangers

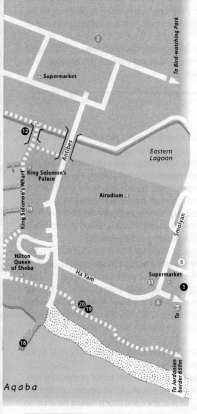

the rest of the country, though on popular routes (Dead Sea, Jerusalem) it is as well to book seats two to four days in advance. See page 361 for details of buses to/from Jordan and Egypt (Sinai).

Getting around Eilat is fairly compact and it's an easy walk between the centre and north beach area. For attractions to the south, bus 15 runs hourly from the Central Bus Station via Dolphin Reef, Coral Beach and the Underwater Observatory, to the Egyptian border at Taba (first bus 0800, last at 1800, restricted service Friday/Saturday).

Tourist information The **Eilat Tourist Office** ① *Bridge House, North Beach Promenade T08-6309111, eilatinfo@tourism. gov.il, Sun-Thu 0830-1700, Fri 0800-1300,* has lots of brochures in many languages, free maps, *Welcome Eilat* and *Sea and Sun* mags (which include discount vouchers for restaurants, etc). They also have a book swap that's worth browsing. There is a commercial **Information Office** ① *T08-6340404, Sun-Thu 0900-1800, Fri 0900-1300,* just in front of the bus station which hands out free maps and is quite helpful.

Background

Ancient history Though the modern town of Eilat was established less than 50 years ago, the advantages of this location – with its fresh water supply, natural anchorage, and commanding position on the trade crossroads between Egypt, Arabia and on to the Mediterranean – have been recognized since antiquity. When Moses led the wandering Children of Israel out of Sinai into the wilderness of Moab, he passed through here (*Deuteronomy 2:8*), and the port here was established some 3000 years ago to serve the copper mines at Timna (see page 368). During Solomon's reign (965-928 BCE), the port of Ezion-Geber had a firmly established ship-building industry (*I Kings 9:26*), and it is often speculated that the Queen of Sheba landed here on her way to visit Solomon in Jerusalem (*I Kings 10:1-2*). The Ptolemies, Nabateans, Romans, Crusaders and Mamluks all ruled Eilat, though few left any permanent mark.

The problem for archaeologists has been the positive identification of the sites of biblical Elath and Ezion-Geber. It is likely that any remains have long since been built over during the construction of the modern towns of Eilat and Aqaba, or been completely washed away by the flash-floods that periodically inundated the area. What this means for the visitor to Eilat is that there are no ancient sites in the town itself to divert you away from the beach.

Modern history The modern history of Eilat begins as recently as 1949, when the settlement was little more than a hostelry for camel caravans and a British Mandate police station. Recognising the strategic and economic importance of access to the Red Sea, the Israeli army occupied a strip of land adjacent to the Gulf of Eilat during the closing stages of the 1948-1949 War of Independence. This territorial gain was confirmed in the Armistice Accords of 1949, a kibbutz was founded (Eilot, later moved a couple of kilometres inland), and in 1951 a port was opened. It was not until 1956 that the Israelis were able to establish the right of innocent passage through the Straits of Tiran into the Gulf of Aqaba, though Israeli ships were constantly harassed by her Arab neighbours, contrary to international law. Attempts by the Egyptians in 1967 to block the Straits to Israeli shipping was one of the factors that led to the Six Day War.

Eilat has developed considerably since then (permanent population around 50,000), and though the port remains Israel's major link to the Far East and the southern hemisphere, it is tourism that represents the town's major earner.

Sights

Beaches

Though Eilat's beaches are considered its main attraction, unless you intend exploring the underwater world or partaking in the various watersports on offer, you may think that the hype is a little overdone. Most beaches are free, charging just for sun-lounge chairs (10-15NIS per day), though some do charge an admission fee. Women rarely go topless in Eilat.

The nearest beach to the town centre (and the most crowded) is North Beach, which is subdivided into a number of smaller beaches generally named after a nearby landmark such as a hotel (Neptune Beach, Royal Beach, etc). They have freshwater showers, bed-chairs for hire, and are generally supervised by lifeguards. A stroll along the promenade and around the lagoon/marina is a popular early evening entertainment.

Quieter beaches are to be found by heading out along the Eilat–Taba road towards the Egyptian border. Village Beach is undoubtedly one of the nicest, though it isn't large; entry and sun-beds are free. A good place for watersports is Veranda Beach, part of the Reef Hotel but if you order a drink you are left in peace. Eilat's underwater attractions are best explored at the Coral Beach Reserve (see below) and Princess Beach, where the best corals and largest variety of fish are to be seen.

Coral Beach Nature Reserve

ⓘ *Winter daily 0900-1700, summer daily 0900-1800. Adult 30NIS, student 26NIS, child 18NIS. There's a short DVD about the reef, with Dos and Don'ts.*

By far the most spectacular attraction in Eilat is the underwater world of the coral reef, populated by a diverse collection of garishly coloured fish, sharks, octopuses, crustaceans and sea-urchins. The best place to view the reef is at the Coral Beach Nature Reserve, on the Eilat–Taba road. Potential snorkellers can hire masks and snorkels here (18NIS, deposit 100NIS) and follow underwater trails through the highlights of the 1-km long coral bed. The private beach has hot showers, sun-beds (10NIS) and a snack-bar. Note that 'Aqua-Sport' Beach (at the northern end) is free.

Warning There are a number of rules to bear in mind. Don't touch anything. Not only is it illegal to damage or remove anything, you may also be putting yourself at considerable risk of injury. Some of the creatures, whether plant or animal (or perhaps simply appearing to be a rock) are venomous, and an encounter with one of these may be an experience that you remember long after the glorious underwater colours have faded from your memory. It is recommended that you always wear some form of footwear in the water (also available for hire). If you do have an accident, even if it is just a scratch, seek immediate medical advice at the dive-shops and equipment hire places, and then consult a doctor.

Dolphin Reef

ⓘ T08-6300111, www.dolphinreef.co.il. Daily 0900-1700, pub/restaurant open later, occasional evening activities (open bar nights with good music, free entry). Beach admission adult 64NIS, student/child 44NIS. Snorkelling/diving with dolphins 280/320NIS (book in advance, includes use of beach). Relaxation pools are open from 0900-0300, over 18s only; 30/45 mins is 300/350NIS (in the actual pools, includes refreshments and use of beach).

In addition to an extremely pleasant beach with loungers, sunshades, freshwater showers and a popular pub/restaurant, Dolphin Reef also offers the opportunity to observe and swim with eight dolphins. The centre was seemingly founded for 'scientific purposes', though it is sometimes argued that this is little more than the commercial exploitation that can be found in dolphinariums the world over. However, the intentions of the centre's staff are certainly sincere and honourable. A 'supportive experience with dolphins' scheme has also proved a valuable form of therapy for emotionally disturbed children.

The admission fee entitles you to use the beach, see a natural history film and observe the dolphins from the floating observation piers. Feeding takes place a few times daily, with trainers on hand to answer questions. The other (almost secretive) activity here involves three relaxation pools (saltwater, Red Sea water, freshwater) where you can float, listening to music, at around 30 C. Numbers are limited to 20 people, and the pools are within a beautiful glorified beach hut where refreshments and further relaxing can be enjoyed, day or night.

Underwater Observatory Marine Park

ⓘ T08-6364200, www.coralworld.com/eilat. Daily 0830-1600. Park and Oceanarium adult 89NIS (no student discount).Glass-bottomed boat 35/25NIS (not on Sun). Park only 79NIS/69NIS. Restaurants, souvenir shops.

If you don't want to get wet, this is the best way to see Eilat's coral world and the creatures that live within it. The Underwater Observatory comprises two large, glass-windowed rooms submerged 5 m below the sea's surface. Spectacular coral grows all around the observatory, with thousands of brightly coloured fish flitting in and out of the reef. There's a circular café within the Underwater Observatory, as well as an observation deck at the top of the tower. At over 20 m high, not only does the deck give a great view down through the clear blue sea to the coral bed below, there is also a 360° vista that takes in four countries (Israel, Egypt, Jordan, Saudi Arabia). From the pier, the **Coral 2000** glass-bottomed boat takes visitors on a 20-minute tour past the Observatory and along the reef, with explanations given in a string of languages.

Back on dry land is the **Oceanarium**, which shows a 20-minute adventure film with some 'virtual' effects (not especially exciting). There are shark, turtle and stingray pools, with set feeding times, as well as a darkened room where you can view phosphorescent fish. The Amazonians exhibition is also interesting, albeit in the wrong geographical location, plus there are rare fish aquariums and the opening of pearl oysters!

Coral Island

A popular cruise destination from Eilat is Coral Island (also known as 'Pharaoh's Island', about 13 km south in the Gulf of Aqaba. It has been suggested that this is Solomon's port of Ezion-Geber. The lagoon on the west side of the island is not natural, and the island was used as an anchorage in later years, with fortified remains from the Hellenistic (332-37 BCE) and Byzantine periods (324-638 CE) as well as the remnants of a Crusader castle (built in 1116). The Crusader fortress was subsequently lost to Salah al-Din in 1170, recovered by Reynald of Châtillon, and lost again to the Mamluks in the 13th century.

Eilat Museum and Art Gallery.

ⓘ 2, Yotam, T/F08-6340754, www.eilat-history.co.il. Mon-Thu 1000-2000, Fri 100-1400, Sat/hols 1200-2000, adult 10NIS, child 5NIS.
This small museum is only for people particularly fond of the development of modern Israel, although items are well displayed and there is some tourist information available. There's a short history of Eilat, from possession of the land in 1949, development of infrastructure, to present day reliance on tourism. The Art Gallery, opposite (entrance free), shows work by over 70 regional artists in ceramics, photos, paintings, jewellery, and more.

Kings City

ⓘ Eastern Lagoon, T08-6304444, www.kingscity.co.il. Mon-Sat 1000-2000 (summer and hols 0900-2200), Sun 1000-1800. Adult 118NIS, student/child 95NIS. Free 48-hr re-entrance. Bags aren't permitted on some rides; use cloakroom outside.

South of Eilat: the Eilat–Taba road

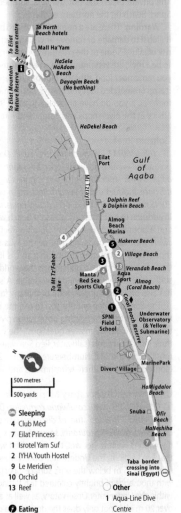

500 metres
500 yards

🛌 Sleeping
4 Club Med
7 Eilat Princess
1 Isrotel Yam Suf
2 IYHA Youth Hostel
9 Le Meridien
10 Orchid
13 Reef

🍴 Eating
5 Last Refuge
3 Sabrest, Baruch Fish, supermarket
1 Sheikh Yousuf's Bedouin Tent
2 Village Beach Bar

⭕ Other
1 Aqua-Line Dive Centre
2 Marina Divers, Parasailing, Glass-bottom boats
4 Camel Ranch
5 Tourist Centre

This monumental 'palace' is as visually startling as Herod's hotel nearby, and it's a must if you have children. There are four sections that highlight Biblical stories (mainly about King Solomon) in various interactive ways, plus a giant food court on the lower level. The 20-minute boat ride through the life of Solomon is rather dull until you are plunged vertically downstream, while the Journey to the Past of the pharaohs is an impressive 4D experience. The Cave of Illusions takes some time, with 70 different activities testing logical powers, games and optical illusions, plus quite terrifying dry-slides. Enquire on entry about timings of shows in English; they tend to be every two hours.

Eilat listings

For Sleeping and Eating price codes and other relevant information, see Essentials pages 26-31.

● Sleeping

The price categories quoted here are for the regular season, though at certain times of the year (Jewish and Christian holidays, weekends, etc) rooms must be booked well in advance (and prices sky-rocket to double or treble). Note that there are significant discounts to be had by booking through a travel agent. Eilat's budget accommodation is almost entirely confined to the area north of the Central Bus Station. NB This area can feel slightly seedy at night, particularly the eastern end of Al Mogim. Most of the dorm beds are 50NIS (unless it is a holiday or summer), with private doubles costing 150-200NIS (depending upon your negotiating skills). Few hostels have curfews.

Central Eilat

LL Dan Eilat, North Beach, T08-6362222, www.danhotels.com. One of Israel's most luxurious hotels but still manages to retain an informal atmosphere. 8 categories of room from standard to Presidential suite, all facing the sea. Dairy, Oriental, Brazilian restaurants, good sports facilities and sumptuous spa, 3 beautiful pools set in landscaped gardens, off season prices surprisingly good value. Recommended.
LL Herod's Palace/Herod's Vitalis, North Beach, T08-6380000, www.herodshotels.com. This place almost makes it into the 'sights' section! Herod's Palace features

luxurious rooms and suites, opulent Salome Lobby built in the style of a Nabatean Temple, Four Winds 'quiet lobby' (including romantic candlelit terrace), Officer's Club bar, Tamarind restaurant, and countless other options, Scardo shopping arcade running down to the beach, several pools, kid's pool, swim-up bar. Herod's Vitalis is a 53-room self-contained boutique spa hotel with separate check-in: over 18s only, no smoking, plus full spa facilities (not open to non-Vitalis guests). If you can afford it, stay here. If you can't, at least come and have a look. Recommended.
LL Isrotel Agamim (Water Garden), North Beach, T08-6300300, www.isrotel.co.il. Laid-back, young hotel that aims to replicate the mellow atmosphere of a Sinai beach in the heart of Eilat. Some rooms are literally "on the water". Lovely pool with bar, hammocks, spa. Good choice.
LL Isrotel Lagoona, King Solomon's Wharf, T08-6366666, www.isrotel.com. Isrotel-run 'all inclusive' hotel (all food and drink), supplement for pool views, family rooms available. Good for families, nice pool. Not a bad deal.
LL Isrotel Sport Club, North Beach, T08-6303333, www.isrotel.co.il. Noted for its sports facilities this all-inclusive hotel has 2 outdoor pools (1 heated), kid's pool, tennis, squash, raquetball, handball, baseball, gym, jacuzzi, sauna, health centre, plus nightly entertainment.
LL Le Meridien, HaPalmah, North Shore, T08-6383333/1700-700-103, www.fattal.co.il. Right on the airport flight-path. 2-3

room suites, fairly grand furnishings, all rooms have part sea-view and big balcony (extra for full sea-view and pool-view); garden rooms with direct access on to beach and jacuzzi are most costly. Pool is appealing surrounded by spindly palms. Lobby restaurant has dairy food, or meat at the pool bar. 790NIS and up B&B.

LL-L Dan Panorama, Lagoon, T08-6389999, www.danhotels.com. Fairly large rooms with marina views (no sea views), balconies, plus some suites with jacuzzi on balcony. Considerable price hike at weekends and holidays. Looks rather dated but has all the amenities you require.

L Club, HaArava, T08-6361666, www.clubhotels.co.il. Enormous place (7 pools!), white and blue nautical exterior feeds into the interior. Rooms face pool or sea, studios for couples or suites sleeping up to 6. Don't expect service with a smile (staff are too busy), but it's a good location and lively for families.

AL Nova, Hativat HaNegev, T08-6382444, www.atlashotels.co.il. Large Atlas hotel set around a decent-sized pool. Good for children, not for those after peace and quiet. Energetic vibe. Rooms are large enough but rather drably furnished. Worth paying extra for a balcony.

AL-A Red Sea, HaTemarim, T08-6372171, www.redseahotel.co.il. Away from beach, bit of a noisy location in city centre. Small pool. Discounts for longer stays.

A Pierre, 123 Ofarim Alley, T/F08-6326601/2, www.scuba.co.il. Double and triple a/c rooms with freshly painted white walls and new linens, flatscreen TVs (bathrooms being remodelled at time of writing). Shared balconies on each floor and a couple of good seating areas – particularly the breezy 5th-floor terrace. Good discounts with Marina Divers, or hotel-diving packages can be arranged. Price includes continental breakfast, free internet/wireless. Well managed, friendly, recommended.

A Red Mountain, 137 Hativat HaNegev, T08-6363222, F6363200, www.2eilat.co.il, redmountain@012.net.il. Reasonable

value for typical hotel room, though smells slightly fusty. Central location, a/c, TV, OK pool. 280NIS.

A-D IYHA Guest House and Youth Hostel, HaArava, T02-5945605, www.iyha.org.il. Clean single-sex a/c dorms with TV, fridge, kettle (100NIS), or private singles/doubles/triples (245/320/495NIS), reservations recommended, price hike in high season and at weekends. Clean and well run. Couple of nice seating areas on balconies looking out to sea. Charges for internet/wi-fi.

B Aviv Motel, 128 Ofarim Alley, T08-6374660, www.avivhostel.co.il, avivhostel88@bezeqint.net. Bright light rooms, many with big balcony (some sea views) or cheaper without; a/c, TV, fridge, kettle, sink, plates. Small pool with dusty loungers. Continental breakfast included. Very good value.

B-D Sunset Motel, 130/1 Retamim, T08-6373817, www.sunsetmotel.co.il, motelsunset@gmail.com. Good-value decent double rooms with fridge, TV, attached bath, around a small but quiet back garden. Single rooms less appealing as they're tiny and open out on to rather noisy bar area, but for 100NIS not bad. Two buildings: the one on the north side of the street has superior rooms though they are same price.

C Fawlty Towers Motel, 116/1 Ofarim Alley, T08-6325578. Some of the cheapest doubles around, at 150NIS, singles 120NIS, simple and clean, a/c, attached bath. Definitely demand an upstairs room with tiny balcony not downstairs which feels dingy. Wi-fi access, no breakfast or kitchen.

C-E Arava, 106 HaAlmogim, T08-6374687, www.a55.co.il. Clean popular dorms and fairly priced private rooms (doubles 160-180NIS depending on season) with a/c, fridge, TVs; singles and triples also available. Luggage storage (10NIS per day), laundry service, cheap snorkelling equipment rental, 2 kitchens, charge for tea/coffee, breakfast available, free wi-fi or internet 12NIS per hr. Owner, Aron (T052-3445027) also has a couple of large apartments for rent which are excellent value, sleeping 2-6 people, with garden, kitchen, TV.

C-E Corinne, 127/1 Retamim, T08-6371472, www.corinnehostel.com. Reasonable a/c mixed sex 8-bed dorms with attached bath (though a little dark, as in the basement) attract long-stayers. Plenty of storage space, free sheets, fridge. Cosy a/c wooden cabins (160-180NIS) weirdly have reindeer cut-outs galloping across the roof, attached bath, TV, clean and quiet. No breakfast but little kitchen is adequately equipped. Jolly management.

C-E Dolphin, 99/1 Almogim, T08-6326650/050-7904594. Don't get too excited about the pool/jacuzzi (it's the size of a bathtub) but 6-bed dorms are large, mainly with single (rather than bunk) beds, and have fridge, microwave, TV. A bit scruffy but cheerful. Small backyard. Double room 150NIS.

C-E The Shelter, 149/1 Eshel, T08-6332868, www.shelterhostel.com, pex@actcom.co.il. Run by Jews who believe that Jesus was the Messiah, this villa converted into an appealing guesthouse is split into male and female halves. Rooms/dorms are small and cheap (150/50NIS), free sheets, towels, tea and coffee, no breakfast but use of kitchen, delightful succah set up in the garden with comfy sofas as well as plenty of space to chill outside. Unmarried couples can't share rooms, curfew 2400, Bible studies at 1100, no drugs/alcohol/smoking permitted.

South of Eilat

Shady camping is available at the (**F**) SPNI Field School at Coral Beach, with good amenities to hand. Camping on the beach is legal away from the town centre, though is perhaps unsafe for lone women, and a noisy road runs right next to the beach.

LL Eilat Princess, Eilat–Taba Rd, T08-6365555, www.eilatprincess.com. One of Eilat's best hotels. Real sense of luxury, all rooms with extra large beds, some beautiful suites and themed 'club' rooms (Indian, Thai, Moroccan, Russian, etc), 3 restaurants, Moscow-New York Bar, Elixir nightclub,

series of swimming pools connected by waterfalls and slides, gym and health centre, tennis, private beach. Good choice if you can afford it. Recommended.

LL Isrotel Yam Suf, Coral Beach, T08-6382222, www.isrotel.co.il. Busy, comfortable hotel with the Red Sea Sports Club and Manta Diving Centre on site, great pools and plenty of sun-loungers, kiddie club, happy families everywhere, decent restaurants and well located.

LL Orchid, Coral Beach, Eilat–Taba Rd, T08-6360360, www.orchidhotel.co.il. Beautiful Thai-style resort village featuring a variety of charming chalets, older wooden ones among little gardens, larger (newer) Shangri La chalets moving up the hillside, peaking in an incredible villa with private pool. All have sea-facing balconies and are tastefully furnished with immense beds. Picturesque pool area, lovely loungers, private beach (a walk away), bike rental, free shuttle to city, supervised kids' entertainment. Chao-Phya Thai restaurant is unfortunately closed indefinitely; dairy restaurant only. A good choice, but staff rather off-hand.

LL-L Club Med, Coral Beach, T08-6350000, www.fattal.co.il. Usually booked through travel agencies (and cheaper too). Lots of entertainment such as nightclub, billiards, tennis, volleyball, minigolf, health club, and daily programme of activities.

AL Reef, Eilat–Taba Rd, T08-6364444, www.reefhoteleilat.com. Beach-side location is excellent, spacious rooms all have balconies with sea views, decent pool. Rather old fashioned decor, almost to the point of being retro-chic. Not bad value (unless it's Israeli holidays). Reasonably priced spa. Junior suites and suites also available.

A-F SPNI Field School, Coral Beach, Eilat–Taba Rd, T6371127, www.teva.org.il, eilat_re@spni.org.il. Private a/c rooms, breakfast included, sleep up to 8 people; prices go up Jul-Aug and hols. Camping (**F**) in pleasant shady picnic area with clean shower blocks (breakfast 40NIS), convenient for beach.

✦ Eating

Central Eilat

Most of the falafel/shwarma stands and bakeries are located along HaTemarim. The nearest big supermarket to the hostels area is at the junction of HaTemarim and Eilot; there is also a Supersol at the back of the Red Canyon Mall.

K2, T08-6337222. Gets the prize for Eilat's funkiest lighting. Brand new restaurant with 5 types of Asian food. Highly recommended. Impressively chic, but do diners really want a TV at their table? Daily 1200-2400.

Ranch House, Royal Beach Promenade, T08-6368989. Expensive American steak house using beef imported from the US. Wang's Grill next door has sophisticated interior and excellent, but expensive, Asian-American cuisine. Open 1900-2300, except Fri.

Casa Do Brasil, T08-6323032. Popular Brazilian grill restaurant has a mellow outdoor terrace filled with plants and a themed indoor area. Carnivores come for a meat feast, the all-you-can-eat deal for 144NIS involves 11 kinds of meat including lamb, chicken, veal, chorizo, liver and heart. The pizza/pasta is a tamer option (58NIS) or salmon steaks (89NIS) and burgers (78NIS) are generous. Daily 1200-2400. Good music and professional staff.

Eddie's Hide-A-Way, 68 Almogim (off Eilot), T08-6371137. Perennial favourite since 1979, best known for its steaks and fish dishes. Reservations recommended. Decor is unfussy: smart white table cloths and simple wooden furniture. Open Mon-Thu 1800-2300, Fri 1730-2330, Sat 1400-2330.

Ginger Asian Kitchen and Bar, T08-6372517, www.gingereilat.com. Excellent, busy restaurant mixing Asian cuisines: Japanese rice dishes and sushi, Thai noodles and fish mains, Malay and Indonesian noodles, good soups. Prices from 18-108NIS. Interior of clean lines and black furniture. Popular for take-aways. Daily 1200-2400.

La Cuccina, Royal Beach Promenade, T08-6368932. Very good Italian food and not grossly overpriced considering the location: pizzas (45-55NIS), steaks, fish (82-92NIS), interesting pastas (69-77NIS). Make sure to book a seat in the elegant outdoor area as the interior is rather 80s by comparison. Daily 1830-2300.

Pago Pago, Lagoon, T08-6376660. Floating restaurant and bar, seafood and grill main dishes. A top choice for many years, though it had been burnt down (accidentally) 2 weeks before our visit! However, there is talk that it will reopen.

Santa Fe, T08-6338081, www.santa-fe.co.il. Fusing Israeli favourites with vaguely Mexican-influenced cuisine, this restaurant has become a popular place of late. Comfortable interior, pretty laid back, decent background tunes.

Little Brazil, 3 Eilot, T08-6372018. "Meet: A lot of Meat", says it all really, though they do actually recognise vegetarianism. All-you-can-eat meat deals: adults 146NIS, children (up to 12 years) 55NIS, veggies 65NIS, fish 98NIS, stews and salads, mains 62-90NIS. Cosy front room preferable to larger rear restaurant. Sun-Fri 1800-2300, Sat 1300-2300.

Gulf Restaurant, T08-6374545. A busy old-school restaurant lit by fairy lights. Pleasant terrace. Wide menu that is not overpriced (good special offers), kosher grilled meat and fish, lots of kebabs, steaks and skewers; for vegetarians it's pasta, pizza, salads. Open 1200-late.

Il Pentolino, 112 HaTemarim, T08-5343430, www.ilpentilino.com. Huge choice of (kosher) pasta, bagels, salads, pizza etc. Always busy with a mix of customers. Relaxed terrace, warm and casual indoor area, candle-lit in the evening but also a good spot for breakfast. Does take-away. Sun-Thu 0800-2400, Fri 0800-1500, Sat end of Shabbat-2400.

Shibolim, Eilot, T08-6323932. Dairy kosher restaurant that is attractively rustic in decor and menu, with wide choice

of borekas (22NIS), salads, sandwiches, excellent breakfasts (30-35NIS). Sun-Thu 0700-2130, Fri 0700-1400. Recommended.
ﾔﾔ-ﾔ HaLev HaRahav, HaTemarim, T08-6371919. "The Wide Heart" serves excellent Middle Eastern food, felafel, kebab, schwarma. Extremely popular – look for the tables outside packed with locals day and night.
ﾔ Pizza Lek, 134 HaTemarim, T08-6341330. Perfect for that emergency pizza slice, green olive particularly delicious, kosher, take-way or eat in. Open 1100-0230.

South of Eilat
ﾔﾔﾔ Sabrest, Coral Beach, T08-6379830. Seafood with Middle Eastern and almost French twists, plus Israeli grill, fish (89-102NIS), aged steaks (102-159NIS), seafood stew. Lovely large terrace or contemporary ambiance inside, padded orange leather sofas mixed with Asian design. Intimately laid out with partitions between some tables, makes the most of an essentially bland square space. Daily 1230-2230.
ﾔﾔﾔ The Last Refuge, Coral Beach, T08-6373627, www.hamiflat.co.il. Considered by Israelis (local and holiday-makers) to be the best seafood restaurant in town. Main dishes 60-90NIS, plenty of choice on the menu. Appealingly decked out with nautical equipment, fishing nets on the ceiling and gingham tablecloths. Daily 1230-2300.
ﾔﾔﾔ-ﾔﾔ Baruch Fish Restaurant, Coral Beach, T052-2769749. Catch of the day – ask for advice – and requests (such as roasted veg accompaniments or salad) are catered for. A cosier place than most, small and narrow and with a personal touch. Sun-Thu 1200-1530 and1800-2300, Fri and Sat 1200-2400.
ﾔﾔ-ﾔ Aroma, next to Isrotel Yam Suf, Coral Beach. Reliable old Aroma for good salads, sandwiches, drinks; a/c. Daily 0730-2300.

⊙ Bars and clubs

There is a density of pubs around the Tourist Centre, all much of a muchness (backpacker/ budget orientated, they get going late).

Swankier options are along the promenade of North Beach or those along the Eilat–Taba Road (particularly Coral Beach area) which are chiefly beach bars. For nargila and snacks head to Sheikh Yousuf's **Bedouin Tent**, near Coral Beach, a good places to be at sunset. Open till midnight.
Neviot Restobar, North Beach, T08-6379989. Attractive central bar area, decking, cane furniture, shaded by sheets of sails, 1+1 deals from 1900-2100, serves breakfast 0900-1400. Nice atmosphere. Open till 2400 or later.
Taverna, Tourist Centre. 'The first and oldest pub in Eilat.' Backpackers bar. Beer and meals reasonably cheap. Rather raucous. Live music. Open 24 hours.
The Three Monkeys, Royal Beach Promenade. 'Plastic' English pub (makes a change from 'plastic' Irish pubs), nevertheless one of the most popular. Live music; shows football games. Daily 0830-0230.
Underground, Tourist Centre. Popular with backpackers. Cheap beer and food, loud music and hard drinking, sports shown on giant screen. Open 24 hours.
Unplugged, Tourist Centre, T08-6326299. Cosy sofas, very busy in the evening, beer cheap, good value meals, shows movies or plays loud music; pool table is a feature. Quite nice.
Village Beach Bar, Coral Beach, T08-6375410. Great little beach with palm shades and mellow music, where you can hit the beers (16-20NIS) from your sun-lounger. Also decent (if limited) food menu. Sun-Thu 0830-2100, Fri/Sat 0830-0400

The top hotels have fairly unatmospheric nightclubs. A more enjoyable time is likely at the various beach parties that are usually held near Coral Beach (ask around in hostels). Nothing gets going in Eilat much before midnight. 'Club nights' come and go at places in the Industrial Area; ask young locals or hostel staff what's 'in'.

☻ Entertainment

Casinos
You will have to cross the border to Egypt for gambling, to the **Hilton Taba** casino, www.tabapoker.com, passport required.

Cinemas
Red Canyon, Red Canyon Centre, HaTemarim. The triangular landmark of IMAX-3D unfortunately has screenings chiefly in Hebrew with only the occasional English film. Tickets are 79NIS which includes a stroll through the mini wax museum.

Festivals and events

For further details and precise dates contact the **Tourist Information Office** (T08-6309111, eilatinfo@tourism.gov.il). **Red Sea Classical Music Festival**: an international festival held late Dec/ early Jan. **Chamber Music Festival** each Feb. **Jazz on the Red Sea**: extremely popular 4-day jazz festival, last week in August. **Teymaniyada**: 3-day celebration of the Middle East (music, singing, dancing, food) in August.

◐ Shopping

Books
Steimatzky have branches on the Promenade and in Mall Ha'Yam.

Jewellery
Jewellery Caprice, 3 Hatushiya, T08-6336363. Largest jewellery shop in Israel. Free pick-up from hotel. H Stern can be found at all the top hotels.

Market
There's a market every Thu on Hatmarim, opposite the bus station.

Shopping centres
Mall Ha'Yam, North Shore, eclipses Eilat's older malls and is conveniently located.

Significantly cheaper, however, is the BIG Shopping Centre in the industrial area north of the city centre, a 20 NIS taxi ride away. There are plenty of designer shops along the Promenade of North Beach.

▲ Activities and tours

Bird-watching
Eilat is on the main migration route between Africa and Europe, via the Great Syrian-African Rift Valley, with about 430 species of migratory birds having been observed in the region. 40 different species of raptors alone have been noted here. The main bird-watching area is the **Bird Sanctuary**, a disused rubbish tip turned into a nature park with indigenous flora. Guided tours and various birding trips are available, contact the International **Birding and Research Centre**, T08-6335339, www.geocities.com/ibrce. International bird-watching week runs from mid-March.

Cycling
Holit Desert Tours, office at Khan Centre (opposite Dan Panorama), T08-6318318, www.holit.co.il. Guided tours (for families also), or quality bikes for rent, maps provided.

Diving
There are numerous companies offering diving and dive equipment rental. Note that you have to pay for mandatory insurance. Experienced divers must have had at least 1 dive in the last 6 months, otherwise will have to do a refresher dive (around 200NIS). Most dive centres offer SSI or PADI certification. Yoseftal Hospital has a decompression chamber. Most of the dive companies also hire out snorkelling gear for 30-40NIS per day, though hiring from a hostel is cheaper (eg Arava Hostel has equipment for 15NIS per day). The prices below are the going rate at the time of writing: Full equipment rental (including unlimited air refill) 150NIS; introductory dive 220-240NIS; private guided dive

Excursions into Sinai and Jordan from Eilat

Many visitors to Eilat (particularly those on package tours) like to book short trips across Israel's borders into Jordan and Sinai (Egypt). A one-day trip to Petra in Jordan (allowing you around four hours at Petra) will cost around $160-180 excluding visas (available on the border, $14) and border taxes (about $20 total). Four hours is nowhere near enough time at Petra (one-two full days is really the minimum to fully appreciate it), but if this is your only chance to visit then you must go for it. A two-day tour to Petra and Wadi Rhum will cost around $400-450, including accommodation and food but excluding visas/border taxes.

A one-day trip to St Catherine's Monastery at the foot of Mount Sinai costs around $135 (a 'Sinai permit' is available on the border) plus border taxes (under $30 total). For those wanting to book a tour to Egypt (and not just Sinai), they will require a full tourist visa (not available on the border but easily available at the Egyptian Consulate in Eilat).

If you are good at planning in advance, booking a trip before you get to Eilat could be cheaper. You can book a one-day tour through **Fun Time**, based in Jerusalem, 24-hour T054-4904105, www.fun-time.org.il.

160-180NIS, 2 dives 200NIS, 3 dives 290NIS, including equipment; guided night dive 300NIS; boat dive to Japanese Gardens 170NIS; boat trip to Coral Island (including 2 dives, full equipment, lunch) 390NIS; dive with dolphins 225-300NIS; SSI Open Water 5 day course 295euro (1500NIS) not including student record (maximum 80euro extra); 2 Star Advanced 2 day course 600NIS.

The following operators are long-established and provide English instruction (with plenty of advance warning): **Aqua Sport**, Coral Beach, T08-6334404, www.aqua-sport.com; **Coral Sea Divers**, Coral Beach, T08-6370337, www.coralsea.co.il; **Isrotel Manta Diving Club**, Yam Suf Hotel, T08-6382240, www.redseasports.co.il; **Lucky Divers**, 5 Tzukim, T08-6335990, www.luckydivers.com; **Marina Divers**, near Reef Hotel, Eilat–Taba Rd, T08-6376787, www.scuba.co.il. **Snuba**, South Beach, T08-6372722, www.snuba.co.il. 'Snuba' is similar to diving except that the tank remains on a small raft on the surface (ages 8 and above, max depth 6 m, approx 1 hr, 180NIS). Good location by the Caves Reef which is rich in marine life.

Glass-bottom boat tours
Coral 2000, Underwater Observatory, T08-6373214, Israel-Yam, T08-6332325, www.israel-yam.co.il. Daily cruises at 1030, 1130 and 1530 for 2 hrs to the Jordan and Egypt borders via Coral Reserve and Japanese Gardens. Bar; upper deck for sunbathing.

Hiking
SPNI Field School, Coral Beach, Eilat–Taba Rd, T08-6326468, office on the 1st floor, Sun-Thu 0800-1800. The best source for information on hiking in the region. They also sell the 1:50,000 map of the Eilat Mountain Reserve (the only sheet that has been translated into English).

Horse and camel riding
Camel Ranch, Wadi Shlomo, T08-6370022, www.camelranch.co.il. Morning and late afternoon excursions along the wadi, or you can try "Solomon's Chariots" (a chariot being a donkey-cart ride).

Water-sports
There are numerous companies in Eilat offering a variety of watersports. The following prices are about the going rates. Boating:

canoe 60NIS per hour; motor boat 200NIS per hour; speed boat 650NIS per hour. Parasailing: 140NIS per 10 minutes. Water-skiing: 120NIS per 10 minutes; 200NIS per 20-min lesson.

Tour operators

Kite X Club, Veranda Beach, T08-6373123, www.kitexeilat.co.il. Courses and equipment for potential and experienced kite-surfers.

Paradise Tours, T08-6323300, www. reservation.co.il. Daily tours to Petra, St Catherine's (everything included except border tax and tips), Masada/Dead Sea ($150), Jerusalem ($150), and all Eilat's activities (fair prices).

Red Sea Sports Club, office at Bridge House, North Beach, T08-6382240, and Manta Diving Centre at Isrotel Yam Suf, www.redseasports. co.il. Full range of diving and water-sport options, as well as jeep safaris, tours etc.

Thru Us Travel, T08-6316886. www. thruustravel.com. Range of options including 1-day tours to Petra ($139 excluding visa fees and border taxes, service described as 'impeccable' by one reader), 2-day tours to Cairo ($170), cheaper if booked online.

Yacht Venus, T050-8444770, www. yachtvenus.com. Tours to Coral Island and Taba, with drinks and BBQ.

⊖ Transport

Air

Airline offices Arkia, Red Canyon Mall, T08-6384888, www.arkia. IsrAir, Shalom Centre, T08-6340666.

Air'Uvda (Ovda) Airport, T08-6375880, T03-9723302, is located some 60 km north of Eilat (1 hour along Route 12), and handles most international flights. Since it is primarily a military airport it is not shown on some maps. Bus 392 passes the airport 5 times per day (only twice on Fri), or a taxi between the airport and Eilat will cost around 300NIS. If arriving on a package tour, transfers are usually arranged for you. There is a tourist information counter, caféteria and a bank.

Eilat Airport, T08-6373553, T03-9723302, is slap bang in the city centre (the travel brochures don't mention the noise when they describe Eilat), and handles mainly domestic flights run by **Arkia, IsrAir** and **El Al**. You can probably walk there from most hotels (otherwise it's a short taxi ride or bus 15 stops outside).

Bus

The Central Bus Station is on HaTemarim (information T08-6368111, 2800*). During holidays and high season tickets should be reserved at least 2 days in advance. There is an information office and phone information service. There are toilets, left luggage and snack places.

Be'er Sheva via **Mitzpe Ramon** (Route 12): Bus 392, Sun-Thu 5 per day 0630-1700, Fri/Sat 2 per day, 3 hrs. **Haifa** (via Be'er Sheva, Hadera and Netanya): Bus 991, Sun-Thu 0900, 2400, Fri 0900, Sat 1530 and 2400, 6 hrs. **Jerusalem** via **'En Boqeq, Masada** (2 hours 20 minutes), **Ein Gedi** (3 hours): Bus 444, Sun-Thu 0700 1000 1415 1700, Fri 0700 1000 1300, Sat 1630 and 2130 (peak season), 5 hrs. **Tel Aviv** via Arava: Bus 393 and 394, Sun-Thu 11 per day from 0500-0100, Fri 5 per day 0500-1500, Sat 11 per day 1130-0100.

For details on getting to **Jordan** and **Sinai** (Egypt), see box on page 361, and the relevant 'Getting there – overland' section on pages 23.

Car hire

The following firms are all found in the Shalom Centre: **Avis**, T08-6373164, www. avis.co.il. **Budget**, T08-6374124, www. budget.co.il. **Eldan**, T08-6374027, www. eldan.co.il. **Sixt**, T08-6373511, www.sixt.co.il.

Taxis

Drivers must always use their meters, although in Eilat they often refuse. Fares are the same whatever the number of passengers (maximum 4). There's an extra charge 2100-0500. They can charge 2NIS per piece of luggage (and are entitled to charge 2NIS extra for telephone call-outs). **King Solomon's**, T08-6332424. **Taba**, T08-6333339.

ⓘ Directory

Banks There are numerous banks with ATMS on HaTemarim and along the Promenade as well as a number of money changers (all offer no commission). The post office offers commission-free foreign exchange. Hotels are bad places to change money. **Embassies and consulates** For a full list of consulates and embassies in Eilat, see www.embassiesabroad.com/embassies-in/israel. **Egypt**, 68 Efroni, T08-6376882. In an unassuming villa west of Eilat centre. Visa services Sun-Thu 0900-1430, but get there by 1400. Visas (single or multiple) take only 15 mins and cost from 65-110NIS (depending on nationality), 1 x passport photo required. **Hospitals** Yoseftal Hospital, Yotam, T08-6358011. The hospital has a decompression chamber. **Internet** There's an internet café at the Central Bus Station, and hostels all have facilities. **Post offices** Main branch for poste restante and foreign exchange is in Red Canyon Centre, HaTemarim, T08-6372302.

Hikes around Eliat

The area above Eilat has been declared the Eilat Mountain Nature Reserve, and provides some excellent hiking ground. The reserve extends as far north as Timna Park, bounded on the west by the Egypt/Israel border, and on the east by the Edom Mountains in Jordan. With the three major rock types found here being dark hard igneous, red stained sandstone, and lighter yellow sandstone, the area is marked by some stunning rock formations in bright, vivid colours.

Ins and outs

The only drawback to hiking here is that few of the trail-heads can be reached by regular public transport. The usual rules about hiking in the desert apply (see page 17). None of the routes described below has drinking water en route, so you must bring your own (minimum 2-3 litres per person). It is not recommended that you walk during the middle of the day, so an early start is necessary, and summer is certainly not a good time to undertake these hikes. Sun-block and a sun-hat are essential. It is a good idea to tell someone exactly where you are going, and what time you are due back. **NB** The hiking maps below are for general information only, and should not be seen as a substitute for the SPNI 1:50,000 hiking map of the area around Eilat. This is the only sheet of the series that has been translated into English, and it is strongly recommended that you buy it if you intend making any of these hikes.

Mt Tz'Fahot hike

This hike offers good views of the Gulf of Aqaba, with the advantage that it is accessible by public transport. The trail is fairly easy, taking two to three hours. To reach the trail-head, take bus 15 from Eilat to the turn off for Wadi Shlomo camel ranch (see map 'South of Eilat: the Eilat-Taba road').

The trail begins at the estuary of the Shlomo River, at the turning for the camel ranch. The path leads upstream for some 2 km, where it meets the Wadi Tz'Fahot (1). Continue along the path of the Wadi Tz'Fahot, with its numerous Acacia trees in its bed, in a southerly direction. The valley becomes narrower, and is joined by a small waterfall to the right (west) (2). About 250 m beyond here the path forks (3). A black-marked path leads right (west) towards the Gishron River, though we take the left, green trail. The path starts to climb up the ravine quite steeply (4), before a narrow valley joins from the right (south) (5). It's a tough slog up this last stretch, until you eventually reach the top of 278-m Mt Tz'Fahot (6). The views down to the Gulf of Aqaba are particularly attractive in the late afternoon light, though the temptation to wait around for the sunset must be avoided, since this will require a difficult descent in the dark. The trail is marked down the east side of the mountain, joining the Garinit River, and reaching the beach area at the Coral Beach Nature Reserve. Bus 15 runs back to Eilat from here.

Mt Shlomo hike

This is quite a long hike (five to six hours), beginning from Route 12 to the northwest of Eilat, and finishing on Route 90 (Arava Road) to the north of Eilat. Unless you want an uninspiring walk back into town, you'll have to arrange for someone to pick you up from where the hike finishes. The hike features an excellent view from the top of Mt Shlomo, as well as passing numerous waterfalls of varying size. The trail-head is reached by leaving Eilat to the west, on Route 12. After 7km, a sign indicates right for Mt Shlomo (Solomon's Mountain). Irregular bus 392 from Eilat runs along Route 12 (see 'Eilat – transport' on page 362).

Leaving the parking lot (1), head north along the course of the Solomon River. The cleave through which the river runs was formed as a result of the process that created the Great Syrian-African Rift Valley. Continue north along the river bed until you come to a point where two stream beds join the Solomon River (2). Follow the course of the stream to the

Mt Tz'Fahot hike

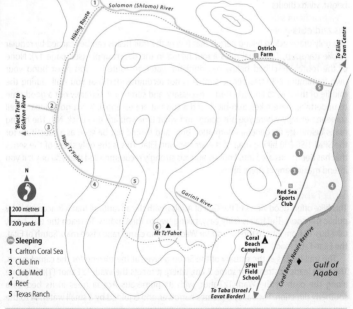

200 metres
200 yards

N

Sleeping
1 Carlton Coral Sea
2 Club Inn
3 Club Med
4 Reef
5 Texas Ranch

east (right) until you reach the mountain's saddle (3). A path leads up to the observation point at the top of Mt Shlomo (4), from where there are terrific views of the surrounding area. Particularly impressive is the view into Moon Valley, in the Sinai to the west.

Descend Mt Shlomo on the path to the east, dropping down to the bed of the Mapalim River (5). The walk north along the river bed is most attractive, passing a number of waterfalls. The height and power of the water will depend upon the season (they may be dry in summer), though it's usually possible to walk through them all. You eventually reach a point where there are two falls together (6). Turn right (east) here, and follow the trail until you reach the Netafim River (7). After walking for a half-hour or so, you reach a point that is accessible by vehicle from Route 90 (8). If you are not being picked up here, it is a 4 km walk down to Eilat.

Ein Netafim and Mt Yoash hike

This short hike is in two parts. The first section visits Ein Netafim, a perennial spring above Eilat, where there is a good chance of seeing some bird and animal life. The second section of the hike visits the Mt Yoash Observation Point, from where there are excellent views of the surrounding area, with the option of continuing down to the Gishron River. Total walking time is around 2 ½ hours for the two early sections, five to six hours if you continue on to the Gishron River hike. The trail-head is reached by leaving Eilat to the west on Route 12. After 10.5 km, a sign on the left indicates Mt Yoash whilst a sign on the right points towards Ein Netafim. Bus 392 from Eilat runs along Route 12.

Turning right off Route 12, there is a sort of parking lot (1). It is possible to drive further down towards Ein Netafim and park there, but you will almost certainly be reluctant to take a hire car down here. It's a 20-minute walk down the twisting dirt path and across a dry wadi, to the lower parking lot (2). Having arrived at the head of the waterfall (dry), it is a treacherous descent to the spring below. You often see mountain goats here, who apparently assemble to have a good laugh at the humans attempting the narrow paths.

Mt Shlomo Hike

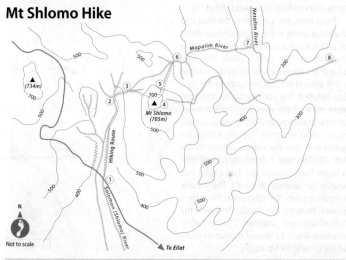

Having reached the bottom of the waterfall, hopefully in one piece, take the path marked in black along the right bank of the Netafim River (**3**). The path is marked by green powdered shards that, when wet, form a clayey substance from which pottery is made. After several minutes walking, a series of rock-cut steps lead down to a section of superbly coloured sandstone, with a collection of hues from pale yellow, through deep reds, to purple. Crossing the river bed, you turn left, after several minutes reaching the head of the spring (**4**). It is not uncommon to see wildlife assembled around the spring. In addition to the goats, rabbits and rodents, quite a lot of bird-life congregates here, including the Desert Swallow and the Onychognathus Tristami, with its orange-tipped wings. Though Ein Netafim is a perennial spring, this does not mean that the flow of water will be much more than a trickle flowing into a muddy puddle during the hotter months of the year. The pool here is not natural, having been built by the British in 1942, and later refurbished.

From here, you can either retrace your steps, or follow the green trail signs back up to the lower parking lot (**2**).

To do the second section of the hike, return to the upper parking lot (**1**), and drive diagonally across Route 12 to the turning marked 'Mt Yoash'. About 100 m along this trail is a parking lot (**5**), from where it is a 20-minute walk along the path on the left to the top of the 734-m Mt Yoash (**6**). (You can take a 4WD vehicle all the way up here). The observation point here has great views over the whole Gulf of Aqaba, with Jordan and Saudi Arabia clearly visible across the water. The Sinai Desert, in Egypt, is to the west, whilst the dark mountain to the north is Mt Shlomo (Solomon). On the return to the parking lot, it is possible to make a left turn and walk down to the Gishron River Observation Point (**7**).

From here, you can follow the blue trail markings down to the Upper Gishron River, or return to your car. If you descend to the river, about 1km further along the river course is a 20-m high waterfall (**8**). You can climb around the falls on a path to the right just before it. The path continues along the right bank of the river, passing a number of rock drawings illustrating ships, camels, goats and a mounted rider (**9**). Follow the green trail into the narrow crevice to the left (**10**). This pass is reputedly named after a larger than average girl, Tsafra, who was unable to squeeze through! The narrow canyon reaches the Yehoshafat River, then passes through the saddle between the Yehoshafat and Solomon Rivers, before reaching Route 12 several kilometres south of the turning for Mt Yoash.

Ein Netafim & Mt Yoash hike

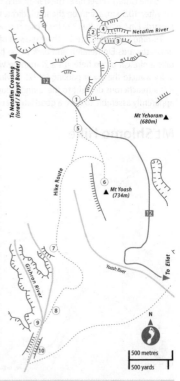

Mt Hizqiyyahu Observation Point and Moon Valley

This is not really a hike, but the observation point here is worth visiting for the fine views it offers, particularly of Moon Valley. The observation point is 300 m east of Route 12, at a point 18 km from Eilat (and 6 km from the Netafim crossing point into Egypt). Irregular bus 392 from Eilat runs along Route 12. Information boards at the two viewpoints here explain the topography of the land. The view into the moonscape of Moon Valley, across the border in Sinai, is amazing. It is also possible to see the Egyptian military guard post across the border, as well as the UN base that was used to monitor the international border.

Red Canyon hike

This is one of the best short hikes in the Eilat Mountain Nature Reserve and is suitable for all ages, though there are a couple of steep descents using ladders, and one steep ascent. Total walking time is 2-2½ hours. The trail-head is reached by leaving Eilat to the west, on Route 12, to the junction for the Netafim border crossing point into Egypt after 11.5km. Irregular bus 392 from Eilat runs along Route 12 (see 'Eilat – transport' on page 362). The road bears right (northeast) here, and after a further 10 km a sign indicates right for Red Canyon. Take this unpaved road (but reasonably good, even for a hire car), taking the right fork after 1 km (the left fork, indicated as Old Petra Road emerges back on to Route 12 about 11 km further on). After 1.5 km, you reach the parking spot (1).

Follow the path leading from the parking lot. After five minutes walking, there is the option of dropping down into the ravine on your left, or continuing along the path above it. The upper path eventually drops down into the ravine (2). There are some stunningly coloured rocks here, including some very vivid purples. Turning right, after several minutes walking, the ravine is joined from the left by the course of the Shani River (3). This is a seasonal wadi, dry for most of the year, though its bed is the habitat of a number of plants adapted to the seasonal drought and extreme temperatures. These include the Raetam bush, identifiable by its stork-like branches, which are bare for most of the year but sprout small green leaves and then flower after the rains. (It is forbidden to touch or pick any plants).

As you continue along the ravine, another small wadi joins from the right. The ravine begins to narrow significantly, until you reach the Red Canyon (4). The Red Canyon was created by the cutting action of the Shani River. Ferrous acids give the rock its deep red colour, with higher concentrations of acid producing the darker reds. Water and wind action created the beautiful shapes in the canyon. Where the canyon narrows, there are a series of metal hand rails to help you down. (**NB** After a couple of hours in the sun, the metal rails can become red-hot to touch.) The canyon subsequently becomes even narrower, with some metal steps placed to help your descent. Further metal steps drop down another level, where the canyon walls provide some deliciously cool and welcome shade.

Red Canyon hike

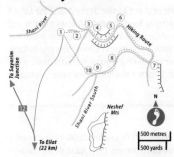

The narrow canyon emerges into a wider one, where a sign (5) offers you the option of climbing back above the Red Canyon and returning to the parking lot (about one hour), or continuing on the green route along the Shani River. The latter is recommended. The Shani River takes a sharp southeast turn (6), marked by a green clay wall to the left. The river bed is dotted with numerous Tamarisk trees that not only sink deep roots into the ground, but have also evolved a system whereby salt is excreted onto their leaves, collecting the night dew and then feeding off the dew as it drops to the ground. The salt left on the ground around the tree deters competitors for the water nearby.

After a further 500 m, the Shani River is joined by another ravine from the right (west) (7). Turn right into this narrow ravine, and follow its gently uphill sloping course (marked by black trail signs). Numerous rock rabbits (Procavia capanis) can be seen scuttling about here. After several hundred metres, the black trail markers indicate an ascent to the left, above the dry waterfall (8). The path here is very steep and care must be taken. Follow the black trail markers past the large Acacia tree (9) until a junction is reached (10). The black route bears left, following the course of the Shani River South towards the dark bulk of the Neshef Mountains, before reaching the main road (Route 12) near to the turn-off for Red Canyon. The better route, however, is to turn right at the junction (10) and follow the red trail markers back to the parking area. This last section is quite up and down, and frustrating in that you keep thinking that the parking lot will be just over the next rise. It's easy to feel disorientated, but keep to the main path and it will lead to the parking lot.

Amran's Pillars hike

This hike begins from Route 90, about 12 km north of Eilat, where a sign (with blue-and-white and green-and-white trail markers) indicates the hiking routes. Going north, you cannot turn left at this point but have to continue on to Be'er Ora Jct. From there, you can backtrack to the south and the turn-off for Amran's Pillars. The track leads 5.5 km to Amran's Pillars (though it is sign-posted as '6.5 km').

The track is unpaved, though with care you should be able to get a car along. After 2.5 km the path forks (with the route to the left following the green-and-white trail along the Nahal Shehoret for the Black Canyon hike) and the right fork following the blue-and-white trail to Amran's Pillars. After about 2.5 km, the rock formations become stunning, with the lines of faulted and folded strata displayed at the surface in beautiful blacks, reds, browns and greens. Less than 500 m further on you reach Amran's Pillars. Yellow buttressed cliffs top the huge eroded red columns of sandstone that form the pillars. They may not be as large or domineering as Solomon's Pillars in Timna National Park, but the colouration of the rock here is certainly more strident.

Arava

From the Gulf of Aqaba to the Dead Sea is a strip of desert known as the Arava, the largest region in Israel but home to just 3000 people. The Arava Road (Route 90) follows the course of the great Syrian-African Rift Valley, an extension of the East African Rift Valley (see boxed text above). Here exist isolated yet vibrant kibbutzim, each with a distinct atmosphere and outlook, which are interesting places to stop for a night or two. Hiking is good in several areas, while the pink Edom mountains of Jordan against the hazy desert plains make for some spectacular vistas. See www.arava.co.il.

Timna Park → *Colour map 4, grid C3.*

ⓘ *T08-6316756, www.timna-park.co.il. Sat-Thu 0800-1600, Fri and hols 0800-1500. Last entry is at 1600 but the exit gates are not locked so you can leave any time. Adult 44NIS, student/*

The Arava

The Arava is part of the Syrian-African Rift Valley, formed in antiquity when this whole region lay under the ocean, with only the granite peaks of Sinai protruding above sea-level, and great deposits of limestone laid upon the ocean-bed. Early in the Miocene epoch, pressure on the earth's surface from both east and west caused the limestone to rise above the water in two long, north–south running folds. The violent rupture of the strata between the two folds, and the subsequent slumping of the land between the two north–south linear faults, created the Syrian-African Rift Valley.

The northern section of the Rift Valley (north of the Dead Sea) is dominated by the Jordan River. The southern section (south of the Dead Sea to the Gulf of Aqaba) is occupied by the Wadi Arava (Arabic 'Arabah); a highly braided stream that only occasionally has water. The two sections are separated by a diagonal ridge of limestone that contrived to shut in a section of the old ocean-bed complete with a large quantity of salt water; hence the Dead Sea. The Jordan River and the Wadi Arava form Israel's eastern border with Jordan.

The Wadi Arava is a wide wadi in the north, with several broad lateral valleys. The western, Israeli, side of the wadi is defined by the ranges of the Tih, and the eastern side by the west-facing scarp of the Jordanian Heights. Throughout the northern Wadi Arava the indigenous vegetation is sparse, according with the highly saline and alkaline nature of the soils, especially in the area of the plains around Sodom. Further south, beginning some 50 km north of Eilat (near the mines of Timna) the valley bottom looks like a poor savannah area with a scattering of acacia and tamarisk and indigenous salt bushes and grasses surviving throughout the year.

Above the valley itself the land rises steeply to the west, with elevations immediately adjacent standing at 476 m at Yahel and elsewhere at 200-400 m, rising inland west of Yotvata to 710 m.

child 39NIS, separate entry for Tabernacle 15NIS (last tour at 1530), night tours 69/59NIS (Jul, Aug and hols). Tickets valid for 3 days. An A4 map (showing touring trails) is provided, however, the Easy Guide booklet (10NIS, 15NIS with CD) lists 16 walking trails, has much clearer maps and is strongly recommended. A 15-min "multi-media" video about the park is shown at the entrance. Ask about timings in English.

Timna Park covers 60 sq km and is an expanse of unusual rock formations, stunning views, archaeological sites, and the oldest known copper mines in the world. The contrasting colours of pink canyons, cream cliffs, black mountains and white-sand wadi beds give Timna a powerful beauty. A variety of hiking and driving trails are marked through the park, taking in the most spectacular and unusual sights, and requiring different levels of physical exertion, from seven hours walking to no more than 30 minutes away from the car.

Ins and outs

Getting there and away Timna Park is 27 km north of Eilat on Route 90, Egged buses 393 and 444 from Eilat (20 mins, 15NIS) can drop you at the turning to the site (from where it's 3 km to the entrance). NB Get off by the brown sign for Timna Park, and not the first blue sign for Timna Mines. Returning to Eilat requires standing by the main road and flagging down any passing vehicles. Most Eilat travel agents run tours to Timna Park.

Getting around The driving tour can also be undertaken on foot, though hikers should be aware that most of the attractions are 3-4 km apart. It is possible to hitch rides between sites if you don't have a car. Bikes can be rented at the lake, where you can also buy a map of trails or check (and photograph) the map board displayed at the start of the trails. If you intend undertaking any walking routes, you must be suitably equipped with a plentiful water supply, sun-block and a wide-brimmed hat. It is advisable that you inform the park staff at the entrance where you intend going, how long you plan to take, and to check in with them when you complete your trip. The staff will also give you a map and advice on the walking trails. Keep to the marked paths, and beware of unmarked (and very deep) mine shafts.

Geology
The park is encircled on three sides by the high Timna Cliffs, formed of light-coloured geologically continental sandstone, overlaid with marine sedimentary rock stacked in distinct layers of dolomite, limestone and marl. Copper carbonate ore nodules, mixed with azurite, cuprite and paratacamite, as well as copper silicate deposits, are located at the base of the cliffs and provided the basis of the substantial copper mining and smelting industry that developed here. The Timna Cliffs are open on the east side, from where the four wadis of the valley (Wadi Timna, Nehustan, Mangan and Nimra) drain into the Arava depression. At the centre of the park stands the Mt Timna plateau, a darker igneous intrusion of granite and syenite.

Background
The copper mines at Timna were once popularly known as 'King Solomon's Mines', with the Bible relating how Solomon (965-928 BCE) derived great wealth from the export of this valuable commodity. However, copper mining and production at Timna predates Solomon by a considerable period and, further, there is no archaeological evidence that suggests that the people of Israel or Judah were engaged in any form of mining in this area. In fact, the Bible makes no actual reference to King Solomon's Mines, and it is probably true that throughout the period of the United Monarchy and the subsequent Kingdoms of Judah and Israel, the mines at Timna lay abandoned.

Timna Park

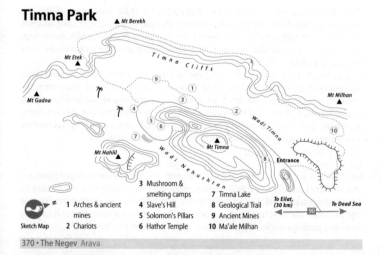

Sketch Map

1 Arches & ancient mines
2 Chariots
3 Mushroom & smelting camps
4 Slave's Hill
5 Solomon's Pillars
6 Hathor Temple
7 Timna Lake
8 Geological Trail
9 Ancient Mines
10 Ma'ale Milhan

Excavations suggest that quarrying for copper ore and primitive copper-smelting began at Timna around 6000 years ago. The most intense period of activity at the site was during the 19th and 20th dynasties of the Egyptian New Kingdom (c. 1320-1085 BCE), with mining continuing through the Iron Age IA-IIB (c. 1200-700 BCE), and periodically through to the second century CE of the Roman period. Production in the region has subsequently continued from the beginning of the Early Arab period (638 CE) until present day.

Sights

This is the main marked route, total tour time is about four hours (on foot) or an hour if you whip round in a car. Head out along the bed of the Wadi Timna, passing the Mt Timna plateau to your left. After 3.5 km, turn right at the sign for the Mushroom, Chariots and Arches. Follow the road for 5.5 km to the arches (other sights you will visit on the way back).

The arches and ancient mines From the car park, follow the blue-and-white arrow up the steps. These lead to a series of attractive rock formations in the white sandstone at the foot of the cliffs, most notably the arches created by wind and water erosion. This area was one of the major mining centres, with approximately 10,000 shafts found in the immediate vicinity. The Late Chalcolithic shaft-and-gallery system mines found here (c. 3300 BCE) are the earliest known examples of such copper mining techniques, while many of the Egyptian New Kingdom shaft-and-gallery mines (c. 1550-1000 BCE) display a level of sophistication only known previously in Roman or later period mine engineering. You can follow a red trail through the arch (using metal rungs at times) and on past the 'cave of the Egyptian miner', until the trail forks. The black trail leads to a observation point with panoramic views, via a ladder, and then rejoins the red trail. The red trail continues down the wadi, then look for the blue trail which climbs out on to a low hill. Here is a mine shaft 37 metres deep (which you can enter) plus an all-round view of the area. The saucer-shapes that are visible all around are actually silt-filled mining shafts that were dug through the rock cover into the sandstone below. The route descends back towards the car park. It takes no more than one hour. Return to the road, and turn left at the sign for the Chariots (2.5 km).

The Chariots A steep, marked path leads to a cliff-face that contains a number of drawings thought to date from the Egyptian/Midianite era. The Midianites, along with the Kenites, were a northern Arabian people who operated many of the Egyptian mines in the region. The drawings on the sandstone cliffs feature deer and ostriches, plus a chariot drawn by ibexes. A walkway leads into a canyon where it is possible to see the better preserved chariot drawings. On the right are oxen-drawn chariots containing Egyptian soldiers armed with shields and axes. In the centre a group of hunters handle dagger, bows and arrows. This short walk takes around 20 minutes.

The Mushroom and the smelting camps Although the Mushroom, a perfect example of desert erosion, is the main photo opportunity, the importance of this site lies in the New Kingdom smelting camp located here (c. 13th-12th centuries BCE). Within a fenced-off area lie the remains of a number of buildings that were formerly accommodation units and storerooms around the main courtyard of the smelting camp. Four furnaces were discovered here, now in the Eretz Israel Museum in Tel Aviv. Amongst the many finds at this site was a corbeled vault containing the remains of two Proto-Boskopoid skeletons of African origin. In a fenced-off area, 70 metres to the west of the smelting camp, is a sacred ceremonial place, used by miners of ancient times.

Returning to the junction on the main road from the park entrance, turn right (west). Take the first left, leading to Slave's Hill, Solomon's Pillars and the Hathor Temple.

Slave's Hill Approximately 500 m along this road, to your right, is a low hill labelled Slave's Hill (though there is no explanation as to why this name has been given). This is the site of a large smelting camp dating to the 14th-12th centuries BCE, with some evidence of a brief period of reoccupation in the 10th century BCE. The camp was surrounded by a strong defensive wall, parts of which remain, with two towers guarding the entrance gateway.

Solomon's Pillars Further along the road (1 km), you come to Timna Park's most outstanding natural phenomenon: huge eroded columns of Nubian sandstone known as Solomon's Pillars. It is thought that the 'pillars' here were created by water seeping into deep cracks that formed in the sandstone cliffs of Mt Timna during the creation of the Great Syrian-African Rift Valley. The pillars are particularly attractive in the late afternoon light (if they're not obscured by tour coaches that is). Metal steps up the rock to the right lead through an arch to some Egyptian rock carvings, though it's very difficult to make them out (look through the nearby "telescope" to locate the hieroglyphs on the rock face). The view alone, however, is worth the climb. The path descends via steps to the Hathor Temple.

Hathor Temple The discovery of the Hathor Temple by Rothenberg in 1966 proved conclusively that the copper mining activities in the southern Negev region were controlled by the Egyptian pharaohs, in collaboration with the Midianites (though local people were employed as workers). An open shrine was built here on the site of Chalcolithic remains during the reign of the Egyptian pharaoh Seti I (1318-1304 BCE). The temple appears to have been rebuilt numerous times, having been severely damaged by earthquakes on at least one occasion. Vast quantities of votive offerings, both Egyptian and Midianite, were found within the site.

Timna Lake and Tabernacle (7) Going back to the main road, it's then 3.5 km on to Timna Lake. By foot, it's quicker to follow the gravel track past the temple and around the edge of Mt Timna (about 40-mins walk). The attractive man-made lake provides a welcome splash of blue in the parched, semi-arid environment. The park entry ticket includes use of the pedalos on the lake, plus plastic bottles to fill with coloured sand as a memento. Next to the lake are shaded picnic tables, a souvenir and snack shop, and the pleasant **King Solomon's Inn** which serves simple but good food until 1700, e.g.Middle Eastern meal for 2 (69NIS), pitta and hummus (15NIS), salad plates (18-25NIS). You can hire bikes at the lake and get a trail map from the shop (see Getting Around, page 370). A 5-minute walk away is the Tabernacle, a reconstruction of the 'portable dwelling place for the divine presence' that accompanied the Israelites as they wandered the desert (*Exodus 25:8-10*). Entrance is with a guide only (set times displayed outside, last entrance 1530), though you may be permitted a quick look having come all this way. It is also possible to camp at the lake (44NIS per person).

Walking Trails The trails can be used to link some of the main sites, or done just for their own sake. The Easy Guide lists 16 trails and it is strongly recommended to buy a copy if you are intending to do some trekking. Three of the best trails are listed below:

The Geological Trail begins at the park entrance, and climbs up the east side of Mt Timna for breathtaking views of the surrounding valley from the granite plateau. The trail follows red markers and Israel National Trail markers, simultaneously, while boards explain geological features on the way. It descends at Solomon's Pillars after around three hours, from where it's an hour's walk back to the park entrance.

The Arches, Ancient Mines and Canyons Trail is a three- to four-hour hike begins at the arches car park (though this is actually 7 km from the park entrance). Follow the blue signs until you come to the sign-post marked 'Roman Cave, White and Pink Canyons, Solomon's Pillars'. The trail then follows black-and-white trail markers along the course of the Wadi Timna bed, via the sites known as Roman Cave, White Canyon and Pink Canyon, before arriving at Slave's Hill and Solomon's Pillars. The hike can be done just as well in reverse, and is especially attractive and scenic.

The Ma'ale Milhan, Timna Cliffs and Mt Berekh hike is the most demanding of all the trails, taking around seven hours but providing some excellent views. The hike begins at the park entrance, heading north, skirting the bases of Sasgon Hill and Mt Mikhrot. There is then a steep ascent, Ma'ale Milhan to Mt Milhan. The route passes along the top of Timna Cliffs, providing great views into the valley below, before making a descent between Mt Berekh and Mt Etek. The trail then joins up with the latter stages of the Arches, Ancient Mines and Canyons trail.

Hai-Bar Yotvata Wildlife Reserve

ⓘ *Route 90, T08-6376018. Sun-Thu 0830-1700, Fri and Sat 0830-1600. Adults 25NIS, children 13NIS, Predator Centre additional 25/13NIS or combination ticket 39/18NIS. Call ahead to book tours. Camping 50/40NIS.*

This reserve is located off Route 90 (Arava Road) about 35 km north of Eilat. It has its origins in the Hai-Bar Society, founded in the 1960s with the twin aims of reintroducing populations of wild animals indigenous to Israel, and to protect existing endangered species. Under the administration of the Nature Reserves Authority, Hai-Bar has developed significantly, and reintroduced many animals mentioned in the Bible, such as the Arabian oryx, African wild ass and onagers. Some species not indigenous to Israel, such as addax and Scimitar-horned oryx, are being bred for reintroduction into their original habitats abroad. A successful predators breeding centre, featuring canines, felines, hyenas, raptors and reptiles, was established in 1986.

There are three sections to the reserve. The first section is the open area, where the various species are left to wander in a quasi-natural space. The Predators Centre features a number of endangered species, plus an 'unpleasant' collection of rodents and scorpions. There is also a large enclosure housing a variety of vultures. The reserve also features a Desert Night Life Exhibition Hall, where it is possible to observe nocturnal and semi-nocturnal wildlife. Feeding time is a must. To tour the reserve "safari-style" you need a vehicle. A CD which gives information about the animals (in English) is available.

Kibbutz Lotan

Formed in 1983, Lotan was founded in the collective spirit by young idealists of mixed nationalities. Unlike early kibbutzim, members are religious, although it is a Reform Judaism that is practised here with strong egalitarian values. Lotan trod an ecological path, which has branched into successful eco-tourism ventures, as well as setting a standard for the region in green living. The kibbutz is now a member of the Global Ecovillage Network. It is a pretty, peaceful and intriguing village, with low homes hidden by flowering shrubs and bikes on the pathways being the main form of transport. The Eco-khef (eco-fun) centre is a working model of organic gardening, composting and water recycling where tours and workshops take place. Other activities include hiking, watsu (see Activities, page 376) or admiring the large herd of dairy goats. A nature and bird reserve on the southern edge of the village attracts migratory species; early morning is a good time to observe the birds from hides. Near the reserve is one of Israel's last remaining sand dunes, best at sunset when the light is particularly romantic.

The seven-week Green Apprenticeship course (usually starting December), attracts overseas students to study organic gardening, ecological design, alternative building methods and permaculture. Volunteers of all ages and creeds are also welcomed, and find it an extremely satisfying episode in their lives, learning skills to carry into a greener future as well as experiencing communal life. Students and volunteers live in the Bustan (Arabic for 'garden'), a prototype for sustainable living in "adobe igloos" built of straw, tyres and mud by the students themselves, See www.kibbutzlotan.com for details of the GA and also about the Peace, Justice and the Environment programme.

Ins and outs
Getting there and away   Lotan is 50 km north of Eilat, about 2 km east of Route 90. Egged buses 394/444 to/from Eilat pass by the turning to Lotan, though you will have to flag down a lift to get you to the kibbutz gate.

Neot Semadar

The kibbutz of Neot Semadar (population 160) seems to be crammed with talented craftspeople from both the artistic and culinary realms. Located 65 km north of Eilat, the community was established in 1989 by a group of friends, and now a constant stream of volunteers boosts their numbers. Fifteen years of hard work have resulted in the creation of an Arts and Crafts Centre to provide workshop space for the local artisans. The resultant building is quite a sight to behold: a fluid structure in the spirit of Gaudi, towering above a garden of roses and painted a distinctive salmon-pink colour, incorporating wrought iron, stained glass, ceramics and mosaics. The "passive" air-conditioning tower is central to the design, plus walls nearly a metre thick also serve to keep the building cool. There are wood-workers and metal-workers, weavers, potters, silk-screen artists and more. The shop sells pieces by the different artists and it's an interesting mix of conventional and innovative design, with items that are useful as well as decorative. You need to call in advance to arrange a **guided visit** ① *T08-6358111/170, www.neot-semadar.com, 35NIS per person including visit to the winery, lasts 1-1½ hrs, no tours during Shabbat or on holidays).* The kibbutz is also famed for its high-quality organic produce (especially from the herd of dairy goats). This can be sampled in their vegetarian restaurant (see Eating below) which is justifiably famous.

Ins and outs
Getting there and away   Neot Semadar is located just off Route 40, about 60 km due north of Eilat. Bus 382/392 passes Shizafon Junction (five to six times per day) from where someone can pick up. From Neot Semadar, the drive east down the Shayarot Cliffs towards the Arava (along Rd 40) is a spectacular one.

Arava listings

For Sleeping and Eating price codes and other relevant information, see Essentials pages 26-31.

Sleeping

A Kibbutz Lotan Guesthouse, T08-6356935/054-9799030, www.kibbutzlotan.com. The original kibbutz houses have been clad in mud and turned into charming guest rooms, decorated with desert colours (request one of the newly refurbished ones), fridge, sink, hot drinks, and lots of space outside to hang around. Wireless connection, a/c, no TV. Communal meals are taken in the dining hall at set hours. Prices go up Thu-Sat and hols. Breakfast is included, meals 25-35NIS, Shabbat dinner 45NIS. Guests get a free eco-tour and use of the seasonal swimming pool (Passover-Sep). The kibbutz pub is open Wed and Fri from 2200.

A-D Desert Inn (Khan Aviran), Peran, T08-6581821/052-3868938, www.han-aviran.co.il. Around a central grassy garden with palm trees and a water feature, 3 rooms have en-suites, a/c, TV and can fit families. A further 5 rooms have just mattresses, pillows, clean sheets, air cooler, and sleep up to 15 (sleeping bag/towel provided in emergencies). These can be taken as dorm beds (though groups aren't mixed together). Big kitchen (limited equipment), good shared bathroom facilities. Large outdoor jacuzzi under a palm shelter is attractive, space for campfires, tables and chairs. Impressive and delicious buffet breakfast taken in the farmhouse-style dining room (dinner only for groups over 10). Owners Amos and Shuli are immensely likeable. Current prices posted on website. Moshav bar is open on Fri nights and use of swimming pool is free. Turn at brown sign for Khan Avitan/Peran from Rd 90, 1 hr north of Eilat. Pick up from bus stop, or from INT trail.

Eating

The **grocery shop** in moshav Peran is open Sun-Thu 0800-1400 and 1730-2100, Fri 0800-1400.

Café Cartouch, Kibbutz Yahel, T052-4564089. Light meals, quiches, nice setting. Wed and Thu 1700-2300, Fri 0900-1600, Sat 0900-1400 and 1700-late.

Pundak Ne'ot Semadar (Inn), Shizafon Junction, Ne'ot Semadar, T08-6358180. Vegetarian organic restaurant (virtually all ingredients made on the kibbutz), breakfasts, light mains, divine frozen yoghurt, fresh juices, salads (35-45NIS). They've managed to create a special atmosphere that is unpretentious and relaxing. The pretty interior has a wood stove for winter evenings, in daytime the sunlight filters through the leaves of many plants, no music, heavenly garden at the back. Also ideal for an evening drink – the kibbutz wine is excellent. Store sells dates, olives, wine, yogurt, etc. Open Sun-Thu 0700-2100, Fri 0700-1600, Sat 1800-2100 (kitchen closes 1 hr earlier than times shown).

The Teahouse, Kibbutz Lotan, T054-9799050. Healthy vegetarian food, soufflés, pies, sandwiches, soups (mushroom if you're lucky); all home-made right down to the bread. As far as possible, Minna uses produce from Lotan, be it dairy or veg from the garden. Local beer available. The unusual octagonal building has windows in all walls and is nicely decorated with piles of cushions, rattan rugs and local artwork on display. There is a little shop, selling further works by artists from the community. Sun-Wed 1000-1600, Thu 1000-1600 and 2000-2300, Fri 1000-1300.

Yotvata Inn, Yotvata, T08-6357449. Most people visiting Yotvata see little more than this roadhouse, made famous by its fabulous selection of dairy products produced at the kibbutz and sold throughout the country. Meat meals, snacks, sandwiches and of course ice-cream and awesome chocolate milk. Sun-Thu 24 hrs, Fri -1700, Sat from 1000.

Activities and tours

Camel Riders, Sharahut, T08-6373218/054-4956030, www.camel-riders.com. A desert tours company based at Sharahut, 22 km south of Shizzafon Jct, i.e. in the middle of nowhere. Tours explore the southern tip of the Negev, from 90 mins (75NIS) to 6 days, allowing you to reach places otherwise inaccessible and following ancient routes. Vegetarian food and sleeping bags are provided, as well as English-speaking guides. Jeep tours also available.

From Sharahut it is also possible to hike to Yotvata, if you are feeling particularly adventurous; you will need maps, overnight equipment, a lot of water and the advice of locals.

Khan Aviran, Peran, T08-6581821/052-3868938, www.han-aviran.co.il. Hire a 4WD plus guide, or take a guided hike. Tours are tailored to suit each group/individuals (from low-key half-day tours with kids, to extreme full-day treks). Amos will sort you out: he's an expert in the region and knows all the canyons and trails. He is also happy to give advice to those who are doing it alone.

Kibbutz Lotan, www.kibbutzlotan.com, can arrange guided nature trails in 6 languages, and birding tours during the spring and autumn migrations, for half-day or longer.

Watsu, Kibbutz Lotan, www.kibbutzlotan. com. Shiatsu in water within a self-constructed building. Individual (50 mins, 210NIS) and family sessions available, plus 6-day courses.

Contents

Footprint features

Gaza

One of the most densely populated places on earth, it seems the Gaza Strip is rarely out of the news, what with Israeli air-strikes, Hamas rockets, and the tunnels under the Egyptian border. But to the 1.5 million Palestinians living there, it feels as though they have been forgotten.

Currently tourists are not permitted to visit the Gaza Strip, and there are no indicators that this situation will change any time soon. The only internationals who can pass through the notorious Erez checkpoint are the journalists, NGO and UN workers who maintain some sort of link between Gaza and the outside world. However, not wishing to delete Gaza from a travel guide, and in the hope that restrictions on tourists' entry will be lifted at some point, this chapter remains and has been updated.

The closure of Gaza's borders began after the June 2006 capture of IDF soldier Gilad Shalit (who is still being held by Hamas). Restrictions were further tightened after Hamas took control of Gaza in 2007, with access denied to all except humanitarian cases and all but essential goods.

The biggest population centre is Gaza City with about 400,000 inhabitants, about half of whom are refugees. And it's a very young population – about 75% of Gazans are under the age of 25. Here in Gaza City are all the hotels, restaurants and cultural activities, though elsewhere in the Strip are ancient remains from the Byzantine empire that shed light on Gaza's illustrious past.

Like many of the world's 'trouble-spots' it has a perverse attraction, where the depth of human kindness and personal generosity of a people who have so little to give, but are so prepared to share, is a deeply humbling experience.

Ins and outs

Getting there and away Most people take a private taxi from Jerusalem (300NIS) or Tel Aviv to Erez. Another option is to take Egged bus 437 from Jerusalem to Ashkelon (1½ hours) and then a taxi to Erez (70NIS). Coming from Tel Aviv, a bus to Ashkelon is in fact the best way to reach Erez (Egged 300/301, 28NIS). Returning from Gaza is 300NIS in a private taxi from Erez to Jerusalem. The last bus from Ashkelon to Jerusalem is at 2050 and to Tel Aviv at 2245.

Geography Geographically, the Gaza Strip is the part of the Mediterranean coastal strip of Israel known in antiquity as the Plain of Philistia (after its Philistine population). Like the coastal plain to the north, the land is agriculturally productive though its soils tend to be somewhat sandier. Despite its population of over 1.5 million Palestinians, the Gaza Strip is just 40 km long, 10 km wide, with a total land area of around 360 sq km.

Climate Gaza is located in a climatic transition zone between a typical Mediterranean climate of dry, hot summers and mild, humid winters, and a steppe climate where diurnal and seasonal fluctuations in temperature are much greater. Generally, however, the Mediterranean exerts a moderating effect on temperature extremes.

Background

The area known today as the 'Gaza Strip' is actually an artificial creation of Israel's independence war of 1947-1948, though the main urban conurbation of Gaza City and its rural hinterland represent an ancient trading centre marking the nexus between the continents of Africa and Asia. The earliest literary reference to Gaza City (the list of Pharaoh Thutmose III's conquests from the 15th century BCE), gives a clue as to the esteem within which the city was held: 'Gazat' is described as being "a prize city of the governor". Its position as the last major town through which travellers and traders must pass before entering the Sinai desert en route to Egypt has ensured a long and eventful history (see 'Gaza City', page 383).

Given the reputation that Gaza has been saddled with in the last 60 years, it is difficult to imagine its former status as a "prize city". Palestinian intellectual Edward W Said describes Gaza as "the essential core of the Palestinian problem, an overcrowded hell on earth largely made up of destitute refugees, abused, oppressed, and difficult, always a center of resistance and struggle" (*Peace and Its Discontents*, 1995). Though Gaza's degeneration into this "hell on earth" is usually attributed to events surrounding the birth of the State of Israel, noted social scientist Sara Roy (who has probably written the best informed assessments of the impact of Israeli occupation of the Gaza Strip), observes that the British Mandate government was largely responsible for sowing the seeds of the territory's underdevelopment. The systematic 'de-development' of the Gazan economy, according to Roy, has been a result of successive Israeli governments' policy ever since (see box on next page).

The 1947-1948 war The first major turning point in Gaza's recent history was the war of 1947-48 that accompanied the establishment of Israel. In a three-month period between November 1948 and January 1949, the influx of Palestinian refugees who had fled in the wake of Israel's military successes in the northern Negev and Mediterranean coastal plain saw the Gaza district's population rise from 60,000 to some 230,000. Most were accommodated in the eight large camps that developed (Jabaliyah, Beach, Nuseirat, Bureij,

Gaza Strip development

Sara Roy is amongst the most authoritative writers on the political economy of the Gaza Strip and the effects of Israeli occupation there. Roy's conclusions in *The Gaza Strip: the political economy of de-development* (Institute for Palestine Studies, Washington, 1996) brought Israel's political ideology and economic rationale into critical focus. Roy defined the results of Israel's role in Gaza as a process of 'de-development', or the "deliberate, systematic deconstruction of an indigenous economy by a dominant power." Her most recent book, *Failing Peace: Gaza and the Palestinian-Israeli Conflict* (London: Pluto Press, 2007) tracks the rise of Hamas in Gaza and the complete collapse of any formal economy,

up to Israel's withdrawal in 2005. It ends on a depressingly pessimistic note that sees Gazans stigmatised as terrorists and sinking further into economic stagnation.

It might be of interest to know that Sara Roy is in fact Jewish, the daughter of two Holocaust survivors whose mother was in the Lodz ghetto and Auschwitz death camp, whilst her father was only one of two Jewish survivors from the Polish town of Chelmnow. It is unlikely that her family history has influenced her writings, except in as much as it exposed her to the conflict during visits to Israel; this information is given here since it now appears customary to delve into the background of anyone who writes anything that criticizes the State of Israel.

Maghazi, Deir al-Balah, Khan Yunis and Rafah), with a disproportionate number of Gazans still living in these camps today. Though the tents and temporary shelters have been replaced by concrete structures, the image of these camps today still remains one of a transitory nature. Pro-Israeli commentators note how an equal number of Jewish refugees expelled from Arab countries after the 1947-48 war have been absorbed into Israeli society, whilst the Palestinians remain in camps. In the words of Benjamin Netanyahu, "Israel's attempts to dismantle the remaining camps and rehabilitate their residents have been continually obstructed by the PLO and the Arab world" (*A Place Among the Nations*, 1993). Whilst the refugees have been used as a tool in the hands of regional Arab power players, the point that Netanyahu chooses to ignore is that the refugees in the camps represent to the Palestinians a physical reminder of Palestinian dispossession, and thus constitute a powerful symbol.

Israel's offer to take Gaza Strip (including its refugees) under her suzerainty, following the armistice with her Arab neighbours, was rejected by Egypt. Thus, the present territorial division known as the Gaza Strip is largely the area of which Egypt assumed control throughout the period 1948-67. The strip was never formally annexed by Egypt "as it was believed that one day Gaza would be re-absorbed into a renascent Arab Palestine on the ruins of the State of Israel" (Joffe, Keesing's *Guide to the Middle-East Peace Process*, 1996).

Six Day War and Israeli occupation

The Gaza Strip was briefly occupied by Israel during the Suez Crisis of 1956, though it was returned to Egypt later that same year. The second major turning point in Gaza's recent history came with the Six Day War of 1967, and the subsequent Israeli military occupation. Israeli statistics indicate that in the Gaza Strip significant steps were taken in reducing infant mortality and adult morbidity during the period 1970-90, whilst both living conditions and agricultural production were improved. NGOs and human rights organizations, however,

Security concerns

Most foreigners wandering around Gaza City will be hospitably greeted, if regarded as something of an oddity. You will almost certainly be invited to discuss the plight of Palestinians and give your ideas and opinions, though it is generally more interesting to listen. Remember that having no opinion on the matter is rather insulting, and a sign that the outside world does not care about, or is ignorant of, the Arab-Israeli conflict.

Visitors to Gaza should remember to dress conservatively, with upper arms and legs covered. Women should also consider bringing some form of headscarf.

Since Hamas took control, internally Gaza is much safer. If there is anything that everyone living here (local or foreigner) agrees on, it's that today it's safe to walk the streets. However, as long as tensions between Israel and Hamas remain high – which will continue as long as Hamas hold Gilad Shalit and Israel continues its blockade – there is always the possibility of air strikes by Israel. Airplanes can often be heard overhead, but it's by no means a daily occurrence and gaps between any bombings can be a month or more. But, everything depends on the current level of tensions between Israel and Hamas – things can change in an instant.

recall a régime of systematic abuse and torture of Palestinians by the Israeli military, whilst the Gazan economy was made subservient to, but not integrated with, the Israeli economy. In effect, Gaza became a source of cheap labour and a market for Israeli produced goods. Sara Roy suggests that this 'de-development' of the Gazan economy (see box above) led to a situation where the GNP per capita in 1992 was in the region of $600 (compared with $13,760 in Israel in 1994), and recalls a situation in 1992 when the United Nations Relief and Works Agency (UNRWA) advertised eight garbage collectors' jobs and received 11,655 applications (see Said's *Peace and Its Discontents*, 1995).

Limited autonomy The First Intifada, which effectively began in the Jabaliyah refugee camp on 9 December 1987, forced Israeli society to examine its role and objectives in Gaza more closely. As Joffe observes, "Popular unease grew over the hardship imposed on young Israeli conscripts who had to guard the area. Similarly, as the heartland for Hamas, some Israeli analysts felt that bequeathing Gaza to PLO jurisdiction was a clever way of handing them a poisoned chalice" (*ibid*). Gaza was also seen as easier to relinquish than the West Bank for two key reasons. Firstly, unlike the West Bank, it was never really part of biblical Eretz Yisrael, and though Jewish settlements have existed in Gaza since antiquity they have always been seen as removed from the mainstream of the Jewish Commonwealth. "The biblical phrase 'eyeless in Gaza' refers to the plight of Samson, blinded and forced into exile in Gaza. But it also implies a region considered by Jews as unfriendly and hostile, populated as it was then by their Philistine enemies" (Joffe, *ibid*). Secondly, the signing of the peace treaty with Egypt in 1979 largely negated the argument that the Gaza Strip was required as a buffer zone.

Thus, in 1993, Israel and the PLO signed the Declaration of Principles (known as Oslo I) that provided for an immediate transfer to Palestinian self-rule in Gaza (and Jericho). A form of limited autonomy was granted to the Palestinian Authority in some 60% of the Gaza Strip, and Israeli troops withdrew from Gaza City in 1994. However, one of the key features of the agreements signed between the Israelis and the Palestinians was that

The Erez Crossing

The only way to cross from Israel to Gaza is through the Erez checkpoint on the northern border (T08-6741411). It is currently not possible for tourists to visit Gaza. The only internationals allowed are those who have special permission, including journalists, diplomats and NGO workers. Journalists need an Israeli GPO card, UN employees use their UN passport and NGO workers will have permits arranged by their employers. Should you be crossing with a press pass or with some other form of permission, the procedure is as follows:

On the Israeli side of the checkpoint there are one or two passport control booths, where your passport will be examined. Because you are leaving Israel, your passport will be stamped; however, note that visas are not renewed on return to Israel. Then there's a 1-km walk through a newly constructed covered/fenced-in walkway until you reach the PA passport check (where they check passports/

papers) From here, there are taxis to Gaza City (around 50NIS) or to anywhere else in Gaza. The taxi then drives on to the Hamas-run checkpoint where there is a further passport control. Here, Hamas search your bag and confiscate any alcohol and other non-permitted items (such as any material they consider pornographic, which could be an advert in an international magazine).

On exiting Gaza it is the same process, in reverse: pass through Hamas passport control, then drive to PA passport control (where they check your papers and coordinate with the Israeli side), before giving you the go-ahead to walk the 1 km back to Israel. On leaving Gaza, the Israeli security at the checkpoint is more intense. You pass through a couple of turnstiles and have a full body-scan, and all bags are x-rayed. Anyone passing through here will have to go through these procedures, which can take between 20 minutes to an hour.

Israel remained responsible for all movements in and out of Gaza (and the West Bank). Therefore, at any time it chose, Israel could close the border between Gaza and Israel, which happened for prolonged periods on numerous occasions following terrorist attacks inside Israel (including, in some instances, acts of Jewish terrorism against Palestinians). Israel still exercises this control over Gaza's land borders (apart from the southern border at Rafah), as well as over its territorial waters and airspace.

One result of the Second Intifada, which began in 2000, was that in 2005 Israel pulled out all their troops from Gaza, along with around 6000 Jewish settlers. However, this did not exactly result in a new and positive beginning. As part of the disengagement plan it was stated that Gazans could no longer work in Israel, and the 20,000 or more workers who used to travel daily to Israel were left unemployed and frustrated. This frustration, alongside various other factors, not least of all the corruption and embezzlement charges levied against Fatah and the PA, increased the popularity of the Islamist militant group Hamas who went on to win the legislative elections of 2006. Thus, in June 2007, Hamas took over full control of the Gaza Strip, effectively splitting it from the West Bank in terms of administration. Under Hamas rule, law and order has undoubtedly improved, though their popularity ebbs and flows. As Hamas refuse to recognize Israel's right to exist, the economic blockade and border controls have remained harsh. Naturally, the economy has been devastated by the blockade. Food prices have risen dramatically, nothing can be exported to the world market, and unemployment now stands at around 40% and rising.

After a six-month ceasefire was broken by Hamas, in December 2008 Israel commenced 'Operation Cast Lead' which comprised an airstrike and a land invasion, lasting for three weeks. Between 1,160-1,400 Palestinians were killed in the conflict, depending on whose statistics you look at, and thousands of buildings were damaged throughout the Gaza Strip.

Gaza City

→ *Colour map 2, grid C1.*
It has to be said that there is not really a great deal to see in Gaza City, with precious few reminders of its long and eventful past. The bombed out shells of city centre areas plus the (understandable) proliferation of ugly concrete block buildings is not very pleasing to the eye. However, it is very interesting to see at first hand the contrast between Gaza City and an average Israeli town, and this is perhaps above all a place where the people are the prime 'attraction': a place to talk and listen to Palestinians explaining their lives.

Ins and outs

Getting there Gaza City is usually reached in a private taxi from the Erez crossing (see 'Ins and outs' on page 379 for full details). Service taxis are few and far between as there is so little traffic at the border but, should you get lucky, they arrive at Palestine Square (Midan Filastin) in Gaza City, as do those to/from other Palestinian towns in the Gaza Strip (see 'Transport', page 388). Gaza's airport (located near to the Rafah border post) was in operation between 1998 and 2001, but was destroyed by Israeli forces after the Al-Aqsa intifada, and will not be running anytime soon.

Getting around There are two foci of interest in Gaza: the 'Old City' area around Palestine Sq, and the beach area that is one of Gaza's most desirable residential addresses. The two districts are linked by Omar al-Mokhtar St, Gaza City's main thoroughfare. You can easily walk between these two districts, or take one of the service taxis that run up and down Omar al-Mokhtar (2NIS).

Tourist information The best place to get information and advice is probably the **French Cultural Centre**, and you could also try **Al-Deira Hotel** (see listings, page 387). The **UNRWA office** has maps of Gaza which they will give out. Hamas are very helpful to visitors, though they don't really have anything in the line of 'tourist' information. And of course local people are always helpful and happy to see foreigners, since it's not very common.

Background

The importance of Gaza in antiquity as a strategically placed trading centre is best emphasized by the fact that, following its capture in the 15th century BCE by Pharaoh Thutmose III, more than 50 military campaigns were conducted in this area by the Egyptians.

Gaza is mentioned in biblical sources as being allotted to the tribe of Judah (*Joshua 15:47; Judges 1:18*), though in reality Israelite influence here was minimal. In fact, from the beginning of the 12th century BCE Gaza was the southernmost city of the Philistine Pentapolis that also included Askalon (AshKelon), Ashdod, Ekron and Gath (*Joshua 13:3; I Samuel 6:17; Jeremiah 25:20*). It was here that Samson met the 'harlot' Delilah, got the haircut, was imprisoned by the Philistines, then pulled down their temple of Dagon (*Judges 16:1-31*).

Gaza City

Gaza Port · Mediterranean Sea

To **3** (50m) · President's Palace · UN Beach Club · al-Rasheed/Ahmad Orabi
al-Rasheed/Ahmad Orabi · **1 6 2 4** · **7** · al-Rasheed

BEACH (ALSHATI) CAMP

Governor's Palace

RIMAL

Palestine Centre for Human Rights

2 1

European Commission

Palestine Rent-a-Car

French Cultural Centre

(Pol)

Al-Shifa Hospital

Orabi

Ez el-Deer el-Qassam

Jamed el-Dowel el-Arabia · al-Majdal

Al-Azhar University

al Jundi Sq · al-Nasser

Alnasrah

Islamic University

UNRWA Embroidery Shop

Mustafa Hafez

al Azhar

UNRWA

Omar al-Mokhtar

al-Ozyez

al-Welda

NORTH RIMAL

Palestine

Yousef el-Abdamu

Khaled

SOUTH RIMAL

Jamal Abdel Nasser

al-Kanal

(Pol)

al-Saraya

UNDP

✉

Ministeries Complex

al-Jalaa

Yarmouk

Yarmouk

al-Mugrabi

Omar al-Mokhtar

Municipal Park

🅼 Yarmouk Market

ALDARAJ

🕌 Fras Market

Municipality · Service Taxis (most destinations)

Al-Fuakher

Sayed Hashem Mosque

Baptist Church · Ahli Hospital · Palestine Square

K Welayat Mosque

Greek Orthodox Church of St Porphyrius

OLD CITY

Great Mosque

🅼 Gold Market

Omar al-Mokhtar

Roman Catholic Church

Al-Shajaia Square

(Pol)

Napoleon's Citadel

Salah al-Din

Service Taxis (to Erez)

🅼 Al-Shajaia Market

Bagdad

Yafa

Salah al-Din

To Rafah & Khan Yunis

To Erez Crossing

To British War Cemetery 500m

400 metres
400 yards

🏨 Hotels		🍴 Eating
1 Adam	5 Marna House	1 Al-Mankal Chicken Tikka
2 Al-Amal	6 Palestine	2 Love Boat/Al-Andalus/
3 Al-Quds International	7 Al-Deira	La Mirage
4 Cliff		3 Roots

Though Gaza was conquered by the Assyrian king Tiglath-pileser III in 734 BCE, and by the Judean king Hezekiah shortly afterwards (*II Kings 18:8*), Gaza undoubtedly remained a Philistine city. The city was subsequently occupied by the Persians, who turned it into an important royal fortress. Alexander the Great's arrival in 332 BCE saw Gaza as the only city in the region to resist the introduction of Hellenistic rule, though this resistance was short lived and Gaza was swiftly conquered and its inhabitants sold into slavery. Gaza became a northern outpost of the Ptolemies until 198 BCE, when it fell to the Seleucid king Antiochus III. Early Hasmonean attempts to take the city were unsuccessful and it wasn't until 96 BCE that Alexander Jannaeus conquered it for the Jews. However, rather than occupying the city, Alexander Jannaeus chose largely to destroy it, hence the reference to "desert Gaza" in the New Testament (*Acts 8:26*).

The city's fortunes were revived under Roman rule, with a number of splendid temples built here. In fact pagan practices continued long after Byzantine Christian rule was established, only ceasing in the fifth century CE. The famous school of rhetoric that was established in the Roman period flourished under the Byzantines, whilst Palestine's reputedly largest church (the Eudoxiana) was built here. No trace of it has ever been found. Though predominantly a Christian city, it is believed that Jews began to settle in Gaza during the Roman and Byzantine periods. Remains of the mosaic floor of an early sixth-century CE synagogue were excavated at a spot 300 m south of the present harbour, subsequently transferred to the Israel Museum in Jerusalem.

Gaza fell to the Arabs in 635 CE, shortly after they had defeated the Byzantine army in battle nearby. The small Jewish and Samaritan communities in Gaza both flourished under Arab rule. The Crusaders captured the city in 1149, turning it into a Templar stronghold. The 12th-century CE Crusader cathedral dedicated to St John the Baptist is preserved in the Djami el-Kebir, or Great Mosque (see below). Salah al-Din captured Gaza in 1170, and under later Mamluk rule it became the administrative capital of the Mediterranean coastal plain as far as 'Atlit. Gaza retained its administrative duties under the Ottomans, continuing in its role as a trading station on the route between Syria and Egypt. Napoleon passed through briefly in 1799 before embarking on his Egypt campaign, before Ottoman rule was brought to an end during the First World War by the British Palestine campaign of 1917-18. Gaza's subsequent history is dealt with in the general introduction to the Gaza Strip above.

Sights

Great Mosque (Djami el-Kebir) The Great Mosque (also referred to as Djami el-Kebir or Great Umari Mosque) preserves the 12th-century CE Crusader cathedral of St John the Baptist. Its façade, complete with grand arched entrance, is a typical piece of Crusader ecclesiastical architecture. The original church was a basilical building with rows of double columns separating the nave from the aisles, though the south and southeast sides were enlarged when it was converted into a mosque. The octagonal minaret was probably built on the site of the Crusader belfry. Though not certain, it is thought that the Crusader church was built on the site of the Byzantine Eudoxiana. Modestly dressed non-Muslims may be escorted round, outside of prayer times (except on Fridays).

Old City The label 'Old City' is slightly misleading since the bazaar area around Palestine Square can hardly compete with Jerusalem for character. Some of the older buildings around the Great Mosque use the ablaq style of decoration, prevalent in the Mamluk period, that features bands of red and white masonry. The short, vaulted gold market is rather similar to the medieval souq in Jerusalem's Old City (though on a far smaller scale).

Napoleon's Citadel (Qasr Al-Basha) The Mamluk period villa that Napoleon used as his headquarters during his brief sojourn in Gaza in 1799 was subsequently a police station during the British Mandate. For a period after this it served as a school for girls, but now has been restored and turned into a museum which is open until 1400. It is located on al-Wehda Street to the east of the Great Mosque.

Al-Jundi (Square of the Unknown Soldier) Heading down al-Mokhtar Street towards the sea you reach al-Jundi, or the Square of the Unknown Soldier. A small park has been developed here, sometimes known as Norwegian Gardens in deference to the Scandinavians' role in the Israeli-Palestinian peace negotiations. It's popular with unemployed Gazans during the day and promenading families in the evenings. The offices of UNRWA and the Islamic University lie just to the southwest of here on Jamal Abdel Nasser street.

Beach area The focus of Gaza's hotels and upmarket restaurants is along the strip of coast next to Gaza's incomplete port development and rather forlorn UN Beach Club. The beach here is rather dirty and miserable and will probably not appeal to visitors, though the sand itself is of a finer quality than you find further north along the Israeli coast. Note that women in Gaza go to the beach and bathe fully clothed. The fishing market here is interesting, located 0.5 km south of the port daily approx 0700-0900. A road block on Ahmad Orabi/al-Rasheed Street prevents those without an appointment visiting Arafat's palace and offices, while little is left of his compound save for a large garage which contains his helicopter and some old military vehicles.

Al-Mathaf Recreational Culture House ① *Sodaniya, Beach Road, T+970-08-2858444, www.almathaf.ps.* Opened in 2008, the brainchild of a prominent Palestinian businessman/collector, this little museum (Arabic: Al-Mathaf) displays artefacts spanning Gaza's rich and varied history. Dating from the Bronze Age to the Roman-Byzantine era, through the Islamic and Crusader periods, and up to the time of Egyptian occupation, relics are displayed in a hall created in part from the stones of old houses, railway sleepers and marble columns uncovered by construction workers. It is said the Hamas government has forbidden the display of some pieces adorned with Jewish menorahs as well as a small statue of Aphrodite in an indecent gown. The museum is on the beachfront near the Shati (Beach) refugee camp, and has a nice restaurant-café on site with a pleasant terrace to while away the time.

British War Cemetery In the Altofah East district of Gaza City (about 2 km east of Palestine Square) is the British War Cemetery, maintained by the Commonwealth War Graves Commission, containing the graves of Commonwealth soldiers killed in the 1917 Palestine campaign. There are also the graves of some soldiers who were brought to Gaza hospital for treatment during the Second World War North Africa campaign. It is a very attractive and restful place.

Gaza City listings

For Sleeping and Eating price codes and other relevant information, see Essentials pages 26-31.

Sleeping

There's not a wide range of accommodation in Gaza, with nothing at the cheaper end of the market, though demand for rooms is not great anyway. However, most of the hotels in Gaza are used to dealing with journalists, foreign delegations and NGO workers.

AL Al Deira Hotel, Al Rasheed, T08-2838100, www.aldeira.ps. As the best hotel in town Al-Deira is naturally the most popular choice for aid workers and journalists. It's efficiently managed with tasteful rooms, all unique, with arched ceilings and Arabesque furniture. Has wi-fi, though it doesn't always work in the room. The restaurant also has a great view of the beach, with decent food but a much better setting. It gets very busy on Thu evenings during the summer.

A-B Al-Quds International, Omar al-Mokhtar, Almena's Roundabout, T970-08-2825181, F2823240. This skyscraper at the beach end of the main street has sea-view rooms with balcony, TV, phone, fridge, carpet (**A**), land-facing rooms with same facilities (**B**), plus cheaper rooms with no balcony, fridge or TV (**C**); breakfast and short orders available from room service; restaurant.

B Cliff, al-Rasheed, Gaza Beach, T2861353, F2820742. Comprises 4 blocks of 3 storeys, all rooms with a/c, cable TV, phone, fridge, attached bath, at cheaper end of B price category. Love Boat restaurant adjacent.

C Adam, al-Rasheed, Gaza Beach, T2823521, F2823519. Rooms a/c with cable TV, attached bath, breakfast included. Restaurant serves reasonable meals at $10-12 a head, or $16 for fish.

C Marna House, al-Ozyez, 1 block east of Omar al-Mokhtar, T2822624, F2823322. Attractive private villa. Rooms have balconies and TV, there are English books to browse in the little library, and a garden. A friendly choice, breakfast included.

C Palestine, al-Rasheed, Gaza Beach, T970-08-2823355, F2860056. Tower-block structure with rooms that are clean and comfortable; all have cable TV, a/c, fridge, some suites in **B** price category; restaurant and large function hall popular for wedding receptions.

D Al-Amal, Omar al-Mokhtar, T/F2861832. Good-value 28-room hotel, most rooms with a/c, TV, attached bath, some cheaper with shared bath, intimate restaurant plus outdoor dining area, very friendly. Recommended.

Eating

Gazan cuisine is typically very spicy (beware the liberal use of chilies). Traditionally, dishes are often cooked in clay-pots in the oven (like a casserole). Seafood was always a staple, but current restrictions on fishing mean that prices have soared for shrimps and fish. All the big hotels have restaurants, where the food is OK, but the dining experience is more about the great views. There are a number of 'upmarket' (by Gaza standard) places to eat down by the beachfront on al-Rasheed St. These include the **Love Boat**, **Al-Andalus** and **La Mirage**, and tend to specialize in fish dishes for around $15-20 per head. **Roots**, Cairo Street, T08-2888666, is the most expensive restaurant in town, but it's worth a visit as the food and atmosphere are especially nice. It's south of the Islamic University; any passerby will be able to give directions. The **French Cultural Centre** has a nice little café, see below

A form of Indian food can be found at **Al-Mankal Chicken Tikka** on al-Mokhtar St, next to Al-Amal Hotel. Very cheap falafel, shwarma and grilled meat and chicken places can be found around Palestine Sq.

Entertainment
Cultural centres

Since the British Council and the Goethe Institute have closed down, the only foreign cultural centre left is the **French Cultural Centre**, on a street between Omar al-Mokhtar and Nasser (see map page 384), T08-2867883, F2828811. Housed in a villa with a garden, the centre is a real blessing for visitors and residents of Gaza City. Not only can you use the computers and library, they have concerts and a cine-club, plus there is gallery space for regular art exhibitions. "La Terrasse" café is a lovely place to have a meal.

Gaza Theatre, T2824870, F2824860.
Qattan Foundation, Palestinian arts charity. Recently opened a centre for arts/drama.
Rashad Al-Shawwa Cultural Centre, T08-2864599, F2868965, hosts occasional exhibitions and events.

Shopping

Fras Market, selling fruit and vegetables, is just northwest of the Municipality building. Al-Shajaia clothes market is southeast of Palestine Square. Traditional Palestinian garments and decorative pieces can be bought at the **UNRWA Embroidery Shop** located close to the UNRWA HQ. All profits go to refugee welfare programmes. Palestinian, Hamas and Islamic Jihad-related souvenirs can be found at a small store to the east of al-Jundi Square, where you can find T-shirts, mugs, flags and other souvenirs which no doubt emit a certain kudos.

Transport

Taxis

Al-Nasser, T08-2861844; Azhar, T08-2868858; **Central**, T08-2861744; Cairo Cab, T059-9332240. Or enquire at your hotel about hiring a vehicle (usually with driver).

Palestine Square is the place to pick up a service taxi to most places on the Gaza Strip, including **Khan Yunis** (25 mins) and **Rafah** (45 mins). You can also can find services leaving for locations outside

Gaza City on the south side of the Al-Shifa Hospital, on Ez el-Deer el-Qassam street. For details of getting to the Gaza Strip from Israel see Ins and outs, page 379.

Directory

Banks There are money-changers around the gold market in the Old City, plus various banks on Palestine Square; there are functioning ATMs at some of the local banks. Most banks will cash US$ TCs and some will give advances on Visa cards (with a hefty commission). It's probably best to bring sufficient funds with you. **Hospitals** Al-Shifa, off Ez el-Deer el-Qassam (see map), T08-2865520; Al-Ahli Al-Arabi Hospital, Palestine Sq, T08-2820325. **Embassies and consulates** The European Commission have offices just off Omar al-Mokhtar (see map). **Egypt**, T2824290, F2820718; **India**, T2825423, F2825433; **Jordan**, T2825134, F2825124; **Morocco**, T2824264, F2824104; **Norway**, T2824615, F2821902; **Qatar**, T2825922, F2825932; **Russian Federation**, T2821819, F2821819; **Tunisia**, T2825018, F2825028; **United Kingdom**, 1st Fl, Al-Riyad Tower, Jerusalem St, Al-Rimal South, T+970-08-2837724, http://ukinjerusalem. fco.gov.uk/en/. **Internet** You can find internet (wireless) at many coffee shops and restaurants. **Police** There are police stations on al-Mokhtar south of Palestine Square and on al-Mokhtar north of al-Jundi Square. **Post offices** Main post office is at the **Ministry of Post and Telecommunications**, 'Ministries Complex', al-Mokhtar, opposite Municipal Park. Little mail goes in or out of Gaza these days so it's probably best not to send anything important. **Telephone** International calls can be made from most hotels; cell phones are on the Jawwal network.

UNRWA

The United Nations Relief and Works Agency (UNRWA) was created in December 1949 by UN General Assembly resolution 302 [IV], having evolved through a series of improvised organizations that sought to take active responsibility for Palestinian refugees displaced during the war that marked the creation of the State of Israel. The temporary nature of the UNRWA's mandate is an affirmation that the 'refugee problem' was still perceived as being a transitory one. It was initially given a three-year life-span, but for the past 60 years the UN General Assembly has dutifully gone through the process of extending its mandate on a yearly basis. Despite this, the UNRWA has grown to become by far the UN's largest organization, its 30,000 employees constituting more than the entire work force of all the other UN agencies combined.

The W in the acronym provides an insight into the duties that the UNRWA was expected to perform, the term 'Works' relating to the implementation of economic development schemes centred on labour provision and economic infrastructure.

The reluctance of refugees to accept long-term infrastructural projects led the UNRWA to reassess its targets, and it has chosen to focus its resources on the provision of education (52%) and health care (19%). About two-thirds of its employees are teachers, with the UNRWA's schooling system amongst the most admired education systems in the Arab world. An organisational reform of the UNRWA is being undertaken, begun in 2007, looking into internal processes, management and human resources.

For more information see www.unrwa.org.

Rest of the Gaza Strip

Beyond Gaza City there are a few other attractions in the Gaza Strip. Tell Umm Amer in the village of Al-Nuseirat, about 9 km south of Gaza City along the beach road, is well worth visiting. Set on a hill overlooking the Mediterranean and covering around 2 acres, the Byzantine remains are being excavated by a French team. The ruins include a chapel, crypt, bath complex and dining rooms, as well as the main St Hilarion's monastery (named after the saint born here in 291 CE). Tell Umm Amer appears on the Madaba map, where it is referred to as 'Tabatha'. The chief attractions are some beautiful mosaic floors which were uncovered in 2001, depicting flora and fauna. A taxi from Gaza will cost about 50NIS with waiting time.

The site of **Tell el-'Ajjul**, some 6 km southwest of Gaza City, features remains from ancient Egyptian settlements dating from c. 1670 BCE to 1450 BCE, though the earliest settlement here dates from 2100 BCE. Excavations at **Deir el-Balah**, 13 km southwest of Gaza City, have revealed remains from the Late Bronze Age (c. 1550 BCE) to the Byzantine period (324-638 CE), including the largest group of anthropoid coffins thus far discovered in Palestine as well as alabaster vessels and gold jewellery. The site is now largely abandoned, however, and the artefacts are housed in the Israel Museum in Jerusalem. Likewise, the remains of **Ruqeish** on the coast near to Deir al-Balah (18 km southwest of Gaza City) require a lot of imagination, though in fact it was the scene of a flourishing Phoenician settlement in the late Iron Age and Persian period.

The two other major towns in the Gaza Strip are Khan Yunis (population c200,000, with unemployment rates the highest in Gaza at nearly 50%) and **Rafah** (population c150,000). Though neither has a great deal to see, both have lively weekly markets (Khan Yunis on Wednesday; Rafah on Saturday and Sunday). Previously an international border crossing for travellers to/from Egypt, these days Rafah is now most renowned for its network of underground tunnels that link Gaza to the outside world. Since Israel's blockade of Gaza intensified in 2007, with only humanitarian supplies being permitted in, these tunnels have served not only as a means to smuggle in weapons but also other profitable commodities, such as petrol. So wide have some of these tunnels become that cars are now coming through the system whole rather than in pieces. Attempts to block off the tunnels, such as a subterranean metal fence that is being constructed by the Egyptians, do little to deter the smugglers who just dig deeper shafts to circumvent any barriers.

The Jewish settlements in Gaza that were evacuated in 2005 were previously home to around 6000 settlers (occupying some 25%of the land). The largest ex-settlements of **Nezarim**, **Kfar Darom** and the **Gush-Katif** bloc in the south have not seen any urban development since the settlers left, though some of the land is used and occupied by people who farm it.

Refugee camp visits

Contrary to popular belief, UNRWA does not 'run' the refugee camps in the Gaza Strip, but instead takes responsibility for them. With advance notice it may be possible to arrange a guided visit to one of the camps: contact UNRWA at its offices on al-Azhar St (opposite the Islamic University) in Gaza City, T08-6867044. Alternatively it is possible to visit the camps on your own (though it is courteous to inform UNRWA first). The largest camp, Jabaliyah, is conveniently located between the Erez crossing point and Gaza City. To some visitors it merely resembles a regular Indian or Pakistani town, though the contrast with neighbouring towns in Israel puts this image into perspective. Beach camp (Alshati) is a short walk along the beach from the sea end of al-Mokhtar Street in Gaza City. The other camps are in Nuseirat, Bureij, Maghazi, Deir al-Balah, Khan Yunis and Rafah.

Contents

Tel Aviv/Jaffa

The 'White City' is a dynamic metropolis on the Mediterranean Sea, incorporating the ancient port of Jaffa and blending almost imperceptibly into the surrounding towns of the coastal plain. Few foreign visitors to Tel Aviv would describe it as a beautiful city on first sight, with its urban sprawl, muggy atmosphere, and apparent absence of history in a land that is steeped in the past. But its vibrancy will appeal in an instant. Glassy modern skyscrapers rise between boulevards lined with leafy trees, spotless beaches echo with the sound of bat against ball, trend-setting youths and classic old-timers mingle in the thousand cafés, while fine Bauhaus buildings lend the city a class of its own.

Plus Tel Aviv has attitude – bags of it. The city's residents, and indeed visitors from the rest of Israel, adore its pavement cafés, bars and nightclubs, its fashion districts and sandy shores, and revel in the very fact that it is not a city dominated by ancient history. Tel Aviv is seen as a city where money is made, and then spent; if you want religion or history, the sentiment goes, then Jerusalem is just 45 minutes away.

Those who take their time in Tel Aviv will find that there is more to do than just lie on the beach, or relax in restaurants and bars. There is a rich cultural life, with innumerable museums, galleries, theatres and concert halls, and attractive old neighbourhoods in the process of being tastefully restored. Visitors used to just pass through Tel Aviv on their way to or from Israel's international airport nearby, but now it's a destination that attracts travellers in its own right, a dazzling and shiny 'bubble' that has much to offer any visitor to Israel.

Ins and outs

Getting there and away Most visitors arrive in Israel through Ben-Gurion Airport, some 22 km southeast of Tel Aviv at Lod (see box on page 19 for details on getting to/from the airport). The Central Bus Station is located southeast of the city centre, and has good connections throughout Israel. Tel Aviv also forms the central hub of the country's limited train network.

Getting around Although most of Tel Aviv's hotels and hostels are 5-10 minutes walk from the beaches, and most of the key sights are clustered in one or two areas, it is still something of a sprawling city. It is possible to walk to the Central Bus Station or the central railway stations, but not with heavy bags. At some stage it will almost certainly be necessary to take a bus. The main routes of use to tourists are buses 4 and 5. Sheruts run along the same routes, and white metered taxis are everywhere.

The four bus terminals in Tel Aviv are: **Reading Terminal** (north of city, of little relevance to tourists); **Arlozorov Terminal** (can be useful: it's a major hub and is closer to the city centre); **Carmelit Terminal** (near Carmel Market); and the main terminal at the **Central Bus Station** (also the departure and arrival point of most inter-city buses). See 'Transport', page 422 for full details on bus travel.

Tourist information Tel Aviv Tourism Association ⓘ *Promenade, 46 Herbert Samuel (cnr Geula St), T03-5166188. Office Sun-Thu 0930-1730, Fri 0930-1300*. Copies of *Hello Israel*, *Time Out*, the *'City Pass'* booklet (good for discounts at museums/restaurants), maps of Tel Aviv/ Jaffa are available. Four free walking tours to different parts of the city per week check website, www.visit-telaviv.com.

Tel Aviv-Jaffa Municipality ⓘ *City Hall, Rabin Square, T1599-588888/03-5218438, www.tel-aviv.gov.il. Sun-Thu 0900-1400.*

Background

The origins of the modern city Tel Aviv's modern history is probably best appreciated whilst admiring the panoramic view from the top of the Azrieli tower. It is only then, as the skyscrapers and suburbs stretch before you, that you realize how rapid the development has been: 100 years ago, you would still have seen the predominantly Arab city of Jaffa to the south, but the area that Tel Aviv stood upon was little more than sand dunes and isolated Palestinian villages.

In 1909, a group of 66 Jewish families selected this spot to build a new Jewish settlement, having decided to leave the overcrowded confines of Jaffa. Thus, work on the construction of Tel Aviv began, financed by the Jewish National Fund, but ironically using predominantly Arab labour. Early Jewish neighbourhoods such as Neve Tzedek and Neve Shalom had been established just outside Jaffa since the end of the 19th century, but it was the gathering of the 66 families on the sand dunes of Jibalis Vineyard that heralded the foundation of modern Tel Aviv.

The early growth of Tel Aviv By the 1920s the population of Tel Aviv stood at some 35,000, thanks largely to the third Aliya (1919-1923) and the arrival of Jews attempting to avoid the increasingly violent Jewish-Arab conflict in nearby Jaffa. Some of these bloody confrontations had their origins in events seemingly unrelated to the Jewish-Arab conflict (the battles of 1 May 1921, for example, actually had their origins in clashes between Jewish communists parading on May Day in support of a Soviet Palestine, and Jewish

Ancient city – modern name

Though the history of the city of Tel Aviv dates only to this century, there is considerable evidence of previous periods of occupation on this site. The history of nearby Jaffa can be traced back to the 15th century BCE, whilst a variety of sites now largely buried under Tel Aviv date from the fifth millennium BCE onwards. Few remains can be seen today, with the best example easily being Tell Qasileh, now within the grounds of the Eretz Israel Museum in Northern Tel Aviv (see page 407).

Tel Aviv derives its name from the title of the Utopian novel by the 'father of political Zionism', Theodor Herzl (1860-1904). The novel, published in 1902 but set in 1923, describes the visit of the two narrators to an imaginary modern Jewish state in Palestine. The title, *Altneuland*, means 'Old-New Land', with Nahum Sokolov's translation into Hebrew bearing the title 'Tel Aviv'. This was also the name of a Babylonian town mentioned in the Bible (*Ezekiel 3:15*).

socialists who opposed them), though as the decade progressed they became more bitter and more violent. The British Mandate authorities were slow to respond, being reluctant to commit their own troops.

With continued Jewish immigration into Palestine, Tel Aviv's population (including Jaffa) stood at around 46,000 in 1931, increasing to 135,000 by 1935. The Arab Revolt of 1936, comprising increased Arab-Jewish fighting as well as strikes and civil disobedience, led to the closing of Jaffa's port and the construction of a new harbour facility at Tel Aviv.

The town continued to grow rapidly, by now far beyond the expectation of the early urban planners. Many fine buildings from this period remain, most notably those in the International Style of Bauhaus, Mies van der Rohe, Le Corbusier and Mendelsohn, though this generally unplanned expansion has today made Tel Aviv a city associated with urban sprawl. By 1947, Tel Aviv's population stood at around 200,000, with a further 30,000 Jews in Jaffa comprising about one-third of the population there. The UN vote on the partition of Palestine in 1947 led to more bitter Arab-Jewish fighting and, just prior to the expiry of the British Mandate, Jaffa fell to the Jewish forces. Almost the entire Arab population of the town fled.

Independence and the 1948/1949 war On 14 May 1948, David Ben-Gurion announced the foundation of the State of Israel from the former home of one of Tel Aviv's founding fathers, Meir Dizengoff. At the conclusion of the subsequent War of Independence, Jaffa was incorporated within the municipality of Tel Aviv. The city was the country's first capital, with the original parliament building standing on what is now the site of the Opera Tower. The subsequent decision to declare Jerusalem as the undisputed and eternal capital of Israel is a move that has not been recognized by most nations, with the majority of foreign embassies still located in Tel Aviv.

Modern town As the city expanded outwards, it all but swallowed up its former outer suburbs. Though the population of Tel Aviv is now given as around 391,000, it should be noted that there are some sizeable satellite towns joined to the outer municipal limits. These include Bat Yam (population 143,000), Holon (population 163,000), Ramat Gan (population 123,000), Petah Tiqva (population 151,000) and Bnei Brak (population 125,000), to name just five. Tel Aviv is happy to allow Jerusalem the title of spiritual, cultural and political capital of Israel, but it remains the business and entertainment centre, as well as the major international gateway.

Tel Aviv: overview

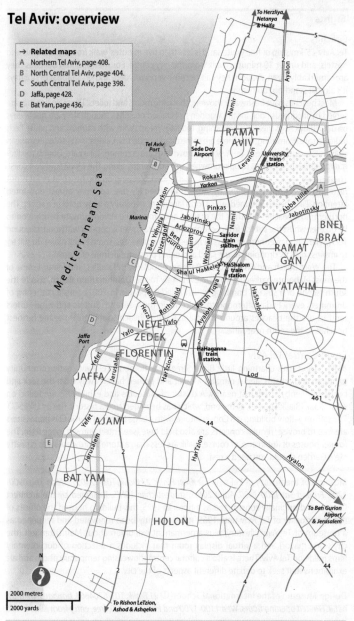

→ **Related maps**

A   Northern Tel Aviv, page 408.
B   North Central Tel Aviv, page 404.
C   South Central Tel Aviv, page 398.
D   Jaffa, page 428.
E   Bat Yam, page 436.

To Herzliya,
Netanya
& Haifa

RAMAT
AVIV

Tel Aviv
Port

Sede Dov
Airport

University
train
station

Rokakh

Yarkon

Mediterranean Sea

Pinkas

ABBA HILLEL

Jabotinsky

Marina

HaYarkon

Jabotinsky

Arlozorov

BNEI
BRAK

Ben Yehuda

Dizengoff

Ben
Gurion

Ibn Gvirol

Weizmann

Namir

Savidor
train
station

RAMAT
GAN

Sha'ul HaMelekh

HaShalom
train
station

GIV'ATAYIM

Allenby

Herzl

Rothschild

Petah Tiqva

Ayalon

HaShalom

Yafo

NEVE
ZEDEK

Yafo

Jaffa
Port

FLORENTIN

HaTiqva

HaHaganna
train
station

Yefet

Jerusalem

JAFFA

Lod

461

AJAMI

Yefet

Jerusalem

HaTiqva

Ayalon

4

BAT YAM

To Ben Gurion
Airport
& Jerusalem

HOLON

44

N

2000 metres
2000 yards

To Rishon LeTzion,
Ashod & Ashqelon

44

Namir

Levanon

5

2

Ayalon

Beaches

Tel Aviv's 5-km strip of fine white sand is less than five minutes' walk from most hotels and hostels, and under 10 minutes' walk from the city centre. For metropolitan beaches they are remarkably clean, though they can become very crowded, and on Shabbat or holidays it's almost standing room only.

Most beaches have freshwater showers, changing rooms and toilets. The main beaches are served by lifeguards (look for the wooden huts raised on stilts), though they are not always on duty. **Black** flags mean **no swimming, red** flags mean **swim with caution,** and **white** flags indicate **safe swimming. NB** There are some deadly undertows along Israel's Mediterranean coastline, including here at Tel Aviv, and **drownings** are common. Take care. During the lifeguards' strike of 1999, 20 people drowned in two months along the Mediterranean coast. **Theft** is also rife: do not leave valuables unattended. Sleeping on the beach at night is **not** recommended. Topless bathing by women is extremely rare and may attract unwanted attention. Each beach is named after a local landmark, generally a large hotel or a street. The northernmost beaches (north of the marina) and around the Hilton's private beach tend to be quieter, whilst the stretch from Gordon to the Opera Tower is popular with tourists, young Tel Avivians, and over-hormonal Israeli males on the make. Yes, some Israeli males do still try to impress girls by dropping to the sand and doing press-ups in front of them!

The **West Beach** and **Charles Clore Park** are popular with families, and feature some of the most elaborate barbecues you are ever likely to see. **Dolphinarium Beach**, also to the south (scene of a suicide bombing which killed 21 people in 2001), sees a gathering of drummers every Friday afternoon to 'welcome in the weekend'. Surfers and wind-surfers tend to use the beaches around the marina, Hilton beach to the north, or the furthest beaches to the south near Jaffa.

South Central Tel Aviv

Bialik Street This charming little Bialik Street was home to Tel Aviv's early community of literati and artistes, and it remains a quiet and refined haven away from the tack and bustle of Allenby Street just nearby. A cluster of museums and exhibitions are found on Kikar Bialik (Bialik Square), at the end, which has been declared a historic site by UNESCO. The saffron yellow building is a Conservatoire, with a large library of music CDs that visitors are free to browse; regular concerts are also held here (see Entertainment, page 418). The former houses of Rubin and, of course, Bialik are less than a stone's throw away, as is pretty Me'ir Garden should you need a rest.

Museum of the history of Tel Aviv ① *Kikar Bialik, 27 Bialik, T03-7240311. Mon-Thu 0900-1700, Fri and Sat 1000-1400. Adult 20NIS, student/child 10NIS.* Designed by the architect Czerner and originally constructed as a hotel in 1925, this building housed the offices of the Municipality of Tel Aviv until 1965. It has recently been renovated and reopened as a museum of Tel Aviv's history, plus a permanent exhibition about Meir Dizengoff (the city's first mayor) and a virtual display room that includes a selection of documentary films made on Tel Aviv. There is also a cultural centre showcasing temporary photo and art exhibitions that seek to debate different aspects of the city.

Design Museum of the International School ① *21 Bialik, T03-6204664, bauhaust@zahav. net.il. Limited opening hours, Wed 1100-1700 and Fri 1000-1400, free, entry from Kikar Bialik.*

Bauhaus: international style in an international city

When Tel Aviv began expanding in the 1920s, it initially developed to an East European design. But with the exodus of Jews from Europe in the 1930s came the functional Bauhaus style from Germany, which was to make an indelible print on the cityscape. Now, somewhat ironically, Tel Aviv has the highest concentration of Bauhaus buildings remaining anywhere in the world. You can recognize the Bauhaus (AKA International) style from the short but wide horizontal windows, the ubiquitous shaded (and often curving) balconies, restrained lines and unornamented façades, and perhaps a long vertical window over the central stairwell.

The Bauhaus buildings of Tel Aviv number over 400 and, despite having been granted UNESCO status in 2003, not all have been restored to their former glory. To see the finest examples stroll the pedestrianized promenade of Rothschild Boulevard, especially beautiful at night when the classic buildings are lit up, looking out for numbers 67-91. Another high density collection encircles Kikar Dizengoff, and don't miss secretive Maze Street or arty Bialik Street.

A good place to get more information on the International Style is the Bauhaus Center on Dizengoff Street, www.bauhaus-center.com, and the tiny Design Museum of the International School on Bialik Street, which shows other aspects of Bauhaus design such as furniture, tableware and lighting. The municipality also gives a free tour of the White City every Saturday at 1100.

Neatly tapping into Bauhaus fever, this new gallery-museum comprises just a single room showcasing the furniture, lighting and other accoutrements of the International Style. It's unique in the city in being the only collection to focus on this aspect of the design, as opposed to the architecture. And it's easy to see how relevant the style has remained: many of the furnishings look so familiar because the 1920s designs are being reproduced in Ikea to this day.

Bialik House ① *22 Bialik, T03-5254530. Mon-Thu 1100-1700, Fri and Sat 1000-1400. Tours booked in advance. Adult 20NIS, student 10NIS. Giftshop*. This beautifully designed and furnished house, built in 1925, was for eight years the home of Israel's national poet, **Chaim Nachman Bialik** (1873-1934). Bialik was not just a great Hebrew poet, he was also an essayist, a noted storyteller, a writer of children's stories, a translator into Hebrew of noted works such as Don Quixote and Wilhelm Tell, a researcher into the field of Jewish folklore, as well as being a religious scholar who worked on an important compilation of rabbinic law.

Following his death in 1934, his wife bequeathed the house and its contents to the City. The renovated house has wonderful tiled floors, beautiful colour schemes and is a very pleasant place to while away an hour or so.

Rubin House ① *14 Bialik, T03-5255961, www.rubinmuseum.org.il. Mon Wed Thu Fri 1000-1500, Tue 1000-2000, Sat 1100-1400. Adult 20NIS, student 10NIS, children free*. Former home of **Reuven Rubin** (1893-1974), one of Israel's most renowned artists, the museum displays selections from the permanent collection of Rubin's work, as well as temporary exhibits featuring early Israeli paintings. It is a gorgeously restored building dating from 1930, and the artist's studio remains as he left it, on the third floor.

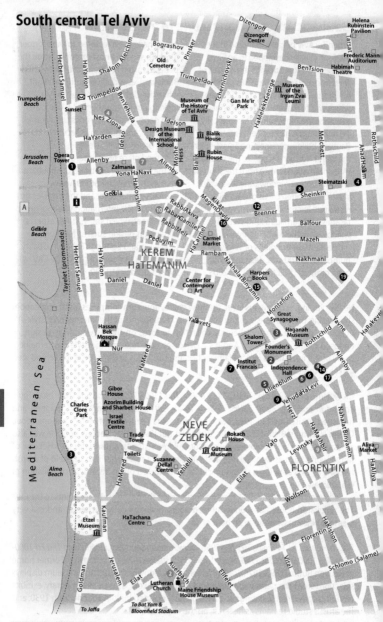

South central Tel Aviv

Dizengoff
Dizengoff Centre

Helena Rubinstein Pavilion

Tarsat

Frederic Mann Auditorium

Habimah Theatre

Bograshov

Pinsker

BenTsion

Old Cemetery

Shalom Aleichm

HaYarkon

HerbertSamuel

Trumpeldor

Trumpeldor

Tchernichovski

HaMelekhGeorge

Museum of the Irgun Zvai Leumi

Gan Me'ir Park

Trumpeldor Beach

Sunset

Trumpeldor

Nes Ziona

Benyehuda

Idelson

Museum of the History of Tel Aviv

Meicheit

Rothschild

HaYarden

Design Museum of the International School

Bialik House

Rubin House

AhadHa'am

Jerusalem Beach

Opera Tower

Allenby

Zalmania

Yona HaNavi

Moshe Hess

Bialik

Steimatzski

Sheinkin

Kikar MagenDavid

Brenner

Balfour

Mazeh

Nakhmani

Ge'ula

Hakovshim

RabbiAkiva

RabanGamliel

RabbiMeir

Peduyim

KEREM HaTEMANIM

HaCarmel

Rambam

NakhalatBinyamin

Carmel Market

Ge'ula Beach

Tayelet (promenade)

HerbertSamuel

HaYarkon

Daniel

Daniel

Center for Contemporary Art

Yavets

Harpers Books

Montefiore

Great Synagogue

Yavne

HaRekevet

Mediterranean Sea

Hassan Bek Mosque

Nur

Shalom Tower

Haganah Museum

Founder's Monument

Institut Francais

Independence Hall

Rothschild

Gibor House

Azorim Building and Sharbet House

Israel Textile Centre

Lilienblum

YehudaHaLevi

Herzl

NahalatBinyamin

Alma Beach

Charles Clore Park

Trade Tower

Toilets

Suzanne Dellal Centre

Yehieli

NEVE ZEDEK

Rokach House

Gutman Museum

Yafo

Levinsky

Aliya Market

FLORENTIN

HaAliya

Etzel Museum

Kaufman

HaTachana Centre

Eilat

Wolfson

HaKishon

Florentin

Viral

Schlomo (Salame)

Jerusalem

Eilat

Auerbach

Elifelet

Lutheran Church

Maine Friendship House Museum

To Jaffa

To Bat Yam & Bloomfield Stadium

A

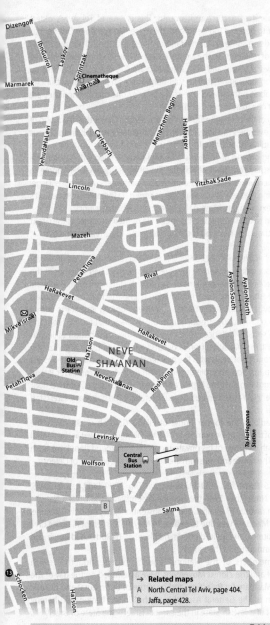

200 metres

200 yards

Sleeping

2 Beit Immanuel Messianic
Congregation & Guesthouse
3 David Inter-
Continental
10 Eden TLV
4 Gilgal
5 Hayarkon 48
7 Mugraby
9 Sub Kuch Milega

Eating

13 24 Rupee
16 Agadir
15 Birnbaum
9 Buddha Burgers
19 Café Noir
4 Café Tamer
17 City Cafeteria
1 Gojo
3 Manta Ray
7 Nana Bar
6 North Abraxas
8 Orna & Ella's
2 Shmaya
12 Sus Etz
14 Turk Lahmacun

Bars

2 9 Rothschild
6 Abraxas
3 Betty Ford
4 Lima Lima
1 Joey's Bar
5 Mish Mish

→ **Related maps**
A North Central Tel Aviv, page 404.
B Jaffa, page 428.

Kerem HaTemanim (Yemenite Quarter) and around This is one of Tel Aviv's oldest districts – and it shows. Yet to become too gentrified, the maze-like Yemenite Quarter has some fine old buildings housing some excellent traditional restaurants and unpretentious bars, with a bohemian mix of residents. To the west, the district borders the Carmel Market, the most exciting of Tel Aviv's 'souqs' and an authentic place full of locals snapping up bargains (see also 'Shopping' on page 419). The stall-holders are an entertaining bunch - listen out for cries of 'bal habeit hish tagaia!' (the stall holder's gone mad!) when they are selling the fruit and veg off cheap at the end of the day.

On the northeast margin of the Yemenite Quarter is Kikar Magen David, the major hub of six converging streets that resembles the Star ('magen') of David. Here you will find a curious smattering of society, including hobos, would-be messiahs and hipsters on their way to Sheinkin Street, the hunting ground of Tel Aviv's 'beautiful people', lined with fashionable shops and cafés. The pedestrianized street of **Nahalat Binyamin** is equally lively, home to pavement cafés, street entertainers, craft-stalls and general sightseers. At No 8 is Degel House, a beautiful old building that serves as a reminder of Kerem HaTemanim at its peak. It's a good idea to allow some extra time to browse this area and maybe have lunch.

Just off Nahalat Binyamin to the southeast is the imposing domed structure of the **Great Synagogue**, built in 1926, though it has a bit too much concrete to be really attractive.

Haganah Museum ① *23 Rothschild, T03-5608624. Sun-Thu 0800-1600, adult 15NIS, student/child 10NIS.* Take your passport, and be prepared for stringent bag searches at the entrance. This museum traces the development of the Jewish Defence Force, Haganah, that later evolved into the Israeli army (IDF). Information is imparted via audios, visuals and displays rather than by collections of artefacts. On three floors, a visit starts with a 20-minute film that is a recommended introduction to the displays that follow. From the establishment of the early settlers' defence movements and the contribution of Jewish Brigades during World War I, the transition from a defensive to an offensive organization was made by 1936. The second floor deals with the procurement of arms during the 1930s and 1940s, clandestine immigration, the role of the Jewish Brigade in World War II, and the resumption of the struggle against the British at the war's conclusion. The third floor finishes with the Independence War and an audio-visual detailing the battle at Castel (staff will need to activate this for you).

The museum building adjoins the former home of **Eliahu Golomb** (1893-1945), the unofficial defence minister of the yet-to-be born State of Israel. His house served as the Central Headquarters of the Haganah, and two of his private rooms on the ground floor have been left as they were in his day. The house and museum are now run by the Ministry of Defence.

Independence Hall ① *16 Rothschild, T03-5173942. Sun-Thu 0900-1400, adult 20NIS, student/child 16NIS.* On 29 November 1947 the General Assembly of the United Nations voted by a margin of 33 in favour, 13 against, and 10 abstentions, to partition Palestine. On the day that the British Mandate was due to expire, 14 May 1948, members of the Civil Administration, People's Council, and invited guests, met here at 16 Rothschild Boulevard to hear David Ben-Gurion announce to the world:

'Accordingly we, the members of the National Council, representing the Jewish people in the Land of Israel and the Zionist Movement, have assembled on the day of the termination of the British Mandate for Palestine, and by virtue of our natural and historic right and of the resolution of the General Assembly of the United Nations, do hereby proclaim the establishment of a Jewish State in the Land of Israel – the State of Israel'.

Tel Aviv attitude

No guidebook to Israel would be complete without that old cliché, "Haifa works, Jerusalem prays, Tel Aviv plays". Comparisons with New York, including references to the 'Big Orange', are stretching reality a little, but visitors and residents alike are certainly spoilt for choice in terms of entertainment and action. In addition to the pavement cafés and bars, restaurants, cinemas, pubs and nightclubs, plus the beaches, Tel Aviv is also home to the 'higher' cultures of theatre, art and orchestra. Apparently there are more museums per capita than anywhere else in the world.

But it is not just the presence of such entertainment facilities that appeals to many who live here: it's also 'Tel Aviv attitude'. Tel Aviv is seen as the symbol of the new Jewish state and, though many of the early Zionist pioneers spoke of a return to Zion and Jerusalem, there was also the desire to begin anew. Too much history was attached to Jerusalem; too much tragedy in the memory of the Jewish people. Places such as Tel Aviv offered the opportunity of a fresh start and a new vision. Israel's national poet Chaim Nachman Bialik (1873-1934), who revived the literary use of Hebrew, preferred Tel Aviv to Jerusalem because "our hands have built it from its foundations to the roof. This after all is the purpose of our national renaissance: to cease being indebted to others, to be our own masters, in body and spirit".

So whilst Tel Avivians enthuse about the city's nightlife, its beaches where you can wear and do what you like, and talk of this 'secular city' that is so different from 'boring' and 'constraining' Jerusalem, you should look beyond these symbols of a materialistic culture. They are not symbols of moral decline or frivolity: they represent confidence and, above all, normality.

The flip-side of this focus on 'normality' is the oft-levied accusation that Tel Aviv exists as a self-centred "bubble", a place where the reality of the political situation is hidden and, on the whole, forgotten. As a tourist, this can certainly be the case. Which is why many find that time in Tel Aviv acts as a refreshing counter-weight to the oppressive remorse and frustration that can start to absorb people after a spell in Jerusalem.

The 'Independence Hall' where this historic announcement took place has been preserved as it was on that day. The rest of the building serves as a small museum detailing a pro-Zionist view of history.

The shell of the building that houses Independence Hall is one of Tel Aviv's original structures, formerly occupied by **Meir Dizengoff**, the city's first mayor, and some artefacts from his home are also on display.

Neve Tzedek Tel Aviv's oldest residential district, Neve Tzedek, was established in 1887 by Jewish families moving out of the congested Jaffa neighbourhood. Many fine old buildings remain (eg 11 Lilienblum) and, following substantial renovation work, Neve Tzedek has become a much sought-after address. It's difficult not to be charmed by the relaxed 'Mediterranean' ambience and narrow streets of quaint buildings. Shalom Shabazi Street has sleek wine-bars, designer clothes shops and balconies dripping with bougainvillea; after dark Lilienblum Street becomes a truly cool place for a night out.

In the southern part of the quarter is the **Suzanne Dellal Centre** ① *5 Yehielli, T03-5105656, see page 419.* The restored hall is now a centre for dance and drama, and the plaza is used for open-air performances (check listings magazines or pick up their leaflet for the current programme). With its dwarf trees, benches and coffee shop, the plaza is a pleasant place to hang out. The restaurant is popular with 'theatrical' types and serves excellent food (the stuffed vegetables are recommended).

Nearby, housed in an historic building that has been artfully renovated and extended, is the **Gutman Museum** ⓘ *21 Shimon Rokach, T03-5161970, www.gutmanmuseum.co,il. Sun-Wed 1000-1600, Thu 1000-2000, Fri 1000-1400, Sat 1000-1500. Adult 24NIS, student/ child 12NIS.* Nahum Gutman (1898-1980) painted Tel Aviv-Yafo as the city developed and is considered one of the fathers of classic Israeli art. His naïve and nostalgic works are beautiful, bold and approachable. Gutman's paintings and sketches are shown alongside works by modern artists, which change every three months or so. A tempting shop has books, prints, etc for sale.

On the same street is the **Rokach House** ⓘ *36 Rokach, T03-5168042, Sun-Thu 1000-1600, Fri, Sat and hols 1000-1400. Adults 10NIS, students/children 5NIS (by donation).* Shimon Rokach was a driving force behind the creation of Neve Tzedek and a leader of the community. This building was one of the first 10 houses built in 1887, and was restored in 1983 by Rokach's granddaughter Lea, an artist. Her sculptures and paintings are woven in amongst the antiques on display in the courtyard and on two floors. There's a little back garden, and the house is worth a stop whilst wandering around the pretty streets.

Standing at the north end of one of Tel Aviv's original roads, Herzl Street, the Shalom Tower occupies the former site of Israel's first secular Hebrew language grammar school, Gymnasia Herzlia. Built in 1959, the Shalom Tower at one time claimed to be the tallest building in the Middle East – though now, at 142 m, it is rather pathetic compared to the 828m Burj Khalifa in Dubai. It functions mainly as an office block, although in the lobby of the western tower look for the vibrant mosaics of Tel Aviv-Jaffo created by Nahum Gutman, 1966 and David Sharir, 1994.

Hassan Bek Mosque Formerly the centrepiece to Jaffa's long-since disappeared Manshieh Quarter, the mosque found fame during the 1948 war when its tall, slender minaret was used as a vantage point by snipers. Neglected for so long, the mosque has now been elegantly restored, though it appears rather incongruous set against the five-star tower-block hotels nearby.

Etzel Museum ⓘ *Charles Clore Park, T03-5172044. Sun-Thu 0830-1600. Adult 15NIS, student/child 10NIS. Take a passport or other official ID.* Devoted to the role of the Irgun, the Etzel Museum is located in an attractively reconstructed building in the area that was once Manshieh. The exhibits here deal primarily with the 1948 battle for control of Jaffa when 32 Arabs lost their lives.

American Colony A small cluster of streets southwest of Florentin, the American Colony is being transformed from a derelict no-man's-land to a prime living location. There are a couple of fine old buildings here and an interesting history. In 1866, 157 Messianic Christians sailed from the state of Maine and arrived in Jaffa. Like many other Christian groups of the time, they believed in the Second Coming and that they should be in Israel to witness it. The Americans purchased this patch of land and began to farm, but the agricultural methods couldn't have been less similar to those used in watery Maine. Their venture failed, and within two years they were forced to head home – leaving the land to be purchased by the Messianic Templars in their place. The Germans lasted at bit longer in the Holy Land (until they became Nazi-sympathizers and the British dispelled them), hence the eye-catching **Lutheran Church** ⓘ *15 Beer Hofman, T03-6829841, www.immanuelchurch-jaffa.com, Tue-Fri 1000-1400*, was built in 1904 and the area became known as the German Quarter. The church now hosts concerts/exhibitions (see website for listings) as well as services, and has unusual stained-glass windows made by a Norwegian artist in the 1970s. Next door, is the wooden **Maine Friendship House** ⓘ *10 Auerbach, T03-6819225, www.jaffacolony.com, Fri 1200-1500, Sat 1400-1600*, now a small museum and heritage centre founded by Jean and Dr Reed Holmes, or call and they will open up. The original house (along with many others) was brought in its entirety on the ship from America to be erected here. Across the street is Beit Immanuel, a grand old building which has seen many incarnations, the latest being a hostel run by a Messianic denomination (and a recommended budget place to stay, see Sleeping page 411). Exotic gardens used to surround the Beit Immanuel, remnants of which can be seen today. Buses 40, 44 and 46 stop at the corner of Auerbach and Eilat.

North Central Tel Aviv

Kikar Dizengoff Dizengoff Square is the centrepiece of the street that's described by Stephen Brook in his book *Winner Takes All: A Season in Israel* as "the street in Israel the haredim would disapprove of most". To many Tel Avivians, the square symbolizes both the secular and fun-loving nature of their city, though unless you visit on a Friday evening as Shabbat gets underway you may be wondering what all the hype is about. At other times the square has more in common with Birmingham's Bullring: a traffic island that happens to have a few shops, restaurants and cafés, with disassociated youth hanging around.

At the centre of the square is the 'unusual' **Agam Fountain Sculpture of Fire and Water**. Created in 1958 by Israeli sculptor Yaacov Agam, the fountain periodically shoots a flame aloft whilst the coloured panels revolve to the sound of music (from classical to The Beatles). The sculpture is a good example of the willingness of Israelis to place daring works of art in public places. On Tuesdays and Fridays, a flea market is held around the square.

The **Kabbalah Centre** ⓘ *14 Ben Ami, T03-2566800, www.kabbalah.com, Sun 0900-2100, Mon-Thu 0900-2200, Fri 0900-1300*, welcomes visitors to browse the books in various languages, and offers a range of kabbalah-related activities.

Bauhaus Center Just along from the square, at 99 Dizengoff Street, this attractive centre has plenty of resources relating to the International Style. It's a good place to browse for excellent coffee-table books, artwork, Israeliana, furniture and gifts. On the upper two levels there is space given over to relevant exhibitions about the city, or about architecture and design, which are invariably interesting. The centre also gives well-regarded two-hour tours of the prominent Bauhaus buildings of the city, every Friday at 1000 (call ahead) or group tours can be arranged. (There are handy toilets upstairs.)

Museum of the Irgun Zvai Leumi ⓘ *1st Floor, 38 Hamelekh George, T03-5287320, www.jabotinsky.org. Sun-Thu 0800-1600, admission free, but take a passport or other official ID*. Housed in the buildings of the Jabotinsky Institute (an Israeli right-wing historical research body) is a small museum presenting the history of the Irgun Tzvai Leumi (National Military Organization). Some see this organization as a freedom movement struggling to end the British Mandate rule, whilst to others it was a vicious terrorist organization that failed to distinguish between the military and civilian non-combatants.

The museum presents the history of the Irgun and its key 'actions'. Perhaps the most notorious of these 'actions' was the attack on the King David Hotel in Jerusalem on 22 July

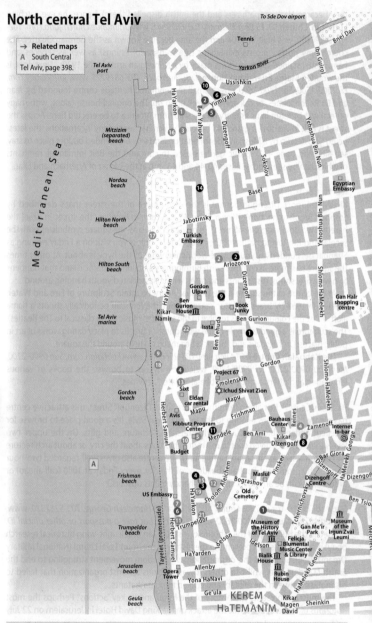

North central Tel Aviv

→ **Related maps**
A   South Central
Tel Aviv, page 398.

To Sde Dov airport

Tennis

Yarkon River

Ussishkin

Tel Aviv
port

10 **6** Yirmiyahu
2 **5**

HaYarkon

Ben Yahuda

Dizengoff

Ibn Gvirol

Bnei Dan

*Mitzizim
(separated)
beach*

Nordau

Sokolov

Yehoshua Bin Nun

*Nordau
beach*

Basel

Egyptian
Embassy

*Hilton North
beach*

Jabotinsky

Turkish
Embassy

2 **2** Arlozorov

Dizengoff

Shlomo HaMelekh

*Hilton South
beach*

Gordon
Ulpan

9

Book
Junky

Gan Hair
shopping
centre

*Tel Aviv
marina*

Kikar
Namir

Ben
Gurion House

Ben Gurion

22 Issta

Ben Yehuda

1

*Gordon
beach*

9
18

4
13
Sixt
Eldan
car rental
Mapu

Project 67
Smolenskin
Ichud Shivat Zion

Gordon

Shlomo HaMelekh

Mediterranean Sea

Herbert Samuel

Avis

Kibbutz Program
Center

5
Budget

10

Frishman

Mendele

Ben Ami

Bauhaus
Center

Reines

Zamenoff

8
8

Kikar
Dizengoff

Bar Giora

Dizengoff

Internet
In-bar
@

HaMelekh George

Dizengoff

*Frishman
beach*

US Embassy

4
16
3
19

7
6

Trumpeldor

Herbert Samuel

HaYarkon

Sholom Aleichem

12

23

Maslul

Bograshov

Pinsker

Tchernichovsky

Dizengoff
Centre

Ben Tsion

A

Tayelet (promenade)

*Trumpeldor
beach*

Old
Cemetery

1

Museum of
the History
of Tel Aviv

Gan Me'ir
Park

HaMelekh George

Melchett

Museum
of the
Irgun Zvai
Leumi

*Jerusalem
beach*

Opera
Tower

HaYarden

Yona HaNavi

Allenby

Idelson

Bialik
House

Felicja
Blumental
Music Center
& Library

Rubin
House

HaMelekh George

*Geula
beach*

Ge'ula

KEREM
HaTEMANIM

Kikar
Magen
David

Sheinkin

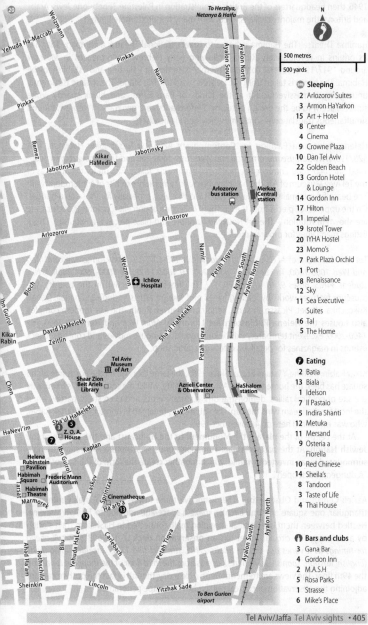

To Herzliya, Netanya & Haifa

N

500 metres

500 yards

Sleeping

2 Arlozorov Suites
3 Armon HaYarkon
15 Art + Hotel
8 Center
4 Cinema
9 Crowne Plaza
10 Dan Tel Aviv
22 Golden Beach
13 Gordon Hotel
   & Lounge
14 Gordon Inn
17 Hilton
21 Imperial
19 Isrotel Tower
20 IYHA Hostel
23 Momo's
7 Park Plaza Orchid
1 Port
18 Renaissance
12 Sky
11 Sea Executive
   Suites
16 Tal
5 The Home

Eating

2 Batia
13 Biala
1 Idelson
7 Il Pastaio
5 Indira Shanti
12 Metuka
11 Mersand
9 Osteria a
   Fiorella
10 Red Chinese
14 Sheila's
8 Tandoori
3 Taste of Life
4 Thai House

Bars and clubs

3 Gana Bar
4 Gordon Inn
2 M.A.S.H
5 Rosa Parks
1 Strasse
6 Mike's Place

Map labels: Weizmann, Yehuda Ha-Maccabi, Pinkas, Namir, Ayalon South, Ayalon North, Remez, Jabotinsky, Kikar HaMedina, Arlozorov, Arlozorov bus station, Merkaz (Central) station, Namir, Petah Tiqva, Ichilov Hospital, Weizmann, Bloch, Ibn Gvirol, David HaMelekh, Zeitlin, Sha'ul HaMelekh, Kikar Rabin, Chen, Tel Aviv Museum of Art, Shaar Zion Beit Ariels Library, Azrieli Center & Observatory, HaShalom station, HaNevi'im, Kaplan, Z.O.A. House, Helena Rubinstein Pavilion, Habimah Square, Frederic Mann Auditorium, Habimah Theatre, Tarsat, Marmorek, Ahad Ha-am, Bilu, Rothschild, Yehuda Halevi, Laskov, Sprintzak, Cinematheque, Ha'arb'a, Carlebach, Petah Tiqva, Sheinkin, Lincoln, Yitzhak Sade, Ayalon South, Ayalon North

To Ben Gurion airport

1946, then headquarters of the British administration in Palestine. Ninety-one Jews, Arabs and Britons (the majority civilians) died, with many hundreds more injured.

Habima Theatre The Habima is home to Israel's National Theatre, a company that has its origins in revolutionary Russia. Following early Hebrew performances in Moscow around 1917/1918, several company members settled in Palestine and established the Habima. The name is taken from the Hebrew word for 'The Stage'. The theatre is currently undergoing a massive facelift at the hands of Ram Karmi, and blank sparkly white surfaces seem to be the design outcome. Performances are generally in Hebrew, though simultaneous translation is sometimes provided via headsets.

Helena Rubinstein Pavilion for Contemporary Art ① *6 Tarsat, Kikar Habimah, T03-5287196, www.tamuseum.com. Mon and Wed 1000-1600, Tue and Thu 1000-2200, Fri 1000-1400, Sat 1000-1600. Entrance free, books/posters for sale. Toilets.* Run under the auspices of the Tel Aviv Museum of Art, this hall plays home to temporary exhibits of contemporary art. The beautiful minimalistic displays make it worth a visit, especially for those on a budget. On the upper level, pieces from the Gertners' collection of porcelain, paintings, Judaica, etc are shown in rotation – the Art Nouveau furniture and glass pieces are exquisite. Check listings magazines for programme.

Tel Aviv Museum of Art ① *27 Sha'ul Hamelekh, T03-6077020, www.tamuseum.com. Mon and Wed 1000-1600, Tue and Thu 1000-2200, Fri 1000-1400, Sat 1000-1600. Adult 42NIS, student 34NIS. Buses 9, 18, 28, 32, 70, 111.* The finest art collection in the country, the museum features works by leading Israeli and foreign artists, including: Chagall, Degas, Kokoschka, Monet, Picasso, Pissarro, Renoir and Reuven Rubin. The airy modern complex also houses the **Helena Rubinstein Art Library** ① *Mon, Wed and Thu 1000-1600, Tue 1400-2000,* excellent temporary exhibitions, regular art-house movies and concerts (check listings in magazines for details), a café and a good shop.

Kikar Rabin/Malkhe Y'Isra'el Plaza Since 1965, the large City Hall on the north side of the square has been the home to the Tel Aviv Municipality, whilst the square itself is frequently the site of political rallies, demonstrations, cultural events, and even street parties when the local football team wins the cup. The square was renamed in honour of **Yitzhak Rabin**, who was murdered here on 4 November 1995.

At the centre of the plaza is the **Monument to the Holocaust and the Rebirth of the Jewish Nation**. At the base of Yigael Tumarkin's unusual sculpture is a yellow triangle surmounted by an inverted pyramid, which together create the form of the Star of David: "A dungeon burst open".

Azrieli Centre and Observatory The distinctive three towers of the Azrieli Centre, one triangular, one square and one circular, make a space-age addition to Tel Aviv's skyline. Nestled between them is a popular shopping mall, connected to HaShalom train station by a walkway. The circular tower has an **observation deck** ① *T03-6081990, call ahead for timings as it varies day-to-day, adults 22NIS, student/child 17NIS, includes audio guide (English, Russian, Spanish, 20 minutes), access from the third floor of the shopping centre,* on the 49th floor. The views are tremendous on a clear day, though in fact the posh restaurant adjoining the observation deck steals all the best seascape panoramas.

Ben-Gurion House ⓘ *17 Ben-Gurion, T03-5221010. Sun, Tue, Wed and Thu 0800-1500, Mon 0800-1700, Fri 0800-1300. Free. Toilets.* This simple town house is maintained more or less as it was when Israel's first Prime Minister David Ben-Gurion, and his wife Paula, lived here. There are original artworks, plenty of quotes from the "Old Man" and many gifts from the Jewish Diaspora, but most impressive is the library of some 20,000 volumes that takes up almost the entire upstairs floor.

Old Cemetery ⓘ *Trumpeldor, Sun-Thu 0930-1430, Fri 0930-1200.* Sometimes referred to as the 'First Cemetery', this Jewish burial ground was established in 1903, and is the final resting place of a number of leading Zionists and Tel Aviv residents, as well as a large number of Jews killed in the 1921 and 1929 riots. Those buried here include Chaim Arlosorov, Max Nordau, Meir Dizengoff, and the poets Chaim Nahman Bialik and Sha'ul Tchernikowsky. Stones scattered across a tomb indicate a recent visit by a relative, a longer-lasting equivalent to the Christian tradition of leaving flowers at a grave.

Northern Tel Aviv

The suburbs of Northern Tel Aviv are divided from the rest of the city by the River Yarqon. In ancient times the river formed a natural boundary between the tribes of Ephraim to the north and Dan to the south. The river also marks a topographical boundary between the Sharon Plain, which runs north of Tel Aviv, and the Shefela Plain, which runs south. The northern suburbs are home to some of Tel Aviv's (and Israel's) leading museums, as well as **Tel Aviv University** (T03-6408111).

Eretz Israel Museum ⓘ *2 Haim Levanon, Ramat Aviv, T03-6415244, www.eretzmuseum. org.il. Sun-Wed 1000-1600, Thu 1000-2000 (NB Ethnography and Folklore Pavillion closes at 1600), Fri and Sat 1000-1400. Adults 40NIS, students 28NIS, children 26NIS. Allow around 3 hrs. Buses 24, 27, 45, 74, 86.* Comprising a number of pavilions and galleries constructed around an ancient archaeological site, the theme of the Eretz Israel Museum is, as the name suggests, "in the land of Israel". Books, hand-woven rugs, ceramics, jewellery, glass, Judaica, and other souvenirs are available at the shop, and there is a decent café. There is always a mix of temporary exhibitions in the galleries, and every year the museum hosts the **World Press Photo exhibition** (see www.worldpressphoto.org for dates).

Central to the museum are the excavations of Tell Qasileh, an overgrown mound with good (and incongruous) views of the skyscrapers and construction of the modern city. At least 12 levels of occupation have been identified here, the oldest dating back to the 12th century BCE. These include brick buildings at Level XII, and dwellings and copper-smelting furnaces that are a century younger at level X. Both are attributed to the Philistines, who also constructed three large temples - each at a different level of occupancy. These are significant in that they provide an insight into Philistine temple architecture through different ages.

Evidence from Level IX-VIII dates to the 10th century BCE and suggests that, following David's conquest of the region, a port was constructed on this site. In fact, some scholars go so far as to suggest that the Lebanese cedars that were used by Solomon to construct the Temple arrived through the port here, and not further down the coast at Jaffa. Four centuries later the process was repeated for the construction of the Second Temple (see *II Chronicles 2:16; Ezra 3:7*).

Other stratum levels indicate occupation in Hellenistic, Roman, Byzantine, Crusader and Islamic times, though it was during the latter occupation that the development of Jaffa led to the decline, and eventual abandonment, of the port at Tell Qasileh. Findings from the tel are displayed in the appropriate pavilions.

Close to the tel, the **Museum Ethnography and Folklore** comprises mainly Jewish religious art, ceremonial objects and clothing. It's an exquisite collection of Judaica (but bear in mind it closes at 1600 on Thursdays). Also nearby, and worth a quick look, is a reconstructed **oil press** and a **flour mill**. Using a 360-degree screen and special effects, the **Planetarium** will offer a "Journey to Space and the Solar System" when renovations are completed in 2010 (extra fee). The **Rothschild Centre** explores the work of the Baron and his family through interactive displays and films, while the Man and his Work Centre contains folk crafts and agricultural tools/techniques. Outside, mosaic fans should be sure not to miss the exquisite sixth-century floors from Beit Guvrin, made up of a fabulous mix of geometry and pastoral life, nor the bird mosaic (in the Yael Garden) with exotic peacocks.

Tracing 3000 years of history, the **Glass Pavilion** houses a superb collection of glassware, said to be amongst the most valuable in the world. Vivid core-formed Persian perfume bottles dating from the sixth century BCE, and pristine glass tableware unearthed from burial tombs of the third century CE, are among numerous highlights. A large collection of ancient coinage, tracing the history and development of currencies of the whole region, is found in the **Kadman Numismatic Pavilion**. The **Ceramics Pavilion** could more correctly be termed a pottery pavilion; here, methods of pottery-making are explained, and items from ancient Israel, Africa, South America and Europe are displayed.

Northern Tel Aviv

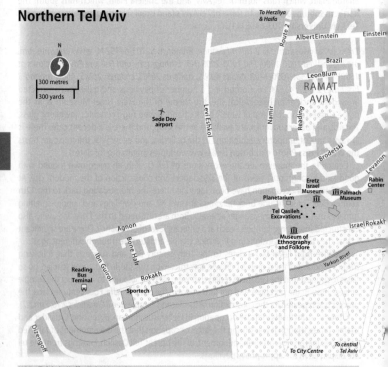

The **Nechushtan Pavilion** concentrates mainly on finds from the Timna Valley copper mines, including colourful jewellery, but look out for the Roman cast-lead coffin from the third century CE decorated with friezes of satyrs and lions. The **Postal and Philatelic Pavilion** traces the history of post and communications back 2,500 years, focussing on Israel's postal system, the centrepiece being a shiny red Ford van with the traditional deer logo.

Palmach Museum ① *10 Haim Levanon, T03-6436393, www.palmach.org.il. Sun, Mon and Wed 0900-1700, Tue 0900-2000, Thu 0900-1400, Fri 0900-1300. Adult 30NIS, student/child 20NIS. Pre-booking is essential, as tours are by group only and individuals need to be assigned into a group. Tours last 90 mins, in Hebrew with English, Spanish, French and Russian translation through headphones. Dairy café.* This museum, next door to the Eretz Israel Museum, explains the history and legacy of the Palmach ('strike force') who were the fighting force of the Haganah. It is an 'experimental' museum, which means there are no information boards but instead 3-D films and special effects, and a 'personal story' to bring events to life. After World War II ended, the Palmach turned their focus to an armed struggle against the British Mandate, and orchestrated such acts as the breakout of 208 Jewish prisoners from Atlit immigration camp in 1945, and the June 1946 'Night of the Bridges', when 10 of the 11 bridges connecting Palestine to its neighbours were blown up. Of the Palmach, 1168 lost their lives fighting the British in the 1940s, and many of its commanders went on to form

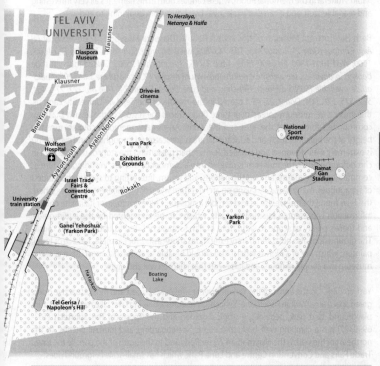

the backbone of the IDF. There is also a Memorial Room, archives, photo gallery and film library (some translated into English) that visitors are welcome to view.

The Israeli Museum at the Yitzhak Rabin Centre ① *14 Haim Levanon, www.rabincenter. org.il. Sun, Mon and Thu 0900–1700, Tue 0900–1900, Fri 0900–1400, Wed and Sat closed. Adults 50NIS, student/child 25NIS, add 10/5NIS for guided tours (phone to book). A visit takes at least 1½ hrs. Audio-guide provided (Arabic, English or Hebrew).* Opened in January 2010, the Rabin Centre uses state-of-the-art museum technology to tell the story of Yitzhak Rabin's life and the story of the State of Israel and Israeli society. Exhibit halls make loops off a main downward-spiralling corridor and a sensory-activated audio-guide is supplemented by a wealth of interesting visual information, including old film footage. Starting with the Haganah's resistance to the British Mandate and Rabin's own military career, there are interesting sections on the difficulties facing new immigrants in the early pioneering years, and later problems between the internal Jewish populations. Displays discuss the State policy regarding settlements, the Lebanon War, the First Intifada, the massacre in Hebron, and the peace treaty with Jordan (amongst many other topics), in a neutral/factual way. As he is oft-quoted, "It is with one's enemies that one makes peace," but when Rabin implemented moves toward Palestinian self-government, images of him wearing a khafiyah were burnt by Israeli right-wingers and ultimately he paid the final price in 1995. A visit ends with footage of Rabin's funeral in the Memorial Room, where candles burn in his name. It's all very interesting and readable stuff, and it can easily take over two hours from beginning to end.

Beth Hatefutsoth, Museum of the Jewish People (Diaspora Museum) ① *University of Tel Aviv Campus (Gate 2), Ramat Aviv, T03-7457808, www.bh.org.il. Sun, Mon, Tue and Thu 1000-1600, Wed 1000-1800, Fri 0900-1300. Adult 35NIS, student/child 25NIS. Guided tours must be booked in advance, see website. English audiovisual display ("Chronosphere") at 1200. Audio-guide available (50NIS deposit). Gift-shop and café. Buses: Egged 74, 74A, 86, 272, 274, 464, 572, 575, 578, 604; Dan 7, 25, 45.* Located in the middle of the Tel Aviv University campus, this impressive museum spread over three floors traces the history of the Jewish Diaspora communities throughout the ages and the world. An elegant 'memorial column' runs the height of the building, study and educational areas are scattered throughout, and everything is extremely well-designed and labelled. Rather than presenting the story of the Diaspora in chronological order, the museum is divided into a number of themes, including the family, community, faith, culture, among the nations, and return. Interesting to see are the models of synagogues, many naturally taking on architectural styles of the different countries where the Jews found themselves, so as to resemble a mosque, Chinese temple or Italianate church. Information is presented in small snippets, which can be augmented by the audio-guide, and there's plenty of scope to sit in front of film footage or listen to traditional folk music. The ground floor also hosts temporary exhibitions showcasing, for example, Judaica or Israeli painters, which are of a high standard. You should be able to appreciate most aspects of the museum in a couple of hours, and it is a visit that children will also enjoy.

Yarkon Park On the banks of the Yarkon River lies Tel Aviv's largest and most attractive open, green space area. Yarkon Park (Ganei Yehoshua') features a boating lake, bike rental, adventure playground, bird park, pedaloes, a tropical garden and the Sportech. The **Sportech** (T03-6990307) has a climbing wall, basketball courts, skateboarding, and football pitches. To the northeast of the park is the **Maymadian Water Park**, and to the north of the park lie the **Israel Trade Fairs and Convention Centre and Luna Park**, which has small-scale fairground rides.

Ramat Gan

Ramat Gan Safari Park ① *T03-6305326/7/8, www.safari.co.il. Times vary seasonally, call to check; summer Sun-Thu 0900-1700, Fri 0900-1400, Sat 0900-1500. Adult 55NIS, student 48NIS.* A selection of African and other wildlife can be seen in this 100-hectare safari park. Some of the inhabitants came here in 1981, when Tel Aviv Zoo. It's the largest collection of animals in the Middle East (numbering around 1,600), with successful breeding programmes of elephants and primates. Closed vehicles only are permitted to drive through, though tours on a 'safaribus' are organized for those without wheels (for an extra charge).

◉ Tel Aviv listings

For Sleeping and Eating price codes and other relevant information, see Essentials pages 26-31.

● Sleeping

Tel Aviv has a large number of hotels, with new ones opening all the time. Whilst most in the top range categories are very fine indeed, there is a distinct lack of good-value places in the mid-price range.

Most of Tel Aviv's budget accommodation is found around the south end of Ben Yehuda and HaYarkon, and can be reached by buses 4 and 5 from the Central Bus Station. Others are 'party places' where a good night's sleep can be hard to find. Most charge around 75NIS per night for a dorm bed, with discounts for longer stays, and private rooms in the **A-C** categories. Breakfast is included, unless otherwise stated. NB Sleeping on the beach is not advised.

South Central Tel Aviv *p396, map p398*
LL David InterContinental, 12 Kaufman, T7951111, www.intercontinental.com/telaviv. Suitably grand foyer with seriously expensive shops. Standard rooms ($320) are plush though no balcony. Various levels of suite cost several hundred dollars a night. Choice of restaurants, pool, health club/spa and conference rooms. Very courteous staff. Good location near the beach and Neve Tzedek's charming streets. Certainly worth considering if you can afford it.
LL Montefiore, 36 Montefiore, T03-5646100, www.hotelmontefiore.co.il. New boutique hotel within a gorgeously restored 1920s

house. There are only 12 rooms and you'll need to book ahead, elegant black and white furnishings, the odd dash of colour in the form of an artfully placed book or cushion. Every detail has been considered and it feels truly luxurious. Prices go up Thu/Fri nights. The painfully stylish restaurant-bar is renowned in its own right, serving brasserie dishes with a Vietnamese twist, open 24 hours. There's also a sunny terrace at the front, but don't even think about going unless you are wearing black and sun-glasses.
L Gilgal, 7 Nes Ziona, T03-5111000, www.hotelgilgal.com. Pleasing hotel with 50 new rooms, blandly but comfortably furnished with picture windows, spacious bathrooms, TV, tea/coffee facilities and Wi-Fi; large library. Excellent roof area with indoor and outdoor decking to sit and admire the views. Sociable atmosphere, peace/love/God are embraced by the management but it doesn't mean you have to. Good restaurant. Short walk to beach. At the lower end of the **L** range.
A Eden TLV Guest House, 27 Kehilat Eden, Yemenite Quarter, T052-7469842, www.edenhousetlv.com. Choice of rooms or apartments. Not fancy but very homely and comfortable, and unique location near Carmel market. Hosts make every endeavour to help you get the best out of Tel Aviv. Reasonable prices.
A-D Beit Immanuel Messianic Congregation & Guesthouse, 8 Auerbach, off Eilat, T03-6821459, www.beitimmanuel.org. Beautiful building (once lived in by Peter Ustinov's grandfather) located in the quaint 'American Colony', an area currently being

redeveloped close to Jaffa and Neve Tzedek. Old-fashioned but light, airy and spacious private rooms with en suite (double 310NIS, single 210NIS), or 10-bed dorms (100NIS), are cleaned daily; no TV, some with balconies. Roof-top terrace with great views, Well run. Good breakfasts are served in the shady garden in summer; coffee shop in the foyer. Checkout 1000, curfew 2300 (not a partying venue). Book ahead. Recommended.

A-E Hayarkon 48, 48 HaYarkon, T03-5168989, www.hayarkon48.com. Probably the best hostel in Tel Aviv, and certainly the most popular. Well run. Large, clean, uncrowded dorms (4-8 beds, 78NIS), some with balcony, some with fans, some with a/c. A selection of light and breezy private rooms (double 375/330NIS with/out en suite, extra person 78NIS), some with semi-private balconies. Plenty of clean and roomy showers (actually space to hang clothes!) with constant hot water. Large, clean kitchen (free tea/coffee, toast in mornings); TV room/bar with pool table; large roof area (in summer) with great views; laundry, lockers, free cell-phone rental, 24-hr service. Buses 4, 16, 30, 31 from bus station to Opera Tower. Friendly and recommended.

B-E Sub Kuch Milega, 22 Hamashbir, Florentin, T077-7771234. A couple of cheap a/c doubles with en suite and balconies; two cheaper ones with fan and shared bathrooms; one a/c dorm with 10 beds - messy and old-school (70NIS). Friendly place with murals on walls and mellow atmosphere. The obvious India vibe means chai, thali and lots more Indian treats (veggie/vegan) are available in the inviting restaurant/bar areas (open pretty much 24/7). There's also a rooftop bar where movies are screened in summer. Decent breakfast; use of the kitchen.

C-E Sky, 34 Ben Yehuda, T03-6200044, www.sky1hostel.com. Single-sex 6-bed dorms (72NIS), plus private rooms (some en suite). Overall a bit grungy. Booking necessary at weekends; popular with Israelis. Use of fridge/microwave; paltry breakfast of coffee/cake. Internet 12NIS per hr.

North Central Tel Aviv *p403, map p404*

LL Crowne Plaza, 145 HaYarkon, T03-5201111, www.h-i.co.il. Variety of rooms and suites are quite grand with modern furnishings and en suites, and scary small glass balconies. Choice of restaurants; new spa, but pool disappointing (half covered).

LL Dan Tel Aviv, 99 HaYarkon, T03-5202552, www.danhotels.com. Long-established classy hotel with reputation for good service. 84 of the 280 rooms are sea-facing (more expensive), 43 luxury suites are much more expensive. Choice of restaurants, health club, lovely indoor heated pool and outdoor seawater pool. Recommended.

LL Hilton, Independence Park, T03-5202222, www.hilton.com. One of Israel's priciest hotels, with standards of service to match. Popular with business travellers. Rooms not especially hip but excellent facilities as you would expect and nice balconies. Excellent King Solomon restaurant; sushi; and lobby bar. Nice pool overlooking sea with lots of loungers. Some say it's the best hotel in the city.

LL Isrotel Tower, 78 HaYarkon, T03-5113636, www.isrotel.co.il. Attractive and luxurious suites suitable for families, or 2-person 'executive' suites, all with sitting rooms, kitchenettes, 2 TVs; supplement for sea views, costly price hike in high season. Bars, business lounges, conference facilities, attractive rooftop pool. Not a bad choice if you can afford it.

LL Renaissance, 121 HaYarkon, T03-5215555, www.renaissancetelaviv.com. Unmemorable rooms (standard double $285) but all have balconies and sea views. Heated indoor pool that is pleasantly quiet; direct access to beach, small gym, sauna, sun deck (though it's visible from the road). Restaurant serves good food. Bit cheaper than the other sea-front options,

LL Park Plaza Orchid, 79 HaYarkon, T03-5197111, www.orchidplaza.co.il. Strange-looking tower in heart of sea-front area, with refurbished studios and suites with kitchenettes; standard rooms cheaper. Free

Wi-Fi and bicycles, LCD-TV; excellent fitness centre, spa and outdoor pool.

LL Gordon Hotel & Lounge, 2 Gordon, T03-5206100, www.gordontlv.com. This brand new 12-room boutique hotel brings Bauhaus to life. Spacious rooms are stylish down to the last detail, and entirely white (save for the black floor), with glass-walled bathrooms (you can see the sea from the shower). 10 rooms have balconies, though some enjoy more of a sea view than others, and come in various shapes and sizes. Downstairs is a Mediterranean bistro. Rooftop soon to be a lounge-bar at night (sun deck by day). Recommended.

LL Sea Executive Suites, 76 Herbert Samuel, T03-7953434, www.sea-hotel.co.il. Extremely stylish 1- ($241) or 2-room ($340) suites, with tasteful kitchen and sofa areas, tones of grey, silent carpets, huge mirrors, jet showers. All have partial/full sea views. The hip foyer sets the tone. Gym, sauna, free internet. Minimum of 3 nights for first reservations.

L Art + Hotel, 35 Ben Yehuda, T03-7971700, www.atlas.co.il. Opened Apr 2009, this bright and breezy hotel with 62 unfussy rooms is very central. It's also a showcase for Israeli art, with video installations in the foyer, huge murals in the corridors and a separate gallery space. Lovely sun deck on the roof and all the amenities necessary. The lobby with its colourful decor, retro-modern furniture and veritable library of books sets the tone for the rest of the experience. Not over-priced at $155 per couple. Free Wi-Fi. Recommended.

L Cinema, 1 Zamenhoff (crn of Kikar Dizengoff), T03-5207100 (reservations T03-5425555) www.atlas.co.il. This was a functioning cinema hall until 1991, as the polished brass, b&w pictures and collection of film cameras testify. Pricier than others in the Atlas chain - chiefly for the memorabilia and time-warp feel – but rooms are fairly small and some even a tad gloomy. Request one with a balcony facing the square. Free Wi-Fi; sauna/jacuzzi open till late.

L Center, 2 Zamenhoff, T03-5266100

(reservations 03-5425555), www.atlas.co.il. Central, remodelled smallish hotel with retro white/bright styling, peppered with murals by Israeli graphic artists. Some rooms have balconies (a couple of which have out-sized mannequins hanging off them); good mid-range facilities; staff very pleasant. Free use of bicycles for 2 hrs. Breakfast is served in the Cinema Hotel (opposite) on a lovely upstairs terrace. Book online for cheaper rate.

L Port Hotel, 4 Yirmiyahu/288 HaYarkon, T03-5445544, www.porthoteltelaviv.com. This little hotel is great value for Tel Aviv ($154 per couple B&B), with a contented mix of international guests. The cool contemporary furnishings of the foyer extend into the rooms, which aren't huge but have very comfortable beds with white linen sheets, sharp black furniture, fridge/flat-screen, b&w tiled shower rooms. No balconies but lovely rooftop terrace (with Astroturf!). A stone's throw from beach and port area. Free bicycles and Wi-Fi. Recommended.

L Tal, 287 HaYarkon, T03-5425500 (reservations 03-5425555), www.atlas.co.il. Part of Atlas chain located near the port area and its nightlife. Pleasant and unassuming, cheerfully decorated in contemporary style, with decent-sized bathrooms and limited sea views from some rooms, but no balconies. Fridge, safe, LCD TVs, coffee/tea facilities.

AL Armon HaYarkon, 268 HaYarkon, T03-6055271, info@armon-hotel.co.il. Rooms ($110 double) have a/c, fridge, TV, pale veneer furniture, but are a little box-like, with lumpy pillows; some face on to noisy road. Ceramic bathrooms newly fitted, however, and it's friendly and small-scale, with free Wi-Fi and use of lobby pc. Not directly on beach, but convenient for a night out in the port area.

AL Golden Beach, 56 Herbert Samuel, T03-5162727, www.goldenbeach.co.il. Not bad value (double 400NIS, plus 50NIS for sea view), facing the beach. Rooms have good-sized balconies (especially corner rooms, and those on 1st floor have sun loungers), fridge, kettle, decent beds, neutral furnishings. Jaffa views and great sunsets. Downsides include busy main road below, slight fusty smell in some rooms, and hand-held shower over tub. Comfy cushioned foyer, rooftop terrace, free internet/Wi-Fi, breakfast included.

AL Imperial, 66 HaYarkon, T03-5177002, www.imperialhotel.co.il. Rooms a little box-like, some with balconies but no real views. Recently remodelled, with nice shower-rooms, but nothing special. Reasonable value by Tel Aviv standards, and close to the beach.

A Arlozorov Suites, 23 Arlozorov, T03-5221064, www.arlozorov-hotel.co.il. Adequate "suites" with kitchenette, but no balcony. Good value at $98 a double. Central location not far from beach.

A The Home, 106 HaYarkon, corner of 6 Frishman, T03-5200800, www.thehome.co.il. Simple studio apartments complete with kitchenette; warmly decorated; mostly sea-facing, some with balcony; TV, free internet, cleaned daily (various configurations 350-480NIS per couple; prices go up slightly high season). Discount monthly rates. It's a decent choice. Advance booking recommended.

A-C IYHA Hostel and Guest House, 36 Bnei Dan, T02-5945655, www.iyha.co.il. Usual clean and orderly a/c dorms (135NIS), plus private rooms (doubles 341NIS); internet facilities, decent kosher breakfast. A little remote on the northern edge of the city, but next to a pleasant park and the port area (buses 5, 24, 25).

A-D Gordon Inn, 17 Gordon, T03-5238239, www.hostelstelaviv.com. This hostel-cum-hotel has reasonable-value private rooms ($20 cheaper with shared bathroom, discounts possible for walk-ins), which are clean with bright white paint, sheets and towels, TV and fridge; single-sex dorms (90NIS) smell fresh but are a bit cramped (as are the shared showers/toilets). Coffee shop with pool table and tiny terrace is a pleasant social space. Lap-top for rent.

A-E Mugraby, 30 Allenby, T03-5102443, www.mugraby-hostel.com. Friendly and more homely than most hostels. Female-only or mixed dorms (76NIS or 490NIS per week) are a little crowded; private rooms with en suite (doubles 290NIS, only 30NIS cheaper with shared bath) have a/c and TV; also 3- and 4-bed rooms. Continental breakfast isn't bad. Internet café (13NIS an hr) and free Wi-Fi.

C-E Momo's, 28 Ben Yehuda, T03-5287471, www.momohostel.com. You'll either love or hate this warren of a place: visitors flee after one night or stay forever. Single-sex and mixed dorms (75NIS) are bog-standard but not too cramped; private rooms (180-240NIS, some with en suite, most with TV) are simple and uninspired; not the cleanest showers/toilets, no curfew and little sleep. Breakfast is tea/cake. A great place to meet people, with a lively bar. Internet 8NIS for 30 mins.

🍴 Eating

Tel Aviv has Israel's best and most diverse selection of restaurants, and a number of distinct 'dining areas'. Little Tel Aviv, at the north end of Dizengoff, has a number of long-established places, while the nearby re-developed Port Area (Hebrew: Namal; www.namal.co.il) is one of the best options for quality dining. Florentine, and to a lesser extent Neve Tzedek, have some smaller cuter eateries, whilst Jaffa has a number of recommended (and not so recommended) restaurants. Unsurprisingly, the Yemenite Quarter (Keren Hataymanim) is home to a number of Yemeni Jewish places, whilst the sea-front promenade is aimed primarily at tourists (foreign and Israeli alike). And, of course, Tel Aviv is famous for its 'café society': sprinkled all over the city are tempting cafés which also serve light meals. Note that most Tel Aviv restaurants are not kosher. There aren't many places aimed primarily at vegetarians, but there's always plenty of options (apart from in speciality meat restaurants). For budget travellers, many of the hostels have kitchens that guests can use for free.

Carmel Market is the cheapest place for fruit and veg, and there are numerous falafel and shwarma places towards the south end of Ben Yehuda, and also around Kikar Dizengoff and on Allenby.

South Central Tel Aviv *p396, map p398*

🍴🍴🍴 **Manta Ray**, Alma Beach, T03-5174773. Upmarket but relaxing beachfront location. Go at sunset. Fabulous seafood and fish dishes. Pricey but highly recommended. Reservations a good idea. Daily 0900-2400.

🍴🍴🍴 **Messa**, 19 Ha'arba'a, Hatichon Tower, T03-6856859, www.messa.co.il. Gourmet dining in a white-on-white room, long tables and over-sized furniture, it all can feel quite intimidating but is worth it to really splash out. The equally monochrome black bar is perfect for aperitifs and has live music on Sun and Wed. Dress up.

🍴🍴🍴-🍴🍴 **Baba Yaga**, 12 HaYarkon, T03-5175179/5167305, www.babayaga.co.il. Somewhere for a special evening out, where fine European cuisine might be accompanied by French Chanson singing. Huge wine goblets on black tablecloths and a sophisticated interior, plus there is a cute garden where you can catch the breeze. The high quality menu is Russian-French, with kreplach (pasta stuffed with beef/onion), classic soups, stroganoff, fois gras, tiger shrimps, and moules (recommended), limited choice for vegetarian. Reserve in advance for Shabbat. Open daily from 1300.

🍴🍴🍴-🍴🍴 **Nana Bar**, 1 Ahad Ha'am, Neve Tzedek, T03-5161915. Hard to know which is better, the bar or the restaurant . The food is excellent, and the cosy bistro with its plant-filled open-air patio is nothing short of romantic (definitely reserve a table). It becomes a lively little bar later on. Daily 1200-0100.

🍴🍴🍴-🍴🍴 **North Abraxas**, 40 Lilienblum, T054-6786560. Simply named after the bar next door, this is one of the hippest new places in town, with a ground-level bar that's got a laid-back feel, and a glamorous upstairs crammed with beautiful people. The food is inventive, by highly regarded restaurateur Eyal Shani, including shrimp pitta and other fish dishes.

🍴🍴-🍴🍴 **Orna & Ellas**, 22 Sheinkin, T03-6204753. Enduringly popular for the quality of its food; one of their signature dishes is yam pancakes – for good reason. Pleasingly simple white and wood decor; big windows look out on to hip Sheinkin Street; lovely terrace at rear; bistro feel. Recommended. Sun-Fri 1000-2400, Sat 1100-2400.

🍴🍴 **Agadir**, 2 Nakhalat Binyamin, T03-5104442. Terrific hamburger place (and veggie burgers), with a swathe of toppings and sides to choose from; also happy hour.

🍴🍴 **Gojo**, Kikar HaKnesset (crn Allenby and Herbert Samuel), T074-7030944. Ethiopian restaurant-bar with "tej" to drink and lots of spicy meat "wats" on the menu (vegetarian: 4-dishes for 59NIS). Follow a bamboo corridor into a bamboo den of mellow music – except Thu-Sat when live singers take to the floor from 2100 and the place doesn't close till at least 0300. Daily from 1100.

🍴🍴-🍴 **24 Rupee**, 1st Floor, 14-16 Shoken, T03-6818066. Like a slice of backpackers' Sinai rather than India, customers relax on cushions and rag rugs amidst walls decked with photos. All-veg thalis are eaten off low tables and, though sadly it's considerably more than 24 rupees (35NIS, in fact), it's extremely fresh and tasty. Lassis or alcohol served. Follow the smell from the motorbike shops downstairs as there's no sign. (Another branch in Kafar Sava). Sat-Thu 1200-2400, Fri 1200-1700. Summer-night dining on the rooftop.

🍴🍴-🍴 **Buddha Burgers**, 21 Yehuda HaLevi, T03-5101222, www.buddhaburgers.co.il. A vegan's delight: download the menu and get very excited. As well as 8 types of burger (medium/double 23/30NIS), there are burritos/tortillas (27/20NIS), rice bowls with toppings (try Seitan), loads of healthy smoothies, and more. Take-away or pavement seating shielded by plants; indoor space is wood and pop-art pix. Very reasonably priced. Sun-Thu 1100-2400, Fri 1100-1700, Sat 1900-

2400. Smaller branch on 86 Ibn Givrol (closed Sat, and 1 hr earlier in week).

♥-♥ City Cafeterria, 44 Yehuda HaLevi, T03-5602266. NY-style retro tiled walls and floors, angle-poise lamps over little tables; coffee is slightly cheaper and more generous than the chains.

♥-♥ Sus Etz, 20 Sheinkin, T03-5287955. Packed pavement tables perfect for watching the parade go by; light meals and salads; cakes are good. Fun on Shabbat.

♥-♥ Tamar, 57 Sheinkin, T03-6852376. Long-standing classic (since 1941): reliable, unpretentious and reasonably priced, with arty clientele.

♥-♥ Turk Lahmacun, 77 Nakhalat Binyamin, T03-5667394. Racks of kebabs, huge rolls of laffa, stuffed peppers, various shwarmas, and fantastic lahmacun (like a pizza piled with minced meat, pron: Lahmajoon) in this Turkish fast-food joint. Watch them with the spices if you don't like it hot. Metal seating out on the pavement; small interior is more salubrious; or take-away (includes mini-cartons for helpings of pickles). Vegetarians will feel left out. Menu in Hebrew, but you can see what's on offer at the counter.

♥ Birnbaum, Nakhalat Binyamin, T03-560066. Since 1969 the friendly sisters have been delighting Birenbaum vegetarians. The small à la carte menu includes bagels, soups and salads, but come for the open buffet: 40 different types of hot/cold dishes including salads, soups, pies, rice and bean stews (45NIS). Sun-Fri 0700-1545 (or until the food runs out – which happens, so make sure you get there in good time).

♥ Shmaya, 2 Vital, Florentin, T03-6829217. Primrose-coloured walls daubed with murals, mixed clientele and their dogs make this a welcoming place to sample Jewish home-cooking. Excellent spicy fish "ktsitsa" (kofta), 1 daily veggie option, meat and lamb ktsitsa also recommended; dishes come with rice and a selection of veg/beans (29NIS). Sun-Fri 1200-2130, but come early to get full choice of dishes – items are crossed off the hand-written menu as they run out.

North Central Tel Aviv *p403, map p404*

♥♥♥-♥♥ Il Pastaio, 27 Ibn Gvirol (crn Rozenbaum), T03-5251166, www.ilpastaio.co.il. Italian-run by a 'wonderful host' who has lived here for 40 years. Great pasta 48-60NIS, meat dishes 75-135NIS. Highly recommended. Mon-Fri 1200-1530 and 1900-2300, Sun 1200-1530.

♥♥♥-♥♥ Sheila, 183 Ben Yehuda, T03-5221224. Trendy, with a resto-bar ambiance that's cool but unpretentious. Sun-Thu 1900-2400, Fri and Sat 1300-2400.

♥♥♥-♥♥ Tandoori, 2 Zamenhof, Kikar Dizengoff, T03-6296185. One of Israel's best for North Indian cuisine; mains 40-50NIS for authentic veg dishes or around 70NIS for meat. Daily 1200-1530 and 1900-2330.

♥♥♥-♥♥ Thai House, 8 Bograshov, junction Ben Yehuda, T03-5178568. Rather lovely and relaxing, with bamboo and beach restaurant feel rather than the austere Thai style common in fancy restaurants. Authentic Thai food, a few tofu options and great for anyone craving pork; mains 60-70NIS, pad thai 50NIS, soups 70NIS, large business lunch available Sun-Thu 1200-1700 (49-72NIS). Daily 1200-2300; reservations necessary on Shabbat.

♥♥ Biala, 14 Ha'arba'a, T03-6240996. For breakfast, healthy shakes and mini-sandwiches; for lunch choose from a plethora of veggie burgers (35-45NIS), salads (root veg is good) and sandwiches (try 5-cheese with salad/tahina); dinner could be a big bowl of noodles or curry. All organic/wholewheat/free-range. Atmosphere is bustling and decor fresh and functional. No English menu but someone will be happy to translate. Daily 1200-2300.

♥♥ Idelson, 110 Dizengoff. Recommended for enormous breakfasts (50NIS), croques madames, salads, excellent pastries and coffee in an unfussy atmosphere. Also branches at 252 Ben Yehuda, 57 Weizman and 2 Malkhay Israel (owned by a chain-smoking lady who went into business at the age of 70 and struck a winning formula).

♥♥ Indira Shanti, 4 Sha'ul HaMelekh, T03-6954437. Small, unfussy, popular, North

Indian and some Chinese dishes 40-60NIS. Lunchtime deals. Daily till 2330.

♥♥ Osteria da Fiorella, 148 Ben Yehuda, T03-5248818. Attractive setting for pleasant family-run place that's not changed much over the years. Hearty Italian fare that is truly authentic.

♥♥ Red Chinese, 326 Dizengoff, T03-5466347. Good-quality Chinese in an unpretentious cosy place that's been around for 30 years. Excellent soups; 65-95NIS main courses, and all encompassing set meals for 85-105NIS. Some Thai dishes. Daily 1230-2400.

♥♥-♥ Batia, junction of 197 Dizengoff and Arlozorov. Family-run place with little concession to modernity. Proper old-school with a photo menu and little bar at the side. Traditional Ashkenazi Jewish food. Open for Shabbat lunch also.

♥♥-♥ Mersand, 70 Ben Yehuda (corner Frishman), T03-5234318. One of Tel Aviv's "originals", this coffee house has existed for over 50 years, and not a morning has passed without the old ladies gathering to re-tell their stories of pioneering days. In recent times, Mersand has grown in its appeal to artists/literati as well, attracted by the genuine retro look and ambiance. Most famed for superb-quality coffee and homemade cakes (some baked by local ladies); also alcohol and light meals. East European in design, and East European prices – a fair few shekels cheaper than most. Daily 0745-2400.

♥ A Taste of Life, 35 Ben Yehuda, T03-5168906, www.tasteoflifeisrael.com. Highly recommended for its vegan burgers (25-27NIS), casseroles, vegetarian steaks and schwarma, tofu dishes and salads. Ingredients are mostly organic, and super healthy. A must for veggies/vegans. Run by the Israelite community of Dimona. Eat-in or take-away. Also run cookery classes. Sun-Thu 0900-2100, Fri 0900-1500 (-1400 winter).

♥ Hummus Askhara, 45 Yirmeyahu. One of Tel Aviv very best hummus joints, no English sign, look for the red lit-up letters on a white background. Open 24 hrs a day, apart from Shabbat (closes at 1500 on Fri to reopen at 1900 on Sat).

♥ Metuka, Carlibach, T1700-702232. Very busy, informal unstylish kosher eatery. Toasts/sandwiches put together in delicious combinations, plus coffee and cakes; cheaper than others; serves alcohol. Take-away. Sun-Fri 0730-2300.

⚙ Bars and clubs

Naturally, Tel Aviv is a great place for bar hopping, and there are mellow, classy, tacky or cutting-edge choices sprinkled all over the city. Florentin is a good place to start, as it has something for everyone. For cheap and sleazy drinking, the north end of Allenby Street is your best bet.

The redeveloped Port Area (Namal) has some lively bars and clubs, which are pretty expensive, but with a fair mix of foreigners and locals. The cooler, harder nightclubs are found out in the industrial part of town. Some of the best club nights in Tel Aviv are gay nights. Stop by the tourist office, which keeps a list of current top venues, and pick up a copy of *Time Out* magazine, which is good for up-to-date hot-spots. **The Block**, 35 David Hachmi, in a warehouse in the industrial area, has the best sound system in the Middle East (if not the world); come here for techno, hip-hop and alternative parties. Another good choice for a club night is **Penguin**, 43 Yehuda HaLevi, which is bit more underground. Also, **Barzilai**, 13 HaRachav, T052-3763935, has different parties for each night of the week ('1984' is their straight-friendly gay night). And **HaOman 17**, 88 Abarbanel, T03-6813636, is a blast Thu-Sat: it's immense and hosts international DJs; 'FFF' is their excellent gay night (also the biggest club in Jerusalem). For a more Indi vibe, head to the hip **Levontin 7**, 7 Levontin, T03-5605084, which also has live performances and is deservedly popular.

South Central Tel Aviv *p396, map p398*
9 Rothschild, 9 Rothschild, T03-5103331. Well-appointed restaurant-café-bar. A bit fussy inside, but the outdoor terrace is a good place to sun yourself, the food is decent, there's a

pleasant atmosphere, and at night it comes into its own as a bar that stays open till 0400.

Abraxas, 40 Lilienblum, T03-5104435. Jammed and laid back, with live DJs. Good for meeting (good-looking) people. Pool table on second floor. Recommended.

Betty Ford, 48 Nakhalat Binyamin, T03-5100650. Long-stayer on the scene, yet keeps its cool mix of people. Classic unfussy décor. Opens at 1900.

Evita, 31 Yavne, T03-5669559. Classic gay night; regular nights include drag and Eurovision Sunday (talented people mime to fun tunes - it sounds dodgy, but it's jolly good). Evita is the starting point for anything else. Put simply: "the best gay bar in Tel Aviv".

Lima Lima, 42 Lilienblum, T03-5600924. Dance bar with 2 areas, and chilling space outside; good DJs. Busy, and a bit tacky, but fun. Free admission; 'ladies' get a free margarita and 'guys' get first beer for 10NIS. Keeps you going all through the night.

Mish Mish, 17 Lilienblum, T03-5168178. Secretive looking place, a bit more exclusive than some: nice with friends. Lots of 'famous' cocktails, good music. Happy hour Sun-Wed 1930-2130 (50% off).

Taxidermy, 18 HaRakevet. You have to love a place called 'Taxidermy', and as the name hints, stuffed animal heads adorn the walls and the decor is wonderfully macabre. Beer is cheap; nibbles available. Recommended.

Tel Aviv Brew House, 11 Rothschild, T03-5168666. Features working micro-brewery at its centre; food is schnitzel, sausage, burgers and the like (good-value business lunch 1200-1800, 38-48NIS). Daily 1230 till the early hours. Mon is Blues night 2100-2330, Fri jazz and 50s/60s 1430-1700. It's not hip but it's reliale and cheery.

North Central Tel Aviv *p403, map p404*

Gana Bar, Gan Ha'ir, 71 Ibn Gvirol, T03-5290507. Might be worth checking out this new-ish place on top of the shopping mall: pretty stylish but hadn't come into its own at the time of writing.

Gordon Inn, 17 Gordon, T03-5238239. Small

and welcoming, with lots of tourists of course; pool table, cheap deals and happy hours.

Joey's Bar, 42 Allenby, T03-5179277. Slice of Americana, popular with tourists, ex-pats and locals, all drinking as much as they can.

M*A*S*H, 275 Dizengoff, T03-6051007. Long-established (1982) bar, with giant screen showing sport and films. Has resisted passing trends and is a haven for English speakers. Pub-grub (all-day breakfast); happy hour; free interent. Daily 1000-0500.

Mike's Place, 88 Herbert Samuel, T0540-8192089, www.mikesplacebars.com. The place to come for proper tacky pub atmosphere. Friendly, and perfect for watching football. Tex-Mex and pub-grub; free buffet on Fri; breakfast (full English with bacon 42IS). Pool tournament every Mon at 2100; happy hour daily 1500-2000, Sat 1100-2000: ½ litre beer 12NIS or two cocktails for price of one.

Rosa Parks, 265 Dizengoff, T054-6439958. Super trendy bar. A place to spot Israeli celebs (though you might not know who they are).

Strasse, 32 Pinsker. Friendly unpretentious pub-style place; happy hour 1600-2000. No English sign (look for the pool table in window).

🎭 Entertainment

Art galleries

Centre for Contemporary Art, 5 Kalisher, T03-5106111, www.cca.org.il. On the edge of HaCarmel Market, this shed-style space promotes up-and-coming artists from contemporary disciplines, be it video art, photography or performance art, plus experimental film screenings and lectures. Exhibitions change every 2 months. Mon-Thu 1400-1900, Fri and Sat 1000-1400. Entrance 10NIS.

Cinemas

Cinematheque, 2 Sprintzak, T03-6917181. Arthouse and world cinema in a rather monstrous red and white building. 50% discount with the City Pass.

Dizengoff, Dizengoff Centre, T03-6200485.

Globus Max, Azrieli Centre, T03-6081130.
Lev, Dizengoff Centre, T03-6212222/*5155.
Rav Chen, Kikar Dizengoff, T03-5282288/*2202.
Rav Chen, Opera Tower, 1 Allenby, T03-5102674/*2202.

Theatres, dance and concert halls

Cameri, 30 Leonardo da Vinci, T03-6060960.
Dance and theatre, often with English subtitles.
**Felicja Blumental Music Centre and
Library**, 26 Bialik, T03-5250499, www.fbmc.
co.il. Small but lovely concert hall which
hosts frequent recitals (almost nightly), often
chamber music. See website for details.
Hasimta, 8 Simtat Mazal Dagim, Old Jaffa,
T03-6812126. Fringe theatre in an intimate
and atmospheric venue .
Mann Auditorium, 1 Huberman, T1-700-
703030/03-6211777, www.ipo.co.il. A
3000-seater concert hall, home to the famed
Israeli Philharmonic Orchestra, founded in
1936. Check listings magazines/website for
details or pick up programme for the whole
season from the Auditorium; tickets 175-
420NIS, students get 50% discount (balcony
seats); go to box office an hour before
performance starts). Box office Sat-Thu
0900-1900, Fri 0900-1300. Buses 5 and 26.
Mayumana, 15 Louis Pasteur, Jaffa,
T03-6811787, www.mayumana.com.
International troupe of performers: dance/
song; high energy show.
Nalaga'at Centre, Retsif Haaliya Hashniya,
Jaffa Port, T03-6330808, www.nalagaat.org.il.
The first of its kind in the world, this unique
cultural centre has performances (Sun, Tue
and Thu) by a deaf-blind acting ensemble
Also see Eating, page 434, about Blackout
restaurant.
National Yiddish Theatre, c/o ZOA
House, 1 Daniel Friesch, T1-800-444660.
Performances in Hebrew or Yiddish, without
English subtitles.
Noga, Noga Sq, 7 Jerusalem, Jaffa, T03-
6816427. AKA Gesher. Contemporary
material, often performed in Russian.
Suzanne Dellal Centre, 5 Yeheli, Neve
Zedek, T03-5105656. See page 401.

The Opera House, Tel Aviv Performing Arts
Centre, 27 Shaul HaMelekh, T03-6927777.
Home of the Israeli opera.
Tmuna Theatre, 8 Shonzino, T03-
5611211/5629462. High-quality dance and
theatrical performances.
Tsavta, 30 Ibn Gvirol, T03-6950156.
A place to hear Israeli folk/pop music.

⊕ Festivals and events

See http://telavivguide.net for details of
festivals and special events.
Feb Jazz Festival, www.jazzfest.co.il.
3-day festival with international and Israeli
musicians, plus free performances in lobby
of the Cinematheque.
Apr (Passover) Tel Aviv Marathon; various
distances up to 21km.
May Documentary Film Festival at the
Cinematheque.
Jun/Jul International Street Theatre
Festival, in Bat Yam, T03-5160259; The Big
Stage, at Suzanne Dellal Centre, 5 Yekheli,
T03-5105656, outdoor dance performances;
The Gay Parade.
Jul-Aug Beach Festivals: various
activities and parties on Tel Aviv's beaches,
T03-5160259.
Aug Hummus Festival, Yarkon Park, with a
Middle Eastern vibe.
Oct Love Parade, by the beach. Plenty of
crazy behaviour.

◯ Shopping

Dizengoff has traditionally been Tel Aviv's
most upmarket shopping street, though
most now agree that it's no longer 'what it
was', with a distinct shift downmarket. This
doesn't mean that generic chain-stores have
taken over, however, and in fact many quirky
little shops have filled in the gaps, and the
northern end is where to find an exclusive
bridal gown. **The Dizengoff Centre** remains
proof that 'hanging out' at the mall is as
popular with the youth of Israel as it is in
the States and, though it now looks shabby

compared to new out-of-town uber-malls, all the main chains are here; on Thu/Fri there is an international food fair. Upmarket shoppers head for the designer shops on **Kikar HaMedina**, while the 'in' place to shop and to be 'seen' whilst shopping is Sheinkin, which is trying a bit too hard but, if it's painfully trendy clothes or an over-priced coffee that you're after, this is the place for you. Up-and-coming Israeli fashion designers (the real cutting-edge stuff) can be found in tiny **Gan HaHashmal** district, in the south of the city just off Allenby street (Levontin and HaRakevet streets). This area is being revived by the entry of young Soho-style fashionistas mingling in with old-school businesses. Home-made jewellery, amongst other things, can be found on the pedestrianized **Nahalat Binyamin**, a popular location for street entertainers, people-watchers, or those wanting an alfresco lunch or coffee.

Bezalel Market, just off King George, is somewhere you can still find a genuinely cheap item of clothing, and is great for those who like poking around for a bargain.

Absolutely unmissable is a visit to **Shuk Hasishpeshim**, or Jaffa's 'flea market', for genuine antiques and genuine junk. Also more authentic is **Carmel Market**, located on the edge of Keren Hataymanim. Though a wide selection of goods are on sale, the market's main produce is fruit and vegetables. It is crowded, raucous, and a lot of fun. If you want organic produce fresh from the Galilee or Golan, go to the **Farmers' Market** in the Port Area, Sat 0700-1600, and in summer also Tue afternoons.

Art
There are an inordinate number of art galleries in Tel Aviv. Those interested in purchasing should pick up the free "Arti" brochure from tourist offices/hotels, which has a comprehensive list.

Bookshops
Book Boutique, 190 Dizengoff, T03-5274527. Second-hand English books.

Book Junky, 167 Dizengoff, T03-5272050. Down an alley (nr Ben Gurion St), second-hand and rare books at a fair price, plus loads of LPs and CDs; Sun-Thu 1000-2000, Fri 1000-1600.

Halper's Books, 87 Allenby, T/F03-6299710, www.halpersbooks.com. Aladdin's Cave of second-hand English books, good for Israeli/Arab fiction. Buying and selling. Sat-Thu 0900-1900, Fri -1500.

M Pollak, 36 & 42 King George. Rare books, antique maps and original David Roberts lithographs.

Steimatzky, www.steimatzky.co.il, have a number of branches across town, including Dizengoff St, inside the Dizengoff Centre, 45 Sheinkin, and a good branch at 107 Allenby. Generally daily 0830-2000, Fri till 1400.

Camping/outdoor gear
Maslul, 47 Bograshov, T03-620350, www.maslul.com. Well-run shop with all the outdoor gear you could need, guidebooks, free tourist information, and frequent lectures. Sadly, their free bikes for loan around the city got stolen so the scheme has been cancelled. Recommended. Sat-Thu 0900-2300, Fri 0900-1600.

Jewellery
H Stern, Israel's prestigious jewellery and diamond merchants, have outlets at the airport and in all the top hotels.
Israel Diamond Centre, 1 Jabotinsky, Ramat Gan, T03-5757979. Diamonds come with appropriate certificates and warrantees; free transport to/from hotel.

For something less serious (and less costly), try the outdoor market on Nahalat Binyamin.

Shopping malls
The Azrieli Centre has all the local and international chains on 3 levels, and a good food hall. It's next to Hashalom train station and has good bus connections.
Dizengoff Centre, junction of Dizengoff and HaMelekh George.

Ramat Aviv Mall, 40 Einstein, Ramat Aviv, T03-6426612, is where you'll find the posh shops.

Souvenirs and gifts
Bauhaus Centre, 99 Dizengoff, T03-5220249, www.bauhaus-center.com. Everything in the International Style so you can take a memory of Tel Aviv home, be it a coffee-table book, print, magnet or game. Sun-Thu 1000-1930, Fri 1000-1430. Toilets. **Zalmania**, 30 Allenby, T03-5177916, www.zalmania.co.il. Photographer Rudi Weissenstein catalogued the development of Israel, recording important events as well as every-day life. He set up his shop here in 1940, and his grandson still runs it. You can buy b&w prints of Tel Aviv, 1936-1960. Sun 0900-1800, Fri 0900-1300.

▲ Activities and tours

Cycling
Cycle, 147 Ben Yehuda, T03-5293037, www.cycle.co.il. Bike rental 25NIS per hr, 55NIS per day. Baby seats and tandems available. Go online to get 10% discount voucher. Sun-Thu 1000-1900, Fri 1000-1500. Helmets, locks. **O-Fun**, 197 Ben Yehuda, T03-5442292. Bike sales (cheap), repairs and rental 25NIS per hr or 60NIS per day (24-hr period). Scooters available. Sun-Thu 1000-1900, Fri 0900-1500. **Sunset** (see Surfing, below) have bikes for 50NIS per day.

Football
International fixtures are played at the Ramat Gan Stadium, whilst domestic fixtures take place at the Bloomfield Stadium in Jaffa (eg Maccabi Tel Aviv) or at the Maccabi Yafo Stadium in Jaffa. Check local press for fixtures (usually Saturday afternoon).

Hiking
Society for the Protection of Nature (SPNI), 2 HaNegev, T03-6388688/057-2003030, Sun-Thu 0900-1400, Fri 0800-1300). Gives advice for potential hikers anywhere in Israel, and arranges guided trips.

Skydiving
Paradive, HaBonim Beach, T1700-702024.

Surfing
Sunset, 59 HaYarkon, T077-3224279. Fair prices on board rental, surf boards, body boards, paddle boards, soft boards, kayaks, all 50-100NIS per day. Sun-Fri 0900-2000, sometimes on Sat in summer (and will open if you call).

Swimming
The best and most affordable option is the **Gordon Pool**, Kikar Atarim, T03-7623300 (60NIS) which is centrally located, large (50m) and next to the beach. The (cold) salt water is chlorine-free. Otherwise, some of the high-end hotels, eg the **David Intercontinental**, allow outside guests (for a hefty charge of around 150-200NIS).

Tour operators
There are numerous tour companies based in Tel Aviv, mainly found at the hotels and along Ben Yehuda. Most offer Israel tours, and some offer tours to Jordan (especially Petra) or Egypt. **Tourism Association Tours**, T03-5166188, www.tel-aviv.gov.il. A choice of 4 city walking tours in English, each about 90 mins; no advance booking required. Jaffa, Wed 0930, meet at the clock-tower; Night-Time Tel Aviv, Tue 2000, meet at corner Rothschild/Herzl; Bauhaus Tel Aviv, Sat 1100, meet at 46 Rothschild/Shadal; Tel Aviv University, Mon 1100, meet at Dyonon bookshop. **Bauhaus Centre Tel Aviv**, 99 Dizengoff, T03-5220249, www.bauhaus-center.com. Tours of Bauhaus buildings in Tel Aviv on Fri 1000-1200, 50NIS (20% discount with City Pass). Recommended. **Tel Aviv-Yafo Panoramic Tour**, T03-6394444, www.dan.co.il. Open-air bus tour (line 100) passing all the highlights of the city and allowing you to "hop on-hop off". Explanations about the sites is given through head-phones (8 languages). Starts from Reading Terminal, daily 0900-1600 on the hour. Pay on board. Full day pass (includes all Dan buses), adult 65NIS, child 56NIS; 2-hr

panoramic tour, adult 45NIS, child 36NIS.

Egged Tours, 59 Ben Yehuda, T1700-707577, www.grayline.com/israel. Variety of tours around Israel, departing daily in 2 languages (always 1 in English), from half-day to 4-days.

Issta, 109 Ben Yehuda/20 Ben-Gurion, T03-5210555, travelhelp@issta.co.il. Sun-Thu 0900-1900, Fri 0830-1300. A reliable place to get flight tickets.

Mazada Tours, 141 Ibn Gvirol, T03-5444454, www.mazada.co.il. Long-established, specializing in trips to Egypt and Jordan. Direct bus to Cairo on Sun and Thu at 1000, around 12 hrs, one-way $90 plus departure tax $55, return $110 plus departure tax; to Amman daily (minimum of 3 persons required) at 0900, 6 hrs, each way $88 plus departure tax $49, see entry under Jerusalem on page for full details.

Sandemans New Tel Aviv, T054-8831447, www.neweuropetours.eu. Free 3-hr city tour by foot every day at 1100 and 1530, starts from next to Opera Tower on Herbert Samuel (tips-only basis); Jaffa tour every day at 1545 (adult/student 75/70NIS, 2 ½ hrs). NB They are also due to establish a drop-in centre, with free computers and lots of free information; it's worth enquiring about this.

United Tours, T03-6173333/15, www.unitedtours.co.il. Long-established (since the 1960s); you see their buses all over Israel. 1-2 day tours to the major sites, run every day, all prices listed online. Departures from Tel Aviv or Jerusalem.

Ophir Tours, 6 Hanatziv, www.ophirtours.co.il, T03-5269777. Agents in charge of processing Indian visas. Also have an office in Jerusalem (42 Agrippas, T02-5398666).

⊙ Transport

Air
Most visitors to Israel arrive at Ben-Gurion Airport, close to Tel Aviv. See page 19.

Domestic flights tend to use **Sede Dov Airport** (see 'Tel Aviv: overview' map), with **Arkia** (T09-8633480/8644444) offering flights to **Eilat** (1 hr), **Rosh Pinna** (30 mins) and **Kiryat Shemona** (40 mins). At the time of going to press El Al had just announced that flights to **Eilat** will be leaving from Ben Gurion Airport. See www.elal.co.il for more information.

Airline offices Air Sinai, 1 Ben Yehuda, T03-5102481; **Arkia**, T09-8644444 or *5758; **El Al**, 32 Ben Yehuda, T03-6716111, www.elal.co.il; **Air Canada**, Azrieli Centre, 132 Menachen Begin, T03-6072111; **Air India**, 23 Ben Yehuda, T03-7951333; **Alitalia**, 25 HaMered, T03-7960700; **Austrian**, 1 Ben Yehuda, T03-5115110; **Cyprus**, 23 Ben Yehuda, T03-7951570; **KLM**, 7 Jabotinsky, Ramat Gan, T03-6112727; **Lufthansa**, 37 She'arit Israel, T03-5135353; **Olympic**, 1 Ben Yehuda, T5110303; Royal **Jordanian**, 5 Shalom Alechem, T03-5165566; **Swissair**, 37 She'arit Israel, T03-5139000; **Turkish**, 78 HaYarkon, T03-5172333. For low-cost flights to the UK, see www.easyjet.com and www.jet2.com.

Bus
Tel Aviv's **Central Bus Station** is on Levinsky, southeast of the city centre. On 7 floors, it features (in addition to the numerous fast-food places) a bank, post office, army surplus store and even a tattoo parlour. Initially confusing, it is actually quite well signposted (though escalators and staircases seem to take the most round-about route). The vast majority of inter-city services are operated by the **Egged Bus Company**. Egged information is on the 6th floor and they will print out timetables in English on request. Electronic information boards show timetables for most destinations. For Egged information call T03-6948888/*2800 or check the website, www.egged.co.il. Tickets are usually bought from the driver on boarding the bus, though you can buy in advance from the counter (essential if using a student card).

Buses running within Tel Aviv are operated by the **Dan Bus Company**. Dan bus information is on the 7th floor. A 'Rav-Kav' card (rechargeable plastic card) saves you at least 20% per ride; ask about this at the

Dan Information Office, where you can also buy the Tel Aviv Centre Bus Routes map. For information on Dan buses call T03-6394444 or check www.dan.co.il. Most services run Sun-Thu 0520-2345, Fri 0530-1730, Sat 2015-2415, and do not run during Shabbat.

NB Security is tight here: bags are searched at the entrance. Do not leave bags unattended. Do not look after bags for anyone else. Left luggage office is on the 6th floor.

For tourists, the most useful local routes are 4 and 5 which run past most of the hotels/hostels. **Line 4**: from the Central Bus Station to Reading Terminal via Allenby, Ben Yehuda and Dizengoff (every 3-10 mins). **Line 5**: from Central Bus Station to Beyt HaHayal, via Allenby, Rothschild, Dizengoff, Ibn Gvirol, Pinkas and Namir (every 3-8 mins, 0450-2415). **Line 10**: from Arlozorov Terminal to Jaffa (and on to Bat Yam) via Ben Yehuda, Allenby and Herbert Samuel (every 10-25 mins). **Line 46**: from the Central Bus Station to Jaffa (and on to Bat Yam), via Jaffa street, Eilat and Yefet (every 5-15 mins).
Long-distance buses Listed below is a small selection of services (those offering the quickest, most direct route). The times listed are for summer. Bear in mind that during winter Shabbat will start and finish earlier, thus affecting times on Fri and Sat.

Arad: 389; Sun-Thu 1010, 1250, 1830, 2015, Fri on the hr 1210-1510, Sat 2110, 38.5NIS, 1¾ hrs. **Ashqelon**: 300/301; 2-3 per hr; 20NIS, 1 hr. **Be'er Sheva**: 370; every 30 mins; Sun-Thu 0600-2200, Fri 0630-1630, Sat 1830-2300, 1 hr. **Eilat**: 394; 10 per day; Sun-Thu 0630-2400, Fri until 1600, Sat 1600-2400; 73NIS, 5½ hrs; can book in advance online. **Haifa**: 910; every hr; Sun-Thu 0630-2305, Fri 0700-1700, Sat 2015-2305; 26NIS, 1½ hrs. **Jerusalem**: 405; every 10 mins; Sun-Thu 0550-2400, Fri 0600-1730, Sat 2015-2400; 20NIS, 55 mins. **Nazareth**: 823; 5 per day; Sun-Thu 0530-1655, Fri 0500, 0945, 1250, Sat 1910; 40.5NIS (also bus 826, more frequent, but to **Pikud Jct** not Nazareth centre), 2½ hrs. **Safed**: 846; Sun-Thu 1700; Fri

1230; 57NIS, 3½ hrs. **Tiberias**: 835/841;every 30 mins; Sun-Thu 0550-2400, Fri 0600-1620, Sat 1530-2400; 47NIS, 2½ hrs.

For buses to **Cairo** and **Jordan**, see Mazada Tours (see opposite).

Sheruts (yellow minibuses operating as shared taxis) run along local bus routes 4 and 5, and are more flexible since you can flag them down and get on or off anywhere along the route. They also run later at night, and on Shabbat. Fares are about the same as the buses (though 25% more on Shabbat). Sheruts leave from outside the Central Bus Station on Levinsky to a number of towns (usually providing a quicker and more convenient service than the buses). Key destinations include: **Akko**; **Haifa**; **Jerusalem** (particularly convenient, arrives near Zion Square); **Lod**; **Nazareth**; **Netanya** and **Ramla**.

Car hire

There are numerous car hire companies in Tel Aviv; those listed below are just a selection. Most have offices at Ben-Gurion Airport, which are open 24 hrs, and on HaYarkon (near the big hotels), Sun-Thu 0800-1700, Fri 0800-1300. **Avis**, 113 HaYarkon, T03-5271752, and at **David Intercontinental**, 115 HaYarkon, T03-5299607, www.avis.co.il; **Budget**, 99 HaYarkon, T03-9350012; **Eldan**, 114 HaYarkon, T03-5271166; **Hertz**, 144 HaYarkon, T03-5223332.

Motorbike hire

Motogo, 103 Hertzel, T03-6811717, www. motogo.co.il. Motorbike hire, 125cc, 20E per day, 125E per week, 480E per month plus taxes.
Motorent, T03-6888851/2, www.motorent. co.il. Daily-monthly scooter hire, up to 50cc.

Taxis

Balfour, 59 Balfour, T03-5604545; **Gordon**, T03-5272999; **HaYarkon**, 101 HaYarkon, T03-5223233; **Nordau**, 16 Nordau, T03-5466222; amongst many others; all 24 hrs.

Train

Tel Aviv has 4 railway stations, **HaHaganna** (near the Central Bus Station), **Azrieli** (near the 3 towers of the same name), **Savidor** (also still referred to as 'Arlozorov' or the 'north' station) and the **University station**. Train is the simplest way (apart from taxi) to get to/ from the airport (24-hr service). Although the network is limited it is a very pleasant way to travel, and not much more expensive than the bus network (especially with a student card which gives 10% discount). An express service runs north to **Nahariyya** every hour or so, stopping at **Binyamina, 'Atlit** and **Haifa** (1 hr 10 mins), with additional slower trains calling at other towns on the way. To **Jerusalem** via **Ramla** it is a slower, but more picturesque journey than the bus (a rapid transit link is being built, but won't materialize in the near future). Trains also go south to **Ashdod** (1 hr) and **Be'er Sheva** (1 ½ hrs) to finish at **Dimona**.

🛈 Directory

Banks

There are numerous banks offering foreign exchange in Tel Aviv (check rates and commission charges). Marked with the '$' bank symbol on the maps are those with useful ATM machines, though they are never far away. Note that post offices offer commission-free foreign exchange. There are numerous money changers on Ben Yehuda, Dizengoff and anywhere else there are tourists.

Embassies and consulates

Most countries have failed to recognize Israel's decision to choose Jerusalem as their capital, and hence embassies and consulates remain in Tel Aviv.

Australia, 37 Sha'ul Ha-Melekh, Europe House, 4th floor, T03-6950451, www. australianembassy.org.il. **Austria**, 9 Mamorek, T03-6855959, www.aussenministerium.at/ telaviv. **Belgium**, 12 HaHazilion, Ramat Gan, T03-6138130, www.diplomatie.be/telaviv.

Brazil, 23 Yehuda HaLevi, T03-6919292. **Canada**, 3 Nirim, T03-6363300, www.israel. gc.ca. **Cyprus**, 50 Dizengoff, Top Tower, T03-5250212, tel_avivembassy@mfa.gov. cy. **Czech Republic**, 23 Zeitlin, T03-6918282, www.mzv.cz/telaviv. **Denmark**, Museum Tower, 4 Berkovitz, T03-6085850, www. ambtelaviv.um.dk. **Egypt**, 54 Basel, T03-5464151. Sun-Thu 0900-1100 for visa services (arrive early). In theory visas can be collected the same afternoon, but don't count on it. Visa fee depends upon nationality; bring 3 photos. Tourist visas are not available on the Eilat border, but non-extendable 14-day 'Sinai permits' are. **Finland**, 40 Einstein, T03-7456600, sanomat.tel@formin.fi. **France**, 112 Herbert Samuel, T03-5208300, www. ambafrance-il.org. **Germany**, 3 Daniel Frisch, T03-6931313, www.tel-aviv.diplo. de. **Greece**, 3 Daniel Frisch, T03-6953060, gremil@netvision.net.il. **India**, 140 HaYarkon, www.indembassy.co.il, but cannot process visas – you have to go through a travel agent. **Ireland**, 3 Daniel Frisch, T03-6964166, telavivembassy@dfa.ie. **Italy**, 25 Hamered Street, T03-5104004, www.ambtelaviv. esteri.it. **Jordan**, 14 Aba Hillel, Ramat Gan, T03-7517722, jordanembassy@barak.net. il. Sun-Thu 0900-1600 for visas (arrive early). Visas can take up to 14 days to be processed. Most nationalities (not Israelis) can get a visa on the border, but not at the Allenby/King Hussein Bridge. **Netherlands**, 4 Weizmann, T03-7540777, www.netherlands-embassy. co.il. **New Zealand**, 3 Daniel Frisch, T03-6956622. **Norway**, 40 Einstein, T03-7441490, www.norway.org.il. **Romania**, 24 Adam HaCohen, T03-5229472, www.telaviv.mae. ro. **Russia**, 120 HaYarkon, T03-5290691, amb_ru@mail.netvision.net.il. **South Africa**, Top Tower, 16th Floor, 50 Dizengoff, T03-5252566, www.safis.co.il/. **Spain**, 3 Daniel Frish, T03-6965210, embespil@mail.mae.es. **Sweden**, 4 Weizmann, T03-7180000, www. swedenabroad.com/telaviv. **Switzerland**, 228 HaYarkon, T03-5464455, vertretung@tel. rep.admin.ch. **Thailand**, 21 Sha'ul HaMelekh, T03-6958980, www.thaiembassy.org/telaviv.

Turkey, 1 Ben Yehuda, T03-5171731. United Kingdom, 192 HaYarkon, T03-7251222, www.britemb.org.il. USA, 71 HaYarkon, T03-5197575, http://telaviv.usembassy.gov.

Hospitals and medical services

Recommended for the best facilities are: Chaim Sheba Medical Centre, Tel Hashomer, 03-5303030, http://eng.sheba.co.il. Tel Aviv Sourasky Medical Centre (Ichilov), 6 Weizmann Street, T03-6974444, www.tasmc.org.il/e. Rabin Medical Centre, Beilinson, 39 Jabotinsky St. Petah Tikva, T03-9377377, www.clalit.org.il/rabin/Content/ContactusEng.asp?cid=36. Schneider Children's Medical Centre, Petah Tikva, T03-9253253, www.schneider.org.il/Eng.

Internet

Available in all the hostels for a charge (usually 12NIS per hour) or free Wi-Fi in numerous cafés and restaurants around the city.

Immigration

Visa extensions at the Ministry of Interior, 125 Menachem Begin, T03-5193305/*3450, info@moin.gov.il,. Call T1700-551111 Sun-Thu 1300-1500 to make an appointment. Bring valid passport, 1 x photo, air ticket (if you have one) and letter explaining the reason you require an extension. Extensions are given for 6-12 months (from original date of entry). Most nationalities have to pay 165NIS. It's actually much quicker to do an extension at one of the regional offices, such as Netanya, Rehovot, Petach Tikva or in any regional centre, than in Tel Aviv.

Language courses

Goldstein-Gore Centre, Ulpan Gordon, 7 LaSalle, T03-5223095, ulpan.gordon@012.net.il. Offers Ulpan (Hebrew classes). For those on a tourist visa the prices are 805NIS for 1-month, 2500NIS for 3½-months (3 hrs, 4 days per week) or 5-months (2 nights per week), max 30 students per class. Office Sun-Thu 0800-1300 and 1600-2100.

Post offices

Central Post Office, with poste restante, 7 Mikve Yisra'el (crn with Levotin), Sun-Thu 0700-1800, Fri 0700-1200; plus numerous branch offices marked on map.

Telephone

Israel Phones, www.israelphones.com. Overseas operator: T188.

Useful addresses and phone numbers

Police T101. Fire T102.

Jaffa

→ Colour map 2, grid B2

Jaffa has a long and incident-packed history, with repeated periods of capture and destruction followed by bouts of reconstruction and prosperity. Only small sections of the old town remain today, though they have been tastefully restored and provide a pleasant contrast to the modern environs of nearby Tel Aviv. The 'Old Jaffa' area is now a concentration of galleries, antique shops and restaurants, and is a popular destination with evening strollers. The Souq HaPishpeshim, or Jaffa's famous 'Flea Market', is another experience that should not be missed.

Ins and outs

Getting there and away Most visitors to Jaffa arrive along Yefet Street, via the clock-tower square area. The seafront promenade walk extends all the way from Tel Aviv to Old Jaffa, a good way to approach. Bus 46 runs from the Central Bus Station or bus 10 runs from downtown Tel Aviv to the clock-tower. Several buses run from the Central Bus Station along Sederot Jerusalem, just inland of Old Jaffa, including 7, 40 and 44.

Getting around There is no single walking route that takes in all the sights of Jaffa in a set order but given the compact size of the district, it is easy and pleasurable just to wander around and still see all the attractions.

Tourist information **Visitors' Centre and Museum** ⓘ *Kedumim Square, T03-5184015, Sun-Thu 1000-1800, Fri 1000-1400 (currently closed Sat for renovations, due to finish end of 2010), museum open Tue, Wed, Thu 1600-2000.* Offers tourist information, map and guided tours on Jaffa. Also note there is a free guided tour in English every Wednesday starting at 0930 at the clock-tower, www.tel-aviv.gov.il.

Background

Ancient history Legend, and Jewish tradition, suggests that Jaffa (**Yafo** in Hebrew and **Joppa** in most biblical references) was founded after the Flood by Japheth, son of Noah. Jaffa also became the setting for the legend of Andromeda, and the supporting cast of the rock, the sea-monster, Perseus and Pegasus (see 'Jaffa legends', opposite).

There are numerous early written references to Jaffa, most notably in the Bible: the port here is mentioned as the landing place for the Cedars of Lebanon that were brought by sea for use in the construction of the First and Second Temples at Jerusalem (*II Chronicles 2:16; Ezra 3:7*).

There is evidence that by 1200 BCE Jaffa was established as a Philistine city, although about 200 years later **David** conquered the city. As with much of the kingdom of Judah, Jaffa was captured by the Assyrian king **Sennacherib** during his successful campaign of 701 BCE. Jaffa became a largely Greek city during the Early Hellenistic period (332-167). In fact, according to Greek legend, Joppa is daughter of the wind god, Aeolus. Jaffa came under control of the Ptolemies until the capture of Palestine by Antiochus III of Syria in 223 BCE. The ethnically Greek population of Syrian-controlled Jaffa came into conflict with the Maccabees during the Hasmonean period, with much of the town being burned by Judas Maccabaeus (*II Maccabees 12:3-7*). This was in response to the deliberate drowning of 200 Jaffa Jews. The port town was subsequently conquered by his brother Jonathan, and annexed to Judea by the older brother Simon (*I Maccabees 12:34*).

Pompey declared the town independent in 63 BCE, though **Julius Caesar** returned it to Jewish control 16 years later. It was reputedly given to **Cleopatra** by a love-struck Mark Anthony, though nominal control was passed to **Herod the Great** following her death in 30 BCE. The port went into serious decline in the first century BCE with Herod's establishment of the port of Sebastos at Caesarea, and was largely destroyed by **Vespasian** in 67 CE. The Roman emperor later rebuilt the town, giving it an independent charter. A biblical reference to Jaffa describes how Peter "tarried many days in Joppa with one Simon a tanner", having raised Tabitha (known as Dorcas) from the dead (*Acts 9:36-43*), and also received a vision here that revealed that pagans should be admitted into the church (*Acts 10:10-48*).

In latter centuries Jaffa was conquered by the **Arabs** (636 CE) and then by the **Crusaders**, with the port becoming a major landing place for pilgrims visiting the Holy Land. After the Mamluk sultan Baibars finally dispatched the Crusaders in 1267, the town was largely abandoned for the next three centuries.

Modern history Jaffa's modern history begins with **Ottoman** rule in Palestine around 1520. **Napoleon** besieged Jaffa in 1799, with the town falling under the control of **Ibrahim Pasha** some years later. Many of the buildings to be seen in Old Jaffa today were built during this period. The mid to late 19th century saw the establishment of new settlements outside

Jaffa legends

There are many legends attached to Jaffa, spanning almost every age in history. Perhaps the most famous biblical reference to Jaffa concerns the story of Jonah, and his experience with the "great fish" (*Jonah 1:17*), or whale. It was from Jaffa that **Jonah** embarked on his ill-fated expedition, ignoring God's commandment to go to the "wicked" city of Nineveh, and instead attempting to sail to Tarshish.

There is also the story of the **Pharaoh Thutmose III**'s capture of the city in the 15th century BCE, when he sent the governor of Jaffa a number of baskets said to contain bounty. Having accepted the gift, the governor discovered too late that the baskets actually contained soldiers, who went on to capture the city from within.

Then there is the legend of **Andromeda**. It seems that Queen Cassiopeia, wife of King Copeus of Ethiopia, boasted that her daughter Andromeda was more beautiful than any mermaid. This seriously pissed off Nireus (father of mermaids), who begged Poseidon (god of the sea) to take revenge for this sleight. Duly obliging, Poseidon sent a sea-monster to terrorize the coast. In an attempt to assuage the fury of Poseidon, King Copeus tied his daughter Andromeda to the rock as a sacrifice to the monster. Fortunately for Andromeda she had a daring suitor in Perseus, who swooped down from the skies on his winged steed Pegasus, slew the monster, and carried her off to safety. Legend doesn't recount what Andromeda later said to her father about the incident.

Jaffa, populated mainly by Christian and Jewish Zionists. Numerous Christian hostelries, churches and monasteries were established in and around Jaffa during this period. The early 20th century saw the tentative beginnings of the new Jewish town of Tel Aviv.

The decade of the 1920s saw increased tension between the Jewish and Arab communities leading to violent clashes. Vast swathes of the town's narrow labyrinthine streets were cleared by the British in order to facilitate military control, though parts have now been restored in the Old Jaffa area. The town's port suffered a terminal blow following its closure during the 1936 Arab Revolt, and the establishment of a new port at Tel Aviv. The UN vote on the partition of Palestine in November 1947 led to prolonged clashes all across Palestine, with Jewish forces capturing Jaffa in April 1948 after a short but bloody battle. The flight of almost the entire Arab population has remained a point of contention ever since.

Following the 1948/1949 War of Independence, Jaffa was amalgamated within the municipality of Tel Aviv. In recent years, parts of Old Jaffa have been substantially restored.

Sights

Ottoman Clock-tower

Built in 1906 to mark the anniversary of the accession to the throne of the Ottoman Sultan Abdul Hamid II, the working clock-tower serves as Jaffa's most recognizable landmark, at one end of Yefet Street. Similar clock-towers were built in Jerusalem, Nablus and Akko to mark the same event. More recent renovations added the plaque commemorating the Israelis killed in the 1948 battle for the town, and the stained-glass windows which date to the mid-1960s.

Also on the clock-tower square stands the '**Kishleh**', a building that dates to the Ottoman period, later used as a detention centre by the British and then as Jaffa Police Station (which is now in a grand new building on Salome Street, nearby). The Kishleh awaits redevelopment, though the seal of Sultan Abdul Hamid II can still be seen above the door.

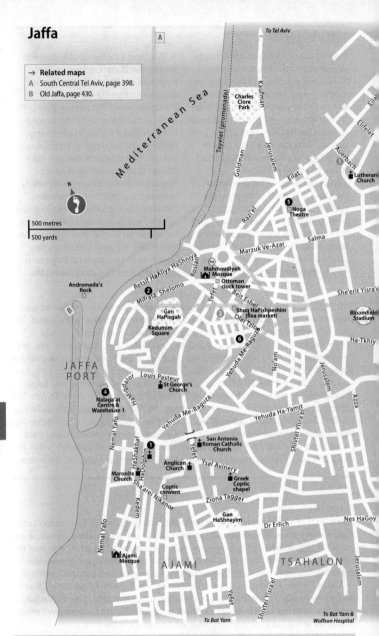

Jaffa

→ **Related maps**
A South Central Tel Aviv, page 398.
B Old Jaffa, page 430.

Mediterranean Sea

To Tel Aviv

Charles Clore Park

Kaufman

Goldman

Jerusalem

Eilat

Elifelet

Auerbach

Lutheran Church

Noga Theatre ⑤

Razi'el

Salma

Marzuk Ve-Azar

Tayelet (promenade)

Retsif HaAliya HaShniya

Roslan

Mahmoudiyeh Mosque

Ottoman clock tower

Sheerit Yisra'e

Bloomfield Stadium

② Mifratz Shelomo

Andromeda's Rock

Beit Eshel

Yefet

Shuq HaPishpeshim (flea market)

Olei Tzion

⑥

Ha-Tkhiy

Gan HaPisgah

Kedumim Square

Yehuda Me-Raguza

No'am

Jerusalem

JAFFA PORT

HaMagdalor

Louis Pasteur

St George's Church

Nalaga'at Centre & Warehouse 1 ④

Yehuda Me-Raguza

Yehuda Ha-Yamit

Azza

Nema Yafo

HaShakhaf

HaDolphin

① San Antonio Roman Catholic Church

Yefet

Ysal Avinery

Shivtei Yisra'el

Anglican Church

Maronite Church

Sha'arei Nikanor

Coptic convent

Greek Coptic chapel

Ziona Tagger

Gan HaShnayim

Dr Erlich

Nes HaGoy

Kedem

Nema Yafo

Ajami Mosque

AJAMI

TSAHALON

Yefet

Shivtei Yisra'el

Jerusalem

To Bat Yam

To Bat Yam & Wolfson Hospital

FLORENTIN

Abarbanel

HaKishon

Herzl

Florentin

Salma

To central
bus station

SHAPIRA

Har Tsion

Salma

Herzl

Har Tsion

Ellfelet

Kibbutz Galuyyot

Shalabim

Lavon

Groningen
Garden

Russian
Monastery
of St Peter

Ben Tsvi

Heine

Shalabim

Herzl

Zoo/
Botanical Gardens

HaHaganah
Garden

Lavon

Nes HaGoyim

Ben Tsvi

Maccabi
Yafo
Stadium

Azza

TEL KABIR
(NEVE OFER)

Heine

DAKAR
(YAFO ALEF)

Sleeping
2 Old Jaffa
   Hostel

🍴 Eating
2 Aladin
1 Ali Caravan/
   Abu Hasan
4 Blackout
5 Le Relais Jaffa
6 Puaa

Mahmoudiyeh Mosque

Located at the southwest corner of the square is the Great, or **Mahmoudiyeh Mosque**. Though dating to 1809, the mosque was extensively renovated just three years later by the Turkish Sultan's representative in Jaffa, Governor Mohammad 'Abu Nabut' Aja, during whose rule Jaffa experienced a period of rejuvenation and expansion. Amongst building materials used on the renovation were columns taken from Ashqelon and Caesarea, and popular legend has it that the masons set them upside down, so that today their capitals stand at the base.

The main entrance to the mosque is in the south wall, though a separate entrance was built in the east wall during the late 19th century for exclusive use of the governor and other notables. Also in the south wall is the marbled **Suleiman Fountain**, which retains something of its former splendour. The mosque has a tall, slender minaret, two white domes and a pleasant interior courtyard, though it is not generally open to non-Muslims.

Other sights along Yefet Street

Before one wanders up the hill into the restored area of Old Jaffa itself, there are a few places of interest in the vicinity of **Yefet Street**. Diagonally opposite the mosque, just off Yefet Street, is the old Jerusalem road (now Beit Eshel Street), the former business

Old Jaffa

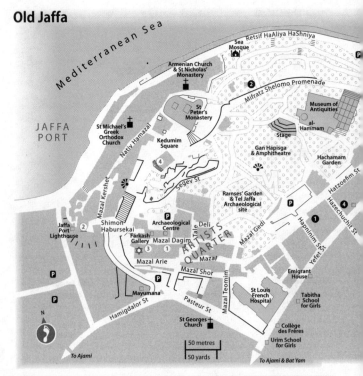

district. At No 11 stands the 19th-century **Manouli Khan**, a caravanserai formerly run by an Armenian family; you can still see something of its previous form as a hostel and stables.

Other buildings of note on Yefet Street include the **Anglo-Palestine House** (site of the first Zionist Bank), **Emigrant House** (a 19th-century hostel for Jewish immigrants), and the **'St Louis' French Hospital**. Named after the leader of the Seventh Crusade, Louis IX, who landed at Jaffa in 1251, this attractive neo-Renaissance building was established as a hospital in the 19th century. These buildings now stand derelict, though perhaps the renovations that are creeping their way up Yefet will encompass them in time.

Further south is the **Tabitha School for Girls**, established and run by the Presbyterian Church of Scotland since 1863. The small graveyard to the rear of the building contains the grave of, amongst other notables, Dr Thomas Hodgkin, the man who diagnosed Hodgkin's Disease, who died in Jaffa in 1866. Next door stands the **Collège des Frères**, a former late 19th-century French catholic school for boys, and further along the turreted **Urim School for Girls**, founded by Catholic nuns in 1882.

Souq HaPishpeshim (Flea Market)
Also located just off Yefet Street, at the clock-tower end, is Jaffa's brilliant flea market. Opinions are divided as to whether you are likely to pick up a bargain or not, but it's certainly worth a visit. In addition to some genuine antiques, there are even more not-so-genuine antiques, plus some real rubbish, particularly amongst those traders whose pitch is just a few square metres of pavement on Olei Zion Street. Odd shoes, electrical equipment that has no hope of ever working, piles of rags that are actually second-hand clothes: the street vendors have them all. The traders with permanent shops have more upmarket wares, particularly furniture, carpets and jewellery, and several very chic vintage shops have opened up in the area. Whoever you are dealing with, bargaining is an essential part of the purchasing process. Closed Saturday.

Eating & Drinking
2 Aladin
3 Dr Shakshuka
4 Jaffa Bar
1 Noa Bistro
5 Yoezer Wine Bar
6 Said Abou Elafia & Sons

Other
5 Bus stop
1 Hasimta Theatre
2 House of Simon the Tanner
3 Ilana Goor Museum
4 Visitors' Centre

St Peter's Monastery
ⓘ *1 Mifratz Shlomo, Old Jaffa, T8222871. Daily 0800-1145 and 1500-1800. Free.*
Old Jaffa's most prominent landmark is the ochre and pale yellow St Peter's Monastery. Franciscans built a monastery on this site in 1654 upon the ruins of a 13th-century Crusader castle, though the present building dates to the late 19th century. It is still possible to see the remarkably intact vaulted chambers of the Crusader halls by descending the stairs in the monastery's courtyard.

The apostle Peter is said to have visited Jaffa, where he performed the Miracle of the Resurrected Tabitha, also known as Dorcas (*Acts 9:36-37, 38-39, 40*). A later guest at the old monastery built in Peter's honour was Napoleon, who is alleged to have stayed there during his 1799 campaign.

Kedumim Square Visitors' Centre
ⓘ *Sun-Thu 1000-1800, Fri 1000-1400 (closed Sat for renovation at time of research). Adult 8NIS, student 6NIS; disabled access.*
The large open plaza in the centre of Old Jaffa, Kedumim Square, is at its most lively during the evening, when it fills up with promenading families, young couples, tourists and restaurant-goers. On the west side of the square is a **viewpoint**, offering exceptional views of the Jaffa port area, and **Andromeda's Rock** (see opposite).

At the centre of the square is a below-ground **Visitors' Centre**, housing a number of excavations and an exhibition detailing the history of Jaffa. The excavations include a three-room subterranean complex dating from the end of the third century BCE, the walls of a Jewish dwelling abandoned in 67 CE, and a number of walls containing inscribed references to Yehuda ben Tozomenos, Jaffa's *agoranomos* (official in charge of weights and measures) during the reign of Emperor Trajan (98-117 CE). A short video (with subtitles in all languages) tells the story of Jaffa's history.

Ramses' Garden and Tel Jaffa
Excavated between 1955 and 1974, Tel Jaffa now forms part of a landscaped lawn, referred to as Ramses' Garden. Though not spectacular, the finds have proved important in piecing together Jaffa's long history. Remains on display include: "stone foundations of a citadel dating to the Hellenistic period (332-140 BCE); a lower wall dating to the Persian period (539-332 BCE); gateway foundations destroyed in a conflagration towards the end of the late Canaanite period (end of 13th, beginning of 12th century BCE); lower section of city's gateway dating to the reign of the Pharaoh Ramses II (1304-1237 BCE), including four jamb-stones of the gateway with incised hieroglyphic inscriptions featuring named titles of Ramses II; beneath the gateway, remains of brick walls dating to the late Canaanite era (16th-14th century BCE); structural remains dating to the Middle Ages, and finally, a soap production building from the British Mandate period".

Artists' Quarter
To the south of Kedumim Square is the Artists' Quarter, a superbly restored labyrinth of narrow alleyways, arched streets and cul-de-sacs. Many buildings are now studios, galleries and upmarket souvenir shops, though the blatantly commercial nature of the quarter does not really detract from its architectural charm. Also in this area is the Hasimta Theatre and the **Ilana Goor Museum** ⓘ *4 Mazal Dagim, Old Jaffa, T03-6837676, www.ilanagoor.com, Sun, Thu and Fri 1000-1400, Sat and hols 1000-1800, hol eves -1300. Adult 15NIS.* The latter building dates to the mid-18th century and was originally used as a hostel for Jewish pilgrims arriving in the Holy Land at Jaffa Port. After 1949 it served as a synagogue for Libyan Jews, and since 1955 it has been the home of self-taught artist and sculptress Ilana Goor. Also a museum displaying her life's work, it is a beautiful building with some interesting pieces on display, and there is a gift shop selling some smaller items of her work.

Jaffa Port

Returning to Kedumim Square, a number of narrow alleys and staircases descend towards the Jaffa Port area. One such path, Shimon Habursekai, passes the House of **Simon the Tanner**, where Peter is said to have stayed following the Miracle of the Resurrection of Tabitha. It is a private house, but the owner may show you around, though there is little of historic interest to see.

Jaffa Port is one of the oldest known harbours in the Middle East, perhaps the world (see above for history), and has many references in the Bible (*Chronicles II 2:16; Zechariah 14:10; 2 Maccabees 12:3-6; Jonah 1:1-3*). Today, it is in the process of being violently remodelled and many citizens disapprove of the blank apartments that now stand empty at the northern end, and the enormous glass 'warehouses' that tower over the marina to the south. There are, however, still fishing boats and pleasure craft, with a few quayside restaurants specializing in seafood, and a fine view of Jaffa can be had by walking out along the breakwater.

There are a number of religious institutions along the quayside, including **St Michael's Greek Orthodox Church**, **The Armenian Church** and **St Nicholas' Monastery**, and the **Jama'a el-Bah'r**, or **Sea Mosque**, where fishermen traditionally came to pray.

Andromeda's Rock

Just beyond the breakwater lies an unspectacular cluster of small rocks (you could hardly call them islands), known collectively as Andromeda's Rock.

South of Old Jaffa

To the south of Old Jaffa stands the **San Antonio Roman Catholic Church**. This modern church, with its red-tile roof and tall steeple was built in 1932, and dedicated to St Antonius of Padua, a contemporary of St Francis of Assisi. Along Ysal Avinery Street, behind San Antonio's, is a Greek Coptic chapel and convent with a small red dome, arched cloisters and squat, square tower. The rather attractive basilica next door is sinking into a state of ruination. Of these, St Antonio's is the only one that is opened on a daily basis.

Opposite San Antonio's is the **Church of St Peter**, though it rather appears now as if somebody is living in the building. The small road beside St Peter's leads to a **Greek Catholic Church and Convent**, built in 1924. Nearby, on HaDolfin, is a **Maronite Church**. The old laneways here still make for a peaceful stroll and there's good local food, though the southern stretch is rapidly being covered by des-res apartments. The promenade stretches onwards to Bat Yam: you can now walk the whole way.

Further to the east, about 2 km inland, and distinguishable by its tall, slender tower, is the **Russian Monastery of St Peter**. Dedicated in 1860 by the Russian government, the chamber beneath the monastery is said to be the site of St Peter's resurrection of Tabitha. The residential district of Ajami (setting for the 2009 Oscar-nominated film of the same name), lies between the sea and the southern reaches of Yefet Street, and this is where the real non-touristy Jaffa is found.

Jaffa listings

For Sleeping and Eating price codes and other relevant information, see Essentials pages 26-31.

🛏 Sleeping

See also Beit Immanuel, page 411, which is only a 10-minute walk from Jaffa's clock-tower.
A-E Old Jaffa Hostel, 13 Amiad St, T03-6822370, telaviv-hostel.com. Popular hostel in excellent location (overlooking the flea market) housed in fine Ottoman-era building. High ceilings, old tiled floors, nice pieces of furniture and photos decorate some rooms: it's atmospheric and full of character. Single-sex 10-bed dorms (68NIS) are spacious, private rooms a mixed bag – some share baths, some have (great) balconies, some with kitchenette, some are tiny. No curfew, lovely roof garden (sleep there in a tent in summer), use of kitchen, TV lounge, internet 10NIS per hr or Wi-Fi, tea/coffee and cookies for breakfast. Management are not to be messed with.

🍴 Eating

Jaffa has a number of appealing restaurants, and it is a great place for eating and drinking on Shabbat, as pretty much everything stays open and there's always a buzz.
₸₸₸ Le Relais Jaffa, 7 Bat Ami, T03-6810637. One of Jaffa's (and Tel Aviv's) most highly recommended restaurants, located in the courtyard of the Noga Theatre. Traditional French cuisine in a beautiful British Mandate building, with high ceilings and Moroccan furnishings. Duck breast in honey sauce, or goose liver with raisins in cognac are typical dishes. Not for vegetarians. Recommended.
₸₸₸-₸₸ Blackout, Nalaga'at Centre, Retsif Haaliya Hashniya, Jaffa Port, T03-6330808, www.nalagaat.org.il. The Nalaga'at Centre is a one-off. The dairy kosher restaurant serves gourmet food, but that's not the only reason why people come. A dinner here is taken in the pitch dark, served by blind waiters. It's a

challenging experience that awakens all your senses, and is fun for a group or romantic for a couple. You can first choose from a menu in the light (1 person 90NIS) but it's recommended to go for the surprise menu (140NIS) - you will be guessing what you are eating (loosely Italian cuisine). Only on Sun, Tue and Thu, sittings at 1900 and 2130. Also on-site and dairy kosher is (₸₸-₸) Café Kapish, with a staff of deaf waiters, where sign language has to get you by. The house salad (sprouted lentils, smoked salmon, vinaigrette) is a winner. Sun, Tue and Thu 1800-2300. (15% discount with City Pass).
₸₸₸-₸ Noa Bistro, Nir Souq Compound, 14 HaZorfim, T03-5184668. This place is a delight: high arches and glass ceilings with numerous pot plants dangling down, to maintain the flea-market feel and beckon you in. Wide and exciting menu fuses Italian with other cuisines; plenty for both meat-eaters (pork shank) and vegetarians; mains 48-82NIS. Very busy on Shabbat. Recommended.
₸₸ Aladin, 5 Mifratz Shlemo Promenade, T03-6826766, aladin.co.il. Pay for the setting and views. Certainly there's a touristy feel at times - but food is great with starters at 25NIS, fish 90NIS, meat 65NIS. Daily (except Yom Kippur) 1100-2400.
₸₸ Puaa, 8 Rabbi Yohanan, near the Flea Market, T03-6823821. Completely fabulous retro shabby-chic interior, nooks and crannies to settle down in, eclectic furniture from the flea market (for sale), menu of light meals, salads, sandwiches, with a slight Middle Eastern edge, great place for breakfast (served all day). Try the curried pumpkin dumplings with rice, a delicious blend of Indian and Thai flavours. Cafe rather than formal restaurant atmosphere, alcohol served. Some people criticise the service, but that's the only downer. Sun-Fri-0900-0100, Sat 1000-1300.
₸₸-₸ Dr Shakshuka, T03-6822842. Meaty mains 40NIS, salad selection 13NIS, and the famed shakshuka and bread 28NIS. Huge business lunch for 2 to sample everything 79NIS. Good

courtyard (views of derelict backstreets), pokey interior. Some consider it the best shakshuka ever, others think they have got too big for their boots and it's overpriced.

† **Ali's Caravan**, 1 HaDolfin, T03-6828255. AKA Abu Hassan, renowned for its hummus, on every Israeli's top ten list. Green and white sign in Hebrew only, some seating, always packed.

† **Said Abou Elafia & Sons**, Yefet. This bakery is famous throughout Israel (so much so that people queue 10 deep on the pavement outside). In addition to fresh bread, baguettes, croissants, etc, they serve an excellent indigenous form of pizza, plus sambusas (baked pitta stuffed with egg, cheese and vegetables) and mean toasted bagels. Take-away only, open 24 hrs including Shabbat (very busy).

⦿ Bars and clubs

Jaffa Bar, 30 Yefet, T03-5184668. Nice location in a typically Jaffan building. Popular, and quite classy without being stuffy or snobbish. Fri afternoons often see live music and people spilling out to fill the alley-way. Respectable clientele.

Margoza Bar, Flea Market, T052-3905091. Happy hour, 2 for 1 on drinks 1900-2100 (except Thu).

Yoezer Wine Bar, 2 Yoezer Aish Habira, Clocktower, T03-6839115. Tucked down an arched alleyway, wine-lovers will find company in this snug place at all hours. It's an old favourite with Tel Avivians, equally renowned for the food as the beverages (the owner was, for many years, a food critic).

Saloona, Jaffa, T03-5181719. Soaring ceilings, comfy seats, retro styling,

⦿ Shopping

Archaeological Centre, 7 Mazal Dagim, Old Jaffa, T03-6826243, www.archaeological-center.com. Should you require a genuine piece of ancient history, be it a Bar Kochba coin or a Roman glass vial. Licensed by the Antiquities Authority.

Farkash Gallery, 5 Mazal Dagim, Old Jaffa, T03-6834741, www.farkash-gallery.com. **Israeliana/Judaica**, photos and books, but the real gems are the vintage posters – both originals and prints. Prices from 35NIS to $2000. Sun-Thu 0900-2030, Fri 0900-1530.

▲ Activities and tours

Kayak 4 All, Jaffa Port, T050-2757076, www.kayak4all.com. Kayaking 'lessons' with a guide; call Rony to arrange in advance.

Around Tel Aviv

There are a number places of interest in the satellite towns around Tel Aviv that are now effectively suburbs of the metropolis. Even using public transport it is possible to visit more than one town in a day.

Bat Yam → *Colour map 2, grid B2.*

Though Bat Yam was initially a separate town established in 1926, Tel Aviv's relentless expansion has virtually incorporated it as one of its larger suburbs (population 160,000). The town has a reputation as being a bit rough around the edges, but its saving grace is the attractive 3.5-km stretch of white sandy beach (Bat Yam is Hebrew for 'Daughter of the Sea'). The promenade along the seafront is attractive, especially as it is lined with cafés and restaurants. The stretch of beach between Jabotinsky and HaAtzma'ut, known as the model beach, has a breakwater so is fairly calm for swimming. There are also showers, changing rooms and beach chairs. Just south of here is a popular area for surfers. A yacht club on the seafront offers boat and board hire, plus the chance to go hang-gliding. The planned Tel Aviv Light Rail system has already started construction of its 'red' terminal in Bat Yam. If you like beaches, then it's a good day out and could be combined with a visit to Jaffa.

Bat Yam listings

For Sleeping and Eating price codes and other relevant information, see Essentials pages 26-31.

Sleeping

L Mercure Suites, 99 Ben-Gurion, T03-5550555, www.mercure.com. Sea views from all rooms, nice balconies, lots of space, little kitchenette. Indoor/outdoor pools (both small), spa; health club in building (30NIS); next to all the nicest restaurants/bars. Good deals online.

AL Armon Yam, 95 Ben-Gurion, T03-5522424, armon-yam@barak.net.il. 66 rooms, majority recently renovated, simply but effectively with funky furniture and decor, and new white en-suites. Breakfast included; TV, a/c and fridge. Lack of natural light the only real critique.

A Colony Beach, 138 Ben-Gurion, T03-5531010/052-2722088. Apartment hotel with well-equipped kitchenettes, min stay 3 days. Studios, 1- and 2-bedroom suites, sea views but no balconies, heated pool. Not truly plush but great value for what you get compared to Tel Aviv.

B Shenhav, 2 Jerusalem, T03-5075231. Rather old fashioned. Little English spoken but decent staff. Some rooms with private 'internal' balcony. No breakfast.

Eating and drinking

There are a number of restaurants and bars along Ben-Gurion, including **Blue Lagoon**, **Dolphin**, **Domino Pizza** and **Dr Fish**, though none is particularly outstanding. **Japanika**, at number 73, has decent sushi in an ultra modern white interior, while Aroma cafe next door is reliable for light meals and salads. **Perchuk's Place**, 15 Ben Gurion, T03-5525334, has jazz in the evenings. Many of the bars reflect the town's sizeable Turkish and North

African populations. **Little Prague**, 83 Ben Gurion, T03-5514623, stays open till at least 0200 and has a happy hour from 1600-2000.

Transport

Bat Yam is located 5.5 km south of Tel Aviv. To reach Bat Yam, continue south through **Jaffa** along either **Yefet** or **Jerusalem**, before turning right (west) on to **Rothschild**. This leads down to the seafront, with all the hotels located here on Ben-Gurion. Dan buses 8, 10, 18, 25, 26 and 46 run to/from **Tel Aviv**, and Egged bus 83 (Central Bus Station to Rishon LeTzion) passes the Colony Beach Hotel or bus 86 from Alozorov goes to the town centre.

Bat Yam

400 metres
400 yards

Sleeping
1 Armon Yam
3 Colony Beach
2 Mercure Suites
4 Shenhav

Eating
1 Dolphin & Blue Lagoon

B'nei B'rak

ⓘ Buses that run from the Central Bus Station to Petah Tiqva (eg 51) pass through B'nei B'rak. There are numerous bus/sherut services between B'nei B'rak and Jerusalem.

The suburb of B'nei B'rak, to the northeast of Tel Aviv, is home to a community of some 150,000 Orthodox Jews, and comparisons are often drawn with Jerusalem's Mea She'arim district. Thomas Friedman notes in his book From Beirut To Jerusalem that "Jewish life in B'nei B'rak today has much more in common with Jewish life in 18th-century Lithuania than anything happening in north Tel Aviv. If they wanted to film the movie 'Hester Street' here, they would not have needed to bring in many props or costumes".

The town was founded in the 1920s by Warsaw Hasidim, though the name B'nei B'rak is mentioned as a city of the Dan tribe in Joshua 19:45, later to become a centre of religious study during the Roman occupation. B'nei B'rak continues this tradition. **NB** If you do decide to visit B'nei B'rak, it is important to dress modestly (men: long trousers, long sleeves; women: long skirt, closed neckline), and not to act as if in a zoo: it's a residential neighbourhood not a tourist site.

Tel Afek and Migdal Afek

ⓘ Daily 0800-1700, winter 0800-1600 (last entry 1 hr before). Adults 25NIS, students 21NIS, children 13NIS; map of the park provided.

The sites of **Tel Afek** (**Antipatris**) and **Migdal Afek** (**Migdal Tsedek**) are located close to **Rosh Ha'ayin** ('Head of the Spring') and, although neither site could be classed as spectacular, they make a pleasant half-day's excursion from Tel Aviv.

Ins and outs

Getting there and away By car, Tel Afek is signed "Antipatris" off Road 483 just before Rosh Ha'ayin. Egged buses 561/ 641 go to Baptist Village Junction from where it's a short walk to the Yarkon Sources entrance to the national park (30 minutes on to Tel Afek). Or from Petah Tikva bus station, Kavim buses 7, 17, 27, 83, 88, 89, 183 go to the Tel Afek turning. For Migdal Afek, take Egged bus 70 from Petah Tikva to Migdal Tsedek Junction.

Background

Excavations at **Tel Afek** have revealed a continuous occupation of the site from the Early Bronze Age (3300-2200 BCE) until the early part of the current century. Afek probably reached its peak in the Middle Bronze Age IIA (2000-1750 BCE) when it covered an area of over 10 hectares, and is listed in the Bible as one of the conquered Canaanite cities (Joshua 12:18). It was at Afek (Aphek), around 1080 BCE, that the Philistines' army gathered before capturing the Ark of the Covenant from the Israelites at Eben-ezer (I Samuel 4:1-11).

A town (called Pegae) developed at the Afek mound during the Early Hellenistic period (332-167 BCE), and was later expanded by **Herod**. He built a fort on the site in 35 BCE, naming the city after his father **Antipatris**. **Paul** spent a night here on his journey from Jerusalem to Caesarea (Acts 23:31). Much of Antipatris was destroyed in a major earthquake in 363 CE. The Crusaders also occupied Afek, as did the Mamluks and Ottoman Turks.

Sights

The dominant structure on the ancient Tel Afek mound is the **Ottoman fortress** (Binar Bashi) that was used to administer and garrison the coastal road from Haifa to Gaza. The large square fortress is strengthened by towers at each corner, of which the one to the southwest is octagonal, whilst the others are square. The main entrance opens on to a large courtyard, around which barracks and stables were built. To the north of the fortress can be seen the **Bronze-Age fortified city walls**.

The main Roman remains date to the Herodian period (37 BCE-70 CE), and comprise a series of buildings built on either side of the **cardo** (main street of Roman city) upon which the deep grooves of cart wheels are visible. The cardo extends down to a small **Roman theatre**, recently re-excavated. The stage, supported by ten arches, remains intact, along with a small section of the spectator seating area. However, the theatre was still unfinished when the earthquake of 363 CE struck.

Also prominent at Tel Afek are extensive remains of a water plant built by the British in 1935, to carry water all the way to Jerusalem. Asides from archaeological remains, the **National Park** is a haven for bird and water life notably six species of frog. There is a walking route (30 minutes) from Tel Afek past pretty water lily pools marking the source of the Yarkon (don't be tempted to swim) to a large picnic area. Shady eucalypts, the ruins of Al-Mir flour mill and plenty of 'mangals' (barbecues) make it a popular weekend spot. The Israel National Trail passes through the park, and hikers who decide to wild-camp here will not be frowned upon.

To the Crusaders, the nearby hill of **Migdal Afek** ① *three kilometres southeast of Tel Afek, 0800-1600 in summer, 0800-1500 in winter, entrance free*, was of far greater strategic value. Though there is evidence to suggest that Byzantine fortifications had previously been built here, almost certainly to protect the source of the perennial River Yarkon, the site is now occupied by the ruins of the Crusader castle of Mirabel ('miraculous beauty'). Though it is certainly not the best preserved Crusader castle in Israel, indeed most of what you see is an Ottoman-era structure built atop the castle, there are good views west to Tel Aviv's skyline and east to the West Bank hills, separated by less than 20 km. The area also encompasses a Sheikh's tomb, lime kilns and quarries linked by signed walking routes.

Tel Afek

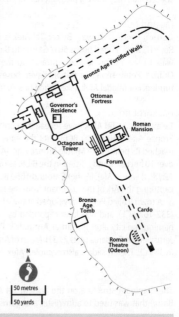

Contents

Footprint features

Mediterranean Coastal Strip

Visitors seeking a sun, sea and sand holiday tend to head to Eilat, at the southern tip of the Negev. This is a great pity, since the beaches along the Mediterranean coast, despite lacking the underwater splendour of the Red Sea's coral reefs, are infinitely superior. Yet there is more to Israel's Mediterranean coast than kilometre after kilometre of golden sand. After all, this coast has been a major zone of transition between Europe and Asia, and the coastal plain is replete with archaeological remains from several millennia of contact and interaction. Indeed, in typical Israeli style, there is often no separation between history and everyday life: in many places, to make your way down to the beach you have to pick your way through the archaeological remains.

Three of the key highlights on the coast contain that combination of beach and archaeology that makes Israel so appealing: Caesarea, Ashkelon, and Dor. This chapter also includes two very different coastal resorts, Herzliya and Netanya, plus the wine-producing region centred around Zichron Ya'akov.

To the south of Tel Aviv, a little inland from the coastal plain, lie a cluster of important archaeological sites in the area known as The Shephelah, including the astonishing underground caves of Beit Guvrin-Mareshah and the atmospheric tel of Lachish. Nearby is the natural wonder of the Soreq Stalactite Cave and the imposing monastery of Latrun, where a couple of interesting sites make for a good stop on the ancient trading route that the Tel Aviv to Jerusalem highway now follows.

Background

Geography The **Mediterranean coast** of Israel is a more or less straight line running north to south. It has neither a sheltered gulf, nor deep estuary for its entire length, and no large islands off-shore. Though harbours were eventually established in places along this coast, none is natural, and it should be noted that no invader from the west ever landed an army on this coast south of Mt Carmel (Haifa) without first having established a presence inland. This holds true for the Philistines, Alexander, Pompey, the Romans, the Crusaders and Napoleon. It could also be said that this section of the Mediterranean coast never produced a maritime people, with even the Phoenicians who settled south of Mt Carmel being predominantly agriculturalists.

The Mediterranean coastal strip, or **Maritime Plain**, is at the very heart of the history of the region. It has seen the march of the armies of Thothmes, Ramses, Sennacherib, Alexander, Pompey, Vespasian, Titus, Salah al-Din and Napoleon, to name but a few. It has also been part of a great trading route: the Great South Road of the famous Via Maris, or Way of the Sea. For millennia, this was the main trading route between Damascus and Egypt.

The Maritime Plain can be broadly divided into two distinct regions. To the north of Tel Aviv, running for 55 km almost all the way to Mt Carmel (Haifa), is the **Plain of Sharon**. In antiquity, much of this area was forested, possibly for almost its entire length, with numerous written references (from the Bible to Josephus, Crusader sources, and even Napoleon) referring to the woodlands here. In subsequent centuries, following years of exploitation and then neglect, much of this land became the malaria-infested swamps that became such a challenge to the early Zionist pioneers. The draining and management of the swamps has turned the Plain of Sharon into a rich agricultural region, though the development of large urban industrial centres here is now unrelenting.

The other section of the Maritime Plain stretches south from Tel Aviv, down to Gaza. Older sources refer to this region as the **Plain of Philistia**, after its early inhabitants, the Philistines. You may also see this region referred to as the **Shephelah** (or Shefela), though strictly speaking this is the region of low hills between the Maritime Plain and the Central Range. The Plain of Philistia is also rich agricultural land, though soils tend to be sandier.

A number of significant cities developed along the Maritime Plain, not least of which were the five chief Philistine cities: Gaza, Askalon (Ashkelon), Ashdod, Ekron and Gath. Further north lie Yavne, Ramla and Lod (Lydda), Jaffa (Joppa) and, most significantly on the Plain of Sharon, Caesarea and Dor. Few of these cities have Jewish origins, though the modern Jewish towns established at the end of the 19th or early 20th centuries have come to dominate the Mediterranean coastal strip. These include Tel Aviv and its 'satellites', plus Herzliya, Netanya and Hadera.

South and Southeast of Tel Aviv

With Arab populations of around 20%, the old towns of Lod and Ramla have a distinctive flavour and medieval architecture that make them stand out in the wider Tel Aviv area. In direct contrast is the Jewish pioneering settlement of Rishon LeTzion, where East European style buildings have been restored in the centre of town.

Rishon LeTzion → Colour map 2, grid B2.

Rishon LeTzion was one of the first of the Jewish agricultural settlements established by the early Zionist pioneers, and is now one of Israel's fastest-growing cities and the fourth largest. The town's history and development is documented in a museum, plus significant buildings from the early years can be seen on a short walking route.

Ins and outs

Getting there and away Rishon LeTzion is a 25-minute bus ride (frequent Dan or Egged services) from Tel Aviv's Central Bus Station, and can be visited as a day trip that also includes Rehovot, Ramla and Lod (if you get up early). Rishon LeTzion's bus station is on the junction of Herzl and Ein HaKore, and has frequent connections to Tel Aviv and other parts of the country (Ashkelon Be'er Sheva: Metropoline 367, 369 and 371; Jerusalem: Egged 431 and 433; Ramla: Superbus 461, 40 minutes, 7.5NIS. There are also sheruts available to Tel Aviv and Jerusalem. All the sights are within walking distance of one another.

Background

The town was founded in 1882 by 17 families of Russian and Romanian immigrants, who were escaping from the pogroms in Eastern Europe. As they were inexperienced in agricultural techniques, beset by disease incubated in the malarial swamps that they were attempting to settle, and occasionally harassed by Arab bandits, the settlement very nearly didn't survive. Without the determination and stubbornness of the founding fathers, and a large measure of financial support from **Baron Edmond de Rothschild**, the infant settlement may well have been stillborn.

Rishon LeTzion claims the distinction of being 'first' in a number of fields of Jewish life. Not only was it the forerunner of other Jewish agricultural settlements ('Rishon LeTzion' meaning 'First to Zion'), it claims to be the site of the first singing of the *Hatikva* (the Jewish national anthem, though this is claimed elsewhere), where the current Israeli flag was first flown, where Hebrew was taught in the first Hebrew school, where the first orchestra played, and where the first 'Hebrew' plough was built. It is also home of the Israeli wine-producing industry, following the introduction of Burgundy and Bordeaux vines in 1887.

Rishon LeTzion Museum

ⓘ *Founders' Square, Rothschild, T03-9598890/9682435, www.rishonlezion-museum.org. Sun, Tue, Wed and Thu 0900-1400, Mon 0900-1300 and 1600-1900. Adult 18NIS, student/child 15NIS, free on first Sat of the month 1000-1600 (but no English tours). Toilets. Shop.*
The town's history is well presented in the compact museum, sited in historical buildings such as the original pharmacy and post office. A guided tour is usually offered (Hebrew, English, plus several European languages, no extra charge, phone ahead to reserve a place) though it is very intense. The museum features mock-ups of homes, shops and artisans

workshops from the early settlement – a recent restoration is "Beit Schalit", the house of the town's founder, beautifully furnished in period style.

Pioneer's Way

A short walking route around the town centre takes the visitor past many of Rishon LeTzion's earliest buildings and most interesting sites (the museum has a leaflet giving further details).

The Great Synagogue The foundations of the synagogue were laid on the hill at the centre of the village in 1885. An Ottoman ordinance in effect at the time banned the construction of new synagogues in Palestine, so the early settlers obtained a permit for the construction of an agricultural warehouse. The two windows at the top of the synagogues façade are said to symbolize the tablet stones of the Ten Commandments, whilst the twelve windows represent the 'Twelve Tribes'.

Founders' Square This site at the top of the hill is where the first 17 families set up their tents on 15 August 1882.

House of Aharon Mordechai and Miriam Freiman Aharon Mordechai Freiman was one of the founding fathers of the town, and he lived in this house after its construction in 1883. It is claimed that the National Hebrew song *Hushu Ahim Hushu* was composed by Yehiel Michel Piress for the house-warming. A Hasidic synagogue and Talmud Torah School were built behind the house on land donated by Freiman, and the house itself was also used as a courthouse. Today it is a kitchen utensils store.

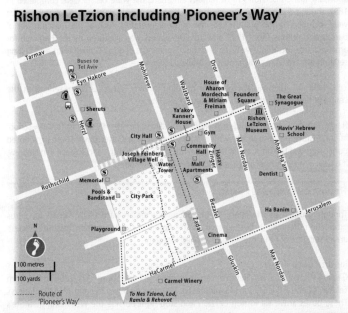

Rishon LeTzion including 'Pioneer's Way'

Ya'akov Kanner's House Built in 1900 by Ya'akov Kanner, one of the more prosperous farmers of the community, this elegant townhouse later housed the Magen David Adom (equivalent of the Red Cross) from 1940 to 1985, and was used as the headquarters of the Haganah during the 1948 war.

Joseph Feinberg Village Well and Water Tower One of the major crises facing the community of settlers in the early days of Rishon LeTzion's existence was the provision of water. With the aid of an 'anonymous' loan from Edmond de Rothschild, who was to become the town's benefactor, the founding fathers were able to construct this village well. Water was eventually found at a depth of 48 m. The image of the well's water tower is now included in the town crest of Rishon LeTzion since it played such a large part in deciding the fate of the settlement. There is a Sound and Light performance at the well (included in museum admission price)

City Hall Originally erected in 1888 to provide accommodation for Rothschild administrators, agronomists, a doctor (and a wine cellar), the building now houses the town's Municipal Offices.

Community Hall The old Community Hall, one third of which is constructed of an intricate wooden design, has been renovated and is back in use. It's situated on the edge of the pleasant park which attracts couples for wedding photo shoots.

Carmel Winery ⓘ *T03-9488802, www.carmelwines.co.il. Tours Sun-Thu 0900, 1100, 1300 and 1500.* Rishon LeTzion's most famous landmark, the wine cellars were completed in 1897, though the building served as more than just a wine producer. Whole workshops were included on the premises for use in auxiliary trades, such as the manufacture of barrels and pumps. From 1929 onwards, the winery was also used by the Haganah for arms practice, including live firing and the manufacture of guns. Guided tours and tasting sessions are available, which must be booked in advance.

Yad HaBanim This was the grandest building in early Rishon LeTzion, serving as the centre of Baron de Rothschild's activities in Palestine.

Haviv Hebrew School Founded in 1886, this is said to be not only the first Hebrew school in Eretz Israel, but also in the whole world. It was named after Haviv Lubman, a noted public figure of the time, and it taught Jewish studies, literature, and science – in Hebrew. It is now a mixed school and a second storey has been added.

Rehovot → *Colour map 2, grid B2.*

Though situated in the heart of an agricultural region particularly famed for citrus production, Rehovot is best known as the home of the **Weizmann Institute**: Israel's greatest centre of fundamental and applied research.

Ins and outs
Getting there and away Rehovot can be reached on Egged buses 201, 226 and 301 from Tel Aviv's Central Bus Station (45 minutes) or Metropoline buses 351 and 371 (30 minutes). These buses arrive via Rishon LeTzion and stop right outside the Weizmann Institute's

Chaim Weizmann (1874-1952)

Born in 1874 near to the border between White Russia, Lithuania and Poland, Weizmann's greatest legacy to the Zionist movement (and the subsequent State of Israel) was the way in which he paved the way for the Balfour Declaration. A great admirer of the British, believing them to be as fair-minded and just as they claimed to be, he used his not inconsiderable charm to win over support amongst the ruling British élite for the establishment of a Jewish homeland. Johnson suggests that, despite teaching biochemistry at Manchester University, Weizmann's life-task was in fact "to exploit the existence of the British Empire, and the goodwill of its ruling classes, to bring the Jewish national home into existence" (A History of the Jews, 1989). By 1948 all his lobbying efforts had paid off, and the following year he became Israel's first President.

main gate. Rehovot's Central Bus Station is a longish walk to the southwest. The Weizmann Institute is also conveniently located near to Rehovot's train station, from where there are regular services to and from Tel Aviv (about one an hour).

Background
The town was established in 1890 by early Zionists from a community of Polish Jews. The name is taken from Rehoboth, a well dug in the Negev by Isaac (*Genesis 26:22*), though the settlement did not expand much beyond a collection of farming villages until it was connected to the Lod-Gaza railway line towards the end of World War I. During the 'Second Aliya', Rehovot became an important social and cultural centre in the history of Jewish resettlement, and the first Hebrew language instruction to the Sephardic community was given here.

It was around this time that **Chaim Weizmann** (see box above) settled in Rehovot, establishing an agricultural research station. In 1944, on the occasion of Weizmann's 70th birthday, the Weizmann Institute of Science was inaugurated. The town of Rehovot now has a population of around 103,000.

Sights
Weizmann Institute of Science ⓘ *Call in advance, T08-9344500, Sun-Thu 1000-1600, adult 30NIS, student/child 20NIS, combination ticket with the Clore Garden 40/30NIS.*
The Weizmann Institute is one of the world's leading research bodies in the fields of physics, chemistry, biology, microbiology and plant genetics. Set in a wonderful park area, comprising over 80 hectares of manicured lawns, gardens and shady paths, the Institute employs almost 2000 staff, researchers and students. Besides the lovely parkland, the attractions include the Wix Auditorium (with an audio-visual presentation), the **Weizmann House** (Weizmann's family home 1949-1952, designed by the renowned architect Erich Mendelsohn) and the simple graves of Weizmann (1874-1952) and his wife (1881-1966). The **Clore Garden of Science** ⓘ *T08-9344401, Mon-Fri 1000-1700 (times change during Jul/Aug, phone to check), adult 30NIS, student/child 20NIS,* is an outdoor science museum, and there is a plaza containing a Holocaust Memorial by sculptor Dani Karavan (adult 15NIS, child 10 NIS).

Ramla (Ramleh) → *Colour map 2, grid B3.*

The name Ramla almost certainly derives from the Arabic word 'raml', meaning 'sand', and is probably a reference to the dunes upon which the town was built. The city became the capital of **Filistin** and is the only city in Palestine that was founded by the **Arabs** (early in the eighth century CE by the Umayyad caliph **Suleiman ibn 'Abd el-Malik**). Ramla owes its strategic importance to its location at the junction of three ancient communication routes. Thus, the town has been fought over and occupied by the Arabs, Crusaders, Mamluks, Napoleon's army, the Ottomans, the British army, Palestinian Arabs, and finally the Israelis. Ramla has a number of interesting remains, and a laid-back feel.

Ins and outs
Getting there and away Ramla can be visited in a day excursion from Tel Aviv that also takes in Lod, Rishon LeTzion and Rehovot. Superbus buses 411, 451 and 455 run direct to Ramla's new Bus Station from Tel Aviv's Central Bus Station. There are plenty of buses/sheruts from Ramla to Lod, and Egged buses to Jerusalem. All the main sights are within easy walking distance of each other, and the souk is an authentic place to stroll (and eat).

Background
Until the conquest of Ramla by the Crusaders in 1099, the town had a long history of religious tolerance, both between faiths, and between different sects of the main faiths. A large number of *Sufis* (from the mystical aspect of Islam, emphasizing the importance of personal spiritual development that is found only through the Qu'ran), came to settle

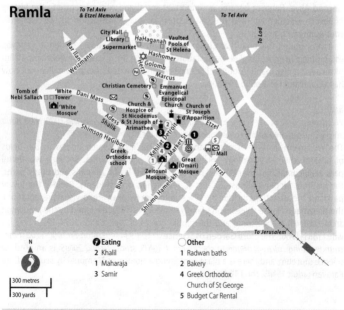

Ramla

To Tel Aviv & Etzel Memorial
To Tel Aviv
To Lod

City Hall
Library
Supermarket
HaHaganah
Vaulted Pools of St Helena
Hashomer
Golomb
Marcus
Christian Cemetery
Emmanuel Evangelical Episcopal Church
Church of St Joseph d'Apparition
Tomb of Nebi Sallach
'White Tower'
'White Mosque'
Dani Mass
Church & Hospice of St Nicodemus & St Joseph of Arimathea
Adess
Shalik
Shimson HaGibor
Bialik
Greek Orthodox school
Zeitouni Mosque
Great (Omari) Mosque
Mall
Bar Ilan
Weizmann
Herzl
Kehilat Detroit
Market St
Etzel
Herzl
Shlomo Hamelekh
To Jerusalem

N
300 metres
300 yards

Eating
2 Khalil
1 Maharaja
3 Samir

Other
1 Radwan baths
2 Bakery
4 Greek Orthodox Church of St George
5 Budget Car Rental

Stealing the White Tower

A popular legend exists in Ramla concerning an attempt by the neighbouring town of Lod to steal the White Tower. A long history of enmity apparently existed between Ramla and Lod, with much of the building material used to construct Ramla being taken from the ruins of Lod. A large section of Lod's population was seemingly forcibly removed to Ramla in order to promote the latter's growth.

Envying Ramla's square tower, the residents of Lod resolved to steal it, and remove it to their town. Borrowing some ropes from an 'old sheikh', the boys from Lod, in the dead of night, tied the ropes to the tower and began to heave it back to Lod. Unbeknown to them, the old sheikh, who was a bit of a wag, had given them rubber cords rather than rope. As the boys arrived in Lod pulling their 'ropes', they cried out "Ramla's tower arrives", at which point the town turned out to greet them. Unfortunately for them, the tower remained in Ramla.

in Ramla during the Abbasid Caliphate (c 750 CE). It is documented that Ramla was already home to members of both the *Sunni* and *Shia* (Shi'ite) branches of Islam, as well as indigenous Jews. Ramla was (and continues to be) centre of one of the main communities of *Karaites*, a Jewish sect dating back to the eighth century. Their centre and synagogue is at **Matsliah** (T08-9249104), 2 km to the south of Ramla.

Much of Ramla's early splendour was destroyed in the 11th century by a series of earthquakes, and in the 12th century by the arrival of the **Crusaders**. Thrice the Crusaders fought the Fatimids for control of Ramla, and in the 90 years or so that they controlled the town it became an important staging post on the pilgrimage route to Jerusalem. Christian tradition relates that Ramla was the site of **Arimathea**, the domicile of **Joseph**, who arranged for Jesus to be brought down from the cross and buried in his family's tomb. Substantial rebuilding took place during the period of Mamluk rule, including the construction of the White Tower.

Later visitors to Ramla have included **Napoleon**, who is alleged to have spent a night at the Church and Hospice of St Nicodemus and St Joseph of Arimathea during his ill-fated 1799 campaign, and General Allenby, who arrived at the head of the British forces during World War I.

During the Arab uprising and riots of 1936, many of the town's Jewish residents left, only to return after the Arab exodus in the wake of the Israeli capture of the town in 1948. Indeed, much has been made recently of David Ben-Gurion's role in this 'population transfer'. The population of Ramla today is around 64,000, 20% of whom are Arabs, with large populations of Russian and Ethiopian immigrants.

Sights

Historical Museum of Ramla ① *112 Herzl, T08-9292650, Sun-Thu 1000-1600, Fri and hols 1000-1300. Adults 6NIS, student/children 5NIS. Combined ticket to museum, arched pool and white tower 12NIS.* Housed in the old town hall, the small museum is a worthwhile first stop; the helpful manager, Yigal also supplies informal tourist information. The most-valued exhibit is a hoard of 376 ancient gold dinars discovered at the White Mosque, from countries ranging from Morocco to Uzbekistan. There are also scale models of the sights in town in their heyday, a section of Byzantine mosaic floor, clay artefacts, and a mock-up of the tent of a 1950s immigrant to Israel.

Great (Omari) Mosque Originally the 12th-century Crusader Church of St John, the Great (Omari) Mosque was converted to its present function during the Mamluk period. A tall, white minaret was built on the foundations of the church's bell-tower, though evidence of the Crusader's aisled basilica can still be seen inside. The mosque is not generally open to casual visitors, though you may be lucky; try between 0800 and 1600.

Old City There are considerable reminders of Ramla's ancient past, and a stroll around the old residential quarter has much to recommend it. Just north of the Great (Omari) Mosque, and beyond the busy bazaar streets, is the main neighbourhood place of worship: the **Zeitouni Mosque**. The mosque contains the tomb of Sheikh Zeitouni. Also to be seen close by are the Ottoman period **Radwan Baths**, in use until 1948. Just to the north of the baths is the **Greek Orthodox Church of St George** ⓘ *T08-9221174, Sat/Sun only*, identifiable by the red dome on its bell-tower and the image of George and the Dragon above the entrance. The traditional houses in this part of town, built as they are around courtyards and clustered together along narrow streets, are rather appealing, though you will find yourself continually coming up against dead-ends.

Church and Hospice of St Nicodemus and St Joseph of Arimathea ⓘ *Main entrance through a gate on Bialik Street, T08-9252917. Mon-Fri 0800-1130; ring the bell if door is closed. Entrance free. Modest dress required.* Originally built by the Franciscans in the 16th century, most of the building actually dates to 1902, with a remarkably simple interior.

'White Tower' and 'White Mosque' ⓘ *Sun-Thu 0800-1430, Fri 0800-1400, Sat and hols 0800-1600. Adults 5NIS, student/child 4NIS (if someone is on duty).* Known as the 'Tower of the Forty Companions of the Prophet' to Muslims and 'Tower of the Forty Martyrs' to Christians (or simply 'White Tower'), this is a later addition to a mosque (**al-Jama'a al-Abyad**) commonly attributed to the Umayyad period. Although an Arabic inscription over the entrance to the tower claims that it was built in 1318 CE by Sultan Mohammad ibn Qala'un, it is known that repairs to the mosque had been carried out earlier, during the reign of the Mamluk sultan Baibars. The 27-m-high square tower is built in Gothic style, and is said to have a fine view from its upper platform (both Napoleon and General Allenby used it as a reconnaissance tower), though it remains closed.

To the south of the tower/minaret are the overgrown remains of a substantial mosque compound (93 m by 84 m), beneath which are a series of deep subterranean cisterns. In the northwest corner of the compound is the Tomb of Nebi Sallach, a Muslim holy man who is reputed to have turned a rock into a camel in the name of Allah.

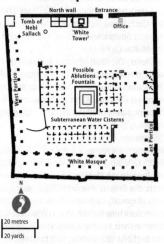

White Tower and White Mosque

North wall · Entrance

Tomb of Nebi Sallach · 'White Tower' · Office

West Portico

Possible Ablutions Fountain

Subterranean Water Cisterns

East Portico

'White Mosque'

N

20 metres
20 yards

Arched Pools of St Helena ① *Sun-Thu 0800-1430, Fri 0800-1400, Sat 0800-1600. Adult 8NIS, student/child 6NIS (includes rowing boat); toilets.* These vaulted pools, located in a garden accessed from HaHaganah Street, are named after the fourth-century CE Roman empress dowager St Helena. She is credited with, three centuries after the event, 'rediscovering' the tomb of Christ, Golgotha, the true cross, the instruments of the passion, the cave of the nativity and the site of the Ascension of Christ. As such, Amos Elon refers to her as "the most successful archaeologist in all history"! The pools have no connection whatsoever with St Helena (except the name), since they were built in 789 CE during the reign of the fifth Abbasid Caliph, Haroun al-Rashid. The reference to the name 'St Helena's Pools' appears for the first time in the books of Christian pilgrims in the early 19th century. The Arab name for the pools is **Birket al-Anzia**.

The large pool is covered by a series of 24 groined vaults with 24 square openings in the roof to allow a large number of people to draw water at one time. The cistern is beautifully cool, and the light reflecting on the rippling pool creates a very pleasing effect. Rowing boats are available for a self-guided tour of the pool.

British War Cemetery ① *T08-9221220, daily. Free.* To the east of Ramla, 2 km beyond the town, is the large World War I cemetery, where the troops of General Allenby's forces, who died fighting the Turks, are buried. The cemetery is cared for by the Commonwealth War Graves Commission.

Ramla listings

For Sleeping and Eating price codes and other relevant information, see Essentials pages 26-31.

Eating

There are plenty of bargain falafel and shwarma places along Herzl, and around the Old City area. In fact, eating anywhere in Ramla is pretty cheap.

₩-₩ Maharaja Restaurant & Indian Sweets on Herzl, T08-9223534. Famed throughout Israel, the Maharaja is run by one of Ramla's 800-strong Indian community. Excellent masala dosas (28NIS) and other South Indian delights, plenty of North India veg dishes, as well as samosas, snacks and sweets. On Fri, however, it's buffet-style (50NIS) rather than the usual menu. Sun-Thu 1000-2100, Fri 1000-1600.

₩-₩ Restaurant Khalil, next to the Greek Orthodox Church of St George; no English sign; diagonally opposite Samir's. All the locals flock here for massive dollops of hummus and a plethora of other Arabic salads (10-15NIS), shishlik, kubeh, fish

(all 35-70NIS); functional canteen-style, rammed with Israelis on Shabbat. Highly recommended.

₩-₩ Samir's, 7 Shafik Adas, T08-9220195, www.rest.co.il/samir. Ramla's first restaurant was established in 1948, and it's still one of the most appealing options in town. Dine under Jerusalem-esque stone arches downstairs, or under the tent on the roof. Very reasonably priced with chicken mains/kebabs/liver 38-40NIS, stuffed vegetables (try the carrots) 25NIS, or selection of salads 10-15NIS, kubeh 10NIS, falafel 5NIS. Daily 0800-2000 (till 2400 in summer).

Transport

From Ramla's bus station there are regular Egged buses to **Jerusalem** via **Latrun** (403, 404 and 433; 22.5NIS, 1 hr); **Rehovot** (248 and 249, 40 mins); **Rishon LeTzion** (433, 50 mins). For **Tel Aviv** Superbus buses 411, 451 and 455; to **Lod** Superbus 461, Veolia bus 150 (15 mins); sheruts to Lod leave from outside Maharaja restaurant on the main street.

Lod (Lydda) → *Colour map 2, grid B3.*

Most visitors to Israel come to Lod (Lydda) without knowing it: Tel Aviv's Ben-Gurion Airport is located on the outskirts. Although the modern town is rather unattractive and has a bit of a bad reputation, it is Lod's association with the Christian martyr St George that draws most visitors. The church/mosque in his name is situated in the old (and rather decrepit) part of town.

Ins and outs

Getting there and away From Tel Aviv take Veolia bus 462 or 475, or Superbus 461, from the sixth floor of the Central Bus Station, they leave frequently from 0520, last one returning to Tel Aviv 2230. Lod's bus station is a small yard in the heart of the Old City, from where the key attractions are a short walk. There are frequent buses and sheruts to/from Ramla (15 minutes), Rehovot and Rishon LeTzion (50 minutes), though to get to Jerusalem you must change at Ramla. Sheruts to Tel Aviv leave when full from outside Dahamash Mosque. There are frequent trains to/from Tel Aviv, though Lod's station is not conveniently located.

Background

The town has its origins in the arrival of the Israelites in the Promised Land (*Chronicles 8:12*), with the first written mention of Lod in the 15th century BCE 'City Lists of Thutmose III'. The town was later occupied by the Greeks in the fourth century BCE ('Lydda'), the Hasmoneans in the second century BCE (*I Maccabees 11:34*), and the Romans in 67 CE ('Diospolis', City of Zeus).

Lod has a lengthy Christian association, dating back to the visit of Paul when he cured Aeneas (*Acts 9: 32-35*), and continued through the town's association with **St George**. Legend suggests that he was born in Lydda, and it was to here that his remains were brought following his martyrdom in 303.

Lod was razed by the Omayyad Caliph Abd el-Malik, and rebuilt by the Crusaders, though its subsequent history is not particularly noteworthy. In fact, it was not until the termination of the British Mandate in 1948 and the creation of the State of Israel that Lod once again came to prominence, when the decision was made to expand the nearby former British airstrip. These days, the city of 68,000 people (69% Jewish, 24% Muslim, 7% Christian/other) suffers from unemployment and unrest. If you are hungry, Abu Michel Oriental Restaurant, between the bus station and St George's, does an excellent hummus.

St George's Church / el-Chodr Mosque, Lod

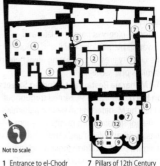

Not to scale

1 Entrance to el-Chodr Mosque
2 Ablutions Fountain
3 Entrance to Prayer Chamber
4 Byzantine Column with Greek inscription (high up)
5 Apse of Byzantine Basilica
6 Mihrab
7 Pillars of 12th Century Crusader Church
8 Entrance to St George's Church
9 Apses of Crusader Church
10 Greek Orthodox Altar
11 Greek Orthodox Altar Screen
12 Staircases to Crypt & Tomb of St George

Sights

St George's Church/el-Chodr Mosque St George's Church, with the saint's sarcophagus, is Lod's main attraction. In addition to being canonized by the Christian church, St George is also revered by Muslims as the 'bright spirit', **el-Chodr**, who will vanquish the demon Dajal on the Day of Judgement. Thus, the complex that houses his remains is shared by the two faiths.

The complex has its origins in a sixth-century Byzantine basilica, remains of which are best seen in the **el-Chodr Mosque** in the southern part of the complex. One of the main columns supporting the prayer hall belongs to the Byzantine church, and can be identified by the Greek inscription. To the north of this column is an apse from the Byzantine structure. Modestly dressed non-Muslims are permitted entry into the mosque (on removal of shoes, and excluding prayer times). Enter through the green-domed gate to the west.

The original **St George's Church** was built by the Crusaders, though much of the present structure was built in 1870 by the **Greek Orthodox church** ① *Mon-Thu 0900-1600, Fri-Sun -1300*. You might have to search out the man with the key. Two apses and two central columns from the Crusader church still form a central component of the present building. The interior is ornately decorated in the style typical of Greek Orthodox places of worship in the Holy Land. The altar screen is particularly intricate, and incense, icons and lamps abound. Two staircases lead down to the crypt, and the simple tomb of St George. The sarcophagus, restored in 1871, is of white, pink and black marble, with an image of the saint holding a spear and a cross. Hanging on a column by the top of the second flight of steps is a chain that is said to be the one that held the martyr as he was tortured; tourists now shackle themselves with it and have their photos taken. The church/mosque is at its busiest (and most interesting) on the saint's burial date (16 November, by the Orthodox liturgical calendar).

Dahamash Mosque This recently refurbished mosque has a contentious history. During fighting between Jordanian and Israeli forces in Lod in 1948, a number of civilians took refuge in the mosque. Local Palestinians tell visitors that Israeli troops deliberately targeted the mosque with mortar fire, killing a hundred or so civilians sheltering inside.

Ashkelon (Ashqelon) → *Colour map 2, grid C1.*

With a natural port site, and a rich hinterland of fertile agricultural land and abundant water, there should be little surprise that Ashkelon developed as an important city, with a history spanning 6000 years. Much of the town's history is presented in an excellent National Park, where substantial remains are set amongst picnic lawns. The town is also attempting to appeal more to holiday-makers, with a refurbishing of the beach area.

Ins and outs

Getting there and away Ashkelon has good bus connections with the rest of the country, notably Tel Aviv and Jerusalem. The Central Bus Station is on Ben-Gurion, with sheruts leaving from the opposite side of the road.

Getting around Bus 6 runs from the Central Bus Station to Ashkelon National Park (or it's a 20-minute walk). Bus 5 runs to Kikar Zefanya (for Antiquities' Courtyard) from the Central Bus Station (or an uphill 20-minute walk), continuing on to Barnea. Buses 1, 2, 4, 4a and 10 run between Migdal and the Central Bus Station, with buses 2 and 3 calling at Barnea.

Tourist Information **Tourist Information Office** ① Ha'Nassi, T08-6749677, Sun-Thu 0830-1300, sometimes on Fri 0830-1000. Helpful kiosk run by volunteers opposite the 'Sundial Square', has good map of Ashkelon and some leaflets in English.

Background

Early rulers Despite an earlier settlement having been established here, it was the movement of the **Sea Peoples** into this area that saw Ashkelon become a **Philistine** city around the 12th century BCE, and there are numerous references in the Bible to 'Ashkelon' as one of the five leading cities of the Philistines (*Joshua 13:3, 3; I Samuel 6:17*). Of the five cities (Gaza, Ashkelon, Ashdod, Ekron and Gath), Ashkelon was perhaps the most important due to its status as a port.

Subsequent centuries saw Ashkelon conquered by a series of rulers, including Assyrians and Egyptians, with the last Philistine ruler of Ashkelon being forced into exile in Babylon around 604 BCE by **Nebuchadnezzar**. The city later came under the rule of the Persians, during whose tenure the maritime **Phoenicians** expanded Ashkelon's commercial wealth. A succession of dynasties followed though, whoever the nominal rulers were, Ashkelon retained a fair degree of autonomy, and by the first century BCE was minting its own silver coins. In subsequent years, most notably during the period of the Mishnah and Talmud (second to fifth centuries CE), Ashkelon was considered to be outside the limits of Eretz Israel ('Land of Israel'), and had resisted Jewish forces during the First Jewish Revolt (66 CE).

Ashqelon

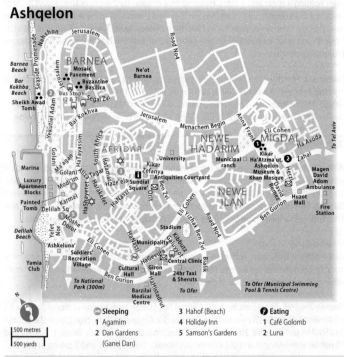

🛏 Sleeping	3 Hahof (Beach)	🍴 Eating
1 Agamim	4 Holiday Inn	1 Café Golomb
2 Dan Gardens	5 Samson's Gardens	2 Luna
(Ganei Dan)		

Roman and Byzantine rule Ashkelon flourished in the Late Roman period (132-324 CE), adding to the splendour that **Herod** had endowed the city with during his earlier period of rule. Josephus (*The Jewish War I: 21, 42*) details Herod's ambitious building projects, and it is suggested in a number of sources that Ashkelon was in fact his birthplace. Trade continued to develop in Byzantine times (324-638 CE), with Ashkelon becoming the major outlet for wine produced in the Levant. The city also became a focus of Christian pilgrimage.

Arab and Crusader periods Muslim rule began in 636 CE and continued until the Crusaders defeated the Fatimids in 1153. The city then changed hands five times between the Christians and the Muslims within the next century. **Salah al-Din** took the city in 1187, only for **Richard Coeur de Lion** to recapture it four years later. In the meantime, Salah al-Din had razed most of the fortifications and attempted to destroy the harbour. Richard subsequently rebuilt some of the fortifications, only to return the city to Salah al-Din by treaty. Once again Salah al-Din dismantled the fortified walls, only for them to be partially rebuilt in 1240 by the Duke of Cornwall. The fortress was finally destroyed in 1265 by the Mamluk sultan **Baibars**. The Ottoman ruler Ahmed el-Jazzer subsequently used stone from the site to help build his sea wall at Akko.

Recent history For most of the last century Ashkelon merely comprised the small Arab village of Migdal, where parts of an old caravanserai and mosque remain. In 1952, following the controversial forced removal of the Arab population, South African Jews founded the settlement of Afridar, from which Ashkelon has grown to a city of some 111,700 people.

Sights
Ashkelon National Park ① *T08-6736444, www.parks.org.il. Summer 0800-2200 (last entrance 2000), winter 0800-1600 (last entrance 1500). Adults 25NIS, student 21NIS, child 13NIS (or admission via the beach). Camping only on Fri/hols (and Thu in Jul/Aug), adult/child 40/30NIS. Bus 6 runs here hourly from the Central Bus Station. Café.*
Set adjacent to the beach, within 80 hectares of sculptured lawns, the Ashkelon National Park contains a number of antiquities that hint at the city's long and distant past. There are remains from most levels of occupation, though those from the Canaanite, Roman, Byzantine, Arab and Crusader periods dominate.

First stop on entering the park is Tel Ashkelon with its mighty fortifying glacis, where the **Canaanite city gate** has been heavily restored. This is the oldest arched gate in the world and you can now pass through it and the corridor beyond.

The park is enclosed within well-preserved **fortified walls**, usually mistakenly attributed to the Crusaders. They were in fact built in the Fatimid period (10th-12th centuries CE) by the Arabs, though they were partially rebuilt and reinforced in 1192 by Richard Coeur de Lion. There were originally gates at each of the cardinal points: Jaffa Gate to the north, Jerusalem Gate to the east, Gaza Gate to the south, and Sea Gate to the west. Today, just the eastern gate remains standing.

The most dramatic view of the surrounding wall can be seen by dropping down on to the beach, and viewing the fortifications from there. Parts of the western wall have succumbed to the years and have been reclaimed by the sea; other parts lie broken on the beach. Much of the debris, including Roman columns, was dumped here by Salah al-Din in an attempt to render the harbour unusable by the Crusaders. In the southwest corner, at the site of the old quay, the ancient **Byzantine wall** remains, buttressed by **Roman columns** that have been likened to the barrels of coastal cannons.

In the centre of the park is the **Roman basilica**, containing Corinthian capitals and column bases, dating to the third century CE when Ashkelon was ruled as a semi-autonomous state by Severius. The building was 110 m long and 35 m wide, with an open central courtyard surrounded by a portico (colonnade) of 24 columns on each side, and 6 at either end. At the southern end is an apse, set at its original level several metres below the current ground level. The area is currently being excavated, and the remarkable marble pillars which were found here are being temporarily stored nearby (see map). One depicts the **goddess of victory**, Victoria-Nike, standing holding a wreath and palm on a globe supported by Atlas. The other is a representation of the Egyptian **goddess Isis**, with the **child-god Horus**.

The park also contains a modern 10,000 seat **amphitheatre** that is used for occasional concerts, plus wells dating to the Ottoman period, one of which has been significantly restored. With ample parking places and large expanses of lawn, the National Park is very popular at weekends with picnicking families. There is a designated **bathing beach** here, though it is rather polluted. It is possible to tour the park on foot, and do a complete circuit of the Arab/Crusader walls.

Tombs To the north of the National Park, close to the seafront, lie two (unconnected) sets of tombs. The first includes a **Roman tomb** and a painted **Hellenistic tomb**, which date from the third or fourth century CE. The barrel-vaulted Hellenistic tomb is decorated with frescoes depicting images from classic Greek mythology, though both are now in a poor state of repair and you will have to seek them out from Yefe Nof Street.

Further north, the 13th-century Mamluk **tomb of Sheikh Awad** stands above the beach, its dome providing an interesting counterpoint to the nearby 'golf-ball' Holiday Inn. The central chamber holds the local saint's tomb, with two later rooms on either side.

Antiquities Courtyard ⓘ *Kikar Zefanya, Afridar. Sun-Thu 0830-1530, Fri 0830-1330. Free.* Located in the heart of the Afridar district is the compact Antiquities Courtyard. An interesting collection of archaeological finds from the Ashkelon area, the key attractions are two third-century CE **Roman sarcophagi**. The first is complete with a cover depicting reclining figures, symbolizing the deceased. You may notice that the faces on these figures are yet to be completed: this suggests that the sarcophagus had not yet been purchased and was still waiting to be completed with a suitable likeness. The superb carvings on one side depict the abduction of Persephone, whilst the two shorter ends show two griffins, and the second side a pitcher between two lions. The other sarcophagus probably had a similar cover, though this was not found when the two items were excavated in 1972. On three sides are carved scenes from a battle between the Romans and the Gauls (or Trojans), whilst on the fourth side there is a depiction of bulls being attacked by lions.

Byzantine basilica and mosaic pavement During the construction of the suburb of Barnea, the remains of a Byzantine basilica church were discovered. The nave is flanked by two side aisles, with a small prayer room to the south. Coloured glass tesserae found on the floor suggest that the walls and floor were decorated with mosaic.

A smaller basilica was found 200 m away, though all you can see now is the uncared for mosaic floor. An inscription in Greek in the *diaconicon* (storehouse in Byzantine churches) dates construction to 499 CE, with a second inscription in the antechamber pavement quoting *Psalm 93:5* ("holiness becometh thine house, O Lord ... "), and a date of 493-494 CE. A third Greek inscription quotes *Psalm 23:1* ("The Lord is My Shepherd ... ").

Migdal district There are a number of interesting things to see in Ashkelon's older district of Migdal, which has a different vibe to the rest of the city. The **Ashkelon Museum** ⓘ *Kikar Ha'Atzmaut, T08-6727002. Sun-Thu 0900-1300 and 1600-1800, Fri 0900-1300, Sat 1000-1300, free*, traces the history of the town from Roman times through to the establishment of the State of Israel. There's an audio-visual presentation, photos,maps, and space given over to local artists. The museum is located within the former Great Mosque of the Arab town of Majdal, adjacent to an old caravanserai on the ancient trading route. Migdal is the town's main market area, best seen on a Monday or Thursday, and is increasingly becoming a place to dine out as the old caravanserai is turned into restaurants and bars.

Beaches

There are a number of distinct beaches along Ashkelon's Mediterranean coast. From north to south they are: **North Beach**, fairly quiet, popular for nude bathing; **Barnea Beach**, becomes quite busy at weekends with residents of this fairly affluent suburb; **Bar Kochba**, the town's religious beach, which has separate bathing hours for men and women; **Delilah Beach**, which has a number of wading pools and is the town's most popular beach, particularly at weekends; finally, on the coastal side of the National Park, is the **HaSela Beach**. **NB** There are very strong undercurrents along this stretch of coastline, and it is advised that you only swim at sanctioned beaches where life-guards are present.

Ashkelon (Ashqelon) listings

For Sleeping and Eating price codes and other relevant information, see Essentials pages 26-31.

Sleeping

Despite its 'resort' reputation there isn't much accommodation choice in Ashkelon.
L Holiday Inn, 9 Yekutiel Adam, T08-6748888, www.holidayinn.co.il. This luxury hotel resembles a giant golf ball from most angles. All rooms face the sea, with some 'business', 'deluxe' and 'chalet' rooms. Full facilities include pleasant pool area, tennis, gym and the Carnival nightclub. Restaurants include Rozmarin and the highly regarded Gazpacho (see Eating). Overall quite plush, though surrounding area is still a little tatty.
AL Dan Gardens (Ganei Dan), 56 Hatayassim, T08-6771777, www.danhotels.com. 250-room hotel, some with sea views; 4 suites, leisure facilities (gym, sauna and tennis), restaurants. The pool-garden area is particularly pleasant, but rooms are a little box-like and few have balconies. Full and half-board also available.

A Agamim, 2 Moshe Dorot, corner of Hatayassim, T08-6710981. Little chalets with pebble-dash and red roofs have a/c, TV, kitchenettes; Butlins-style in private grounds; some comfy outdoor seating. Remodelled rooms are spotless, including shower. Not much English spoken; restaurant; reasonable value at 360NIS per couple.
A Hahof (Beach Hotel), Delilah Beach, T08-6716404. Rather run down (looks abandoned from some angles), rooms have a/c, TV; bare and old fashioned but clean. Staff are friendly, though don't speak much English. No breakfast, but tea/coffee possible. Bottom end of this price range, good sea views.
A Samson's Gardens, 38 Hatamar, T08-6736641. Chalets set around garden in quiet residential neighbourhood. Rooms have a/c, TV, kitchenettes, and are large with decent bathrooms; (religious) family-orientated.

Eating and drinking

There are some reasonable cafés and pubs on **Kikar Zefanya/'Sundial Sq'**, and also a **Supersol** supermarket, plus a collection of cafés, sushi, seafood joints and bars on Delilah Sq (facing the beach). Falafel and shwarma is at its cheapest in **Migdal**. The shopping malls all have fast-food outlets and a couple of café/restaurants.

₪₪₪-₪₪ Luna, 1 Kikar Khan, Migdal, T08-6722220. A kosher fusion restaurant, offers North African kebab, burgers, a great fish falafel, and anything else you can imagine; business lunch deals (54-74NIS). A chic venue in the old caravanserai: dine under the arches. Long bar is well-stocked, mix of seating styles and low red lighting; also outdoor area with sun-shades. Sun-Thu 1200-2300, Sat 2000-0200.

₪₪ Gazpacho, Holiday Inn, T08-6748886. Mediterranean bistro that is highly recommended by locals and visitors alike. Dishes are modern, as is the setting, with tapas, Italian, fish, meat and vegetarian choices. There's also a nice bar area.

₪ Cafe Golomb, Kikar Golomb, Herzl, Migdal. You can't miss the curved glass frontage of this welcoming café, trying to be trendy inside, with tables outside. Free internet and Wi-Fi, snacks and pastries, good iced coffee. Sun-Thu 0700-2200, Fri 0700-1600.

Shopping

The two main shopping malls are **Huzot Mall** on Ben-Gurion, and **Giron Mall**, just west of the Central Bus Station. **Le Ha-Ir Mall** is at the southern end of HaHistadrut.

Activities

Diving Southern Divers, Delilah Beach, T08-6711375. **Tennis** Israel Tennis Centre, Ofer, T08-6725364. 17 all-weather courts.

Transport

Bus

For local buses, see 'Getting around' on page 451. The Central Bus Station is located on Ben-Gurion. **Be'er Sheva**: 363 and 364, at least 1 hour, last at 2030, 1 hr. **Haifa**: change at Tel Aviv. **Jerusalem**: 436 and 437, every 30 mins, last at 2050, 1½ hrs. **Kiryat Gat**: 25, every 30 mins, last at 2130; 301 (continues to Tel Aviv), every 15 mins. **Tel Aviv**: 300 express (also 301 via Rehovot and Rishon LeTzion), every 15 mins, last at 2245, 1-1½ hrs.

Car hire

Eldan, junction of Herzl/Ben-Gurion, T08-6722724, www.eldan.co.il; Mal Mor, 4 Herzl, T08-6750622.

Sherut

Muniyot HaMerkazit, opposite the Central Bus Station, T08-6739977, offer 24-hr services to Tel Aviv via Ashdod.

Train

Trains run north to **Tel Aviv** and onwards every hr, taking 1 hr.

Directory

Banks Several banks with ATM machines are found on Kikar Zefanya/'Sundial Sq'. Banks are also found on Herzl in Migdal. Post offices offer commission-free foreign exchange. **Hospitals** Barzilai Medical Centre, 3 HaHistadrut, T6745555; Central Clinic, Ben-Gurion, just west of Central Bus Station. **Post offices** GPO, 18 Herzl, Migdal (post restante). Branch offices behind Central Bus Station and on Orit, near to Kikar Zefanya.

The Shephelah → *Colour map 2, grid C2-3.*

The Shephelah (Shefela) correctly refers to the region of low hills between the Plains of Philistia and the higher Central Range. This area, broadly inland of Ashdod and Ashkelon, has played a significant role in the history of Palestine/Israel. There are a number of places of interest here, though access by public transport is not always straightforward.

Background

The name Shephelah translates as 'low' or 'lowland', describing a region of low, broken hills scattered amongst areas of plain. This line of hills runs in a gently curving arc, enclosing the Maritime Plain from Jaffa to Gaza. The Shephelah is cut by several wide valleys that run broadly east to west from the foot of the Judean Hills to the Mediterranean. These are the **Ajalon Valley** (see 'Beit Guvrin to Jerusalem road' on page 464), the **Vale of Soreq**, the **Vale of Elah** and the **Wadi el-'Afranj**.

Because of these valleys, the Shephelah has not functioned as a physical barrier between the people dwelling on the plains and those living further east. If anything, the Shephelah has provided a point of contact between the different groups. Many of the great battles between groups contesting this ground either took place in the four valleys that run east to west and cut through the hills, or were facilitated by these valleys acting as lines of communication into the heart of the protagonist's territories.

The **Vale of Soreq**, the modern route of the Tel Aviv to Jerusalem rail link, is the traditional site of the towns of Zorah and Eshtaol, and the Camp of Dan, where a "woman bare a son, and called him Samson: and the child grew, and the Lord blessed him" (*Judges 13:24*). The head of the Vale of Soreq has been suggested as the site where the Philistines captured the **Ark of the Covenant** from the Israelites (*I Samuel 4:1-11*), though neither the exact site of battle nor the "Stone of Help" where they rested the Ark has been definitively identified. The route of the Ark's return, however, is more certain, following the "highway" along the Vale of Soreq from Ashdod up to Beth-Shemesh (*I Samuel 6:1-21*).

The entrance to the Philistine Plain of the **Vale of Elah** is guarded by **Tel Zafit**, site of the Crusader castle of 'Blanche Garde' ('White Citadel'). Though unconfirmed, this site is tentatively described by some scholars as being the location of the great Philistine city of Gath (though there is precious little to see here). As the Vale of Elah winds up into the Shephelah, at the junction of two further wadis, one leading south towards Hebron and the other striking out towards Bethlehem, there is a broad flat plain (along Route 38, just north of Ha'Ela Junction). This is suggested as the scene of the contest between **David and Goliath** (*I Samuel 17:1-52*), and though there is nothing specific to see, the description in the biblical passage does rather match the setting.

The fourth valley running through the Shephelah is cut by the **Wadi el-'Afranj**, running broadly northwest from Hebron to the coast at Ashdod. This route is particularly important since it takes in the sites of **Lachish**, **Mareshah** and **Beit Guvrin** (see below).

Beit Guvrin and Mareshah → *Colour map 2, grid C3.*

The fascinating remains of the two ancient cities of Beit Guvrin and Mareshah make Beit Guvrin National Park an excellent day out. Don't think of typical remnants of walls, gates and citadels, it is the subterranean cave complexes and Sidonian burial caves that are the attraction here. Archaeological digs continue and further sites continue to be opened up to the public, in particular Roman-Byzantine era discoveries. In fact, at Beit Guvrin you can be an archaeologist for a day: contact **Archaeological Seminars** ① T02-5862011, www. archesem.com, about their "Dig-for-a-day" programme ($30 plus 20NIS entrance fee). In reality it's only three hours, but still a good experience for families.

Ins and outs

Getting there and away To reach Beit Guvrin National Park, take Egged bus 446 from Jerusalem, every 30 minutes to Kiryat Gat, from where bus 11 goes to Kibbutz Beit Guvrin (Sunday to Thursday 0810 and 1530 only, Friday 0810 only, 8.5NIS; return Sunday to Friday at 1545. As you can see, these times are not very convenient, and require an early start, though you can always try to hitch. If travelling in your own transport, take Route 35 towards Hebron. The park is signposted 17 km southeast of Kiryat Gat.

Background

Following the end of the United Monarchy (c. 928), Mareshah was one of the cities given to Judah (*Joshua* 15:44), and during the reign of Asa (908-867 BCE) a major battle was fought just to the north of Mareshah (described in some detail in the Bible, *II Chronicles* 14:9; 15:12).

In the Early Hellenistic period (332-167 BCE) Mareshah replaced Lachish (see page 461) as the capital of western Idumaea (Edom), and a sizeable Sidonian community came to settle here.

During the Hasmonean wars it was repeatedly attacked by the Maccabees, and upon its capture by Hyrcanus I the population was forcibly Judaized by the imposition of circumcision (Josephus, *The Jewish War I*, 63). Mareshah remained under Hasmonean rule until its recapture by Pompey (*The Jewish War I*, 156) and was part of the domain granted to Herod (c. 40 BCE), though it was almost immediately destroyed by the Parthians. Once stability returned, Beit Guvrin replaced Mareshah as the district capital. It became a Roman polis in 200 CE under the emperor Septimus Severus, and was granted one of the largest tracts of land in Palestine, stretching from Ein Gedi to the sea. He gave the city the name Eleutheropolis, 'City of Freedom'.

During the Early Arab period (638-1099) the city became known as Bet Jibrin, and in the 12th century the Crusaders built a small city here. The Crusader king Fulk of Anjou built a castle in 1136 as part of the plan to encircle Ashkelon, though once that city

Bet Guvrin National Park

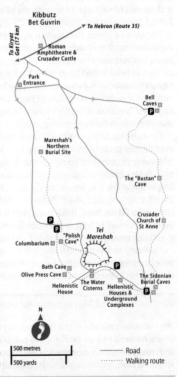

fell in 1153, Beit Guvrin's strategic significance was lessened. The Knights Hospitaller continued to occupy the fortress, perhaps mindful of its location on the Jerusalem road.

Beit Guvrin National Park → *Colour map 2, grid C3.*
ⓘ *0800-1700 (winter -1600), closes 1 hr earlier on Fri. Adult 25NIS, student 21NIS, child 13NIS. The main attractions are well marked on a walking trail. The complete walking tour takes 4-5 hrs, and it's an enjoyable one, though you must take lots of water and sun protection. Most visitors drive between sites and park in the spaces provided, which involves some degree of doubling back on foot, and a visit takes at least 2 hrs. Cold drinks, snacks and toilets are available outside the Sidonian Caves.*

Mareshah's Northern Burial Site Two caves dating back to the third to second centuries BCE are open for viewing, though there are far more impressive caves within the park. There is a parking lot and picnic site nearby, though most visitors drive on to parking lots I and II and begin the tour there.

'Polish Cave' Forty or so steps lead down into this water cistern, cut from the rock in the fourth or third century BCE. The 'artefact' (Latin for 'an installation for the raising of pigeons') niches were added in the late Byzantine/early Arab period. The 'Polish' reference is to the soldiers of General Anders' army who visited the caves in 1943, carving the words 'Warsaw', 'Poland' and the Polish eagle symbol into the cave walls.

Columbarium A large number of columbaria have been found in this area, though this one is probably the finest example. Shaped like a double cross, this large columbarium still has over 2000 niches for nesting pigeons, though initially it may have had many more. Although considered as something of a nuisance by some cultures, pigeons had significant uses in Byzantine times. A source of food, pigeons were also used for ritualistic purposes. Their droppings, which you may well encounter in this cave, were collected and used as fertilizer. After the third century this cave was probably used as a storehouse.

Bath Cave Hip baths from the third to second centuries BCE can be seen in two small chambers cut into the rock. The baths were filled by spouts linked to conduits bringing water from outside. Decorated pottery braziers found nearby were almost certainly used to heat the water.

Olive Press Cave Olive trees contributed significantly to the local economy during the Hellenistic period, and 22 such oil presses have so far been discovered in the Mareshah vicinity. Assuming that there were 30 such oil presses in the area, it has been calculated that annual production would exceed 250,000 kg. To support this industry, substantial areas of olive groves would have occupied the surrounding area. In fact, such was the level of production that surplus was exported to Egypt and to the towns on the coast. A restored oil press is displayed in this cave, along with a description of the production process.

Dwelling House This Hellenistic house has rooms built around a central courtyard, from where a spiral staircase led to the upper floor, probably the living quarters. On the ground floor was a kitchen, reception room and a pantry in which numerous amphorae (two-handled ceramic jars used for transporting grains and liquids) of the Mediterranean, Aegean and Italian-North African type were found. Also, 25 silver coins were found in a juglet under the floor in one of the rooms, the latest dating to 113 BCE. This corresponds to the year in which John Hyrcanus conquered the city, so it is assumed that the house was destroyed then. All the coins were minted at Ashkelon and featured an eagle on one side, and the image of the ruler(s) on the other.

Below the house is located a system of connecting water cisterns, a vast warren of soaring rooms dating from the 4th to 2nd century BCE. Rain water was collected from the roof of the house, the yard, and the surrounding lanes by a series of channels and clay pipes, and then funnelled down into the water cisterns below. A steep staircase descends into these beautifully cool underground storage systems, interconnected by holes and passageways added in later centuries, to emerge via a neighbouring house's cistern. Note the niches carved into the walls for lamps.

Dwelling houses and underground systems Further Hellenistic houses are found nearby (follow signs), using the same pattern of rooms arranged around a central courtyard, with a staircase leading to the upper floor. Beneath each house is a system of water cisterns and storage caves hewn from the rock, where curving steps and a twisting passage cut through endless chambers, including a columbarium and an impressive olive press. After passing from one cistern to the next, you eventually emerge four houses away into blinding sunlight.

Tel Mareshah A path leads up to the 'tel' upon which stood the upper city of Mareshah, where there is an **observation point**. Little remains to be seen of the upper city, bar the square tower at the **northwest corner**, and this is probably best seen from the road below the hill.

The lower city of **Mareshah**, also surrounded by a low wall, was an underground city of several hundred caves below a network of streets, houses and public buildings.

The Sidonian Burial Caves Cave 8 (the 'Apollophanes' cave) is the most impressive, and an outstanding example of how the people of Mareshah buried their dead. It is entered through the large bush (!), from where you emerge into an entrance hall. This large tomb comprises three burial chambers, of which the middle is the most impressive. It features fourteen loculi (rectangular, shelf-like burial niches), and a recess in the far wall leads to a further three burial rooms. The decorative friezes have been well restored, and mainly depict hunting scenes and weird and wonderful animals (read the interesting story of their preservation on the information board). A number of Greek inscriptions were found in the tomb, the most important of which is probably the epitaph of Apollophanes, the head of the Sidonian community in Mareshah for 33 years. Many of the family members were buried in this tomb, and the epigraphic references provide much information on the social and family structure of Mareshah. For example, the fact that the names of the fathers are generally Semitic, whilst those of the sons tend to be Greek, reflect the assimilation of the Sidonian community amongst the population of Mareshah.

Cave 9, referred to as the 'Musicians' Cave', is constructed on a similar plan, with decorated walls featuring a musician in a striped tunic playing a flute, with a woman behind playing a harp. Inscriptions in the tomb are dated between 188 and 135 BCE.

NB From the parking lot outside the Sidonian Burial Caves, it is possible to drive the 2.4 km to the parking lot outside the Bell Caves. Alternatively, you can walk there (only 1.5 km) via site 13.

Crusader Church of St Anne The remains of the apse of a 12th-century Crusader church dedicated to St Anne stands on the earlier site of a Byzantine church. Small portions of elaborately worked mosaics, featuring birds and flowers, were uncovered here, though sadly they are incomplete. The Crusader church is often referred to by its Arabic name of 'Santahanna' (or 'Sandahanna'), and presents a somewhat eerie sight, standing isolated on the hillside. Not far beyond the church is the Bustan (Garden) Cave complex which, though not as spectacular as the Bell Caves (see below), contains a series of bell-shaped caves and a columbarium.

The Bell Caves Originally it was thought that these caves were dug to be used as dwelling places, water holes and storage installations. However, it is now clear that these bell-shaped caves are essentially quarries dug to provide building materials, and that the uses suggested above came only after the quarries were exhausted. The caves in this vicinity date not to the city of Mareshah, but to the later city of Beit Guvrin, and most of the quarrying here was done in the seventh-tenth centuries CE.

The quarrying techniques involved here are remarkably advanced, taking full advantage of the local geological structure. The quarriers begun by digging a hole through the surface crust (nari; 1.5 to 3 m thick) until the softer chalky rock below was reached. The rock below was then gradually scooped out, eventually forming the large 'bell-shaped' quarries. The bell shape provides structural support, maintaining the security of the quarriers below.

In many of the caves there are crucifixes and altars carved into the walls, along with Arabic inscriptions. Connoisseurs of cheesy films may recognize the caves from scenes in *Rambo III* – a film that was set in Afghanistan! Unfortunately, due to structural instability, the southern Bell Caves complex is closed (you can walk around the outside), though the northern complex is open.

Northern complex of Beit Guvrin A number of interesting archaeological finds have been discovered near Kibbutz Beit Guvrin (opposite the National Park entrance) which can be visited on the same ticket. These include the remains of an impressive Roman amphitheatre, a Byzantine church and sections of a Crusader fortress.

Lachish → *Colour map 2, grid C3.*

Tel Lakhish is the mound site of the ancient city of Lachish. The city's strategic location has brought triumph and tragedy to Lachish's population. The city enjoyed the status of being the largest city in Canaan and, in later periods, as the second city of the kings of Judah. Unfortunately, Lachish's importance as a fortified town has also been its downfall. Almost all historical sources, including numerous biblical references, have one reoccurring theme – the city's capture and destruction. Lachish has been destroyed on at least five occasions, and was finally abandoned when the nearby sites of Mareshah and Beit Guvrin rose to prominence. Those who have already visited Mareshah and Beit Guvrin may be disappointed by the neglected state of this site.

Ins and outs

Getting there and getting away To reach Tel Lakhish by public transport is not easy. You can take a Hebron-bound buses from Kiryat Gat (only two per day) that go via Route 35 (plus bus 11 to Kibbutz Beit Guvrin: see page 459), and get off at the junction for Lachish (after 8 km, marked by a brown sign). From here it is 2.5 km to the site. If travelling by your own transport, turn off Route 35 (Kiryat Gat to Hebron road) 8 km southeast of Kiryat Gat on to Route 3415 (Amazya road). Continue for 2.4 km until a sign at the junction points right. The tel is 300 m on the left.

The Sacking of Lachish: the evidence

Part of the significance of Lachish as a major archaeological site is the fact that there are so many different sources of evidence corroborating the historical events. One such example is the sacking of Lachish in 701 BCE by the Assyrian king Sennacherib.

When John L Starkey excavated the site in 1932-36, the discovery of over 1,500 skeletons in a pit dating to the exact period, confirmed the story of the sacking of Lachish as told in the Bible (2 Kings 18:13-17). However, the most graphic description of the sacking is seen in the bas-relief that Sennacherib commissioned for his palace in Nineveh.

In three scenes, the bas-relief tells the story of the battle and its aftermath. Sennacherib's infantry advance on Lachish's fortified walls, the attackers manoeuvring their ladders, battering rams and great siege trains under a hail of arrows and burning torches from the defenders above. The moat and battlefield is littered with corpses. The final scene shows a victorious Sennacherib, seated on a throne viewing his booty. Prisoners are led before him, whilst others are being tortured or executed. The inscription reads "Sennacherib, king of the world, king of Assyria, sat on his throne and the spoil from Lakisu (Lachish) passed in review before him." In the background, the surviving civilian population are being led off into slavery and exile. The original bas-relief from Nineveh can be seen in the British Museum in London, though there is a copy in the Israel Museum in Jerusalem.

Unfortunately, the site of Tel Lakhish itself does not live up to its billing as one of the most important excavations in the area. Today, the site probably looks pretty much as it did after one of its many sackings – totally abandoned. Inside the inner walls you are likely to be confronted by waist-high grass and, given the number of underground passages and tunnel shafts, it is probably not wise to stray off the marked footpath.

Background

The Canaanite city Although there is evidence of much earlier occupation, it was by the Middle Bronze Age IIB (1750-1550 BCE) that one of the major cities of southern Canaan had developed on this site. Remains from this era include fortifications (with the glacis of particular note), a palace, a cult place, plus residential quarters. Most of the Middle Bronze Age city was destroyed in a major conflagration, though precise details of this conflict are unknown.

The city on the mound here slowly recovered, and by the end of the Late Bronze Age (1550-1200 BCE) it may well have been the largest city in **Canaan**. The city was under Egyptian suzerainty during this period; a fact reflected in both architectural style and a number of surviving letters sent between the rulers of Lachish and the Pharaohs (including the 'Hermitage Papyrus 1116A', dated c. 1427-1402 BCE).

The reasons for the city's demise c. 1130 BCE are not entirely clear, though at least two theories are suggested. Some suggest that Lachish became a victim of the 'Sea Peoples' (including the Philistines), whilst others believe the Israelites were the conquerors.

Kingdom of Judah The mound site was unoccupied for a long period, then rebuilt as a fortified city either during the United Monarchy or early in the time of the kings of Judah. Lachish is mentioned as one of the cities that **Rehoboam** (928-911 BCE) built "for the defence of Judah" (*II Chronicles 11:5, 9*), though it could be that Rehoboam was only responsible for beginning the fortification work. Important structures from this period that remain today include the city walls, outer gate, inner gate, palace-fort and 'Great Shaft'.

Assyrian conquest In 701 BCE Lachish was conquered by **Sennacherib**, the king of Assyria, during his invasion of Judah – "he himself laid siege against Lachish, and all his power with him" (*II Chronicles 32:9*).

The Assyrians attacked from the southwest by building a large siege ramp (70-75 m wide, 50-60 m long). Though parts of the siege ramp remain, much of it was removed by early British excavators who failed to identify its true purpose. The defenders of Lachish, meanwhile, constructed a defensive counter-ramp opposite the siege ramp with the purpose of creating a secondary, higher line of defence within the city walls. Numerous remains of arms and ammunition were discovered at this place, reflecting the intensity of battle.

Babylonian conquest Lachish declined rapidly after Sennacherib's murderous assault, and by the time of Josiah's reign over Judah (639-609 BCE) the site had been abandoned. However, within a remarkably short period of time the city was rebuilt, though on a smaller scale than before. The fortified city of Lachish is mentioned as one of the cities that **Nebuchadnezzar** attacked during the Babylonian invasion that brought to an end the rule of the kings of Judah in 586 BCE (*Jeremiah 34:7*).

Important artefacts dating to the period of the last king of Judah, Zedekiah (596-586), were found amongst the burnt ruins of a room in the outer gate. Known as the **Lachish letters**, they are possibly letters exchanged between the military commanders of Lachish and Jerusalem, or signals sent by a subordinate stationed near Lachish "to my lord Yaush", commander of the city's garrison.

Tel Lakhish / Lachish

N

| 800 metres |
| 800 yards |

1 Fosse Temple
2 Assyrian Siege Ramp
3 Ramp Entrance
4 Outer Gate
5 Inner Gate
6 Counter Ramp
7 Acropolis Temple
8 Palace Forts
9 Palace Courtyard

Babylonian, Persian and Hellenistic periods Lachish may have been abandoned for a period after Nebuchadnezzar's assault, though a seal found on the mound that bears the words "belonging to Gedaliah, who is over the house" ties in with biblical evidence that "for the people that remained in the land of Judah, whom Nebuchadnezzar king of Babylon had left, even over them he made Gedaliah the son of Ahikam, the son of Shaphan, the ruler" (*II Kings 25:22*). The Book of Nehemiah also refers to people settling in Lachish following the Babylonian exile.

Lachish was finally abandoned in the Late Hellenistic period (167-37 BCE), when Mareshah and Beit Guvrin (see page 457) became the dominant cities of the region.

Sights

Outer fortifications The entrance to the fortified city is via the outer gate, having ascended a ramp that lies adjacent to Sennacherib's **siege ramp**. The outer gate uses the defensive principle of indirect access, with the orientation of the entrance also meaning that anyone approaching the gate would have to expose their unprotected flank to the city's defenders; swords were carried in the right hand, protective shields in the left.

The **gate area** that you see today is a restoration of the city fortifications built by the early kings of Judah, possibly Rehoboam (928-911 BCE). At the time of construction it was the largest city gate in Israel, exceeding similar examples at Megiddo and Hazor. It was subsequently destroyed by Sennacherib and later reconstructions were on a far less grand scale. The modern restoration used debris found in the immediate vicinity. The outer gate opens into a courtyard, from where you pass through the **inner gate** into the city. It was in one of the small chambers in the gate area that the **Lachish letters** were found.

Immediately to the right, inside the enclosed mound, are the remains of the **counter ramp**, built in an ultimately futile attempt to repel the Assyrian army.

Acropolis Temple Though the Acropolis Temple built as part of the Canaanite city yielded few finds, the temple's plan is well defined. Egyptian hegemony over the region during this period is reflected in the design of the temple, with similar structures having been identified in Egypt.

'Palace-forts' On the east side of the podium-platform lie the superimposed remains of a series of 'palace-forts'. The initial palace-fort was quite possibly built by Rehoboam (928-911), with a later building on the same site serving as the headquarters of the royal-appointed governor. A third palace was built upon the foundations of the earlier buildings during the Persian period (586-332 BCE). Though smaller than its predecessors, the Persian-period palace was impressively built, with imposing porticos giving way to a large inner courtyard. It is hard to make out any such grandeur here now.

Fosse Temple The Fosse Temple, northwest of the mound, can be seen from the viewpoint. Three successive temples were built during the Late Bronze Age (1550-1200 BCE), though each in turn was destroyed. A rich assemblage of temple-related artefacts was found in the immediate vicinity, and the third Fosse Temple is reasonably well preserved despite being destroyed by fire in the late 13th century BCE. Today, the remains are barely visible.

The 'Ghost Tree' and the well Arab local legend had it that this, the only remaining tree on the mound, was inhabited by spirits. The idea was that children sent to fetch water from the nearby well would be too frightened to linger, and would hurry home. The 44-m-deep well, which taps into the Nahal Lakhish, is quite impressive. The path continues down to a 'bustan' (garden) of olive trees, from where you can connect to the road.

Beit Guvrin to Jerusalem

From Beit Guvrin there is an interesting route (largely along Route 38) to Jerusalem that takes in a number of minor places of interest on the journey through the Shephelah into the Judean Hills. Refer to colour map 2 for orientation. Public transport to these sights is not good.

Elah Valley
The Elah Valley is the traditional site of the battle between **David and Goliath**, with the biblical passage (*I Samuel 17:1-58*) rather matching the setting on Route 38 just north of

Ha'Ela Junction. A little way to the south of this junction is **Mitzpe Massu**, an attractive forest watchtower set in an appealing picnic spot, whilst nearby on Route 39 are some **Roman milestones** dating to around 210 CE.

Beth-Shemesh/Beit Shemesh

Getting there and away   There are regular trains from Tel Aviv or Superbus 411; both take about 1 hr. From Jerusalem a train leaves every hour, taking 30 mins, Superbus 415 or Egged 417 take slightly less. You will have to walk or hitch from the town to reach the nearby attractions.

Background The name of this development town recalls the Israelite city of Beth-Shemesh that stood at the head of the route between the Philistine city of Ashdod and Jerusalem. Remains of the Israelite city can be seen at **Tel Beth-Shemesh**, signposted just to the west of the modern town. Though there is not a great deal of interest to see at the site, it does have a long and well-documented history. It was to Beth-Shemesh that the Philistines returned the Ark of the Covenant after finding that it brought nothing but ill fortune to them (*I Samuel 6:8-9*). Beth-Shemesh was the scene of a battle between Joash, king of Israel, and Amaziah, king of Judah (*II Kings 14:11-13; II Chronicles 25:21-23*), and was later captured by the Philistines (*II Chronicles 28:18*).

A little to the south of Beth-Shemesh, is **Beit Jemal Monastery** ① *T02-9917671, Mon-Sat (except hols) 0830-1130 and 1330-1630*, where a walk around the fortress-like building brings you to the modern St Stephen's Church where mosaics are rather badly displayed on the exterior wall. The community produces respectable wine and olive oil, for sale in the shop. More attractive is the adjacent **Monastery of Our Lady of the Assumption** ① *Mon-Sat (except hols) 1030-1630, ring the bell or call T02-9911889*, built on the site of a Byzantine church that supposedly marked the burial place of St Stephen, the first Christian martyr (*Acts 6-7*). Visitors are welcome to view the rock-walled chapel with arabesque lighting and menorahs and the main church, which can only be described as chic. A silent film shows the religious and practical life of the 40 or so white-hooded nuns, who only leave the monastery on Sundays when they go for a communal walk. Days are spent in prayer, gardening, carpentry, domestic chores, painting icons and ceramics. The monastery is in fact renowned for its excellent handmade pottery, which is sold in the shop.

Soreq Cave Nature Reserve

① *T02-9911117, www.parks.org.il. Daily 0800-1700, winter 0800-1600, last entry 1¼ hr before, closes 1 hr earlier on Fri. Adult 25NIS, student 21NIS. During the week, come before 1000 to avoid school groups. NB Photography is only permitted at specific points; and 23 degrees plus humidity means the cave floor is slippery. There is no public transport to the site. Egged bus 180 goes to Nes Harim from Jerusalem, though it's a 7-km walk from there. Alternatively, it's a 10-km uphill climb (or hitch) from Beth-Shemesh along Route 3855. The cave is signed "Stalactite Cave" from Rd 3855. Guided tours only; in Hebrew unless there are a majority of English-speakers.*

The Soreq Stalactite Cave is another of Israel's natural wonders. The cave was discovered during quarrying in 1968, and comprises an awe-inspiring collection of stalactites (growing down) and stalagmites (growing up) condensed into what appears to be a naturally formed auditorium. The whole 'show' began some five million years ago and is an extremely complex process of chemical and physical weathering. Plenty of outrageous shapes and imaginative formations have been created by the dripping and splashing of water in this vast subterranean space, particularly at points where stalagmites 'grow' up to meet descending stalactites.

A short slide show explains the science, with a series of out-of-focus slides showing the more spectacular or amusing formations. A walkway passes around the cave, with the guide pointing out the key sites with a torch. Various points are dramatically lit, though lighting is kept to a minimum since it encourages a destructive algae to grow on the formations.

Latrun → Colour map 2, B3.

The area around Latrun occupies a historically important strategic position on the road from the coastal plain up to Jerusalem. During the 1948 war, the Ayalon Valley was the scene of some of the bloodiest battles between the Israelis and the Arabs, notably for the control of Latrun and Castel. The valley was the main supply route for the beleaguered Israeli forces in West Jerusalem, with the rapidly built so-called 'Burma Road' running largely to the south of the modern Route 1.

To the west of the road lie the Crusader fortress of **Le Toron des Chevaliers**, with the Cistercian 'Monastery of the Silent', **Latrun Monastery**, nearby. More recent attractions to the west are 'Mini Israel' and the Armoured Corps Museum, near to which there is a café and restaurant. To the east of Route 1 lies the former site of the Arab village of Amwas, destroyed in the Six-Day War, identified in some sources as the site of the biblical village of **Emmaus**. A number of remains from different periods can be seen in **Ayalon-Canada Park**, a recreational area. Close to the entrance to the park are the remains of an extensive **Roman/Byzantine bathhouse**, plus the **Churches of Emmaus-Nicopolis** that mark the traditional Byzantine and then Crusader location of Emmaus.

Ins and outs

Getting there and away By car, it's a simple turn off Route 1 at Latrun Junction (clearly signed). Egged buses 403, 404, 433, 434 and 435 run to Latrun from Jerusalem's Central Bus Station; from Tel Aviv get any bus to Beit Dagan Jct then change to Egged bus 432, 433 and 404. Walking between the sites is manageable (although Mini Israel is just far enough to feel too far).

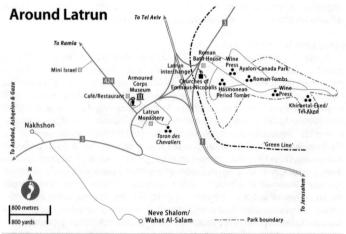

Around Latrun

Jesus' Resurrection appearance on the road to Emmaus

Luke's gospel (Luke 24:13-35) recalls that on the day of the Resurrection, two of the disciples were making their way on foot to the village of Emmaus, some seven miles from Jerusalem. As they discussed the events of this first Easter, "Jesus himself came up and walked with them; but something prevented them from recognizing him." The two disciples and the 'stranger' discussed what had happened in Jerusalem, with Jesus explaining how Christ's martyrdom had been prophesied in the Bible. On reaching their destination the disciples, one of whom was called Cleopas, persuaded the 'stranger' to dine with them. It was only when the 'stranger' broke the bread and said the blessing that they recognized him as Jesus. He subsequently disappeared, leaving the two disciples to rush back to Jerusalem to explain the 'Good News' of the Resurrection to the other disciples.

The location of the gospel Emmaus is unknown, though since the fourth century CE four different sites have been suggested: Abu Ghosh, Latrun ('Imwas),

el-Qubeibeh and Qalunieh. Discrepancies in different gospel manuscripts have led to this confusion, with some reading that Emmaus was located 60 stadia from Jerusalem, whilst others mention 160 stadia. The 60 stadia (11.5 kms) criteria certainly fits both Abu Ghosh and el-Qubeibeh (and would have been sufficiently close for the two disciples to reach Emmaus and return to Jerusalem in one day). Both these identifications, however, are relatively late, dating to the Crusader period. The identification with Latrun is comparatively early, and is mentioned in Eusebius' Onomasticon (c 330 CE). The former Arab village of Qalunieh (abandoned in 1948, located on the ridge above the Jerusalem-Tel Aviv highway below Motza) is the probable site of a village established in the first century CE for 800 Roman veterans of the First Jewish Revolt and named Emmaus. Apart from the fact that it is 30 stadia from Jerusalem, and thus within 'day-trip' range of Jerusalem, this is the only connection with the gospel Emmaus.

Background

A capital of one of the Roman toparchies of Judea by the first century BCE, it was during the third century CE that the fortunes of **Emmaus** changed dramatically, when it was granted the status of a city by the emperor Elagabalus (218-222 CE), subsequently becoming known as Nicopolis. It is thought that the Roman bathhouse here was built after the granting of this imperial charter (see below).

The first Christian basilica found at Emmaus dates to the third century CE, and can be seen as part of the 'Churches of Emmaus-Nicopolis' complex (see below). It is not clear if the gospel event had been localized here at this point, though it certainly had by the time Eusebius had compiled his *Onomasticon* in 330 CE. A further church was constructed on the site in the sixth century CE, though events shortly after the Arab conquest of Palestine were soon to erase the identification of Emmaus from the collective memory. An outbreak of plague here in 639 CE claimed many thousands of lives, with many Arab sources suggesting that Emmaus was the source of the subsequent plague epidemic that swept through the entire Middle East. Though the Crusaders settled in the area in the 12th century CE, building a smaller church within the existing Byzantine basilica, it is not thought that the site was associated with the gospel tradition of Emmaus. In fact, the Crusaders appeared to prefer the association of Emmaus with Abu Ghosh or el-Qubeibeh, and the church here may have been built merely to serve the community that developed around Le Toron des Chevaliers fortress. The name Emmaus is preserved in the name of the Arab village of 'Imwas.

Sights

Churches of Emmaus-Nicopolis ⓘ *www.emmaus-nicopolis.org. Mon-Sat 0830-1200 and 1430-1730 (winter -1700). Ring bell if closed. Entrance 5NIS. Small gift-shop, beer and soft drinks for sale; toilets.*

Aside from the church complex, recent excavation here has revealed several first-century CE Jewish tombs: one is a unique example of a Roman tomb built above the earlier Herodian tomb. In the fourth century CE a Christian **basilica** was built featuring a trefoil-shaped stone baptismal font, which can still be seen. In the sixth century CE a second **basilica** of enormous stone blocks was erected, possibly because the original basilica was destroyed in the Samaritan revolt of 529 CE. In a small museum, the remains of the Byzantine mosaic floor is preserved which includes scenes of a lion devouring a bull, a leopard attacking a gazelle and a number of birds perched on lotus flowers. During the 12th century CE the Crusaders built a Romanesque style **church**, reusing the central apse of the third-century church and adding their own vaulted hall. Also open to visitors is the chapel of the Catholic Community of the Beatitudes, who manage the site.

Ayalon-Canada Park An attractive rugged area, with walking trails and picnic tables among the trees, Ayalon-Canada Park features a number of remains from the Hellenistic, Roman, Byzantine and Crusader periods.

Accessed via the Park, close by the entrance, is the Roman/Byzantine bathhouse. First built as part of the imperial charter that granted Emmaus-Nicopolis city status (after 221 CE, but before the early fourth century CE), the present remains comprise just four rooms preserved to their original ceiling height. They appear to have been damaged in, but survived, the major earthquakes of 498, 502 and 507 CE. In fact, the bathhouse's survival at all is attributed to an unusual series of events. The commander of the Arab armies in Palestine, Abu 'Ubeideh, is believed to have died in the plague epidemic that struck Emmaus in 639 CE. In the 13th century CE, the Mamluks sought to reinforce the site's link with Islam, partially in an attempt to counter the nearby site venerated by the Christians and partially as a means of establishing a religious cause at this strategic crossroads. The baths subsequently became a holy place linked to the memory of Abu 'Ubeideh (with some sources still referring to the baths as Maqam esh-Sheikh 'Ubeid), hence the Islamic tombs dotted around.

Also of note within the park are the remains of a sophisticated Roman aqueduct system, the Hasmonean grave complex, a number of wine-presses from the Byzantine period, plus the site of the Crusader fortress of Castellum Arnaldi.

Latrun Monastery ⓘ *Mon-Sat 0830-1200 and 1430-1700 (winter 0830-1100 and 1430-1600).* The monastery was established here in 1890 by the Trappist Order, subsequently becoming known as the Monastery of the Silent. Though expelled by the Turks during World War I, the monks returned in 1926, building the present monastery. Though very imposing from the outside, the church itself is rather austere, lit by simply patterned stained glass. The Latrun Monastery, as it is now commonly known, produces good-quality wine, available (along with other local produce) from the shop (Monday to Saturday 0800-1700).

Le Toron des Chevaliers This fortress was one of several established along this road by the Order of the Templars some time after 1132. It is in fact claimed that the name 'Latrun' is derived from the original Crusader name Le Toron des Chevaliers (Tower of the Knights), though a counter-claim suggests that Latrun comes from the title *castellum boni latronis*, or 'fortress of the good thief' (since it marked the birthplace of the 'good thief' who was crucified with Jesus). Situated as it is close to the main theatre of confrontation between the Crusaders and the Muslims, the fortress changed hands on a number of occasions, with its guest list including Salah al-Din, Richard Coeur de Lion and the Mamluk sultan Baibars. By 1283 the fortress was in ruins, though a large caravanserai was built nearby in the 14th century CE. Today the fortress is rather forlorn and overgrown, with subterranean rooms hidden beneath the foliage. It is accessed by turning right, then right, then right again from Latrun Monastery (up the track behind the monastery).

Armoured Corps Museum ⓘ *Sun-Thu 0830-1630, Fri 0830-1230, Sat 0900-1630. Adult 30NIS, student/child 20NIS. Free tour in English, call T08-9255186 to arrange, www. yadlashiryon.com. Shop.* This big block of a British fortress was built to guard the Jerusalem road, and now houses a rather scant museum where much of the explanation is only in Hebrew. The chief purpose of the site is to commemorate the 4,800 soldiers of the armoured corps who have fallen in their defence of Israel, who are engraved on the Wall of Names in alphabetical order. It will appeal to fans of tanks, which encircle the museum, and the Memorial Complex has a curious 'Tower of Tears' where steady drips have coated the steel walls in rust and water bubbles beneath your feet forming a new spring of life. Booking a tour with a soldier will enrich the experience.

Mini Israel ⓘ *www.minisrael.co.il. Fri 1000-1400, Sat-Thu Nov-Mar 1000-1800, Apr-May 1000-1900, Jun 1000-2100, Jul-Aug 1000-2200, Sep-Oct 1000-2000. Adult 72NIS, child aged 2-5 19NIS, aged 5-18 59NIS, audio-guide 10NIS. Café, shop.* As the name suggests, here are all of Israel's sights in miniature for you to wander around in 1½ hours rather than 2½ weeks. There are currently 385 scale models (more are being added) arranged vaguely in the shape of the Star of David rather than the shape of Israel. Some of the models could do with a lick of paint (notably the Dome of the Rock), but children really love the dynamics, the voices and the details – the elephant in Ramat Gan Safari Park squirts water from its trunk, Muslims bow in prayer at Al Qasr, and Bonsai olive trees grow in the Galilee. You could come as a first stop between the airport and Jerusalem, but there is a certain satisfaction in visiting at the end of a trip in order to point out the places you have been. In windy weather a visit is not advised, as most of the mechanics have to be switched off. A '4-D' cinema experience is to be completed summer 2010.

Neve Shalom/Wahat Al-Salam In this democratic community, Jews and Palestinian Arabs (with Israeli citizenship) live together and work together in peace. Pretty unique in the region. If you wish to learn about the ethos of the village, it's possible to join a tour or even volunteer, see www.nswas.org. For casual visitors, there's a hotel and restaurant, swimming pool, café and gift shop.

North of Tel Aviv

Herzliya/Herzliya Pituach → *Colour map 2, grid A2.*

Established as an agricultural settlement in 1924, and named after the 'founder' of modern Zionism Theodor Herzl, Herzliya Pituach is Israel's most up-market beach resort. With a beautiful 7-km stretch of fine golden sand, yet just 15 km and a 20-minute drive north of Tel Aviv (barring inevitable traffic jams), it has also become one of the country's most salubrious residential neighbourhoods, favoured by foreign diplomats and the affluent classes. There are actually two parts to the town. The older part of the town, Herzliya itself, is further inland, to the east of Route 2 which connects Tel Aviv to Haifa. Visitors will be more concerned with Herzliya Pituach, or "Herzliya-on-Sea", the resort area on the coast. Herzliya hosts a **Biennale of Contemporary Art** during Sukkot, with DJs, street art and dancing (next in 2011).

Ins and outs
Getting there and away The Central Bus Station (served by Egged and Dan buses from Tel Aviv's Central Bus Station) is located on Wolfson, in Herzliya itself. Egged buses stop at the Central Bus Station, thus the most convenient way to get to Herzliya Pituach is to take Dan bus 90 from Tel Aviv. This goes from Carmelit terminal, via Alozorov, through Herzliya's high-tech ('industrial') area to finish at the Sharon Hotel in Herzliya Pituach. Sheruts from Tel Aviv can drop off on Route 2, and also run on Shabbat. If you are coming by bus from the north, ask to be let down at Accadia Junction (the turn-off from Route 2). The train station is also located in Herzliya.

If you arrive in Herzliya itself, note that bus 13 runs from the Central Bus Station, past the railway station, then along Ramat Yam (past the marina and hotels) to Kikar Shalit, then north to Sidna Ali Beach. Bus 29 does the same in reverse, every 10 minutes, 0600-2200.

Sights
Beaches Herzliya's prime attractions are the beaches, though in summer you must pay to use them. Facilities are good, with showers, changing rooms and toilets, plus a choice of restaurants and cafés. At the southern end of Herzliya is the Marina development, with a large mall and fashionable outdoor eateries overlooking the sailboats. It's a real attraction for Israeli families at weekends, and the stretch of beach immediately south is particularly appealing (in summer there's an area cordoned off for orthodox visitors). Other popular beaches are **Zevulun-Daniel Beach**, opposite the Daniel Hotel, and the **Sharon** and **Accadia** beaches, near to the hotels of the same name. The remote **Shefayim Beach**, 5 km to the north, is favoured by (male) nudists. **Warning** There is danger from the strong undercurrents, and bathers should only swim where life-guards are on duty.

Sidna Ali Beach and Sidna Ali Mosque A number of features make Sidna Ali Beach interesting, though be careful when walking here not to get cut off by tides. Besides the remains of the Crusader fortifications that dot the beach (see below), there is the extraordinary beach house of an eccentric known as the '**Caveman**'. A lesson in recycling, the 'house' is built primarily from materials found washed up on the beach below, and features a number of extravagant sculptures. In the summer the owner operates a small café. Further north along the beach is another small community of people living close to nature.

Herzliya Pituach

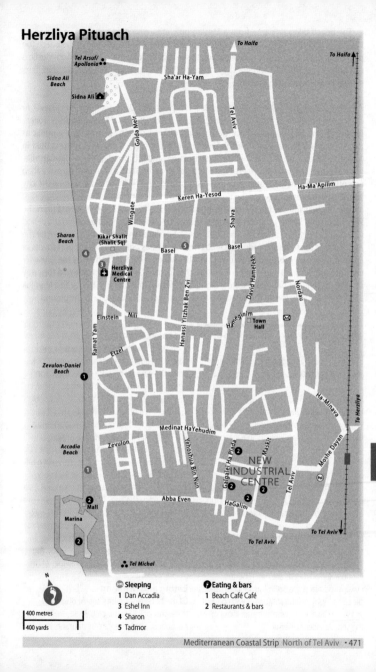

To Haifa

Tel Arsuf/
Apollonia

Sidna Ali
Beach

Sidna Ali

Sha'ar Ha-Yam

Golda Meir

Tel Aviv

To Haifa

Ha-Ma'Apilim

Wingate

Keren Ha-Yesod

Sharon
Beach

Kikar Shalit
(Shalit Sq)

Basel

Shalva

Basel

Herzliya
Medical
Centre

David Hamelekh

Nordau

Einstein

Nili

Hanassi Yitzhak Ben Zvi

Ramat Yam

Etzel

Hameginim

Town
Hall

Zevulon-Daniel
Beach

Ha-Minerva

Accadia
Beach

Medinat HaYehudim

To Herzliya

Zevulon

Yehoshua Bin Nun

Galgalei Ha Plada

Maskit

NEW
INDUSTRIAL
CENTRE

Tel Aviv

Moshe Dayan

Marina

Mall

Abba Even

HaGalim

To Tel Aviv

Tel Michal

To Tel Aviv

N

400 metres

400 yards

🛏 Sleeping
1 Dan Accadia
3 Eshel Inn
4 Sharon
5 Tadmor

🍴 Eating & bars
1 Beach Café Café
2 Restaurants & bars

The beach takes its name from a Muslim holy man who died fighting the Crusaders. His shrine is in the courtyard of the green-domed **Sidna Ali Mosque** above the beach (on polite request the caretaker may allow you to see it; daily 0630-2000, though non-Muslims can only access the roof and not the interiors). Muslims from all over Israel worship here, especially at Friday noon prayers.

Apollonia National Park ① *Apr-Sep 0800-1700, Oct-Mar 0800-1600 (on Fri closes 1 hr earlier; last entrance an hr before closing). Adults 20NIS, students 17NIS, child 9NIS. Toilets.* North of Sidna Ali Mosque is the ancient site of Tel Arsuf, recently opened to the public as the Apollonia National Park. The chief remains of interest are a Crusader fortress built in 1241 (but to last only 24 years before its destruction) and the foundations of a Roman villa. It is a pleasant cliff-top walk (there is also wheelchair access) and a visit takes no more than an hour. An informative leaflet with maps is provided, and sketches showing how the city would have appeared in Crusader times are placed at relevant spots.

The city was founded in the Persian period (586-332 BCE) as Arshof (derived from the Phoenician god Reshef), though it became known as Apollonia during the Hellenistic period (332-37 BCE). It was captured by the Arabs in 638 CE (since when it has been known by the Arab corrupt form, Arsuf). Under the Arabs it developed as one of the major port towns of Palestine, but was captured by Baldwin I in 1101 (when it became known by the Crusader corrupt form, Arsur). It was near here, in 1191, that Richard Coeur de Lion defeated the army of Salah al-Din. The Crusaders were eventually defeated in battle in 1265 by the Mamluk Sultan Baibars, who forced the defenders to raze and burn their own city to the ground.

Herzliya/ Herzliya Pituach listings

For Sleeping and Eating price codes and other relevant information, see Essentials pages 26-31.

Sleeping
LL Dan Accadia, Ramat Yam, T09-9597070, www.danhotels.com. Popular luxury hotel (busy with Israeli families on Shabbat) with 4 classes of room. All are high standard, but the very spacious suites facing the pool and sea are the best (very expensive). Leisure facilities include tennis, an attractive outdoor pool (summer only), kids' pool, health club, plus choice of restaurants. Courteous staff. Recommended.
LL Daniel, 60 Ramat Yam, T09-9528282, www.tamareshotels.co.il. Public areas are lavish but standard rooms disappoint by comparison; expensive club rooms are much better. Luxurious Shizen spa (with indoor pool) and pleasing lobby restaurant (dairy), with perfect sea view. Outdoor pool in summer looks on to the sea. Adjacent cinema.

LL Sharon, 5 Ramat Yam, T09-9525777, www.sharon.co.il. Some rooms have sea-facing balconies; other newly refurbed rooms look on to the garden; or there's lots of space in Bella Vista rooms with kitchenettes. However, the health club is starting to look pretty jaded and there is a bit of a 70s vibe throughout. Indoor and outdoor pools not so appealing.
AL Tadmor, 38 Basel, T09-9525000, F9575124. Built in the international style but far removed from Tel Aviv chic, this place is reasonable at $120 for a double, but very dated. There's a pool (summer only) but it's a little far from the beach.
A Eshel Inn, 3 Ramat Yam, T09-9568208, F09-9568797. This motel-style place is the cheapest in town; a/c rooms with TVs, cramped bathrooms. The exterior is rather shabby, the small rooms are clean. Snacks available 24 hrs.

Eating and drinking
Of the hotel restaurants, the **Al Bustan** at the Dan Accadia is the pick. There are a number of attractive café/restaurants on the

beachfront where 'being seen' is as important as the quality of the food; these are more fun in summertime (try **Beach Cafecafe**, open 24 hrs, near the Daniel hotel). The Marina has a host of choices, from speciality fish to Irish pub. Much of Herzliya Pituach's dining is found in the 'New Industrial Centre', as it's for hi-tech workers by day. Abba Eban in particular has some classy places, or there's **El Gaucho**, 60 Medinat Ha-Yehudim, T09-9555037 (reserve ahead on Shabbat), and **Whitehouse Steakhouse**, Mercazim Building, Maskit, T03-9580402. **Tandoori**, 32 Maskit, T09-9546702, serves high-quality North Indian cuisine, main dishes 39-74NIS. The pick of the bars is **Inga Bar**, 16 Galgalei HaPlada, T09-9510142, which opens Sun-Thu 1800-0200, Fri-Sat 2000-0300 (happy hour Sun-Thu 1800-2100), with funky music and good food.

Entertainment
Art galleries
Herzliya Museum of Contemporary Art, 4 HaBanim, Herzliya, T03-9551011, www. herzliyamuseum.co.il. Mon, Wed, Fri and Sat 1000-14000, Tue and Thu 1600-2000. Adult 10NIS. Work by local and international artists, no permanent exhibition.

Cinema
Herzliya Cinematheque, 29 Sokolov, Herzliya, T09-9513361, www.hcinema.org.il. In the "New Centre" has quality quirky films, third screen planned, Wed-Sat, evenings only. Download the English programme.

Museums
Founders' Museum (Beit Rishonim), 8 HaNadiv, Herzliya, T09-9504270. Sun-Fri 0800-1300, Mon 1600-1830, free. Audio-visual history of Herzliya inside the house; nice botanical garden outside.

Theatre and dance
Stage Arts Centre, 15 Jabotinsky, Beit Cehl HaAvir, Herzliya, T1700-702929, www. hoh-herzliya.co.il. Classical/jazz concerts, theatre, dance and more. A chance to catch performances if you miss them in Tel Aviv.

Transport
Air
Herzliya's airport (T09-9719555) is used primarily by companies offering sight-seeing tours over Israel, private charters, or flying lessons. **Chim-Nir Aviation Service**, T09-9520520, www.cnairways.com; **Moon Air**, T09-9587280, info@moonair.co.il.

Bus
The **Central Bus Station** is on Wolfson, in Herzliya, and is served by Dan and Egged buses. For those travelling to or from Tel Aviv, it is most convenient to use Dan Bus 90, which connects Tel Aviv with Herzliya Pituach. The bus starts outside the **Dan Panorama Hotel** in Tel Aviv, running Kikar Dizengoff – Arlozorov – Namir, before heading north to Herzliya Pituach.

Train
Buses 13 and 29 connect the train station to Herzliya Pituach. Frequent service to **Tel Aviv** (first around 0530, last around 2330) taking only 15 mins, with reduced services on Fri and Sat. To Haifa change at Binyamina (only first and last trains are direct), at least 2 per hour during peak, every hour off-peak, with reduced services on Fri and Sat.

Directory
Hospitals Herzliya Medical Centre, 7 Ramat Yam, T09-9592555, www.hmc.co.il. **Post office** The main post office is just off Route 2, Tel Aviv to Haifa road.

Netanya → *Colour map 2, grid A3.*

By general consensus Netanya is an unpretentious town, perhaps drawing more comfort from comparisons with the English seaside resort of Brighton than more lofty talk of a 'Miami-on-the-Med'. Its prime attraction is over 10 km of sandy beach, with a

Mediterranean climate that remains pleasant throughout the year. The town also prides itself on the variety of activities and entertainment that it sponsors, most of it free. Netanya has a wide selection of hotels and restaurants, and can serve as a good base from which to explore the rest of the Sharon Plain and Mediterranean coastal strip.

In and outs

Getting there and away Netanya is easily accessible from most parts of the country, notably from Tel Aviv and Haifa. The train station is some distance from the town centre (and even further from the beaches), thus making the bus the best way to arrive.

Getting around The town centre is fairly compact, with the bus station being less than 20 minutes walk from the beach (or you can take Bus 12 during July/August). The main tourist activity (sleeping, eating, drinking, shopping) is centred around Kikar Ha'Atzma'ut and the pedestrianized section of Herzl.

Tourist Information The **tourist information office** ① *Kikar Ha'Atzma'ut, T09-8827286. Sun-Thu 0830-1600, Fri 0900-1200,* can help with booking long- and short-term apartment lets, plus plenty of brochures detailing events in and around Netanya.

Background

Founded as an agricultural settlement specializing in citrus production in the 1920s, the town takes its name from the Jewish-American philanthropist Nathan Strauss. World War II saw two new industries spring up in Netanya that continue to sustain the town to this day.

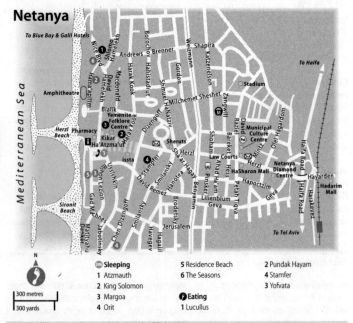

Netanya

To Blue Bay & Galil Hotels

To Haifa

Mediterranean Sea

Amphitheatre

Herzl Beach

Sironit Beach

To Tel Aviv

Hadarim Mall

N

300 metres
300 yards

😴 Sleeping	5 Residence Beach	2 Pundak Hayam
1 Atzmauth	6 The Seasons	4 Stamfer
2 King Solomon		3 Yofvata
3 Margoa	🍴 Eating	
4 Orit	1 Lucullus	

The use of Netanya as a convalescent centre for British officers founded the beginnings of the tourism industry, whilst the setting up of diamond-cutting workshops by immigrants from Antwerp led to the establishment in Netanya of this multi-million-dollar business.

Sights

Beaches Netanya has a number of fine white sand beaches that are clean, with facilities such as deck chairs, showers, changing rooms and elevators that take you up/down the cliffs to the beach! There are also plenty of restaurants and snack-bars, plus basketball courts, children's playgrounds and an outdoor gym for poseur men with large muscles and small swim-suits. Life-guards are on duty most of the year, and it is important to adhere to the warning flags set out for swimmers (see under 'Tel Aviv, beaches' on page 396). Those who want quieter and less crowded beaches should head further north or south from the main town beach area.

Diamond factories and showrooms An interesting diversion from the beach is a visit to Netanya's **National Diamond Centre** (NDC) ⓘ *90 Herzl, T09-T6427790, admission and tour free*. Over 10,000 people are employed directly and indirectly in the diamond trade in Netanya, and at the NDC you will get a chance to see some artisans in action. If easily tempted, leave your credit card at home. **NB** There are other factory/showrooms in town; the tourist office can advise.

The Museum for the Yemenite Jewish Heritage ⓘ *11/4 Kikar Ha'Atzma'ut, T09-8331325, Sun-Thu 0800-1545*. Located just off Kikar Ha'Atzma'ut, this is a small museum tracing the history and culture of the Yemenite Jewish community (in both Yemen and Israel).

Excursions from Netanya

There are a number of attractions in the Sharon Plain around Netanya, although some are not readily accessible by public transport.

Poleg Nature Reserve and Kibbutz Ga'ash The Poleg Nature Reserve stands on land reclaimed from the swamps by the early Zionist pioneer settlers. There are any number of pleasant picnic sites on the banks of the Poleg River, as well as a pleasant walk along the river upstream from where it meets the sea. Many visitors combine a visit here (8 km south of Netanya) with a trip to the superb beach at Kibbutz Ga'ash, a couple of kilometres further south. In addition to the attraction of being quiet and uncrowded, the beach is backed by spectacular cliffs rising to over 60 m. For details of how to get there, see 'Netanya, Transport' on page 477.

Kfar Vitkin and Nahal Alexander National Park The attraction of Kfar Vitkin is the beautiful sandy beach nearby which is popular with windsurfers at weekends (café, lifeguards, toilets, cars have to pay entrance). Also at the moshav, right next to Road 2, there is a 24-hour mall plus the popular Kfar Vitkin Pancake House (see 'Eating' on next page). Just to the north of Kfar Vitkin, on the road to Mikhmoret, is the Nahal Alexander National Park, renowned locally for its turtle population. Inside the park (on elevated ground by the Alexander River) is Khirbet Samara, an Ottoman building on Roman foundations that oversaw taxation on watermelons, brought from the Sharon and Samaria by river or camel then shipped to Egypt and afar.

Netanya listings

For Sleeping and Eating price codes and other relevant information, see Essentials pages 26-31.

Sleeping

There's no lack of hotels in Netanya, many more than the ones listed here. Price categories below are for the 'regular' season; note that during the 'high' season and Jewish holidays rates can double.

LL The Seasons, 1 Nice Blvd, T09-8601555, www.haonot.co.il. Very ugly exterior belies the rather luxurious interior: 'oversized' studios and suites, balconies and sea views, good leisure facilities, 3 restaurants, bar. Tastefully decorated, and much better value out of season.

L Galil, 26 Nice Blvd, T09-8301103/04, www.zyvotel.com. Sea-facing rooms (most with balconies) can accommodate up to 5, a/c, TV, pool, sauna and fitness room, restaurant, nightclub.

L King Solomon, 18 Hamapilim, T09-8338444, www.inisrael.com/kingsolomon. Friendly hotel with high percentage of returning guests. Trendy rooms have sea-facing balconies, a/c, TV; pool, gym, sauna, jacuzzi, restaurant. A good choice.

L Residence Beach, 16 Gad Machnes, T09-8301103/04,www.zyvotel.com. Excellent location, quite small and intimate; choice of studios or suites all with kitchenette, a/c, TV and balcony. Good value out of season; use of the pool, sauna and gym at the Galil.

AL-A Margoa, 9 Gad Machnes, T09-8624434, www.hotelmargoa.co.il. Friendly place close to the beach; some rooms with balconies (though sea-view rather obscured), a/c, TV; good pub, restaurant. Not bad value; breakfast included.

A Orit, 21 Chen, T09-8616818. Simple, friendly, Swedish-run hotel; very clean, en suite rooms with small balconies, communal lounge and fridge. Quiet neighbourhood; reservations recommended. Not a bad deal; breakfast included.

B Atzmauth Hostel, 2 Ussishkin, T09-8621315. Excellent-value hostel-style choice:

very clean double rooms (200NIS), a/c with attached bath, fridge. Very friendly owner. Highly recommended; reservations essential.

Eating

Most of Netanya's restaurants are crowded around Kikar Ha'Atzma'ut and the pedestrianized section of Herzl. The best guide is often the number of diners, although the food is often fairly bland. Most serve pizza, pasta dishes, schnitzel, burgers, etc, with chips and salad for around 25-45NIS. Most of the cheaper falafel and shwarma places are further inland along Herzl and Sha'ar Hagay towards the Central Bus Station.

♥♥♥-♥♥ Lucullus, 8 Nice Blvd, T09-8617831. Lovely French restaurant specializing in seafood and classic dishes; generous servings; beautiful presentation. For a long time it's been considered the nicest place to dine in Netanya and for good reason. Traditional interior and attractive outdoor seating. Kosher. Recommended. Sun-Thu 1200-1500 and1800-2300.

♥♥♥-♥♥ MC2, Rishonim House, Bitan Aharon, T09-8665662, www.2eat.co.il/eng/mc. A magnificently restored 19th-century stone house, impeccably furnished in French country kitchen style with tasteful modern twists, such as the beautiful bulb lamps above the bar. Mon-Wed the chef's special menu (1900-2200; 190NIS) of multiple mini-courses allows you to sample the unique vegetarian dairy dishes; Thu à la carte menu 0800-2400; Fri brunch 0800-1500. Book in advance, especially as you may wish to avoid the Bar Mitzvahs/events hosted here. The restaurant is on the edge of the tiny Bitan Aharon Nature Reserve, featuring Roman and Byzantine caverns, where you can walk off dinner. Located 100 m north of the HaVatselet HaSharon intersection, 5 km north of Netanya. Nateev bus 29.

♥♥ Kfar Vitkin Pancake House, Kfar Vitkin (see previous page). Famous roadside (literally – it's bang next to Route 2) restaurant, originally known for its pancakes

(24-35NIS) and Mexican food (23-26NIS), but the hummus, toasts, kebabs and desserts are also recommended, and the beer is cheap (10-16NIS). Open 24 hrs and worth a stop on the way to Haifa.

†† Stamfer, 6 Stamfer, T09-8844714. A slightly hipper scene is found here, serving up the usual light meals (salads, pastas); later on it turns into a decent bar. Daily 0800-the early hours.

†† Yotvata, Kikar Ha'Atzma'ut, T09-8629141. Very busy branch of the famed kibbutz dairy vegetarian chain. Wonderfully refreshing fruit shakes and, of course, wicked cakes, in addition to a varied and healthy savoury menu. Daily 0800-0100.

††-† Pundak Hayam, 1 Harav Kook, T8615780. No-nonsense Middle Eastern dishes for rock-bottom prices; basically grilled meats and salads. Sat-Thu 1200-2400, Fri 1200-1500.

Bars and clubs
There are a number of bars and clubs along Herzl and around Kikar Ha'Atzma'ut; the language their signs are written in is a clue to the clientele they are aiming at.

Entertainment
Netanya prides itself on its range of public activities and special events. Most of these are listed in a monthly magazine, available from the Tourist Information Office. In summer, the modern amphitheatre in Gan Ha-Melekh Park (by the cliff-side) has film screenings once a week, in addition to musical concerts. Kikar Ha'Atzma'ut is good for watching folk dancing (Sat from 2000).

Shopping
Unless you are in the market for diamonds (see page 475), Netanya is not particularly renowned as a shopping centre. The main shopping districts are on Herzl, Benjamin and Raziel. There is a large open market on Zangwill, near to one of the main diamond workshop areas.

Activities and tours
Fishing
Burgata Fishing Park, T8688075.

Horse riding
Cactus Ranch, T09-8651239. Daily 0800-sunset; pub/restaurant. The Ranch, north of town, T09-8663525; lessons, plus moonlight riding (Bus 17 or 29 from Central Bus Station).

Transport
Bus
The Central Bus Station is found at 3 Benyamin. **Eilat**: 991, 2 daily at 0745 and 2330, 5 hrs, 74NIS; **Haifa**: 947, every 30 mins, 0620-2200, 22.5NIS, 1 ¼ hrs; **Jerusalem**: 947, every 15 mins, 0610-2140, 28NIS, 1¾ hrs; **Kfar Vitkin** and **Mikhmoret** (for Nahal Alexander NP): 29, about 1 every 2 hrs; **Poleg Nature Reserve** (continuing to Kibbutz Ga'ash): 601, every 30 mins; **Tel Aviv**: bus 641 every 15 mins, 17NIS, 2 hrs (with traffic).

Car hire
Avis, 1 Ussishkin, T09-8331619, www.avis. co.il; **Budget**, 2 Gad Machnes, T03-9350018, www.budget.co.il; **Eldan**, 2 Gad Machnes, T09-8821544, www.eldan.co.il.

Sheruts
Sheruts to **Tel Aviv** leave from the junction of Herzl/HaNatziv.

Train
There are 2-4 trains hourly to **Tel Aviv**, and at least 1 per hour to **Haifa**, with some services continuing to **Akko** and **Nahariya**.

Directory
Banks There are a number of banks with ATM machines on Kikar Ha'Atzma'ut, plus several money changers. **Hospitals** Laniado (north of city centre), T09-8604666. **Internet** Solan, 8 Kikar Ha'Atzma'ut, T09-8622131, Sun-Thu 0900-2200, Fri 0900-1400. **Post office** Central Post Office, 57 Herzl; branch post office at 2 Herzl.

Hadera → *Colour map 1, grid C2.*

Hadera is a pleasant small town famed for the fragrant orange blossom perfume that is said to saturate the air every spring. Hadera has an interesting historical museum, telling the story of the early Zionist pioneers' struggle to turn malaria-infested swamps into productive agricultural land. It is also an important transport junction for visitors to Caesarea.

Ins and outs

Getting there and away Hadera's massive factory chimneys are a prominent landmark on the Tel Aviv to Haifa Route 2. The bus station is on Ahad Ha'am to the west of the town centre. For Tel Aviv: Egged buses 852 (quickest), 841 or 921, every 15 minutes (restricted services on Friday/Saturday), 1-1½ hrs, 20NIS. Haifa: 921, every 30 minutes until 2400 (restricted services on Friday/Saturday), 1 hour, 20NIS. For Caesarea: take Bus 76, Sunday-Thursday 0740 1000 1305 1430, Friday 0730 0810 1035 1235 1410 (plus a couple of later ones), 45 minutes (this bus goes right 'round the houses' to Caesarea and Kibbutz Sdot Yam). Last bus back to Hadera Sunday-Thursday at 1949 2134, Friday at 1304 1439. The train station is located about 2 km west of the town centre (15 minutes' walk or Bus 015), and has regular connections south to Tel Aviv and north to Haifa. Hadera is compact enough to get around on foot, though Buses 1/3/7/75 run from the bus station to the town centre.

Background

In 1891 a delegation representing 178 Zionist families in Russia arrived in Palestine seeking land. The delegation eventually purchased a large estate of some 30,000 dunams (3000 hectares) near Caesarea, giving it the name of the old Arab village of Hudaira ('green'), and quickly encouraged their brethren to sell their property in Russia and begin a new life here. The families were heartened by descriptions of abundant land, a plentiful water supply, and by the possibility of raising fish in the "lakes".

It soon transpired that the "vast, open stretch of land flooded with water and rich in greenery" was little more than a swamp: a perfect breeding ground for malarial mosquitoes. As yet, the world had not identified the cause of malaria, and within the first 20 years of settling at Hadera 210 out of the 540 residents died. It soon became apparent that the "lakes" around Hadera, rather than supporting the community, were harbouring disease and death, and thus they had to be drained. This was to be no small task, although the role of Palestinian and Egyptian paid labourers in this endeavour is understated in the 'official' history presented at the town's museum.

As the swamps were slowly brought under control, and the community learned how to farm the land, there were further influxes of settlers. These included not only idealistic Zionists from Poland and Russia, but also 40 families from Yemen. Today, Hadera retains its agricultural base, though the linking of the town to the country's rail network has brought additional industrial employment.

K'han Historical Museum

ⓘ *74 Hagiborim, T0463223300. Sun and Tue 0800-1300 and 1600-1800, Mon, Wed and Thu 0800-1300, Fri 0800-1200. Adult 20NIS, child 18NIS.* The town's early history is well presented in the K'han Historical Museum; certainly worth a visit, particularly if you have time on your hands whilst awaiting a transport connection to Caesarea.

Caesarea is one of Israel's most important historical sites and certainly the premier archaeological attraction on the Mediterranean coast. Stretching for 3.5 km along the sea-shore, and covering some 94 hectares, Caesarea is a large site comprising numerous restored and semi-restored structures from the Herodian, Roman, Byzantine, Arab and Crusader periods. Most of the highlights are contained within the Caesarea National Park. A visit to Caesarea is highly recommended.

Ins and outs

Getting there and away Take a bus from Tel Aviv or Haifa to Hadera bus station, and from there take irregular Bus 76 directly to the site (45 minutes). Although there are only eight buses to Caesarea per day, you can either plan your journey to Hadera so that you connect with Bus 76, or kill time in Hadera by visiting the museum. To return from Caesarea, take Bus 76 from the stops outside either of the main entrances. For full timetable, see 'Transport', above.

Getting around The key attractions are located within the Caesarea National Park. **Ticket offices (1)** are located next to the Roman theatre and at the east gate of the fortified medieval city (this is the main entrance). All other sites are free. **NB** Retain your ticket since this allows access to all sites. A tour of the major attractions takes one-two hrs, a longer tour that takes in more distant sites (eg the high-level aqueduct) can take two-three hours, whilst the grand tour, including all the outlying places of interest, can take four-six hours.

Roman & Byzantine street system, Caesarea

Background

Herodian period Between 22 and 9 BCE, **Herod the Great** built a magnificent new city on the site of the old Phoenician port town of Straton's Tower, naming it after his patron Caesar Augustus: Caesarea. The new harbour that was constructed, **Sebastos**, remains one of the greatest engineering feats of the era, although the question is often asked why Herod didn't simply choose the easier option of refurbishing the more natural port at Jaffa (Joppa). In fact, Herod shrewdly judged that the Jewish population in Jaffa were more nationalistic in their political outlook, whereas at Straton's Tower he could virtually start from scratch in building a truly Herodian city.

Herod's attempt to win over the hearts and minds of his subjects manifested itself in the grandiose scale of the building projects undertaken, and Josephus provides a graphic description of this "exceptional" new city (*The Jewish War, I*, 407-21). It is interesting to note that, although Jews did settle in Caesarea, the city was distinctly pagan, greatly resembling in its municipal functioning the earlier Greek city-states of the Hellenistic period.

Roman rule Following the annexation of Judea in 6 CE by the Romans, Caesarea became the seat of the provincial governor and the de facto capital of Judea (later called *Palaestina*). One of the more famous Roman prefects of Judea, **Pontius Pilate** (26-36 CE), dedicated a temple to the emperor Tiberius during his residence in Caesarea.

It appears that discrimination against the Jewish population of Caesarea in favour of the Greco-Syrian citizens was a continual source of tension between the two communities. Interestingly, both communities claimed the city as their own, the Jews "on the ground that it had been built by a Jew, King Herod", and the Greco-Syrians on the assumption that, although the founder was a Jew, "Herod would not have set up statues and temples if he had meant it for the Jews" (*The Jewish War, II*, 264). When the First Jewish Revolt erupted in 66 CE, "the people of Caesarea had massacred the Jewish colony, in less than an hour slaughtering more than 20,000 and emptying Caesarea of the last Jew" (*The Jewish War, II*, 467). The destruction of the temple in Jerusalem (70 CE) was celebrated by "special games" in the Caesarea amphitheatre in which, according to Josephus, over 2,500 Jews "perished in combats with wild beasts or in fighting each other or by being burnt alive" (*The Jewish War, VII*, 44). During the next couple of centuries of Roman rule, increased trade with the rest of the Roman empire led to a thriving economy in Caesarea, though Jewish leaders continued to shun the city.

Byzantine period There is an early-Christian association with Caesarea, with "a certain man in Caesarea called Cornelius, a centurion" (*Acts 10;1*) perhaps being the first gentile that **Peter** converted to Christianity. **Paul** was imprisoned in Caesarea for two years, before being sent to Rome (*Acts 23-27*). Like the Jewish population of Caesarea, most of the Christian community is presumed to have been massacred by the city's pagan majority on the eve of the First Jewish Revolt (66 CE).

By the end of the second century CE, however, Christians and Jews had begun to return in number to Caesarea, and by 250 CE celebrated rabbinical academies and Christian theological and scholarly centres had been established here. Christian scholarship was centred around the great theologian **Origen**, who assembled a magnificent library and compiled the hexapla text of the Bible. His manuscript collection was added to by Pamphilius, who's own pupil **Eusebius**, (the 'first biblical geographer'), compiled the *Onomasticon*. This classic text has enabled many biblical sites in the Holy Land to be located and identified.

Renovation of the harbour at the beginning of the sixth century CE looked set to add to Caesarea's prosperity. However, the Samaritan revolt of 529-530 CE (and subsequent death, enslavement or banishment of the Samaritan community) destroyed the agricultural base upon which Caesarea was dependent.

Early Arab period Having passed through the hands of the Persians (614 CE) and the Romans again (628 CE), Caesarea fell to the Arabs in 641 or 642. Many commentators seem keen to denigrate the Arabs, suggesting that they "allowed the port to silt up", thus bringing about Caesarea's decline. Though the population declined and older parts of the city began to collapse, the Arab geographer el-Muqaddasi, visiting in the 10th century, describes a flourishing town at the heart of a rich agricultural region.

Arrival of the Crusaders With the return of seafarers, Caesarea's port was rebuilt once more. **Baldwin I** captured the town in 1101 after a brief siege and formed a Crusader principality. A Christian church replaced the Arab mosque on Herod's pagan temple platform. Amongst the booty that Baldwin captured was a hexagonal green glass, believed to be the Holy Grail used by Jesus at the Last Supper. The object is now preserved in the church of San Lorenzo in Genoa (where it has been found to be a glass dish from the Roman period).

Though Caesarea was captured by **Salah al-Din** in 1187 and much of it razed, it was recaptured by **Richard Coeur de Lion** in 1191. Most of the Crusader ruins that you see today date from the reign of the French king **Louis IX**, who, between 1251 and 1252, is said to have "laboured on the fortifications with his own hands, as an act of penance".

The Mamluk sultan **Baibars** captured the city in 1265, though the Crusaders apparently managed to slip away by sea at night to Acre (Akko) whilst surrender negotiations were underway. To prevent reoccupation the Mamluks dismantled many of the fortifications and, perhaps following the precedent set by Louis IX, Baibars is said to have "pick in hand, assisted at its demolition". In 1291 his successors levelled the site.

The site

ⓘ T04-6361358, www.parks.org.il. Daily 0800-1800, winter -1600 (last entrance 1 hr earlier), closes 1 hr earlier on Fri. Adult 36NIS, student 32NIS, child 22NIS, includes entrance to 'Time Trek' audiovisual screenings. Ask at entrance for times of shows in English, as the short films effectively recreate how Caesarea would have looked in Herod's day. Entrance to the restaurants only, during the day, 12NIS. After sunset the park gate remains open so people can dine at the restaurants, of which there are several, plus clusters of shops and galleries.

Roman theatre (2) The Roman theatre is probably Caesarea's best-known attraction, particularly as a venue for concerts by Israel's top performers. Herod built the original theatre and can be said to have introduced this form of entertainment into the region. The theatre that you see today was modified and added to throughout the centuries. At its peak it could seat up to 4000 spectators, with a special box in the central *cuneus* (wedge-shaped block of seating) for the provincial governor.

Remains from Herod's theatre include the *cavea* (spectators' section) and stairways, euripus (channel for removing water from the orchestra), and the concentric gangways. The floor of the orchestra was decorated with painted plaster, depicting floral, fish-scale and geometric patterns. Behind the stage stood the *scaenae frons*, a wall three storeys high that provided the stage backdrop. Built in Hellenistic style, it had a central square *exedra* (recess) flanked by smaller concave niches. The front of the stage facing the audience (*pulpitum*) was painted to match the plasterwork in the niches.

In the third century CE a semi-circular platform was added behind the stage, and a century later the orchestra area was converted into a large basin that could be flooded (*columbetra*), suitable for nautical games and mock naval battles.

A stone being used as a step in the theatre was found to bear an inscription mentioning Pontius Pilate as prefect of Judea, and the temple in Caesarea that he dedicated to the emperor Tiberius. A replica of the stone is nearby, between the theatre and the promontory palace.

In the Byzantine period (324-638 CE) the theatre is thought to have become a victim of the puritanical church elders who disapproved of lascivious and bloody entertainment, and banned gladiatorial contests. It subsequently became part of the **Byzantine fortress**, or *kastron*, that is referred to in some texts from the period. Remains of the Byzantine **fortifications (3)** can be seen continuing west from the theatre.

Promontory 'palace' (4) Early visitors to Caesarea mention a set of ruins on the promontory just to the west of the Roman theatre. Though wave action has severely eroded the rock upon which these ruins stand, there is just enough remaining for some archaeologists to surmise that this could be Herod's palace, as mentioned by Josephus.

The large pool at the west end of the promontory is believed to have been a decorative swimming pool, later modified and used as the city's fish market, connected to the sea by a series of open channels and pools.

The best-preserved part of the promontory complex, to the east of the pool furthest from the sea, contains a number of rooms with mosaic floors. Though some of the floors have been damaged in a conflagration that may have destroyed the entire complex, the mosaic carpet in the middle room is preserved in its entirety. The mosaic, comprising geometric patterns in red, black, yellow and white, is almost identical to one found in the triclinium (dining room) at Herod's winter palace in Jericho.

Numerous sections of the Byzantine system of **streets** (5) have been discovered in this area (which continues to be excavated), though no sections of Herod's grid-plan city have been uncovered (as described by Josephus). However, its plan can almost certainly be deduced from the remains of the Roman and Byzantine streets that were laid out on the same grid. 'Street II' (see map opposite) was flanked by colonnades on either side, covering mosaic pavements that are now being revealed.

Among the structures excavated in the Byzantine commercial and administrative district is the **Archives (or Tax) Building** (6). Greek inscriptions found on the mosaic floor include one that reads 'Christ help Ampelios, the keeper of the archives, and Musonius, the financial secretary, and the other archivists of the same depository'. With further references to chartoularioi (secretaries), noumerarios (accountants) and a skrinion (bureau), it is almost certain that this building was a government building, probably attached to the palace of the imperial governor of Palestine. A building with a well-preserved **mosaic floor** (25), named the 'Ibex Hall' after the deer depicted, lies just to the east.

Along the sea-front, for a long time concealed by a sand dune, stands a complex of barrel-vaulted horrea (warehouses) dating to the Herodian period. Artefacts and containers used for shipping wine, oil and other commodities were found here, suggesting strong trade links with North Africa, Spain, Italy, Greece and Gaul. The northernmost horreum was converted into a **Mithraeum** (7) in the first century CE, and used as a sanctuary in the cult worship of the god Mithras. A hole was cut into the roof of the horreum, allowing a shaft of light to illuminate the altar near the eastern end. Frescoes depicted Mithraic scenes on the walls, whilst a marble medallion found in the vault shows Mithras slaying the sacred bull. Few Mithraeums were built in the Middle East, and this is the only one that has been found in Israel.

The well-preserved marble remains of a **Byzantine bathhouse complex** (26) lie under a shelter, whilst the 10,000-seater **Herodian hippodrome** (27) where horse-races were held has a newly built sea-promenade running alongside, between the Crusaders' south gate and the promontory palace.

Medieval city walls and gates Of all the towns built at Caesarea, the Crusader city is the smallest, covering less than nine hectares. The city was originally walled on all four sides but almost the entire seaward wall has been lost, though the defensive walls on all other sides remain impressive (8). The architectural features suggest that the majority of the medieval city walls were built by Louis IX.

Though the fortifications still look formidable, most of what you see today is just the *glacis*, the sloping base of the defensive wall. The glacis was previously surmounted by a 10-m-high wall, parts of which remain only along the south wall. A seven-m-wide fosse (ditch or trench) provided extra security.

The **south wall** is approximately 275 m long, with four towers providing additional strength. Though the Crusader city walls are at their most complete here, with parts of the main defensive wall rising above the glacis, it seems that the **South Gate (9)** was never completely finished and only the outer gateway was constructed in full.

Caesarea

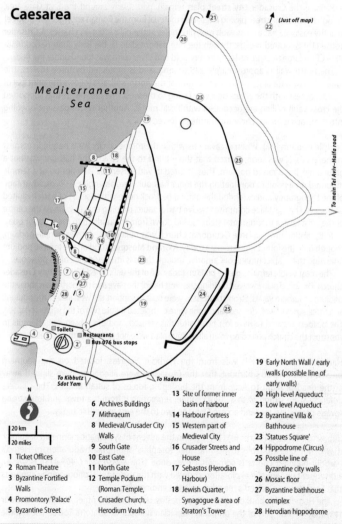

1 Ticket Offices
2 Roman Theatre
3 Byzantine Fortified Walls
4 Promontory 'Palace'
5 Byzantine Street
6 Archives Buildings
7 Mithraeum
8 Medieval/Crusader City Walls
9 South Gate
10 East Gate
11 North Gate
12 Temple Podium (Roman Temple, Crusader Church, Herodium Vaults)
13 Site of former inner basin of harbour
14 Harbour Fortress
15 Western part of Medieval City
16 Crusader Streets and House
17 Sebastos (Herodian Harbour)
18 Jewish Quarter, Synagogue & area of Straton's Tower
19 Early North Wall / early walls (possible line of early walls)
20 High level Aqueduct
21 Low level Aqueduct
22 Byzantine Villa & Bathhouse
23 'Statues Square'
24 Hippodrome (Circus)
25 Possible line of Byzantine city walls
26 Mosaic floor
27 Byzantine bathhouse complex
28 Herodian hippodrome

20 km
20 miles

The **east wall** is fortified by nine towers that project beyond the wall. The **East Gate (10)** was the main entrance, accessed via a bridge over the fosse, the supporting pillars and arches of which are still in place. The doorway of the gatehouse is protected by loopholes and gaps through which burning oil could be poured. The hall of the gatehouse contains a well and a basin, a stone bench, and a doorway in the west wall leading to the town. All of these features were added by Louis IX when he modified the existing fortifications. 30 m north of the East Gate is a secret passage leading from the town into the fosse.

Parts of the **Crusader city street plan** remain, particularly around the East Gate area, though much of the street paving is recycled material from the Roman era. A section of street near the east wall has a cross vault roof, plus holes in the pillars for tying horses. A **Crusader house (16)** is located nearby, though the foundations date to the Early Arab period (638-1099 CE). A large treasure of 10th-century gold and silver coins was found under the floor.

The north wall is approximately 275 m-long, and is protected by three towers. The square **North Gate (11)** stands in the centre of the north wall, and follows the principal of indirect access with the actual doorway facing to the west. The four pillars that supported the cross vault ceiling are decorated with floral motifs. Another secret passage opening into the glacis is located near the northeast tower.

Temple podium (12) When excavations within the medieval city walls begun in earnest in the 1960s, it was soon realized that the mound to the east of the harbour was not a natural hill, but a raised podium. Thus, it fitted in with Josephus' description of a temple mounted on a podium dominating the inner harbour. Herod's engineers took advantage of the topography and extended the natural bedrock ridge with a series of barrel-vaulted chambers. The west face comprises twelve barrel vaults running east to west. At the centre of the west face, a monumental staircase led down from the podium to the harbour quay.

In Byzantine times, a large **Octagonal Church** was built on the former temple podium, though only the foundations remain today. A **Grand Mosque** stood on the temple podium following the Arab conquest of Caesarea, though there is little evidence of its presence.

The most visible remains on the podium today are of the unfinished 13th-century **Crusader church**. The initial plan involved building the west half of the nave and the north aisle above the podium's southern vaults. Strong buttresses were built to support the west side of the podium, and three apses of well-dressed sandstone were completed before two of the vaults collapsed. The builders seemed to have lost heart after this set-back, and the subsequent attempts to construct the church according to an alternative plan were not realized with any real finesse.

Harbour Fortress (14) It was from the Harbour Fortress, located on the southern breakwater of Herod's harbour, that the Crusaders were alleged to have slipped away in the dead of night to Acre, from the besieging forces of sultan Baibars. The citadel's defences were strong, with a 20-m channel separating it from the town and four strong towers protecting the land access. Only the two to the east are visible today.

Sebastos (Herodian harbour) (17) Prior to the advent of systematic marine archaeology, it was not unreasonable to assume that Josephus' triumphant adoration of Herod's harbour-building efforts is somewhat over-done (*The Jewish War I, 408-415*). However, subsequent underwater exploration, coupled with the use of aerial photography, suggests that Sebastos was indeed a miracle of marine engineering.

The Herodian harbour comprises three basins, one inside the other. The **inner harbour (13)** may well be part of the original Phoenician harbour of Straton's Tower. The **middle** basin was part of a natural bay, protected to the north and south by rocky promontories. The **outer basin**, formed by building two long breakwaters thus enclosing a large expanse of open sea, is Herod's construction miracle.

The main body of the breakwater was in fact made of conglomerate blocks poured into a wooden frame and then lowered on to a bed of rubble. The average size of these blocks was 1.8 m by 3.9 m by 3.9 m, with the outer edge of the breakwater resting on 5-m-long ashlar blocks. Not quite the dimensions that Josephus refers to, but evidence from the sea-bed does confirm the overall scale of the harbour and the existence of the huge towers that he describes. Tectonic faulting has caused the sea-bed to subside five to seven metres, causing the outer harbour constructions to sink several metres below their original level. As a result Herod's breakwater became a major danger to shipping and the remains of several ships have been found. Though it is not entirely clear when the final submergence of the Herodian harbour took place, dating of samples from the ships wrecked attempting to sail over the sunken breakwater suggest a date early in the fourth century CE.

Western part of medieval city (15) Extensive excavation in the western part of the medieval city revealed remains that pre-date the Crusader occupation. The second stratum of the dig contained evidence of a flourishing settlement dating to the middle and late **Arab period** (9th to 10th centuries CE). Large houses built around private courtyards, with numerous alleys and culs-de-sac, conform to classic Islamic city design. Water delivery and storage systems are technologically advanced, though archaeologists were disappointed by the paucity of artefacts found.

The lower, fourth stratum revealed extensive remains from the **Byzantine period** (324-638 CE), including an 8-m-wide paved street. An unidentified large public building was also uncovered, complete with sections of mosaic floor and two marble pillars; one has the Hebrew word shalom carved into it.

Jewish quarter (18) Excavations to the north of the medieval city walls have provided evidence that this area was almost certainly the main Jewish quarter of the Herodian, Early Roman, and later, Byzantine period cities. Finds from the Hellenistic period in lower levels of stratum also suggest that the site of **Straton's Tower** was centred here, though the lack of pottery finds seems to confirm Josephus' assertion that the town was in decline when Herod chose the site for his new city.

Talmudic sources mention a synagogue in Caesarea near to the sea, and in the 1920s a capital carved with a seven-branched menorah was found on the sea-shore. A number of synagogues from different periods are superimposed upon one another, reflecting periods of persecution and then tolerance of the Jewish community. The best-preserved is a fifth-century synagogue, paved with a mosaic floor bearing the inscription: "Beryllus, archisynagogus and administrator, son of Ju[s]tus, made the pavement work of the hall from his own money". One of the marble columns in the building refers to "The gift of Theodorus son of Olympus for the salvation of his daughter Matrons", whilst other columns bear the seven-branched menorah.

Early north wall (19) This segment of perimeter wall includes two round towers and one that is polygonal, similar to those found at Samaria that date from the Hellenistic period. Their drafted sandstone block construction is similar to work found in the vault excavated at the southwest corner of the temple podium, and it is suggested that this early north wall formed part of the city walls of Straton's Tower. Other sources, however, date the wall to the Herodian period with Roman period additions, noting how well it fits in with the Roman and Byzantine street pattern.

High-level aqueduct and low-level aqueduct The water supply system that served Caesarea was one of the most technically advanced and efficient in the country, and the Roman aqueducts here are the best preserved in Israel. Caesarea was fortunate to have two sources of water. The **high-level aqueduct** (20) brought water from the springs of Mt Carmel, possibly providing the town's drinking water. The **low-level aqueduct** (21) brought water from a dam on the Zarqa River (Nahal Tanninim), possibly for use in irrigation.

There is some dispute as to who built the 9-km-long high-level aqueduct, with some sources claiming that it was built by Herod, and later repaired by the Roman Second Legion (Traina Fortis) and the Tenth Legion (Fretensis) during Hadrian's reign (117-138 CE). There is evidence that the Roman legions worked on the aqueduct, with at least eight Latin inscriptions set in the masonry referring to their work. Others suggest that the plaster-lined 'channel A' furthest from the sea was built by Herod, whilst the western 'channel B' was built circa 130 CE by Hadrian. With channel A delivering 900 cubic metres per hour, more than enough for a city of over 50,000, there is some question as to why the additional 1,600 cubic metres per hour provided by channel B was necessary. The date and builder of the low-level aqueduct are not known.

Byzantine street and square Just to the east of the medieval city's East Gate excavations have revealed a large public square dating to the Byzantine period (324-638 CE). Paved with large marble slabs, the square contains a number of large statues, giving it the popular name '**Statues Square**' (23). The porphyry statue features a man seated on a green granite throne, perhaps the emperor Hadrian, whilst the subject of the white marble statue, also a man seated on a throne, has not been identified. It is clear, however, that the upper and lower parts of the two statues do not match, suggesting that the second- or third-century statues were moved to this square at a later date in the Byzantine period.

Hippodrome (circus) To the southeast of the medieval city it is still possible to make out the outline of the second-century **hippodrome** (24), or circus. At its peak, this huge racetrack stadium (450 m north to south, 90 m east to west) could seat over 30,000 spectators, and became renowned for the quality of its racing. The centre of the racetrack (*spina*) was marked by a row of columns, the mightiest of which (a porphyry obelisk 27 metres high) now rests where it fell. The hippodrome has not been reconstructed and now appears somewhat neglected, set amidst the cultivated land. The entrance is marked by a modern arch beside the road.

Sdot Yam Museum of Caesarea Antiquities ① *T04-6364367, Sat-Thu 1000-1600, Fri 0800-1300, 10NIS.* Many items found in the Caesarea area are now on display in the small museum in the grounds of the adjacent Kibbutz Sdot Yam. The kibbutzniks have been responsible for a large number of chance finds over the years; the Byzantine street and square ('Statues Square') was accidently discovered in 1951 when a kibbutz tractor struck a colossal porphyry statue!

Beaches

There are three beaches in the vicinity of Caesarea, though sadly they are often badly polluted by the nearby kibbutz factory. The Old City beach is set within the Herodian harbour, and has facilities including chairs, umbrellas, showers and toilets (admission charged). A free beach is available to the north, with the high-level aqueduct providing a superb backdrop. Life-guards operate in season. To the south of Caesarea is the sandy Shonit beach, with life-guards, showers, toilets, and a small snack-bar/restaurant. The beach is free, though there is a fee for parking. **NB** As per anywhere on Israel's Mediterranean coast, beware of strong currents and undertows. Swim only in marked areas and observe warning flags.

Caesarea listings

For Sleeping and Eating price codes and other relevant information, see Essentials pages 26-31.

Sleeping

L Dan Caesarea, T04-6269111, www. danhotels.com. Luxury 'country-club' style resort set in extensive grounds. Full facilities include choice of restaurants, pool, floodlit tennis, health club, fitness centre, plus a range of activities also available. Recommended. The hotel has its own 18-hole golf course (not cheap).

Eating

There are a number of restaurants in the Caesarea National Park. In fact, it's a very fashionable location for families and couples to go out to dine. **Hametsuda** (the Fort) serves sushi and other Japanese food, as well as more standard Israeli schnitzels and fish. The **Crusaders'** restaurant is popular with families, while Helena is famous for its seafood and meat dishes. All have wonderful locations, with outdoor terraces and views of the sea, though it is quite an intrusive form of development. They remain open in the evening, after the National Park has shut. Kibbutz Sdot Yam has a good value cafeteria.

Caesarea to Haifa: the coastal route

→ *Colour map 1, grid B/C2.*
Heading north from Caesaerea, there are two options for continuing on to Haifa. The coastal route takes in some idyllic beaches and important archaeological sites, and is probably the most popular of the two.

Ins and outs

Getting there and away Most of the sights along this route are located on or just off the two main roads connecting Tel Aviv and Haifa (Route 2 and Route 4). Buses running along these two roads should be able to drop you off at the turnings for the various sights, and you will rarely have to walk for more than 15 or 20 minutes to reach them. With your own transport, access provides no such problems. Even using public transport, all these spots on the coastal route can be visited as excursions from Haifa (or from Tel Aviv with an early start).

Dor → *Colour map 1, grid C2.*

A little over 12 km north of Caesarea is one of the Mediterranean coast's best beaches, in addition to an important archaeological site that has yielded many superb finds from the Iron Age, Persian, Hellenistic, Roman and Byzantine periods.

Ins and outs

Getting there and away There is no direct transport all the way to the beach/site (which perhaps keeps it quieter). The Tel Aviv to Haifa bus 921 passes the turn-off for Dor ('Dor Junction', look for the Kibbutz Nahsholim sign), from where it is a half-hour walk to the beach. **NB** Make sure you inform the driver in advance where you wish to get off.

Background

A 13th-century BCE Nubian inscription lists Dor as one of the major cities of the Via Maris, with further references in the biblical description of the Israelite conquest of Canaan (*Joshua 12:1, 23*). Excavations now suggest that the maritime site was first inhabited in the Middle

Bronze Age IIA (2000-1750 BCE), and was continually occupied until at least the third century BCE. Though Dor was abandoned in the Late Roman period (132-324 CE), evidence suggests that shipping continued to use the natural anchorage here until the end of the 19th century CE. In fact, it was on the beaches of Dor (Tantura) that Napoleon's army awaited in vain the arrival of the French evacuation fleet following defeat at Acre (Akko) in 1799. Large quantities of French ordnance, including cannons, rifles and daggers, have been found on the sea-bed.

Sights

Hamizgaga Museum ⓘ *Kibbutz Nahsholim, T04-6390950, Sun-Thu 0830-1400, Fri 0830-1300, Saturday 1030-1500, adult 18NIS, student/child 12NIS.* The Nahsholim Museum is the home of the Centre of Nautical and Regional Archaeology, and features an impressive collection of local finds. A visit is highly recommended prior to exploring the remains of ancient Dor. The building was originally intended for use as a glass factory, established by Baron Edmond de Rothschild to supply the wineries at Zichron Ya'akov. Unfortunately, the project failed due to the poor quality of the sand.

Tel Dor The Tel Dor mound has been extensively excavated. A massive wall 3 m high and 2.5 m wide, presumably built in the 12th-11th century BCE by the Sikil (one of the tribes of the Sea Peoples/Philistines), is considered to be the most impressive Philistine fortification yet discovered in Israel. The tel has provided a large number of cult objects from the Persian period (586-332 BCE), including clay figurines and masks. The Hellenistic period (332-37 BCE) is also well represented, with numerous examples of pottery vessels. The Roman period (37 BCE-132 CE) has provided extensive remains of a medium-sized town, with several large piazzas, streets, drainage channels, and part of the aqueduct that brought water from the springs in the Mt Carmel range. Portable items found include moulded drinking vessels in the shape of a Negroid head and a dog. A number of artefacts from Dor are displayed at the Reuben and Edith Hecht Museum, University of Haifa.

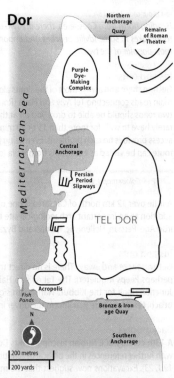

Byzantine church To the east of the Tel Dor mound, close to Kibbutz Nahsholim, stand the remains of a Byzantine church (324-638 CE). The church was probably built during two separate periods, possibly on the site of a Hellenistic cult worship temple. The original church was probably destroyed in the late fourth or early fifth century CE, rebuilt, then destroyed again in the seventh century CE.

Purple dye factory The purple dye factory to the north of the mound is considered to be the best-preserved example in the eastern Mediterranean. The dye was extracted from the murex sea snail, and subsequently used to produce the purple garments that symbolized royal and religious authority in Hellenistic, Roman and Byzantine times (see *The Jewish War VII, 149*).

Maritime Dor Maritime Dor owes its significance to the off-shore reefs and rocky islands that act as natural breakwaters, providing one of the few natural anchorages along Israel's Mediterranean coast. It was in the Middle Bronze Age IIA that the harbour city was first established. Ironically, the instability of the underwater sand dunes at the entrance to the main port claimed many victims, and it is through the cargoes of these wrecks that much of the information about maritime Dor has been gathered. Major finds include 140 stone anchors dating from 1900 BCE to the sixth century BCE, a complete Persian war helmet dating to the fifth century BCE, a number of sixth- or seventh-century bronze steelyards inscribed with crosses and bearing the words (in Greek) "Jesus Christ the Saviour", plus a number of less-important finds dating to the period when the Crusaders established the stronghold of Merle on the summit of the mound.

Dor Beach ① *Daily 24/7, 10NIS entrance, children free. Also accessible through the grounds of the Nahsholim resort*. Variously referred to as Dor Beach, Tantura Beach or Nahsholim Beach, the stretch of fine white sand here is clean and uncrowded during the week, though it gets pretty busy at weekends. Four small, rocky islands just off-shore act as breakwaters and form natural lagoons. Each island also functions as a bird sanctuary. A walk north along the beach leads you to the archaeological site of Tel Dor (see opposite), and continuing north brings you to HaBanim beach, another attractive spot. It is easy enough to escape the crowds on the main beach by walking a short way.

Dor listings

For Sleeping and Eating price codes and other relevant information, see Essentials pages 26-31.

Sleeping
LL Nahsholim Resort, T04-6399533, www. nahsholim.co.il. Very popular beachside chalets with a/c, kitchenettes and TV; plus zimmers in the kibbutz nearby. Substantial discounts are offered in winter, though prices go up on Jewish holidays. Half-board (in the decent Rozmarin self-service kosher restaurant) is 120NIS extra.

A cheaper option is the campsite in the nearby Moshav Dor; or camp on the beach (though this may be risky).

Wadi Me'arat Nature Reserve ('Carmel Caves') → *Colour map 1, grid C2.*

① *T04-9841750, daily 0800-1700, winter 0800-1600 (last entrance 1 hr before closing), Fri closes 1 hr earlier. Adults 20NIS, student 17NIS, child 9NIS. Shop with snacks, toilets.*
The Mt Carmel range comprises mainly hard limestone and dolomites and is extensively pitted with caves, many providing evidence of habitation dating back to Prehistoric times. Four main caves here have been excavated and are open to visitors. The wooded hill-side has a dramatic aspect, and the trails between the caves afford some good views. The 'geological' trail (black markers) takes around 30 minutes while the 'botanical' trail (blue markers) is around 1-1½ hours. Staff can provide you with a map and there are information boards outside the caves.

Ins and outs

Getting there and away The 'Carmel Caves' are located within the Wadi Me'arat Nature Reserve, roughly equidistant from Dor and Haifa (just east of Route 4). Bus 921 will drop you on Route 4 about 1 km away (make sure the driver knows where you want to get off). The caves are well labelled, and marked trails lead through the Nature Reserve, with numerous attractive picnic spots.

Tabun Cave

This cave (Cave of the Oven) has revealed remains from the Lower and Middle Palaeolithic periods, with radio-carbon (carbon-14) dating suggesting that the cave was abandoned around 40,000 years ago. It is speculated that the cave may have been first occupied around 500,000 years BP, though there is insufficient evidence to confirm a continual sequence of occupation. The discovery of the body of a woman of the Neanderthal type, perhaps over 120,000 years old, has suggested that both Neanderthal (Homo erectus) and Cro-Magnon (*Homo sapiens sapiens*) may have coexisted for a while in this region, since the woman's body antedates numerous specimens of Homo sapiens sapiens found in the nearby Skhul Cave.

During Tabun Cave's period of occupation, sea-level was considerably higher, though environmental change led to a substantial drop in sea-level and an expansion of the coastal plain in front of the cave. Tabun Cave was probably abandoned when the chimney at the rear of the cave opened up, though this provided an trap into which animals could be driven.

El-Wad (Nahal) Cave

This cave (Cave of the Valley) is approximately 90 m long and comprises two large chambers and a corridor. Though the site had been mentioned in the writings of 19th-century travellers, it was not until stone-quarrying began in 1928 for use in Haifa harbour that the archaeological wealth of the site was uncovered. The site was probably first occupied in the Upper Palaeolithic (45,000-30,000 BP), though it is the finds from the Natufian period (12,950-10,300 BP) that are considered to be the most interesting. A number of attractive necklaces, made of dentalium and bone pendants, have been found, in addition to Natufian burials with skulls decorated with necklaces of dentalia.

'Atlit → *Colour map 1, grid C2.*

Standing on this promontory jutting out into the Mediterranean are the remains of one of the most important Crusader castles in the Holy Land. It was one of the last strongholds to be abandoned after the fall of Acre in 1291, and the Mamluks were so impressed by the fortifications they ordered much of it to be dismantled for fear that it may be reoccupied. The ancient site around the castle is rich with remains from both ancient and medieval periods. However, the area is a heavily fortified naval base and the castle is enclosed by barbed wire fences and high security (do not take photographs). There is a decent curve of beach with good views of the castle, though it is probably not worth the effort of getting here by public transport. If you're in a car, perhaps stop for a swim and admire the view, and you can also visit the '**Atlit Illegal Immigrants Camp** ① *T04-8841980, Sun-Thu 0900-1530, Fri 0900-1300, adult 20NIS, student 15NIS*, on the way. This was the site of a detention camp during the British Mandate period, used for holding illegal Jewish immigrants. A number of the original camp structures remain and the camp is now used as a museum. Models, photographs, reconstructions and a short audio-visual presentation give some idea of conditions inside the camp. On 10 October 1945, three units of the Palmach (the proactive wing of the underground Jewish self-defence organisation, the Haganah) successfully attacked the camp, freeing a large number of detainees. One of the three units was led by Yitzhak Rabin, future Prime Minister of Israel.

Ein Hod

Ins and outs
Getting there and around Take bus 202 or 921 from Haifa that follow the old Haifa to Hadera road (Route 4) and get off at the Ein Hod Junction (20 minutes). From here it is a 2 km walk (uphill) to the village. **NB** There's no transport here on Shabbat, and generally no public transport back to Haifa after the concerts. Those with their own vehicles should note that they must be parked outside the village.

A popular excursion from Haifa, Ein Hod is an attractively located artists' colony. The colony was established in 1953 by the one of the founders of the Dadaist movement, Marcel Janco (1895-1984), on the site of an Arab village that had been abandoned during the 1948 war. There are a number of attractions, beside the use of bronzes and sculptures in open spaces. The **Ein Hod Artists' Gallery** ① T04-8842548, daily 0930-1600, 4NIS, features exhibitions of the village artists' work. The **Janco-Dada Museum** ① T04-9541961, Sun-Thu 0930-1700, Fri 0930-1400, Sat 1100-1500, adult 20NIS, student 10NIS, contains works by Janco, contemporary Israeli Dadaists, and a short audio-visual show explaining the movement. A small amphitheatre hosts evening concerts, most weeks. Ein Hod has a whole host of lovely accommodation options. For information on these and on other galleries in the village, see www.ein-hod.info/.

Caesarea to Haifa: the inland route

→ *Colour map 1, grid B/C 2.*
Though the majority of visitors take the coastal route between Caesarea and Haifa, this inland route is a very pleasant alternative, passing through the beautiful undulating scenery of Israel's wine country, and taking in a number of fascinating places of interest. Many of the settlements on this route were founded with the financial assistance of Baron Edmond de Rothschild (1845-1934) and bear the name of his family members.

Ins and outs
Getting there and away This route is undoubtedly at its best if you have the flexibility of your own transport. Having said that, it is certainly possible to appreciate this area using public transport. The places of interest to the north (**Daliyat el-Carmel**, **Isfiya**, **Mukhraka**) can easily be visited by a combination of bus and walking, as an excursion from Haifa. Bearing in mind that the southernmost places of interest (**Shuni**, **Ramat HaNadiv** and **Zichron Ya'akov**) are less than 8 km apart, it is perfectly feasible, and very pleasant, to walk between the main sites.

Shuni
Shuni (Miyamas) stands on a gently sloping hill at the southern end of the Carmel Range, and the key attractions have now been incorporated within **Jabotinsky Park**. The park takes its name from the leader of the Irgun Zvai Leumi (Irgun) underground/terrorist organisation, Ze'ev Jabotinsky (1880-1940), whose units used this remote area as a base for attacks. Inside the park, the key attraction is the partially restored Roman theatre. The

theatre is reasonably large, with 20 rows of seats divided in two by a narrower row of seats, and two lines of steps separating the audience from the orchestra. The floor of the orchestra was paved with smooth slabs of limestone quarried nearby on Mt Carmel, with the remains of what is thought to be an altar to Dionysus or Asclepius (see below) at its centre. The theatre was destroyed by an earthquake in the fourth century CE.

In the Byzantine period (324-638 CE), remains from the Roman theatre were reused, though the standard of workmanship on the subsequent Byzantine theatre was not high. Later in the Byzantine period, and continuing into the Early Arab period, the theatre area was used as an oil press and threshing floor.

The **springs** at Shuni were also the source of water that fed the high-level aqueduct to Caesarea. A marble statue of **Asclepius** (the god of healing) was found near the high-level aqueduct, providing a link with a reference in the writings of the Bordeaux Pilgrim (333 CE), who refers to a mountain called Mons Syna close to Caesarea from which a miraculous spring enabled barren women to become pregnant. Ritualistic bathing was an important element of this cult, and a system of small pools fed by an aqueduct (dating to the Early Byzantine period) were found to the south of the Roman theatre. Other pools to the west of this aqueduct were decorated with intricate mosaic floors. The statue of Asclepius now resides in the Rockefeller Museum in Jerusalem.

Ramat HaNadiv → Colour map 1, grid C2.

Located on a southern ridge of Mt Carmel, Ramat HaNadiv, literally 'the Benefactor's Heights', has been developed into a beautiful park containing the family tomb of Baron Edmond de Rothschild. Also lying within the park are a number of important archaeological sites. Ramat HaNadiv can be reached by sherut taxi on the Zichron Ya'akov-Binyamina route. Alternatively, it is not far to walk from either Zirchon Ya'akov (2 km) or Binyamina and Shuni (see previous page).

Rothschild Memorial Gardens and Tomb The centre-piece of the 450-hectare parkland is the **Rothschild Memorial Gardens** ① T06-3697821, Sun-Thu 0800-1600, Fri 0800-1400, Sat 0800-1600, free, 2 km along the unpaved road from the park entrance. The gardens are beautifully maintained and feature separate rose, palm and fragrance gardens set between manicured lawns shaded by Cedars of Lebanon. The bodies of Baron Rothschild and his wife, Baroness Adelaide, were brought here from France in 1954 aboard an Israeli warship and placed in the crypt beneath a single slab of black marble. It's a fine place to be buried, whilst the living can appreciate a magnificent view of the Sharon Plain and the Mediterranean coast from Dor to Caesarea.

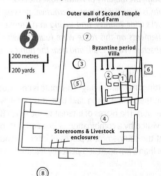

Second Temple period & Byzantine period remains, Ramat Hanadiv

N

200 metres
200 yards

Outer wall of Second Temple period Farm

Byzantine period Villa

Storerooms & Livestock enclosures

1 Second Temple period bathtub
2 Second Temple period stepped Mikveh (Ritual Bath)
3 Oil Press
4 Byzantine period Cistern
5 Wine Press
6 Wine Press
7 Threshing floor area
8 Byzantine period Wine Press

Kebara Cave The prehistoric Kebara Cave is one of several such sites on Mt Carmel. The cave entrance opens on to a spacious chamber 26 m by 20 m. Excavations have revealed at least ten layers of occupation, dating back to the end of the Middle Palaeolithic period (c. 45,000 BP). The most significant finds date to the Natufian culture (Late Mesolithic, c. 12,950-10,300 BP), and include a large number of bone implements and tools. Also of great interest to archaeologists was the discovery of skeletons belonging to a baby and a young Neanderthal male, similar to those found at Tabun Cave (see page 490). Follow the marked trail from the main parking lot. **NB** Further excavation means that the cave is not always open to visitors.

Second Temple period farm A large agricultural estate dating to the end of the Second Temple period has been excavated at Ramat HaNadiv. The farm was owned by a Jewish family, though the reason for its abandonment are unclear. Dating of pottery remains found at the site suggest that it was not abandoned during the First Jewish Revolt (66-70 CE), when the Jewish population at nearby Caesarea suffered greatly. A more likely date for the abandonment would be the Bar Kokhba Revolt (Second Jewish Revolt) of 132-135 CE.

The L-shaped estate covers less than a third of a hectare and is surrounded by a wall one metre thick. A large tower has been identified at the northern part of the compound, with storerooms and livestock enclosures to the south. The residential area of the compound has revealed an oval bathtub and a stepped *mikveh* (Jewish ritual bath). Winepresses are located to the west of the residential area, and to the east, just outside the eastern wall.

Byzantine period villa Some time at the beginning of the sixth century CE, a Byzantine villa was built on the site of the abandoned estate (see plan). The villa's design, with the eastern wing roofed by three parallel vaults and numerous windows in the supporting walls, is common in Roman-Byzantine buildings throughout other parts of Israel, but almost unique to this area. Water was supplied by the cistern just to the south. A large Byzantine winepress is also located nearby.

The villa was abandoned at the beginning of the Early Arab period (638 CE), but remained in fairly good condition up until the beginning of this century. In fact the vaulted structures were still standing when Conder and Kitchener visited the site on behalf of the British Palestine Exploration Fund in 1873.

Zichron Ya'akov → *Colour map 1, grid C2.*

This small hill-top town sits at the heart of arguably Israel's best wine-producing country. A tasting session at the Carmel Oriental Wine Cellars is top of most visitors' priorities here, though there are a couple of other attractions, plus galleries, shops and cafés to while away the time.

Ins and outs
Getting there and away From Tel Aviv, bus 872 runs to Zichron Ya'akov eight times per day (1¾ hours); from Haifa, bus 202 leaves about once an hour (30 minutes). A very limited number of trains on the Tel Aviv to Haifa line serve Zichron Ya'akov (see 'Transport' on page 424).

Background
The settlement here was founded in 1882 by Jewish immigrants from Romania. The early pioneers, however, fell into immediate difficulty with high mortality rates compounded by little experience in farming such land. The population of this early settlement, along with others in the immediate area, were saved from ruin by a wealthy benefactor,

Baron Edmond de Rothschild. He purchased the entire valley (subsequently HaNadiv, or Benefactor's Heights), and the pioneers became salaried employees. The settlement was named Zichron Ya'akov, 'In Memory of Jacob', after Rothschild's father.

A telling contribution of Rothschild was his decision to bring expert agronomists into the area for an assessment of the land's productive potential. The soil and climate were found to be suitable for vine cultivation, and so began Israel's wine-producing industry.

Sights

Carmel Oriental Wine Cellars ① *T04-6391788, www.carmelwines.co.il. Book tours in advance.* Not surprisingly, one of Zichron Ya'akov's main attractions is a tour of the Carmel Oriental (Carmel Mizrachi) Winery. 'Carmel' is often translated as 'God's Vineyard' (Kerem El), and some fine wines are produced here (connoisseurs, however, will tell you that the wines from the Golan are the nation's best). The tour finishes with a tasting, and the opportunity to make purchases at discount prices. The winery also produces a selection of spirits.

Aaronson Museum ① *Beit Aaronson, 40 Hameyasdim, T04-6390120, www.nili-museum. org.il, Sun-Thu 0830-1600, Fri 0830-1200, adult 16NIS, student 12NIS.* The Aaronson Museum serves a dual function. Part of the exhibits emphasize the work of **Aaron Aaronson** (1876-1919) as a leading botanist and agronomist, with a small natural history museum displaying examples of Palestinian flora. The rest of Aaronson's former home is devoted to his role as a spy-master, controlling a spy-ring (that included his sisters), dedicated to the termination of Ottoman rule in Palestine. Working closely with British intelligence, Aaronson and his sisters Sarah and Rebecca led an organisation called **NILI** (an acronym for "The Eternal One of Israel will not prove false", a quote from the *Book of Samuel*) in spying operations against the Turks. Sarah was later imprisoned and tortured by the Turkish police before committing suicide. Aaron survived the British victory in Palestine, but was presumed killed when his plane disappeared on the way to the Paris Peace Conference.

Old town Much of the original town remains, and refurbishment has included attractive cobbled streets lined with old-fashioned lamp-posts. The original synagogue, **Beit Ya'akov**, built in 1885, still remains, as does the water-tower, **Binyamin Pool**, and the old **Town Hall**.

Beit Daniel In 1938, following the suicide of her 18-year-old son Daniel (a former child prodigy), Lillian Friedlander built this 'artists' retreat', on the western edge of Zichron Ya'akov, overlooking the Carmel coast. Amongst those who stayed here are Leonard Bernstein and Toscanini. This small complex of buildings is now a museum, featuring Daniel's Steinway piano, and is also the venue for a chamber music festival held twice yearly on the Jewish Pesach and Sukkot holidays.

Zichron Ya'akov listings

For Sleeping and Eating price codes and other relevant information, see Essentials pages 26-31.

Sleeping

AL Beit Maimon, 4 Zahal, T04-6290999, www. maimon.com. Small, family-run hotel, with highly recommended **Casa Barone** terrace restaurant (see menu on www.casa-barone. co.il). Short walk to town, swimming pool (seasonal), sun deck and jacuzzi. Wonderful sea views from the 25 rooms; breakfast included, half-board and full-board available. Be aware that at weekend prices can go up by 50%!

Contents

Footprint features

Haifa & the North Coast

The port city of Haifa tends to divide opinion, as it has all the potential to be one of Israel's most attractive cities yet it is cursed with a reputation as a sleepy place full of hard-working high-tech grads. Extending down the western slopes of Mt Carmel to the sweep of Haifa Bay, cut by the green swathe of the beautiful Baha'i gardens and the golden shrine of the Bab, Haifa certainly has an attractive aspect. Viewed from Mt Carmel at night, when the twinkling lights lead the way down past the German Colony to the bars and pubs near the Port, it doesn't feel like a place that's snoozing at all. Within the city itself there is a broad selection of galleries and museums, a rich mix of religions and cultures – and a richly varied choice of cuisine to match.

An unmissable attraction on the northern coast are the labyrinth-like quarters of Old Akko (Acre), the last bastion of Crusader rule in the Holy Land, where a subterranean city is still being uncovered and you can explore secret tunnels leading to the sea.

For those who prefer a rural environment, there's the opportunity to walk your socks off in Mt Carmel National Park or around the idyllically located castle of Montfort. Back on the coast, Akhziv enjoys a beautiful stretch of beach, complete with lagoons and natural pools, while further north on the Lebanese border are the jagged cliffs of Rosh Ha-Nikra.

Background

The section of coastline between Haifa and the Israeli border with Lebanon is dominated by Mt Carmel, which has played an important role in the cultural and religious life of Israel (see under 'Haifa, History', next page). It has a history of occupation dating back to the Middle Palaeolithic (120,000-45,000 years BP) and has featured heavily in the three great monotheistic faiths: Judaism, Christianity and Islam. It is most noted as the scene of Elijah's battle with the 450 priests of Baal (*I Kings 18:17-40*).

The lower hills that separate Mt Carmel from the Central Range have historically allowed access to one of the most important routes in Palestine/Israel: the **Plain of Esdraelon** and the **Jezreel Valley**. This has represented an important trading and invasion route since antiquity. Even the Philistines, based on the coast far to the south, marched this far north in order to follow the easy passage of the Plain of Esdraelon to fight the Israelites at Gilboa. Likewise, the Egyptians used this route to reach the Euphrates (see page 570 for full details of the Jezreel Valley).

The stretch of coastline to the north of Mt Carmel has been known since antiquity as the **Phoenician coast**, after the great sea-faring peoples who settled here and further north in modern-day Lebanon. The Bay of Akko (Acre) is the only real sheltered gulf on the whole of Israel's Mediterranean coast, and it can be little wonder that major harbours have been established at its northerly and southerly headlands (Akko and Haifa). The coastal strip north of Haifa has also served as an important contact point between the peoples of the eastern and western Mediterranean. Though there are ancient sites along this coast, such as Akhziv (Achziv) to the north of Nahariya, perhaps this history of contact with the Western world is best seen at Akko (Acre), the last bastion of Crusader power in the Holy Land.

Haifa

→ *Colour map 1, grid B2.*
Haifa is a city of sweeping panoramic views, with distinct and characterful neighbourhoods, fine museums and easy access to nearby beaches, in addition to being a convenient base from which to explore the surrounding area.

Haifa may not quite be San Francisco, but there is some justification for the comparison. Physically, the city resembles its Californian counterpart by sprawling down the slopes of the wooded Mt Carmel in a series of switchbacks and winding roads, to the sandy coastline below. In terms of temperament, the allusion also works. Despite Haifa's reputation for being a city of hard work, the town does have a laid-back atmosphere where all are welcome. Despite some set-backs, there is a relatively stable relationship between the Jewish and Arab communities, plus the city has become home to two formerly persecuted groups, the Baha'is and the Ahmadies. Add to these the Christians and the Druze communities, and Haifa is proud to proclaim "six faiths – one city".

Ins and outs

Getting there and away Haifa has good transport links with the rest of the country. For those travelling up and down the Mediterranean coast, the train is the most enjoyable and fastest way of getting around. Haifa has several train stations, though most visitors will only use Haifa Merkaz. Southbound, there are express services to Tel Aviv every hour or so, plus one to three slower services per hour that also stop at 'Atlit, Binyamina, Hadera, Netanya and Herzliya. Northbound, trains go to Nahariya via Akko about once per hour. 'Express' and 'regular' buses run from one of two main bus stations, on the north and south edges of the city. Although the bus stations are closed on Shabbat, most bus services still run, plus sheruts that operate on the main routes (see 'Transport' on page 516 for full details).

Getting around Due to the hilly nature of Haifa, seeing all of the town's attractions on foot can be rather hard work unless you limit yourself to viewing groups of places of interest that are on the same level. Buses around town are numerous, though the system does take some getting used to due to the city's unusual one-way system. Many of the attractions are, however, within reach of a Carmelit stop (underground rail system, though really a funicular. The Carmelit does not run during Shabbat, though many of the buses around town do.

Tourist information **Haifa Tourist Board and Visitors' Centre** ① *48 Ben-Gurion, T04-8535606, www.tour-haifa.co.il, Sun-Thu 0900-1630, Fri 0900-1300, Sat 1000-1500. Located in refurbished German Colony house; extremely helpful staff. Free maps (or 4NIS for a more extensive map), and brochures. Also, there's a short film about the city, in particular the German Colony.* Regular guided tours can be arranged through your hotel/hostel; book a day in advance (to Haifa four hours, Akko six hours, Carmel six hours, Nazareth-Sea of Galilee eight hours).

Background
Mt Carmel In comparison with many other cities in Israel, the name Haifa is not particularly ancient; there is, however, a long history of occupation of the site, with Mt Carmel featuring as a symbol throughout Old Testament writing (usually as both a symbol of God's munificence, and as a sanctuary, eg *Songs of Solomon 7:5*; *Isaiah 35:2*). The karstic caves on Mt Carmel's escarpment were used as far back as the Middle Palaeolithic period (120,000-45,000 BP), and have revealed evidence of occupation by *Homo sapiens and Homo erectus*.

Carmel's status as a sanctuary comes primarily from the Old Testament story of the prophet **Elijah**'s battle with the priests of **Baal**. The cave on Mt Carmel in which the prophet is said to have sought sanctuary (Elijah's Cave, see page 508) is today venerated as a place of worship by Jews, Christians and Muslims alike.

Ancient history Remains pre-dating Elijah's exploits have been found at **Tel Shiqmona**, 1 km southwest of Carmel Cape (near to the present-day National Institute of Marine Research). Almost all periods from the beginning of the Late Bronze Age I (c. 1550 BCE) through to the reign of Hoshea (724 BCE) are represented.

Elijah's defeat of Baalism was short-lived, and the cult worship of Baal was reintroduced following the **Assyrian** conquest in 732 BCE. During the **Persian period** (586-332 BCE) a Phoenician town occupied the site at Shiqmona. The Greeks also occupied this site during the **Hellenistic period** (332-37 BCE), identifying the cult of Baal with the worship of Zeus, whilst the **Romans** (37 BCE-324 CE) celebrated the derived forms of Deus Carmelus and Jupitor of Heliopolis here. A series of fortresses stood at Shiqmona during the latter three periods.

In the fourth century BCE, the settlement at Shiqmona is referred to by Eusebius (in his *Onomasticon*) as **Hefa** – subsequently **Haifa**. The origin of the name is unclear, though it may be derived from the Hebrew *hof yafe*, or 'beautiful coast'. The name may, alternatively, have come from Caiphas, a high priest in the Temple at Jerusalem, who was born in the city.

Crusaders, Mamluks and Ottomans There is a large gap in the recorded history of Haifa during the Early Arab period (638-1099 CE). The implication is that the city entered into an era of relative decline, having been bypassed in favour of Acre, 'Atlit and Caesarea. The **Crusaders** captured Haifa ('Cayfe') in 1099/1100, but also preferred to develop alternative sites. **Salah al-Din** recaptured the city in 1187, though it subsequently fell again to **Richard Coeur de Lion** in 1191. It was around this time that the early forebears of the Carmelite Order began to settle on Mt Carmel.

The Mamluk **Sultan Baibars** razed the city in 1265, expelling first the Crusaders and then the Carmelites. The town was rebuilt and refortified in 1740 by the rebel Arab chief, the self-declared Lord of Galilee **Dahr el-Omar**. His successor, the great **Ahmed el-Jazzar**, further developed the town and was in turn responsible for expelling **Napoleon**'s invading troops in 1799.

Haifa at the turn of the 20th century Preceded by years of prolonged stagnation and periodic conflagration, the approach of the 20th century marked an important new era in Haifa's development. Jewish immigration into Haifa began to increase steadily, augmented by the arrival of the German Templars (see 'German Colony', below). The early 20th century also saw two other religious reform groups, the Baha'is and the Ahmadies, settle in Haifa. The port facilities were expanded to enable steamships to dock, whilst the connection of the city to the Hejaz Railway (via a branch line to Damascus) proved to be the major catalyst in the town's development.

British Mandate British forces finally captured the city from the Ottoman Turks in September 1918, after a prolonged and bloody battle. With the British awarded the Mandate over Palestine at the conclusion of World War I, Haifa was further developed to suit British strategic interests. A new rail line linking Haifa to Egypt was completed, and in 1933 a major new port was constructed. Two years later, the British finished laying a pipe that connected their oil-fields in northern Iraq to the port facility at Haifa. In June 1940, the oil refinery in Haifa was largely sustaining the British war effort in North Africa and the Mediterranean.

The late 1920s and early 1930s saw increasing antagonism between **Jews** and **Arabs** all across Palestine, as Jewish immigration expanded rapidly. Haifa did not escape this rivalry, and the tensions across Palestine that culminated in the **Arab Revolt** of 1938 were felt in Haifa, where Arab attacks on Jews were reciprocated with equal ferocity.

Rather than discouraging **Jewish immigration**, Britain's '1939 White Paper' actually encouraged 'illegal/clandestine' immigrants to attempt to beat the British blockade. Many of the major, and most tragic, scenes of these attempts were seen in and around Haifa.

The 1948 War Following Israel's declaration of independent statehood, and the subsequent war between the Arab armies and the fledgling Jewish state, Haifa fell to the Haganah after just 24 hours of intense fighting. Much of the Arab population of Haifa fled, though the circumstances surrounding this flight remain controversial. Israel has maintained that the civilian population was ordered to leave by Arab radio broadcasts, so as to make way for the all-conquering Arab armies. Evidence of this has remained elusive, suggesting that a climate of fear had been installed instead, by stories of the massacre at Deir Yassin (see page 710). Most families, however, left expecting to return shortly in the wake of the victorious Arab forces. There is evidence, though, that in Haifa attempts were made by the Jewish community to reassure the Arabs of the town that it was safe to stay.

Collins and Lapierre (1978, *O Jerusalem*) claim that special permission was granted by the Chief Rabbi for the city's Jewish bakers to break the Sabbath, and bake bread for the Arab community in the quarter captured by the Haganah.

Modern town Haifa is now Israel's third largest city with a population of about 267,000 people. With the country's number one port and the major concentration of oil, chemical, textile, glass, cement and other heavy industrial plants, the city makes a major contribution to the economy of Israel. With two universities, including the leading technology institute at the Technion (see page 510), it is also one of the country's key educational centres. Haifa is stratified into three main levels, with affluence increasing as you ascend. The lower town area around the port is the poorest and seediest. Above this stands the Hadar HaCarmel ('Glory of the Carmel') or Hadar for short. Standing proudly on the upper slopes of Mt Carmel, looking down physically and metaphorically on the rest of the city, is the Carmel Centre district, home of the upper classes, the upmarket hotels and the trendier shops, cafés and bars.

Sights

For convenience, the sights below have been divided into the following six sections: Carmel Centre, Central Haifa, Hadar District, Lower town and port area, Western Haifa and Outskirts/suburbs of Haifa.

Carmel Centre

Baha'i Shrine and Persian Gardens ⓘ *www.ganbahai.org.il. Garden tours in English daily except Wed, about 50 mins (if there has been rain tours are cancelled) at 1200, but go 15 mins early to register and check website, entrance from 45 Yefe Nof. Shrine of the Bab daily 0900-1030 and inner gardens till 1200, entrance from 80 HaZiyyonut. Yefe Nof viewing platform daily 0900-1700, entrance from 61 Yefe Nof. The Shrine and gardens are holy places: modest dress and behaviour is therefore essential. Do not wear shorts, short sleeves, or revealing tops (both men and women). No photos inside the Shrine itself. Buses 23, 30, 31 to Yefe Nof.*

Designed by the Persian architect who also created the Lotus Temple in Delhi, these extraordinary gardens were opened to the public in 2002 and placed on the UNESCO World Heritage list in July 2008. The manicured, geometrically planned lawns and cypress trees stretch down via 19 terraces from Carmel Centre to the German Colony. Each terrace circulates and recycles its water, and it takes teams of 70 Israelis plus 35 volunteers to maintain such pristine beauty. The multiple shades of green against the orange pathways are extremely striking in the symmetrical areas, whilst wilder informal areas to the sides encourage wildlife. All followers of the Baha'i faith donate money to the maintenance of the gardens and headquarters in Haifa; no funds are accepted from outside the community and nor are souvenirs sold.

The magnificent **Shrine of the Bab** is without doubt Haifa's most beautiful building, dominating all others, not in size, but in style. It is a subtle synthesis of classical European and Eastern styles, culminating in a golden dome glistening under 12,000 gold-leaf tiles. The mausoleum is built of Italian-cut Chiampo stone, with supporting columns of Rose Baveno granite. Floodlit at night, it is an inspiring sight. At the time of research it was undergoing construction work to make it earthquake proof and was under scaffolding; this is due to finish in 2010.

The mausoleum contains the remains of the **Bab**, the Martyr-Herald who foretold the coming of **Baha'ullah**, the founder of the Baha'i movement (see box on page 506).

The Bab was martyred in Tabriz in 1850 (it is said they had to execute him twice) and his mortal remains kept hidden until a suitably splendid place of burial could be found. In 1909, followers of the Baha'i secretly brought his remains to Palestine and constructed this shrine. The site is said to have been selected as the place where Baha'ullah pitched his tent, following his enforced exile from Persia. The shrine was completed in 1953 by the addition of the monumental dome. The interior of the tomb is a place of tranquil contemplation, comprising two small rooms. The first is a simple carpeted prayer chamber, from which you look through the low arch to the second chamber containing the shrine. The tomb is located beneath the red carpet under the chandelier. The candles and flowers have no religious significance and are merely a means of beautification. (The tomb of Baha'ullah can be seen at **Bahji**, 3 km north of Akko, see page 532.) **NB** This is a place of worship so it is important to act with decorum in your behaviour and dress. Remove shoes before entering the Shrine, and remain quiet once inside.

Above the Shrine of the Bab, on the other side of HaZiyyonut, are five other splendid Baha'i buildings, though these are not open to the general public. The **Universal House of Justice** is the home of the co-ordinating body of the Baha'i faith's worldwide activities; a marvellous white, neoclassical building supported by a colonnade of 58 Corinthian columns. Nearby stands the **International Baha'i Archives** building, the administrative headquarters of the faith, built in classic Ionic style and modelled on the Parthenon.

Gan HaPesalim (Ursula Malbin Sculpture Garden) ⓘ *112 HaZiyyonut. Free. Buses 23, 26 and 115.* Located just to the west of the Baha'i Shrine is the Sculpture Garden, a small, pleasant garden overlooking the Bay of Haifa, and enhanced by bronze sculptures by Ursula Malbin, a former refugee from Nazi Germany. The garden now closes at 1800 (a result of problems with statue thieves).

Louis Promenade, Panorama Garden and Wilhelm's Obelisk The social and economic stratification of Haifa is in evidence up on Carmel Centre, from where you can gaze down upon the poorer folk down the hill. The top hotels and restaurants are generally located on these upper slopes of Mt Carmel, along with the better residential neighbourhoods. The whole sweep of Haifa Bay (and up to Lebanon) can be seen from the Louis Promenade and Panorama Garden on Yefe Nof, with the beautiful Baha'i Shrine, and the not so beautiful Dagon grain silo, in the foreground. This is an ideal spot at any time of the day, though the view is particularly attractive at sunset.

In the corner of the Panorama Garden stands a small obelisk, known as 'Wilhelm's Obelisk', built to commemorate the visit of Kaiser Wilhelm II of Germany on 25 October 1898. The Kaiser, along with his wife the Kaiserin Augusta Victoria, landed in Haifa at the beginning of their tour of the Holy Land, and came to this spot to view the German Colony.

This elevated position was used by the Turkish artillery against the British forces during World War I, with the cannon displayed here forming part of the Turkish defences.

Numerous buses reach Carmel from the downtown area, including 22, 23, 28, 31 and 37, though the Carmelit is equally convenient. Also, many of Haifa's 'thousand steps' lead up to Carmel, though it is certainly easier to descend than ascend.

Mane Katz Museum ⓘ *89 Yefe Nof, T04-8383482. Sun, Mon, Wed and Thu 1000-1600, Tue 1400-1800, Fri 1000-1300, Sat/hols 1000-1400. Adult 12NIS, student/child 6NIS.*
The Ukranian-born Expressionist painter Mane Katz (1894-1962) lived and worked in this house for a brief phase during the latter years of his life. The attractive building is now a

Haifa centre

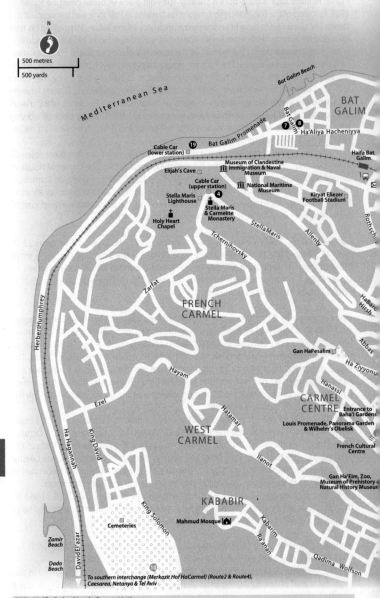

N

500 metres
500 yards

Mediterranean Sea

Bat Galim Beach

BAT GALIM

Bat Galim Promenade

7 8 Ha'Aliya Hacheniyya

Cable Car (lower station) 19

Haifa Bat Galim 1

Museum of Clandestine Immigration & Naval Museum

Elijah's Cave

Cable Car (upper station)

National Maritime Museum

Kiryat Eliezer Football Stadium

Stella Maris Lighthouse

Stella Maris & Carmelite Monastery 4

Holy Heart Chapel

Stella Maris

Allenby

Rothschild

Tchernihovsky

Zarfat

HaBare Hirsh

FRENCH CARMEL

Abbas

Gan HaPesalim

Ha Ziyyonu

Hayam

Hanassi

HerbertHumphrey

CARMEL CENTRE

Entrance to Baha'i Gardens

Hatamar

Louis Promenade, Panorama Garden & Wilhelm's Obelisk

WEST CARMEL

Ezel

Ilanot

French Cultural Centre

Gan Ha'Eim, Zoo, Museum of Prehistory & Natural History Museum

KABABIR

King Solomon

Kabarim

Cemeteries

Mahmud Mosque

Ra'anan

King David

Qadima Wolfson

Zamir Beach

Dado Beach

David El'azar

Ha Haganah

10

To southern interchange (Merkazit Hof HaCarmel) (Route2 & Route4), Caesarea, Netanya & Tel Aviv

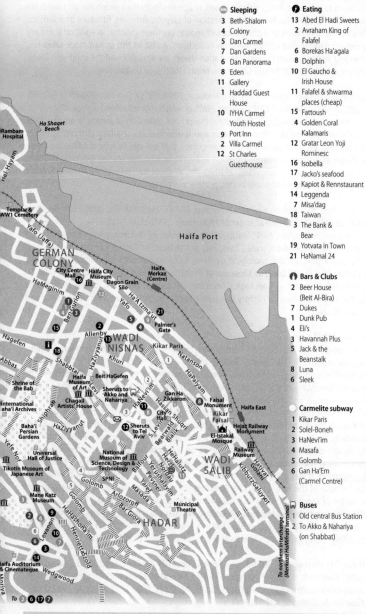

museum that houses Katz's paintings and sculptures, with their emphasis on Jewish life in Eastern Europe, plus his private collection of carpets, antiques, furniture and Judaica. Exhibitions of his work and possessions change every three months; in addition there are guest exhibitions that complement his collections. A visit to this quaint place takes less than half an hour, good English information sheets are available and the shop sells lovely reproductions (33-60NIS) and silk-screen prints (300NIS) of his paintings.

Tikotin Museum of Japanese Art ① *89 Hanassi, T04-8383554. Sun-Thu 1000-1600, Fri 1000-1300, Sat 1000-1500. Adult 29NIS, student 22NIS, or with combined ticket (see page 504).*
This museum has developed far beyond the private collection of Japanese art that Felix Tikotin gifted to the city almost 40 years ago. It now features regularly changing exhibits of Japanese art, both ancient and contemporary, that are said to adhere to the Japanese tradition of displaying beautiful objects in harmony with the season. Exhibitions might include graphic art, lacquerware, ceramics etc, all presented beautifully against suitably simplistic backdrops. Shop sells books, pottery and posters.

Gan Ha'Em, zoo and museums ① *Hanassi, T04-8371833. Sun-Thu 0800-1600, Fri 0800-1300, Sat 0900-1600, July and Aug until 1800. Adults 29NIS, child 23NIS.*
Gan Ha'Em, or 'Mothers' Park', features entertainment for children (playground, etc), plus entertainment for adults (cafés, bars, etc) at the heart of Carmel Centre. On the north side of the park are the zoological gardens, focusing primarily on animals indigenous to Israel, plus the **M Stekelis Museum of Prehistory** ① *Mon-Thu and Sat 1000-1500, Fri 1000-1300*, featuring archaeological finds from Mt Carmel and illustrating prehistoric life in the region. The Natural History Museum and Biological Museum present the flora and fauna of Israel.

Central Haifa
German Colony The German Colony was founded in 1868 by the German religious reform movement, the Pietist Society of the Temple. The community believed the Messiah was coming and that they needed to gather in the land of God to prepare the way for him. Many of the Templars' fine stone buildings still stand today, chiefly on Ben-Gurion Avenue, and the whole street has been very appealingly restored. Now perfectly aligned with the Baha'i Gardens, the view up the hill to the terraces from Ben-Gurion is the classic image of Haifa, and especially magical when lit by 2,200 lamps at night. Some buildings have received a new lease of life as up-market restaurants, whilst others still retain the original Germanic family names on the door lintels. Prior to substantial land reclamation, the former sea-shore came up to what is now the junction of Ben-Gurion and Ha'Atzma'ut. It was at this point in 1898 that the German Kaiser Wilhelm II disembarked for his tour of the Holy Land. The Templars did much to enhance Haifa's development in terms of construction, agricultural methods, and professional skills. However, most of the community began to associate with rising German nationalism and thus they were expelled by the British during World War II. The Tourist Office has a leaflet detailing the buildings along Ben-Gurion and their history, which is worth picking up.

Haifa City Museum ① *Beit Ha'am, 11 Ben-Gurion, T04-9115888. Adult 30NIS, student/child 20NIS. Combined ticket gives access to Tikotin, Art and Maritime museums, valid for 3 days, adult 45NIS student/child 33NIS. Mon-Thu 1000-1600, Fri 1000-1300, Sat 1000-1500. Guided tours can be arranged, T04-9115944.*

Beit Ha'am was the first of the buildings built by the Templars, and was used as a conference hall and then a school. Now it is the city's history museum, beautifully renovated, with a range of temporary exhibitions.

Wadi Nisnas and Wadi Salib Not all of Haifa's Arab population fled or were expelled during the 1948 war, and a number still live in the Wadi Nisnas ('mongoose') neighbourhood. This is certainly no Cairo, Damascus, or even East Jerusalem, but you can still feel something of the Arab world in its narrow, twisting streets. Particularly pleasing is Yohanan (St John) Street, with its fruit and veg markets, and cheap restaurants. Also look out for the Arabic and Jewish poetry decorating the walls of Al-Farabi Street. Though you may not be able to understand it, it is still an attempt at coexistence. Bear in mind that the area is quieter on Sundays, as the population is chiefly Christian, but it's a good place to visit on Shabbat when the market is in full swing.

To the east of Wadi Nisnas is the Wadi Salib/old city district. Most of these magnificent three- and four-storey buildings have been abandoned, and the stepped paths between them blocked off. Only a few on the edge have been gentrified and converted into offices, and sadly it looks like these typical Arab-style houses will continue to fall into dereliction. At the centre of Wadi Salib is the **el-Istakal Mosque**, one of Haifa's main Muslim places of worship, and nearby is the **Hejaz Railway Monument** (commemorating the completion of the Damascus to Mecca rail line in 1904).

Hadar district

Hadar is Haifa's midtown area, with several key shopping and business districts, plus a few hotels and sights. Many buildings along **Nordau Mall** and parallel streets are in the Bauhaus style, but only now are a few beginning to be restored, Tel Aviv style – the Science Museum is a fine example of one that is beautifully maintained.

Mada Tech, National Museum of Science, Technology and Space ① *Old Technion Building, 12 Balfour/ 25 Shmariyahu Levine, T04-8614444, www.madatech.org.il. Sun 1200-1600, Mon, Tue, Wed and Fri 1000-1600, Thu and Sat 1000-1800. Adult 50NIS, student 25NIS, child 50NIS (under 5s free).*
Forget notions of trudging around boring exhibits at traditional museums: this is hands-on science in action. Housed in the old Technion building, this is less of a museum and more of a 'science activity centre'. Seemingly complex principles of physics and chemistry are explained through interactive displays, suitable for old and young alike. The museum also works hard to emphasize technological advances in Israeli industry. The state-of-the-art Cinematrix allows you to 'interact' with the cinema screen (for English book in advance).

Haifa Museum of Art ① *26 Shabbtai Levi, T04-8523255. Sun-Wed 1000-1600, Thu 1600-1900, Fri 1000-1300, Sat 1000-1500. Adult 30NIS, student/child 20NIS. Combined ticket gives access to Tikotin, City and Maritime museums, valid for 3 days, adult 45NIS student/child 33NIS. Buses 10, 12, 21, 28 and 41.*
The art museum is devoted to contemporary works, with a huge collection shown in revolving exhibitions. Paintings and sculptures, all by Israeli artists (with a focus on artists from Haifa and the north), and graphic works form the bulk of the collection. There is also great emphasis on new media, making this is a place to catch up-to-the-moment video installations.

The Baha'i Faith

Described as a Universalist world religion, the Baha'i faith claims around four million adherents worldwide. Presenting a syncretist view of world religions, its basic ethos is that all religions are essentially the same, merely differing in unimportant aspects of dogma. Thus, Baha'ism is the logical progression since it encompasses them all. God is manifested to men and women by divine revelation through a succession of prophets (Moses, Jesus and Mohammad included), of which Baha'ullah is the latest. The Baha'i look forward to a single world government, language and faith. For further details (in the UK) call T020-7584-2566, or see www.bahai.org.

Beit HaGefen Arab-Jewish Cultural Centre ⓘ *2 HaGefen, T04-8525252. Sun-Thu 0800-1600, Fri and Sat 1000-1300. Free. Buses 10, 12, 22, 41 and 42.*
This cultural centre seeks to promote greater understanding between the Arab and Jewish communities. Various interchanges are promoted by the centre, with regular exhibitions by Arab and Jewish artists on display in the gallery, plus it's the home of the Arab Theatre (call ahead for forthcoming programmes). Look on the outside of the building for the symbol that they have devised to represent their organisation, as it's rather beautiful.

Chagall Artists' House ⓘ *24 HaZiyyonut, T04-8522355. Sun-Thu 1030-1600, Sat 1000-1300. Free.*
Features a selection of temporary exhibits, and is used primarily as a show-case for contemporary artists and new immigrant artists to sell their work.

Lower town and port area

Harbour/port area Approaching the coast at Haifa by sea, there are magnificent views of Mt Carmel and the whole sweep of the bay up to Akko. As you get closer, the view becomes dominated by the unattractive port installations and the massive Dagon grain silo (see below). The modern harbour was finished by the British in 1933, built primarily to ship oil from the British-controlled fields in Iran and Iraq without having to use the Suez Canal.

The harbour area is like any other port in the world, in that it's a bit seedy and a bit edgy. This is changing, however, as the municipality seeks to overhaul the port's negative image and is aiding the rejuvenation of the area. There are several cafés and restaurants here now and it's increasingly seen as a good place to go out, especially known for its student pub-life.

Dagon grain silo ⓘ *Plumer Square, T04-8664221. Guided tours Sun-Thu 1030-1130; closed for renovation at time of writing.*
Whilst the Baha'i Shrine dominates the middle level of Haifa, and the twin towers of the Dan Panorama Hotel in Carmel dominate the sky-line above the city, the Dagon grain silo is the most conspicuous building in the lower town. With a capacity of over 100,000 tonnes and standing almost 70 m high, this is the largest industrial building in the country. The silo is always covered in flocks of pigeons who profit from the industry inside.

Railway Museum ⓘ *Old Haifa East Station, Hativat Golani, near Kikar Feisal, T04-8564293. Sun-Thu 0830-1530. Adult 20NIS, student/child 15NIS. Buses 17, 103, 108.*
Train enthusiasts will enjoy this collection of railway paraphernalia and rolling stock dating primarily from Britain's construction of the Damascus-Cairo railway.

Templar and World War I cemetery On Yafo Street lies the Templar, the World War I and the World War II cemeteries. The latter are superbly maintained by the Commonwealth War Graves Commission, honouring those killed in the Palestine campaign of 1917-18 and victims of the early years of World War II. The Commonwealth Regiments are represented, with two separate compounds for Hindu and Muslim soldiers of the Indian Army. Behind the World War I cemetery is the Templarfriedof, the graveyard of Haifa's Templar community. First impression suggests that this cemetery is getting overgrown, particularly when compared with the manicured lawn of the World War I cemetery. However, closer inspection reveals that it is a living, thriving garden, with graves located between shady trees and beautiful flowering plants.

Beaches/Bat Galim Promenade There are a number of beaches in and around Haifa, though the most pleasant ones are a bus ride away. **HaShaqet Beach**, or 'Quiet Beach', is closest to the town centre. This is a 'religious beach', with separate bathing days for men (Monday, Wednesday and Friday) and women (Sunday, Tuesday and Thursday); Saturdays are mixed. Though free, with showers, changing rooms and restaurants, it's only about 100 m long, with a hospital directly behind, a large car park to the left, and the main port to the right.

Bat Galim Beach is a renowned surfing beach and, due to its small size, can become very crowded. It's free, with life-guards, showers, changing rooms, and a café. On the down side, the sand is similar to that found on building sites and it is enclosed on one side by a closed military area complete with machine-gun towers! The **Bat Galim Promenade** extends for several hundred metres along the sea-shore, and the area has a couple of pleasant seafood restaurants and an interesting mix of houses in varying styles and states of repair.

Haifa's more attractive beaches are at the base of the western slopes of Mt Carmel, near to the main highway south to Caesarea and Tel Aviv. These include the **HaCarmel**, **Zamir** and **Dado beaches** that are, in reality, just the beginning of the long stretch of sand south to 'Atlit and Dor. These beaches have a number of facilities, though the further south you go the more it is just sea and sand. It is only 10 minutes by train from Merkaz station to the Hof HaCarmel terminal.

Western Haifa
Stella Maris Church, Stella Maris Lighthouse and Carmelite Monastery ① *T04-8337758. Daily 0600-1230 and 1500-1800, entrance free. Buses 30A, 31,115, or cable car (see below).*
The Stella Maris Church, belonging to the Carmelite Order on Mt Carmel, is a circular chapel with a beautifully painted dome. It illustrates Elijah elevated to Heaven in his chariot, David playing the harp, the saints of the Carmelite order, plus the prophets Isaiah, Ezekiel, Daniel, and the Holy Family, and was completed in the late 1920s by a member of the order. Unusually, beneath the altar is a grotto, believed to be the dwelling place or tomb of Elijah. Above the altar is a magnificent statue of Our Lady of Mt Carmel. The head was carved by Caraventa of Genoa in 1820, and crowned three years later in the Vatican in the presence of Pope Pius VII. The body is a century younger and is carved from Cedar of Lebanon.

A tiny **museum** is attached to the church, containing an unspectacular collection of artefacts. There is a model of the grotto of the Nativity, plus marble and stone fragments of the Byzantine church and ancient lighthouse that previously stood on the site.

The present Stella Maris Lighthouse ('Star of the Sea') was built in 1821 as Abdallah Pasha's summer palace, using masonry from the Carmelite monastery that he had ordered destroyed (see box on page 509). After two years, however, the building was passed to the Carmelite order who subsequently used it as a pilgrims' hostel. The British Army took it over in 1927, ever since which it has remained in military hands. It is now occupied by the Israeli military, and photography is forbidden. Outside the lighthouse stands a delicate bronze statue of the Virgin Mary, known as Our Lady of Mt Carmel.

Behind the lighthouse, a winding path leads down past the **Holy Heart Chapel** (formerly a windmill, converted into a chapel in the 1960s but seemingly disused), and down to Elijah's Cave. **NB** The path is steep in places and very slippery when wet. Views are good, there is some shade, and it feels like a brief immersion in the countryside. Alternatively, you can take a **cable car** ⓘ *Upper Station Carmelite Monastery, Lower Station Bat Galim Promenade, T04-8335970. Daily 1000-1800. Adult 28/19NIS return/one-way*, though it is not an enormously exciting experience. A commentary (Hebrew/English) gives sparse details on sites seen during the brief ride, though the view from the cable car is no better than the view from the upper station platform.

Elijah's Cave ⓘ *230 Allenby, T04-8527430. Sun-Thu 0800-1800 (winter -1700), Fri/hol eves 0800-1300, Sat closed. Free. Buses 3, 5, 43, 44 and 45.*

Ascending some steps above Allenby Street, opposite the National Maritime Museum, a small path leads to an enlarged chamber cut from the rock. The cave is ascribed with miraculous healing powers and has served as a place of pilgrimage for generations. Jews and Christians believe that the prophet Elijah sheltered in this cave from King Ahab, having slain the prophets of Baal on Mt Carmel (*I Kings 18:20-46; 19:9-13*). Later Christian tradition suggests that the Holy Family rested here on their return from Egypt. Muslims revere the site as the Cave of el-Khader, the 'green prophet' (Elijah). In past times, Elijah's Cave was somewhere you could see Jews, Muslims and Christians worshipping in the same place, at the same time. Nowadays, the whole cave is used by those of the Jewish faith praying for Elijah's return as the harbinger of the Messiah. Men pray in the right hand half, which used to be the Muslim section (the mihrab was located behind the curtain at the end). Women pray in the left half, where the ceiling of a large hollow is dressed with scarves, plastic bags, and lengths of tissue paper.

From the picnic area beneath the cave, a steep but shady path leads up to the Stella Maris Lighthouse and Carmelite Monastery. **NB** This is a religious site: modest dress and behaviour is essential.

Museum of Clandestine Immigration and Naval Museum ⓘ *204 Allenby, T04-8536249. Sun-Thu 0830-1600, adult 15NIS student/child 10NIS. Buses 3, 5, 43 and 44.*

During the period of the British Mandate, quotas were placed on the number of Jewish immigrants who were allowed to enter and settle in Palestine. This museum tells the story of those Jews who attempted to bypass the British blockade and enter illegally/clandestinely. The museum may be considered by some to be controversial – it tells one version of history – but the exhibits are well presented, with labels and commentaries in Hebrew and English. More importantly, the courage of the refugees on board the ships and in the detention camps is not diminished by the need to make a political point. A visit is recommended.

The tour of the museum usually begins with a short audio-visual presentation detailing the clandestine immigration operations, chronicling the number of ships and refugees attempting to run the blockade, and describing the fate of those who were unsuccessful. Exhibits from the clandestine operations are displayed in an area under the keel of an old tank landing craft, the *Af-Al-Pi*, that was itself used to bring illegal Jewish immigrants ashore. Further displays and reconstructions give some idea of the fate of those immigrants

The Carmelite Order at Mount Carmel

The Catholic Carmelite Order have a long, though not continuous, history of occupation on the mountain from which they draw their name. Imitation of the life of the prophet Elijah first brought Crusaders to this site in the 12th century and, early in the next century, under the tutelage of their Prior Brocard (later St Berthold), the Carmelite Order was born.

The spread of the order throughout Europe was contemporary with the withdrawal of the Carmelites from the Holy Land, following the Crusaders' defeat at Acre (Akko) in 1291. The Discalced ('barefoot') Carmelites returned to Mount Carmel in 1631 and built a small monastery on the site near to the ancient Stella Maris lighthouse.

Once again the Carmelites were driven out, this time by the Muslim Dahr el-Omar in 1767, though they returned shortly after, building a large church and monastery over a grotto where Elijah is said to have lived. A previous Byzantine (324-638 CE) chapel and the medieval Greek Abbey of St Margaret had occupied this site.

During Napoleon's ill-fated Palestine campaign in 1799, wounded French soldiers were left at the monastery, though they were massacred by the Turks once the main body of French soldiery had withdrawn. A small memorial to the fallen French, in the form of a forged iron cross atop a pyramid, stands outside the main entrance today. Twenty-one years after the massacre, Abdallah Pasha of Akko had the ruined monastery completely destroyed. The present church and monastery dates to 1836, and was granted the status of 'Minor Basilica' by Pope Gregory XVI three years later.

who were unsuccessful, and found themselves interred in camps in Cyprus, having just fled from the Holocaust in Europe. Inside the hull of the *Af-Al-Pi* is a reconstruction of immigrants' quarters on board ship.

The rest of the exhibits form part of the Naval Museum, telling the story of the foundation and development of the Israeli Navy. Pride of place goes to items from the Ibrahim el-Awal, an Egyptian destroyer captured intact by the Israeli Navy during the 1956 war.

National Maritime Museum ① *198 Allenby, T04-8536622. Sun-Thu 1000-1600, Fri 1000-1300, Sat 1000-1500. Adult 29NIS, student/child 22NIS, or with combined ticket (see page 504). Buses 44 and 114.*

The permanent maritime exhibits here are well explained and surprisingly interesting, with themes designed to intrigue children. The basement has an exhibition about pirates alongside examples of "Mariners' Crafts" including scrimshaw – carvings on whales' teeth by sailors seeing Inuit or Siberian cultures for the first time. There are storage jars dating from Solomon's time that have been dredged from Israel's northern Mediterranean coast by fishermen. Ancient maps, globes and model ships ranging from those in bottles to ones 3 m long maintain the nautical theme.

The upper floor has findings from under the water, including the 2000 year old hull of a boat from the Sea of Galilee – a contemporary of Jesus. An exhibition on Maritime Discovery details the maritime exploits of the Phoenicians, Greeks, Romans and Crusaders, plus there's a selection of navigational aids such as maps, compasses and sextons. The ground floor has changing exhibitions, though one that is likely to stay for some time displays Byzantine mosaic floors from Shikmona with formal geometric/foliate designs.

Outskirts/suburbs of Haifa

Castra ① *8 Fliman, T04-8590001, www.castra.co.il. Sun-Thu 1000-2100, Fri/hol eves 1000-1400, Sat 1000-2100. Entrance free.*

An art, shopping and entertainment centre all rolled into one, built on the site of the 2000-year-old city of Castra. Inside, a swish Archaeological Museum displays artefacts from the ancient city, and a Doll Museum with over 1000 figurines tells the story of the Jewish people from the Diaspora to the modern day. You can't miss the world's largest ceramic wall painting, which illustrates scenes from the Bible and the Judgements. Galleries sell sculpture, glass, Judaica, ceramics, jewellery and more, alongside restaurants, bars and boutiques. It is suitable for a Saturday afternoon when most other entertainments are closed.

Technion, Israel Institute of Technology ① *Kiryat HaTechnion, T04-8293863. Sun-Thu 0800-1530. Free. Call ahead for information and tour details. Buses 17, 19 and 31.*

Israel's leading institute of technology moved to its present campus in the 1980s, having outgrown its previous site in the Old Technion Building in downtown Hadar. Many of Israel's engineers, architects and town planners have graduated from here, with faculties for medicine and life sciences having been added in recent years. The work and achievements of the various departments is presented in the Coler-California Visitors' Centre, which utilizes the "tools of high technology in a dynamic and interactive" way in their permanent and evolving exhibitions. These include a multimedia presentation, a simulator and hands-on exhibits.

University of Haifa ① *Mt Carmel, T04-8240111, www.haifa.ac.il.* Serving as the centre for higher education in the north, the University of Haifa offers a broad range of studies, including a unit that looks at the socio-economic function of the kibbutz, plus a special centre studying interaction between Jews and Arabs.

Most visitors to the university come to admire the stunning views from the observatory at the top of the 27-storey **Eshkol Tower** ① *Abba Khushi, Eshkol Tower Observatory, T04-8240007.* On clear days, the view extends up to the Lebanese coast and sometimes to the snowy peak of Mt Hermon. The building was designed by Oscar Niemeier, who was also responsible for the United Nations building. The basement of the tower is the site of the **Reuben and Edith Hecht Museum** ① *T04-8257773, http://mushecht.haifa.ac.il. Sun, Mon, Wed and Thu 1000-1600, Tue 1000-1900, Fri 1000-1300, Sat 1000-1400; entrance free; buses 24, 37 and 46,* which contains a remarkable array of artefacts from the 'Land of Israel', many of which were found locally. The exhibits are beautifully presented in a light and airy setting. A visit is certainly recommended, particularly for those on a budget. The small art wing has some Impressionist pieces (including Monet, Pissaro) as well as works from the Jewish School of Paris. Nearby is an open-air exhibition of reconstructed ancient buildings from around Israel, including Herbat Castra from western Haifa where the Castra Mall now stands.

Mahmud Mosque, Kababir ① *Ra'anan, Kababir, T02-8385002, www.alislam.org. Daily 0900-1200 and 1700-1900 (summer), 0900-1100 and 1300-1500 (winter), though not during Friday prayers. Bus 34.*

The Druze and the Baha'i are not the only religious sects found within Haifa. In the suburb of Kababir, west of Carmel Centre, lives a community of around 1,500 **Ahmadies**; a religious reform movement that may be best described as a messianic sect of Islam (see box above).

Ahmadiyya

The Ahmadiyya is a religious reform movement founded in Qadian, India, by **Mirza Ghulam Ahmad** (1835-1908). A devout and pious Muslim scholar, Mirza Ghulam Ahmad announced in 1889 that he was Mahdi, the promised Messiah foretold in the Qu'ran (Koran) and the second coming of Christ foretold in the Bible. To many Muslims such a statement is heretical, and many subsequent followers of the Ahmadiyya have faced discrimination and persecution.

However, the Ahmadiyya is not a new religion and the founder was quick to point out that he was a follower of the Prophet Mohammad and the basic tenets of the Qu'ran. The purpose of the movement was to re-establish true Islamic values and restore Islam to its pristine form, lost over the centuries.

Another interesting aspect of Ahmad's teaching was revealed in one of his eighty published books, Jesus in India: being an account of Jesus' escape from death on the cross and his journey to India. Ahmadis reject the Christian account of the crucifixion, insisting that Jesus ('Yus Asaf') escaped from the cross, settled in Kashmir, married, had children, continued his prophetic vocation, and died at the age of 120. He was buried in Srinagar, where the 65th generation of his descendants still live. That is not to say that Ahmad saw a contradiction between the Ahmadiyya and other revealed religions such as Christianity; rather he emphasized what he saw as wrongly perceived interpretations by man.

Today the movement has more than 10 million adherents spread across the world, with the operational headquarters in London where the current leader of the movement, Mirza Masroor Ahmad, resides. His predecessor had to flee Pakistan, where the Ahmadi community faces considerable persecution and are not recognised as Muslims. Pressure on the Ahmadi community in Pakistan seems generally to be mounted by fundamentalist sections, though the government frequently acquiesces. In addition, the government of Saudi Arabia has been known to make it difficult for the Ahmadiyya to make the haaj. The Ahmadi community in Israel (which has no formal diplomatic relations with Pakistan) faces no such persecution.

Finally, note should be taken of the source of the name of the movement. It is not a reflection of the ego of Mirza Ghulam Ahmad: it is in fact the Prophet Mohammad's second name.

For more information about the Amhadiyya, see www.alislam.org.

The Ahmadiyyat was first established in Kababir in 1929 by Jalaludin Shams, an early missionary of the movement, with the foundation stone of the first Ahmadiyya mosque in the Middle East being laid here in 1931. Over 30 years ago, the **Mahmud Mosque** was built in Kababir using funds raised by the local community. The mosque has handsome, twin minarets and a grand white dome. The interior is simply furnished in plain white, with much light coming through the yellow glass windows. Casual callers are welcome (if modestly dressed), but it's better to call ahead; a local adherent (willing to explain the beliefs of the movement) will show you around.

Haifa listings

For Sleeping and Eating price codes and other relevant information, see Essentials pages 26-31.

⊜ Sleeping

Haifa does not have a huge number of hotels, though (with the exception of the budget end) there is a fairly good spread. Presume breakfast to be included unless stated otherwise.

LL Dan Carmel, 85-87 Hanassi, T04-8303030, www.danhotels.com. Recently renovated and still considered the best in town. Standard rooms are $280; it's worth paying the extra $20 for a bay-view, or a further $10-20 for the deluxe rooms (huge beds) – though suites might be a bit steep at $400-1,500! Outdoor pool (summer only), spa, tennis, squash, dairy restaurant Very professional staff.

LL-L Dan Panorama, 107 Hanassi, T04-8352222, www.danhotels.com. Looking a bit dated these days (the retro foyer is a genuine blast from the past), standard rooms are not huge so it's worth an extra $30 for the spacious 'superior bay-view' rooms, and if you're paying this much keep going for the 'excecutive bay' rooms. Outdoor pool, fitness centre, adjacent shopping mall, 'Danpano' restaurant always busy.

LL-L Villa Carmel, 1 Heinrich Heine, T04-8375777/8, www.villacarmel.co.il. Luxurious and refined, this individual boutique hotel is situated off Moriya Blvd, one of Carmel Centre's most desirable areas. Standard rooms ($190 db) are elegant, all tonal greys, soft carpets, original art-work, pillow-laden beds, classy bathrooms, HD-TV; while the 3 further categories ($210-260) have jacuzzis, balconies and more space. Restaurant is charming; lovely terrace and sun deck, spa. Staff are excellent. Only 15 rooms; booking essential.

L Colony Hotel, 28 Ben-Gurion, T04-8513344, info@colony-hotel.co.il. Gorgeous

period building artistically restored, opened as a 40-room hotel in 2008. Larger deluxe rooms have views ($183, standard $163), upstairs rooms have balconies, some have jacuzzi, bathrooms are marble. Stylish public areas, original tiles on floors, lovely roof terrace with views up the Baha'i gardens. Sensibly priced, especially when compared to the equivalent elsewhere in Israel.

L-AL Dan Gardens, 124 Yefe Nof, T04-8302020, dangardenshaifa@danhotels. com. Standard rooms have simple pleasing decor, beds a little small. Those at the back have balconies but not much of a view ($144), bay-view suites are significantly bigger with sofas ($164). No restaurant. Nice front terrace for breakfast. Free use of pool at Dan Panorama.

AL Beth-Shalom, 110 Hanassi, T04-8377481/2, www.beth-shalom.co.il. 29 spotless, functional a/c rooms in this Swiss-Christian-run hotel; decent shower rooms, TV; carpet-covered doors are an odd touch. At the bottom end of this price bracket ($110 double, $85 single). Very quiet, pleasant staff, little café in foyer. Checkout 1000.

AL Gallery, 61 Herzl, T04-8616161, www.haifa.hotelgallery.co.il. Recently reopened as the Gallery, this hotel is a bit of a bargain in this category (doubles $120). In a Bauhaus building, each floor showcases paintings by up-and-coming artists, there's a mini-gym, and port views from the sun deck. Classically furnished rooms aren't huge, but have wooden floors and stick to neutral fabrics; feather pillows, new white bathrooms, TV, fridge, safe, kettle. Suites for $180. Once inside it's very quiet; only the East Europeans swigging afternoon beers in the bars immediately outside are off-putting.

A Haddad Guest House, 26 Ben-Gurion, T07-72010618, www.haddadguesthouse. com. Well located in the German Colony, catering mostly to Baha'i pilgrims. 11 rooms (350NIS per double, 300NIS single, for stays over 5 days deduct 50NIS), cleaned daily, a/c, TV, sandwich-maker, kettle, fridge, modern showers. Common area upstairs, balcony in planning stages when we visited. Free internet, no breakfast.

A St Charles Guest House, 105 Jaffa, T04-8553705, www.pat-rosary.com. Supervised by the Catholic Rosary Sisters. Convenient location (though the street can be a bit creepy at night). A/c rooms are unadorned save for flowery bedspreads and ill-matched modern furniture (single $45, double $80, triple $105). Public spaces include TV lounge, wide cool corridors, crucifixes, and some fabulous pieces of old furniture. Also an apartment for 5-8 people ($35 per person) with 2 rooms, kitchen, TV: good for families.

A-B Eden, 8 Shemaryahu Levin, junction with HaHalutz, T04-8664816, F8642633. Old-style basic rooms are about the cheapest you can get in Haifa at 200NIS (shared bath). More expensive rooms (250NIS) have showers literally 'in' the room (toilet outside), or ones for 300NIS have ensuite. All have TV, a/c and are clean. Central (noisy) location, no breakfast. It would be an unusual choice.

A-C IYHA Carmel Youth Hostel, Kfar Zamir, Hof HaCarmel, T02-5945544, www.iyha.co.il. Great location for the beach and tennis centre, though restaurant-wise you're restricted to what's on offer at nearby Haifa Mall. Very peaceful out here. 12 rooms have a/c, TV, mini-bar; dorm bed 97.5NIS, doubles 290NIS (includes breakfast). Good choice if you can cope with the remoteness. Egged buses 43, 44 and 114.

A-E Port Inn, 34 Jaffa, T04-8524401, www.portinn.co.il. Popular with Baha'i pilgrims, welcoming to everyone, always busy, essential to book the modern private rooms (breakfast included) in advance, and wise to book dorm beds (105/75NIS with/out breakfast). All a/c. Some private rooms share baths, others are en suite (340NIS). Also triple/4-beds available. Staff extremely helpful, with maps, advice and info. Little back garden full of potted plants is good for socialising, plus there's a comfy lounge with

TV, well-equipped kitchen, no curfew. All-in-all a very pleasant atmosphere, and a very popular place. Laundry service, internet 5NIS for 15 mins. Short walk from Merkaz train station, or Bus 103 from bus stations.

🍴 Eating

There's a good range and choice of restaurants in Haifa, though be aware that some pride themselves on their views and ambience as much as their food. Popular dining areas include Carmel Centre and the German Colony (where the restaurants, to a degree, become less exclusive as you ascend Ben-Gurion Street). Eating cheaply and well in Haifa is not difficult. Many of the restaurants mentioned below offer good value meals, particularly at lunch-time. For falafel and shwarma, head to the junction of HaNevi'im and HeHalutz for some of Israel's cheapest. There are also a number of similar establishments near the junction of Allenby and HaZiyyonut, including **Avraham**, **King of Falafel**, one of Israel's oldest and best. Kikar Paris (Paris Square) and the Wadi Nisnas neighbourhood have cheap Middle Eastern restaurants, which are very good value if you stick to hummus, falafel and fuul. Fruit and veg can be bought in **Wadi Nisnas market**, and in the market below HeHalutz in Hadar (where you can also buy cheap alcohol). If you head out to **Haifa University**, in addition to fine views, there is a very cheap self-service cafeteria.

Carmel Centre

🍴 **Rennstaurant**, 99 Yefe Nof, T04-8375602, www.rest.co.il/renns. Quality restaurant serving gourmet French/Italian (vegetarians will feel hard done by). Pretty pricey, fab cocktails and 'sours' (34NIS), definitely for a special occasion, the interior is slickly decorated without being too fussy. Daily 1200-last customer.

🍴-🍴 **El Gaucho**, 120 Yefe Nof, T8370997. Recently renovated branch of the Argentinian steakhouse chain. The Irish

House is handily next door for drinks.

Ψ†-Ψ† Jacko's Seafood, 11 Moriya. A real institution: a suave yet back-to-basics fish restaurant. Saturdays see the place packed with people dipping into piles of mussels dripping with garlic and washed down with fine wine, or there are endless choices including St Peter's Fish, bream, salmon and even shark.

Ψ† The Bank, 119 Hanassi, T8389623. Popular with 'oldies' during the day and a younger crowd at night; especially busy Sat mornings. Coffee, toasts, salads, pasta.

RR Mandarin, 129 Hanassi, T04-8380691. Truly sumptuous desserts/cakes/pies, imaginative sandwiches, good Israeli breakfasts (shakshouka), and pretty much anything else. Platter plus beers for 2 isn't a bad deal (84NIS) and the frozen lemon/vodka is great. Daily 0900-2400 or later; good for Shabbat mornings. The original Mandarin is further along Moriya Blvd, heading out of Carmel Centre.

Ψ† Kapiot, 99 Yefe Nof, T04-8383745. Nicely located café/bar that is utterly unpretentious; families in the mornings and relaxed atmosphere in evenings. Live music (mellow, folky) on Sat nights. Daily 0800-0400. Perfect for a Shabbat morning session: there's a breakfast deal with delicious juices, omelette, salad etc (42NIS). No English sign: look for "free internet" and "coffee 8NIS" advertised outside.

Ψ†-Ψ Leggenda, 129 Hanassi. The famed ice cream and frozen yoghurt people do a roaring trade from these 2 stores (next door to each other) in Carmel Centre, and it's not surprising as they have every combination of flavours under the sun. Simply delicious. Look for the play-school coloured chairs out on the pavement. Prices start at 17NIS. Daily. Also in City Mall, German Colony (but not so many flavours).

Ψ Borekas Ha'agala, 52 Moriya (crn of), T04-8388662. Renowned fast-food stop for borekas (hot filled pastry parcels) – spinach, cheese, mushroom, etc, all delicious. Also branch nr the Merkazit HaMifrats bus

station on Route 60. No English sign: look for red and white signage.

Central Haifa

Ψ† Fattoush, 38 Ben-Gurion, Germany Colony, T04-8524930. Lovely pavement seating under citrus trees; interior like an Arabic mansion. Mix of Middle Eastern and international dishes, but try the excellent kanefe (even though it's twice the price you would pay in a traditional kanafe shop).

Ψ† Isobella, City Centre mall, German Colony, T04-8552201. Hugely popular venue for excellent Italian food and, though it's located in a mall, at least there's a terrace on to the street and a central bar area. Meat/fish-focussed (bacon!) for the mains, also pasta/pizza (try stuffed). Recommended.

Ψ† Taiwan, 59 Ben-Gurion, T04-8532082. Pretty much Haifa's oldest Chinese restaurants. Good value. Sat-Thu 1200-1500 and 1900-2400.

Ψ Abed El Hadi Sweets, 3 Shahada Shelach, Wadi Nisnas, T04-8521905. Locals from all communities flock here to buy seriously good sticky Arab sweets by the kilo. No English sign: look for the neon red/green letters in Arabic and Hebrew. Daily until 2300.

Ψ Gratar Leon Yoji Rominesc, 31 HaNevi'im, T04-8675073. Small and easy to miss, but considered the best Romanian restaurant in Israel. Full and generous meals; menu includes calves foot jelly and spinal cord, and more approachable dishes such as bean soup or liver. Cheap booze. Recommended.

Lower Town

Ψ†-Ψ Hanamal 24, 24 Hanamal, Port Area, T057-9442262. On one of the up-and-coming 'cool' streets in the port area, Hanamal is a reincarnation of '1837', the famed restaurant that used to grace the German Colony. Blending French cuisine with more Mediterranean flavours, this is a gourmet experience in warm and rustic surroundings, with pieces imported from Tuscany to adorn the space. There are lots of little corners in which to hide away, and can feel quite like a romantic trattoria.

Dolphin, 13 Bat Galim, T04-8523837. Noted seafood menu, mussels 85NIS, fish main course 80-95NIS, or lobster comes at 150NIS per 1/2kg, good Middle Eastern salads to accompany. Trattoria-meets-maritime décor, it's rather like being onboard, decked with suitable pictures and sea-shells, very pleasant atmosphere. Daily 1200-2200.

Misa'dag, 29 Bat Galim, T04-8524441. Apart from fried/grilled fish of all kinds (68-78NIS), they are big on shrimp and calamari dishes. Sea views, simple modern environment. Daily 1200-2200; no English sign: look for the fish logo and name in red letters on black. Recommended.

Mayan Habira, 4 Natanzone, T04-8623193. Eastern European food at its best, this is considered to be one of the top 10 restaurants in Israel. On Tue nights there's live music. Daily until 1600, Tue -2330.

Pata Carola, 37 HaAtzmaut. Italian vegetarian restaurant, great pizza their speciality. Daily till 2200.

Farag, 29 HaMegenim, T04-8621276. Lebanese food, excellent falafel and pickles. Majedera and burgol come with every dish you order. Daily 0700-1800.

Western Haifa

Yotvata in Town, Bat Galim Promenade, near cable car station, T04-8526835. Part of kibbutz chain of popular dairy restaurants, and vegetarian heaven: Thai tofu, Balkan bagels, oven-baked pizza, huge variety of sandwiches and pastas (30-50NIS), plus smoked salmon. Enormous windows on to the surf, Ikea-style white chairs and functional tiling; family atmosphere. Don't be put off by the shabby life-size Friesian cows (and gnomes) in the entrance. Alcohol served; reasonable prices. Daily 0900-2400.

Kalamaris, Sendyan & Golden Coral, Stella Maris (upper cable car station). Mediterranean dishes and fish on offer in three similar establishments which have great views.

🔊 Bars and clubs

Bars

Those who like their bars seedy will be attracted to the various drinking establishments around Plumer Gate (near the docks). More salubrious watering holes are found up in Carmel Centre and in the German Colony. Note that none really get going before 2230.

Bear, 135 Hanassi, Carmel Centre, T04-8381703. Ex-pats and lashings of beer.

Beit Al-Bira ("Beer House"), Gan Ha'em Park, Hanassi, Carmel Centre, T04-8229750. 120 different beers and very friendly service.

Dukes, 107 Moriah, Popular Irish pub/ restaurant, daily from 1200.

Dunk Pub, 94 HaMeginim, T04-8532836/050-6398200. Looks like a 'real' pub, with lots of draught beers and cosy atmosphere (shame about the slogan "You've Been Butt-Plugged" displayed outside). Daily 1200-0400.

Eli's, 35 Jaffa, T04-8525550. Loud music, live on Mon/Wed and sometimes Thu. Good burgers and schnitzels. 25% off the whole menu if you say you're staying at the Port Inn. Every day 2130-last customer (around 0400 at weekends).

Havannah Plus, Ben-Gurion. Good place to go for a drink earlier on, if you don't keep Haifan hours, as it's always busy. Lots of apple sheesha smoking, nice staff, huge and reasonably priced menu. Daily until 0500.

Irish House, 120 Yefe Nof, T04-810377. Good for watching sports on the big screens; big menu, happy hour 2000-2100 25% off.

Jack and the Beanstalk, 44 Jaffa, T04-8535668. Coloured glass windows beckon you inside, where the wooden bar is lined with racks of spirits and miniatures. Large tapas menu (16-18NIS per dish), good calamari/capers/olives, some have a Jewish slant (herring/onion) and vegetarian (try eggplant/sweet tomato jam or baked yams/ yoghurt/vinaigrette). Live acoustic music on Sat nights, open-mike night on Tue, very nice staff. Weekends 2030-0400, weekdays till about 0200. No English sign. Outdoor tables.

Sleek, Moriya. Bar/restaurant, attracts a young crowd; happy hour 1900-2130 (25% discount).

Clubs

A number of pubs and clubs are utilising former warehouses in the semi-derelict area of Wadi Salib, though you'll have to ask around as to where is 'in'. **Luna**, HaPalyam (entrance from the alley at the rear) 2300-late at weekends, is a long-stayer that is recommended. Locals tend to head to the nightspots out in the residential neighbourhoods of Romena and Danya. During Jul/Aug there are a lot of events organized on the various beaches.

Entertainment

Cinemas

Cinemall, next to the Merkazit HaMifrats bus station. Multiple screens at the big orange mall.

Cinematheque, 142 Hanassi, Carmel Centre, T04-8383424. Has shown classic movies, world cinema, and hosted lectures since 1975.

Concert halls

Bruce & Ruth Rappaport Art & Culture Centre, 138 Hanassi, T04-8101558, www.ipo. co.il. Arts and cultural centre where the Israel Philharmonic Orchestra play.

Haifa Symphony Orchestra, 50 Pevzner, T04-8599499, www.haifasymphony.co.il.

Theatres

Haifa Meyerhoff Municipal Theatre, 50 Pevzner, T04-8600500.

Festivals and events

Festivals

For further details check with the Haifa Tourist Board, T04-8535605/6, www.tour-haifa.co.il.

Apr: International Children's Theatre Festival (usually during Pesach).
Jul/Aug: Dado events.

Sep/Oct: International Film Festival at the Cinematheque.
Nov-Dec: 'Festival of Festivals' in Wadi Nisnas, starts the last Sat of Nov and then each Sat of Dec until New Year: cultural events, parades, street art, celebrating the 3 festivals of Hannukah, Christmas and Eid Al-Adha.

Shopping

Bookshops

Steimatzky Steimatzky have branches at 82 Ha'Atzma'ut, 130 Hanassi, in HaNevi'im Tower and at 16 Herzl

Shopping Malls

Castra, 8 Fliman, focus on galleries and artworks, T04-8590001; **City Centre**, Ben-Gurion, German Colony; **Grand Canyon Mall**, Simcha Golan, Neve Sha'anan; **Haifa Mall**, 4 Fliman, near Haifa Congress Centre, T04-8550360; **Horev Centre**, 15 Horev; **Lev Hamifratz**, 55 Hahistadrut, Haifa Bay, T04-8416090; **Panorama Centre**, 109 Hanassi, T04-8375011.

Transport

Air

Haifa's airport is located to the east of the city in the industrial zone. There are **Arkia** and **Israir** flights to **Eilat** (1 hr 15 mins), and to **Tel Aviv** (30 mins), plus some charter flights abroad.

Airline offices Arkia T03-6903333/1700-700255. Israir, T03-7955888/03-7955777.

Bus

Haifa has two central bus stations, one on the west of town (Merkazit Hof HaCarmel) serving ṣouthern destinations, and another on the east (Merkazit HaMifrats) serving northern destinations. When taking a local bus to either of the central bus stations to travel onwards, it's possible to buy a ticket through to your final destination (eg Tel Aviv) on the local bus; ask for a "pass ticket", valid for 1 hr, which will cut out the cost of a separate ticket for the local bus. **NB** From centre of town to Merkazit Hof HaCarmel, bus 103 is quicker than 114

Below is a selection of services to other towns. Though exact departure times may change during the lifespan of this book, you will still have an idea of the frequency of the service.

From Merkazit HaMafrits to: **Afula**: Bus 301, 0550-2335, 1 hr; **Akko**: Bus 251/271, every 15 mins, 0535-2345, 13NIS, 35 mins; **Bet She'arim**: Bus 301 and 331, 0540-2330, 30 mins; **Jerusalem**: Bus 960, every hour til 1800, 44NIS; **Kiryat Shemona**: Bus 500 (direct), every hr, 0600-1930, 2 hrs, (via Safed, bus 501, 3 per day); **Nahariya**: Bus 271 0545-2330, every 10 mins, 1 hr; **Nazareth**: Bus 331 (also picks up at Merkaz Hashmona train station); **Tiberias**: Bus 431, every 30 mins, 0625-2210, 1 hr 15 mins; **Safed**: Bus 361, 0540-1930, 2 hrs (and bus 501); **Zichron Ya'akov**: Bus 202, around 1 per hr, 0610-2155, 30 mins.

From Merkazit Hof HaCarmel: **Atlit**, buses 202/221/921, 0545-2235, 15 mins; **Beer Sheva**, change in Tel Aviv; **Beit Shean**, change at Afula; **Caesarea**: Bus 910/947, get off at Or Akiva Jct. **Dor**: Bus 921/922, 0540-2230, 15 mins, ask to be let off at Dor Jct; **Hadera**: Bus 921, 0545-2235, 1 hr; **Jerusalem**: Bus 940/947, every 30 mins, 0550-2100, 2 hrs, and bus 947 (not direct), 3 hrs; **Netanya**: Bus 947, every 30 mins, 0550-2100, 45 mins; **Tel Aviv**: Bus 910, every hr, 0550-2335, 1½ hrs.

For **Daliyat el-Carmel** and **Isfiya**: Bus 37A, from downtown and Carmel Centre (Yefe Nof).

Car hire

Avis, 99 Hahistadrut, T04-8493366, www. avis.co.il. Budget, 7 Ha'ashlag, T03-9350019, www.budget.co.il. Eldan, 84 Hahistadrut, T04-8410910, www.eldan.co.il.

Sheruts

To Ben-Gurion Airport, Amal, T04-8662324, 1½ hrs. Frequent services to **Tel Aviv**, **Akko** and **Nahariya** (11NIS), including **Shabbat**, depart from near the junction of HeHalutz/ HaNevi'im, see map. **Nahariya**; **Isfiya** and **Daliyat el-Carmel** from Eliyahu HaNavi (near Kikar Paris); to **Nazareth** from Kikar Paris.

Subway

The subway runs from Kikar Paris (port area), via **Solel-Boneh** (Hassan Shukri), **Ha Nevi'im** (Hadar area), **Masada**, **Golomb** to Gan Ha'Em (Carmel Centre). Sun-Thu 0600-2400, Fri 0600-1500, Sat 1 hr after sundown-2400.

Train

Train is the quickest and easiest way to travel along the coast. Haifa has three railway stations, though most visitors will only use Haifa Merkaz HaShmona (AKA Centre HaShmona) . Southbound, there are direct services to **Tel Aviv** every hour (1 hr 10 mins), plus 1-3 slower services per hour (1½ hrs) that also stop at **'Atlit**, **Binyamina**, **Hadera**, **Netanya** and **Herzliya**. hr. To **Be'er Sheva** services every hr, 2½ hrs. Northbound, trains go to **Nahariya** (40 mins) via Akko (30 mins) about once per hour. **NB** Holders of ISIC student cards get a 10% discount.

⏱ Directory

Banks As always, check exchange rates and commission charges before changing money at banks. Post offices offer commission-free foreign exchange (including TCs) at good rates. There are numerous banks around Haifa; those marked on the map have an ATM machine. **Cultural centres** Rappaport Art and Cultural Centre, 7 Mahanayim, T04–8353506. Hosts regular cultural events, concerts and exhibitions. **Hospitals and medical services** Rambam Medical Centre, 8 Aliya, Bat Galim, T04-85432222. Haifa's main hospital. Carmel Medical Centre, 7 Michal, T04-8250211. **Internet** Monski Store & Internet, 15 Nordau, one of few open every day

0900-2100, 15NIS per hr; **Net Station**, 125 Hanassi; plus many cafés have free Wi-Fi. **Post offices** The main post office at the junction of Shabetai Levi and HaNevi'im offers full services, including foreign exchange. Other branches are at 19 HaPalyam (for poste restante), 152 Yafo, and elsewhere in the city. **Visas and immigration** Visa extensions: 11 Hassan Shukri, T04-8667781. Call T1700-551111, Sun-Thu 1300-1500, to make an appointment.

Around Haifa

Mt Carmel National Park
① *T04-8228983, www.parks.org.il. Daily 0800-1700. Buses 22, 24 and 37 from Haifa go close to the main park entrance, as does bus 192 to Beit Oren. Free entrance for pedestrians, cars 33NIS. Camping 10NIS per person.*

The Mt Carmel National Park is the largest park in Israel, covering some 21,000 acres of forest and woodland slopes which stay green all year round. There are some well-marked trails through the pine, cypress and eucalyptus forest, of varying length and requiring differing degrees of fitness. Trail descriptions are marked at the park's main entrance, where the helpful staff can suggest walks suited to your ability, and you can buy a map showing the trails. The scenery is beautiful here, as are the views, and the sense of tranquillity certainly makes a visit worthwhile, even if just for a picnic.

Druze villages → *Colour map 1, grid B2.*
Another popular short excursion from Haifa is a visit to the Druze community villages of 'Isfiya and Daliyat el Carmel. (**NB** For further details of Druze beliefs and practices, see the 'Religion' section on page 727). It is also possible to combine an excursion to these villages with a walk down to the monastery at Muhraqa.

Getting there and away Public bus services to 'Isfiya and Daliyat el Carmel are fairly limited. Bus 192 runs from Haifa's Central Bus Station at 1215, 1400, 1530 and 1630 (about 40 minutes, 15NIS), though the service is not that reliable (and doesn't run on Saturday). Sheruts offer the better option, running from Eliyahu HaNavi, near Kikar Paris and Ha'Atzma'ut.

'Isfiya This is the smaller of the two villages, though it is pushing it nowadays to describe either as a village and they are still expanding. Most people concur that 'Isfiya is less attractive than its neighbour further down the road, Daliyat el Carmel. However, it does have the advantage of being quieter and less commercialized. The village is associated with the former Jewish village of Husifah that dates to the Roman and Byzantine periods, and a fifth- or sixth-century CE synagogue was excavated here, though next to nothing remains in the village today.

Taboun Zeman restaurant ① *T04-8399585*, on the main road, is recognizable by the large black sign with pictures of food and flames on it. It is an excellent and authentic place to sample local food (hummus with meat is recommended).

Daliyat el Carmel The village is located slightly further on from 'Isfiya (though the two, in fact, have merged together), and has become such a popular day trip from Haifa that some feel that what you see now is more of a Druze community theme-park. Visitors are attracted by the clothes, art and handicrafts on display, but potential purchasers should be aware that not all the goods are made locally and most are quite tacky. The village is quieter and more attractive on weekdays, away from the Shabbat crowds. **NB** Most of the shops in the bazaar are closed on Friday.

There is genuinely great Druze food to be sampled, however, in several restaurants. Recommended is **Abu Antar** ① *T04-8393537, daily 0800-2300*, on the main street who do great varieties of hummus (try 'Abu Antar hummus' with pine nuts and tahina), meat on the charcoal grill, excellent salads etc in generous portions. The main restaurant is quite glitzy; they also do simpler shwarma/falafel in their stall next door. Daliyat el Carmel was also the home of **Sir Lawrence Oliphant**, a late 19th-century British Christian Zionist, until his death in 1886. An unusual 'Christian mystic', Oliphant not only established close links with the Druze, he is also credited with sheltering both Arab and Jewish insurgents. His old stone home, **Beit Oliphant** ① *open daily 24 hours, in the Old Town, ask for directions*, has been renovated and turned into a memorial to Druze members of the security forces and IDF; their photos date from 1939 to the previous few weeks. There is also a library, a room with his desk where it is said the National Anthem was composed, and a memorial house to Rabin with weaponry on display. Close to Beit Oliphant (signed) is the **Maqam of Abu Ibrahim**, a pretty white-washed building marked by a small red dome. Though the saint is not buried here, it is where he is known to have come to pray (in the dank underground room), thus followers come and do likewise. Head-coverings are provided.

Muhraqa (Camelite chapel) ① *T052-8779686. Daily 0900-1630 (except hols), admission 3NIS. Toilets, souvenirs.*

Some 4 km beyond Daliyat el Carmel is Muhraqa. You may be able to take a taxi from Daliyat el Carmel, though the chances are that if you don't have your own transport, you will have to walk or hitch. The turn is signed as you leave Daliyat el Carmel; keep straight on the side road to reach Muhraqa.

This is believed by some to be the site where Elijah defeated the 450 priests of Baal (*I Kings 18:17-40*). Although open to conjecture, with no archaeological evidence to confirm either the story or its actual location, circumstantial evidence here does fit the biblical text. The site does stand at the entrance to the Jezreel Valley, as described in the First Book of Kings (*I Kings 18:46*); it is possible to see the sea (*I Kings 18:43*); and the Kishon Brook does run along the base of the hill (*I Kings 18:40*).

The Carmelite order built a **chapel** here in the late 19th century, from whose roof terrace there is a superb panoramic view. Close to the entrance, a red/white trail leads to another good viewpoint (10-minute walk).

North of Haifa

The 'Phoenician coast' to the north of Haifa has a number of attractions, as well as a few sights of interest lying a little inland in Western Galilee. Many of these places can be visited from Haifa as day trips, although there is accommodation to suit the majority of budgets most of the way along this coast.

Akko (Acre) → *Colour map 1, grid B2.*

The 'Old City' of Akko is one of the highlights of the Mediterranean coast. Although the town has a long and ancient history, it is the remains from the medieval period that delight most visitors. This was the last bastion of Crusader rule in the Holy Land, and many of the structures they built can be seen on a short walking tour of the labyrinth-like winding streets of 'Old Akko'. The Crusader buildings were added to during the Fatimid and Mamluk periods, and again by the Ottomans, and the quarter continues to be a living-breathing Arab town. 'Old Akko' certainly fits that cliché of being a 'living museum'. In 2000 its unique appeal was recognized when it was designated a UNESCO World Heritage site. Note that 'Acre' is the Crusader name; it's Akka in Arabic and Akko in Hebrew.

Ins and outs

Getting there and away There are two parts to the city: most of the attractions are confined to the Old City area (Acre/Akka), whilst the transport connections are found in the New City (Akko). Akko's railway station is located one block behind the bus station, with regular services north to Nahariya and south to Haifa and Tel Aviv. The Central Bus Station is on Ha-Arba'a; many services run on Shabbat and sheruts also ply the main routes going south.

Getting around The Old City is less than 15 minutes' walk from the main bus station, 20 minutes from the train station or 10-12NIS in a taxi. The Old City area is fairly small, making it pleasant to just wander around at will. Most people enter the Old City along Weizmann, beginning their tour at the el-Jazzar Mosque and Subterranean Crusader city. The subsequent sights below are listed in a more or less clockwise tour of the Old City, though the twisting lanes and culs-de-sac mean that some backtracking is inevitable. Visitors should note that substantial restoration work is in progress around the Subterranean Crusader City and the Citadel, and subsequently the entrances and exits to these sites may now have changed.

Tourist Information Your first point of call should be the **Visitors' Centre** ① *1 Weizmann, T04-9551088, www.akko.org.il, Thu, Sat and Sun 0830-1715, Fri 0830-1615, closes 1 hr earlier in winter, in the Enchanted Gardens*, where there is a short documentary about the Old City, good maps, brochures and free internet. Also located in the gardens is the Box Office (closes 1615) from where you buy tickets for most of Akko's attractions (though not the Prisoners Museum or El-Jazzar Mosque). "Combined tickets" are valid for the duration of your stay, basically the Subterranean Crusader City plus whichever other sites you tag on. An eight-language audio guide for the Crusader City (and Templar Tunnel) is included in the price of a ticket.

Background

Early history Though dominated by buildings from the Crusader, Late Arab and Ottoman periods, the ancient city of Akko (Acco) was established as a major coastal settlement as early as the beginning of the second millennium BCE. The original settlement was located on a mound to the east of the present city, referred to as **Tel Akko** (Tell el-Fukhar, or the Mound of Potsherds), although there is precious little to see at the site today.

Just about anybody who was anybody in history passed through Akko at some stage, including the **Egyptian** pharaohs, the **Israelites**, the **Phoenicians** (who developed a major port city here), the **Assyrian** king Sennacherib, the **Greeks** (Alexander the Great founded a coin mint here in 332 BCE that was to remain in operation for almost 600 years), the **Seleucids** (who renamed it Antiochia Ptolemais), and the **Romans** (who annexed Akko in 63 BCE). Subsequent important visitors to Akko included **Julius Caesar** in 47 BCE, **King Herod** in 39 BCE (who began his process of legitimating the lands granted to him by the Romans from here), **Paul** (who passed through 'Ptolemais' on his third voyage; Acts 21:7), and finally the future emperor **Vespasian**, who used Akko as his base from which to suppress Galilee during the First Jewish War (66-73 CE). Akko continued to prosper under the Romans and under the subsequent **Byzantine empire** (324-638 CE).

Arab and Crusader periods With the arrival of the Arabs in 636 CE, the city reverted to its former name Akko, and saw its harbour facilities expand rapidly as it became the main port of the Umayyad capital at Damascus. The decline of Caesarea's harbour further south made Akko the key port in the Holy Land, and an obvious target for the sea-faring Crusaders. However, it was not until 1104, five years after the conquest of Jerusalem, that the Crusaders were able to take the city. **Baldwin I** was assisted by the Genoese fleet in capturing Akko, with the key European maritime powers and city-states instrumental in the town's development (Genoese, Venetian, Amalfi and Pisan quarters all developed within the city). The various military-religious orders all established headquarters here, including the Order of the Knights of St John (Hospitallers), the Knights Templar, the Teutonic Knights and the Order of St Lazarus. The city was renamed after St Jean d'Acre and became known as **Acre**.

Akko

Sleeping
1 Palm Beach Club
2 Zipi's Place

Eating
1 El Gaucho
2 Leonardo & Panorama

Other
2 Sheruts (transport)
1 Petrol stations

250 metres
250 yards

Following the loss of Jerusalem, Acre briefly became the capital of the Latin kingdom in the Holy Land, though the Crusaders were obliged to surrender the city without a fight to **Salah al-Din** in 1187. The town was recaptured in 1191 by **Richard Coeur de Lion** and **Philip Augustus of France**, and restored to its position as the capital of the Latin Kingdom (the Crusaders being excluded from Jerusalem). **St Francis of Assisi** and **Marco Polo** both visited Acre.

However, disputes soon arose between the various merchant communities of Acre, and between the various military-religious orders. The Venetian and Genoese fleets even fought a sea battle off the coast of Acre in 1259, despite the fact that the invading Mongol army were at the city walls. The warring factions managed to unite long enough to repel the Mongols, and the Mamluks who attacked in 1265, but perhaps the writing was on the wall for the Crusader city. Despite the efforts of **Henry II of Cyprus** to unite the city under his claim to the throne in 1285, Acre's defences were ill prepared to resist the numerically superior forces of the Mamluk forces in 1291. Nevertheless, despite being outnumbered ten to one, the Crusaders held the city for two months before it finally fell to the sultan **el-Malik el-Ashraf**. Though between 30,000 and 40,000 of the city's inhabitants managed to flee to Cyprus, the Mamluks took a bloody revenge on the remaining Christian population, who a year previously had slaughtered a large number of the city's Muslims. The town was razed, and left uninhabited for over 300 years.

Recent history It was the self-declared ruler of Galilee **Daher al-Omer** who initiated the city's revival. Between 1750 and 1775, he substantially rebuilt the city's defences (what is now the city's inner wall), making Akko one of the key towns in the fiefdom that he carved out of the Ottoman empire. He was succeeded in 1775 by **Ahmed el-Jazzar** ('The Butcher'), who engineered his succession by murdering his predecessor. Restoration of the town continued, despite a brief interlude in 1799 in which the British fleet intervened on el-Jazzar's behalf and repelled **Napoleon**'s attempts to conquer the city. El-Jazzar's building programme continued, and he is responsible for restoring much of the harbour, and for building the Great Mosque and the Turkish baths.

Ibrahim Pasha took the city from the Turks in 1832 with his Egyptian army, though within eight years the British had pressurized him into retiring back to Egypt. The **British** themselves captured the city from the Turks in 1918, and continued to rule Akko throughout the Mandate period. The former Citadel was converted into a prison and used to house Jewish underground fighters (or 'terrorists', according to your viewpoint). Arab opposition to Zionism was vociferous locally, and the prison was also used to hold those involved in the Arab revolt of the 1930s. In May 1948 the Israelis captured the city.

Sights
City walls and gates The stout city walls surrounding Akko today, together with the deep fosse and counterscarp, were built mainly by el-Jazzar, following the defeat of Napoleon's forces in 1799. Very small portions of the original Crusader city walls can be seen on Weizmann as you approach the Old City. The city enclosed by the Crusader city walls was considerably larger than el-Jazzar's fortified town, and possibly extended as far north as Ben Ammi Street and as far east as the present Naval Academy. By climbing up the ramparts to the **'Land Wall Promenade'** behind the **Moat Garden**, it is possible to walk along a section of the city walls. Information boards describe Napoleon's failed attack on the city, and in the late afternoon this is a popular location for newly-weds to be photographed.

Ahmed el-Jazzar Mosque/Great Mosque ① *Daily 0800-1900, though closed during prayers. Entrance 10NIS. Wear modest dress (though the doorkeeper may provide you with additional coverings if he feels that your dress is not modest enough). Remove shoes before entering the mosque. Guides may offer their services, though they are highly variable in ability.* Occupying the former site of a Crusader church, the Ahmed el-Jazzar Mosque (or Great

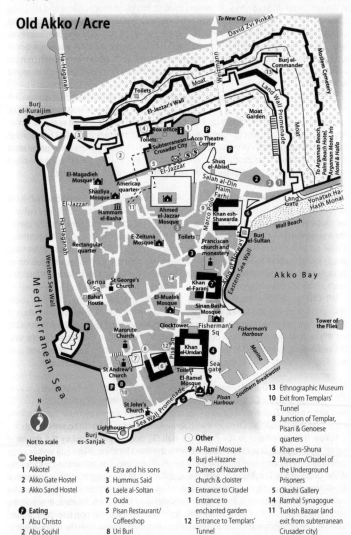

Old Akko / Acre

To New City
David Zvi Pinkas
To Argaman Beach, Palm Beach Hotel, Argaman Motel, Iris Hotel & Haifa
Burj el-Commander
Moslem Cemetery
Moat
Weizmann
Ha-Haganah
Toilets
El-Jazzar's Wall
Land Wall Promenade
Moat
Burj el-Kuraijim
Box office
Toilets
Subterranean Crusader City
Moat Garden
Acco Theatre Center
Shuq el-Abiad
El-Jazzar
Salah al-Din
Haim Farhi
American quarter
El-Magadieh Mosque
Shazliya Mosque
Hammam el-Basha
Ahmed el-Jazzar Mosque
Marco Polo
Khan esh-Shawarda
Land Gate
Wall Beach
Yonatan Ha-Hash Monai
Burj el-Sultan
Eastern Sea Wall
Akko Bay
El-Jazzar
Rectangular quarter
E-Zeituna Mosque
Toilets
Franciscan church and monastery
Khan el-Franji
Khan of Norway
Western Sea Wall
Ha-Haganah
Genoa Sq
St George's Church
Baha'i House
El-Mualek Mosque
Sinan Basha Mosque
Tower of the Flies
Maronite Church
Clocktower
Fisherman's Sq
Fisherman's Harbour
Marina
St Andrew's Church
Pisa St
Khan el-Umdan
Sea gate
El-Ramel Mosque
Southern Breakwater
Mediterranean Sea
St John's Church
Sea Wall Promenade
Pisan Harbour
Lighthouse
Burj es-Sanjak
Not to scale
N

Sleeping
1 Akkotel
2 Akko Gate Hostel
3 Akko Sand Hostel
4 Ezra and his sons
3 Hummus Said
3 Laele al-Soltan
7 Ouda
5 Pisan Restaurant/ Coffeeshop
8 Uri Buri

Eating
1 Abu Christo
2 Abu Souhil

○ **Other**
9 Al-Rami Mosque
4 Burj el-Hazane
7 Dames of Nazareth church & cloister
1 Entrance to Citadel
1 Entrance to enchanted garden
12 Entrance to Templars' Tunnel

13 Ethnographic Museum
10 Exit from Templars' Tunnel
8 Junction of Templar, Pisan & Genoese quarters
6 Khan es-Shuna
2 Museum/Citadel of the Underground Prisoners
5 Okashi Gallery
14 Ramhal Synagogue
11 Turkish Bazaar (and exit from subterranean Crusader city)

Mosque) is a fine example of Ottoman period building style. In front of the entrance to the complex is the ritual ablutions fountain, resembling an elegant pavilion with a green copper roof supported by slim columns. A short flight of steps leads into the mosque's beautiful courtyard, enhanced by palms, flower beds and shady trees. Many of the columns in the courtyard were 'recycled' from Caesarea. The arcade around three sides of the courtyard opens on to small rooms used to accommodate pilgrims and religious students. To the right of the mosque is a simple domed mausoleum containing the sarcophagi of Ahmed el-Jazzar (died 1804) and his adopted son and successor, Suleiman (died 1819). The interior of the mosque itself is fairly simple, with a plain white dome supported by brown, black and white stone decorated with verses from the Qu'ran on a blue background. Galleries on three sides above the main prayer floor are reserved for women.

To the east side of the courtyard is the entrance to an underground reservoir. The mosque is built on the quarter of the city occupied in the Crusader period by the Order of the Knights of St John (Hospitallers), and it is believed that this structure was part of the original Crusader church of St John. When el-Jazzar built the mosque in 1781, he turned the former church into an emergency water cistern and reservoir. Water was supplied from the Pasha Gardens via ceramic pipes, and from rainfall, and was integrated within the city's main water supply system. It still fills with rain water, and is open to the public.

Subterranean Crusader City ⓘ *Sun-Thu 0800-1700, Fri 0800-1400, Sat 0900-1800. Adult 25NIS, student 22NIS (or combined ticket, prices listed at the Box Office).*
The moniker of 'subterranean' or 'underground' to describe this part of the former Crusader city is something of a misnomer; what was street level during the 12th and 13th centuries is now up to 8 metres below the present surface level. Successive occupiers of the site simply found it easier to fill in the Crusader halls with rock and earth filler, and build over them. Now that these 'subterranean' structures have been largely excavated, the fact that much of the site is underground makes it even more interesting to visit.

NB Due to ongoing excavations, you may find there are changes from the route description here. Numbers on this Handbook map will not match those on the maps on the walls. Nor will all the numbers on the audio-guide have matching numbers on the wall, but it is certainly worth picking it up as there are very few written descriptions at the site. The audio-guide is included in the price of a ticket (you will need to leave some form of ID to collect it). Soon to open to the public are the Southern Road and Beautiful Hall.

Tour of the complex The Subterranean Crusader City is entered from the Enchanted Gardens. In the **courtyard** (1) the Citadel built by Daher al-Omer and el-Jazzar looms up above you. To the south is a **hall** (2) where the upper arches of the Crusader columns protrude from the floor, suggesting that the original Crusader level is some 4 metres or so below the current one.

Follow the stairs down to the **Prisoners' Hall** (3), originally accessed by the opposite (south) opening. It is as yet undetermined what the exact function of this hall was, but it is known as the Prisoners' Hall because there were no windows. The entrance to the fortress of the Order of the Knights of St John (Hospitallers), and the Knights' Halls, is through a large Ottoman Gate (it is said that the Turkish rulers used to hang the condemned from the main beam of this gateway). The original Crusader gate is probably located some metres below the surface. Follow the passageway, lined with concrete supports, to the **Knights' Halls** (4). The impressive series of barrel-vaulted chambers are now used to hold banquets during the fringe theatre festival (see listings, page 532).

An interesting story relates to the patch of modern concrete that is still visible in the ceiling of the third chamber. During a jailbreak from the British-run prison in the Citadel, a number of prisoners tunnelled out through the floor of their cells. To their surprise, they emerged into these rubble-strewn halls. However, the rubble fill was so dense, they could make no further progress, and were forced to return to their cells. Their escape tunnel was only discovered when the halls were being excavated. This chamber is also the only one which retains its original Crusader entrance. The tour now emerges from the western end of the excavated Knights' Halls into the **Great Pillared Hall** (5), which has been heavily restored and rebuilt. The principal architectural style here is very different to that of the Knights' Halls, which suggests that the Pillared Hall was built during a different period, with the vaults of the Knights' Halls probably dating to the Ottoman period.

In the **Citadel courtyard** (6) note the granite pillars that el-Jazzar brought from the ruins of Caesarea, and the Crusader latrines at the northwest edge. This courtyard was

Subterranean Crusader City

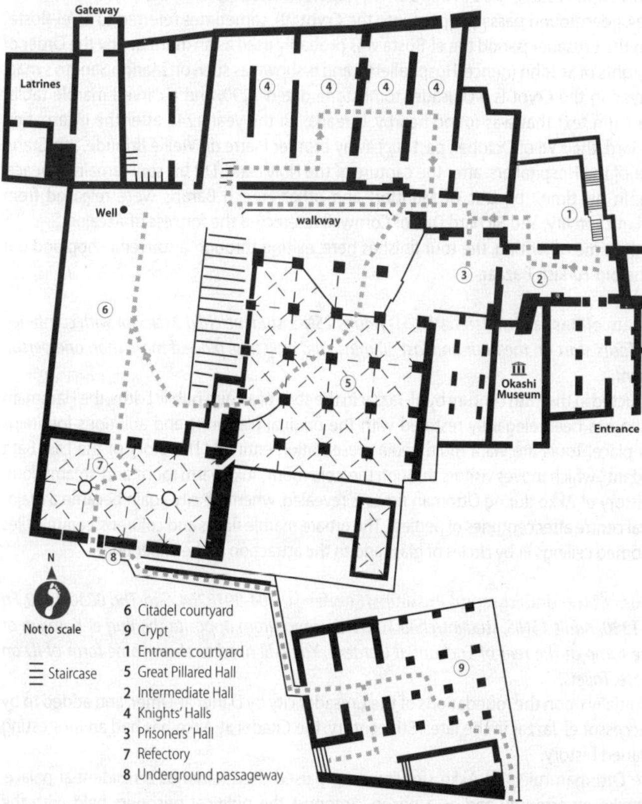

Not to scale

☰ Staircase

6 Citadel courtyard
9 Crypt
1 Entrance courtyard
5 Great Pillared Hall
2 Intermediate Hall
4 Knights' Halls
3 Prisoners' Hall
7 Refectory
8 Underground passageway

once completely filled in with rubble, and the level of the courtyard of the fort that was built on top can be seen above. A few steps descend into the **Refectory (7)**, the most impressive of all the halls thus far excavated. Two carved fleurs-de-lis, one in the northeast corner and one in the southeast corner, suggest that the hall was built around 1148, when Louis VII (leader of the Second Crusade) established the lily as the emblem of the French kingdom. The architectural style of the refectory is interesting, the elegant arches marking a transition from Romanesque to Gothic. The Crusader's stone-masons cut the stone on the spot, evidenced by the discovery of a quarry on the west side of the refectory. As its name suggests, the refectory was used as a grand dining room and guest hall, though the suggestion that Marco Polo was entertained here is pure conjecture.

Some 350 m of underground passages have so far been excavated, some leading north to the city walls, others leading south towards the port. A section of the **underground passageway (8)** has been lit, and leads to the final section of the tour. The exact function of the 'secret tunnel' is unclear. Some speculate that it was part of an elaborate Crusader sewerage system, though it was probably intended as part of a secret escape route; that's certainly what el-Jazzar had in mind when Napoleon was attacking the city.

The underground passage opens into the **Crypt (9)**, sometimes referred to as 'el-Bosta'. During the Crusader period the el-Bosta was probably used as an infirmary by the Order of the Knights of St John (hence 'Hospitallers'), and is shown as such on Marino Sanuto's map. Displayed in the Crypt is a Crusader tombstone dated 1290, and a carved marble tablet with a Latin text that was found nearby. It reads: "In the year 1242 after the incarnation of our lord, the XVII of October, past [*sic*] away brother Pierre de Vieille Brioude, 8th Grand Master of the Hospitallers, after the capture of the Holy Land. Let his soul remain in peace, Amen. In his time, the Duc of Montfort and other French Barons were released from Egyptian captivity, and Richard Duc of Cornwall re-erected the fortress of Ascalon."

At the time of writing, the tour finishes here, exiting through a souvenir shop and out into the old Turkish Bazaar.

Hammam el-Basha (Turkish bath) ① *Adults 25NIS, student/child 21NIS, or with combined ticket. Tours start on the hour and last 30 mins, and only take place if more than one person is present.*

Constructed in the 18th century by el-Jazzar in the style of a Cairo public baths, the Hammam el-Basha has been elegantly restored with the original platforms and ablutions fountains still in place. Tours are via a multimedia presentation entitled "The Story of the Last Bath Attendant", which moves visitors through the 'cold room', 'lukewarm room' and 'steam room'. The history of Akko during Ottoman times is revealed, when the city again became a major cultural centre after centuries of neglect. The ornate marble floors and columns, ceramic tiles and domed ceilings lit by circles of glass add to the attraction of the experience.

Museum of the Underground Prisoners/Citadel ① *T04-9918264. Sun-Thu 0830-1630, Fri 0830-1330. Adult 15NIS, student/child 10NIS. Entrance from opposite the Burj el-Kuraijim or via the ramp at the rear of Enchanted Gardens. You will need to show some form of ID on entrance. Toilets.*

Built initially upon the foundations of the Crusader city by Daher al-Omer, and added to by his successor el-Jazzar in the late 18th century, the Citadel at Akko has had an interesting and varied history.

The Ottoman rulers of Akko simultaneously used the Citadel as a residential palace, a barracks, an armoury and as a prison. Amongst the political prisoners held with the common criminals was **Baha'ullah**, the founder of the Baha'i faith (see page 506). The British also made use of the jail facilities, eventually developing it into the largest prison in Palestine. Amongst the first Jewish prisoners held here was Ze'ev Jabotinsky, in 1920, who later went on to found the Irgun 'terrorist/freedom fighters' organization. At its peak, the prison was holding political prisoners from both the Jewish and Arab communities, common criminals from both communities, and clandestine Jewish immigrants who had been captured by the British. On 4 May 1947, the prison was the scene of a spectacular prison breakout that saw 41 Jewish and 214 Arab detainees initially escape. The breakout featured prominently in Leon Uris' book *Exodus* (with the film scene shot on location here). Until 1982, part of the building was still being used as a mental hospital.

The museum has been undergoing an extensive reorganisation and renovation (not complete at the time of our visit but due to finish summer 2010). Entrance is across a British-built bridge over the dry moat. Below, note the large blocks at the base of the fortress. These are Crusader foundations, while the smaller blocks date to the fortress's 18th-century construction. At the time of writing, many rooms merely contain mock-ups of life in the prison (which don't make it look like a particularly tough ordeal) plus some information outlining the history of the Jewish resistance groups. The Remembrance Room is also open.

The northwest wing houses the cells where Jabotinsky and Baha'ullah were held; the latter is a place of pilgrimage for Baha'is. Interesting displays tell Jabotinsky's story and that of the Jewish Brigade, a silent movie rolls, and soon to come is an audio-visual presentation. It is also possible to see the gallows where nine Jewish prisoners were executed. When the 40-m high Burj el-Hazane (Tower of the Treasury) re-opens, climb to the top for a prime view of Old Akko and along the coast to Haifa.

Okashi Gallery ① *Sun-Thu 0830-1700, Fri 0830-1400. Adult 10NIS, students/child 7NIS, or with a combined ticket.*
This attractive gallery displays the work of the Jewish abstract painter Avshalom Okashi (1916-1980). He was a resident of Akko from 1948 until his death, and many of his paintings feature scenes from the city. About half of the gallery space is given over to temporary exhibitions of paintings/photos.

Tour of Akko

The following tour of Akko follows a more or less clockwise route around the Old City, beginning from the el-Jazzar Mosque. However, much of the delight of Akko is in just wandering and, should you need them, signs on walls and posts accurately point the way to the sights.

Ethnographic Museum ① *T04-9911004, www.ozarot.net. Sat-Thu 0930-1700, Fri 0930-1500. Adult 15NIS, student/child 12NIS, or with a combined ticket.*
Located in the Burg el-Commander (where the Ottoman garrison lived) in the northeast corner of the walls, this museum recreates typical Galilean artisans' workshops of a century ago. Beautifully assembled from private collections, shops include a pharmacy, hatmakers, potters and pharmacy (complete with baby-weighing scales). Information sheets are provided to illuminate objects on display. The right-hand section of the arched barracks houses a random selection of artefacts, ranging from toys to wonderful Syrian furniture inlaid with bone and shell. There's also a little garden, located within the outer city walls.

Shuq el-Abiad Built by Daher al-Omer in the mid- to late 18th century, this low arcade stands opposite the entrance to the main bazaar. Today, the Shuq el-Abiad (White Market) houses a number of cheap foodstalls.

Land Gate Though now standing as the eastern entrance to el-Jazzar's fortified city, it should be remembered that the original Crusader walls extended considerably further east, possibly as far as the Naval Academy. However, until the breach in the wall was made to accommodate Weizmann Street in 1910, this gate provided the only land access to the fortified town. The impressive studded iron doors remain.

Khan esh-Shawarda Built on the site of the Franciscan Convent of St Clare, whose nuns are said to have preferred suicide to dishonour when Acre fell to the Mamluks in 1291, only parts of the Khan esh-Shawarda (Merchants' Inn) remain today. It is also believed that, in Crusader times, an inner anchorage penetrated the city here, perhaps related to the fact that the arsenal was located here.

Burj el-Sultan The Burj el-Sultan (Sultan's Tower) is the last Crusader city tower that still stands to its full height. The tower is shown on Marino Sanuto's map of the Crusader city as being at the edge of the Venetian Quarter and, until its incorporation into the 18th-century Turkish sea-wall, it was enclosed by water on three sides. Inside the tower is a guardroom and a subterranean dungeon, though it is kept locked.

Khan el-Faranj Directly to the south of the 18th-century Franciscan church and monastery is the Khan el-Faranj, or 'Inn of the Franks'. This was initially the heart of the Venetian Quarter during the Crusader period, though European ('Franks') traders established themselves on this site at the beginning of the Ottoman period (1516). The caravanserai (khan) was built by the Druze emir Fakhr ed-Din around 1600 and, as such, is the oldest khan in Akko.

Ramhal Synagogue Visits may be arranged in advance through the Visitors' Centre or by calling T04-050-5377132, to see if someone can come and open up.

This small synagogue was constructed with the permission of Dahar al-Omer, after he turned the original synagogue into the El-Mualek mosque. It has been renovated and the short tour is very interesting.

Khan el-Umdan The caravanserai Khan el-Umdan (Khan of the Pillars) was built by el-Jazzar in 1785 on the site of a former Crusader period Dominican order monastery. It takes its name from the splendid row of granite and porphyry columns that el-Jazzar 'recycled' from Caesarea, laid out in alternating colours. The tall clock-tower above was built in 1906 to mark the 30th year of the rule of the Ottoman Sultan, Abdul Hamid II. A similar clock-tower in Jaffa marks the same event. The Khan is undergoing restoration work to become a functioning caravanserai once more – in the reincarnation of a boutique hotel – though this is not expected to be completed for at least a couple of years.

Templars' Tunnel ⓘ *Summer Sat-Thu 0930-1830, Fri 0930-1730, winter daily 0830-1730. Adult 10NIS, student/child 7NIS, or with combination ticket.*
The audio-guide from the Subterranean City in fact continues here, but be sure to return the audio ASAP after a visit in order to make it available to other visitors.

Near the Khan el-Umdan is the entrance to the Templars' Tunnel, discovered in 1994 when a blocked sewer in the building above led workmen to the 700-year-old shaft. The tunnel does undoubtedly smell strongly of sewage, but this was never its purpose. It served as a strategic connection from the Templars' fortress in the west to their port in the east, a distance of 350 m. Be prepared to stoop in parts of the tunnel, the bottom half of which is hewn out of the bedrock whilst the upper reaches are neatly bricked. In fact, two parallel tunnels make up the first part of the journey, and note that a further tunnel runs above. This section open to the public extends for some 350 m to come out near the lighthouse.

Fisherman's Harbour and Marina Since Persian times at least (586-332 BCE), Akko's ancient harbour has been located where the Fisherman's Harbour and Marina now lie. During dredging work on the harbour in 1983, ancient cargo from two boats sunk in the fourth or fifth century BCE and the first century CE respectively, was discovered. The foundations of the southern breakwater in use today were probably laid during the late sixth or early fifth centuries BCE, though the Romans raised its height, perhaps reflecting a change in sea-level. The Crusaders also made alterations to the harbour plan, again perhaps due to a drop in sea-level (possibly 1.5 metres). There may well have been an inner basin, possibly an anchorage for the Genoese fleet, as well as the separate anchorage that the Pisans built (see below). Dhar el-Amr and Ahmed el-Jazzar both substantially repaired the harbour, the latter again 'recycling' marble and porphyry columns from Caesarea.

Today, the harbour is filled with fishing boats and pleasure craft, with a few seafood restaurants lining the quay.

The Tower of the Flies The Tower of the Flies stands on an artificially created island 70 m east of the tip of the breakwater. Its function is unknown, though it may have served as 'a kind of emporium or free port for foreign trading vessels' (Raban, 1993). During early Arab rule, a 400-m-long eastern breakwater probably connected the Tower of the Flies to the shore to the north (near to the Naval Academy).

Sea Gate This gate, which dates to the Crusader period, is thought to stand at the point where a 9-m-wide channel used to extend from the Crusader harbour in to what may have been an inner basin used by the Genoese.

Pisan Harbour and Khan es-Shuna This inner anchorage, though outside the main harbour, was created by the Pisans on the site of the former western anchorage of the Phoenician port. It allowed small vessels to sail up to the commercial centre of the Pisan Quarter around the Khan esh-Shuna. A couple of restaurants now sit on the quay of the Pisan harbour.

Formerly the 'Inn of the Pisans', the Khan esh-Shuna is now used as a workshop area. Just to its north is the former site of a Templar tower that controlled the **junction** of the Templar, Pisan and Genoese quarters.

Sea wall promenade At the southern tip of the mini peninsula on which Akko stands, it is possible to take a walk along the ramparts. At the centre of the sea wall promenade is **St John's Church**, built by the Franciscans in 1737. The **Lighthouse** is thought to mark the former site of the Burj es-Sanjak (Flag Tower) Crusader tower.

The section of 18th-century sea wall to the north of the lighthouse was destroyed in an earthquake in 1837. This whole area, now the 'lighthouse parking lot', was formerly occupied by the Templars' fortress. Renowned for its beauty as much as for its strength, it was destroyed by the Mamluks following the Crusader departure in 1291, to ensure that the Christians would not return. No trace remains today.

Western section of Old Akko The western section of Old Akko has a number of interesting features, most notably the Crusader street plan. Continuing north from the lighthouse, take the steps to your right opposite the viewpoint to the north of the 'lighthouse parking lot'. Located here are the **Dames of Nazareth Church and Cloister** and a **Maronite Church**, though the former looks derelict and the latter is generally locked. Behind these buildings is the former junction of the Templar, Pisan and Genoese quarters. The narrow street that heads north from here has a number of interesting Crusader houses to the left.

The street leads to Genoa Square, where the fortified gate at the entrance to the Genoese Quarter used to stand. On the west (sea) side of the square, at the junction of HaHaganah, is the **Baha'i House** where Baha'ullah spent 12 years of his exile. The large house – identifiable by its whitewashed walls, blue doors and frames, and red tiled roof – is not open to the public, only to pilgrims.

At the east side of the square is the Greek Orthodox **St George's Church**. Built on medieval foundations, the church is usually dated to the 17th century, though the carving over the door lintel of St George slaying what appears to be people, as opposed to a dragon, is dated 1845. Behind the church a tablet bears dedications to a number of British officers who fell in action here.

Two small streets lead north from behind the Baha'i House into the so-called 'Rectangular quarter'. Much of the original Crusader street pattern is retained, with houses set forward every 50 m or so in order to make the city more defensible. Likewise, the sharp turns at the north and south ends of the street prevent the enemy from having a clear line of fire. The street to the east (right) was a 'neutral street', dividing the Genoese quarter from the area controlled by the Dominicans. It has Crusader buildings on both sides, though the lower storeys to the west are the best preserved.

Akko listings

Sleeping

There isn't much accommodation in Akko, so many people stay in Haifa and just visit for the day. In addition to the options listed here, a couple of new places are being developed – one to be very boutique, complete with Italian frescoes. Ask at the Visitors' Centre for the latest information.
L Akkotel, T04-9877100, www.akkotel.com. Charmingly renovated Ottoman building that was once the checkpoint of the Land Gate, and has also been used as the courthouse and a boys' school. Creamy stone walls, arched ceilings, tastefully furnished, big beds and modern fixtures – flat screen TVs, electric shutters, double glazing. Bathrooms the best in town. Family rooms have mezzanines. Attractive restaurant (♥♥) and plans for a café on the roof (which extends on to the city walls). Seasonal price increases. Breakfast included.
AL Palm Beach Club, Argaman Beach, T04-9877777, www.palmbeach.co.il. Facilities include pool, indoor pool, spa, health club, tennis, squash, basketball, beach access, plus comfortable (if dated) rooms (doubles $140). Very much an Israeli family atmosphere. 10-15% discount when you book online.
AL Zipi's Place, 10 Bilu, New Akko, T04-9915220/050-7901447, zipi503@walla.com. Outside the old city walls in the Jewish part of town. Spotless, cute, tasteful and homely, with the garden an added bonus. Double

rooms are 450NIS, breakfast included, kitchen facilities, disabled access, Wi-Fi and laundry facilities. A very pleasant place.

A-B Akko Sand Hostel, T04-9918636, sand. hostel@hotmail.com. New hotel scene, with a big emphasis on cleanliness. Private rooms with a/c, fridge, TV, modern Arab style decor (lots of gold trim), piles of blankets, quality sheets. 2 family rooms (350NIS), 1 single with outside bath (200NIS), 3 doubles (250NIS). Upstairs seating area with great view of Al-Jazzar mosque, but not for those who are bothered by the call to prayer. Use of well-appointed kitchen, free tea/coffee. Internet 10NIS per hr. Large dorm with cubicles around beds planned for the future. Can pick up from station with advance warning. Management somewhat overpowering.

B-E Akko Gate Hostel, Salah al-Din, T04-9910410/052-6834649, www.akkogate.com. Walid has been in the business over 20 years and knows the ropes. Three mixed 8-bed dorms (70NIS) with TV: not huge but clean and bathrooms adequate. Private rooms with shared bathrooms, plus 6 large modern doubles with tv, a/c, en suite (250NIS). Run by a friendly family, use of kitchen, back terrace, free pick-up from station possible, no curfew, tours to the Golan (full day including Safed, Nimrod Castle, Druze villages etc, space for 5-12 people) and to Rosh Ha-Nikra (2-3 hrs). Internet 20NIS per hr, breakfast 25NIS, beer 10-12NIS.

Eating

Some good value meals (hummus, pita, etc) can be had in the friendly restaurants opposite Haim Farhi Square (see map). For coffee, pizza, fast food and people-watching, try the pedestrianized section of Ben Ammi in the new city, and the hang-outs opposite the bus station.

††††-†† Abu Christo, Pisan Harbour, T9910065. An Akko institution. On the quay with outdoor seating or inside the high bright interior, selection from the daily catch (around 80NIS), draught beer (18NIS), good halloumi, mix of mezze (30NIS). Daily 1200-2300 or later.

††††-†† El Gaucho, 5 Ben Ammi, T04-9917577, www.elgaucho.co.il. If you are tiring of fish and hummus then head here for steaks, skewers, etc. It's not Tel Aviv chic but it is bustling and friendly.

†††-†† Uri Buri, near the lighthouse, T04-9552212. An excellent restaurant, where you are welcome to have a smorgasbord of dishes to sample as much as possible, or you can take half-portions for half-price. Inventive twists include wasabi, but simple shrimps with lemon and chilli (33NIS) hit the mark. Menu covers all varieties of fish (95NIS) and seafood plus kebabs. Decor is artfully non-existent with peeling paint revealing stone walls, plain table cloths, bottles of wine. Booking essential on Shabbat. Daily 1200-2200 or later.

†† Ezra and his sons, Fisherman's Harbour. Usual 'catch of the day' and selections from the grill, but can be closed out of season.

†† Ouda, Khan el-Faranj, T04-9912013, www.ouda-ltd.com. Middle Eastern salads, shashliks and hummus are specialities here in this friendly dining hall.

† Abu Souhil, T04-9817318. Claims to be "number 1" in the country for hummus and fuul, and it's a valid proposition. Add your oils, lemon, flavourings from the condiment selection on the table, plus the pickles are particularly awesome. Two clean tiled rooms or tables outside the back. Daily till 1630. No English sign.

† Hummus Said, Benjamin of Tuleda (in the souq). Packed out from dawn with locals, this hummus haven in the centre of the old market is a classic. But starts shutting down by 1400.

Coffee shops

Laele al-Soltan, Khan es-Shawarda. Great coffee shop with cavernous interior featuring draperies, cushions, grizzled men and Um Khaltoum on the wall. Traditional Arabic drinks or cheap Nescafé in a latte glass. Nargilla 12NIS. No sign, look for the giant coffeepot outside. Open 24/7.

Leonardo & Panorama, Argaman Beach. Adjacent bar-coffee shops which are open late, slightly sleezy.

Pisan Restaurant/Coffee shop, Pisan Harbour. Right on the water's edge, this slightly scruffy place has a more local feel; good for salads, a beer (12-20NIS) and nargillah. Fish dishes from 50-90NIS. Daily 0830-0400.

Entertainment
Acco Theater Centre, 1 Weizman, T04-9913834/9919634, www.acco-tc.com. Social theatre involving Arab and Jewish artists, which seeks to stimulate Israeli engagement with the political situation. Performances in Arabic/English/Hebrew, check website for programme.
American Corner, A-Saraya, (near Al-Jazzar mosque), T04-9558277, http://aca.usac.gov. A nicely renovated little community centre in the old city. Mon and Wed 0800-1400, Thu 0800-1800. Free library with magazines, books, DVDs, use of internet (for educational searches).

Festivals and events
During Sukkot (Oct) the **Akko Festival** takes place over 5 days with theatrical and other events in the streets and subterranean city; fun, food and fringe theatrical events.

Activities and tours
Though primarily for use by residents, there are a number of sports facilities available at the **Palm Beach Hotel and Country Club** (see 'Sleeping' on page 530).

Short boat tours are also available from Fisherman's Harbour, during high seasons, weekends and holidays.

There is a fishing tackle shop close to El-Mualek Mosque.

Transport
Bus
Akko's Central Bus Station is on Ha-Arba'a. Southbound buses 271, 361 and 500 every 10 mins or so to **Haifa** (13NIS, 45 mins). For destinations further south change at Haifa. Northbound, Bus 271 goes to **Nahariya** (8.5NIS, 35 mins). There is also regular bus 361 from Akko to **Safed** (1½ hrs, 29.5NIS) via Karmi'el.

Sherut/service taxi
The main sherut stand for services to **Haifa** (11NIS), **Nahariya** and sometimes **Safed** is opposite the bus station (including Shabbat).

Train
Akko's train station is one block behind the bus station, www.rail.co.il. Train is the most enjoyable and quickest way to go south to **Haifa** (30 mins), **Tel Aviv** (1¾ hrs) etc, departing every half hour Sun-Thu 0500-2200, Fri 0500-1420, Sat 2115-2315, and north to **Nahariya** (10 mins) every 15 mins.

Directory
Banks Most of the banks (with ATM machines also) are located along Weizmann and Ben Ammi. Post offices offer good-value foreign exchange. **Hospitals** The main hospital is north of the New City (see map), though there is a first-aid post at the junction of Ben Ammi and HaHaganah. **Internet** Hostels are the best place to access the internet, see sleeping above. **Post offices** The main post office is at 11 Ha'Atzma'ut, and offers post restante and foreign exchange. There are branch offices on Ben Ammi and on El-Jazzar (Sun-Fri 0800-1800).

Around Akko

Bahje House and Baha'i Gardens
ⓘ *T04-9811569. Shrine Fri-Mon 0900-1200; Persian Gardens daily 0900-1600. Free. Bus 271 from Akko; tell the driver where you want to get off.*
About 3 km north of Akko is Bahje, the holiest pilgrimage site to followers of the Baha'i faith. Baha'ullah, founder of the religion, lived here under house arrest in the red tile-roofed

Josephus in Jotapata

Though little remains to see today, the former location of Jotapata (now Yodfat, 20 km southeast of Akko) was the site of a key battle in the First Jewish Revolt (66-73 CE). Scene of one of the historian Josephus' greatest moments (in his eyes at least), it is one of those sites where it really pays to stand with a copy of Josephus' *The Jewish War* in your hand and read the relevant passages of text (III, 158; III, 383).

Yodfat was perhaps the strongest of the fortified Galilean villages controlled by Josephus, prior to his switch of allegiance to the Romans. Such was the strength of Jotapata that it took 47 days of bitter fighting before the Romans finally overran the town. Josephus estimates that 40,000 were killed in the battle, with many of the defenders preferring suicide to surrender.

Josephus himself managed to escape this grisly end, hiding in a cave with some 40 others. Against his wishes, his 40 companions entered a suicide pact, rather than submit to the Romans. In an excellent passage that sums up the author, Josephus describes how lots were drawn to establish who would kill whom (so that nobody would have to die by their own hand). Miraculously, by 'divine providence', it was Josephus who was left as last man alive! Yet, perhaps unsurprisingly, an early Slavonic translation dispels this notion of 'divine providence' interceding on Josephus' behalf. Referring to the lottery, it says of Josephus, "he counted the numbers cunningly and so managed to deceive the others"!

Bahje House following his release from Akko prison. He died here in 1892 and is buried in a small shrine, where there is also a little museum. The beautiful Persian Gardens, laid out in the 1950s, are considered by many people to be more enchanting than their more famous counterparts in Haifa. For more information on the Baha'i faith, see page 506. **NB** Main entrance gate is for Baha'is only: other visitors must enter through the side gate 500 m beyond. This is a holy religious shrine and visitors must be modestly dressed.

Beit Lohamei Ha-Geta'ot and el-Jazzar's aqueduct
ⓘ *T04-9958052. Sun-Thu 0900-1600 (last entry 1500). Admission 25NIS.*
Several kilometres north of Bahje is the kibbutz of Lohamei Ha-Geta'ot (Hebrew for 'fighters of the ghetto'), founded in 1949 by survivors of the Nazi Holocaust. A small museum has been set up to commemorate those who died in the camps and ghettoes. The museum contains the booth in which Adolf Eichmann sat during his 1961 trial in Jerusalem. Next door is the **Yad Layelad Museum** ⓘ *T04-9958044*, in remembrance of the 1.5 million child victims of the holocaust; a visit is a moving experience.

Standing just to the south of the museum is a superbly preserved section of Ahmed el-Jazzar's aqueduct, built in 1780 to supply Akko with water from the Kabri spring to the north. Large sections of the aqueduct can be seen almost the whole way from Akko to Nahariya.

Shavei Zion
This settlement has a beautiful setting, amongst orange groves and avocado orchards, fronting on to an uncrowded stretch of Mediterranean beach (fee paying). This part of the coastline has been a rich hunting ground for marine archaeologists, with the wreck of a fifth-century CE ship off the coast of Shavei Zion revealing an interesting cargo.

In 1955 a **Byzantine church** was discovered amongst the groves of Shavei Zion, complete with an extensive **mosaic pavement**. The designs are reasonably simple, featuring crosses, pomegranates and fish, though they are quite well executed. A ten-line Greek inscription in the narthex (antechamber to the nave) mentions the name of the donor, and the date 485-486 CE. The kibbutz is 7 km north of Akko; bus 271 stops at the turning for Shavei Zion from where it's a short walk.

North and inland of Akko

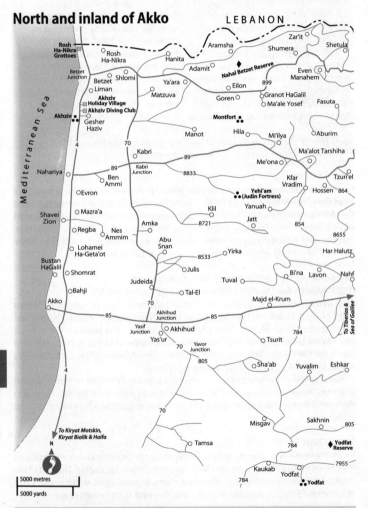

There are few reminders of Nahariya's ancient past (the biblical Helbah/Heleph), with the modern town presenting itself as a laid-back beach resort. It's a pleasant enough place, although the beach isn't quite nice enough, nor the range of accommodation quite broad enough, to make it a really outstanding holiday spot.

Ins and outs

Getting there and away The whole town is compact enough to get around on foot. The train station is at the eastern end of the main road, HaGa'Aton, with all trains running to Akko, Haifa, Netanya and Tel Aviv. The Central Bus Station, also on HaGa'Aton, has regular connections to Akko and Haifa, and is also the transport hub for excursions to Akhziv, Montfort, Peki'in and Rosh Ha-Nikra.

Tourist Information The **Municipal Tourist Office** ⓘ *Ground Floor, Municipality Building, T04-9879800, Sun-Thu 0900-1300 and 1600-1900, Fri 0900-1200,* has free maps, brochures, plus advice on renting rooms.

Background

Nahariya's Canaanite origins, plus its Persian/Hellenistic remains, are largely buried beneath the modern town, and there are few remains from its Roman and Byzantine periods. The modern town takes its name from the Nahal Ga'Aton (river) that still flows along the centre of the main street (HaGa'Aton).

The town was the first Jewish settlement in Western Galilee, and was founded in 1933 by German Jews fleeing Hitler. Attempts at agriculture were not particularly successful and thus, taking advantage of Nahariya's clean beaches and rural setting, the idea was born of turning the town into a tourist resort. The rest, as they say, is history, though the tourism industry was hit badly in the 1970s and early 1980s when the town became the occasional target for Katyusha rockets fired from inside Lebanon. Being just 10 km from the border, Nahariya suffered the same fate during the 2006 Hezbollah rocket attacks but, despite this, tourism forms a major sector of the town's economy, though light industry is probably a larger employer. About 50,000 people now live in Nahariya.

Sights

Beaches on northern coast Nahariya's prime attraction is its beaches, though it must be said there are better beaches on Israel's northern coast. The main strip of sand, Galei Galil Beach, has showers, life-guards and a breakwater just off shore. Other facilities include a large outdoor pool, kids' pool and heated indoor pool (daily 0800-1700, entrance fees apply). A popular past-time is taking a horse and cart around town; you will have no trouble spotting one should you wish to take a ride. There are free beaches north and south of Galei Galil, but take care in the heavy surf.

Canaanite temple The scant remains of a Canaanite temple and bamah (cultic high place or altar platform) are located 20 minutes' walk north of Galei Galil Beach. Most remains date to the Middle Bronze Age IIB (1750-1550 BCE), though some are older. When the earlier temple fell into disuse, the bamah was constructed, with offerings brought to honour the goddess of the sea, Asherah. A second temple was then erected to the north of the bamah. There is little to see today, though some artefacts from the site are displayed in the Municipal Museum.

Municipal Museum ① *5th-7th floors, Municipality Building, HaGa'Aton, T04-9879863. Sun-Fri 1000-1200, Sun and Wed also 1600-1800. Free.*

This small museum has four themes: 'archaeology of Western Galilee', 'art', 'malacology' and 'history of Nahariya', with the collection of sea-shells (malacology) and artefacts from the surrounding area (archaeology) being the most interesting exhibits.

Byzantine church mosaic pavement ① *Bielefeld, near Giv'at Katzenelson School: see map. Arrange a visit through the Tourist Information Office, T04-9879800, admission 4NIS.*

In the early 1970s, the remains of a Byzantine basilical triapsidal church were excavated in the Giv'at Katzenelson neighbourhood. The church has a beautiful mosaic pavement, with typical Byzantine flora and fauna designs in addition to hunting scenes, and is certainly worth the effort of arranging a visit.

Nahariya listings

For Sleeping and Eating price codes and other relevant information, see Essentials pages 26-31.

Sleeping

For a town billing itself as a seaside resort there are surprisingly few hotels, and a pretty poor spread across the price categories (nothing for budget travellers). Note that prices sky-rocket during weekends and Jewish holidays, especially the 'honeymoon season' that follows Lag Ba'Omer.

L Carlton, 23 Ha Ga'Aton, T04-9005555, www.carlton-nahariya.com. Used to be the biggest and best in town; rooms spacious,

Nahariya

To Canaanite Temple remains

To Akhziv, Rosh Ha-Nikra, & Lebanese border

GIV'AT KATZENELSON

Steinmetz Max

Galei Galil Beach

Hama'apilim

Ha Aliya

Jabotinsky

Indoor Pool

Hameyas Dim

Weizmann

Pinsker

David Eliezer

Ha Aliya

Reich Shimon

Golomb

Ha Haganah

Wolfson

Byzantine Church

Kibbutz Galuyot

Struma

Yechiam

HaGilad

HaSharon

To hospital, Mi'ilya Montfort, Yehi'am & Pek'in

Mediterranean Sea

Bike Shop

HaGa'aton

Ben Zvi Hanussi

GIV'AT USSISHKIN

Playground

Amphitheatre and playground

Sinai

Municipality Building & Municipal Museum

Sokolov Nachum

Balfour

David Remez

Szold Henrietta

Weizmann

Agnon Shai

Ahad Ha'am

Herzl

Keren Hayesod

Lochamei HaGetaot

Ha'Atzma'ut

- - - - Possible boundary of Canaanite settlement

- - - - Possible boundary of Persian/Hellenistic settlement

To Mini-golf, Akko & Haifa

N

200 metres
200 yards

🛏 **Sleeping**
2 Carlton
3 Erna
4 Frank
1 Park Plaza
5 Rosenblatt

🍴 **Eating**
1 Kapulsky
2 Pengiun & El Gaucho
3 Singapore

⭕ **Other**
1 Supermarket
2 Steimatzky (bookshop)

some more attractive with sun terrace and garden/pool view ($45 extra), a/c, TV, large pool (covered and heated in winter), health club, sauna and spa, restaurant; reputation for good service.

L Park Plaza, 17 HaAliya, T04-9000248. Nahariya's newest hotel is a real blessing, with good beach views from the upper storeys. Modern facilities aren't especially stylish, but rooms have kitchenettes, there's good food in the restaurant, free use of the adjacent country club's large pool, tennis courts, and other sports and leisure facilities. Bonus is free access to their private beach. Recommended.

A Erna, 29 Jabotinsky, T04-9920170, www.hotelerna.info. In quiet residential neighbourhood, small hotel with 30 rooms, newly remodelled, nice sunny patio, short walk to the beach, bar, breakfast included; very clean with good service, rooms have a/c, TV, fridge.

A Frank, 4 HaAliya, T04-9920278, www.hotel-frank.co.il. Rooms are quite large with picture windows, a/c, TV. Though old-fashioned and rather shabby it's very clean. There's a bar, free Wi-Fi; buffet breakfast nothing special, and the staff can be lack-lustre.

B Rosenblatt, 59 Weizmann, T04-/9923469, jael@wall.co.il. Chalet rooms with a/c, TV, popular with returning guests, reasonable value - one of the more affordable at 250NIS for a double (no breakfast).

Apartment rental and B&Bs

Signs advertising 'rooms for rent' (Tzimerrim) can be found all over town, though your best bet is to go to the Municipal Tourist Office and obtain their list of registered places. Most have 8 to 12 double rooms with en suite, sharing a common kitchen. Discounts are available for longer stays, and bargaining may be in order.

Eating

The usual collection of falafel, shwarma and pizza places are located along HaGa'Aton. There are a couple of supermarkets opposite the bus station.

¶¶-¶¶ **El Gaucho**, Ha Ga'Aton, T04-9928635. The popular Argentinian grill chain, serving big lunches and a wide-ranging meaty menu. The interior takes the cow-theme rather too far, there's also a nice terrace area. Daily 1200-2400.

¶¶ **Penguin**, 31 Ha Ga'Aton, T9928855. Popular informal atmosphere, excellent schnitzels, blintzes, light meals, salads etc. This is 'the' place everyone eats in Nahariya, and has been for many years. There's also the Penguin Café outside. Daily 0800-2300.

¶¶ **Singapore**, corner of Jabotinsky and Hameyasdim, T04-9924952. A reliable Chinese restaurant, with set meals that are good value. Daily 1200-1500 and 1900-2400.

¶ **Kapulsky** has a restaurant serving cakes and light meals on the promenade at the end of HaGa'Aton.

Bars and clubs

There are a number of bars in the blocks opposite the bus station and the Municipality, plus several places on the seafront at the western end of Ha Ga'Aton.

Entertainment
Folkdancing

On the promenade every Wed and Sat at 2100 in Jul and Aug.

Transport
Bus

Nahariya's Central Bus Station is at 3 Ha Ga'Aton; the main bus service is the 271 to **Haifa** (every 10-15 mins, 0500-2245, 40 mins, 16.5NIS) via **Akko** (20 mins, 8.5NIS).

Nahariya is also the transport junction for visiting a number of places inland and to the north:

Akhziv: Nateev bus 22, 24, 27, 28, 32 and 33, 0705-1430, 15 mins. **Montfort**: Nateev buses 41, 44 and 45 to Mi'ilya (then walk), approximately hourly 0715-1430, 15 mins. **Peki'in**: Nateev bus 44 and 45, every hour or so 0715-2210, to Peki'in Jct. **Rosh Ha-Nikra**: Nateev bus 20, 32 and 33, every 45 mins Sun-Thu 0900-1900, Fri 0900-1500, Sat 2130, to Bezet junction then 3km uphill walk to the site. **Yehi'am**: Nateev bus 39 and 42 at 1200, 1700, 2000 and 2120.

Sheruts

Run from outside the Central Bus Station, and from the junction of Ha Ga'Aton and Ha'Atzma'ut, north to Bezet junction (via Akhziv), and south to Akko.

Train

Nahariya's train station is at 1 Ha Ga'Aton, at the junction with Ha'Atzma'ut. All trains stop at **Akko** (10 mins), **Haifa** (30 mins) and **Tel** Aviv (1½-2 hrs), slower ones call at stations in between: Sun-Thu every half hr, 0500-2200; Fri last at 1430, Sat 4 trains 2115-2315.

Directory

Banks There are several ATMs in the centre of town. **Hospital** The Municipal Hospital is on Ben Zvi Hanassi (T9850505) to the east of town, across from the main Rosh Ha-Nikra to Akko road (Ha'Atzma'ut). **Post offices** The main branch is at 40 Ha Ga'Aton, T9920180, and offers poste restante and commission-free foreign exchange.

Montfort → *Colour map 1, B3*

Though not the most spectacular Crusader castle in the Holy Land, Montfort has a very picturesque setting, and a visit can be combined with a short hike through an attractive nature reserve.

Ins and outs

Getting there and away There are two ways of getting to Montfort – from the north or the south – both of which involve some very pleasant walking. The easiest approach is via the Christian Arab village of **Mi'ilya** to the south, on Route 89. From the sign-post announcing Mi'ilya, head uphill, following the main road through the village, and out and down the other side. Beyond Mi'ilya the paved road takes a sharp 90-degree bend to the right (20 minutes' walk). From here you have two choices. If you follow the paved road turning right at the 90-degree bend, after 200 m on your left is a **lookout point** and car park. From here it is possible to make a four-hour walking loop down to the castle and back up to Mi'ilya. Follow the black-and-white marked trail down to **Nahal Keziv**, then take the green-and-white trail along the river (Nahal Keziv/Wadi Qurein), before joining the red-and-white trail up to the castle and back to Mi'ilya. There is plenty of shade *en route*, though you should make sure that you have a hat/sunblock and plenty of drinking water.

The alternative approach from Mi'ilya is by turning left at the 90-degree bend after the village, and heading along the dirt track. About 100 m down the track the path forks. The left fork is part of the black-and-white trail to **Horbat Bilton** and **Nahal Sha'ar**, whilst the right fork follows the red-and-white trail down to **Nahal Keziv** and **Montfort**. Following the red-and-white trail downhill, it branches to the right after ten minutes' walking. Follow this path down into **Nahal Keziv Nature Reserve**, where the trail becomes lined on either side by trees. After walking through this avenue of trees for 10 minutes, a set of stone steps leads off to your right. You can either take the steps or walk for another 100 m and scramble up the rocks marked by the red-and-white trail. Both routes lead to a narrow path, before you get your first glimpse of the castle ruins ahead. You approach the castle close to the smaller, additional moat from where you can scramble up the castle walls to the keep. Return to Mi'ilya by the same route (though it's now uphill all the way), or continue along the red-and-white trail to **Goren Park**.

The approach to Montfort from the north is via **Goren Park**, which is on Route 899 from Rosh HaNikra. The red-and-white trail descends from Goren Park, and after an hour's walk you reach Montfort. From here you can continue on to Mi'ilya. You ideally need a car to reach the access points to Montfort, but you can try hitching. If you wish to arrive at the castle by one route and leave by another, it is recommended that you arrive via Goren Park and leave through Mi'ilya.

Background

Today, much of Montfort lies in ruins following its surrender to the Mamluk sultan **Baibars** in 1271, after a brief siege in which the Muslim forces breached the outer walls and much of the inner western defences. The Crusaders were permitted to surrender and retreat to Acre, though without their arms. Baibars dismantled much of Montfort to prevent its reoccupation.

However, when constructed in 1226 it was the main Crusader fortress in Palestine of the **Knights of the Teutonic Order** (Teutonic Knights). The castle stands on a narrow ridge running east to west above the Nahal Keziv (Arabic: *Wadi Qurein*). The literal meaning of the French name Montfort is 'strong mountain', with its Latin (Mons fortis) and German (Starkenberg) names meaning the same. The fortress was part of a defensive chain protecting the Plain of Acre (Akko) that included the Chateau du Roi (formerly at Mi'ilya) and the Judin Fortress (at Yehi'am, see below). Roads were cut linking the fortresses, and connecting Montfort to Acre via the Nahal Keziv.

Sights

Walls, gates and moats Only parts of the outer defensive walls remain, though the best-preserved parts to the north and west can be seen almost in their entirety. The wall is about 2 m thick, and, like the rest of the fortress, is built with stone quarried and cut less than 1 km from here. A path runs along the top of the wall, from where the Crusaders could fire arrows through loopholes in the wall. The western fortifications look particularly impressive, though according to the Arab writer Ibn Furat (who may have witnessed the battle and describes the siege in some detail), the Muslims breached this area in some strength.

Montfort Castle

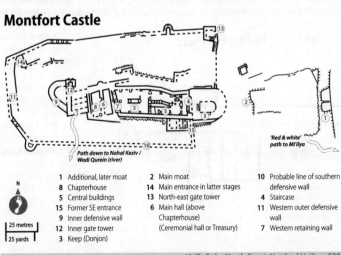

N

25 metres
25 yards

1	Additional, later moat	2	Main moat	10	Probable line of southern defensive wall
8	Chapterhouse	14	Main entrance in latter stages	
5	Central buildings	13	North-east gate tower	4	Staircase
15	Former SE entrance	6	Main hall (above Chapterhouse) (Ceremonial hall or Treasury)	11	Western outer defensive wall
9	Inner defensive wall		7	Western retaining wall
12	Inner gate tower		
3	Keep (Donjon)		

'Red & white' path to Mi'ilya

Path down to Nahal Keziv / Wadi Qurein (river)

The main moat, 20 m wide and 11 m deep, protects the east flank of the fortress. About 50 m further east, a narrow, deep depression was expanded to form a second moat. A number of modern ladders and walkways allow you to get a better view of this additional moat.

Montfort had three main gates, and possibly a number of secondary entrances. The **main entrance gate** from the latter stages of the castle's occupation is well preserved, standing to the northwest. The path from this entrance leads to the inner gate tower, also well preserved. The **inner gate tower** is 17 m high and comprises three storeys. A gallery at the top allowed a free arc of fire for the Crusaders, whilst the bowmen could also fire through the loopholes in the storey below. The gate's entrance formed the lower floor. It is thought that this was formerly the main entrance, prior to the later construction of the northwest entrance gate. Little remains of the **southeast entrance gate**, though parts of the northeast gate tower still stand.

Keep The strongest part of the fortress, the keep (or 'donjon', as it is described when referring to Crusader architecture) is on the east side. By climbing up here you can get great views of the rest of the fortress, and the surrounding wooded hills. The keep's cellar forms a large cistern.

Central buildings Only sections of the central buildings remain, though archaeologists have been able to make guesses as to the various buildings' functions. The situation is confused, however, because several stages of construction are discernible. A row of seven Gothic columns probably supported a Gothic roof on a two-storey building. A large section of the **western retaining wall** still stands. Some sources identify this area as containing 'knights' houses', with the discovery of pieces from a stained-glass window suggesting that a church also stood here. A wine press was discovered, with other artefacts indicating workrooms and a kitchen.

Prior to the construction of the outer walls, this was the western defensive position, with the original fortress just comprising the keep and central buildings. Located amongst the later fortifications to the immediate west are two halls, preserved in

Yehi'am (Judin) Fortress

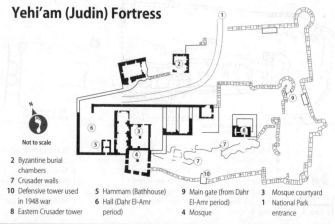

Not to scale

2 Byzantine burial
chambers
7 Crusader walls
10 Defensive tower used
in 1948 war
8 Eastern Crusader tower

5 Hammam (Bathhouse)
6 Hall (Dahr El-Amr
period)

9 Main gate (from Dahr
El-Amr period)
4 Mosque

3 Mosque courtyard
1 National Park
entrance

entirety (including ceilings). Labelled by some as the **chapterhouse**, above them stood the fortress's **main hall**. This may have been a ceremonial hall or possibly the treasury.

Cisterns A number of rock-cut cisterns for water storage have been found throughout the fortress, in addition to cellars used as reservoirs.

Outlying building A stepped path leads down to the Nahal Keziv from the southwest side of Montfort (this is how you will arrive if coming via the Goren Park or Nahal Keziv hike routes). A two-storey building on the river bank originally served the Crusaders as a flour mill, though, when the splendid Gothic ribbed-vault roofed upper storey was added, it probably served as a pilgrims' hostel.

Nahal Betzet Nature Reserve North of Goren is the beautiful Nahal Betzet Nature Reserve. There are several trails marked through the reserve, taking in giant maple forests, bathing pools, and a number of ancient ruins. The red-and-white trail leads to the hanging **Bow Cave**, a natural arch that provides stupendous views of rural Galilee. Those intending to hike in the park are advised to contact the offices of the SPNI at the field school located in Akhziv (T04-4-9522599, matan@spni.org.il).

Yehi'am (Judin) Fortress National Park ① *T04-9856004. Summer 0800-1700, winter 0800-1600, closes 1 hr earlier on Fri. Adult 13NIS, student/child 7NIS.*
The Judin Fortress was built early in the 13th century by the Templars, and subsequently bought and occupied by the Teutonic Knights. It formed part of the defensive line of fortresses protecting the Plain of Acre (Akko). Following its capture by the Mamluk sultan **Baibars** in 1265, most of the fortress was destroyed. The most impressive Crusader ruins visible today are parts of the walls and the **eastern tower**.

In the 18th century the site was occupied by a local sheik, **Mahd el-Hussein**, who rebuilt some of the fortress and turned it into his stronghold. In 1738, the stronghold was captured by **Daher al-Omer**, who substantially rebuilt the fortress, with most of the main structures visible today due to his building efforts. These include the **mosque, bathhouse** and **main hall**.

In 1946 **Kibbutz Yehi'am** was established near to the Judin Fortress. Initially occupying parts of the fortress, the kibbutz took its name from Yehi'am Weitz, one of the members of the Palmach unit killed during the 'Night of the Bridges' (see Akhziv Bridge, page 543).

Attractive trails are marked through the Yehi'am forest; there is a designated campsite (adults/children 40/30NIS), plus Kibbutz Yehi'am also has accommodation. To get there, take the Nahariya to Safed road, Route 89, turn off at Ga'aton junction and take Route 8833.

Peki'in (Bke'ah) → Colour map 1, grid B3.

① *Bus 44 from Nahariya goes about once an hour (45 mins). Disembark at Peki'in Atika, not Peki'in Hadasha one stop before.*
Peki'in (Arabic: *Bke'ah*) is an attractive hillside village in the heart of rural Galilee. Jewish sources claim that it is the only village in Israel with an uninterrupted Jewish presence since the time of the Second Temple (destroyed 70 CE). Today, the village has a mixed population (though predominantly Druze), with the diversity of beliefs reflected in the range of religious institutions; a Druze Hilwes (House of Prayer), a Greek Catholic church, a Greek Orthodox church (built in 1894 on the ruins of the ancient church of St Gregory), several mosques, and a 19th-century synagogue.

The village is particularly important to Jews as it is believed to be the spot where **Rabbi Shimon Bar Yochai**, and his son **Eliezer**, fled from Roman persecution during the second century CE. A Roman decree banned the study of the Torah, but for 12 years the pair hid in a small cave in the hillside and continued their study. It was during this period of contemplation that the rabbi produced a number of thoughts and teachings that later found their way into the *Zohar*, the treatise on Jewish mysticism first written down in the 1280s CE.

The **Cave of Rabbi Shimon Bar Yochai** is the village's main attraction today, though it can be a little hard to find, and is sure to disappoint. Despite signs announcing that the cave is a holy religious site, it is poorly cared for.

Though the key site in Peki'in is rather unexciting, this is a pleasant village to visit, without such commercial trappings of Druze villages such as Isfiya and Daliyat el-Carmel (see 'Around Haifa' section on page 518). There are a couple of friendly café/restaurants at the western entrance to the village.

Akhziv National Park → *Colour map 1, grid B2.*

ⓘ *T04-9823263. Summer 0800-1900, winter 0800-1700. Adult 30NIS, child 18NIS.*
The Akhziv National Park is an excellent place to come for a picnic and a bathe, with a small stretch of beach that must rank as one of the most attractive along this stretch of coastline. A natural breakwater shelters the beach, forming a shallow wading pool and a deeper 'natural' swimming pool, plus there is an artificial pool. As a backdrop to the beach there are a number of 'antiquities' that hint at Akhziv's long and historical past, plus modern facilities such as showers, toilets, changing rooms, picnic tables and cafés. Ancient Akhziv (Achziv) dates back to the beginning of the Middle Bronze Age (c. 2200 BCE), and was settled continuously until the Crusader period, when it was called Castle Humbert. Camping is permitted at the national park (adults/children 60/50NIS).

Just to the north of the National Park, an old Arab mansion stands at the centre of a

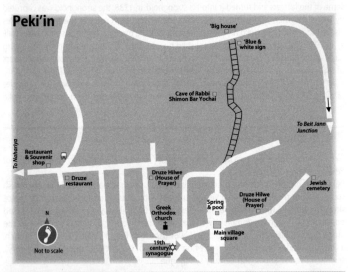

plot of land. An eccentric by the name of Eli Avivi settled here in 1952, making a unilateral declaration of independence! Now you can visit the 'state' of Akhzivland, even getting a stamp in your passport if you wish. A small collection of finds from the local area are displayed in Eli's museum (admission 10NIS). It's possible to stay here overnight, though some horror stories exist concerning lone females who have stopped here.

Akhziv listings

For Sleeping and Eating price codes and other relevant information, see Essentials pages 26-31.

Sleeping
Achziv Holiday Village, just north of the National Park, T04-9823602, F9826030. Attractive wooden a/c huts on the beach, all with sea views, some suited to couples and others to families. Has all the rural ambiance

of a campsite but with a bit of luxury (jacuzzis, spa), and the sea is very clean here. Go during the week or at the beginning of summer, when it feels quite romantic (at other times you will get little peace). Prices drop in winter. The restaurant is nothing special.
AL-A SPNI Field School, 4 km north of Nahariyya, T04-9522599, matan@spni.org. il. Attractive a/c rooms, kosher dining hall, lovely views of Rosh HaNikra's cliffs and the Mediterranean, prices include breakfast.

Akhziv Bridge and Yad Le-Yad Memorial

Just to the north of Akhziv is the Yad Le-Yad Memorial, a monument to a bizarre incident during the 'Night of the Bridges' in the British Mandate period. On the night of 17 June 1946, in an attempt to disrupt the communication lines of the British, a unit of the Palmach

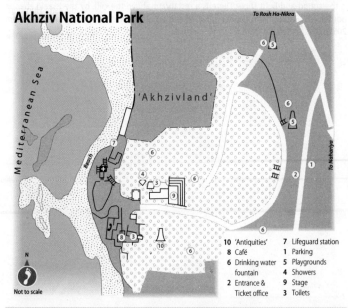

Akhziv National Park

To Rosh Ha-Nikra

Mediterranean Sea

'Akhzivland'

Beach

To Nahariyya

Not to scale

N

10 'Antiquities'	7 Lifeguard station
8 Café	1 Parking
6 Drinking water fountain	5 Playgrounds
	4 Showers
2 Entrance & Ticket office	9 Stage
	3 Toilets

(the striking arm of the Jewish resistance) attempted to blow up the railway bridge at Akhziv. The 14 members of the demolition team were spotted by a British sentry, who then fired a flare to illuminate the scene. By bizarre chance the flare ignited the team's explosives, blowing up the bridge but also killing all the members of the Palmach unit. The Yad Le-Yad Memorial ('memorial to the fourteen') stands near to the site of the incident.

Rosh Ha-Nikra

ⓘ *T04-9857109, www.rosh-hanikra.com. Sat-Thu 0900-1800 (winter 0900-1600), Fri 0900-1600. Adult 43NIS, student/child 35NIS. Ride on the toy-train to Akhziv (40 mins), Sat/hols only, 1100-1500, 20NIS. Sheruts from Nahariya go directly to the site, leaving from Lohamei HaGettaot Street.*

Straddling Israel's border with Lebanon are spectacular chalk cliffs from which thousands of years of wave action have cut a series of grottoes and blow-holes. Referred to in antiquity as the 'Ladders of Tyre', the wave-cut caverns are said to have been expanded by **Alexander the Great** in 323 BCE to allow passage for his army during the siege of Tyre (31 km north). Following the Arab conquest, the site became known as A-Nawakir ('the grottoes') and subsequently Ras-A-Nakura. The present name is the Hebraicized version.During World War I the tunnels were widened by the **British** to allow the passage of motor vehicles, and during World War II further tunnels were dug to accommodate the Beirut to Haifa railway.

The **sea grottoes** are now marketed as a tourist attraction, with a very brief cable car ride providing access. A walk through the grottoes takes no more than 5-10 minutes, though it can be an exhilarating experience, particularly if the sea is rough. **NB** Swimming here is both illegal and highly dangerous. Also included in the price of your entrance ticket is the sound-and-light show There is a restaurant above the cliff, by the Israel/Lebanon border. **NB** Photography is not permitted at the border, except in front of the "Jerusalem 205km, Beirut 120 km" sign.

Contents

Galilee

With the possible exception of Jerusalem, there are probably more 'unmissable' places in the Galilee than in any other part of Israel. This is not just a function of the region's long and eventful human history and importance within Judaism and Christianity, but also a reflection of the Galilee's supreme natural beauty. Places where Jesus preached and Jewish sages compiled their treatises on the Law compete for attention with lush waterscapes, rolling hills and rugged mountains.

Time is well-spent by the hazy blue of the Sea of Galilee, in Hebrew the 'Kinneret', where cliffs and ancient settlements meet the magical shores. Another highlight is exploring the timeless streets of living cities, be it the maze-like Arab markets of old Nazareth dotted with churches or the winding alleys of the Jewish quarter of Tzfat with its picturesque synagogues and artists shops.

Those who like their history can choose from the Bronze Age, Iron Age, Hellenistic, Roman, Byzantine or medieval periods, with some sites conveniently providing remains from all six. Be it the perfectly preserved mosaics of Zippori, the grandiose Roman theatre of Bet Shean or the elaborate Israelite water system of Armageddon (Megiddo), this is another area that deserves extensive exploration.

A further major draw of the Galilee is the wide variety of interesting and beautifully located guest-houses; whether you are after a one-off zimmer with all the trimmings, or a simple tent in a moshav, there really is something for everyone. And this focus on quality accommodation comes hand-in-hand with some of the best dining opportunities in the country – many Israelis seem to come here simply to eat fabulous food!

Geography

The Galilee has clearly defined geographical boundaries. To the south is the Jezreel Valley (or Plain of Esdraelon), forming the boundary with the northern hills of the West Bank (Samaria), whilst to the west is the former Phoenician coast of the Mediterranean. The geographical boundary to the north is formed by the Litani River, though the political boundary is the border with Lebanon. And in the east the Syrian-African Rift Valley, through which the Jordan River flows, forms both a physical and political boundary.

Galilee is characterized by a number of low mountain ranges, with rolling hills interspersed by fertile valleys that afford easy passage. Most of the bedrock is chalk, limestone and dolomite, with basalt-covered areas to the east and into Golan. Upper Galilee is quite mountainous, dominated by the chalk and limestone Meiron range to the west of Safed. The rest of Upper Galilee comprises the 'Galilee Finger' of the Hula Valley running from the Sea of Galilee up to the Lebanese border at Metulla. Terrain has dictated the pattern of human settlement and movement throughout the Galilee, with the most densely populated areas being the plains of Lower Galilee, and the Jezreel Valley in particular. The Sea of Galilee has also been a major focus of the region.

Climate

Galilee has a Mediterranean climate, moderated by altitude. Average temperatures are higher and levels of rainfall lower in Lower Galilee when compared with Upper Galilee. The best time to visit is in spring and autumn, thus avoiding the winter rains (60 days per year in Upper Galilee, mainly in January and February), and the excesses of summer heat in the lower areas (Tiberias is particularly muggy in summer). Though bear in mind that elevated towns, such as Safed, get pretty chilly in the winter months, and snow is not unknown.

Vegetation

The abundant water (both precipitation and ground water), plus the relatively low levels of population density, has allowed the Galilee to retain the country's richest diversity of vegetation. The natural vegetation is Mediterranean forest, a surprising amount of which has been preserved by the establishment of protected nature reserves. The Jezreel Valley provides the country's richest agricultural land. The impression of the Galilee that most people take away with them is one of green valleys dividing wooded rolling hills.

Background

Galilee's long and rich history has been largely influenced by its physical geography. In particular, wide valleys such as the Jezreel became integral parts of international trading routes such as the Via Maris, connecting Egypt to Babylonia via the Galilee. It has also become a major theatre of war, with the first written account of a military battle (Pharaoh Thutmose III's defeat of the Canaanites in 1468 BCE) taking place in the Jezreel Valley before Megiddo. The Israelites' return to the Promised Land saw the tribes of Naphtali, Zebulun and Asher settled in the Galilee (Joshua 19), with the tribe of Dan arriving later (Judges 18). However, despite Deborah's victory in 1125 BCE, many of the fortified cities still remained under the control of the Canaanites. The first king of the United Monarchy, Saul, also suffered defeat in Lower Galilee before his successors David and Solomon conquered the region. Israelite control was short-lived, however, with the Assyrian king Tiglath-pileser III sweeping through the region in 733-32 BCE, with no new significant Jewish settlement in the region until the Hasmonean era of Alexander Jannaeus (103-76 BCE).

The Early Roman period saw much of Galilee controlled by Herod the Great, and subsequently his successors, and witnessed the establishment of predominantly Jewish towns such as Sepphoris and Tiberias. Peace in the Galilee was short-lived, however, the region being the scene of many key events in the early stages of the Jewish Revolt (66-67 CE) against Rome that Josephus describes so colourfully. A number of ancient synagogues that have been found across the Galilee hint at the conscious separation of the Jewish and pagan communities from the mid-third century onwards. This is a reflection of the growing importance of Galilee to the Jews following the destruction of the Temple at Jerusalem in the first century CE, with the shifting of the Sanhedrin to Bet She'aram, and then Zippori and Tiberias.

The Byzantine period (324-638 CE) was a time of great prosperity in the Galilee, with the expansion of existing settlements and the founding of new ones. It also saw the development of religious and economic competition, as Christianity became established. In Upper Galilee Christianity does not appear to have encroached into Jewish areas, though in Lower Galilee it certainly did. The bitter rivalry between the competing communities is perhaps best reflected in the Persian invasion of 613-14 CE, when the Galilee's Jews assisted the invading army in persecuting the region's Christian community. Roles were reversed when the Byzantine army reasserted its authority 15 years later.

The Arab invasion of 638 CE dealt a serious blow to the Christians, though the Jewish communities appear to have been left unmolested. Subsequent Christian-Muslim rivalries, in particular the Crusades, dominate the medieval history of the Galilee. Many great battles were fought here (most notably the crushing defeat of the Crusaders by the army of Salah al-Din at the Horns of Hattin in 1187) and have left a legacy of spectacular fortresses perched on high mountain tops. The Galilee was subsequently in Muslim hands for the next six centuries until the final defeat of the Ottoman Turks during the Palestine campaign of World War I (1918). The British ruled Galilee for the next 30 years or so until the expiry of their Mandate for Palestine. The United Nations Partition Recommendation (1947) envisaged a divided Galilee, with the eastern and western blocks apportioned to the Jews, and a wide swathe through the centre from Nazareth to Lebanon to be part of a future Arab state. The Arab rejection of this plan, and the subsequent war, saw the whole of the Galilee fall into Israeli hands. The Galilee is now home to 17% of Israel's population, including a sizeable Arab minority, with an economy based largely upon agriculture, tourism and light industry.

Lower Galilee

In Nazareth and the surrounding countryside lie some of Christendom's most significant and beautiful churches, ruins from Canaanite, Jewish and Byzantine cities, and some splendid walking along the route of the 'Jesus Trail'. Reckon on about four days for a thorough and leisurely exploration of the area.

Nazareth → *Colour map 1, grid B3.*

The large Arab town of Nazareth is one of the most important Christian pilgrimage destinations in the Holy Land. Though the place of Jesus' childhood, plus later scenes in his life (including an appearance before his disciples following his resurrection), Nazareth is most revered as the site of the Annunciation: the Archangel Gabriel's appearance before the Virgin Mary at which he announced the impending birth of Jesus. A number of churches mark the traditional sites of the key Christian events in Nazareth.

Ins and outs

Getting there and away The majority of visitors arrive as part of a tour, but Nazareth is easy to visit independently and can even be a day trip from Haifa or Tiberias (both just one hour away on the bus). But then you would miss out on Nazareth's famed dining culture and interesting selection of accommodation.

Getting around Most of Nazareth's key attractions are within walking distance of each other, though visitors should be prepared for some steep climbs if they wish to visit all the various churches and monasteries on the hillside above the town centre. The focus of the downtown area is the Basilica of the Annunciation, also Nazareth's most

Nazareth

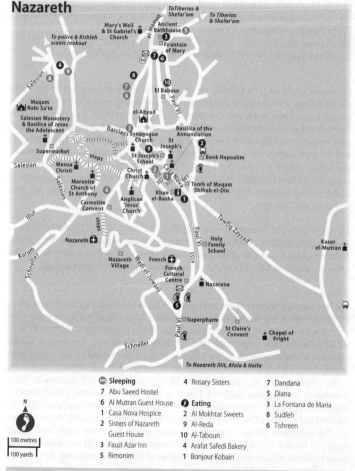

🛏 Sleeping	4 Rosary Sisters	7 Dandana
7 Abu Saeed Hostel		5 Diana
6 Al Mutran Guest House	🍴 Eating	3 La Fontana de Maria
1 Casa Nova Hospice	2 Al Mokhtar Sweets	8 Sudfeh
2 Sisters of Nazareth	9 Al-Reda	6 Tishreen
Guest House	10 Al-Taboun	
3 Fauzi Azar Inn	4 Arafat Safedi Bakery	
5 Rimonim	1 Bonjour Kobain	

Jesus of ... Nazareth?

Christian scholars are still divided as to whether Joseph and Mary actually lived in Nazareth prior to the birth of Jesus. It is suggested that were Nazareth their home town, they would be more likely to have fled there, rather than Egypt, when Herod began to implement his infanticide. With Joseph being of a Judean family, and Egypt being a common refuge for fleeing Judeans, circumstantial evidence could be said to support the interpretation of Matthew's gospel (*Matthew 2*) that the couple were from Bethlehem. The family could well have moved north to Nazareth to escape the potentially murderous attentions of Herod's successor, his son Archelaus (4 BCE-6 CE). Murphy-O'Connor (*The Holy Land*, 1992) also suggests that Joseph may well have been encouraged north by Herod Antipas' recruitment drive for artisans to work on his new capital at Sepphoris. Luke's clear assertion that the family were originally from Nazareth (*Luke 2:4*) may have been based on the premise that since Jesus was brought up there as a child (*Matthew 13:54; Luke 4:16*), and had relatives there (Matthew 13:55-56), his parents were actually born there.

prominent landmark. The twisting alleyways of the old Arab souq just to the north can be initially confusing, and it may take some wandering back and forth to find the various sites located in this area (the map is vastly over-simplified). It can also be a little frustrating if you are attempting to find the right path/flight of steps up to the various sites on the hillside above the town; you can often see the church/monastery but can't find the path leading there. Locals will point you in the right direction. **NB** Remember, you will be denied access to most sites unless you are suitably dressed (no shorts for either sex, no bare shoulders, etc). A number of women have complained of harassment whilst visiting Nazareth. Dressing conservatively may go some way towards reducing this unwanted attention.

Tourist information **Tourist Information Office** ① *Bishara, T04-6573003/6570555, Mon-Fri 0830-1700, Sat 0900-1300.* Brochure and maps available, pick up a copy of *What's Up in Nazareth* which is useful for phone numbers/restaurants rather than current events. The office can also book tickets for church services during the main Christian festivals.

Background

The first written references to Nazareth appear in the New Testament, though excavations in the vicinity of the Basilica of the Annunciation have unearthed at least one cave containing a number of artefacts dating to the Middle Bronze Age II (2000-1550 BCE), whilst a second cave shows remarkable similarity to the Bronze Age caves at nearby Megiddo. A fairly large necropolis from the Roman/Byzantine periods has been discovered, mainly across the hill to the west of the Basilica of the Annunciation.

Despite Nazareth's importance within Christianity, the picture of the early-Christian community here is rather confused. **Eusebius** suggests that until the sixth century CE Nazareth was a small village inhabited solely by Jews, though some sources point to the existence of a Judaeo-Christian community in the second and possibly third centuries CE. The settlement became a minor pilgrimage site in Byzantine times, with **Egeria** noting in his visit c. 380 CE that the cave (later the 'Grotto of the Annunciation') had been consecrated with an altar, and the **Pilgrim of Piacenza** mentioning the presence of two churches in his visit of c. 570 CE. Our first detailed reference to Nazareth following the **Arab** conquest of the Holy Land (c. 638 CE) comes from the pilgrim Arculf, who describes two substantial churches during his visit c. 670 CE, though later visitors during the Early Arab period (638-1099 CE) claim that the Christian community had frequently to pay bribes to the Muslims not to destroy the early Church of the Annunciation. The **Crusader** conquest of the Holy Land saw Nazareth become a major pilgrimage site, with a proliferation of church construction and the establishment of several European monastic orders.

The defeat of the Crusader Latin Kingdom at the Horns of Hattin in 1187 saw the expulsion of the Christian population of Nazareth, though a subsequent treaty between Emperor Frederick II and el-Malik el-Kamil allowed access to the city for pilgrims, and a return for a part of the permanent Christian population. When the Crusaders finally left the Holy Land in 1291 Nazareth went into a seemingly terminal decline, with one early 14th-century source describing the Muslim population of the town as being "wicked of heart, cruel and fanatical, who wreaked havoc upon all the Christian churches".

The **Ottoman** conquest of Palestine saw little change in the status of Nazareth until the Druze emir **Fakhr ed-Din** allowed a significant Christian population to return to the town. In 1620 the Franciscans established a monastery and began the reconstruction of a church on the traditional site of the Annunciation. The respite was short lived, however, and following the execution of the emir a period of persecution and discrimination resumed.

The Bedouin sheikh **Dahr el-Amr**, in the 18th century, was reasonably well disposed towards Christians and allowed considerable construction of churches and monasteries within Nazareth. The church that the Franciscans built over the site of the Annunciation stood until work on the present basilica began in 1955. Despite persecution and the threat of genocide under **Ahmed el-Jazzar** ('The Butcher') towards the end of the 18th century, Nazareth continued to grow. Greater stability in the mid-19th century saw a major increase in the volume of visitors from Europe, notably Russia, and a return to the status of a major pilgrimage site.

The Allied forces under General Allenby captured Nazareth in September 1918 as part of the campaign that saw the rout of the German-Turkish forces across the Plain of Esdraelon. The **British** made Nazareth their Galilean administrative headquarters, and, following their withdrawal from Palestine at the end of the Mandate period, the **Israelis** captured the town on 16 July 1948.

Today, Nazareth (En-Nasra) is the largest Arab town in Israel with a population split at about 40/60 between Christianity and Islam. This has led to some friction in recent years. The local council's plan to build a large piazza just below the Basilica of the Annunciation to receive the huge numbers of visitors expected in the year 2000 was scuppered by a Muslim group who claimed a mosque once stood here and demanded it should be rebuilt. The scene turned particularly ugly over Easter 1999, when a Muslim mob attacked Christian worshippers leaving the Basilica. Today this area is adorned with many pro-Islam posters, though plans to construct a mosque have been halted and the controversy has finally died down.

A large Jewish town, **Nazareth Illit** (Upper Nazareth), has developed on the hills above the Arab town; the combined population of the two towns is around 65,000. Though there is substantial industry within Nazareth, and the surrounding area is an important agricultural region, tourism remains a major sector of the local economy. Although at first sight, Nazareth is not a picture-postcard vision that conjures up Christ's early years, most tourists agree that an old-world charm lingers in the bazaars.

Sights

Basilica of the Annunciation ⓘ *04-T6554170, daily: Grotto 0545-2100, Upper Basilica 0800-1800, free; toilets available.* Dominating the lower town, the modern Basilica is built over the reputed site of the home of the Virgin Mary, the scene of the Annunciation (*Luke 1:26-38*). Consecrated in 1969, the Basilica is said to be the largest church built in the Holy Land for the best part of 800 years. The exterior design is not to everybody's liking, with it being variously likened to a giant lantern or a lighthouse. This is compensated for inside, however, by the skill of the architects in incorporating parts of the earlier places of worship that stood on this site into the bold and modern structure seen today. An evening visit is a powerful experience, when the interior is quiet and serene with those at prayer. It's also worth asking at the entrance whether any services/processions are happening on the day of your visit.

Extensive excavations were undertaken in 1955 by the Franciscan Institute for Biblical Research, unearthing a network of granaries, caves and vaulted storage cells dating to the Roman period at least. One such granary cave has subsequently been venerated as the Grotto of the Annunciation. The 1955 investigations also revealed the plan of a large three-

Grotto of the Annunciation

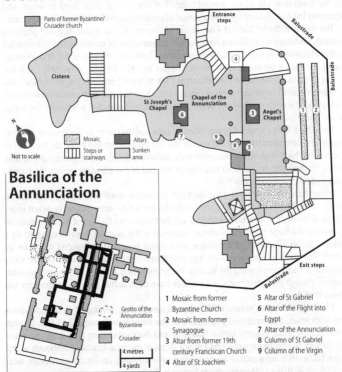

Not to scale

- Parts of former Byzantine/ Crusader church
- Mosaic
- Altars
- Steps or stairways
- Sunken area

Cistern

Entrance steps

Balustrade

Balustrade

St Joseph's Chapel

Chapel of the Annunciation

Angel's Chapel

Exit steps

Balustrade

Basilica of the Annunciation

- Grotto of the Annunciation
- Byzantine
- Crusader

4 metres

4 yards

1 Mosaic from former Byzantine Church
2 Mosaic from former Synagogue
3 Altar from former 19th century Franciscan Church
4 Altar of St Joachim
5 Altar of St Gabriel
6 Altar of the Flight into Egypt
7 Altar of the Annunciation
8 Column of St Gabriel
9 Column of the Virgin

The Jesus Trail

First – don't be put off by the name! You don't need to be clutching a Bible to enjoy this beautiful and beautiful and challenging four to five day hike following the route of Jesus' ministry. If you have the time, the Jesus Trail is one of the most rewarding ways to see the Galilee, while if your schedule is tight it's possible to choose a short section and walk just for a day, finishing at a suitable guesthouse for the night.

The 'classic' trail starts in Nazareth and goes from village-to-village via Zippori, Cana, Arbel and Tabgha to finish 62 km later at Capernaum on the Sea of Galilee. Asides from numerous sites important to Christianity, the route traverses historical remains from ancient Judaism and Islam, while also giving plenty of scope to get back to nature and be immersed in the flora and fauna of the Galilee.

This trail is feasible for everyone, from the budget-backpacker to those who want to enjoy idyllic guesthouses and gourmet restaurants on the way. Interestingly varied accommodation is hosted by folk from all walks of life be it Jew or Christian, kibbutznik or Arab, goat farmer or olive presser. Alternatively, just carry your stuff and camp, using the maps and information freely provided on www.jesustrail.com. Another option is to book a package that includes bag transportation between the guesthouses, packed lunches, a guide, entry fees and a rescue car on call .

The *Hiking the Jesus Trail* book (available in Steimatzsky's or ordered through the website) details all the sights along the way, plus it provides details on extensions/diversions to the route – including a full circuit of the Sea of Galilee.

wing Byzantine church that incorporated the Grotto within its design. Several mosaic floors have survived from the Byzantine church, and have subsequently been relaid.

The basilica that the Crusaders built in the late 12th century is considered to have been one of the most magnificent structures that they created in the Holy Land. Built on the ruins of the Byzantine church, and incorporating the Grotto and crypt, the interior was elaborately decorated by French masons as well as local craftsmen. Work was probably not yet complete when the Christian community was expelled from Nazareth following Salah al-Din's victory at Hattin in 1187. The present basilica largely follows the line of the Crusader church.

The main entrance is on Casa Nova Street, from where it is possible to admire the superb **west façade**. At the apex stands a statue of Jesus, below which in bas-relief is a representation of the angel Gabriel bringing the message to Mary. Matthew, Mark, Luke and John, together with their traditional symbols (man, lion, bull and eagle), are depicted below, along with quotations from Genesis (*3:14-15*) and Isaiah (*7:14*). Above the door is a line from the New Testament: "The Word was made flesh, and dwelt among us" (*John 1:14*).

The Basilica is built on two levels with the main entrance leading to the **Grotto of the Annunciation**. A low balustrade surrounds the sunken enclosure that contains the Grotto, where parts of the Byzantine and Crusader churches are clearly visible. Of the two parallel strips of **mosaic** opposite the cavern, the one nearest the balustrade is thought to belong to a synagogue that previously stood on this site. The second strip is from the Byzantine church. The **central altar** in this chapel comes from the 18th-century Franciscan church that previously occupied the site.

Passing the coloured glass windows that spread shafts and patterns of brightly coloured light across the lower level of the Basilica, ascend the spiral staircase into the main body of the church. The cupola of the Basilica represents an inverted lily, its roots stretching up to heaven and its petals enveloping the site of the Annunciation. The floral association is derived from the Semitic name 'Nazareth', meaning flower. Above the high altar is a huge yet unattractive mosaic depicting Jesus, arms outstretched, flanked by St Peter and a seated Virgin Mary. The ceramic reliefs and mosaics around the walls, gifts from Christian communities throughout the world, are equally hit-and-miss. Leaving the Basilica through a small side door, you come to the **Baptistry**, traditionally separated from the Basilica by a custom that forbade those who were not baptized from entering the church. Below can be seen some of the **network of caves**, oil presses, dwellings, cisterns and granaries discovered during the excavations of 1955. Some contained potsherds dating to the Israelite period (Iron Age: 1200-586 BCE), though most of the remnants found are from the Roman and Byzantine periods. The adjacent museum, displaying finds from the excavations, is only opened for groups, though individuals are welcome to tag along. Within the same compound, past the museum and monastery, is St Joseph's Church.

St Joseph's Church ① *Daily 0700-1800, free.* Identification of this site with Joseph's carpentry shop is thought to be a 17th-century tradition. The present church, built on the lines of a Crusader structure, dates to 1914. The rock-hewn grotto beneath can be viewed through a grille in the floor of the crypt. Lower levels have revealed a granary cave and a pit. Artefacts from this site have been dated to Israelite (1200-586 BCE), Hellenistic (332-37 BCE), Roman (37 BCE-324 CE), Byzantine (324-638 CE) and medieval periods. In the crypt, a 2 m by 2 m basin lined with mosaics has been cut into the floor, accessible by seven steps. Similar in style to an early baptistry found beneath the Basilica of the Annunciation, it is tentatively identified as an early baptismal pool, possibly pre-Constantine (ie prior to the fourth century CE).

Opposite the entrance to St Joseph's, the remains of a well and two-room house have recently been uncovered – ask the tourist office what the current status of this site is.

Sisters of Nazareth Convent ① *No 3, St 306, T04-6554304, F6460741, accueilnasra@live.fr. Make prior appointment, at least 48 hrs in advance.* Those staying at the Sisters of Nazareth Convent (see 'Sleeping', page 556) will already appreciate the tranquil confines of the convent's walled courtyard. By appointment it is also possible to view sections of the first-to fourth-century Jewish necropolis located beneath the convent, where there is one of the best examples in the country of a tomb sealed by a rolling stone. It is thought that the burial chamber was used as a storeroom during medieval times, with remains of a Crusader monastery or convent on this site clearly visible.

Bazaar area Despite its narrow winding streets and labyrinth-like properties, Nazareth's 'old' bazaar area is certainly not the stuff of *1001 Nights*. Most of the produce is the simple everyday essentials of a modern town: fruit and vegetables, clothing and household utensils, with the odd smattering of mass-produced junk for the pilgrim/tourist market. Many shop fronts are closed as businesses were relocated to the outskirts of town in the smartening-up process prior to the millennium, never to return. However, you can still track the rich aroma of fresh coffee through the streets and find the odd little café to hide away in.

Synagogue Church/Church of Greek Catholic Community ① *04-T6568488, daily 0830-1800.* Located within the bazaar area is a small church run by the Greek Catholics referred to as the 'Synagogue Church'. Tradition has it that this is the site of the synagogue in

Nazareth where the young Jesus was taught, and to where, as an adult, he returned to read from the scriptures, thus fulfilling their prophesy (*Luke 4:16-21*). Such a site is first mentioned in the writings of the Pilgrim of Piacenza around 570 CE, though the simple barrel-vaulted room that you see inside the courtyard to the left of the church dates only to Crusader times. Indeed, the Pilgrim of Piacenza was even shown the bench upon which Jesus sat learning the scriptures as a child, and notes that whilst Christians were able to lift it and move it about, Jews were unable to budge it at all!

To reach the Synagogue Church, head up Casa Nova Street from the Basilica. Where the road bears right, head left through the new stone arch into the paved old bazaar. After about 100 m take the first left turn. Walk to the end of the street, turn right, and the pillar-flanked archway leading into the Synagogue Church's courtyard is 20 m on your right.

Mensa Christi Church A large slab of stone measuring 3.6 m by 3 m, reputed to be the table at which Jesus is said to have dined with his disciples shortly after his resurrection, is the centrepiece of the small Mensa Christi (Latin: '*Table of Christ*') Church. Built by the Franciscans in 1860, the church is located to the northwest of the bazaar area (the huge brass key can be obtained from the first door on the right up the alley opposite the church gate, for a small donation). Close by is the 18th-century **Maronite Church of St Anthony** ⓘ *T04-6554256, Sun 0800-1200*, whilst to the south is the 19th-century **Anglican ('Jesus') Church**, built in the shape of a cross.

Salesian Basilica of Jesus the Adolescent ⓘ *Mon-Fri 0800-1500, Sat 0800-1200. Accessed through the corridors of the Don Bosco School.* Dominating the hillside above Nazareth is this beautiful church belonging to the French Salesian order. This Gothic-style basilica, built in 1918, features a large statue above the high altar of Jesus as an adolescent. The soaring white marble interior and simple stained-glass window are appealing. Although it is a fairly steep and winding climb up to the monastery from the bazaar area, it is worth making the effort in order to enjoy the view across Nazareth (alternatively take bus 5 or 15).

The hill in the middle distance, just beyond the edge of town, is the '**Mount of Precipitation**' ('Mount of the Leap of the Lord'), from which the people of Nazareth are reputed to have attempted to throw Jesus, having rejected his teachings (see 'Chapel of Fright/Notre Dame de l'Effroi', next page). Above the Salesian Monastery you can make out the rocket-like minaret of the **Maqam Nabi Sa'in Mosque**.

Mary's Well and St Gabriel's Church/Greek Orthodox Church of the Annunciation ⓘ *T04-6569349, daily 0700-1200 and 1300-1800, closes 1 hr earlier in winter. A small donation is appreciated; toilets.* Greek Orthodox tradition holds that the Archangel Gabriel's first appearance to Mary took place at the village well (see the second-century *Protoevangelium of James*, or *Apocryphal Gospel of St James*) and not inside a house. This mid-18th-century church is built over the site of Nazareth's fresh-water spring ('Mary's Well'), though the site has been revered since Byzantine times; the Pilgrim of Piacenza visited around 570 CE the spring from which Mary is said to have drawn water, whilst the pilgrim Arculf mentions a church on this site during his visit around 670 CE.

Like most Greek Orthodox churches, St Gabriel's has a lavishly decorated interior, with painted screens (iconostasis) shielding the altar, icons and hanging lamps. Seven steps descend into an atmospheric vaulted chamber built by the Crusaders, where, on the left, you can drink (treated) water drawn from the spring. The spring, strewn with coins, can be seen 2 m down at the end of the chamber.

Close to St Gabriel's Church, just off the traffic roundabout, is Mary's Well, though it is now dry. Just next to the spring is the **Ancient Bath House at Cactus** ① T04-6578539, www.nazarethbathhouse.org, where you can tour the cavernous baths only uncovered when the owners began work on their shop in 1993. Tours cost 28-30NIS per person depending on group size; refreshments are provided afterwards.

Nazareth Village ① El-Wadi El-Jawani (next to the YMCA), T04-6456042, www. nazarethvillage.com, Mon-Sat 0900-1700 (last tour at 1530), adults 50NIS, student 32NIS, child 25NIS. Tours last about 1½ hrs. Gift shop, toilets. Aiming to bring to life a Galilean village as it was 2000 years ago in the time of Christ, Nazareth village is situated among the actual remains of a Roman period farm and its terraced fields. A tour starts with some interactive history to give visitors the context of the times, before moving outside to the "village" and terraces, where an olive press, homesteads, villagers and sheep, a reconstructed first-century synagogue and the like are explained. Jesus' life and message is brought up at every opportunity, which can be a bit tiresome.

Chapel of Fright (Notre Dame de l'Effroi) Following Jesus' preaching in the synagogue at Nazareth (see Luke 4:16-21, and Synagogue Church on page 554), the people of the town grew agitated, "rose up, and thrust him out of the city, and led him unto the brow of the hill whereon their city was built, that they might cast him down headlong. But he passing through the midst of them went his way" (Luke 4:29-30). The hill mentioned in Luke's narrative, the '**Mount of Precipitation**' (or 'Mount of the Leap of the Lord'), is supposedly located just to the south of Nazareth, on the edge of the modern town. The Franciscan's Chapel of Fright, or Notre Dame de l'Effroi, is built on the site from which Mary is said to have witnessed this scene. The Orthodox community have their own chapel, **Kaser el-Mutran**, on a different site (see map). A wealthy Russian pilgrim is said to have donated the funds for the chapel's construction in 1862.

The Franciscan's Chapel of Fright can be reached by heading south on the road opposite the **Galilee/HaGalil Hotel** on Paul VI Street (next to the Nazarene Church), and continuing beyond St Claire's Convent. The 'Mount of Precipitation' is about 2 km outside the town centre.

Nazareth listings

For Sleeping and Eating price codes and other relevant information, see Essentials pages 26-31.

● Sleeping

Nazareth has an interesting choice of accommodation. Advance booking is recommended at all times, and essential around the main Christian festivals. Group discounts are often available.
AL Rimonim, Paul VI, T04-6500000, www. rimonim.com. Inexpensive, "normal" hotel of a fairly high standard; rooms don't smell like a monastery. Carpets, fridge, TV, etc. Some rooms have balcony with town views.

Expansive basement bar, soulless restaurant.
AL St Gabriel Monastery, PO Box 2448, off Salesian, T04-6572133, F04-6554071. Excellent location above town; frumpy furnishings, but get a front-facing room with large picture window and you won't mind, a/c not necessary in this stone building; very attractive terrace and gardens. Excellent restaurant serves unique local dishes, try stuffed zucchini or the lamb mixed with parsley and onion. Staff are friendly. Recommended.
AL Al Mutran Guest House, Al-Mutran Sq, T04-6457947, www.al-mutran.com. Charming, lofty old building with 11 rooms

in a variety of layouts (doubles 450NIS), 3 suites, plenty of space for families. Same management as the Fauzi Azar but more sophisticated; furnishings new and comfortable. Attractive, old Arabic-style lobby. Breakfast 35NIS.

A **Casa Nova Hospice**, Casa Nova, T04-6456660, casanovanazareth@yahoo.com. Reasonably good value ($39 per person) in plain doubles or triples with en suite; advance booking essential, check-out an unpalatable 0830, curfew 2300. Cafeteria, attractive public areas with old tiled floors. Mainly pilgrim groups.

A **Rosary Sisters**, T04-6554435, www.rsisters.com. Located high on the hill, with splendid views. Rooms are very clean and simple, if a bit flowery, with new tiled bathrooms some with doors on to the garden; relaxed atmosphere. 1-4 bed rooms available, includes breakfast around long communal table, Wi-Fi, TV lounge and laundry service.

A **St Margaret's Anglican Pilgrim Hostel**, Orfaneg, T04-6573507, F04-6567166. Formerly a 19th-century orphanage for girls, this beautiful building is set around a charming flagged courtyard with white-clothed tables and a welcoming bar. Rooms are well furnished in a non-descript way; the best are at the rear as those in the main building open on to the arched breakfast hall. Good views; independent travellers welcome (doubles 320NIS B&B).

A-E **Fauzi Azar Inn**, T04-6020469/054-4322328, www.fauziazarinn.com. There are few places in Israel as pleasing as the courtyard of the Fauzi Azar at night, with the old arches of the Ottoman house soaring above and the sound of water trickling in the well. Private rooms all unique (numbers 6 and 11 especially nice), some with rock walls, cute lighting and modern bathrooms, others with original painted Ottoman ceilings, charm and shared bathrooms. The 10-bed dorm is roomy and clean (mixed sex), as are the shared showers (70NIS). Nice touches like home-made cake with your coffee and free internet/Wi-Fi. Excellent breakfast. Highly recommended; book rooms in advance.

A-E **Abu Saeed Hostel**, T04-6462799/050-5703880, hajmosmar.ramzi@gmail.com. An old Ottoman house that's still very much Ramsi's home, furniture is fusty and there's a lack of natural light (best in summer), but mattresses new and it's thoroughly clean, antiques on the walls and the functioning old cistern that collects rainwater is a feature. 5 rooms, 3 with shared bath, 1 has kitchenette (dorm-style 70NIS, doubles 300NIS). Tea/coffee/communal fridge. Breakfast 35NIS.

B-E **Sisters of Nazareth Guest House**, No 3, St 306, T04-6554304, F6460741, accueilnasra@live.fr. The renovated Guest House positively sparkles. Centrally heated private rooms are plain and pristine (single/double 185/220NIS), with excellent shower rooms. Cheap single-sex dorms (female with 6 beds, male with 16, 60NIS) also brand new, single beds rather than bunks, shower and toilet off the little hallway, towels provided. Set around a tranquil cloistered courtyard where you can sit sipping beer on wicker chairs among bougainvillea. Add 25NIS per person for breakfast. The downside is the 2230 curfew.

🍴 Eating

Many visitors come to Nazareth purely for the food, which is as famed as the hospitality, and there are several chic restaurants to choose from.

Casa Nova Street and Paul VI Street are thick with restaurants selling hummus, falafel, shwarma, grilled chicken, etc, though none is exceptional. Bonjour Kobain is probably the pick of the bunch, daily 0800-late, with seating.

ᵀᵀᵀ-ᵀᵀ **Al-Reda**, El-Bishara, T04-6084404. A splendid Arab mansion that's been turned into a top-notch restaurant, Al Reda is intimate and inviting. Middle Eastern salads and mezze, shrimp and calamari

(64-69NIS), meat dishes (50-80NIS, try the sesame-coated fried chicken), great choice for vegetarians. Also perfect for a nightcap. Like everywhere else it Nazareth, it's packed with Israelis on Shabbat so best book ahead. Mon-Sat 1300-0200, Sun 1900-0200.

₮₮-₮₮ Diana, Paul VI, T04-6572919. An institution, especially with Israeli day-trippers. The menu isn't expansive but the quality is outstanding, and the mezze memorable. Don't be put off by the somewhat scruffy façade. Daily 1200-1800.

₮₮-₮₮ Sudfeh, Restaurant Bar & Gallery, T04-6566611. Fantastically chic bistro with outsize lampshades and vaulted stone surrounds; attractive smokers' courtyard, Italian-Arab fare, Mon-Sat 1300-2300.

₮₮-₮₮ Tishreen, 56 El-Bishara/Mary's Well, T04-6084666, www.rest.co.il/tishreen. If you like things buzzing and social, Tishreen is the place. It collects Nazarenes and foreigners together to wine and dine from a menu of mezze, steak, calamari, chicken, stir fries and stuffed veggies. The interior is classy while the feeling is cosy and rustic. Booking essential on Fri and Sat nights. Mon-Sat 1200-2400.

₮₮ La Fontana de Maria, 3 Paul VI St, just to the east of Mary's Well, T04-6460435, www.lafontana.co.il. An old-fashioned but relaxing cave adorned with plants, photos and fish tanks, serving Arab staples (grills, fish, salads). Also good for a quiet pre-dinner beer (10-20NIS), especially in winter. Daily 1300-2300.

₮₮-₮ Al-Taboun, Paul VI, T04-6578852. Reliable and cheap hummus and dips, plus shwarma and shish kebab in a simple sit-down eatery.

₮ Al Mohhtar Sweets, Paul VI. Amazingly good knaffeh is turned out trayload after enormous trayload. Full of feasting locals and people coming to buy baklava in bulk. Daily 0930-2400.

₮ Arafat Safedi, T04-6466568. Fresh pastries that you can smell from streets away, located way up on top of the hill near the Salesian Church. Daily 0400-1900.

⊛ Festivals and events

Easter Week is marked by a **Sacred Music Festival**, with similar musical performances over the Christmas period (tickets for church services should be arranged in advance through the tourist office). The **Feast of the Annunciation** (25 March 2011) is the most exciting (and busiest) time to visit Nazareth.

◐ Shopping

El Babour, El-Bishara, T04-6455596. This 100-year-old spice mill is cavernous, unlike the unsigned tiny door though which you enter. In the back rooms, in amongst the vintage machinery, you will find workers sifting and grinding spices using age-old methods. Dried fruits, nuts, oils, tea, coffee and more, in addition to every spice under the sun.

Fahoum Spices, Old Market, T04-6081055. Follow the smell of coffee (and ask any local) to find this time-warp spices shop hidden in the bazaar.

▲ Activities and tours

Fauzi Azar Inn organize a daily tour around the old market, starting at 1000 and costing 15NIS per person. The guides are well informed and interesting, and visit places that you would never find on your own. A good introduction.

Holy Land Tours, arrange through Fauzi Azar Inn. Tours to the Christian sites on the northern shore of the Sea of Galilee, 0900-1600, for 4 persons 900NIS, with multilingual local guide.

◎ Transport

Bus

There is no bus station as such in Nazareth; simply a series of bus stops on either side of Paul VI. **Afula**: Kavim bus 354 and 356, Sun-Thu frequent service from 0600, Fri until 1650, also **Tel Aviv** bus 823 and 841. **Akko**:

Egged bus 343, Sun-Thu every 90 mins 0640-1700, Fri until 1540, Sat no service(1¼ hrs, 28NIS). **Amman**, Jordan: **Nazarene Tours** bus (T04-6010458), leaving from **Nazareth Hotel** on Sun, Tue, Thu and Sat at 0830 (5 hrs, 75NIS). **Cana** (Kafr Kanna): **Nazarene Tours** buses 28, 29 and 30, frequent service, 15 mins. **Haifa**: Nazarene tours bus 331 every 30 mins 0510-1900 (45 mins, 17NIS). **Jerusalem**: Egged bus 955, Sun-Thu 0545 and 0845, Fri 0850, Sat 1845 and 2015 (2 hrs, 47NIS). **Megiddo**: Egged bus 823 (see Tel Aviv below) stops at Megiddo Jct. **Tabor**: Kavim bus 354 and 356 to **Afula**, then change to bus 350 to **Daburiya**. **Tel Aviv**: Egged bus 826 from Pikod Junction (near Nazareth Hotel), Sun-Thu every 45 mins 0500-1800, Fri until 1445, Sat 1545-2115 (2 hrs, 40.5NIS); also bus 823 (via Afula and Petah Tiqva), Sun-Thu about 1 per hr 0520-1720, Fri limited service until 1430, Sat 4 buses after sundown (3 hrs, 40.5NIS). **Tiberias**: Nazarene Tours bus 431, Sun-Thu 1 per hr 0645-2030, Fri limited service until 1630, Sat 2100 (45 mins, 21.5NIS). **Zippori**: Egged bus 343 (see Akko, above) passes the intersection, 4 km from the site.

Car hire

Most hotels can arrange car (and driver) hire, notably for excursions to Mt Tabor (see page 561).

Sheruts

There are sheruts (T04-6571140) to **Tel Aviv** every hr until 1700 (30NIS), from Paul VI, across from the Basilica.

Taxis

Abu el-Assal, T04-6554745, near junction of Paul VI and Casa Nova.

ⓘ Directory

Banks Bank HaPoalim and Bank Leumi have ATMs on Paul VI St. There are several moneychangers around town. **Hospitals** French, off Wadi el-Juwani, T04-6574530. **Post offices** Central Post Office (including poste restante) is a couple of blocks to the west of Mary's Well. There's also a small post office on Paul VI, close to the Galilee Hotel.

Cana → Colour map 1, grid B3.

The friendly Arab village of Kafr Kanna, some 9 km northeast of Nazareth, is claimed as the site of the biblical town of Cana, where Jesus performed his first miracle by turning

Franciscan Church of the Wedding Feast, Cana

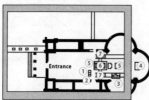

1 Mosaic featuring Aramaic inscription	4 Altar
2 Translation of inscription	5 Byzantine water pot
3 Well	6 Steps to crypt
	7 Stairs to upper floor

Not to scale

water into wine at a wedding feast (John 2:1-11). There is no archaeological evidence to sustain this belief, though there is a long tradition dating back to the early-Christian era associating this site with the miracle. Sceptics might like to note that another village in Western Galilee is also called Kafr Kanna (near to Yodfat) and claims the same distinction, whilst cynics will enjoy the numerous souvenir shops selling 'Cana wedding wine'. Further, two different factions of the Christian church compete to claim the event as their own.

Ins and outs Cana is best reached by bus from Nazareth. Nazarene buses 28, 29 and

30 run frequently from Nazareth, while it is also possible to take Tiberias bus 431, and ask to be let off as it passes through Cana. Many of Nazareth's hotels will arrange taxi tours to Cana, usually also including a visit to Mt Tabor (see page 561).

Franciscan Church of the Wedding Feast ① *T04-6517011, Mon-Sat 0800-1200 and 1400-1800 (winter -1700), Sun closed 1400-1700. Free.* This Roman Catholic church is located in the centre of the village along a rather attractive alley lined with souvenir shops, aptly named Churches Street. Though it was built in the late 19th century, parts of earlier Crusader and Byzantine churches can be seen within the crypt. The church's green dome and twin bell-towers are the village's main landmark. The interior of the church is fairly simple, with the main points of interest being in the crypt. Before descending, note the section of third- or fourth-century CE mosaic beneath the perspex grille to the right. A translation of the Aramaic is given on the adjacent wall, and it is suggested that the inscription was originally part of a synagogue bench, with the Joseph mentioned being a Christian convert and founder of several new churches in Galilee during the early Byzantine period.

The crypt contains a Byzantine fountain and water pot, plus the remains of ancient cisterns. Some claim that this crypt is the actual site of the miracle, with an altar commemorating the spot and a pictorial representation of Jesus blessing the wine. The numerous jars and pots just off the passageway to the left are not claimed to be the original vessels used at the wedding, simply replicas.

Around Nazareth

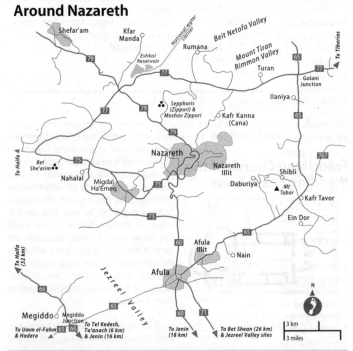

Greek Orthodox Wedding Church ⓘ *Mon-Sat 0800-1500, Sun 0800-1130; you may have to wait for someone to open up. Free.* Opposite the Roman Catholic church is the Greek Orthodox version, set in a little garden. Built in 1885 in the shape of a Greek cross, the church features a central chandelier, a large number of icons and an impressive iconostasis. The most important artefacts are two stone jars, protected by glass, that are rather improbably claimed to have featured in the miracle itself. They are more likely to be around 300 years old rather than 2000.

Nathanael Chapel Cana was also the home of Nathanael, a man whose initial suspicions of Jesus led to his oft-quoted expression "Can there be anything good come out of Nazareth?" (*John 1:46*), but who later became one of the early disciples and was present when the resurrected Christ appeared at the Sea of Galilee (*John 21:2*). Also on Churches Street, just north of the other churches, is a Franciscan chapel over the supposed site of his former home. It is opened only once a year, so, unless you are very lucky, you will have to look over the wall at the austere exterior.

Cana listings

For Sleeping and Eating price codes and other relevant information, see Essentials pages 26-31.

Sleeping and eating

A-D Cana Wedding Guest House, Kfar Kanna, T04-6412375/050-4007636. Range of double and twin rooms, some share bathrooms, plus dorm beds for 100NIS, in 2 buildings belonging to a friendly Arab Christian family. Everything new and fresh; lovely terrace with direct views on to church bells; kitchenette, TV, a/c and heater. Great resting place for those on the Jesus Trail and a good choice all round. Breakfast available (25NIS for those in dorm). To find it, turn left off Churches St just before the Franciscan Church.

D-F Yarok Az, Ilaniyya (northeast of Cana on Rd 77), T054-2558791/2. This working farm is a unique place to stay, with two geometric domes that can sleep 15+ people in each (about 100NIS). It's 5 mins from the Jesus Trail and there's lots of space for campers (30NIS per person), hot showers, open kitchen, breakfast available. Very down-to-earth, eco-conscious hosts; you can join in with farm work (dairy goats, veg garden, chickens, cooking, picking) or even do a course in organic farming. The name means "Deep" and/or "Green Goat", a play on words that must work better in Hebrew. From the gate of Ilaniyya, follow the goat pictures.

Ⱡ **Al-Mokhtar Bakery**, Kfar Cana, on the right as you leave the village travelling north. Famous (well, locally); opens at dawn and is a total bargain.

Mt Tabor → *Colour map 1, grid C3.*

Since the fourth century CE, Mt Tabor has been identified with the "high mountain apart" (*Matthew 17:1; Mark 9:2*), the scene of Christ's **Transfiguration**. Rising above the surrounding countryside to a height of 588 m, the distinctive curve of Tabor is a suitable location for such an important event in the Christian tradition: "Jesus took Peter, John and James and went up a mountain to pray. And while he was praying the appearance of his face changed and his clothes became a brilliant white. Suddenly there were two men talking with him – Moses and Elijah – who appeared in glory and spoke of his departure, and the destiny he was to fulfil in Jerusalem ... there came a cloud which cast its shadow over them; they were afraid as they entered the cloud, and from it a voice spoke: 'This is my son, my chosen; listen to him.' After the voice had spoken, Jesus was seen to be alone. The disciples kept silence and did not at that time say a word to anyone of what they had seen." (*Luke 9:28-36*).

Ins and outs Public transport to Mt Tabor is not particularly good. From Tiberias, Egged buses 835, 841 and 962 bound for Afula pass the base of the mountain, stopping at Kfar Tavor, from where it's still 8 km uphill. From Nazareth it is possible to take Kavim buses 354 or 356 to Afula, then bus 350 to the "terminal" at Shibli village. It is still a steep climb to the summit from here, so white mini-vans wait to ferry people to the summit for 100NIS per vehicle including waiting time (20NIS per person in a group), or less if you haggle hard. Most visitors to Mt Tabor arrive on tour buses, which park in Shibli at the terminal. Those in a car can just wind on up to the car park at the top of the hill.

Background Early-Christian scholars vacillated in their placement of the scene of the Transfiguration, with Eusebius unable to decide between Mt Tabor and Mt Hermon, and the Pilgrim of Bordeaux (c. 333 CE) suggesting the Mount of Olives as the true site. Mt Tabor finally became the first choice after Cyril, Bishop of Jerusalem, decided in its favour in 348 CE. The appeal of Mt Tabor as a "high mountain apart" was recognized as long ago as the second millennium BCE, when the **Canaanites** created a 'high place' here for the worship of Baal. It was also from the top of Mt Tabor c. 1125 BCE that **Deborah** and Barak swept down upon the 900 iron chariots of Sisera and vanquished the Canaanite army (*Judges 4:4-24*). A similar feat was achieved by Antiochus III of Syria in 218 BCE, who lured the Egyptian garrison down from their position of strength atop the mountain and slaughtered them to a man.

Mt Tabor remained a stronghold in Roman times with **Josephus**, the Jewish commander of the Galilee, fortifying the mountain-top prior to the advance of Vespasian's army (although he later embraced the Roman cause). Josephus describes how the huge defensive rampart around the summit was built in just 40 days, though he also describes Mt Tabor as being "no less than 20,000 feet high" (*Jewish War, IV*, 55)! Nevertheless, parts of a large defensive wall dating to this period can still be seen. The **Crusaders** built new churches and monasteries on the Byzantine ruins following their conquest of the Holy Land in 1099, though the small community of Benedictine monks that they installed were murdered by the Turks in 1113. Subsequent Crusader-built places of worship on Mt Tabor were more akin to fortresses, withstanding Salah al-Din's attack in 1183. Following their defeat at the Horns of Hattin four years later, the Crusaders abandoned Mt Tabor, though the threat of their return (the Fourth Crusade, 1202-04) forced the sultan of Damascus **Melek el-Adel** to re-fortify the site. Many of the defences still visible today were built by the sultan and his son **Melek el-Moudzam**.

The presence of this Muslim-built stronghold on the site of the Transfiguration inspired the Fifth Crusade and, though the Crusaders failed to capture the mountain, Melek el-Adel dismantled much of his

Mount Tabor

Steep road to Daburiya, Shibli & Route 65 (8 km)

Ancient walls

Ancient walls

Melek el-Adel's 13th century walls

N

Not to scale

1 Church of St Elias
2 Church of the Transfiguration
3 Chapel
4 Gate of the Wind
5 Graveyard
6 Parking

fortress in order to placate the Christians. Pilgrims and monastic orders were permitted a presence on the mountain-top, though they were subsequently banished by the sultan Baibars in 1263.

The Druze emir Fakhr ed-Din allowed the Franciscans to build a monastery on Mt Tabor in 1631 and they have remained ever since. In 1911 the Greek Orthodox built a church dedicated to St Elias (Elijah) on the north side of the summit.

Sights An extremely steep and winding road climbs up from the base of the mountain. Close to the top the road forks, with the path to the left leading to the Greek sector and the right to the Franciscan-owned area. The right fork leads through the **Gate of the Wind**, part of Melek el-Adel's medieval fortress. It is possible to trace the line of the 13th-century defensive walls (with their 12 towers) around the summit of Mount Tabor. Continuing along the tree-lined avenue of the Franciscans' estate, a medieval graveyard lies to the left of the path whilst a small **chapel** stands to the right. Little is known about the Byzantine structure that forms the building's foundations, though the chapel itself is a Crusader commemoration of the conversation between Jesus and his disciples following his Transfiguration. The graveyard dates to the first century CE whilst the surrounding ruins are probably part of the Benedictine monastery complex destroyed by the Turks in 1113.

Beyond the car park, behind wrought-iron gates, is the piazza of the **Franciscans' complex** ① *Sun-Fri 0800-1145 and 1400-1800, closes 1700 in winter, Fri -1130. Free. Shop with snacks. Modest dress essential.* A modern monastery and hospice stands opposite the 12th-century ruins of the Benedictine monastery. At the end of the path is the splendid **Church of the Transfiguration**. Completed in 1924, the Italian architect Antonio Barluzzi incorporated the monumental building style of the early-Christian church in Syria into the design. Everything is on a grand scale, including the twin projecting towers marking the façade, whilst the nave is separated from the aisles by wide arches and is at a middle level between the altar and crypt. A large mosaic in the vaulting depicts the Transfiguration of Christ. The colourful crypt reveals parts of the earlier Crusader and Byzantine churches through holes in the floor, as well as evidence of the Canaanite occupation of the summit. Two chapels in the west towers are dedicated to Elijah and Moses respectively, the latter containing a mosaic floor dating to before 422 CE (after that date the Emperor Theodosius II banned the representation of crosses on church floors).

On leaving the church turn sharp left up the stairs to the **viewpoint**. On a clear day there are unprecedented views north across the Galilee, east to the Jordan Valley, and south across the Jezreel Valley.

Leaving the Franciscans' property, head over to the Greek Orthodox sites on the north side of the summit. These include the **Church of St Elias** (Elijah), built in 1911 upon the ruins of a Crusader church. The church stands above the '**Cave of Melchisedek**' (enter through small iron door outside) dubiously supposed to be the site where Melchisedek, king of Salem, received Abraham (*Genesis 14:18-20*). The church gates are generally only opened to orthodox pilgrims.

Sights around Mt Tabor
There are a number of minor places of interest in the vicinity of Mt Tabor, though none really merits a special trip. The Arab village of **Daburia** at the western foot of Mt Tabor is named after the Israelite Prophetess and Judge, Deborah. Tradition holds that upon coming down from the mountain, after the Transfiguration, Jesus healed an epileptic boy here (*Luke*

9:37-42). The Bedouin village of Shibli on the slopes of Mt Tabor has a **Bedouin Heritage Centre** ① *Sat-Thu 0900-1600, 10NIS*. The Jewish village of Kfar Tavor has a **museum** ① *T04-6765844, Sun-Thu 0900-1400, Sat 1030-1500 (closed Sat in summer), adult 16NIS, student/child 13NIS*, telling the story of local pioneering efforts; a marzipan museum; and excellent winery. Further south, closer to Afula along Route 65, is Nain, supposed site of the miracle at which Jesus restored to life the only son of a widow (*Luke 7:11-17*). A small church marks the site.

Mt Tabor listings

For Sleeping and Eating price codes and other relevant information, see Essentials pages 26-31.

Sleeping
A-D Khaled's Place, Shibli, T04-6701812/052-2698513. Brand new guestrooms halfway up Mt Tabor; 2 big double rooms with bathrooms, kitchen, quality fixtures and fittings. Breakfast and authentic meals can be arranged, and his wife's lemon juice is memorable. Those on a budget can sleep on the roof. Call for directions: it's not far from the 'terminal' in Shibli.

AL-C HooHa Cyclists House, Kfar Tavor, T054-8070524, www.hooha.co.il. This modern building is architecturally interesting and brightly decorated, with the capacity to sleep 25 people on 3 floors. Primarily (but not only) for cyclists, lovely dorm with 8 beds (150NIS), 4 x double/twins (400-480NIS), suite with poolside patio and private jacuzzi (650NIS during week). Open-plan kitchen, lovely heated outdoor pool and jacuzzi in garden, lots of communal space with DVDs, music and comfy sofas. Free internet/Wi-Fi, library, laundry room; bicycles to rent (90-120NIS per day) and good-value packages available (see website for details).

Zippori (Sepphoris)

→ *Colour map 1, grid B3.*
① *T04-6568272, daily 0800-1700, winter -1600, Fri closes 1 hr earlier. 25NIS adult, 21NIS student, 13 child. Short movie (English/German), shop, snacks.*

The city of Sepphoris was a major Jewish town in Galilee during the Roman and Byzantine periods. Known by its Hebrew name of Zippori, there are substantial remains of the successive cities built on the mound. Zippori National Park is noteworthy particularly for its superbly preserved Roman and Byzantine mosaics and its rather idyllic setting. The adjacent moshav makes a great stop for a night.

Ins and outs
Getting there and away Zippori is not the easiest place to get to by public transport. Bus 343 between Nazareth and Akko travels along Route 79, and there is a bus stop at the turn-off for the site. From this junction it is a 4-km walk. See 'Around Nazareth' map on page 560.

Background
Roman rule The ancient city of Sepphoris has played a major role in the history of Roman Galilee. During the Hasmonean period (152-37 BCE) Sepphoris was probably the administrative centre of the whole of Galilee, with Josephus mentioning the town during the reign of Alexander Jannaeus (103-76 BCE). Eight years after the Roman conquest of Palestine in 63 BCE, the proconsul Gabinius declared Sepphoris the capital of the district, and **Herod the Great** took the city without opposition as one of his first acts after gaining power in 37 BCE (Josephus, *Jewish War I*, 304).

Following Herod's death the townspeople rose up and attempted to sever links with Rome. The rebellion was short lived and, under the command of Varus, governor of Syria, Sepphoris was razed and its inhabitants enslaved (*Jewish War II*, 68). Thus, when Herod the Great's kingdom was partitioned, the Sepphoris that his son **Herod Antipas** inherited was an uninhabited ruin. Some scholars argue that the ambitious reconstruction plan that Herod Antipas initiated drew artisans and craftsmen from far and wide, including a certain Joseph who chose to settle in nearby Nazareth (see page 548). Herod Antipas' city became known as Autocratoris, though it soon receded in importance around 20 CE when the capital was shifted to the new city of Tiberias.

During the **First Jewish Revolt** (66-73 CE), when the Roman army arrived, the population of Sepphoris surrendered their city without a fight, **Josephus** noting that the inhabitants of Sepphoris were "the only people in Galilee who desired peace" (*ibid, III, 33*). Relations with the Romans following the revolt appear to have been stable, with the Jewish local government even minting coins in honour of the Roman emperor Trajan (98-117 CE) and the Romans glorifying the city. But though there are no records of events during the Bar Kokhba Uprising (132-135 CE), the resulting fate of Sepphoris suggests that the Romans did not enjoy the support of the local people; the Jewish local government was abolished and replaced with a gentile one, and the city was given the Roman name Diocaesarea.

Jewish renaissance Sepphoris' Jewish renaissance really dates to the second and third centuries CE. Towards the end of the second century CE, **Rabbi Judah I ha-Nasi** shifted the **Sanhedrin** from Bet She'arim to Sepphoris (or Zippori), and it was here c. 200 CE that the codification of Jewish law, Mishnah, was completed. With the restoration of local government, Jewish life flourished and the town is subsequently mentioned many times in Talmudic literature. Indeed, the Hebrew name of Zippori is explained in the *Babylonian Talmud*: "Because it is perched on the top of a mountain like a bird [zippor]" (*Megillah 6:a*). The Sanhedrin continued to sit in Zippori until the middle of the third century, when it was shifted to Tiberias by Rabbi Yohanan.

Byzantine period With Christianity becoming the state religion of the Roman empire, a Jewish convert named Joseph received permission from the emperor to build Sepphoris' first church, though it was probably never completed and the town remained almost exclusively Jewish. The massive **earthquake** that hit Palestine in 363 CE totally destroyed Sepphoris, and the subsequent rapid reconstruction of the town saw an influx of Christians. But though the town became the seat of a bishop it remained predominantly Jewish until the mid-sixth century at least.

Later history Sepphoris' history during the Early Arab period (638-1099) is unremarkable, and even the Crusader fortress built here (Le Sephorie) would be little remembered if it were not from the spring near here (Ein Zippori) that the Crusader army set out on 3 July 1187 for their fateful battle at the Horns of Hattin (see page 608).

In the 18th century the Bedouin ruler of Galilee, Dahr el-Amr, fortified the Arab village of Saffuriyyeh at the site; it later became an Arab base during the 1936-39 revolt and the 1948 War of Independence. A year after its capture by the Israelis a moshav was founded here, taking the ancient Hebrew name of Zippori. Though the British had undertaken some excavations in the 1930s, a series of major digs in the 1970s, 80s and 90s revealed most of what is visible today.

Sights

A short film is shown in the **pavilion shop (4)**, nearby which are some well-placed picnic tables under ancient (replanted) olives. Excavation work continues at Zippori, and new mosaics and sections of street are being uncovered all the time. A tour takes about two hours, excluding the reservoir/water supply system.

Ancient reservoir (1) A worthwhile first stop is the ancient water reservoir, just to the left on entering the park. The town's main water supply came from springs located in the hills around Nazareth, with water being brought on two aqueducts built in the first and second centuries CE. The northern one leads to the **Mashad Pool (2)**, whilst the southern one leads to the **subterranean reservoir (3)**.

The reservoir is carved out of the soft chalk, taking advantage of a natural fault line. It measures 260 m long, between 2-4 m wide, is up to 10 m deep, and has a storage capacity of some 4,300 cubic metres. As you enter the reservoir at the top of the 36 steps, note the layers of plaster over the walls, in places several layers thick. The north wall here is of hard limestone whilst the south wall is softer. When you reach the bottom of the steps note how the floor is also plastered to prevent seepage. Water exited the reservoir via a lead pipe at the far end. Flow was controlled by a valve and ran through a 240-m-long man-made tunnel towards the city. An above-ground stone aqueduct then fed water into the municipal water system, though it should be noted that houses on the summit were dependent upon rainwater filling their rock-cut cisterns. It's possible to explore the first section of the reservoir, and its size and ingenuity is most impressive.

Colonnaded streets (5) Much of the lower market of Zippori that is mentioned in the Talmud can be seen here. Two colonnaded streets bisected the town, forming a cross. A large section of the upright (*cardo*, forming the north to south axis) is well preserved. The limestone pavement slabs of the street still bear the ruts made by wagon wheels, and

Zippori National Park

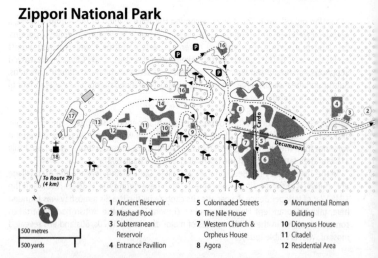

1 Ancient Reservoir	5 Colonnaded Streets	9 Monumental Roman
2 Mashad Pool	6 The Nile House	Building
3 Subterranean	7 Western Church &	10 Dionysus House
Reservoir	Orpheus House	11 Citadel
4 Entrance Pavillion	8 Agora	12 Residential Area

some mosaics on the colonnaded walkways (*stoae*) on either side commemorate those who built it. The *decumanus* (east to west axis) is still being uncovered, and excavations in this area recently unearthed a Byzantine church, possibly built over an earlier temple. The foundations of shops are clearly visible on the left side of the street, while a grand public building is emerging on the right side.

Nile mosaic building (6) This large Byzantine building occupies almost an entire insula, or city block. The mosaic floors are of exceptional workmanship, picturing dynamic Amazonians wielding spears and participating in festivities.

The mosaic in the largest room particularly stands out, featuring the unusual combination of the Nile festival illustrated alongside hunting scenes. The central image depicts the Nile River flowing from the mouth of a Nilotic beast. Above the river is a nilometer, bearing the numbers IE, IS, and I2 (referring to 15, 16 and 17 cubits). A man standing on a woman's back engraves the number I2, indicating the river's level that year. The reclining female form in the upper left corner personifies Egypt, one arm resting on a fruit-laden basket with her other hand holding a fruit-filled cornucopia. The male personification of the Nile sits astride an animal from whose mouth the river flows. Beneath is the Pharos lighthouse and Pompei's Pillar in Alexandria and, below that, scenes of predators hunting and eating their prey.

Western Church and Orpheus House (7) On the west side of the Cardo, a Roman-period four-panel mosaic has been revealed. The main image is of Orpheus playing a stringed instrument to calm the wild beasts and birds around him, the other three panels illustrate the life of the times, showing wrestling, board-games and a slave carrying water. On descending from the viewing platform of the Orpheus house, cross the cardo and inspect the flags on the far side for a little carving of a menorah.

Agora (8) This large (40 m by 60 m) complex was located at the intersection of two of the town's main thoroughfares. Comprising a central pillared courtyard surrounded by rooms of various sizes, it is thought to have served as the market place (agora) from the first to fourth centuries CE. A large geometric mosaic is currently being uncovered on its floor, which can be viewed from a platform above.

Dionysus House (10) The prime location of this third-century CE palatial mansion on the summit of the mound suggests that the occupier was a person of some means. The pagan nature of the mosaic pavements suggests that it housed a gentile, possibly the city governor, though the possibility of the owner being a wealthy Jewish citizen has not been ruled out. The building was apparently destroyed in the earthquake of 363 CE.

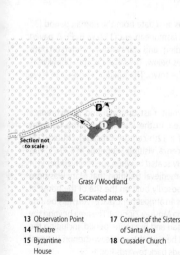

Section not to scale

Grass / Woodland

Excavated areas

13 Observation Point
14 Theatre
15 Byzantine House
16 Synagogue
17 Convent of the Sisters of Santa Ana
18 Crusader Church

The central hall served as a triclinium (dining room) and is embellished with one of the best mosaic pavements found thus far in Israel. Comprising 1.5 million tiles in 28 hues, the central mosaic features scenes from the life of the Greco-Roman god Dionysus. Though all aspects of his life are depicted, including his victorious procession after conquering India and his marriage to Ariadne, it is his revelry that is best celebrated. Scenes include his drinking competition with Hercules, and are labelled with inscriptions in Greek, such as "Dionysus' drunkenness" and "Merriment". Another fine panel is the head of an attractive woman known as the "Israeli Mona Lisa", who may well be familiar from the ubiquitous pictures on tourist literature. Acquaintance with the image, however, does not diminish the subtle details or delicate use of colours and tones which give it an almost painterly quality.

Citadel (11) The dominant building on the mound, the square block of the Citadel, was probably built by the Crusaders as a watch-tower, though they used materials from earlier structures in its construction. Note, for example, the rubble-filled Roman sarcophagus incorporated as the southwest corner-stone. Dahr el-Amr rebuilt it in the 18th century, the Ottomans added an additional storey in the 19th century and at one time it was used as a school for the Arab children of Saffuriyyeh.

On entering, note the incredibly thick walls with their deeply recessed windows on the ground floor. The **museum** on the first floor provides explanations about the influence of Hellenism on Jewish life, and how the sages debated and adapted to this threat. There's also some interesting stories relating to the *Mishnah* (compilation of oral law) that was completed at Zippori.

The **viewpoint** on the roof should not be missed. Picture boards describe the key sites in all directions. The village beyond the Eshkol Reservoir, Kafr Manda, is said to be the burial place of Moses' wife Zipporah, whilst the Rimmon Valley to the east may be the "field of corn" of the Gospels (*Matthew 12:1; Luke 6:1*).

Residential area (12) Most of the buildings in this area date from the Roman period (37 BCE-324 CE), though parts of some date to the Hasmonean era (152-37 BCE). A paved street 2.2 m wide runs through the area, with buildings and courtyards adjoining on both sides, most having rock-cut cisterns or storehouses below. The large number of mikvehs (ritual baths) attests to the Jewish character of the town. The buildings appear to have been in use until the fourth century CE.

Observation point (13) From the observation point, past the cacti and pomegranate trees, a number of interesting points can be seen. In the foreground is the **Convent of the Sisters of Santa Anna (17)**, with parts of a 12th-century **Crusader church (18)** incorporated into its west side. The Pilgrim of Piacenza, visiting Sepphoris in 570 CE, was shown a chair that the Virgin Mary was supposedly seated in when she received her visit from the Archangel Gabriel, and thus began the medieval tradition that Mary was born in Sepphoris. The ruinous Crusader church is supposedly built on the site of the home of Anne and Joachim, the Virgin Mary's parents, and is an atmospheric place (you may be able to squeeze through the fence here, otherwise go via Moshav Zippori). The area beyond the Convent is dotted with burial caves from the Roman and Byzantine period, including the presumed **tomb of Rabbi Yodan Nessiya**. This can be visited as you leave Zippori National Park, immediately to the right of the road that heads back towards Route 79.

Theatre (14) Of traditional Roman design, the theatre was originally built in the first century CE and remained in use until the Early Byzantine period. Most of the cavea (spectator seating area) is cut from the bed-rock, while much of the limestone slab seating has been looted (though some reconstruction using original slabs has been done). The large stone stage had a wooden cover, with the actors' dressing rooms located beneath it. The presence of the pagan institution of theatre in an essentially Jewish city did not go unnoticed, with contemporary commentators criticizing theatre-goers in the Babylonian Talmud (*Avoda Zara, 18:b*). Nearby are the overgrown remains of a **Byzantine house**.

Synagogue (16) In recalling the funeral of Rabbi Judah I ha-Nasi, the Talmud speaks of eighteen synagogues in Zippori. The first complete synagogue to be discovered here is housed in a new pavilion with good explanatory diagrams. It has a hall featuring a central mosaic with a Zodiac motif, surrounded by geometric designs incorporating Aramaic inscriptions. There are also many Jewish symbols such as the menorah and the Holy Ark, as well as depictions of Biblical stories.

Zippori (Sepphoris) listings

For Sleeping and Eating price codes and other relevant information, see Essentials pages 26-31.

Sleeping and eating

Moshav Zippori, next to the historical site of Zippori, is a restful place with very attractive and interesting accommodation suited to all budgets. Still primarily an agricultural village, many locals have branched out into tourism: there's a spa (see Sleeping, below), a riding stables (T04-6556550, closed Sun, 25% discount for walk-ins) and an interesting medicinal plant farm worth visiting, which has the largest selection of medicinal/culinary herbs in Israel (call in advance T04-6464848, www.supherbs.co.il; shop). Apart from anything else, the moshav is a perfect place for a meal after exploring the ruins.

AL-A Zippori Spa, T04-6468317, www.zippori-spa.co.il. Wooden throughout (it was once a stables), this spa-cum-guesthouse has 8 slightly kitsch but very homely chalets (1 with disabled facilities), all excellently equipped and set in attractive grounds. Mini-suites and suites are a fair price (350-500NIS per couple, includes an enormous breakfast). At weekends Mira only takes 2- night bookings. To visit the spa as a day-guest, a 4-hr session costs 590/670NIS week/weekend for a couple, which includes jacuzzi, sauna, massage and a generous (dairy) meal.

AL-C Zippori Village Country Cottages, T04-6462647, www.zipori.com. Split-level units with good views can sleep 2 adults and 6 kids; kitchenette, TV, wood stove. The grounds contain a winery, olive grove, play area, pool (heated from spring-time on, with no chemicals used in the water). Just constructed is a replica of the stone fortress atop the nearby hill, containing 3 rooms with fabulous arched windows and terraces. Mitch and Suzy really have thought of everything to make a stay comfortable and fun. From 400NIS per couple B&B, it's real value for money. Backpackers can sleep 4 per room for 150NIS.

A Place to Dream (Makom La'khlom), T04-6554725/050-3002501, www.hamakom.co.il. Three stylish wooden zimmers around an old Roman pool, with huge jacuzzi (of course) and excellent organic breakfast. Two romantic chalets for couples; other suits a family. Set within in a peaceful garden.

D-E Rish Lakish, T04-6555245/052-8454663, rishlakisholiveoil@gmail.com. Set in an organic, flower-filled garden, Israel/Jesus trailers are welcome to pitch up here and pay by working on the land for a couple of hours. Or a tent is available (showers, toilets) and newly built budget accommodation (indoor). The interesting family runs an olive press, and 'picking days' in the olive season (end-Oct to end-Dec) and workshops are organized. Best of all is the amazingly fresh, simple food (all vegetarian) served in the quaint rustic café made from hay bales – a stop-off here is highly recommended. Weekends all day; during the week call ahead.

ΨᵀΨ Tzon-El Dairy (Ellis Farm), T04-6464787. This farm is reckoned to produce the best (goat and sheep) cheese in the country. Wander into the cosy little restaurant/café and find out. Good light meals and pizza, or stop by for a coffee and to admire the goats. Daily 0900-1600.

Jezreel Valley/Plain of Esdraelon

→ *Colour map 1, grid C3-4.*

The Jezreel Valley (Hebrew: Ha'Emeq Yizre'el) is a series of several plains that run broadly northwest to southeast from Mt Carmel on the coast to the Jordan Valley, dividing the hills of Samaria from those of Galilee. Known in the Bible as the Plain of Esdraelon, such has been this region's importance in history that the great biblical geographer George Adam Smith was moved to call this plain "the classic battle ground of Scripture" (Historical Geography of the Holy Land, 1894). Smith is not far from the truth in describing Esdraelon as a "vast theatre" for the "spectacle of war", since its flatness presents a "clearly-defined stage" and the strategic passes that enter the plain act as "exits and entrances".

The topography of the valley provides the easiest passage between the Mediterranean coast and the east, and thus Esdraelon fell naturally into the great trading route, the Via Maris (Way of the Sea). Coupled with the plain's great fertility, little wonder that Esdraelon was so regularly fought over.

The valley is the largest in Israel and today is a major contributor to the agricultural economy of the country. For the tourist, there are several major places of interest, most notably the ancient city of Megiddo to the west and the country's best-preserved Roman-Byzantine city, Bet Shean, to the southeast. Those with a little more time should not miss the Crusader castle of Belvoir, or delightful Gan HaShlosha Park.

Bet She'arim → *Colour map 1, grid B3.*

ⓘ *T04-9831643, main tombs Sun-Thu 0800-1700, winter -1600, close 1 hr earlier on Fri. Adult 20NIS, student 17NIS, child 9NIS. Catacombs 1-4 and 11 only as part of a group tour, Fri and Sat 1030 and 1230 (advance reservations on *3639, no extra charge).*

Located at the western end of the Jezreel Valley, Bet She'arim was formerly the seat of the highest Jewish religious and judicial body in the country, and as such was the spiritual centre of Jewry. At the time when the Romans had closed Jerusalem to Jews, Bet She'arim became the most desirous alternative burial site and it is possible to visit the impressive rock-cut tombs of the necropolis within Bet She'arim National Park. Part of this vast subterranean network of catacombs is open to the public, including one tomb that has been converted into a museum containing a number of Jewish burial artefacts.

Ins and outs

Getting there and away Bet She'arim is best reached by public transport as an excursion from Haifa (19 km to the northwest), though some walking is necessary. Egged buses 301 and 75 from Haifa pass the town of Kiryat Tiv'on along Route 75, as does Nazarene Tours bus 331. Ask the driver to let you off at Kiryat Tiv'on junction, stressing you want to visit Bet She'arim National Park and not the kibbutz of the same name further on. It's about a 15-minute walk from the main road.

Getting around The main tombs that are accessible to visitors are fairly close together, and a leaflet is provided mapping out a short route around. Make sure to also take the new map (Hebrew only) which shows the newly opened tombs outside the park. Display boards outside the kiosk provide good background information on the history and the meaning of inscriptions found within the catacombs.

Background

Following the failure of the First Jewish Revolt (66-73) and the destruction of the Temple in Jerusalem, the focus of Jewish life gravitated first to Yavne then subsequently to Lower Galilee. By the second century CE Bet She'arim was already home to many important Jewish scholars, and its status was further enhanced by the arrival of the Jewish patriarch **Judah I ha-Nasi** (c. 135-217), leader of the Sanhedrin and teacher in the celebrated rabbinical academy. With Jews totally excluded from Jerusalem following Hadrian's suppression of the Second Jewish (Bar Kochba) Revolt (135 CE), Bet She'arim expanded rapidly under ha-Nasi's influence. It was here that he compiled much of the *Mishnah* (the written code of 'Oral Law' that is central to Judaism).

Though ha-Nasi moved to Sepphoris during the illness of his latter years, following his death (c. 217 CE) he was brought for burial to Bet She'arim. Whilst Jerusalem remained forbidden, Bet She'arim became the central Jewish necropolis with communities from all over Palestine and the diaspora wishing to have their dead interred here.

Bet She'arim

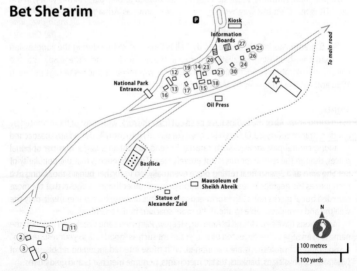

Esdraelon: battleground of the famous

The cast of characters who have performed their acts of warfare upon this stage reads like a Who's Who of the Middle East. The earliest written evidence of a battle refers to the confrontation between the Pharaoh Thutmose III and an alliance of Canaanite and Syrian cities that took place on the Plain of Esdraelon in 1468 BCE. The Israelites fought one of their first great battles here during the time of the Judges, the divinely inspired Deborah and Barak defeating the Canaanites. Gideon drove the Midianites from the valley, whilst Saul was less successful with the Philistines; his head and body parted company c. 1004 BCE. David and Solomon regained the valley for the Israelites, but the Egyptians were back in 925 BCE in the all-conquering form of the Pharaoh Shishak. The Assyrians came and captured in the eighth century BCE, whilst the Bible's last righteous king descended from David, Josiah, was killed here in the seventh century BCE.

In later years, the Roman legions of Pompey, Mark Anthony, Vespasian and Titus marched this way, whilst later still the Christian armies of the Crusaders fought the Muslim Arabs in a series of great battles. Many an ambitious emperor or general came a cropper here, with Napoleon suffering the first great retreat of his career here in 1799. And to prove that the Plain of Esdraelon has retained its strategic importance up until contemporary times, it formed one of General Allenby's major military objectives during the 1918 Palestine campaign.

Smith's summary is no over-statement: "What a Plain! Upon which not only the greatest empires, races, and faiths, east and west, have contended, but each has come to judgement – on which with all its splendour of human battle, men felt there was fighting from heaven, the stars in their courses were fighting" (*Historical Geography of the Holy Land*, 1894). Little wonder then that the final battle between the forces of good and evil that will herald the second coming (*Revelation* 16:16) is scheduled to take place in this valley, at a site known as 'Armageddon'.

Bet She'arim was largely destroyed by Gallus Caesar in 351 CE during the suppression of a third Jewish uprising. Excavations began at the site in 1871 under the auspices of the Palestine Exploration Fund, though most progress was made in a series of digs between 1936 and 1959 led primarily by Mazar and Avigad.

Sights

Main tomb area All of the tombs have been cut from the rock, with most of them fronted by a wide entrance courtyard. Others have been cut directly into the hillside and are approached by a long central passageway. Such catacombs tend to contain a larger number of burial places, though the reason for this is not entirely clear. The inference is that the popularity of Bet She'arim as a Jewish final resting place eventually led to further burial space being at a premium as the necropolis reached saturation point. Another theory suggests that the more crowded burial places reflect the socio-economic status of those buried there, with only the wealthy and prominent able to afford the more spacious burial chambers.

Inscriptions have been found in Aramaic, Hebrew, Palmyrene and Greek, and mention the name and lineage of the deceased plus a sentiment such as "good luck in your resurrection". A wide range of professions are mentioned, with those interred including rabbis, heads of synagogues, physicians, bankers, textile merchants, perfume merchants and goldsmiths.

Many of the tombs fell victim to grave robbers who smashed the sarcophagi in search of plunder. Some remained intact, however, and revealed objects such as jewellery, coins, pottery and vessels. This enabled archaeologists to reconstruct burial practices of the period.

Museum One of the main chambers of **Catacomb 20** houses a small museum of finds associated with Bet She'arim. These include details of Jewish burial practices and a model of a tomb and accompanying mausoleum. In the centre of the museum is a large slab of glass, considered to be the biggest single glass object to have been made in ancient times (over 8000 kg) though it resembles more a slab of pottery than of glass. A film can be viewed (in English), though you may need to ask staff for help in operating the DVD.

Catacomb 20 Referred to as the 'Cave of the Coffins', over 130 limestone sarcophagi were found in this catacomb, though (like all others at Bet She'arim) grave robbers had preceded the archaeologists. However, many coffins remain intact, with the Hebrew inscriptions and decorations providing some clue as to who was buried in this tomb. Common features include menorahs, heraldic eagles, hanging wreaths and tabulae *ansatae* (a tablet with triangular handles, intended to carry an inscription), with the quality of workmanship suggesting that this catacomb contains the tombs of Jewish notables. Avigad and Mazar point to a number of sarcophagi decorations that seemingly depict likeness to Greek gods, suggesting that this is an indication of the tolerant attitude of Jewish leaders of the day, interpreting potentially idolatrous themes as simply sculpture and decorative art.

The best-preserved sarcophagi are all lit, with low-key lighting illuminating the rest of the catacomb.

Catacomb 14 This tomb features the common architectural form of a three-arch façade fronting on to a large courtyard. It is one of the most important at Bet She'arim due to the Hebrew inscriptions that mention **Rabbi Simon**, **Rabbi Gamaliel** and **Rabbi Anina**. Avigad and Mazar suggest that these could be the men referred to by Patriarch Judah I ha-Nasi: "Simon my son shall be *hakham* [president of the Sanhedrin], Gamaliel my son Patriarch, hanina bar Hama shall preside over the great court". It has also been suggested that this is the burial vault of ha-Nasi's family, with the tomb built to the rear of the chamber being that of Patriarch Judah I ha-Nasi himself. The tomb is generally kept locked in order to preserve it, but staff will open it on request.

Above both Catacombs 20 and 14 there are remains of open-air structures that were surrounded by benches. These are thought to have been used as places of assembly for prayer and sermons during burial and mourning, and were so designed to add aesthetic beauty to the necropolis.

Other catacombs The entrance to **Catacomb 23** has collapsed, though this enables us to see one form of the burial patterns at Bet She'arim. A passage entrance to the left gives some indication of the extent of 'burrowing' into the hillside. Just inside the main entrance to the National Park is the 'Cave of the Ascents', or **Catacomb 13**. By descending 30 or so steps it is possible to climb through the small one-metre-square doorways that are hewn from the rock-face. Inscriptions inside declare that "This is the resting place of Yudan, son of Levi, forever in peace. May his resting place be [set] in peace." Like many other chambers here, Catacomb 13 is the site of multi-burials, with this catacomb actually being carved into two storeys.

Catacombs 1-4 and 11 Just before the entrance to Bet She'arim National Park, at the hairpin bend in the road, a road leads southwest towards a number of other catacombs. The recently restored tombs are particularly rich in wall inscriptions, reliefs and carvings (open Sat and Sun only). Generally referred to as the 'Menorah Caves', they feature depictions of men and animals, architectural designs, plus Jewish symbols such as menorahs, shofars, ritual objects and images of the Ark of the Law. Cave 3, of the 'Warrior and his Menorah' and next door Cave 4 (split into two halves) containing the 'Torah Ark' are noteworthy for their wall reliefs.

A large, elaborate mausoleum previously stood above Catacomb 11, probably dating to the third century. Part of the arch and the mosaic forecourt remain, though sections of the frieze above the arch, featuring scenes of lions hunting, wolves fighting, and an eagle, are now in the museum in Cave 20.

Synagogue On the left of the road leading to the National Park, you pass the remains of an ancient synagogue dating to the third or fourth century CE. The walls of the synagogue were previously decorated with marble tablets and inscriptions in plaster honouring those who contributed towards the construction. The synagogue and surrounding buildings were destroyed by the major conflagration that consumed the city in 351 CE. The precise dating of the city's destruction is provided by a hoard of some 1,200 coins discovered in the area. All the coins date to the reigns of Constantine I and Constantius II, with none minted later than 351 CE. Just past the synagogue are the remains of a two-room **oil press** and the city gate.

Basilica At the top of the hill stands a large basilica dating to Byzantine times (324-638 CE). There are remains beneath the basilica, however, that suggest an almost continuous occupation of the site from the ninth century BCE until the Late Arab period (1291-1516 CE). The basilica was constructed of large ashlars (hewn stone laid in horizontal courses) and was divided by rows of columns into a nave and two aisles. It was probably destroyed around 351 CE when Gallus Caesar razed the city.

Statue of Alexander Zaid Near to the basilica is a statue of Alexander Zaid, one of the founders of 'The Shomer' and a guardian of the Jewish settlers living in this area. He was killed by Arabs during the uprising of the late 1930s. He is featured in the statue sitting on his horse, gazing into the distance: you can't blame him, for it is a fine view.

Tomb of Sheik Abreik A little further down the hill is the small, twin-domed mausoleum of Sheik Abreik; the man who gave his name to the Arab village formerly on see the green cloth-shrouded sarcophagi.

Megiddo → *Colour map 1, grid C3.*

ⓘ *T04-6590316, daily 0800-1700, winter -1600 (last entry 1 hr before), closes 1 hr earlier on Fri, adult 25NIS, student 21NIS, child 17NIS. Cafeteria Sun-Fri 0800-1600 (meal deals 49NIS), gift shops, toilets.*

One of the most important archaeological sites in the north of the country, Megiddo owes its long and violent history to its strategic position on that great trade route between Egypt, Asia Minor and Babylon, the Via Maris (Way of the Sea). The earliest written record of a major military encounter refers to a battle that took place here, whilst history is replete with the names of armies who fought on the Plain of Esdraelon (Jezreel Valley) before Megiddo. Consequently, Megiddo has come to symbolize the apocalyptic battle to end all

'Armageddon' and the 'End of Days'

Just one single line in the *Revelation* of St John the Divine (*Revelation*) has given Megiddo worldwide fame and ensured a constant flow of Christian pilgrims to the site. Indeed, such is the importance of the site to Christians that Pope Paul VI chose to meet the Israeli prime minister Levi Eshkol at Megiddo.

Revelation is a visionary description of the apocalypse; the 'End of Days' that leads to the second coming. Attributed to the apostle John (though some scholars claim it to be a composite work written c. 90 CE), *Revelation* describes the army of righteousness of God Almighty as it prepares to meet the forces of evil in battle: "And he gathered them together into a place called in the Hebrew tongue Armageddon" (*Revelation*

16:16). Subsequently 'Armageddon', a corruption of the Hebrew 'Mount (Har) of Megiddo', has come to represent this final conflagration.

Whether this line in *Revelation* is to be taken literally or not is a considerable point of dispute within Christian theology. Many evangelical groups follow the 'premillennialist' argument, believing that the actual final battle will take place at Megiddo. The 'amillennialists', on the other hand, see Revelation as an allegorical work drawing attention to the seemingly endless succession of battles fought at Megiddo throughout its history, and pointing out the symbolism of line 16:16 in much the same way as there are symbolic references to 'Babylon' and 'Rome'.

battles: 'Armageddon' (Revelation 16:16). This connection is what brings most visitors to Megiddo, though when they get here they find the complex and unsubstantial remains rather confusing.

Ins and outs

Getting there and away Megiddo is located approximately 35 km southeast of Haifa, on Route 66 at Megiddo Junction. Public transport poses few problems, though look out for the signs and tell the driver where you want to get off. From Haifa HaMifrats: bus 302, two early morning services. From Nazareth via Afula: bus 823, every 30-60 minutes until 1730. From Tiberias via Afula: buses 835/ and 841 en route to Tel Aviv. These buses all stop at Megiddo Junction, 2 km from the site. To return: if in doubt head to Afula from where connections are pretty good.

Background

Such is the complex nature of Megiddo's history that archaeologists have identified 25 levels of occupation on the tel. Whilst lowest levels of stratum suggest settlement in the Chalcolithic period (4500-3300 BCE) or earlier, it is in the period between the Late Bronze Age (c. 1550 BCE) and the latter stages of the Iron Age IIC (700-586 BCE) that the city experienced the key events in its history.

Bronze Age (Canaanite period) The first written reference to Megiddo dates to the 15th century BCE, when **Thutmose III** describes in his inscription at the Temple of Karnak a detailed account of the crushing blow that he dealt the Canaanites on the plain below Megiddo in May 1468 BCE. This testimony represents the earliest-known record of a military engagement.

Megiddo subsequently became a vassal state of Egypt, with the high quality of buildings and artefacts excavated from this period confirming that it was the pharaoh's major base in the Jezreel Valley. The city is mentioned in a number of documents from this period, including the *Taanach letters*, the *el-Amarna letters*, and the *Papyrus Anastasi I*, the latter including a detailed description of the Via Maris route as it passes Megiddo.

Iron Age (Israelite period) How and when the city passed into Israelite hands is still unclear; the various biblical accounts give a confusing picture of the political set-up at the time (compare *Judges 5:19*; *Judges 1:27-28*; *Joshua 17:11-13*; *Joshua 12:7* and *21*; *1 Chronicles 7:29*).

Most commentators conclude that Megiddo was taken by the **Israelites** during the early stages of the United Monarchy, probably by **David** (1004-965 BCE). The violent conflagration that totally destroyed the city at this level is concomitant with David's campaign in the region. What is sure is that Megiddo became one of **Solomon's** fortified northern cities (*1 Kings 9:15*), with a large defensive casement wall enclosing a rich complex of public structures built during his reign (965-928 BCE).

Megiddo

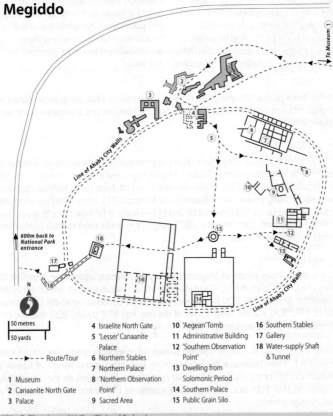

50 metres

50 yards

- - - ▶ - - - Route/Tour

1 Museum
2 Canaanite North Gate
3 Palace
4 Israelite North Gate
5 'Lesser' Canaanite Palace
6 Northern Stables
7 Northern Palace
8 'Northern Observation Point'
9 Sacred Area
10 'Aegean' Tomb
11 Administrative Building
12 'Southern Observation Point'
13 Dwelling from Solomonic Period
14 Southern Palace
15 Public Grain Silo
16 Southern Stables
17 Gallery
18 Water-supply Shaft & Tunnel

(map labels) To Museum ① · Line of Ahab's City Walls · 600m back to National Park entrance · N · Line of Ahab's City Walls

Having been conquered and largely destroyed by the pharaoh Shishak c. 925 BCE, a completely new city was built on the mound by the Israelite king **Ahab** (871-852 BCE). Retaining just the previous main north gate, a new city wall 820 m long and 3.6 m thick was built to encircle the mound, and an extensive complex of buildings was constructed. This included a new stable compound to the north, an extension of the residential district, and the large southern stable complex. The construction of these two stables have led some scholars to suggest that Ahab turned Megiddo into a "chariot city", which survived for a century or more until the arrival of the Assyrian king **Tiglath-pileser III** in 733-732 BCE (*II Kings 15:29*). Having conquered the whole of Galilee, Tiglath-pileser III made Megiddo the administrative capital of the Assyrian province of Magiddu, building his own city on the site on a revolutionary new plan.

The death of the Judean king Josiah at the hands of the Pharaoh Necho at Megiddo in 609 BCE (*II Kings 23:29*; *II Chronicles 35:20-24*) suggests that the city may have passed into Judean hands, though the archaeological evidence suggests an unfortified city clearly in decline. The site may have been partially occupied during the Babylonian/Persian period (586-332 BCE), though from the fourth century BCE Megiddo was abandoned.

Later events Whilst the precise locations of many biblical cities remain in doubt, the same cannot be said for Megiddo; Estori ha-Parhi identified the site here as early as the 14th century CE. **General Allenby** based the British forces here during the latter stages of the Palestine campaign of World War I, later taking the title of Viscount Allenby of Megiddo and Felixstowe! Interestingly, Smith notes how closely Allenby's advance north from Gaza to do battle at the Plains of Esdraelon with the Turks and Germans corresponds with Thutmose III's campaign of 1468 BCE (*Historical Geography of the Holy Land*, 1931 edition). It is also said that Allenby consulted Smith's 1896 edition of this classic work on a daily basis during the 1917-1918 campaign.

The Oriental Institute of Chicago undertook extensive digging at the site in the 1920s and 30s (though some of their conclusions have been challenged, and certainly their brutal methods). Israel's greatest archaeologist Yigael Yadin oversaw the major excavation of Megiddo in the 1960s and early 1970s, and the site was declared a UNESCO World Heritage Site in 2005, along with Hazor and Tel Be'er Sheva.

Sights

Museum A short video sets the scene well and it is recommended that you then begin your tour in the **museum** (1). The centrepiece is the large model of the tel. Different points of interest can be illuminated by touch-buttons, whilst levels of strata that are hidden are revealed by operating the hydraulic lifts built into the model.

North Gate area Exit from the museum past the **reservoir** and on to the excavations. The flight of steps that you pass to your left is part of an outer gate built into the northern wall during the Solomonic period (965-928 BCE), whilst the path above it is part of the Solomonic entrance ramp.

Continuing up the path you arrive at the **Canaanite North Gate** (2), probably built sometime between 1650-1550 BCE. Typical of a Middle to Late Bronze Age city gate, it comprises a straight passageway with a series of three piers projecting from the inner walls, still allowing passage for chariots but reducing the speed at which any traffic could pass through. This gate remained in use for some four centuries.

Immediately inside the gate, are the (very) indistinct remains of a **palace** (3) built during the same period. The building has been identified by the rich treasure of jewellery and carved ivories found there, many of which can now be seen in the Rockefeller Museum in Jerusalem.

Having passed through the Canaanite North Gate, you are greeted on your left by the **Israelite North Gate** (4). A raised wooden walkway enables you to get a better idea of the gate's form, though only the east side has been preserved. This is now thought to have been built by Jeroboam II in the eighth century BCE, rather than Solomon as was previously believed.

Northern observation point From the Israelite Gate follow the marked path left (east) towards the northern observation point. On your left you pass the **northern palace** (7), currently being reconstructed, where you will see stone troughs from the **northern stables** (6) built over the palace during the reign of Ahab.

The **northern observation point** (8) looks down into the **Sacred Area** (9) where the remains of temples from several periods can still be seen. The recently provided isometric drawings at the 'northern observation point' allow a better appreciation of how the 'temple area' looked during various stages of its history. From the northern observation point, retrace your steps to the crossroads and past the '**Aegean Tomb**' (10) towards the public **grain silo** (15). Approximately 8 m deep, the silo is thought to date to the period of Jeroboam (784-748 BCE) and has two flights of circular steps, one for those coming up and one for those going down.

Heading east (left) from the public grain silo, the path divides. The left fork leads to the **southern observation point** (12) from where you can again look down into the Sacred Area (see above). Close to the southern observation point is an **administrative building** (11) from the Israelite period, sometimes referred to as the governor's palace.

The right fork on the path from the public grain silo to the southern observation point leads to a **large dwelling** (13) from the Solomonic period (965-928 BCE), though it was initially thought to date to his predecessor David. Some fine portico pillars are still standing. The very overgrown **southern palace** (14) had thick walls of ashlar masonry, and stood within a large enclosure protected by a gate tower to the north. Unfortunately, it was largely dismantled by the Chicago expedition.

Southern stables Most scholars have agreed that the presence of stone troughs, tethering holes in the stone pillars, as well as the paved halls and courtyards, confirm that these buildings were the **southern stables** (16). The complex was built by Ahab in the ninth century BCE, making Megiddo "Ahab's chariot city", a fact further confirmed by the presence of the Solomon-built administrative building beneath. The southern stables have been reconstructed (complete with 'artistic' iron horses); beyond the stables can be seen a section of the city walls also built during Ahab's reign.

City water-supply system For a city attacked and besieged as many times as Megiddo, a reliable **water-supply** (20) was essential. The city's main source was a spring just to the west of the mound, and several attempts were made to secure this supply. Some time in the 11th-10th century BCE a long narrow passageway built of well-dressed stone (referred to as '**the gallery**' (19) was built from the mound towards the spring, allowing concealed access. Its remains can be clearly seen today.

The gallery was blocked by Ahab's new city wall in the ninth century BCE when work on a new secure access route began. This involved the cutting of a 30-m-deep square shaft into the bedrock within the city's secure walls connected to an 80-m-long horizontal tunnel leading to the spring. It's still possible to walk through the cool but clammy tunnel, though this involves a descent of 183 steps followed by an ascent of 80 steps. You should also note that the tunnel deposits you on a road outside the National Park from where it's a 600-m walk back to the site entrance (or return via the water system). A trip down the remarkable tunnel is in fact the highlight of a visit to Megiddo.

The Harod Valley

Ma'ayan Harod National Park

ⓘ T04-6532211, www.parks.org.il, daily Apr-Sep 0800-1700, Jul-Aug 0800-1800, Oct–Mar 0800-1600, adult/student 36NIS, child 22NIS (50% discount off-season). Kavim buses 411 and 412 between Afula and Bet Shean lead to a junction 1 km from the National Park.

Source of the Harod River, the Harod Spring bubbles up from a point referred to as Gideon's Cave. The spring is associated with the days of the Judges, when Gideon camped here and selected 300 warriors prior to driving the raiding Midianites back across the Jordan, and defeating them there. The small park features a large open-air swimming pool (seasonal), biking trails, BBQ areas and a museum (groups by prior arrangement).

Ein Harod

The kibbutz of Ein Harod is one of few kibbutzim still functioning along truly socialist lines. In 1952, the community split into two, Ein Harod Meuhad and Ein Harod Ihud, as a result of ideological differences. Today the split is in name only, and Ihud makes a perfect base to explore the area. The village itself has several attractions, chiefly **Mishkan Leomanut Museum of Art** ⓘ T04-6485701, www.museumeinharod.org.il, Sun-Thu 0900-1630, Fri 0900-1400, Sat 1000-1430, adult 26NIS, student 13NIS, shop, busy café with garden, the largest art gallery in northern Israel. Lit entirely by natural light, the gallery holds excellent exhibitions and has a permanent collection of beautiful Judaica, themed by the Jewish holidays. Occasionally the gallery's works by Chagall are also on display, while the library has an excellent collection of art books in English. **Bet Sturman Museum** ⓘ T052-3967695, Sun-Thu 0800-1500, Sat 1100-1500, Fri by arrangement, adult 15NIS, student/child 13NIS, houses a collection of archaeological and natural history exhibits (two-headed calf!) related to the local area. It's also possible to arrange horse-riding or visit the dairy farm for night-milking of the 700 cows and 1000 Avasi curly-woolled sheep.

Beit Alpha Synagogue → Colour map 1, grid C4.

The kibbutzim of Beit Alpha and Hefzi-bah were part of the early 20th-century pioneering Jewish settlement of the Jordan Valley region. Whilst digging a new irrigation channel in 1928, members of the kibbutzim stumbled upon the remains of a sixth-century CE synagogue. Though little of the structure of the Beit Alpha Synagogue remains, the splendid mosaic floor is almost entirely preserved and is considered to be one of the best examples from this period in the country. The lively naive designs, with their intriguing mix of subject matter, are memorably unique.

Ins and outs Beit Alpha Synagogue is located at Kibbutz Hefzi-bah (and not Kibbutz Beit Alpha; make sure you get off at the right stop if coming by bus). These kibbutzim are both on Route 669, just south of the HaShitta Junction with Route 71. The site is served by Kavim buses 411 and 412 that run between Afula and Bet Shean.

Synagogue design: the myth of the women's gallery?

Any area that is partitioned from the main hall of an ancient synagogue, for example a balcony, is often described by excavators as being reserved for women. However, an increasing number of scholars are challenging such assumptions. Lee I. Levine, writing in the New *Encyclopedia of Archaeological Excavations in the Holy Land* (1993, p. 1423), points out that though there are plenty of examples that attest to women's participation at the synagogue (*Acts 16:12-13; 17:1-4, 10-12;*

I Corinthians 14-34; Tosefta, Meg. 3:11; J.T. Sot. 1, 4, 16d), there is no mention in rabbinical literature of any physical separation or specific seating area such as a 'women's gallery'. Instead, he argues, the identification of specific areas in ancient synagogues as being designated for women is "purely speculative", adding that the separation of men and women in the synagogue probably only dates to the Middle Ages, perhaps evolving within the influence of Christianity or Islam.

The Synagogue ① *T04-6532004, www.parks.org.il, daily 0800-1700 (last entrance 1630), closes 1 hr earlier on Fri and in winter, adult 20NIS, student 17NIS, child 9NIS.* A 13-min film is shown as you enter the synagogue which does a good job in explaining the history and design elements of the mosaic floor. Aligned to face Jerusalem, the synagogue probably once stood in a residential area of narrow streets, though now it is entirely enclosed within a protective building. Comprising a rectangular hall flanked by two aisles, an **atrium** (courtyard) and a **narthex** (vestibule), it is assumed that the narthex supported a second-storey gallery, possibly for use by women (see box above). The walls of the synagogue were built of undressed stone, and plastered on the inside and out. On the southern wall an apse (raised a little above the level of the nave) housed the Ark of the Covenant. The shallow depression in the floor of the apse, usually used as a depository for sacred texts, revealed a hoard of 36 Byzantine coins.

A walkway allows visitors to walk around and view the mosaic carpet. While the geometric designs in the western aisle are well executed, it is the ornate scenes in the nave made up of 22 different colours that catch the eye. Three panels dominate the floor of the nave. The first, as you enter through the modern doorway, is a panel depicting the **Offering of Isaac**. A sausage-armed Abraham is shown bearing the child Isaac in one hand and a sword in the other, with their names inscribed above. An inscription in Aramaic at the base of the mosaic mentions the artists who laid the floor, dating it to the reign of Emperor Justin, though crucially the floor is broken where the year of his reign is mentioned. Scholars agree that this must be Justin I (518-527 CE), though the building itself is probably older (possibly late fifth century CE).

The central panel is the most intriguing, depicting the cycle of the **zodiac** around a vibrant image of the sun god Helios driving his chariot across the sky. At the four corners the busts of winged women represent the seasons. For the record, the twelve signs are (proceeding anti-clockwise from the '3 o'clock' position): *Taleh*, Aries; *Shor*, Taurus; *Teomin*, Gemini; *Sartan*, Cancer; *Aryeh*, Leo; *Betulah*, Virgo; *Meoznayim*, Libra; *Aqrab*, Scorpio; *Kashat*, Sagittarius; *Gedi*, Capricorn; *Deli*, Aquarius; *Dagim*, Pisces. This representation of pagan-influenced symbols in a synagogue is perhaps surprising, particularly adjacent to the image of the Offering of Isaac. It has been suggested by some scholars that by the sixth century CE the connection in the Jewish consciousness between the zodiac and idol worship had long since disappeared, and that this design was therefore used solely for decorative purposes. However, others are not so sure and Murphy-O'Connor argues that "the very human desire to look into the future was too strong, and they [the rabbis] were forced to find ways to make the zodiac acceptable" (*The Holy Land*, 1992). One such means was to link the symbolism of the twelve tribes of Israel to the *twelve* signs of the zodiac.

The upper panel, closest to the apse, features the Ark of the Law, two lighted menorahs and a shofar, flanked by guarding lions with their claws out.

Mt Gilboa → *Colour map 1, C4.*

Dividing the Plain of Esdraelon from the biblical land of Samaria to the south is a line of basalt hills that includes the 508-m **Mt Gilboa**. What sets this particular rise apart from the rest of the chain is that this was the site of **Saul**'s disastrous battle against the **Philistines**, c. 1004 BCE. Having consulted the witch at En-dor (who foresaw his grisly fate, see I Samuel 28:7-25), Saul's Israelite army was resoundingly defeated with his three sons Jonathon, Abinadab and Malchi-shua all being killed (*I Samuel 28-31*). Such was the watching Saul's despair that he fell upon his own sword, whilst the jubilant Philistines hung his headless body from the walls of Bet Shean (*I Samuel 31:10*). David's famous lament over Saul's death (*II Samuel 1:17-27*) is the source of the expression "how the mighty have fallen".

There are no archaeological remains to be seen, though the 22-km **Gilboa Scenic Route** provides pleasant views as it snakes its way along the top of the forested hills. The route begins either at the Ma'ale Gilboa (Ascent of Gilboa) Junction on Route 669, or at a point opposite Jezreel (Yizre'el) where a dry-ski slope is close to completion. The hills feature several attractive picnic spots in the forest planted by the Jewish National Fund, with excellent views – especially worthwhile is the detour to Mt Shaul viewpoint. Each spring there is the 'Annual Gilboa Popular Walk' (T6533242, F6533362, for details) when the famed purple Gilboa Iris, unique to the area, is in bloom. A couple of walking trails are marked out; a good place to start these is at Mt Barkan where a look-out tower provides 360-degree views.

Gan HaShlosha (Sachne) Park

① *T04-6586219, www.parks.org.il, daily 0800-1700, winter -1600, closes 1 hr earlier on Fri, adults 36NIS, student 32NIS, child 22NIS. The park is served by Kavim buses 411 and 412 between Afula and Bet Shean.*

A great favourite with weekend-ing Israelis, this beautiful park features landscaped flowering gardens leading down to a series of pools connected by waterfalls that combine to form a beautiful swimming environment. The water is deliciously refreshing in summer, and remains inviting during cooler months. Visibility is good, though you must be prepared to share your bathing experience with millions of tiny fish. Other facilities include a children's pool, changing rooms and toilets, massage, a very good restaurant ('Muzza on the Water', open till 2400), children's playground, picnic tables and a first-aid station. Other attractions are the **Museum of Regional and Mediterranean Archaeology** ① *Sat-Thu 1000-1400*, exhibiting findings from the Bet Shean Valley in addition to rare Etruscan and Greek artefacts, and a restored wooden tower and stockade (though they don't seem to drag many people away from the water). After a hard day of sightseeing in the Jezreel Valley, the park makes a highly recommended break.

The water in the main pools is deep, so children should be supervised. Take care with your possessions whilst swimming since theft is not unknown. The park may become too overcrowded for some during weekends and holidays.

For Sleeping and Eating price codes and other relevant information, see Essentials pages 26-31.

Sleeping

LL-E Ein Harod Country Guest House, Ein Harod Ihud, T04-6486083, www.ein-harod.co.il. A range of accommodation levels, top of which are the romantic 'Iris Suites'. From the giant jacuzzi you can gaze over your private garden to the Gilboa Range; furnishings and fittings are truly high-spec and tasteful; 'cinema' and sound system; shower with 7 settings! 'Ofek' wooden cabins suitable for couples or families, with terraces, kitchenettes, jacuzzi, gardens and views of the Jezreel Valley. The older guestrooms are clean and simple with compact kitchen; dorm beds are available for 100NIS. A restaurant is planned for the near future, and breakfast (included) can be eaten in your room, or at the Beehive Café (see below). Guests are given discount tokens for surrounding attractions/restaurants, and there's a summer swimming pool.

A-C IYHA Ma'ayan Harod Youth Hostel, T04-5945588, www.iyha.org.il. 28 pleasant a/c chalets, with fridge, TV, coffee facilities, meals available, call ahead for reservations. Right next to the National Park, where you get discounted entry.

Alpha Accommodation (Alfa Eru'ah), Kibbutz Beit Alpha, T04-6533026, ba@betalfa.org.il. Some of the cheapest double rooms in Israel, this odd but friendly choice has large grounds at the base of the Gilboa ridge and a rural feel. 15 new rooms are comfy and simple, with kitchenette and terrace (120NIS); old ones are clean, but smell musty; 6-bed dorms (50NIS) are clean but more jaded. Kavim bus 411 and 412, can pick up from bus stop.

Eating

₸₸₸-₸₸ Herb Farm, Mt Gilboa, signposted off the Gilboa Scenic Route 667, T04-6531093, www.herb-farm.co.il. Country-style restaurant that is famed throughout Israel, where you can enjoy quality food made from locally produced ingredients. Salads (try the Gilboa, 48NIS), mains (from 57-110NIS) including ostrich fillets; vegetarians limited to pastas and appetisers; desserts are special (cold baked cheesecake with wildberry sauce); wine from their own vineyards. The large bustling terraces overhang killer views; ceramics workshop adjacent. Weekday lunch menu till 1600 is the best deal. Mon-Sat 1200-2230.

₸₸ Dag Dagan, Kibbutz Hefzi-bah, T04-6534359, www.rest.co.il/dag-dagan. Adjacent to Beit Alpha Synagogue, this excellent fish restaurant seems to have fed every Israeli politician and singer imaginable. Sweet or salt water fish comes grilled or smoked, or in various sauces; several vegetarian options, plus salads. The main room has sawdust floors and was an old cattle shed (dating from 1925); it's preferable to the newer side room. There's a little garden for dining under bougainvillea trees. Mon-Thu 1200-1600 and 1900-2300, Fri and Sat 1200-2300

₸₸-₸ Beehive Café, Ein Harod Ihud, T04-6486263. Terribly cute little café hidden behind an unimposing façade, serving cakes, snacks and breakfasts. Homewares and knick-knacks are for sale and add to the homely feel. Mon-Thu 0900-1700, Fri 0900-1300, Sat 0900-1600.

Bet Shean → *Colour map 1, grid C4.*

ⓘ *T04-6587189, www.parks.org.il, daily 0800-1800 (last entrance at 1630), winter -1700, closes 1 hr earlier on Fri, adult 28NIS, student 21NIS, child 13NIS. Guided night tours Mon, Tue, Thu and Sat Apr-Oct (English not always available), reserve via T*3639, adults 40NIS, child 30NIS. Cardo Café has fine views over the site; large shop; toilets.*

With a history spanning almost 6000 years, the excavations at Bet Shean have provided an important window to the region's past. Long before digging at the site began it was noted by a visitor in 1894 that "few sites promise richer spoil to the first happy explorer with permission to excavate" (Smith, *Historical Geography of the Holy Land*). When excavation work did begin in 1926, the Field-Director was able to write to Smith that "the wonderful truth of your forecast about the richness of the antiquities … has been amply proved".

Today, Bet Shean National Park attracts a large number of tourists to see the best-preserved Roman-Byzantine town in Israel, and the site is very well presented. But though Bet Shean does live up to its billing, and is definitely worth visiting, those who have visited Jerash (in Jordan) may feel something of an anti-climax here.

Ins and outs
Getting there and away From Tiberias, Veolia bus 28 (45 minutes, 14.5NIS), Egged bus 961 at 0700 (Jerusalem-bound). From Afula Kavim buses 411 and 412 (one hour), frequent service Sunday-Thursday 0530-2300, Friday 0530-1700, Saturday from 1700.

Getting around A tour of the site begins at the theatre, and follows a roughly clockwise route. Excavations remain in progress so some areas may be sealed off. It is worth listening to three audio commentaries, positioned at key points of the site. A few less impressive attractions are located outside the National Park (see 'General Plan').

Background
Such has been the strategic importance of the site here that it was more or less continuously occupied from the Late Neolithic period (c. 5000 BCE) until the Early Arab period (638-1099 CE). Bet Shean lies at the junction of two important routes: the *Via Maris* (Way of the Sea), linking Egypt and the Mediterranean coast to Babylon and the east, and the Jordan Valley road, connecting the Sea of Galilee to Eilat. The desirability of this location was enhanced by the abundance of the water supply and the fertility of the surrounding land. Bet Shean's history, and subsequently its archaeology, can be divided into two distinct periods. During its early history, the superimposed settlements occupied the four-hectare mound – **Tel Bet Shean** (Arabic: *Tell el-Husn*) – at the north of the site. Some time in the third century BCE the city moved down to the plain, with very limited building taking place on the mound itself.

Early history From finds excavated on Tel Bet Shean it appears that the site was first settled in the Pottery Neolithic period of the fifth millennium BCE, with numerous finds dating from the later Chalcolithic period (fourth millennium BCE). By the middle of the Late Bronze Age (c. 1550-1200 BCE), Bet Shean was firmly established as an **Egyptian** administrative centre following **Thutmose III**'s successful campaign in the region (see 'Megiddo', page 574). The town is subsequently mentioned in several New Kingdom sources, including Thutmose III's list of cities at Karnak Temple in Luxor.

Following the **Israelite** conquest of the region in the 13th century BCE, Bet Shean is mentioned as one of the Canaanite cities that was perhaps too strong to be taken (*Joshua 17:11*; *Judges 1:27*). The town later became infamous as the place where the **Philistines** hung the headless torso of Saul from the city walls after the Israelite defeat on Mt Gilboa in 1004 BCE (*I Samuel 31:9-10*). Bet Shean came under Israelite control probably during the reign of David (1004-965 BCE) and is listed as one of **Solomon**'s (965-928 BCE) administrative districts (*I Kings 4:12*), though it was also one of the cities captured during Pharaoh **Shishak**'s campaign of 925 BCE.

Later history A substantial gap now appears in the recorded history of Bet Shean. It is not until the third century BCE that Bet Shean reappears, this time under the name of **Scythopolis** and now located at the foot of the tel. It is still unclear how it came to be known as 'City of the Scythians', and few of the explanations offered seem particularly plausible. The picture is further confused by references to the town as 'Nysa', the supposed place where Dionysus (Bacchus) was nursed by the nymphs.

During the **Maccabean (Hasmonean) Revolt** (166-63 BCE), Jewish control over the city was firmly established c. 107 BCE by the uncompromising **John Hyrcanus** (third son of Simon, last of the Maccabee brothers). He offered the citizens of the town the choice of conversion and circumcision, or exile; most chose the latter. During the reign of John's son and successor, the despotic **Alexander Jannaeus** (103-76 BCE), an ageing **Cleopatra** paid a visit to Scythopolis following the conclusion of their peace treaty.

Many of the exiled citizens of Scythopolis returned when the city fell into **Roman** hands following Pompey's conquest of Palestine, and a period of sustained growth ensued. The development of the town was briefly interrupted by the outbreak of the Jewish revolt against Rome (66-73 CE). Josephus records the tragic experience of the Jewish population of Scythopolis during the early days of the revolt. Rather than supporting their compatriots, the Jews "lined up with the Scythopolitans, and treating their own safety as of more importance than the ties of blood, they joined the battle with their countrymen" (*Jewish War, II: 466-8*). However, the Scythopolitans became suspicious of the excessive zeal of their Jewish allies and, in a remarkable display of treachery, lured them to a grove and slaughtered all 13,000 of them.

Following the suppression of the Jewish Revolt by Vespasian, Scythopolis experienced something of a boom, with Josephus describing it as the largest city of the **Decapolis** (the league of ten cities established by Pompey to serve as the bastion of Graeco-Roman influence). By the end of the third century CE Scythopolis was one of the leading textile-producing centres in the Roman Empire, famed for its quality linen. The Christianization of the Roman Empire saw an influx of Christians, with the 'biblical geographer' Eusebius later referring to Scythopolis as "a noble city" (*Onomasticon*). The city also produced the sixth-century CE Christian historian Cyril of Scythopolis. Inevitably, the decay of the **Byzantine Empire** saw a decline in the city's fortunes, most notably after the exodus of the skilled linen workers. (Those who believe that history is cyclical will note the current plight of Bet Shean. A development town almost totally dependent on the textile industry, the recent closure of the Kitan clothing factory has pushed unemployment levels in the town well above the national average.)

In 634 CE the town fell to the **Arabs** following a major tactical blunder by the Byzantine army. Having fallen back upon Scythopolis, the Byzantines took advantage of the plentiful local water supply to flood the surrounding plain, making it an impenetrable marshland. However, as the Arab army prepared for a long and potentially futile siege, the Byzantine army rashly attacked, suffering a complete defeat. The victorious Arabs revived the old Semitic version of the city's name (Arabic: *Besian*), with this battle celebrated in the annals of Islam as the 'Day of Besian'. Though the name was revived the city's fortunes were not, and this once great urban centre's fate was sealed by the devastating **earthquake** of 749 CE.

The **Crusaders** briefly occupied Bet Shean, though they preferred to concentrate their fortifications at Belvoir, to the north (see page 588). This was to prove a fateful mistake, ignoring the glaringly obvious strategic location of Bet Shean in favour of a remote, and thus ineffectual, position. Smith suggests that "when the Crusaders left Bet Shean to its fate, they sealed their own".

The site

Theatre Bet Shean's Roman **theatre** (1) is spectacular, despite the fact that only one of three tiers of seating is preserved; at its peak, it could probably accommodate in the region of 7000 spectators. One of the theatre's most remarkable features is the ornately decorated scaenae frons (several-storey-high stage back-drop), built with imported marble and granite (in the process of being restored). The date of construction is placed tentatively within the reign of the Roman Emperor Septimius Severus (193-211 CE), though an earlier theatre could well have stood on this site. Alterations and repairs were made throughout the Roman and Byzantine periods, indicating that the theatre remained in use. It was largely destroyed in the great earthquake of 749 CE.

Western bathhouse Though built upon Roman foundations, the **bathhouse** (2) standing today was built over several periods of the fifth and sixth centuries CE. The heating system

Roman & Byzantine remains, Bet Shean

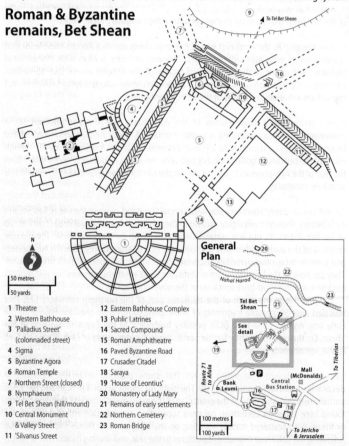

50 metres
50 yards

N

1 Theatre
2 Western Bathhouse
3 'Palladius Street' (colonnaded street)
4 Sigma
5 Byzantine Agora
6 Roman Temple
7 Northern Street (closed)
8 Nymphaeum
9 Tel Bet Shean (hill/mound)
10 Central Monument & Valley Street
11 'Silvanus Street

12 Eastern Bathhouse Complex
13 Public Latrines
14 Sacred Compound
15 Roman Amphitheatre
16 Paved Byzantine Road
17 Crusader Citadel
18 Saraya
19 'House of Leontius'
20 Monastery of Lady Mary
21 Remains of early settlements
22 Northern Cemetery
23 Roman Bridge

General Plan

To Tel Bet Shean

Nahal Harod

Tel Bet Shean

See detail

Route 71 to Afula

To Tiberias

Bank Leumi

Central Bus Station

Mall (McDonalds)

To Jericho & Jerusalem

100 metres
100 yards

(hypocaust) that provided hot air to the *caldaria* (hot rooms) and *tepidaria* (tepid rooms) can be clearly seen. Here the citizens would socialize at any time of day or night.

Palladius Street This 180-m-long **colonnaded street (3)** running from the foot of the tel (mound) to the theatre takes its name from an inscription discovered in the *stoa* (roofed portico that served as a sidewalk) that mentions the city's governor, Flavius Palladius. This street was probably first laid in the mid-fourth century CE though it was repaired several times subsequently. Roman cities were always built to the same design, so that strangers could easily orientate themselves on arrival, and so it is with the street plan of Bet Shean, though modifications had to be made to account for the local topography. The street is paved with basalt slabs in a herring-bone pattern with a 2-m-deep sewage channel running down the centre. The west side of the street was flanked by a raised stoa paved with mosaics, with a roof supported by columns topped by Ionic capitals.

About half-way along the street, to the west, is a semi-circular **sigma (4)**, or plaza. Some of the buildings that open on to the sigma have their original mosaic floors.

Roman temple At the northeast end of Palladius Street stands a **Roman temple (6)** that is speculatively associated with worship of Dionysus or Tyche. A 20-m-wide monumental stairway rises to the *prostyle* (columned façade of the temple) where four 15-m-high columns once stood on high pedestals. The two immense columns lying broken on the ground are a dramatic reminder of the 749 CE earthquake.

Nymphaeum Also a major victim of the earthquake was the **nymphaeum (8)**, a monumental structure featuring a public fountain. A Greek inscription on one of the beams attributes construction to a Flavius Artemidorus in the fourth century CE, though much of the building is quite obviously two centuries older. A conduit brought water from the rear of the nymphaeum to a small pool at the front. Archaeologists plan to rebuild this structure eventually.

Tel Bet Shean Steep stairs take you back several thousand years, to the site of Bet Shean's early history. Though thoroughly excavated there is little of great visual impact on the top of **Tel Bet Shean (9)**, but it is certainly worth the climb for the view alone. The meagre **remains of the early settlements (21)** belie the rich treasure troves from the Nineteenth and Twentieth Egyptian dynasties discovered here: the most important such finds in Israel. They are now in the Israel Museum in Jerusalem, and what you see here are just replicas enclosed within a mud-brick mock-up of the governor's house.

The low rise to the north of the tel forms part of the **northern cemetery (22)** that revealed over 50 sizeable fragments of anthropoid coffins from the Late Bronze to the Early Iron Age (c. 1300-1150 BCE), possibly belonging to the Egyptian garrison at Bet Shean. On the next hill slightly further north stands the **Monastery of Lady Mary (20)** (Tell Istaba, see opposite).

Central monument and Valley Street This stone platform originally supported a **decorative columnar monument (10)**. The platform stands about 4 m high and has been partially restored, and, though the exact plan of the monument is unclear, the varied debris found here suggests Corinthian columns supporting an elaborate *entablature* (cornice or frieze) with scattered statues standing on marble pedestals. Damn that earthquake. Adjoining the columnar monument platform to the rear, and sharing its southwest wall, is a large basilica (28 m by 65 m). A hexagonal altar dedicated to Dionysus with an inscription dating it to 142 CE was excavated from the basilica. A Roman colonnaded street ('Valley Street') runs northeast towards the remains of a **Roman bridge** (23) over the Nahal Harod. The basalt paved street is an impressive 11 m wide, though including the colonnaded sidewalks on either side it measures 24 m across in places.

Silvanus Street The 56-m-long **Silvanus Street** (11) incorporated a Roman colonnade of 18 limestone columns standing on pedestals and topped with Ionic capitals. A superb marble statue of Dionysus (now housed in the Israel Museum) was found in the debris of the stoa. An ornamental stepped pool once reflected the columns fronting the stoa, but was filled in and topped by a row of shops in the Arab period. At the east end of the stoa are a number of artist's reconstructions of 'Silvanus Street' in the Roman (second to fourth centuries CE) and Early Arab (seventh to eighth centuries CE) periods.

Eastern bathhouse Returning towards the theatre, recent excavations have now revealed the full glory of the **eastern bathhouse complex** (12). It appears that this structure was built during the Roman period and later renovated in Byzantine times. It is possible to make out the *caldarium* to the north and the *frigidarium* to the south. The public latrines (13), always an attraction, could seat up to 40 on the communal marble bench which is in a particularly fine state of preservation. The **sacred compound** (14) consists of a small temple with altars and a fountain, where goddesses to death and nature were discovered.

Other sites outside the National Park

The **Roman amphitheatre** (15) is located to the south of the National Park, just off the main road between the bus station and park entrance. Its external measurements are 102 m by 67 m, though only three out of perhaps twelve rows of stone seats remain. Dating construction is not precise, though it may well have been built whilst the Sixth Legion (Ferrata) was stationed here in the second century CE. The seats were placed a good 10 m higher than the arena in order to prevent the wild animals from mauling any of the spectators. It fell out of use in the fourth century, with the decline in support of gladiatorial conquests between man and beast, and man and man, amongst the increasingly Christian population.

Alongside the amphitheatre runs a section of **paved Byzantine road** (16) (c. 522 CE according to an inscription) lined with shops, suggesting that this was a densely populated residential area by the Byzantine period. Many gold coins, including some dating to the succeeding Early Arab period, were found in the ruins of the buildings destroyed by the earthquake.

The **Crusader citadel** (17) now houses the tourist office, and the adjacent **Saraya** (18) has been beautifully restored; note that the Ottomans incorporated a couple of capitals from the nearby ruins into the entrance. Worth a visit are the 'House of Leontius' and the Monastery of Lady Mary, though before setting out ensure at the National Park ticket office that they are open. The **'House of Leontius'** (19) is a Byzantine-period synagogue located several hundred metres west of the Byzantine bathhouse. The floor of the building features some particularly fine mosaics, with some cryptic Greek inscriptions suggesting that the synagogue may have been part of an inn.

A particularly fine calendar mosaic can be seen in the floor of the **Monastery of Lady Mary** (20) (Arabic: *Tell Istaba*), built to the north of Bet Shean (and visible from the tel) in 567 CE.

Border crossing into Jordan

There is a recognized land border crossing between Israel and Jordan just 6 km east of Bet Shean. It is known as the **Jordan River Border Crossing** or **Jisr Sheikh Hussein** (Sheikh Hussein Bridge) according to which side of the border you are on and, unlike the crossing point closest to Jerusalem (Allenby/King Hussein Bridge), it is possible to get a Jordanian visa on the border. This crossing point is closer to Jerusalem than the Arava crossing point near Eilat.

You can take an over-priced taxi from Bet Shean (30NIS), or Nazarene Tours runs four buses per week to Amman (75NIS, T1-599-599-599, www.ntt-buses.com) from Nazareth, with a pick-up in Afula on the way (not at the Central Bus Station in Afula, but from Rd 71 just north of the bus station, ask for directions). From the Jordanian side irregular minibuses run to Irbid from where regular buses run to the capital Amman. Aim to cross the border as early in the day as possible. Information on this border crossing can be found at www.iaa.gov.il. For full details on border crossing formalities (departure tax, visas, opening times, etc) see the 'Getting there, overland' section on page 21.

Belvoir (Kokhav HaYarden National Park) → Colour map 1, grid C4.

① T04-6581766, daily 0800-1700, winter -1600, closes 1 hr earlier on Friday, adult 20NIS, student 17NIS, child 9NIS. Toilets.

Belvoir remains one of the best-preserved Crusader castles in Israel, though as the name suggests the splendour of the setting is part of the attraction.

Though Belvoir was partially dismantled in the 13th century, the substantial remains give a vivid picture of a concentric ring castle, making it well worth the effort of getting here. If nothing else you can appreciate the superb view of the Jordan Valley below you, and across to Mount Gilead in Jordan. On a clear day you can see north across the Sea of Galilee to the snowy peaks of Mt Hermon.

Ins and outs

Getting there and away Belvoir is not really accessible by public transport. Buses that run between Tiberias and Bet Shean (Veolia 28, Egged 961) pass the turn-off for the site (though the nearest official bus stops are 1 km on either side). From the turn-off, it is a very steep 6.5-km twisting climb up Route 717 to Belvoir. I cannot emphasize enough how steep and long this climb is. Take plenty of water. By car, turn off Route 90 about halfway between the Sea of Galilee and Bet Shean. An alternative route approaches along Route 717 from the west, via Ein Harod and Moledet, though the road is only suitable for 4WDs, and officially it's private.

Background

The **Order of the Knights Hospitaller** constructed the black basalt castle here in 1168 on the site of a fortified farm established some 30 years earlier. It was built to defend a number of important routes, most notably the Jordan Valley road, the route via Mount Tabor and Nazareth to Acre (Akko), and the ancient Via Maris through the Jezreel Valley. However, as we shall see, the fortress was probably too isolated to fulfil this role. Its name Belvoir ("fine view") requires no explanation. In 1182-83 the superbly constructed fortress easily withstood **Salah al-Din**'s assault, yet four years later the garrison stood by impotently as Salah al-Din's troops by-passed Belvoir on their way to defeating the Crusader army at the Horns of Hattin, just 25 km to the north (see page 608). One of Belvoir's strengths, its remoteness, became a weakness, succinctly put by Smith: "The

Christian banner at Belvoir waved a mere signal, remote, ineffectual above the Arab flood that speedily covered the land" (*Historical Geography of the Holy Land*, 1894).

Following the defeat of the Latin Kingdom at the Horns of Hattin, Salah al-Din's army laid siege to Belvoir. The Crusaders held out for 18 months, a testament to the resolution of the garrison and the fortress's superb construction. The Crusaders were eventually forced to sue for peace when the Arab army, having tunnelled under the outer fortification wall, undermined the east tower and brought about its collapse. In recognition of the garrison's courage, and an indication of the integrity of Salah al-Din, the Crusaders were allowed free passage to Tyre. Though the Arab army dismantled the church, the fortress itself was left largely intact.

It was not until the early 13th century when, fearing the return of the Christian armies, the then ruler of Damascus, **el-Malik el-Mu'azzam**, ordered Belvoir to be dismantled. In effect only the upper storey was removed but, though the Crusaders regained Belvoir by treaty in 1241, their stay was too short to effect any restoration. The fortress remained abandoned until the early 19th century when Bedouins established the village of Kaukab el-Hawa ("Star of the Winds") amongst the ruins. This too was abandoned in 1948.

Tour of the site
Belvoir comprises two concentric rings, a building style common in the late Latin Kingdom period. The knights, including the commander of the order and the priesthood, were housed within the inner keep (or *donjon*), whilst the ordinary soldiery, auxiliaries and mercenaries occupied the area between the donjon and the outer fortification wall. This was seen as a safeguard against treachery when the loyalty of the mercenaries could not be guaranteed.

The tour of the site begins at the viewpoint just outside the southeast tower, and is adequately explained on noticeboards throughout the fortress and in the leaflet from the ticket office. A Panoramic Trail (clearly signed) takes you on a 30-minute circular walk, and is certainly worthwhile for the views.

Tiberias and the Sea of Galilee

→ Colour map 1, B4.
Not only is the Sea of Galilee (Heb: Kinneret) central to the physical geography of Galilee, regulating the micro-climate and providing a source of drinking water, irrigation and food, it is also central to the cultural and religious geography of the region. Most visitors use the Jewish holy city of Tiberias as a base from which to explore the beautiful surrounding countryside and numerous archaeological sites, most notably the locations associated with the Galilean Ministry of Jesus.

Background
Geography Located in the Jordan Valley some 209 m below sea level, the Sea of Galilee is the largest reservoir of fresh water in Israel, and second only in the Middle East to Lake Nasser. As such it is a vital component of the water economy of Israel, supplying around 25 percent of the country's water requirement through the National Water Carrier. At its widest points it is 21 km north to south and 12 km east to west, with a maximum depth of 46 m. In addition to providing water for agriculture and municipal functions, the Sea of Galilee generates income through tourism and fishing, the latter revolving mainly around an indigenous species of perch known locally as St Peter's fish.

Physically, the basin in which the lake lies is said to remind some of a poorly wooded Scottish loch (Smith, 1894), though Mark Twain was less impressed. Visiting the Holy Land in 1867, Twain describes the Sea of Galilee region as "an unobtrusive basin of water, some mountainous desolation, and one tree" (*The Innocents Abroad*, 1911). It's remarkable how Twain's derogatory remarks have been used by Zionists to forward their argument that the land was unoccupied and uncared for. He came to mock, not make a political statement.

Tiberias and the Sea of Galilee

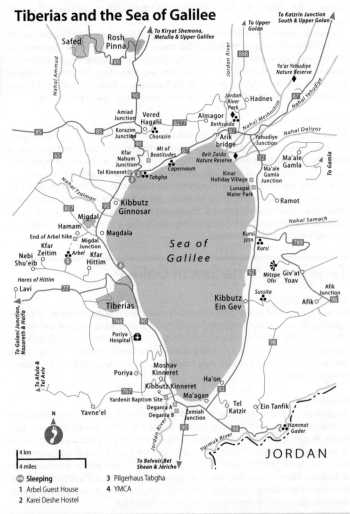

Sleeping
1 Arbel Guest House
2 Karei Deshe Hostel
3 Pilgerhaus Tabgha
4 YMCA

Biblical history It is for its biblical history that most people know the Sea of Galilee. In the 'Fourth Book of Moses, called Numbers' (*Numbers 34:11*) the 'Sea of Chinnereth' (or 'Kinnereth') is first mentioned in the account of the distribution of land amongst the tribes of Israel. The name 'Kinnereth' is said to be derived from the Hebrew word kinnor, or harp, which the shape of the lake is said to resemble. Tiberias, the only one of the large cities built around the lake that still exists, became a great centre of Jewish learning and remains one of the four holy cities of the Jews.

For Christians also there is a deep attachment to the Sea of Galilee as the theatre in which so many events in the life of Jesus were acted out. Capernaum, on the northwest shore, became Jesus' "own city" where he performed several miracles. It was also the place at which he called Matthew, Peter, Andrew, James and John to follow him, the latter four of whom made their living as fishermen on the lake. Indeed, it was for these fishermen that he "stilled the storm" (*Matthew 8:23-27; Mark 4:35-41; Luke 8:22-25*), and walked on the water to give them faith (*Matthew 14:22-32; Mark 6:47-51; John 6:16-21*). The "Sermon on the Mount", delivered on the Mt of Beatitudes just above the northwest shore, has become one of the basic tenets of Jesus' teachings.

Tiberias → *Colour map 1, grid B4.*

The largest town on the shores of the Sea of Galilee, Tiberias is a natural base from which to explore the Galilee and Golan region. The atmosphere is relaxed, accommodation is good value, there's nightlife to suit all tastes, and the hot springs have been a major attraction since Roman times. Many visitors seem to assume that there is a strong link between the city's history and Christianity but, though Tiberias is mentioned in the New Testament (*John 6:1, 23*), there is no evidence that Jesus ever visited here. In fact, it is within Judaism, and not Christianity, that Tiberias finds its significance. To Jews it is one of the four holy cities (with Jerusalem, Safed and Hebron) and features several important pilgrimage sites.

Ins and outs

Getting there and away Tiberias has good transport connections with the rest of the country. Buses connect Tiberias to Tel Aviv (three hours) (sherut is faster), Jerusalem, Nazareth (45 minutes) and Haifa (1¼ hours), as well as all the major sites in Upper Galilee and the Golan. There are several car-hire firms based in Tiberias, with a rented car being easily the most convenient way to explore the Sea of Galilee, Upper Galilee and the Golan.

Getting around The town centre is compact enough to get around on foot, and even the sites to the south can easily be reached by walking (though bus five runs as far as the hot springs). Bikes are a perfect way to explore further afield, readily available from hostels (see Activities, page 606).

Tourist information **Tourist Information Office** ① *Archaeological Garden, HaBanim, T06-6725666, Sun-Thu 0800-1600, Fri 0800-1200.* Excellent information and advice, good for brochures and maps. Also see www.tiberias-hotels.com for good listings of attractions and restaurants.

Background

Founding of the city The city was founded between 17 and 20 CE by a son of Herod the Great, **Herod Antipas**, and named after his patron Tiberias Caesar. The new city, which soon replaced Sepphoris as the district capital, was built by Herod Antipas primarily to revive the process begun by his father, namely creating a progressive, Hellenized version of the Jewish state. Ironically, the new city had difficulty attracting Jewish residents since it was built on the site of an ancient cemetery and thus violated Jewish law. Josephus suggests that Herod Antipas attracted new settlers by "equipping houses at his own expense and adding new gifts of land" (*Antiquities XVIII*, 36-38), though force and coercion were more likely inducements to settle here. Tax exemptions were offered and even the poor and runaway slaves were given citizenship, though many Jews living in the surrounding area were forced off their land and relocated to Tiberias.

Josephus presents a picture of a magnificent city built in the Roman style, with a large royal palace, baths, cardo and a large synagogue "capable of accommodating a large crowd" (*Life*, 277). Ironically, by the middle of the first century CE Herod Antipas' new Graeco-Roman city had a Jewish majority, though the king's Judaism was often questioned. Not only did he decorate his palace and the gates of the city with idolatrous images, he also broke Mosaic law by marrying his brother's wife. It was John the Baptist's condemnation of such marriage practices that led to his beheading.

Roman Tiberias and Jewish Renaissance In the build-up to the Roman advance into Galilee during the **First Jewish Revolt** (66-73 CE), Tiberias was a pawn in the struggle for control of the opposition armies between Josephus, Governor of Galilee, and his rival John (though it should be noted that the main source of detail of this rivalry is Josephus himself!). When the city revolted against his command, Josephus felt himself compelled to hand it over to his soldiers to pillage, though he later "collected all the plunder and gave it back to the townspeople to … give the citizens a sharp lesson by pillaging it, and then giving back their possessions to recover their good will" (*Jewish War, II*, 647; see also Sepphoris, page 564). Perhaps fearing that the Roman commander would not be so magnanimous, Tiberias surrendered to Vespasian without incident, the town's zealots fleeing to Tarichaeae (see Migdal, on page 614). Tiberias was ruled by Agrippa II until his death c. 96 CE, after which the city came under direct Roman rule. A period of economic prosperity followed, notwithstanding the Jewish Bar Kokhba Uprising of 132-35 CE, though Tiberias' role in this revolt is unclear.

Despite the construction early in the second century CE of a large pagan temple honouring the Roman Emperor Hadrian, the city was 'cleansed' of ritual impurity by Rabbi Simeon Bar Yochai (c. 145 CE), thus making it acceptable for Jews to settle here in numbers. Tiberias became the centre of Jewish life in Israel (Jerusalem still being designated off-limits to Jews). **Rabbi Yohanan ben Nappaha** (c. 180-279 CE) established the Great Study House (Bêth HaMidrash HaGadol) in Tiberias c. 220 CE, where he continued his study of the oral code of law (Mishnah) that had been compiled by his teacher and mentor, **Rabbi Judah I ha-Nasi**. The work that Yohanan began in testing the logical consistency of the Mishnah manifested itself in the Gemara, finally completed by his disciples c. 400 CE. With the Mishnah, the Gemara forms the Palestinian (Jerusalem) Talmud, with the system of Hebrew punctuation developed in Tiberias becoming the accepted standard for the Torah. The Jewish renaissance in Tiberias was highlighted by the shifting here from Sepphoris (Zippori) of the Sanhedrin (the highest judicial and ecclesiastical council of the ancient Jewish nation), c. 235 CE.

Byzantine period Despite the adoption of **Christianity** by the Roman empire, Galilee remained predominantly Jewish during the early years of the Byzantine period (324-638 CE). However, the gradual conversion of the pagan population to Christianity brought them into conflict with the Jews. The Persian invasion in 614 CE saw the Jews support the invaders, with many Christians massacred and their churches destroyed. When the Roman Byzantine army retook the region in 628 CE, the massacres were reciprocated. Despite this, Tiberias remained for a time the seat of Jewish study, with the Academy (Yeshiva) of Eretz-Israel that succeeded the Sanhedrin continuing to function here well into the 10th century CE.

Early Arab and Crusader periods When the **Arabs** defeated the Byzantine army at Yarmuk River in 636 CE, they established Tiberias as their northern capital, though later shifted it to Bet Shean. The importance of Tiberias to the Jews declined, not due to Muslim persecution but to the Arab decision to allow Jews to re-occupy Jerusalem. The earthquake that destroyed Bet Shean in 749 CE effectively revitalized Tiberias, establishing it again as the Arab capital of the province of Jordan. Ironically, a major earthquake in 1033 largely destroyed Tiberias.

When Tancred conquered the Galilee for the **Crusaders** in 1099 a new city was built at Tiberias, just to the north of the original site. The city was encircled by **Salah al-Din** in 1187, and it was on the way to relieving the city that the forces of the Latin Kingdom were defeated at the Horns of Hattin 10 km to the west (see page 608), thus bringing to an end Crusader rule in the Holy Land. Though the Crusaders returned to the Galilee, they were finally expelled by the **Mamluks** in 1265.

Ottoman period Turkish rule was established in Palestine following the defeat of the Mamluks in 1516. Keen to attract Jewish entrepreneurial skill, the early Ottoman sultans encouraged the Jews recently expelled from Spain and Portugal to settle in Palestine. In 1562 Suliman the Magnificent granted tax collection rights in Tiberias to **Joseph Nasi**, a Marrano Jew from Portugal, and his mother-in-law **Donna Gracia**. They were permitted to rebuild the city walls and to establish a silk industry, with a view towards establishing a safe haven for Jews that may later become an independent Jewish enclave. Their plans were thwarted by the failure of the Ottomans to retain effective control over this part of their empire.

Tiberias became a relative backwater once more until the Druze war-lord **Fakhr al-Din** briefly revived the city's fortunes when he established his capital here between 1595 and 1635. After another period of Ottoman rule, Tiberias once again became semi-autonomous under the rule of the Bedouin sheikh **Dahr el-Amr**. Relative stability was brought to Tiberias under Dahr el-Amr, though in 1742, just two years into his period of rule, annoyed by his refortification of the city the Turkish army marched from Damascus to teach him a lesson. After a siege lasting 85 days the Turks captured Tiberias and, having admonished Dahr el-Amr marched directly back to Damascus. He didn't seem to learn from this example and 33 years later the Turks assassinated this 'upstart'.

The subsequent Turkish governor of the Galilee, **Ahmed el-Jazzar**, known affectionately as 'The Butcher', ruled with an iron fist, though fear of his excesses served to bring peace to the region. He was succeeded briefly by the invading Egyptians, headed by Ibrahim Pasha. In 1837 Tiberias was once again levelled by a major earthquake.

British rule and the War of Independence At the conclusion of World War I Britain assumed the Mandate for Palestine. Relations between the Jewish and Arab communities seem to have been relatively good, with few incidents reported during the Arab uprising of 1929. The Arab riots of 1936-38 were considerably more bloody.

The UN Partition Plan of 1947 envisaged Tiberias as part of the Jewish state. This decision was partially influenced by the pattern of Jewish landholding in the region that had resulted from the establishment here of pioneering Jewish agricultural communities in the late 18th and early 19th centuries. The population of Tiberias was approximately 52.5 percent Jewish and 47.5 percent Arab. Following a series of battles in and around the town, the Golani Brigade entered the city in mid-April 1948, cutting the city in two. Under the protection of the British Army, most of the Arab population was evacuated east to Jordan. A mounted "Davidka" (home-produced mortar) outside the Post Office on HaYarden now tells the story of how Tiberias was the first mixed town to be "liberated" by the Israelis.

Modern Tiberias The modern town, with a population of around 45,000, has expanded rapidly since independence. It now markets itself as a seaside resort and holiday centre, though it has to be said that much of the development has been unattractive. However, the promenade area has had a face-lift and several new buildings have been constructed in the Ottoman style, clad in basalt stone. As well as Roman/Byzantine remains, there are several sites of particular note related to Tiberias' rich Jewish history. **NB** In the months of July and August, the town can become unpleasantly hot and sweaty.

Sights

Archaeological Garden The 'Archaeological Garden' that now stands in the heart of the modern town was once the northern residential quarter of Byzantine Tiberias, and the centre of the Crusader period city. Insubstantial remains of the '**northern synagogue**', probably one of Tiberias' 13 synagogues mentioned in the Talmud, can still be seen, most notably parts of a mosaic containing an inscription in Greek to "Procolus son of Crispus". It's not clear whether this refers to the synagogue's founder or the mosaic's craftsman.

The Archaeological Garden also contains a **Crusader/Mamluk-period building** (now home to the Tourist Information Centre), some small sections of the **Byzantine residential quarter**, and a modern open-air theatre.

Greek Orthodox Monastery of the Apostles The fourth-century church and monastery here was destroyed during the Persian invasion of 614 CE and has subsequently been rebuilt several times; the most recent renovations were just 30 years ago. The monks may admit you if you ring the bell, but don't count on it (best to try 0900-1200). There are four small chapels within the walled courtyard dedicated to St Peter, St Nicholas, Mary Magdalene and the disciples. The foundations of St Nicholas' chapel, also visible to the east outside the courtyard, are thought to belong to a Crusader period tower. The views over the Sea of Galilee from the church are very fine indeed.

Running between the monastery and HaBanim is a short stretch of the black basalt **city walls** built by Dahr el-Amr in the mid-18th century. Next door to the monastery is the charmingly built orthodox pilgrim's hostel (religious guests only) and opposite is a water-level gauge, shaped like the Sea of Galilee. Water runs through the display every 15 minutes and the water level (said to be a direct reflection of Israeli morale) is constantly shown.

The Galilee Experience ① *T06-6723620, www.thegalileeexperience.com, Sun-Thu 0900-2100, restricted hrs on Shabba, adult US$6, shows run every hr, 12 languages available but it's essential to phone to confirm. Adult US$6, student/child over 7 yrs US$5.*
A 36-minute show that features 2000 slides illuminated by 27 computer-sequenced projectors claims to make "4000 years of Galilee history come alive before your eyes". The commentary is a bit cheesy, and the Zionist element is blatant propaganda (with no mention of the Arabs, who comprise over 50% of the region's population). However, the film is scheduled to be re-made by the end of 2010 so perhaps these elements will be

revised. There is a good souvenir shop in the complex and a renovated coffee shop with views over the Kinneret from the enormous windows.

Al-Bahri Mosque Tucked away on the promenade is the small late-19th-century al-Bahri Mosque, complete with a short stubby minaret and two low white domes. It is adjoined by a barrel-vaulted hall. For many years it has been suggested that this is to become the new **Municipal Museum**, though work doesn't appear to have begun on its transformation as yet.

Synagogues There are three synagogues situated in the Court of the Jews area, just off the promenade. The **Karlin-Stolin Synagogue** is built on the site of the former home of Rabbi Menachen Mendel of Vitebsk (d. 1788), who is buried in the cemetery to the south of the city centre (see page 598). The **Etz Chaim** ('tree of life') **Synagogue**, located close

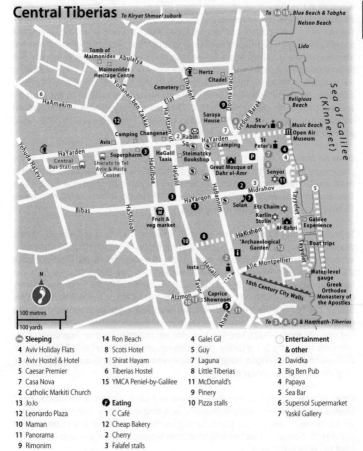

Central Tiberias

To Kiryat Shmuel suburb

To 14 15, Blue Beach & Tabgha
Nelson Beach
Lido

Sea of Galilee (Kinneret)

Tomb of Maimonides
Abulafya
Maimonides Heritage Centre
Cemetery
HaAmakim
Yohanan ben Zakkai
Elhadeff
Hertz
Citadel
Donna Gracia
Elat
Saraya House
Religious Beach
Changenet
Camping
Rabin Sq
HaYarden
St Andrew's
Music Beach
Open Air Museum
Avis
Superpharm
HaGalil Taxis
Sheruts to Tel Aviv & Haifa Centre
HaGalil
Steimatzky Bookshop
HaYarden
Camping
St Peter's
HaYarden Central Bus Station
Yehuda Halevi
Great Mosque of Dahr el-Amr
Senyor
HaGilboa
HaBanim
HaYarqon
Midrahov
Tayyelet
Bibas
HaShiloah
Fruit & veg market
Solan
Etz Chaim
Karlin Stolin
Galilee Experience
Al-Bahri
HaKishon
'Archaeological Garden'
Boat trips
Tayyelet
issta
HaGalil
Alle Montpellier
Water-level gauge
Tayor
18th Century City Walls
Caprice Showroom
Atzmon
Greek Orthodox Monastery of the Apostles
Ahawza

100 metres
100 yards

To 3, 4, 9 & Hammath-Tiberias

Sleeping
4 Aviv Holiday Flats
3 Aviv Hostel & Hotel
5 Caesar Premier
7 Casa Nova
2 Catholic Markiti Church
13 JoJo
12 Leonardo Plaza
10 Maman
11 Panorama
9 Rimonim
14 Ron Beach
8 Scots Hotel
1 Shirat Hayam
6 Tiberias Hostel
15 YMCA Peniel-by-Galilee

Eating
1 C Café
12 Cheap Bakery
2 Cherry
3 Falafel stalls
4 Galei Gil
5 Guy
7 Laguna
8 Little Tiberias
11 McDonald's
9 Pinery
10 Pizza stalls

Entertainment & other
2 Davidka
3 Big Ben Pub
4 Papaya
5 Sea Bar
6 Supersol Supermarket
7 Yaskil Gallery

by, is named after a book by the Hebron-born Rabbi Chaim Abulafia (d. 1744, and buried in the same cemetery). It was Rabbi Abulafia whom Dahr el-Amr invited to re-establish the Jewish presence in Tiberias. The present synagogue is an inconsequential looking cube, dating to 1949 and standing on the site of several previous buildings. The mid-19th-century **Senyor Synagogue**, squeezed between the Caesar hotel and McDonalds, is in a run-down state, although money has been donated to restore it.

St Peter's Catholic Church ① *T04-6720516, daily 0800-1230 and 1430-1900; ring the bell if the door is shut. Mass in English weekdays at 1800, Sun at 0830 (English) and 1800 (Russian). Entrance from Tayyelet next to Galei Gil restaurant. Toilets.*
A church was established here by the Crusaders in the 12th or 13th century, almost certainly to commemorate the ministry of Jesus in the Galilee. The nave of the Crusader church, designed in the shape of an upturned fishing boat to symbolize Peter relinquishing his profession to follow Jesus, forms part of the current church (best seen from the outside). The lack of Crusader churches on long-established sites of Christian worship around the Sea of Galilee (eg Tabgha, Capernaum) suggests that these places of pilgrimage were not identified by the Crusaders: hence the decision to celebrate Jesus' ministry in a city that he probably never visited. The church has had a mixed history. A mihrab (niche indicating the direction of Mecca) in the south wall suggests that the church was converted into a mosque, whilst the Turks later used it as a caravanserai. In addition to the Crusader sections, parts of the church date to 1870, 1903 and 1944 respectively. In the courtyard outside is a monument built by Polish soldiers billeted in Tiberias during World War II, and a bronze statue of St Peter that once stood behind the altar.

Open Air Museum A collection of sculptures are dotted around the north end of the promenade, enlivening the steps that lead down to Music Beach. The works all relate in some way to Tiberias and its history; explanations in English are given next to each one. This open-air museum culminates in the eye-catching metal sail-boat sculpture by native Tiberian, Ilana Gour, next to the water's edge.

St Andrew's Church and the Scots Hotel Visitors are welcome at St Andrew's Church, though the interior is suitably plain and austere as befits the Scottish tradition. The door is left open when the vicar is in residence, generally in the afternoons. The Scottish Church also owns the magnificent Scots Hotel across the road (see Sleeping, page 602). The hotel was originally built in 1885 as the region's first hospital by the Scottish missionary **Dr David Torrance**. Jewish critics of Torrance claim that he was on a proselytizing mission, though the fact that he converted only two Jews and a few Muslims whilst treating thousands of people of all denominations suggests that his motives were humanist. In fact, upon his death in 1923, Tiberias' chief rabbi was moved to say that "Tiberias was blest with three things: the Sea of Galilee, the hot springs and Dr Torrance". In 1959 the hospital was converted into a pilgrim hostel, with major renovations in 1992 making it one of the most attractive places to stay in town.

Hotel Tiberias Another 19th-century building of historic interest is the former Hotel Tiberias (due to be restored and reopened as a boutique hotel). Formerly a luxurious establishment serving the sea planes landing on the Sea of Galilee, it later became the British HQ in Tiberias and was the subject of bitter fighting between Jews and Arabs in the 1948 War of Independence.

Great Mosque of Dahr el-Amr This was obviously once a splendid building, now in a shameful state of repair and located rather incongruously at the centre of an unsuccessful shopping plaza. Dahr el-Amr, the Bedouin sheikh who carved a semi-autonomous fiefdom out of the Ottoman empire in Galilee in the mid-18th century, encouraged Jews to resettle in Tiberias, and it is suggested that in gratitude they funded the construction of this mosque.

Donna Gracia Street A couple of historic buildings are found on Donna Gracia Street, named after the wealthy Marrano Jewess who funded so much of the Jewish settlement in Tiberias. Although the buildings are unfortunately inaccessible, the street makes a quaint little detour. The Saraya House was used as the governor's residence and a prison during Ottoman times; all that can be seen now from the street are the stables for the postal horses. Further along, the Citadel, erroneously referred to on some maps as 'Crusader castle', was built during the reign of Dahr el-Amr (though it is usually attributed to his son Chulabi). It remains an impressive two-storey edifice, with four corner towers, and was part of the wall that once encircled the Ottoman city.

On HaShiloah street, the Donna Gracia Hotel (near the bus station, T04-6700930) has a 'museum' telling the lady's story in the lobby area (wander around on your own or pay 45NIS to borrow leaflets and watch a film).

Tomb of Rabbi Moses ben Maimon and Maimonides Heritage Centre ⓘ *Ben Zakkai Street, tomb open 24 hrs, modest dress required. Heritage Centre, T04-6790632, www. maimonidesheritage.org, Sun-Thu 1030-1600.*
Rabbi Moses ben Maimon (known commonly as Rambam or Maimonides) was born in Spain in 1135. Maimonides fled persecution to Morocco at an early age, passing briefly through Israel before settling in Egypt. In addition to being one of the leading Jewish sages of the 12th century (as well as a noted Aristotelian philosopher), he was the personal physician to Salah al-Din's vizier Al-Fadi al-Baisami, and later Salah al-Din's son. Such was his reputation as a doctor, that he was apparently offered the position of court physician to the 'Frankish King' (either England's Richard Coeur de Lion, or Amalric, King of Jerusalem), though he declined the invitation. Upon his death in 1204 it is said that an unled camel brought him from Egypt to this spot for burial. His major life's work was the 14 books of the Mishne Torah, represented by the 14 black stones that line the path to his tomb. A tall, red iron structure stands above the cenotaph (marking the position from some distance away). A new Heritage Centre has opened in the renovated basalt-stone house close to the tomb. It gives interesting information about his attitudes, rulings, medical practices and responses to challenges, and shows a short film (English and Hebrew).

The camel that brought Maimonides' body here selected a place of burial next to the first-century CE leader of the Sanhedrin, **Rabbi Yohanan ben Zakkai**. During the siege of Jerusalem in the Second Jewish Revolt (66-73 CE), ben Zakkai is said to have approached the commander of the besieging forces, Vespasian, and addressed him as Caesar (Emperor). As Vespasian ordered the rabbi killed, a messenger from Rome announced the death of Caesar and declared Vespasian's succession. A stunned Vespasian, believing ben Zakkai to be a prophet, spared his life and granted the rabbi's request that the Jews be allowed to continue Torah study at Yavne. Interestingly, the Jewish historian Josephus tells us a similar story, though the version of this event that he tells takes place at Jotapata and the prophet is ... Josephus! Ben Zakkai temporarily took charge of the Sanhedrin, but took to his grave the terrible doubt as to whether he should have been more ambitious in his request to Vespasian and asked for the Temple in Jerusalem to be spared, at the risk of losing everything.

Amongst others buried in the ancient cemetery is Rabbi Isaiah ben Abraham haLevi Horowitz (d. 1630), author of the Shnei Luchot haBrit, and former head of Jerusalem's Ashkenazi Jewish community.

Tomb of Rabbi Akiva To reach the tomb, head northwest along Elhadeff, bearing left where it turns into Yehuda haNasi. Take the fifth left on to Trumpeldor just before the police station/government offices and head southwest. At the loop in the road take the third left along HaGevura and continue straight until the Hebrew sign points to the tomb; bus 4 goes as far as the police station/government offices, otherwise it's a hell of a walk.

An illiterate shepherd until the age of 40, Rabbi Akiva (c. 50-135 CE) went on to become one of the most knowledgeable Torah scholars of the age, and teacher and mentor to Rabbi Me'ir Ba'al Ha-nes (see page 601). During the Bar Kokhba Revolt against Rome of 132-35 CE, Rabbi Akiva proclaimed Bar Kokhba as the messiah and was executed by the Romans for his trouble. His cave-like grave is covered by a small white dome.

Beaches If the definition of a beach is where water meets land, then yes, Tiberias does have beaches. However, the rocky shoreline can make getting in and out of the water rather difficult. Tiberias' best beaches are privately run with admission fees charged, though facilities generally include showers and changing rooms, chairs and umbrellas, and cafés/restaurants (but not towels). The majority only open for the summer, between Pesach and Sukkot (roughly April-October). The recently created Music Beach, at the north end of the promenade, has imported sand, life-guard, sun-shades and is very clean. It is a welcome addition to central Tiberias and entrance is free; the downside is that it's terribly small. Several other sections of beach are free, such as below the Greek Orthodox church, next to the Rimonim Hotel and past the hot springs. **Blue Beach** ⓘ *T04-6720105, daily 0900-1700, 25NIS*, is a good choice to the north of the centre.

To the south of the city centre, well-maintained **Gai Beach** ⓘ *T04-6700713, daily 0930-1700, 70NIS, kids under three free*, is a water-park featuring giant water-slides, a variety of nice pools, wave machine and a veritable forest of umbrellas. **Sironit (Turtle) Beach** ⓘ *T04-6721449, daily 0900-1700, 25NIS*, has rough sand, plenty of grassy areas and seating, and chalets for rent at the weekend. Though not hugely attractive, the summer parties and bar here might be a draw. Next along, **Ganim Beach** ⓘ *municipal, 0900-1700, 25NIS*, has a rocky half and a 'sandy' half; it's a bit institutional-looking but allows camping (55NIS per person, includes use of the facilities and beach the following day). The pebbly **Separated Beach** ⓘ *opposite Royal Plaza Hotel, daily 0900-1700, 25NIS or 20NIS in the afternoon*, though not glamorous, is actually a good choice for lone women and has plenty of space.

Southern Tiberias
Graves of 18th- and 19th-century rabbis The southern boundaries of the modern town centre are marked by a small Muslim cemetery and a larger **Jewish cemetery**. Several 18th- and 19th-century rabbis, who led Jewish followers to Tiberias to precipitate the arrival of the messiah, are buried here. The most notable are Rabbi Chaim Abulafia (d. 1744), Rabbi Nachman of Horodenka (d. 1780), Rabbi Menachem Mendel of Vitebsk (d. 1788) and Rabbi Yisrael ben Shmuel of Shklov (d. 1839). These can be interesting places to observe the faithful at prayer, especially at dusk and during religious holidays. Further up the hill (signed from the road) is the Tomb of Rachel, wise wife of Rabbi Akiva, whose clever reasoning led him to study the Torah at the advanced age of 40.

Mt Berenice ① *Head south on Ahawa, turning right on to the winding Toledano, before turning left on to the dirt road that leads 1.5 km to the site.* This small hill is known by popular tradition as Mt Berenice (Bereniki), after the sister of Agrippa II. However, during Agrippa's period of rule over Galilee (c. 61-96 CE) it seems clear that Berenice remained at his court in Caesarea-Philippi (Banias) and there is no archaeological evidence to connect her with this hill. Nor has excavation of Mt Berenice located the magnificent palace of Herod Antipas that Josephus describes in such detail. Excavations have, however, revealed the remains of a triapsidal **Byzantine church** built on the site of a former Canaanite *bimah* (high place). There are good views, and if you feel like a short hike it's a good one for sunset, but the remains of the basilica are not spectacular in themself. From the site you can also continue on a trail (black and white) up to the Switzerland Forest or follow it down the other side of the hill back to the lake road, bearing right to finish by the Holiday Inn.

Roman/Byzantine city and Hammat-Tiberias

Roman/Byzantine city ① *Access 24 hrs, free.* The remains of Tiberias' Roman and Byzantine city are as yet an untapped tourist resource, with excavations not yet complete and the site surrounded by fences. It is possible to wander around, though prospective visitors should be careful when visiting the area, not just for your own safety but for the preservation of the site. The most substantial remains are from a large **bathhouse** (1) (42 m by 31 m) adjacent to the *cardo* (main north to south street) and the market place. Built in the fourth century CE and remaining in use until the 11th century CE, its size and location suggest that it is the central Tiberias bathhouse that is mentioned in Talmudic literature. The east wing contains dressing rooms, with a large hall possibly used for social or ceremonial functions, whilst the west wing housed the bathing rooms. Both wings feature mosaic floors, though those in the west wing are particularly fine and in a good state of preservation.

The municipal **marketplace** (2), a sixth-century CE columned structure covering some 800 sq m, is located just to the north. Adjoining both the bathhouse and the

Sleeping
1 Gai Beach
2 Kinneret Spa
3 Royal Plaza

Eating
1 Galileo

Sights
1 Bathhouse
2 Municipal Market Place
3 Cardo
4 Southern Gate
5 Basilica Complex
6 HaGadol of Yohanan ben Nappaha

marketplace to the west is the **cardo (3)**, the 12-m-wide paved main street flanked on both sides by a colonnaded sidewalk. Probably initially paved in the second century CE, short stretches still remain. The street originally ran 370 m south, down to the **southern gate (4)**. This gate, protected by two round towers whose bases are clearly visible, may well date to the foundation of the city at the beginning of the first century CE.

Also visible to the east of the market place (close to the road, roughly between Sironit and Ganim Beaches), are the insubstantial remains of a second-century CE **basilica complex (5)** that was converted for Christian use in the fifth to sixth centuries CE. Next to be uncovered at the site are the remains of a 5000 seat Roman theatre, one of the largest of its kind in Israel.

A large public **building (6)** dating to the Roman period has been excavated at the foot of Mt Berenice, with the presence of an adjoining stepped pool (probably a mikveh) suggesting to some that this may be the Great Study Centre (Beth HaMidrash HaGadol) that Rabbi Yohanan ben Nappaha established in Tiberias c. 220 CE for the study of the Mishnah, and culminated in the writing of the Gemara. If so, this is a significant find, though there is not really a great deal to see.

Berko Park ① *Entry free, snack bar and toilets. Entrance is just before (north of) the Holiday Inn Hotel.* Not fully complete at the time of research, this new park has a challenging adventure playground (3-15 years, 0800-1800, entrance charge), kiddies playground, landscaped areas for picnics and an open-air stage where free events and concerts are held. In time, it will also encompass the Roman-Byzantine remains to the north within the "Oz Berkovich Tiberias Archaeological Park".

Tiberias Hot Springs (Hamme Teverya) ① *T04-6728500/580, www.chameytveria.co.il, sun 0800-1800, Mon and Wed 0800-2000, Tue and Thu 0800-2200, Fri 0800-1600, Sat 0830-1600, adults 69NIS, children 40NIS; Tue and Thu from 1600 adults 37NIS. Cafeteria.* Legend has it that King Solomon created the hot springs here by ordering demons to bring the water up to the surface from the bowels of the earth. Because he then made the demons deaf it appears that the demons have not heard the news that Solomon died in 928 BCE, so they're still working away like mad. Sometimes referred to as the 'Young' Mineral Hot Springs', the entrance fee includes use of the indoor and outdoor thermo-mineral pools (murky), jacuzzi, half-Olympic-sized outdoor swimming pool, dry sauna, fitness room, children's pool and the private beach (in summer). But not towels or a robe. There are also numerous massages, water therapies, mud treatments, and other delights offered in the swanky spa section. If you take, for example, a 50-minute massage (260NIS) it also allows entrance to the 'therapeutic pool' plus all other facilities (and a robe and towel!). On the opposite side of the road, the 'Old' hot springs offer a separate-sex bathing experience but, unless you are a religious Jew, you will not feel at home here.

Hammat-Tiberias National Park ① *T04-6725287, daily 0800-1700; Fri, hols and winter closes 1 hr earlier. Adult 13NIS, student 12NIS, child 7NIS. Bus 5 is the most regular service, though it's an easy walk or bike ride.* Though initially developing as a separate walled town, Hammat-Tiberias eventually merged with Tiberias sometime in the first century CE. Its independent development can perhaps be explained by the reluctance of the priestly order to settle in Tiberias itself since it was built on the site of an ancient cemetery. The presence of the **hot springs**, almost certainly a deciding factor in Herod Antipas' decision to build his new city here, has supported the economy of the city from Roman times right through to today.

The notable sight here is the synagogue, most probably built in the late fourth to fifth centuries CE, with alterations and rebuilding continuing into the eighth century CE. It was most likely destroyed in the earthquake that hit the region in 749 CE. Its plan is unique, comprising a broadhouse (15 m by 13 m) orientated southeast to northwest, with an entrance facing Jerusalem. A separate room outside the main hall provided a permanent platform for the Ark of the Law, though this is believed to be part of a later second synagogue.

The most remarkable feature is the **mosaic pavement**, now protected by a canopy roof. The central panel has a representation of the zodiac, pre-dating the one at Beit Alpha and better executed (though not as large or complete). For the details of the symbols see under Beit Alpha Synagogue (page 579), though the sequence here begins at '12 o'clock' as opposed to '3 o'clock'. The busts of four women (representing the seasons) appear in the corners of the panel, whilst the central image of the sun god Helios riding in his chariot has been partially destroyed. The top panel depicts two flaming menorahs flanking the Ark of the Law, whilst the bottom panel features a long dedicatory inscription flanked by two beautiful lions. The Greek inscription, mentioning a Severus as the builder of the synagogue, is the first to mention the patriarchies of the Sanhedrin. (For a discussion on the incongruity of a representation of the pagan zodiac in a synagogue, refer again to Beit Alpha Synagogue on page 579).

To the south and west of the synagogue are insubstantial remains of the **Byzantine city walls**, including parts of the southern city gate and tower. The remnants here only hint at the size of the Byzantine city, when Hammat-Tiberias covered almost 20 hectares. A Hammam Sultan **museum**, located within the former Ottoman period bathhouse, traces the history of the hot springs here and displays a few pertinent artefacts.

Tomb of Rabbi Me'ir Ba'al Ha-nes Standing just above the Hammat-Tiberias National Park is the Tomb of Rabbi Me'ir Ba'al Ha-nes. The Rabbi Me'ir ("he who brings light") Ba'al Ha-nes ("the miracle worker") was a second-century CE Jewish sage who is attributed with producing the Mishnah's anonymous rulings: a commentary on the code of the oral law. A Jewish patriot, the Rabbi was forced to flee Israel following the Bar Kokhba Revolt of 132-135 CE when Roman prohibitions banned Torah study, though he later returned to Tiberias to complete his work.

The tomb is marked by two domes, the smaller (c.1898) belonging to the Ashkenazi community, whilst the larger white-domed building (c.1873) is the domain of Sephardic Jews. Both are said to be built over the burial cave where the Rabbi was apparently buried standing up, anticipating the arrival of the Messiah. Though one of Judaism's most important sites, the plaza in front of the tomb has been the victim of a particularly ugly restoration programme. Although there's not much to see, the tomb is always a lively and interesting place heaving with a real mix of devotees. It is particularly fascinating on the anniversary of the Rabbi's death (14th Iyar), when thousands of pilgrims come to pray. Lag B'Omer (18th Iyar) is also an excellent time to visit. Visitors must be modestly dressed (cardboard yarmulkes and headscarfs for women are provided).

Tiberias listings

For Sleeping and Eating price codes and other relevant information, see Essentials pages 26-31.

⏺ Sleeping

Tiberias has a broad spread of hotels and hostels. Prices rise at weekends, in the summer, and during Jewish holidays. Finding accommodation here during Pesach can be a nightmare; hotels double or treble their prices.

There is also plenty of 'rural accommodation' in the Sea of Galilee and Galilee area. For a good listing, pick up the Galilee brochure at the tourist office.

LL Caesar Premier, Tayyelet/Midrahov, T04-6727272, www.caesarhotels.co.il. One of the town centre tower-blocks. Airy sociable foyer is always bustling with Israeli families. Furnishings a bit old-fashioned but not unattractive, plenty of marble in rooms and public spaces. Direct lake views (rooms $240 B&B, suites $150 extra), nice outdoor pool, heated indoor pool, excellent spa facilities.

LL Rimonim Galei Kinnereth, 1 Eliezer Kaplan, T04-6728888, www.rimonim.com. Tiberias' original hotel (older than the State of Israel itself) is now part of the Rimonim chain and is quite luxurious. Private beach, outdoor pool plus mineral water jet steam pool, spa with 13 treatment rooms. Pretty pricey: $350 mid-week for a couple.

LL The Scots Hotel, corner of HaYarden/ Gedud Barak, T04-6710710, www. scotshotels.co.il. Genuine 5-star heaven. 'Unique' rooms in the main (modern) block are certainly swish, though it's the 'Antique' rooms in the 19th-century hospital buildings that appeal more (and cost more). Lake views from the upper floors only. Terraced garden, large and lovely pool, gourmet restaurant (buffet allows you to sample), lovely Scottish Bar, 2 massage rooms; spa and private beach planned for 2011. Musical evenings are a big attraction at weekends. The old hospital storeroom has

been transformed into a fabulous wine cellar, housing the best boutique wines of the Galilee and Golan. Advance reservations essential. Recommended.

L Gai Beach, Eliezer Kaplan, T04-6700700, www.gaibeachhotel.com. Well-equipped rooms with expansive beds are airy and inviting, even if the decor is uninspired. Most look on to the beautiful pool and landscaped gardens (though no balconies on 3rd floor). Admission to the water park next door is included, there's a spa, attractive lobby café serving light meals, and everything is refreshingly spick and span. Recommended.

L Leonardo Plaza, Habanim, T04-6713333, www.fattal.co.il. Another of the ugly hotels dominating town, but newly renovated rooms/bathrooms have all mod cons and fair-sized balconies facing the lake ($190 B&B); also suites (**LL**). Lobby restaurant-bar and buffet dining hall, spa and gym, attractive outdoor pool. Good value compared to similar hotels.

L Ron Beach, Gedud Barak, T04-6791350, www.ronbeachhotel.com, sf_ronbeach@ bezeqint.net. Nice waterfront location north of town. Spacious rooms off an endless corridor have all the necessary amenities, larger than average bathrooms, inoffensive furnishings. 2 upper floors with balconies are preferable to garden-level terraces; ask for pool/lake view not side view. Attractive pool in shady garden; private beach. Dinner $30 extra per person. Not a bad choice at all, though popular with tour groups.

L Royal Plaza, Ganei Menora Blvd, off Eliezer Kaplan (south of town), T04-6700000, www. royal-plaza.co.il. Unattractive exterior, but standard rooms are a good size (plus 16 suites with jacuzzi) with pale wooden furnishings and a Mediterranean feel. No balconies; request a lake view. The large pool would be nicer if the area were landscaped; fitness room, decent spa, sauna, restaurant, Red Lion pub. Better rates online.

L Shirat Hayam, HaYarden/Igal Alon Promenade, T04-6721122, www.shirathayam.org.il. Intimate boutique hotel well located on Music Beach, in an historic building (1850). Rooms incorporate basalt stone into the walls and have bright, white furnishings, Ottoman arched windows and chic bathrooms. Some face the lake, most have jacuzzi, one has 2 balconies (**LL**), others just the one. There's a delightful roof terrace with loungers and swing chairs. Because they are still getting established, discounts are possible off-season. Breakfast included, massage available. Recommended.

AL YMCA Peniel-by-Galilee, Rd 90 (3 km north of town), T04-6720685, www.ymca-galilee.co.il, ymca_galilee@hotmail.com. Gorgeous setting in flower-filled gardens leading to the lake; no other buildings around save for the orthodox church next door. The lounge with antique painted wooden walls is wonderful, as is the back terrace for dining. Most rooms are in a Jerusalem stone building next to the original 1931 house; some have delightful balconies with lake views. Beach area is overgrown, but the natural warm water bathing pool is very inviting. Doubles 450NIS, singles 250NIS, 25NIS weekend price rise.

A Kinneret Spa, off Eliezer Kaplan (2 km south of town), T04-6723444, www.kspa.co.il. Unpretentious small hotel that is very welcoming. Standard rooms a bit boxy with small windows and carpets, decent-sized bathrooms. De luxe are bigger with jacuzzi on balcony (extra $30), modernised decor, white wood floors, flat-screen TV. Bar-restaurant's nothing special. Good lake views with no obstructions, especially from roof terrace where there's a small sauna and sun-beds. Use of hot springs included in the price.

A-E Aviv Hotel & Hostel, HaGalil, T04-6723510/6720007, www.aviv-hotel.co.il, avivhotel@walla.com. Large holiday flats (300NIS) with kitchenette, 6 with jacuzzi (50NIS extra), all have balcony and are cleaned daily. Dorms in separate hostel

sleep 4-7 (single beds not bunks, mixed and female, 70NIS), attached bath, fridge. Also private rooms (doubles 250NIS): if you don't mind noise the balconied ones at the front are great for hanging out. All rooms/dorms have a/c and TV. No curfew, 24-hr reception, free internet/Wi-Fi, left luggage service. Buffet breakfast 30NIS. Quality bikes for rent (see activities, page 606). (New 4-star hotel section with swimming pool due to complete 2011.) Recommended.

A-E Tiberias Hostel, Rabin Sq, T04-6792611, m11111@012.net.il. Spotless double rooms aren't huge (250-350NIS depending on season), dorms with 4-5 beds (bunks) either mixed or female (75NIS), attached shower. All rooms a/c, carpeted, with TV and fridge, but no balconies. Kitsch lobby, with 100 seats and kitchen; a good place to hang out. Surprisingly quiet, considering the location on a main road - it's a minute from the bus station. Bike rental 60NIS per day. Internet 10NIS per ½ hr, laundry next door. Free tea, coffee and (small) breakfast.

B-E Casa Nova, 1 HaYardon, T04-6712281, F6712278. Pilgrim accommodation (crucifixes on the wall), yet rather attractive with super clean bathrooms and austere rooms with twin beds ($60), dorms on the cloister by the courtyard of St Peter's ($20, 6 single beds, male/female). A/c throughout, no TV or fridge in rooms; breakfast included. Unmarried couples allowed, but don't advertise it. Curfew 2300.

B-E Maman Guest House, Atzmon, T04-6792986, F6791240. Good travellers place, spacious a/c dorms (4-8 beds, single sex or mixed) with clean attached bath. Private rooms (250NIS) are quite retro-style, but fresh and white. Kitchen, bar, small outside pool (area being remodelled at time of our visit), no curfew, bike rental, breakfast 35NIS. Well-kept and cared for. Recommended.

C Catholic Melkite Church, T052-7249329. Within the church compound are a few rooms, newly created from the run-down old building by sociable Nahmeh Mazowi, who hails from Nazareth. Shiny and clean, with pretty bedlinen; reasonable (flexible) prices. Upstairs rooms share a kitchenette, and there's also an outdoor kitchen/TV area for hanging out. The plain quaint adjoining church is in memory of St Peter (though St George is depicted) and is gladly opened to visitors.

C Panorama, HaGalil, T04-6720963, F6790146. Simple family-style hotel. Small rooms with a/c, fridge and TV; 2 front rooms with balconies are the best. No breakfast, guest kitchen available; cheap with room for negotiation.

D-E JoJo, 8 Atzmon, T04-6791042. One of the bottom-rung hostels. A few rooms sleep 2-4 persons, double room 100NIS. Outdoor area for socializing has TV.

❻ Eating

Those on a tight budget, and hence on a diet of falafel, pizza and shwarma, are well served by the numerous stalls along HaGalil, along HaYarden towards the bus station, and at the junction of HaBanim and the Midrahov. There's a convenient **Supersol** supermarket on HaBanim, and a larger (cheaper) one on HaAmakim, near the bus station. One of the most popular dishes served in Tiberias is St Peter's Fish. If you're part of a pilgrim/tour group visiting the Sea of Galilee, it's inevitable that you will be brought to a restaurant on Tiberias' Tayyelet and made to try the dish. It tastes like bass, though it's of the perch family.

♙♙♙ Galileo, opposite Tiberias hot springs, T04-6725123. Restaurant-bar serving inventive meals that make a change from the standard Tiberian offerings. Veal, salmon, fillets, might come on a bed of mint and cashews. Unfussy modern interior, some outside tables. Attracts the young moneyed crowd. Sun-Thu 1230-2300, Sat from 2000.

♙♙♙ Torrance Restaurant, Scots Hotel, T04-6710730. Breakfast and dinner (buffet – but don't let that put you off) open to non-residents. A true gourmet experience blending Galilean traditions with Mediterranean cuisine. The restaurant is not exactly chic, but the garden-level terrace is lovely for Fri and Sat brunch, 1130-1430. Highly recommended.

♙♙♙-♙♙ Decks, Lido, T04-6721538. Restaurant-bar nicely located on a pier over the lake, recommended for steaks and BBQ meats, but also do good starters for 2 or 4 (hummus, pitta, labeneh, etc), grilled fish, Middle Eastern fusion food. Extensive wine list. Sun-Thu 1200-2300, Sat from 2000.

♙♙♙-♙♙ Galei Gil, Tayyelet, T04-6720699. An old favourite with locals and tourists alike, this meat and fish restaurant has an appealing terrace right on the water; the indoor area is equally pleasant (note the ancient trees incorporated into the outside wall). Fried and grilled fish of all varieties from 58-85NIS. Daily 1200-2330. Recommended.

♙♙♙-♙♙ Pagoda, Lido, T04-6725513, www.lido-galilee.com. Consistently rated amongst the best Chinese/Thai restaurants in Israel. No silly big menus here, it is kept simple with red/green curries, soups, excellent choice of appetizers and dumplings (17-36NIS), sushi, duck, chicken, fish fillet, etc. Some scope for vegetarians. The setting is particularly attractive - the restaurant looks like a pagoda - and there's a small garden. Reservations recommended despite its large capacity. Sun-Thu 1200-2400, Fri 1200-1400, Sat from 2000.

♙♙ Cherry, T04-6790051, Midrahov. Excellent dairy dishes, breakfasts, pasta, pizza, sandwiches, plus diet-busting cakes. Kosher le'mehadrin and popular with the young religious crowd.

♙♙ Laguna, Midrahov. Doesn't look much, but it packs people in for excellent grilled fish at affordable prices (56-60NIS); fixed menus 42-52NIS. Always busy. Daily 1200-2400.

♙♙ Little Tiberias, HaKishon, T04-6792806. Popular tavern, warm and wooden inside plus terrace outside in quiet setting. The menu sounds pedestrian with typical meat and pasta dishes, plus seafood and oven-baked fish, but the standard is high and it's highly recommended.

☰ Pinery (Ya'ar HaOren), Donna Gracia, T04-6790242. Cosy Chinese restaurant, warmly decorated, friendly staff. Set menus are recommended (90-120NIS per person) or an enormous range of à la carte meat and fish dishes (54-62NIS), plus plenty for vegetarians (28-30NIS). Also take-away/delivery. Sun-Thu 1100-2300.

☰-☰ C Café, HaYarkon, T04-6712321. Popular little café with good coffee, naughty cakes, and light meals. Wi-Fi. Daily 0830-2000, or till the early hours at weekends when it becomes a cool place to hang out.

☰-☰ Guy Restaurant, HaGalil, T04-6723036. One of the best-value places in town serving simple home-cooked Sephardic ('Oriental Jewish') meals of generous proportions. Try the eggplant stuffed with meat (27NIS), spicy meat balls with nuts (15NIS), stuffed vine leaves (10NIS) plus a whole host of salads (10-15NIS). You might not be so tempted by heart, spleen and lungs. Friendly and authentic. Sun-Thu 1200-2030, Fri 1200-1500.

☊ Bars and clubs

Tiberias' night-life revolves around the promenade, which only really comes to life in the summer months.

Big Ben, Midrahov, T04-6722248. A popular meeting place, with an English-style pub inside and waitress-service tables outside. Varied food menu, nice ambiance, and friendly staff. Beer 22-25NIS for a half-litre. One of few to stay open throughout the winter. Daily 0900-2400.

The Ceilidh Bar (Scottish Pub), Scots Hotel, T04-6710731 (see Sleeping, page 602). Non-residents are welcome to prop up the semi-circular bar or rest on a comfy sofa, where tartan tablecloths and old pictures aid a wee whisky or two.

Kibbutz Afiqim, about 10 km south of Tiberias, runs a popular disco on Fri, as does Kibbutz Degania a km or so closer to Tiberias (about 60NIS by taxi, or by sherut, cheap drinks and entry). Some of the more expensive hotels have 'nightclubs'.

Papaya, Tayyelet, is a long-stayer and in summer has loud music, a small dance floor and the 'beautiful people' of the young Israeli crowd. Nothing gets going much before 2230, and they don't close until 0200-0400.

Sea Café, behind the Galilee Experience block. Refurbished place, with a good location at the end of the pier, evenings only.

Sironit (Turtle Beach), south of city centre, T04-6721449. Parties at the weekend in summer (Thu, Fri and Sat) until around 0400, entrance is free or 10NIS at most.

✹ Festivals and events

Jacob's Ladder Spring Festival, Nof Ginnosar, www.jfestival.com. Now in its 34th season, this festival offers 3 days of concerts, workshops, yoga and many other activities (suitable for families). In 2011, the festival will be 19-21 May; tickets cost 210-380NIS for adults depending how many days you wish to attend. They also hold a **Winter Weekend** festival, which is a scaled-down indoor version of events (10-11 Dec 2010).

Scottish Festival, The Scots Hotel (see Sleeping, page 602). In May a 1-week festival is held with different daily events of dance, music, whisky and food.

The hotels also puts on weekend musical events and concerts in their gorgeous gardens (opera, jazz and more). Call to see what's on.

☋ Shopping

Books
Steimatzky, 3 HaGalil, T04-6791288. Small selection of English fiction and travel books. Sun-Thu 0800-1930, restricted hrs on Shabbat.

Camping
Camping, HaGalil, T04-6723350.
Camping Centre, 38 HaYarden, T04-6721406.

Souvenirs
Sea of Galilee Treasures, 'Galilee Experience' block, T04-6725610. For all your souvenir needs.

▲ Activities and tours

Cycling
Bikes are an excellent way to explore the area. The road encircling the lake involves few hills and it's possible to cycle to the Christian sites to the north, or even complete a circuit of the lake (around 6 hrs). The first Shabbat in Nov, the road around the Kinneret is closed to cars and cyclists take over.

Aviv Hotel and Hostel (see Sleeping, page 603). Most reliable place to hire bikes with over 300 mountain/road bikes available (60/100NIS per day), free call-out service. Recommended for their quality bikes. Other hostels can arrange bicycle hire.

Tennis
Tennis Centre, off Ohel Ya'akov, T04-6731564.

Tour operators
Mantan Tours, T054-4616148, or through Aviv Hotel (see Sleeping, page 603). Day tours to north Galilee and Golan (Tabgha-Katzrin-Tel Dan-Banias-Nimrod-Metulla-Kiryat Shimona-Tavor), min 5 persons, 250NIS per head (entrance fees included).
Moshe Friedman, T050-5417651. Registered guide, leads 2-hr city tours of Tiberias' historical and religious sites, minimum 5 persons, 50NIS per head.
The Scots Hotel (see Sleeping, page 602) organises walking tours of Tiberias which anyone can join, Sun-Thu. Phone in advance to register. 45 mins, 20-25NIS per person depending on numbers.

Watersports/boating
Holyland Sailing, in the Galilee Experience building, T04-6723006/7. Wooden boat, aimed at pilgrim groups who want to sail to

Capernaum, etc; phone to see if you can join a group.
Lido Company, T04-6721538. Several white wooden boats, usually a half-hour trip; phone at 0930 for timings. In holidays and high season they leave when full from the Lido.
Water Sport Centre, Marina, T052-3491461. The usual motor-boats and banana boats for rent, plus water-skiing, at fair prices. Closed on Shabbat.

◉ Transport

Bus
The **Central Bus Station**, T6729222, occupies a block on HaYarden. There's an electronic departure board and phone information booth. **NB** During the life-span of this book, exact departure times are bound to change. However, the times given here will at least give an idea of frequency of services. Double-check exact times for yourself.

Egged buses serve: **Haifa** (Merkazit haMifrats bus station): bus 430, Sun-Thu every half hr 0500-2100, Fri until 1600, Sat 1645-2200 (1 hr, 26NIS). **Jerusalem**: buses 962 and 963 via Rd 6, Sun-Thu 1 per hr 0630-2045 (2¾ hrs, 47NIS), Fri until 1500, Sat 1700-2200; bus 961 via the Jordan Valley (armoured vehicle, 0630 and 1820). **Katzrin**: buses 15 and 19 at 1200, 1335, 1600 and 1835. **Kiryat Shemona**: buses 63, 841 and 963, Sun-Thu about 1 per hr 0650- 0220, Fri until 1730, Sat from 1820 (1½ hrs, 28NIS). **Tel Aviv** via **Afula**: bus 835, Mon-Thu at least every half hr, Fri until 1630, Sat 1530-2200 (3 hrs, 47NIS); via **Afula**, **Hadera** and **Petah Tiqva**: bus 841 (4 hrs). To **Capernaum** and **Tabgha**: buses 63, 841 and 963 to **Kfar** Nahum Junction ('Tabgha Junction') and walk (4 km to Capernaum, 2 km to Tabgha), 20 mins, 14NIS.

Veolia buses go locally within Tiberias and around the **Kinneret**; bus 5, to the hot springs; **Kafr Tavor**, bus 32; Veolia also serves **Bet Shean**, bus 28, Sun-Thu around every hr 0630-2100, Fri until 1500, Sat 2050 and 2230 (45 mins, 14.5NIS); **Safed** (via Kfar Nahum Jct, for Capernaum and Tabgha): bus 450, Sun-Thu hourly 0700-1900, Fri until 1500, Sat at 2230 (1 hr).

Nazareth Tours and Transport serve **Nazareth**, bus 431 to Nazareth, Sat-Thu almost hourly 0630-1900, Fri until 1615 (40 mins).

Car hire

Avis, 2 HaAmakim, opposite Central Bus Station, T04-6722766, www.avis.co.il. **Eldan**, 1 HaBanim, below Leonardo Club, T04-6715091, www.eldan.co.il. **Hertz**, Elhadeff, T04-6723939.

Sherut

Sheruts to **Tel Aviv** (2 hrs, 40NIS) and Haifa leave from in front of the Central Bus Station. On Sat, sheruts start at 1400.

Taxis

HaEmeq, HaYarden, T04-6720131. **Kinneret**, T04-6792505. Around 120NIS per hr.

ⓘ Directory

Banks Bank HaPoalim, HaBanim, and Bank Leumi, corner of HaYarden/HaBanim, have ATMs. There are money changers around Rabin Square. **Hospitals** Poriya Hospital, south of town (off map), T04-6652211. **Internet** Solan Express, 8 Midrahov, T04-6726470, internet 10NIS per 30 mins; also sells stamps and rents phones, Sun-Thu 0900-2200, Fri 0900-1600, Sat after 1700. **Post office** The post office on Rabin Square (Sun and Thu 0800-1800, Mon and Tue 0800-1230 and 1530-1800, Wed 0800-1330, Fri 0800-1200), offers poste restante and foreign exchange.

Excursions from Tiberias

Arbel

ⓘ *Daily 0800-1700, winter -1600 (closes 1 hr earlier on Fri and hol eves), adult 20NIS, student 17NIS, child 9NIS. The site leaflet has footpaths marked on the map, useful even though it's in Hebrew.*

The ancient Jewish settlement of Arbel (biblical 'Beth-Arbel', Hosea 10:14) stands at the top of a dramatic cliff about 6 km northwest of Tiberias, looking down on the Sea of Galilee 390 m below. The caves that riddle the cliff beneath the village have been the site of two significant battles in Jewish history, the latter being colourfully recorded by Josephus. The walk down the Arbel cliff is an enjoyable one, and it's possible either to make a circuit (seeing the caves on the way, and returning to the car park at the top of the cliff), or to carry on to the Ginnosar plains below.

Getting there and away For those with their own transport, it is possible to explore Arbel and the Horns of Hattin in the same day. To reach the synagogue and cliff above the fortress, head west out of Tiberias on Route 77, turning right on to Route 7717 shortly after clearing the city limits. Follow the brown signs for Arbel National Park. The closest you can get to Arbel by public transport is Buses 8, 9, 10, 835 and 841 from Tiberias to Kfar Hattin Jct, then walk or hitch the rest of the way. A taxi from Tiberias costs about 50NIS. To return to Tiberias from the foot of the cliff trail you will have to walk to Migdal Junction (2 km) and stop a bus there, or try to hitch.

Background The settlement was probably founded by the **Hasmoneans** (Maccabees) in the second century CE, with its 10-hectare size suggesting a population rising to around 2500. The caves in the cliff-face below the village were fortified by the Hasmoneans, though the Syrian commander Bacchides captured them during his campaign of 161 CE

(*I Maccabees 9:2*). When **Herod the Great** first attempted to exercise his newly acquired power during the early years of his reign (c. 38 BCE), the Hasmoneans once again returned to their fortified caves. Josephus vividly describes Herod flushing them out: "These caves opened out on to almost vertical slopes and could not be reached from any direction except by winding, steep and very narrow paths; the cliff in front stretched right down into ravines of immense depth dropping straight into a torrent bed. So for a long time the king was defeated by the appalling difficulty of the ground, finally resorting to a plan fraught with the utmost danger. He lowered the toughest of his soldiers in cradles till they reached the mouths of the caves; then they slaughtered the bandits with their families and threw firebrands at those who proved awkward ... Not a man voluntarily surrendered, and of those who were brought out forcibly many preferred death to captivity" (*Jewish War I, 303-313*, though Josephus' description in *Antiquities 14: 423-6* is even more gruesome). The settlement overcame this set-back and later flourished as a centre of Jewish learning. A *Beth Midrash*, or 'house of study', was built in Arbel, whilst Rabbi Nittai, a member of the Sanhedrin, resided here.

Sights A short way before the car park, look for a sign with big blue Hebrew letters on the right side. This track leads to the synagogue and old town.

The remains of the fourth-century limestone-built **synagogue** stand out against the dark basalt walls of the other village buildings. A hoard of 140 coins, some dating back to the second century CE, was found on the floor of the synagogue, though scholars are now largely agreed on the later date as the period of construction. The significant features of this synagogue include its easterly as opposed to southerly entrance (a rare feature in synagogues in the Galilee), plus its unique main entrance, with threshold, door jambs and lintel carved from a single stone. The village and synagogue were probably destroyed in the earthquake of 749 CE.

From the top of the cliff a red-and-white marked **hiking trail** descends past the **caves** and the **Arbel Fortress** to the Nahal Arbel (Wadi Hamam) below. The views are excellent. The caves, containing carved cisterns and mikvehs (ritual baths), were incorporated into a fortress built into the cliff-face by the Bedouin sheikh Fakhr al-Din in the early 17th century CE. From the caves, you can then return to the top car park following the black trail. Or if you carry on to the bottom it's a real bitch to climb back up, so if you have your own transport it's advisable to get someone to drive to the base of the cliff to pick you up. Those on 'shank's pony' will have to continue on foot to Migdal Junction. Both the circular or the one-way walk take about 2 hours. **NB** The path is very steep and can be rather tricky in places. The trail can get busy with school groups during the week, which might mean queuing at the places where you climb the metal rungs in the cliff-face.

Horns of Hattin
① *The Horns of Hattin are located just to the north of the Tiberias to Nazareth road (Route 77), approximately 8 km west of Tiberias. You could take any bus that passes along this road and ask to be let off about 2 km east of the turn-off to Kibbutz Lavi.* From a distance, it doesn't really look much: a grassy summit with the peaks at either end vaguely resembling a pair of horns. Yet this is the scene of the crushing defeat of the Crusader army on 4 July 1187 at the hands of Salah al-Din, bringing an end to the Latin Kingdom in the Holy Land.

The area takes the name Horns of Hattin (Arabic: Qarne Hittim) from the form of the hills created by the collapse of an extinct volcanic crater. An "open air" museum to the left of the road on the ascent to the Shrine of Nabi Shu'eib explains the geology of

Kingdom of Heaven

Having encircled the Crusader garrison at Tiberias, Salah al-Din encamped most of his 12,000-strong army of mounted bowmen at Ein Sabt (close to the modern-day moshav of Sde Ilan). This provocative gesture was designed to lure the Crusader army into battle, but on the Muslim commander's terms. All Salah al-Din needed now was for the Christians to accept the bait.

Meeting at Ein Zippori, Raymond of Tripoli, lord of Tiberias, urged restraint, whilst the Grand Master of the Templars, Gerard of Ridfort, egged on by the reckless Reynald of Châtillon, had the scent of battle in his nostrils. The king, Guy de Lusignan, by all accounts a weak-willed man, ruled against the procrastinators and ordered the troops to ready themselves to march the next morning. It was to be a fateful decision, though, in fairness to the king, the threat of withdrawal of the Templars' support left him with little option. At 0400 the following morning 1200 mounted knights, protected by 16,000 infantry, set out for Tiberias, 22 km to the east.

Almost as soon as they began their march the Crusader army came under attack. The Muslim troops took care not to become embroiled in a full-scale confrontation, preferring to severely harass the Crusader rearguard with lightning strikes on their swift, manoeuvrable ponies. By midday the Crusader army, dressed in full armour and toiling under the heat of a scorching July sun, had covered little over half the distance to Tiberias. Having passed

no water sources on their march, the desperate Crusader army diverted north to the spring at Hittim but found their path blocked by one of Salah al-Din's regiments. By mid-afternoon the commander of the rearguard, Balian of Ibelin, having borne the brunt of Salah al-Din's deadly sorties, told the king that they could proceed no further. The Crusader army, still water-less, set their camp for the night and prepared for one last defiant stand.

Contrary to Crusader expectations, Salah al-Din failed to attack at dawn. Instead, he waited until the July sun was high in the sky, then set fire to the scrub around the besieged army. Then he attacked. The first assault was beaten off, but sustained charges against the bewildered and disorientated knights, without water for over 24 hours and still in full armour, soon turned the tide in Salah al-Din's favour. Faced by the inevitability of defeat, the remaining knights made a last stand around the red tent of the king. They were swiftly overrun, and the 'True Cross' was captured from the hands of the dead Bishop of Acre. As Smith describes it, "A militant and truculent Christianity, as false as the relics of the 'True Cross' round which it rallied, met its judicial end within view of the scenes where Christ proclaimed the Gospel of Peace, and went about doing good" (*Historical Geography of the Holy Land*, 1894). The chivalrous Salah al-Din spared the king, though many of the knights (most notably Reynald of Châtillon) were executed for past misdeeds.

the area. Though there are remains here of a Late Bronze-Age fortress and an Iron-Age II city, there are no physical reminders of the Crusaders battle with the Muslim army. However, the views of the Galilee from the top of the hill can be inspiring, particularly if you are holding in your hand a copy of Beha ed-Din's *Life of Saladin*, open at the page that describes the battle.

Shrine of Nabi Shu'eib ⓘ *Daily, free. Modest dress; head-coverings for both men and women are provided. No photos permitted of the tomb itself.* All are welcomed at the grave of Nabi Shu'eib, the most sacred Druze shrine in the country. The large complex comprises an older eastern wing, constructed at the behest of Salah al-Din in 1187 CE after his victory over the Crusaders. The shrine itself is located above the Ayyubid building, in an impressively renovated prayer room with spectacular modern chandeliers. The Druze sect identify Nabi Shu'eib with Jethro, father-in-law of Moses, and each year on his Urs (death anniversary, 25 April) they hold an elaborate feast here. The tomb is draped with green cloth and adorned with the green, yellow, white, blue and red flag of the Druze. The faithful come to kiss the tomb and see Jethro's footprint in stone, preserved in the niche nearby.

Around Tiberias listings

For Sleeping and Eating price codes and other relevant information, see Essentials pages 26-31.

Sleeping

A-D Arbel Guesthouse (Shavit Family B&B), T04-6794919, www.4shavit.com. Perfectly located near the top of the Arbel Cliff, Israel and Sara have 6 comfortable rooms with plenty of privacy. Each is unique and thoroughly homely, with terraces, jacuzzi and fully equipped kitchenette; 2 on upper storey have views. Garden with 70 species of tree. 350NIS during the week or 560NIS weekend/high season, extra bed 50NIS. Budget travellers will be happy in the new dorm (100NIS), with kitchen, and enjoy the sizable swimming pool. The snug country-style restaurant is a delight: signature dishes include the leg of lamb marinated in wine and slow cooked with herbs, or the veal or lamb casserole; there's also St Peter's Fish and the freshest of soups. Those on a budget should treat themselves to dinner or to the delicious and vast breakfast (40NIS per person). It's right on the Jesus Trail; they'll pick up from Tiberias bus station. Highly recommended.

Hammat Gader

→ *Colour map 1, grid B5.*
A visit to Hammat Gader is one of the most enjoyable ways of spending a day/half-day in Galilee; it has just about a bit of everything. In addition to the hot springs and sulphur pool which first attracted the Romans, this large park also features a fascinating alligator farm and mini zoo, as well as the remains of the best-preserved Roman baths in the country.

Ins and outs

Getting there and away Hammat Gader is about 17 km southeast of Tiberias as the crow flies. Head south on Route 90 around the shore of the lake and, when Route 90 bears south (right) at Zemiah Junction, continue round the lake on Route 92. Take the first right on to Route 98 and follow the winding road above the Yarmuk River (and international border) to the park. Bus 24 runs to Hammat Gader from Tiberias only once per day (0915, 30 minutes) and not at all on Saturday. **NB** Though bus 24 is scheduled to return from Hammat Gader at 1410, it often leaves early if the driver feels like it. Arrive at least 15 minutes early. If you do get stuck, it's often possible to hitch a lift with an Israeli family. Hammat Gader gets impossibly crowded during Jewish holidays.

Background

The history of Hammat Gader is really the history of the baths here. They were built to serve the Roman town of **Gadara** (one of the cities of the Decapolis), just across the Yarmuk River. The baths and the city are now divided by the international border between Israel and Jordan, so the remains of Gadara (Umm Qais) can only be visited from the Jordanian side. The ancient geographer Strabo mentions the hot springs close to Gadara at the end of the first century BCE, though he doesn't refer to Hammat Gader by name. The historian Origen, writing in the mid-third century CE, suggests that visitors came from as far away as Athens to be treated. The fact that an Eudocia inscription found in the baths mentions the emperor Antoninus Pius (138-161 CE) suggests that the original baths may well have been constructed in the late second/early third century CE. By the end of the fourth century CE the baths were being described by the Greek writer Eunapius as being second only in beauty to those at the imperial resort at Baia, on the Bay of Naples, though his contemporary Epiphanius is more critical in his assessment, with acerbic references to the fact that men and women bathed together. There are also several mentions of the baths in Talmudic literature, and it seems that many of the learned rabbis of Tiberias (including Rabbi Me'ir Ba'al ha-Nes, Judah I ha-Nasi and Judah ha-Nasi II) visited the baths, though the inference is that they were not here for recreational purposes, but rather to discuss the Sabbath boundary between the baths and Gadara town!

The baths were at the height of their fame during the fifth-seventh centuries CE, as attested to by a number of inscriptions in the Hall of Fountains, though the period of

Hammat Gader

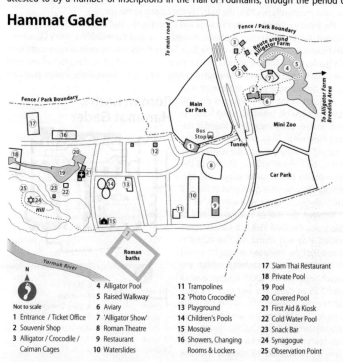

1 Entrance / Ticket Office
2 Souvenir Shop
3 Alligator / Crocodile / Caiman Cages
4 Alligator Pool
5 Raised Walkway
6 Aviary
7 'Alligator Show'
8 Roman Theatre
9 Restaurant
10 Waterslides
11 Trampolines
12 'Photo Crocodile'
13 Playground
14 Children's Pools
15 Mosque
16 Showers, Changing Rooms & Lockers
17 Siam Thai Restaurant
18 Private Pool
19 Pool
20 Covered Pool
21 First Aid & Kiosk
22 Cold Water Pool
23 Snack Bar
24 Synagogue
25 Observation Point

Not to scale

uncertainty that accompanied the collapse of the Byzantine empire may have seen considerable damage inflicted on the building. The Umayyad Caliph Mu'awiya (661-680 CE) instituted a refurbishment of the complex, with an inscription in the Hall of Fountains announcing the baths' reopening in 662 CE. Less than a century later, however, they had entered a terminal decline, possibly another victim of the great earthquake of 749 CE. Though their existence has always been known, and it seems certain that sick people continued to bathe in the ruins here throughout the centuries, it was not until 1979 that the Roman baths were systematically excavated.

Sights

Roman baths The bathhouse complex at Hammat Gader is particularly large, covering an area in excess of 5000 sq m. It was built using coarsely dressed basalt stones, with the exception of the Hall of Fountains where finer limestone blocks were used. The long, high retaining wall to the southwest featured a line of windows that supplied both light and ventilation. Water was channelled to the bathing pools via conduits and an intricate system of lead pipe plumbing, examples of which can be clearly seen. Seven main bathing halls have been identified, with the temperature of the water generally regulated by the distance from the hot spring source. Lead and clay pipes carrying cooler water were also used to moderate temperatures. It is suggested that visitors to the baths would enter through the **Entrance Corridor** (2) to the northwest, then move from one bathing hall to the next, eventually reaching the hotter water closest to the spring.

The Entrance Corridor leads to a large hall known as the **Hall of Pillars** (3). A 1.5-m-deep stepped pool in the centre of the hall remained in use until the mid-fifth century CE, when it was filled in and covered with a marble floor. The hall was subsequently used as some form of a 'games room'. The hall takes its name from the two rows of pillars along its east and west sides that helped to support the vaulted ceiling some 18 m above. Three smaller pools are located between the pillars on the west side.

Adjacent to the Hall of Pillars is the **Hall of Inscriptions** (4), taking its name from the 40 or so dedicatory inscriptions found in the floor. Most are in Greek and are probably the legacy of wealthy patrons who wished their visit to be commemorated. All date to the latter period of the baths' usage (late fifth century CE), when the main pool in this hall had been filled in and paved with marble.

Between the Hall of Inscriptions, Hall of Pillars and the Oval Hall is a narrow space divided into two chambers. The northern chamber of this **Passage Corridor** (5) served as a connecting passageway, whilst the antechamber to the south housed a small pool 1.25 m deep. The fact that this pool was seemingly sealed off from the rest of the complex, and that the remains of numerous clay oil lamps dating to the fourth and fifth centuries CE were found here, has led some commentators to suggest that this

Roman baths, Hammat Gader

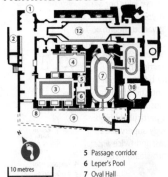

	5 Passage corridor
	6 Leper's Pool
10 metres	7 Oval Hall
10 yards	8 Stone Drainage Pipe
1 Modern entrance	9 Service Hall
2 Entrance corridor	10 Hot Spring
3 Hall of Pillars	11 Spring Pool
4 Hall of Inscriptions	12 Hall of Fountains

is the 'lepers' pool' (6) as described by Antoninus of Placentia. It appears that lepers were encouraged to fall asleep in the pool, whilst the one that saw a vision would be cured.

The **Oval Hall** (7) features a large, stepped bathing pool in an excellent state of preservation. Being so close to the hot spring source the water in this pool would have been particularly warm. The water was moderated by a flow of cool water via lead pipes from the four small baths in the semi-circular alcoves in each of the hall's corners. Large decorative windows provided the light. The **Service Area** (9) contained the drainage channels and pools that took away the waste water. A 9-m-long stone drainage pipe was found in situ.

The **Hot Spring** (10) fed water to all parts of the complex, with water from this source being in the region of 50°C. The **Spring Pool** (11) close by was probably the ultimate destination of visitors to the baths. The pool was originally rectangular but was altered to its present shape in the late fifth century. The five marble fountains around the pool fed in cooler water.

The large pool in the **Hall of Fountains** (12) served as the frigidarium, or cold room, with a large cold-water pool (1.3 m deep) at its centre. The pool was fed by a network of lead pipes, with the water emerging from 32 carved marble fountains. The figures that decorated these fountains were seemingly defaced during the Muslim period. This hall was almost certainly open to the sky, in keeping with other such baths of the period. To the east and south of the Hall of Fountains, only partially excavated, are several other small bathing chambers, and possibly a number of dressing rooms.

Hot springs/sulphur pool ⓘ *T04-6659999, www.hamat-gader.com/eng, Mon-Wed and Sat 0930-1700, Fri 0830-2230 (but call to check, as there are seasonal variations), adult 74NIS during week, 85NIS weekend, evening entry after 1700 56NIS, students 25% discount, children under 1m free. There are spa treatments and massages; various packages are available.* Bathing in the pools of the Roman bathhouse is now forbidden for fear of damaging them, though potential bathers are more than compensated for by the modern facilities. There is a large, warm bathing pool, particularly welcome when air temperatures drop significantly in winter, plus hot and cold pools. Take advice from staff on the maximum length of time that you should remain in the water. There is also a 'massage waterfall', a covered pool, plus various health and beauty treatments available.

Alligator farm The original residents of this farm were imported from Florida as a tourist attraction, but such has been the success of the breeding programme that alligators are now being exported. When it's warm, and the beasts come out to sun themselves, it's a fantastic (though slightly terrifying) sight. A wooden walkway runs through the main enclosure, though the fact that it's only 3 m or so above the pool, and the railings are not particularly high, makes it a rather unnerving experience. (**NB** Children need to be closely supervised.) A number of crocodiles and caimans are to be found in the caged areas, and twice a day there is a show featuring a parrot (1100 and 1300). The mini zoo nearby features ostrich, ibex and turkeys, amongst other creatures.

Other features On the tel, or mound, above Hammat Gader lie the remains of an early fifth-century **synagogue**, standing on the site of two earlier buildings. There is not a great deal to be seen, with the impressive mosaic floors having been removed to the museum at nearby Degania (see page 629). Also within the park area stand the insubstantial remains of Hammat Gader's 2000-seater **Roman theatre**.

Sea of Galilee (Lake Kinneret) → *Colour map 1, grid B 4-5.*

Tour around the Sea of Galilee

The description below describes a **clockwise** circumnavigation of the lake beginning at Tiberias (since this seems to be the most popular route). It should be noted that it is impossible to see and appreciate all the sites described below in one day, even if you have your own transport and make an early start. The key sites, and also the most crowded, are the ones with the major Christian interest, on the northwest shores: Tabgha, Mt of Beatitudes and Capernaum. That said, the east side of the lake is blissfully traffic-free, and a fine place for cycling.

Getting there and away The easiest way to tour the lake is by car. The most enjoyable way, despite the high levels of traffic in places, is by **bicycle**. For details of bike hire see the 'Tiberias' section on page 606. Cyclists should note that one lap is nearer to 65 km, and not 55 km as you may be told seven to nine hours). It's generally pretty flat, though there are a few killer hills around Tabgha. Traffic (especially tourist coaches) can be heavy around Tabgha and Capernaum, and again in the 'home-stretch' from Zemiah Junction to Tiberias. Take protection against the sun and plenty of drinking water. You should not drink the water in the lake. **NB** Although shorts may seem like a good idea for cycling, they are not suitable for visiting any holy sites, where modest dress is required. Irregular **bus** services (15, 18, 19 and 22) also run around the lake, though you should be prepared for some long waits. Almost all of the settlements around the Sea of Galilee offer some form of 'country accommodation'.

Routes Head north from Tiberias on Route 90, passing the YMCA, to arrive at **Migdal Junction** after 5.6 km. The left turn (Route 807) leads northwest, with the left fork after 1 km leading to the base of the cliff below Arbel (see 'Excursions from Tiberias', page 607). The right turn at Migdal Junction leads to Hawaii Beach and Migdala Beach (entrance fee). Also on the sea-shore is the site of ancient **Migdal**.

Migdal

The ancient settlement of Migdal (as opposed to the modern moshav of the same name to the west of Route 90) is located down on the lakeside. Sometimes referred to as either **Magdala**, or by its Greek name of **Tarichaeae**, this is the reputed birthplace of **Mary Magdalene**, one of the New Testament's most famous repentant sinners, who washed Jesus' feet with her tears and wiped them with her hair (*Luke 7:37-50*). A small fenced-off area belonging to the Franciscans is associated with the tradition, though it's not generally open.

Josephus describes Tarichaeae during the Roman period as being a city of some 40,000 people, and describes in some detail the battle between the Jewish zealots who had fled Tiberias during the Second Jewish Revolt (66-73 CE), and Vespasian's Roman army. The zealots on the land were swiftly defeated, whilst others put out in their boats on to the lake. The Roman army built rafts and followed, routing the Jewish navy: "A fearful sight met the eyes – the entire lake stained with blood and crammed with corpses; for there was not a single survivor. During the days that followed a horrible stench hung over the region. The beaches were thick with wrecks and swollen bodies which, hot and steaming in the sun, made the air so foul that the calamity not only horrified the Jews but revolted even those who had brought it about … The dead, including those who had earlier perished in the town, totalled 6,700" (*Jewish War, III, 532*). Parts of the key and harbour ('Migdal Nunya') were excavated in the 1970s, though there's little to see today.

Route Continuing north on Route 90 from Migdal Junction, the road passes several turnings on the right for various beaches before arriving at **Ginnosar** (2.2 km).

Kibbutz Ginnosar → *Colour map 1, grid B4.*

Founded originally as an agricultural community, Kibbutz Ginnosar now makes a sizeable amount of its income from tourism. The **beach** ① *adult 30NIS, child 20NIS, open 0800-1800*, is about as good as you get on the Sea of Galilee, with a nice pool and seating area. Sailing, wind-surfing and kayaking are available, as well as fishing trips. The kibbutz also hosts the very popular **Jacob's Ladder Spring Festival** and the **Winter Weekend** (see page 605).

The Beit Yigal Allon Museum ① *T04-6727700. Sat-Thu 0830-1700, Fri -1400, adult 15NIS*, details the history of 'Man in the Galilee', though by far its most famous exhibit is a 2000-year-old fishing boat, discovered just south of the kibbutz beach. During the major drought that the region suffered in 1986, the level of the Sea of Galilee dropped considerably, revealing the frame of the old boat lying on its port side in the mud

Carbon-14 dating, as well as analysis of the construction technique and style, has suggested that the boat was built some time between 100 BCE and 70 CE. Obviously this date leads to speculation about the type of boats Jesus' fishermen disciples would have used, or suggestions that the boat may have been involved in the great naval battle of 67 CE between the Jews and the Romans that Josephus describes in such gory detail (see 'Migdal' on page 614). Unfortunately, the truth is more mundane. Two of the boat's excavators, Wachsmann and Raveh, write that after a long work life and numerous repairs, "its usable timber --- including the mast step, stempost, and the sternpost – were removed; the remaining hull, old and now useless, was then pushed out into the lake, where it sank into the silt" (*New Encyclopedia of Archaeological Excavations in the Holy Land*, 1993). Appreciate it for what it is: a well-preserved 2000-year-old boat.

Kibbutz Ginnosar listings

For Sleeping and Eating price codes and other relevant information, see Essentials pages 26-31.

Sleeping
L-AL Nof Ginosar Hotel, Kibbutz Ginnosar, T04-6700320, www.ginosar.co.il. All rooms a/c and comfortable, standard rooms ($156) in the older wing have flowery decor, newer deluxe (additional $50) have balcony and contemporary decor, wood floors, and huge beds. Restaurant, bar, dairy cafeteria, pool (seasonal), admission to private beach, tennis, breakfast included. The Nof Ginosar Village just next door shares the same facilities but has cheaper ($102) rows of cabins, more simply furnished but with kitchenettes, BBQ, suited to families. Prices go up high season.
A-D Karei Deshe Youth Hostel, Karei Deshe Beach, T04-6720601, www.iyha.org.il. Sparkling building around a central courtyard; plenty of clean single-sex dorms, with fridge, TV, coffee; breakfast included. Some private rooms, 2 kosher dining halls, TV room, nice views, best bit is the private beach. Internet 10NIS for 30 mins. Large bands of youth predominate. Seasonal price hike. The hostel is signed to the right off Rd 90, 3.5 km after Nof Ginnosar, 1.5 km walk from the bus stop.

Route
Returning to Route 90, after 5 km the road leads to Kfar Nahum Junction ('Tabgha Junction'). There are several options here. The tour around the lake continues on the road to the right,

now Route 87. The road to the left, Route 90, heads directly north as far as Metulla in Upper Galilee (near the Lebanese border). The majority of visitors who are touring the lake take a short excursion up Route 90 to the Mt of Beatitudes (3.4 km), possibly also to Chorazin/Korazim National Park (9 km), before returning to Route 87 to visit Tabgha (2 km) and Capernaum (4 km). The route described here firstly details the attractions on Route 87 (Tabgha and Capernaum), before returning to the loop that includes Mt of Beatitudes and Chorazin, then back again to Route 87. Confused? Look at the 'Tiberias and Sea of Galilee' map on page 590 and all will become clear.

Tabgha → *Colour map 1, grid B4.*

Tabgha is the reputed site of Jesus' miracle of the multiplication of the loaves and fishes: "the feeding of the 5000" (*Matthew 14:13-21*; *Mark 6:30-44*; *Luke 9:10-17*; *John 6:1-13*). Matthew and Mark also report a second feeding – "the feeding of the 4000" (*Matthew 15:32-39*; *Mark 8:1-10*) – that took place at Tel Hadar on the northeast shore of the lake, whilst Luke and John combine both events into one. A church has stood on this site at Tabgha since the fourth century CE, whilst another chapel at the water's edge marks the traditional site where Jesus appeared to his disciples after his Resurrection (*John 21:1-24*). Tabgha is a major Christian pilgrimage site and can become a little too busy for some, particularly when several coachloads of visitors arrive at the same time.

Ins and outs
Getting there and away Buses 63, 450, 841 and 963 go from Tiberias to Kfar Nahum Junction (20 minutes, 14NIS), from where they continue north on Route 90. Get off at the junction and walk the last 2 km. Alternatively, take one of the slower local buses that circumnavigate the lake.

Background
The name 'Tabgha' is an Arabic derivative of the Greek "(Land of) the Seven Springs", or **Heptapegon** (Hebrew: *Ein Sheva*). The springs were described by the pilgrim Egeria in 383 CE, and can still be seen today to the east of the Church of the Primacy of St Peter. Their warmth and high sulphur and salt content are said to help sustain an environment suitable for the 'St Peter's fish' that live in the lake. Egeria mentions that the rock upon which Jesus placed the five loaves and two fish had become an altar within a small chapel, and subsequent archaeological investigations have revealed the presence of such a structure built c. 350 CE. Later visitors to Tabgha such as St Sabas (late fifth century CE), Theodosius (c. 530 CE) and Antoninus Placentius (c. 570 CE) all mention the church that replaced the chapel, though by the time Bishop Arculf

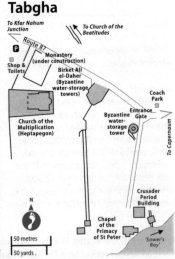

Tabgha

To Kfar Nahum Junction
To Church of the Beatitudes
Route 87
P
Shop & Toilets
Monastery (under construction)
Birket Ali el-Daher (Byzantine water-storage towers)
Coach Park
Byzantine water-storage tower
Entrance Gate
Church of the Multiplication (Heptapegon)
N
To Capernaum
Crusader Period Building
Chapel of the Primacy of St Peter
'Sower's Bay'
50 metres
50 yards

visited the site in 670 CE the church lay in ruins. This could have been as a result of the Persian invasion of 614 CE or the Arab invasion of 636 CE. It appears that the site then disappeared from view for the next 1200 years or so, until initial exploration was carried out in 1892, and full excavations in 1932. Though there are Crusader remains in the vicinity, it is not certain that they managed to identify the site, perhaps explaining why aspects of Jesus' Galilean ministry are celebrated in churches in Tiberias.

Sights

Church of the Multiplication ① *T04-6678100, Mon-Fri 0800-1700, Sat 0800-1500, last entry 15 mins before closing. Sun closed except for mass. Admission free, though donations welcome. Parking, toilets, shop. Modest dress required and guides are not permitted to give commentaries inside the church.* The present church was consecrated in 1982, replacing a more modest effort built in the mid-20th century. It is built on the same plan as the fifth-century Byzantine church, a basilica with north and south transepts, and incorporated as many original features as possible. Throughout the centuries the venerated stone under the altar that Jesus is said to have laid the bread and fishes upon has shrunk in size as pilgrims chipped off pieces to take home. Modern visitors use a camera or video-recorder to take their souvenir home.

The key feature of the Church of Heptapegon is its **mosaics**, parts of which are preserved in the current church. The two most complete floors are those in the transepts, where wispy Galilean trees and elegant birds mix with lotus flowers and peacocks. The dominant motif of the nilometer suggests the mosaics may have been the work of an Egyptian. However, it is the restored mosaic in front of the altar that is most famous. The image of the two fish flanking a basket carrying the loaves can be seen on postcards, t-shirts and all forms of souvenir throughout the Holy Land. Notice how the basket only contains four loaves; a real loaf is usually placed on the altar to complete the five. As pilgrims pray and sing, tourists jostle to photograph the mosaic. It's not very dignified.

A new monastery is beginning its construction next to the church, under the auspices of the German Association of the Holy Land which owns this site.

Church of the Primacy of St Peter ① *T04-6724767, daily 0800-1650, admission free, donations accepted. Toilets. Modest dress required.* Close to the Church of the Multiplication, down on the lake's shore, is the Church of the Primacy of St Peter. To reach it you have to go back out on to Route 87 and walk a couple of hundred metres along the road to the gate.

Tradition has it that this was the site of Jesus' appearance to the disciples following his Resurrection *(John 21:1-24)*, when he commissioned Peter to "feed my sheep". The large stone inside the present chapel is said to be the 'Mensa Christi' ('Table of Christ') upon which Jesus prepared the breakfast for the disciples prior to commissioning Peter. The pilgrim nun Egeria did not mention a church on the site during her visit c. 383 CE, though a later document suggests that a small chapel may have been built over the 'Mensa Christi' during the Byzantine period, and the large heart-shaped blocks that you can see down by the water's edge may have been part of the early-Christian settlement here. Known as the **Twelve Thrones**, they may have been placed here to commemorate the Twelve Apostles. There is evidence of a church being here in the Crusader period, though it appears to have been destroyed, rebuilt, then destroyed again.

The present church was built from basalt stone by the Franciscans in 1933, and the interior is attractively lit by stained-glass windows. Outside is a communal prayer area and a bronze statue of Jesus commissioning Peter with his crook. Also within the grounds, along the path between the entrance and the church, are the remains of Byzantine water-storage towers, Crusader period buildings, and some later water mills. A steep path, between the Church of the Primacy and the Church of the Multiplication, leads up the hill to the Mt of the Beatitudes. The path is visible from the Church of the Multiplication, accessed from the main road to the left of the water tower. The walk is perhaps more enjoyable, however, going downhill to the lake.

Tabgha listings

For Sleeping and Eating price codes and other relevant information, see Essentials pages 26-31.

Sleeping
L Pilgerhaus Tabgha, T04-6700100, pilgerhaus@tabgha.org.il. More of a boutique hotel than a pilgrim hospice, the original building in this tranquil place dates from 1889. New sections, built in keeping with the old style, hide 70 rooms with modern fittings and furnishings, There's a rocky private beach (swimming is possible) and numerous delightful spots to sit and relax, indoors and out. The restaurant comes recommended. Doubles 680NIS B&B. Run by the German Association of the Holy Land. Turn off to the right, just after Kfar Nahum Jct, and before the Church of the Multiplication.

Route
From Tabgha it is 2 km along Route 87 to the turn-off for Capernaum (just beyond the 'St Peter's Fish Restaurant'). From the turn-off it is 500 m to the site.

Capernaum → *Colour map 1, grid B5.*

ⓘ *T04-6721059, daily 0830-1630, adult 3NIS. Souvenir shop, toilets, parking. Modest dress essential.*
Though the references to Capernaum in the gospels are frequent, the origin of the name (Hebrew: *Kfar Nahum*, or Village of Nahum) is unclear..It is an important site of Christian pilgrimage as the scene of many events during the Galilean Ministry of Jesus. It became "his own city" (*Matthew 9:1*) when he was driven out of Nazareth. It was here that he called Peter, Andrew, James, John and Matthew to be his disciples, and he performed many miracles at Capernaum. Parts of the first-century CE town can still be seen, including a house that compelling evidence suggests was the home of St Peter. Capernaum is also renowned for the remains of one of the most splendid synagogues in Galilee.

Ins and outs
Getting there and away Unless you have your own transport, you'll have to follow the instructions for getting to Kfar Nahum Junction (see 'Tabgha' on page 616), and then walk the 4 km from there (about 40 minutes).

Background
Though there are numerous ancient literary references to Capernaum, there are still several aspects of the town's history that remain unexplained. There is no mention of Capernaum in the Old Testament, though archaeologists have discovered some evidence of occupation from the second millennium BCE. It was during the Early Roman period (37 BCE-132 CE) that the settlement really developed, almost certainly as a result of its position on the Via Maris trading route. Yet the inference is that this was such a poor community that it had to rely on a Gentile, the centurion commanding the garrison, to

build the synagogue (*Luke 7:5*). What has yet to be satisfactorily explained is why the magnificent fourth-century CE synagogue that you see today was built in this relatively poor community, particularly since the decline in importance of the Via Maris in later years must have hastened Capernaum's own decline.

The structure of Capernaum's population in the centuries following Jesus' crucifixion also remains unclear. Epiphanius (writing in 374 CE) claims that until the fourth century CE the Jews of Capernaum forbade Christians, Samaritans and gentiles from living in their midst, yet the archaeological and written evidence attests to the permanent presence of Jesus' followers from the first century CE onwards. This small minority of converts would be more accurately described as a Judeo-Christian community, or *Minim* ('followers of Jesus'), and probably still considered themselves to be essentially Jewish. The acceptance of Christianity as the state religion by the Roman emperor Constantine at the beginning of the fourth century CE may have fuelled tension between the communities, although both continued to live in Capernaum. Indeed, rather than manifesting itself in a violent form, this rivalry between the two could have been the driving force behind the building efforts that produced so ornate a synagogue, and the expansion of Peter's house through the stage of *domus ecclesia* (house church) to a basilica.

Both the synagogue and church had been destroyed prior to the Arab conquest of Palestine in 636 CE, though how and by whom is not clear. It's not unlikely that the church was destroyed by the Jews during the Persian invasion of 614 CE, and that the synagogue was razed by the Christians when the Byzantines retook the land 15 years later. It was initially thought that this was the end for Capernaum, but more recent excavations to the east of the main site (towards the present-day Church of the Seven Apostles) have uncovered significant remains from the Arab period. Not much is known about Capernaum's subsequent history, though the traveller Burchardus, writing in 1283, describes the town as being a poor village of just seven fishermen's houses. The lack of construction during the Crusader period on this important Christian site may be explained by the vulnerability to attack of this location. The site was first tentatively identified by the American explorer Robinson in 1838, though it wasn't until the Franciscans acquired the site in 1894 that extensive excavations began.

Sights

House of St Peter In 1990 the Franciscans built a modern church above the traditional site of the House of St Peter. The exterior is considered by some to be extremely unattractive, though the interior is rather nice and provides a fine view through the glass floor of the house below. The lake shore near the church is a particularly attractive spot. (**NB** The church is not always open to visitors and is primarily reserved for pre-booked tour groups who wish to celebrate Catholic mass).

The House of St Peter is characteristic of the other first-century CE residencies that can be seen here, most notably **Insula II** between the House of St Peter and the synagogue. The term 'insula' refers to the city block form containing multiple dwellings that was characteristic of this period, each block occupied by up to 15 related families (as many as 100 persons) sharing a communal courtyard. The insula that contains St Peter's house is referred to as **insula sacra** (sacred quarter).

Sceptics who may doubt the authenticity of the claim that this is the actual house of St Peter would do well to bear in mind the compelling evidence that supports it. From as early as the first century CE, a small room (5.8 m by 6.45 m) at the centre of the 'insula sacra' has been accorded special treatment. Though artefacts found here (including fish-hooks) attest to general usage in the first half of the first century CE, by the second half of the century the room was put to some kind of public use. It is the only one in the block that has plastered walls and floors, whilst 131 inscriptions in Greek, Aramaic, Syriac and Latin have been carved into the walls. Some of this graffiti mentions 'Jesus', 'Lord', 'Christ' and 'Peter', and suggests that Peter's house was used as a domus ecclesia (house church). By the fourth century CE an enclosure wall separated this house from the rest of the town, with a central arch supporting a more permanent roof structure (see *Mark 2:3-4*) and a polichrome pavement laid on the floor. The pilgrim nun Egeria, visiting c. 383, describes in some detail how the "house of the prince of Apostles was changed into a church".

By the mid-fifth century a small central octagon had been built around the house, with an ornate mosaic carpet replacing the polichrome pavement. The peacock centrepiece of the mosaic symbolizes immortality (now displayed outside the building). A larger concentric octagon and an outer semi-octagon enclosed the site, with a baptismal font added to the east apse. The church is described by the anonymous pilgrim of Placentia c. 570 CE, but was destroyed at some stage in the seventh century. The early stage from which this site was venerated gives much credence to the suggestion that this was indeed St Peter's house.

The synagogue The history behind the synagogue is more complex. The key question is why such a fine building, constructed of imported limestone as opposed to the locally found basalt used for residential quarters, was built in what by all accounts was a relatively poor town? It is also far from clear who built it, whilst its date of construction remains contentious. It is now generally agreed that the synagogue was built at the end of the fourth century CE, with the court to the east completed in the fifth century. A cache of 25,000 Late Roman period coins and some pottery finds buried in the foundations seem to support this date. However, the style of the building is very different to other synagogues built in Galilee during the same period. Whereas the synagogues at Hammat- Tiberias and Beit Alpha (albeit the latter belonging to the sixth century CE) have plain exteriors and elaborate mosaic floors inside, Capernaum's synagogue had an impressive ornamental façade and exterior, but a relatively plain stone floor inside. Further, the period when the synagogue was built was a time of considerable tension between the Jewish and Christian communities, and it would have been unusual for the Byzantine authorities to allow the construction of such a large synagogue so close to a church. More speculative theorists suggest that the synagogue was actually built by the Christian community in order to create a spectacular reminder of some of the scenes from Jesus' time in Capernaum.

The synagogue comprises three main sections: a large prayer hall, the courtyard to the east, and the porch along the façade. Despite the wealth of remains discovered here it has not been possible to reconstruct the complete plan of the synagogue. For example, experts still disagree as to whether there was an upper gallery, possibly for use by women. The floor plan is that of a basilica, with the rectangular prayer hall divided by a stylobate into a wide nave and three aisles to the west, north and east. The prayer hall was joined to the east by a court which had roofed porticoes to the north, east and south. This would probably have served as some form of community centre/meeting place. The hall and court were both paved with stone slabs. The interior of the synagogue was plastered and decorated with reliefs.

The synagogue faces south, towards Jerusalem, and is entered by one of three doorways up a flight of steps. The reference to a synagogue where the "way in is up many steps, and it is made of dressed stone" by Egeria c. 383 has been one factor in the argument for dating the construction somewhat earlier. Sections of the intricately carved lintels, cornices, capitals and gables remain in situ, whilst fallen sections are displayed in the "open air museum" just inside the entrance to the site.

Excavations beneath the synagogue have revealed the remains of a large public building dating to the first century CE (you can see the lines of black basalt beneath the white limestone of the present synagogue). It has been suggested that this could be the synagogue where Jesus taught and performed some of his miracles. Against this argument is the fact that the lower remains here are at the same level as the first-century CE Insula II buildings, and thus this cannot belong to the synagogue that "is up many steps", as described by Egeria. However, the counter-argument is that these lower remains are just the foundations of the first-century CE synagogue, and the building itself would have been somewhat higher.

Greek Orthodox Church of the Seven Apostles ① *T04-6722282, daily 0830-sunset; if locked, knock on the monastery door (to the left of the church), free. Shop, toilet. Modest dress only.* The land to the east of the Capernaum site is the property of the Greek Orthodox Church, and contains the remains of the town from around the late seventh century CE until the mid-11th century CE. The most notable finds have been the remains of a large square building that may have served as some form of fish storage facility, and a long lakeside quay.

The Greek Orthodox Church of the Seven Apostles, just to the east of Capernaum, is one of the loveliest spots in the area. The small church, built in 1931, is distinguished by its red domes which can be seen from some distance. The interior of the church is elaborately decorated in the Greek Orthodox tradition, with numerous icons and images of Jesus and the Apostles.

Route
From Capernaum, Route 87 continues along the north shore of the Sea of Galilee to the junction with Route 8277. This is where the short excursion from the lakeside road via the **Mt of Beatitudes** and **Chorazin** rejoins Route 87 (see next page).

Mt of Beatitudes → *Colour map 1, grid B4.*

The Mt of Beatitudes is the traditional site of the 'Sermon on the Mount' (*Matthew 5:1* to *7:27; Luke 6:17-49*) and, though there is no archaeological evidence to support this claim, this is most surely an appropriate spot for one of Jesus' most important lessons.

Ins and outs
Getting there and away Buses 63, 450, 841 and 963 from Tiberias, get off at the Italian Monastery Junction (give the driver plenty of warning, 25 minutes). On foot, the church can be reached by taking the steep path from Tabgha (see page 616). By car, take the steep, winding Route 90 heading upwards from Kfar Nahum Junction. After 2.4 km of switchback turns, a road sign-posted "Hospice of the Beatitudes" heads off 1 km to the right. There can be coach jams on this road.

Church of the Beatitudes
① *T04-6790978, daily 0800-1145 and 1430-1645, free, or car 5NIS. Parking, toilets, café, souvenir shop (the battle for souvenirs can be brutal). Modest dress required.* The original fourth-century CE Monastery of the Sermon on the Mount was built close to Tabgha, but fell out of

use in the seventh century CE. The modern Church of the Beatitudes is one of the more attractive churches in the Holy Land, set in one of the prettiest locations. Built in 1937, the church is constructed of local basalt, with white Nazareth stone used in the arches and columns. Designed by the renowned Italian architect Antonio Barluzzi, the eight sides of its octagonal plan represent the eight Beatitudes (which bless the poor in spirit, those that mourn, the meek, those that hunger and thirst after righteousness, the merciful, the pure in heart, the peacemakers, and those who are persecuted for righteousness), whilst the dome symbolizes Christ's promise of reward in heaven. There are clear views of the area of Jesus' Ministry through the narrow horizontal windows, or from the arcaded ambulatory around the church. The interior is frequently cordoned off for Catholic masses. Despite the crowds, the landscaped gardens provide a fine setting for quiet contemplation.

Route

If you wish to continue on this excursion away from the lakeside, return to Route 90 and continue north. After 4.5 km turn right at Korazim Junction on to Route 8277. Immediately on your left is Vered HaGalil (see below). Shortly after, on your right, is the Domus Galilaeae Roman Catholic Church, a striking modern edifice commanding fabulous views over the Sea of Galilee. There is a guesthouse here (pilgrims only) or it's possible to visit the **church** ① *Mon-Sat 0900-1200 and 1500-1630, entrance free.*

Proceeding east on Route 8277, passing the turn off on the left for the settlement of Korazim, continue for 2.5 km until you come to Korazim National Park (Chorazin) on your right. Beyond the National Park, Route 8277 continues east towards the kibbutz at Almagor (3.3 km), site of a four-day battle between the Israelis and Syria in 1951, and where there is a lovely guesthouse (see below). The road then bears south, after 5.7 km rejoining the lake ring-road, Route 87.

Korazim (Chorazin) → *Colour map, B4.*

① *T04-6934982, daily 0800-1700 (closes 1 hr earlier in winter), Fri 0800-1500, adult 20NIS, student 17NIS, child 9NIS.*

The fine remains of this ancient Jewish town, most notably the fourth-fifth-century CE synagogue, stand on a low hill above the Sea of Galilee amongst a barren landscape littered with black basalt stones. Many dolmens (upright stones supporting a horizontal slab, used for burial) are located in the area around the town. Though the remains are not extensive, this must rate as one of the best presented sites in the region.

Background

The ancient Jewish settlement of **Korazim** (Chorazin) is best known as one of the three towns (also Capernaum, Bethsaida) that Jesus cursed for rejecting his teachings (*Matthew 11:20-24; Luke 10:12-16*). Excavations suggest that the town was founded in the first or second century CE, and concentrated mainly on the upper side of the hill (north of Route 8277, labelled on map as '**Northern Quarter**'). The settlement expanded over the centuries, and by the Talmudic period of the late third-early fourth centuries CE it extended over most of the hill.

Some time in the early fourth century CE the town was destroyed, and is described in Eusebius' *Onomasticon* as being "a village in Galilee, cursed by the messiah, [that] lives in ruins today". The causes of this calamity are unknown, though an earthquake is a more likely explanation than the sometimes mentioned theory of Christian-Jewish communal strife. The town, including the impressive synagogue, was swiftly rebuilt pretty much on the same plan as the earlier settlement. The site continued to be occupied for the next few hundred years, with alterations and repairs made to all the major buildings. The town began to decline in the eighth century CE and may even have been abandoned completely until the area was resettled (on a far smaller scale) in the 12th or 13th century CE. A small community of Jewish fishermen were still reported to be living here in the 16th century CE. Bedouins occupied the site intermittently until 1948.

The site was first identified in 1869, though early commentators (most notably St Jerome) confused Korazim with Kursi on the east shore of the Sea of Galilee (see page 627).

The park

Grave of Sheikh Ramadan (1) Located just in front of the **ticket office** (2), the grave was originally built during the Mamluk period. Believed by the Bedouin to be the grave of one of Salah al-Din's generals, they used to gather here to make vows and settle disputes, believing that guilt or innocence could be established beyond doubt.

Ritual bath complex (3) Gravelled pathways lead south from the ticket office. To the right of the path is the ritual bath complex (3), enclosed within a walled courtyard paved with flagstones. Nine steps (two above ground, seven below) lead down into the mikveh (ritual

Korazim National Park (Chorazin)

Synagogue detail

To Korazim Junction & Route 90 / Route 87
Route 8277

To Almagor & Route 87

Northern Quarter

Central Quarter

Eastern Quarter

Western Quarter

N

Not to scale

- - - - Tour Route

a Entrance Court
b Bedrock
c Central Hall

d Aisles
e Site of Ark of the Law
f 'Seat of Moses'
1 Grave of Sheikh Ramadan

2 Ticket Office
3 Ritual Bath Complex
4 'Building A'
5 'Building B'
6 Synagogue

7 Open Square at Entrance to Synagogue
8 'House of Arches'
9 Subterranean Chamber
10 Oil Presses

bath) itself. The pool was fed by the subterranean cistern close by. Both are partly cut from the rock and partly built with stone. A central column in the cistern supported a stone roof.

Central Quarter Head south along the main north–south road of the town to the '**Central Quarter**' of the residential area, built on the wide natural platform on the top of the hill. This quarter comprises two main buildings ('A' and 'B'), both of which feature a central courtyard surrounded by a row of rooms. A large cistern in the courtyard of '**Building B**' probably served both residential units. Despite minor alterations to both buildings in the late sixth and eighth centuries CE, they pretty much conform to their original late fourth-early fifth-century CE plan.

Synagogue The **Synagogue** (6), with its reconstructed façade, is Korazim's most impressive sight. In contrast to Capernaum's synagogue it is built of local black basalt, though the plan and design are similar. Notice how remnants of the large slab of rock to the northwest were left in situ. A monumental staircase leads up from the **large open square** (7) to the synagogue's three entrance doorways. These lead into the central prayer hall, with a U-shaped arrangement of 12 columns dividing it into a central hall and two aisles. Just inside the entrance, to the left, stands a decorated column that may well have been part of a structure designed to hold the Ark of the Law. To the right, is an aedicula (small niche) in which was discovered a stone chair bearing the inscription "Seat (Cathedra) of Moses" (the original is in the Israel Museum in Jerusalem). There are also substantial remains from the decorative elements of the synagogue, including sections of friezes, cornices and capitals. A carved conch, possibly part of a window, is particularly fine.

Western Quarter Though fragments of earlier periods are visible, the houses in the 'Western Quarter', most notably the '**House of Arches**' (8), date from the medieval period. It is possible to see here how the double row of arches supported the stone beam roof. To the south of the 'House of Arches' is a **subterranean chamber** (9) that probably served as a storeroom or cistern in the Talmudic period. To the west of the 'House of Arches' are the remains of several **oil presses** (10), one of which appears to have been in use from the fourth century CE until the 17th century CE. Sections of the '**Southern Quarter**' and '**Eastern Quarter**' can also be seen from the pathways, though they resemble little more than heaps of rubble.

Korazim (Chorazin) listings

For Sleeping and Eating price codes and other relevant information, see Essentials pages 26-31.

Sleeping and eating
AL Vered HaGalil Guest Farm, Korazim Junction, T04-6935785, www.veredhagalil. co.il. The 'Rose of Galilee' has a choice of very pleasant accommodation: in cabins, studios (with kitchenette), cottages with living room, or the 2-room bunkhouse for those on a budget. Built of stone and wood, dotted around established gardens, there's a rustic-alpine feel about the place. Seasonal pool,

games room, sauna and lovely spa (massages from 235NIS). The American-style country restaurant here is highly recommended: it's a lovely open space with great terraces and something for everyone on the menu, daily 0800-late. Another attraction is the riding stables (T6800407) where you can take lessons or a ride to explore the surrounding countryside, from 1 hr to a few days!
AL-D Sea of Galilee Guesthouse, Almagor, T04-6930063/052-3493700, www. seaofgalileeguesthouse.com. Six spotless homely private rooms have nice touches (herbs in jars), modern tiled shower-rooms, fridge, sink, lots of space, little tables and

chairs outside among the fruit trees; can sleep 2-6. Excellent dorm with a lovely wooden veranda, 7 beds, kitchen, free internet and Wi-Fi; reasonably priced laundry service. The grassy lawn with Kinneret views and hammocks is the perfect place for sunsets and down-time. Homemade breakfast in the sunny breakfast room decorated with pioneering photos (jams, creams and yogurts just a few of many marvellous items spread out); very friendly hosts. Disabled room available. Recommended.

Route

Continuing northeast along the lakeside road (Route 87) from its junction with Route 8277, after 2 km you come to the **Ariq Bridge**. Several km beyond here is the turning for the **Jordan River Park**.

Jordan River Park → Colour map 1, B5.

ⓘ Entry for car 55NIS, motorbike 20NIS; camping with car 70NIS, motorbike 25NIS.

This short section of the Jordan River has been turned into a wonderful recreation site that's an excellent camping spot. In addition to the nature trails and bird-watching opportunities, and the archaeological remains of the ancient Jewish settlement of Bethsaida, the park's most notable attraction is the opportunity to paddle down the Jordan in a kayak or float down in an inner tube.

Ins and outs

Getting there and away There's no public transport directly to the park, though buses that circumnavigate the lake may be able to drop you off at the junction just past the Ariq Bridge.

Tel Bethsaida

This low tel (mound) to the east of the Jordan River Park is the remains of the ancient Jewish settlement of **Bethsaida** (Beth Zaida). It was founded by Herod Philip upon the territories inherited from his father Herod the Great, and named Julius-Bethsaida after the wife of the Roman Emperor Augustus. **Herod Philip** was buried here upon his death in 33 CE.

Jordan River Park

Bethsaida is also the reputed birthplace of the Apostles Peter and Andrew, but was one of the towns (with Capernaum and Chorazin) that was upbraided by Jesus for rejecting his teachings (*Matthew 11:20-24; Luke 10:12-16*). The town was destroyed by the Romans during the First Jewish Revolt (66-73 CE), leaving little to be seen today.

Kayak/inner tube hire

ABU-Kayak ⓘ T04-6921078, daily 0900-1700, rent out two- and three-seater inflatable kayaks (148NIS per couple, trip takes 40 minutes-1½ hrs), or inflated inner tubes (only when the current is not strong, in summer-time), for a very enjoyable one-hour float along the Jordan. Hire fee includes transportation back to the starting point.

Walking trails

There are two marked hiking trails (blue and red), both of which begin at the restored flour mills. The short red trail involves walking through the streams and thickets, and takes around half an hour to complete. The blue trail takes about one hour, the highlight of which is a fine panoramic viewpoint over the Jordan River.

Route

At 1.2 km beyond the turning for the Jordan River Park, Route 87 bears left in a northeast direction at Yehudiye Junction towards the fabulous Ya'ar Yehudiye Nature Reserve. Beyond Yehudiye Junction, the road running along the east side of the Sea of Galilee becomes Route 92. About 1.5 km south of Yehudiye Junction, between the 25 and 24 km stones, a dirt road heads west into the Beit Zaida Nature Reserve.

Beit Zaida Nature Reserve → Colour map, B5.

The Beit Zaida Nature Reserve (also known as Majrasse) is a low, flat delta area where a number of streams flow into the northeast corner of the Sea of Galilee. Several lagoons have been created, the extent of which depends upon the seasonal variation of the Jordan River, Meshushim, Yehudiye, Daliyyot and Shfamnun streams. The area attracts migratory birds, and is also the home of many other creatures, including over 20 different types of fish. There is an excellent hike through part of the reserve, though for much of its length it involves swimming through deep water and hence is recommended in summer only. (**NB** Do not drink the water.)

Hike

To reach the starting point, turn west off Route 92 on to the dirt road (1) about 1.5 km south of Yehudiye Junction. After about 800 m take the fork to the right (northwest) (2) for a further 800 m, and where it bears left stop at the eucalyptus tree: the hike begins here. After a couple of minutes walking, the path crosses the Nahal Yehudiye (3). The depth here

Beit Zaida Nature Reserve hike

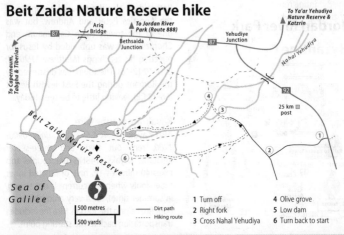

1 Turn off	4 Olive grove
2 Right fork	5 Low dam
3 Cross Nahal Yehudiya	6 Turn back to start

depends upon the season. Bear left towards the olive grove (about 100 m) (**4**), then follow the trail markers. These soon lead you into the water, which you will now be in for the next couple of hours. Though there are occasional trail markers in the water, it is just a matter of following the course of the stream. **NB** It is very deep in places. Depending upon the season, the stream will open out into a number of deep pools. Having walked and swum for over 1 km through the water, you reach a low dam (**5**). Beyond this point the Nature Reserve is a protected area, and visitors are excluded. Leave the water and head left towards the eucalyptus trees. A track to the left (**6**) heads back to the start point, running parallel to the stream through which you hiked. The total length of the hike is less than 4 km, though it can easily take 2 hrs, depending upon how much time you spend resting/swimming.

Route

A couple of km further south along Route 92, at Ma'ale Gamla Junction, Route 869 heads northeast towards Gamla (see page 685). Route 93 continues and, after 4 km, brings you to **Luna Gal Water Park** ① *T04-6678000/1, daily 0930-1800, adult 75NIS for whole day, kayak and inner tube hire extra*. This recreational park features the Sea of Galilee's best beach, plus the added attractions of giant water-slides, kayak hire, inner tube rides, several pools (one is Olympic-sized) and waterfalls, plus gourmet restaurant, zimmers and picnic areas. Irregular buses 15, 22 and 843 from Tiberias pass the entrance.

Continuing south on Route 92, passing Zeelon Beach to the right, after 2.6 km you come to Kursi Junction. Turn left here on to Route 789, and then turn immediately right into the car park of Kursi National Park. Continuing east up the steep and winding Route 789 leads to Mitzpe Ofir Observation Point and the start of the Mitzpe Ofir to Ein Gev hike.

Kursi National Park → *Colour map, B5.*

① *T04-6731983, www.parks.org.il, daily 0800-1700, winter -1600, closes 1 hr earlier on Fri, adult 13NIS, student 12NIS, child 7NIS. It is recommended to visit first thing in the morning, when the area is utterly serene; at other times coach tours can be a distraction. Buses 15, 18 and 22 from Tiberias.*

The Byzantine monastery and church complex stands on the traditional site of the Miracle of the Swine, where Jesus exorcised a man tormented by devils, and transferred the evil spirits to a nearby herd of pigs who subsequently rushed headlong down into the lake and drowned (*Matthew 8:28-33; Mark 5:1-20; Luke 8:26-39*). A sign just before the actual church entrance directs you to an 'energy bench' where, it is said, magnetic forces from an underground chamber below can cure your ills.

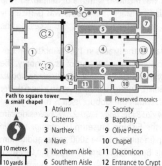

Byzantine Church, Kursi

Path to square tower & small chapel →

N

10 metres
10 yards

■ Preserved mosaics

1 Atrium
2 Cisterns
3 Narthex
4 Nave
5 Northern Aisle
6 Southern Aisle
7 Sacristy
8 Baptistry
9 Olive Press
10 Chapel
11 Diaconicon
12 Entrance to Crypt

Byzantine church and monastery

The identification of the site has been problematic since each gospel refers to the place of the miracle by a different name: Matthew, Gadara; Mark, Gerasa; Luke, Gergesa. All agree, however, that it took place on the "other side" (east) of the Sea of Galilee.

The name 'Kursi' may have been derived from the Aramaic word *kursa*, meaning 'chair' (a reference to the rock formation above the church). 'Kursi' is also similar to the Greek word for swine, as well as possibly being a derivative of Chorozain (see page 622), which for a long time was mistakenly identified with this site. However, the excavations of the **square tower** and **small chapel** on the hillside above the church have revealed the presence of a natural cave, thus closely matching the topographical features mentioned in the gospel narrative.

It appears that construction began on the monastery and church complex at the end of the fifth century CE, though major alterations were made to the church at the end of the sixth century CE. The entire complex was badly damaged in the Persian invasion of 614 CE, and all but destroyed in the earthquake of 741 CE. Though the church has been largely restored, little remains of the **monastery**, bar a large section of the dressed basalt stone wall that surrounded the complex.

The Byzantine **church** is the largest basilica yet excavated in Israel. The mosaic floors of the aisles in the main hall have survived remarkably well, with fruits of the Galilee being a popular theme, though the representations of living forms have been systematically obliterated. The mosaics' colours are especially strong in the chamber south of the apse, where Greek letters tell us that this was converted into a *baptistry* in 585 CE. An olive press was found just north of the central hall, whilst the two chambers to the south of the main hall were used as a chapel and a *diaconicon* (storage room). Beneath here were found a number of burial troughs containing the remains of 30 men, presumably the priests or monks attached to the complex.

A path leads east from the church up to the remains of a square tower, built around a natural rock pillar. The small chapel attached to the east was built by enlarging a natural cave. It appears to have been cut at the same time as the church was built.

Route
Continuing south on Route 92 from Kursi Junction, the road passes a number of beaches to the right, before arriving at Kibbutz Ein Gev (3.2 km).

Ein Gev → *Colour map 1, B5.*

The modern history of Kibbutz Ein Gev begins in 1937, when the "tower and stockade" became the first Jewish settlement on the east side of the Sea of Galilee. One of its founders was Teddy Kollek, the famous long-time major of Jerusalem. Following the armistice at the end of the 1948 War of Independence, Ein Gev was included within a demilitarized strip of land along the east side of the lake controlled by Israel. The kibbutz was particularly vulnerable to attack from the Syrian positions on the heights above, and access to the outside world was by boat only.

Since the capture and occupation of the Golan by the Israelis in 1967, Kibbutz Ein Gev has diversified from fishing and agriculture to include tourism as part of its economy. The **Ein Gev Resort** ① *T04-6659800, www.eingev.com, about 1.5 km to the south of the kibbutz entrance*, offers **AL** price category accommodation (**L** during holidays), set on a lawn under palm trees by the lakeside with excellent views. Within the kibbutz itself is the huge and hugely popular **Ein Gev Fish Restaurant** ① *T04-6658136, daily 1200-2200*, a lakeside café and bar, a 'mini-train' that tours the grounds, the **Fishing Museum** ① *arrange visits in advance*, and the chance to arrange a fishing trip (in summer). The 5000-seater auditorium is also the venue for concerts and music festivals. Buses 15, 18 and 22 run to Ein Gev from Tiberias (every two hours or so).

Route

Returning to Route 92, heading south from Kibbutz Ein Gev there are a number of beaches along the shore of the lake, including Shittim, Rotem and Shizaf. A further 9 km south, you come to a T-junction. The road left (Route 98) heads down to the excellent attractions at Hammat Gader (about 12 km southeast, see page 610). The right fork continues around the lake for 1 km to bring you to the major intersection at the southern tip of the Sea of Galilee. From Zemiah Junction, one branch of Route 90 heads south down the Jordan Valley, passing Belvoir and Bet Shean on its way to Jericho. The other branch of Route 90 continues around the lake, passing Kibbutz Degania Alef (2.6 km) and Yardenit (400 m) before continuing along the 'home straight' for the 11 km back to Tiberias. **NB** Traffic along this final section can get quite heavy: cyclists beware.

Bet Gabriel Cultural Centre

ⓘ *Zemiah Junction, T04-6751175 ext 0, www.betgabriel.co.il, cars 5NIS during daytime, 1000-2400).* The Bet Gabriel Cultural hosts exhibitions, cultural events (theatre, dance, music) and has two cinemas (call for schedule). There is also a noted **Italian restaurant-café** ⓘ *kosher, open till 2200 except on Shabbat*, with a terrace by the lake-shore. You can visit the **'Peace Chamber' mini-museum** ⓘ *Tuesday only 1000-1130*, where the peace accord between Rabin and King Hussein of Jordan was signed in November 1994.

Kibbutz Degania

The two small kibbutzim here, Degania Alef (Degania A) and Degania Bet (Degania B), often simply referred to collectively (no pun intended) as Kibbutz Degania, played a pivotal role in the establishment of the kibbutz system. There are several exhibits here that recall Degania's past.

Ins and outs

Getting there and away Buses 15, 18, 26 and 28 from Tiberias all pass Kibbutz Degania.

Background

It is not strictly true that Kibbutz Degania was the world's first kibbutz: rather, it was the first kvutza, the forerunner of the kibbutz system. This collective settlement had its origins in a labour dispute between Jewish agricultural workers in Kinneret and their manager. As a means of resolving the dispute the head of the Palestine Office, Dr Arthur Ruppin (considered by many to have been the great unsung hero of the Zionist colonization movement), gave the green light to what can best be described as "an experiment in self-management" (W. Laqueur, 1989, *A History of Zionism*). Thus, in 1910, ten men and two women settled permanently on the land that became Degania. Degania struggled through its early years, and even the members of Degania themselves had no clear idea of the direction in which their movement was heading, with disputes arising over marriage, child care, the role of women, the status of children, to name but a few. There were even members of Degania who wished to move on to a new pioneering settlement once Degania became 'established'.

Yet Degania's relative success became a role model for other collective settlements, perhaps too much so: the fact that Degania started with 12 members was merely an accident, but it became the conventional wisdom that the new settlements should mimic the experience on Degania in every detail, whether it was suitable or not. It was only the arrival of greater numbers of immigrants needing to be absorbed after 1919 that put paid to this dogma of the 12.

Amongst the new arrivals in Palestine from Eastern Europe were members of the Hashomer Hatzair (Young Watchman). Their view of collective settlement was far more radical than that of the generation that had established Degania, most notably in the education, care and upkeep of children. The family unit was replaced by a system of collective responsibility, with children being educated as a group and even sleeping in a special children's house, rather than with their parents. However, whilst Beit Alpha in the Jezreel Valley is really the first true kibbutz (see page 579), Degania is still considered to be the 'mother' of the movement.

Sights

Within Degania Alef's grounds is **Beit Gordon** ⓘ T04-6750040, Sun-Thu 0900-1500, Fri 1000-1300, adult 13NIS, student/child 7NIS, a small museum dedicated to the memory of Aaron David Gordon (1856-1922, one of the pioneering fathers of the kibbutz system, who spent his last days at Degania), containing one wing dedicated to the history of the region and a second wing featuring aspects of Galilee's natural history and stuffed animals.

Yardenit Baptismal Site

ⓘ T04-6759111, www.yardenit.com, daily Mar-Nov 0800-1800, baptismal ceremonies until 1700; Dec-Feb 0800-1700, baptismal ceremonies until 1600; Fri and hol eves 0800-1600, baptismal ceremonies until 1500, entrance free.

Just to the west of Kibbutz Degania, on land owned by Kibbutz Kinneret, the Jordan River exits the Sea of Galilee. With an eye on the pilgrim dollar, Kibbutz Kinneret has built the Yardenit Baptism Site. This is not the site where John the Baptist is reputed to have baptized Jesus (*Matthew 3:13-17; Mark 1:9-11; Luke 3:21-22*); tradition holds that this event occurred at al-Maghtes, to the southeast of Jericho. Nor is this a site identified with John's baptisms in the Jordan River (*Matthew 3:1-12; Mark 1:2-8; Luke 3:2-17*). However, with al-Maghtes being on the sensitive border between Israel and Jordan, and therefore out of bounds to visitors except on one day per year, Yardenit provides a convenient alternative. The setting is attractive enough, though very close to the road, and steps have been built to make the approach to the water easier. The cleanliness of the water is approved by the Ministry of Tourism every two weeks, contrary to Israeli rumours. There is a well-stocked souvenir shop and large restaurant, making Yardenit a bit too commercialized for some. Still, over half a million pilgrims come here each year to baptise themselves symbolically in the Jordan River. Some only venture in ankle deep, but Orthodox visitors make full body submersions even in winter time. Changing facilities are $1.50, or free with towel and white robe rental which costs $10 and includes a baptismal certificate, or to buy the robe is $25 (including certificate – but not the towel!).

Upper Galilee

In addition to some diverse and dramatic scenery, the Upper Galilee has a rich history, which is presented in a number of sites that should not be missed.

Highlights include the mystical Jewish holy city of Safed, the lush green Hula Nature Reserve, and the ancient settlement of Tel Dan. The attractions in Western Galilee are included in the 'Haifa and the North Coast' chapter.

Ins and outs

Getting there and away In recent years, there have been significant improvements in accommodation options in Upper Galilee, particularly in the budget price bracket. Backpackers no longer have to use Tiberias as a base for touring the region and can find dorm beds in all sorts of interesting places. The majority of towns and sites of Upper Galilee detailed below lie on, or close to, the main highway that heads directly north from the Sea of Galilee (Route 90). Yet, in spite of this, transport is not straightforward. Though there are plenty of buses up and down Route 90, it is more difficult to access the sites not directly on this main highway, and visiting to these places requires hitching, walking or long waits for transport connections. For this reason, many visitors choose to hire a car in Tiberias; a sensible option, particularly when the expense is shared between a group. That said, don't let these minor obstacles deter you from exploring Upper Galilee.

Safed (Tzfat) → *Colour map 1, grid B4.*

Of the four holy Jewish cities that represent the principal elements of creation – Jerusalem (fire), Hebron (Earth), Tiberias (water) and Safed (air) – it is Safed that perhaps has the most appropriate association. At 834 m it is Israel's highest city, with the clean air, cooling climate and tranquil atmosphere making Safed somewhat reminiscent of an Indian hill-station. Many of the visitors to Safed are religious Jews making a 'pilgrimage' to the spiritual capital of Jewish mysticism, though the town is equally attractive to the secular and gentile, who come to admire the views, wander around the narrow streets, browse the galleries of the Old City and Artists' Colony, or set off for some good walking in the surrounding area.

Ins and outs

Getting there and away Safed is located just to the northwest of the Sea of Galilee, and is often visited as a day-trip from Tiberias or Haifa.

Getting around It can be a little difficult to orientate yourself when you first arrive in Safed. The low hill with the remains of the Citadel perched on the top is circled by the town's main road, Jerusalem St. The Central Bus Station is located at the east base of the hill, with the suburb of Mt Cana'an further east. The Old Jewish Quarter cascades down the west side of the hill, towards the various cemeteries. Adjoining the Old Jewish Quarter to the south is the Artists' Colony, and to the south of here is Southern Safed. The sights listed below have been grouped by neighbourhood.

Tourist information Tourist Administration Office ① *Saraya, T04-6801465, Mon-Thu 0800-1600, Fri 0900-1500.* New office (no sign at time of writing, but it's the first door on the right when entering Saraya building), good stock of brochures and maps.

Livnot U'Lehibanot ① *Alkabetz, T04-6924427, www.livnot.com, daily 0830-1600.* Maps and leaflets; 10-minute movie on history of Tzfat; free access to excavations underneath the building. Laurie is very helpful, and can advise on accommodation.

A highly recommended aid to your tour of Safed is Yisrael Shalem's *Safed: Six Self-Guided Tours In and Around the Mystical City* (1991). It should be available from most branches of Steimatsky's.

NB Safed is a religious city, and visitors should be modestly dressed (shorts and bare shoulders are permitted but you will feel horribly conspicuous). Cardboard yarmulkes and scarves are provided at most sites, though it may be as well to bring your own as supplies can run out. Women are well advised to carry a light shawl to wrap around yourself if wearing a T-shirt. Synagogues are generally open Sunday-Thursday 0930-1700 and Fri 0930-1230 (later in summer); donations are encouraged: 2NIS is a perfectly acceptable sum.

It is requested that you refrain from smoking in the Old Jewish Quarter during Shabbat. Photography is permitted, except on Shabbat, though it is generally recommended that you seek permission before photographing people. Be warned, large groups of teens getting in touch with their religious and cultural heritage, plus the coach loads that come to visit the galleries, can make the narrow streets quite congested and noisy. Visitors to Safed should also note that its relatively high altitude can make it chilly at night, even in summer, so it may be an idea to bring some warmer clothing.

Background

Safed has its origins in the Second Temple period (c. 520 BCE-70 CE) as one of the chain of *masu'ot*, or beacon villages, that spread all across the land from Jerusalem to Babylonia. This chain of hill-top bonfires was used to announce the beginning of the new month or religious holidays (the Jewish religious calendar is lunar-solar), as decided by the Sanhedrin at Jerusalem.

Safed's location at 834 m was also instrumental in Josephus' decision to fortify the settlement in anticipation of the Roman legions' advance into Galilee (though no reference to the city is made in Josephus' account of the campaign), and in the Crusader choice of the site for a citadel some 1100 years later. This Crusader period, when the town was a commercial point on the trade route between Damascus and Akko, first brought Safed prosperity and significance. The Crusader citadel was surrendered to Salah al-Din in 1188, regained by treaty and rebuilt in 1240, and subsequently surrendered again in 1266, this time to the Mamluks. The prominence of Safed was increased by the Mamluk destruction of Akko, making it the important regional centre of the north.

However, it is in the 16th century that Safed really reached its zenith, when the city became the recognized centre of Jewish mysticism: **kabbalah** (see box on page 634). Persecution of European Jewry, followed by expulsion from Spain in 1492 and uncertainty in North Africa thereafter, saw an influx of Jews into Safed, many of whom were attracted by the growing school of kabbalistic thought emerging from here. **David ben Solomon ibn abi Zimra**, known as Radbaz, was perhaps the first notable mystic to establish himself in Safed, though he was quickly followed by **Moses ben Jacob Cordovero** (1522-70), who is credited with compiling the first systematic codification of the kabbalah. A subsequent arrival from Egypt, **Isaac ben Solomon Luria** ('the Ari'), was the rabbi who turned the kabbalah into a mass movement whilst based in Safed.

The 18th century saw a major influx of Hasidic Jews from eastern Europe, though the 19th century was more catastrophic, with a violent Arab attack in 1834, a devastating earthquake in 1837 that killed up to 5000, and a sacking by the Druze three years later.

The first half of the 20th century was equally violent, with Safed deeply affected by the nationwide riots of 1929 and the Arab revolt of 1936-39. On both occasions the Old Jewish Quarter was sacked.

Safed was also the scene of a pivotal battle in the 1948 War of Independence. In a surprise move, the **British** forces withdrew from Safed at very short notice one month before the termination of the Mandate. The main military positions in the town – the police fortress on Mt Cana'an, the Citadel, Shalva House, and the police post overlooking the Jewish and Arab quarters – were all taken over by the majority **Arab** population (some 90 percent of Safed's occupants). Realizing that leaving Safed in Arab hands could jeopardize Israeli operations all across Galilee, the commander of the Jewish Palmach, Yigal Allon (a military hero from World War II, who later went on to hold the civilian posts of Deputy Prime Minister and Foreign Minister), launched 'Operation Yiftah' to capture Safed. Following several failed attacks, by the morning of 10 May 1948 the Jewish forces had captured all the strategic sites after a series of bloody battles. The entire Arab population fled and Safed has been a **Jewish** city ever since.

Recent years have seen a further influx of Jews into Safed from Ethiopia, eastern Europe, and the former Soviet Union, who now account for around a quarter of the city's population of just over 22,000.

Citadel Park (Gan HaMetzuda) area

There are several minor points of interest in and around the Citadel Park area that occupies the hill at the centre of Safed.

Beit Busel This fine stone building was constructed in 1904 as part of a hospital complex established by Scottish missionaries. It is reported that Jews boycotted the hospital for fear of forced baptism, eventually persuading the Jewish financier Baron Rothschild to fund a Jewish hospital in Safed. Following its use by the Turkish army during World War I, the missionaries returned at the end of the war, converting the building into a college. Again war intervened, with this time the British using the building as their military headquarters. Towards the end of World War II, the building was purchased by the Jewish Labour Union's Sick Fund, ostensibly for use as an hotel, but in reality to act as a base for the Jewish underground. More recently the building has served as an absorption centre for Ethiopian immigrants, though it is currently derelict.

On Hativat Yiftah, the road that leads up to the citadel, look out for the former residence of the Ottoman governor. The attractive building was used for a time as the Bible Art Museum, but now stands derelict.

Citadel Though the setting and the view from the top of the hill is impressive, precious little remains of the Citadel. Its foundations are said to be solid and well preserved, but have been hidden from view since the British sealed them off to use as reservoirs for the city's water supply. The first **Crusader** fortress was built here in 1102 and managed to withstand **Salah al-Din**'s siege of 1188, though the garrison eventually agreed to surrender it in exchange for free passage to the coast at Tyre. The Crusaders regained the site by treaty in 1240, with the **French Templars** constructing a formidable new citadel on the hill. It comprised three concentric walls around a central keep. The outer wall would have roughly followed the line of the current Jerusalem Street, whilst parts of the **second wall** and a **tower** can still be seen close to the road. Once again the citadel withstood a lengthy siege, this time by the Mamluk sultan **Baibars** in 1266, though again it had to be

Kabbalah

In the Talmud, the term *kabbalah* simply means 'received doctrine' or 'tradition', referring to the later books of the Bible (ie after the Torah, or first five books) and the oral teachings. However, the term subsequently came to mean "esoteric teaching, enabling the privileged few either to make direct communication with God or to acquire knowledge of God through non-rational means" (Johnson, *A History of the Jews*, 1987). The most interesting feature of *kabbalah* is the code used to unlock these 'secrets'. Kabbalists argue that since the Torah is holy, the words and numbers contained within it must be holy also, and thus once the 'key' could be found, the secret knowledge contained within the text could be unravelled. Each letter and accent of every word in the holy books has a numerical value, with calculations based on these values revealing things such as secret names for God. These 'passwords' in turn facilitate access to the secrets of the universe.

Kabbalah has become 'fashionable' in US celebrity circles in recent years, with Madonna, Lindsay Lohan, Sandra Bernhard, Britney Spears and Roseanne Barr all expressing a deep interest in the subject (the latter once declaring on a visit that she felt very Israeli with her "big mouth" and "horribly opinionated nature"!).

---

surrendered in exchange for safe passage to the coast. It is suggested that Baibars did not keep to his word, and slaughtered all but two of the garrison after they had surrendered. Whilst appreciating the view across to Mt Meiron (west), Mt Tabor (south), and the Sea of Galilee (southeast), it is easy to see why this hill-top was used as part of the chain of *masu'ot* (beacon) villages, from which the lighted bonfires announced the beginning of the Jewish month. Renovation schemes are in the planning stages, but for now the park on the summit of the hill is rather neglected and rubbish-strewn.

British Mandate period police station There are several former British police stations scattered around Safed (including one close to Beit Busel), all of which saw a great deal of action in 1948. When the British withdrew from Safed in April of that year, some weeks before the Mandate expired, the police station was handed over to the Arabs, a fact that still rankles with the Jews. It's not easy to look impartially at events surrounding the creation of the State of Israel and Safed's experiences are no exception. The British decision to hand over all the key military installations to the Arabs may have been based on the fact that the Jews comprised just 11% of the town's population, making Safed in British eyes an Arab town. This, however, ignores Safed's ancient Jewish history, but perhaps more seriously ignores the fact that advance British intelligence reports warned that the British withdrawal would be a signal for an Arab attack. Safed highlights the dilemma facing the British all across Palestine in 1948. Their offer of safe passage out of the city for the Jewish population was not surprisingly rejected by a community that had existed here for many generations. The building still bears the bullet pock-marks of the subsequent battle. Outside the former police station is a **Davidka**, a homemade mortar used extensively by the Jews during the 1948 War of Independence, that now serves as a war memorial.

The monumental staircase opposite the police station, **Ma'alot Olei HaGardom**, was built by the British after the riots of 1929 to keep the two communities apart, dividing the Jewish Quarter from the Arab Quarter (the current Artists' Colony area).

Cave of Shem and Ever This is the reputed place where Noah's son (**Shem**) and grandson (**Ever**) either: a) studied the Torah (though it was written generations later by Moses!); b) lie buried; c) established a yeshiva where Jacob studied. The cave is holy to Jews, Christians and Muslims alike, with the latter group referring to the cave as the 'Place of Mourning', since they believe that it is here that Jacob learnt of the death of his son Joseph.

The Old Jewish Quarter

The Old Jewish Quarter is the most attractive feature of Safed: a densely packed area of winding streets, narrow alleyways and simple, attractive housing. Its sheer number of synagogues has led some to dub it 'Synagogue Quarter'. Getting lost is a certainty, though its small size means that you will soon find your way out again.

Ari Ashkenazi Synagogue ① *Daily 0900-1300 and 1400-1800.* In the 16th century this location was on the very edge of town, so the synagogue is built on the reputed site where **Ari** and the other Kabbalists used to hold the *Kabbalat Shabbat* service to greet the Sabbath. The original synagogue, built after Ari's death, was destroyed by an earthquake in the mid-19th century, and was subsequently replaced with the building that you see today. The key features of the synagogue include the central *bimah*, or platform, where the Torah is read. The small hole in the *bimah* (facing the door) was caused by a piece of flying shrapnel during the 1948 war. Fortuitously, the assembled congregation had their heads bent in prayer at this moment, thus narrowly avoiding any injuries. Pilgrims place papers inside the hole, as they do in the Western Wall in Jerusalem. To the rear of the bimah is 'Elijah's Chair', used during the circumcision ceremony. Legend has it that couples who sit on this bench will produce a baby boy within a year. The 150-year-old hand-carved Ark of the Law is also notable, one of very few left of this style and era (as the East European synagogues were destroyed in World War II).

Close to the Ari Ashkenazi Synagogue are a couple of buildings of some interest. One of them, marked by a small plaque, served as the **Haganah Command Post** during the 1948 war. The building next door is on the reputed site of the **Beit Midrash Ha'Ari**, where study of the Pentateuch took place during Ari's time, in order to make clear points of law. The **Avritch Synagogue** is also close by (marked by a blue door halfway down a flight of steps, though the synagogue is not open to tourists). In 1840 the Avritch rabbi was instrumental in persuading Sir Moses Montifiore to buy land in the Galilee to establish Jewish agricultural settlements.

Yosef Caro Synagogue This synagogue is located along Beit Yosef, a street lined with art and craft shops and stalls. The Yosef Caro Synagogue has a number of features not usually found in a synagogue, suggesting that its original function was as a house of study (*beit midrash*), as opposed to a house of worship. In particular, the windows are not placed high in the wall as at most synagogues (where they prevent worshippers being distracted by goings-on outside as well as permitting a glimpse up to the heavens). In fact, the first Chief Ashkenazi Rabbi of Israel, Rabbi Kook, went so far as to suggest that this was a welcome feature since it allowed the praying congregation to be brought into contact with their fellow man outside.

The building was restored around 1847 by an Italian Jew by the name of Guetta, following the destruction caused by the earthquake 10 years earlier. The three **Torah scrolls** in the Ark of the Law are of considerable antiquity: the scroll on the left, from Spain, is said to be over 500 years old; the central scroll, from Iraq, is around 300 years old; and the Persian scroll to the left dates from the 18th century.

The nearby **Beit Caro** ① *7 Alsheikh, usually open during the day,* is the attractively restored former home of Rabbi Yosef Caro, and probably the place where much of the Shulhan Arukh was written. Sky blue paint (against the evil eye) and the cave containing his holy books lit by candles make it an appealing little stop.

Alsheikh Synagogue This is the only original 16th-century building still standing in Safed (though it is only open during the Welcoming of Shabbat ceremony). **Rabbi Moses Alsheikh** was a student under Yosef Caro and went on to become a leading Torah authority, though he was deemed by the Ari as not being suitable for the study of the Kabbalah. The walls on either side of the street on which the synagogue stands are painted a very attractive shade of light blue, said to suggest the heavens and concentrate your mind on God.

Old Jewish quarter & artists' colony, Safed

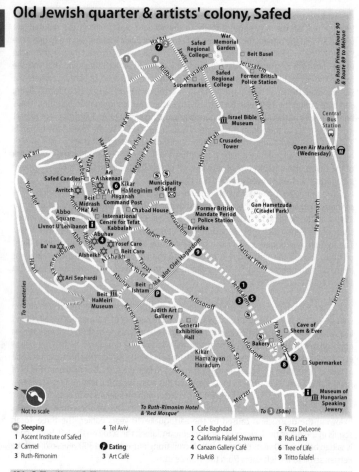

Sleeping		
1 Ascent Institute of Safed	4 Tel Aviv	
2 Carmel		
3 Ruth-Rimonim	**Eating**	
	3 Art Café	

1 Cafe Baghdad	5 Pizza DeLeone	
2 California Falafel Shwarma	8 Rafi Laffa	
4 Canaan Gallery Café	6 Tree of Life	
7 HaAri8	9 Tritto falafel	

Noted Safed Rabbis

Rabbi Isaac (Yitzhak) ben Solomon Luria: The Ari

The son of an Ashkenazi from east-central Europe, Isaac ben Solomon Luria (1534-72) was brought up by a tax-farmer uncle in Egypt. Though conducting a successful business in spice trading, as a young man Luria was recognized as an expert in orthodox non-mystic halakhah, though he also thoroughly absorbed the kabbalah legends. Just three years before his death he moved to Safed, and the impact that he had there in such a short time was staggering. He was not a prolific writer (there is only one book attributed to him), but his students assiduously memorized his teachings so that they later became a written form. He was referred to by his followers as the 'Ari'; an acronym of the words "our master Rabbi Isaac (Yitzhak)", but also meaning 'lion' in Hebrew.

Rabbi Yosef Caro (1488-1575)

Born in Spain shortly before the expulsion, Rabbi Yosef Caro spent 32 years of his life compiling the Shulhan Arukh ('The Set Table'), the condensed version of which has become the standard guide on how to live your everyday life according to Jewish law. With Rabbi AlKabetz, Rabbi Yosef Caro helped develop the tradition of studying the Torah all night on Shavuot, the holiday when Jews celebrate the giving of the Torah.

Abuhav Synagogue ① *Open throughout the day.* There are several traditions surrounding the Abuhav Synagogue. One has it that the synagogue was designed in Toledo, Spain by the 15th-century Spanish rabbi Yitzhak Abuhav, and built in Safed the following century by his followers. Another suggests that it was originally built in Spain, then miraculously moved to Safed when the Jews were expelled *en masse*. It was largely destroyed in the earthquakes of 1759 and 1837.

The synagogue was designed to incorporate a number of Kabbalistic symbols, most notably the four supporting pillars that represent the four elements of creation: fire, water, earth and air. The six steps up to the *bimah* represent the six days of the week, whilst the ultimate, the Sabbath, is where the Torah is read. The painting of the Dome of the Rock is not just a reminder of the destruction of the Temple, but also a call to tolerance.

The three Arks of the Law stand against the only original 16th-century wall. One of the Torah scrolls in the ark to the right was written by Rabbi Abuhav. The picture of the Western Wall between the arks has something of the 'Laughing Cavalier' quality about it: from whichever side of the picture you view it, the street at the bottom is always facing you. On the pillar next to 'Elijah's Chair' is a small plaque commemorating the victims of the Holocaust.

International Centre for Tzfat Kabbalah ① *18 Alkabetz, T04-6821771, www.tzfat-kabbalah.org.* Established in 2006, the Visitors' Centre (0900-1600) shows a film introducing the world of kabbalah, organizes lectures and workshops, takes guided Kabbalah tours of the old city (see www.kabbalahtour.com), and hosts popular Klezmer concerts in the evenings which are accompanied by dinner. It aims for a pluralistic approach, but you might end up feeling brainwashed just the same.

The Artists' Colony

The 'Artists' Colony' occupies much of the former Arab quarter of Safed. It was to here in the 1950s and '60s that Israel's beatniks were attracted, by a relaxed ambiance and the creative momentum of the times. When Safed became the home of orthodox Judaism in the 1970s and 1980s, the artistic community went into something of a decline, bolstered slightly by the wave of immigration from Russia and the former Soviet States and more recently by the boom business in Kabbalah art. The quarter's former mosque now houses the **General Exhibition Hall**, a gallery featuring work by members of the Artists' Colony Association (see previous page), and it is around here that the areas few galleries and studios are concentrated.

The **Ruth-Rimonim Hotel** was built as a station of the postal network linking Cairo to the Euphrates during the Mamluk period. A little further along the same road is a black and white **mausoleum** belonging to a former Mamluk governor of the town, ironically now used as the 'Zohar' Freemasons Lodge. Just beyond, is the **'Red Mosque'** built by Sultan Baibars in 1276. Classic Mamluk architecture includes the stalactite-vaulted porch. The building has been renovated and now serves as a cultural and art centre, complete with fitted carpet and a cloth to cover the inscription of the Waqf on the green stone above the main mihrab.

Beit HaMeiri Museum ① *T04-6971307/6921939, Sun-Thu 0800-1430, Fri 0800-1330, adult 14NIS, student/child 9NIS, toilets.* Established by a fifth-generation Safed Jew, Yehizkel Hameiri, this museum is housed in an old building that he painstakingly restored over 30 years. It is a typical Safed edifice, with stone floors and passages, and arched windows with stained glass, now full of nostalgic paintings and photos, old antique furnishings and collections of utensils. There are explanation boards in English, a lovely rooftop courtyard, and many reconstructed rooms to explore; it is worth a visit.

The Cemeteries From the HaMeiri museum, turn right, taking the next set of stairs down on the left. A right turn at the bottom leads to the **Ari Sephardi Synagogue**. This synagogue serves the Sephardic community: descendants of the Jews expelled from Spain into North Africa and the Middle East in 1492, and sometimes referred to erroneously as 'Oriental Jews'. The Ari is said to have prayed here to demonstrate the equality of all traditions of worship, and legend suggests that he once studied here with the prophet Elijah. In fact, whilst his father had an Ashkenazi background, the Ari's mother was a Sephardic Jew from Jerusalem, perhaps partially explaining why his teachings were so readily accepted by both communities.

From the steps a path leads down into Safed's **Military Cemetery**. The most notable monument here is the shrine to the seven members of the Irgun (IZL: a Jewish underground movement that blurs the line somewhat between 'freedom-fighters' and 'terrorists') who were hanged by the British Mandatory government in Akko Citadel Prison. The monument is designed to resemble a gallows. Just below the platform is the **Grave of Rabbi Leib Ba'al HaYisurim**, a disciple of the first Lubavitcher Rebbe.

A path from the Military Cemetery leads to the **Ancient Cemetery** where many of Safed's Kabbalists are buried. These include the following: Rabbi Isaac (Yitzhak) ben Solomon Luria (the Ari) (whose *mikveh*, or ritual bath is located a little further up the hill); Rabbi Moses ben Jacob Cordovero (1522-70), known as 'Remak', and probably the provider of the first complete and systematic theology of the kabbalah; Rabbi Shlomo AlKabetz, whose hymn *L'cha Dodi* forms part of the *Kabbalat Shabbat*; and Rabbi Yosef Caro.

The domed tomb in the cemetery was built by the Karaites of Damascus, and is said to mark the **grave of the prophet Hosea**. Also buried on the hill, legend tells, are Hannah and her Seven Sons, whose martyrdom is recounted in the Apocrypha (two books of the Maccabees). The victims of the terrorist atrocities at Avivim in 1970 and Ma'alot in 1974 are also buried here.

Southern Safed

There are several sites of minor interest in the area of Southern Safed. The **Saraya** was originally built as a caravanserai in the Ottoman period, though it was later used by both the Turks and the British as an administrative building. Members of the Jewish community took refuge here during the riots of 1929. It now serves as the **Wolfson Community Centre** and houses the new Tourist Administration office. Nearby is a tall sculpture by Victor Halvani titled 'Chariot of Fire' and depicting Elijah's ascent into heaven (*II Kings 2:11*). Next to the Saraya is the **Memorial Museum of Hungarian Speaking Jewry** ① *T04-6925881, www.hmj.org.il. Sun-Fri 0900-1300, entrance 15NIS, tours 30NIS*, the only one of its kind in the world. The tiny museum features artefacts depicting aspects of the life of the Hungarian Jewish community, both in Hungary before the Holocaust and Israel in the last 60 years. Audios in English give information and there are photos, documents, clothing and religious items, as well as an interesting room about the labour camps of World War II.

Safed listings

For Sleeping and Eating price codes and other relevant information, see Essentials pages 26-31.

● Sleeping

Safed accommodation options are fairly limited: there are a couple of top-range hotels, and a good hostel that's a lifesaver for budget travellers. An alternative to the hotels and hostels are private guest rooms in flats and apartments around town, generally run by families, and often religious. It's best to contact them through the Tourist Information Centre and use ones that are registered there. Prices in Safed sky-rocket on Shabbat and Jewish holidays.

LL Canaan Spa, Mt Canaan, T04-6993000, www.canaanspa.com. Crazily opulent 120-room hotel; standard rooms around 1,600NIS, suites 2,600NIS, or day-use with meals 1,300NIS. 2 beautiful indoor pools, gym, spa, stunning Turkish bath. Workshops on art and spirituality if you've the inclination. No children under 14.

LL Mizpe Hayamim, Route 89, T04-6994555, www.hayamim.com. Categorically "the" place to stay if you can afford to. Spa with fabulous treatments and divine range of rooms, all in a very attractive setting. Designed to get you back into shape via special diet, massage, shiatsu, etc. Separate vegetarian and meat restaurants, both

highly recommended. Outside Safed, on the way to Rosh Pina.

LL-L Villa Galilee, 106 Hagdud HaShlishi, Mt Canaan, T04-6999563, www.villa-galilee.com. Sweet spa hotel with classic style, the bar-lounge is a lovely place to relax on leather armchairs surrounded by dim lighting, flock wallpaper and old master prints. Standard rooms ($180) are a little small, but you can upgrade via the superior and deluxe rooms all the way to penthouse ($350) with balcony, jacuzzi and tonnes of space. Delightful outdoor pool, and good views from the terrace.

L Ruth-Rimonim, Artists' Colony, T04-6994666, www.rimonim.com. The hotel is split between the 'authentic' building (formerly the post house and then caravanserai), which has stone walls, high ceilings and has just been renovated, and the attractive modern section, built around a garden courtyard; rooms have huge beds, excellent bathrooms, there's a sauna, spa, gym, pool, restaurant. However, the attitude of the staff could be improved.

AL-D Safed Inn (AKA Ruckenstein B&B), Mt Cana'an, T04-6971007, www.safedinn.com. A range of rooms from cosy new suites with jacuzzi (robes and slippers), to spotless cheery dorm beds (soap, lockers), and plenty of other configurations in between. By far the best option for budget

travellers, it's 100NIS in the 3-bed dorms, kitchen facilities, free internet, very cheap laundry – everything's been thought of! There's a lovely sauna, outside hot tub, plenty of space in the alpine garden to have BBQs. Double-act Rikki and Dubi take the hotel business seriously whilst being entertaining company, and they're full of good information and advice. The downside is it's not in the old city but on the east side, up the hill. It's a taxi ride going up or bus 3 from the town centre leaves every 30-40 mins (ask for Pikud Tzafon); walking down to Safed old town takes about 20 mins. Recommended.
A Berenson House (Tel Aviv Hotel), off Ha'Ari/Ridbaz, T04- 6972555. Fine stone building built in 1858 to house the Austrian Consulate, now converted into a functional hotel. Rooms have a/c, TV, garden, glatt kosher dining room; breakfast included.
A Carmel, 8 HaAri, T04-6920053. In an attractive old fashioned building, the 12 old fashioned rooms all have balconies (best views from nos 10 and 13), quaint shutters, some with original Syrian tiled floors, plenty of character. Coffee corner, fridge, hot plates on Shabbat ('platter Shabbat') for observers.
A-C IYHA Beit Binyamin Youth Hostel, 1 Lohamei HaGeta'ot, near Amal Trade School, South Safed, T04-6921086, www.iyha.co.il. Fairly long walk from the Central Bus Station (25 mins, or Bus 6 or 7), reception open 0800-1600, 20 private rooms (D) with a/c, , breakfast included, TV room; very clean and well maintained.
B-E Ascent Institute of Safed, 2 HaAri, T04-6921364, www.ascent.co.il. Jews only (secular or otherwise). This is a Jewish experience programme and hence cheaper than your usual hostel (dorms 60NIS, private 180NIS, incl breakfast) – except on Shabbat when prices rocket out of all proportion (dorm 200NIS, single 350NIS, double 550NIS, includes meals). However, it's attractive and well-run, though private rooms are small and getting scuffed; two terraces have great sunset views. Small

rebate for attending classes on Jewish mysticism, Shabbat dinners with families, reservations advised.

Apartment rental and B&Bs
Several families offer accommodation, apartment-style; enquire at the tourist office.

Eating

It is worth remembering that most restaurants close for Shabbat (particularly Fri night), and at others Shabbat meals must be ordered in advance. Strangely, on the main (Jerusalem) street they also close on Tue afternoons. Almost all are small café-style places, and almost all are kosher. There's plenty of falafel and shwarma by the bridge, and a decent supermarket at the far end of Jerusalem Street and another on HaPalmach.

There is little in the way of night-time entertainment in Safed, but Rosh Pina isn't far away.
¶¶¶-¶¶ Gan Eden, Mt Cana'an, T04-6972434. Quality restaurant in historic building. Outside terrace on hillside is perfect for a leisurely lunch, though an evening spent in the warm interior is equally appealing (white table cloths, old tiles, lace curtains, chandeliers, but not formal). Pasta (artichoke ravioli 51NIS), fish (bream 81NIS, kebab with cranberries and herb salad 69NIS) and other interesting dishes, but no meat. The desserts and cakes are exquisite: leave room. Sun-Thu 0900-2330, Fri 0900-1400, Sat from 1800 (summer only).
¶¶¶-¶¶ HaAri8 Kitchen & Bar, 8 Ari St, T04-6920053, www.haari8.com. This meat restaurant (kosher) has been welcomed on the scene. Steaks and snitzels etc. Sun-Thu 1000-2300.
¶ Art Café, 72 Jerusalem St, T04-6820928. Dairy restaurant with a cosy interior that's more restaurant-like than most; nice views from the unadorned outside patio; expansive menu includes pasta, salads, noodles, omelettes, pancakes, pizza, toasts,

and more (29-48NIS), alcohol available (beers 12-16NIS). Sun-Thu 0830-2330, Fri 0830-1430, Sat after 2000.

Café Baghdad, Jerusalem St, T04-6794065. Tiny vaulted room with trendy lighting, art on walls, and some clutter. Outdoor music and tables across the street (with views), good for hanging out. Excellent dairy vegetarian food, vast menu of breakfasts, blintzes, pizza, salads, borek, pasta and toasts. Recommended. Sun-Thu 0800-2100, Fri 0800-1600.

Canaan Gallery Café, Bet Yosef, T04-6974449. There are grand views from this cosy bistro café, and the light meals, soups, sandwiches etc are made with care. There's also a weaving studio and art gallery to add to the appeal. Daily 1000-2000.

Pizza Da Leone, Jerusalem St, T04-6827833. The sign doesn't lie – this is the best pizza in Israel. Recommended.

Thai Bar, City Gate Mall, T04-6920992. Tasty Chinese and Thai dishes; nothing revolutionary but good quality and generous portions, soups 15-20NIS, pad thai 28NIS, lots of choice for carnivores. Makes a pleasant change from light-dairy-kosher. Business lunch available till 1800 (wide selection, 37-40NIS) and good for take-away. Sun-Thu 1200-2300, Fri 1200-1500, Sat 1900-2300. On the south side of town, up the hill, in the Canyon mall.

Tree of Life, T050-6907476. Sun-Thu 0930-2100, Fri 0930-1445 (get there early on Fri). A vegetarian café; lentil stew, salads, quiches, stir fry with tofu (all 38-48NIS) are regulars on the menu, or there's a specials board with loads more. Cute courtyard seating or a tiny interior with stencilled decoration. Excellent spot to watch the Orthodox world go by.

California Falafel and Shwarma, 92 Jerusalem St. Probably the best place on the strip to eat falafel.

Felafel Tritto, Jerusalem St, T04-9621490. Mon-Thu 1000-2000, Fri 1000-1400.

M Bagel, Jerusalem St. Canteen-style interior with murals on the walls. American-style bagels (18-20NIS) are good and fresh, soups for 20NIS, pizza slice 9NIS. Sun-Thu 0800-2300, Fri 0800-1500, Sat 1830-2300.

RafiLaffa, Jerusalem St. Another falafel place, but better for shwarma which comes wrapped in enormous 'lafah' bread, Sun-Thu 0830-2300, Fri 0830-1430.

● Entertainment

Art galleries
There are more art galleries in Safed than you can shake a paint brush at. Beit Yosef Street is lined with fairly tacky showrooms, though in amongst the mediocre efforts there are quality works that shine out. Kabbalah-inspired art is what is in demand here. In the Artists' Colony, a former mosque now houses the **General Exhibition Hall**, T04-6920087, www.artistcolony.co.il (Sun-Thu 1000-1700, Fri, Sat and hols 1000-1400), and a permanent exhibition of work. The staff here can direct you to the galleries of members of the Artists' Colony Association, or you could just wander in this area. Artists here work in mediums such as oils, water colours, copper relief, ceramics, woodcuts, pen and ink, bronze, etc.

Cultural centres
Yigal Allon Theatre and Cultural Centre, HeHalutz, near Kikar Ha'Atzma'ut, T04-6971990. Features occasional theatre, concerts, cinema (there is a more active Cinemateque in Rosh Pina).

Ascent Institute, 2 HaAri, T04-6921364, www.ascent.co.il. English-language lectures on Kabbalah at 1200 daily (go 15 mins early), for Jews and non-Jews.

Livnot U'Lehibanot (To Build and To Be Built), Alkabetz, T04-6924427, www.livnot. com. Programmes for English-speaking Jews (1 week, 5 months) that feature community service, kibbutz work, hiking, restoration work in Safed's Old Jewish Quarter, etc. Also accepts volunteers (no cost, room and board).

⊛ Festivals and events

There are two annual festivals in Safed that should not be missed if at all possible (though accommodation becomes a nightmare and there are major traffic jams in and out of the city). **Lag b'Omer** (usually end-Apr-early May) is possibly Israel's best-attended annual event, with around 250,00 Jews making the pilgrimage from Safed to Rabbi Shimon bar Yochai's grave at Meiron, where they dance with the Torah scrolls. The 3-day **Klezmer Festival**, held in July or August, attracts thousands for a series of concerts of Jewish soul music, a combination of Eastern European and Druze influences. Accommodation in Safed is scarce during both events (though you could always commute from Tiberias). The Classical Music Concerts event, usually of chamber music, will be held 7-12 Jul 2010.

⊙ Shopping

There is an open air market every Wed 0700-1530 just opposite the Central Bus Station, which is a good mix of cultures and cheap goods.
Eliezer's House of Books, Jerusalem St, has mainly religious books (in English and other languages), Sun-Thu 0930-1400, Fri 0930-1300. The Jerusalem Post can only be found in the **Minimarket** across the road from Judith Gallery.
Safed Candles, next to Ashkenazi Ari synagogue, T04-6822068, www.safedcandles. com. The famous beeswax candles are handmade from natural products. The Havdalah braids of colourful interwoven strands of wax (lit to mark the beginning of a new week) can be beautiful and intriguing souvenirs; or the smiley Hasids might amuse. Sun-Thu 0900-1900, Fri 0900-1300.
HaMeiri Dairy (Tzfat Cheese), next to HaMeri museum, T052-3721609. Tours of the oldest dairy in Israel on Fri at 1200, producing salty sheep cheese (it's good!); shop sells their products, 0800-1500.

⊖ Transport

Bus
The Central Bus Station is on Ha'Atzma'ut Sq. **Akko** and **Haifa**: Bus 361 via Carmel, every 30 mins, Sun-Thu 0700-2045, last on Fri 1700, first on Saturday 2100. **Alma** (and Rehania): Bus 45, 4-5 buses per day. **Jerusalem**: Bus 982 every 2 hrs, 4 hrs, or go to Rosh Pina for further services. **Kiryat Shemona**: Bus 501 or 511 via Rosh Pina, every 2 hrs. **Meiron**: Bus 361 (see Akko). **Rosh Pina**: All Tiberias and Kiryat Shemona buses go through Rosh Pina. **Sasa**: Bus 43 or 367, about 10 per day. **Tel Aviv**: Bus 846 via Carmel and coast road, 3 per day, 3 ½ hrs, or it's quicker to go to Akko and catch the train. **Tiberias**: Bus 45, Sun-Thu hourly until 1900, Fri last around 1500, Sat first around 1700, 1 hr.

⊕ Directory

Banks There are at least 3 banks on Jerusalem Street, but for ATM in English go to **Bank HaPoalim** at no 72. All offer foreign exchange (check rates and commission), as does **Central Post Office** (see below). There are also several money changers on/around Jerusalem Street. **Hospitals** Rebecca Ziev (Sieff) Hospital, Henrietta Szold, Ammami, T04-6828811, Safed's best (only) hospital. **Post office** Central Post Office, HeHalutz (look for communications tower to southwest of town) offers poste restante and commission-free foreign exchange; there is also a more convenient branch post office at 37 Jerusalem Street.

Safed to Meiron

There are several minor points of interest on the road west from Safed to Meiron (Route 89). Shortly after leaving Safed you pass on your left the **tomb of Rabbi Yehuda bar Ilai**, one of the spiritual leaders of the Jewish people following the Roman response to the Bar Kokhba Revolt (132-135 CE) whose work led to the re-establishment of the Sanhedrin. People come here to ask for good health, and also they gather the rocks and dirt from around the area, which are considered holy. The tomb nearby is that of **Rabbi Yossi Saragossi**, one of the 16th-century CE rabbis whose presence in Safed led to it becoming such a major centre of Jewish learning.

Route 89 continues west, passing the former Jewish settlement of Ein Zeitim, abandoned since the Arab riots of 1929. Route 886 (to Alma and Rehania, see page 650) heads north from Ein Zeitim Junction here, passing the pleasant Ein Zeitim recreation park. Visit the **Rimon Winery** ① *T04-6822325, www.rimonwinery.com, Sun-Thu 1000-1700, Fri 1000-1400*, at Kerem Ben Zimra, if you didn't know that wine could be made from pomegranates (Hebrew: Rimon). It is a scenic location, with outdoor seating by the orchards, where they make port, dessert (light not syrupy) and spritzer-style wines, as well as an excellent dry red. Also on sale is pomegranate seed oil, thick with antioxidants and known for its medicinal and cosmetic benefits. Tours lasting 40 minutes are free if you show a Footprint Handbook, and include a tasting session.

Continuing west on Route 89, the large red sculpture on the top of the hill to your right (north) is the **Armoured Corps Memorial**, a war memorial to the tank brigade that formed up here in preparation for the assault on the Golan Heights in the 1967 war. Just beyond this point, on the left (south), a marked path leads off towards the Nahal Ammud Nature Reserve. There are a number of attractive hikes through here, most notably a leg on the Yam L'Yam (Mediterranean to Sea of Galilee) three-day hike. The main entrance to the Nature Reserve is actually off Route 866, south of Moshav Meiron, and details are included below. Route 89 continues on to the T-junction opposite Meiron then bears right (north) to Jish, Sasa, Bar'am and Avivim, whilst the road left (south) heads via Nahal Ammud Nature Reserve towards Carmel and the coast.

Meiron (Meron) → *Colour map 1, B4.*

Standing on the eastern foothills of Mt Meiron, this small Orthodox Jewish settlement lies close to the site of an ancient Jewish settlement that flourished during the third to fourth century CE. Parts of the lower city have been excavated, as has a splendid synagogue from this period. However, most visitors to Meiron come as pilgrims, to visit the graves of a number of important rabbis who are buried here. During any week of the year, the Tomb of Shimon is busy 24 hours, and is an atmospheric place. Of course the village is completely closed during Shabbat.

Ins and outs

Getting there and away Buses 361 between Safed and Haifa pass Meiron (every 30 minutes, Sunday-Thursday 0700-2045, last on Friday 1700, first on Saturday 2100).

Background

Excavations at Meiron suggest that settlement here dates to the Late Hellenistic period (167-37 CE), though it was not until the two major Jewish revolts against Rome (66-73

CE and 132-135 CE) were concluded that the village expanded to the size of a town. The settlement of Khirbet Shema' (known as Tekoa of Galilee) just to the south probably formed one of the suburbs of Meiron. Meiron reached its peak during the third and fourth centuries CE when it was a noted centre of olive oil production, though the town's economic orientation was probably to the north, towards the port at Tyre. Meiron was seemingly abandoned in 363 CE following the devastating earthquake of that year, though a process of systematic abandonment seems to have preceded this catastrophe in response to harsh taxes imposed under the Roman Emperor Constantius II (337-361 CE).

It was not until the late medieval period that occupation of Meiron began again in earnest, following the publication of the *Sefer-ha-Zofar*, or *Zohar*. Compiled by the leading Spanish kabbalist **Moses ben Shem Tov of Guadalajara** in the 1280s, this treatise on kabbalistic lore contained many of the sayings and teachings of Rabbi Shimon bar Yochai and his colleagues, and led to a revival in interest in the second-century CE sage. In fact, it is not uncommon to still find claims that the *Zohar* was written by bar Yochai. His grave at Meiron subsequently became a major centre of pilgrimage, and was also a deciding factor in the decision of the leading kabbalist thinkers to settle in nearby Safed.

Sights

Tomb of Rabbi Shimon bar Yochai Rabbi Shimon bar Yochai was one of the leading Jewish opinion-makers during the period immediately following the Roman crushing of the Bar Kokhba Revolt (132-135 CE). In fact, his vocal opposition to Roman rule led to a death warrant being issued against him, and he was forced to seek refuge for 12 years in a cave in the village of Peki'in, on the western side of Mt Meiron. This period of contemplation resulted in the series of teachings that found their way into print over 1100 years later, in the form of the *Zohar*: the central text of kabbalah. Each year his death is commemorated on the holiday of *Lag b'Omer*, when hundreds of thousands of Jews from all over the world congregate at the tomb for three days of celebrations. A procession carrying the Torah scrolls used to dance its way from Safed to Meiron; however, in recent years, vehicles have taken over this journey. And though it becomes unbelievably packed with people and cars, it is an excellent time to visit Meiron. It is also traditional for three-year-old boys to have their first haircut at Meiron during *Lag b'Omer*, in the style specified by *Leviticus 19:27*: "Ye shall not round the corners of your heads, neither shalt thou mar the corners of thy beard". Another particularly busy time at the grave is the first day of the month (according to the Jewish calendar), though it tends to be very active at any time of day or night. The rabbi's simple tomb is painted white and has a curtain over it, so that half appears in the women's section and half in the men's. Bar Yochai's son Ele'azar, who also hid for 12 years in the cave at Peki'in, is also buried here (his tomb is clad in white cloth).

Tomb of Rabbi Hillel the Elder Leaving bar Yochai's tomb and turning right, a path leads down to the burial cave of Rabbi Hillel the Elder. A famous teacher during the first century CE, Hillel preached a message of humility and humanity that later found an outlet in the teachings of Jesus; in fact some scholars believe that Jesus may have been a pupil of Rabbi Hillel. Hillel's message was in direct contrast to the rigorous orthodoxy preached by Hillel's comtemporary, Rabbi Shammai the Elder, who is reputedly buried nearby (see Khirbet Shema', below).

Lower city Two major insulae, or settlement-blocks, from the settlement at Meiron have been excavated, located on either side of the dirt track leading from the car park.

On the east (right) side of the road lies a well-preserved section of the **lower city**. Of particular interest is the former two-storey building, which served as a **cooperage** during Meiron's peak (c. 250-363 CE). This was a major centre of olive oil production, and Josephus describes how his rival, John of Gischala (see nearby 'Jish/Gush Halav', page 649), cornered the market in this trade, making an eight-fold profit on the supplies he appropriated. A *mikveh*, or ritual bath, was also discovered in the courtyard here, linked to an elaborate system of rock-cut cisterns. There is also evidence of a sophisticated sewerage system serving the settlement.

On the opposite (west) side of the track excavations have revealed several finely constructed houses that suggest that this was the wealthy or upper class district of the town. One house, labelled the **'Patrician House'** by the excavators, is particularly well built and contains a number of interesting features. The room in the northwest corner of the house had no visible means of access (except perhaps a trap-door in the roof). A number of finds from this room included storage jars containing food remains (nuts, wheat, barley and beans) that had been charred so as to make them inedible. One jar was inscribed with the words "fire" and another with "belonging to Julia [or Julian]". Nearby was found a small bell minus its clapper and a handle-less sickle. It has been speculated that the room was used as a repository by the pious family occupying the house, with these items found here being consecrated offerings. All had been deliberately rendered unusable. The **'Lintel House'** just to the east shares its foundations with the 'Patrician House', and is noted for its fine lintel above the door in the north wall.

Synagogue Little of the late-third-century CE synagogue remains, it becoming a victim of the 363 CE earthquake less than a hundred years after it was built. Most of the façade is reasonably well preserved. A tradition based on mysticism and numerology claims that the collapse of this gate will herald the Messianic era, perhaps the reason why the visitors on *Lag b'Omer* stomp and dance so vigorously! Stylistically, the synagogue is very different to the one just 1 km away at Khirbet Shema' (see below).

Khirbet Shema' (Tekoa of Galilee)

Excavations suggest that this site was settled mainly between the mid-second and early fifth centuries CE, and it is most likely that it developed from a suburb of Meiron into an isolated village. Its most notable features are the synagogue and the mausoleum. It has been identified as **Tekoa** (of Galilee, as distinct from the ancient settlement of the same name in the Judean Desert, close to Chariton).

The small settlement at Khirbet Shema' on the foothills of Mt Meiron is separated from Meiron, 1 km to the north, by the Nahal Meiron. To reach the site walk from Meiron along Route 866 (towards Carmel), and then take the steep uphill path to the right (west) at the first hairpin bend in the road.

Synagogue The ancient synagogue at Khirbet Shema' has a number of interesting features, not least of which is the fact that several aspects of its construction seem to contradict halachah (Jewish religious law). Whether this is deliberate or just a reflection of the nature of the terrain on the construction is not clear. For example, it is not built on the highest point of the settlement, as was the custom, but was in fact entered through a number of steps leading down into the sanctuary. Further, it is located unusually close to the mausoleum and a number of rock-cut caves, the latter of which would almost certainly have been used for burial. It appears that the builders have gone to great lengths, however, to make sure that the synagogue is orientated towards Jerusalem. It is assumed that the mikveh (ritual bath) beneath the northeast corner pre-dates the synagogue and was built some time after 180 CE.

Mausoleum Excavation of the mausoleum has produced next to no evidence to indicate for whom it was built, or indeed when it was built, though some circumstantial evidence suggests the fourth century CE. However, since medieval times, it has been venerated as the **Tomb of Rabbi Shammai the Elder**. This creates a certain amount of symmetry since Shammai's great rival, Hillel the Elder, is reputedly buried on the opposite hillside in Meiron. Whilst Hillel preached humility and humanity and was renowned for his gentle demeanour, Shammai is portrayed as an impatient man who did not suffer fools gladly and who preached a rigorous interpretation of the law. Perhaps this rigorism about cleanliness and ritual purity was beyond the bounds of ordinary people, resulting in the Shammai school vanishing altogether. On the hillside above the tomb is the **Messiah's Chair/Rock**; traditionally the site where the Messiah will sit whilst the prophet Elijah announces the arrival with a blast on the trumpet.

Mt Meiron → *Colour map 1, B4.*

The peak of Mt (Har) Meiron is just to the west of the village of that name, and at 1208 m it is the highest mountain in the Galilee. Much of the mountain lies within the Har Meiron Reserve, and there are a number of hikes of various lengths that can be made in this area.

Ins and outs
Getting there and away From Safed take the early Bus 43 to Kibbutz Sasa (departs 0703 and 1248, returns 0745, 1345 and 1800,) or bus 367 at 0815 and 1130 to Sasa Junction. From Kibbutz Sasa, follow the signs to the left for 1 km and then take the road to the right for 1 km up to the **Mt Meiron Field Study Centre** ⓘ *T04-6980022, www.aspni.org*. You can get advice on the hikes here as well as a copy of the (Hebrew only) trail map of the area (84NIS).

Getting around The shortest hike is the Summit Trail, which follows red-and-white trail markers around the summit of Mt Meiron. The steep path leading up from Meiron village can take you there. You must stick to the trail, since the top of the mountain itself is a closed military area. The best, though longest, hike takes in much of the Har Meiron range, though if you do not want to complete the entire 18 km hike it is possible just to walk certain sections. The starting point for both hikes listed below is the Mt Meiron Field Study Centre, close to Kibbutz Sasa (to the northwest of Meiron).

Har Meiron Reserve hike
This eight-hour, 18-km hike begins at the parking lot behind the **Mt Meiron Field Study Centre** (1). Follow the black-and-white trail markers heading southeast from the parking lot. The trail leads to the look-out point on **Har Nerriya** (2), from where there are fine views to the north and northeast. Continuing northeast, passing the small Iron-Age look-out tower at the beginning of the forest, the trail soon meets up with the red-and-white Summit Trail around **Mt Meiron** (3). Follow the trail in a clockwise direction around the summit, past the **Lebanon** (4) and then **Safed** (5) look-out points. The trail descends towards the picnic area, then follows the paved road towards Har bar Yochai. Follow the road until a blue-and-white trail heads off to the right. Continue along the blue-and-white

trail (ignoring the green-and-white trail that heads off towards the Druze settlement of Beit Jann), passing through **Khirbet Bek (6)**. This former Druze village (Germak) was later selected as the site of a Jewish settlement, following the destruction of most of Safed in the 1837 earthquake. The settlement only lasted four years. The blue-and-white trail continues west, reaching a wadi and dirt road that cross the trail after 1 km. If you follow the dirt road down to the left you will come across one of the best examples of the **karst sink-holes (7)** that are a feature of this region. This landscape is created by the process of carbonic acid eroding the limestone, creating spectacular and unusual rock formations. It is claimed that the Druze residents of Germak used to dispose of Ottoman tax collectors down this particular hole!

Returning to the blue-and-white trail, and following it down through the forest, you pass the first of a number of ancient wine presses. Eventually you reach the Nahal Zeved, where you turn right towards the bed of the Nahal Keziv. Cross to the west bank of the Nahal Keziv towards the spring at **Ein Sartava (8)**. The trail heads northwest along the course of the Nahal Keziv, following black-and-white trail markers. As the river bed becomes narrower (after about 2 km), continue along the east bank. You soon come to a point where the route of the Har Meiron Reserve hike intersects with the final leg of the Nahal Moran and Nahal Neriyya hike (see below) **(9)**. Follow the green-and-white trail to the right (east), and then join the red-and-white trail that heads east along the course of the Nahal Neriyya. After 3 km of walking through pleasant shady forest, the trail hits the road just below the Mt Meiron Field Study Centre.

Nahal Moran and Nahal Neriyya hike

This shorter, four-hour hike begins at the turn-off to the **Mt Meiron Field Study Centre (1)**. The trail marked green-and-white heads off northwest, then west, into the forest, before

Har Meiron Reserve hikes

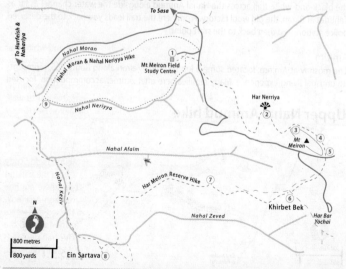

following the course of the Nahal Moran along its south bank. This is a particularly pleasant route, most notably in spring when the flowers are in bloom. Look out especially for the marjoram plant and wild garlic. The trail eventually begins to bear southwest and then meets up with the final section of the **Har Meiron Reserve hike (9)**. Turn left (east) and follow the red-and-white trail along Nahal Neriyya through this lovely forest. After 3 km the trail hits the road just below the Mt Meiron Field Study Centre.

Nahal Ammud Nature Reserve

This pleasant, easy-going hike begins 2.5 km south of Meiron on Route 866 (that heads towards Carmel). There is the option of a 4-km loop that leads you back to where you started, or a 5-km trail leading all the way to Safed. There is also the far longer alternative of following the course of the Nahal Ammud all the way down to the Sea of Galilee (20 km or more).

South of Meiron on Route 866 an orange sign indicates **Nahal Ammud Nature Reserve** to the left (east) **(1)**. Follow the track across the cattle-grid and through the forest to the **parking lot (2)**. From here follow the red-and-white trail along the water-pipe for 500 m, as far as the former **British police station (3)**. The station was built to protect the pumping station at Ein Yakim (Arabic: *Ein a Tina*) below **(4)**. Follow the path down to the pumping station and then proceed along the trail that follows the water carrier along the south bank of the Nahal Meron. After 100 m cross the stream over the bridge to the north bank, re-crossing the stream again shortly afterwards. Slightly further on a **tributary** joins from the north **(5)**. Follow the blue-and-white trail markers in a southerly direction along the east bank of the stream. At the next bridge over the stream you meet the **trail junction (6)**. The easterly route heads towards Safed, emerging close to the cemeteries. The black-and-white trail heads south along the course of the Nahal Ammud all the way to the Sea of Galilee. Many hikers continue a short distance along the black-and-white trail as far as the flour mill and the Sekhvee pools. This makes an ideal spot for a dip on a hot day. To return back to the starting point on the loop trail, head west from the trail intersection, following the black-and-white trail across the Nahal Ammud alongside the water channel as far as Tahunet el-Batan, the old wool factory. From here the trail leads you back to the deserted police station, and then back to the start point.

Amirim

The moshav at Amirim, located some 5 km south of Meiron along Route 866, represents an unusual living experience. Many families here offer zimmer accommodation, focused

Upper Nahal Ammud hike

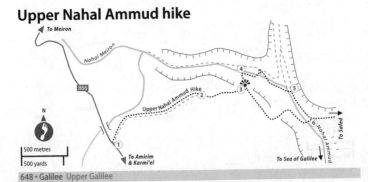

on a 'back-to-nature' experience in a very tranquil setting (many have pools). All of the moshav's members are vegetarians, and there are about eight veggie restaurants or delivery services from which to choose (Indian, vegan, Arabic, kosher, etc). For further details see http://amirim.com.

Jish/Gush Halav

Jish is mentioned in ancient texts as the site of the city of Gush Halav, transliterated into Greek as **Gischala**. The *Mishnah* refers to Gush Halav as one of Joshua's fortified cities, though more is known about the settlement from the early Roman period when the town was fortified in preparation of the Roman advance (Josephus, *Jewish War, II*, 575). Though **Josephus**, as Governor of Galilee, was responsible for preparing many of the defences against the Romans in the north, it was his great rival **John of Gischala** who built the defences here. John was to survive the Roman conquest of Jerusalem, though he ended up as a chained prisoner in Titus' victory parade. Jerome was later to claim that Gush Halav was the home town of Paul's parents, though his suspect grasp of the geography of the Holy Land means that this assertion should be treated with extreme caution. Gush Halav was famed for its silk and olive oil production, and like Meiron saw most of its trade linking it with Tyre to the northwest.

The main attraction at Jish/Gush Halav is the remains of the **ancient synagogue**. Archaeologists are unable precisely to place the date of construction, though it is now widely assumed that there were four main phases of construction (250-306 CE; 306-63 CE; 363-460 CE; 460-550 CE). Those familiar with the history of the Galilee will note that the final dates of at least two phases (306 and 363 CE) coincide with the dates of two major earthquakes that hit the region. Construction techniques employed, most notably the particularly strong foundations at the four corners, suggest that the builders knew that Gush Halav was located on the fault line of the Safed epicentre but were still unable to build a structure that could completely withstand the tremors. It is still possible to make out the ground plan of the synagogue today, the most unusual features of which are the two storage rooms to the east of the main hall and the long corridor along the west side. Also of note in Jish/Gush Halav is the mausoleum, with its well-built antechamber at the entrance to the rock-cut burial cave. It is part of the huge Gush Halav necropolis of the Mishnaic and Talmudic period. The church on top of the hill (with a huge neon cross that is impressive at night) serves the population of Maronite Christians who are the majority here, in addition to a 20% Muslim minority. Wandering around this Arab village is very pleasant, and there is an excellent restaurant (see below). To reach Jish/Gush Halav take Bus 43 from Safed (see page 642 for details).

Bar'am synagogues

Ins and outs The synagogues at Bar'am are located about 2 km north of Hiram Junction (Route 89 meets Route 899), and about 1 km south of Moshav Dorev (and not at Kibbutz Bar'am slightly further north). Take Bus 43 from Safed (see page 642 for details).

The site The remains of the two synagogues at the site of the former third-century CE Jewish settlement of Bar'am suggest that in its day this must have been a wealthy and flourishing community. Though little remains of the **small synagogue** (it was described in some detail in the 16th, and again in the 19th centuries CE, and decorative parts of it can be seen in the Louvre in Paris), the **large synagogue** is in a particularly fine state of repair and gives some idea of how the similar Galilean synagogues at Capernaum and Chorazin must have looked at their peak.

The most notable feature is its much-photographed façade, largely intact. Facing south towards Jerusalem, like its contemporaries at Capernaum and Chorazin it has a large central doorway flanked by two smaller entrances. The lintel of the central doorway featured the figure of a winged Nike bearing a wreath, though at some stage it has been deliberately defaced. A frieze above the lintel features a twisting vine branch above which is a cornice and an arched window. The sill of the east window of the façade has a Hebrew inscription that reads "Built by El'eazar son of Yudan", though the exact dating of the synagogue is unsure. Several medieval visitors ascribed the synagogue to the second-century CE Rabbi Shimon bar Yochai (see 'Meiron' on page 643), though this is far from certain.

The unique feature of the synagogue is the porch that ran the length of the façade. The porch was supported by six columns at the front and one on either side between the corner column and the building. A triangular pediment with an arch at the centre almost certainly rested above the porch. The interior of the synagogue is divided into a nave and two narrow aisles by a U-shaped row of 14 columns, with a floor paved using heavy flagstones. A number of sections of the decorative frieze have also been discovered. The building remains close to the synagogue belong to a former Maronite Christian village abandoned in 1948.

Alma Cave

One of the few attractions in the area around Safed that does not involve a visit to an ancient synagogue is a trip down into the Alma Cave. What it does involve is getting very wet, muddy and sweaty. The cave is part of the chain of caverns and tunnels that have been carved out of the chalk and limestone by the sustained processes of chemical and physical erosion. The trip involves a steep descent (slide) into the subterranean chambers, followed by several hours of walking and crawling through narrow, muddy passages up to 100 m below the surface. The tour finishes with a steep and slippery climb back up to the surface.

Obviously, there are a number of safety precautions that should be borne in mind. 1) You should never attempt this alone (three is a good number to have in your party); 2) You should inform somebody of your plans, including what time you expect to return, and should make sure that you 'check-in' with them when you have completed the trip; 3) You should be confident that you are not going to freak out at the prospect of being in a small, dark, muddy tunnel 100 m below ground for several hours; 4) One reliable torch per person is the minimum (head-torches are ideal); 5) Bring drinking water, but not much else; 6) Do not deviate from the marked trail (white leads you in, red leads you out); 7) Do not leave any litter, or touch the stalagmites and stalactites; 8) You will have to be reasonably fit and supple – the climb out is particularly challenging when you're tired; 9) You will get very, very muddy.

Tour The cave is located between the villages of **Alma** and **Rehania**, to the north of Safed. Take Bus 45 from Safed and get off at the entrance to Rehania. The path to the caves can be a little tricky to find (ask around). You head along the dirt paths opposite the entrance to Rehania village (some of them disappear) for about 1.5 km until you come to a large rock with a crack down the centre. The white markers lead you down into the hole in the ground at its base. Slide down the slope, keeping to the right. About halfway down the slope, two large rock columns mark the entrance to the cave complex. Follow the white trail markers in and don't lose sight of them. Towards the end of the trip the caverns are full of stunning stalagmite and stalactite formations. (An old English joke explains the difference: tites/'tights' come down). The subsequent climb out is steep, slippery and quite tiring (though the metal hand-rails assist your progress).

Mt Meiron listings

For Sleeping and Eating price codes and other relevant information, see Essentials pages 26-31.

Eating

♈♈ **Cedars Restaurant** (Hebrew: HaArazim), Jish (Gush Halav), T04-6987762. Top-quality Lebanese food at bargain prices, and such a staggering selection of salads to start (20NIS per head, best fattoush in the area) that it's hard work fitting in a main (eg kufta 48NIS, or fish, shrimp, lamb shishlik). It's a plain, unpretentious place with great views from huge windows. Classic menu also offers "portions of children". As you pass the village sign "Jish", the restaurant is immediately on your left, less than 15 mins' drive from Tzfat. Daily 1000-2200. Show your Footprint Handbook for a 10% discount.

♈ **Sambusek of the Cedars**, Hurfeish, T04-9972276. In the 100% Druze village of Hurfeish you will find a special sambusek (Turkish: 'a kiss'), where the flattened dough is filled with lamb,ground spices, and traditional Druze 'kishk' – a mix of labaneh, bulgar wheat, seame seeds and nuts – before being popped into the open flame oven. It's an unimposing authentic place, mostly for take-away (though there are some seats), open on 3 sides. Daily 1000-2300, and costs 7-12NIS. Look for the large sign with 3 cedar trees between coca-cola logos, near the roundabout on Route 89 on the west edge of town (or just ask).

If in Hurfeish, you should also seek out some of the region's best kanafe and baklava in **Bara Lial** sweet shop, on the south side of the main road (T054-8354910; daily 0900-2100); look for the Adar gift shop sign, Bara Lial is next door.

North of Safed

The majority of sites in Upper Galilee lie either on, or very close to Route 90, the main road that heads due north from the Sea of Galilee, all the way to Metulla on the Lebanese border.

Rosh Pina

Rosh Pina is one of the oldest settlements established in Palestine in the 19th century by the Zionist pioneers. It has a few reminders of its past, but is now most known for its appealing gourmet restaurants and small galleries selling art, jewellery and ceramics. The quality is good and prices are reasonable.

Getting there and away Rosh Pina is an important transport junction on Route 90 between Tiberias (27 km) and Metulla (38 km), and Route 89 that heads west to Safed (5 km) and on to the coast at Akko. Rosh Pina is on the bus route between Tel Aviv and Kiryat Shemona (Bus 841 and 842), Haifa and Kiryat Shemona (Bus 500), Tiberias and Safed (Bus 450) and Kiryat Shemona and Jerusalem (Bus 963), with a further service to Jerusalem (Bus 964). The bus stops are by the roundabout at the bottom of the hill that leads to the old part of town.

Background The original settlement here of Gai Oni was founded by religious Jews from Safed in 1878, though their project aimed at Torah study combined with agricultural work collapsed just three years later. The land was subsequently sold to Romanian Jews escaping persecution in Europe and renamed Rosh Pina, 'cornerstone' in Hebrew. This settlement too would have floundered were it not for financial support from the Jewish philanthropist **Baron Edmond de Rothschild**.

Sights Though there is not a great deal to see, the **Rosh Pina Pioneer Settlement Site**, straight up the hill from the modern centre, has preserved a number of original buildings, most notably the synagogue. The **information centre** ① *T04-6936913, Sun-Thu 0830-1400*, has a map of the old town and its buildings (5NIS) and a 20-min audio-visual presentation about the settlement which is relatively interesting (adults 15NIS, student/child 10NIS); book ahead for English (also Friday till 1400).

Rosh Pina listings

For Sleeping and Eating price codes and other relevant information, see Essentials pages 26-31.

Eating

The most attractive pubs and restaurants are found in the old part of town. There are also two malls at the bottom of the hill: closest to the bus station is the HaGalil Centre which has cheap falafel/shwarma/hummus; slightly further up is the Khan which has **Café café**, sushi, and others.

⑪⑪⑪ Rafa's Restaurant, T04-6936192. Highly recommended meat restaurant – casseroles, aged steaks, schnitzel, some fish, veg casserole, all come with sweet/baked potato or rice; children's menu. Small and simple, inside and out; Moroccan lights about the only adornment. Daily 1230-2230, reservations necessary on Shabbat.

⑪⑪⑪-⑪⑪ Pina Ba'Rosh, HaHalutzim, T04-6936582. Comprising Nili Friedman's B&B and Shiri's gourmet bistro, this is truly a delightful place with a prime setting on the edge of the hills. 7 quirky guest rooms have stained-glass doors, artwork and vaulted ceilings; some are enormous. The restaurant has a glorious terrace for breakfast (served till 1300), and the evening menu offers something for everyone, from goose liver to simple pasta dishes. Couples can try the 'dégustation' of 7 light courses (recommended for meat-eaters). There's a lovely bottle-coated bar area, and (if you don't opt for the veal fillet, 135NIS), prices are surprisingly reasonable for a place like this. Daily 0830-2230; book on Shabbat.

⑪⑪-⑪ Blues Brothers Pub, T04-6937788. Sloped garden full of shrubs with cute metal seats, hammocks hanging in trees and beer bottles on strings. Perfect place for a drink or few. Weekends 2100 until late, and also summer week nights.

Entertainment

Cinematheque, Community Centre, David Shuv St, T04-6801453. Recent films, frequent screenings.

Hazor

① *T04-6937290, daily 0800-1700, winter -1600, closes 1 hr earlier on Fri, adult 20NIS, student 17NIS, child 9NIS, same ticket for museum at Kibbutz Ayelet HaShahar.*

The ancient 'tel' (mound) of Hazor is the largest and most important archaeological site in Upper Galilee, though it is not necessarily the most visually impressive. The fact that there are at least 21 separate strata of occupation has necessitated some considerable detective work on the part of the site's excavators in determining the historical sequence here. Site-plans and labels bring some order to the chaos plus, on Fridays and Saturdays, volunteers give guided tours of the site (up to 1½ hrs) which adds immeasurably to the experience. The site comprises two main areas, the upper city and the lower city, although only the former is open to the public.

The small museum at Kibbutz Ayelet HaShahar (500 m further north) features a few of the original finds from the site, plus replicas of pieces that have been removed to the major museums in Jerusalem and Tel Aviv. Here there is also a weekend volunteer who will explain the significance of finds; the displays are well presented and will increase your understanding of the site at Hazor by 200%. Same ticket for Hazor National Park and same opening hours.

Ins and outs

Getting there and away From Rosh Pina go 5 km north along Route 90 to turn right at the sign to Ayelet HaShahar, and then it's 3 km down the side road to the turning. Note that the turning left into the site is particularly tight, and located right on the bend. Buses 511 and 522 between Safed and Kiryat Shemona stop at the entrance to Kibbutz Ayelet HaShahar, 500 m north of the site, and buses 841, 842, 845, 500 and 963 stop on Route 90.

Background

The first recorded reference to Hazor is in the Egyptian Execration texts of the 19th to 18th centuries BCE, though excavations here have revealed evidence of occupation by the Khirbet Kerak culture of the 29th-28th centuries BCE. It was in the **18th century BCE** that Hazor reached its first peak, when the large lower city was founded. Why the city expanded so rapidly at this point is still not clear, though it is obvious that Hazor must have experienced a sudden and dramatic influx of settlers (up to 20,000) who could not be accommodated in the upper city. Hazor's position on the great *Via Maris* trade route between Babylon and Egypt explains the city's importance, as attested to in the city lists of pharaoh Thutmose III's conquered cities, and the city lists of Amenhotep II and Seti I.

During the Late Bronze Age period (c. 1550-1200 BCE) Hazor was repeatedly destroyed and rebuilt, though its peak was undoubtedly in the **14th century BCE**, when it was the largest city in the whole of Canaan. Documents from this period, most notably the **'el-Amarna letters'**, suggest that the king of Hazor was one of the few Canaanite rulers who was justified in proclaiming himself 'king'. A major conflagration destroyed Hazor in the mid-13th century BCE; an event evidenced in both archaeological and written sources. The thick layer of ash in stratum XIII of both the upper and lower cities could be a result of the conquest of Hazor by the **Israelites**, described in vivid detail in the *Book of Joshua (11:10-13)*. The special emphasis in this passage on the burning of Hazor suggests the importance of this Canaanite city.

The Israelite rebuilding of Hazor was not immediate, with most remains from the 12th and 11th centuries BCE suggesting a limited, perhaps semi-nomadic settlement of the site. However, in the mid-10th century BCE **Solomon** used some of the levy of "six score talents of gold" sent from Hiram, king of Tyre, to rebuild Hazor along with Megiddo and Gezer (I Kings 9:14-15). The Solomonic city was considerably smaller than Canaanite Hazor, occupying just the western half of the upper city area. **Ahab** (871-852 BCE) considerably expanded Hazor, though still within the confines of the upper city mound. In 732 BCE Hazor was captured and destroyed by the Assyrian king **Tiglath-pileser III** (II Kings 15:29) and, with a few minor exceptions, has been unoccupied ever since.

Sights

The Solomonic Gate Still visible here are the foundations of the Solomonic period city gate (10th century BCE), just inside which are six rooms (three on each side) that would have housed soldiers and tax collectors. The gate was built over the site of the entrance to a Late-Canaanite-period temple, which confuses the plan somewhat, though a diagram of the two structures on the sign-board here clarifies their respective positions.

To make the picture clearer, two of the buildings excavated here have been physically removed to a new position some 80 m to the west (a diagram shows their position in situ).

The fine columned building is in fact a storehouse and was probably destroyed during the earthquake in Jeroboam II's reign (784-48 BCE). The adjacent building ('Beit Yael', after the archaeologist who excavated it) served as private dwelling and would have had two storeys, with the extended family living on the upper floor. Some inscriptions found on various sherds have even provided the names of some of the occupants of this dwelling.

The Canaanite Palace This palace, perhaps where the king lived, has been partially reconstructed using mud-bricks and cedar wood (as it would have been in Canaanite times). The cobbles of the interior may well have been laid over with cedar floor. The ornamental slabs of basalt lining the large interior would have to have been brought from 40 km away, and display cracks that must be the result of an intense conflagration (some suggest, the sacking of the city by Joshua). A statue 70 cm high was unearthed here, with its hands and head removed, something apparently practised by victorious Israelites.

The Water System This is one of the most exciting discoveries made at Hazor, with the entrance structure, vertical shaft and tunnel taking a full year to excavate. Clues to the source of the city's water-supply were suggested by the large dip in the ground, opposite the point at the foot of the mound where the Wadi Waqqas springs were found, and the archaeologist Yigael Yadin located the exact spot from aerial photos. Steps have been built to allow visitors to descend into the complex, though the original access was via two ramps of crushed limestone and then a series of five flights of rock-cut steps (clearly visible). The shaft is 30 m deep, with the top half supported by retaining walls (still visible) and the lower section hewn directly from the rock. A 25-m-long, 4-m-high vaulted tunnel slopes down gently to the underground pool. The bottom seven steps are made of hard basalt, rather than carved from the chalky bedrock, in order to prevent water corrosion. The genius of the engineers is that they dug the tunnel into the aquifer itself, rather than the springs, thus saving the need to dig an additional 75 m through the rock, and managing to enclose the water-source within the mound itself (unlike Megiddo and all other tels so far excavated in Israel). The entire complex is dated to the period of king Ahab (871-852 BCE).

Hazor listings

For Sleeping and Eating price codes and other relevant information, see Essentials pages 26-31.

Sleeping
C **Hotel Ayelet HaShahar**, Kibbutz Ayelet HaShahar, T6932611. Very attractive setting, and good facilities including pool, tennis, TV room, dining hall; breakfast included. Recommended.

Hula Nature Reserve → *Colour map 1, grid A5.*

ⓘ *T04-6937069, www.parks.org.il, daily 0800-1700 (all year round), no admission after 1600, adult 30NIS, student 26NIS, child 18NIS. Binocular rental 10NIS. Visitors' Centre, snack-bar and shop, toilets, picnic area.*

The Hula Nature Reserve is one of the last remaining areas of natural wilderness in the north of the country, and serves as a reminder of how much of Palestine must have looked when the early Zionist pioneers arrived in the late 19th century. The marshland and swamps that formerly occupied most of the Mediterranean coast have long since been drained, as has all of the Hula Valley bar this small pocket. Declared a protected area in

1964, the Hula Nature Reserve is a delightful place to visit, even if you manage to miss all the wildlife (early morning is best). From November-January it is an excellent place to see migratory birds, when it attracts ornithologists from all over the globe.

Ins and outs

Getting there and away Around 6 km north of Tel Hazor along Route 60 a road is sign-posted right (east) to HaHula. Buses 500, 511, 841, 842 and 963 stop at this turn off. Follow the road for 2 km to Hula Nature Reserve.

Getting around A Visitors' Centre introduces you to the indigenous flora and fauna; there is also a 20-min film but whether you can see it in English depends on other visitors' preferences. A 1.5-km marked trail leads you through the reserve, some sections of which are along a raised wooden walkway through the heart of the swamp's papyrus thickets. It's not unusual to come across furry critters (all harmless) sharing the path with you. A covered section extends out over the lake, providing an excellent 'hide' from which to observe the bird-life. A high observation tower further along the trail fulfils a similar function.

Background

The Palestinian (Jerusalem) Talmud describes seven ancient seas that surround the Land of Israel. Included amongst these is the '**Sea of Hula**' (Lake Semechonitis), a huge body of water that once occupied the Hula Valley roughly between the modern day settlements of Kiryat Shemona and Rosh Pina. In the 1900s, this swamp and marshland covered somewhere in the region of 6000 hectares, representing an almost untouched wetlands ecosystem. However, draining the swamps became a priority for the Jewish settlers who arrived in Palestine in the late 19th and early 20th centuries. The reasons for wanting to drain the Hula Valley were twofold: in addition to the desire to employ the land for agricultural purposes, there was also a pressing need to eliminate the malaria that was endemic in the swamps. Cynics may argue that there was also a political motive behind this programme: an agriculturally productive Hula Valley would show how the newly founded Jewish state "cared" for the land, "rescuing" it from the neglected state perpetuated by the ambivalence of its previous occupants. Three years after Israel became independent, the Jewish National Fund implemented a massive eight-year programme to drain the Hula Valley.

In terms of eradicating malaria and establishing productive agricultural land, the drainage programme was remarkably successful. However, there was a high price to pay. Many migratory birds ceased nesting and feeding here, and some such as the darter have never returned. Several mammal species moved out altogether, whilst others 'invaded' in disastrous numbers. The same process also occurred in the plant world. Even the small pocket of the 'Sea of Hula' that scientists and conservationists had managed to exempt from the drainage programme was affected as fertilizers and pesticides from the agricultural sector seeped into the reserve, whilst over-use of water resources caused sections to dry up.

Fearing the total disappearance of this unique wetlands ecosystem, the remaining area was declared a protected reserve in 1964 (the first in Israel), and a long-term management plan was drawn up. New pools connected by a network of drainage channels were constructed, and constant monitoring of water levels and quality was introduced. To help finance the programme the reserve was opened to tourists in 1978. To the relief of the scientists and conservationists, many, though not all, of the migratory birds have returned. The inherent dynamism of the ecosystem means that nature is not static, so it is foolish to suggest that the original form of the 'Sea of Hula' has been 'recreated' here. However, the Hula Nature Reserve has been a remarkable exercise in conservation (as opposed to 'preservation'): long may it continue.

Dubrovin farm
ⓘ *T04-6937371, Mon-Thu and Sat 1030-1600, Fri 1030-1400, adult 10NIS, child 7NIS.*
Shortly before reaching the Hula Nature Reserve you will see signs for Dubrovin Farm, a reconstruction of an early-20th-century agricultural estate. This particular farm was established in 1909 by the Christian Dubrovin family from Russia who converted to Judaism and moved to the Holy Land. The small museum in the farmhouse tells the family's story, reconstructs their rooms, and displays their agricultural equipment. Presentation is aided by a short video, whilst **The Restaurant** ⓘ *T04-6934495, Sun-Thu 1200-2200, Fri closes 1 hr before Shabbat*, receives excellent reviews for its country-style kosher food (fixed meaty menu). Entrance to the museum is deducted from the price of the main course. The pretty setting includes a waterwheel in the flowering gardens, and old stone buildings; it's in the middle of the orchards of the 127-year old moshava of Yesod Hama'ala.

Agamon Lake (Hula Lake)
ⓘ *T04-6817137, www.agamon-hula.co.il, Sun-Thu 0900-1 hr before sunset, Fri and Sat 0630-1 hr before sunset. Donation of 3NIS requested. Audio-guide and binocular rental 20NIS. Shop, café, toilets.*
If you want more of a guarantee of seeing birdlife, then Agamon Lake will be of interest. Dug by the Jewish National Fund in the 1990s, the lake is 40-80 cm deep and attracts about 500 million birds passing through twice a year (peak season Oct-Mar). The most famous visitors are the cranes, pelicans, ibis and white storks, while permanent terrestrial guests are water buffalo. Unlike the Hula Nature Reserve (see above) the birds are apparently encouraged to stay here by regular feeding and the creation of a mud wall to aid the mating process (which can be observed in spring).

At the visitiors' centre you can see a short film (in English) before following the 10-km route around the park. This is possible on foot, by bike (bring your own or rental is 52NIS), golf cart (145NIS for two persons) or by 'hidden' wagon which gets closer to the wildlife (adult/child 52/47NIS). If you choose to walk, it is a pleasant easy-going route, with regular look-out points with telescopes. In the summer months they run night safaris (2½ hrs, 77NIS; must reserve in advance especially if an English speaker).

NB Bring plenty of drinking water, as it is not available once inside the park. Mosquitos are rife at sunset and in the early morning: bring repellent.

Hula Nature Reserve to Kiryat Shemona: alternative route
Route 90 continues due north along the Hula Valley to Kiryat Shemona (14 km). However, those with their own transport may like to make a short diversion along a road that runs parallel to Route 90, just to the west. At Koah Junction, 6 km north of the turning to Hula Nature Reserve, turn left on to Route 899. The road climbs steeply for 4.2 km to Yesha' Junction where you turn sharp right into the car park of the military base. This is the **Nebi Yusha Fortress** (Hebrew: *Metzudat Koach*), located on the strategic heights of the Hills of Naftali. During the 1948 war in the prelude to the operation to capture Safed, attacks on the Arab held Nebi Yusha Fortress by both the Palmach and Haganah were repulsed with heavy loss of life. The fortress was finally captured by the 'Yiftach' Palmach Brigade under Colonel 'Mula' Cohen on the night of 16 May, and was subsequently used in the defence of the Galilee

'finger'. A path leads round behind the current IDF base to a war memorial and, though there is not a great deal to see here, the viewpoint down to the Hula Valley is superb.

Continuing west along Route 899, after 700 m take the road to your right, heading due north (Route 886). You are now running parallel to the Lebanese border to the west and to Route 90 to the east. At Margaliot (14 km) you come to the former site of the Crusader fortress of **Chateauneuf**, built in 1107 by Hugh of St Omer. The fortress has subsequently been destroyed and rebuilt a number of times, and most of what you see today dates from the Mamluk period.

Having passed Margaliot, take the winding road down to the right (sign-posted 'Kiryat Shemona', 'Metulla', 'Tel Hai'). As it continues down to the junction with Route 90 (just to the north of Kiryat Shemona) it passes several places of interest, including Kibbutz Kfar Gil'adi, with its Beit Hashomer Museum, and then the settlement of Tel Hai.

Kibbutz Kfar Gil'adi **The Beit Hashomer Museum** ① T04-6941565, Sun-Thu 0800-1600, Fri groups by prior arrangement, adults 15NIS, student/child 10NIS, was established at Kfar Gil'adi to tell the story of the 'Hashomer', an organization of 'watchmen' or 'guardians' whose purpose was the defence of the early Jewish pioneers who were settling in remote places all across Palestine. Its members comprised refugees from pogroms in Russia and Eastern Europe who formed the Second Aliyah (mass immigration) of Jews into Palestine at the turn of the 20th century. The Hashomer evolved from the clandestine Bar-Giora organization founded in Jaffa in 1907, though its roots were in the self-defence associations founded in Eastern Europe. Many members of the Hashomer were instrumental in founding the Haganah, the forerunner of the IDF. The museum at Kibbutz Kfar Gil'adi has an interesting collection of exhibits, though not all are labelled in English. Make sure that you pick up the free explanatory brochure.

Tel Hai → Colour map 1, grid A5.

Following the withdrawal of the British from the region towards the end of World War I, the military outpost of Tel Hai, sitting on the low promontory just above the Hula Valley, along with the settlements at Kfar Gil'adi and Metulla, seemingly lapsed into the sphere of control of French-administered Syria and Lebanon. In 1920 a group of Arab farmers gathered here to protest that the Jewish settlers were aiding and abetting the French in expropriating their land. There are several versions of what happened next. One version tells how the leader of Tel Hai, **Yosef Trumpeldor**, allowed a delegation of Arabs inside the compound at Tel Hai to search for French agents, only for them to turn on the settlers, killing eight. A second version suggests that the Arabs simply over-ran Tel Hai, killing six men and two women, Trumpeldor included. Whatever the truth of events, Trumpeldor's alleged last words, "It is good to die for your country", became a rallying cry of the early Zionists. The eight victims (whose sacrifice is commemorated at the nearby town of Kiryat Shemona, or 'Town of Eight' in Hebrew) are buried in the military cemetery just up the road from the hostel. A statue of the 'Lion of Judah', a nickname for Trumpeldor, inscribed with his last words, looks down into the Hula Valley. The settler's original tower and stockade has been turned into a small **museum** ① T04-6951333, signed 'Tel Hai Yard' off Route 90, telling the story of Tel Hai and Yosef Trumpeldor, which offers guided tours in Hebrew.

A further attraction in the Tel Hai Industrial Park, opposite Tel Hai on the east side of Route 90, is the **Museum of Photography** ① T04-6816700, Sat-Thu 0800-1600, Fri 1000-1700, adult 18NIS, child 14NIS, featuring temporary exhibitions of Israeli photographers' work and occasionally international artists.

Tel Hai listings

For Sleeping and Eating price codes and other relevant information, see Essentials pages 26-31.

Sleeping

A-C IYHA Tel Hai Youth Hostel, T02-5945666, www.iyha.co.il. Typically spotless 4-6-bed dorms (bunks, 130NIS) which can also be taken as private rooms, with a/c, TV, cheerful curtains and sheets, plenty of space, tea/coffee facilities, fridge. Also more salubrious hotel-style rooms (60-80NIS extra) with balcony or terrace. Lovely quiet setting with views to the Golan; no fires allowed; breakfast included; dinner available only when enough people; prices go up high season and weekends. Offers discounts at the Canada Centre (see Metulla, page 661). Reservations recommended in summer. It's signed to the right from Route 90, 3 km north of Kiryat Shemona. Buses 20, 21 and 24 stop nearby; 300-m walk.

Kiryat Shemona

Though Kiryat Shemona (spelt with any combination of the words Kiryat, Qiryat, Shemona, Shmona) is a relatively obscure town, with no real attractions, accommodation or places of interest, many people who have never even visited Israel appear to have heard of it. Kiryat Shemona's fame, or infamy, is a direct by-product of its position close to the border with Lebanon. No doubt this small town of around 22,000 people would prefer to be referred to as the gateway to Upper Galilee and the Golan, with its administrative and transport functions, though most visitors only know it by its troubled past.

Ins and outs

Getting there and away Buses run to Kiryat Shemona from all the major cities, though they're often packed to bursting point with young soldiers. It is the main transport hub for northern destinations, standing at a crossroads which leads east to the Golan or north to Metulla.

Background

From the 1970s the town has been a victim of persistent attacks. In 1974, Palestinian terrorists infiltrating from Lebanon murdered 18 Israeli civilians here. Attacks in subsequent years generally came in the form of katyusha rockets fired from southern Lebanon (so much so that the town became nicknamed Kiryat Katyusha!). The prolonged attacks of 1981, when Kiryat Shemona was bombed for 12 days solid, caused 80 % of the population to flee. Such rocket attacks were Israel's justification for launching its bloody invasion of southern Lebanon in 1982 ('Operation Peace for Galilee'), though – as many commentators point out – early 1982 was one of the quietest years for cross-border rocket attacks. Continued Hizbollah rocket attacks nearby led to the Israeli 'Operation Grapes of Wrath' offensive that culminated in the massacre at the UN camp at Qana in early 1996. After the 2000 withdrawal of Israeli troops from south Lebanon, Kiryat Shemona got a few years of peace and quiet, though the 2006 Second Lebanon War saw the resumption of daily rocket launches. Fortunately, since then the border has been quiet and in theory Kiryat Shemona should remain safe.

Manara Cliff

① *T04-6905830, www.cliff.co.il, summer 0900-1730, winter 1030-1600 (call to check times).*
Just off Route 90, 1 km south of Kiryat Shemona, this leisure complex offers rides on Israel's

Yosef Trumpeldor (1880-1920)

Yosef Trumpeldor was an extraordinary character. Born in Russia in 1880, he lost an arm serving in the Czar's army during the Russo-Japanese war and was subsequently decorated for gallantry by the Russian empress.

A committed Zionist, Trumpeldor believed that young Jewish pioneers should receive training in the diaspora in preparation for a life of manual work in Palestine. His experiences upon his arrival in Palestine in 1912 convinced him even more that advance preparation was essential, and the conversations that he had with Jabotinsky during World War I led to the formation of such an organization, *Hehalutz*, in Russia towards the end of the war.

Despite his handicap, Trumpeldor served the Allies with distinction during World War I, helping in the creation of several specifically Jewish units including the Zion Mule Corps and three battalions of the Royal Fusiliers. Amongst the places where he saw action was the disastrous Allied landings at Gallipoli. Following the war he helped to establish the settlement at Tel Hai, as well as being instrumental in the formation of his pre-war pet project, the *Gdud Ha'avoda* or 'Legion of Labour'. Trumpeldor was killed before the 'Legion of Labour' officially came into being, but, though it only survived for six years, it was at the vanguard of the pioneer movement. Thus, Trumpeldor fully deserves his place in the annals of Labour Zionism.

---

longest cable car up to Kibbutz Manara at the top of the Naftali range. The ride is 10 minutes each way (60NIS) and affords excellent views. Ask if the 'tractor carriage' tour at the top is available in English yet (further 30/10NIS adult/child, 40 minutes). Other activities include the mountain slide (a kind of toboggan on a track) that reaches speeds of 40 km per hour, and a trampoline-dome (both 26NIS), while at the mid-way station you can try rappelling (AKA abseiling), take a 200-m long zip-wire (60NIS) or do climbing on an artificial wall (experienced climbers only, 30NIS). Packages combining various activities offer better value. There is also a kosher restaurant at the top of the cliff. Buses stop on Route 90 just outside the complex.

Kiryat Shemona listings

For Sleeping and Eating price codes and other relevant information, see Essentials pages 26-31.

Transport
Bus
The Central Bus Station is on the main road, Tel Hai Blvd. Because bus travel in Upper Galilee and Golan is limited, check departure and return times carefully. **Hazor**: take a Tel Aviv, Tiberias, Rosh Pina or Safed bus; buses 026, 027 and 036 run infrequently, 8NIS. **Katzrin**: buses 55 and 58 run twice a day in a long loop via Upper Golan, via Horshat Tal, Tel Dan, Banias, Neve Ativ and Majdal Shams. **Metulla**:

bus 20 and 21, at least 5 per day. **Rosh Pina**: take a Tiberias or Tel Aviv bus. **Safed**: bus 501 and 511, every hr. **Tel Aviv**: buses 840, 841, 842 and 845, hourly, 3½ hrs. **Tel Dan**: buses 026 and 035, limited service, 8NIS. **Tel Hai**: buses 20 and 21, 5 per day. **Tiberias**: Buses 840, 841 and 963 via Rosh Pina.

Directory
Most of Kiryat Shemona's other 'necessities', such as post office, restaurants, supermarkets and banks are located just south of the Central Bus Station. The large mall just north of the city centre has a **Steimatzky** bookshop, **Aroma** coffeeshop, **Superpharm** and **Supersol** supermarket.

Nahal Iyyoun (Ayoun) Nature Reserve

ⓘ *T04-6951519, daily 0900-1600 (last entrance 1 hr before closing), adult 25NIS, student 21NIS, child 17NIS.*

The Nahal Iyyoun Nature Reserve provides the opportunity for a very pleasant 2-2½-hour walk along the course of the Iyyoun Valley. Though there is lush green vegetation all year round, the reserve comes into its own out of the summer season when the full streams produce a number of spectacular waterfalls. The area is teeming with bird life, and you may be lucky enough to spot kingfishers, wallcreepers, long-tailed wagtails, rock doves and kestrels (winter and spring are best for bird-watching).

Ins and outs

Getting there and away There are two entrances to the reserve: one just off Route 90 some 4 km north of Kiryat Shemona, and one just north of Metulla (see page 661). The once-hourly (8 per day) bus 020 from Kiryat Shemona to Metulla can drop you at the southern trailhead, or in Metulla town itself from where the northern trailhead is a short sign-posted walk. Alternatively, you can walk to the southern trailhead from Kiryat Shemona. The brief route description here follows a south to north course going uphill, thus taking longer than north to south.

South to north hike

A 10-minute walk from the southern entrance to the reserve brings you to the 30-m-high **Tanur Falls**. This is the reserve's best-known landmark, the name being a corruption of 'Tabor', the chimney-like oven that Arab peasants used to use and which the falls are said to resemble. A different school of thought suggests that the falls resemble the long skirt, 'Tanura', that Arab women wear. The falls are a spectacular sight when gushing, but rather an anti-climax in summer when bone dry.

Crossing to the west bank of the river you can see how the canyon begins to narrow. There are several waterfalls along this section, with the two biggest examples, the **Cascade Falls** at 10 and 5 m respectively, being about one hour's walk away. Continuing north you come to an old flour mill at the base of the 21-m-high **Mill Falls**. The mill was purchased early in this century by Baron Edmond de Rothschild and continued serving the local Jewish settlers until it was abandoned following the fighting at Tel Hai in 1920 (see page 657).

The path continues north along the course of the Nahal Iyyoun, crossing several

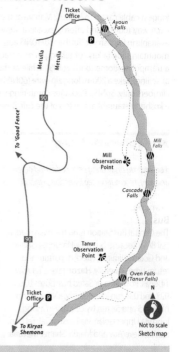

Nahal Ayoun Nature Reserve

Ticket Office

Ayoun Falls

P

Metulla

Metulla

To 'Good Fence'

90

To Kiryat Shemona

Mill Falls

Mill Observation Point

Cascade Falls

Tanur Observation Point

Ticket Office P

90

Oven Falls (Tanur Falls)

N

Not to scale
Sketch map

times depending upon the season until reaching **Iyyoun Falls**. The wall built by the British above the 9-m falls was used to create a reservoir that could supply the troops based here. There is a camping and picnic ground at the northern entrance to the reserve on the edge of Metulla (though this isn't much good if you have parked your car at the southern entrance).

Metulla → *Colour map 1, grid A4.*

Israel's most northerly town (though 'large village' may be a more apt description), Metulla was one of the string of settlements that Jewish pioneers established in Upper Galilee at the end of the last century. Like so many others, it owed its continued existence to financial support from Baron Edmond de Rothschild. Sometimes referred to as 'Israel's Little Switzerland', it is still best known for the defunct 'Good Fence' to the west of town.

Ins and outs

Getting there and away The town of Metulla itself is rather attractive (certainly when compared to Kiryat Shemona). Though little more than one main street (HaRishonim), it features some very pleasant hotels and pensions and is a relaxing place to unwind. Buses 20 and 21 run to and from Kiryat Shemona around five times per day.

The 'Good Fence' and Dado Viewpoint

This was the border crossing point between Lebanon and Israel until the 2000 withdrawal of Israeli troops from south Lebanon. It took its name (in Hebrew: *HaGader HaTova*) in the days when Lebanese villagers were allowed to pass through in order to seek free medical services in Israel, as well as visiting relatives and commuting to jobs in Metulla. There's not a great deal to see at the border these days, bar camouflage netting and a padlock; long gone are the falafel stands and entwined Lebanese and Israeli flags. Photography is a bad idea here.

On the way to the Good Fence, you will see signs for Dado viewpoint, which gives an excellent perspective on the topography of the Hula Valley and Golan Heights. It is worth the short detour.

Canada Centre

Those with excess energy to burn should head for the **Canada Centre** ① *T04-6098701, www.canada-center.co.il, admission (adult 87NIS, student/child 67NIS) includes skate-hire and free use of most facilities (daily 1000-2200)*, one of the best sports centres in the country. It features a skating rink, a pool with a large jacuzzi, sauna (30NIS), gym, bowling and shooting range (T04-6951514, daily 1000-1900).

Metulla listings

For Sleeping and Eating price codes and other relevant information, see Essentials pages 26-31.

Sleeping

Although there are only 4 or so 'proper' hotels in Metulla, there are numerous zimmers, with almost every house having a 'rooms for rent' sign outside. Most of the hotels and zimmers can provide meals, and there are half-a-dozen café/restaurants in the town centre.

LL Beth Shalom, 28 HaRishonim, T/F04-6940767. A boutique hotel in an old stone building, with unique, immaculate suites; an in-house spa; dairy vegetarian restaurant; and a warmly lit and very welcoming garden.

AL Alaska Inn, T04-6997111. A nice hotel with well-furnished rooms, attractive dining area and facilities including pool (summer only, which starts later in Metulla: around June). Good value, includes breakfast.

AL-A Arazim, T04-6997143. Attractive pension; rooms have TV and central heating, and there's a pool. Outside the centre of town, breakfast included.

Eating

¶¶¶-¶¶ Tachana, south end of HaRishonim, T04-6944810. Ask anyone in the north what the best restaurant is and Tachana will always feature top of their list. The cow decorations everywhere provide the clue: lots of steak (140NIS), burgers (66-99NIS), grills, plus casseroles (78NIS), lamb, pullet. It's all quite pricey, but go on a weekday for the business lunch and it's good value for money. On Shabbat, book a table for late evening to avoid crying children. Cosy cluttered decor is very appealing, plus a few nice outdoor tables, excellent waiters. Daily 1200-2300.

Sam's Neighbourhood Shop, north end of HaRishonim, sells groceries and booze and is open on Shabbat. They also have Wi-Fi, and the owner (Samuel) is a mine of information on the area. Daily 0700-2200.

Horshat Tal National Park → *Colur map 1, A5.*

ⓘ *T04-6942360, www.parks.org.il, daily 0800-1700 (winter -1600) closes 1 hour earlier on Fri, adult 36NIS, student 32NIS, child 22NIS. Toilets, grocery/snack shop. The park is located 6 km east of Kiryat Shemona on Route 99 (buses 35, 36, 55 and 58).*

This large National Park is one of Upper Galilee's most popular recreational spots, dreadfully busy on weekends and holidays with noisy groups, it's only advisable to visit during the week. The Dan River has been diverted to create an (ice-cold) swimming pool, whilst the landscaped picnic lawn is shaded by a forest of ancient Tabor oaks. Legend has it that 10 companions of the prophet Mohammed (PBUH) rested here, and finding neither shade nor posts to tether their horses they drove their staffs into the ground. When they awoke the following morning their staffs had sprouted into a forest of magnificent oaks. Camping is permitted (adult/child 60/50NIS) or there are three concrete bungalows with air conditioning that sleep four (extortionate, week/Friday 450/650NIS) or endless huts (expensive, 300/400NIS) with shared bath, sheets, and no air conditioning so must be killer-hot in summer.

Horshat Tal listings

For Sleeping and Eating price codes and other relevant information, see Essentials pages 26-31.

Sleeping

Kibbutz Hagoshrim Resort, Kibbutz Hagoshrim (next to Horshat Tal National Park), T04-6816000, www.hagoshrim-hotel-co.il. Nicely located large resort with modern rooms, 2 pools, and Country Club with fitness classes, gym, other sporting activities and a spa. The kibbutz's kosher Gosh Restaurant is particularly recommended for its vegetarian meals, fish, soups and salads, as well as its location for an end-of-day beer (or 10).

Eating

¶¶¶-¶¶ Focaccia, Gannat Zafon shopping area, T04-6904474/052-5556061. Another of the north's restaurant 'musts', Focaccia has become quite an empire, renowned for Mediterranean/Italian dishes that are cooked to perfection. Main courses are mostly meaty, plus pizza and delicious pasta; business lunch available weekdays till 1800 (60NIS). Decor is unfussy, dark wood and maroons, no English sign (look for purple and white painted exterior). Their adjacent diner has a more casual atmosphere and menu (think American, burgers, etc) and is more for a quick bite; there's a frozen yogurt joint as well. Sat-Thu 1200-2300, Fri 0900-2300. Diner is open till 0200 on Fri nights. The turning is marked with a brown sign for HaZafon Gardens about 4 km along Route 99 from Kiryat Shemona (you will see the McDonalds arches).

♥♥♥-♥♥ Nahalim. Gannat Zafon shopping area, T04-6904875. In the same shopping area is charming Nahalim restaurant, where the riverside garden is as much a pull as the fantastic French-inspired menu. Trout, shrimps, veal, liver, plus some vegetarian options; mains are 79-129NIS, or set menus from 69NIS. Interior is fresh and white, and the terrace in the garden lovely. Specialist range of wines from the region. Daily 1200-2300.

At the junction there is also a memorial to the 70-plus killed in 1997 in Israel's worst ever military aviation accident, when two helicopters ferrying troops to Israel's self-declared security zone in southern Lebanon collided and crashed in poor weather.

♥♥-♥ Cookia, Kibbutz Dafna, T04-6945800. Famously high-quality cakes and sweets (eg pear tart, chocolate volcano, mousses and tiramisu); also excellent light meals in this cute and simple café. Breakfast till 1300 (shakshuka, stack of 5 pancakes, 28NIS), salads and sandwiches in mouth-watering combinations, meals such as quiche or lasagne. Top-notch coffee, boutique beers and Galilee wine, Wi-Fi, indoor and outdoor seating. Daily 0900-2330. Dafna is 3.5 km east of Horshat along Route 99; turn immediately right on entering the kibbutz.

Tel Dan → Colour map 1, grid A5.

ⓘ *T04-6951579, www.parks.org.il, daily 0800-1700 (winter 1600), Fri closes 1 hr earlier, adult 25NIS, student 21NIS, chld 13NIS, self-service restaurant, toilets.*

Tel Dan Nature Reserve compares favourably for beauty with any of Israel's nature reserves. The perennial Dan River, the major source of the Jordan River, flows through the reserve supporting a dense mix of vegetation that is unrivalled in the rest of the country. On a hot day it is pleasantly cool under the trees, and the small size makes it easy to take in the floral and faunal highlights as well as exploring the evidence of mankind's sojourn here. Dan is most commonly known through the numerous biblical references used to express the boundaries of the ancient Land of Israel: "from Dan to Be'er Sheva" (*I Samuel 3:20; II Samuel 3:10, 17:11, 24:15; I Chronicles 21:2*). The ancient site, built upon the Canaanite city of Laish (Leshem), is now a minor attraction within an area most appreciated for its natural charms.

Ins and outs

Getting there and away Along Route 99 is Kibbutz Dan, and immediately after there is a difficult turning left (across the traffic and on a slight bend) towards the Tel Dan Nature Reserve. The site is 1.5 km down this road, passing Beit Ussishkin (see page 666) on the way. Buses 35, 36, 55 and 58 from Kiryat Shemona run to Kibbutz Dan, from where it's a 1.5-km walk.

Getting around There are marked walking routes around the reserve, the shortest (45 minutes) of which is partly accessible by wheelchair. Other trails go to the Dan Springs or Ancient Dan, but if time allows, the 'combined trail' is the best option (2 ½ hrs). Armed with the map a detailed route description is not necessary, though some details of the natural and man-made sites are included below. You are reminded that it is illegal to pick any plants or flowers or disturb the wildlife. You must stick to the paths, and note that paddling is allowed at the wading pool (marked) only. The flour mill has been restored to working order, but operation must be supervised by staff.

Background

It is not difficult to see why this site was selected for human habitation. Two groupings of springs, **Ein Dan** and **Ein Leshem**, feed the Dan River, themselves drawing water from a deep aquifer that collects snow-melt from Mt Hermon. The water is extremely potable with a remarkably low mineral content. This water source was able to support the large Canaanite city of Laish (or Leshem) that is mentioned in the Egyptian Execration texts of the 18th century BCE, and in the lists of cities captured by the pharaoh Thutmose III in the 15th century BCE. Its defining moment came following the conquest and subsequent division of the Land of Israel by Joshua. Unable to hold the coastal plain against the Philistines, the tribe of the children of Dan headed north: "[they] went up to fight against Lesham, and took it, and smote it with the edge of the sword, and possessed it, and dwelt therein, and called Lesham, Dan, after the name of Dan their father" (Joshua 19:47).

During the period of the United Monarchy (c. 1020-928 BCE) Dan marked the northern boundary of the kingdom;, however, the death of Solomon saw the splitting of the kingdom between Judah in the south and Israel in the north. In a direct challenge to the first King of Judah Rehoboam (928-911 BCE), who was custodian of the Temple at Jerusalem, the first King of Israel **Jeroboam I** (928-907 BCE) built his own "house of high places" in Dan, even setting a golden calf there and offering sacrifices to it (I Kings 12:28-33). One of the cultic high places built by Jeroboam I can still be seen (note that it is the one closest to the southern gate; the other cultic high place was built later by Ahab).

During the reign of Jehu (842-814 BCE) we have a description of the golden calf still standing at Dan (II Kings 10:29), and the city also appears to have been the administrative

Tel Dan Nature Reserve

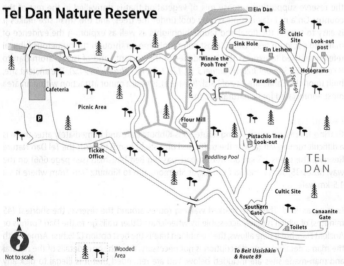

and military centre of Jeroboam II's northern kingdom (784-748 BCE). The city's subsequent history is not entirely clear. The inference is that Dan was captured by the Assyrian king Tiglath-pileser III in 732 BCE, though it may not have been destroyed (*II Kings 15:29*) since there are later references to Dan during the rule of Hezekiah (King of Judah 727-698 BCE, see *II Chronicles 30:5*) and Josiah (King of Judah 639-609 BCE, see *Jeremiah 4:15, 8:16*). Archaeological evidence suggests that the mound was occupied in the Hellenistic period (332-37 BCE) and also in the Roman period, before finally being abandoned in the fourth century CE.

Flora and fauna

If it is rainy, do not despair. This greatly enhances your chances of seeing the bright yellow and black spotted salamander (*Salamandra salamandra*), who comes to the pools to spawn in winter. There is also a wide variety of birdlife and butterflies, including jays and warblers. However, you are far more likely to see stuffed examples of these creatures at Beit Ussishkin (see next page) than live ones here. Notable tree species include the Syrian Ash, at the southernmost margins of its distribution, tall Laurels, magnificent Tabor Oaks, plus several Atlantic Pistachios, one 2000-year-old example of which has been sadly killed by fire.

Sights

Southern (Israelite) gate The fortifications along the southern side of the tel are generally attributed to Jeroboam I (10th century BCE), who may have been keen to protect his golden calf. The following century saw the construction of the gate complex, which comprises two towers with two guard rooms on either side. The large paved square outside resembles the description of the one in which Hezekiah assembled his "captains of war" at Jerusalem (*II Chronicles 32: 6*).

Canaanite gate This gate is extremely well preserved, perhaps to its full height of 47 courses. It is built of sun-baked bricks and comprises three arches (the outer one of which is the only one that you can see beneath the modern protective roof). Ceramic finds have dated its construction to the Middle Bronze Age IIA-IIB (c. 2000-1550 BCE), though the fact that it was only used for 50 years or so and then filled in with earth has ensured its excellent state of preservation. Parts of the great earthen rampart, preserved up to a height of 10 m, though originally higher, can also be seen in this area. At its base the rampart is up to 50 m wide, with a 6-m-thick stone core running through its centre.

Cultic site There are two cultic high places thus far excavated at Tel Dan. The one closest to the southern gate appears to have been constructed by Jeroboam I, perhaps the one referred to in *I Kings 12:31*. The charred stones are possibly the result of its destruction at the hands of Ben-Hadd (see opposite). The site appears to have been recycled as a high place in later years, with some of the construction here being Hellenistic. The second cultic site, to the north of the mound closer to Ein Leshem, appears to be an Iron-Age cult precinct from the ninth century BCE, possibly built by Ahab.

Look-out post When Britain and France divided up the Levant between them at the end of World War I, Dan was right on the border between the two spheres of influence. In fact in 1964 the Syrians, as successors to the French, used the thickness of the pencil-drawn line on the map that accompanied the 1923 treaty as a justification for drawing water from the Dan. Continued disputes over the boundaries of the respective states escalated into a major battle in November 1964, which Israel won.

Beit Ussishkin ① *T04-6941704, Sun-Thu 0800-1600, Fri/Sat phone ahead to arrange a visit, adult 20NIS, student/child 15NIS. Same buses as Tel Dan, though it's only 500 m from main road.* This attractive building 1 km south of Tel Dan houses a museum that presents in great detail the biogeography and geomorphology of the area. There is a film about the area, displays of stuffed creatures (all well labelled), and finds from the ruins of Tel Dan.

Contents

Footprint features

The Golan

The Golan Heights, or Ramat HaGolan in Hebrew, is a high basalt plateau extending from Mt Hermon in the north to the Yarmuk River in the south, bounded on the west by the Hula Valley and Sea of Galilee and on the east by the Raqqad River. Captured from the Syrians by Israel in 1967, the status of the Golan dominates bilateral relations between the two states. Though the fate of the Golan is uncertain, it is clear that it will not be returned to Syria in the immediate future.

In the meantime, a growing number of visitors, Israelis and foreigners alike, are ignoring the transport shortfalls and exploring the Golan's many attractions and interesting accommodation options. The region has a rugged, almost desolate beauty, coupled with a number of exceptional historical sites. Also of interest are the Druze villages of the Upper Golan, clustering around the slopes of Mt Hermon, Israel's highest peak at 2,814 m, which indeed feel like another country.

Highlights of the Golan include the rich waterscape at Banias, the superbly preserved medieval Nimrod Fortress, some challenging hiking opportunities in the Ya'ar Yehudiya Nature Reserve, and the combination of stunning views and enthralling history at Gamla. And if you really want to immerse yourself in nature and get to know these hills and valleys, the trans-Golan trek takes you through the heart – from Mt Hermon to the Sea of Galilee. This is a region not to be missed.

Ins and outs

Getting there and away There are three main points of access into the Golan Heights: (a) travelling east on Route 99 from Kiryat Shemona in Upper Galilee into Upper Golan; (b) travelling east on Route 91 across the B'not Ya'akov Bridge, roughly to the northeast of Safed; (c) travelling northeast on Route 87 from the northeast corner of the Sea of Galilee.

Accommodation options in the Golan Heights have been more limited than elsewhere in the country (especially in the budget price range), though this is happily now changing. A further constraint on tourism is that transport connections to the Golan's relatively isolated sites is poor – this is a region where hitch-hiking is commonly accepted as a means of travelling around. Renting a car and sharing the expense between a group of people is undoubtedly the best way to get the most out of the Golan.

Warning Syrian and Israeli land mines still litter the Golan Heights, and whilst the slightest prospect remains that any part of the Golan is to be handed back to Syria there is understandably little incentive on the part of the Israelis to clear them. Suspect areas are fenced off, with a yellow and red sign warning of the danger in English, Hebrew and Arabic. However, the best advice is not to cross any fences whether signposted or not.

Climate The Golan experiences a Mediterranean climate that is considerably moderated by altitude. The Mt Hermon range heavily influences levels of precipitation in the north, where the peak levels of 1,200 mm per annum are double the levels recorded in the southern Golan, less than 50 km away. Heavy snowfall is often recorded in Upper Golan. Likewise, temperatures are influenced by the changes in altitude, averaging around 9°C in the north but almost 20°C in the south. **NB** Visitors to the Golan should be aware of the climatic differences between the Golan and, say, Tiberias (particularly in autumn and winter). It may be sunny with clear skies when you leave Tiberias in the morning, but a one-hour drive up to the Golan can leave you amongst low cloud with rain, and a very noticeable drop in temperature. Take appropriate clothing.

Background

Geography Though the Golan is part of a larger area of volcanic basalt fields that stretch north and east, the 1,200 sq km of the Golan Heights plateau that Israel controls has distinct geographical boundaries. In the north the limestone bedrock of Mt Hermon is separated from the basalt of the Golan by the Nahal Sa'ar. At its western margins, the plateau slopes down steeply to meet the Sea of Galilee. The southern margins, known in the Bible as the land of Geshur, are bounded by the Yarmuk River and the biblical lands of Gilead, the latter now part of Jordan. The eastern boundary is formed by the Raqqad River, still controlled by Syria.

The basalt that covers most of the Golan was created in a series of volcanic eruptions that began almost four million years ago; a relatively recent process that is still continuing. Notable features in the eastern Golan, particularly prominent from the 'Quneitra Viewpoint' (see page 678), are the small volcanic cones and 'tuffs', or volcanic particles, created by violent eruptions. Those in the south have been largely eroded into a series of low hills.

Vegetation In antiquity, the Golan was covered by thick Mediterranean vegetation, with considerable forested areas. Today, just 3% of the Golan is forested, concentrated in a number of reserves such as Odem and Yehudiya. Most of the vegetation cover is now scattered grasslands, with extensive cultivation of the more fertile plain to the south.

Across the Golan

The Cross Golan trek (in Hebrew, 'Chotze Golan') is an unforgettable experience for those who like their walking a bit hardcore and their scenery a bit wild. Starting from Mt Hermon (in the very north) and finishing 120 km later at Ein Taufik (south of the Sea of Galilee) this hike takes in the magnificent vistas of the eastern Golan plateau, passing Druze villages, pre-historic settlements and the ruins of ancient synagogues. White-blue-green trail markers lead the way.

The minimum time required for the whole trek is seven days – and those are full days of walking. However, to choose a short section and make night stops in villages is entirely possible. Many people carry a tent, food supplies, camping equipment and 'rough it', while others arrange for someone to transport their luggage from base to base. There are villages on the way where you can stock up on supplies.

The best time to do the trek is spring, when the land is green and flowering and there is water in the creeks. In summer it is simply too hot, while Golan winters can be freezing cold and wet.

For full advice on the route and the finer details, contact a Golan SPNI field school (listed in text). It is also essential to arm yourself with the SPNI 1:50,000 map number 1 for the Golan Heights, which is in Hebrew (staff can translate the route). They can also advise on transport to the start of the trek and about the volunteer 'path angels' who provide support along the way.

Remember, there are still uncleared land-mines in the Golan, and areas that are fenced off and adorned with yellow signs bearing a red triangle and the word "Danger" are to be respected. Stick to the path and don't cross any fences. Another potential hazard are the plentiful cows.

Those who are feeling particularly adventurous can always consider doing the route by bike or horse.

The political future of the Golan Heights Standing on the edge of the Golan plateau looking west into the Hula Valley and Upper Galilee, or down upon the Sea of Galilee, it is easy to see the strategic advantage of occupying the high ground, and why Israel is so reluctant to enter into any negotiations on the Golan's future. Throughout the 1960s the Syrian army took advantage of this elevated position randomly to shell Israeli settlements in Upper Galilee and the Sea of Galilee region, but since the Israelis captured the Golan in 1967, as Israeli prime minister Benjamin Netanyahu puts it, "Israel has looked down at the Syrians, rather than the other way around" (A Place Among the Nations, 1993). In fact, whilst many Israelis are willing to concede parts of the West Bank to the Palestinians, you meet few who advocate a return of the Golan Heights to Syria.

However, the Syrian government have a similar argument. During the Yom Kippur War of 1973 armoured Syrian divisions initially broke through Israeli defences on the Golan, almost reaching the bridges across the Jordan into Upper Galilee. In a campaign graphically described in Chaim Herzog's The Arab-Israeli Wars (1982), the Israeli counter-attack reached within 40 km of the Syrian capital at Damascus before the Israeli Military High Command felt that they had made their point and withdrew. Thus, the Golan is also seen by the Syrians as crucial to the defence of their capital.

It is clear that the issue of the Golan must be resolved if there is to be any normalization of relations between Israel and Syria. However, it seems unlikely that any progress will be made on the issue in the near future, as Netanyahu is far less likely to surrender the

Golan than his predecessors. Israel's stated minimum requirement, forward monitoring and listening bases, is totally rejected by Syria, whilst Damascus' call for a unilateral Israeli withdrawal as a pre-condition for any future peace deal is unthinkable for Israel. Thus, the Golan Heights remain in Israeli hands, annexed by Begin's Likud government in December 1981 in a move not recognized by the international community.

Upper Golan

This most northerly corner of Israel has looming mountains and a rugged wildness quite unlike the landscape of the rest of the country. The road ends at southern slopes of Mt Hermon, where seasonal snows are a glorious sight attracting skiers during the winter months. Other places that make the journey worthwhile are the magnificent ruins of Nimrod Fortress, perched on a hilltop like a fairytale castle, and the Banias Nature Reserve where the remains of ancient acropolises sit alongside gushing waterfalls and streams. Also of interest are the Druze villages surrounded by cherry and apple orchards and dotted by the shrines of saints, which offer excellent food to travellers to the upper Golan.

Banias (Nahal Hermon Nature Reserve) → *Colour map 1, grid A5.*

ⓘ *T04-6902577, www.parks.org.il. Daily 0800-1700 (winter -1600), Fri closes 1 hr earlier; last entry 1 hr before closing. Adult 25NIS, student 21NIS, child 13NIS, one ticket valid for both entrances, combined ticket with Nimrod 32NIS/21NIS/18NIS. Toilets, café, souvenir shop available at both entrances.*

At the southwest foot of Mt Hermon is an area of natural beauty that is also of considerable historical and archaeological interest. The site of one of the sources of the Jordan River, and the point where several streams collecting melted snow from Mt Hermon converge, the reserve is an area of running water, cascading waterfalls and a dense mix of vegetation types. Several marked walking trails wind their way through the natural wonders of the reserve, passing en route an ancient cultic cave site dedicated to the worship of the god Pan, remains of a city established in the first century BCE, plus medieval fortifications dating to the period of the Crusades. Banias also receives a significant number of Christian visitors, since tradition holds that it is here that Jesus referred to Peter as the "rock" upon which he would build his church. It is very busy at the springs and attractions close to the main car park, but you won't meet so many people walking along the trails.

Ins and outs

Getting there and away Transport to Banias is not that regular. Buses 55 and 58 run there from Kiryat Shmona, but the last bus back leaves at noon. If you walk the 5 km back to Kibbutz Dan, you can get a later bus (35 or 036, last at 1930). There are two entrances to the reserve: the first is 3 km to the northeast of Tel Dan along Route 99 and is signposted as "Banias Waterfalls"; the second (busier) entrance is 2 km further east along Route 99 and is signposted "Banias".

Getting around A walking trail links the two entrances to the reserve (about one hour in each direction), with a variety of diversions available en route. Other circular walks, starting at the eastern car park, take less than 45 minutes. The map provided marks the trails clearly. Perhaps the best route if you have the time, is a combination of trails beginning at the westerly entrance. Go first to Banias Falls, via the recently constructed 'suspended' trail

'Banias': Etymology of a name

The name Banias (sometimes spelt Banyas) is a corruption of the ancient Greek and Latin name Panias (or Paneas, Paneias), an obvious reference to the cult worship here of Pan. The change from a 'P' to a 'B' can be dated to the arrival of the Arabs and has stuck ever since (the French Crusaders using the 'B' in their version, Belinas). However, Banias has had a variety of names throughout its long history. The polis built here in 2 BCE by Herod the Great's son Philip was named Caesarea, in honour of the emperor Augustus, with 'of Philip' being added to distinguish it from the city of the same name on the Mediterranean coast. Although the Gospels refer to the city as Caesarea Philippi (Matthew 16:13-20; Mark 8:27-30), the name does not appear to have been in common usage. Neither did Agrippa II's attempt to rename the city after the emperor Nero (Neronias) have much lasting impact. Most 2nd- and 3rd-century sources refer to the city as Caesarea Panias, and subsequently as simply Panias then Banias.

(red and white markers). This involves an 80 m section along a wooden walkway above the Banias stream, following the curve of the rock walls above the crashing clear water. After viewing the attractive Banias Waterfalls (20 minutes' walk), continue up to the Officers' Pool (Breichat Haketzinim, 25 minutes). This is a large concrete pool built for the Syrian officers formerly stationed here, and fed by the warmer waters of Ein Khilo (spring). If time is short, and you have your own transport, return to the westerly entrance and drive up to the second entrance to see the cave and spring. Otherwise continue along the trail. Shortly after crossing the Nahal Nimrod (stream), the path divides. After taking the route to the right, you then have two choices. Either via the Crusader fortifications and past the Grave of Sheikh Sidi Ibrahim (not accessible from here) and on to the springs. Or more interestingly through the remains of Agrippa II's palace, part of which were turned into a bathhouse in Byzantine times, and on to the springs. After a rest, you can return via the Temple of Pan, the Roman bridge and the Druze flour mill to rejoin the trail back to the Banias Falls. In total this will take around 2½ hours. Note that there is an excellent, but tiring walking route from the main parking lot via Banias Observation Point up to Nimrod Fortress (over two hours).

Background

In 200 BCE, the defeat of the Ptolemy forces of Egypt here brought the whole of Palestine under the control of the **Seleucids** of Syria. A subsequent reference to the battle by Polybius mentions a grotto dedicated to *Paneion*, suggesting that a cult place dedicated to Pan as part of the Ptolemaic dynastic cult of Dionysus had been established here as early as the third century BCE. Pan worship was common throughout Ptolemic Egypt, and the Pan site may have been built here as a rival to the Semitic cult site at nearby Dan (see 'Tel Dan', page 663). The Ptolemies returned to this area, though the subsequent conquest of the entire region by Pompey saw the district of Panias divided into smaller and smaller units. In 20 BCE the land was granted to Herod the Great, who built a temple close to the Pan cave in honour of his patron Augustus.

Following the death of Herod in 4 BCE, Panias and its territory passed to his son **Philip**. A new polis was built to serve as the capital of Philip's tetrarchy, **Caesarea Philippi**, with Gospel sources claiming that Jesus and his disciples visited here (*Matthew 16:13-20; Mark 8:27-30*). After Philip's death in 34 CE the city eventually came under the control of Agrippa II, though his attempts to refound the city in 61 CE as Neronias do not appear to have caught on. The First Jewish Revolt (66-73 CE) saw the small Jewish community of Caesarea Philippi imprisoned and subsequently murdered. The city during this period must have been fairly extensive with impressive amenities, since **Titus** rested here for some time with his troops following the capture of Jerusalem in 70 CE. From Josephus' account it appears that Titus' R&R comprised "shows of every kind" in which "many of the prisoners perished … some thrown to wild beasts, others forced to meet each other in full-scale battles" (*Jewish War, VII, 23-24*).

Following Agrippa II's death in 93 CE, Caesarea Philippi came under Roman control. Its subsequent history is sketchy, with evidence from coins, inscriptions and the few written references suggesting a predominantly pagan population, but with Jewish and later Christian minorities. By the fourth century CE a small Christian community was well established here, as attested to by Eusebius. The name Caesarea Philippi appears to have disappeared completely by this stage, with most references being to Panias.

The Early Arab period (638-1099 CE) saw Banias as capital of a district within the province of Damascus, though the town appears to have been devastated by the earthquake of 1033 CE. By 1126 Banias was in the hands of an Isma'ili sect known as the **Assassins**. Though they heavily fortified Banias in anticipation of an attack from Damascus, the Assassins instead chose to offer the city to the Crusader king **Baldwin II** in exchange for asylum. The offer was accepted in 1129 and Banias and its domain was conferred upon Rainier of Brus. Despite considerable fortification, Shams el-Mulk captured it for Damascus in 1132, though the local ruler installed here by Damascus, Ibrahim ibn Turghut, subsequently rebelled and offered Banias to Zengi, ruler of Mosul. This action resulted in an extraordinary turn of events. Now given a common cause, the Christian and Muslim armies combined to retake Banias in 1140, the town then becoming a place for Frankish and Muslim nobles to meet for hunting and sport.

Seventeen years later Zengi's son **Nur ed-Din** laid siege to Banias, succeeding in breaking through the outer fortifications and forcing the Crusader garrison to retreat into the inner fortress. The precise location of this inner fortress is still unknown, though it is now clear that it was not the castle now known as Nimrod's Fortress (see page 674). Reinforcements sent by Baldwin II forced Nur ed-Din's army to withdraw temporarily and, though much of the defensive fortifications was rapidly rebuilt, Nur ed-Din succeeded in capturing Banias in 1164. The subsequent history of Banias saw the city captured, destroyed, and rebuilt a number of times, until it eventually drifted into insignificance. When the Israelis captured the Golan from Syria in 1967 Banias was just a poor village occupied by some 200 inhabitants.

Sanctuary of Pan

The centrepiece of the sanctuary dedicated to honouring Pan is a small niche quarried out of the rock face. This '**grotto of Pan**' was formerly plastered, housing a statue of Pan playing the flute to three goats that share a single head. The statue has never been found and this description has been determined by images found on third-century CE coins. Three other decorated niches have been cut into the rock face, with Greek inscriptions dating some of the work to 148-49 CE. A number of architectural fragments such as Attic bases and Corinthian columns were found in the area in front of the cave (and can still be seen today).

Close to the grotto is a large **cavern**, part of a phreatic cave (created below water level). Josephus describes how the source of the Jordan River flowed from the cave. Subsequent seismic action has now forced the water from the underground springs to emerge from a crack below the cave. The collapse of the cave's roof in the 1837 earthquake has prevented the excavation of the Hellenistic and Roman remains inside.

Medieval buildings

Both the Crusader and Muslim towns followed the plan of the ancient town. The **curtain wall** to the west and south can be seen in a number of places, as can the dry ditch that defended the east side. The best-preserved of the medieval buildings is probably the **Gate Tower** to the south, which is preserved to a height of around 25 m. Some Roman columns and blocks are incorporated in secondary use in the gate's construction, with research suggesting that the Frankish masonry may be of secondary use too. This, along with the fact that the overall fortification plan is somewhat irregular, has led some of the site's main excavators to suggest that the defences seen here are not Crusader at all, but instead belong to the Ayyubid or Fatimid Arabs.

Banias listings

For Sleeping and Eating price codes and other relevant information, see Essentials pages 26-31.

Sleeping and eating
A-D SPNI Hermon Field Study Centre,

T04-6941091, www.aspni.org. Located close to Kibbutz Snir, the Field School provides dorm and private room accommodation, though it is essential to book in advance. Anyone contemplating hiking in the Golan region should call here first.

Nimrod Fortress

ⓘ *T04-6949277, www.parks.org.il, daily 0800-1700 (winter -1600), last entrance at least 1 hr before, Fri closes 1 hr earlier. Adult 20NIS, student 17NIS, child 9NIS, combined ticket with Banias (see page 671). Toilets, snack-bar. NB you are strongly advised to keep to the marked path, and supervise children closely.*

Nimrod is the best-preserved castle in Israel, how you imagine a Crusader castle should look: magically perched along a narrow ridge and attracting the eye from every direction. But in fact Nimrod was not built by the Crusaders at all, and the historical and architectural evidence suggests that they never even occupied it. The Arabic name of Qalat Es-Subeiba would be

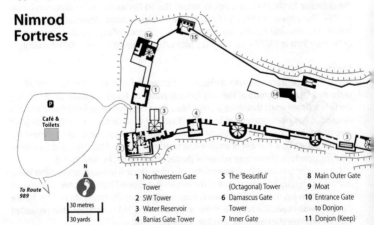

Nimrod Fortress

1 Northwestern Gate Tower	**5** The 'Beautiful' (Octagonal) Tower
2 SW Tower	**6** Damascus Gate Tower
3 Water Reservoir	**7** Inner Gate
4 Banias Gate Tower	**8** Main Outer Gate
	9 Moat
	10 Entrance Gate to Donjon
	11 Donjon (Keep)

To Route 989

N

30 metres
30 yards

more appropriate, as it was built by the Ayyubids in the 13th century CE to protect the road to Damascus from the Crusader threat. History aside, not only are the sweeping views from here the best in the whole of the north of the country, but the thrill of being in such a dramatic setting is enough to bring out the Errol Flyn in those who are old enough to know better.

Ins and outs

Getting there and away Unfortunately, Nimrod Fortress is not easy to get to without your own transport. Buses 55 and 58 runs from Kiryat Shemona to Neve Ativ at 1330, passing the road leading up to the fortress (30 minutes' walk). If it's wet, snowy or cloudy, this road is a real bugger. Note that the bus back from Neve Ativ leaves at noon; this is where hitching comes in.

Background

The controversy in identifying the builder of this monumental work and assigning a date lie in the fact that the Crusader fortress at Banias (see previous page) has yet to be located. Thus references to the "Banias Fortress" have mistakenly been applied to Nimrod Fortress. However, Nimrod features many characteristic Arab styles, whilst key features of the Crusader style of construction are entirely absent. The current school of thought suggests that the construction of the castle was initiated in 1227 by Ayyubid brothers **el-Moatis** and **el-Malik el-'Aziz 'Uthman**, with substantial building work being done between 1228 and 1230. A number of Arabic inscriptions, very well preserved, list building work completed by him and others. Further restoration work during the period 1239-1240 is confirmed by inscriptions found in situ. It appears that the Crusaders attempted to take the fortress in 1253 but were unsuccessful. An account of this campaign refers to the fortress as **Qal'at es-Subeiba**; almost certainly a name derived from the Arabic word for 'cliff' (*subeib*). The name Nimrod (*Nimrud*) evolved later from the Arab legend that the "mighty hunter" Nimrod (*Genesis 10:8-9*) used to sit on the mountain here, 815 m above sea level, and cup his hand to draw water from the Banias spring below.

A subordinate of the Mamluk sultan **Baibars** carried out rebuilding work at Nimrod between 1260 and 1277, leaving beautiful inscriptions attesting to the sultan's glory, but the final departure of the Crusaders from the Holy Land after the fall of Acre in 1291 reduced the strategic importance of the castle. It was subsequently used as a jail for political prisoners before being finally abandoned.

Sights

At the site, several boards are very informative and there are isometric drawings of how the castle would have looked in its prime. A walking route marked on the map ensures you take in all the main sights. The water reservoirs are worth locating, and from the base of the southwestern tower a (dark) spiral staircase leads down to embrasures (through which archers could fire their arrows). Also note

12 Barbican Tower
13 Reception Hall
14 'Guest House'
15 Northern Tower
16 Secret Passage

the lion carving displayed outside the southwestern gate, which was unearthed by a tractor clearing a new pathway to the fortress and hence has a chunk of his tail missing. These lions usually come in pairs, but as yet no one has been able to discover the whereabouts of his partner. Either leave the fortress by descending a steep path down the east slope to end up at the ticket office, or by retracing your steps back through the ruins to exit via the secret passage (where stalactites are developing) back to the car park.

Wadi Hazor trek

This 1½-hour trek along Wadi Hazor is an invigorating rocky scramble that should only be attempted in dry weather. It is unsuitable for children, as longer legs are required to climb down high boulders at some points on the wadi bed. During winter months, it is really too cold to enjoy this trek, plus water in the wadi is unpleasant to walk through and makes the rocks dangerously slippery.

The trek starts 1 km north of the entrance to Nimrod Fortress, signed left off Route 989 to Wadi Hazor and Nabi Hazuri's tomb. From the car park follow the blue and white trail down the slope (not the red and white trail to the left of the sheikh's tomb), shortly to cross a little Roman bridge. You will soon be following the course of the wadi, always going down. Even in summer, during this first part there remain a few pools of stagnating water (though you won't get your feet wet). After less than 15 minutes, the wadi opens into a v-shaped valley. A rocky descent follows, after which the path criss-crosses the wadi, following its course under the shade of small trees for 30-40 minutes. You will see flashes of Nimrod through the trees, directly ahead and above you. Reaching a crossroads, where blue meets a black and white trail, turn left to keep with the blue and white markers. It should take about an hour to reach this point. Now follows a fairly steep 15-minute climb, up a dusty dirt path (lethal if it is wet), finishing in a grove of ancient olives. Follow the blue sign which points left and the trail brings you out on Route 989 again, next to the ticket office of Nimrod Fortress. From here it is a 15-20-minute walk up the road, back to the car park by Nabi Hazuri's tomb. The guardians may let you in to view the sheikh's carpeted tomb, draped with the Druze flag (head-coverings available outside).

Neve Ativ/Mt Hermon Ski Centre

From Nimrod Fortress, Route 989 winds northeast to the town of **Neve Ativ**. The moshav, established here shortly after the Israelis captured the Golan from Syria in 1967, has developed itself into something of a resort, serving the **Mt Hermon Ski Centre**. The skiing facilities here, on the less than 10% of Mt Hermon (Arabic: Jebel al-Sheikh) that Israel controls, get mixed reviews, though they remain extremely popular with Israelis. There are 25 km of ski runs, though the sensitive nature of the setting means that there is no facility for skiing off-piste (the Israelis and Syrians fought major battles here in 1967 and 1973, and it remains a strategic military position). There are three beginners' runs, six graded as 'easy', five 'difficult' and two 'extremely difficult'. A chair-lift is also provided for non-skiers to visit the viewing point (adult/child 40/35NIS return); entry to the area costs an additional 45/40NIS. **NB** It is best to avoid this place on Shabbat or holidays if possible. The season lasts from December until late April. For details on snow conditions and full prices of rental and equipment see www.skihermon.co.il. For an idea, one-day ski pass for an adult is 230NIS, full equipment rental is 150NIS, lesson for three persons is 200NIS. Calling ahead is a good idea: lack of snow is a genuine threat!

Recently opened is a downhill mountain bike trail, very extreme (probably the most extreme in Israel), which gives cyclists a reason to visit Hermon during the summer months. A new cable car takes you and your equipment up the slopes to the start of the trail. In fact, visiting Hermon in summer rather than in the snowy season can be a wise decision, as the area is still scenic but is relatively uncrowded, and you just pay for the cable car and the views (rather than having to pay a charge for merely entering the area, as you do in the winter months).

Ski passes and equipment rental Though the ski centre has 2000 sets of skis and boots, most Israelis prefer to hire rather than own their equipment and thus it's not unusual to find all the equipment rented out at weekends. Arrive early to avoid disappointment and to ensure that you get a pair of boots that fit properly. Drivers should note that at weekends it is obligatory to park several kilometres away and take the free shuttle bus to the ski centre. There are also a number of transport packages available.

Neve Ativ listings

For Sleeping and Eating price codes and other relevant information, see Essentials pages 26-31.

Sleeping
For skiers, there are a number of package deals in Neve Ativ hotels that are worth considering, (with or without skiing equipment rental), see www.skihermon. co.il for details of these. If you are a non-skier but take one of these packages, free skiing lessons are provided.

L Rimonim Hermon Holiday Village, Neve Ativ, T04-6985888, www.rimonim.com. 44 stylish wooden chalets with a/c, shower, TV and views. Can sleep up to 6 in each. Other facilities include health club and spa, heated indoor pool, restaurant and bar.

Transport
Buses 55 and 58 each run once a day from **Kiryat Shmona**, via **Banias**, to **Neve Ativ**, **Nimrod Jct**, **Majdal Shams**, **Mas'ade**, **Ein Zivan**, and on to **Katzrin**.

South of Mt Hermon

Druze Villages
From Neve Ativ Route 989 continues east to **Majdal Shams**, the largest of several Druze villages in the area. The name means 'Tower of the Sun', though on a cold and wet winter's day this can appear a bleak town indeed. The Druze are a fiercely independent people (for details of the Druze religion see page 727), and, unlike their brethren in the villages around Haifa, they do not want (or have) Israeli citizenship. Instead, they have been given a blue Israeli ID card which states their country of birth as 'Ramat HaGolan', and should they wish to travel abroad they are issued with special papers. It is usually written that the Druze villagers here would prefer to be part of Syria, though this is only true to a certain extent. Many wish to be reunited with family and friends across the disengagement zone in Syria, though they would prefer to be left to their own devices under the broad umbrella of nominal Syrian authority. The Druze are in fact the largest single community on the Golan plateau, numbering some 20,000 as opposed to 17,000 Jews.

A white UN building on the opposite hillside marks the border, acting as an observation point. Below this is *Givat Ha-Tza'akot*, or "Shouting Valley" where, in the past, each Friday and Saturday Majdal Shams' Druze came to shout through megaphones across to their relatives and co-religionists on the Syrian-controlled side of the border. Nowadays, this only really happens in the event of a death or for something of great importance, and Druze families who have been split by the border periodically meet in Jordan.

Smaller Druze villages in the area include little-visited **Ein Quniya**, to the south of Nimrod Fortress, and **Mas'ada** (pronounced 'Ma-sa-day'), south of Majdal Shams on Route 98. The main reason to come here is to eat in the excellent Nedal's restaurant (see eating, below), from whose pavement seating you can observe the new Druze fashions evolving amongst the youth of the town.

Just to the east of the settlement of Mas'ada is the lake of **Birket Ram**. The perfectly round shape of the lake suggests volcanic origins, though it was in fact formed by the action of underground springs breaking through the surface stratum. It was believed for a long time that the lake was the source of the Jordan River, after Philip, founder of Caesarea Philippi (Banias, see page 671) "proved" this fact in the first century CE. Josephus recounts how chaff was thrown into "Phiale", or "the Bowl" here, later appearing at Caesarea Philippi (Josephus, *Jewish War III, 512-13*). What Josephus does not explain is that this was a trick: a courtier dropped more chaff in at Caesarea Philippi so as not to disappoint his patron.

Mt Bental and Quneitra viewpoint

The only mountain of the Golan which you are permitted to ascend (the others all have military posts on top) has 360-degree views, encompassing Mt Hermon, the Sea of Galilee, the mountains of Lebanon and straight into Syria. The viewpoint here looks down upon the deserted town of **Quneitra** (Kuneitra), located in the Disengagement Zone between Israel and Syria. This is a good spot to stand with a detailed map of the Golan and to take out a copy of Chaim Herzog's *The Arab-Israeli Wars* (1984). The former President of Israel describes in great detail the major battles that took place here in 1967 and 1973. Prior to the Six Day War (1967), Quneitra was a modest-sized Syrian town inhabited largely by Circassians. It was captured without a fight by the Israelis on 10 June 1967, though the armoured brigade that rolled in under the command of Col. Albert Mandler had been involved in some of the heaviest fighting for the Golan Heights, as they fought their way down from the northwest. The ceasefire that concluded the Six Day War left Quneitra on the Israeli side of the 'Purple Line'.

In October 1973 (the Yom Kippur War), Syrian tanks and artillery crossed the 'Purple Line', concentrating their attack at Rafid, 20 km to the southeast of Quneitra. After initial early gains the Syrian forces were routed. Herzog estimates that of the 1,400 Syrian tanks that crossed the 'Purple Line' on 6 October, not a single one remained in fighting condition to the west of that line four days later. The subsequent ceasefire, and the disengagement agreement negotiated the following year, saw Quneitra returned to Syrian control, but located in a demilitarized zone between the two states. The Syrians have made no attempt to redevelop Quneitra, and today it stands as a ghost-town. It can only be visited from the Syrian side. Through Quneitra checkpoint, only the UN peace-keeping forces, Druze students and Golan apples can cross.

South of Mt Hermon listings

For Sleeping and Eating price codes and other relevant information, see Essentials pages 26-31.

Sleeping

L-C Chalet Nimrod Castle, Nahal Nimrod, T04-6984218. Wood against white linen,

herbs and flowers, each room unique with plenty of privacy, jacuzzi, balcony: so much more than just huts. Chalet Nimrod also leads the way in eco-design, with clever recycling, old wood crafted into new uses, organic produce and the first flowering-roof in Israel. Also have dorm beds in a room that has original art on the wall, a kitchen, pretty quilts, wood stove, CD-player, mezzanine, veranda, Wi-Fi in the lobby. Hearty dinners available, fantastic breakfasts that will keep you full all day. Camping in the cherry orchard (45NIS per person) with shower block and lots of space. They also have 2 huts in the orchards with pool. Can do a package for hikers including transport of luggage between destinations on the Golan trek. Lilah has created a dream environment indeed.

AL-A Narkis, Majdal Shams, T04-6982961, www.narkis-hotel.co.il. Colourful new hotel on the western edge of town, a short drive away from the ski-slopes of Mt Hermon. Rather fancy double rooms, with TV, a/c and heater, some with jacuzzi, all have balcony. Free Wi-Fi available.

Eating

₮₮₮-₮₮ The Witch and the Milkman, Nahal Nimrod, T04-6870049, www.witch.co.il. A highly regarded restaurant in a spectacular location, with views to Birket Ram and 1110 m down the hills. The menu delivers with tasty, rich dishes that suit the chilly climes of a Golan winter. The countless figurines of witches suspended around the place are perhaps a bit much, but the environment is warm and pleasing. Daily from 1000, the kitchen closes at 2030.

₮₮-₮ Coffee Anan, T04-6820664, On the summit of Mt Bental, the "highest coffee shop in Israel" Coffee Anan (get it?) has lofty windows and outdoor picnic tables to make the most of the view. Light dairy meals and sandwiches made to order, salads, soups in winter and professional coffee. They also have a clean toilet and aren't funny about non-diners using it. Daily 0930-1800 (winter -1700).

₮₮-₮ Nedal, main street, Mas'ada, T04-6981066. For some of the best labaneh, falafel and hummus EVER (10-15NIS), come to Nedal's restaurant. They have been here for 64 successful years, which says something: it's now run by the son and grandson of the original owner. Also main grills, lamb shishlik chicken shishlik, kebab, etc, 45-55NIS. Daily 0730-2030, queues on to the street on Shabbat.

₮ De Karina, Ein Zivan, T04-6993622, www.de-darina.co.il. If you haven't indulged in the Israeli chocolate fetish yet, seize this opportunity. Tucked away in a frontier-feel kibbutz (the first in the country to be privatised), this slick operation still makes every choc by hand to a secret recipe under the guidance of Karina, a 3rd-generation chocolatier from Argentina, The bustling terrace café is an excellent spot for the gourmet tastings and a hot Choc HaFuch drink (or, if you are chocolated-out, coffees or soft drinks). They also do interesting tours (and specialized tours for the blind); phone ahead for English, adult 20NIS, child 16NIS. Sun-Thu 0900-1700, Fri 0900-1500.

B'not Ya'akov Bridge

This bridge on the Jordan River is a major communications junction, effectively marking the boundary between Upper Golan and Lower Golan. This has been a strategic crossing point of the Jordan for several thousand years, with the indistinct remains of the fort of 'Ateret being identified with the Antiochia that the Seleucids built following their victory over the Ptolemies at Banias in 200 BCE. In fact the name of this crossing point, meaning 'Daughters of Jacob', is far older, referring to the crossing of the Jordan into Canaan by the family of Jacob. There have subsequently been battles to control this crossing point between the Crusaders and the Arabs, Napoleon and the Ottoman Turks (1799), the Turks and the British (1918), and the Israelis and the Syrians (1948 and 1967).

Lower Golan

The plateau of the lower Golan is enlivened by scenic valleys and hides little villages where interesting accommodation, good restaurants and quality produce are in abundance. Hiking is particularly rewarding in the Yehudia Forest Nature Reserve, while the regional capital Katzrin and dramatically-located Gamla both contain the remains of ancient Jewish settlements.

Ins and outs

Getting there and away From the Sea of Galilee, several turns off Route 92 head east towards the lower Golan. Route 789 leads to Givat Yoav and other interesting moshavim along Routes 98 and 808. For Katzrin, the regional centre, take Route 87 then Route 9088. From Tiberias, buses 15, 18 and 19 make infrequent loops through the villages on the way to and from Katzrin. Again, this is an area where hitch-hiking can be the most convenient way to travel.

Katzrin → *Colour map 1, grid B5.*

Katzrin (Katsrin, Qasrin, Qazrin) is a modern settlement established in 1977 in order to project an impression of permanence on the Israeli occupation of the Golan Heights. It now has a population of around 7000, as generous government resettlement grants help the town to 'fill out' to the planned size of around 10,000. It has already established itself as the de facto administrative 'capital' of the Golan Heights. Recent excavations, however, confirm that Jewish settlement on the Golan doesn't just date to post-1967: just to the east of the new town, Ancient Qasrin Park displays the reconstructed remains of a Talmudic (fourth to eighth century-CE) village.

Ins and outs

Getting there and away There are three main approaches to Katzrin: (a) from the west via Route 90, then Route 91 across the B'not Ya'akov Bridge; (b) from the northeast, via Routes 98/91 from Upper Golan; (c) from the south, via Route 87 from the northeast corner of the Sea of Galilee. All three routes are served by a very limited bus route. Buses 55 or 58 run twice daily in a huge loop from Kiryat Shemona, via Banias and Mas'ada to Katzrin (approach 'b'); Buses 15 or 19 run to Katzrin from Tiberias (approach 'c', 50 minutes). All the buses arrive in the Commercial Centre area.

Tourist information

Tourist information ① *T04-6962885, www.tour.golan.org.il, Sun-Thu 0900-1545, Fri 0900-1245*, is in the mall next to Ancient Katzrin, at the eastern entrance to town. They have a good free map of the Golan, and Pocket Guide to the region, 10NIS.

Ancient Qasrin Park

① *T04-6962412, Sun-Thu 0900-1600, Fri 0900-1400, Sat 1000-1600, admission 24NIS, student/child 16NIS, also includes entrance to Golan Archaeological Museum. Site is located just to the east of the modern town of Katzrin, off Route 9088.*

Though the site of the ancient village here was identified in 1913, it was not until the Israelis established control over the Golan Heights in 1967 that Qasrin was systematically excavated. Approximately 10% of the village has been cleared, including a finely preserved synagogue. Village life during the Talmudic period (fourth to eighth centuries CE) has been recreated by placing models and replicas of everyday utensils, tools and furniture in two of the restored houses. A free brochure from the ticket office gives details of the articles displayed in the '**House of Uzi**' and '**House of Rabbi Abun**'.

The pattern of the village follows the *insulae* form, with separate extended family units divided from neighbours by narrow paths. The basic nuclear family unit comprises a large multi-purpose room, or *triclinium*, divided from a large storage room by a 'window wall', above which stands a sleeping loft. The rooms open on to a courtyard, with additional extended family units joined on to form a self-contained *insula*. The village seen today was probably established in the fourth to fifth centuries CE and continued in use until the mid-eighth century CE earthquake that struck the region. The site was resettled during the Mamluk period (13th-15th centuries CE) and a mosque built on the ruins of the synagogue. There is also evidence of Bedouin settlement in the 20th century CE.

The **synagogue** is the best-preserved example in the Golan. It appears to have gone through three stages of construction, four different architectural phases, and five floors. Most of what you see today dates from the second synagogue (sixth to seventh century CE) and hints at the economic prosperity of a village economy based upon olive oil production. Many of the artefacts found at the site are displayed in the Golan Archaeological Museum in the new town, where there is also an audio-visual show on the "story of Gamla" (in English, Hebrew, French, Russian, Spanish, German and Italian). Note that the same ticket gains you admission to both sites.

Golan Magic Visitors' Centre

Next to the open mall near Ancient Katzrin is the Visitors' Centre, where you can view the Golan Magic audio-visual show: English tours on the half-hour, first show 0930, last show 1730 (in winter 1630), adult 25NIS, student/child 18NIS. The initial movie is about images/effects rather than facts, but the topographical model of the Golan is a great visual aid accompanied by a short history of the region, and helps get the valleys, plateaus and mountains in perspective. The adjacent **Golan Brewery** ① *T04-6961311*, gives group tours Sunday-Thursday, and is worth a visit in any case to sample the brew (see Eating, below).

Golan Heights Winery

① *T04-6968409/435, www.golanwines.co.il, Sun-Fri, admission, including tour and tasting 15NIS.*

Located behind the Golan Magic Visitors' Centre is the Golan Heights Winery. It is generally agreed that some of Israel's best wines are produced here, most notably Hermon Red and Yarden cabernet sauvignon. Tasting tours can be arranged in advance. **NB** wines bought at the shop here are not necessarily cheaper than elsewhere in the country.

Talmudic Village & Synagogue, Ancient Qasrin Park

To Amphitheatre & Sculpture Park

Route

Entrance

N

10 metres
10 yards

1 'House of Uzi'
2 'House of Rabbi Abun'
3 Viewpoint
4 Spring
5 Synagogue

Katzrin listings

For Sleeping and Eating price codes and other relevant information, see Essentials pages 26-31.

Sleeping
A-D SPNI Golan Field School, Katzrin, Zavithan, T04-6961352/6961234, www.aspni. org. A/c dorms plus some private rooms. There is also space to pitch a tent. Advance reservations are highly recommended. This is also an indispensable source of hiking information for the Golan region.

Eating
♥♥♥-♥♥ Suzana, Ani'am, T04-6999855, see www.suzana.co.il for menu and gallery. Sun-Thu 1200-2230, Fri -1500. Fashioned from wood and decorated with wine bottles and dramatic metal chandeliers, there's veranda seating and a mezzanine inside. Meat is their speciality, amnum/musht fish from the Kinneret, steak tricot, chicken poullet, and the mezze are excellent (all kosher) or you are welcome for drinks at the eucalyptus wood bar.. Located in the pretty artist's village of Ani'am (off the 808, around 11 km from Katzrin), which has colourful galleries built to an old style and makes for a pleasant browse post-lunch (shops closed Sun).
♥ Golan Brewery Pub, Katzrin, T04-6961311, www.golanbeer.co.ils. For a night out, this pub is excellent, with four fantastic beers brewed on the premises and pumped directly into your glass (the wheaty 'Galilee' was our favourite). The food menu is equally decent, with an East European slant, and good value for money. There's live music Wed/Thu from 2000, and Fri 1500-1800. Open daily from 1130-last customer.

Ya'ar Yehudiya Nature Reserve → *Colour map 1, B5.*

ⓘ *T04-6962817, www.parks.org.il, daily 0800-1700, winter -1600, closes 1 hour earlier on Fri, adult 20NIS, student 17NIS, child 9NIS. Ticket is valid for all 3 treks for 1 day only.*
At the risk of repetition, it is fair to say that the Ya'ar Yehudiya Nature Reserve offers some of the best hiking possibilities in Israel. There are several options, all of which are fairly challenging, but offering sweeping views, spectacular rock formations, waterfalls and attractive waterscapes. Details of the three best hikes are included here, plus information on how to reach the amazing Brekhat HaMeshushim, or Hexagon Pools.

Getting there and away The reserve is located on Route 87, about half-way between Yehudiye Junction on the northeast corner of the Sea of Galilee, and Katzrin Junction South.
   Getting to the reserve by public transport is a hassle since buses that pass the site from Tiberias (15) do not leave early enough, though the 843 from Katzrin to Tel Aviv passes the entrance, leaving Katzrin at 0745. Another option is to camp at the Yehudiya Campground overnight, and hike the next day. It costs 15NIS per person to pitch a tent in the designated campground, with bathroom facilities, shaded areas, and a snack-bar. Those with their own transport have no such problems. **NB** Note that there is separate travel information for taking the short route to Brekhat HaMeshushim (see page 685).

Getting around NB It is strongly recommended that you consult with the helpful staff before commencing any hikes. They are able to provide up-to-date information on local conditions, as well as tips on routes and journey times. After rain, trails here are generally closed, although the Upper Zavitan only closes after very heavy rainfall. The map in this Handbook should be suitable for all the hikes, likewise, the free map given out when you enter the park should be good enough. On most of the hikes there is no drinking water en route, so you should make sure that you are carrying an adequate supply (at least two litres per person). On some of these hikes you will get wet, and in some places you need to be able to swim.

Nahal Yehudiya hike

This excellent hike takes around three to four hours, with the option of extending it into a loop trail that adds about another two hours. **NB** This hike involves a very steep 9-m descent down a ladder, plus swimming across pools of deep water. You will need a swimming costume plus waterproof bags for valuables/maps, etc. Only do this trek in hot weather.

The hike begins at the entrance to Ya'ar Yehudiya Nature Reserve (1). Cross to the east side of Route 87, following the red trail markers (away from the main entrance). Almost immediately you come to the ruins of an ancient town identified as **Sogane** (Tell Khushniyye). It is described by Josephus as one of the towns that he fortified against the approaching Romans (*Jewish War II, 572*), though it appears that, unlike Gamla (see below), Sogane surrendered to Rome's representative Agrippa II at the beginning of the revolt (66 CE). Its subsequent history is not entirely clear, though it is known that Turcomans from Central Asia settled here in the 19th century CE.

Ya'ar Yehudiya Nature Reserve hikes

Nahal Yehudiya hike:
1, 2, 3, 4, 5, 6, 7, 8, 1

Upper Zavitan hike:
1, 9, 10, 11, 12, 13, 14, 1, or
continue to Lower Zavitan
hike

Lower Zavitan hike:
1, 14, 15, 14, 1

As you skirt the site to the south the trail divides (2), with the red trail heading northeast and the green trail heading southwest. Take the red trail to the left, along the top of the canyon. After a kilometre or so the trail descends into the Nahal Yehudiya at the foot of the waterfall (3). You can stop for a swim at the pretty pool here, though there is plenty of opportunity for getting wet later! Follow the red trail along the river. After 500 m you reach a second waterfall (4). Climb down to the pool 9 m below using the steep metal ladder. Officially it is not permitted to jump from the top of the ladder into the pool, though many hikers ignore this rule. Swim across the (deep) pool. Several further pools have to be negotiated as you follow the course of the Nahal Yehudiya towards the Sea of Galilee. The trail crosses the stream from bank to bank a number of times. About a kilometre below the pools, a green trail heads off to the right (northwest) (5). This trail returns to Sogane (2), completing the shorter circuit.

If you want to complete the longer circuit, continue to follow the red trail along the course of the Nahal Yehudiya. The trail encounters a series of waterfalls and pools, though you pass these to your left. You have to swim across the final deep pool (6). About a kilometre further on look out for the red trail markers as the path climbs the bank to the right (7), about a 20-minute ascent. Once you reach the plateau it can be a little difficult to follow the red trail markers through the Yehudiya Forest of Tabor oaks, though if you head in a northwest direction after less than a kilometre you should hit Route 87 (8). From here it should not be more than 1-2 km back to the Nature Reserve entrance (1).

Upper Zavitan hike

This hike takes around three to four hours, though it can be extended if you combine it with the Lower Zavitan hike (add four hours). It's a fairly easy walk, with one tricky descent, and features some interesting rock formations, a waterfall, and a swimming pool.

The hike begins at the reserve entrance (1). Head north through the gate along the old semi-paved road for 1.5 km. If you have a car you can drive this section. At the foot of the lava flow, near the electricity pole (9), head to the left (west) along the blue marked trail. After 1 km the trail divides (10). Take the black trail to the right and head northwest for 1.5 km. When the trail meets the Nahal Zavitan (11) descend to the west bank and follow the canyon downstream. After a short walk you arrive at two small pools (12). The unusual rock formations here were created some three million years ago by the rapid cooling of the lava flow, with the basalt cracking into these hexagonal shapes. The red trail continues along the canyon, crossing the Nahal Zavitan several times, in part following the course of the old abandoned Arab-built aqueduct. You reach another pool featuring hexagonal rock formations above the 25-m-high Zavitan Waterfall (13). The red trail bypasses the waterfall by turning to the left. After a few minutes' walking, a treacherous blue trail descends to the swimming pool below the waterfall. From here, there are two options. It's possible to retrace your footsteps back up the blue trail, and follow it back to the intersection with the black trail (10), and the starting point (9). Alternatively, you can continue on to the Lower Zavitan hike.

NB If you continue on to the Lower Zavitan hike, note that it is illegal to enter the dangerous 'Black Gorge' that leads down from the swimming hole at the end of the Upper Zavitan hike (13). Instead you must follow the red trail along the southeast side of the Black Gorge. After a kilometre or so it meets the green trail that marks the beginning of the Lower Zavitan hike (14) (see below).

Lower Zavitan hike

The Lower Zavitan hike takes around four hours and can be started either from the entrance to the reserve (1), or from the finish of the Upper Zavitan hike (14). If you begin your hike from the reserve entrance, head west on the green trail through the Tabor oaks and cattle grazing area. After 1.5 km the green trail meets the red trail at a cliff viewpoint above the Nahal Zavitan (14). Follow the red trail for a very short distance to the right, then look out for the black trail markers that lead left down the stepped path into the canyon. Turn left into the stream bed and follow its course. Passing one attractive pool, the trail leads to a deep circular swimming pool at Ein Netef (spring) (15). This is a great stop for a break.

If you are continuing on to Brekhat HaMeshushim (16), cross the river bed and follow the red trail in a westerly direction (see below). Note that these hexagonal pools are another 2 hours away at least. To complete the Lower Zavitan hike, cross to the southeast side of Nahal Zavitan, then follow the red trail to the northeast above the canyon. After a short distance you will reach the intersection with the green trail (14), from where you return to the reserve entrance (1).

Brekhat HaMeshushim (Hexagon Pools)

The Brekhat HaMeshushim, or Hexagon Pools, are located on the Nahal Meshushim shortly before it meets the Nahal Zavitan (16). Though these rock formations are found elsewhere in this area, they are at their most spectacular here, as perfectly formed six-sided basalt columns (3-5 m high) line either side of the stream. It's certainly worth the effort of getting here.

If you have your own transport the Hexagon Pools can be reached after just two hours' walking (plus the same time back again); note that last entrance is at 1400 and taking food inside is forbidden. At Beit Hameches/Custom House Junction, between Katzrin and B'not Ya'akov Bridge, Route 888 runs south towards the Jordan River Park. Just to the south of this junction a road heads southeast to the Meshushim parking lot. (Alternatively, Custom House Junction can be reached by heading north along Route 888 from the Jordan River Park and the Sea of Galilee). From the parking lot it takes 2 hours to reach the pools along the red trail along the southwest bank of the Nahal Meshushim.

The longer approach to the Hexagon Pools is by continuing along the red trail from Ein Netef (15) on the Lower Zavitan hike. **NB** It is six hours one-way from the Nature Reserve entrance (1) to Brekhat HaMeshushim (16).

Gamla → Colour map 1, grid B5.

ⓘ *T04-6822282, www.parks.org.il, daily 0800-1700 (-1600 in winter), 1 hr earlier on Fri and hol eves, adult 25NIS, student 21NIS, child 13NIS. Binocular rental 10NIS. Toilets, well-stocked kiosk, picnic area.*
Making an early start, it's not impossible to complete all four walks in one day. NB Do not underestimate the blazing heat of summer: there is little shade, and there are gruelling uphill climbs. Take plenty of water (available at the site, tap or bottled) plus sunscreen and a hat. Alternatively, after winter rains the Golan mud is sticky beyond belief and children get messy.

Ins and outs

Getting there and away Unfortunately there is no public transport to Gamla, with the nearest bus stops being quite some distance away. Bus 18 from Tiberias goes to Ramat Magshimim, 8 km to the southeast, whilst bus 22 goes to Ma'ale Gamla, a similar distance to the southwest. Another alternative is to go to Katzrin and hitch. A hire-car from Tiberias is the best option.

Most scholars agree that this magnificent site is the ancient town of Gamla (Gamala), scene of one of the most dramatic battles in Josephus' account of the First Jewish Revolt against the Romans (66-73 CE). Though certain aspects of the terrain do not entirely match Josephus' description, it is a setting worthy of the human tragedy that unfolded at Gamla. Whether viewed from the Sea of Galilee looking due east, or from the cliff above with the Sea of Galilee in the background, Gamla is an impressive sight. The remains of the town and citadel stand on a hump-shaped hill ('gamal' is Hebrew for camel), connected to the higher Golan plateau by a narrow saddle. The cliff face above Gamla is a major breeding ground for birds of prey, so as you look down on an amazing panoramic vista towards the Sea of Galilee, huge vultures effortlessly glide pass you in the foreground, soaring and swooping on the air currents. And if all that were not enough, a walking trail takes you to the dramatic waterfalls of Nahal Gamla, dropping from the plateau into the valley and down to the Sea of Galilee. Though Gamla is difficult to reach without your own transport, it is recommended that you make every effort to get here.

Background

The bulk of Gamla's history has been gleaned from the writings of **Josephus** (quotes from whom are stuck on rocks throughout the site), though almost all points are backed up by archaeology. The town is first mentioned in the context of Alexander Jannaeus' campaign in the region c. 83-80 BCE, though Talmudic sources refer to a walled city here dating back to the time of Joshua. The earliest coins found here date only to 280 BCE, but excavations on the east side of the hill have unearthed remnants from the Early Bronze Age (c. 3300-2200 BCE).

The Hellenistic settlement that Alexander Jannaeus captured appears to have been populated by Jews during the reign of Herod the Great in the first century BCE. At the beginning of the **First Jewish Revolt** (66 CE) it was within the kingdom of Agrippa II and appears to have kept its allegiance to Rome. However, it switched allegiance during the struggle against the Romans and became one of the northern cities that the Jewish commander Josephus fortified (before he too switched allegiance). Agrippa II's seven-month siege of Gamla failed to break the town and it is was only after a severe setback

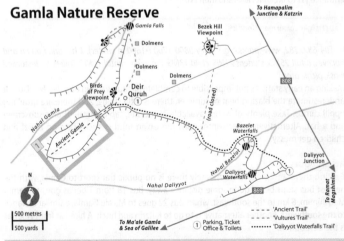

The Roman capture of Gamla

Gamla was the last of the major fortified towns in the north to fall to Vespasian's all-conquering Roman army and, given the town's formidable natural defences, coupled with the defensive walls, trenches and underground passages that the inhabitants had built, it is easy to see why the occupants were reluctant to surrender. In fact it was to take three legions of the Roman army, and a stunning setback, before the Roman might eventually prevailed. After the siege-engines had battered the walls, the Romans "poured in through the breaches with a great blare of trumpets and din of weapons, and shouting themselves hoarse flung themselves upon the defenders of the town." With the scent of victory (and blood) in their nostrils the usually disciplined Roman army surged forwards, pursuing the defenders towards the upper part of the town. As Vespasian was to concede later, the Romans should have withdrawn at this point and consolidated their hold on the lower town. Instead they pushed on, falling into the trap set for them. The Jewish defenders "swung round and counter-attacked vigorously. Swept down the slope and jammed inextricably in the narrow alleys, the Romans suffered fearful casualties ... they climbed on to the roofs of the houses ... [but] crowded with men and unequal to the weight these quickly collapsed ... many were buried under the debris, many while trying to escape found one limb or another pinned down ... the debris furnished them [the Jews] with any number of great stones, and the bodies of the enemy with cold steel: they wrenched the swords from the fallen and used them to finish off those who were slow to die ... unacquainted with the roads and choked with the dust, they [the Romans] could not even recognize their friends, but in utter confusion attacked each other." Even Vespasian himself had succumbed to the excitement of the assault, and only a disciplined retreat had prevented his capture.

The demoralized Roman army withdrew and regrouped outside the town. Morale was boosted by Vespasian's pep-talk, who sought not to apportion blame for the ill-discipline that had precipitated the disaster (himself not being wholly blameless). Instead he pointed out how Roman victories were attained by adhering to a tactical battle-plan. Some days later, when the walls had been breached by three members of the Fifteenth Legion undermining a projecting tower, Vespasian's son Titus led an ordered advance into the town at the head of 200 cavalry. The Romans pressed forward relentlessly "as men were slaughtered on every side, and the whole town was deluged with the blood that poured down the slopes." Mindful that the Roman army would be in no mood to take prisoners, those trapped in the citadel "despairing of escape and hemmed in every way, they flung their wives and children and themselves too into the immensely deep artificial ravine that yawned under the citadel"; a scene that was to be repeated several years later at Masada. In fact, as at Masada just two women survived, with Josephus succinctly pointing out that "the fury of the victors seemed less destructive than the suicidal frenzy of the trapped men; 4000 fell by Roman swords, but those who plunged to destruction proved to be over 5000." (Josephus, *The Jewish War*, IV, 27-83)

that **Vespasian**'s legions were able to capture the town in late 67 CE (see box on previous page). The site does not appear to have been occupied after the Roman conquest.

The Ancient Trail

Though it is only about 500 m down to the ancient town on the hill below the plateau, it's a killer climb on the way back, so you should allow at least two hours for this walk. The trail begins by the Gamla Lookout. Descending to the defensive city walls, it is possible to see the breach made by the Romans during the first assault on Gamla. The walls extend for around 350 m on the east side, whilst the other approaches are protected by natural steep cliffs.

Close to the point where the walls were breached is a large rectangular structure built on a northeast to southwest axis. It is usually identified as a **synagogue** dating to the period of Herod the Great, though some commentators challenge this viewpoint. Gutman, who largely excavated the site, is certain that it is a synagogue, pointing out that its unusual orientation (not facing Jerusalem) is determined by the topography of the ground. If it is indeed a synagogue, it is one of the oldest ones found in the Holy Land and the only one built within city limits whilst the Temple at Jerusalem was still standing. The synagogue is adjoined by a mikveh (ritual bath), a study room and a courtyard, and would have been the centre of community life.

From the synagogue it is possible to wander through the remains of the town to the **wealthy residential area** at the western tip. Many of the buildings in the town are labelled, including several well-preserved oil presses.

The Vultures' Trail

This green marked trail is a short wheelchair-friendly stroll along the cliff top and back, and should not be missed. Passing above the main breeding grounds of the Griffon vultures (who are permanent residents), you are likely to glimpse soaring **birds of prey** above the ravine of the Nahal Gamla to your left, as they "flap lazily overhead, then plunge into the ravine in search of lunch" (Stephen Brook, *Winner Takes All*, 1990). At the observation point, cameras watch the progress of mating birds, and staff are on hand to explain the

Ancient Gamla

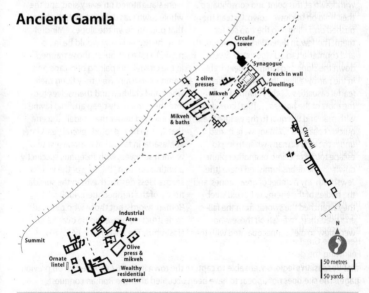

Circular tower

'Synagogue'

Breach in wall

2 olive presses

Mikveh

Dwellings

Mikveh & baths

City wall

Industrial Area

Summit

Olive press & mikveh

Ornate lintel

Wealthy residential quarter

N

50 metres
50 yards

breeding process. When eggs are laid they are air-lifted to Jerusalem for incubation, and then the adolescent birds spend 3½ years being raised in large cages in Gamla before being released into the wild. With the camel-hump hill of Gamla in the foreground, the waterscape of the Beit Zaida Nature Reserve beyond, and the Sea of Galilee in the distance, the planing birds complete the scene nicely. **NB** It is illegal to descend the cliffs or to the river-bed, or to disturb the birds in any way. Keep to the paths.

The Dolmen Trail
This trail leads from the Byzantine settlement of Deir Quruh to **Gamla Waterfall**, Israel's highest perennial waterfall at 51 m. On either side of the trail **dolmens** are scattered: 4000-year-old megalithic blocks stacked together which possibly served as burial sites. The trail ends at a viewpoint, from where it is possible to look back at the nesting sites in the cliff face. Do not go beyond the final viewpoint because an IDF firing zone begins here. Return by the same route.

The Daliyyot Waterfalls Trail
This red-and-white trail can be completed in either direction, beginning at either the main entrance to Gamla Nature Reserve, or at the southerly entrance on Route 869 (the road down to Sea of Galilee at Ma'ale Gamla Junction) close to Daliyyot Junction. The walk takes about two hours in either direction (four hours return). The highlights of this walk are the sweeping views down towards Gamla and beyond, and the waterfalls on the Nahal Daliyyot and its tributary, Nahal Bazelet. However, bear in mind that during summer months you are unlikely to see any actual water on this walk; then it is more about the views and the exercise.

Sussita and around → Colour map 1, B5.

Founded by the Seleucids in the Early Hellenistic period (332-167 BCE), the town is best known by its Greek name, **Hippos**. The promontory upon which it stands is said to resemble the shape of a horse (Greek: 'hippos'), with its Aramaic name Sussita having the same meaning. Ongoing excavations are uncovering ever more buildings and sections of Roman road in the ancient town. The dramatic craggy landscape, a lack of tourists, and the fact that there is no entrance charge make for a rewarding visit. **Warning**: There are **mines** near the area so it is important to stick to the path and not to cross any fences.

Ins and outs
Getting there and away You can reach Sussita from Route 92 on the Sea of Galilee, almost opposite the entrance to Ein Gev, where an unmarked road heads off to the east. After a steep and winding climb of 3.7 km, a sign to the left of the road indicates the site of Sussita. It is also accessible via a fairly rough road that leads west off Route 98 on the Golan plateau, about 3 km southwest of Afiq Junction.

Background Despite its stout defensive wall around the summit, the city was captured by **Alexander Jannaeus** for the Maccabees c. 80 BCE, though **Pompey** subsequently recaptured it in 63 BCE. According to the writings of Pliny it became one of the cities of the Decapolis, though the decision by the Roman Emperor Augustus to grant the city to Herod the Great in c. 30 BCE was not one that went down well with the city's population. Following the death of Herod, the town once more became part of the Province of Syria. Despite considerable trade between Hippos and Tiberias, the towns were deadly enemies, and the Jews attacked Hippos during the **First Jewish Revolt** (66-73 CE).

The town here developed substantially during the second and third centuries CE, primarily due to its location on the road between Damascus and Scythopolis (Bet Shean, see page 582); at its peak its population may have reached 20,000. The town enjoyed a great deal of prosperity during the **Byzantine period**, becoming the seat of a bishop. It was peacefully occupied by the **Arabs** following their conquest of Palestine in 636 CE, though it had to be abandoned when the elaborate aqueduct system that brought the city its water from a point 25 km to the south was destroyed in the earthquake of 749 CE.

Sights

The tour begins at the east of the promontory, where a black trail leads between two fences that mark the minefields. You enter past the southern pier of the **east gate** from the Roman period (though it was rebuilt in the Byzantine period); scattered blocks from the aqueduct lie around. Here begins the **cardo maximus** (main street) of the Roman period; large stretches of paving stones remain both here and on perpendicular streets. Passing a number of abandoned buildings dating to the military occupation, you come to the remains of the Byzantine **cathedral**. The two rows of nine columns that divided the basilica into a nave and two aisles lie on the floor, along with a number of pink and white marble Corinthian capitals, victims of the earthquake. An inscription in the southern aisle mentions the two Syrian philanthropist brothers, St Damian and St Cosmas, whilst another inscription in the baptistry dates the construction of this room to 591 CE. Three other churches have been discovered (their mosaics were covered for protection at the time of research), along with a forum; basalt pillars litter the site. To the west of here a small amphitheatre has recently been excavated and there is a fine view across the Sea of Galilee. The black marked trail continues down the slope to Ein Gev, suitable for 4WD as well as trekking, passing by the southern church on the way.

Mitzpe Ofir Observation Point

ⓘ *From Route 92 on the Sea of Galilee, turn east on to Route 789. After 8.9 km on the right, a brown sign indicates Mitzpe Ofir. A further 1.2 km leads to the car park.*

Mitzpe Ofir must be the best vantage point from which to view the Sea of Galilee, 400 m below. Prior to the Six Day War in 1967, the border between Israel and Syria ran along the base of this cliff, with Israel occupying a narrow strip of land around the east side of the lake. In fact, Mitzpe Ofir was a Syrian gun position, and it's easy to see just how easy it was to drop a few shells into Kibbutz Ein Gev. In spring (Feb-Mar) there are carpets of purple Tumus flowers in this area, which move slightly year by year as they are re-seeded by the wind. A hiking trail leads down from Mitzpe Ofir to Kibbutz Ein Gev. It's possible to do this as a night walk at full moon, as the path to Ein Gev viewpoint is along white rock rather than on typical local basalt and is clearly visible. Warning Keep to the trail: there are still uncleared mine fields in the area.

Mitzpe Ofir to Ein Gev hike

The trail (marked by blue and white) descends to the south from the viewpoint, passing an uncleared minefield beyond the fence to the left. Continue on to the dirt track, and follow the path to the **Bir esh-Shikum** (spring), which is now dry. This was the site of the agricultural community of B'nei Yehuda (Sons of Judah), established by religious Jews from Safed in the late 19th century CE next to the Arab village. The settlement was not a success, and dwindled from 52 families in 1888 to just one by 1920 (the mother and son of whom were killed in the uprisings). One of the houses has been reconstructed to give an idea of how the village would have looked, and the olive trees growing around serve as a reminder of the lost communities. The marked trail continues along the ridge, before striking off down towards the lake. Ein Gev viewpoint provides a final place to rest before tackling the steep descent: be prepared for much scrambling. Pass through the outer fields of Kibbutz Ein Gev, along a narrow wadi, until you hit the main road (Route 92). The whole hike takes three to four hours from the start point, but with stops to enjoy the views it can easily be five hours.

Sussita and around listings

For Sleeping and Eating price codes and other relevant information, see Essentials pages 26-31.

Sleeping
L-D Gengis Khan in the Golan, Givat Yoav, T052-3715687, www.gkhan.co.il. 5 Mongolian tents arranged around a lawn with picnic tables, each sleep 10 and attract adventurous types from all corners of the globe. 'Dorm' beds are 100NIS, or private (up to 5 persons) is 590NIS. Groups of 6-10 pay 100NIS each. Sheet/pillow/blanket/towel 30NIS extra per person, or just bring your sleeping bag. There's a well-equipped kitchen, BBQs, each tent has a private bathroom and a/c-heater. But it's Sara and Benzi's warmth and attitude to life that make a stay all the more special. You'll get excellent advice on the local area and its hidden gems. Highly recommended.

Eating and drinking
Cafe Galeria, Ne'ot Golan, T04-6600132/050-4060999, www.cafegaleria.com. A cafe-cum-gallery with a unique atmosphere, you can eat among eclectic works of art ranging from Czech glass candles to life-size figurines from the terracotta army. Also groups of seating in the shady garden full of rustling shrubs and trees. Characterful owner Lior keeps the menu simple, with hearty breakfasts, quiches, salads, crepes and cakes (just don't ask him for an omelette). Popular with locals as well as out-of-towners, it's not very kid-friendly. Don't miss the bathroom, it's a work of art in itself. Essential to book on Shabbat in summertime. To get here, follow the coffee-cup signs through the attractive moshav. Daily except Mon 1000-2300 (in winter -2100).

Cowboy Valley, T04-2419966, near Givat Yoav (4.5 km along Road 789 from Kursi Jct). There are awesome views down to the Kinneret through panoramic windows in this ranch-style wooden restaurant – best enjoyed as the sun sets in the west. Generous steaks, burgers and chicken meals form the uncomplicated menu (choice of quiche for vegetarians), are best washed down with a beer. There's a riding school on site. Open Sun-Thu 1300-2200, Fri Sat –1900.

La-Morse, Givat Yoav, T04-6762021. The last thing you expect in Givat Yoav is an Irish-style pub, and certainly not one so pleasant. Dark green walls, a mix of music, bar to prop up, a whole host of beers to choose from. It's a good evening out or a welcome break on hike. Open daily till the last customer leaves (and at weekends that can be 0600).

Activities and tours
Cycling, hiking and jeep tours
Gil Mualem, T050-3206786 or **Elad Harris** 050-2880440, are mountain bike enthusiasts based in Givat Yoav. They can arrange bike hire or take guided trips, and also offer hiking and jeep tours in the area. Can give advice on the 3-4 hr mountain bike trail recently marked out from Givat Yoav.

Horse-riding
Cowboy Valley, T04-2419966, www.habokrim.co.il. You get a whole new perspective on the Lower Golan from the back of horse. Cowboy Valley rides give supreme views of the Sea of Galilee and the lava folds of the valleys while you trot through olive groves and fruit plantations. A 1.5 hr session with instruction is 125NIS. Located 4.5 km along Road 789 from Kursi Jct, on the left side.

Boutique Golan

Kibbutzim and moshavim are reinventing themselves in the Golan and, in addition to the central agricultural way of life, they are welcoming visitors to see the production process and to taste the fruits of their labour. 'Boutique' is the by-word, with a focus on quality not quantity. One wonders what the founding fathers of Dagania would make of it all. These are by no means the only ones, but they have English speakers.

Kibbutz Gshur

Eretz-Gshur, T04-6764169/052-3965348, www.eretz-gshur.co.il, Sunday-Thursday 0800-1600, Friday 0800-1400. Free. Long famed as grape-growers, in 2002 the kibbutz decided to apply the principles of wine-making to producing unique single-variety olive oils. Visitors are welcome at the high-tech cold-press; there's a short movie, information boards and staff on hand to show you around. Taste-testing olive oil is a curious experience, and there are nine different oils on offer all with unique flavours and aromas. They are the first in Israel, and they are award-winners. More virgin than extra virgin due to the low acidity level. Environmentally minded, they ensure the polluting by-products of water and pulp from the olives is recycled.

Kidmat Zvi

Sara's Jam House, Kidmat Zvi, T052-6485803. This gingerbread house surrounded by flowers and filled with 70 kinds of jam is straight out of a fairytale. Shiny pots line the walls and a central tasting table has an array of colourful jams. Sara does the whole process by hand and with her heart. Ingredients are entirely natural, the flavours are unbelievably intense and fresh: passion fruit, pomello (giant grapefruit) and fig with ginger to name but a few. Little tables and chairs

in the garden allow you to relax outside listening to the wind-chimes. Open every day, but ring ahead to check she's at home.

At the entrance to the moshav (the right turn immediately before the gate) is **Bazelet HaGolon Winery**, T04-6965010/050-8485010, www.bazelet-hagolan.co.il, a small-scale venture that makes a mellow alternative to busier wine-tastings, with a scenic setting and fabulous 20-month aged Cab Sauv Reserve. Call in advance for English tours, 25NIS per person, Sunday-Friday 0900-1500.

Avnei Eitan

Robotic Cow Shed/Farm, Avnei Eitan, T04-6763563/050-4060311. Sunday-Friday 0900-1600 (in winter -1400). Adult/child 28NIS for movie and tour. It's not the cows that are robotic but the milking machine to which they bring themselves to be milked, fed and checked for fertility by the computer. Leora is an amusing guide and makes a visit surprisingly fascinating, and children get a kick out of bottle-feeding the calves. This is a religious village hence all products are kosher le'mehadrin – though the robotic milker doesn't rest on Shabbat. On passing the kibbutz gate, take immediate left, then immediate right, to find the farm.

Givat Yoav

Golan Heights Honey, T04-6763413/050-5356662. Charmingly British David Alin (originally Allingham) and his daughter have a visitor centre/shop at their modest honey factory; visitors are welcome (no charge) every day of the week (but call in advance). The bees feed on Golan wildflowers, making honey that has traces of thyme and differing intensities of colour and aroma. Chunks of honeycomb, medicinal propolis, balms, and syrupy honey are for sale, and David is a mine of information.

Contents

Footprint features

Background

History

It is very difficult to present the history of this land (whether you call it Israel, Palestine, the Holy Land, or something else) in just a few pages. Events that took place here some 4000 years ago, and would be considered 'pre-history' elsewhere, are as fresh in the collective memory as the defining moments of the 20th century. Thus, the history of Israel begins not with the establishment of the State of Israel in 1948, but with the beginning of Jewish history around 1650 BCE.

Likewise, there are different interpretations of history. The authors of this book have attempted to be impartial in the following presentation of history, striving to present together dichotomous views of the same events. Yet the history of Israel/Palestine, even the nomenclature, is a veritable minefield of contrary positions and interpretations, and it is inevitable that a few explosions will be set off in attempting to guide readers through it. For this reason, at the end of each section a small selection of further reading is included that may help provide a greater understanding of the opposing viewpoints.

Ancient Israel

Early settlement

Though Jewish history can be said to have begun some 4000 years ago when Abraham made the purchase of the Cave of Machpelah at Hebron, the Patriarchs and their descendants the Israelites were by no means the first peoples to settle the land here. The move from food-gatherers to food-producers by members of a Pre-Pottery Neolithic culture some time in the ninth millennium BCE, and the subsequent construction of a defensive wall around their settlement, gives rise to Jericho's claim as the oldest city in the world.

At some point in the Early Bronze Age, around 3300 BCE, a civilization known as **Canaanite** established itself on the coastal strip that now roughly corresponds to present-day Israel, sandwiched between the more highly advanced civilizations of Egypt and Mesopotamia. The Canaanites belonged to the northwest Semitic peoples of northern Mesopotamia and Syria, a region that was also to produce the group subsequently known as Jews. The land that became known as Canaan was in fact a series of city-states, all subject to the power and influence of generally stronger neighbouring civilizations. At some point in the Middle Bronze Age (circa 18th or 17th century BCE) other groups began to settle in Canaan, notably the **Philistines** on the coast, and in the hills a nomadic people known as the **Habiru**.

The Patriarchs

The Habiru, including the 'early Hebrews', were led into Canaan by the patriarch of the tribe, **Abraham** of Ur (in present day Iraq). The Bible/Torah recalls how God made a covenant with Abraham, calling upon him to lead God's chosen people, and telling him that "I will give unto thee, and to thy seed after thee, the land wherein thou art a stranger, all the land of Canaan, for an everlasting possession" (Genesis 17:8). Abraham is thus the first true believer in the one God, with this belief in a single god evolving into the monotheism that underlies Judaism, Christianity and Islam. Abraham's tribe called themselves 'B'nei Israel' (the people or tribe of Israel), subsequently known as the **Israelites** and now the **Jews**. Archaeology, plus various literary archives that have emerged from Bronze-Age Syria and

Mesopotamia, has allowed a rough dating of the Patriarchs (Abraham, his son Isaac, and grandson Jacob) to the first half of the second millennium BCE, with Abraham's purchase of the Cave of Machpelah in Hebron usually dated to around 1650 BCE.

Exodus

The spread of famine throughout Canaan saw Abraham's grandson Jacob and his twelve sons and their families establish themselves to the east of the Nile delta in Egypt. The reproductive rate of the Israelite community in Egypt was such that the new pharaoh, fearing that they may soon out-number his own subjects, had the Israelite community enslaved and pressed into forced labour. There is considerable evidence, too, that a sizeable Israelite population remained in Canaan during this period.

After some 400 years of enslavement in Egypt, according to the biblical narrative, **Moses** was called upon by God to lead his people out of slavery and back to the "promised land": the **Exodus**. It was during the 40 years of wandering in the Sinai desert that the Israelites received the Law of Moses (including the Ten Commandments) and, though the sojourn

Genealogy of the Patriarchs

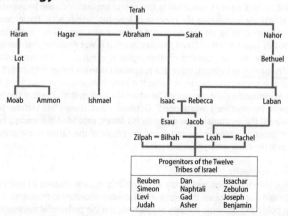

Progenitors of the Twelve Tribes of Israel		
Reuben	Dan	Issachar
Simeon	Naphtali	Zebulun
Levi	Gad	Joseph
Judah	Asher	Benjamin

in Egypt and then the desert involved only part of the Israelite community, it effectively forged them into a nation. As Johnson observes, "Before they went to Egypt, the Israelites were a small folk almost like any other, though they had a cherished promise of greatness. After they returned, they were a people with a purpose, a programme and a message to the world" (*A History of the Jews*, 1987).

In the 200 years or so that followed the Exodus, the various tribes of the Israelites abandoned their nomadic ways and set about conquering much of Canaan. The tribes functioned through an institution dating back to Abraham and Moses: prophetship (the '**judges**'), an essential part of the Israelite theocracy since this was the medium through which God communicated with his "chosen people"; prophets also became political and military leaders.

United Monarchy

Though the Israelites continued to have significant military success in dispossessing the Canaanites, the **Philistines** proved to be far more formidable opponents. In fact, it was in response to the threat of Philistine power that the Israelites turned to a new institution: kingship. It was the prophet/judge **Samuel** who eventually anointed **Saul** as king. The loose confederation of Israelite tribes now became joined under the United Monarchy.

Despite early successes against the Canaanites, Saul's period of kingship can hardly be considered a success, and within a year his Israelite army was comprehensively defeated by the Philistines at Mt Gilboa (and Saul himself killed). However, Saul's lasting legacy was a mercenary that he had recruited to their cause: **David**. It is beyond the scope of this brief introduction to delve exhaustively into David's background, though suffice to say the popular image of King David encountered today appears a long way from reality. As Johnson notes, though David's reign (1004-965 BCE) has been regarded by Jews as the 'golden age' for more than 2000 years now, "At the time ... his rule was always precarious ... His most dependable forces were not Israelites at all but his personal guards of foreign mercenaries ... The tribes [of Israel] were still separatist by instinct ... They resented the cost of David's campaigns ... and the apparatus of oriental kinship he introduced" (*ibid*).

Despite the revolts against his regime and the successional dispute that continued all through his reign, he was still a great king, carving out a huge empire through a combination of conquests and alliances. One of his conquests included Jerusalem, where David effectively legitimated the concept of kingship. Significantly, David designated his son **Solomon** to be his successor; not a warrior or a general but a scholar-judge. Perhaps this was a result of David's realization that it was essential that the Israelites were ruled by someone capable of discharging religious as well as temporal duties. Solomon appears to be much more of a pragmatist than his father, with one of his first acts upon assuming the throne, building the Temple at Jerusalem, effectively being a means of instituting royal absolutism "in which the king controls the sole shrine where God could be effectively worshipped" (Johnson, *ibid*). During his lifetime Solomon consolidated the territorial gains made by his father, expanded the trading networks with neighbouring economies, and raised the profile of the nation to the status of an equal with the other great regional powers.

Divided Monarchy

However, Solomon's reign was hardly an unqualified success. Towards its end there was considerable discontent over the high levels of taxation necessary to finance his ambitious foreign policy and domestic building programme, and the preferential treatment that he

Kings of Judah and Israel

THE UNITED MONARCHY
Saul c.1020-1004 BCE
David 1004-965
Solomon 965-928

JUDAH		ISRAEL	
Rehoboam	928-911	Jeroboam	928-907
Abijam	911-908	Nadab	907-906
Asa	908-867	Baasha	906-883
Jehoshaphat	867-846	Elah	883-882
Jehoram	846-843	Zimri	882
Ahaziah	843-842	Tibni	882-878
Athaliah	842-836	Omri	882-871
Joash	836-798	Ahab	871-852
Amaziah	798-769	Ahaziah	852-851
Uzziah	769-733	Jehoram	851-842
Jotham	758-743	Jehu	842-814
Ahaz	733-727	Jehoahaz	814-800
Hezekiah	727-698	Jehoash	800-784
Manasseh	698-642	Jeroboam	784-748
Amon	641-640	Zechariah	748/747
Josiah	639-609	Shallum	748/747
Jehoahaz	609	Menahem	747-737
Jehoiakim	608-598	Pekahiah	737-735
Jehoiachin	597	Pekah	735-733
Zedekiah	596-586	Hoshea	733-724

showed the members of his own tribe. Upon his death in 928 BCE, the northern tribes rejected the principle of hereditary succession through the family of David, and the monarchy divided on regional lines: a northern kingdom of **Israel** and a southern kingdom of **Judah**.

The Kingdom of Israel, comprising the ten northern tribes, survived a little over 200 years before being crushed by the expanding **Assyrian** empire in 722 BCE. Though many refugees fled from Israel to Judah, notably to Jerusalem, the majority of the ten tribes were sent into exile (and subsequent oblivion).

The Kingdom of Judah, based upon the tribes of Benjamin and Judah, fared a little better, lasting until 586 BCE when the invading **Babylonian** army (led by Nebuchadnezzar II) captured Jerusalem, razed the Temple, and sent the population into exile. This conquest marked the end of the First Jewish Commonwealth (and the end of the 'First Temple Period').

The Exile and Return
Though relatively brief (less than 50 years), the **Babylonian Exile** represents one of the most significant events in Jewish history. During the Exile the Jews never forgot their connection to the homeland, but more importantly this period raised the questions of the evolution of Judaism as a religion and the formation of a diaspora mentality amongst Jews.

Hasmoneans

Jonathon	152-142 BCE	Salome Alexandra	76-67
Simeon	142-134	Aristobulus II	67-63
John Hyrcanus	134-104	Hyrcanus II	63-40
Aristobulus	104-103	Matthias Antigonus	40-37
Alexander Jannaeus	103-76		

Paul Johnson's *A History of the Jews* (1987) is a very thorough examination of these issues. To paraphrase his thesis, the Exile saw the Jews first become disciplined into the regular practice of the given laws of their religion (for example circumcision; the Sabbath; and the study of the Law) as they sought to preserve their unique spiritual identity. The voluntary nature of the submission to the Law is significant.

The defeat of the Babylonian empire by the Persian Achaemenid dynasty in 539 BCE saw Cyrus the Great deliver a proclamation that allowed the Jews to return to their historic homeland. Though work began almost straight away on building a new Temple (and thus ushering in the '**Second Temple period**'), it took fully four waves of returnees before Jewish recolonization could be said to be successful. The fourth wave was led by Ezra the Scribe and the prominent Persian official Nehemiah in 445 BCE, and saw the re-emergence once more of Jerusalem as a major city. This time, however, it represented the centre of a new version of the Israelite faith that had evolved during the exile: **Judaism**. In the centuries subsequent to the Return, this new 'religion' recieved a legal and official sanction in the form of a written document: the Old Testament.

Further reading: Paul Johnson, *A History of the Jews*.

Early Hellenistic period

Alexander the Great's successful foreign campaigns of the early fourth century BCE saw Greek colonists arrive in great number in West Asia, bringing with them the concept of the *polis*, or Greek city-state. The effect on the population of the land that is now Israel ranged between two extremes. On the one hand, the process of Hellenization saw fundamentalist groups emerge within Judaism, often retreating into isolated communities to preserve their spiritual purity. On the other hand, many Jews embraced the Greek culture, seeking to rush through Hellenizing reforms. Perhaps such a reaction is inevitable when one race is preaching a message of universal monotheism and the other the notion of universalist culture. Inevitably, the two competing cultures were to clash.

Hasmonean Dynasty

The emerging conflict was brought to a head during the reign of the Seleucid king Antiochus IV Epiphanes (the **Seleucids** being Alexander's Syrian-based successors, as opposed to the Egypt-based successors, the **Ptolemies**). His Hellenizing reforms effectively sought to abolish Mosaic law and turn the Temple into an interdenominational place of worship. The spark that lit the fire of revolt occurred in Modi'im, a small town in the Judean foothills, with members of the priestly Hasmonean family leading the successful uprising which became known as the **Maccabean Revolt**. By 152 BCE the Seleucids had recognized

Herodian dynasty

Herod (the Great)	37-4 BCE	Philip	4 BCE-34 CE
Archelaus	4 BCE-6 CE	Herod Agrippa I	37-44 CE
Herod Antipas	4 BCE-39 CE	Agrippa II	53-100 CE (?)

the head of the Hasmonean family, Jonathon, as high priest. His successor, Simeon (Simon Maccabee) became both high priest and ruler; the Jews were once more ruled by a Jew.

Summarizing the **Hasmonean** dynasty, Johnson suggests that "They began as the avengers of martyrs; they ended as religious oppressors themselves. They came to power at the head of an eager guerilla band; they ended surrounded by mercenaries. Their kingdom, founded on faith, dissolved in impiety" (*ibid*). So what went wrong? In many ways the Hasmoneans raised many of the old dichotomies that had been a feature of David's rule, notably the question of religion and temporal power. Indeed, this was perhaps inevitable when John Hyrcanus revived the concept of rule through kingship. He was also on a mission, divinely inspired as he believed, to restore the Davidic kingdom, and like his role model he did it by creating a large mercenary army. His son Alexander Jannaeus continued the policy of expansion and forced conversion, though unlike his father whose reputation remained relatively untarnished, Alexander Jannaeus is remembered as a bully and despot who split rather than united the Jewish people.

By the time of Alexander Jannaeus' death, the **Romans** had established themselves as the successors to the Seleucid empire in the region and, following the successful campaign of the Roman governor of Syria **Pompey** in 63 BCE, Judea effectively became a Roman client-state. Jewish efforts to reassert their independence under Hyrcanus II were ultimately futile, and by 37 BCE the Romans had appointed a new King of Judea: **Herod the Great**. The Jews were not to become fully independent again in the Land of Israel for another 2000 years.

Roman period

Early Roman period

In many respects the Early Roman period (37 BCE-132 CE) is the most interesting era in the history of this land. It saw the Temple rebuilt and destroyed, the coming of a man known as Jesus Christ, and two major Jewish revolts against Roman rule.

Despite rebuilding the Temple in Jerusalem into one of the most magnificent structures of its time, Herod's Idumean background and admiration for Greco-Roman culture meant that his Jewishness was always open to question amongst his subjects. Yet despite being a puppet-king of the Romans, Herod enjoyed real executive power in domestic affairs and was effectively one of the most powerful monarchs in the region. A summary of his rule produces many contradictions: a ruthless barbarian but brilliant politician; an admirer of Solomon (his idol) but an instigator of Hellenizing reforms; the consummate diplomat with more than a touch of insanity. Herod's successors generally proved incapable of following his act (perhaps unsurprisingly), and by 44 CE the province was under direct Roman rule.

First Jewish Revolt

In 66 CE the Jews rose up in open revolt against Rome. The causes of this uprising were many and complex: Johnson suggests that the revolt "should be seen not just as a rising by a colonized people, inspired by religious nationalism, but as a racial and cultural conflict between Jews and Greeks" (*ibid*). Though the Greeks had submitted physically to the Roman military machine, they had in fact taken it over intellectually, with Greek culture effectively being the cornerstone of the Roman empire. Thus, the First Jewish Revolt was effectively a re-run of the Maccabean uprising that had begun two centuries earlier.

The story of the First Jewish Revolt is graphically told through the writings of Josephus, despite his unreliability as a historian (see 'Further Reading' below). Though the revolt lasted the best part of seven years, only concluding with the mass suicide of the Jewish Zealots holding out at Masada, it was effectively over in 70 CE when the Romans took Jerusalem and destroyed the Temple.

Bar Kokhba Revolt

The Second Jewish Revolt against Rome took place from 132 to 135 CE, led by the charismatic **Simon bar Kokhba**. Inevitably the might of the Roman empire prevailed and recriminations were harsh. Jerusalem was effectively levelled and refounded as '**Aelia Capitolina**' along the lines of a Greek polis, standing as the capital of the new Roman province of Filistina ('Palestine', derived from the word 'Philistine').

Late Roman period

Many of the Jews who survived the revolt were either sold or forced into exile, marking another key stage in the diaspora experience. The failure of the revolts of 66-73 CE and 132-135 CE had two significant consequences: firstly it led to the final separation from Judaism of a nascent reform movement that ultimately manifested itself in the doctrine of Christianity; and secondly it led to a fundamental change in the nature and practice of Judaism itself. In fact, it was this period of introspection, in which study of the religious texts replaced attempts to assert Jewish independence through nationalist uprisings, that perhaps ensured the survival of the Jews as a distinct race. The next couple of hundred years saw the formation of the Sanhedrin, or supreme legislative and judicial body of the Jews, the completion of the Mishnah (the first written compilation of the Oral Law) and the Talmud (the commentary on Jewish law and lore), thus effectively enlarging the Torah from a religious text into a logical and consistent code of moral theology and community law.

Further reading: Josephus, *The Jewish War*; Paul Johnson, *A History of the Jews*.

Byzantine period

Byzantine rule

The conversion of the Roman emperor **Constantine the Great** to Christianity in 313 CE, and his unification of the West and East empires in 324 CE, brought Christian Byzantine rule to Palestine. Churches were established on the key holy sites, notably in Jerusalem, Bethlehem and the Galilee, accompanied by a phenomenon that has continued to sustain the economy to this day: religious tourism. Large Christian communities developed primarily as a result of pagan converts, and the population of the land may well have become predominantly Christian. Christian rule saw Jewish communities have many of their privileges withdrawn, such as the right to hold state office, serve in the army, proselytize or inter-marry with Christians. Such discriminations had their origin in the charge of deicide levelled against the Jewish people as a whole (for having crucified

Jesus), though the idea that the Jews were somehow part of 'God's great plan' prevented them from being ethnically cleansed. Instead their communities were marginalized from mainstream life.

By the early seventh century CE, the Byzantine empire was in an advanced state of decline, exacerbated by early splits within the Church. The Persians, assisted by the Jews, invaded in 614 CE, destroying numerous Christian places of worship and massacring Christian communities. Though the Byzantine army rallied to expel the Persians in 629 CE (and take their revenge on the Jews), the empire was tottering precariously on its last legs.

The Arabs and the spread of Islam

Early Arab period
Significantly, the same year that the Byzantine army expelled the Persians, **Mohammad** conquered Mecca. Just two years after his death, the Arab army comprehensively defeated the Byzantines at the Battle of Yarmuk, and by 638 CE the whole of Palestine was in Muslim hands.

The status of the non-Muslim communities in Palestine were determined by the Islamic concept of *dhimmis*, whereby Jews and Christians were considered to be inferior, having received but failed to adhere to God's law, but nevertheless entitled to protection upon payment of a special tax known as jizya. Jews were treated better by the Muslims than they had been under the Byzantine Christians, whilst the Christians felt particularly aggrieved at having been 'reduced' to the same status as Jews.

As with the Christian church before it, Islam became riven by disputes, in this case over the succession of the Caliphate. The four Orthodox Caliphs were succeeded in 661 CE by the **Umayyads**, who in turn were succeeded by the **Abbasids**, with the capital being shifted from Damascus to Baghdad. Around 975 CE the **Fatimids**, who had conquered Egypt some six years earlier, came to power in Palestine. Christian pilgrims continued to visit the Holy Land throughout this period, though this all changed under the second Fatimid Caliph **al-Hakim**, who systematically persecuted the non-Muslim population of Palestine, particularly the Christians. This persecution culminated in his destruction of the central shrine in Christendom, the Church of the Holy Sepulchre. The **Seljuk Turks**, who had come to power in the region in 1055, continued where al-Hakim had left off, generally harassing Christian pilgrims to the Holy Land and eventually slamming the gates of Jerusalem firmly shut. Such a provocation put the Muslim world on a collision course with Christian Europe. Although the Seljuk Turks were defeated by the Fatimids, it was too late: the Christian armies were on their way.

Battle for the Holy Land

The Crusades
In 1095 at the Council of Clermont, Pope Urban II called upon all Christians to take up arms to recover the holy places from the infidels. Four years later, at midday on 15 July 1099, the **Crusaders** eventually captured Jerusalem, slaughtering most of its Muslim and Jewish inhabitants in the process. Godfrey de Bouillon, who led the campaign, declared himself 'Protector of the Holy Sepulchre', to be replaced upon his death one year later by his brother Baldwin, who crowned himself king of Jerusalem.

During the 12th-century CE Crusader expansion across the Holy Land, power was mainly confined to a series of isolated castles and fortified cities. The securing of main routes, however, allowed the Christian pilgrimage trade to flourish in a way that Jerusalem hoteliers can only dream about today.

The Crusades

First Crusade	1095-1099	Fifth Crusade	1217-1221
Second Crusade	1147-1149	Sixth Crusade	1288-1229
Third Crusade	1189-1192	Seventh Crusade	1248-1254
Fourth Crusade	1202-1204	Eighth Crusade	1270

Of course the Crusader kingdom was in reality a house of cards, riven by internal factional fighting, and it can be of little surprise that the Crusaders were eventually defeated and driven from the Holy Land by **Salah al-Din**, at the Horns of Hittim in 1187 (see page 608). A series of Crusades throughout the rest of the 12th and 13th centuries saw the Crusaders regain a measure of control over the Holy Land, though again their influence was confined to a network of fortified castles. Eventually, in 1291, the Crusaders were finally driven from the Holy Land by the Mamluks.

Mamluk period

A dynasty arising from freed slaves of Turkish or Circassian origin, the **Mamluks** came to power in Egypt in 1250, though a rival elite based itself in Damascus. Palestine was effectively a province administered from the latter, though Jerusalem was considered to be a separate entity under the jurisdiction of Cairo, where the sultan was charged with protecting the Islamic holy places. A notable feature of the Mamluk period was a large influx of Jewish immigrants, a result of their mass expulsion from Spain and Portugal in 1492.

Ottoman Empire

Ottoman rule

The defeat of the Mamluks in 1516 by the **Ottoman Turks** saw Palestine come under Ottoman rule for the next four centuries. Palestine never constituted a political administrative unit in its own right, but was divided into districts known as *sanjaks* and incorporated into a province (*vilayet*) of greater Syria that was ruled from Damascus. After 1841 it was further divided, with the northern section going to the *vilayet* of Beirut. The *sanjak* of Jerusalem remained important as a source of revenue through levying taxes on pilgrims. The Islamic *dhimmis* system applied to non-Muslims, and it is fairly safe to say that Jews in particular were afforded better protection by the Ottomans than their brethren in medieval and early modern Europe.

However, unsupervised Ottoman officials often lined their own pockets with exorbitant tax demands, and the *Tanzimat* laws passed in Istanbul in 1858 allowed land in Palestine to pass into private ownership. Wealthy families acquired huge properties, with the result that tenant farmers now became share-croppers, and heavily indebted to absentee landlords.

Palestine in the 19th century

The importance of finding an accurate picture of Palestine under the Ottomans (and in the 19th century in particular) will soon become apparent. Pick up any pro-Israeli or Zionist account of history and a familiar pattern emerges. The references are to a land "brought to a state of widespread neglect", bedevilled by "capricious" taxation and "absentee landlords", with the land "denuded of trees" and where "swamp and desert

Ottoman Palestine & Syria, 1910

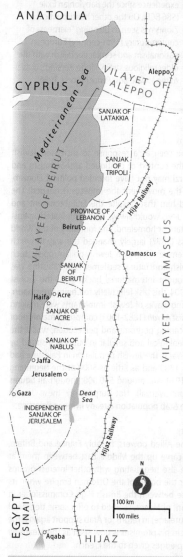

ANATOLIA

CYPRUS

Mediterranean Sea

VILAYET OF ALEPPO

Aleppo

SANJAK OF LATAKKIA

SANJAK OF TRIPOLI

Hijaz Railway

VILAYET OF BEIRUT

PROVINCE OF LEBANON

Beirut

Damascus

VILAYET OF DAMASCUS

SANJAK OF BEIRUT

Haifa
Acre
SANJAK OF ACRE

SANJAK OF NABLUS

Jaffa

Jerusalem

Gaza

Dead Sea

INDEPENDENT SANJAK OF JERUSALEM

Hijaz Railway

EGYPT (SINAI)

Aqaba

HIJAZ

N

100 km
100 miles

encroached on agricultural land" (*Facts About Israel*, Israel Information Centre, 1995). Accounts of travels in the region are trotted out (Chateaubriand, Mark Twain, Lamartine, Nerval, Disraeli, etc), all seeming to confirm this picture of a land in decline. The purpose of course is to present an image that fits the popular Zionist slogan of the time, "A land without people for a people without a land."

Of course, such a sentiment ignores one indisputable point: the land here was already home to a significant Arab population. As the Palestinian intellectual Edward W. Said observes, "No matter how backward, uncivilized, and silent they were, the Palestinian Arabs were on the land" (*The Question of Palestine*, 1979), with Said also pointing out that the 19th-century travellers that are so often quoted by the Zionists all carry accounts of the Arab inhabitants here. The question of whether the 19th-century Arabs had any sense of national identity, whether they thought of themselves as Palestinians, is also a starting point for debate. As late as 1969 Israeli Prime Minister Golda Meir was asserting that the Palestinians "did not exist", whilst Yitzhak Rabin's usual expression was "the so-called Palestinians". In many ways the argument is irrelevant as long as it is recognized that the land (whether you call it 'Palestine' or not) was overwhelmingly occupied by Arabs when the early Jewish Zionists began to arrive in the late 19th century. In fact, it would not be far from the truth to suggest that Palestinian Arab nationalism and identity were direct products of the perceived threat of Jewish immigration. But, as Johnson observes, the Arabs rather missed the boat (*A History of the Jews*, 1987). The Jews' head start was to prove catastrophic for the Palestinians.

Further reading: Edward W. Said, *The Question of Palestine*; Samuel Katz, *Battleground: Facts and Fantasy in Palestine*.

Zionism

The term 'Zionism' derives from the word 'Zion', a synonym for the Land of Israel that acknowledges Jewish attachment to this particular piece of land.

Whilst Zionism implies the redemption of the Jewish people in their ancestral homeland, some identify a distinction between spiritual Zionism and political Zionism. The former is seen as an inherent part of Jewish existence that has underpinned the Jewish Diaspora experience since the Babylonian Exile (586 BCE). On the other hand, political Zionism is seen as blending "elements of contemporary [19th-century] European nationalism and secular liberalism with the older religious strain" (Joffe, *Keesing's Guide to the Middle-East Peace Process*, 1996).

Zionism

European Jewry and the rise of Zionism

Whilst Palestinian Arab nationalism may be seen as a response to increased Jewish immigration, political Zionism emerged in the context of continued anti-Semitism and persecution of Jews in Europe. **Theodor Herzl** may not have founded political Zionism, but it was without doubt Herzl who gave the movement the impetus it needed. The infamous Dreyfus trial in France convinced him that despite the Enlightenment and attempts to integrate into European society, Jews would always be discriminated against and persecuted unless they had their own state or homeland. The founding of the World Zionist Organization at the Zionist Congress (1897) largely changed the way in which a 'return to Zion' was approached. The system of relying on Jewish philantropists such as the Rothschilds to support fledgling Jewish agricultural settlements in Palestine was supplemented by political lobbying that sought international backing for the Zionist cause. Following Herzl's untimely death in 1904, this task fell chiefly to **Chaim Weizmann**.

Away from the capitals of Europe, increasing waves of Jewish immigrants were making Aliyah (literally 'going up') to Palestine. The *First Aliyah* (1882-1903) comprised mainly poor farmers from Russia and eastern Europe escaping pogroms and persecution, whilst the *Second Aliyah* (1904-14) was much more ideological and secular in outlook, inspired by political Zionism. By the outbreak of World War II, the Jewish population in Palestine had risen to around 85,000, from just 24,000 in 1880 and as little as 5000 at the beginning of Ottoman rule. (The Arab population in 1914 was around 500,000; though all figures concerning the Arab:Jew ratio remain controversial). Not surprisingly these Jewish immigrants soon came into conflict with the Arab population already living in Palestine.

World War I and the peace settlements

No sooner had World War I begun than the Allied powers, notably France and Britain, began planning how they were going to carve up the Middle East between them at the conclusion of the war. The British were also negotiating with other interest groups so as to be in a better position to pick over the bones of the Ottoman Empire when its inevitable defeat came. The correspondence between the British High Commissioner in Cairo, Sir Henry McMahon, and Husayn, Sharif of Mecca, seemed to offer some degree of 'independence' to the Arabs (under British tutelage) in return for Arab support against the Ottomans. McMahon's failure to be specific in his promises is now seen as the means by which the British could avoid contradicting pledges given to the French.

The Balfour Declaration: Bob's your uncle

Here's one for trivia fans: Arthur Balfour (he of the 'Declaration') is the source of the English expression "Bob's your uncle" (implying that a simple action can achieve something rather easily). The saying originated in 1886 when British Prime Minister Lord Salisbury (first name Robert, or Bob) appointed Balfour to a senior government post. Popular lore suggests that Balfour received this post because he was Salisbury's nephew; ie Bob was his uncle!

Meantime, in London, Chaim Weizmann was lobbying hard on behalf of the Zionists. The eventual outcome was the **Balfour Declaration** of 2 November 1917: "His Majesty's Government view with favour the establishment in Palestine of a national home for Jewish people, and will use their best endeavours to facilitate the achievement of this object, it being clearly understood that nothing shall be done which may prejudice the civil and religious rights of existing non-Jewish communities in Palestine, or the rights and political status enjoyed by Jews in any other country." Whole books have been written about the Balfour Declaration, with some suggesting that it was just another example of British wartime expediency: it was seen as an attempt to keep post-revolutionary Russia in the war (with Jews seen as being influential amongst the Bolsheviks), or as an appeal to American Jewry to back US involvement in World War I. Zionists saw the Balfour Declaration as a recognition of Britain's moral obligation to the Jews, thus enabling them to claim betrayal when the British reversed their policy on Palestine with the issue of the 1939 White Paper (see page 706). Perhaps the best summary can be left to Johnson: "The Allies, for their part, issued during the war a lot of post-dated cheques to countless nationalities whose support they needed. When the peace came some of the cheques bounced and the Arabs, in particular, found that they had been handed a stumer" (*A History of the Jews*, 1987).

Further reading Walter Laquer, *A History of Zionism*; Edward W. Said, *The Question of Palestine*; Charles D. Smith, *Palestine and the Arab-Israeli Conflict*; Shlomo Avineri, *The Making of Modern Zionism: The Intellectual Origins of the Jewish State*; Ibrahim Abu-Lughod, *Transformation of Palestine*; Walid Khalidi, *From Haven to Conquest: Readings in Zionism and the Palestine Problem until 1948*; Maxime Rodinson, *Israel: A Colonial-Settler State?*

British Mandate

Jewish and Arab resistance to the British Mandate

Ottoman rule in Palestine was effectively brought to an end in December 1917 when General Edmund Allenby, at the head of the British forces, marched into Jerusalem. The conclusion of World War I saw a whole host of conferences at which the post-war territorial carve-up began. The San Remo Conference of 1920 granted the British the 'Mandate' for Palestine (confirmed by the League of Nations in 1922) but, though the **Mandate for Palestine** included the Balfour Declaration in its preamble, it was open to interpretation and seemed to promise the same thing to Jews and Arabs alike. Later that same year the area of Transjordan to the east of the Jordan River (now Jordan) was exempted from the provisions given in the Balfour Declaration, making it a separate entity within the Mandate and effectively banning Jewish settlement there.

The period between the two World Wars saw three further major influxes of Jews into Palestine. The *Third Aliyah* (1919-1923) saw some 35,000 or so Jews arrive from eastern Europe (notably Russia), many of whom went on to establish the kibbutz and moshav communal system. The Fourth Aliyah (1924-1928) brought around 60,000 new immigrants mainly from Poland; many from this influx were artisans and middle-class immigrants who settled in towns where they established small businesses and light industry. The Fifth Aliyah (1929-1939) reflected sinister developments in Europe, with some 165,000 immigrants, mainly from the academic and professional classes, escaping the rise of Hitler and Nazi power.

Fears amongst the Arab majority of the 'Jews taking over' were manifested in a number of ways, though an increasingly common feature of the 1920s was the series of physical attacks on individual Jews or isolated Jewish communities. These attacks culminated in the 'riots' of 1929, when the attacks on the Jewish communities of Safed, Jerusalem and notably Hebron can be described as effectively being pogroms. The immediate effect of the 1929 'riots' upon the Arabs was the lost chance to be represented politically in the Mandate structure (in which they were already discriminated against, in spite of their numerical superiority). Despite the clear sympathies towards the Palestinian Arabs of the British military officials in Palestine, Arabs were not represented in government posts in ratio to their population size, Jewish salaries were higher for identical posts and Jews had greater access to officials in high places. Arab unemployment was also exacerbated by the problem of a growing landless class, resulting from Arab land sales and Jewish land purchases. The classic colonial-style exploitation of Palestine worked totally to the disadvantage of Arab smallholders, who had to sell increasing amounts of their land just to survive.

Peel Partition Plan and the 1939 White Paper

Arab opposition to Jewish expansion in Palestine led in 1936 to a call to 'revolt' by the Higher Arab Committee. This 'revolt' took many forms including a general strike by all Arab workers and government officials (not particularly effective since Arab labour was simply replaced by Jewish labour), a boycott of Jewish goods and sales to Jews, plus attacks on Jews and Jewish settlements and British forces.

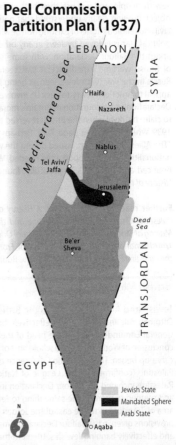

Peel Commission Partition Plan (1937)

LEBANON

SYRIA

Mediterranean Sea

Haifa

Nazareth

Nablus

Tel Aviv/
Jaffa

Jerusalem

Dead
Sea

Be'er
Sheva

TRANSJORDAN

EGYPT

N

Jewish State
Mandated Sphere
Arab State

Aqaba

In many ways the 'revolt' was a failure, even counter-productive, though it did force the British to face the unpalatable truth that the mandate was not working. The British response was the **Peel Commission**, which in 1937 presented a partition plan that envisaged an Arab State, a Jewish State and a (British) Mandated Sphere that would include Jerusalem and a corridor to the port at Jaffa (see map below). The Jewish leadership accepted the idea of partition, but the Arabs were vehemently opposed to it. There can be little doubt that the Jewish acceptance was based upon the assumption that the borders of the Jewish state would be expanded at some later date (as Ben-Gurion's speech to the World Zionist Congress that year makes clear). However, it is important to examine the reasons for the Arab rejection: though the Jewish state would only be allotted 20% of Palestine, it effectively included almost all of the most fertile agricultural land, and would require the 'evacuation' of some 250,000 Arabs from Galilee. And whilst the Arab state would be 90% Arab in ethnic composition, the proposed Jewish state would still feature a roughly 50-50 Arab-Jew population split.

The partition plan, however, was swiftly overtaken by events in Europe as the continent geared up for war. From 1939 onwards British policy in Palestine became inextricably linked to the strategic importance of the Middle East to the war effort. Thus, as Smith so succinctly puts it, "Resolving the Palestinian crisis in a manner favourable to the Arab population came to be seen as a means of acquiring the cooperation of the Arab world once the war began" (*ibid*). This was done by issuing a **White Paper** on 17 May 1939 that outlined future British policy on Palestine. Restrictions were to be placed upon Jewish immigration, whilst there was the promise of some sort of independent Arab Palestine within which a 'Jewish National Home' could be established. Not surprisingly, the Jews were devastated by this betrayal of the promises made in the Balfour Declaration (and subsequently the principles of the Mandate), and ever since the White Paper has been presented as "denying European Jewry a place of refuge from Nazi persecution" (*Facts About Israel*, 1995). The reaction of the Jewish community in Palestine was perhaps best summed up by David Ben-Gurion, who declared that "We will fight the war as if there were no White Paper, and the White Paper as if there were no war."

World War II and the Holocaust
World War II saw Nazi Germany's systematic attempt to destroy European Jewry. Some six million Jews, or two-thirds of the pre-war European Jews, were victims of the **Holocaust**, reducing the world's largest and most vibrant Jewish community to a remnant. (**NB** It is too difficult here to do justice to the Holocaust, the memory of its victims and survivors, and its impact on world Jewry, so it is highly recommended that you conduct some further reading of your own, see below.)

Further reading Paul Johnson, *A History of the Jews*; Martin Gilbert, *The Holocaust: The Jewish Tragedy*; *Auschwitz and the Allies*; *Atlas of the Holocaust*; Daniel Goldhagen, *Hitler's Willing Executioners*; Charles D. Smith, *Palestine and the Arab-Israeli Conflict*.

End of the Mandate
British policy in Palestine at the conclusion of World War II continued as before, with restrictions on Jewish immigration. Jewish underground groups continued to smuggle Jewish immigrants into the country whilst the British navy mounted a blockade. Some 85,000 Jews arrived clandestinely between 1945 and 1948, and British immigration policy resulted in the ridiculous (and tragic) situation in which those caught trying to

enter Palestine were interned in camps: a public relations disaster since many of those interned were former prisoners in Nazi death camps.

The British administration was also deeply affected by the increasingly violent opposition that it was meeting from the Jewish underground groups that had been established in the 1930s. Some restricted their targets to military personnel and positions, but others were less discriminating. A corollary today would perhaps be between Palestinian groups that targeted Israeli soldiers only, and those that targeted Israelis in general. Of course both groups are branded "terrorists" by Israel, though attempts to brand the Jewish underground groups of the 1930s and 1940s as terrorists gets the Israeli right-wingers crying "foul".

The general failure of British policy in Palestine, coupled with the inability to reconcile the conflicting demands of the two communities, led to Britain placing the problem before the newly created United Nations.

Partition

The 11-member United Nations Special Committee on Palestine (UNSCOP) toured Palestine for five weeks in 1947, fêted by the Zionists and boycotted by the Palestinian Arab leadership. Their conclusion was that the British Mandate should end, with the partition of Palestine into a Jewish State and an Arab State, with Jerusalem being internationalized (see map). At the time of the partition recommendation Arabs outnumbered Jews by two to one, with Jews owning 20% of the cultivable land and 6% of the total land area. On 29 November 1947 the UN General Assembly voted by 33 to 13 in favour of the UNSCOP partition plan (with 10 abstentions).

In the light of the subsequent Cold War, the timing of Israel's push for independence was remarkable. As Johnson observes, "If British evacuation had been postponed another year, the United States would have been far less anxious to see Israel created and Russia would almost certainly have been hostile. Hence the effect of the terror campaign on British policy was perhaps decisive to the entire enterprise. Israel slipped into existence through a fortuitous window in history which briefly opened for a few months in 1947-48. That too was luck: or providence" (*ibid*).

Arab-Israeli War 1948-1949

Of course, the UN vote on partition did not guarantee the creation of the Jewish state;

UN Partition Recommendation (Resolution 181) 1947

LEBANON

SYRIA

Mediterranean Sea

Haifa

Nazareth

Nablus

Tel Aviv/ Jaffa

Jerusalem

Dead Sea

Be'er Sheva

TRANSJORDAN

EGYPT

Aqaba

Jewish State
International Zone
Arab State

N

instead it triggered an increase in armed conflict as the Palestinian Arabs attempted to prevent the Jewish state coming into being, whilst Jews sought to consolidate their hold on the land allocated to them. It is difficult to find impartial sources on the events that followed, though Smith summarizes as follows: "Terror and atrocities were committed by both sides, with little regard for non-combatants or women and children when avenging an attack … The British were accused by both sides of favouring the other" (*ibid*).

On the eve of the termination of the British Mandate, on 14 May 1948, David Ben-Gurion proclaimed the **State of Israel**. The declaration brought de facto recognition from the US, *de jure* recognition from the Soviet Union, and prompted the regular armies of Egypt, Syria, Jordan, Lebanon and Iraq to invade with the intent of "driving the Jews into the sea". Tthe war fell into two distinct phases. From May 1948 until mid-June 1948 the Israelis tenaciously (but precariously) hung on to the areas granted to them under the UN partition plan, though the millennia-old Jewish presence in the Old City of Jerusalem was to end. The brief truce between 11 June and 6 July, despite the supposed arms embargo, saw the Israelis receive huge new stockpiles of heavy weaponry. Despite considerable numerical reinforcements to the Arab armies, the tide of the war had been turned and the Israelis made considerable advances before an Armistice was agreed in the second half of 1949. The West Bank (including part of Jerusalem) was subsequently annexed by King Abdullah of Jordan in a move recognized only by Britain and Pakistan.

Of course one of the key unresolved consequences of Israel's independence is the fate that befell the Palestinian Arabs: what they term as Al-Naqba or 'The Catastrophe'. Indeed, one of the most controversial aspects of the war was the way in which somewhere in the region of 500,000 to 725,000 (the figures are disputed) Arabs left or were driven out of the land that became the State of Israel (see 'Deir Yassin' box on page 710, for example).

For the two opposing perspectives of this period, readers can compare the case presented in Edward W Said's *The Question of Palestine* with the Israeli viewpoint in Benjamin Netanyahu's *A Place Among the Nations* or Samuel Katz's *Battleground: Facts and Fantasy in Palestine*. If nothing else, it will show just how far apart the two positions are.

Further reading Chaim Herzog, *The Arab-Israeli Wars*; Paul Johnson, *A History of the Jews*; Edward Tivnan, *The Lobby: Jewish Political Power and American Foreign Policy*; John Snetsinger, Truman, *The Jewish Vote and the Creation of Israel*; Edward W Said, *The Question of Palestine*.

Israel's early years

Nation building
Jewish immigration remained (as today) a priority, formalized in the passing of the Law of Return in 1950 (see page 736). Many of these new arrivals (up to 600,000) arrived in Israel as a result of mounting discrimination and insecurity in Muslim countries in which they had resided for generations. Infrastructural development was a major challenge, as was the expansion of the agricultural and industrial base, particularly within the constraints of bellicose and belligerent neighbours. There was also the not unimportant question of what sort of state Israel should be: a state for Jews or a Jewish state? (See the Modern Israel' section on page 727).

The Suez Crisis
One of the first challenges to the fledgling Israeli state came in the so-called Suez Crisis of 1956. Of the four states participating in the events following Nasser's nationalizing of

Deir Yassin

A key event in the fighting of 1947-1949 occurred at Deir Yassin, a small Arab village strategically located on the road to Tel Aviv to the west of Jerusalem. The attack on the village was undertaken by the Irgun and Stern Gang, though such was the resistance from the villagers that 'regular' Palmach forces had to be summoned. What happened next is a source of considerable controversy. The consensus of opinion is that the Jewish forces subsequently massacred up to 250 Arab villagers (the figures are still disputed), engaging in acts of rape and torture during the process (see for example Collins and Lapierre, *O Jerusalem*; Paul Johnson, *A History of the Jews*, both of whom include detailed accounts that they say were exhaustively researched). An alternative view is presented in Samuel

Katz's *Battleground: Facts and Fantasy in Palestine*. He claims that: "The Arab leaders seized on the opportunity to tell an utterly fantastic story of a 'massacre', which was disseminated throughout the world by all the arms of British propaganda. The accepted 'orthodox' version to this day, it has served enemies of Israel and anti-Semites faithfully." Katz's message is clear: to criticize Israel is to be anti-Israel, and to be anti-Israel is to be anti-Semitic.

The significance of Deir Yassin is the impact it had on the war. Whether the massacre happened or not, the threat of 'further Deir Yassins' was no doubt a major factor in the resulting flow of Palestinian refugees into neighbouring states. Again, whether the refugees were encouraged to flee by the Jews or by Arab leaders remains a bitter point of debate.

the Suez Canal, there were two winners and two losers. Britain confirmed that it was no longer a dominant imperial power in the Middle East, with the French invasion ending in fiasco. Ironically, despite the military defeat, Nasser emerged as a hero in the Arab world (though this was to be short-lived). The greatest beneficiary of the Suez Crisis was Israel. It is now claimed that Israel was acting in response to Egyptian provocation in closing the Straits of Tiran to Israeli shipping, though Ben-Gurion's comments to the French and British during the planning stages of the operation suggest that he had greater designs involving Israeli territorial gains in Lebanon, the West Bank and the Sinai (see Michael Bar Zohar's 1978 biography *Ben-Gurion*). By the end of the Suez campaign Israel controlled the entire Sinai peninsula and Gaza Strip, though they were forced to withdraw under US pressure, while still obtaining a commitment from Egypt to allow free navigation in the Gulf of Aqaba/Eilat).

Six Day War of 1967

The Six Day War of 1967 is often depicted as an act of Israeli aggression since they technically 'fired the first shot', though this is stretching the truth somewhat. With Egypt having ordered the UN observers out of Sinai and massed their troops on the border (and then closed the Straits of Tiran to Israeli shipping), they may be said to have already been in a state of war with Israel. However, the Israeli politicians and military planners appear to have looked favourably upon the prospects of war.

Israel opted to make a pre-emptive strike against Egypt. At 0745 on 5 June 1967 the Israeli air-force undertook a mission that was to decide the course of the war. Within three hours, 309 out of Egypt's 340 serviceable combat aircraft had been destroyed, largely on the ground. Syria, Jordan and Iraq, meanwhile, believing the reports of crushing victories for Egypt emanating out of Cairo, launched their own attacks on Israel's eastern flank. By the end of 5 June, the entire Jordanian air force had been wiped out, along with two-thirds of Syria's military aircraft.

Though a series of bitter infantry, artillery and tank battles were to follow, the outcome of the war was almost certainly settled by Israel's early attainment of complete aerial supremacy. Within six days Israel had defeated the combined might of the Arab armies. By the time the UN-brokered ceasefire was imposed on 10 June, Israeli controlled the whole of the Sinai peninsula, the Gaza Strip, the entire West Bank (including Jerusalem) and the Golan Heights.

Further reading Chaim Herzog, *The Arab-Israeli Wars*.

Israel after the Six Day War

Perhaps more important than the military details of the war itself is the effect that the war had not just on Israel and her Middle East neighbours, but on world Jewry. To appreciate the euphoria that the victory created in the Jewish world it is necessary to recall the mood in Israel prior to the war, when many were privately preparing for another Holocaust. Indeed, such was the 'intoxication' that this transformation from vulnerability to strength brought, that many considered it to be divinely inspired. A new, radical nationalist variant of religious Zionism emerged after Israel's acquisition of the West Bank, the heart of the biblical Land of Israel, with groups claiming that it was an obligation to settle there if the Jews were to strive for redemption. The new territories that Israel now occupied afforded increased security against future attack, though they came with a price: a large and resentful Palestinian population, many of whom were themselves refugees from the earlier war of 1947-49. Subsequent negotiations on the status of territories occupied by Israel since 1967 must be seen within the context of US-Soviet superpower rivalries. The **UN Resolution 242** that sought to resolve this question is notoriously vague, but it has remained the basis for negotiations ever since. Israel tends to quote the lines that refer to the "right to live in peace within secure and recognized boundaries free from threats or acts of force", whilst Palestinians emphasize the illegality under international law of conquering and settling territory through acts of war, highlighted in the resolution's call for "all parties to the conflict to withdraw from territories occupied by them after June 4 1967." It should also be noted that the draft version of this resolution referred to "the territories", with "the" being withdrawn from the final resolution at Israel's request. It has subsequently allowed a completely new interpretation of the resolution.

Ceasefire lines after Six-Day War

1 Golan Heights
2 West Bank
3 Gaza

War of Attrition

The ceasefire that concluded the Six Day War of 1967 effectively inaugurated a 'war of attrition' against Israel, with Arab countries maintaining their stance of "no recognition of Israel". In 1969 the **Palestinian Liberation Organization** (PLO) was relaunched under a charismatic new chairman, **Yasser Arafat**. The Palestinian National Charter was amended, calling for "armed struggle" to liberate Palestine and "liquidate the Zionist and imperialist presence", and guerrilla attacks were launched on Israel from neighbouring countries. Such attacks soon spread beyond the Middle East, including perhaps the most infamous terrorist incident of this period: the attack on Israeli athletes at the 1972 Munich Olympics, in which 11 Israelis died.

Yom Kippur War of 1973

The fragile ceasefire brokered between Israel and her Arab neighbours in 1967 was broken on 6 October 1973, when Egypt and Syria launched a surprise attack on Israel. The fact that the attack was timed to take place on Yom Kippur, the holiest day of the Jewish year, is usually presented as a double-blow to Israel since most reservists were off-duty. However, Israel's lack of preparedness is often attributed to the over-cockiness that emerged from the stunning victory of six years earlier. Chaim Herzog suggests that not only was Israeli intelligence assessment poor, but the Israeli military stubbornly assumed that "the unrealistic and unfavourable ratio of forces along the borders was adequate to hold any Egyptian or Syrian attack" (*The Arab-Israeli Wars*, 1984).

Unlike the Six Day War of 1967, this war was not an attempt to destroy the State of Israel (though had the opportunity arisen, there is no doubt that Syria and Egypt would have taken it), but an attempt to break the deadlock in the Arab-Israeli conflict before proceeding to a peace conference at which, it was hoped, the superpowers would pressurize Israel to return to her pre-1967 borders. Such a scenario would avoid forcing any Arab country to sign a formal peace treaty with Israel (thus granting her any recognition of legitimacy). Egypt and Syria's early successes in the 1973 war allowed them to claim victory, thus partially erasing the memory of the humiliation that they had suffered six years earlier, though both Arab states were relieved at the opportunity to accept the UN's ceasefire proposals on 22 October, as the Israelis had fought back to make a series of major gains. The subsequent **UN Security Council Resolution 338** called for direct talks based upon the principles of the earlier Resolution 242.

Camp David Accords

Likud returned to power at the 1977 elections, largely as a result of Sephardi and Mizrachi dissatisfaction with the Ashkenazi-dominated establishment.

It is ironic that the first full peace treaty signed between an Arab state and Israel should take place during the term of office of Israel's most reactionary prime minister, **Menachem Begin**. The **Camp David Accords** that US President Carter hosted in 1978 were perhaps more an indication of Egyptian President Sadat's desperation to sign a deal, and the American willingness to facilitate it, than Begin's desire for peace. Begin brought a new interpretation to Resolution 242, suggesting that it did not apply to the West Bank, and continually reminded anyone who would listen that the PLO was a Nazi organization, and even if they accepted 242 he would never deal with them. All references to 242's application to the West Bank were withdrawn, and thus Begin was able to sign a document that included the term "the legitimate rights of the Palestinian people" because he considered it to be meaningless in the light of Israel's guaranteed occupation of the region (Smith, *ibid*). Having been excluded from the negotiating process, the PLO (since 1974 recognized by the Arab world as the "sole legitimate representatives of the Palestinian people") rejected the plans for their future that were included within the Israel-

Egypt deal. Thus, when the peace treaty between Egypt and Israel was finally signed on 26 March 1979, only the proposals related to bilateral relations were implemented. The treaty worked on the principle of relinquishing territory for peace, with Israel agreeing to a phased withdrawal from the Sinai in return for Egypt's commitment to peace and the recognition of Israel's "right to exist". Whilst Begin and Sadat received the Nobel Peace Prize for their efforts, Egypt was expelled from the Arab League and Sadat subsequently assassinated (in 1981).

Israeli invasion of Lebanon, 1982

Israel presents its 1982 invasion of Lebanon as 'Operation Peace for Galilee', claiming that its desired aim was to stop once and for all the shelling and rocket attacks on Israel from PLO bases in southern Lebanon (where the PLO had effectively created a mini-state). Ironically, early 1982 was a relatively quiet year for PLO rocket attacks across the border, and thus Israel used the attempted murder of their ambassador to London on 3 June 1982 as the 'excuse' to invade three days later. Such was the scale of the invasion, however, that its planning must have begun long before the shooting in London. Israel was always to claim that 'Operation Peace for Galilee' was "not directed against the Lebanese or Palestinian peoples ... The terrorists are responsible for any civilian casualties since they were the ones who had placed their headquarters and installations in populated civilian areas" (Israeli press release, 21 June 1982). Yet, on 4 July the Israeli army cut off water and power supplies to West Beirut, ostensibly to put pressure on the PLO. When the UN Security Council condemned this action, Israel denied it, though it was later forced to retract this denial.

Most objective historians now believe that the purpose of 'Operation Peace for Galilee' was to terminate the PLO once and for all, and to install a pro-Israeli Christian government in Lebanon. Thus, the invasion proceeded all the way to Beirut. Begin's attempts to get some sort of peace treaty with Lebanon to secure Israel's northern border ignored one crucial point: there was no person or group in Lebanon capable of signing and implementing any such agreement.

Israel after the Camp David Accords (present de facto borders)

1 Golan Heights
2 West Bank
3 Gaza

Like many foreign armies before them (and after them), the Israelis found that it was easier to get into Lebanon than to get out. Indeed, it was not until 1985 that the Israeli army substantively withdrew, though they maintained a unilaterally declared 'security zone' of 1550 square km in southern Lebanon occupied by an undisclosed number of Israeli troops and the SLA, a proxy army, until 2000. In many ways, the invasion of Lebanon changed fundamentally the way many Israelis saw themselves, and the way Diaspora Jews viewed Israel. Between September 1982 and June 1983, 60 Israeli soldiers were imprisoned for refusing to do reserve duty in Lebanon, whilst the Peace Now movement was able to bring between 200,000 and 400,000 people on to the

The Sabra and Chatila massacres

Perhaps the most controversial of all the episodes in the 1982 invasion occurred after the PLO had been escorted out of Beirut: the massacres at the Sabra and Chatila camps. Ironically, as Fisk observes, most of the civilians of west Beirut, including these camps' residents, "would have been as happy as the Israelis to see the PLO leave, providing the guerrillas were not replaced by Phalangist militiamen from east Beirut" (*ibid*). Yet this is exactly what happened.

Again, compare the reporting of this atrocity: "This horrifying massacre was not perpetrated by Israeli forces but by Arabs … Israeli forces did not participate in the massacre, did not enable it, did not even know about it" (Netanyahu, *ibid*); "The guilty were certainly Christian militiamen … but the Israelis were also guilty. If the Israelis had not taken part in the killings, they had certainly sent the militia into the camp. They had trained them, given them uniforms, handed them US army rations and Israeli medical equipment. Then they had watched the murderers in the camps, they had given them military assistance – the Israeli air force had dropped all those flares to help the men who were murdering the inhabitants of Sabra and Chatila – and they had established military liaison with the murderers in the camps" (Fisk, *ibid*); "The goyim are killing the goyim and they want to hang the Jews for it" (Menachem Begin to his Cabinet); "The Israeli soldiers did not see innocent civilians being massacred and they did not hear the screams of innocent children going to their graves. What they saw was a 'terrorist infestation' being 'mopped up' and 'terrorist nurses' scurrying about and 'terrorist teenagers' trying to defend them, and what they heard were 'terrorist women' screaming. In the Israeli psyche you don't come to the rescue of 'terrorists'. There is no such thing as 'terrorists' being massacred" (Thomas Friedman, who won a Pulitzer Prize for his reporting of the Sabra and Chatila massacres).

streets in opposition to the war in Lebanon. In the wider world many Diaspora Jews began to make a distinction between the wars that Israel had been forced to fight (1947-49, 1967, 1973) and this war that Israel had 'chosen' to fight.

Intifada

It is all too easy to ignore the significant strides that Israel made in the late 1980s in bringing the economy under control. However, Israel's rapid GDP growth and mastery of run-away hyper-inflation in this period is overshadowed by the next phase in her conflict with the Palestinians: the *intifada*. The *intifada* (literally 'shaking off' in Arabic) was in fact a "spontaneous eruption of hatred and frustration incited by a specific incident" (Smith, *ibid*), that is, a traffic accident in Gaza on 8 December 1987 that killed four Palestinians. However, the protest that followed soon took on a life force of its own, rapidly developing into a general uprising against Israel.

The effects of the *intifada* were manifold. Not only did it bring the Palestinian struggle back on to the world stage, it fundamentally altered the world's perception of the Palestinians. No longer were they seen as the plane-hijacking terrorists of the 1970s, but now they were the victims: stone-throwing children being shot by Israeli soldiers (though in the period 1987-1991 nearly as many Palestinians were killed by other Palestinians as 'collaborators', as were killed by the Israeli army). The more the Israelis imposed the 'iron fist' to crack down on the *intifada*, the more the image of Israel suffered. It was not just the international community who were bringing pressure on Israel to resolve the 'Palestinian issue'; Israelis themselves (notably on the 'left') began to question the price of holding on to the territories. The Israeli right, notably the settler movements, became more vocal in their determination to retain all of Eretz Yisrael whatever the cost, thus polarizing Israeli society even more.

With hindsight, the intifada can be seen as the catalyst for change that made the current peace process possible. One of the first people to recognize the need to come to some sort of accommodation with the Palestinians of the West Bank and Gaza Strip was Yitzhak Rabin, who was Minister of Defence at the height of the intifada.

Algiers Declaration, 1988
The seemingly moribund PLO was revitalized by the *intifada*. The Algiers Declaration of November 1988 represented a declaration of Palestinian statehood that envisaged a bi-national state, with negotiations to take place on the basis of Resolutions 242 and 338; effectively the PLO were going back to the 1947 UN partition plan (Resolution 181). Although recognition of Israel was implicit in this declaration it was not specified, and so Arafat was forced explicitly to renounce terrorism and recognize Israel at the United Nations. At the first attempt, he changed the speech that had been 'approved' by the Americans, and what he offered certainly did not meet US conditions for an opening of dialogue with the PLO. Fortunately for him he got a second chance, the following evening (14 December 1988), when he read from a speech 'approved' by the US, recognizing "the right of all parties in the Middle East conflict to exist in peace and security", and emphasizing that "we totally and absolutely renounce all forms of terrorism".

The US subsequently put pressure on Israel to negotiate with the Palestinians (but not necessarily the PLO), though many in Israel doubted the PLO's commitment to peace (pointing out that their National Covenant still called for the destruction of Israel). Nevertheless, Israeli prime minister Yitzhak Shamir put forward his own peace plan in April 1989 - one he knew would be unacceptable to the Palestinians. Thus, Israel would be able to claim that they were striving for peace, yet the Palestinians were rejecting the offer. However, the opportunity to break the log-jam in the Arab-Israeli conflict was in fact brought about by the perceived 'New World Order' that emerged from the Gulf War of 1991.

The Gulf War
Though diplomatically and morally on the side of the US-led coalition, Israel was requested to refrain from taking a proactive role in the military action against Iraq for fear of splitting the coalition. Thus, Israel had to sit by silently as Iraq rained Scud missiles down on its cities. The PLO appeared to have shot itself in the foot somewhat with Yasser Arafat seemingly supporting Iraq's stance, with the effect that most of Kuwait's Palestinian migrant worker population were expelled in the wake of the 'Allied' victory.

Further reading Robert Fisk, *Pity the Nation: Lebanon at War*; Thomas Friedman, *From Beirut to Jerusalem*; Chaim Herzog, *The Arab-Israeli Wars*; Andrew Gowers and Tony Walker, *Yasser Arafat and the Palestinian Revolution*; Zachary Lockman and Joel Beinin (editors), *Intifada: The Palestinian Uprising Against Israeli Occupation*; Don Peretz, *Intifada: The Palestinian Uprising*; Ze'ev Schiff and Ehud Ya'ari, *Intifada: The Palestinian Uprising – Israel's Third Front*; Robert Hunter, *The Palestinian Uprising: A War by Other Means*.

Madrid, Oslo and the Middle East peace process

At the conclusion of the Gulf War in 1991, US President Bush highlighted the need to resolve the Israeli-Palestinian question. US Secretary of State James Baker subsequently began a prolonged bout of 'shuttle diplomacy' between the various capitals of the Middle East, which led to a conference in Madrid. The price of Israeli participation appears to have been an agreement to allow them to 'vet' the Palestinian delegation, with no members of the PLO being admitted and the Palestinian delegation effectively coming under the 'umbrella' of the Jordanian team. The deadlock was broken in June 1992 by the election of a Labour government in Israel that had campaigned largely on a 'peace ticket'. Although the Madrid conference progressed through 10 rounds of talks (November 1991-July 1993), the newly elected Labour government realized that a new approach was needed. It was obvious that, despite the pretence, the Palestinian delegation at Madrid were in fact taking orders direct from the PLO in Tunis. Thus, despite contacts with the PLO still being a criminal offence in Israel, a direct channel of talks was initiated. The 'secret talks' began in January 1993 in a town close to Oslo, eventually 'going public' on 30 August 1993. These talks resulted in the **Declaration of Principles On Interim Self-Government Arrangements** (DOP, or 'Oslo I'), signed in Washington on 13 September 1993 following the famous handshake between Rabin and Arafat on the White House lawn. The DOP envisaged a three-stage process: i) immediate self-rule in Jericho and Gaza; ii) 'early empowerment' for Palestinians in the rest of the West Bank; and iii) an Interim Agreement on the West Bank and Gaza.

The DOP was in turn ratified by the UN, the PLO Central Council, and eventually the Israeli Knesset, though opposition remained strong. In February 1994 a right-wing Israeli extremist massacred Muslim worshippers in Hebron in an attempt to sabotage the fragile peace process, whilst *Hamas* responded with a series of suicide bomb attacks within Israel. The **Israeli-Palestinian Interim Agreement on the West Bank and Gaza Strip** ('Oslo II') was eventually thrashed out and signed in Washington on 28 September 1995. 'Oslo II' covered a multitude of issues, though its key issues were Israeli troop withdrawal, elections to a Palestinian Council, preventing terrorism, economic cooperation, plus other matters such as education, human rights, religious sites and the special status of Hebron. However, all the key sticking points (and potential flashpoints) were deferred to Final Status Talks. Such issues included the seemingly irreconcilable questions of refugees, settlers, water, borders and the future status of Jerusalem.

Further reading Lawrence Joffe, *Keesing's Guide to the Middle-East Peace Process*; Edward W Said, *Peace and Its Discontents; The Politics of Dispossession*.

Post-Oslo

With the ink barely dry on the 'Oslo II' deal, the whole peace process came to a shuddering halt with the murder of Yitzhak Rabin at the hands of a right-wing Jewish extremist. At the general election that followed Rabin's murder the Israeli electorate indicated their doubts about the peace process by narrowly returning the Likud bloc to power and **Benjamin Netanyahu** (nicknamed "Bibi" by Israelis) became the country's youngest prime minister. Netanyahu had always stressed his dissatisfaction with 'Oslo II', and sought to bring a very narrow interpretation to the agreements already signed. Meanwhile, the Clinton administration in the US, generally perceived to be the most pro-Israeli US government in history, perpetuated the charade of acting as the 'honest broker' in the 'peace process'.

In 1999, Labour's **Ehud Barak** (running under a 'One Israel' coalition ticket) won a landslide in elections, with a commitment to the peace process that was encouraging. However, the break-down of his coalition government meant Barak had to call early elections in 2001 and the resultant 'national unity' coalition headed by Ariel Sharon in turn broke down just two years later. The government that then formed under Sharon in 2003 was more right wing, with an emphasis on Israeli security and the 'fight against terror'. However, Sharon's process of unilateral disengagement from Gaza (in 2005) and from four settlements in the northern West Bank was more than some of the right-wing elements in the government could take, and thus Sharon formed the Kadima (Forward) party. Following a more liberal, centrist policy than the socialist Labor (Avodar) and right-wing Likud parties, Kadima won 29 seats in the 2006 parliamentary elections. Kadima held power until 2009, with Ehud Olmert taking over as Prime Minister when Sharon's medical problems became overwhelming (he remains in a coma after suffering a massive stroke). Since 2009, Netanyahu has been Prime Minister, for the second time, heading the Likud party. Policies have therefore been right-wing again, with the Jewish settlement programme in East Jerusalem and the West Bank continuing largely unabated, the peace process stalled and instances of disagreement between Israel and the Obama government in the US regarding how to move forward with peace negotiations.

Land and environment

Israel is a small country, measuring some 470 km north to south and 116 km at its widest east to west point. Within its present de facto boundaries it occupies 27,870 sq km (this figure includes East Jerusalem, 5,879 sq km of the West Bank, and 1,150 sq km of the Golan Heights). Within its de jure boundaries Israel occupies just 20,770 sq km, and in places is less than 15 km wide. It has a recognized land border with Egypt to the southwest, a recognized land border with Jordan to the southeast and east, a disputed border with Syria to the northeast (demarcated by a ceasefire line) and a recognized land border with Lebanon to the north.

Topography

Israel is characterized by four broad topographical features: a large arid and semi-arid zone to the south (the Negev), with three parallel strips running north to south above it: coastal plain, mountain spine, and the Jordan rift valley. More details of the regional landscape are given in the relevant chapters of this book.

Negev

The arid and semi-arid triangular wedge that occupies the southern half of Israel is referred to as the Negev. Home to just 12% of the population of Israel (but occupying about 55% of the land area), the Negev is usually classified as desert, though the northwest section is more of a steppe climatic zone, allowing significant agricultural activity through careful use of irrigation. The wide swathe through the centre of the Negev is closer to desert, also featuring examples of a spectacular geological feature known as a *makhtesh* (erosion crater). An extremely arid zone subject to catastrophic flash-flooding borders the Wadi Arava area and the southern section of the Negev. Outcrops of Nubian sandstone create a number of extraordinary landscapes.

Coastal plain

Israel's Mediterranean coast stretches for some 270 km in a gently curving arc, comprising mainly sandy shorelines and dunes (though there are cliffs in places, notably to the north). The coastal plain that borders the shoreline is between just 16 km and 40 km in depth, though it has subsequently become home to some 50% of Israel's population, most of its industry and a sizeable proportion of its agriculture.

Mountain spine

Israel's mountain ranges broadly run in a north to south direction. In places tectonic fault-lines have produced broad transverse valleys, the most notable of which is the Jezreel Valley. The mountain areas in the north comprise the rolling hills and wide valleys of Galilee, consisting primarily of limestone and dolomite and rising to a maximum height of 1,208 m. A separate upland area in the northeast is the high basalt plateau of the Golan, a geologically young feature. The mountain spine of Israel is formed by the central ranges of the hills of Samaria in the north (maximum height 1,108 m) and the Judean Hills in the south (maximum elevation 1,020 m).

Jordan rift valley

Israel's eastern border is largely defined by the Jordan River, running through a section of the Great Syrian-African Rift Valley. The Jordan River rises in the Mt Hermon area to the north, with its northern reaches for many years passing through the swamp land of the Hula Valley. This area has now been extensively drained. It then enters the rift valley as it exits the Sea of Galilee. This upper section of the rift valley between the Sea of Galilee and the Dead Sea is often referred to as the Ghor (literally "hollowed out"). The topography of the rift valley has a profound effect upon the microclimate, most notably because of its great depth below sea-level culminating at the lowest point on earth, the Dead Sea, at some 420 m below sea level. To the south of the Dead Sea the rift valley continues through the Wadi Arava depression all the way to the Red Sea.

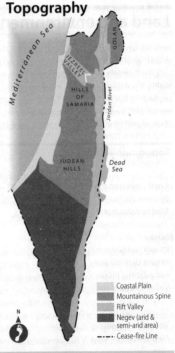

Topography

Mediterranean Sea

GOLAN

JEZREEL VALLEY

HILLS OF SAMARIA

Jordan River

JUDEAN HILLS

Dead Sea

Coastal Plain
Mountainous Spine
Rift Valley
Negev (arid & semi-arid area)
- - - - Cease-fire Line

N

Rivers and water

Israel's principal river (and water source) is the **Jordan River**, which winds for some 330 km in a 700-m descent from its source near Mt Hermon to the Dead Sea. Three streams form its source (Banias, Dan, Hazbani) and it is joined by several tributaries, notably the **Yarmuk**. Because of the long dry summers that Israel experiences (and the high rate of evaporation) many of the rivers are in fact seasonal streams (*nahal* in Hebrew, *wadi* in Arabic), flowing for only part of the year. Spectacular but catastrophic flash-floods are often a winter and spring feature of these streams.

Israel's principal freshwater reservoir is the **Sea of Galilee**. As a means of countering the imbalance between the well-watered north and the semi-arid south, Israel constructed the **National Water Carrier**, completed in 1964. However, despite leading the world in arid and semi-arid irrigation techniques, Israel still faces a potential chronic water deficit, as does the whole of the region.

The Palestinians regularly claim that the Israelis are stealing their water in the West Bank, and a 2009 World Bank Report found that four fifths of the water in the shared aquifer that runs the length of the West Bank hills was taken by Israel (though the Israeli water authorities dispute this). Israel naturally interprets the 'security' aspects of the Oslo peace agreement as including the need to secure water supplies, but the result is that the Palestinians have had little or no say in how resources are allocated. The water situation in Gaza is far more dire, with pollution and heavy salination affecting the only natural water supply, and a lack of sewage management exacerbating the problem. The Jordanians, however, were rewarded for signing a peace treaty with Israel with improved access to waters from the Jordan, Yarmuk and Arava.

Climate

Israel has four broad climatic zones, though as a general classification, Israel marks a transition zone between Mediterranean and desert climate. Much of the country falls within a **Mediterranean climate** zone, characterized by hot, dry summers (April-October) and mild, wet winters (November-March). Proximity to the coast has a marked moderating effect on this zone, as does the change in altitude as you move inland. Much of the Northern Negev comprises a **desert climate**, with this zone extending in a narrow finger along the Jordan Valley largely as a result of the rift valley's great depth below sea-level. Bordering the desert climate zone to the southeast is a region of **extreme desert climate**, where rainfall is negligible, daytime temperatures are very high, and where there is a wide diurnal temperature range. The Mediterranean and desert zones are bordered by a species of transition zone that may effectively be described as a **steppe climate**.

Vegetation

Israel's wide range of plant and animal life is a direct function of its location at the junction of three continents (Europe, Asia, Africa), and its status as a transition zone between the Mediterranean and desert climatic zones. Over 2800 types of plants have been identified. In many areas the natural vegetation has been radically modified by human action. Medieval accounts of the Mediterranean coastal plain, for example, describe a thickly wooded area, though subsequent deforestation led to much of this area becoming swampland. This was in turn drained and turned into rich agricultural land, thanks mainly to the efforts of the early Zionist pioneers (late 19th and the 20th century). The same is also true of the Hula Valley in Upper Galilee, with the loss of an irreplaceable swampland ecology.

Mediterranean zone

Though remnants of Tabor oak (*Quercus ithaburensis*) can still be found in parts of the Mediterranean vegetation zone (notably Lower Galilee), much of the vegetation is secondary, particularly the scrub forests of calliprinos oaks and pistachios. Other species of oaks, laurels, cypresses, Aleppo pines and a number of evergreens occupy more upland areas. Most of the lower areas in this zone have been given over to agriculture.

Irano-Turanian zone
A transition zone occupying much of the north and northwest Negev, and bordering the drier climatic zones to the south and east, this zone comprises a savannah-like mix of grasses, low-growing trees and bushes, plus a number of dwarf species.

Saharo-Sindinian zone
This vegetation zone occupies the desert regions of the Negev, Arava depression, Jordan rift valley and the Judean Desert, and reflects the constraints imposed by low levels of rainfall. Many species here have developed sophisticated methods of reducing water loss through surface evaporation (such as leaf shape and size, waxy leaf texture, deep roots, etc). The tamarisk tree, for example, secretes a salty residue on to the ground surrounding it, thus discouraging other plants from competing with its roots for the water resource. Many species are found in seasonally dry wadi beds, flowering only after the stream is in flow. In some areas, remnants such as the Atlantic terebinth (*Pistacia atlantica*) and Mesopotamian poplars (Populas euphratica) serve as living reminders of the process of environmental change.

Sudano-Deccanian zone
There are a number of oases in Israel's arid and semi-arid zone where favourable groundwater reserves, coupled with high temperatures, allow the growth of certain tropical and sub-tropical species (such as date palms). These oases represent pockets of the Sudano-Deccanian vegetation zone, the two most notable of which are Ein Gedi and Jericho.

Wildlife

Israel and the Palestinian Territories have an extremely diverse collection of wildlife, again reflecting its geographical position as a European-African-Asian transition zone. Over 510 different species of birds can be seen, though the vast majority are just temporary visitors. Israel stands on the main migratory flight-path between Europe and Africa, with notable 'twitching' spots being in the Eilat region and around the Hula Nature Reserve in Upper Galilee. Gamla National Park in Lower Golan provides a spectacular back-drop for a key nesting area for birds of prey. Some 116 mammal species can be found in Israel and the Palestinian Territories, though many are elusive due to nocturnal habits and the need to retreat to more remote locations away from predatory man. The Negev is the best area to see larger mammals such as the Nubian ibex (*Capra ibex*), striped hyena (*Hyaena hyaena*) and the ubiquitous rock hyrax (Procavia capensis), though your chances of seeing one of Israel's handful of remaining leopards (*Panthera pardus jarvisi*) are slim indeed. Wild pigs (*Sus scrofa*) are occasionally encountered in the Galilee. There are 97 different reptile species native to Israel, including lizards, snakes, scorpions and chameleons. Few are dangerous and they are rarely encountered, though the Palestinian viper (Vipera palaestinensis) should be avoided. (You are much more likely to encounter a gecko in your hotel room.) Visitors to Israel should make every effort to view the spectacular marine life that lives on the coral bed of the Red Sea. An underwater observatory and glass-bottomed boats mean that visitors to Eilat need not get their feet wet in the process, though snorkelling and scuba-diving remain more adventurous options. In addition to the vivid colours of the smaller fish, it is also possible to see larger creatures such as sharks, dolphins and rays.

Religion

Judaism

Judaism is the first great revealed religion of the Middle East, arguably the world. The Judaic tradition grew up from the teachings of the prophets in the belief that God was the God of the Jews. Later, Jews came to the belief that God had a universal and supreme role. Judaism is seen to be founded on five great principles:

(1) that God needs no intermediary in the form of an incarnation of himself in his dealings with man;
(2) that all Jews have equal rights and responsibilities before God and that the rabbis are teachers only – not a priesthood (**NB** the concept of man's equality before the law is arguably the Jews' greatest legacy to mankind);
(3) that justice and living by the law are obligations for all Jews;
(4) that learning and reason (and in some societies mystical powers) are great virtues and the scholar is to be respected in Jewish society;
(5) that the honourable and upright will be rewarded in this world, with the implication that there is no life after death (the body instead returning to God to await physical resurrection on the Day of Judgement, hence no cremation and the reluctance to submit a body for autopsy).

Written texts

The sacred Jewish texts are based upon the **Torah**: the five books of Moses (*Genesis, Exodus, Leviticus, Numbers, Deuteronomy*) that in the Christian tradition are known as the first five books of the Old Testament (the Greek *Pentateuch*). The Torah contains God's laws as laid down to **Moses**, including guidelines and regulations that determine how Jews must behave in their everyday life, and forms the basic text upon which all else rests. In its written form, the Torah was almost certainly completed before the Babylonian Exile (586 BCE), though some subsequent editing appears to have taken place.

However, the Torah is just the foundation stone of Jewish sacred literature. The second layer comprises the books of the prophets, the psalms and the wisdom literature, which appears to have been canonized by **Rabbi Yohanan ben Zakkai** between 70 and 132 CE. A third, non-canonical layer aids in the study of Jewish religion and history, and comprises works such as the *Septuagint* (Greek translation of the Bible), the Apocrypha, and even records such as Josephus.

The next layer represents an attempt to codify the Oral Law that has accumulated through countless generations of study and commentary. Such a practice is referred to as *Mishnah*, literally 'repeat' or 'study' since the Oral Law was learnt by rote, memorized, and then repeated orally to future generations. *Mishnah* comprises three distinct elements: *midrash*, which involves making clear points of law through study of the Torah; *halacha* (or *halakhah*), which is the body of accepted legal decisions on individual points; and *aggadah*, which is an anecdotal system of conveying the technical points of law in everyday terms to ordinary people. By about 210 CE the code of Oral Law had found a written form, largely completed through the efforts of Rabbi Judah Ha-Nasi. Later scholars sought to provide a commentary on the Mishnah based largely upon judgements in actual legal cases: the result was the Talmud (meaning 'learning' or 'study'). Two main schools of commentary evolved: the **Jerusalem (Palestine) Talmud** was produced in Israel around 390 CE, with the **Babylonian Talmud** being produced around a century later. In subsequent centuries, further great scholars produced additional commentaries aimed primarily at simplifying the sheer mass of material accumulated.

Branches of Judaism

The majority of Jews belong to the **Orthodox** stream (with others being considered ultra-Orthodox, see page 731), but a sizeable proportion of Jews are choosing to affiliate with more liberal streams, particularly in the Diaspora (notably the US). **Reform (Reconstructionist and Progressive)** Judaism emerged in Germany in the 19th century, almost certainly in light of European emancipation and enlightenment. It soon became established in the US (by 1880 some 90% of America's 200 or so synagogues were Reform), with the **Conservative (Masorti)** stream also rising to prominence. The split between Orthodox, Reform and Conservative streams remains a thorny issue to this day.

There are also a number of sub-sects within Judaism that reflect the historical experience of the Jews. Such groups include the **Samaritans**, who regard themselves as descendants of the tribes of Joseph and his sons Menasseh and Ephraim. Another faction within Judaism are the **Karaites**, who emerged in the eighth century and profess adherence to the Torah alone as the source of religious law. Today they number around 15,000, living mainly in Ramla, Ashdod and Be'er Sheva.

Everyday practices

Formal worship is conducted in a **synagogue**, though there is an argument that this institution plays a far greater role in community life in the Diaspora than in Israel itself. A quorum of 10 adult males (a minyan) is required for traditional Orthodox worship. Prayers are conducted three times a day, generally led by a rabbi. Men and women are seated separately and their heads are covered. The Holy Ark containing the Torah scrolls is the focal point of the synagogue, with a prescribed Torah portion being read cyclically throughout the Jewish year. It is not uncommon to see prayers being conducted in public places (notably the Western Wall, but sometimes in shopping precincts) where men strap a small leather box to their head, with leather straps wrapped around their arms. These implements are known collectively as **tefillin**, with the box containing a prescribed portion of the Torah. The purpose is to remind Jews that the heart, mind and body has been given to perform good, not evil, with the straps and box symbolically binding the mind and body.

The Torah prescribes that male children should be **circumcised** on the eighth day after birth. Jewish males reach adulthood at 13, at which age they become subject to Jewish law. On the first Shabbat after his 13th birthday, a Jewish male reads from a portion of the Torah in the synagogue for the first time. This rite of passage is known as **bar mitzvah**, and is generally an occasion for family celebration (particularly exuberant when held at the Western Wall). Further details on Jewish **dietary** practices can be found in the 'Food and drink' section. For details of Jewish **festivals** and **holidays** see page 32.

Christianity

Christian theology has its roots in Judaism, with its belief in one God, the eternal Creator of the universe. Judaism saw the Jewish people as the vehicle for God's salvation, the 'chosen people of God', and pointed to a time when God would send his Saviour, or Messiah. **Jesus**, whom Christians believe was 'the Christ' or Messiah, was born in the village of Bethlehem some 20 km south of Jerusalem. Very little is known of his early life except that he was brought up in a devout Jewish family. At the age of 29 or 30 he gathered a small group of followers and began to preach in the region between the Dead Sea and the Sea of Galilee. Two years later he was crucified in Jerusalem by the authorities on the charge of blasphemy that he claimed to be the son of God.

Christians believe that all people live in a state of sin, in the sense that they are separated from God and fail to do his will. They believe that God is personal, 'like a father'. As God's son, Jesus accepted the cost of that separation and sinfulness himself through his death on the cross. Christians believe that Jesus was raised from the dead on the third day after he was crucified, and that he appeared to his closest followers. They believe that his spirit continues to live today, and that he makes it possible for people to come back to God.

The New Testament of the Bible, alongside the Old Testament, is the text to which Christians refer as the ultimate scriptural authority. It consists of four 'Gospels' (meaning 'good news') and a series of letters by several early Christians referring to the nature of the Christian life.

Christian worship

Although Christians are encouraged to worship individually as well as together, most forms of Christian worship centre on the gathering of the church congregation for praise, prayer and the preaching of God's word, which usually takes verses from the Bible as its starting point. Different denominations place varying emphases on the main elements of worship, but in most church services today the congregation will take part in singing hymns (songs of praise), prayers will be led by the minister, priest or a member of the congregation, readings from the Bible will be given and a sermon preached. For many Christians the most important service is the act of Holy Communion (Protestant) or Mass (Catholic) which celebrates the death and resurrection of Jesus in sharing bread and wine, which are held to represent Christ's body and blood given to save people from their sin.

Christian sects in the Holy Land

Numerous sects and sub-sects of Christianity operate in the Holy Land, largely reflecting the theological, political and physical separation of the Eastern and Western churches. Though international power politics in the 18th and 19th centuries have played a role in this inter-denominational rivalry, the first split was considerably earlier (451 CE in fact), arising primarily out of the condemnation of Monophysitism as heresy at the Fourth Ecumenical Council held in Chalcedon. Almost all the sects are nationalistic in outlook, yet the balance of power between the various denominations in the Holy Land does not reflect global realities. The rivalry between the various sects is often bitter, sometimes violent, and seriously calls into question the concept of Christian brotherhood.

Islam

The word Islam translates roughly as 'submission to God'. The two central tenets of Islam are embodied in the creed "There is no god but Allah and Mohammad is his Prophet" (*"Lah*

Main branches of the Christian Church in the Holy Land

The four main branches of the Church operating in the Holy Land today are the **Eastern Orthodoxy** (Greek, Russian, Serbian, Bulgarian Orthodox); **Oriental Orthodoxy** (Armenian, Coptic, Ethiopian, Syrian Orthodox); **Catholicism** (Roman/Latin, Maronite, Greek Catholic); and **Protestantism** (various denominations).

Eastern Orthodoxy The dominant Eastern Orthodox church (and the main ecclesiastical body in Israel) is probably the Greek Orthodox Church, despite the fact that its worldwide constituents are few in number and drawn from a limited geographical area. The Greek Orthodox Church established a Patriarchate in Jerusalem in 451 CE, and now 'owns' the major portions of the Church of the Holy Sepulchre in Jerusalem and the Church of the Nativity in Bethlehem. The priesthood is almost exclusively Greek-speaking, despite the fact that the vast majority of its congregation are Arabs. The Russian Orthodox Church also has a notable presence in the Holy Land, though again this mission is divided in two by competing claims as to who is the legitimate successor to the 19th-century Russian government mission.

Oriental Orthodoxy The main Oriental Orthodox churches include the **Armenian Orthodox Church**, which established a presence in Jerusalem in the 4th century CE and whose continuity in the Holy Land has far from reflected the experiences of the Armenian state. The **Syrian Orthodox Church** (sometimes referred to as the Jacobites) also have a significant presence in the Holy Land, with the seat of an archbishop in Jerusalem. The **Copts** (Egyptian Christians) are also represented in Israel. Their long-time rivals are the **Ethiopians**, who claim a line of descent through Solomon's union with the Queen of Sheba.

Catholicism The **Latin (Catholic) Church** became established in the Holy Land only in the medieval period, as a result of the Crusades. Thus papal influence on Christians in Israel nowhere near reflects the global influence of the Pontiff. In fact, relations between the Holy See and the State of Israel have always been rather strained, with full diplomatic links only being established in 1994. Until 1965 (when the charge against the Jews of deicide was formally dropped) only one serving Pope had ever visited the Holy Land. Since then, Pope John Paul II visited in March 2000 and Pope Benedict XVI came in May 2009. The **Greek Catholic (Melkite) Church** still observes the Greek rite, though it has been united with Rome since 1709 and recognizes the Pope as head of the church.

Protestantism Another late arrival in the Holy Land was the **Protestant Church**, whose ministry began largely in the 19th century. Numerous sub-sects of the Protestant church are active in Israel, with the largest one possibly being the Anglicans (comprised mainly of Arabs).

Illaha illa 'llah Mohammad Rasulu 'llah") which affirms the belief in the oneness of God and recognizes Mohammad as the divinely appointed messenger of God.

The *Qur'an* (generally referred to as the Koran in English) is Islam's holiest book. The word translates literally as 'recitation', and unlike the Bible is considered to be the *uncreated* (ie direct) word of God, as revealed to **Mohammad** through *Jibril* (the angel Gabriel). The text consists of 114 chapters, each known as a sura. Each sura is classified as Meccan or

Medinan, according to whether it was revealed to Mohammad in Mecca or Medina. Most of the text is written in a kind of rhymed prose known as saj, and is considered by Muslims to be inimitable. Each chapter of the Koran begins with the words *"Bismillah al-Rahman al-Rahim"* ("In the name of Allah, the Merciful, the Compassionate"), an invocation which can also be heard being uttered by Muslims in numerous everyday situations, for example when boarding a bus or before eating food.

In addition to the Qur'an, there is the *Hadith* body of literature, a record of the sayings and doings of Mohammad and his followers that forms the basis of Islamic laws (*Shariat*) and precepts. Unlike the Qur'an, the Hadiths are recognized to have been written by men and are therefore potentially flawed and open to interpretation. Thus they are commonly classified into four major categories according to their trustworthiness: *Sahih* (sound, true, authentic), *Hasan* (fair, good), *Da'if* (weak) and *Saqim* (infirm). The two most revered compilations of Hadiths are those of *al-Bukhari* and *Muslim*. It is in the interpretation of the Hadiths that most of the controversy surrounding certain Islamic laws and their application originates.

While Mohammad is recognized as the founder of the Islamic faith and the principle messenger of God, Muslims also regard him as having been the last in a long line of Prophets, starting with Adam and including Moses, Abraham and Jesus (who they consider simply another of God's Prophets). Both Jews and Christians are considered *Ahl-e-Kitab* ('People of the Book'), the Torah and the Gospels being completed in Islamic belief by the Qur'an.

Nearly all Muslims accept six basic articles of the Islamic faith: belief in one God, in his angels, in his revealed books, in his Apostles, in the Resurrection and Day of Judgement, and in his predestination of good and evil. Heaven is portrayed in Muslim belief as a paradise filled with sensuous delights and pleasures. Hell, on the other hand, is portrayed as a place of eternal terror and torture, which is the certain fate of all who deny the unity of God.

Islam has no ordained priesthood or clergy. The authority of religious scholars, learned men, Imams, judges, etc derives from their authority to interpret the scriptures, rather than from any defined status within the Islamic community.

The development of Islam

Mohammad, the founder of the Islamic faith, was born around 570 CE in the city of **Mecca** in present-day Saudi Arabia. His family were of noble descent, members of the house of **Hashim**, belonging to the **Abd Manaf** clan which had a semi-priestly status, being responsible for certain functions during the annual pilgrimage to the *Ka'ba* in Mecca. (Muslims believe the Ka'ba, the cube-shaped building to which they face when praying, was established by Adam, and revere it as a sanctuary where closeness to God can be achieved.)

At the age of 40 Mohammad received his first revelations of the *Qur'an* and began preaching his message. He encountered stiff opposition, and was eventually forced to flee to **Medina**, known then as Yathrib (the famous *Hijra*, or 'flight', which marks the beginning of the Islamic calendar). There he established himself and achieved a position of power, fighting three major battles with the Meccans before finally returning there in triumph two years before his death in 632 CE.

In his lifetime he had become recognized as a prophet and founded the Islamic faith. Part of his success was in incorporating many aspects of the ancient Arabian religion, such as the pilgrimage to Ka'ba, as well as aspects of Judaism and Christianity. But his success was not purely in religious terms. He was also an accomplished statesman who laid the foundations for what would later become a great Islamic empire.

The Five Pillars of Islam

There are five practices or *Akran*, known as the Five Pillars of Islam, which are generally accepted as being obligatory to Muslims.

Shahada The profession of faith ("There is no god but Allah ... "), which also forms the basis of the call to prayer made by the *muezzin* of the mosque.

Salat The ritual of prayers, carried out five times a day at prescribed times; in the early morning before the sun has risen above the horizon, in the early afternoon when the sun has passed its zenith, later when the sun is halfway towards setting, immediately after sunset and in the evening before retiring to bed. Prayers can be carried out anywhere, whether it be in a mosque or by the roadside, and involves facing towards the *Ka'ba* in Mecca and prostrating before God while reciting verses of the Qur'an.

Zakat The compulsory payment of alms. In early times this was collected by officials of the Islamic state, and was devoted to the relief of the poor, debtors, aid to travellers and other charitable purposes. In many Muslim communities, the fulfilment of this religious obligation is nowadays left to the conscience of the individual.

Sawm The 30 days of fasting during the month of Ramadan, the ninth month of the Muslim lunar calendar. It is observed as a fast from sunrise to sunset each day by all Muslims, although there are provisions for special circumstances.

Hajj The pilgrimage to Mecca. Every Muslim, circumstances permitting, is obliged to perform this pilgrimage at least once in their lifetime and having accomplished it may assume the title of *Hajji*. The lack of diplomatic relations between Israel and Saudi Arabia makes performing the *Hajj* all but impossible.

Islamic sects

Islam is divided into two major sects, **Sunni** and **Shia**, formed out of the opposing groups who fought for political power in the century following Mohammad's death. (Mohammad left no sons and therefore no obvious heir, and gave no instructions as to who should succeed him.) Followers of the Sunni sect, generally termed 'Orthodox', account for around 80% of Muslims globally, and almost all Muslims in Israel/Palestine. They base their Sunna (path, or practice) on the 'Six Books' of traditions. They are organized into four orthodox schools or rites, named after their founders, each having equal standing. The Hanafi is the most moderate. The others are the **Shafii**, **Maliki** and **Hanbali**, the latter being the strictest. Many Muslims today prefer to avoid identification with a particular school, preferring to call themselves simply Sunni.

The other main Islamic group is the **Shia** sect which, though important in southern Lebanon, has next to no presence in Israel/Palestine. Aside from the dispute over the succession of Mohammad, Sunnis and Shias do not generally differ on fundamental issues since they draw from the same ultimate sources. However, there are important differences of interpretation, which partly derive from the practice of *ijtihad* ('the exercise of independent judgement') amongst Shias, as oppose to *taqlid* (the following of ancient models) as adhered to by Sunnis. Thus Shias divest far more power in their *Imams*, accepting their role as an intermediary between God and man, and basing their law and practice on their teachings. (**NB** The term Imam is also used more generally by both Shias and Sunnis to refer to the prayer leader of a mosque.) The majority of Shias are known as *Ithna asharis* or 'Twelvers', since they recognize a succession of 12 Imams. They believe that the last Imam, who disappeared in 878 CE, is still alive and will reappear soon before the Day of Judgement as the *Mahdi* (one who is rightly guided), who will rule by divine right.

A further sect of Islam found within Israel is the **Ahmadiyyat**, though many Muslims believe that this group is heretical (see page 511 for full details).

Other faiths

Druze
Very few details are known about the true nature of the Druze faith, largely because not all Druze are initiated into the precepts of the faith themselves. Those who are aware of the doctrines are referred to as *uqqal* ('intelligent'), whilst the 'ignorant' members are *juhhal*. Some of the basic dogma is known, however, and is related to a Western audience as a form of Gnostic mysticism. The key point of the doctrine involves 'the oneness of God', reflecting the Druze roots in Islam from which it split in the reign of the Caliph al-Hakim (996-1021 CE). God is believed to reveal himself through a number of human incarnations, the last of whom was al-Hakim himself

Baha'i
Israel is also home of the Universalist Baha'i faith. For further details see the 'Haifa' section on page 506.

Modern Israel

Population and society

Analysing Israeli society is a little more complicated than dividing the population into 'Jews' and 'non-Jews'. For example, despite having the common bond of Judaism, the Jewish faith does have a number of different streams (see under 'Religion' above), whilst Israel's Jewish society can be divided into three broad groupings.

Ashkenazi Jews This group comprises mainly Jews of European origin (Ashkenaz deriving from the Hebrew word for Germany), though in Israel it often includes those who arrived from Europe via North and South America, South Africa and Australia. The early Zionist movement and the early years of the State of Israel were largely shaped by the Ashkenazi community.

Sephardi Jews The term 'Sephardi' is frequently wrongly applied to describe all Middle Eastern and North African Jews. The word Sephard does in fact refer to the ancient Hebrew word for Spain, and when correctly applied refers to those descended from the 200,000-strong Jewish community expelled from Spain (and Portugal) by King Ferdinand of Aragon and Queen Isabella of Castile in 1492. They eventually settled in such places as Turkey, Holland, Italy, Bulgaria, Greece, and in parts of North Africa, with the latter group probably being the reason for the continued misuse of the term Sephardi.

Mizrachi Jews This is the grouping that is usually wrongly referred to as 'Sephardi'. Mizrachi Jews are in fact the 'Oriental' or 'Eastern' Jews that originate from the very

Basics

Capital Jerusalem (though this is not recognized by the UN or most nations, with most retaining embassies in Tel Aviv).

Flag White background with pale blue horizontal band at top and bottom (to symbolize the tallit, or Jewish prayer shawl) and a pale blue Star of David at the centre.

National Anthem "Hatikva" ("The Hope").

Population 7.51 million (including East Jerusalem and Golan, but excluding areas under Palestinian Authority control).

Language Hebrew; Arabic (around 15%); European languages.

Ethnic divisions Jews 75.4%; Arabs 20.3%; other 4.3%.

Religion Jewish 76%; Muslim 16%; Christian 2.5%; Druze 1.5%; other 4%.

ancient Jewish communities in the Islamic countries of North Africa and the Middle East. The term may also be applied to the Jewish community from Cochin in India, since this group actually arrived on the sub-continent from the Middle East. Though many arrived in Palestine during the late 19th and early 20th centuries, the majority arrived in Israel in the period 1948-72 having left (or been expelled from) Islamic countries that became enemies of Israel following the latter's independence. A number, such as the Ethiopian Jews, arrived in a series of spectacular airlifts/rescue operations (for example 'Operation Moses' in 1984 that brought 15,000 and 'Operation Solomon' in 1991 that brought the rest of the community). Such operations had their precedent in 'Operation Magic Carpet' that brought some 46,000 Jews out of Yemen in the years 1949-50. For details on the struggle of the Sephardi and Mizrachi groups to adapt to life in Israel, see 'Unity in diversity?' on page 730.

Other groups Amongst the most visible of the Jewish communities in Israel (and the world in general) are the **Haredim**, or ultra-Orthodox Jews. The word *haredim* literally means 'those who fear heaven', and is the usual designation given to those belonging to the stream of strict ('ultra') orthodox Judaism that opposes accommodation with both the non-Orthodox trends within Judaism (Reform, Conservative) and secularism. Their attitudes to Zionism and the State of Israel in general range from outright hostility to ambivalence. A small but volatile sector of the community believe that Jewish sovereignty in the Land of Israel, even a state founded according to Jewish religious law (halacha), cannot be established before the coming of the Messiah. Thus, they oppose, and refuse to participate in, the State of Israel. Other groups are more pragmatic, using their considerable voting potential to win concessions and benefits for their community.

Other branches, or sub-sects, of Judaism found in Israel are the small communities of **Samaritans** and **Karaites**, though numerically they are insignificant.

Minority communities in a Jewish State

Approximately 24% of the population of Israel (excluding the territories occupied by Israel since 1967 and the Palestinian Authority areas) is non-Jewish; around 1.5 million people. They are generally referred to collectively as **Israeli Arabs**, though this is a gross over-simplification. Whilst standards and access to education and healthcare have improved since this group became included within the State of Israel, and the status of women in society has undergone a number of liberalizing trends, it is widely accepted that Israeli Arabs have faced considerable discrimination when compared to their Jewish Israeli counterparts. On the other hand, Israel would argue with some justification that Israeli Arabs have far greater democratic and legal rights than most of their brethren in neighbouring Arab states. This issue is further explored in 'Pluralism and segregation' on page 732.

Muslim Arabs account for around 85% of Israel's non-Jewish population, almost all of whom belong to the Sunni branch of Islam. **Christian Arabs** are Israel's second largest minority group, comprising about 120,000 people. They are concentrated mainly in the Nazareth, Shefar'am and Haifa area, plus smaller communities in Jerusalem. Christian Arabs belong mainly to the Greek Catholic, Greek Orthodox and Roman Catholic denominations of Christianity.

Bedouins represent around 12% of the Muslim Arab population of Israel (around 170,000 people). In common with nomadic groups across the world, the 30 or so Bedouin tribes in Israel have been pressured into adopting a sedentary lifestyle. Seven permanent settlement towns with education and healthcare facilities have been built, though they tend to be located in peripheral areas of the Negev where a secure economic base is uncertain. Some tribes, such as the Jahalin, have been forcibly removed from their traditional homes more than once to accommodate the expansion of Israeli settlements.

Druze communities number approximately 120,000 members, mainly in the Haifa (80%) and Upper Golan (20%) regions. Those concentrated in the Haifa and Western Galilee region tend to participate fully in Israeli society (including the army), whilst those in the Golan look more to their co-religionists in neighbouring Lebanon and Syria.

Circassians belong to a distinct ethnic group that migrated to Palestine in the 19th century from the Caucasus region of Central Asia. They number around 3000, living in two small villages in Upper Galilee. They are Sunni Muslim and tend to use Arabic as their everyday language. In keeping with the request of their community leaders, their young men are liable for the Israeli military draft. Other small religious communities in Israel include the **Ahmadies** (see page 511) and members of the **Baha'i faith** (see page 506).

Israel's significant non-Jewish population is sometimes referred to as its "demographic demon", implying that because of their higher birth rate, Arabs will become a majority in Israel in the next 30 years or so. However, birth rate must be considered alongside death rate, emigration and immigration; the last of which is, of course, the key. Thus, Israel does all that it can to facilitate the immigration of Jews from the Diaspora; it is one of very few countries that encourages a species normally turned away by other nations – the 'economic migrant' (see page 735).

Immigration: the continued ingathering

The whole *raison d'être* of the creation of the modern State of Israel is the "ingathering of the exiles" (*Genesis 15:13-16*), to provide a homeland and refuge for the Jewish people. This concept is the essence of the Zionism founding philosophy, and is enshrined within the Law of Return (see page 736).

Within about 80 years Israel has absorbed around 3.4 million immigrants, around five times the size of its population at independence. In this regard, Israel is perhaps unique in relying on substantial immigration to increase its population. The number of Palestinians who left or were forced out during the war that accompanied Israel's independence in 1948 (a contentious figure that is placed at anywhere between 550,000 and 725,000) is roughly matched by the number of Jewish immigrants into Israel who left or were forced out of Arab countries during the period 1948-1972 (around 570,000 *Mizrachi* or 'Oriental' Jews, see page 727).

At independence, the majority of Jews living in the newly created State of Israel came from three main sources: the *Yishuv*, or ancient Jewish community of Palestine; the early Zionist pioneers, who were predominantly *Ashkenazi* Jews (see page 727) from eastern and central Europe; and refugees from the Nazi Holocaust in Europe, mainly Ashkenazi, but also a sizeable portion of Sephardi Jews (see page 727). The rapid influx of *Mizrachi* Jews in the period 1948-1972 drastically altered the nature of the state within just one generation of its independence.

The continued ingathering perpetuates the process of social change in Israeli Jewish society. Since 1990 Israel has absorbed over 900,000 new immigrants from the **former Soviet Union**. This large, and highly visible, community has had a major impact on contemporary life in Israel. Aside from the economic impact, the 'Jewishness' (or lack of it) of these immigrants is questioned, and links to the Russian mafia and other criminal groups have been further causes for concern.

An interesting case is that of the Falasha Mura, the Ethiopians whose ancestors were Jews but at some point in the past converted to Christianity. When the Beta Israel (Ethiopian Jews) were dramatically airlifted out of the country and brought to Israel in 1985 and 1991, the Falasha Mura began gathering in Addis Ababa in the hope of also immigrating to Israel. After initially refusing to recognise them as Jews (and predicting – correctly – that the floodgates would open if they allowed them in) the Israeli government bowed to pressure and allowed around 4000 to enter between 1997 and 1998. By 2001, however, over 20,000 more Falasha Mura had congregated at the camps (where living conditions were life-threatening) and Israel again agreed to accept them, but this time in quotas of 300 per month. Limited numbers are still accepted (who fit certain criteria) to this day. Falasha Mura women can sometimes be recognised by the Coptic crosses that have been tattooed on to foreheads or necks, though many seek to have these removed after arrival in Israel.

Unity in diversity?

Although around 76% of Israel's population are Jews, this figure actually represents a community drawn from some 80 countries around the world, and not surprisingly represents a very broad collection of ethnic, cultural and social backgrounds. Israel has many anomalies, such as "a vibrant multi-party democracy, but also a strong military establishment; a socialist state structure, married to a highly entrepreneurial industrial sector; strongly secular political mores, but a solid religious political grouping always in the wings" (Joffe, 1996).

Divisions in Israeli society are over many things. The most obvious of course is the relationship with the Palestinians, and notably the idea of withdrawing from the West Bank, or the concept of exchanging land for peace. Perhaps of greater threat to Israel as a cohesive unit, however, are the divisions within Jewish society itself. Many such divisions are a direct result of the way in which Israel came into being, and the means by which this 'New Society' was created.

At independence the Israeli population comprised mainly Ashkenazi and Sephardi Jews. Their tastes and customs reflected their European origins, with the early ideals of these immigrants dictating the way in which Israel developed. The sudden arrival within the first 25 years or so of Israel's existence of over half a million Mizrachi Jews (see above) presented a grave challenge to the new Jewish State. On the whole, the Mizrachi Jews were more patriarchal in their social organization, unfamiliar with the 'Western' ideals through which the state functioned, with their generally lower levels of education acting

Secular vs Orthodox

Opening on Shabbat in Jerusalem (apart from in predominantly Arab areas) is unheard of, and the Municipality even employ Druze inspectors specifically for the task of implementing these rules (since Jewish inspectors are unable to work on the Sabbath). Shabbat opening hours are just one illustration of the gulf that exists between secular and Orthodox in Israel. When the glitzy Mamilla retail avenue opened in 2007, it was out of the question that any of the stores would be opening on Shabbat. However, the car park that's located below the shops was opened on a Saturday morning, and even this action caused Orthodox Jews to demonstrate on the street outside in protest.

Likewise, when it was decided in 2010 to extend the emergency room of the Barzilai Medical Centre in Ashkelon, the two sides were at loggerheads. Initial construction work uncovered graves in the area proposed for the site, and to move the remains of Jewish bodies is considered a sacrilegious act. So archeologists were called in, who proved that they were in fact the graves of a Byzantine community and were not Jewish remains. However, the Haredim still objected to the bones being moved just in case a Jewish body or two had ended up in the Byzantine cemetery. Serious discussions ensued as to whether the ER should be built 1-km distant from the main hospital or even in a bunker beneath the graves. Eventually (after severe public pressure) the government decided to go ahead and move the graves. The Orthodox communities in Jerusalem, Ashkelon and Bnei-Brak rioted in protest, burning garbage bins, throwing stones, and leading to the arrest of several. For the same reason, Route 6 (the main arterial road connecting the north to the south) will only ever have two lanes and never three, as graves would have to be moved in order to expand it.

as a constraint upon employment opportunities and political advancement. In effect, Israel's early years were characterized by an Ashkenazi Israel and a Mizrachi Israel. The Mizrachi community is now largely integrated within Israeli society, being well represented in government, military and business spheres, whilst the most recent Ashkenazi influx (from the former Soviet Union) have struggled to become acculturated and accepted. Israel's 120,000 Falasha feel that their 'Jewishness' is often questioned, and that efforts to integrate them have not produced the generous grants and welfare programmes that the later Russian émigrés have enjoyed.

A further division within Israeli society is often classified under the heading of 'religious versus secular Jew'. This issue has largely risen out of the Diaspora experience, where some communities chose to integrate with their host societies whilst others chose to (or were forced to) turn in upon themselves (notably in the ghettos of eastern Europe). Thus Jewish society comprises observant, non-observant and secular Jews. It is rather difficult to put figures to the categories of 'religious' and 'secular' Jews, though it is widely accepted that 20% of the Jewish population of Israel fulfil all religious precepts, 60% follow some combination of Jewish religious laws and practices, whilst 20% are totally non-observant (*chilonim*). These divisions come into sharp focus when the nature of the State of Israel is discussed. Though religion and state are effectively separated, there is no formal basis to this separation: just a *modus vivendi* that has operated since Israel's inception. In some quarters there is the call for a halacha state based upon the precepts of Jewish religious law. Currently, *halacha* is binding in the areas of marriage, divorce and the personal status of Jews, whilst the law of the state applies to all other fields (though the courts may, at their discretion, take account of *halacha* where no secular legislation is applicable). It is often said that most of Israel wants to live in a Jewish Sweden, whilst the rest want to live in a Jewish Iran.

Pluralism and segregation

The extent of segregation within Israeli society is another topic of hot debate. Many communities choose to segregate voluntarily in order to maintain their cultural, religious and ethnic identity. Notable amongst this group are the ultra-Orthodox Jews.

The true test of Israel's pluralist credentials is the way in which it deals with minorities. For example, Muslim and Christian Arabs, plus Bedouins, who live in the areas that became part of Israel after 1948 constitute almost 1.5 million people. Although they are granted Israeli citizenship (and can thus vote in elections, and have some of their own parties and Knesset members) it is widely accepted that they are discriminated against, with their commitment as Israeli citizens often questioned. On the other hand, it may be argued that levels of education, women's rights, and general economic conditions have improved significantly amongst most Arab Israeli communities.

The subject is far more complex (and controversial) when discussing the Palestinian residents of areas that Israel has occupied (or 'administered', according to your viewpoint) since 1967. The segregation of the West Bank Palestinians behind the separation wall (or apartheid wall, as Palestinians call it) began in 2001 and is ongoing (see boxed text, page 741). The construction of the wall has generally brought condemnation from the international community, although the great majority of Israelis seem to feel that it is justified (and effective) in preventing terrorist attacks. Of further concern to Palestinians is the way in which Jerusalem continues to be ringed by new Jewish suburbs, effectively further disconnecting 'Arab' East Jerusalem from its Arab hinterland.

The kibbutz and moshav system

Growing out of the pioneering Zionist programme that saw Jewish redemption through working the land, the *kibbutz* and *moshav* system had a disproportionately larger impact on Israel's early development than the number of kibbutzniks (kibbutz members) suggested. The percentage of Israelis living on a kibbutz has never risen above 8%, and has tended to settle at the present figure of around 4%, but, as Stephen Brook points out, kibbutzniks' impact on civil life has been immense: "One third of the young state's first constituent assembly in 1948 was composed of kibbutzniks. For the first 20 years of Israel's existence, a third of all cabinet members were kibbutzniks. The number of kibbutznik officers in the IDF is six times greater than their proportion of the population would lead one to expect, and during the Six Day War, one quarter of the casualties were kibbutzniks" (*Winner Takes All*, 1990).

Today the kibbutz system is often labelled as an institution in crisis. The decline in the contribution to the national economy of the agricultural sector has seen many kibbutzim turn to light industry and tourism as a means of survival. Meanwhile, the transfer to the government and Israeli mainstream of functions such as immigration, settlement, defence and agriculture has seen the kibbutz movement become marginalized to the fringes of society.

There are divisions within the kibbutz movement too, with many suggesting that the eroding of the collective ethos is shifting the institution away from its founding principles, whilst others argue the need to be pragmatic and make fundamental changes if the kibbutz is to survive.

The role of the military in Israeli society

Another key Israeli institution is the **Israeli Defence Forces**, or IDF. Israel's standing army is in the region of 175,000 men and women (with reserves of around 445,000). All eligible men and women are drafted at the age of 18, with men serving three years and women serving two (including Druze and Circassian men). Women are eligible for over half of the job categories in the services, including the Caracal combat unit, and have recently been permitted to sign up for service as pilots, though the image of women soldiers that most visitors to Israel take away with them is of soldiers wearing lipstick, make-up and nail varnish!

Upon completion of service, all soldiers are assigned to a reserve unit, with 30 days being the average amount of reserve duty expected each year (though this can be increased when necessary). Men serve reserve duty up to the age of 40 (officers up to age 45), with unmarried women liable to the draft up to 24. National service conscription is in fact considered to be an essential rite of passage and national unifying factor. Israeli Arabs and Bedouins are exempt from national service, though there are options for them to join if they wish. Ultra-Orthodox Jews, notably men involved in Torah and religious study, are also exempt, though there is considerable animosity about this amongst many sectors of Israeli society, who resent the political and economic benefits that the ultra-Orthodox community enjoy without sending their sons to the army.

A more recent development has seen a significant rise in the numbers of religious Zionists signing up for combat units in the IDF, and disproportionately high numbers of religious nationalists in the elite units. Many observers feel this has the potential to tear the IDF apart, as well as further jeopardizing any future peace process. Part of any peace deal will involve evacuation of at least some Jewish settlements in the West Bank, and the very soldiers supposed to enforce such an evacuation are ideologically and religiously opposed to the idea (or even residents of the very settlements they would be required to evacuate).

Government, politics and institutions

Israel is a parliamentary democracy that comprises three main bodies: the legislature (the Knesset, or parliament); the executive (the elected government); and the judiciary (the court system). The structure is based upon the separation of powers, with a number of checks and balances built into the system. Despite the number of political parties with a religious platform, Israel follows the liberal model used in the West of separating Church (or rather, Synagogue) and State.

The political system

Israel has a multi-party political system that is probably the most democratic in the Middle East. The legislative assembly is the **Knesset**, which takes its name from the *Knesset Hagedolah* (Great Assembly of the Jewish Commonwealth) that Ezra and Nehemiah convened in Jerusalem in the 5th century BCE.

Like the British model, the elected prime minister enjoys real executive authority at the head of a Cabinet of his or her choice. The President is largely a titular head of state, though, unlike the monarchy system in Britain, the Israeli president is elected every five years by popular mandate. Israel's election process uses the system of proportional representation. To date, no party has ever received enough (ie 61) seats to allow it to form a government on its own, and thus all Israeli governments have been a coalition of groups often representing very different viewpoints.

Israel's Prime Ministers and political groupings

David Ben-Gurion (1948-1954) – Labour
Moshe Sharett (1954-1955) – Labour
David Ben-Gurion (1955-1963) – Labour
Levi Eshkol (1963-1969) – Labour
Yigael Allon (1969 acting) – Labour
Golda Meir (1969-1974) – Labour
Yitzhak Rabin (1974-1977) – Labour
Shimon Peres (1977 acting) – Labour
Menachem Begin (1977-1983) – Likud
Yitzhak Shamir (1983-1984) – Likud
Shimon Peres (1984-1986) – Labour

Yitzhak Shamir (1986-1992) – Likud
Yitzhak Rabin (1992-1995) – Labour
Shimon Peres (1995-1996) – Labour
Benjamin Netanyahu (1996-1999) – Likud
Ehud Barak (1999-2001) – Labour ('One Nation')
Ariel Sharon (2001-2006) – Likud, then Kadima (from 2006)
Ehud Olmert (2006-2009) – Kadima
Benjamin Netanyahu (2009-) – Likud

An electoral reform that came into effect in 1996 was the introduction of a threshold designed to exclude extremely small extremist groups from enjoying access to power (such as the neo-fascist Kach). The only problem with this commendable measure is that there are in fact some extremely large extremist groups who continue to enjoy power in Israel (parties need only win 2% of the vote to enter the Knesset).

Political parties

The origins of the main political parties lie in the political groupings found in Zionist circles in east and central Europe at the beginning of the 20th century, with political Zionism dividing into three main trends by the 1930s: "Labour Zionism, essentially nationalist but with a strong socialist component; Revisionist Zionism, which originated as a revolt against the former, and which stressed free market values and strong defence; and finally Religious Zionism, which combined Jewish faith with an acceptance of the renaissance of a Jewish secular state" (Joffe, 1996, *ibid*). Newer elements represent Israeli Arabs as well as ultra-orthodox Jewish groups, and, in a more recent development, the establishment of parties to represent ethnic groupings, like Sephardi/Mizrachi Jews, or communities such as recent Russian immigrants.

A glance at the list of Israel's prime ministers indicates how politics in this country has been dominated by two main political groupings: **Labour** and **Likud**. **Labour** has traditionally been a myriad of socialist groups from the Labour Zionism trend, while **Likud** is the direct successor to the Revisionist Zionism movement, favouring free-market economics and being 'hawkish' on defence and security issues. In 2005, the Kadima (Forward) party was founded by Ariel Sharon and went on to win 29 seats in the 2006 Parliamentary elections. Kadima is a more liberal, centrist party made up of moderates from Likud who were then joined by Labour politicians with the same agenda. Kadima held power until 2009, with Ehud Olmert becoming Prime Minister in early 2006 when Sharon's medical problems became overwhelming. The current leader of the party is Tzipi Livni.

Pressure groups

The Israeli political scene is also notable for the high number of pressure groups that lobby on a number of platforms. Perhaps best known is the **Peace Now** (Shalom Akhshav) group, organizers of the pro-peace demonstration in Tel Aviv at which Yitzhak Rabin was

Israel's Presidents

Chaim Weizmann (1949-1952)
Yitzhak Ben-Zvi (1952-1963)
Zalman Shazar (1963-1973)
Ephraim Katzir (1973-1978)
Yitzhak Navon (1978-1983)

Chaim Herzog (1983-1993)
Ezer Weizman (1993-2000)
Moshe Katsav (2000-2007)
Shimon Peres (2007-)

assassinated, and recent organizers of demonstrations against the actions of the IDF in the May 2010 Gazan flotilla episode. **B'tselem**, a human rights group, was established in 1989 in order to document and educate the Israeli public and policy-makers about human rights violations in the Paelstinian Territories. Other movements seek to promote settlement (which they see as being a religiously ordained duty) throughout the whole of biblical Eretz Yisrael.

Legal system and judiciary

When Israel became independent, it passed the Law and Administration Ordinance (1948) that saw all prevailing laws prior to independence remain in force as long as they did not contradict the principles embodied in the Declaration of the Establishment of the State of Israel. The irony of this is that laws created during the British Mandate period (1922-48) to suppress Jewish and Arab resistance (armed or otherwise) to British rule, and against which Jews fought because they were deemed unjust and illegal, have in turn been used to deal with Palestinians in the West Bank and Gaza Strip.

The judiciary is designed to be entirely independent of the political system. Jurisdiction in matters of marriage and divorce have been delegated to the religious courts: rabbinical courts for Jews, sharia courts for Muslims, and ecclesiastical courts for Christians.

The rabbinical courts have become a considerable source of controversy in recent years, dominated as they are by the Orthodox and ultra-Orthodox. The debate over the "conversion law" and its relevance to the Law of Return continues. Currently the Law of Return determines that someone is Jewish if they have at least one Jewish grandparent, though halacha (Jewish religious law) defines Jewishness as coming exclusively from a Jewish mother. If passed, the so-called "conversion law" will see the Orthodox establishment effectively hold a veto over conversions to Judaism performed by their rival Reform and Conservative movements, also casting doubts on the eligibility of converted Reform and Conservative Jews to become Israeli citizens under the Law of Return. The issue brings Israel into conflict with the large US Jewish community, much of which is Conservative or Reform.

Economy

Key characteristics

There are a number of key features that dominate Israel's economic performance. A major drain on the economy is the high level of **defence spending**, though given Israel's situation this is seen as a necessary evil. Whilst most 'Western' countries spend around 3-5% of GDP on defence, Israel spends about 15% (currently about $13.3 billion annually). This actually marks a huge drop from the 'cold war' of the 1970s when defence spending accounted for around 25% of the annual budget.

The Law of Return and the Law of State Lands

The Law of Return, passed in 1950, is one of the cornerstones of the State of Israel, and in fact underlies the very concept of the "ingathering of the exiles". Under this law every Jew is granted the right to return to Israel, and, upon entry, automatically to acquire citizenship (subject to a number of checks that seek to deter criminals and undesirables). New arrivals are also provided with monetary support (part of which is bestowed in the airport on arrival; the rest, as monthly payments), immediate access to ULPAN classes (to learn Hebrew), payment of rent for one year and lower taxes.

The 1960 Law of State Lands determines the status of the land in Israel. Both laws frequently come under attack, though for completely different reasons.

One case against these laws is perhaps most eloquently argued by the Palestinian intellectual Edward W. Said: "Whereas the moral and political right of a person to return to his place of uninterrupted residence is acknowledged everywhere, Israel has negated the possibility of return, first by a series of laws declaring Arab-owned land in Palestine absentee property, and hence liable to expropriation by the Jewish National Fund (which legally owns the land in Israel 'for the whole Jewish people', a formula without analogy in any other state or quasi state), and second by the Law of Return, by whose provision any Jew born anywhere is able to claim immediate Israeli citizenship and residence (but no Arab can, even if his residence and that of his family for numerous generations in Palestine can be proved). These two exclusionary categories systematically and juridically make it impossible, on any grounds whatever, for the Arab Palestinians to return, be compensated for his property, or live in Israel as a citizen equal before the law with a Jewish Israeli." (*The Question of Palestine*, 1979).

A second major drain on the economy is the huge **external debt** (currently estimated at around $55.8 billion), which along with defence spending accounts for about 50% of the country's budget. Foreign aid that Israel has received since its inception has come in a variety of forms. Foreign government grants and loans (mainly from the US) form a large proportion of this aid, though Israel has also received aid in the form of funds brought by immigrants, restitution payments to victims of the Nazis, and donations from Jewish fund-raising organizations abroad.

A number of other crucial factors have largely determined the way in which Israel's economy has performed. One such factor has been the need to absorb large scale **immigration**, put somewhere in the region of 3.4 million people in the last 60 years. This challenge was brought sharply into focus once again in the 1990s, when some 900,000 immigrants arrived from the former Soviet Union. The need to provide jobs, housing, healthcare and education has been a further drain on Israel's delicately poised economy. Though the standard of Israel's public services is probably the envy of the region, it is not without its economic cost. Vast resources have also been invested in a modern economic infrastructure.

Recent performance

The key characteristic of the Israeli economy in the 1980s was three-digit **inflation**, reaching 445% per annum in 1984. Emergency measures introduced by the government, including the introduction of the New Israeli Shekel (NIS), slashed annual rates to around 14%. The key feature of the 1990s was an economy running at full speed, with Israel achieving the highest **GDP growth rate** of all OECD countries. Since 2000, the high-tech industry has gone from strength to strength, as has the manufacturing sector (see below). The recent economic crisis has not hit Israel to the same degree as it has affected Europe and the US, as Israeli banks are notoriously cautious and such investment risks were not taken. In 2009, **unemployment** was estimated at 7.4%.

Agriculture

It is easy to think of Israel as being a country dominated by agriculture; after all, the process of "turning the desert green" is one of the key claims made by Zionism. Dramatic advancements have been made in agriculture in Israel since its independence some 60 years ago, with the total area under cultivation increasing by a factor of 2.6 to 440,000 hectares, and land under irrigation rising by an astonishing factor of 8. However, although the absolute value of agricultural production and exports has risen dramatically, its share of GDP, exports and employment have all decreased.

Israel meets most of its domestic food needs, with its main food imports (grain, oilseeds, meat, coffee and sugar) easily financed by agricultural exports. Such exports include winter fruit, vegetables and flowers, plus dairy and poultry exports. Israel may be said to lead the world in arid and semi-arid agriculture research and development (R&D).

Industry

A lack of natural resources has forced Israel to concentrate industrial output on manufactured products with high added value (though in 2009 significant natural gas reservoirs were found in Israel's Mediterranean waters, which are expected to have a dramatic impact on the economy and enable the country to be much more independent in terms of its energy sources). Israel is the world leader in the field of diamond polishing (producing 40% of the world's polished diamonds) despite the fact that no diamonds are actually mined in the country! Israel's investment in **research and development** (R&D) sees it now rank amongst the world's leading players in the field of **high technology**. Notable advances in the world of **electronics**, communications, electro-, laser- and fibre-optics, computer technology, aeronautics, robotics, plus **medical**, **energy** and agricultural R&D can be attributed to Israeli scientists and researchers. Much of the foreign investment in Israel is in the high-tech sector. Israel is ranked eighth in the world in **conventional-weapons** exports (2009, Stockholm International Peace Research Institute).

Tourism

Israel markets itself as a major tourist destination, with tourism comprising a significant source of foreign exchange earnings. However, the Al-Aqsa Intifada saw tourism grind to a virtual halt throughout the country, and security concerns still scare many potential visitors away. Yet, pilgrims are back in force these days and the volume of independent travellers is increasing. In 2008, tourist arrivals numbered over 2.5 million which was up by 500,000 from the year before. Around 75-80% of foreign tourists to Israel come from North America and Western Europe, with USA (23%), France (10%), Russia (8%), UK (7%), Germany (5.5%), and Italy (4.5%) being the main sources.

International relations

United States

Israel's relationship with the United States is extraordinary: full of contradictions, and beset by rocky patches, but incredibly enduring. Israel is the largest beneficiary of US overseas aid and also the recipient of substantial US loan guarantees that allow Israel to secure loans for projects such as absorbing immigrants. One-third of world Jewry lives in the United States, and thus it is little surprise that the US is Israel's champion in the outside world and defender at the United Nations.

However, at the time of going to press good-will between Israel and the US is at the lower end of the scale. The Obama administration is frustrated by the lack of movement towards peace talks, whilst international pressure to end the blockade of Gaza is mounting and the US insistence on a freeze on settlements is being disregarded.

Arab neighbours

Egypt The turning point came in 1977 when Egyptian President Anwar Sadat made a ground-breaking visit to Jerusalem. This event led to the Camp David Accords signed between the two states in September 1978, and the subsequent peace treaty signed in March of the following year. Israel completed its withdrawal from the Sinai in April 1982 in a deal based upon the principle of exchanging land for peace. As a result of signing this treaty Egypt was expelled from the Arab league, and Sadat subsequently assassinated. The impact of this treaty on relations between the two states has been mixed. Whilst the threat of war has subsided, a legacy of decades of mutual distrust and hostility still has not been overcome, and the goals of economic and cultural integration remain a long way off. In many regards, the description of relations between Israel and Egypt as a 'cold peace' is remarkably apt.

Jordan Though outwardly enemies, secret talks remained a major feature of Israeli-Jordanian relations throughout the period of the Arab boycott of Israel. These talks were perhaps the result of King Hussein's pragmatism, though any agreements reached between the negotiating teams were usually scuppered by domestic opposition. The Israeli-PLO Declaration of Principles signed in 1993 effectively allowed Israel and Jordan to sign a mutually beneficial peace treaty in 1994. Both sides have gained from the treaty: Israel through increased security on her eastern border, and Jordan through a larger share of water resources of the Yarmuk and Jordan rivers, plus the financial incentive to sign given by the United States (that saw Jordan's $480 million debt to the US wiped off at the stroke of a pen). Within Jordan there was widespread opposition to a normalization of ties with Israel, not least amongst the considerable Palestinian refugee population.

Syria Of course relations between Israel and Syria are dominated by the issue of the Golan Heights. Syria is maintaining its stance that Israel must withdraw completely before the two states can even begin negotiating a peace treaty, whilst Israel believes that it needs either the Golan Heights or a satisfactory peace treaty (or both) to secure its safety from the Syrian military threat. Even if Israel did agree to withdraw from the Golan, its demands for early warning stations on Mt Hermon, plus a demilitarized zone complete with UN or US observers on the Golan itself, remain unacceptable to Syria.

The 'Jewish lobby' in the USA

Israel divides public opinion on many issues, especially the question of the 'Jewish lobby' in the United States. Opinions on the matter range from those who believe that Jews determine the outcome of US elections and US foreign policy, to those who deny that any such lobby exists.

It is not unreasonable to argue that the State of Israel came into being partly through the lobbying efforts of Theodor Herzl and Chaim Weizmann in the capitals of Europe, and it could be said that the Balfour Declaration is perhaps the greatest achievement of Jewish lobbying this century.

But just how effective is the 'Jewish lobby' in the modern era, particularly in the US? Firstly, it can be quite clearly stated that the Jewish vote in the US does not determine who becomes US President; its constituency is just too small. However, there is considerable evidence to suggest that financial pressure is brought to bear on potential political candidates to make pro-Israeli statements and policy. Further, the main Jewish lobbying groups in the US – eg American Israel Public Affairs Committee (AIPAC, often described as the most effective lobbying group in the US), the Anti-Defamation League of B'nai B'rith

(ADL), and the Conference of Presidents of Major American Jewish Organizations – have all sought through a variety of means to influence US foreign policy, particularly in areas related to Israel and the Arab world. One vital point that is often forgotten is that this is surely the whole point of the lobbying process: to direct public opinion and government policy towards the aims of the constituency that you are representing. It is the means that the 'Jewish lobby' uses that is so objectionable to some commentators.

It is beyond the scope of this book to attempt to explore this issue fully, though there are any number of books on the subject. Whether you agree with the authors' conclusions or not, such books never fail to make an absorbing read. Try: John Snetsinger, *Truman, The Jewish Vote and the Creation of Israel*, 1974, Hoover Institution Press; Edward Tivnan, *The Lobby: Jewish Political Power and American Foreign Policy*, 1987, Simon & Schuster; Paul Findley, *They Dare To Speak Out: People and Institutions Confront Israel's Lobby*, 1985, Lawrence Hill; John J Mearsheimer & Stephen M Walt, *The Israel Lobby and US Foreign Policy*, 2008, Farrar, Straus and Giroux.

Lebanon In May 2000, Israel withdrew troops from the narrow strip of southern Lebanon that it had occupied, largely due to public pressure at home and various military setbacks. Hezbollah then took control of the area whilst regional tension increased further with the first intifada in September 2000. Various incitements by Hezbollah, chief of which was the abduction of Israeli soldiers in order to prompt a prisoner exchange, led to the 2006 Lebanon War. Israel was widely criticized by the international community for a disproportionate use of force in their response (about 1200 Lebanese civilians were killed). The prospect for an equitable peace between the two countries was set back once again.

United Nations

Israel has had a fractious relationship with the United Nations, largely as a result of the 'automatic majority' of Arab and Muslim nations, the non-aligned movement and the former Soviet bloc guaranteeing the adoption of resolutions condemning Israel. However, it should be noted that not all resolutions condemning Israel are passed solely because of this bloc (many such resolutions are opposed by just three nations: Israel, USA, and the USA-dependent Micronesia).

Perhaps the most famous (or infamous) such incident at the United Nations concerning Israel occurred on the 10 November 1975, when the General Assembly voted by a majority of 72-35 (with 32 abstentions) to condemn Zionism as "a form of racism and racial discrimination". Benjamin Netanyahu suggests that "Such an achievement had eluded even the great anti-Semitic propagandists of our millennium like Torquemada and Joseph Goebbels" (*A Place Among the Nations*, 1993), adding that "for the first time in history, a world body had given its stamp of approval to the libelling of an entire people", whilst the US Ambassador to the UN at the time, Daniel Moynihan, declared "The US will not abide by, it will not acquiesce in, this infamous act. A great evil has been loosed upon the world. The abomination of antisemitism [sic] has been given the appearance of international sanction". Others disagree. Edward W. Said, whilst suggesting that "Israel's Jewish achievements ... are considerable achievements, and it is right that they not sloppily be tarnished with the sweeping rhetorical denunciation associated with 'racism' ... " declares that "*Racism* is too vague a term: Zionism is Zionism. For the Arab Palestinian, this tautology has a sense that is perfectly congruent with, but exactly the opposite of, what it says to Jews" (*The Question of Palestine*, 1979). Said also goes out of his way to explain that "To write critically about Zionism in Palestine has therefore never meant, and does not mean now, being anti-Semitic ... all liberals and even most 'radicals' have been unable to overcome the Zionist habit of equating anti-Zionism with anti-Semitism". A 'free' vote took place on the resolution in the UN in December 1991, with the General Assembly voting to revoke the equation by a margin of 111-25 (with 13 abstentions).

Other important relationships

A significant step was taken in 1994 when diplomatic relations were formally established between Israel and the **Holy See** (Vatican). It is remarkable to think that it was only in 1965 that Pope Paul VI issued *Nostra Aetate*, which formally dropped the charge of deicide against the Jewish people.

The diplomatic relationship between Israel and Turkey has taken a battering recently, most particularly after the Israeli navy killed eight Turkish nationals aboard one of the ships in the aid flotilla headed for Gaza in May 2010. Israel had an arrangement to use Turkish airspace for training flights (by the time you've gone supersonic over Israel you're out of its airspace), and joint manoeuvres between Turkey and Israel had become a matter of course.

Israel currently has full diplomatic relations with 157 states, of which over half were established or renewed following the signing of the Declaration of Principles between Israel and the PLO in 1993. Two notable additions to this list are **China** and **India**. Israel now has a total of 99 embassies, consulates or special missions abroad.

The Palestinian Territories

The Palestinian Authority (PA) was created by the 'Oslo I' agreement of 1993 to administer the areas granted limited autonomy under that deal (Gaza and Jericho), and to act as a mechanism through which the Israelis and Palestinians could negotiate future and final

The Separation Barrier – '*Geder Hafrada*' in Hebrew

Since 2001 Israel has been building the separation barrier around the West Bank. The finished length will be over 700 km. By the end of 2009 about 70% was finished, much of it cutting deep into the West Bank to enclose major settlement blocks on the Israeli side. The barrier is an 8-m/25-ft-high wall for about 10% of its length, and a fence for the remainder. Over 450,000 thousand dunams of Palestinian land is on the Israel side of the barrier, isolating almost 30,000 Palestinians in 17 communities.

Additional walls and fences have been built around many of these communities creating enclosed ghettos, whose only exit is by special 'Arab only' roads, which in some cases are enclosed by fences along each side. The segregated transportation system also applies to Israelis, who can easily access the settlements via 4-lane highways, with the Palestinian roads going though tunnels underneath.

The barrier also encloses about 70 sq km of West Bank into Israeli-controlled 'Greater Jerusalem'. About 9.5% of the West Bank is on the Israeli side of the barrier. Many olive groves, and over 200 homes and shops, were destroyed to make way for the barrier, and thousands of acres of Palestinian land are now inaccessible to farmers. According to the United Nations Relief and Works Agency (UNRWA), 15 communities have been directly affected, numbering approximately 138,593 Palestinians, including 13,450 refugee families, or 67,250 individuals.

While the barrier is an effective way to block Palestinians without permits from entering Israel, Israelis and tourists can usually cross freely, even during the 'closures', which occur at major Jewish holidays. Tourists can pass through the barrier at checkpoints via Israeli or Palestinian public transport. Israeli transport connects Tel Aviv and Jerusalem to all the major settlements and many smaller ones. Their routes follow the "Israeli only" roads and also the roads that are still shared with Palestinians.

Palestinian transportation networks can be accessed in East Jerusalem, and reach all parts of the West Bank, often transferring at the bus stations in Ramallah for the north, and Bethlehem for the south. Sometimes a combination of settler buses and Palestinian busses or taxis is the most efficient method of reaching a West Bank destination. Take your passport. There are checkpoints on all roads leading through the barrier.

Fred Schlomka
Green Olive Tours
www.greenolivetours.com

Sources
www.btselem.org/english/Separation_Barrier/Statistics.asp
unispal.un.org/UNISPAL.NSF/0/2DB345FABA654D4585256EB60066C514
blog.toursinenglish.com/2010/01/ghettos-of-jerusalem.html
www.jewishvirtuallibrary.org/jsource/Peace/fence.html

issues. (**NB** The PA is also referred to as the Palestinian National Authority (PNA), though Israeli references prefer to drop the 'National' component. This Handbook uses the term found in the 'Oslo I and II' documents, ie PA.)

The PA was intended to be a temporary institution lasting five years, designed to bridge the gap between early self-rule and final status, though what the ultimate nature of the

Palestinian entity will be (autonomy, confederation, statehood) is still to be negotiated. According to the terms of the agreements signed between Israel and the Palestinians, the PA was due to hand over its powers to its elected successor body, the **Palestinian Legislative Council**, which would ultimately look after the well-being of Palestinians in the area under its remit. The timetable for 'Oslo II' envisaged 'final status' negotiations being concluded by May 1999; in fact this date came and went without them having even begun. Indeed, at one stage Yasser Arafat threatened to declare an independent Palestinian state on 4 May 1999, although he eventually backed down when it was realized that such a move would almost certainly serve to re-elect the right-wing Netanyahu government at the general election later that month. In the event of the Al-Aqsa intifada (2000-2005), the peace process obviously ran aground completely, and final status negotiations were never reached. Hence the PA effectively took over all military and civil responsibilities in the urban areas (Area A) and civil administration in the rural areas (Area B) until parties reach the negotiating table again. Since elections in 2005 where he won 62% of the votes, the PA President has been Mahmoud Abbas (AKA Abu Mazen). He is also the Chairman of the PLO and a member of the Fatah party, the oldest political party in the Palestinian Territories, founded by Arafat in the 1950s.

In January 2006 (just five months after Israel evacuated its settlements in the Gaza Strip), Fatah lost the Palestinian Legislative Council elections to Hamas, who took full control in Gaza in June 2007. This effectively split Gaza from the West Bank in terms of administration. Hamas are a radical Islamic party and refuse to recognize Israel's right to exist, hence an all-encompassing economic blockade was imposed against Gaza in an effort to destroy their power base. The capture of Gilad Shalit, an Israeli soldier who has been held captive by Hamas since June 2006, plus the continued firing of rockets into Israel, ensured that restrictions were not lifted. Meanwhile, the rest of the world began to become critical of the hardline policy which appeared merely to cause great hardship to the civilian population without achieving the stated aim.

After a six-month ceasefire was broken by Hamas, Israel commenced 'Operation Cast Lead' in December 2008 which comprised an air strike and a land invasion, lasting for three weeks and killing between 1160 and 1400 Palestinians. Since May 2010, Israel has come under heightened pressure from the international community to revoke the economic embargo of Gaza. This comes in the wake of the navy raid on a flotilla which was sailing to Gaza to bring aid. Eight Turkish activists and one American were killed in the night-time raid. At the time of going to press, there were suggestions that Israel was planning to loosen up the restrictions over what goods are/are not permitted into Gaza under the terms of the blockade.

Further reading

Where to begin? There is a vast array of literature available that is related to Israel and Palestine, and it has to be said that the following list is somewhat personal and subjective.

History and politics

Josephus, *The Jewish War*, various reprints and translations.

Norman G Finkelstein, *Beyond Chutzpah: On the Misuse of Anti-Semitism and the Abuse of History*, Verso Books, 2005. Unemotional, scholarly and original account of the Israel-Palestine conflict.

Paul Johnson, *A History of the Jews*, 1987. A monumental work. Anyone interested in Israel should read this; very accessible.

Walter Laqueur, *A History of Zionism*, Schocken Books, New York, 1989. Probably the definitive general history of the Zionist movement; reasonably accessible. Described as "sympathetic yet critical".

Charles D. Smith, *Palestine and the Arab-Israeli Conflict*, St Martin's Press, New York, 1992. Good, general reader, with no noticeable bias.

Edward W Said, *The Question of Palestine, 1992; The Politics of Dispossession: The Struggle for Palestinian Self-Determination 1969-1994, 1995; Peace and its Discontents: Gaza-Jericho 1993-1995*, 1995, Vintage, London. All essential reading for those who wish to understand fully the Palestinian-Israeli conflict.

Lawrence Joffe Keesing, *Guide to the Middle-East Peace Process*, Catermill, 1996. Unravels the 'peace process' in comprehensive yet fathomable detail, with valuable biographies of principal participants.

Simon Goldhill, *Jerusalem: City of Longing*, Harvard University Press, 2008. Informal and warm account of the city, examining the architecture and history without getting too heavy.

Benjamin Netanyahu, *A Place Among the Nations: Israel and the World*, Bantam, 1993. Clear presentation of Israeli version of

history, though rather patronizing towards its audience. Netanyahu's views and programme clearly laid out.

Richard Ben Cramer, *How Israel Lost: The Four Questions*, Simon & Schuster, 2004. Chaim Herzog *The Arab-Israeli Wars*, Random House, 1984.

A number of seminal texts presenting a pro-Palestinian interpretation of Zionism and its impact can be found in the following:

Ibrahim Abu-Lughod, *Transformation of Palestine*, Northwestern University Press, 1971.

Sami Hadwani, *Bitter Harvest, Palestine 1914-67*, New World Press, 1967.

Avi Shlaim, *The Iron Wall: Israel and the Arab World*, 2000, Penguin History. One of the most informative accounts of the Israeli position on "Palestine".

Maxime Rodinson, *Israel: A Colonial-Settler State?*, Monad Press, 1973.

Elia T Zurayk, *The Palestinians in Israel: A Study in Internal Colonialism*, Routledge, 1979.

Sabri Jiryis, *The Arabs in Israel*, Monthly Review Press, 1976.

Socio-political travelogues

Robert Fisk, *Pity the Nation: Lebanon at War*, OUP, 1991. Superb, but immensely depressing work by one of the Middle East's most respected reporters.

Thomas Friedman, *From Beirut to Jerusalem*, Harper and Collins, 1993. Very readable; particularly interesting for its examination of the relationship between Israel and the USA and the 'who is a Jew?' question, though Edward Said sees it as a classic example of 'Orientalism'. Friedman is reviled as a 'self-hating Jew' by the Israeli right.

Amos Oz, *In The Land of Israel*, 1985; The Slopes of Lebanon, 1989; Israel, Palestine and Peace, 1989, various reprints. The doyen of

Josephus' *The Jewish War*

One of the best accompaniments to a visit to Israel is a copy of Josephus' *The Jewish War* – the key source of information about the First Jewish Revolt against Rome (66-73 CE). Born of a well-connected Jewish family, Joseph ben Matthais famously switched sides during the Revolt, taking the Romanized version of his name (Josephus Flavius) before retiring to an apartment in Imperial Rome to write his memoirs. As a historian Josephus is, in the words of Johnson, "tendentious, contradictory and thoroughly unreliable" (*A History of the Jews*, 1987), yet his work is never less than absorbing.

One of the key criticisms of Josephus is the number of inconsistencies between *The Jewish War* and his later work, *Antiquities of the Jews*. As Johnson points out, however, his motives for producing these works changed between the writing of the two: "he was an example of a Jewish phenomenon which became very common over the centuries: a clever young man who, in his youth, accepted the modernity and sophistication of the day and then, late in middle age, returned to his Jewish roots. He began his writing career as a Roman apologist and ended it close to being a Jewish nationalist" (*ibid*).

Perhaps the last word on Josephus should be left to PJ O'Rourke, who sees many similarities between the events described in *The Jewish War* and those in evidence today: "Here, 60 generations ago, is nearly the same cast of characters engaged in exactly the same obsessive, vicious and fatal behaviour for the same terrifying reasons on the same cursed, reeking, ugly chunk of land." (*Give War A Chance*, 1992).

(There are several translations of *The Jewish War*, though one of the most accessible is G.A. Williamson's translation, revised and annotated by E Mary Smallwood, published by Penguin Books, London, 1981.)

---

the Israeli left eloquently presents the case for an Israeli-Palestinian compromise, as well as providing an insight into Israeli society.

Stephen Brook, *Winner Takes All: A Season in Israel*, Picador, London, 1990. Interesting political and social journey through Israel.

Amos Elon, *Jerusalem: City of Mirrors*, 1989. Very informative and entertaining read.

PJ O'Rourke, *Holidays in Hell*, Picador, 1988 and *Give War a Chance*, Picador, 1992. Ascerbic wit and no concessions to political correctness.

Howard Jacobson, *Roots Schmoots*, 1993. Non-observant Jewish intellectual does for Israel what he did for Australia with "In the Land of Oz", ie came along and took the piss.

Saul Bellow, *To Jerusalem and Back*, Secker & Warburg, 1976.

Mark Twain, *The Innocents Abroad*, various reprints, 1871. The PJ O'Rourke of the 19th century.

Amira Hass, *Drinking the Sea at Gaza: Days and Nights in a Land Under Siege*, Picador, 2000. Unusually from the perspective of a female Israeli journalist.

Adina Hoffman, *House of Windows: Portraits from a Jerusalem Neighbourhood*, 2001, Ibis Editions. Sketches of life in Jerusalem, with poignant and personal stories about 'both sides'.

Biography

Robert Slater, *Rabin of Israel: Warrior for Peace*, Robson Books, London, 1996. Interesting biography, though not over-critical.

Andrew Gowers and Tony Walker, *Yasser Arafat and the Palestinian Revolution*, Corgi, London, 1990. Gives an insight into how difficult it is to 'get inside' the man, and you perhaps learn more about the history of the PLO than Arafat himself.

Robert I Friedman, *Zealots for Zion*, Random House, 1992. Rather frightening exposé of the West Bank settler movement.

Michael Bar-Zohar, *Ben-Gurion*, Delacorte, 1978. Regarded as the definitive biography.

Alan Hart, *Arafat*, Sidgwick and Jackson, London, 1994. Incredibly absorbing work; certainly proves the notion that there are twoxs sides to every story.

Archaeology

Ephraim Stern (ed.), *The New Encyclopedia of Archaeological Excavations in the Holy Land*, Simon & Schuster, 1993. The ultimate reference work, though at four volumes and 4kg, it's not the book to take into the field!

Jerome Murphy-O'Connor, *The Holy Land: An Archaeological Guide from Earliest Times to 1700*, OUP, 1998. Excellent, portable guide, concentrates on sites where there is "something significant to see". Father Jerry is extremely entertaining.

Kay Prag, *Blue Guide: Jerusalem*, Black & Norton, London and NY, 1989. Unbeatable reference for anyone exploring Jerusalem in depth.

George Adam Smith, *Historical Geography of the Holy Land*, various reprints, 1894 and 1931. 'Colonial' style, infinite detail and a lovely turn of phrase.

General

Raja Shehadeh, *Palestinian Walks: Notes on a Vanishing Landscape*, Profile Books, 2007. *Palestine and Palestinians, Alternative Tourism Group*, 2005. An alternative guidebook that allows for a thorough exploration of the West Bank.

Mariam Shaheen, *Palestine: A Guide*, Interlink Books 2005. History, sites and culture all rolled into one.

Azaria Alon, *Israel National Parks and Nature Reserves*. A Carta Guide, 2008. Useful introduction to all the National Parks with good colour photos; will help you make a decision on which to visit as well as provide information when you are there.

Larry Collins and Dominique Lapierre, *O Jerusalem*, 1978. A gushing account of the 1948 Arab-Israeli battle for Jerusalem that reads like a racy novel, though there's a strong pro-Jewish bias.

Victor Ostrovsky, *By Way of Deception*, 1990; *The Other Side of Deception*, 1994, St Martin's Press. Spy enthusiasts will love the revelations about life in the Mossad in the first book, whilst the sequel is a must for all conspiracy-theorists.

Michael Baigent and Richard Leigh, *The Dead Sea Scrolls Deception*, Corgi, 1991. Very entertaining and convincing account of the cover-up that accompanied the discovery of the Dead Sea Scrolls.

Other works for the conspiracy-theorists include **Edwin Black**, *The Transfer Agreement: The Untold Story of the Secret Pact Between the Third Reich and Jewish Palestine*, MacMillan, 1984;

Edward Tivnan, *The Lobby: Jewish Political Power and American Foreign Policy*, Simon & Schuster, 1987;

John Loftus and Mark Aarons, *The Secret Wars Against the Jews*, St Martin's Press, 1994. When this was reviewed in one journal, the reviewer reminded readers of the authors' own warning, ie only fools take what they are told at face value!

Joel Roskin, *A Guide to Hiking in Israel*, Jerusalem Post, 1994. Excellent hiking guide featuring 40 one-day walks.

Anna Dintaman and David Landis, *Hiking the Jesus Trail, and other Biblical Walks in the Galilee*, Village To Village Press, 2010. Clear instructions and maps, plus interesting historical info allowing trekkers to make the most out of the Galilee.

Fiction

Sayed Kashua, *Dancing Arabs*, Grove Press, 2002. Darkly satirical look at Israel-Palestine through the eyes of a dysfunctional Israeli-Arab male.

The Selected Poetry of Yehuda Amichai, University of California Press, 1996. Inspiring, sad, emotional words translated from the Hebrew.

Matt Rees, *Omar Yussef Mystery Series*, Atlantic Books. Palestine mystery/crime novels set in Gaza and Bethlehem; a good read.

A B Yehoshua, *The Lover*, Dutton. Israel's best-selling novel.

James A Michener, *The Source*, Random House. Excellent read that brings archaeology quite literally to life, spanning the whole of human history (and pre-history) in Israel. Written before the 1967 war from a perspective that sounds terribly out-moded in 2010; beware reaching the

1820s as a very skewed Zionist version of events is presented that some will find nauseating. Despite that, it is a truly gripping read, particularly the Crusaders section.

Muriel Spark, *The Mandelbaum Gate*, Penguin Books. Spies, archaeology and abduction in the Holy City.

Linda Grant, *When I Lived in Modern Times*. Fascinating story set in the late 1940s about a young Jewish woman's time in Israel. Illuminates the last days of the Mandate, early days in Tel Aviv, life on a kibbutz and the role of the Irgun.

Contents

Footnotes

Glossary of archaeological and architectural terms

A

acropolis fortified part of upper city, usually containing political, administrative, religious centre

AD Anno Domini ('after Christ', see *CE*)

agora marketplace, place of assembly

ambulatory usually covered passageway around sanctuary or church nave

Apocrypha books included in the Septuagint (Greek) and Vulgate (Latin) versions of Hebrew Bible, but excluded from Jewish and Protestant versions

architrave horizontal beam resting above an entrance, beam spanning space between two columns, mouldings decorating exterior of an arch

ashlar square or rectangular hewn stone laid in regular horizontal courses

atrium central court in Roman house, forecourt of Christian church

attic upper horizontal piece above a cornice

B

bab gate (Arabic)

bamah/bimah cultic high place, synagogue platform for reading Torah

barbican outer fortification

basilica church with nave and lateral (colonnaded) aisles, rectangular structure with two or more internal colonnades, often ending in an apse

BC/BCE Before Christ/Before the Common Era

beth midrash Jewish house of study (Hebrew)

bir well (Arabic)

BP Before Present

broadhouse rectangular building with entrance in one of the long walls

C

caldarium(-ia) hot room in Roman baths

caravanserai see *khan*

cardo main street of Roman/Byzantine city, generally running N-S and intersecting main E-W street (decumanus) at right-angles

casement wall double fortification wall with partitioned compartments between

cavea spectator seating area in theatre or amphitheatre

CE Common Era (AD)

corbel projecting or overlapping stone blocks supporting a vault

D

dado column pedestal or lower panel of wall

decumanus(-i) main E-W street in Roman/ Byzantine city (see cardo)

deir monastery (Arabic)

derekh street (Hebrew)

dolmen megalithic (burial) monument comprising two upright stones supporting a horizontal stone

donjon keep or strongest part of Crusader fortress

Doric austere Greek architectural style

E

entablature collective architectural term to describe *architrave*, *frieze* and *cornice*

Execration texts figurines or tablets from 20-19th century BCE Egypt, generally inscribed with names of actual or potential enemies (in Syria/Palestine), rather like the voodoo doll principle

exedra semi-circular or rectangular recess

F

fosse ditch or trench outside city walls

frigidarium cold room in Roman baths

G

gadrooned voussoirs *voussoirs* decorated with sets of convex curves at right-angles to the architrave

Gemara rabbinic commentary of the *Mishnah*

genizah repository for discarded books and sacred objects in a synagogue

glacis sloping defensive fortification wall

H

hamman/hammam bath house (Arabic)

har mountain (Hebrew)

Haram sanctuary (Arabic) holy of holies innermost chamber of temple or sanctuary

hypocaust space beneath floor of Roman house or bath house through which hot air is passed

I

insula(-ae) quadrangular city block featur- ing multiple dwellings

Ionic Greek architectural style

J

jebel/jabal hill (Arabic)

joggled voussoirs joined by notches and corresponding projections

K

khan accommodation for caravans featuring single-gated courtyard, surrounded by rooms and stables; see caravanserai

khanqah monastery for Sufi mystics (Arabic)

khirbet ruin (Arabic)

L

loculus(-i) rectangular, shelf-like burial niche in tomb

M

madrasa/madrassa Islamic religious school

Mar Christian saint (Arabic)

mazar shrine of (Muslim) pilgrimage (Arabic)

menorah seven-branched candelabrum used in Jewish ritual

mihrab niche in mosque, indicating direction of prayer (Mecca)

mikveh/miqveh Jewish ritual bath

minbar freestanding pulpit in mosque

Mishnah collection of oral Jewish law and traditions, forming a basic part of the *Talmud*

N

nahal river (Hebrew)

narthex antechamber to nave of church (after 5th century CE)

nave elongated central hall in basilica or church

necropolis extensive or important cemetery (from Greek for `city of the dead')

nymphaeum(-a) monumental structure in Roman city, generally a public fountain

O

onomasticon alphabetical list of identified sites from the Bible, most famous version written by Eusebius, bishop of Caesarea, in 4th century CE

ossuary receptacle used for secondary burial of bones once flesh has decayed

P

palaeography study of ancient alphabets and writing styles

pediment triangular space beneath a gabled roof in Greek and Roman architecture

peristyle open courtyard surrounded by columns

portico colonnade or covered ambulatory at entrance to a building

postern small opening in fortification wall

propylaeum(-a) monumental structure marking entrance to a sanctuary

proto-Aeolic capital common in Israelite/ Judean architecture, a decorated stone capital

Q

qanatir arcade (often stepped), eg Dome of the Rock platform

qibla marking direction of prayer (Arabic)

qubba/qubbat dome (Arabic)

S

sabil public fountain (Arabic)

Sanhedrin highest court and supreme council of Jews (1st century BCE-6th century CE)

saray palace (Arabic)

scaenae frons façade of Roman stage building used as backdrop

Septuagint pre-Christian Greek translation of Hebrew Bible, supposedly written simultaneously by 70 scholars in 70 days, c. 3rd-2nd century BCE

sha'ar gate (Hebrew)

shari'a street (Arabic)

stela(-ae) upright slab of pillar, usually with an inscription

stoa roofed portico, or Greek free-standing 1-storey building with long rear wall and row of columns bearing a sloping roof at the front

stucco high-quality plaster coating

stylobate continuous base supporting a row or rows of columns

suq market or bazaar (Arabic)

T

Talmud interpretation of *Mishnah* and *Gemarah*

tel/tell artificial mound (Hebrew/Arabic)

tepidarium warm room in Roman baths

transept space between nave and apse of a church

triclinium(-ia) Roman dining room

turba mausoleum (Arabic)

V

Via Maris Way of the Sea, one of the two main routes linking Egypt and Mesopotamia, via Canaan/Israel coast

voussoir wedge-shaped stone blocks forming an arch

W

wadi seasonal stream(bed) (Arabic)

wali Muslim saint or holy man

waqf Islamic endowment

Y

yad memorial (Hebrew)

yeshiva rabbinical seminary

Yishuv pre-20th century CE Jewish population of Palestine

Z

zawiya Muslim religious dwelling, place of devotion or burial (Arabic)

zuqaq alley

Principal source: *New Encyclopaedia of Archaeological Excavations in the Holy Land, 1993, Simon and Schuster.*

Index

Notes

Credits

Footprint credits

Project Editor: Jen Haddington
Text editor: Catherine Charles
Layout, production and colour section: Angus Dawson
Maps: Kevin Feeney, Gail Townsley
Series design: Mytton Williams
Cover design: Pepi Bluck

Managing Director: Andy Riddle
Commercial Director: Patrick Dawson
Publisher: Alan Murphy
Publishing Managers: Jo Williams, Felicity Laughton, Jen Haddington
Digital Editor: Alice Little
Marketing and PR: Liz Harper
Sales: Jeremy Parr
Advertising: Renu Sibal
Finance and administration: Elizabeth Taylor

Photography credits

Front cover: Dome of the Rock, Jerusalem: John Frumm / hemis.fr
Back cover: Wailing Wall, Jerusalem: Bruno Perousse / hemis.fr
Page 1: Eitan Simanor/PCL Travel
Page 2-3: Mond Image/PCL Travel
Montage: Eitan Simanor/PCL Travel; Bluerain/ Shutterstock; vblinov/Shutterstock; Vanessa Betts; Dmitry Pistrov/Shutterstock; Karen McCunnall/PCL Travel.
Page 8: Vanessa Betts

Manufactured in India by Nutech.
Pulp from sustainable forests.

Footprint feedback

We try as hard as we can to make each Footprint guide as up to date as possible but, of course, things always change. If you want to let us know about your experiences – good, bad or ugly – then don't delay, go to **footprinttravelguides. com** and send in your comments.

Publishing information
Footprint Israel
3rd edition
© Footprint Handbooks Ltd
September 2010

ISBN: 978 1 907263 07 1
CIP DATA: A catalogue record for this book is available from the British Library

® Footprint Handbooks and the Footprint mark are a registered trademark of Footprint Handbooks Ltd

Published by Footprint
6 Riverside Court
Lower Bristol Road
Bath BA2 3DZ, UK
T +44 (0)1225 469141
F +44 (0)1225 469461
footprinttravelguides.com

Distributed in the USA by Globe Pequot Press, Guilford, Connecticut

Footprint Mini Atlas
Israel

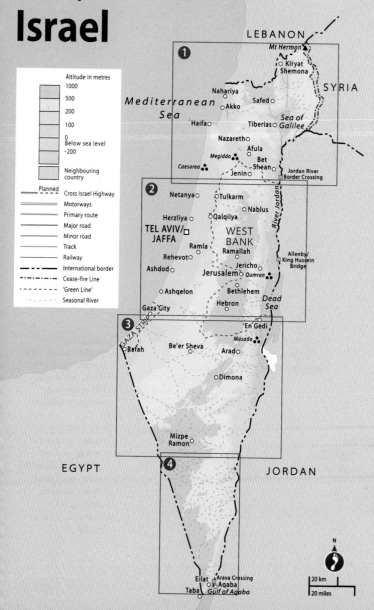

LEBANON

Mt Hermon

① Kiryat Shemona

SYRIA

Mediterranean Sea

Nahariya

Akko

Safed

Haifa

Tiberias

Sea of Galilee

Nazareth

Afula

Megiddo

Bet Shean

Caesarea

Jenin

Jordan River Border Crossing

② Netanya

Tulkarm

Nablus

Herzliya

Qalqilya

TEL AVIV/ JAFFA

Ramla

WEST BANK

Ramallah

Rehevot

Jericho

Allenby/ King Hussein Bridge

Ashdod

Jerusalem

Qumran

Ashqelon

Bethlehem

Gaza City

Hebron

Dead Sea

③ GAZA STRIP

'En Gedi

Masada

Rafah

Be'er Sheva

Arad

Dimona

Mizpe Ramon

EGYPT

④

JORDAN

Eilat

Arava Crossing

Aqaba

Taba

Gulf of Aqaba

Altitude in metres

1000
500
200
100
0
Below sea level
-200

Neighbouring country

Planned	Cross Israel Highway
	Motorways
	Primary route
	Major road
	Minor road
	Track
	Railway
	International border
	Cease-fire Line
	'Green Line'
	Seasonal River

N

20 km
20 miles

Map 1

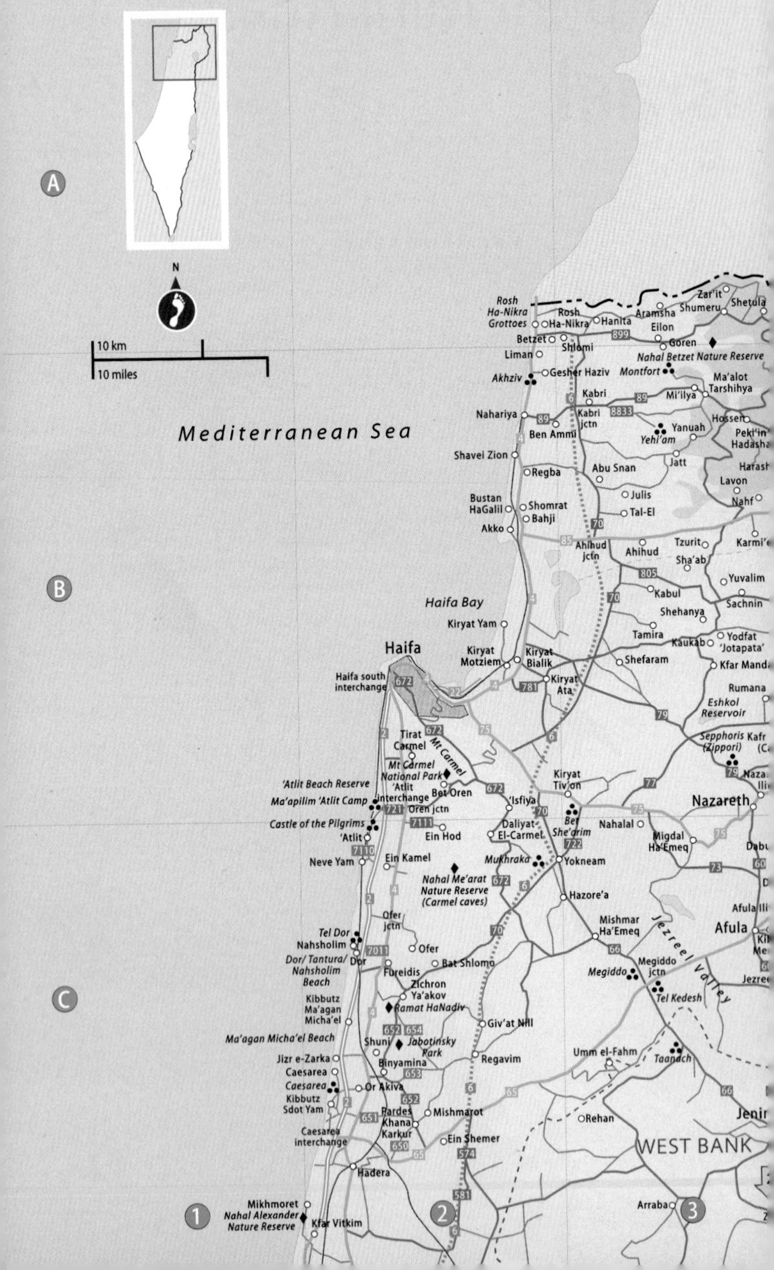

A

N

10 km
10 miles

Mediterranean Sea

B

Rosh
Ha-Nikra Rosh   Aramsha Shumeru   Shetula
Grottoes Ha-Nikra Hanita   Zar'it
          Betzet   Shlomi   Eilon   Goren
          Liman   Nahal Betzet Nature Reserve
          Akhziv   Gesher Haziv   Montfort   Ma'alot
                                             Tarshiha
                   Kabri   Mi'ilya
Nahariya   Kabri   Hosset
                  jctn   Peki'in
          Ben Ammi   Yehi'am Yanuah   Hadasha
Shavei Zion   Jatt   Harash
          Regba   Abu Snan   Lavon
Bustan   Julis   Tal-El   Nahf
HaGalil Shomrat
         Bahji   Tal-El
Akko
         Ahihud jctn Ahihud   Karmi'e
                               Tzurit Sha'ab
                      Kabul   Yuvalim
Haifa Bay   Shehanya   Sachnin
         Kiryat Yam   Tamira   Yodfat
Haifa   Kiryat   Kaukab   'Jotapata'
         Motziem Kiryat   Kfar Manda
Haifa south   Bialik Shefaram   Rumana
interchange   Kiryat   Eshkol
              Ata   Reservoir
         Tirat   Sepphoris Kafr
         Carmel   (Zippori)
         Mt Carmel Kiryat   Naza
         National Park Tiv'on Ilit
'Atlit Beach Reserve 'Isfiya   Nazareth
Ma'apilim 'Atlit Camp Bet Oren Daliyat
Castle of the Pilgrims Oren jctn El-Carmel Nahalal
         'Atlit   Ein Hod Bet   Migdal
Neve Yam Ein Kamel She'arim Ha'Emeq
         Mukhraka Yokneam   Dabu
         Nahal Me'arat
         Nature Reserve
         (Carmel caves) Hazore'a
Ofer   Mishmar   Afula Ili
jctn   Ha'Emeq   Afula
Tel Dor Ofer   Megiddo Kli
Nahsholim Bat Shlomo   jctn   Me
Dor/ Tantura/ Zichron   Jezre
Nahsholim Ya'akov Megiddo
Beach   Ramat HaNadiv Tel Kedesh
Kibbutz
Ma'agan Shuni Jabotinsky
Micha'el   Park
Ma'agan Micha'el Beach Giv'at Nili
Jizr e-Zarka Regavim Umm el-Fahm Taanach
Caesarea
Caesarea
Kibbutz Or Akiva
Sdot Yam Pardes
Caesarea Khana/ Mishmarot
interchange Karkur Ein Shemer Rehan Jenir
                                WEST BANK
         Hadera
Mikhmoret
Nahal Alexander
Nature Reserve Kfar Vitkim Arraba

C

1   2   3

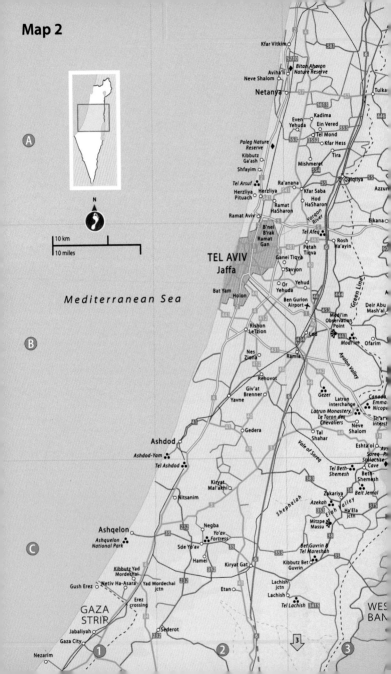

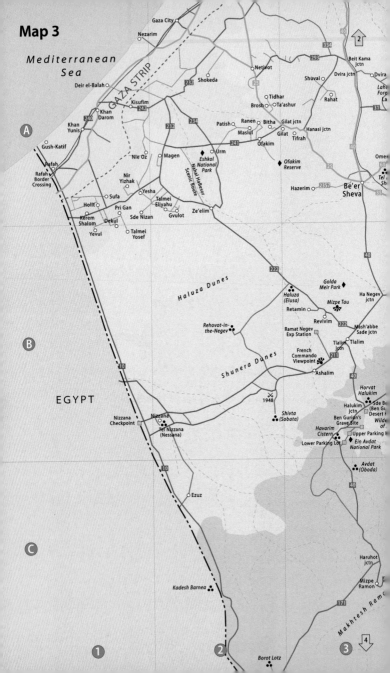

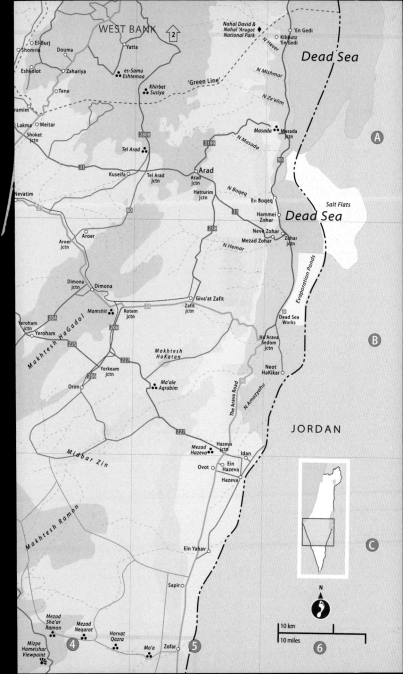

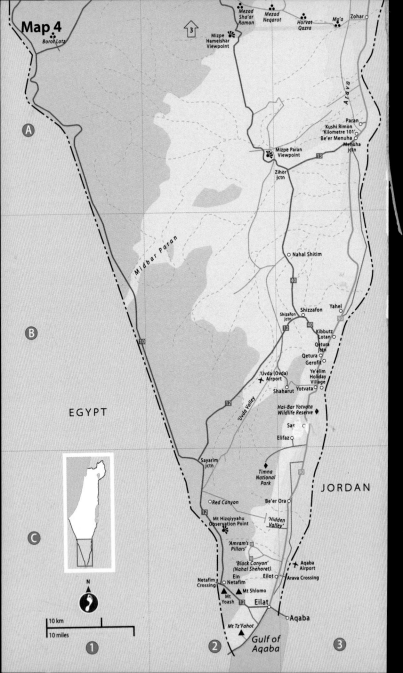

Map 4

Borot Lotz

Mezad Sha'ar Ramon

Mezad Neqarot

Horvat Qazra

Mg'a

Zohar

Mizpe Hameishar Viewpoint

A

Arava

Paran

Kushi Rimon

'Kilometre 101'

Be'er Menuha

Menuha jctn

13

Mizpe Paran Viewpoint

Zihor jctn

Midbar Paran

Nahal Shitim

40

B

Shizzafon

Yahel

Shizafon jctn

90

40

12

Kibbutz Lotan

Qetura jctn

Qetura

Gerofit

'Uvda (Ovda) Airport

Ye'elim Holiday Village

Shaharut

Yotvata

Hai-Bar Yotvata Wildlife Reserve

EGYPT

Uvda Valley

Samar

Elifaz

Sayarim jctn

Timna National Park

90

JORDAN

C

Red Canyon

Be'er Ora

12

Mt Hizqiyyahu Observation Point

'Hidden Valley'

'Amram's Pillars'

'Black Canyon' (Nahal Shehoret)

Netafim Crossing

Ein Netafim

Aqaba Airport

Eilot

Arava Crossing

N

Mt Yoash

Mt Shlomo

Eilat

12

10 km

10 miles

Mt Tz'Fahot

Aqaba

Gulf of Aqaba

1

2

3

About the authors

Vanessa Betts A writer and editor from England, Vanessa has spent most of the last 13 years living and working overseas. What was supposed to be a round-the-world trip turned into a round-Asia trip when life there proved just too exciting. She is co-author of Footprint *India*, *Northeast India*, and *Indian Himalaya* and author of Footprint *Egypt*. Since October 2010, she has been living in Jerusalem and Tel Aviv to research and update this book. After thinking it would be a breeze compared to an India update, she discovered that a great deal can be packed into a very small space.

Dave Winter Having spent much of his twenties travelling through the Middle East, South Asia and Southeast Asia, Dave was subsequently lured back to college and graduated with a first-class degree from London University's School of Oriental and African Studies (SOAS). He then joined the Footprint team, co-authoring Footprint *Pakistan* before writing the first and second editions of Footprint *Israel*.

Acknowledgements

Vanessa Betts A huge thank you goes to Maoz Inon and Yaron Burgin of the ILH Israel Hostels Association for all their help and enthusiasm for this project – without them I could never have done it! Also, many thanks to Ted Neiters for his invaluable knowledge of life in Gaza, and to Gili Greenbaum for sharing his experience of the country's trekking trails. I am also infinitely grateful to the following people for their input, time, patience and generosity: Jane and Mike Betts, Simon Boas, Katharine Bowerman, Kevin Eisenstadt, Eran and Michal Horn, Andreas Indregard, Samer Kokaly, Suraida Nasser, Sanna Negus, Eran Shaham, Toni and Avi Shaham, Fred Shlomka, and Sara Zafrir. Thank you also to everyone at Footprint, particularly Jen Haddington and Alan Murphy. And my enduring gratitude, of course, to Mr Dave Winter.